Law of
Capital Acquisitions Tax

11th edition   Finance Act 2009

Edited by

Tony Fitzpatrick

Irish Taxation
Institute

Irish Taxation Institute
South Block
Longboat Quay
Grand Canal Harbour
Dublin 2

Telephone: +353 1 6631700
Fax: +353 1 6688387
E-mail: info@taxireland.ie
Web: www.taxireland.ie

First edition 1999
Seventh edition 2005
Eighth edition 2006
Ninth edition 2007
Tenth edition 2008
Eleventh edition 2009

A catalogue record for this book is available from the British Library.

The objects of this book are set out in the Editor's Foreword and might be summarised as an effort to bring together in one volume the main legislation which has, or has had, a direct or indirect bearing on capital acquisitions tax.

While every effort has been made to ensure the accuracy of the material in this book, neither the Institute nor the Editor accepts any responsibility for loss or damage occasioned by any person acting, or refraining from acting, as a result of this material. Any views or opinions expressed are not necessarily subscribed to by the Institute. Professional advice should always be sought before acting on any interpretation of the legislation in this book.

ISBN 978-1-84260-183-9

10 9 8 7 6 5 4 3 2 1

Printed and bound in Ireland by Spectrum Print Logistics, Unit 4044, Citywest Business Campus, Naas Road, Dublin 24

PRESIDENT'S FOREWORD

It is with great pleasure that I present the eleventh edition of the Irish Taxation Institute's *Law of Capital Acquisitions Tax*, in which one of our leading editors, Tony Fitzpatrick, guides readers through the various changes made to CAT legislation since its inception in 1976 through to its current standing.

For many years now, this five-part book has proved invaluable to readers with an interest in this area: Part I contains the CAT Consolidation Act 2003 as amended by Finance Acts 2003 to 2009; Part II provides the editor's consolidation of CAT legislation in force on 2003; Part III features all CAT legislation as the provisions were originally enacted; Part IV details other general tax provisions impacting on CAT prior to the Taxes Consolidation Act 1997; and Part V covers probate tax, now repealed. Cross-references to all relevant case law, *Tax Briefings*, *Irish Tax Review* articles and the *Revenue CAT Manual* are also included.

I wish to offer my sincere gratitude to Tony for his excellent work on the book, which I highly recommend to all members and students, as well as those with a general interest in the tax.

JIM RYAN
President
Irish Taxation Institute

EDITOR'S FOREWORD

The Capital Acquisitions Tax Act, 1976, which was enacted on 31st March, 1976, imposed a gift tax on a gift taken by a donee on or after 28th February, 1974, and an inheritance tax on an inheritance taken by a successor on or after 1st April, 1975. The date when a gift or an inheritance is taken is referred to respectively as the date of the gift or the date of the inheritance, which date is the date when the donee or successor becomes beneficially entitled in possession to the property in the gift or inheritance.

Since gift tax and inheritance tax were enacted, the legislation has been extensively amended, the amendments applying to gifts or inheritances taken on or after specified dates.

In addition, a once-off discretionary trust tax was imposed by the Finance Act, 1984, in the form of an inheritance tax on an absolute inheritance of property in a discretionary trust deemed to be taken by the trust. This was followed by the imposition, by the Finance Act, 1986, of an annual 1% discretionary trust tax in the form of an inheritance tax on an absolute inheritance of property in a discretionary trust deemed to be taken by the trust. Later, probate tax was imposed by the Finance Act, 1993, in the form of an inheritance tax on an absolute inheritance in a deceased person's estate deemed to be taken by his personal representatives. Again, the legislation relating to the two discretionary trust taxes, and to probate tax (now abolished), has been amended extensively, the amendments applying to deemed inheritances taken after specified dates.

Finally, the Capital Acquisitions Tax Consolidation Act 2003 was enacted on 21st February, 2003. This Consolidation Act has effect in relation to gifts and inheritances taken on or after 21st February, 2003, and embodies provisions relating, *inter alia*, to the once-off and annual discretionary trust tax charges imposed on or after that date. However, the Capital Acquisitions Tax Act, 1976, and its amendments, continue to apply to gifts and inheritances, including the two discretionary trust tax charges, arising prior to 21st February, 2003.

It is therefore essential, in order to assess gift tax on a particular gift, or inheritance tax on a particular inheritance, to apply the relevant legislation existing at the date of the gift or the inheritance. The object of this book is to enable the reader to do so, irrespective of when the particular gift or inheritance is taken. With this in mind, the book has been divided into five parts:

First Part   This Part should be consulted where the gift or inheritance is taken on or after 21st February, 2003. It sets out the capital acquisitions tax legislation, including the Capital Acquisitions Tax Consolidation Act 2003, and ancillary legislation, as currently in force after the enactment of the Finance Act 2009 on 3rd June, 2009. The footnotes to each section, where necessary, will show any amendments made to the section between 21st February, 2003, and 3rd June, 2009. Amendments contained in the Finance (No. 2) Act 2008, and in the Finance Act 2009, are shown in bold print. By using these footnotes, and knowing the date of the relevant gift or inheritance, the reader should be enabled to consult, in the Third Part, the legislation in operation at any time between those two dates.

In addition, a commentary has been added to certain sections in this Part, which it is hoped will assist the reader in the interpretation of these sections.

Second Part This Part should be consulted where the gift or inheritance is taken before 21st February, 2003. It sets out a non-statutory consolidation of the capital acquisitions tax legislation, including the Capital Acquisitions Tax Act, 1976, and ancillary legislation, in force immediately before 21st February, 2003.

However, sections of the Taxes Consolidation Act, 1997, refer to gift tax and inheritance tax, and it should be noted that amendments to this Act, contained in the Finance Acts 2003, 2004, 2005, 2006, 2007, 2008 and 2009, may affect gifts and inheritances taken before 21st February, 2003. Amendments contained in the Finance (No. 2) Act 2008, which in this Second Part affect only the Taxes Consolidation Act, 1997, are shown in bold print. In addition:

(i) section 81 of the Finance Act 2004 has amended section 55(3) of the Capital Acquisitions Tax, 1976, dealing with the exemption of heritage objects taken before 21st February, 2003, and

(ii) section 145(6) of the Finance Act 2005 has repealed section 41 of the Capital Acquisitions Tax Act, 1976, dealing with interest on tax with effect from 1st April, 2005.

The footnotes to each section, where necessary, will show what amendments have been made to the section. By using these footnotes, and knowing the date of the relevant gift or inheritance, the reader should be enabled to consult, in the Third Part, the legislation in operation at the relevant date.

Again, a commentary has been added to certain sections in this Part, which it is hoped will assist the reader in the interpretation of these actions.

Third Part This Part sets out, usually in their original unamended form, the Acts, Rules, Regulations and Orders which have a bearing on capital acquisitions tax.

Fourth Part Because the Taxes Consolidation Act, 1997, consolidated certain general tax provisions which also applied to capital acquisitions tax, it has been necessary to include a Fourth Part. This Fourth Part sets out a full consolidation of these general tax provisions in force on 6th April, 1997, on which date they were repealed and re-enacted in the Taxes Consolidation Act, 1997. Again, footnotes show how these general tax provisions evolved from the time they were enacted up to the time they were repealed on 6th April, 1997.

Fifth Part   Probate tax had effect in relation to persons dying after 17th June, 1993, but has been abolished in relation to persons dying on or after 6th December, 2000, by section 225 of the Finance Act, 2001. The Fifth Part sets out a full consolidation of the probate tax legislation as it existed immediately before its abolition. Once again, footnotes show how the probate tax legislation evolved from the time it was enacted up to the time it was abolished. A commentary has also been added to certain sections to assist in their interpretation.

It should be noted, however, that the rate of interest on unpaid probate tax, dealt with in section 117(b) of the Finance Act, 1993, has been amended by section 129(5) of the Finance Act, 2002, with effect from 1st September, 2002, to 31st March, 2005, and by section 145(6) of the Finance Act 2005 with effect from 1st April, 2005. Section 115 of the Finance Act, 1993 (incidence of tax) has also been amended by section 16 of the Courts and Court Officers Act, 2002, which, at the date of publication of this book, has not yet become operative.

The term "the Principal Act" is used in Finance Acts to denote various Acts. To avoid confusion, where "the Principal Act" appears in legislation, this book will show in its place the actual Act involved, for example, "[the Capital Acquisitions Tax Act, 1976]", "[the Capital Acquisitions Tax Consolidation Act 2003]" or "[the Taxes Consolidation Act, 1997]".

CONTENTS

TABLE OF CASES

TABLE OF STATUTORY REFERENCES

DESTINATION TABLE

LIST OF ABBREVIATIONS

FIRST PART

SECOND PART

THIRD PART

FOURTH PART

FIFTH PART

CONTENTS

TABLE OF CASES

The cases following are referred to in the footnotes and commentaries to the provisions of the Capital Acquisitions Tax Consolidation Act 2003 contained in the First Part of this book.

Each provision of the Capital Acquisitions Tax Consolidation Act 2003 contained in the First Part shows, under the section or Schedule number, the corresponding legislation source of that section or Schedule.

By using this source, one may trace where a case is referred to in the Second Part of this book. For example, *Balfour v Balfour* is referred to in section 28 of the Capital Acquisitions Tax Consolidation Act 2003, and in section 18 of the Capital Acquisitions Tax Act, 1976.

TABLE OF STATUTORY REFERENCES

The statutes following are referred to in the provisions of the Capital Acquisitions Tax Consolidation Act 2003 contained in the First Part of this book.

Each provision of the Capital Acquisitions Tax Consolidation Act 2003 contained in the First Part shows, under the section or Schedule number, the corresponding legislation source of that section or Schedule.

By using this source, one may trace where a statute is referred to in the Second Part of this book. For example, the Central Bank Act, 1971, s.2, is referred to in section 109 of the Capital Acquisitions Tax Consolidation Act 2003, and in section 61 of the Capital Acquisitions Tax Act, 1976.

NAME OF STATUTE   **SOURCE**

NAME OF STATUTE   **SOURCE**

NAME OF STATUTE.. **SOURCE**

DESTINATION TABLE

The table following shows the location, in the Capital Acquisitions Tax Consolidation Act 2003, of the earlier legislation applicable directly to capital acquisitions tax as it existed immediately before such earlier legislation was repealed on 21st February, 2003.

CAPITAL ACQUISITIONS TAX ACT, 1976

Provision of Earlier Act	Provision of CATCA	Remarks
s.1	s.1	Short title
s.2	s.2	Definition of "Collector" inserted in s.2, CATCA
		Section 2(5)(b), CATA, omitted from CATCA
s.3	s.3	
s.4	s.4	Section 4, CATA, shortened in s.4, CATCA
s.5	s.5	Section 5(1), CATA, restated in s.5(1), CATCA
		Section 121(1), FA 1993, as modified by s.147, FA 1994, contained in s.5(7), CATCA
s.6	s.6	Section 6(1), CATA, restated in s.6(1) and (2), CATCA
s.7	s.7	
s.8	s.8	
s.9	–	Repealed by s.110(2), FA 1984
s.10	s.9	Section 10, CATA, shortened in s.9, CATCA
s.11	s.10	Section 11(1), CATA, restated in s.10(1), CATCA
		Section 123(1), FA 1993, as modified by s.148, FA 1994, contained in s.10(4), CATCA
s.12	s.11	Section 12(1), CATA, restated in s.11(1) and (2), CATCA
s.13	s.12	
s.14	s.13	
s.15	s.26	
s.16	s.27	
s.17	–	Repealed by s.134, FA 1993
s.18	s.28	
s.19	s.89	
s.20	s.29	
s.21	s.30	
s.22	s.31	
s.23	s.32	
s.24	s.33	

Provision of Earlier Act	Provision of CATCA	Remarks
s.25	s.34	
s.26	s.35	
s.27	s.36	
s.28	s.37	
s.29	s.38	
s.30	s.39	
s.31	s.40	
s.32	s.41	
s.33	s.42	
s.34	s.43	
s.34A	s.105	
s.35	s.45	Section 81, FA 1989, contained in s.45(1)(b)(i), CATCA
s.36	s.46	
s.37	s.47	
s.38	s.48	
s.39	s.49	
s.40	s.50	
s.41	s.51	Section 76(2), FA 1989, contained in s.51(5), CATCA Section 41(7), CATA, unnecessary Section 41(9), CATA, substituted in s.64(2), CATCA
s.42	s.52	
s.43	s.54	
s.44	s.59	
s.45	s.56	
s.46	s.57	
s.47	s.60	
s.48	s.61	
s.49	s.63	
s.50	s.65	
s.51	s.66	

Provision of Earlier Act	Provision of CATCA	Remarks
s.52	s.67	
s.52A	s.68	
s.53	s.69	
s.54	s.76	
s.55	s.77	Section 39(1) and (1A), FA, 1978, contained in s.77(6) and (7), CATCA
s.56	s.80	
s.57	s.81	
s.58	s.82	
s.59	s.83	
s.59A	s.84	
s.59B	s.85	
s.59C	s.86	
s.59D	Sch. 2	Section 59D, CATA, contained in para. 9, Sch. 2, CATCA
s.59E	Sch. 2	Section 59E, CATA, contained in para. 10, Sch. 2, CATCA
s.60	s.108	
s.61	s.109	Section 61(6), CATA, omitted (obsolete)
s.62	s.110	
s.63	s.58	
s.64	s.111	
s.65	s.112	
s.66	s.106	
s.67	s.107	
s.68	s.113	
s.69	s.115	
s.70	s.114	
s.71	s.116	
s.72	s.117	
First Sch.	Sch. 1	

Provision of Earlier Act	Provision of CATCA	Remarks
Second Sch.	Sch. 2	

FINANCE ACT, 1978

Provision of Earlier Act	Provision of CATCA	Remarks
s.39	s.77	Section 39(1) and (1A), FA 1978, contained in s.77(6) and (7), CATCA

FINANCE ACT, 1982

Provision of Earlier Act	Provision of CATCA	Remarks
s.98	s.87	

FINANCE ACT, 1984

Provision of Earlier Act	Provision of CATCA	Remarks
s.104	s.14	Definition of "the Principal Act" unnecessary in s.14, CATCA
s.106	s.15	
s.107	s.16	
s.108	s.17	Section 17(1)(b), CATCA, contains s.129, FA 1990
s.109	s.18	Section 109, FA 1984, extended by s.143, FA 1994

FINANCE ACT, 1985

Provision of Earlier Act	Provision of CATCA	Remarks
s.59	s.71	
s.60	s.72	

Provision of Earlier Act	Provision of CATCA	Remarks
s.61	s.103	Section 61(3) and (4), FA 1985, unnecessary
s.63	s.104	

FINANCE ACT, 1986

Provision of Earlier Act	Provision of CATCA	Remarks
s.102	s.19	Definition of "the Principal Act" unnecessary in s.19, CATCA
s.103	s.20	
s.104	s.21	Section 104(f), FA 1986, unnecessary
s.105	s.22	
s.106	s.23	
s.107	s.24	
s.108	s.25	

FINANCE ACT, 1989

Provision of Earlier Act	Provision of CATCA	Remarks
s.75	s.49(8)	
s.76(2)	s.51(5)	
s.79	s.53	
s.81	s.45(2)(b)(i)	
s.85	s.75	Section 85(1) and (2), FA 1989, contained in s.75(1) and (2), CATCA
s.90	s.44	Section 90(11), FA 1989, unnecessary
		The provisions of s.127, FA 1993, (i) are included in the definition of "specified amount" in s.44(1), CATCA, and
		(ii) necessitate the insertion of s.44(2), CATCA, dealing with a "company controlled by the disponer"

FINANCE ACT, 1990

Provision of Earlier Act	Provision of CATCA	Remarks
s.127	s.70	
s.129	s.17(1)(b)	
s.130	s.72	

FINANCE ACT, 1991

Provision of Earlier Act	Provision of CATCA	Remarks
s.118	s.72	
s.119	s.73	
s.129	s.64	

FINANCE ACT, 1993

Provision of Earlier Act	Provision of CATCA	Remarks
s.121	s.5(7)	Section 121(1), FA 1993, as modified by s.147, FA 1994, contained in s.5(7), CATCA
s.123	s.10(4)	Section 123(1), FA 1993, as modified by s.148, FA 1994, contained in s.10(4), CATCA
s.127	s.44	
s.133	s.74	

FINANCE ACT, 1994

Provision of Earlier Act	Provision of CATCA	Remarks
s.124	s.90	
s.125	s.91	
s.126	s.92	
s.127	s.93	
s.128	s.94	
s.129	s.95	
s.130	s.96	

Provision of Earlier Act	Provision of CATCA	Remarks
s.131	s.97	
s.132	s.98	
s.133	s.99	
s.134	s.100	
s.135	s.101	
s.135A	s.102	
s.143	s.18	
s.146	s.62	
s.147	s.5(7)	Section 121(1), FA 1993, as modified by s.147, FA 1994, contained in s.5(7), CATCA
s.148	s.10(4)	Section 123(1), FA 1993, as modified by s.148, FA 1994, contained in s.10(4), CATCA

FINANCE ACT, 1995

Provision of Earlier Act	Provision of CATCA	Remarks
s.164	s.55	
s.165	s.79	
s.166	s.78	

FINANCE ACT, 1997

Provision of Earlier Act	Provision of CATCA	Remarks
s.142	s.88	

FINANCE ACT, 2001

Provision of Earlier Act	Provision of CATCA	Remarks
s.224	s.75	

LIST OF ABBREVIATIONS

CABA .... Criminal Assets Bureau Act, 1996

CAT .... capital acquisitions tax

CATA .... Capital Acquisitions Tax Act, 1976

CATCA .... Capital Acquisitions Tax Consolidation
Act 2003

DCITPA .... Disclosure of Certain Information for
Taxation and Other Purposes Act, 1996

FA .... Finance Act

ITA... Income Tax Act, 1967

para.. paragraph

s.. section

Sch .... Schedule

S.I... Statutory Instrument

TCA .... Taxes Consolidation Act, 1997

WCTIPA .... Waiver of Certain Tax, Interest and
Penalties Act, 1993

FIRST PART

This Part relates to gifts and inheritances taken on or after 21st February, 2003, and contains capital acquisitions tax legislation, as amended and extended, in force on 3rd June, 2009, the date of enactment of the Finance Act 2009. The legislation has been grouped under the following headings:

(I) CAPITAL ACQUISITIONS TAX CONSOLIDATION ACT 2003

PART 1
Preliminary

PART 2
Gift Tax

PART 3
Inheritance Tax

CHAPTER 1
General

PART 6
Returns and Assessments

PART 7
Payment and Recovery of Tax, Interest and Penalties

PART 10
Reliefs

CHAPTER 1
Agricultural Relief

CHAPTER 2
Business Relief

CHAPTER 2A
Clawback of Agricultural Relief or
Business Relief: Development Land

CHAPTER 3
Miscellaneous Reliefs

PART 11
Miscellaneous

(II) FINANCE ACT 2006

(III) DOUBLE TAXATION CONVENTIONS

(IV) MISCELLANEOUS PROVISIONS OF THE TAXES
CONSOLIDATION ACT, 1997

SECOND PART

This Part relates to gifts and inheritances taken before 21st February, 2003, and contains capital acquisitions tax legislation, as amended and extended, in force immediately prior to that date.
However:

(i)   section 81 of the Finance Act 2004 extends section 55(3) of the Capital Acquisitions Tax Act, 1976, to include the Commissioners of Public Works in Ireland as a body to whom a sale of heritage objects does not result in a clawback of tax where the sale to such body occurs on or after 1st August, 1994, and

(ii)   section 145(6) of the Finance Act 2005 has repealed section 41 of the Capital Acquisitions Tax Act, 1976, with effect from 1st April, 2005, to the extent that such section 41 applies to interest chargeable or payable on gift tax and inheritance tax that has not been paid before that date, regardless of when that tax became due and payable.

In addition, as shown below at (vii), miscellaneous provisions of the Taxes Consolidation Act, 1997, apply to gift tax and inheritance tax, and amendments to these provisions, contained in the Finance Acts 2003, 2004, 2005, 2006, 2007 and 2008, may affect gifts and inheritances taken before 21st February, 2003.

For ease of reference, the legislation in this Part has been grouped under the following headings –

(I) GIFT /INHERITANCE TAX

CAPITAL ACQUISITIONS TAX ACT, 1976

PART I
Preliminary

PART II
Gift Tax

PART III
Inheritance Tax

PART IV
Value of Property for Tax

PART V
Provisions relating to Gifts and Inheritances

PART VI
Returns and Assessments

PART VII
Payment and Recovery of Tax

THIRD PART

This Part contains, in order of enactment, Acts, Rules, Regulations and Orders dealing directly or indirectly with capital acquisitions tax. It includes the Capital Acquisitions Tax Act, 1976, the Capital Acquisitions Tax Consolidation Act 2003, and other legislation up to and including the Finance (No. 2) Act 2008, which was enacted on 24th December, 2008. The Finance Act 2009 has no effect on this Part. These Acts, Rules, Regulations and Orders are as enacted and before subsequent amendments, save in relation to a small number of pre-CAT enactments, which are in their final form.

(I) ACTS

FINANCE ACT, 2001

FOURTH PART

This Part contains sections enacted in various Finance Acts, which sections are relevant to taxes in general, including capital acquisitions tax as contained in the Capital Acquisitions Tax Act, 1976. These sections are shown, as and where amended, as they existed on 6th April, 1997, on which date they were repealed and re-enacted in the Taxes Consolidation Act, 1997.

FIFTH PART

Probate tax was introduced in Chapter I, Part VI, of the Finance Act, 1993, and had effect in relation to persons dying after 17th June, 1993. The tax was imposed in the form of an inheritance tax on an absolute interest in a deceased person's estate deemed to be taken by his personal representatives, and was governed by the Capital Acquisitions Tax Act, 1976.

This Fifth Part contains sections of the various Finance Acts relating to probate tax, as and where amended, as they existed immediately before probate tax was abolished by section 225 of the Finance Act, 2001, in relation to persons dying on or after 6th December, 2000. However:

(i)   section 117(b) of the Finance Act, 1993, dealing with the rate of interest on unpaid tax, has been amended by section 129(5) of the Finance Act, 2002, with effect from 1st September, 2002, to 31st March 2005, and by section 145(5) of the Finance Act, 2005, with effect from 1st April, 2005, and

(ii)   section 115 of the Finance Act, 1993, dealing with the incidence of probate tax, has been amended by section 16 of the Courts and Court Officers Act, 2002, which, at the date of publication of this book, has not yet become operative.

PROBATE TAX

CAPITAL ACQUISITIONS TAX ACT, 1976

FIRST PART

This Part relates to gifts and inheritances taken on or after 21st February, 2003, and contains capital acquisitions tax legislation, as amended and extended, in force on 3rd June, 2009, the date of enactment of the Finance Act 2009, The legislation has been grouped under the following headings:

For Contents of this Part, see page xxxv

(c)   in the case of a benefit under Part IX or section 56 of the Succession Act 1965, the date of death of the relevant testator or other deceased person, and correspondingly in the case of an analogous benefit under the law of another territory,

(d)   in the case of a disposition which consists of the failure to exercise a right or a power, the date of the latest time when the disponer could have exercised the right or the power if that disponer were *sui juris* and not under any physical disability, and

(e)   in any other case, the date on which the act (or where more than one act is involved, the last act) of the disponer was done by which that disponer provided or bound that disponer to provide the property comprised in the disposition;

"date of the gift" means the date of the happening of the event on which the donee, or any person in right of the donee or on that donee's behalf, becomes beneficially entitled in possession to the benefit, and a reference to the time when a gift is taken is construed as a reference to the date of the gift;

"date of the inheritance" means—

(a)   in the case where the successor or any person in right of the successor or on that successor's behalf becomes entitled in possession to the benefit on the happening of any such event as is referred to in section 3(2), the date of the event,

(b)   in the case of a gift which becomes an inheritance by reason of its being taken under a disposition where the date of the disposition is within 2 years prior to the death of the disponer, the date which would have been the date of the gift if the entitlement were a gift, and

(c)   in any other case, the date of the latest death which had to occur for the successor, or any person in right of the successor or on that successor's behalf, to become beneficially entitled in possession to the benefit,

and a reference to the time when an inheritance is taken is construed as a reference to the date of the inheritance;

"discretionary trust" means any trust whereby, or by virtue or in consequence of which—

(a)   property is held on trust to accumulate the income or part of the income of the property, or

(b)   property (other than property to which for the time being a person is beneficially entitled for an interest in possession) is held on trust to apply, or with a power to apply, the income or capital or part of the income or capital of the property for the benefit of any person or persons or of any one or more of a number or of a class of persons whether at the discretion of trustees or any other person and notwithstanding that there may be a power to accumulate all or any part of the income;

"disponer", in relation to a disposition, means the person who, for the purpose of the disposition, directly or indirectly provided the property comprised in the disposition, and in any case where more than one person provided the property each is deemed to be the disponer to the extent that that disponer so provided the property; and for the purposes of this definition —

(a) the testator is the disponer in the case of a disposition referred to in paragraph (k) of the definition of "disposition",

(b) the intestate is the disponer in the case of a disposition referred to in paragraph (l) of that definition,

(c) the deceased person referred to in paragraph (m) of that definition is the disponer in the case of a disposition referred to in that paragraph, and

(d) a person who has made with any other person a reciprocal arrangement by which that other person provided property comprised in the disposition is deemed to have provided that property;

"disposition" includes —

(a) any act or omission by a person as a result of which the value of that person's estate immediately after the act or omission is less than it would be but for the act or omission,

(b) any trust, covenant, agreement or arrangement, whether made by a single operation or by associated operations,

(c) the creation of a debt or other right enforceable against the disponer personally or against any estate or interest that disponer may have in property,

(d) the payment of money,

(e) the allotment of shares in a company,

(f) the grant or the creation of any benefit,

(g) the grant or the creation of any lease, mortgage, charge, licence, option, power, partnership or joint tenancy or other estate or interest in or over any property,

(h) the release, forfeiture, surrender or abandonment of any debt or benefit, or the failure to exercise a right, and, for the purpose of this paragraph, a debt or benefit is deemed to have been released when it has become unenforceable by action through lapse of time (except to the extent that it is recovered subsequent to its becoming so unenforceable),

(i) the exercise of a general power of appointment in favour of any person other than the holder of the power,

(j) a *donatio mortis causa*,

(k)   a will or other testamentary disposition,

(l)   an intestacy, whether total or partial,

(m)   the payment of a share as a legal right under Part IX of the Succession Act 1965, to a deceased person's spouse, or the making of provision for a widow or child of a deceased person under section 56 or section 117 of the Succession Act 1965, or an analogous share or provision paid or made on the death of a deceased person to or for the benefit of any person under the law of another territory, and

(n)   a resolution passed by a company which is deemed by subsection (3) to be a disposition;

"donee" means a person who takes a gift;

"entitled in possession" means having a present right to the enjoyment of property as opposed to having a future such right, and without prejudice to the generality of the foregoing a person is also, for the purposes of this Act, deemed to be entitled in possession to an interest or share in a partnership, joint tenancy or estate of a deceased person, in which that person is a partner, joint tenant or beneficiary, as the case may be, but that person is not deemed to be entitled in possession to an interest in expectancy until an event happens whereby this interest ceases to be an interest in expectancy;[2]

"general power of appointment" includes every power, right, or authority whether exercisable only by will or otherwise which would enable the holder of such power, right, or authority to appoint or dispose of property to whoever the holder thinks fit or to obtain such power, right or authority, but exclusive of any power exercisable solely in a fiduciary capacity under a disposition not made by the holder, or exercisable by a tenant for life under the Settled Land Act 1882, or as mortgagee;

"gift" means a gift which a person is by this Act deemed to take;

["the Income Tax Acts" has the meaning assigned to it by section 2 of the Taxes Consolidation Act 1997;][6]

"inheritance" means an inheritance which a person is by this Act deemed to take;

"interest in expectancy" includes an estate in remainder or reversion and every other future interest, whether vested or contingent, but does not include a reversion expectant on the determination of a lease;

"limited interest" means—

(a)   an interest (other than a leasehold interest) for the duration of a life or lives or for a period certain, or

(b)   any other interest which is not an absolute interest;

"local authority" has the meaning assigned to it by section 2(1) of the Local Government Act 2001 and includes a body established under the Local Government Services (Corporate Bodies) Act 1971;

"market value", in relation to property, means the market value of that property ascertained in accordance with sections 26 and 27;

"minor child" means a child who has not attained the age of 18 years and is not and has not been married;

"personal property" means any property other than real property;

"personal representative" means the executor or administrator for the time being of a deceased person and includes –

(a) any person who takes possession of or intermeddles with the property of a deceased person,

(b) any person having, in relation to the deceased person, under the law of another country, any functions corresponding to the functions, for administration purposes under the law of the State, of an executor or administrator;

"property" includes rights and interests of any description;

"real property" means real and chattel real property;

"regulations" means regulations made under section 116;

"relative" means a relative within the meaning of subsection (4);

"return" means such a return as is referred to in section 46;

"share"[3], in relation to a company, includes any interest whatever in the company which is analogous to a share in the company, and "shareholder" shall be construed accordingly;

"special power of appointment" means a power of appointment which is not a general power of appointment;

"successor" means a person who takes an inheritance;

"tax" means any tax chargeable under this Act;

["the Tax Acts" has the meaning assigned to it by section 2 of the Taxes Consolidation Act 1997;][7]

"valuation date" has the meaning assigned to it by section 30;

"year of assessment" has the meaning assigned to it by section 2 of the Taxes Consolidation Act 1997.

(2) For the purpose of the definition of "general power of appointment" contained in subsection (1), a person is deemed to have a general power of appointment –

(a) notwithstanding that the person is not *sui juris* or is under a physical disability,

(b) over money which the person has a general power to charge on property, and

(b)   under a disposition where the date of the disposition is the date of the death of the disponer,

(c)   under a disposition where the date of the disposition is on or after 1 April 1975 and within 2 years prior to the death of the disponer, or

(d)   on the happening, after the cesser of an intervening life interest, of any such event as is referred to in subsection (2).

(2)   The events referred to in subsection (1)(d) are any of the following –

(a)   the determination or failure of any charge, estate, interest or trust,

(b)   the exercise of a special power of appointment,

(c)   in the case where a benefit was given under a disposition in such terms that the amount or value of the benefit could only be ascertained from time to time by the actual payment or application of property for the purpose of giving effect to the benefit, the making of any payment or the application of the property, or

(d)   any other event which, under a disposition, affects the right to property, or to the enjoyment of that property.

Cross-Reference

1   S.3(2) is referred to in the definition of "date of the inheritance" in s.2(1), CATCA.

PART 2

Gift Tax

Section 4

[S.4, CATA - part]

Charge of gift tax.

4.   A capital acquisitions tax, to be called gift tax and to be computed in accordance with this Act, shall, subject to this Act and any regulations made under the Act, be charged, levied and paid on the taxable value of every taxable gift taken by a donee.

Section 5

[S.5, CATA, as amended, s.121, FA 1993, and s.147, FA 1994]

Gift deemed to be taken.

5.   (1)   For the purposes of this Act, a person is deemed to take a gift, where, under or in consequence of any disposition, a person becomes beneficially entitled in possession, otherwise than on a death, to

---

any benefit (whether or not the person becoming so entitled already has any interest in the property in which such person takes such benefit), otherwise than for full consideration in money or money's worth paid by such person.

(2) A gift is deemed —

    (a) to consist of the whole or the appropriate part, as the case may be, of the property in which the donee takes a benefit, or on which the benefit is charged or secured or on which the donee is entitled to have it charged or secured, and

    (b) if the benefit is an annuity or other periodic payment which is not charged on or secured by any property and which the donee is not entitled to have so charged or secured, to consist of such sum as would, if invested on the date of the gift in the security of the Government which was issued last before that date for subscription in the State and is redeemable not less than 10 years after the date of issue, yield, on the basis of the current yield on the security, an annual income equivalent to the annual value of the annuity or of the other periodic payment receivable by the donee.

(3) For the purposes of section 6(1)(c) and 6(2)(d), the sum referred to in subsection (2)(b) is deemed not to be situate in the State at the date of the gift.

(4) Where a person makes a disposition under which a relative of the person becomes beneficially entitled in possession to any benefit, the creation or disposition in favour of the person of an annuity or other interest limited to cease on the death, or at a time ascertainable only by reference to the death, of the person, shall not be treated for the purposes of this section as consideration for the grant of such benefit or of any part of such benefit.

(5) For the purposes of this Act, "appropriate part", in relation to property referred to in subsection (2), means that part of the entire property in which the benefit subsists, or on which the benefit is charged or secured, or on which the donee is entitled to have it so charged or secured, which bears the same proportion to the entire property as the gross annual value of the benefit bears to the gross annual value of the entire property, and the gift shall be deemed to consist of the appropriate part of each and every item of property comprised in the entire property.

(6) (a) Where a contract or agreement was entered into, under or as a consequence of which a person acquired the right, otherwise than for full consideration in money or money's worth, to have a benefit transferred to that person, or to another in that person's right or on that person's behalf, and an act or acts is or are done, on or after that date, in pursuance of, or in performance or satisfaction, whether in whole or in part, of such contract or agreement, then the gift or inheritance, as the

case may be, taken by or in right or on behalf of that person, is deemed to have been taken, not when the right was acquired, but either—

    (i)   when the benefit was transferred to that person or to another in that person's right or on that person's behalf, or

    (ii) when that person or another in that person's right or on that person's behalf became beneficially entitled in possession to the benefit,

whichever is the later.

  (b) In this subsection, a reference to a contract or agreement does not include a reference to a contract or agreement—

    (i)   which is a complete grant, transfer, assignment or conveyance, or

    (ii) which was enforceable by action.

(7) (a) In paragraph (b), the expression "shares in a private company" shall be construed by reference to the meanings that "share" and "private company" have, respectively, in section 27.

    (b) Where a person becomes beneficially entitled in possession to a benefit, and the property in which the benefit is taken consists wholly or partly of shares in a private company and where the consideration referred to in subsection (1), being consideration in relation to a disposition, could not reasonably be regarded (taking into account the disponer's position prior to the disposition) as representing full consideration to the disponer for having made such a disposition, subsection (1) is deemed to apply as if "otherwise than for full consideration in money or money's worth paid by such person" were deleted in that subsection.

Commentary

A   As to "full consideration in money or money's worth paid by the disponer", see *AG v Boden* [1912] IKB 539 and *AG v Ralli* [1936] 15 ATC.

B   As to successive interests in a trust fund received by the same beneficiary, see *Jacob v Revenue Commissioners* 3 ITR 104.

C   See Part 19.18 of the *Revenue CAT Manual* in relation to Co-Directors and Business Partners Assurance. These are policies effected purely for commercial purposes and agreed between the individual shareholders/partners on an arm's-length basis, without any intention of conferring a benefit. The approach to such policies, written in the form of own life in trust for others, is to treat the proceeds as exempt from gift tax on the basis of "full consideration".

Cross-References

1   The "sum" in s.5(2)(b) is also the "sum" for the purposes of s.37(2)(ii), CATCA.

2   The definition of "appropriate part" in s.5(5) is also used in s.37(1), CATCA, s.86(1)(a), CATCA and para. 7(1), Part 1, Sch. 2, CATCA.

Section 6

[S.6, CATA, as amended]

Taxable gift.

6. (1) In relation to a gift taken under a disposition, where the date of the disposition is before 1 December 1999, "taxable gift" in this Act means—

   (a) in the case of a gift, other than a gift taken under a discretionary trust, where the disponer is domiciled in the State at the date of the disposition under which the donee takes the gift, the whole of the gift,

   (b) in the case of a gift taken under a discretionary trust where the disponer is domiciled in the State at the date of the disposition under which the donee takes the gift or at the date of the gift or was (in the case of a gift taken after that [disponer's]¹ death) so domiciled at the time of that [disponer's]¹ death, the whole of the gift, and

   (c) in any other case, so much of the property of which the gift consists as is situate in the State at the date of the gift.

   (2) In relation to a gift taken under a disposition, where the date of the disposition is on or after 1 December 1999, "taxable gift" in this Act means—

   (a) in the case of a gift, other than a gift taken under a discretionary trust, where the disponer is resident or ordinarily resident in the State at the date of the disposition under which the donee takes the gift, the whole of the gift,

   (b) in the case of a gift taken under a discretionary trust where the disponer is resident or ordinarily resident in the State at the date of the disposition under which the donee takes the gift or at the date of the gift or was (in the case of a gift taken after the death of the disponer) so resident or ordinarily resident at the date of that death, the whole of the gift,

   (c) in the case where the donee is resident or ordinarily resident in the State at the date of the gift, the whole of the gift, and

   (d) in any other case, so much of the property of which the gift consists as is situate in the State at the date of the gift.

   (3) For the purposes of subsections (1)(c) and (2)(d), a right to the proceeds of sale of property is deemed to be situate in the State to the extent that such property is unsold and situate in the State.

   (4) For the purposes of subsection (2), a person who is not domiciled in the State on a particular date is treated as not resident and not ordinarily resident in the State on that date unless—

   (a) that date occurs on or after 1 December 2004,

   (b) that person has been resident in the State for the 5 consecutive years of assessment immediately preceding the year of assessment in which that date falls, and

        (c)   that person is either resident or ordinarily resident in the State on that date.

(5)   (a)   In this subsection—

"company" and "share" have the same meaning as they have in section 27;

"company controlled by the donee" has the same meaning as is assigned to "company controlled by the donee or successor" by section 27.

[(b)   For the purposes of subsection (2)(d), so much of the market value of any share in a private company incorporated outside the State (which after taking the gift is a company controlled by the donee) as is attributable, directly or indirectly, to property situate in the State at the date of the gift shall be deemed to be a sum situate in the State.][2]

(c)   Paragraph (b) shall not apply in a case where the disponer was domiciled outside the State at all times up to and including the date of the gift or, in the case of a gift taken after the death of the disponer, up to and including the date of that death or where the share in question is actually situate in the State at the date of the gift.

Footnotes

1   Substituted for "donee's" by para. 2(b), Sch. 3, FA 2004, with effect as on and from 21st February, 2003, under para. 5(b) of that Sch.

2   As substituted by s.113, FA 2006, in relation to gifts taken on or after 2nd February, 2006.

Commentary

A   For analysis of "taxable gift", see the decision of the Appeal Commissioner under reference 25 AC 2000. Before that appeal was reheard in the Circuit Court, the taxpayer paid the tax due.

B   See an article on the Scope of Capital Acquisitions Tax by Ann Williams in the *Irish Tax Review* of May 2001, page 269.

Section 7

[S.7, CATA]

Liability to gift tax in respect of gift taken by joint tenants.

7.   The liability to gift tax in respect of a gift taken by persons as joint tenants is the same in all respects as if they took the gift as tenants in common in equal shares.

Section 8

[S.8, CATA]

Disponer in certain connected dispositions.

8.   (1)   Where a donee takes a gift under a disposition made by a disponer (in this section referred to as the original disponer) and, within the period commencing 3 years before and ending 3 years after the date of that gift, the donee makes a disposition under which a second donee takes a gift and whether or not the second donee makes a disposition within the same period under which a third donee takes a gift, and so on, each donee is deemed to take a gift from the original disponer (and not from the immediate disponer under whose disposition the gift was taken); and a gift so deemed to be taken is deemed to be an inheritance (and not a gift) taken by the donee, as successor, from the original disponer if —

(a)   the original disponer dies within 2 years after the date of the disposition made by that original disponer, and

(b)   the date of the disposition was on or after 1 April 1975.

       (2)   This section shall not apply in the case of any disposition (in this subsection referred to as the first-mentioned disposition) in so far as no other disposition, which was connected in the manner described in subsection (1) with such first-mentioned disposition, was made with a view to enabling or facilitating the making of the first-mentioned disposition or the recoupment in any manner of the cost of such first-mentioned disposition.

Commentary

A   See Part 19.16 of the *Revenue CAT Manual*. In cases, for example, where a gift (the first gift) is taken by a married child of the disponer and consists of a house, or a site for a house, and that married child, in raising a mortgage on that property finds that the lending institution, as a requirement for the mortgage, demands that the property is placed in the joint names of the spouses (the second gift), then, provided adequate evidence of that requirement is forthcoming, Revenue will accept that such gifts are not connected for the purposes of s.8.

and 20(1)) is resident or ordinarily resident in the State at the date of the inheritance, the whole of the inheritance, and

(c)   in any case, other than a case referred to in paragraph (a) or (b), where at the date of the inheritance –

(i)   the whole of the property –

(I)   which was to be appropriated to the inheritance, or

(II)   out of which property was to be appropriated to the inheritance,

was situate in the State, the whole of the inheritance;

(ii)   a part or proportion of the property –

(I)   which was to be appropriated to the inheritance, or

(II)   out of which property was to be appropriated to the inheritance,

was situate in the State, that part or proportion of the inheritance.

(3)   For the purposes of subsections (1)(b) and (2)(c) –

(a)   "property which was to be appropriated to the inheritance" and "property out of which property was to be appropriated to the inheritance" shall not include any property which was not applicable to satisfy the inheritance, and

(b)   a right to the proceeds of sale of property is deemed to be situate in the State to the extent that such property is unsold and situate in the State.

(4)   For the purposes of subsection (2), a person who is not domiciled in the State on a particular date is treated as not resident and not ordinarily resident in the State on that date unless –

(a)   that date occurs on or after 1 December 2004,

(b)   that person has been resident in the State for the 5 consecutive years of assessment immediately preceding the year of assessment in which that date falls, and

(c)   that person is either resident or ordinarily resident in the State on that date.

(5)   (a)   In this subsection –

"company" and "share" have the same meaning as they have in section 27;

"company controlled by the donee" has the same meaning as is assigned to "company controlled by the donee or successor" by section 27.

[(b)   For the purposes of subsection (2)(c), so much of the market value of any share in a private company incorporated outside the State (which after taking the inheritance is a company controlled by the successor) as is attributable, directly or indirectly, to property situate in the State at the date of the inheritance shall be deemed to be a sum situate in the State.][1]

(c) Paragraph (b) shall not apply in a case where the disponer was not domiciled in the State at the date of the disposition under which the successor takes the inheritance or where the share in question is actually situate in the State at the date of the inheritance.

Footnote

1   As substituted by s.114, FA 2006, in relation to inheritances taken on or after 2nd February, 2006.

Commentary

A   The Appeal Commissioner decision (reference 25 AC 2000), dealing with a "taxable gift", is also relevant to a "taxable inheritance". Before that appeal was reheard in the Circuit Court, the taxpayer paid all the tax due.

B   See an article on the Scope of Capital Acquisitions Tax by Ann Williams in the *Irish Tax Review* of May 2001, page 269.

Section 12

[S.13, CATA]

Disclaimer.

12.   (1)   If—

(a)   (i)   a benefit under a will or an intestacy, or

(ii)   an entitlement to an interest in settled property,

is disclaimed;

(b)   a claim—

(i)   under a purported will in respect of which a grant of representation (within the meaning of the Succession Act 1965) was not issued, or

(ii)   under an alleged intestacy where a will exists in respect of which such a grant was issued,

is waived; or

(c)   a right under Part IX of the Succession Act 1965, or any analogous right under the law of another territory, is renounced, disclaimed, elected against or lapses,

any liability to tax in respect of such benefit, entitlement, claim or right shall cease as if such benefit, entitlement, claim or right, as the case may be, had not existed.

(2)   Notwithstanding anything contained in this Act—

(a)   a disclaimer of a benefit under a will or intestacy or of an entitlement to an interest in settled property;

(b) the waiver of a claim—

    (i) under a purported will in respect of which a grant of representation (within the meaning of the Succession Act 1965) was not issued, or

    (ii) under an alleged intestacy where a will exists in respect of which such a grant issued; or

(c) (i) the renunciation or disclaimer of,

    (ii) the election against, or

    (iii) the lapse of,

a right under Part IX of the Succession Act 1965, or any analogous right under the law of another territory,

is not a disposition for the purposes of this Act.

(3) Subsection (1) shall not apply to the extent of the amount of any consideration in money or money's worth received for the disclaimer, renunciation, election or lapse or for the waiver of a claim; and the receipt of such consideration is deemed to be a gift or an inheritance, as the case may be, in respect of which no consideration was paid by the donee or successor and which was derived from the disponer who provided the property in relation to which the benefit, entitlement, claim or right referred to in subsection (1), arose.

Commentary

A   Contrast s.142, UK Inheritance Tax Act, 1984.

B   As a general rule, a beneficiary may disclaim one of several separate legacies but a part of one legacy may not be disclaimed – see *Parnell v Boyd* [1896] 2 IR 571.

C   As to a disclaimer on intestacy, see s.72A, Succession Act, 1965, inserted by s.6, Family Law (Miscellaneous Provisions) Act, 1997, reproduced on page 678.

D   See Part 19.3 of the *Revenue CAT Manual* which deals with the Revenue practice where the State, as the ultimate intestate successor under s.73, Succession Act, 1965, waives its right in favour of a person.

E   See two articles on the Post Death Variation of Estates by Finola O'Hanlon and Anne Stephenson in the *Irish Tax Review* of May 2004 (page 232) and July 2004 (page 311).

F   See an article on disclaimers by Lorna Gallagher at page 78 of the *Irish Tax Review* of July 2007.

Section 13

[S.14, CATA]

Surviving joint tenant deemed to take an inheritance, etc.

13. (1) On the death of one of several persons who are beneficially and absolutely entitled in possession as joint tenants, the surviving joint tenant or surviving joint tenants is or are deemed to take an inheritance of the share of the deceased joint tenant, as successor or successors from the deceased joint tenant as disponer.

(2) The liability to inheritance tax in respect of an inheritance taken by persons as joint tenants is the same in all respects as if they took the inheritance as tenants in common in equal shares.

CHAPTER 2
Initial Levy on Discretionary Trusts

Section 14

[S.104, FA 1984]

Interpretation (Chapter 2).

14. In this Chapter—

"object", in relation to a discretionary trust, means a person for whose benefit the income or capital, or any part of the income or capital, of the trust property is applied, or may be applied;

"principal objects", in relation to a discretionary trust, means such objects, if any, of the trust for the time being as are—

(a) the spouse of the disponer,

(b) the children of the disponer, or

(c) the children of a child of the disponer where such child predeceased the disponer.

Commentary

A   See an article on discretionary trust tax by Eamon O'Connor in the *Irish Tax Review* of November 1997, page 561.

Section 15

[S.106, FA 1984, as amended]

Acquisitions by discretionary trusts.

15. (1) Where, on or after 25 January 1984, under or in consequence of any disposition, property becomes subject to a discretionary trust, the trust is deemed, on—

(a) the date on which that property becomes or became subject to the discretionary trust,

(b) the date of death of the disponer, or

(c) where there are principal objects of the trust, the date on which there ceases to be a principal object of the trust who is —

    (i) under the age of 25 years, where the property became subject to the trust on or after 25 January 1984 and before 31 January 1993, or

    (ii) under the age of 21 years, where the property becomes or became subject to the trust on or after 31 January 1993,

whichever date is the latest, to become or to have become beneficially entitled in possession to an absolute interest in so much, if any, of that property or of property representing that property and of accumulations of income of that property or of property representing those accumulations as remains subject to the discretionary trust on that latest date, and to take or to have taken an inheritance accordingly as if the trust, and the trustees as such for the time being of the trust, were together a person for the purposes of this Act, and that latest date shall be the date of the inheritance.

(2) Property which, under or in consequence of any disposition, was subject to a discretionary trust on 25 January 1984 is, for the purposes of subsection (1), deemed to have become subject to the trust on that date.

(3) Property which, under or in consequence of any disposition, was subject to a discretionary trust on 31 January 1993 is, for the purposes of subsection (1), deemed to have become subject to the trust on that date.

(4) For the purposes of this section —

(a) an interest in expectancy is not property until an event happens whereby the interest ceases to be an interest in expectancy or is represented by property which is not an interest in expectancy,

(b) an interest in a policy of assurance on human life is not property until, and then only to the extent that, the interest becomes an interest in possession under section 41 or is represented by property which is not an interest in expectancy.

(5) Where, apart from this subsection, property or property representing such property would be chargeable under this section, or under this section and the corresponding provisions of the repealed enactments, with tax more than once under the same disposition, such property is so chargeable with tax once only, that is, on the earliest occasion on which such property would become so chargeable with tax.

Commentary

A   See an Irish High Court case, *Revenue Commissioners v Executors and Trustees of the will of Jeannie Hammett Irvine, deceased* [2005] No. 172 R, which decided that the bequest of the residue of an estate to a discretionary trust does not become subject to the trust until the residue is ascertained. This case is discussed by Paraic Madigan at page 70 of the *Irish Tax Review* of September 2007.

Cross-Reference

1   See s.44(11) CATCA, which extends to "related shares" the charge for tax arising under s.15.

Section 16

[S.107, FA 1984, as amended]

Application of this Act.

16.   In relation to a charge for tax arising by reason of section 15 —

(a)   a reference in section 27 to a company controlled by the successor and the definition in that section of "group of shares" is construed as if (for the purpose of that reference) the list of persons contained in subsection (3) of that section and (for the purpose of that definition) the list of persons contained in that definition included the following, that is, the trustees of the discretionary trust, the living objects of the discretionary trust, the relatives of those objects, nominees of those trustees or of those objects or of the relatives of those objects, and the trustees of a settlement whose objects include the living objects of the discretionary trust or relatives of those living objects,

(b)   section 30 shall apply, with the modification that the valuation date of the taxable inheritance is —

(i)   the date of the inheritance, or

(ii)   the valuation date ascertained in accordance with that section,

whichever is the later, and with any other necessary modifications;

(c)   a person who is a trustee of the discretionary trust concerned for the time being at the date of the inheritance or at any date subsequent to that date is a person primarily accountable for the payment of the tax;

(d)   an object of the discretionary trust concerned to whom or for whose benefit any of the property subject to the trust is applied or appointed is also accountable for the payment of tax the charge in respect of which has arisen prior to the date of the application or appointment of the property to that person or for that person's benefit, and this Act shall apply, in its application to that charge for tax, as if that object of the discretionary trust were a person referred to in section 45(2); and

(e)   section 45(1), sections 50, 56 and 81 and Schedule 2 shall not apply.

---

relevant period to an absolute interest in the entire of the property of which that inheritance consisted on and at all times after the date of that inheritance (other than property which ceased to be subject to the terms of the appropriate trust by virtue of a sale or exchange of an absolute interest in that property for full consideration in money or money's worth), then, in relation to all such earlier relevant inheritances, all such settled relevant inheritances, all such will trust relevant inheritances or all such later relevant inheritances, as the case may be, the tax so chargeable is computed at the rate of 3 per cent.][4]

(4) Where 2 or more persons are together beneficially entitled in possession to an absolute interest in property, those persons shall not, by reason only that together they are beneficially so entitled in possession, be regarded for the purposes of subsection (3) as beneficially so entitled in possession.

[(5) Notwithstanding section 57, interest shall not be payable on any repayment of tax which arises by virtue of subsection (3).][1]

Footnotes

1   Deleted by s.145(1)(a), FA 2003, which section will come into effect by Ministerial Order. S.I. No. 515 of 2003 (see page 1379) appoints 1st November, 2003, as the date on which s.145(1)(a), FA 2003, comes into operation. See also s.153, FA 2003.

2   As substituted by s.113(1)(a), FA 2007, which applies to inheritances deemed to be taken on or after 1st February, 2007.

3   As substituted by s.113(1)(b), FA 2007, which applies to inheritances deemed to be taken on or after 1st February, 2007.

4   As substituted by s.113(1)(c), FA 2007, which applies to inheritances deemed to be taken on or after 1st February, 2007.

CHAPTER 3
Annual Levy on Discretionary Trusts

Section 19
[S.102, FA 1986, as amended]

Interpretation (Chapter 3).

19.   In this Chapter —

["chargeable date", in relation to any year, means —

(a)   in respect of the year 2006, 5 April and 31 December in that year, and

(b)   in respect of the year 2007 and subsequent years, 31 December in the year concerned;][1]

"chargeable discretionary trust" means a discretionary trust in relation to which —

(a)   the disponer is dead, and

(b) none of the principal objects of the trust, if any, is under the age of 21 years;

"object" and "principal objects", in relation to a discretionary trust, have the meanings respectively assigned to them by section 14.

Footnote

1   As substituted by s.116(1)(a), FA 2006, as respects the year 2006 and subsequent years.

Commentary

A   See an article on discretionary trust tax by Eamon O'Connor in the *Irish Tax Review* of November 1997, page 561.

Section 20

[S.103, FA 1986]

Annual acquisitions by discretionary trusts.

20. (1) Where, in any year commencing with the year 2003, under or in consequence of any disposition, property is subject to a chargeable discretionary trust on the chargeable date, the trust is deemed on each such date to become beneficially entitled in possession to an absolute interest in that property, and to take on each such date an inheritance accordingly as if the trust, and the trustees as such for the time being of the trust, were together a person for the purposes of this Act, and each such chargeable date shall be the date of such inheritance.

(2) (a) In this subsection, "property" includes property representing such property.

(b) Where—

(i) under or in consequence of any disposition, property was subject to a discretionary trust prior to a chargeable date,

(ii) that property is not on that chargeable date subject to that discretionary trust (being on that date a chargeable discretionary trust) because such property is on that date property to which for the time being a person is beneficially entitled for an interest in possession, and

(iii) on that chargeable date that property is property which is limited to become subject again to that chargeable discretionary trust, or will do so by the exercise of a power of revocation,

that property is deemed to be subject to that chargeable discretionary trust on that chargeable date if that interest in possession is an interest which is revocable or which is limited to cease on an event other than—

(I) the death of that person, or

Section 24

[S.107, FA 1986]

Values agreed.

24. (1) Where—

    (a) under or in consequence of any disposition, a charge for tax arises by reason of section 20 on a chargeable date (in this section called the first chargeable date),

    (b) an accountable person has furnished all the information necessary to enable the Commissioners to ascertain the market value of—

        (i) real property, or

        (ii) shares which are not dealt in on a stock exchange,

        comprised in the taxable inheritance so taken on the valuation date of that taxable inheritance,

    (c) pursuant to an application in writing to the Commissioners on that behalf, the market value of such property on that valuation date is agreed on between that person and the Commissioners,

    (d) under or in consequence of the same disposition, a charge for tax arises by reason of section 20 on either or both of the 2 chargeable dates in the years next following the year in which the first chargeable date occurs (in this section called the subsequent chargeable dates), and

    (e) the same property at subparagraph (i) or (ii) of paragraph (b) is comprised in the taxable inheritances so taken on the subsequent chargeable dates,

the value so agreed on is treated for the purposes of this Chapter as the market value of such property on that valuation date and on the valuation dates of the taxable inheritances so taken on the subsequent chargeable dates.

[(1A) Where the market value of property is on a valuation date determined in accordance with subsection (1) and that valuation date is 5 April 2006, then that market value as so determined shall be treated as the market value of the property on the valuation date that is 31 December 2006.][1]

(2) Notwithstanding subsection (1), the market value so agreed is not binding—

    (a) in any case where there is failure to disclose material facts in relation to any part of the property comprised in the taxable inheritances taken on the first chargeable date or on the subsequent chargeable dates, or

    (b) where, at any time after the first chargeable date and before the third of those chargeable dates—

> > (i) in the case of real property, there is any alteration in the tenure under which the property is held or let, or
> >
> > (ii) in the case of shares, there is any alteration in the capital or the ownership of the capital of the company concerned or of the rights of the shareholders inter se,
>
> or
>
> (c) where, at any time after the first chargeable date and before the third of those chargeable dates –
>
> > (i) in the case of real property, there is any change whatever, whether affecting that or any other property, which would materially increase or decrease the market value over and above any increase or decrease which might normally be expected if such a change had not occurred, or
> >
> > (ii) in the case of shares, there has been any material change in the assets of the company or in their market value over and above any such change which might normally be expected,
>
> and in such cases the market value of the real property, or of the shares, may be ascertained again by the Commissioners for each of the relevant valuation dates, but in the case of any change referred to in paragraph (c), the market value may be ascertained again by the Commissioners only at the request of the person primarily accountable for the payment of the tax arising by reason of section 20 on that relevant valuation date.

(3) Any agreement made under this section shall be binding only on the persons who as such are accountable for the payment of the tax arising by reason of section 20 on the first chargeable date and on the subsequent chargeable dates.

Footnote
1   Inserted by s.116(1)(c), FA 2006, as respects the year 2006 and subsequent years.

Section 25

[s.108, FA 1986]

Penalty.

25.   ......[1]

Footnote
1   This section, which was amended by s.146(1)(a), FA 2003, and by para. 2(a), Sch. 4, FA 2007, has been deleted by s.98(1), and by para. (a), Part 4 of Sch. 5, of the F(No. 2)A, 2008, and comes into effect after 24th December, 2008.

the date of the gift or on the date of the inheritance, a company controlled by the donee or successor, deemed to be –

(i) such benefit as would be appropriate to the ownership of that interest if the second-mentioned company were under the control of the first-mentioned company in the same manner as (on the date on which the market value is to be ascertained) the second-mentioned company is under the control of the following, that is, the first-mentioned company, the donee or successor, the relatives of the donee or successor, nominees of the donee or successor, nominees of relatives of the donee or successor, and the trustees of a settlement whose objects include the donee or successor or relatives of the donee or successor, or

(ii) the actual benefit appropriate to the ownership of that interest,

whichever is the greater.

(3) In this section, a reference to a company controlled by the donee or successor is a reference to a company that is under the control of any one or more of the following, that is, the donee or successor, the relatives of the donee or successor, nominees of the donee or successor, nominees of relatives of the donee or successor, and the trustees of a settlement whose objects include the donee or successor or relatives of the donee or successor; and for the purposes of this section, a company which is so controlled by the donee or successor shall be regarded as being itself a relative of the donee or successor.

(4) For the purposes of this section –

(a) a company is deemed to be under the control of not more than 5 persons if any 5 or fewer persons together exercise, or are able to exercise, or are entitled to acquire control, whether direct or indirect, of the company and for this purpose –

(i) persons who are relatives of any other person together with that other person,

(ii) persons who are nominees of any other person together with that other person,

(iii) persons in partnership, and

(iv) persons interested in any shares or obligations of the company which are subject to any trust or are part of the estate of a deceased person,

shall respectively be treated as a single person, and

(b) a person is deemed to have control of a company at any time if –

(i) that person then had control of the powers of voting on all questions, or on any particular question, affecting the company as a whole, which, if exercised, would have yielded a majority of the votes capable of being exercised on such questions or question, or could then have obtained such control by an exercise at that time of a power exercisable by that person or at that person's direction or with that person's consent,

(ii) that person then had the capacity, or could then by an exercise of a power exercisable by that person or at that person's direction or with that person's consent obtain the capacity, to exercise or to control the exercise of any of the following powers, that is:

(I) the powers of a board of directors of the company,

(II) powers of a governing director of the company,

(III) power to nominate a majority of the directors of the company or a governing director of the company,

(IV) the power to veto the appointment of a director of the company, or

(V) powers of a like nature;

(iii) that person then had a right to receive, or the receipt of, more than one-half of the total amount of the dividends of the company, whether declared or not, and for the purposes of this subparagraph, "dividend" is deemed to include interest on any debentures of the company, or

(iv) that person then had an interest in the shares of the company of an aggregate nominal value representing one-half or more of the aggregate nominal value of the shares of the company.

Footnote

1   Reproduced on page 191.

Commentary

A   See an article on Share Valuations by B. H. Giblin in the *Irish Tax Review* of July 2000, page 377.

B   See two articles on the Valuation of Shares by Denis Cremins in the *Irish Tax Review* of September 2006, page 60, and January 2007, page 55.

Cross-References

1   The definition of "group of shares" in s.27(1) is construed by s.16(a), CATCA, in connection with the once-off discretionary trust tax, and by s.21(a), CATCA, in connection with the annual discretionary trust tax.

2   The definition of "nominee" in s.27(1) is also used in para. 7(1), Part I, Sch. 2, CATCA.

3   The definition of "private company" is s.27(1) is also used in s.5(7), CATCA, s.6(5), CATCA, s.10(4), CATCA, s.11(5), CATCA, s.38(4), CATCA, s.43(2), CATCA, s.44(1), CATCA, s.78(1), CATCA, s.80(3), CATCA, s.83(3), CATCA, and para. 7(1), Part 1, Sch. 2, CATCA.

4   The definition of "share" in s.27(1) is also used in s.5(7), CATCA, s.6(5), CATCA, s.10(4), CATCA, s.11(5), CATCA, and s.43(2), CATCA.

5 The definition of "company controlled by the donee or successor" in s.27(3) is also used in s.6(5), CATCA, s.11(5), CATCA, s.16(a), CATCA, s.21(a), CATCA, s.44(2), CATCA, s.93(1), CATCA, and s.95(3), CATCA.

6 "Control of a company" within the meaning of s.27(4)(b) is also referred to in s.38(4), CATCA, s.80(3), CATCA, s.95(3), CATCA, and para. 7(1), Part 1, Sch. 2, CATCA.

Section 28

[S.18, CATA, as amended]

Taxable value of a taxable gift or inheritance.

28. (1) In this section, "incumbrance-free value", in relation to a taxable gift or a taxable inheritance, means the market value at the valuation date of the property of which the taxable gift or taxable inheritance consists at that date, after deducting any liabilities, costs and expenses that are properly payable out of the taxable gift or taxable inheritance.

(2) Subject to this section (but except where provided in section 89), the taxable value of a taxable gift or a taxable inheritance (where the interest taken by the donee or successor is not a limited interest) is ascertained by deducting from the incumbrance-free value of such a taxable gift or a taxable inheritance the market value of any bona fide consideration in money or money's worth, paid by the donee or successor for the gift or inheritance, including —

 (a) any liability of the disponer which the donee or successor undertakes to discharge as that [donee or successor's][2] own personal liability, and

 (b) any other liability to which the gift or inheritance is subject under the terms of the disposition under which it is taken,

and the amount so ascertained is the taxable value, but no deduction shall be made under this subsection in respect of any liability which is to be deducted in ascertaining the incumbrance-free value.

(3) Where a liability (other than a liability within the meaning of subsection (9)) for which a deduction may be made under subsection (1) or (2) is to be discharged after the time when it is to be taken into account as a deduction under either of those subsections, it is valued for the purpose of making such a deduction at its current market value at the time when it is to be so taken into account.

(4) The taxable value of a taxable gift or a taxable inheritance, where the interest taken by the donee or the successor is a limited interest, is ascertained as follows —

 (a) the value of the limited interest in a capital sum equal to the incumbrance-free value is ascertained in accordance with the Rules contained in Schedule 1, and

 (b) from the value ascertained in accordance with paragraph (a) a deduction is made in respect of the market value of any bona fide consideration in money or money's worth paid by the donee or the successor for the gift or the inheritance and the amount remaining after such deduction is the taxable value, but no deduction is made under this paragraph in respect of any liability which is to be deducted in ascertaining the incumbrance-free value.

(5) A deduction shall not be made under this section—

(a) in respect of any liability the payment of which is contingent on the happening of some future event, but if the event on the happening of which the liability is contingent happens and the liability is paid, then, on a claim for relief being made to the Commissioners and subject to the other provisions of this section, a deduction is made in respect of the liability and such adjustment of tax as is appropriate is made; and such adjustment is made on the basis that the donee or successor had taken an interest in possession in the amount which is to be deducted for the liability, for a period certain which was equal to the actual duration of the postponement of the payment of the liability,

(b) in respect of any liability, costs or expenses in so far as the donee or successor has a right of reimbursement from any source, unless such reimbursement can not be obtained,

(c) in respect of any liability created by the donee or successor or any person claiming in right of the donee or successor or on that donee or successor's behalf,

(d) in respect of tax, interest or penalties chargeable under this Act in respect of the gift or inheritance, or of the costs, expenses or interest incurred in raising or paying the same,

(e) in respect of any liability in so far as such liability is an incumbrance on, or was created or incurred in acquiring, any property which is comprised in any gift or inheritance and which is exempt from tax under any provision of this Act or otherwise,

(f) in the case of any gift or inheritance referred to in section 6(1)(c), 6(2)(d), 11(1)(b) or 11(2)(c) in respect of—

(i) any liability, costs or expenses due to a person resident outside the State (except in so far as such liability is required by contract to be paid in the State or is charged on the property which is situate in the State and which is comprised in the gift or inheritance), or

(ii) any liability, costs or expenses in so far as the same are charged on or secured by property which is comprised in the gift or inheritance and which is not situate in the State, except to the extent that all the property situate outside the State and comprised in the gift or inheritance is insufficient for the payment of the liability, costs or expenses,

(g) for any tax in respect of which a credit is allowed under section 106 or 107.

[(5A) Notwithstanding section 57(3), relief shall be given under subsection (5)(a) on a claim which shall be made within 4 years after the liability referred to in that paragraph has been paid.]¹

(6) In the case of a gift or inheritance referred to in subsection (5)(f), any deduction to be made under subsection (2) or (4)(b) is restricted to the proportion of the consideration which bears the same proportion to the whole of the consideration as the taxable gift or taxable inheritance bears to the whole of the gift or the whole of the inheritance.

(7) A deduction shall not be made under this section—

(a) more than once for the same liability, costs, expenses or consideration, in respect of all gifts and inheritances taken by the donee or successor from the disponer, or.

(b) for any liability, costs, expenses or consideration, a proportion of which is to be allowed under section 89(2)(ii) or (iii) in respect of a gift or inheritance taken by the donee or successor from the disponer.

(8) Where a taxable gift or a taxable inheritance is subject to a liability within the meaning of subsection (9), the deduction to be made in respect of that liability under this section shall be an amount equal to the market value of the whole or the appropriate part, as the case may be, of the property, within the meaning of section 5(5).

(9) For the purpose of subsection (8), "liability", in relation to a taxable gift or a taxable inheritance, means a liability which deprives the donee or successor, whether permanently or temporarily, of the use, enjoyment or income in whole or in part of the property, or of any part of the property, of which the taxable gift or taxable inheritance consists.

(10) Where—

(a) bona fide consideration in money or money's worth has been paid by a person for the granting to that person, by a disposition, of an interest in expectancy in property, and

(b) at the coming into possession of the interest in expectancy, that person takes a gift or an inheritance of that property under that disposition,

the deduction to be made under subsection (2) or (4)(b) for consideration paid by that person is a sum equal to the same proportion of the taxable value of the taxable gift or taxable inheritance (as if no deduction had been made for such consideration) as the amount of the consideration so paid bore to the market value of the interest in expectancy at the date of the payment of the consideration.

(11) Any deduction, under this section, in respect of a liability which is an incumbrance on any property, is, so far as possible, made against that property.

Footnotes

1   Inserted by para. 2(a), Sch. 6, FA 2008, and under s.137(2), FA 2008, applies as on and from 31st January, 2008.

2   As substituted for "disponer's" by s.99 and by para. 3, Sch. 6, F(No. 2)A, 2008, and is deemed under para. 7(c) of that Sch. to have come into force and have taken effect as on and from 21st February, 2003.

Commentary

A   S.11, CATCA, has provisions for determining when an inheritance which consists of non-Irish property shall not be a taxable inheritance. According to Part 19.12 of the *Revenue CAT Manual*, the Revenue view has been upheld by the Appeal Commissioner and by the Circuit Court that, for the purposes of s.28(5)(e), CATCA, this is an exemption of an inheritance.

B   As to a liability consisting of a claim for wages against an estate by a family member, see Part 19.1 of the *Revenue CAT Manual* which quotes two cases, *Jones v Padavatton* [1961] 1 WLR 328 and *Balfour v Balfour* [1919] 2KB 571. Such claims are disallowed.

C   See Part 19.5 of the *Revenue CAT Manual*. Where the worldwide property of a deceased person is taxable in the State under s.11, CATCA, arrears of income tax, capital gains tax, etc., due to the British Revenue by the deceased person, are allowed as a liability of the deceased for CAT purposes, provided such tax is actually paid and whether or not the deceased person died possessed of assets in the UK.

D   See Part 19.11 of the *Revenue CAT Manual*. Where it is shown, by evidence from the Inspector of Taxes, that a beneficiary of the estate of a person was charged to income tax on income which accrued in relation to the deceased person's estate during the period between the date of death and the valuation date of the beneficiary's inheritance, that income is not taken into account in calculating the taxable value of the beneficiary's taxable inheritance. The proportion of any liabilities, costs and expenses which is payable out of the part of the estate represented by such increase will, if the figures justify apportionment, be disallowed accordingly.

Cross-Reference

1   "Liability" in s.28(9) is also dealt with in s.34(2), CATCA, and in s.37(2), CATCA.

Section 29

[S.20, CATA]

Contingencies affecting gifts or inheritances.

29. (1) Where, under a disposition, a person becomes beneficially entitled in possession to any benefit and, under the terms of the disposition, the entitlement, or any part of the entitlement, may cease on the happening of a contingency (other than the revocation of the entitlement on the exercise by the disponer of such a power as is referred to in section 39), the taxable value of any taxable gift or taxable inheritance taken by that person on becoming so entitled to that benefit is ascertained as if no part of

PART 5

Provisions Relating to Gifts and Inheritances

Section 31

[S.22, CATA]

Distributions from discretionary trusts.

31. (Where a person becomes beneficially entitled in possession to any benefit —

(a) under a discretionary trust, other than a discretionary trust referred to in paragraph (b), otherwise than for full consideration in money or money's worth paid by the person, that person is deemed to have taken a gift,

(b) under a discretionary trust created —

(i) by will at any time,

(ii) by a disposition, where the date of the disposition is on or after 1 April 1975 and within 2 years prior to the death of the disponer, or

(iii) by a disposition *inter vivos* and limited to come into operation on a death occurring before, on or after the passing of this Act,

otherwise than for full consideration in money or money's worth paid by the person, that person is deemed to have taken an inheritance.

Section 32

[S.23, CATA]

Dealings with future interests.

32. (1) In subsection (2), "benefit" includes the benefit of the cesser of a liability referred to in section 37.

(2) Where a benefit, to which a person (in this section referred to as the remainderman) is entitled under a disposition, devolves, or is disposed of, either in whole or in part, before it has become an interest in possession so that, at the time when the benefit comes into possession, it is taken, either in whole or in part, by a person (in this section referred to as the transferee) other than the remainderman to whom it was limited by the disposition, then tax is payable, in respect of a gift or inheritance, as the case may be, of the remainderman in all respects as if, at that time, the remainderman had become beneficially entitled in possession to the full extent of the benefit limited to that remainderman under the disposition, and the transferee is the person primarily accountable for the payment of tax to the extent that the benefit is taken by that transferee.

(3) Subsection (2) shall not prejudice any charge for tax in respect of any gift or inheritance affecting the same property or any part of it under any other disposition.

Cross-Reference

1   The "remainderman" in s.32(2) is referred to in s.111(2)(b), CATCA.

2   The "transferee" in s.32(2) is referred to in s.45(1), CATCA, s.54(4), CATCA, s.86(2), CATCA, s.89(7), CATCA, and s.90(4), CATCA.

Section 33

[S.24, CATA]

Release of limited interests, etc.

33. (1) In this section, "event" includes —

(a) a death, and

(b) the expiration of a specified period.

(2) Where an interest in property, which is limited by the disposition creating it to cease on an event, has come to an end (whether by another disposition, the taking of successive interests into one ownership, or by any means whatever other than the happening of another event on which the interest was limited by the first-mentioned disposition to cease) before the happening of such event, tax is payable under the first-mentioned disposition in all respects as if the event on which the interest was limited to cease under that disposition had happened immediately before the coming to an end of the interest.

(3) Subsection (2) shall not prejudice any charge for tax in respect of any gift or inheritance affecting the same property or any part of it under any disposition other than that first-mentioned in subsection (2).

(4) Notwithstanding anything contained in subsection (3), if —

(a) an interest in property which was limited to cease on an event was limited to the disponer by the disposition creating that interest, and

(b) on the coming to an end of that interest, subsection (2) has effect in relation to a gift or inheritance which was taken by a donee or successor under that disposition and which consists of the property in which that interest subsisted, then —

a further gift or inheritance taken by the same donee or successor under another disposition made by the same disponer (being the disposition by which that interest has come to an end) is not a taxable gift or a taxable inheritance in so far as it consists of the whole or any part of the same property.

Cross-Reference

1   "Event" in s.33(1) has the same meaning in s.34(1), CATCA.

not to be situate in the State at the date of the gift or at the date of the inheritance.

Cross-Reference
1   A "benefit" in s.37(2) is also governed by s.32(1), CATCA.

Section 38

[S.29, CATA]

Disposition enlarging value of property.

38.   (1)   In subsection (4), "company" means a private company within the meaning of section 27.

(2)   In this section, "property" does not include any property to which a donee or successor became beneficially entitled in possession prior to 28 February 1969.

(3)   Where the taking by any person of a beneficial interest in any property (in this section referred to as additional property) under any disposition made by a disponer has the effect of increasing the value of any other property (in this section referred to as original property) to which that person is beneficially entitled in possession, and which had been derived from the same disponer, the following provisions shall apply —

(a)   the increase in value so effected is deemed to be a gift or an inheritance, as the case may be, arising under that disposition and taken by that person, as donee or successor, from that disponer, at the time that donee or successor took the beneficial interest in the additional property,

(b)   the original property is treated as having been increased in value if the market value of that property at the time referred to in paragraph (a) would be greater if it was sold as part of an aggregate of the original property and the additional property rather than as a single item of property, and the increase in value for the purposes of this section is the amount by which the market value of the original property if sold at that time as part of such aggregate would be greater than the amount of the market value of that property if sold at that time as a single item of property,

(c)   the additional property is, for the purpose of determining its market value, deemed to be part of an aggregate of the original property and the additional property, and

(d)   the market value of any property which is to be valued as part of an aggregate of property is ascertained as being so much of the market value of such aggregate as may reasonably be ascribed to that part.

(3) Subsection (2) shall not prejudice any charge for tax in respect of any gift or inheritance affecting the same property or any part of it under any other disposition.

Cross-Reference

1   The "remainderman" in s.32(2) is referred to in s.111(2)(b), CATCA.

2   The "transferee" in s.32(2) is referred to in s.45(1), CATCA, s.54(4), CATCA, s.86(2), CATCA, s.89(7), CATCA, and s.90(4), CATCA.

Section 33

[S.24, CATA]

Release of limited interests, etc.

33.   (1)   In this section, "event" includes —

(a)   a death, and

(b)   the expiration of a specified period.

(2)   Where an interest in property, which is limited by the disposition creating it to cease on an event, has come to an end (whether by another disposition, the taking of successive interests into one ownership, or by any means whatever other than the happening of another event on which the interest was limited by the first-mentioned disposition to cease) before the happening of such event, tax is payable under the first-mentioned disposition in all respects as if the event on which the interest was limited to cease under that disposition had happened immediately before the coming to an end of the interest.

(3)   Subsection (2) shall not prejudice any charge for tax in respect of any gift or inheritance affecting the same property or any part of it under any disposition other than that first-mentioned in subsection (2).

(4)   Notwithstanding anything contained in subsection (3), if —

(a)   an interest in property which was limited to cease on an event was limited to the disponer by the disposition creating that interest, and

(b)   on the coming to an end of that interest, subsection (2) has effect in relation to a gift or inheritance which was taken by a donee or successor under that disposition and which consists of the property in which that interest subsisted, then —

a further gift or inheritance taken by the same donee or successor under another disposition made by the same disponer (being the disposition by which that interest has come to an end) is not a taxable gift or a taxable inheritance in so far as it consists of the whole or any part of the same property.

Cross-Reference

1   "Event" in s.33(1) has the same meaning in s.34(1), CATCA.

Section 34

[S.25, CATA]

Settlement of an interest not in possession.

34. (1) In this section, "event" has the same meaning as it has in section 33(1).

(2) Where any donee or successor takes a gift or an inheritance under a disposition made by such donee or successor then, if at the date of such disposition such donee or successor was entitled to the property comprised in the disposition, either expectantly on the happening of an event, or subject to a liability within the meaning of section 28(9), and such event happens or such liability ceases during the continuance of the disposition, tax is charged on the taxable value of the taxable gift or taxable inheritance which such donee or successor would have taken on the happening of such event, or on the cesser of such liability, if no such disposition had been made.

(3) Subsection (2) shall not prejudice any charge for tax in respect of any gift or inheritance affecting the same property or any part of it under the disposition referred to in that subsection.

Section 35

[S.26, CATA]

Enlargement of interests.

35. (1) Where a person, having a limited interest in possession in property (in this section referred to as the first-mentioned interest), takes a further interest (in this section referred to as the second-mentioned interest) in the same property, as a taxable gift or a taxable inheritance, in consequence of which that person becomes the absolute owner of the property, the taxable value of the taxable gift or taxable inheritance of the second-mentioned interest at the valuation date is reduced by the value at that date of the first-mentioned interest, taking such value to be the value, ascertained in accordance with the Rules contained in Schedule 1, of a limited interest which—

(a) is a limited interest in a capital sum equal to the value of the property,

(b) commences on that date, and

(c) is to continue for the unexpired balance of the term of the first-mentioned interest.

(2) For the purposes of subsection (1)(a), "value" means such amount as would be the incumbrance-free value, within the meaning of section 28(1), if the limited interest were taken, at the date referred to in subsection (1), as a taxable gift or taxable inheritance.

(3) This section shall not apply where the second-mentioned interest is taken under the disposition under which the first-mentioned interest was created.

Section 36

[S.27, CATA]

Dispositions involving powers of appointment.

36. (1) Where, by virtue of or in consequence of the exercise of, or the failure to exercise, or the release of, a general power of appointment by any person having such a power, a person becomes beneficially entitled in possession to any benefit, then, for the purposes of this Act, the disposition is the exercise of, or the failure to exercise, or the release of, the power and not the disposition under which the power was created, and the person exercising, or failing to exercise, or releasing, the power is the disponer.

(2) Where, by virtue of or in consequence of the exercise of, or the failure to exercise, or the release of, a special power of appointment by any person having such a power, a person becomes beneficially entitled in possession to any benefit, then, for the purposes of this Act, the disposition is the disposition under which the power was created and the person who created the power is the disponer.

Section 37

[S.28, CATA]

Cesser of liabilities.

37. (1) In this section, "appropriate part" has the meaning assigned to it by section 5(5).

(2) The benefit of the cesser of —

(a) a liability within the meaning of section 28(9), or

(b) any liability similar to that referred to in paragraph (a) to which the taking of a benefit which was a gift or inheritance was subject,

is deemed to be a gift or an inheritance, as the case may be, which is deemed —

(i) to the extent that the liability is charged on or secured by any property at the time of its cesser, to consist of the whole or the appropriate part, as the case may be, of that property, and

(ii) to the extent that the liability is not charged on or secured by any property at the time of its cesser, to consist of such sum as would, under section 5(2)(b), be the sum the annual income of which would be equal to the annual value of the liability.

(3) For the purposes of sections 6(1)(c), 6(2)(d), 11(1)(b) and 11(2)(c), the sum referred to in subparagraph (ii) of subsection (2) is deemed

not to be situate in the State at the date of the gift or at the date of the inheritance.

Cross-Reference
1   A "benefit" in s.37(2) is also governed by s.32(1), CATCA.

Section 38

[S.29, CATA]

Disposition enlarging value of property.

38. (1) In subsection (4), "company" means a private company within the meaning of section 27.

(2) In this section, "property" does not include any property to which a donee or successor became beneficially entitled in possession prior to 28 February 1969.

(3) Where the taking by any person of a beneficial interest in any property (in this section referred to as additional property) under any disposition made by a disponer has the effect of increasing the value of any other property (in this section referred to as original property) to which that person is beneficially entitled in possession, and which had been derived from the same disponer, the following provisions shall apply—

(a) the increase in value so effected is deemed to be a gift or an inheritance, as the case may be, arising under that disposition and taken by that person, as donee or successor, from that disponer, at the time that donee or successor took the beneficial interest in the additional property,

(b) the original property is treated as having been increased in value if the market value of that property at the time referred to in paragraph (a) would be greater if it was sold as part of an aggregate of the original property and the additional property rather than as a single item of property, and the increase in value for the purposes of this section is the amount by which the market value of the original property if sold at that time as part of such aggregate would be greater than the amount of the market value of that property if sold at that time as a single item of property,

(c) the additional property is, for the purpose of determining its market value, deemed to be part of an aggregate of the original property and the additional property, and

(d) the market value of any property which is to be valued as part of an aggregate of property is ascertained as being so much of the market value of such aggregate as may reasonably be ascribed to that part.

(4) For the purpose of this section, the donee or successor is deemed to be beneficially entitled in possession to any property notwithstanding that within 5 years prior to such a disposition as is referred to in subsection (3) that donee or successor has divested such donee or successor of such property, or any part of such property, otherwise than for full consideration in money or money's worth or has disposed of it to a company of which such donee or successor is, at any time within that period of 5 years, deemed to have control within the meaning of section 27(4)(b).

Section 39

[S.30, CATA]

Gift subject to power of revocation.

39. Where, under any disposition, a person becomes beneficially entitled in possession to any benefit and, under the terms of the disposition, the disponer has reserved to such disponer the power to revoke the benefit, such person is, for the purposes of this Act,. deemed not to be beneficially entitled in possession to the benefit unless and until the power of revocation is released by the disponer, or otherwise ceases to be exercisable.

Cross-Reference

1   A power of revocation in s.39 is not a "contingency" for the purposes of s.29, CATCA.

Section 40

[S.31, CATA]

Free use of property, free loans, etc.

40. (1) In subsections (2) and (4), "relevant period", in relation to any use, occupation or enjoyment of property, means the period of 12 months ending on 31 December in each year.

(2) A person is deemed to take a gift in each relevant period during the whole or part of which that person is allowed to have the use, occupation or enjoyment of any property (to which property that person is not beneficially entitled in possession) otherwise than for full consideration in money or money's worth.

(3) A gift referred to in subsection (2) is deemed to consist of a sum equal to the difference between the amount of any consideration in money or money's worth, given by the person referred to in subsection (2) for such use, occupation or enjoyment, and the best price obtainable in the open market for such use, occupation or enjoyment.

(4) A gift referred to in subsection (2) is treated as being taken at the end of the relevant period or, if earlier, immediately prior to

the time when the use, occupation or enjoyment referred to in subsection (2) comes to an end.

(5) In any case where the use, occupation or enjoyment of property is allowed to a person, not being beneficially entitled in possession to that property, under a disposition –

   (a) made by will,

   (b) where the date of the disposition is on or after 1 April 1975 and within 2 years prior to the death of the disponer, or

   (c) which is a disposition *inter vivos* and the use, occupation or enjoyment is had by that person after the cesser of another person's life interest,

subsections (2), (3) and (4) shall apply in relation to that property as if a reference to an inheritance were substituted for the reference to a gift wherever it occurs in those subsections, and for the purpose of this subsection "relevant period" in subsections (2) and (4), in relation to the use, occupation or enjoyment of property, means the period of 12 months ending on 31 December in any year.

(6) For the purposes of sections 6(1)(c), 6(2)(d), 11(1)(b) and 11(2)(c), the sum referred to in subsection (3) is deemed not to be situate in the State at the date of the gift or at the date of the inheritance.

Commentary

  A   As to "best price" in s.40(3), see Part 19.14 of the *Revenue CAT Manual*.

Section 41

[S.32, CATA]

When interest in assurance policy becomes interest in possession.

41. (1) For the purposes of this Act, an interest in a policy of assurance on human life is deemed to become an interest in possession when either –

   (a) the policy matures, or

   (b) prior to the maturing of the policy, the policy is surrendered to the insurer for a consideration in money or money's worth, but if during the currency of the policy the insurer makes a payment of money or money's worth, in full or partial discharge of the policy, the interest is deemed to have come into possession to the extent of such payment.

  (2) This section has effect in relation to a contract for a deferred annuity, and for the purposes of this section such a contract is deemed to mature on the date when the first instalment of the annuity is due.

Commentary

  A   See an article on Policies of Assurance by Brian Bohan in the *Irish Tax Review* of December 1990, page 263.

Section 44

[S.90, FA 1989, as amended, and s.127, FA 1993]

Arrangements reducing value of company shares.

44. (1) In this section –

"arrangement" means an arrangement which is made on or after 25 January 1989, and includes –

(a) any act or omission by a person or by the trustees of a disposition,

(b) any act or omission by any person having an interest in shares in a company,

(c) the passing by any company of a resolution, or

(d) any combination of acts, omissions or resolutions referred to in paragraphs (a), (b) and (c);

"company" means a private company within the meaning of section 27;

"event" includes –

(a) a death, and

(b) the expiration of a specified period;

"related shares" means the shares in a company, the market value of which shares is increased by any arrangement;

"related trust" has the meaning assigned to it by subsections (3) and (5);

"specified amount" means an amount equal to the difference between –

(a) the market value of shares in a company immediately before an arrangement is made, and ascertained under section 27 as if each share were a share in a company controlled at that time by the disponer concerned and that share was the absolute property of that disponer at that time, and

(b) the market value of those shares, or of property representing those shares, immediately after the arrangement is made, and ascertained under section 26,

and such specified amount is deemed to be situate where the company is incorporated.

(2) In this section, a reference to a company controlled by the disponer concerned is a reference to a company that is under the control of any one or more of the following, that is, that disponer, the relatives of that disponer, nominees of relatives of that disponer, and the trustees of a settlement whose objects include that disponer or relatives of that disponer, and for the purposes of this section, a company which is so controlled by that disponer is regarded as being itself a relative of that disponer.

(3) Where—

    (a)   a person has an absolute interest in possession in shares in a company, and

    (b)   any arrangement results in the market value of those shares, or of property representing those shares, immediately after that arrangement is made, being less than it would be but for that arrangement,

then, tax is payable in all respects as if a specified amount which relates to that arrangement were a benefit taken, immediately after that arrangement is made, from that person, as disponer, by—

    (i)   the beneficial owners of the related shares in that company, and

    (ii)   so far as the related shares in that company are held in trust (in this section referred to as the "related trust") and have no ascertainable beneficial owners, by the disponer in relation to that related trust as if, immediately after that arrangement is made, that disponer was the absolute beneficial owner of those related shares,

in the same proportions as the market value of the related shares, which are beneficially owned by them or are deemed to be so beneficially owned, is increased by that arrangement.

(4) Where—

    (a)   an interest in property is limited by the disposition creating it to cease on an event,

    (b)   immediately before the making of an arrangement to which paragraph (c) relates, the property includes shares in a company, and

    (c)   the arrangement results in the market value of those shares, or of property representing those shares, immediately after that arrangement is made, being less than it would be but for that arrangement,

then, tax is payable under that disposition in all respects—

    (i)   where the interest in property is an interest in possession, as if such property included a specified amount which relates to that arrangement,

    (ii)   where the interest in property is not an interest in possession, as if it were an interest in possession and such property included a specified amount which relates to that arrangement, and

    (iii)   as if the event on which the interest was limited to cease under that disposition had happened, to the extent of the specified amount, immediately before that arrangement is made.

(5) Where—

    (a)   shares in a company are, immediately before the making of an arrangement to which paragraph (b) relates, subject to a discretionary trust under or in consequence of any disposition, and

    (b)   the arrangement results in those shares, or property representing those shares, remaining subject to that discretionary trust but, immediately after that arrangement is made, the market value of those shares, or of property representing those shares, is less than it would be but for that arrangement,

then, tax shall be payable under that disposition in all respects as if a specified amount, which relates to that arrangement, were a benefit taken immediately after that arrangement is made—

    (i)   by the beneficial owners of the related shares in that company, and

    (ii) so far as the related shares in that company are held in trust (in this section referred to as the "related trust") and have no ascertainable beneficial owners, by the disponer in relation to that related trust as if, immediately after that arrangement is made, that disponer was the absolute beneficial owner of those related shares,

in the same proportions as the market value of the related shares, which are beneficially owned by them or are deemed to be so beneficially owned, is increased by that arrangement.

  (6) Subsections (3), (4) and (5) shall not prejudice any charge for tax in respect of any gift or inheritance taken under any disposition on or after the making of an arrangement referred to in those subsections and comprising shares in a company, or property representing such shares.

  (7) Where shares in a company, which are held in trust under a disposition made by any disponer, are related shares by reason of any arrangement referred to in this section, any gift or inheritance taken under the disposition on or after the arrangement is made and comprising those related shares, or property representing those related shares, are deemed to be taken from that disponer.

  (8) In relation to the tax due and payable in respect of any gift or inheritance taken under paragraph (ii) of subsection (3) or paragraph (ii) of subsection (5), and notwithstanding any other provision of this Act—

    (a)   the disponer in relation to the related trust is not a person primarily accountable for the payment of such tax, and

    (b)   a person who is a trustee of the related trust concerned for the time being at the date of the gift or at the date of the inheritance, or at any date subsequent to that date, is so primarily accountable.

  (9) A person who is accountable for the payment of tax in respect of any specified amount, or part of a specified amount, taken as a

gift or an inheritance under this section shall, for the purpose of paying the tax, or raising the amount of the tax when already paid, have power, whether the related shares are or are not vested in that person, to raise the amount of such tax and any interest and expenses properly paid or incurred by that person in respect of such tax, by the sale or mortgage of, or a terminable charge on, the related shares in the relevant company.

(10) Tax due and payable in respect of a taxable gift or a taxable inheritance taken under this section shall be and remain a charge on the related shares in the relevant company.

(11) Where related shares are subject to a discretionary trust immediately after an arrangement is made in accordance with the provisions of this section, the amount by which the market value of such shares is increased by such arrangement is property for the purposes of a charge for tax arising by reason of section 15.

(12) Where, immediately after and as a result of an arrangement, shares in a company have been redeemed, the redeemed shares are, for the purpose of the references to property representing shares in subsection (1) and subsection (3), (4) or (5), except a reference in relation to which the redeemed shares are actually represented by property, deemed, immediately after the arrangement, being an arrangement made on or after 6 May 1993, to be represented by property, and the market value of the property so deemed to represent the redeemed shares is deemed to be nil.

PART 6

Returns and Assessments

Section 45

[S.35, CATA, as amended, and s.81, FA 1989]

Accountable persons.

45. (1) The person primarily accountable for the payment of tax shall be—

(a) except where provided in paragraph (b), the donee or successor, as the case may be, and

(b) in the case referred to in section 32(2), the transferee referred to in that subsection, to the extent referred to in that subsection.

(2) Subject to subsections (3) and (4), the following persons shall also be accountable for the payment of any amount of the tax for which the persons referred to in subsection (1) are made primarily accountable—

(a) in the case of a gift—

(i) the disponer (other than a disponer in relation to a disposition where the date of the disposition was prior to 28 February 1974), and

(ii) every trustee, guardian, committee, personal representative, agent or other person in whose care any property comprised in the gift or the income from such property is placed at the date of the gift or at any time after that date and every person in whom the property is vested after that date, other than a bona fide purchaser or mortgagee for full consideration in money or money's worth, or a person deriving title from or under such a purchaser or mortgagee,

(b) (i) in the case of an inheritance, taken [....]¹ before the death of the disponer, the disponer (other than a disponer in relation to a disposition, where the date of the disposition was prior to 1 May 1989), and

(ii) in the case of any other inheritance, every trustee, guardian, committee, personal representative, agent or other person in whose care any property comprised in the inheritance or the income from such property is placed at the date of the inheritance or at any time after that date and every person in whom the property is vested after that date, other than a bona fide purchaser or mortgagee for full consideration in money or money's worth, or a person deriving title from or under such a purchaser or mortgagee.

(3) No person referred to in subsection (2)(a)(ii) or (b)(ii) is (unless that person is a person who is also primarily accountable under subsection (1)) liable for tax chargeable on any gift or inheritance to an amount in excess of —

(a) the market value of so much of the property of which the gift or inheritance consists, and

(b) so much of the income from such property,

which has been received by that person, or which, but for that person's own neglect or default, would have been received by that person or to which that person is beneficially entitled in possession.

(4) A person who acts solely in the capacity of an agent is not liable for tax chargeable on a gift or inheritance to an amount in excess of the market value of so much of the property of which the gift or inheritance consists and of the income from such property which that person held, or which came into that person's possession, at any time after the serving on that person of the notice referred to in subsection (5).

(5) The Commissioners may serve on any person who acts solely in the capacity of agent in relation to any property comprised in a gift or an inheritance a notice in writing informing that person of that person's liability under this section.

(6) The tax shall be recoverable from any one or more of —

(a) the accountable persons, and

(b) the personal representatives of any accountable persons who are dead,

on whom the Commissioners have served notice in writing of the assessment of tax in exercise of the power conferred on them by section 49, but the liability of a personal representative under this subsection shall not exceed the amount for which the accountable person, of whom that person is the personal representative, was liable.

(7) Any person referred to in subsection (2)(a) or (b) or in subsection (6)(b) who is authorised or required to pay, and pays, any tax in respect of any property comprised in a gift or in an inheritance may recover the amount paid by that person in respect of tax from the person primarily accountable for that tax unless —

(a) the latter person is the donee or successor referred to in paragraph (a) of subsection (1) and the interest taken by that latter person is a limited interest, or

(b) in the case referred to in paragraph (b) of subsection (1), the latter person is the transferee and the interest taken by the remainderman is a limited interest.

(8) A person—

    (a) who is primarily accountable for the payment of tax, or

    (b) referred to in subsection (2)(a) or (b) or in subsection (6)(b) who is authorised or required to pay tax,

in respect of any property shall, for the purpose of paying the tax, or raising the amount of the tax when already paid, have power, whether the property is or is not vested in that person, to raise the amount of such tax and any interest and expenses properly paid or incurred by that person in respect thereof, by the sale or mortgage of, or a terminable charge on, that property or any part of that property.

(9) If a person, who is primarily accountable for the payment of tax in respect of a gift or inheritance (in this subsection and in subsection (11) referred to as the first gift or inheritance) derived from a disponer, has not paid the tax on the first gift or inheritance, the Commissioners may serve a notice in writing in accordance with subsection (11) on any person who is, by virtue of paragraph (a)(ii) or (b)(ii) of subsection (2), accountable for the payment of tax on any other gift or inheritance (referred to in subsections (10) and (11) as the second gift or inheritance) taken by the same donee or successor from the same disponer, and the person on whom the notice is served shall at that time become accountable for the payment of tax in respect of the first gift or inheritance.

(10) Subsections (3), (4), (5), (6), (7) and (8) shall apply in relation to a person made accountable under subsection (9) as they apply in relation to a person referred to in paragraph (a)(ii) or (b) of subsection (2) and, for the purposes of this subsection—

    (a) references in subsections (3) and (4) to the property of which the gift or inheritance consists, and

    (b) the second and third references to property in subsection (8),

shall be construed as references to the property of which the second gift or inheritance consists, in so far as the last-mentioned property had not been duly paid out at the date of the service of the notice under subsection (9).

(11) A notice under subsection (9) shall refer expressly to the first and the second gift or inheritance, and shall inform the person on whom it is served of that person's accountability in respect of the first gift or inheritance.

(12) Every public officer having in such person's custody any rolls, books, records, papers, documents, or proceedings, the inspection of which may tend to secure the tax, or to prove or lead to the discovery of any fraud or omission in relation to the tax, shall at all reasonable times permit any person authorised by the Commissioners to inspect the rolls, books, records, papers, documents and proceedings, and to take notes and extracts as that person may deem necessary.

Footnote

1   The words "on or" deleted by para.2, Sch.6, FA 2005, which is deemed by para.4(b) of that Schedule to have come into force and have taken effect as on and from 21st February, 2003.

Cross-References

1   S.45(7) or (8) does not derogate from the relief given under s.111, CATCA.

2   See s.44(8), CATCA, as to the persons accountable for payment of tax under that section.

3   See s.16(c) and (d), CATCA, as to the persons accountable for payment of the once-off discretionary trust tax, and s.21(c) and (d), CATCA, as to the persons accountable for payment of the annual discretionary trust tax.

Section 45A[1]

Obligation to retain certain records.

45A. (1)   In this section -

"records" includes books, accounts, documents, and any other data maintained manually or by any electronic, photographic or other process, relating to -

(a)   property, of any description, which under or in consequence of any disposition, a person becomes beneficially entitled in possession to, otherwise than for full consideration in money or money's worth paid by that person,

(b)   liabilities, costs and expenses properly payable out of that property,

(c)   consideration given in good faith, in money or money's worth, paid by a person for that property,

(d)   a relief or an exemption claimed under any provision of this Act, and

(e)   the valuation, on the valuation date or other date, as the case may be, of property the subject of the disposition.

(2)   Every person who is an accountable person shall retain, or cause to be retained on his or her behalf, records of the type referred to in subsection (1) as are required to enable -

(i)   a true return, additional return or statement to be made for the purposes of this Act, or

(ii)   a claim to a relief or an exemption under any provision of this Act to be substantiated.

(3)   Records required to be retained by virtue of this section shall be retained -

(a)   in written form in an official language of the State, or

(b)   subject to section 887(2) of the Taxes Consolidation Act 1997, by means of any electronic, photographic or other process.

(4) Records retained for the purposes of subsections (2) and (3) shall be retained by the person required to retain the records -

(a) where the requirements of [........]² section 46(2), requiring the preparation and delivery of a return on or before the date specified in each of those provisions, are met, for the period of 6 years commencing on the valuation date of the gift or inheritance, or

(b) notwithstanding paragraph (a), where an accountable person fails to comply with the requirements of the provisions referred to in paragraph (a) in the manner so specified, or, where any person is required to deliver a return, additional return or statement under this Act other than the provisions referred to in paragraph (a), for the period of 6 years commencing on the date that the return, additional return or statement is received by the Commissioners.

(5) Any person who fails to comply with subsection (2), (3) or (4) in respect of the retention of any records relating to a gift or inheritance is liable to a penalty of €1,520; but a penalty shall not be imposed under this section on any person who is not liable to tax in respect of that gift or inheritance.

Footnotes

1   This section was inserted by s.146(1)(b), FA 2003, which section will come into effect by Ministerial Order. S.I. No. 466 of 2003 (see page 1377) appoints 1st October, 2003, as the date on which s.146(1)(b), FA 2003, comes into operation. See also s.153, FA 2003.

2   The words "section 21(e) or" deleted by para.2(b), Sch. 4, FA 2007, which is deemed by para. 6(b) of that Schedule to have come into force and have taken effect as respects the year 2006 and subsequent years.

Section 46³

[S.36, CATA, as amended]

Delivery of returns.

46. (1) In this section —

(a) notwithstanding anything contained in sections 6 and 11 a reference, other than in subsection (13) or (14), to a gift or a taxable gift includes a reference to an inheritance or a taxable inheritance, as the case may be, and

(b) a reference to a donee includes a reference to a successor.

(2) [Any person who is primarily accountable for the payment of tax by virtue of paragraph (c) of section 16, paragraph (c) of section 21, or section 45(1),]⁴ shall, within 4 months after the relevant date referred to in subsection (5) —

(a) deliver to the Commissioners a full and true return of —

(i) every gift in respect of which that person is so primarily accountable,

(ii) all the property comprised in such gift on the valuation date,

(iii) an estimate of the market value of such property on the valuation date, and

(iv) such particulars as may be relevant to the assessment of tax in respect of such gift;

(b) notwithstanding section 49, make on that return an assessment of such amount of tax as, to the best of that person's knowledge, information and belief, ought to be charged, levied and paid on that valuation date, and

(c) duly pay the amount of such tax.

(3) [Subsection (2)(c) (other than in respect of tax arising by season of section 20)]⁵ shall be complied with —

(a) where the tax due and payable in respect of any part of the gift is being paid by instalments under section 54, by the due payment of —

(i) an amount which includes any instalment of tax which has fallen due prior to or on the date of the assessment of the tax referred to in subsection (2)(b), and

(ii) any further instalments of such tax on the due dates in accordance with that section;

(b) where the tax due and payable is inheritance tax which is being wholly or partly paid by the transfer of securities to the Minister for Finance under [section 56]², by —

(i) delivering to the Commissioners with the return an application to pay all or part of the tax by such transfer,

(ii) completing the transfer of the securities to the Minister for Finance within such time, not being less than 30 days, as may be specified by the Commissioners by notice in writing, and

(iii) duly paying the excess, if any, of the amount of the tax referred to in subsection (2)(b), or in paragraph (a)(i), over the nominal face value of the securities tendered in payment of the tax in accordance with subparagraph (i).

(4) Subsection (2) applies to a charge for tax arising by reason of [section 15 or 20]⁶ and to any other gift where —

(a) the aggregate of the taxable values of all taxable gifts taken by the donee on or after 5 December 1991, which have the same group threshold (as defined in Schedule 2) as that other gift, exceeds an amount which is 80 per cent of the threshold amount (as defined in Schedule 2) which applies in the computation of tax on that aggregate, or

(b) the donee or, in a case to which section 32(2) applies, the transferee (within the meaning of, and to the extent provided for by, that section) is required by notice in writing by the Commissioners to deliver a return, and for the purposes of this subsection, a reference to a gift includes a reference to a part of a gift or to a part of a taxable gift, as the case may be.

(5) For the purposes of this section, the relevant date shall be—

(a) the valuation date, or

(b) where the donee or, in a case to which section 32(2) applies, the transferee (within the meaning of, and to the extent provided for by, that section) is required by notice in writing by the Commissioners to deliver a return, the date of the notice.

(6) Any person who is accountable for the payment of tax by virtue of subsection (2) or (9) of section 45 shall, if that person is required by notice in writing by the Commissioners to do so, comply with paragraphs (a), (b) and (c) of subsection (2) (as if that person were a person primarily accountable for the payment of tax by virtue of section 45(1)) within such time, not being less than 30 days, as may be specified in the notice.

(7) (a) Any accountable person shall, if that person is so required by the Commissioners by notice in writing, deliver and verify to the Commissioners within such time, not being less than 30 days, as may be specified in the notice—

(i) a statement (where appropriate, on a form provided, or approved of, by them) of such particulars relating to any property, and

(ii) such evidence as they require,

as may, in their opinion, be relevant to the assessment of tax in respect of the gift.

(b) The Commissioners may authorise a person to inspect—

(i) any property comprised in a gift, or

(ii) any books, records, accounts or other documents, in whatever form they are stored, maintained or preserved, relating to any property as may in their opinion be relevant to the assessment of tax in respect of a gift,

and the person having the custody or possession of that property, or of those books, records, accounts or documents, shall permit the person so authorised to make that inspection at such reasonable times as the Commissioners consider necessary.

[(7A) The making of enquiries by the Commissioners for the purposes of subsection (7)(a) or the authorising of inspections by the Commissioners under subsection (7)(b) in connection with or in relation to a relevant return (within the meaning given in section 49(6A)(b)) may not be initiated after the expiry of 4 years commencing on the date that the relevant return is received by the Commissioners.

(7B) (a) The time limit referred to in subsection (7A) shall not apply where the Commissioners have reasonable grounds for believing that any form of fraud or neglect has been committed by or on behalf of any accountable person in connection with or in relation to any relevant return which is the subject of any enquiries or inspections.

(b) In this subsection "neglect" means negligence or a failure to deliver a correct relevant return (within the meaning given in section 49(6A)(b)).][1]

(8) The Commissioners may by notice in writing require any accountable person to —

(a) deliver to them within such time, not being less than 30 days, as may be specified in the notice, an additional return, if it appears to the Commissioners that a return made by that accountable person is defective in a material respect by reason of anything contained in or omitted from it,

(b) notwithstanding section 49, make on that additional return an assessment of such amended amount of tax as, to the best of that person's knowledge, information and belief, ought to be charged, levied and paid on the relevant gift, and

(c) duly pay the outstanding tax, if any, for which that person is accountable in respect of that gift,

and

(i) the requirements of subparagraphs (ii), (iii) and (iv) of subsection (2)(a) shall apply to such additional return required by virtue of paragraph (a), and

(ii) subsection (3) shall, with any necessary modifications, apply to any payment required by virtue of paragraph (c).

(9) Where any accountable person who has delivered a return or an additional return is aware or becomes aware at any time that the return or additional return is defective in a material respect by reason of anything contained in or omitted from it, that person shall, without application from the Commissioners and within 3 months of so becoming aware —

(a) deliver to them an additional return,

(b) notwithstanding section 49, make on that additional return an assessment of such amended amount of tax as, to the best of that person's knowledge, information and belief, ought to be charged, levied and paid on the relevant gift, and

(c) duly pay the outstanding tax, if any, for which that person is accountable in respect of that gift, and

(i) the requirements of subparagraphs (ii), (iii) and (iv) of subsection (2)(a) shall apply to such additional return required by virtue of paragraph (a), and

(ii) subsection (3) shall, with any necessary modifications, apply to any payment required by virtue of paragraph (c).

(10) Any amount of tax payable by an accountable person in respect of an assessment of tax made by that accountable person on a return delivered by that accountable person (other than an amount of that tax payable by the transfer of securities to the Minister for Finance under section 56) shall accompany the return and be paid to the Collector.

(11) Any assessment or payment of tax made under this section shall include interest on tax payable in accordance with section 51.

(12) The Commissioners may by notice in writing require any person to deliver to them within such time, not being less than 30 days, as may be specified in the notice, a full and true return showing details of every taxable gift (including the property comprised in such gift) taken by that person during the period specified in the notice or, as the case may be, indicating that that person has taken no taxable gift during that period.

(13) As respects a taxable gift to which this subsection applies, any accountable person who is a disponer shall within 4 months of the valuation date deliver to the Commissioners a full and true return—

(a) of all the property comprised in such gift on the valuation date,

(b) of an estimate of the market value of such property on the valuation date, and

(c) of such particulars as may be relevant to the assessment of tax in respect of the gift.

(14) Subsection (13) applies to a taxable gift, in the case where—

(a) the taxable value of the taxable gift exceeds an amount which is 80 per cent of the group threshold (as defined in Schedule 2) which applies in relation to that gift for the purposes of the computation of the tax on that gift,

(b) the taxable value of the taxable gift taken by the donee from the disponer increases the total taxable value of all taxable gifts and taxable inheritances taken on or after 5 December 1991 by the donee from the disponer from an amount less than or equal to the amount specified in paragraph (a) to an amount which exceeds the amount so specified, or

(c) the total taxable value of all taxable gifts and taxable inheritances taken on or after 5 December 1991 by the donee from the disponer exceeds the amount specified in paragraph (a) and the donee takes a further taxable gift from the disponer.

(15) Where, under or in consequence of any disposition made by [a person who is resident or ordinarily resident in the State][7] at the date of the disposition, property becomes subject to a discretionary trust, the disponer shall within 4 months of the date of the disposition deliver to the Commissioners a full and true return of —

    (a) the terms of the discretionary trust,

    (b) the names and addresses of the trustees and objects of the discretionary trust, and

    (c) an estimate of the market value at the date of the disposition of the property becoming subject to the discretionary trust.

[(16) For the purposes of subsection (15), a person who is not domiciled in the State at the date of the disposition is treated as not resident and not ordinarily resident in the State on that date unless —

    (a) that person has been resident in the State for the 5 consecutive years of assessment immediately preceding the year of assessment in which that date falls, and

    (b) that person is either resident or ordinarily resident in the State on that date.][8]

Footnotes

1   As inserted by s.145(1)(b), FA 2003, which section will come into effect by Ministerial Order. S.I. No. 515 of 2003 (see page 1379) appoints 1st January, 2005, as the date on which s.145(1)(b), FA 2003, comes into operation. See also s.153, FA 2003.

2   Substituted for "section 58" by para. 2(C), Sch. 3, FA 2004, with effect as on and from 21st February, 2003, under para. 5(b) of that Sch.

3   See S.I. No. 443 of 2003 at page 1375, dealing with the Electronic Transmission of Capital Acquisitions Tax Returns. S.46 (apart from subsections (3), (7), (13) and (15)) is specified for the purposes of Chapter 6, Part 38, of the TCA in relation to returns to be made on or after 29th September, 2003.

4   As substituted by s.117(1)(b), FA2006, as respects the year 2006 and subsequent years.

5   Substituted for "Subsection(2)(c)" by s.117(1)(c), FA 2006, as respects the year 2006 and subsequent years.

6   Substituted for "section 15" by s.117(1)(d), FA 2006, as respects the year 2006 and subsequent years.

7   Substituted for "a person who is living and domiciled in the State" by s.117(1)(e), FA 2006, as respects the year 2006 and subsequent years.

8   Inserted by s.117(1)(f), FA 2006, as respects the year 2006 and subsequent years.

Section 46A[1]

Expression of doubt.

46A. (1) Where an accountable person is in doubt as to the correct application of law to, or the treatment for tax purposes of, any matter to be included in a return or additional return to be delivered by such person under this Act, then that person may deliver the return or additional return to the best of that person's belief but that person shall draw the Commissioners' attention to the matter in question in the return or additional return by specifying the doubt and, if that person does so, that person shall be treated as making a full and true disclosure with regard to that matter.

(2) Subject to subsection (3), where a return or additional return, which includes an expression of doubt as to the correct application of law to, or the treatment for tax purposes of, any matter contained in the return or additional return, is delivered by an accountable person to the Commissioners in accordance with this section, then section 51(2) does not apply to any additional liability arising from a notification to that person by the Commissioners of the correct application of the law to, or the treatment for tax purposes of, the matter contained in the return or additional return the subject of the expression of doubt, on condition that such additional liability is accounted for and remitted to the Commissioners within 30 days of the date on which that notification is issued.

(3) Subsection (2) does not apply where the Commissioners do not accept as genuine an expression of doubt as to the correct application of law to, or the treatment for tax purposes of, any matter contained in the return or additional return and an expression of doubt shall not be accepted as genuine where the Commissioners are of the opinion that the person was acting with a view to the evasion or avoidance of tax.

(4) Where the Commissioners do not accept an expression of doubt as genuine they shall notify the accountable person accordingly within the period of 30 days after the date that the expression of doubt is received by the Commissioners, and the accountable person shall account for any tax, which was not correctly accounted for in the return or additional return referred to in subsection (1) and section 51(2) applies accordingly.

(5) An accountable person who is aggrieved by a decision of the Commissioners that that person's expression of doubt is not genuine may, by giving notice in writing to the Commissioners within the period of 30 days after the notification of the said decision, require the matter to be referred to the Appeal Commissioners.

Footnote

1   This section was inserted by s.146(1)(c), FA 2003, which section will come into effect by Ministerial Order. S.I. No. 466 of 2003 (see page 1375) appoints 1st October, 2003, as the date on which s.146(1)(c), FA 2003, comes into operation. See also s.153, FA 2003.

Commentary

A   An expression of doubt under s.46A, CATCA, is not a "protective notification" for the purposes of s.811A(3), TCA.

Section 47

[S.37, CATA, as amended]

Signing of returns, etc.

47. (1)   A return or an additional return required to be delivered under this Act shall be signed by the accountable person who delivers the return or the additional return and shall include a declaration by the person signing it that the return or additional return is, to the best of that person's knowledge, information and belief, correct and complete.

(2)   The Commissioners may require a return or an additional return to be made on oath.

(3)   The Commissioners may, if they so think fit, accept a return or an additional return under this Act that has not been signed in accordance with this section and such return or additional return is deemed to be duly delivered to the Commissioners under this Act.

(4) (a)   A return or additional return delivered under this Act shall−

    (i)   be made on a form provided, or approved of, by the Commissioners, or

    (ii)   except in a case to which subsection (2) relates but in a case where subsection (3) applies, be in a form approved of by the Commissioners and delivered by any electronic, photographic or other process approved of by them and in circumstances where the use of such process has been agreed by them and subject to such conditions as they may impose.

(b)   An affidavit, additional affidavit, account or additional account, delivered under this Act, shall be made on a form provided, or approved of, by the Commissioners.

(5)   Any oath or affidavit to be made for the purposes of this Act may be made−

    (a)   before the Commissioners,

    (b)   before any officer or person authorised by the Commissioners in that behalf,

    (c)   before any Commissioner for Oaths or any Peace Commissioner or Notary Public in the State, or

"Table" means the Table to this subsection.

(ii) The interest payable in accordance with paragraph (a), shall be—

(I) where one of the periods specified in column (1) of Part 1 of the Table includes or is the same as the period of delay, the amount determined by the formula—

$$T \times D \times P$$

where—

T   is the tax due and payable which remains unpaid,

D   is the number of days (including part of a day) forming the period of delay, and

P   is the appropriate percentage in column (2) of the Table opposite the period specified in column (1) of Part 1 of the Table within which the period of delay falls or which is the same as the period of delay,

and

(II) where a continuous period formed by 2 or more of the periods specified in column (1) of Part 1 of the Table, but not (as in subparagraph (I)) only one such period, includes or is the same as the period of delay, the aggregate of the amounts due in respect of each relevant period which forms part of the period of delay, and the amount due in respect of each such relevant period shall be determined by the formula—

$$T \times D \times P$$

where—

T   is the tax due and payable which remains unpaid,

D   is the number of days (including part of a day) forming the relevant period, and

P   is the appropriate percentage in column (2) of Part 1 of the Table opposite the period specified in column (1) of Part 1 of the Table into which the relevant period falls or which is the same as the relevant period.

[TABLE

Part 1

(Period)	(Percentage)
(1)	(2)
From 31 March 1976 to 31 July 1978	0.0492%
From 1 August 1978 to 31 March 1998	0.0410%
From 1 April 1998 to 31 March 2005	0.0322%
From 1 April 2005 to 30 June 2009	0.0273%
From 1 July 2009 to the date of payment	0.0219%

Part 2

(1)	(2)
From 8 February 1995 to 31 March 1998	0.0307%
From 1 April 1998 to 31 March 2005	0.0241%
From 1 April 2005 to 30 June 2009	0.0204%
From 1 July 2009 to the date of payment	0.0164%

]³

(2A) For the purposes of calculating interest on the whole or the part of the tax to which section 55 applies, subsection (2) shall apply as if references in that subsection to Part 1 of the Table were references to Part 2 of the Table.]²

(3) Notwithstanding subsection (2), interest is not payable on the tax—

    (a) to the extent to which section 89(4)(a) applies, for the duration of the period from the valuation date to the date the agricultural value ceases to be applicable,

    (b) to the extent to which section 77(3) and (4) applies, for the duration of the period from the valuation date to the date the exemption ceases to apply,

    (c) to the extent to which section 101(2) applies, for the duration of the period from the valuation date to the date the reduction which would otherwise fall to be made under section 92 ceases to be applicable,

    (d) to the extent to which section 78(6) applies, for the duration of the period from the valuation date to the date the exemption ceases to apply,

    [(e) to the extent to which section 86(6) or (7) applies, for the duration of the period from the valuation date to the date the exemption ceases to apply,

(f)   to the extent to which section 102A(2) applies, for the duration of the period from the valuation date to the date the development land is disposed of.][4]

(4)   Notwithstanding subsection (2), interest is not payable on tax which is paid within 3 months of the valuation date, and where tax and interest, if any, on that tax is paid within 30 days of the date of assessment of that tax, interest shall not run on that tax for the period of 30 days from the date of the assessment or any part of that period, but, in relation to an assessment of tax made by an accountable person on a return delivered by that accountable person, interest is not payable on tax which is paid within 4 months of the valuation date.

(5)   A payment on account of tax shall be applied—

(a)   if there is interest due on tax at the date of the payment, to the discharge, so far as may be, of the interest so due, and

(b)   if there is any balance of that payment remaining, to the discharge of so much tax as is equal to that balance,

and a payment by an accountable person of tax is treated as a payment on account of tax for the purposes of this section, notwithstanding that the payment may be conditional or that the assessment of tax is incorrect.

(6)   Subject to subsections (2), (4) and (5), payments on account may be made at any time, and when a payment on account is made, interest is not chargeable in respect of any period subsequent to the date of such payment on so much of the payment on account as is to be applied in discharge of the tax.

(7)   In the case of a gift which becomes an inheritance by reason of its being taken under a disposition where the date of the disposition is within 2 years prior to the death of the disponer, this section has effect as if the references to the valuation date in subsections (1), (2), (3) and (4) were references to the date of death of the disponer.

(8)   Where the value of a limited interest is to be ascertained in accordance with rule 8 of Schedule 1 as if it were a series of absolute interests, this section has effect, in relation to each of those absolute interests, as if the references to the valuation date in subsections (1), (2), (3) and (4) were references to the date of the taking of that absolute interest.

Footnotes

1   See s.55, CATCA, in relation to interest on tax chargeable on agricultural and business assets.

2   As substituted for subsection (2) by s.145(4)(a), FA 2005, and applies, under s.145(8)(d), FA 2005, to any unpaid gift tax or inheritance tax, as the case may be, that has not been paid before 1st April, 2005, regardless of when that tax becomes due and payable and notwithstanding anything to the contrary in any other enactment.

3   This Table is substituted by s.29(3), FA 2009, with effect from 3rd June, 2009. Since s.145(4), FA 2005, amends s.51, CATCA, the latter Act applying to gifts and inheritances taken on or after 21st February, 2003, it is not clear to the Editor how interest on such gifts and inheritances may arise prior to that date under this Table.

4   As substituted by s.115, FA 2007, which applies where the event which causes the exemption to cease to apply or the tax to be re-computed, as the case may be, occurs on or after 1st February, 2007.

Commentary

A   See a Revenue Statement of Practice (SP-CAT/1/90) in relation to the postponement of payment of tax in exceptional circumstances. See also Part 17.3 of the *Revenue Tax Manual* regarding the registration of outstanding tax as a voluntary judgement mortgage.

Section 52

[S.42, CATA]

Set-off of gift tax paid in respect of an inheritance.

52.   Where an amount has been paid in respect of gift tax (or interest on such gift tax) on a gift which, by reason of the death of the disponer within 2 years after the date of the disposition under which the gift was taken, becomes an inheritance in respect of which inheritance tax is payable, the amount so paid is treated as a payment on account of the inheritance tax.

Section 53

[S.79, FA 1989]

Surcharge for undervaluation of property.

53.   (1)   In this section "ascertained value" means the market value subject to the right of appeal under section 66 or section 67.

(2)   Where—

(a)   an accountable person delivers a return, and

(b)   the estimate of the market value of any asset comprised in a gift or inheritance and included in that return, when expressed as a percentage of the ascertained value of that asset, is within any of the percentages specified in column (1) of the Table to this section,

then the amount of tax attributable to the property which is that asset is increased by a sum (in this section referred to as the "surcharge") equal to the corresponding percentage, set out in column (2) of that Table opposite the relevant percentage in column (1), of that amount of tax.

(3) Interest is payable under section 51 on any surcharge as if the surcharge were tax, and the surcharge and any interest on that surcharge is chargeable and recoverable as if the surcharge and that interest were part of the tax.

(4) Any person aggrieved by the imposition on that person of a surcharge under this section in respect of any asset may, within 30 days of the notification to that person of the amount of such surcharge, appeal to the Appeal Commissioners against the imposition of such surcharge on the grounds that, having regard to all the circumstances, there were sufficient grounds on which that person might reasonably have based that person's estimate of the market value of the asset.

(5) The Appeal Commissioners shall hear and determine an appeal to them under subsection (4) as if it were an appeal to them against an assessment to tax, and the provisions of section 67 relating to an appeal or to the rehearing of an appeal or to the statement of a case for the opinion of the High Court on a point of law shall, with any necessary modifications, apply accordingly.

TABLE

Estimate of the market value of the asset in the return, expressed as a percentage of the ascertained value of that asset	Surcharge
(1)	(2)
Equal to or greater than 0 per cent but less than 40 per cent	30 per cent
Equal to or greater than 40 per cent but less than 50 per cent	20 per cent
Equal to or greater than 50 per cent but less than 67 per cent	10 per cent

Section 54

[S.43, CATA]

Payment of tax by instalments.

54.   (1) Subject to the payment of interest in accordance with section 51 and to the provisions of this section, [the tax due and payable (other than tax arising by reason of section 20)][2] in respect of a taxable gift or a taxable inheritance may, at the option of the person delivering the return or additional return, be paid by 5 equal yearly instalments, the first of which is due at the expiration of 12 months from the date on which the tax became due and payable and the interest on the unpaid tax shall be added to each instalment and shall be paid at the same time as such instalment.

(2) An instalment not due may be paid at any time before it is due.

(3) In any case where and to the extent that the property of which the taxable gift or taxable inheritance consists is sold or compulsorily acquired, all unpaid instalments shall, unless the interest of the donee or successor is a limited interest, be paid on completion of the sale or compulsory acquisition and, if not so paid, shall be tax in arrear.[1]

(4) This section shall not apply in any case where and to the extent to which a taxable gift or a taxable inheritance consists of personal property in which the donee, or the successor, or the transferee referred to in section 32(2), as the case may be, takes an absolute interest.[1]

(5) In any case where the interest taken by a donee or a successor is an interest limited to cease on that person's death, and that person's death occurs before all the instalments of the tax in respect of the taxable gift or taxable inheritance would have fallen due if such tax were being paid by instalments, any instalment of such tax which would not have fallen due prior to the date of the death of that donee or successor shall cease to be payable, and the payment, if made, of any such last-mentioned instalment is treated as an overpayment of tax for the purposes of section 57.

Footnotes

1   But see s.55, CATCA, in relation to the payment by instalments of tax chargeable on agricultural and business assets.

2   Substituted for "the tax due and payable" by s.117(1)(g), FA 2006, as respects the year 2006 and subsequent years.

Commentary

A   See Part 17.2 of the *Revenue CAT Manual* in relation to the payment of tax by non-statutory instalments where the tax cannot be paid without causing excessive hardship.

Section 55

[S.164, FA 1995, as amended]

Payment of tax on certain assets by instalments.

55. (1) In this section—

"agricultural property" has the meaning assigned to it by section 89;

"relevant business property" has the same meaning as it has in section 93, other than shares in or securities of a company (being shares or securities quoted on a recognised stock exchange) and without regard to sections 94 and 100(4).

(2) Where the whole or part of the tax which is due and payable in respect of a taxable gift or taxable inheritance is attributable to either or both agricultural property and relevant business property—

(a) section 54 shall apply to that whole or part of the tax notwithstanding subsection (3) or (4) of that section but where all or any part of that agricultural property or relevant business property, or any property which directly or indirectly replaces such property, is sold or compulsorily acquired and, by virtue of subsection (4) of section 89 or section 101, that sale or compulsory acquisition causes the taxable value of such a taxable gift or taxable inheritance to be increased, or would cause such increase if subsection (2) of section 89 or section 92 applied, all unpaid instalments referable to the property sold or compulsorily acquired shall, unless the interest of the donee or successor is a limited interest, be paid on completion of that sale or compulsory acquisition and, if not so paid, shall be tax in arrear, and

[(b) notwithstanding subsection (2) of section 51, the interest payable on that whole or part of the tax shall be determined –

(i) in accordance with that subsection as modified by subsection (2A) of that section, or

(ii) in such other manner as may be prescribed by the Minister for Finance by regulations,

instead of in accordance with subsection (2) of that section, and that section shall apply as regards that whole or part of the tax as if the interest so payable were determined under that section, but the interest payable on any overdue instalment of that whole or part of that tax, or on such part of the tax as would represent any such overdue instalment if that whole or part of the tax were being paid by instalments, shall continue to be determined in accordance with subsection (2) of section 51.][1]

(3) For the purposes of this section reference to an overdue instalment in paragraph (b) of subsection (2) is a reference to an instalment which is overdue for the purposes of section 54 (as it applies to this section) or for the purposes of paragraph (a) of subsection (2).

(4) For the purposes of this section the value of a business or of an interest in a business shall be taken to be its net value ascertained in accordance with section 98.

(5) This section shall not apply in relation to an inheritance taken by a discretionary trust by virtue of section 15(1) or section 20(1).

(6) Every regulation made under this section shall be laid before Dáil Éireann as soon as may be after it is made and, if a resolution annulling the regulation is passed by Dáil Éireann within the next 21 days on which Dáil Éireann has sat after the regulation is laid before it, the regulation shall be annulled accordingly, but without prejudice to the validity of anything previously done under that regulation.

Footnote

1   S.55(2)(b) was amended by s.148, FA 2003, the amendment applying on and from 1st September, 2002, to the rate of interest payable under s.55(2)(b) in respect of an amount to be paid whether before, on or after that date in accordance with that provision.

S.55(2)(b) is substituted by s.145(4)(b), FA 2005, the substitution applying, under s.145 (8)(d), FA 2005, to any unpaid gift tax or inheritance tax, as the case may be, that has not been paid before 1st April, 2005, regardless of when that tax becomes due and payable and notwithstanding anything to the contrary is any other enactment.

Section 56

[S.45, CATA]

Payment of inheritance tax by transfer of securities.

56.   Section 22 of the Finance Act 1954[1] (which relates to the payment of death duties by the transfer of securities to the Minister for Finance) and the regulations made under that Act shall apply, with any necessary modifications, to the payment of [inheritance tax (other than tax arising by reason of section 20)][2] by the transfer of securities to the Minister for Finance, as they apply to the payment of death duties by the transfer of securities to the Minister for Finance.

Footnotes

1   Reproduced on page 673.

2   Substituted for "inheritance tax" by s.117(1)(h), FA 2006, as respects the year 2006 and subsequent years.

Commentary

A   Revenue have accepted that, if a testator bequeaths qualifying National Loan to one legatee and the residue of the estate to another, the inheritance tax on the residue may be paid by a transfer of the National Loan if the two legatees involved agree to this.

B   At the date of publication of this book, the last security available to pay inheritance tax was 6½% Exchequer Stock, 2000/05, which was redeemed on 27th June, 2000.

Section 57

[S.46, CATA]

Overpayment of tax.

[**57.**   (1)   In this section –

"relevant date", in relation to a repayment of tax means –

(a)   the date which is [93 days][4] after the date on which a valid claim in respect of the repayment is made to the Commissioners, or

(b)   where the repayment is due to a mistaken assumption in the operation of the tax on the part of the Commissioners, the date which is the date of the payment of the tax which has given rise to that repayment;

"repayment" means a repayment of tax including a repayment of –

(a)   any interest charged,

(b)   any surcharge imposed,

(c)   any penalty incurred

under any provision of this Act in relation to tax;

"tax" includes interest charged, a surcharge imposed or a penalty incurred under any provision of this Act.

(2)   Where, a claim for repayment of tax made to the Commissioners, is a valid claim, the Commissioners shall, subject to the provisions of this section, give relief by means of repayment of the excess or otherwise as is reasonable and just.

(3)   Notwithstanding subsection (2), no tax shall be repaid to an accountable person in respect of a valid claim unless that valid claim is made within the period of 4 years commencing on [the valuation date or the date of the payment of the tax concerned (where the tax has been paid within 4 months after the valuation date)].[5]

(4)   Subsection (3) shall not apply to a claim for repayment of tax arising by virtue of section 18(3), Article VI of the First Schedule to the Finance Act 1950,[1] or Article 9 of the Schedule to the Double Taxation Relief (Taxes on Estates of Deceased Persons and Inheritances and on Gifts) (United Kingdom) Order 1978 (S.I. No. 279 of 1978).[2]

(5)   Subsection (3) shall not apply to a claim for repayment of tax arising on or before the date of the passing of the Finance Act 2003, where a valid claim is made on or before 31 December 2004.

(6)   Subject to the provisions of this section, where a person is entitled to a repayment, the amount of the repayment shall, subject to a valid claim in respect of the repayment being made to the Commissioners and subject to section 1006A(2A) of the Taxes Consolidation Act 1997, carry simple interest at the rate of 0.011 per cent, or such other rate (if any) prescribed by the Minister for Finance by order under subsection (11), for each day or part of a day for the period commencing on the relevant date and ending on the date upon which the repayment is made.

(7)   A claim for repayment under this section shall only be treated as a valid claim when -

(a)   it has been made in accordance with the provisions of the law (if any) relating to tax under which such claim is made, and

(b)   all information which the Commissioners may reasonably require to enable them determine if and to what extent a repayment is due, has been furnished to them.

(8)   Interest shall not be payable under this section if it amounts to €10 or less.

(9)   This section shall not apply in relation to any repayment or part of a repayment of tax in respect of which interest is payable under or by virtue of any provision of any other enactment.

(10) Income tax shall not be deductible on any payment of interest under this section and such interest shall not be reckoned in computing income for the purposes of the Tax Acts.

(11) (a) The Minister for Finance may, from time to time, make an order prescribing a rate for the purposes of subsection (6).

(b) Every order made by the Minister for Finance under paragraph (a) shall be laid before Dáil Éireann as soon as may be after it is made and, if a resolution annulling the order is passed by Dáil Éireann within the next 21 days on which Dáil Éireann has sat after the order is laid before it, the order shall be annulled accordingly, but without prejudice to the validity of anything previously done under it.

(12) The Commissioners may make regulations as they deem necessary in relation to the operation of this section.][3]

Footnotes

1   Reproduced on page 175.

2   Reproduced on page 183.

3   As substituted by s.145(1)(d), FA 2003, which section will come into effect by Ministerial Order. S.I. No 515 of 2003 (see page 1379) appoints 1st November, 2003, as the date on which s.145(1)(d), FA 2003, comes into operation, in so far as it relates to s.57, CATCA (other than subsections (2) to (5)) as respects repayments made on or after that date (except repayments in respect of claims for repayment made before that date not being claims for repayment made under s.18(3), CATCA). In so far as s.145(1)(d), FA 2003, relates to s.57(2) to (5), CATCA, S.I. No. 515 of 2003 appoints 31st October, 2003, as the date on which s.145(1)(d), FA 2003, comes into operation. See also s.153, FA 2003.

4   Substituted for "183 days" by s.121(4), FA 2007, which applies to interest payable on repayments made on or after 2nd April, 2007.

5   Substituted by s.127(1), FA 2008, for "the later of the valuation date or the date of the payment of the tax concerned". The substitution applies to claims for repayment of tax made on or after 31st January, 2008.

Section 58

[S.63, CATA, as amended]

Penalties.

58. (1) (a) Any person who contravenes or fails to comply with any requirement or provision under section 46 shall be liable to a penalty of **[€3,000]**[4].

(b) Where the contravention or failure referred to in paragraph (a) continues after judgment has been given by the court before which proceedings for the penalty have been commenced, the person concerned shall be liable to a further penalty of €30 for each day on which the contravention or failure so continues.

[(1A) Where a person **[deliberately or carelessly]**[6] fails to comply with a requirement to deliver a return or additional return under subsection (2), (6) or (8) of section 46 **[......]**[6] that person is liable to a penalty of -

(a) **[€3,000]**,[4] and

  (b) the amount [...][3] of the difference specified in subsection (5A).][1]

(2) Where, under, or for the purposes of, any of the provisions of this Act, a person is authorised to inspect any property for the purpose of reporting to the Commissioners the market value of that property and the person having custody or possession of that property prevents such inspection or obstructs the person so authorised in the performance of that person's functions in relation to the inspection, the person so having custody or possession is liable to a penalty of [€3,000][5].

(3) Where an accountable person [deliberately or carelessly][7] –.

  (a) delivers any incorrect return or additional return,

  (b) makes or furnishes any incorrect statement, declaration, evidence or valuation in connection with any property comprised in any disposition,

  (c) makes or furnishes any incorrect statement, declaration, evidence or valuation in connection with any claim for any allowance, deduction, exemption or relief, or

  (d) makes or furnishes any incorrect statement, declaration, evidence or valuation in connection with any other matter,

on the basis of which the amount of tax assessable in respect of a taxable gift or taxable inheritance would be less than it would have been if the correct return, additional return, statement, declaration, evidence or valuation had been delivered, made or furnished, that person is liable to a penalty of –

  (i) €6,345, and

  (ii) the amount [...][3] of the difference specified in subsection (5).

(4) Where any such return, additional return, statement, declaration, evidence or valuation as is mentioned in subsection (3) was delivered, made or furnished neither [deliberately nor carelessly][8] by a person and it comes to that person's notice that it was incorrect, then, unless the error is remedied without unreasonable delay, such matter is treated, for the purposes of this section, as having been [carelessly][8] done by that person.

(5) The difference referred to in subsection (3) is the difference between –

  (a) the amount of tax payable in respect of the taxable gift or taxable inheritance to which the return, additional return, statement, declaration, evidence or valuation relates, and

  (b) the amount which would have been the amount so payable if the return, additional return, statement, declaration, evidence or valuation as made or submitted had been correct.

[(5A) The difference referred to in paragraph (b) of subsection (1A) is the difference between -

(a) the amount of tax paid by that person in respect of the taxable gift or taxable inheritance to which the return or additional return relates, and

(b) the amount of tax which would have been payable if the return or additional return had been delivered by that person and that return or additional return had been correct.][2]

(6) For the purpose of subsection (3), where anything referred to in that subsection is delivered, made or furnished on behalf of a person, it is deemed to have been delivered, made or furnished by that person unless that person proves that it was done without that person's knowledge or consent.

(7) Any person who assists in or induces the delivery, making or furnishing for any purposes of the tax of any return, additional return, statement, declaration, evidence or valuation which that person knows to be incorrect shall be liable to a penalty of [€3,000][9].

(8) This section shall not affect any criminal proceedings.

[(9) Subject to this section —

(a) sections 987(4), 1062, 1063, 1064, 1065, 1066 and 1068 of the Taxes Consolidation Act 1997 shall, with any necessary modifications, apply to a penalty under this Act as if the penalty were a penalty under the Income Tax Acts, and

(b) sections 1077E (inserted by the Finance (No. 2) Act 2008) of the Taxes Consolidation Act 1997 shall, with any necessary modifications, apply to a penalty under this Act as if the penalty were a penalty relating to income tax, corporation tax or capital gains tax, as the case may be.][10]

Footnotes

1   As inserted by s.146(1)(d)(i), FA 2003, which section will come into effect by Ministerial Order. S.I. No. 466 of 2003 (see page 1377) appoints 1st October, 2003, as the date on which s.146(1)(d), FA 2003, comes into operation. See also s.153, FA 2003.

2   As inserted by s.146(1)(d)(ii), FA 2003, which section will come into effect by Ministerial Order. S.I. No. 466 of 2003 (see page 1377) appoints 1st October, 2003, as the date on which s.146(1)(d), FA 2003, comes into operation. See also s.153, FA 2003.

3   The words ", or in the case of fraud, twice the amount," deleted by s.132, FA 2005, which applies to returns, additional returns, statements, declarations, evidence or valuations delivered, made or, as the case may be, furnished on or after 25th March, 2005.

4   As substituted for "€2,535" by s.98(1), and by para. (b)(i), Part 4 of Sch. 5, of the F(No. 2)A, 2008, and comes into effect after 24th December, 2008.

5   As substituted for "€1,265" by s.98(1), and by para. (b)(ii), Part 4 of Sch. 5, of the F(No. 2)A, 2008, and comes into effect after 24th December, 2008.

6   As inserted by s.98(1), and by para. (b)(iii), Part 4 of Sch. 5, of the F(No. 2)A, 2008, which also deleted the words", by reason of fraud on neglect by that person," both amendments coming into effect after 24th December, 2008.

7   As substituted for "fraudulently or negligently" by s.98(1), and by para. (b)(iv), Part 4 of Sch. 5, of the F (No. 2) A, 2008, and comes into effect after 24th December, 2008.

8   "deliberately nor carelessly" substituted for "fraudulently nor negligently", and "carelessly" for "negligently", both by s.98(1), and by para. (b)(v), Part 4 of Sch. 5, of the F(No. 2)A, 2008, and comes into effect after 24th December, 2008.

9   As substituted for "€1,265" by s.98(1), and by para. (b)(vi), Part 4 of Sch. 5, of the F(No. 2)A, 2008, and comes into effect after 24th December, 2008.

10   As substituted by s.98(1), and by para. (b)(vii), Part 4 of Sch. 5, of the F(No. 2)A, 2008, and comes into effect after 24th December, 2008.

Commentary

A   See an article on interest and penalties at page 3, Issue 55, of the *Revenue Tax Briefing* of April 2004.

Section 59

[S.44, CATA]

Postponement, remission and compounding of tax.

59. (1) Where the Commissioners are satisfied that tax leviable in respect of any gift or inheritance can not without excessive hardship be raised at once, they may allow payment to be postponed for such period, to such extent and on such terms (including the waiver of interest) as they think fit.

(2) If, after the expiration of the relevant period immediately following the date on which any tax became due and payable, the tax or any part of that tax remains unpaid, the Commissioners may, if they think fit, remit the payment of any interest accruing after such expiration on the unpaid tax; and in this subsection, "relevant period" means the period at the end of which the interest on an amount payable in respect of tax would, at the rate from time to time chargeable during that period in respect of interest on tax, equal the amount of such tax.

(3) If, after the expiration of 20 years from the date on which any tax became due and payable, the tax or any part of that tax remains unpaid, the Commissioners may, if they think fit, remit the payment of such tax or any part of that tax and all or any interest on that tax.

(4) Where, in the opinion of the Commissioners, the complication of circumstances affecting a gift or inheritance or the value of that gift or inheritance or the assessment or recovery of tax on that gift or inheritance are such as to justify them in doing so, they may compound the tax payable on the gift or inheritance on such terms as they shall think fit, and may give a discharge to the person or persons accountable for the tax on payment of the tax according to such composition.

Commentary

A   See a Revenue Statement of Practice (SP-CAT/1/90) in relation to the postponement of payment of tax in exceptional circumstance. See also Part 17.3 of the *Revenue CAT Manual* regarding the registration of outstanding tax as a voluntary judgement mortgage.

B   According to Part 19.9 of the *Revenue CAT Manual*, the hardship provisions of s.59, CATCA, may apply when the financial position of surviving common-law spouses (who are treated as strangers to the disponer) and their children is particularly difficult.

Section 60

[S.47, CATA]

Tax to be a charge.

60. (1) Tax due and payable in respect of a taxable gift or a taxable inheritance shall, subject to this section, be and remain a charge on the property (other than money or negotiable instruments) of which the taxable gift or taxable inheritance consists at the valuation date and the tax shall have priority over all charges and interests created by the donee or successor or any person claiming in right of the donee or successor or on that donee or successor's behalf, but where any settled property comprised in any taxable gift or taxable inheritance shall be subject to any power of sale, exchange, or partition, exercisable with the consent of the donee or successor, or by the donee or successor with the consent of another person, the donee or successor shall not be precluded by the charge of tax on that donee or successor's taxable gift or taxable inheritance from consenting to the exercise of such power, or exercising any power with proper consent, as the case may be; and where any such power is exercised, the tax shall be charged on the property acquired, in substitution for charging it on the property previously comprised in the gift or inheritance, and on all moneys arising from the exercise of any such power, and on all investments of such moneys.

(2) Property comprised in a taxable gift or taxable inheritance shall not, as against a bona fide purchaser or mortgagee for full consideration in money or money's worth, or a person deriving title from or under such a purchaser or mortgagee, remain charged with or liable to the payment of tax after the expiration of 12 years from the date of the gift or the date of the inheritance.

(3) Tax shall not be a charge on property under subsection (1) as against a bona fide purchaser or mortgagee of such property for full consideration in money or money's worth without notice, or a person deriving title from or under such a purchaser or mortgagee.

Commentary

A   See Part 4.4 of the *Revenue CAT Manual* in relation to the issue of a letter of clearance from inheritance tax, where there is a sale in course of administration before the valuation date, and the charge for tax applies to the proceeds of sale.

Cross-Reference

1   The priority of the charge in s.60(1) is qualified by s.111(2)(d) and (f), CATCA.

Section 61

[S.48, CATA, as amended]

Receipts and certificates.

61. (1) [......][1]

(2) [......][1]

(3) The Commissioners shall, on application to them by a person who is an accountable person in respect of any of the property of which a taxable gift or taxable inheritance consists, if they are satisfied that the tax charged on the property in respect of the taxable gift or taxable inheritance has been or will be paid, or that there is no tax so charged, give a certificate to the person, in such form as they think fit, to that effect.

(4) Where a person who is an accountable person in respect of the property of which a taxable gift or taxable inheritance consists has –

(a) delivered to the Commissioners, a full and true return of all the property comprised in the gift or inheritance on the valuation date and such particulars as may be relevant to the assessment of tax in respect of the gift or inheritance,

(b) made on that return an assessment of such amount of tax as, to the best of that person's knowledge, information and belief, ought to be charged, levied and paid, and

(c) duly paid the amount of such tax (if any),

the Commissioners may give a certificate to the person, in such form as they think fit, to the effect that the tax charged on the property in respect of the taxable gift or taxable inheritance has been paid or that there is no tax so charged.

(5) A certificate referred to in subsection (3) or (4) shall discharge the property from liability for tax (if any) in respect of the gift or inheritance, to the extent specified in the certificate, but shall not discharge the property from tax in case of fraud or failure to disclose material facts and, in any case, shall not affect the tax payable in respect of any other property or the extent to which tax is recoverable from any accountable person or from the personal representatives of any accountable person, but a certificate purporting to be a discharge of the whole tax payable in respect of any property included in the certificate in respect of a gift or inheritance shall exonerate from liability for such tax a bona fide purchaser or mortgagee for full consideration in money or money's worth without notice of such fraud or failure and a person deriving title from or under such a purchaser or mortgagee.

(6) Subject to subsection (7), where tax is chargeable on the taxable value of a taxable gift or taxable inheritance and –

(a) application is made to the Commissioners by any person (in this section referred to as "the applicant") –

(i) who is a person accountable, but not primarily accountable, for the payment of the whole or part of the tax, or

(ii) who is the personal representative of any person referred to in subparagraph (i),

and

    (b) the applicant –

        (i) delivers to the Commissioners a full and true return of all the property comprised in the gift or inheritance and such particulars as may be relevant to the assessment of tax in respect of the gift or inheritance, and

        (ii) makes on that return an assessment of such amount of tax as, to the best of that person's knowledge, information and belief, ought to be charged, levied and paid,

the Commissioners may, on payment of the tax assessed by the applicant, give a certificate to the applicant which shall discharge the applicant from any other claim for tax in respect of the gift or inheritance.

(7) A certificate by the Commissioners under subsection (6) shall not discharge the applicant in the case of fraud or failure to disclose material facts within that applicant's own knowledge and shall not affect any further tax that may be payable by the applicant if any further property is afterwards shown to have been comprised in the taxable gift or taxable inheritance to which the certificate relates and in respect of which further property the applicant is liable for the tax.

Footnote

1   Repealed by Part 1 of the Table to Sch. 4, F(No. 2)A, 2008, which, under para. 6 of that Sch., comes into effect and applies as respects any tax that becomes due and payable on or after 1st March, 2009.

Commentary

A   See Part 4.4 of the *Revenue CAT Manual* in relation to the issue of a letter of clearance from inheritance tax, where there is a sale in course of administration before the valuation date, and the charge for tax applies to the proceeds of sale.

Section 62

[S.146, FA 1994, as amended]

Certificate relating to registration of title based on possession.

62. (1) In this section –

["Act of 1964" means the Registration of Title Act 1964, as amended by the Registration of Deeds and Title Act 2006;][1]

[....][2]

["Authority" means the Property Registration Authority established by section 9 of the Registration of Deeds and Title Act 2006;][3]

"relevant period", in relation to a person's application to be registered as owner of property, means the period commencing on 28 February 1974 and ending on the date as of which the registration was made, but –

(a)   where the certificate referred to in subsection (2) is a certificate for a period ending prior to the date of the registration, the period covered by the certificate shall be deemed to be the relevant period if, at the time of the registration, the [Authority]⁴ had no reason to believe that a death relevant to the application for registration occurred after the expiration of the period covered by the certificate, and

(b)   where the registration of the person (if any) who, at the date of that application, was the registered owner of the property had been made as of a date after 28 February 1974, the relevant period shall commence on the date as of which that registration was made;

"the Rules of 1972" means the Land Registration Rules 1972 (S.I. No. 230 of 1972).

(2)   A person shall not be registered as owner of property in a register of ownership maintained under the Act of 1964 on foot of an application made to the [Authority]⁵ on or after the date of the passing of this Act which is—

(a)   based on possession, and

(b)   made under the Rules of 1972, or any other rule made for carrying into effect the objects of the Act of 1964,

unless the applicant produces to the [Authority]⁵ a certificate issued by the Commissioners to the effect that the Commissioners are satisfied—

(i)   that the property did not become charged with gift tax or inheritance tax during the relevant period, or

(ii)   that any charge for gift tax or inheritance tax to which the property became subject during that period has been discharged, or will (to the extent that it has not been discharged) be discharged within a time considered by the Commissioners to be reasonable.

(3)   In the case of an application for registration in relation to which a solicitor's certificate is produced for the purpose of rule 19(3), 19(4) or 35 of the Rules of 1972, the [Authority]⁵ may accept that the application is not based on possession if the solicitor makes to the [Authority]⁵ a declaration in writing to that effect.

(4)   Where, on application to them by the applicant for registration, the Commissioners are satisfied that they may issue a certificate for the purpose of subsection (2), they shall issue a certificate for that purpose, and the certificate and the application for that certificate shall be on a form provided by the Commissioners.

(5)   A certificate issued by the Commissioners for the purpose of subsection (2) shall be in such terms and subject to such qualifications as the Commissioners think fit, and shall not be a certificate for any other purpose.

(6) In subsection (2), the reference to a certificate issued by the Commissioners shall be construed as including a reference to a certificate to which subsection (7) relates, and subsection (2) shall be construed accordingly.

(7) (a) In this subsection—

"the relevant particulars" means the particulars of title to the relevant property which are required to be produced to the [Authority][5] for the purposes of paragraph 2 of Form 5 of the Schedule of Forms referred to in the definition of "Forms" contained in rule 2(1) of the Rules of 1972;

"the relevant property" means the property in respect of which the application for registration is being made.

(b) A certificate to which this subsection relates is a certificate by the solicitor for the applicant for registration in which it is certified, on a form provided by the Commissioners, that the solicitor—

(i) is satisfied—

(I) in a case where the applicant is a statutory authority within the definition of "statutory authority" contained in section 3(1) of the Act of 1964, that the market value of the relevant property at the time of the application does not exceed €127,000, or

(II) in any other case, that—

(A) the area of the relevant property does not exceed 5 hectares, and

(B) the market value of the relevant property at the time of the application does not exceed €19,050,

and

(ii) having investigated the title to the relevant property, has no reason to believe that the relevant particulars, in so far as relating to the relevant property at any time during the relevant period, are particulars which related at that time to significant other real property, that is, real property which, if combined with the relevant property for the purposes of subparagraph (i), would cause a limit which applies to the relevant property by virtue of that subparagraph to be exceeded.

(8) Notwithstanding subsection (7), a certificate by the solicitor for the applicant for registration shall be a certificate to which subsection (7) relates if it certifies, on a form provided by the Commissioners, that the solicitor is satisfied that—

(a) the area of the property in respect of which the application for registration is being made does not exceed 500 square metres,

(b) the market value of that property at the time of the application does not exceed €2,540, and

(c) the application is not part of a series of related applications covering a single piece of property the total area of which exceeds 500 square metres or the market value of which at the time of the application exceeds €2,540.

Footnotes

1 Substituted for "the Act of 1964" by s.128(1)(a)(i), FA 2008, in respect of applications to register property made on or after 4th November, 2006.

2 Definition of "the Registrar" deleted by s.128(1)(a)(ii), FA 2008, in respect of applications to register property made on or after 4th November, 2006.

3 Definition of "Authority" inserted by s.128(1)(a)(iii), FA 2008, in respect of applications to register property made on or after 4th November, 2006.

4 "Authority" substituted for "Registrar" by s.128(1)(a)(iv), FA 2008, in respect of applications to register property made on or after 4th November, 2008.

5 "Authority" substituted for "Registrar" by s.128(1)(b), FA 2008, in respect of applications to register property made on or after 4th November, 2008.

Section 63

[S.49, CATA]

Recovery of tax and penalties.

63. (1) [......][1]

(2) [......][1]

(3) If any accountable person is liable under section 46 to deliver to the Commissioners a return or an additional return and makes default in so doing, ...[2] the Commissioners may sue by action or other appropriate proceeding in the Circuit Court for an order directing the person so making default to deliver such return or additional return or to show cause to the contrary; and the Circuit Court may by order direct such accountable person to deliver such return or additional return within such time as may be specified in the order.

(4) Whenever property is subject to a charge by virtue of section 60, [......][2] the Commissioners may sue by action or other appropriate proceeding in any court of competent jurisdiction for, and the court may make, an order directing the owner of the property to pay the tax with which the property is charged.

Footnotes

1 Repealed by Part 1 of the Table to Sch. 4, F(No. 2)A, 2008, which, under para. 6 of that Sch., comes into effect and applies as respects any tax that becomes due and payable on or after 1st March, 2009.

2 The words "the Attorney General or the Minister for Finance or" deleted by Part 1 of the Table to Sch. 4, F(No. 2)A, 2008, which, under para. 6 of that Sch., comes into effect and applies as respects any tax that becomes due and payable on or after 1st March, 2009.

Section 64[1]

[S.129, FA 1991, as amended]

Application of certain income tax provisions in relation to the collection and recovery of capital acquisitions tax, etc.

64. ......

Footnote

1   Repealed by Part 1 of the Table to Sch. 4, F(No. 2)A, 2008, which, under para. 6 of that Sch., comes into effect and applies as respects any tax that becomes due and payable on or after 1st March, 2009.

Section 65[1]

[S.50, CATA]

Evidence in proceedings for recovery of tax.

65. ......

Footnote

1   Repealed by Part 1 of the Table to Sch. 4, F(No. 2)A, 2008, which, under para. 6 of that Sch., comes into effect and applies as respects any tax that becomes due and payable on or after 1st March, 2009.

PART 8
Appeals

Section 66

[S.51, CATA]

Appeals regarding value of real property.

66. (1) If a person is aggrieved by the decision of the Commissioners as to the market value of any real property, that person may appeal against the decision in the manner prescribed by section 33 of the Finance (1909-10) Act 1910[1], and the provisions as to appeals under that section of that Act shall apply accordingly with any necessary modifications.

(2) The particulars of any transfer or lease which are presented to or obtained by the Commissioners under section 12(2) of the Stamp Duties Consolidation Act 1999 shall, in any appeal under this section, be received as prima facie evidence of all matters and things stated in such particulars.

Footnote

1   Reproduced on page 655.

Section 67

[S.52, CATA, as amended]

Appeals in other cases.

67. (1) In this section—

"Appeal Commissioners" has the meaning assigned to it by section 850 of the Taxes Consolidation Act 1997;

"appellant" means a person who appeals to the Appeal Commissioners under subsection (2).

(2) Subject to the other provisions of this Act, a person who is called on by the Commissioners to pay an assessment of tax in respect of any property and who is aggrieved by the assessment may, in accordance with this section, appeal to the Appeal Commissioners against the assessment and the appeal shall be heard and determined by the Appeal Commissioners whose determination shall be final and conclusive unless the appeal is required to be reheard by a judge of the Circuit Court or a case is required to be stated in relation to it for the opinion of the High Court on a point of law.

(3) An appeal shall not lie under this section in relation to the market value of real property.

(4) A person who intends to appeal under this section against an assessment shall, within 30 days after the date of the assessment, give notice in writing to the Commissioners of that person's intention to appeal against the assessment.

(5) (a) Subject to this section, the provisions of the Income Tax Acts relating to—

(i) the appointment of times and places for the hearing of appeals,

(ii) the giving of notice to each person who has given notice of appeal of the time and place appointed for the hearing of that person's appeal,

(iii) the determination of an appeal by agreement between the appellant and an officer appointed by the Commissioners in that behalf,

(iv) the determination of an appeal by the appellant giving notice of that appellant's intention not to proceed with the appeal,

(v) the hearing and determination of an appeal by the Appeal Commissioners, including the hearing and determination of an appeal by one Appeal Commissioner,

(vi) the publication of reports of determinations of the Appeal Commissioners,

(vii) the determination of an appeal through the neglect or refusal of a person who has given notice of appeal to attend before the Appeal Commissioners at the time and place appointed,

(viii) the extension of the time for giving notice of appeal and the readmission of appeals by the Appeal Commissioners and the provisions which apply where action by means of court proceedings has been taken,

(ix) the rehearing of an appeal by a judge of the Circuit Court and the statement of a case for the opinion of the High Court on a point of law,

(x) the payment of tax in accordance with the determination of the Appeal Commissioners notwithstanding that an appeal is required to be reheard by a judge of the Circuit Court or that a case for the opinion of the High Court on a point of law has been required to be stated or is pending,

(xi) the procedures for appeal,

(xii) the refusal of an application for an appeal hearing,

shall, with any necessary modifications, apply to an appeal under this section as if the appeal were an appeal against an assessment to income tax.

(b) The Commissioners shall, subject to their giving notice in writing in that behalf to the appellant within 10 days after the determination of an appeal by the Appeal Commissioners, have the same right as the appellant to have the appeal reheard by a judge of the Circuit Court.

(c) The rehearing of an appeal under this section by a judge of the Circuit Court shall be by a judge of the Circuit Court in whose circuit the appellant or one of the appellants resides or (in the case of a body corporate) has its principal place of business, but—

(i) in any case where no appellant is resident in or (in the case of a body corporate) has a place of business in the State, or

(ii) in any case where there is a doubt or a dispute as to the circuit,

the appeal shall be reheard by a judge of the Circuit Court assigned to the Dublin Circuit.

(6) (a) Where a notice or other document which is required or authorised to be served by this section is to be served on a body corporate, such notice shall be served on the secretary or other officer of the body corporate.

(b) Any notice or other document which is required or authorised by this section to be served by the Commissioners or by an appellant may be served by post and in the case of a notice or other document addressed to the Commissioners, shall be sent to the Secretaries, Revenue Commissioners, Dublin Castle, Dublin 2.

(c) Any notice or other document which is required or authorised to be served by the Commissioners on an appellant under this section may be sent to the solicitor, accountant or other agent of the appellant and a notice thus served shall be deemed to have been served on the appellant unless the appellant proves to the satisfaction of the Appeal Commissioners, or the Circuit Court, as the case may be, that that appellant had, before the notice or other document was served, withdrawn the authority of such solicitor, accountant or other agent to act on that appellant's behalf.

(7) Prima facie evidence of any notice given under this section by the Commissioners or by an officer of the Commissioners may be given in any proceedings by the production of a document purporting—

(a) to be a copy of the notice, or

(b) if the details specified in the notice are contained in an electronic, photographic or other record maintained by the Commissioners, to reproduce those details in so far as they relate to that notice,

and it shall not be necessary to prove the official position of the person by whom the notice purports to be given or, if it is signed, the signature, or that the person signing and giving it was authorised to do so.

(8) (a) The Commissioners may serve notice in writing, referring expressly to this subsection, on any person whom they have reason to believe to be accountable for the payment of tax, of any decision they have made which is relevant to such tax.

(b) Any person who is informed of a decision in accordance with paragraph (a) may appeal to the Appeal Commissioners against the decision.

(c) The Appeal Commissioners shall hear and determine an appeal to them under this subsection as if it were an appeal to them against an assessment to tax, and the provisions of this section relating to an appeal or to the rehearing of an appeal or to the statement of a case for the opinion of the High Court on a point of law shall, with any necessary modifications, apply accordingly.

Cross-Reference

1   An appeal under s.67 may be made against a "determination" under s.30(6), CATCA, against a "decision" under s.46A(5), CATCA, against the imposition of a surcharge under s.53(4), CATCA, against a "decision" under s.80(4), CATCA, against an "opinion" under s.811(7), TCA, against a "failure" under s.917EA(4), TCA, and against a "refusal" under s.917G(7), TCA.

Section 68

[S.52A, CATA]

Conditions before appeal may be made.

68. No appeal shall lie under section 66 or 67 until such time as the person aggrieved by the decision or assessment (as the case may be) complies with section 46(2) in respect of the gift or inheritance in relation to which the decision or assessment is made, as if there were no time-limit for complying with section 46(2) and that person were a person primarily accountable for the payment of tax by virtue of section 45(1) and required by notice in writing by the Commissioners to deliver a return.

PART 9

Exemptions

Section 69

[S.53, CATA]

Exemption of small gifts.

69. (1) In this section, "relevant period" means the period of 12 months ending on 31 December in each year.

(2) The first [€3,000][1] of the total taxable value of all taxable gifts taken by a donee from any one disposer in any relevant period is exempt from tax and is not taken into account in computing tax.

(3) In the case of a gift which becomes an inheritance by reason of its being taken under a disposition where the date of the disposition is within 2 years prior to the death of the disposer, the same relief is granted in respect of that inheritance under subsection (2) as if it were a gift.

Footnote

1   "€3,000" substituted for "€1,270" by s.149, FA 2003, as respects relevant periods ending after 31st December, 2002.

Section 70

[S.127(1), FA 1990]

Exemption for spouses (gifts).

70. Notwithstanding any other provisions of this Act, a gift taken by a donee, who is at the date of the gift the spouse of the disposer, is exempt from tax and is not taken into account in computing tax.

Commentary

A   This exemption does not apply to a common-law spouse, who is treated as a stranger to the disposer. However, according to Part 19.9 of the *Revenue CAT Manual*, the hardship provisions of s.59, CATCA, may apply where the financial position of surviving common-law spouses and their children is particularly difficult.

Section 71

[S.59(1), FA 1985]

Exemption for spouses (inheritances).

71. Notwithstanding any other provisions of this Act, an inheritance taken by a successor, who is at the date of the inheritance the spouse of the disponer, is exempt from tax and is not taken into account in computing tax.

Commentary

A   This exemption does not apply to a common-law spouse, who is treated as a stranger to the disponer. However, according to Part 19.9 of the *Revenue CAT Manual*, the hardship provisions of s.59, CATCA, may apply where the financial position of surviving common-law spouses and their children is particularly difficult.

B   See Part 19.8 of the *Revenue CAT Manual*. In cases where there is an interval between the death of the disponer and the taking of an inheritance from the disponer by the disponer's spouse, the surviving spouse is still regarded as being the disponer's spouse at the date of the inheritance even if the surviving spouse has then re-married.

Section 72

[S.60, FA 1985, as amended, s.130, FA 1990, and s.118, FA 1991, as amended]

Relief in respect of certain policies of insurance.

72. (1) In this section—

["approved retirement fund tax" means tax which a qualifying fund manager is obliged to deduct in accordance with the provisions of section 784A(4)(c) of the Taxes Consolidation Act 1997;][3]

"insured" means an individual or, in relation to a qualifying insurance policy where—

(a) the insured is an individual and the spouse of that individual at the date the policy is effected,

(b) annual premiums are paid by either or both of them during their joint lives, and by the survivor of them during the life of such survivor, and

(c) the proceeds of the policy are payable on the death of such survivor, or on the simultaneous deaths of both such spouses,

means—

(i) where the proceeds of the policy are so payable on the death of such survivor, that survivor, and the proceeds of the policy [are deemed][1] to have been provided by such survivor, as disponer, or

(ii) where the proceeds of the policy are so payable on the simultaneous deaths of both such spouses, each of the spouses, and each such spouse is deemed to have provided the proceeds of the policy—

(I) to the extent that such proceeds are applied in paying the relevant tax of the insured who is that spouse, and

(II) where the proceeds of the policy are not applied in paying relevant tax, to the extent that the proceeds not so applied are comprised in an inheritance taken under a disposition made by that spouse;

"qualifying insurance policy" means a policy of insurance—

(a) which is in a form approved by the Commissioners for the purposes of this section,

(b) in respect of which annual premiums are paid by the insured during the insured's life, and

(c) which is expressly effected under this section for the purpose of paying relevant tax;

"relevant tax" [means approved retirement fund tax and inheritance tax][4] payable in respect of an inheritance (excluding, in the computation of such tax, an interest in a qualifying insurance policy) taken—

(a) on the death of the insured,

(b) under a disposition made by the insured, where the inheritance is taken on or after the date of death of the insured and not later than one year after that [death, or][2] and

(c) under a disposition made by the spouse of the insured where the inheritance is taken only in the event of the insured not surviving the spouse by a period of up to 31 days,

and the relevant qualifying insurance policy is—

(i) a policy of insurance within the meaning of paragraphs (a), (b) and (c) of the definition of "insured" in this subsection, or

(ii) a policy of insurance where the insured is an individual and the proceeds of the policy are payable only on the contingency of the insured surviving that spouse.

(2) (a) An interest in a qualifying insurance policy which is comprised in an inheritance taken under a disposition made by the insured is, to the extent that the proceeds of the policy are applied in paying relevant tax, exempt from tax in relation to that inheritance and is not taken into account in computing tax.

(b) An interest in a qualifying insurance policy which is comprised in an inheritance taken under a disposition made by the insured is, to the extent that the proceeds of the policy are not applied in paying relevant tax, and notwithstanding the provisions of this Act, deemed to be taken on a day immediately after—

(i) the date of the death of the insured, or

(ii) the latest date (if any) on which an inheritance is taken in respect of which that relevant tax is payable,

whichever is the later.

[(c)   For the purposes of this section, an amount of the proceeds of a qualifying insurance policy equal to the amount of approved retirement fund tax shall be treated as applied in paying relevant tax of that amount.]⁵

Footnotes

1   Substituted for "is deemed" by para. 2(d)(i), Sch. 3, FA 2004, with effect as on and from 21st February, 2003, under para. 5(b) of that Sch.

2   Substituted for "death, and" by para. 2(d)(ii), Sch. 3, FA 2004, with effect as on and from 21st February, 2003, under para. 5(b) of that Sch.

3   Inserted by s.133(1)(a)(i), FA 2005, in relation to "relevant tax" payable in respect of inheritances taken on or after 3rd February, 2005.

4   Substituted for "means inheritance tax" by s.133(1)(a)(ii), FA 2005, in relation to "relevant tax" payable in respect of inheritances taken on or after 3rd February, 2005.

5   As inserted by s.133(1)(b), FA 2005, in relation to "relevant tax" payable in respect of inheritances taken on or after 3rd February, 2005.

Commentary

A   See the Revenue Statement of Practice (SP-CAT/1/04) which sets out Revenue guide-lines in relation to policies effected under s.72, formerly s.60, FA 1985.

B   See an article on Section 60 Life Assurance Policies by John Caslin in the *Irish Tax Review* of May 1991, page 406.

C   See articles, on different types of Section 60 policies, by John Crowe in the *Irish Tax Review* of November 1996, page 385, and by Owen Morton in the *Irish Tax Review* of July 1998, page 436.

D   See Part 15 of the *Revenue CAT Manual* in relation to these policies.

Section 73

[S.119, FA 1991]

Relief in respect of certain policies of insurance relating to tax payable on gifts.

73.   (1)   In this section—

"appointed date" means—

(a)   a date occurring not earlier than 8 years after the date on which a relevant insurance policy is effected, or

(b)   a date on which the proceeds of a relevant insurance policy become payable either on the critical illness or the death of the insured, or one of the insured in a case to which paragraph (b) of the definition of "insured" relates, being a date prior to the date to which paragraph (a) of this definition relates;

"insured" means—

(a)   where the insured is an individual, that individual, or

(b)   where the insured is an individual and the spouse of that individual at the date the policy is effected, that individual and the spouse of that individual, jointly or separately, or the survivor of them, as the case may be;

"relevant insurance policy" means a policy of insurance—

(a) which is in a form approved by the Commissioners for the purposes of this section,

(b) in respect of which annual premiums are paid by the insured,

(c) the proceeds of which are payable on the appointed date, and

(d) which is expressly effected under this section for the purpose of paying relevant tax;

"relevant tax" means gift tax or inheritance tax, payable in connection with an inter vivos disposition made by the insured within one year after the appointed date, excluding gift tax or inheritance tax payable on an appointment out of an inter vivos discretionary trust set up by the insured.

(2) The proceeds of a relevant insurance policy are, to the extent that such proceeds are used to pay relevant tax, exempt from tax and are not taken into account in computing such tax.

(3) Subject to sections 70 and 76, where the insured makes an inter vivos disposition of the proceeds, or any part of the proceeds, of a relevant insurance policy other than in paying relevant tax, such proceeds are not exempt from tax.

(4) A relevant insurance policy is a qualifying insurance policy for the purposes of section 72 where the proceeds of such relevant insurance policy become payable on the death of the insured or one of the insured in a case to which paragraph (b) of the definition of "insured" relates, if such relevant insurance policy would have been a qualifying insurance policy if it had been expressly effected under that section.

(5) A qualifying insurance policy for the purposes of section 72 is a relevant insurance policy where the proceeds of such qualifying insurance policy are used to pay relevant tax arising under an inter vivos disposition made by the insured within one year after the appointed date.

Commentary

A See the Revenue Statement of Practice (SP-CAT/1/04) which sets out Revenue guidelines in relation to policies effected under s.73, formerly s.119, FA 1991.

B See Part 15 of the *Revenue CAT Manual* in relation to these policies.

Section 74

[S.133, FA 1993]

Exemption of certain policies of assurance.

74. (1) In this section—

"assurance company" has the meaning assigned to it by section 706 of the Taxes Consolidation Act 1997;

"new policy" means a contract entered into by an assurance company which is a policy of assurance on the life of any person issued on or after 1 January 2001;

"old policy" means a contract entered into by an assurance company in the course of carrying on a foreign life assurance business within the meaning of section 451 of the Taxes Consolidation Act 1997 and issued on or after 1 December 1992 and before 1 January 2001.

(2) Where any interest in a new policy or in an old policy is comprised in a gift or an inheritance, then any such interest—

(a) is exempt from tax, and

(b) is not taken into account in computing tax on any gift or inheritance taken by a donee or successor,

if it is shown to the satisfaction of the Commissioners that—

(i) such interest is comprised in the gift or inheritance at the date of the gift or at the date of the inheritance,

(ii) at the date of the disposition, the disponer is neither domiciled nor ordinarily resident in the State, and

(iii) at the date of the gift or at the date of the inheritance, the donee or successor is neither domiciled nor ordinarily resident in the State.

(3) Where—

(a) an interest in a new policy or in an old policy, as the case may be, which is comprised in a gift or inheritance came into the beneficial ownership of the disponer or became subject to the disposition prior to 15 February 2001, and

(b) the conditions at [paragraphs][1] (i) and (iii) of subsection (2) are complied with,

then that subsection shall apply to that interest in a new policy or in an old policy, as the case may be, if, at the date of the disposition, the proper law of the disposition was not the law of the State.

Footnote

1   Substituted for "subparagraphs" by s.151(a), FA 2003, with effect from 28th March, 2003.

Section 75

[S.85, FA 1989, as amended, and s.224, FA 2001]

Exemption of specified collective investment undertakings.

75.   [(1) In this section—

"common contractual fund" has the meaning assigned to it by section 739I of the Taxes Consolidation Act 1997;

"investment undertaking" has the meaning assigned to it by section 739B of the Taxes Consolidation Act 1997;

"unit", in relation to a common contractual fund, has the meaning assigned to it by section 739I of the Taxes Consolidation Act 1997;

"unit", in relation to an investment undertaking, has the meaning assigned to it by section 739B of the Taxes Consolidation Act 1997.][1]

(2) Where any unit of an investment undertaking or of a [common contractual fund][2] is comprised in a gift or an inheritance, then such unit—

    (a) is exempt from tax, and

    (b) is not taken into account in computing tax on any gift or inheritance taken by the donee or successor,

if it is shown to the satisfaction of the Commissioners that—

    (i) the unit is comprised in the gift or inheritance—

        (I) at the date of the gift or at the date of the inheritance, and

        (II) at the valuation date,

    (ii) at the date of the disposition, the disponer is neither domiciled nor ordinarily resident in the State, and

    (iii) at the date of the gift or at the date of the inheritance, the donee or successor is neither domiciled nor ordinarily resident in the State.

[(3) Where—

    (a) any unit of an investment undertaking which is comprised in a gift or inheritance came into the beneficial ownership of the disponer or became subject to the disposition prior to 15 February 2001, and

    (b) the conditions at subparagraphs (i) and (iii) of subsection (2) are complied with,

then that subsection shall apply to that unit of an investment undertaking comprised in a gift or inheritance, if at the date of the disposition, the proper law of the disposition was not the law of the State.][3]

Footnotes

1   As substituted by s.134(1)(a), FA 2005, with effect in relation to gifts and inheritances taken on or after 25th March, 2005.

2   As substituted by s.134(1)(b), FA 2005, with effect in relation to gifts and inheritances taken on or after 25th March, 2005.

3   As substituted by s.134(1)(c), FA 2005, with effect in relation to gifts and inheritances taken on or after 25th March, 2005.

Section 76

[S.54, CATA, as amended]

Provisions relating to charities, etc.

76.   (1) Where any person takes a benefit for public or charitable purposes that person is deemed—

(a)   for the purposes of sections 5(1) and 10(1), to have taken that benefit beneficially, and

(b)   for the purposes of Schedule 2, to have taken a gift or an inheritance accordingly to which the group threshold of €19,050 applies.

(2)   A gift or an inheritance which is taken for public or charitable purposes is exempt from tax and is not taken into account in computing tax, to the extent that the Commissioners are satisfied that it has been, or will be, applied to purposes which, in accordance with the law of the State, are public or charitable.

(3)   Except where provided in section 80(5), a gift or inheritance which a person takes on becoming entitled to any benefit on the application to public or charitable purposes of property (including moneys provided by the Oireachtas or a local authority) held for such purposes is exempt from tax and is not taken into account in computing tax.

Commentary

A   See an article on the Law and Taxation of Charities by John H. Hickson in the *Irish Tax Review* of November 1996, page 377.

B   The Minister for Finance (Charles McCreevy) stated in the Dáil on 17th November, 1998, that "a gift or inheritance taken by a political party would qualify for exemption from capital acquisitions tax (s.54, CATA) on the grounds that it was applied for public purposes" – *Irish Tax Review*, January 1999, page 18. The tax treatment of political donations is now set out in a Revenue Statement of Practice (SP-CAT/1/02).

C   Under s.11(6), Health (Repayment Scheme) Act 2006, any "prescribed repayment" under that Act is to be treated as taken by a person as a benefit for public or charitable purposes under s.76(2).

Section 77

[S.55, CATA, as amended, and s.39, FA 1978, as amended]

Exemption of heritage property.

77.   (1)   This section applies to the following objects, that is, any pictures, prints, books, manuscripts, works of art, jewellery, scientific collections or other things not held for the purposes of trading—

(a)   which, on a claim being made to the Commissioners, appear to them to be of national, scientific, historic or artistic interest,

(b)   which are kept permanently in the State except for such temporary absences outside the State as are approved by the Commissioners, and

(c)   in respect of which reasonable facilities for viewing are allowed to members of the public or to recognised bodies or to associations of persons.

(2)   (a)   Any object to which this section applies and which, at the date of the gift or at the date of inheritance, and at the valuation date, is comprised in a gift or an inheritance taken by a person is exempt from tax in relation to that gift or inheritance, and the value of

that gift or inheritance is not taken into account in computing tax on any gift or inheritance taken by that person unless the exemption ceases to apply under subsection (3) or (4).

(b) Section 89(5) shall apply, for the purposes of this subsection, as it applies in relation to agricultural property.

(3) If an object exempted from tax by virtue of subsection (2) is sold within 6 years after the valuation date, and before the death of the donee or successor, the exemption referred to in subsection (2) shall cease to apply to such object, but if the sale of such object is a sale by private treaty to the National Gallery of Ireland, the National Museum of Science and Art or any other similar national institution, [the Commissioners of Public Works in Ireland,][1] [the Trust (within the meaning of section 1003A of the Taxes Consolidation Act 1997),][2] any university in the State or any constituent college of such university, a local authority or the Friends of the National Collections of Ireland, the exemption referred to in subsection (2) shall continue to apply.

(4) The exemption referred to in subsection (2) shall cease to apply to an object, if at any time after the valuation date and –

(a) before the sale of the object,

(b) before the death of the donee or successor, and

(c) before such object again forms part of the property comprised in a gift or an inheritance (other than an inheritance arising by virtue of section 20) in respect of which gift or inheritance an absolute interest is taken by a person other than the spouse of that donee or successor,

there has been a breach of any condition specified in paragraph (b) or (c) of subsection (1).

(5) Any work of art normally kept outside the State which is comprised in an inheritance which is charged to tax by virtue of section 11(1)(b) or 11(2)(c) is exempt from tax and is not taken into account in computing tax, to the extent that the Commissioners are satisfied that it was brought into the State solely for public exhibition, cleaning or restoration.

(6) Subsections (2) to (4) shall apply, as they apply to the objects specified in subsection (1), to a house or garden that is situated in the State and is not held for the purpose of trading and –

(a) which, on a claim being made to the Commissioners, appears to them to be of national, scientific, historic or artistic interest,

(b) in respect of which reasonable facilities for viewing were allowed to members of the public during the 3 years immediately before the date of the gift or the date of the inheritance, and

(c)   in respect of which reasonable facilities for viewing are allowed to members of the public,

with the modification that the reference in subsection (4) to subsection (1)(b) or (c) shall be construed as a reference to paragraph (c) of this subsection and with any other necessary modifications.

(7)   Without prejudice to the generality of subsection (6), the provision of facilities for the viewing by members of the public of a house or garden is not regarded as reasonable in relation to any year which is taken into account for the purposes of paragraphs (b) and (c) of subsection (1), unless —

    (a)   [the National Tourism Development Authority][3] has, on or before 1 January in that year, been provided with particulars of —

        (i)   the name, if any, and address of the house or garden, and

        (ii)   the days and times during the year when access to the house or garden is afforded to the public and the price, if any, payable for such access,

    and

    (b)   in the opinion of the Commissioners —

        (i)   subject to such temporary closure necessary for the purpose of the repair, maintenance or restoration of the house or garden as is reasonable, access to the house or garden is afforded for not less than 60 days (including not less than 40 days during the period commencing on 1 May and ending on 30 September of which not less than 10 of the days during that period shall fall on a Saturday or a Sunday or both) in that year,

        (ii)   on each day on which access to the house or garden is afforded, the access is afforded in a reasonable manner and at reasonable times for a period, or periods in the aggregate, of not less than 4 hours,

        (iii)   access to the whole or to a substantial part of the house or garden is afforded at the same time, and

        (iv)   the price, if any, paid by members of the public in return for that access is reasonable in amount and does not operate to preclude members of the public from seeking access to the house or garden.

Footnotes

1   As inserted by s.81, FA 2004, as respects sales on or after 1st August, 1994.

2   Inserted by s.115, FA 2006, with effect from 31st March, 2006.

3   Substituted for "Bord Fáilte Éireann (in this section referred to as "the Board") by para. 2, Sch. 2, FA 2006, which is deemed by para. 9(b) of that Schedule to have come into force and have taken effect from 28th May, 2003.

Commentary

A   See the Revenue Information Leaflet CAT8 in relation to this section.

B   See an article on the Favourable Treatment of Heritage Objects by Anne Corrigan and Marie Griffin in the *Irish Tax Review* of March 2002, page 179.

Section 78

[S.166, FA 1995]

Heritage property of companies.

78.   (1)   In this section—

"relevant heritage property" means any one or more of the following—

(a)   objects to which section 77(1) applies,

(b)   a house or garden referred to in section 77(6);

"private company" has the meaning assigned to it by section 27;

"subsidiary" has the meaning assigned to it by section 155 of the Companies Act 1963.

(2)   Where a gift or inheritance consists in whole or in part—

(a)   at the date of the gift or at the date of the inheritance, and

(b)   at the valuation date,

of one or more shares in a private company which (after the taking of the gift or inheritance) is, on the date of the gift or on the date of the inheritance, a company controlled by the donee or successor within the meaning of section 27, then each such share is, to the extent that its market value for tax purposes is, at the valuation date, attributable to relevant heritage property, exempt from tax and the value of such relevant heritage property is, to that extent, not to be taken into account in computing tax on any gift or inheritance taken by that person unless the exemption ceases to apply under subsection (5) or (6), subject to the condition that the relevant heritage property was in the beneficial ownership of the company on 12 April 1995, or in the beneficial ownership on that date of another company which was on that date a subsidiary of the first-mentioned company.

(3)   Section 89(5) shall apply, for the purposes of subsection (2), as it applies in relation to agricultural property.

(4)   Where in relation to a gift or inheritance—

(a)   a part of a share in a private company is exempt from tax by virtue of subsection (2), and

(b) such share is relevant business property within the meaning of Chapter 2 of Part 10,

then the relevant heritage property to which the market value of such share is partly attributable is disregarded in determining for the purposes of that Chapter what part of the taxable value of that gift or inheritance is attributable to such share; but the amount of the reduction (if any) which would but for subsection (2) fall to be made under that Chapter in respect of such share shall not otherwise be restricted notwithstanding subsection (2).

(5) If a share in a private company which is exempted in whole or in part from tax by virtue of subsection (2) is sold within 6 years after the valuation date, and before the death of the donee or successor, the exemption referred to in subsection (2) shall, subject to subsection (7), cease to apply to such share.

(6) Where the whole or part of the market value of a share in a private company which is comprised in a gift or inheritance is on the valuation date attributable to an item of relevant heritage property and—

(a) that item of relevant heritage property is sold within 6 years after the valuation date, and before the death of the donee or successor, or

(b) at any time after the valuation date and—

(i) before the sale of such share or such item of relevant heritage property,

(ii) before the death of the donee or successor, and

(iii) before such share or such item of relevant heritage property forms part of the property comprised in a subsequent gift or inheritance in respect of which gift or inheritance an absolute interest is taken by a person other than the spouse of that donee or successor,

there has been a breach of any condition specified in section 77(1)(b) or (c) or section 77(6)(c),

then the exemption referred to in subsection (2) shall, subject to subsection (7), cease to apply to such share to the extent that that market value is attributable to such item of relevant heritage property.

(7) Notwithstanding subsections (5) and (6), the exemption referred to in subsection (2) shall continue to apply if the sale of the share referred to in subsection (5), or the sale of the item of relevant heritage property referred to in subsection (6), is a sale by private treaty to the National Gallery of Ireland, the National Museum of Science and Art or any other similar national institution, any university in the State or any constituent college of such university, a local authority or the Friends of the National Collections of Ireland.

Commentary

A   See the Revenue Information Leaflet CAT8 in relation to this section.

B   See an article on the Favourable Treatment of Heritage Objects by Anne Corrigan and Marie Griffin in the *Irish Tax Review* of March 2002, page 179.

Section 79

[S.165, FA 1995]

Exemption of certain inheritances taken by parents.

79.   Notwithstanding any other provision of this Act, an inheritance taken by a person from a disponer is, where—

   (a)   that person is a parent of that disponer, and

   (b)   the date of the inheritance is the date of death of that disponer,

exempt from tax and is not taken into account in computing tax if that disponer took a non-exempt gift or inheritance from either or both of that disponer's parents within the period of 5 years immediately prior to the date of death of that disponer.

Section 80

[S.56, CATA]

Payments relating to retirement, etc.

80.   (1)   In this section—

     "superannuation scheme" includes any arrangement in connection with employment for the provision of a benefit on or in connection with the retirement or death of an employee;

     "employment" includes employment as a director of a body corporate and cognate words shall be construed accordingly.

   (2)   Subject to subsection (3), any payment to an employee or former employee by, or out of funds provided by, that employee's or former employee's employer or any other person, bona fide by means of retirement benefit, redundancy payment or pension is not a gift or an inheritance.

   (3)   Subsection (2) shall not apply in relation to a payment referred to in that subsection, and any such payment is deemed to be a gift or an inheritance where—

     (a)   (i)   the employee is a relative of the employer or other disponer, or

         (ii)   the employer is a private company within the meaning of section 27, and of which private company the employee is deemed to have control within the meaning of that section;

(b) the payment is not made under a scheme (relating to superannuation, retirement or redundancy) approved by the Commissioners under the Income Tax Acts; and

(c) the Commissioners decide that in the circumstances of the case the payment is excessive.

(4) The Commissioners shall serve on an accountable person a notice in writing of their decision referred to in subsection (3) and the accountable person concerned may appeal against such decision and section 67 shall apply with any necessary modifications in relation to such appeal as it applies in relation to an appeal against an assessment of tax.

(5) Any benefit taken by a person other than the person in respect of whose service the benefit arises, under the provisions of any superannuation fund, or under any superannuation scheme, established solely or mainly for persons employed in a profession, trade, undertaking or employment, and their dependants, is (whether or not any person had a right enforceable at law to the benefit) deemed to be a gift or an inheritance, as the case may be, derived under a disposition made by the person in respect of whose service the benefit arises and not by any other person.

Cross-Reference

1   A benefit under s.80(5) is excluded from the exemption given by s.76(3), CATCA.

Section 81

[S.57, CATA, as amended, s.135, FA 1997 and s.219, FA 2001]

Exemption of certain securities.

81. (1) In this section −

"security" means any security, stock, share, debenture, debenture stock, certificate of charge or other form of security issued, whether before, on or after the passing of this Act, and which by virtue of any enactment or by virtue of the exercise of any power conferred by any enactment is exempt from taxation when in the beneficial ownership of a person neither domiciled nor ordinarily resident in the State;

"unit trust scheme" means an authorised unit trust scheme within the meaning of the Unit Trusts Act 1990, whose deed expressing the trusts of the scheme restricts the property subject to those trusts to securities.

(2) Securities, or units (within the meaning of the Unit Trusts Act 1990) of a unit trust scheme, comprised in a gift or an inheritance are exempt from tax (and are not taken into account in computing tax on any gift or inheritance taken by the donee or successor) if it is shown to the satisfaction of the Commissioners that −

    (a) the securities or units were comprised in the disposition continuously for a period of [15 years][1] immediately before the date of the gift or the date of the inheritance, and any period immediately before the date of the disposition during which the securities or units were continuously in the beneficial ownership of the disponer is deemed, for the purpose of this paragraph, to be a period or part of a period immediately before the date of the gift or the date of the inheritance during which they were continuously comprised in the disposition;

    (b) the securities or units were comprised in the gift or inheritance –

        (i) at the date of the gift or the date of the inheritance, and

        (ii) at the valuation date;

        and

    (c) the donee or successor is at the date of the gift or the date of the inheritance neither domiciled nor ordinarily resident in the State,

and section 89(5) shall apply, for the purposes of this subsection, as it applies in relation to agricultural property.

(3) Subsection (2)(a) shall not apply where –

    (a) the disponer was neither domiciled nor ordinarily resident in the State at the date of the disposition, or

    (b) the securities or units concerned came into the beneficial ownership of the disponer before 26 March 1997, or became subject to the disposition before that date, and the disponer was neither domiciled nor ordinarily resident in the State at the date of the gift or the date of the inheritance.

(4) Where the securities or units concerned came into the beneficial ownership of the disponer, or became subject to the disposition prior to 15 February 2001, then subsection (2) shall apply as if the reference to the period of [15 years][2] in that subsection were construed as a reference to a period of 3 years.

Footnotes

1   Substituted for "6 years" by s.150(1)(a), FA 2003, which has effect where the date of the gift or the date of the inheritance is on or after 24th February, 2003, and the securities or units (i) come into the beneficial ownership of the disponer on or after 24th February, 2003, or (ii) become subject of the disposition on or after that date without having been previously in the beneficial ownership of the disponer.

2.   Substituted for "6 years" by s.150(1)(b), FA 2003, with effect as on and from 24th February, 2003.

Commentary

A   See Part 19.19 of the *Revenue CAT Manual*. Where s.81 (formerly s.57, CATA) securities are held in a unit trust which is being wound up but certain of the securities are not sold but are distributed in specie to the unit-holders, then provided all other conditions laid down by s.81 (formerly s.57, CATA) are fulfilled, and the direct ownership of the securities commences at the instant the ownership of the units by the unit-holders ceases, the period of time unit-holders held the units will be treated as aggregable with the period they directly hold the securities.

Section 82

[S.58, CATA, as amended]

Exemption of certain receipts.

82. (1) The following are not gifts or inheritances:

(a) the receipt by a person of any sum bona fide by means of compensation or damages for any wrong or injury suffered by that person in that person's person, property, reputation or means of livelihood;

(b) the receipt by a person of any sum bona fide by means of compensation or damages for any wrong or injury resulting in the death of any other person;

(c) the receipt by a person of any sum bona fide by means of winnings from betting (including pool betting) or from any lottery, sweepstake or game with prizes;

(d) any benefit arising out of —

(i) the payment to the Official Assignee in Bankruptcy of money which has been provided by, or which represents property provided by, friends of a bankrupt, or

(ii) a remission or abatement of debts by the creditors of a bankrupt,

to enable the bankrupt to fulfil an offer of composition after bankruptcy in accordance with section 39 of the Bankruptcy Act 1988; and

(e) any benefit arising out of —

(i) the payment to the Official Assignee in Bankruptcy of money which has been provided by, or which represents property provided by, friends of an arranging debtor, or

(ii) a remission or abatement of debts by the creditors of an arranging debtor,

to enable the debtor to carry out the terms of a proposal made by that debtor under section 87 of the Bankruptcy Act 1988, which has been accepted by that debtor's creditors and approved and confirmed by the High Court.

(2) Notwithstanding anything contained in this Act, the receipt in the lifetime of the disponer of money or money's worth —

(a) by —

(i) the spouse or child of the disponer, or

(ii)   a person in relation to whom the disponer stands *in loco parentis,*

for support, maintenance or education, or

(b)   by a person who is in relation to the disponer a dependent relative under section 466 of the Taxes Consolidation Act 1997, for support or maintenance,

is not a gift or an inheritance, where the provision of such support, maintenance or education, or such support or maintenance —

(i)   is such as would be part of the normal expenditure of a person in the circumstances of the disponer, and

(ii)   is reasonable having regard to the financial circumstances of the disponer.

(3) (a)   In this subsection "incapacitated individual", "trust funds" and "qualifying trust" have the meanings assigned to them, respectively, by section 189A (inserted by the Finance Act 1999) of the Taxes Consolidation Act 1997.[1]

(b)   The receipt by an incapacitated individual of the whole or any part of trust funds which are held on a qualifying trust, or of the income from such a qualifying trust, is not a gift or an inheritance.

(4)   The receipt by a minor child of the disponer of money or money's worth for support, maintenance or education, at a time when the disponer and the other parent of that minor child are dead, is not a gift or an inheritance where the provision of such support, maintenance or education —

(a)   is such as would be part of the normal expenditure of a person in the circumstances of the disponer immediately prior to the death of the disponer, and

(b)   is reasonable having regard to the financial circumstances of the disponer immediately prior to the death of the disponer.

Footnote
1   See s.189A, TCA (inserted by s.12, FA 1999) on page 1006 for definitions.

Commentary
A   As to s.82(2) and (4), see *Bennett v Inland Revenue Commissioners* [1995] STC 54 in relation to s.21, UK Inheritance Tax Act, 1984, and "normal expenditure out of income".

Section 83

[S.59, CATA]

Exemption where disposition was made by the donee or successor.

83.   (1)   In this section, "company" means a body corporate (wherever incorporated), other than a private company within the meaning of section 27.

(2) Tax is not chargeable on a gift or an inheritance taken by the donee or successor under a disposition made by that donee or successor.

(3) Where, at the date of the gift, 2 companies are associated in the manner described in subsection (4), a gift taken by one of them under a disposition made by the other is deemed to be a gift to which subsection (2) applies.

(4) For the purposes of subsection (3), 2 companies shall be regarded as associated if—

    (a) one company would be beneficially entitled to not less than 90 per cent of any assets of the other company available for distribution to the owners of its shares and entitlements of the kind referred to in section 43(1) on a winding up, or

    (b) a third company would be beneficially entitled to not less than 90 per cent of any assets of each of them available as in paragraph (a).

Section 84

[S.59A, CATA]

Exemption relating to qualifying expenses of incapacitated persons.

84. (1) In this section, "qualifying expenses" means expenses relating to medical care including the cost of maintenance in connection with such medical care.

(2) A gift or inheritance which is taken exclusively for the purpose of discharging qualifying expenses of an individual who is permanently incapacitated by reason of physical or mental infirmity is, to the extent that the Commissioners are satisfied that it has been or will be applied to such purpose, exempt from tax and is not taken into account in computing tax.

Section 85

[S.59B, CATA]

Exemption relating to retirement benefits.

85. (1) In this section, "retirement fund", in relation to an inheritance taken on the death of a disponer, means an approved retirement fund or an approved minimum retirement fund, within the meaning of section 784A or 784C of the Taxes Consolidation Act 1997, being a fund which is wholly comprised of all or any of the following, that is—

    (a) property which represents in whole or in part the accrued rights of the disponer, or of a predeceased spouse of the disponer, under an annuity contract or retirement benefits scheme approved by the Commissioners for the purposes of Chapter 1 or Chapter 2 of Part 30 of that Act,

(b)   any accumulations of income of such property, or

(c)   property which represents in whole or in part those accumulations.

(2)   The whole or any part of a retirement fund which is comprised in an inheritance which is taken on the death of a disponer is exempt from tax in relation to that inheritance and the value of that inheritance is not taken into account in computing tax, where—

(a)   the disposition under which the inheritance is taken is the will or intestacy of the disponer, and

(b)   the successor is a child of the disponer and had attained 21 years of age at the date of that disposition.

Section 86

[S.59C, CATA, as amended]

Exemption relating to certain dwellings.

86.   (1)   In this section—

"dwelling-house" means—

(a)   a building or part (including an appropriate part within the meaning of section 5(5)) of a building which was used or was suitable for use as a dwelling, and

(b)   the curtilage of the dwelling-house up to an area (exclusive of the site of the dwelling-house) of one acre but if the area of the curtilage (exclusive of the site of the dwelling-house) exceeds one acre then the part which comes within this definition is the part which, if the remainder were separately occupied, would be the most suitable for occupation and enjoyment with the dwelling-house;

"relevant period", in relation to a dwelling-house comprised in a gift or inheritance, means the period of 6 years commencing on the date of the gift or the date of the inheritance.

(2)   In this section any reference to a donee or successor is construed as including a reference to the transferee referred to in section 32(2).

(3)   Subject to subsections (4), (5), (6) and (7), a dwelling-house comprised in a gift or inheritance which is taken by a donee or successor who—

(a)   has continuously occupied as that donee or successor's only or main residence—

(i)   that dwelling-house throughout the period of 3 years immediately preceding the date of the gift or the date of the inheritance, or

(ii)   where that dwelling-house has directly or indirectly replaced other property, that dwelling-house and that other property for periods which together comprised at least 3 years falling within the period of 4 years immediately preceding the date of the gift or the date of the inheritance,

(b) is not, at the date of the gift or at the date of the inheritance, beneficially entitled to any other dwelling-house or to any interest in any other dwelling-house, and

(c) continues to occupy that dwelling-house as that donee or successor's only or main residence throughout the relevant period,

is exempt from tax in relation to that gift or inheritance, and the value of that dwelling-house is not to be taken into account in computing tax on any gift or inheritance taken by that person unless the exemption ceases to apply under subsection (6) or (7).

[(3A) For the purposes of subsection (3)(a), in the case of a gift—

(a) any period during which a donee occupied a dwelling house that was, during that period, the disponer's only or main residence, shall be treated as not being a period during which the donee occupied the dwelling house unless the disponer is compelled, by reason of old age or infirmity, to depend on the services of the donee for that period,

(b) where paragraph (a)(i) of subsection (3) applies, the dwelling house referred to in that paragraph is required to be owned by the disponer during the 3 year period referred to in that paragraph, and

(c) where paragraph (a)(ii) of subsection (3) applies, either the dwelling house or the other property referred to in that paragraph is required to be owned by the disponer during the 3 year period referred to in that paragraph.][1]

(4) The condition in paragraph (c) of subsection (3) shall not apply where the donee or successor has attained the age of 55 years at the date of the gift or at the date of the inheritance.

(5) For the purpose of paragraph (c) of subsection (3), the donee or successor is deemed to occupy the dwelling-house concerned as that donee or successor's only or main residence throughout any period of absence during which that donee or successor worked in an employment or office all the duties of which were performed outside the State.

(6) If a dwelling-house exempted from tax by virtue of subsection (3) is sold or disposed of, either in whole or in part, within the relevant period, and before the death of the donee or successor (not being a donee or successor who had attained the age of 55 years at the date of the gift or inheritance), the exemption referred to in that subsection shall cease to apply to such dwelling-house unless the sale or disposal occurs in consequence of the donee or successor

requiring long-term medical care in a hospital, nursing home or convalescent home.

(7) The exemption referred to in subsection (3) shall cease to apply to a dwelling-house, if at any time during the relevant period and —

(a) before the dwelling-house is sold or disposed of, and

(b) before the death of the donee or successor,

the condition specified in paragraph (c) of subsection (3) has not been complied with unless that non-compliance occurs in consequence of the donee or successor requiring long-term medical care in a hospital, nursing home or convalescent home, or in consequence of any condition imposed by the employer of the donee or successor requiring the donee or successor to reside elsewhere.

(8) Where a dwelling-house exempted from tax by virtue of subsection (3) (in this section referred to as the "first-mentioned dwelling house") is replaced within the relevant period by another dwelling house, the condition specified in paragraph (c) of subsection (3) is treated as satisfied if the donee or successor has occupied as that donee or successor's only or main residence the first-mentioned dwelling-house, that other dwelling-house and any dwelling-house which has within the relevant period directly or indirectly replaced that other dwelling-house for periods which together comprised at least 6 years falling within the period of 7 years commencing on the date of the gift or the date of the inheritance.

(9) Any period of absence which would satisfy the condition specified in paragraph (c) of subsection (3) in relation to the first-mentioned dwelling-house shall, if it occurs in relation to any dwelling-house which has directly or indirectly replaced that dwelling-house, likewise satisfy that condition as it has effect by virtue of subsection (8).

(10) Subsection (6) shall not apply to a case falling within subsection (8), but the extent of the exemption under this section in such a case shall, where the donee or successor had not attained the age of 55 years at the date of the gift or at the date of the inheritance, not exceed what it would have been had the replacement of one dwelling house by another referred to in subsection (8), or any one or more of such replacements, taken place immediately prior to that date.

Footnote

1   As inserted by s.116, FA 2007, which applies to gifts taken on or after 20th February, 2007.

Commentary

A   See an article in relation to s.86 (formerly s.59C, CATA) by Ann Williams in the *Irish Tax Review* of January 2001, page 13.

B   See page 32, Issue 40, of the *Revenue Tax Briefing* of June 2000, in relation to a partial clawback where a replacement dwelling-house is involved.

C   See the Revenue Information Leaflet CAT10 in relation to gift/inheritance tax exemption for dwelling-house.

D   See an Irish Circuit Court case, *Paul Danaher v The Revenue Commissioners* [2005] No. 8 RA, which decided, in relation to s.59C, CATA, now s.86, CATCA, that a house was not replaced property to qualify for relief.

E   In relation to s.86(3)(b), see Part 19.15 of the *Revenue CAT Manual* which refers to a Circuit Court decision that a beneficiary, who inherited two houses, did not qualify for relief.

Section 87

[S.98, FA 1982]

Exemption of certain benefits.

87.   Where a gift or an inheritance is taken, by direction of the disponer, free of tax, the benefit taken is deemed to include the amount of tax chargeable on such gift or inheritance but not the amount of tax chargeable on such tax.

Commentary

A   See Part 14 of the *Revenue CAT Manual*.

Section 88

[S.142, FA 1997, as amended]

Exemption of certain transfers from capital acquisitions tax following the dissolution of a marriage.

88.   (1)   Notwithstanding any other provision of this Act, a gift or inheritance taken by virtue or in consequence of an order to which this subsection applies by a spouse who was a party to the marriage concerned is exempt from tax and is not taken into account in computing tax.

   (2)   Subsection (1) applies —

       (a)   to a relief order or an order under section 25 of the Family Law Act 1995, made, following the dissolution of a marriage, or

       (b)   to a maintenance pending relief order made, following the granting of leave under section 23(3) of the Family Law Act 1995, to a spouse whose marriage has been dissolved,

       (c)   to an order referred to in section 41(a) of the Family Law Act 1995, or an order under section 42(1) of that Act made in addition to or instead of an order under section 41(a) of that Act, in favour of a spouse whose marriage has been dissolved,

       (d)   to an order under Part III of the Family Law (Divorce) Act 1996, and

       (e)   to an order or other determination to like effect, made on or after 10 February 2000, which is analogous to an order referred to in paragraph (a), (b), (c) or (d), of a court under the law of another territory made under or in consequence of the dissolution of a marriage, being a dissolution that is entitled to be recognised as valid in the State.

PART 10
Reliefs

CHAPTER 1
Agricultural Relief

Section 89

[S.19, CATA, as amended]

Provisions relating to agricultural property.

89. (1) In this section —

["agricultural property" means —

(a) agricultural land, pasture and woodland situate **[in a Member State]**[6] and crops, trees and underwood growing on such land and also includes such farm buildings, farm houses and mansion houses (together with the lands occupied with such farm buildings, farm houses and mansion houses) as are of a character appropriate to the property, and farm machinery, livestock and bloodstock on such property, and

(b) a payment entitlement (within the meaning of Council Regulation (EC) No. 1782/2003 of 29 September 2003);][3]

"agricultural value" means the market value of agricultural property reduced by 90 per cent of that value;

"farmer" in relation to a donee or successor, means an individual [....][4] in respect of whom not less than 80 per cent of the market value of the property to which the individual is beneficially entitled in possession is represented by the market. value of property **[in a Member State]**[6] which consists of agricultural property, and, for the purposes of this definition —

[(a) no deduction is made from the market value of property for any debts or encumbrances (except debts or encumbrances in respect of a dwelling house which is the only or main residence of the donee or successor and which is not agricultural property), and][5]

(b) an individual is deemed to be beneficially entitled in possession to —

(i) an interest in expectancy, notwithstanding the definition of "entitled in possession" in section 2, and

(ii) property which is subject to a discretionary trust under or in consequence of a disposition made by the individual where the individual is an object of the trust.

(2) Except where provided in subsection (6), in so far as any gift or inheritance consists of agricultural property —

(a) at the date of the gift or at the date of the inheritance, and

(b) at the valuation date,

and is taken by a donee or successor who is, on the valuation date and after taking the gift or inheritance, a farmer, section 28 (other than subsection (7)(b) of that section) shall apply in relation to agricultural property as it applies in relation to other property subject to the following modifications—

(i) in subsection (1) of that section, the reference to market value shall be construed as a reference to agricultural value,

(ii) where a deduction is to be made for any liability, costs or expenses in accordance with subsection (1) of that section only a proportion of such liability, costs or expenses is deducted and that proportion is the proportion that the agricultural value of the agricultural property bears to the market value of that property, and

(iii) where a deduction is to be made for any consideration under subsection (2) or (4)(b) of that section, only a proportion of such consideration is deducted and that proportion is the proportion that the agricultural value of the agricultural property bears to the market value of that property.

(3) Where a taxable gift or a taxable inheritance is taken by a donee or successor subject to the condition that the whole or part of that taxable gift or taxable inheritance will be invested in agricultural property and such condition is complied with within 2 years after the date of the gift or the date of the inheritance, then the gift or inheritance is deemed, for the purposes of this section, to have consisted—

(a) at the date of the gift or at the date of the inheritance, and

(b) at the valuation date,

of agricultural property to the extent to which the gift or inheritance is subject to such condition and has been so invested.

(4) [(a) Where—

(i) all or any part of the agricultural property (other than crops, trees or underwood) comprised in a gift or inheritance is disposed of or compulsorily acquired within the period of 6 years after the date of the gift or inheritance, and

(ii) the proceeds from such disposal or compulsory acquisition are not fully expended in acquiring other agricultural property within a year of the disposal or within 6 years of the compulsory acquisition,

then, except where the donee or successor dies before the property is disposed of or compulsorily acquired, all or, as the case may be, part of the agricultural property shall, for the purposes of subsection (2) and in accordance with paragraph (aa), be treated as property comprised in the gift or inheritance which is not agricultural property, and the taxable value of the gift or inheritance shall be determined accordingly (without regard to whether the donee or successor has ceased to be a farmer by virtue of the disposal or compulsory acquisition) and tax shall be payable accordingly.

(aa) For the purposes of paragraph (a) –

   (i)   the market value of agricultural property which is treated under paragraph (a) as not being agricultural property is determined by the following formula –

$$V1 \ \text{X} \ \frac{N}{V2}$$

where –

V1 is the market value of all of the agricultural property on the valuation date without regard to paragraph (a),

V2 is the market value of that agricultural property immediately before the disposal or compulsory acquisition of all or, as the case may be, a part thereof,

and

N is the amount of proceeds from the disposal or compulsory acquisition of all the agricultural property or, as the case may be, a part thereof, that was not expended in acquiring other agricultural property,

and

   (ii)   the proceeds from a disposal include an amount equal to the market value of the consideration (not being cash) received for the disposal.][1]

(b)   If an arrangement is made, in the administration of property subject to a disposition, for the appropriation of property in or towards the satisfaction of a benefit under the disposition, such arrangement is deemed not to be a [disposal][2] or a compulsory acquisition for the purposes of paragraph (a).

(c)   The agricultural value in relation to a gift or inheritance referred to in subsection (2) shall cease to be applicable to agricultural property, other than crops, trees or underwood, if the donee or successor is not resident in the State for any of the 3 years of assessment immediately following the year of assessment in which the valuation date falls.

(5)   For the purposes of subsection (2), if, in the administration of property subject to a disposition, property is appropriated in or towards the satisfaction of a benefit in respect of which a person is deemed to take a gift or an inheritance under the disposition, the property so appropriated, if it was subject to the disposition at the

date of the gift or at the date of the inheritance, is deemed to have been comprised in that gift or inheritance at the date of the gift or at the date of the inheritance.

(6) Subsection (2) shall apply in relation to agricultural property which consists of trees or underwood as if the words "and is taken by a donee or successor who is, on the valuation date and after taking the gift or inheritance, a farmer," were omitted from that subsection.

(7) In this section, any reference to a donee or successor includes a reference to the transferee referred to in section 32(2).

Footnotes

1   As substituted for para. (a) by s.135(1)(a), FA 2005, in relation to disposals or compulsory acquisitions of agricultural property occurring on or after 3rd February, 2005.

2   Substituted for "sale" by s.135(1)(b), FA 2005, in relation to disposals or compulsory acquisitions of agricultural property occurring on or after 3rd February, 2005.

3   As substituted by s.118(1)(a)(i), FA 2006, and is deemed to have applied as regards gifts and inheritances of agricultural property taken on or after 1st January, 2005.

4   The words "who is domiciled in the State and" deleted by s.118(1)(a)(ii), FA 2006, in relation to gifts and inheritances taken on or after 2nd February, 2006

5   As substituted by s.117, FA 2007, which applies to gifts and inheritances taken on or after 1st February, 2007.

6   Substituted for "in the State" by s.89(1), F(No. 2)A, 2008, and applies to gifts and inheritances taken on or after 20th November 2008. "Member State" is defined in Part 2 of the Sch. to the Interpretation Act 2005 - see page 1279.

Commentary

A   See Part 19.13 of the *Revenue CAT Manual* citing a case where the owner of a dwelling house, a PAYE employee, inherited land situated three miles from the dwelling house. The Appeal Commissioners upheld a Revenue argument that the dwelling house was not "agricultural property" for the purpose of the "farmer test" as it was not of a character appropriate to the land.

B   See *Starke v IRC* [1995] STC 689 in relation to the definition of "agricultural property" contained in s.115(2), U.K. Inheritance Tax Act, 1984. There a 2.5 acre site, containing a substantial house and outbuildings, was held not to be "agricultural property".

C   See articles in relation to Agricultural Property Relief/Business Property Relief (dealing with both reliefs applying to agricultural property post FA 2000) by Brian Bohan in the *Irish Tax Review* of May 2000, page 279, and by Fergus McCarthy in the *Irish Tax Review* of July 2000, page 342.

D   See the Revenue Information Leaflet CAT5 in relation to agricultural relief.

E   See a discussion by Frank Carr at page 40 of the *Irish Tax Review* of March 2006 on a UK Land Tribunal case of *Lloyds TSB Private Banking plc., as personal representative of Rosemary Antrobus, deceased v Inland Revenue* [2005] DET/47/2004. The issue involved the definition of a "farmhouse".

E   See page 7, Issue 61, of the *Revenue Tax Briefing* of November 2005 which refers to the EU Single Payment Scheme for farmers and its implication for agricultural relief.

F   See a discussion by Frank Carr at page 25 of the *Irish Tax Review* of January 2007 on a UK Special Commissioners case of *McKenna, deceased, executors v Revenue Commissioners* [2006] SPC 565. The case decided that a listed medieval house attached to a farm did not qualify for agricultural relief.

G   As to a residence "being of a character appropriate to the property", see a Northern Ireland case of *John Sidney Higginson, deceased, executors v Commissioners of Inland Revenue* [2002] STC (SCD) 483.

Cross-References

1   The definition of "agricultural property" in s.89(1) is used in s.55(1), CATCA, and in s.90(1), CATCA.

2   The provisions of s.89(5) are applied to s.77(2), CATCA, s.78(3), CATCA, and s.81(2), CATCA.

CHAPTER 2
Business Relief

Section 90

[S.124, FA 1994, as amended]

Interpretation (Chapter 2).

90.   (1)   In this Chapter—

"agricultural property" has the meaning assigned to it by section 89;

"associated company" has the meaning assigned to it by section 16(1)(b) of the Companies (Amendment) Act 1986;.

"business" includes a business carried on in the exercise of a profession or vocation, but does not include a business carried on otherwise than for gain;

"excepted asset" shall be construed in accordance with section 100;

"full-time working officer or employee", in relation to one or more companies, means any officer or employee who devotes substantially the whole of such officer's or employee's time to the service of that company, or those companies taken together, in a managerial or technical capacity;

"holding company" and "subsidiary" have the meanings assigned to them, respectively, by section 155 of the Companies Act 1963;

"quoted", in relation to any shares or securities, means quoted on a recognised stock exchange and "unquoted", in relation to any shares or securities, means not so quoted;

"relevant business property" shall be construed in accordance with section 93.

(2)   In this Chapter a reference to a gift shall be construed as a reference to a taxable gift and a reference to an inheritance shall be construed as a reference to a taxable inheritance.

(3)   For the purposes of this Chapter a company and all its subsidiaries and any associated company of that company or of any of those subsidiaries and any subsidiary of such an associated company are members of a group.

(4)   In this Chapter any reference to a donee or successor is construed as including a reference to the transferee referred to in section 32(2).

Commentary

A   Part 12 of the *Revenue CAT Manual* deals with business relief.

B   See the Revenue Information leaflet CAT4 in relation to business relief.

C   According to Appendix I to Part 12 of the *Revenue CAT Manual*, business relief may be claimed for shares and securities quoted on the Unlisted Securities Market (USM) on the basis that they are "unquoted" within the meaning of that definition.

D   According to Appendix I to Part 12 of the *Revenue CAT Manual*, "securities" may be treated as including any debt which is either charged on property or is evidenced by a document under seal. Debts such as debentures and loan notes, even if described as "unsecured", may therefore rank as "securities".

E   See articles on business relief by Kieran Twomey in the *Irish Tax Review* of July 1994, page 979, by Jim Muddiman in the *Irish Tax Review* of March 1997, page 169, and by John Quinlan in the *Irish Tax Review* of March 1998, page 194.

Section 91

[S.125, FA 1994]

Application (Chapter 2).

91.   This Chapter shall apply in relation to gifts and inheritances, but shall not apply in relation to an inheritance taken by a discretionary trust by virtue of sections 15(1) or 20(1).

Section 92

[S.126, FA 1994, as amended]

Business relief.

92.   Where the whole or part of the taxable value of any taxable gift or taxable inheritance is attributable to the value of any relevant business property, the whole or that part of the taxable value is, subject to the other provisions of this Chapter, treated as being reduced by 90 per cent.

Commentary

A   As to the calculation of business relief, see Part 12.6 of the *Revenue CAT Manual*.

B   See Taxfax (Irish Taxation Institute) dated 31st May, 1996, confirming a Revenue concession which applies only where a sole-trader business or partnership interest, and other property, are comprised in the one acquisition, and not where company shares and other property are so comprised. Liabilities affecting the business should be deducted from the value of the business property, but other liabilities and consideration should, as far as possible, be deducted from the value of the other property (see page 1 of the Revenue form I.T.5 for use where business relief is claimed).

Section 93

[S.127, FA 1994, as amended]

Relevant business property.

93.   (1)   In this Chapter and subject to the following provisions of this section and to sections 94, 96 and 100(4) "relevant business property" means, in relation to a gift or inheritance, any one or more of the following, that is:

(a) property consisting of a business or interest in a business,

(b) unquoted shares in or securities of a company whether incorporated in the State or otherwise to which paragraph (c) does not relate, and which on the valuation date (either by themselves alone or together with other shares or securities in that company in the absolute beneficial ownership of the donee or successor on that date) give control of powers of voting on all questions affecting the company as a whole which if exercised would yield more than 25 per cent of the votes capable of being exercised on [all such questions][2],

(c) unquoted shares in or securities of a company whether incorporated in the State or [otherwise][3] which is, on the valuation date (after the taking of the gift or inheritance), a company controlled by the donee or successor within the meaning of section 27,

(d) unquoted shares in or securities of a company whether incorporated in the State or otherwise which do not fall within paragraph (b) or (c) and which on the valuation date (either by themselves alone or together with other shares or securities in that company in the absolute beneficial ownership of the donee or successor on that date) have an aggregate nominal value which represents 10 per cent or more of the aggregate nominal value of the entire share capital and securities of the company on condition that the donee or successor has been a fulltime working officer or employee of the company, or if that company is a member of a group, of one or more companies which are members of the group, throughout the period of 5 years ending on the date of the gift or inheritance,

(e) any land or building, machinery or plant which, immediately before the gift or inheritance, was used wholly or mainly for the purposes of a business carried on by a company of which the disponer then had control or by a partnership of which the disponer then was a partner and for the purposes of this paragraph a person is deemed to have control of a company at any time if that person then had control of powers of voting on all questions affecting the company as a whole which if exercised would have yielded a majority of the votes capable of being exercised on all such questions,

(f) quoted shares in or securities of a company which, but for the fact that they are quoted, would be shares or securities to which paragraph (b), (c) or (d) would relate on condition that such shares or securities, or other shares in or securities of the same company which are represented by those shares or securities, were in the beneficial ownership of the disponer immediately prior to the disposition and were unquoted at the date of the commencement of that beneficial ownership or at 23 May 1994, whichever is the later date.

(2)   Where a company has shares or securities of any class giving powers of voting limited to either or both—

(a)   the question of winding-up the company, and

(b)   any question primarily affecting shares or securities of that class,

the reference in subsection (1) to all questions affecting the company as a whole has effect as a reference to all such questions except any in relation to which those powers are capable of being exercised.

(3)   A business or interest in a business, or shares in or securities of a company, is not relevant business property if the business or, as the case may be, the business carried on by the company consists wholly or mainly of one or more of the following, that is, dealing in. currencies, securities, stocks or shares, land or buildings, or making or holding investments.

[(4)   Subsection (3) shall not apply to shares in or securities of a company if—

(a)   the business of the company consists wholly or mainly in being a holding company of one or more companies whose business does not fall within that subsection, or

(b)   the value of those shares or securities, without having regard to the provisions of section 99, is wholly or mainly attributable, directly or indirectly, to businesses that do not fall within that subsection.]¹

(5)   Any land, building, machinery or plant used wholly or mainly for the purposes of a business carried on as mentioned in subsection (1)(e) is not relevant business property in relation to a gift or inheritance, unless the disponer's interest in the business is, or shares in or securities of the company carrying on the business immediately before the gift or inheritance are, relevant business property in relation to the gift or inheritance or in relation to a simultaneous gift or inheritance taken by the same donee or successor.

(6)   The references to a disponer in subsections (1)(e) and (5) include a reference to a person in whom the land, building, machinery or plant concerned is vested for a beneficial interest in possession immediately before the gift or inheritance.

(7)   Where shares or securities are vested in the trustees of a settlement, any powers of voting which they give to the trustees of the settlement are, for the purposes of subsection (1)(e), deemed to be given to the person beneficially entitled in possession to the shares or securities except in a case where no individual is so entitled.

Footnotes

1   As substituted by s.78, FA 2004, in relation to gifts or inheritances taken on or after 25th March, 2004.

2   Substituted for "those shares" by para. 2(f)(i), Sch. 3, FA 2004, with effect as on and from 21st February, 2003, under para. 5(b) of that Sch.

3   Substituted for "othewise" by para. 2(f)(ii), Sch. 3, FA 2004, with effect as on and from 21st February, 2003, under para. 5(b) of that Sch.

Commentary

A   See the Revenue Information Leaflet CAT4 in relation to what is "relevant business property".

B   See Part 12.5, and Appendix II to Part 12, of the *Revenue CAT Manual* in relation to the interpretation of "relevant business property".

C   In Appendix II to Part 12 of the *Revenue CAT Manual*, see a query dated 12th August, 1994, and the Revenue reply, in relation to the operation of s.93(3).

D   In Appendix II to Part 12 of the *Revenue CAT Manual*, see a query dated 22nd November, 1994, and the Revenue reply, in relation to the operation of s.93(3) and (4).

E   In Appendix II to Part 12 of the *Revenue CAT Manual*, see a query dated 28th March, 1995, and the Revenue reply, in relation to multiple holding companies and s.93(3) and (4). Business relief is available for a holding company (Company A) which owns (say) 100% of the shares of a second holding company (Company B) which in turn owns (say) 100% of the shares of a trading company (Company C). It is also understood that Revenue agree that business relief is available where more than two holding companies (Companies C and D) are involved.

F   In Appendix II to Part 12 of the *Revenue CAT Manual*, see a query dated 21st April, 1995, and the Revenue reply, in relation to s.93(3) and property developers who deal in land.

G   In Appendix II to Part 12 of the *Revenue CAT Manual*, see a query dated 1st July, 1997, and the Revenue reply, in relation to s.93(3) and forested land owned by a company.

H   In Appendix II to Part 12 of the *Revenue CAT Manual*, see a query dated 15th August, 1997, and the Revenue reply, in relation to s.93(3).

I   As to the operation of a caravan park, see page 420 of the *Irish Tax Review* of September 1997 which refers to a UK Special Commissioners case of *Powell and Another v IRC* [1997] STC (SCD) 181 (where business relief was not granted) and page 573 of the *Irish Tax Review* of November 1999 which refers to a UK Special Commissioners case of *Furniss v IRC* [1999] SpC 202, STC(SCD) 232, where business relief was granted. A further case involving a caravan park (where relief was not granted) is *Weston v IRC* [1999] SpC 222, STC(SCD) 321, referred to at page 227 of the *Irish Tax Review* of May 2000 and at page 135 of the *Irish Tax Review* of March 2001. Again, the matter was considered by the UK Special Commissioners in the case of *Stedman, deceased* – see page 427 of the *Irish Tax Review* of November 2002. The *Stedman case* (*IRC v George and Another, executors of Stedman, deceased,* [2004] STC 147) is discussed by Frank Carr at page 232 of the *Irish Tax Review* of May 2003, and at page 111 of the *Irish Tax Review* of March 2004.

According to page 240 of the *Irish Tax Review* of May 2002, the Minister for Finance (Charles McCreevy) stated at the Select Committee stage of the Finance Bill, 2002 – "Revenue's approach is to look at the type of letting activity which takes place at caravan sites, that is, how much of the letting relates to the provision of furnished caravans owned by the business and how much involves letting of pitched sites. As a general guideline, where the operator's own caravans account for at least half of the total number of lettings, the caravan park is likely to qualify for business relief. Parks where the letting of pitched sites predominates will not qualify for the relief as the business primarily involves an exploitation of an interest in land."

See page 15, Issue 55, of the *Revenue Tax Briefing* of April 2004 which now clarifies the Revenue position on "caravan sites" contained at Part 12.5 of the *Revenue CAT Manual*.

J   See page 224 of the *Irish Tax Review* of May 2000 which refers to a UK Special Commissioner case of *Beckman v IRC* [2000] SpC 226. This case decided that business relief did not apply to the capital account of a retired partner who had died before the amount of the capital account was paid, since on retirement the capital account had become merely a debt.

K   See articles in relation to Agricultural Property Relief/Business Property Relief (dealing with both reliefs applying to agricultural property post FA 2000) by Brian Bohan in the *Irish Tax Review* of May 2000, page 279, and by Fergus McCarthy in the *Irish Tax Review* of July 2000, page 342.

L   See *Hardcastle v CIR* [2000] SpC 259, which held that Lloyds underwriting activities constituted a business consisting of the net funds held by Lloyds at a deceased person's death, but that money owing to Lloyds on open account (that is, amounts owed on account for which a result had not been notified before the death) was not a liability incurred for the purposes of the business.

M   See an article *Hertford v CIR* [2004] SpC 444, at page 23 of the *Irish Tax Review* of January 2005. The UK Special Commissioner accepted that a heritage house, 78% of which was open to the fee-paying public, was a business. He also held that the remaining 22% was not an excepted asset (see s.100, CATCA).

N   See a discussion by Frank Carr at page 40 of the *Irish Tax Review* of March 2006 on a UK Special Commissioners case of *Clark and Another v Revenue* [2005] STC (SCD) 823. The case involved the shares in a private company which rented out some properties and managed others, while retaining a substantial labour force to refurbish etc. the properties.

O   See page 8, Issue 61, of the *Revenue Tax Briefing* of November 2005 which refers to the EU Single Payment Scheme for farmers and its implications for business relief.

P   See a discussion by Frank Carr at page 22 of the *Irish Tax Review* of January 2007 on a UK Special Commissioners case of *Phillips, deceased, executors v Revenue Commissioners* [2006] SpC 555. The case involved the shares of a private company whose business consisted wholly or mainly of lending money to related family companies. Business relief was refused.

Q   See *Nelson Dance Family Settlement, trustees v Commissioners for Revenue and Customs* [2008] SpC 682, which decided that a transfer of business assets, rather than the business itself, qualified for business relief.

R   See *Piercy, deceased, executors v Commissioners for Revenue and Customs* [2008] SpC 687, as to whether shares in a company were shares in a company "whose business consisted wholly or mainly ...... in making or holding investments" (no exemption) or whether the company was a property development company whose holdings of land ranked as stock (exemption).

Cross-Reference
1   The definition of "relevant business property" in s.93 is used, with modifications, in s.55(1), CATCA.

Section 94

[S.128, FA 1994]

Minimum period of ownership.

94.   In relation to a gift or an inheritance, property shall not be relevant business property unless it was comprised in the disposition continuously—

(a)   in the case of an inheritance, which is taken on the date of death of the disponer, for a period of 2 years immediately prior to the date of the inheritance, or

(b)   in any other case, for a period of 5 years immediately prior to the date of the gift or inheritance,

and any period immediately before the date of the disposition during which the property was continuously in the beneficial ownership of the disponer, or of the spouse of the disponer, is deemed, for the purposes of this Chapter, to be a period or part of a period immediately before the date of the gift or inheritance during which it was continuously comprised in the disposition.

Commentary

A   See the Revenue Information Leaflet CAT4, and Part 12.5 and Appendix II to Part 12, of the *Revenue CAT Manual,* in relation to this section.

B   In Appendix II to Part 12 of the *Revenue CAT Manual,* see a query dated 4th July, 1994, and the Revenue reply, which involves the operation of s.94(b). The query concerns a gift by a private trading company, owned 100% by a husband and wife, of shares in its 100% owned subsidiary private trading company to children of those parents, and involves s.43, CATCA.

Section 95

[S.129, FA 1994]

Replacements.

95. (1) Property shall be treated as complying with section 94 if –

(a) the property replaced other property and that property, that other property and any property directly or indirectly replaced by that other property were comprised in the disposition for periods which together comprised –

(i) in a case referred to at paragraph (a) of section 94, at least 2 years falling within the 3 years immediately preceding the date of the inheritance, or

(ii) in a case referred to at paragraph (b) of section 94, at least 5 years falling within the 6 years immediately preceding the date of the gift or inheritance,

and

(b) any other property concerned was such that, had the gift or inheritance been taken immediately before it was replaced, it would, apart from section 94, have been relevant business property in relation to the gift or inheritance.

(2) In a case to which subsection (1) relates, relief under this Chapter shall not exceed what it would have been had the replacement or any one or more of the replacements not been made.

(3) For the purposes of subsection (2) changes resulting from the formation, alteration or dissolution of a partnership, or from the acquisition of a business by a company controlled (within the meaning of section 27) by the former owner of the business, are disregarded.

Commentary

A   See the Revenue Information Leaflet CAT4, and Part 12.5 and Appendix II to Part 12, of the *Revenue CAT Manual,* in relation to the interpretation of this section.

B   See *Dugan-Chapman v Commissioners for Revenue and Customs* [2008] SpC 666, as to whether shares acquired by a deceased could be identified with shares already owned by the deceased.

Section 96

[S.130, FA 1994]

Succession.

96. For the purposes of sections 94 and 95, where a disponer became beneficially entitled to any property on the death of another person the disponer is deemed to have been beneficially entitled to it from the date of that death.

Section 97

[S.131, FA 1994]

Successive benefits.

97. (1) Where —

(a) a gift or inheritance (in this section referred to as "the earlier benefit") was eligible for relief under this Chapter or would have been so eligible if such relief had been capable of being given in respect of gifts and inheritances taken at that time, and

(b) the whole or part of the property which, in relation to the earlier benefit was relevant business property became, through the earlier benefit, the property of the person or of the spouse of the person who is the disponer in relation to a subsequent gift or inheritance (in this section referred to as "the subsequent benefit"), and

(c) that property, or part, or any property directly or indirectly replacing it, would, apart from section 94, have been relevant business property in relation to the subsequent benefit, and

(d) the subsequent benefit is an inheritance taken on the death of the disponer,

then the property which would have been relevant business property but for section 94 is relevant business property notwithstanding that section.

(2) Where the property which, by virtue of subsection (1), is relevant business property replaced the property or part referred to in subsection (1)(c), relief under this Chapter shall not exceed what it would have been had the replacement or any one or more of the replacements not been made, and section 95(3) shall apply with the necessary modifications for the purposes of this subsection.

(3) Where, in relation to the earlier benefit, the amount of the taxable value of the gift or inheritance which was attributable to the property or part referred to in subsection (1)(c) was part only of its value, a like part only of the value which, apart from this subsection, would fall to be reduced under this Chapter by virtue of this section is so reduced.

Commentary

A   See the Revenue Information Leaflet CAT4, and Part 12.5 of the *Revenue CAT Manual*, in relation to the interpretation of this section.

Section 98

[S.132, FA 1994]

Value of business.

98.   For the purposes of this Chapter —

(a)   the value of a business or of an interest in a business is taken to be its net value,

(b)   subject to paragraph (c), the net value of a business shall be taken to be the market value of the assets used in the business (including goodwill) reduced by the aggregate market value of any liabilities incurred for the purposes of the business,

(c)   in ascertaining the net value of an interest in a business, no regard is had to assets or liabilities other than those by reference to which the net value of the entire business would fall to be ascertained.

Commentary

A   See the Revenue Information Leaflet CAT4 in relation to this section, and also Part 12.5 of the *Revenue CAT Manual*.

B   In Appendix II to Part 12 of the *Revenue CAT Manual*, see a query dated 15th August, 1997, and the Revenue reply, as to the deduction of borrowings charged on excepted assets from the value of those assets.

C   As to a liability in s.98(b) incurred for the purposes of the business, see footnote L under s.93, CATCA, in relation to *Hardcastle v CIR* [2000] SpC 259.

Section 99

[S.133, FA 1994]

Value of certain shares and securities.

99.   (1)   Where a company is a member of a group and the business of any other company which is a member of the group falls within section 93(3), then, unless that business consists wholly or mainly in the holding of land or buildings wholly or mainly occupied by members of the group whose business does not fall within section 93(3), the value of shares in or securities of the company is taken for the purposes of this Chapter to what it would be if that other company were not a member of the group.

(2)   (a)   In this subsection "shares" include securities and "shares in a company" include other shares in the same company which are represented by those shares.

(b)   Where unquoted shares in a company which is a member of a group are comprised in a gift or inheritance and shares in another company which is also a member of the group are quoted on the valuation date, the value of the first-mentioned shares is taken, for the purpose of this Chapter, to be what it would be if that other company were not a member of the group, unless those unquoted shares were in the beneficial ownership of the disponer immediately prior to the disposition and those quoted shares were unquoted –

(i) at some time prior to the gift or inheritance when they were in the beneficial ownership of the disponer or a member of that group, while being a member of such group, or

(ii) at 23 May 1994,

whichever is the later date.

Commentary

A   See Part 12.5 of the *Revenue CAT Manual* regarding the operation of this section.

B   In Appendix II to Part 12 of the *Revenue CAT Manual*, see a query dated 12th August, 1994, and the Revenue reply, in relation to (i) interest-free loans between companies of a group resulting in some companies of the group being dormant, and (ii) a company in a group owning property from which other companies in the group trade.

Section 100

[S.134, FA 1994, as amended]

Exclusion of value of excepted assets.

100. (1) In determining for the purposes of this Chapter what part of the taxable value of a gift or inheritance is attributable to the value of relevant business property, so much of the last-mentioned value as is attributable to –

(a) any excepted assets within the meaning of subsection (2), or

(b) any excluded property within the meaning of [subsection (8),][1]

is disregarded.

(2) An asset is an excepted asset in relation to any relevant business property if it was not used wholly or mainly for the purposes of the business concerned throughout the whole or the last 2 years of the relevant period; but where the business concerned is carried on by a company which is a member of a group, the use of an asset for the purposes of a business carried on by another company which at the time of the use and immediately prior to the gift or inheritance was also a member of that group is treated as use for the purposes of the business concerned, unless that other company's membership of the group is to be disregarded under section 99.

(3) The use of an asset for the purposes of a business to which section 93(3) relates is not treated as use for the purposes of the business concerned.

(4) Subsection (2) shall not apply in relation to an asset which is relevant business property by virtue only of section 93(1)(e), and an asset is not relevant business property by virtue only of that provision unless either—

(a) it was used in the manner referred to in that provision—

(i) in the case where the disponer's interest in the business or the shares in or securities of the company carrying on the business are comprised in an inheritance taken on the date of death of the disponer, throughout the 2 years immediately preceding the date of the inheritance, or

(ii) in any other case, throughout the 5 years immediately preceding the date of the gift or inheritance,

or

(b) it replaced another asset so used and it and the other asset and any asset directly or indirectly replaced by that other asset were so used for periods which together comprised—

(i) in the case referred to at paragraph (a)(i), at least 2 years falling within the 3 years immediately preceding the date of the inheritance, or

(ii) in any other case, at least 5 years falling within the 6 years immediately preceding the date of the gift or inheritance,

but where section 97 applies paragraphs (a) and (b) are deemed to be complied with if the asset, or that asset and the asset or assets replaced by it, was or were so used throughout the period between the earlier and the subsequent benefit mentioned in that section, or throughout the part of that period during which it or they were in the beneficial ownership of the disponer or the disponer's spouse.

(5) Where part but not the whole of any land or building is used exclusively for the purposes of any business and the land or building would, but for this subsection, be an excepted asset, or, as the case may be, prevented by subsection (4) from being relevant business property, the part so used and the remainder are for the purposes of this section treated as separate assets, and the value of the part so used shall (if it would otherwise be less) be taken to be such proportion of the value of the whole as may be just.

(6) For the purposes of this section the relevant period, in relation to any asset, is the period immediately preceding the gift or inheritance during which the asset or, if the relevant business property is an interest in a business, a corresponding interest in the asset, was comprised in the disposition (within the meaning of section 94) or, if the business concerned is that of a company, was beneficially owned by that company or any other company which

immediately before the gift or inheritance was a member of the same group.

(7) For the purposes of this section an asset is deemed not to have been used wholly or mainly for the purposes of the business concerned at any time when it was used wholly or mainly for the personal benefit of the disponer or of a relative of the disponer.

(8) Where, in relation to a gift or an inheritance –

(a) relevant business property consisting of shares in or securities of a company are comprised in the gift or inheritance on the valuation date, and

(b) property consisting of a business, or interest in a business, not falling within section 93(3) (in this section referred to as "company business property") is on that date beneficially owned by that company or, where that company is a holding company of one or more companies within the same group, by any company within that group,

that company business property shall, for the purposes of subsection (1), be excluded property in relation to those shares or securities unless it would have been relevant business property if –

(i) it had been the subject matter of that gift or inheritance, and

(ii) it had been comprised in the disposition for the periods during which it was in the beneficial ownership of that first-mentioned company or of any member of that group, while being such a member, or actually comprised in the disposition.

(9) In ascertaining whether or not company business property complies with paragraphs (i) and (ii) of [subsection (8),][2] section 95 shall, with any necessary modifications, apply to that company business property as to a case to which subsection (1) of section 95 relates.

Footnotes

1 Substituted for "subsection 7" by s.152(a), FA 2003, with effect from 28th March, 2003.

2 Substituted for "subsection 7" by s.152(b), FA 2003, with effect from 28th March, 2003.

Commentary

A See the Revenue Information Leaflet CAT4 in relation to this section. It should be noted, however, that agricultural property may also qualify for business relief – see s.102, CATCA.

B See Part 12.5, and Appendix II to Part 12, of the *Revenue CAT Manual* in relation to the interpretation of this section. It should be noted, however, that agricultural property may also qualify for business relief – see s.102, CATCA.

C In Appendix II to Part 12 of the *Revenue CAT Manual*, see a query dated 12th August, 1994, and the Revenue reply, in relation to (i) interest-free loans between companies of a group resulting in some companies of the group being dormant, and (ii) a company in a group owning property from which other companies in the group trade.

D   In Appendix II to Part 12 of the *Revenue CAT Manual*, see a query dated 15th August, 1997, and the Revenue reply, in relation to s.100(2).

E   With regard to s.100(2) and cash balances held by a trading company, see page 344 of the *Irish Tax Review* of July 1998 which refers to a case of *Barclays Bank v IRC* [1998] ST1 738, heard before the UK Special Commissioners.

F   See Commentary M to section 93, CATCA.

Section 101

[S.135, FA 1994, as amended]

Withdrawal of relief.

101. (1) In this section "relevant period", in relation to relevant business property comprised in a gift or inheritance, means the period of 6 years commencing on the date of the gift or inheritance.

(2) The reduction which would fall to be made under section 92 in respect of relevant business property comprised in a gift or inheritance shall cease to be applicable if and to the extent that the property, or any property which directly or indirectly replaces it—

(a) would not be relevant business property (apart from section 94 and the conditions attached to paragraphs (d) and (f) of subsection (1) of section 93 and other than by reason of bankruptcy or a bona fide winding-up on grounds of insolvency) in relation to a notional gift of such property taken by the same donee or successor from the same disponer at any time within the relevant period, unless it would be relevant business property (apart from section 94 and the conditions attached to paragraphs (d) and (f) of subsection (1) of section 93) in relation to another such notional gift taken within a year after the first-mentioned notional gift,

(b) is sold, redeemed or compulsorily acquired within the relevant period and is not replaced, within a year of the sale, redemption or compulsory acquisition, by other property (other than quoted shares or securities or unquoted shares or securities to which section 99(2)(b) relates) which would be relevant business property (apart from section 94 and the condition attached to section 93(1)(d)) in relation to a notional gift of that other property taken by the same donee or successor from the same disponer on the date of the replacement,

and tax is chargeable in respect of the gift or inheritance as if the property were not relevant business property, but—

(i) any land, building, machinery or plant which are comprised in the gift or inheritance and which qualify as relevant business property by virtue of section 93(1)(e) shall, together with any similar property which has replaced such property, continue to be relevant business property for the purposes of this section for so long as they are used for the purposes of the business concerned,

    (ii)   this section shall not have effect where the donee or successor dies before the event which would otherwise cause the reduction to cease to be applicable.

[(3) Notwithstanding subsection (2), where relevant business property (in this section referred to as "original property") comprised in a gift or inheritance has been replaced directly or indirectly by other property and the market value of the original property is greater than the market value of that other property, then the reduction which would fall to be made under section 92 in respect of the original property shall be reduced in the same proportion as the market value of the other property bears to the market value of the original property.][1]

Footnote

1   As inserted by s.136(1), FA 2005, with effect in relation to relevant business property which has been replaced by other property on or after 3rd February, 2005.

Commentary

A   See Part 12.7, and Appendix II to Part 12, of the *Revenue CAT Manual* in relation to the interpretation of this section.

B   See the Revenue Information Leaflet CAT4 in relation to this section.

Section 102

[S.135A, FA 1994]

Avoidance of double relief.

102.   Where the whole or part of the taxable value of any taxable gift or taxable inheritance is attributable to agricultural property to which section 89(2) applies, such whole or part of the taxable value is not reduced under this Chapter.

CHAPTER 2A

Clawback of Agricultural Relief or Business Relief: Development Land

Section 102A[1]

Agricultural and business property: development land.

102A.(1)   In this section—

    "agricultural property" has the meaning assigned to it by section 89;

    "current use value" —

    (a)   in relation to land at any particular time, means the amount which would be the market value of the land at that time if the market value were calculated on the assumption that it was at that time and would remain unlawful to carry out any development (within the meaning of section 3 of the Planning and Development Act 2000) in relation to the land other than development of a minor nature, and

(b)   in relation to shares in a company at any particular time, means the amount which would be the value of the shares at that time if the market value were calculated on the same assumption, in relation to the land from which the shares derive all or part of their value, as is mentioned in paragraph (a);

"development land" means land in the State, the market value of which at the date of a gift or inheritance exceeds the current use value of that land at that date, and includes shares deriving their value in whole or in part from such land;

"development of a minor nature" means development (not being development by a local authority or statutory undertaker within the meaning of section 2 of the Planning and Development Act 2000) which, under or by virtue of section 4 of that Act, is exempted development for the purposes of that Act;

"relevant business property" shall be construed in accordance with section 93;

"valuation date" shall be construed in accordance with section 30.

(2)   Where—

(a)   relief has been granted by virtue of section 89(2) or section 92 in respect of a gift or inheritance of agricultural property or, as the case may be, relevant business property,

(b)   the property is comprised, in whole or in part, of development land, and

(c)   the development land is disposed of in whole or in part by the donee or successor at any time in the period commencing 6 years after the date of the gift or inheritance and ending 10 years after that date,

then tax shall be re-computed at the valuation date of the gift or inheritance as if the amount by which the market value of the land disposed of exceeds its current use value at that date was the value of property which was not—

(i)   agricultural property, or

(ii)   relevant business property,

as the case may be, and tax shall be payable accordingly.

Footnote

1   This section was inserted by s.118(1)(b), FA 2006, in relation to gifts and inheritances taken on or after 2nd February, 2006.

CHAPTER 3
Miscellaneous Reliefs

Section 103

[S.61, FA 1985]

Relief from double aggregation.

103. (1) Property in respect of which tax is chargeable more than once on the same event is not included more than once in relation to that event in any aggregate referred to in Schedule 2.

(2) Paragraph 5 of Part 1 of Schedule 2 shall not have effect in ascertaining the tax payable in respect of property which is chargeable to tax as being taken more than once on the same day.

Section 104

[S.63, FA 1985, as amended]

Allowance for capital gains tax[1] on the same event.

104. (1) Where gift tax or inheritance tax is charged in respect of property on an event happening on or after the date of the passing of this Act, and the same event constitutes for capital gains tax purposes a disposal of an asset (being the same property or any part of the same property), the capital gains tax, if any, chargeable on the disposal is not deducted in ascertaining the taxable value for the purposes of the gift tax or inheritance tax but, in so far as it has been paid, is deducted from the net gift tax or inheritance tax as a credit against the same; but, in relation to each asset, or to a part of each asset, so disposed of, the amount deducted is the lesser of—

(a) an amount equal to the amount of the capital gains tax attributable to such asset, or to the part of such asset, or

(b) an amount equal to the amount of the gift tax or inheritance tax attributable to the property which is that asset, or that part of that asset.

(2) For the purposes of any computation of the amount of capital gains tax to be deducted under this section, any necessary apportionments are made of any reliefs or expenditure and the method of apportionment adopted is such method as appears to the Commissioners, or on appeal to the Appeal Commissioners, to be just and reasonable.

[(3) The deduction by virtue of subsection (1) of capital gains tax chargeable on the disposal of an asset against gift tax or inheritance tax shall cease to apply to the extent that the asset is disposed of within 2 years after the date of the gift or, as the case may be, the date of the inheritance.][2]

Footnotes

1   Under s.730GB, TCA, inserted by s.70(1)(f), FA 2001, capital gains tax includes "appropriate tax" payable as a result of the death of a person.

Under s.739G(5), TCA, inserted by s.74(1)(e)(ii), FA 2001, capital gains tax includes "appropriate tax" payable as a result of a death of a person.

Under s.747E(5), TCA, inserted by s.72(1), FA 2001, capital gains tax includes tax payable under s.747E(1), TCA.

2   Inserted by s.119, FA 2006, in relation to gifts and inheritances taken on or after 2nd February, 2006.

Commentary

A   See Part 13 of the *Revenue CAT Manual*.

B   See Part 19.4 of the *Revenue CAT Manual*. Where there is a disposition of a house charged with a mortgage, or subject to partial consideration, the entire of the capital gains tax attributable to the disposal (being a disposal of the whole house) is deductible from the entire of the CAT attributable to the disposition (being a disposition of the entire house).

C   See Part 19.17 of the *Revenue CAT Manual* confirming that Revenue will allow a temporary credit for capital gains tax until such time as it is paid.

Section 105

[S.34A, CATA]

Allowance for prior tax on the same event.

105.   Where tax is charged more than once in respect of the same property on the same event, the net tax payable which is earlier in priority is not deducted in ascertaining the taxable value for the purposes of the tax which is later in priority, but is deducted from the tax which is later in priority as a credit against the same, up to the net amount of the same.

Section 106

[S.66, CATA]

Arrangements for relief from double taxation.

106.   [(1) If the Government by order declare that arrangements specified in the order have been made with the government of any territory outside the State in relation to —

(a)   affording relief from double taxation in respect of gift tax or inheritance tax payable under the laws of the State and any tax imposed under the laws of that territory which is of a similar character or is chargeable by reference to death or to gifts *inter vivos*, or

(b)   exchanging information for the purposes of the prevention and detection of tax evasion in respect of the taxes specified in paragraph (a),][1]

[and that it is expedient that those arrangements should have the force of law and the order so made is referred to in the Table to this

section, the arrangements shall, notwithstanding anything in any enactment, have the force of law as if each such order were an Act of the Oireachtas on and from the date of –

    (i)   the insertion of the Table, or

    (ii) the insertion of a reference to the order in the Table,

whichever is the later.][2]

(2) Any arrangements to which the force of law is given under this section may include provision for relief from tax charged before the making of the arrangements and provisions as to property which is not itself subject to double tax, and the provisions of this section shall apply accordingly.

(3) For the purposes of subsection (1), arrangements made with the head of a foreign state are regarded as made with the government of that foreign state.

(4) Where any arrangements have the force of law by virtue of this section, the obligation as to secrecy imposed by any enactment shall not prevent the Commissioners from disclosing to any authorised officer of the government with which the arrangements are made such information as is required to be disclosed under the arrangements.

(5) (a) Any order made under this section may be revoked by a subsequent order and any such revoking order may contain such transitional provisions as appear to the Government to be necessary or expedient.

    (b) Where an order is proposed to be made under this section, a draft of such order shall be laid before Dáil Éireann and the order shall not be made until a resolution approving of the draft has been passed by Dáil Éireann.

[TABLE

Part 1

ARRANGEMENTS MADE BY THE GOVERNMENT WITH THE GOVERNMENT OF ANY TERRITORY OUTSIDE THE STATE IN RELATION TO AFFORDING RELIEF FROM DOUBLE TAXATION AND EXCHANGING INFORMATION IN RELATION TO TAX

1. The Double Taxation Relief (Taxes on Estates of Deceased Persons and Inheritances and on Gifts) (United Kingdom) Order 1978 (S.I. No. 279 of 1978).[4]

Part 2

ARRANGEMENTS IN RELATION TO THE EXCHANGE OF INFORMATION RELATING TO TAX AND IN RELATION TO OTHER MATTERS RELATING TO TAX][3]

Footnotes

1   As substituted by s.79, FA 2004, with effect from 25th March, 2004.

2   Substituted by s.129(1)(a), FA 2008, with effect from 31st January, 2008, for "and that it is expedient that those arrangements should have the force of law, the arrangements shall, notwithstanding anything in any enactment, have the force of law." The substituted words were already an amendment to s.106(1) contained in s.79, FA 2004, with effect from 25th March, 2004.

3   Inserted by s.129(1)(b), FA 2008, with effect from 31st January, 2008.

4   Reproduced on page 178.

Commentary

A   Two such "arrangements" have been made, (i) with the USA, the provisions of s.10, FA 1950, being treated as applicable to US Federal Estate Tax, and to Irish inheritance tax (not gift tax) (see page 171), and (ii) with the UK in relation to UK inheritance tax, and to Irish gift tax and inheritance tax (see page 178).

B   See an article on CAT and Double Taxation Relief by Ann Williams in the *Irish Tax Review* of September 2000, page 437.

C   See an article on Capital Acquisitions Tax Issues for Non-Irish Domiciled Persons (dealing with persons dying on or after 1st December, 2004) by Ann Williams at page 405 of the *Irish Tax Review* of September 2004.

Section 107

[S.67, CATA, as amended]

Other relief from double taxation.

107. (1) (a)   In this section—

"foreign tax" means any tax which is chargeable under the laws of any territory outside the State and is of a character similar to estate duty, gift tax or inheritance tax;

"event" means—

(i)   a death, or

(ii) any other event,

by reference to which the date of the gift or the date of the inheritance is determined.

(b)   For the purposes of this section, a reference to property situate in a territory outside the State is a reference to property situate in that territory at the date of the gift or the date of the inheritance, as the case may be, or to property representing such property.

[(2) Where the Commissioners are satisfied that a taxable gift or taxable inheritance, taken under a disposition by a donee or successor on the happening of any event, is reduced by the payment of foreign tax which is chargeable in connection with the same event under the same disposition in respect of property which is situate in any territory outside the State, they shall allow a credit in respect of that foreign tax against the gift tax or inheritance tax payable by that donee or successor on that taxable gift or taxable inheritance; but such credit shall not exceed—

(a) the amount of the gift tax or inheritance tax payable in respect of the same property by reason of such property being comprised in any taxable gift or taxable inheritance taken under that disposition on the happening of that event, or

(b) in so far as it has been paid, the amount of that foreign tax,

whichever is the lesser.][1]

(3) This section is subject to any arrangement to which the force of law is given under section 106 and, if any such arrangement provides for the allowance of the amount of a tax payable in a territory outside the State as a credit against gift tax or inheritance tax, the provisions of the arrangement shall apply in relation to the tax payable in that territory in lieu of the provisions of subsection (2).

(4) Where the foreign tax in respect of property comprised in a taxable gift or a taxable inheritance taken under a disposition on the happening of an event is, under the terms of the disposition, directed to be paid out of a taxable gift or a taxable inheritance (taken under that disposition on the happening of the same event) other than the taxable gift or taxable inheritance out of which it would be payable in the absence of such a direction, then, for the purposes of subsection (2), the taxable gift or taxable inheritance out of which the foreign tax would be payable in the absence of such a direction, and no other taxable gift or taxable inheritance, is treated as reduced by the payment of the foreign tax.

Footnote

1   As substituted by s.137(1), FA 2005, in relation to gifts or inheritances taken on or after 1st December, 2004.

Commentary

A   See an article on Capital Acquisitions Tax Issues for Non-Irish Domiciled Persons (dealing with persons dying on or after 1st December, 2004) by Ann Williams at page 405 of the *Irish Tax Review* of September 2004. The comment there on unilateral relief is now dealt with in the revised s.107(2) above.

PART 11

Miscellaneous

Section 108

[S.60, CATA]

Certificates for probate.

108. (1) In this section "Inland Revenue affidavit" has the meaning referred to in section 48(1).

(2) Where an Inland Revenue affidavit has been delivered to the Commissioners and they are satisfied –

(a) that an adequate payment on account of inheritance tax in respect of the property passing under the deceased person's will or intestacy or Part IX or section 56 of the Succession Act 1965 has been made, or

(b) that the payment of inheritance tax in respect of such property may be deferred for the time being,

they shall certify in writing –

(i) that the Inland Revenue affidavit was delivered to them, and

(ii) (I) that a payment referred to in paragraph (a) has been made, or

(II) that the payment referred to in paragraph (b) has been deferred for the time being,

as the case may be.

(3) If, in the opinion of the Commissioners, the payment of inheritance tax in respect of the property passing under the deceased person's will or intestacy or Part IX or section 56 of the Succession Act 1965 can not be deferred for the time being without serious risk of such tax not being recovered, they may refuse to issue the certificate referred to in subsection (2) until the tax has been paid, or until such payment as is referred to in paragraph (a) of that subsection has been made.

(4) The certificate required by section 30 of the Customs and Inland Revenue Act 1881[1], to be made by the proper officer of the court, shall not be made until a certificate of the Commissioners issued under subsection (2) has been produced to such officer and shall (instead of showing that the affidavit, if liable to stamp duty, has been duly stamped) show that the Commissioners have issued a certificate under subsection (2) and shall state the substance of the certificate so issued by the Commissioners.

(5) The form of certificate required to be given by the proper officer of the court under section 30 of the Customs and Inland Revenue Act 1881[1] may be prescribed by rule of court in such manner as may be necessary for giving effect to this Act.

Footnote

1   Reproduced on page 651.

Section 109

[S.61, CATA, as amended]

Payment of money standing in names of 2 or more persons.

109. (1) In this section –

"banker" means a person who carries on banking business in the State and includes a friendly society, an industrial and provident society, a building society, the Post Office Savings Bank, a trustee savings bank and any person with whom money is lodged or deposited;

"pay" includes transfer in the books of a banker and any dealings with any moneys which were lodged or deposited in the name of a person who died after the time of the lodgment or deposit and any other person or persons;

"current account" means an account which is customarily operated on by means of a cheque or banker's order;

"banking business" has the meaning assigned to it by section 2 of the Central Bank Act 1971;

references to moneys lodged or deposited include references to shares of a building society, friendly society or industrial and provident society.

(2) Where, either before or after the passing of this Act, a sum of money exceeding €31,750 is lodged or deposited (otherwise than on a current account) in the State with a banker, in the joint names of 2 or more persons, and one of such persons (in this section referred to as the deceased) dies on or after the date of the passing of this Act, the banker shall not pay such money or any part of such money to the survivor or all or any of the survivors of such persons, or to any other person, unless or until there is furnished to such banker a certificate by the Commissioners certifying that there is no outstanding claim for inheritance tax in connection with the death of the deceased in respect of such money or any part of such money or a consent in writing by the Commissioners to such payment pending the ascertainment and payment of such tax.

(3) Notwithstanding anything contained in this Act, tax chargeable on the death of the deceased is deemed for the purposes of this section to become due on the day of the death of the deceased.

(4) A banker who, after the passing of this Act, pays money in contravention of this section is liable to a penalty of €1,265.

(5) Where a penalty is demanded of a banker under this section, the onus of proving that such certificate or such consent as is mentioned in this section was furnished to such banker before that banker paid such money shall lie on such banker.

(6) Where a penalty is demanded of a banker under this section, it shall be a good defence to prove that, at the time when such banker paid such money, that banker had reasonable ground for believing that none of the persons in whose joint names such money was lodged or deposited with that banker was dead.

(7) This section shall not apply where the sum of money referred to in subsection (2) is lodged or deposited in the joint names of 2 persons, one of whom dies on or after the date of the passing of this Act and is at the time of that person's death the spouse of that other person.

Section 110

[S.62, CATA]

Court to provide for payment of tax.

110. Where any suit is pending in any court for the administration of any property chargeable with tax under this Act, such court shall provide, out of any such property which may be in the possession or control of the court, for the payment to the Commissioners of any of the tax or the interest on that tax which remains unpaid.

Section 111

[S.64, CATA]

Liability to tax in respect of certain sales and mortgages.

111. (1) In this section –

"death duties" has the meaning assigned to it by section 30 of the Finance Act 1971[1], and

"purchaser or mortgagee" includes a person deriving title from or under a purchaser or mortgagee in the case of such a sale or mortgage as is referred to in this section.

(2) Where an interest in expectancy has, prior to 1 April 1975, been bona fide sold or mortgaged for full consideration in money or money's worth, and that interest comes into possession on a death occurring on or after the date of the passing of this Act, the following provisions shall apply, that is –

(a) the purchaser or mortgagee shall not be liable in respect of inheritance tax on the inheritance referred to in paragraph (b) for an amount greater than that referred to in paragraph (c);

(b) the inheritance referred to in paragraph (a) is the inheritance of property in which the interest so sold or mortgaged subsists and which arises in respect of the interest of the remainderman referred to in section 32 so coming into possession;

(c) the amount referred to in paragraph (a) shall be the amount that would then have been payable by the purchaser or mortgagee in respect of death duties on the property in which the interest subsists as property passing under the same disposition as that under which the inheritance is taken, if the property, on so coming into possession, had been chargeable to death duties –

(i) under the law in force, and

(ii) at the rate or rates having effect,

at the date of the sale or mortgage;

(d) where such an interest is so mortgaged, any amount of inheritance tax payable in respect of the inheritance referred to in paragraph (b), and from the payment of which the mortgagee is relieved under this section, shall, notwithstanding the priority referred to in section 60(1), rank, in relation to property charged with such tax under that section, as a charge subsequent to the mortgage;

(e) any person, other than the purchaser or mortgagee, who is accountable for the payment of so much of the inheritance tax as is not the liability of the purchaser or mortgagee by virtue of the relief given by this section, shall not be liable for the payment of any amount in respect of such inheritance tax in excess of the amount which is available to that person for such payment by reason of there being, at the time when the interest comes into possession, other property, or an equity of redemption, or both, subject to the same trusts, under the disposition referred to in paragraph (c), as the property in which the interest in expectancy subsists; and

(f) nothing in section 45(7) or (8) or section 60(1) shall be construed as derogating from the relief given by this section to a purchaser or mortgagee.

Footnote
1   Reproduced on page 679.

Section 112

[S.65, CATA]

References in deeds and wills, etc. to death duties.

112.   In so far as a provision in a document refers (in whatever terms) to any death duty to arise on any death occurring on or after the date of the passing of this Act, it shall apply, as far as may be, as if the reference included a reference to inheritance tax—

(a) if that document was executed prior to 31 March 1976, and the reference is to legacy duty and succession duty or either of them,

(b) if that document was so executed, and the reference is to estate duty, and it may reasonably be inferred from all the circumstances (including any similarity of the incidence of inheritance tax to that of estate duty) that the inclusion of the reference to inheritance tax would be just, and

(c) whether the document was executed prior to, on or after 31 March 1976, if the reference is to death duties, without referring to any particular death duty.

Section 113

[S.68, CATA]

Tax, in relation to certain legislation.

113. (1) Inheritance tax shall not be a duty or a death duty for the purposes of section 9 of the Succession Act 1965, but it shall be a death duty for the purposes of —

(a) section 34(3) of that Act,

(b) the definition of pecuniary legacy in section 3(1) of that Act, and

(c) paragraph 8 of Part II of the First Schedule to that Act.

(2) Section 72 of the Registration of Title Act 1964 shall apply as if gift tax and inheritance tax were mentioned in that Act as well as estate duty and succession duty.

Section 114

[S.70, CATA]

Delivery, service and evidence of notices and forms, etc.

114. (1) Any notice which under this Act is authorised or required to be given by the Commissioners may be served by post.

(2) A notice or form which is to be served on a person may be either delivered to that person or left at that person's usual or last known place of abode.

(3) Prima facie evidence of any notice given under this Act by the Commissioners or by an officer of the Commissioners may be given in any proceedings by production of a document purporting —

(a) to be a copy of that notice, or

(b) if the details specified in that notice are contained in an electronic, photographic or other record maintained by the Commissioners, to reproduce those details in so far as they relate to that notice,

and it shall not be necessary to prove the official position of the person by whom the notice purports to be given or, if it is signed,. the signature, or that the person signing and giving it was authorised so to do.

(4) In any case where a time limit is specified by or under this Act, other than Part 8 of this Act, for the doing of any act required by or under this Act, other than Part 8 of this Act, to be done by any person other than the Commissioners, the Commissioners may, in their discretion, extend such time limit.

Section 115

[S.69, CATA]

Extension of certain Acts.

115. (1) Section 1 of the Provisional Collection of Taxes Act 1927[1] is hereby amended by the insertion of "and gift tax and inheritance tax" before "but no other tax or duty".

(2) Section 39 of the Inland Revenue Regulation Act 1890, is hereby amended by the insertion of "gift tax and inheritance tax," before "stamp duties".

Footnote

1   Reproduced on page 658.

Section 116

[S.71, CATA]

Regulations.

116. (1) The Commissioners shall make such regulations as seem to them to be necessary for the purpose of giving effect to this Act and of enabling them to discharge their functions under the Act.

(2) Every regulation made under this section shall be laid before Dáil Éireann as soon as may be after it is made and, if a resolution annulling the regulation is passed by Dáil Éireann within the next 21 days on which Dáil Éireann has sat after the regulation is laid before it, the regulation shall be annulled accordingly, but without prejudice to the validity of anything previously done under that regulation.

Section 117

[S.72, CATA]

Care and management.

117. (1) Tax is hereby placed under the care and management of the Commissioners.

(2) Subject to the direction and control of the Commissioners, any power, function or duty conferred or imposed on the Commissioners by this Act may be exercised or performed on their behalf by an officer of the Commissioners.

PART 12

Repeals, etc.

Section 118

Repeals.

118. (1) Subject to subsection (2), the Capital Acquisitions Tax Act 1976 is hereby repealed.

(2) This Act shall not apply in relation to gifts and inheritances taken before the date of the passing of this Act, and the repealed enactments shall continue to apply in relation to such gifts and inheritances to the same extent that they would have applied if this Act had not been enacted.

(3) Notwithstanding subsection (1), any provision of the repealed enactments which imposes a fine, forfeiture, penalty or punishment for any act or omission shall, in relation to any act or omission which took place or began before the date of the passing of this Act, continue to apply in substitution for the provision of this Act to which it corresponds.

(4) Anything done under or in connection with the provisions of the repealed enactments which correspond to the provisions of this Act shall be deemed to have been done under or in connection with the provisions of this Act to which those provisions of the repealed enactments correspond; but nothing in this subsection shall affect the operation of section 120(3) and (4).

Section 119

Consequential amendments to other enactments.

119. Schedule 3, which provides for amendments to other enactments consequential on the passing of this Act, shall apply for the purposes of this Act.

Section 120

Transitional provisions.

120. (1) The Commissioners shall have all the jurisdictions, powers and duties in relation to capital acquisitions tax under this Act which they had before the passing of this Act.

(2) The continuity of the operation of the law relating to capital acquisitions tax shall not be affected by the substitution of this Act for the repealed enactments.

(3) Any reference, whether express or implied, in any enactment or document (including this Act and any Act amended by this Act) —

(a) to any provision of this Act, or

(b) to things done or to be done under or for the purposes of any provisions of this Act,

shall, if and in so far as the nature of the reference permits, be construed as including, in relation to the times, years or periods, circumstances or purposes in relation to which the corresponding provision in the repealed enactments applied or had applied, a reference to, or, as the case may be, to things done or to be done under or for the purposes of, that corresponding provision.

(4) Any reference, whether express or implied, in any enactment (including the repealed enactments and enactments passed after the passing of this Act) —

(a) to any provision of the repealed enactments, or

(b) to things done or to be done under or for the purposes of any provisions of the repealed enactments,

shall, if and in so far as the nature of the reference permits, be construed as including, in relation to the times, years or periods, circumstances or purposes in relation to which the corresponding provision of this Act applies, a reference to, or as the case may be, to things done or to be done under, or for the purposes of, that corresponding provision.

SCHEDULE 1
Valuation of Limited Interests
[First Schedule, CATA]

PART 1
Rules relating to the valuation of limited interests utilising Tables A and B in PARTs 2 and 3 of this Schedule

1. The value of an interest for a single life in a capital sum shall be that sum multiplied by the factor, contained in column (3) or (4) respectively of Table A, which is appropriate to the age and sex of the person in respect of the duration of whose life the interest is to be valued.

2. The value of an interest in a capital sum for the joint continuance of 2 lives shall be the value of an interest in that sum for the older life, ascertained in accordance with rule 1, multiplied by the joint factor in column (2) of Table A which is appropriate to the younger life.

3. The value of an interest in a capital sum for the joint continuance of 3 or more lives shall be the value of an interest in that sum for the joint continuance of the 2 oldest of those lives, ascertained in accordance with rule 2, multiplied by the joint factor of the youngest of those lives.

4. The value of an interest in a capital sum for the longer of 2 lives shall be ascertained by deducting from the total of the values of an interest in that sum for each of those lives, ascertained in accordance with rule

1, the value of an interest in the capital sum for the joint continuance of the same 2 lives, ascertained in accordance with rule 2.

5.   Where an interest is given for the longest of more than 2 lives, it shall be valued, in accordance with rule 4, as if it were for the longer of the 2 youngest of those lives.

6.   The value of an interest in a capital sum for a period certain shall be the aggregate of—

(a)   the value of the capital sum, multiplied by the factor in Table B which is appropriate to the number of whole years in that period (or zero if that period is less than a whole year); and

(b)   where the period is not an integral number of years, a fraction (of which the numerator is the number of days in excess of the number of whole years, if any, in that period and the denominator is 365) of the difference between—

(i)   the value of an interest in the capital sum for one year longer than the number of whole years, if any, in the period; and

(ii)   the value ascertained under the provisions of paragraph (a) (or zero, where so provided in that paragraph).

7.   In the case of a limited interest where the interest is for a life or lives, but is guaranteed for a period certain, the value shall be the higher of—

(a)   the value of an interest for such life or lives, ascertained in accordance with the appropriate rule in this Part of this Schedule; and

(b)   the value of an interest for the period certain, ascertained in accordance with rule 6.

8.   The value of a limited interest for which the other rules in this Part of this Schedule provide no method of valuing shall be ascertained as if the interest taken were a series of absolute interests in the property applied in satisfaction of the interest from time to time, taken as separate gifts or inheritances as the case may be.

PART 2

TABLE A

Years of age	Joint Factor	Value of an interest in a capital of €1 for a male life aged as in column 1	Value of an interest in a capital of €1 for a female life aged as in column 1
(1)	(2)	(3)	(4)
0	.99	.9519	.9624
1	.99	.9767	.9817
2	.99	.9767	.9819
3	.99	.9762	.9817
4	.99	.9753	.9811

Years of age	Joint Factor	Value of an interest in a capital of €1 for a male life aged as in column 1	Value of an interest in a capital of €1 for a female life aged as in column 1
(1)	(2)	(3)	(4)
5	.99	.9742	.9805
6	.99	.9730	.9797
7	.99	.9717	.9787
8	.99	.9703	.9777
9	.99	.9688	.9765
10	.99	.9671	.9753
11	.98	.9653	.9740
12	.98	.9634	.9726
13	.98	.9614	.9710
14	.98	.9592	.9693
15	.98	.9569	.9676
16	.98	.9546	.9657
17	.98	.9522	.9638
18	.98	.9497	.9617
19	.98	.9471	.9596
20	.97	.9444	.9572
21	.97	.9416	.9547
22	.97	.9387	.9521
23	.97	.9356	.9493
24	.97	.9323	.9464
25	.97	.9288	.9432
26	.97	.9250	.9399
27	.97	.9209	.9364
28	.97	.9165	.9328
29	.97	.9119	.9289
30	.96	.9068	.9248
31	.96	.9015	.9205
32	.96	.8958	.9159
33	.96	.8899	.9111
34	.96	.8836	.9059
35	.96	.8770	.9005
36	.96	.8699	.8947

Years of age	Joint Factor	Value of an interest in a capital of €1 for a male life aged as in column 1	Value of an interest in a capital of €1 for a female life aged as in column 1
(1)	(2)	(3)	(4)
37	.96	.8626	.8886
38	.95	.8549	.8821
39	.95	.8469	.8753
40	.95	.8384	.8683
41	.95	.8296	.8610
42	.95	.8204	.8534
43	.95	.8107	.8454
44	.94	.8005	.8370
45	.94	.7897	.8283
46	.94	.7783	.8192
47	.94	.7663	.8096
48	.93	.7541	.7997
49	.93	.7415	.7896
50	.92	.7287	.7791
51	.91	.7156	.7683
52	.90	.7024	.7572
53	.89	.6887	.7456
54	.89	.6745	.7335
55	.88	.6598	.7206
56	.88	.6445	.7069
57	.88	.6288	.6926
58	.87	.6129	.6778
59	.86	.5969	.6628
60	.86	.5809	.6475
61	.85	.5650	.6320
62	.85	.5492	.6162
63	.85	.5332	.6000
64	.85	.5171	.5830
65	.85	.5007	.5650
66	.85	.4841	.5462
67	.84	.4673	.5266
68	.84	.4506	.5070

Years of age	Joint Factor	Value of an interest in a capital of €1 for a male life aged as in column 1	Value of an interest in a capital of €1 for a female life aged as in column 1
(1)	(2)	(3)	(4)
69	.84	.4339	.4873
70	.83	.4173	.4679
71	.83	.4009	.4488
72	.82	.3846	.4301
73	.82	.3683	.4114
74	.81	.3519	.3928
75	.80	.3352	.3743
76	.79	.3181	.3559
77	.78	.3009	.3377
78	.76	.2838	.3198
79	.74	.2671	.3023
80	.72	.2509	.2855
81	.71	.2353	.2693
82	.70	.2203	.2538
83	.69	.2057	.2387
84	.68	.1916	.2242
85	.67	.1783	.2104
86	.66	.1657	.1973
87	.65	.1537	.1849
88	.64	.1423	.1730
89	.62	.1315	.1616
90	.60	.1212	.1509
91	.58	.1116	.1407
92	.56	.1025	.1310
93	.54	.0939	.1218
94	.52	.0858	.1132
95	.50	.0781	.1050
96	.49	.0710	.0972
97	.48	.0642	.0898
98	.47	.0578	.0828
99	.45	.0517	.0762
100 or over	.43	.0458	.0698

PART 3
TABLE B

(Column (2) shows the value of an interest in a capital of €1 for the number of years shown in column (1))

Number of years (1)	Value (2)	Number of years (1)	Value (2)
1	.0654	26	.8263
2	.1265	27	.8375
3	.1836	28	.8480
4	.2370	29	.8578
5	.2869	30	.8669
6	.3335	31	.8754
7	.3770	32	.8834
8	.4177	33	.8908
9	.4557	34	.8978
10	.4913	35	.9043
11	.5245	36	.9100
12	.5555	37	.9165
13	.5845	38	.9230
14	.6116	39	.9295
15	.6369	40	.9360
16	.6605	41	.9425
17	.6826	42	.9490
18	.7032	43	.9555
19	.7225	44	.9620
20	.7405	45	.9685
21	.7574	46	.9750
22	.7731	47	.9815
23	.7878	48	.9880
24	.8015	49	.9945
25	.8144	50 and over	1.0000

SCHEDULE 2

Computation of Tax

[Second Sch., CATA, as amended, s.59D and s.59E, CATA]

PART 1
Preliminary

1. In this Schedule—

   "group threshold", in relation to a taxable gift or a taxable inheritance taken on a particular day, means—

   (a) **[€304,775]**[1], where—

      (i) the donee or successor is on that day the child, or minor child of a deceased child, of the disponer, or

      (ii) the successor is on that day a parent of the disponer and—

         (I) the interest taken is not a limited interest, and

         (II) the inheritance is taken on the death of the disponer;

   (b) **[€30,478]**[1], where the donee or successor is on that day, a lineal ancestor, a lineal descendant (other than a child, or a minor child of a deceased child), a brother, a sister, or a child of a brother or of a sister of the disponer;

   (c) **[€15,239]**[1], where the donee or successor (who is not a spouse of the disponer) does not, on that day, stand to the disponer in a relationship referred to in subparagraph (a) or (b);

   "the consumer price index number", in relation to a year, means the All Items Consumer Price Index Number for that year as compiled by the Central Statistics Office and expressed on the basis that the consumer price index number at mid-November 1996 is 100;

   "Table" means the Table contained in Part 2 of this Schedule;

   "threshold amount" in relation to the computation of tax on any aggregate of taxable values under paragraph 3, means the group threshold that applies in relation to all of the taxable gifts and taxable inheritances included in that aggregate but, in computing under this Schedule the tax chargeable on a taxable gift or taxable inheritance, that group threshold shall, for the purposes of this definition, be multiplied by the figure, rounded to the nearest third decimal place, determined by dividing by 104.8 the consumer price index number for the year immediately preceding the year in which that taxable gift or taxable inheritance is taken.

2. In the Table "Value" means the appropriate aggregate referred to in paragraph 3.

3.	The tax chargeable on the taxable value of a taxable gift or a taxable inheritance (in this Schedule referred to as the first-mentioned gift or inheritance) taken by a donee or successor shall be of an amount equal to the amount by which the tax computed on aggregate A exceeds the tax computed on aggregate B, where—

(a)	aggregate A is the aggregate of the following:

(i)	the taxable value of the first-mentioned gift or inheritance, and

(ii)	the taxable value of each taxable gift and taxable inheritance taken previously by that donee or successor on or after 5 December 1991, which has the same group threshold as the first-mentioned gift or inheritance,

(b)	aggregate B is the aggregate of the taxable values of all such taxable gifts and taxable inheritances so previously taken which have the same group threshold as the first-mentioned gift or inheritance, and

(c)	the tax on an aggregate is computed at the rate or rates of tax applicable under the Table to that aggregate, but where—

(i)	in a case where no such taxable gift or taxable inheritance was so previously taken, the amount of the tax computed on aggregate B shall be deemed to be nil, and

(ii)	the amount of an aggregate that comprises only a single taxable value shall be equal to that value.

4.	In the Table any rate of tax shown in the second column is that applicable to such portion of the value (within the meaning of paragraph 2) as is shown in the first column.

5.	For the purposes of this Schedule, all gifts and inheritances which have the same group threshold and which are taken by a donee or successor on the same day shall count as one, and to ascertain the amount of tax payable on one such gift or inheritance of several so taken on the same day, the amount of tax computed under this Schedule as being payable on the total of such gifts and inheritances so taken on that day shall be apportioned rateably, according to the taxable values of the several taxable gifts and taxable inheritances so taken on that day.

6.	Where any donee or successor is, at the date of the gift or at the date of the inheritance, the surviving spouse of a deceased person who, at the time of that deceased spouse's death, was of nearer relationship than such donee or successor to the disponer, then such donee or successor is, in the computation of the tax payable on such taxable gift or taxable inheritance, deemed to bear to the disponer the relationship of that deceased person.

7.	(1)	In this paragraph—

"company" means a private company which, for the relevant period—

(a) is a private company controlled by the disponer and of which the disponer is a director, and

(b) is not a private non-trading company;

"control", in relation to a company, is construed in accordance with section 27(4)(b);.

"investment income", in relation to a private company, means income which, if the company were an individual, would not be earned income within the meaning of section 3 of the Taxes Consolidation Act 1997;

"nominee" has the same meaning as it has in section 27;

"private company" has the meaning assigned to it by section 27;

"private company controlled by the disponer" means a private company that is under the control of any one or more of the following, that is—

(a) the disponer,

(b) nominees of the disponer,

(c) the trustees of a settlement made by the disponer;

"private non-trading company" means a private company—

(a) whose income (if any) in the 12 months preceding the date at which a share in that company is to be valued consisted wholly or mainly of investment income; and

(b) whose property, on the date referred to in paragraph (a), consisted wholly or mainly of property from which investment income is derived;

"relevant period" means—

(a) the period of 5 years ending on the date of the disposition; or

(b) where, at the date of the disposition,

　　(i) an interest in possession in—

　　　　(I) the property referred to in subparagraph (2)(a), or

　　　　(II) the shares referred to in subparagraph (2)(b),

　　　　as the case may be, is limited to the disponer under the disposition, and

　　(ii) such property is not, or such shares are not, property consisting of the appropriate part of property, within the meaning of section 5(5), on which is charged or secured an annuity or other annual right limited to cease on the death of the disponer,

　　the period of 5 years ending on the coming to an end of that interest, subject, in relation to work, to the exclusion of reasonable periods of annual or sick leave from that period of 5 years.

(2) For the purpose of computing the tax payable on a gift or inheritance, the donee or successor is deemed to bear to the disponer the relationship of a child in any case where the donee or successor is a child of a brother, or a child of a sister, of the disponer and either—

    (a) the donee or successor has worked substantially on a full-time basis for the disponer for the relevant period in carrying on, or in assisting in carrying on, the trade, business or profession of the disponer, and the gift or inheritance consists of property which was used in connection with that business, trade or profession; or

    (b) the donee or successor has worked substantially on a full-time basis for a company for the relevant period in carrying on, or in assisting in carrying on, the trade, business or profession of the company, and the gift or inheritance consists of shares in that company.

(3) Without prejudice to the generality of subparagraph (2), a donee or successor is not deemed to be working substantially on a full-time basis for a disponer or a company unless—

    (a) where the gift or inheritance consists of property which was used in connection with the business, trade or profession of the disponer, the donee or successor works—

        (i) more than 24 hours a week for the disponer, at a place where that business, trade or profession, is carried on, or

        (ii) more than 15 hours a week for the disponer, at a place where that business, trade or profession is carried on, and such business, trade or profession is carried on exclusively by the disponer, any spouse of the disponer, and the donee or successor,

    or

    (b) where the gift or inheritance consists of shares in the company, the donee or successor works—

        (i) more than 24 hours a week for the company, at a place where the business, trade or profession of the company is carried on, or

        (ii) more than 15 hours a week for the company, at a place where the business, trade or profession of the company is carried on, and such business, trade or profession is carried on exclusively by the disponer, any spouse of the disponer, and the donee or successor.

(4) This paragraph shall not apply to a gift or inheritance taken by a donee or successor under a discretionary trust.

8. (a) In this paragraph "specified disposition" means a disposition –

    (i) the date of which is a date prior to 1 April 1975,

    (ii) in relation to which the disponer is a grandparent of the donee or successor, and

    (iii) in which the marriage of the parents of the donee or successor was, at the date of the disposition, expressed to be the consideration.

    (b) Where, on the cesser of a limited interest to which a parent of the donee or successor was entitled in possession, the donee or successor takes a gift or an inheritance under a specified disposition, then, for the purpose of computing the tax payable on the gift or inheritance, the donee or successor is deemed to bear to the disponer the relationship of a child.

9. (1) In this paragraph –

"the appropriate period" means periods which together comprised at least 5 years falling within the 18 years immediately following the birth of the donee or successor.

(2) Where, on a claim being made to them in that behalf, the Commissioners are, subject to subparagraph (3), satisfied –

    (a) where the inheritance is taken by a successor on the date of death of the disponer, that the successor had, prior to the date of the inheritance, been placed in the foster care of the disponer under the Child Care (Placement of Children in Foster Care) Regulations 1995 (S.I. No. 260 of 1995), or the Child Care (Placement of Children with Relatives) Regulations 1995 (S.I. No. 261 of 1995), or

    (b) that throughout the appropriate period the donee or successor –

        (i) has resided with the disponer, and

        (ii) was under the care of and maintained by the disponer at the disponer's own expense,

then, subject to subparagraph (3), for the purposes of computing the tax payable on that gift or inheritance, that donee or successor is deemed to bear to that disponer the relationship of a child.

(3) Relief under subparagraph (2) shall not apply where the claim for such relief is based on the uncorroborated testimony of one witness.

10. Where, on a claim being made to them in that behalf, the Commissioners are satisfied that –

    (a) the donee or successor had at the date of the gift or the date of the inheritance been adopted in the manner referred to in paragraph (b) of the definition of "child" contained in section 2(1), and

(b) the disponer is the natural mother or the natural father of the donee or successor,

then, notwithstanding section 2(5), for the purpose of computing the tax payable on that gift or inheritance, that donee or successor is deemed to bear to that disponer the relationship of a child.

11. For the purposes of this Schedule, a reference to a gift or an inheritance, or to a taxable gift or a taxable inheritance, includes a reference to a part of a gift or an inheritance, or to a part of a taxable gift or a taxable inheritance, as the case may be.

PART 2

TABLE

Portion of Value	Rate of tax Per cent
The threshold amount	Nil
The balance	[25]²

Footnotes

1   Under s.27(1)(a), FA 2009, in relation to gifts and inheritances taken on or after 8th April, 2009, a group threshold of "€304,775" was substituted for "€381,000", a group threshold of "€30,478" was substituted for "€38,100", and a group threshold of "€15,239" was substituted for "€19,050". Indexation produced the following results in relation to the original and substituted group thresholds -

Calendar Year	Indexation Factor	Group Threshold	
2003, on or after 21st February	1.158	€441,198	(a)
		€44,120	(b)
		€22,060	(c)
2004	1.198	€456,438	(a)
		€45,644	(b)
		€22,822	(c)
2005	1.225	€466,725	(a)
		€46,673	(b)
		€23,336	(c)
2006	1.255	€478,155	(a)
		€47,815	(b)
		€23,908	(c)
2007	1.304	€496,824	(a)
		€49,682	(b)
		€24,841	(c)
2008	1.368	€521,208	(a)
		€52,121	(b)
		€26,060	(c)
2009, before 8th April	1.424	€542,544	(a)
		€54,254	(b)
		€27,127	(c)
2009, on or after 8th April	1.424	€434,800	(a)
		€43,400	(b)
		€21,700	(c)

2   "22" substituted for "20" by s.90(1), F(No. 2)A, 2008, which applies to gifts and inheritances taken on or after 20th November, 2008 and before 8th April 2009. "25" substituted for "22" by s. 27(1)(b), FA 2009, which applies to gifts and inheritances taken on or after 8th April 2009.

Commentary

A   As to the definition of "child" in s.2, CATCA, including a "stepchild", see Part 19.17 of the *Revenue CAT Manual* dealing with "lineal descendants" involving stepchildren.

B   With regard to para.6, Part I of Sch.2, Part 19.10 of the *Revenue CAT Manual* provides that this paragraph applies to a surviving spouse even if the surviving spouse has re-married before the date of the gift or inheritance.

C   With regard to para.7, Part I of Sch.2, see a Circuit Court decision in *A.E. v Revenue Commissioners* [1984] ILRM 301, in relation to a niece working on a farm.

SCHEDULE 3

Consequential Amendments

In the enactments specified in column (1) of the following Table for the words set out or referred to in column (2), there shall be substituted the words set out in the corresponding entry in column (3).

Enactment Amended (1)	Words to be replaced (2)	Words to be substituted (3)
....		
Taxes Consolidation Act 1997:		
section 8(1)(c)	Capital Acquisitions Tax Act 1976	Capital Acquisitions Tax Consolidation Act 2003
section 176(1)(b)(i)(I)	section 21 of the Capital Acquisitions Tax Act 1976	section 30 of the Capital Acquisitions Tax Consolidation Act 2003
....		
section 730GB	section 63 of the Finance Act 1985	section 104 of the Capital Acquisitions Tax Act 2003
section 739G(5)	section 63 of the Finance Act 1985	section 104 of the Capital Acquisitions Tax Consolidation Act 2003
section 747E(5)(a)	section 63 of the Finance Act 1985	section 104 of the Capital Acquisitions Tax Consolidation Act 2003
section 811(1)(a), in paragraph (iv) of the definition of "the Acts".	Capital Acquisitions Tax Act 1976	Capital Acquisitions Tax Consolidation Act 2003

Enactment Amended (1)	Words to be replaced (2)	Words to be substituted (3)
section 818(c)	Capital Acquisitions Tax Act 1976	Capital Acquisitions Tax Consolidation Act 2003
section 825(1)(c)	Capital Acquisitions Tax Act 1976	Capital Acquisitions Tax Consolidation Act 2003
section 858(1)(a), in paragraph (vi) of the definition of "the Acts"	Capital Acquisitions Tax Act 1976	Capital Acquisitions Tax Consolidation Act 2003
section 859(1), in paragraph (f) of the definition of "the Revenue Acts"	Capital Acquisitions Tax Act 1976	Capital Acquisitions Tax Consolidation Act 2003
section 887(1), in paragraph (d) of the definition of "the Acts"	Capital Acquisitions Tax Act 1976	Capital Acquisitions Tax Consolidation Act 2003
section 912(1), in paragraph (f) of the definition of "the Acts"	Capital Acquisitions Tax Act 1976	Capital Acquisitions Tax Consolidation Act 2003
section 917D(1), in paragraph (e) of the definition of "the Acts"	Capital Acquisitions Tax Act 1976	Capital Acquisitions Tax Consolidation Act 2003
section 1002(1)(a), in paragraph (vi) of the definition of "the Acts"	Capital Acquisitions Tax Act 1976	Capital Acquisitions Tax Consolidation Act 2003
section 1003(1)(a), in paragraph (iii) of the definition of "the Acts"	Capital Acquisitions Tax Act 1976	Capital Acquisitions Tax Consolidation Act 2003
section 1006(1), in paragraph (d) of the definition of "the Acts"	Capital Acquisitions Tax Act 1976	Capital Acquisitions Tax Consolidation Act 2003
section 1006A(1), in paragraph (e) of the definition of "the Acts"	Capital Acquisitions Tax Act 1976	Capital Acquisitions Tax Consolidation Act 2003
section 1078(1), in paragraph (f) of the definition of "the Acts"	Capital Acquisitions Tax Act 1976	Capital Acquisitions Tax Consolidation Act 2003

Enactment Amended	Words to be replaced	Words to be substituted
(1)	(2)	(3)
section 1079(1), in paragraph (f) of the definition of "the Acts"	Capital Acquisitions Tax Act 1976	Capital Acquisitions Tax Consolidation Act 2003
section 1086(1), in paragraph (d) of the definition of "the Acts"	Capital Acquisitions Tax Act 1976	Capital Acquisitions Tax Consolidation Act 2003
section 1089(2)	section 41 of the Capital Acquisitions Tax Act 1976	section 51 of the Capital Acquisitions Tax Consolidation Act 2003
section 1104(5)	Capital Acquisitions Tax Act 1976	Capital Acquisitions Tax Consolidation Act 2003
....		

FIRST PART

(II) FINANCE ACT 2006

For Contents of this Part, see page xl

FINANCE ACT 2006

Number 6 of 2006
(Enacted on 31st March, 2006)

PART 6
Miscellaneous

Section 123

Prescribing of forms, etc.

123. (1) In this section—

"the Acts" means—

(a) the Tax Acts,

(b) the Capital Gains Tax Acts,

(c) the Capital Acquisitions Tax Consolidation Act 2003, and the enactments amending or extending that Act,

(d) the Stamp Duties Consolidation Act 1999, and the enactments amending or extending that Act, and

(e) Chapter IV of Part II of the Finance Act 1992,

and any instruments made thereunder;

"form or other document" includes a form or other document for use, or capable of use, in a machine readable form.

(2) Where a provision of the Acts requires that a form or other document used for any purpose of the Acts is to be prescribed, authorised or approved by the Revenue Commissioners, such form or other document may be prescribed, authorised or approved by—

(a) a Revenue Commissioner, or

(b) an officer of the Revenue Commissioners not below the grade or rank of Assistant Secretary authorised by them for that purpose.

(3) Nothing in this section shall be read as restricting section 12 of the Interpretation Act 2005.[1]

Footnote
1   Reproduced on page 1269.

Commentary
A   See s.47(4), CATCA, in relation to this section.

FIRST PART

(III) DOUBLE TAXATION CONVENTIONS

For Contents of this Part, see page xl

FINANCE ACT, 1950

Number 18 of 1950
(Enacted on 5th July, 1950)

PART III
Death Duties

Section 10

Confirmation of Convention set forth in First Schedule.

10. (1) The convention set forth in the First Schedule to this Act and concluded on the 13th day of September, 1949, between the Government and the Government of the United States of America (in this section referred to as the Convention) is hereby confirmed and shall have the force of law.

(2) Subsection (4) of section 7 of the Finance Act, 1894[1] (which provides for relief in respect of duty payable in a foreign country) shall not have effect in relation to estate tax chargeable under the laws of the United States of America to which the provisions of the Convention apply.

Footnote
1   Reproduced on page 653.

Commentary

A   The Convention is treated as applying to Irish inheritance tax (not gift tax). It does not apply to any death taxes imposed by individual U.S.A. States.

B   See an article on CAT and Double Taxation Relief by Ann Williams in the *Irish Tax Review* of September 2000, page 437.

C   See an article on Capital Acquisitions Tax Issues for Non-Irish Domiciled Persons (dealing with persons dying on or after 1st December, 2004) by Ann Williams at page 405 of the *Irish Tax Review* of September 2004.

FIRST SCHEDULE
Convention between Ireland and the United States of America.

Convention between the Government of Ireland and the Government of the United States of America for the avoidance of double taxation and the prevention of fiscal evasion with respect to taxes on the estates of deceased persons.

The Government of Ireland and the Government of the United States of America,

Desiring to conclude a Convention for the avoidance of double taxation and the prevention of fiscal evasion with respect to taxes on estates of deceased persons. Have appointed for that purpose as their Plenipotentiaries:

> The Government of Ireland:
> Patrick McGilligan, Minister for Finance;
> Sean MacBride, Minister for External Affairs;

and

> The Government of the United States of America:
> George A Garrett, Envoy Extraordinary and Minister Plenipotentiary of the United States of America at Dublin;

Who, having exhibited their respective full powers, found in good and due form, have agreed as follows:-

ARTICLE I

(1)   The taxes which are the subject of the present Convention are:

(a)   In the United States of America, the Federal estate tax, and

(b)   In Ireland, the estate duty imposed in that territory.

(2)   The present Convention shall also apply to any other taxes of a substantially similar character imposed by either Contracting Party subsequently to the date of signature of the present Convention.

ARTICLE II

(1)   In the present Convention, unless the context otherwise requires:

(a)   The term "United States" means the United States of America, and when used in a geographical sense means the States, the Territories of Alaska and of Hawaii, and the District of Columbia.

(b)   The term "Ireland" means the Republic of Ireland.

(c)   The term "territory" when used in relation to one or the other Contracting Party means the United States or Ireland, as the context requires.

(d)   The term "tax" means the estate duty imposed in Ireland or the United States Federal estate tax, as the context requires.

(2)   In the application of the provisions of the present Convention by one of the Contracting Parties, any term not otherwise defined shall, unless the context otherwise requires, have the meaning which it has under the laws of that Contracting Party relating to the taxes which are the subject of the present Convention.

ARTICLE III

(1) For the purposes of the present Convention, the question whether a decedent was domiciled in any part of the territory of one of the Contracting Parties at the time of his death shall be determined in accordance with the law in force in that territory.

(2) Where a person dies domiciled in any part of the territory of one Contracting Party, the situs of any rights or interests, legal or equitable, in or over any of the following classes of property which for the purposes of tax form part of the estate of such person or pass on his death, shall, for the purposes of the imposition of tax and for the purposes of the credit to be allowed under Article V, be determined exclusively in accordance with the following rules, but in cases not within such rules the situs of any such rights or interests shall be determined for those purposes in accordance with the law relating to tax in force in the territory of the other Contracting Party:

   (a) Immovable property shall be deemed to be situated at the place where such property is located;

   (b) Tangible movable property (other than such property for which specific provision is hereinafter made) and bank or currency notes, other forms of currency recognised as legal tender in the place of issue, negotiable bills of exchange and negotiable promissory notes, shall be deemed to be situated at the place where such property, notes, currency or documents are located at the time of death, or, if in transitu, at the place of destination;

   (c) Debts, secured or unsecured, other than the forms of indebtedness for which specific provision is made herein, shall be deemed to be situate at the place where the decedent was domiciled at the time of death;

   (d) Shares or stock in a corporation other than a municipal or governmental corporation (including shares or stock held by a nominee where the beneficial ownership is evidenced by scrip certificates or otherwise) shall be deemed to be situated at the place in or under the law of which such corporation was created or organised; but, if such corporation was created or organised under the laws of the United Kingdom of Great Britain and Northern Ireland or under the laws of Northern Ireland, and if the shares or stock of such corporation when registered on a branch register of such corporation kept in Ireland are deemed under the laws of the United Kingdom or of Northern Ireland and of Ireland to be assets situated in Ireland, such shares or stock shall be deemed to be assets situated in Ireland;

   (e) Moneys payable under a policy of assurance or insurance on the life of the decedent shall be deemed to be situated at the place where the decedent was domiciled at the time of death;

   (f) Ships and aircraft and shares thereof shall be deemed to be situated at the place of registration or documentation of the ship or aircraft;

(g) Goodwill as a trade, business or professional asset shall be deemed to be situated at the place where the trade, business or profession to which it pertains is carried on;

(h) Patents, trade-marks and designs shall be deemed to be situated at the place where they are registered;

(i) Copyright, franchises, and rights or licences to use any copyrighted material, patent, trademark or design shall be deemed to be situated at the place where the rights arising therefrom are exercisable;

(j) Rights or causes of action ex delicto surviving for the benefit of an estate of a decedent shall be deemed to be situated at the place where such rights or causes of action arose;

(k) Judgment debts shall be deemed to be situated at the place where the judgment is recorded;

provided that if, apart from this paragraph, tax would be imposed by one Contracting Party on any property which is situated in its territory, this paragraph shall not apply to such property unless, by reason of its application or otherwise, tax is imposed or would but for some specific exemption be imposed thereon by the other Contracting Party.

ARTICLE IV

(1) In determining the amount on which tax is to be computed, permitted deductions shall be allowed in accordance with the law in force in the territory in which the tax is imposed.

(2) Where tax is imposed by one Contracting Party on the death of a person who at the time of his death was not domiciled in any part of the territory of that Contracting Party but was domiciled in some part of the territory of the other Contracting Party, no account shall be taken in determining the amount or rate of such tax of property situated outside the former territory: provided that this paragraph shall not apply as respects tax imposed-

(a) In the United States in the case of a United States citizen dying domiciled in any part of Ireland; or

(b) In Ireland in the case of property passing under a disposition governed by the law of Ireland.

ARTICLE V

(1) Where one Contracting Party imposes tax by reason of a decedent's being domiciled in some part of its territory or being its national, that party shall allow against so much of its tax (as otherwise computed) as is attributable to property situated in the territory of the other Contracting Party, a credit (not exceeding the amount of the tax so attributable) equal to so much of the tax imposed in the territory of such other Party as is attributable to such property; but this paragraph shall not apply as respects any such property as is mentioned in paragraph (2) of this Article.

(2) Where each Contracting Party imposes tax by reason of a decedent's being domiciled in some part of its territory, each Party shall allow against so much of its tax (as otherwise computed) as is attributable to property which is situated, or is deemed under paragraph (2) of Article III to be situated,

(a) in the territory of both Parties, or

(b) outside both territories,

a credit which bears the same proportion to the amount of its tax so attributable or to the amount of the other Party's tax attributable to the same property, whichever is the less, as the former amount bears to the sum of both amounts.

(3) Where Ireland imposes duty on property passing under a disposition governed by its law, that Party shall allow a credit similar to that provided by paragraph (1) of this Article.

(4) For the purposes of this Article, the amount of tax of a Contracting Party attributable to any property shall be ascertained after taking into account any credit, allowance or relief, or any remission or reduction of tax, otherwise than in respect of tax payable in the territory of the other Contracting Party; and if, in respect of property situated outside the territories of both parties, a Contracting Party allows against its tax a credit for tax payable in the country where the property is situated, that credit shall be taken into account in ascertaining, for the purposes of paragraph (2) of this Article, the amount of the tax of that Party attributable to the property.

ARTICLE VI

(1) Any claim for a credit or for a refund of tax founded on the provisions of the present Convention shall be made within six years from the date of the death of the decedent in respect of whose estate the claim is made, or, in the case of a reversionary interest where payment of tax is deferred until on or after the date on which the interest falls into possession, within six years from that date.

(2) Any such refund shall be made without payment of interest on the amount so refunded, save to the extent to which interest was paid on the amount so refunded when the tax was paid.

ARTICLE VII

(1) The taxation authorities of the Contracting Parties shall exchange such information (being information available under the respective taxation laws of the Contracting Parties) as is necessary for carrying out the provisions of the present Convention or for the prevention of fraud or

the administration of statutory provisions against legal avoidance in relation to the taxes which are the subject of the present Convention. Any information so exchanged shall be treated as secret and shall not be disclosed to any person other than those concerned with the assessment and collection of the taxes which are the subject of the present Convention. No information shall be exchanged which would disclose any trade secret or trade process.

(2) As used in this Article, the Term "taxation authorities" means, in the case of the United States, the Commissioner of Internal Revenue or his authorised representative; in the case or Ireland, the Revenue Commissioners or their authorised representative.

ARTICLE VIII

(1) The present Convention shall be ratified and the instruments of ratification shall be exchanged at Washington, District of Columbia, as soon as possible.

(2) The present Convention shall come into force on the date of exchange of ratifications and shall be effective only as to

(a) the estates of persons dying on or after such date; and

(b) the estate of any person dying before such date and after the last day of the calendar year immediately preceding such date whose personal representative elects, in such manner as may be prescribed, that the provisions of the present Convention shall be applied to such estate.

ARTICLE IX

(1) The present Convention shall remain in force for not less than three years after the date of its coming into force.

(2) If not less than six months before the expiration of such period of three years, neither of the Contracting Parties shall have given to the other Contracting Party, through diplomatic channels, written notice of its intention to terminate the present Convention, the Convention shall remain in force after such period of three years until either of the Contracting Parties shall have given written notice of such intention, in which event the present Convention shall not be effective as to the estates of persons dying on or after the date (not being earlier than the sixtieth day after the date of such notice) specified in such notice, or, if no date is specified, on or after the sixtieth day after the date of such notice.

IN WITNESS WHEREOF the above-named Plenipotentiaries have signed the present Convention and have affixed thereto their seals.

Done at Dublin, in duplicate, this 13th day of September, 1949.

For the Government of Ireland:
(Signed)
PATRICK McGILLIGAN

SEAN MacBRIDE

For the Government of the United States of America:
(Signed)
GEORGE A GARRETT

S. I. No. 279 of 1978

Convention between Ireland and the United Kingdom.

DOUBLE TAXATION RELIEF (TAXES ON ESTATES OF DECEASED PERSONS AND INHERITANCES AND ON GIFTS) (UNITED KINGDOM) ORDER, 1978

WHEREAS it is enacted by section 66 (1) of the Capital Acquisitions Tax Act. 1976 (No. 8 of 1976), that if the Government by order declare that arrangements specified in the order have been made with the government of any territory outside the State in relation to affording relief from double taxation in respect of gift tax or inheritance tax payable under the laws of the State and any tax imposed under the laws of that territory which is of a similar character or is chargeable by reference to death or to gifts inter vivos and that it is expedient that those arrangements should have the force of law, the arrangements shall, notwithstanding anything in any enactment, have the force of law:

AND WHEREAS it is further enacted by section 66(5) of that Act that, where such an order is proposed to be made, a draft thereof shall be laid before Dáil Eireann and the order shall not be made until a resolution approving of the draft has been passed by Dáil Eireann:

AND WHEREAS a draft of this Order has been laid before Dáil Eireann and a resolution approving of the draft has been passed by Dáil Eireann:

NOW, the Government, in exercise of the powers conferred on them by section 66 of the Capital Acquisitions Tax Act, 1976, hereby order as follows:

1. This Order may be cited as the Double Taxation Relief (Taxes on Estates of Deceased Persons and Inheritances and on Gifts) (United Kingdom) Order, 1978.

2. It is hereby declared –

    (a) that the arrangements specified in the Convention set out in the Schedule to this Order have been made with the Government of the United Kingdom in relation to affording relief from double taxation in respect of gift tax and inheritance tax payable under the laws of the State and any tax imposed under the laws of the United Kingdom which is of a similar character, and

    (b) that it is expedient that those arrangements should have the force of law.

SCHEDULE

CONVENTION BETWEEN THE GOVERNMENT OF IRELAND AND THE GOVERNMENT OF THE UNITED KINGDOM FOR THE AVOIDANCE OF DOUBLE TAXATION AND THE PREVENTION OF FISCAL EVASION WITH RESPECT TO TAXES ON ESTATES OF DECEASED PERSONS AND INHERITANCES AND ON GIFTS

The Government of Ireland and the Government of the United Kingdom;

Desiring to conclude a Convention for the avoidance of double taxation and the prevention of fiscal evasion with respect to taxes on estates of deceased persons and inheritances and on gifts;

Have agreed as follows:

ARTICLE 1

Scope

This Convention shall apply to any person who is within the scope of a tax which is the subject of this Convention, and to any property by reference to which there is a charge to such a tax.

ARTICLE 2

Taxes Covered

(1)   The taxes which are the subject of this Convention are:

    (a) in Ireland

        (i)   the gift tax, and

        (ii)   the inheritance tax;

    (b) in the United Kingdom, the capital transfer tax.

(2)   This Convention shall also apply to any identical or substantially similar taxes which are imposed by either Contracting State after the date of signature of this Convention in addition to, or in place of, the existing taxes.

ARTICLE 3

General definitions

(1)   In this Convention, unless the context otherwise requires:

    (a) the term "nationals" means:

        (i)   in relation to Ireland, all citizens of Ireland and all legal persons, associations or other entities deriving their status as such from the law in force in Ireland;

(ii) in relation to the United Kingdom, citizens of the United Kingdom and Colonies, British subjects under Section 2 of the British Nationality Act 1948 whose notices given under that Section have been acknowledged before the date of signature of this Convention, British subjects by virtue of Section 13 (1) or Section 16 of the British Nationality Act 1948 or Section 1 of the British Nationality Act 1965, and British protected persons within the meaning of the British Nationality Act 1948; and all legal persons, associations or other entities deriving their status as such from the law in force in the United Kingdom;

(b) the term "tax" means the gift tax or the inheritance tax imposed in Ireland or the capital transfer tax imposed in the United Kingdom, as the context requires;

(c) the term "a Contracting State" and "the other Contracting State" mean Ireland or the United Kingdom, as the context requires;

(d) the term "person" includes an individual, a company and any other body of persons;

(e) the term "company" means any body corporate or any entity which is treated as a body corporate for tax purposes;

(f) the term "competent authority" means, in the case of the United Kingdom, the Commissioners of Inland Revenue or their authorised representative, and in the case of Ireland, the Revenue Commissioners or their authorised representative;

(g) the term "event" includes a death.

(2) As regards the application of this Convention by a Contracting State any term not otherwise defined shall, unless the context otherwise requires, have the meaning which it has under the law of that Contracting State relating to the taxes which are the subject of this Convention.

ARTICLE 4

Fiscal domicile

(1) For the purposes of this Convention, the question whether a person is, or was at any material time, domiciled in a Contracting State shall be determined by whether he is, or was at that time, domiciled in that Contracting State in accordance with the law of that Contracting State or is or was treated as so domiciled for the purposes of a tax which is the subject of this Convention.

(2) Where by reason of the provisions of paragraph (1) a person is, or was at any material time, domiciled in both Contracting States, then this question shall be determined in accordance with the following rules:

(a) he shall be deemed to be domiciled in the Contracting State in which he has, or had at the material time, a permanent home available to him. If he has or had a permanent home available to him in both Contracting States, the domicile shall be deemed to be in the

Contracting State with which his personal and economic relations are, or were at the material time, closer (centre of vital interests);

(b) if the Contracting State in which he has or had his centre of vital interests cannot be determined, or if he has not or had not a permanent home available to him in either Contracting State, the domicile shall be deemed to be in the Contracting State in which he has, or had at the material time, an habitual abode;

(c) if he has or had an habitual abode in both Contracting States or in neither of them, the domicile shall be deemed to be in the Contracting State of which he is, or was at the material time, a national;

(d) if he is or was a national of both Contracting States or of neither of them, the competent authorities of the Contracting States shall settle the question by mutual agreement.

ARTICLE 5

Taxing rights

(1) Subject to the following provisions of this Convention, each Contracting State shall retain the right to tax which it would have under its own law apart from this Convention.

(2) For the purposes of paragraph (2) of Article 6 and paragraph (2) of Article 8, the Contracting State with subsidiary taxing rights shall be determined as follows:

(a) in relation to property other than property comprised in a settlement, where a person's domicile has been determined under paragraph (2) of Article 4, that Contracting State shall be the Contracting State in which the person is or was, by virtue of that paragraph, not domiciled;

(b) in relation to property comprised in a settlement:

(i) where the proper law of the settlement as regards that property at the time when the settlement was made was the law of Ireland and the settlor's domicile at the time when the settlement was made has been determined under paragraph (1) of Article 4 as being in the United Kingdom, then that Contracting State shall be the United Kingdom;

(ii) where the proper law of the settlement as regards that property at the time when the settlement was made was not the law of Ireland and the settlor's domicile at that time has been determined under paragraph (1) of Article 4 as being in the United Kingdom but under its own law Ireland would impose tax on property outside its territory because at some later time either the proper law of the settlement as regards that property was the law of Ireland or the settlor's domicile has been determined under the said paragraph as being in Ireland, then that Contracting State shall be Ireland;

        (iii)   subject to paragraph (ii) of this subparagraph, where the proper law of the settlement as regards that property at the time when the settlement was made was not the law of Ireland and the settler's domicile at that time has been determined under paragraph (2) of Article 4, then that contracting state in which the settler was, by virtue of that pargraph, not domiciled at that time.

(3)   In subparagraph (a) of paragraph (2) of this Article, the term "person" means, in Ireland the disponer, and in the United Kingdom the transferor.

(4)   In paragraph (2) of this Article, "settlement" has the meaning which it has under the law of the United Kingdom relating to capital transfer tax and for the purposes of that paragraph a settlement is made when property first becomes comprised in it.

ARTICLE 6

Situs

(1)   For the purposes of this Convention, the situs of any property shall be determined by each Contracting State under its own law, except that, where part of the value by reference to which tax is imposed in the United Kingdom is represented by a liability to tax which is satisfied out of property situated outside the United Kingdom, then that part of the value shall be deemed to be attributable to that property.

(2)   If the situs of any property as determined by one Contracting State under paragraph (1) of this Article is not the same as that so determined by the other Contracting State, and the credit to be allowed under Article 8 is thereby affected, then the question shall be determined exclusively under the law of the Contracting State which, by virtue of paragraph (2) of Article 5, has subsidiary taxing rights or, if there is no such Contracting State, shall be determined by mutual agreement.

ARTICLE 7

Deduction of debts

In determining the amount on which tax is to be computed, permitted deductions shall be allowed under the law in force in the Contracting State in which the tax is imposed.

ARTICLE 8

Elimination of double taxation

(1)   Where a Contracting State imposes tax on an event by reference to any property which is not situated in that Contracting State but is situated in the other Contracting State, the former Contracting State shall allow against so much of its tax (as otherwise computed) as is attributable to that property a credit (not exceeding the amount of tax so attributable) equal to so much of the tax imposed in the other Contracting State on the same event as is attributable to such property.

(2) Where both Contracting States impose tax on an event by reference to any property which is not situated in either Contracting State but is situated in a third territory, the Contracting State which, by virtue of paragraph (2) of Article 5, has subsidiary taxing rights shall allow against so much of its tax (as otherwise computed) as is attributable to that property a credit (not exceeding the amount of tax so attributable) equal to so much of the tax imposed in the other Contracting State on the same event as is attributable to such property.

(3) Any credit to be allowed in Ireland under this Article in relation to gifts or inheritances shall be allowed only so as to relieve the tax imposed in Ireland on the gift or inheritance which is reduced by the payment of the tax in respect of which that credit is to be allowed; and a gift which in the United Kingdom is a chargeable transfer shall be treated as reduced by the amount of tax imposed in the United Kingdom on that gift and borne by the transferor.

(4) For the purposes of this Article:

(a) the tax attributable to any property imposed in a Contracting State is tax as reduced by the amount of any credit allowed by that Contracting State in respect of tax attributable to that property imposed in a territory other than a Contracting State;

(b) tax is imposed in a Contracting State or a territory if it is chargeable under the law of that Contracting State or territory and duly paid; and

(c) property includes property representing property.

ARTICLE 9

Time limit

Any claim for a credit or for a repayment of tax founded on the provisions of this Convention shall be made within six years from the date of the event in respect of which the claim was made.

ARTICLE 10

Non-discrimination

(1) The nationals of a Contracting State shall not be subjected in the other Contracting State to any taxation or any requirement connected therewith which is other or more burdensome that the taxation and connected requirements to which nationals of that Contracting State in the same circumstances are or may be subjected.

(2) The taxation on a permanent establishment which an enterprise of a Contracting State has in the other Contracting State shall not be less favourably levied in that other Contracting State than the taxation levied on enterprises of that other Contracting State carrying on the same activities.

(3)   Enterprises of a Contracting State, the capital of which is wholly or partly owned or controlled, directly or indirectly, by one or more residents of the other Contracting State, shall not be subjected in the first-mentioned Contracting State to any taxation or any requirement connected therewith which is other or more burdensome that the taxation and connected requirements to which other similar enterprises of that first-mentioned Contracting State are or may be subjected.

(4)   Nothing contained in this Article shall be construed as obliging either Contracting State to grant to individuals not domiciled in that Contracting State, any of the personal allowances, relief, and reductions for tax purposes which are granted to individuals so domiciled.

(5)   In this Article the term "taxation" means taxes covered by this Convention.

ARTICLE 11

Mutual agreement procedure

(1)   Where a person considers that the actions of one or both of the Contracting States result or will result for him in taxation not in accordance with the provisions of this Convention, he may, irrespective of the remedies provided by the domestic laws of those Contracting States, present his case to the competent authority of either Contracting State.

(2)   The competent authority shall endeavour, if the objection appears to it to be justified and if it is not itself able to arrive at a satisfactory solution, to resolve the case by mutual agreement with the competent authority of the other Contracting State, with a view to the avoidance of taxation which is not in accordance with the provisions of this Convention.

(3)   The competent authorities of the Contracting States shall endeavour to resolve by mutual agreement any difficulties or doubts arising as to the interpretation or application of this Convention.

(4)   The competent authorities of the Contracting States may communicate with each other directly for the purpose of reaching an agreement in the sense of the preceding paragraphs.

ARTICLE 12

Exchange of information

(1)   The competent authorities of the Contracting States shall exchange such information as is necessary for carrying out the provisions of this Convention and the domestic laws of the Contracting States concerning taxes covered by this Convention in so far as the taxation thereunder is in accordance with this Convention. Any information so exchanged shall be treated as secret and shall not be disclosed to any persons other

than persons (including a Court or administrative body) concerned with the assessment or collection of, or prosecution in respect of, or the determination of appeals in relation to, the taxes which are the subject of this Convention.

(2)   In no case shall the provisions of paragraph (1) be construed so as to impose on the competent authority of either Contracting State the obligation:

(a)   to carry out administrative measures at variance with the laws or administrative practice prevailing in either Contracting State;

(b)   to supply particulars which are not obtainable under the laws or in the normal course of the administration of that or of the other Contracting State;

(c)   to supply information which would disclose any trade, business, industrial, commercial or professional secret or trade process, or information, the disclosure of which would be contrary to public policy.

ARTICLE 13

Diplomatic and consular officials

Nothing in this Convention shall affect the fiscal privileges of diplomatic or consular officials under the general rules of international law or under the provisions of special agreements.

ARTICLE 14

Entry into force

This Convention shall enter into force on the exchange of Notes confirming that the necessary steps have been taken to give it the force of law in Ireland and in the United Kingdom and shall thereupon have effect:

(a)   In Ireland:

(i)   in respect of gift tax, from 28 February 1974;

(ii)   in respect of inheritance tax, from 1 April 1975;

(b)   In the United Kingdom:

(i)   in respect of capital transfer tax other than capital transfer tax on a death, from 27 March 1974;

(ii)   in respect of capital transfer tax on a death, from 13 March 1975.

ARTICLE 15

Termination

This Convention shall remain in force until terminated by one of the Contracting States. Either Contracting States may terminate the Convention, through the diplomatic channel, by giving notice of termination at least six months before the end of any calendar year after the year 1980. In such event the Convention shall cease to have effect at the end of the calendar year in which the notice is given but shall continue to apply in respect of property by reference to which there was a charge to tax which arose before the end of that calendar year.

In witness thereof the undersigned, duly authorised thereto by their respective Governments, have signed this Convention.

Done in two originals at London this 7th day of December, 1977.

For the Government of Ireland: **PAUL J. KEATING**

For the Government of the
United Kingdom: **FRANK JUDD**

Commentary

A   See an article on CAT and Double Taxation Relief by Ann Williams in the *Irish Tax Review* of September 2000, page 437.

B   See an article on Capital Acquisitions Tax Issues for Non-Irish Domiciled Persons (dealing with persons dying on or after 1st December, 2004) by Ann Williams at page 405 of the *Irish Tax Review* of September 2004.

FIRST PART

(IV) MISCELLANEOUS PROVISIONS OF THE
TAXES CONSOLIDATION ACT, 1997

For Contents of this Part, see page xl

TAXES CONSOLIDATION ACT, 1997

Number 39 of 1997
(Enacted on 30th November, 1997)

PART I
Interpretation

Section 7

Application to certain taxing statutes of Age of Majority Act, 1985.

7. (1) Notwithstanding subsection (4) of [section 2 of the Age of Majority Act, 1985][1] (in this section referred to as "the Act of 1985"), subsections (2) and (3) of that section shall, subject to subsection (2), apply for the purposes of the Income Tax Acts and any other statutory provision (within the meaning of the Act of 1985) dealing with the imposition, repeal, remission, alteration or regulation of any tax or other duty under the care and management of the Revenue Commissioners, and accordingly section 2 (4)(b)(vii) of the Act of 1985 shall cease to apply.

(2) Nothing in subsection (1) shall affect a claimant's entitlement to a deduction under section 462 or 465.

Footnote

1   Reproduced on page 782.

Section 8

Construction of certain taxing statutes in accordance with Status of Children Act, 1987.

8. (1) In this section, "the Acts" means-

(a)   the Tax Acts,

(b)   the Capital Gains Tax Acts,

(c)   the [Capital Acquisitions Tax Consolidation Act 2003,][1] and the enactments amending or extending that Act, and

(d)   the statutes relating to stamp duty,

and any instruments made thereunder.

(2) Notwithstanding any provision of the Acts or the dates on which they were passed, in deducing any relationship between persons for the purposes of the Acts, the Acts shall be construed in accordance with [section 3 of the Status of Children Act, 1987].[2]

Footnotes

1   Substituted for "Capital Acquisitions Tax Act, 1976" by s.119, CATCA, with effect from 21st February, 2003.

2   Reproduced on page 799.

PART 6

Company Distributions, Tax Credits, Franked Investment Income and Advance Corporation Tax

CHAPTER 9

Taxation of acquisition by a company of its own shares

Section 176

Purchase of unquoted shares by issuing company or its subsidiary.

176. (1)   Notwithstanding Chapter 2 of this Part, references in the Tax Acts to distributions of a company, other than any such references in sections 440 and 441, shall be construed so as not to include references to a payment made by a company on the redemption, repayment or purchase of its own shares if the company is an unquoted trading company or the unquoted holding company of a trading group and either–

   (a)   (i)   the redemption, repayment or purchase–

              (I)   is made wholly or mainly for the purpose of benefiting a trade carried on by the company or by any of its 51 per cent subsidiaries, and

              (II) does not form part of a scheme or arrangement the main purpose or one of the main purposes of which is to enable the owner of the shares to participate in the profits of the company or of any of its 51 per cent subsidiaries without receiving a dividend,

          and

         (ii) the conditions specified in sections 177 to 181, in so far as applicable, are satisfied in relation to the owner of the shares, or

   (b)   the person to whom the payment is made–

         (i)   applies the whole or substantially the whole of the payment (apart from any sum applied in discharging that person's liability to capital gains tax, if any, in respect of the redemption, repayment or purchase) to discharging–

              (I)   within 4 months of the valuation date (within the meaning of section 21 of the [Capital Acquisitions Tax Consolidation Act 2003][1] of a taxable inheritance of the company's shares taken by that person,

> a liability to inheritance tax in respect of that inheritance, or
>
> (II) within one week of the day on which the payment is made, a debt incurred by that person for the purpose of discharging that liability to inheritance tax,
>
> and
>
> (ii) could not without undue hardship have otherwise discharged that liability to inheritance tax and, where appropriate, the debt so incurred.

(2) Where subsection (1) would apply to a payment made by a company which is a subsidiary (within the meaning of section 155 of the Companies Act, 1963) of another company on the acquisition of shares of the other company if for the purposes of the Tax Acts other than this subsection—

(a) the payment were to be treated as a payment by the other company on the purchase of its own shares, and

(b) the acquisition by the subsidiary of the shares were to be treated as a purchase by the other company of its own shares,

then, notwithstanding Chapter 2 of this Part, references in the Tax Acts to distributions of a company, other than references in sections 440 and 441, shall be construed so as not to include references to the payment made by the subsidiary.

Footnote

1   Substituted for "Capital Acquisitions Tax Act, 1976" by s.119, CATCA, with effect from 21st February, 2003.

Commentary

A   See an article on s.176(1)(b) by Tony Fitzpatrick in the *Irish Tax Review* of September 1991, page 543.

PART 13
Close Companies

CHAPTER 1
Interpretation and General

Section 431[1]

Certain companies with quoted shares not to be close companies.

431. (1) In this section, "share" includes "stock".

(2) For the purposes of this section-

  (a) a person shall be a principal member of a company-

    (i) if such person possesses a percentage of the voting power in the company of more than 5 per cent and, where there are more than 5 such persons, if such person is one of the 5 persons who possess the greatest percentages, or

    (ii) if (because 2 or more persons possess equal percentages of the voting power in the company) there are no such 5 persons, such person is one of the 6 or more persons (so as to include those 2 or more who possess equal percentages) who possess the greatest percentages,

  (b) a principal member's holding shall consist of the shares which carry the voting power possessed by the principal member, and

  (c) in determining the voting power which a person possesses, there shall be attributed to such person any voting power which for the purposes of section 432 would be attributed to such person under subsection (5) or (6) of that section.

(3) Subject to this section, a company shall not be treated as being at any time a close company if-

  (a) shares in the company carrying not less than 35 per cent of the voting power in the company (not being shares entitled to a fixed rate of dividend, whether with or without a further right to participate in profits) have been allotted unconditionally to, or acquired unconditionally by, and are at that time beneficially held by, the public, and

  (b) any such shares have within the preceding 12 months been the subject of dealings on a recognised stock exchange, and the shares have within those 12 months been quoted in the official list of a recognised stock exchange.

(4) Subsection (3) shall not apply to a company at any time when the total percentage of the voting power in the company possessed by all of the company's principal members exceeds 85 per cent.

(5) For the purposes of subsection (3), shares in a company shall be deemed to be beneficially held by the public only if the shares-

  (a) are within subsection (6), and

  (b) are not within the exceptions in subsection (7),

and the reference to shares which have been allotted unconditionally to, or acquired unconditionally by, the public shall be construed accordingly.

(6) Shares are within this subsection (as being beneficially held by the public) if the shares-

(a)   are beneficially held by a company resident in the State which is not a close company, or by a company not so resident which would not be a close company if it were so resident,

(b)   are held on trust for an exempt approved scheme (within the meaning of Chapter 1 of Part 30), or

(c)   are not comprised in a principal member's holding.

(7)   (a)   Shares shall be deemed not to be held by the public if the shares are held-

      (i)   by any director, or associate of a director, of the company,

      (ii)   by any company under the control of any such director or associate, or of 2 or more persons each of whom is such a director or associate,

      (iii)   by an associated company of the company, or

      (iv)   as part of any fund the capital or income of which is applicable or applied wholly or mainly for the benefit of, or of the dependants of, the employees or directors, or past employees or directors, of the company, or of any company within subparagraph (ii) or (iii).

(b)   References in this subsection to shares held by any person include references to any shares the rights or powers attached to which could for the purposes of section 432 be attributed to that person under subsection (5) of that section.

Footnote

1   This section provides a definition of "private company" in s.16(2), CATA, and s.27(1), CATCA.

PART 26
Life Assurance Companies

CHAPTER 5
Policyholders — New Basis

Section 730GB

Capital acquisitions tax: set-off.

730GB.   Where on the death of a person, an assurance company is liable to account for appropriate tax (within the meaning of section 730F (1)) in connection with a gain arising on a chargeable event in relation to a life policy, the amount of such tax, in so far as it does not exceed the amount of appropriate tax to which the assurance company would be liable if that tax was calculated in accordance with section 730(1)(a), shall be treated as an amount of capital gains tax paid for the purposes of [section 104 of the Capital Acquisitions Tax Consolidation Act 2003.][1]

Footnote

1   Substituted for "section 63 of the Finance Act, 1985" by s.119 and Sch. 3, CATCA, with effect from 21st February, 2003, where the reference there was to "the Capital Acquisitions Tax Act 2003." This reference has been corrected to "Capital Acquistions Tax Consolidation Act 2003" by para. 1(o), Sch.8, FA 2008, with effect as on and from 13th March, 2008.

PART 33
Anti-Avoidance

CHAPTER 2
Miscellaneous

Section 811

Transactions to avoid liability to tax.

811. (1) (a)   [In this section and section 811A –][2]

"the Acts" means –

(i)   the Tax Acts,

(ii)   the Capital Gains Tax Acts,

(iii)   the Value-Added Tax Act, 1972, and the enactments amending or extending that Act,

(iv)   the [Capital Acquisitions Tax Consolidation Act 2003,][1] and the enactments amending or extending that Act,

(v)   Part VI of the Finance Act, 1983, and the enactments amending or extending that Part, and

(vi)   the statutes relating to stamp duty,

and any instruments made thereunder;

"business" means any trade, profession or vocation;

"notice of opinion" means a notice given by the Revenue Commissioners under subsection (6);

"tax" means any tax, duty, levy or charge which in accordance with the Acts is placed under the care and management of the Revenue Commissioners and any interest, penalty or other amount payable pursuant to the Acts;

"tax advantage" means –

(i) a reduction, avoidance or deferral of any charge or assessment to tax, including any potential or prospective charge or assessment, or

(ii) a refund of or a payment of an amount of tax, or an increase in an amount of tax, refundable or otherwise payable to a person, including any potential or prospective amount so refundable or payable,

arising out of or by reason of a transaction, including a transaction where another transaction would not have been undertaken or arranged to achieve the results, or any part of the results, achieved or intended to be achieved by the transaction;

"tax avoidance transaction" has the meaning assigned to it by subsection (2);

"tax consequences", in relation to a tax avoidance transaction, means such adjustments and acts as may be made and done by the Revenue Commissioners pursuant to subsection (5) in order to withdraw or deny the tax advantage resulting from the tax avoidance transaction;

"transaction" means—

(i) any transaction, action, course of action, course of conduct, scheme, plan or proposal,

(ii) any agreement, arrangement, understanding, promise or undertaking, whether express or implied and whether or not enforceable or intended to be enforceable by legal proceedings, and

(iii) any series of or combination of the circumstances referred to in paragraphs (i) and (ii),

whether entered into or arranged by one person or by 2 or more persons—

(I) whether acting in concert or not,

(II) whether or not entered into or arranged wholly or partly outside the State, or

(III) whether or not entered into or arranged as part of a larger transaction or in conjunction with any other transaction or transactions.

(b) In subsections (2) and (3), for the purposes of the hearing or rehearing under subsection (8) of an appeal made under subsection (7) or for the purposes of the determination of a question of law arising on the statement of a case for the opinion of the High Court, the references to the Revenue Commissioners shall, subject to any necessary modifications, be construed as references to the Appeal Commissioners or to a judge of the Circuit Court or, to the extent necessary, to a judge of the High Court, as appropriate.

[(c) For the purposes of this section and section 811A, all appeals made under section 811(7) by, or on behalf of, a person against any matter or matters specified or described in the notice of opinion of the Revenue Commissioners that a transaction is a tax avoidance transaction, if they have not otherwise been so determined, shall be deemed to have been finally determined when —

(i) there is a written agreement, between that person and an officer of the Revenue Commissioners, that the notice of opinion is to stand or is to be amended in a particular manner,

(ii) (I) the terms of such an agreement that was not made in writing have been confirmed by notice in writing given by the person to the officer of the Revenue Commissioners with whom the agreement was made, or by such officer to the person, and

(II) 21 days have elapsed since the giving of the notice without the person to whom it was given giving notice in writing to the person by whom it was given that the first-mentioned person desires to repudiate or withdraw from the agreement, or

(iii) the person gives notice in writing to an officer of the Revenue Commissioners that the person desires not to proceed with an appeal against the notice of opinion.][3]

(2) For the purposes of this section and subject to subsection (3), a transaction shall be a "tax avoidance transaction" if having regard to any one or more of the following —

(a) the results of the transaction,

(b) its use as a means of achieving those results, and

(c) any other means by which the results or any part of the results could have been achieved,

the Revenue Commissioners form the opinion that —

(i) the transaction gives rise to, or but for this section would give rise to, a tax advantage, and

(ii) the transaction was not undertaken or arranged primarily for purposes other than to give rise to a tax advantage,

and references in this section to the Revenue Commissioners forming an opinion that a transaction is a tax avoidance transaction shall be construed as references to the Revenue Commissioners forming an opinion with regard to the transaction in accordance with this subsection.

(3) (a) Without prejudice to the generality of subsection (2), in forming an opinion in accordance with that subsection and subsection (4) as to whether or not a transaction is a tax avoidance transaction, the Revenue Commissioners shall not regard the transaction as being a tax avoidance transaction if they are satisfied that—

    (i) notwithstanding that the purpose or purposes of the transaction could have been achieved by some other transaction which would have given rise to a greater amount of tax being payable by the person, the transaction—

        (I) was undertaken or arranged by a person with a view, directly or indirectly, to the realisation of profits in the course of the business activities of a business carried on by the person, and

        (II) was not undertaken or arranged primarily to give rise to a tax advantage,

    or

    (ii) the transaction was undertaken or arranged for the purpose of obtaining the benefit of any relief, allowance or other abatement provided by any provision of the Acts and that the transaction would not result directly or indirectly in a misuse of the provision or an abuse of the provision having regard to the purposes for which it was provided.

(b) In forming an opinion referred to in paragraph (a) in relation to any transaction, the Revenue Commissioners shall have regard to—

    (i) the form of that transaction,

    (ii) the substance of that transaction,

    (iii) the substance of any other transaction or transactions which that transaction may reasonably be regarded as being directly or indirectly related to or connected with, and

    (iv) the final outcome and result of that transaction and any combination of those other transactions which are so related or connected.

(4) Subject to this section, the Revenue Commissioners as respects any transaction may at any time—

(a) form the opinion that the transaction is a tax avoidance transaction,

(b) calculate the tax advantage which they consider arises, or which but for this section would arise, from the transaction,

(c) determine the tax consequences which they consider would arise in respect of the transaction if their opinion were to become final and conclusive in accordance with subsection (5) (e), and

(d) calculate the amount of any relief from double taxation which they would propose to give to any person in accordance with subsection (5) (c).

(5) (a) Where the opinion of the Revenue Commissioners that a transaction is a tax avoidance transaction becomes final and conclusive, they may, notwithstanding any other provision of the Acts, make all such adjustments and do all such acts as are just and reasonable (in so far as those adjustments and acts have been specified or described in a notice of opinion given under subsection (6) and subject to the manner in which any appeal made under subsection (7) against any matter specified or described in the notice of opinion has been finally determined, including any adjustments and acts not so specified or described in the notice of opinion but which form part of a final determination of any such appeal) in order that the tax advantage resulting from a tax avoidance transaction shall be withdrawn from or denied to any person concerned.

(b) Subject to but without prejudice to the generality of paragraph (a), the Revenue Commissioners may –

(i) allow or disallow in whole or in part any deduction or other amount which is relevant in computing tax payable, or any part of such deduction or other amount,

(ii) allocate or deny to any person any deduction, loss, abatement, relief, allowance, exemption, income or other amount, or any part thereof, or

(iii) recharacterize for tax purposes the nature of any payment or other amount.

(c) Where the Revenue Commissioners make any adjustment or do any act for the purposes of paragraph (a), they shall afford relief from any double taxation which they consider would but for this paragraph arise by virtue of any adjustment made or act done by them pursuant to paragraphs (a) and (b).

(d) Notwithstanding any other provision of the Acts, where –

(i) pursuant to subsection (4) (c), the Revenue Commissioners determine the tax consequences which they consider would arise in respect of a transaction if their opinion that the transaction is a tax avoidance transaction were to become final and conclusive, and

(ii) pursuant to that determination, they specify or describe in a notice of opinion any adjustment or act which they consider would be, or be part of, those tax consequences, then, in so far as any right of appeal lay under subsection (7) against any such adjustment or act so specified or described, no right or further right of appeal shall lie under the Acts against that adjustment or act when it is made or done in accordance with this subsection, or against any adjustment or act so made or done that is not so specified or described in the notice of opinion but which forms part of the final determination of any appeal made under subsection (7) against any matter specified or described in the notice of opinion.

(e) For the purposes of this subsection, an opinion of the Revenue Commissioners that a transaction is a tax avoidance transaction shall be final and conclusive –

(i) if within the time limited no appeal is made under subsection (7) against any matter or matters specified or described in a notice or notices of opinion given pursuant to that opinion, or

(ii) as and when all appeals made under subsection (7) against any such matter or matters have been finally determined and none of the appeals has been so determined by an order directing that the opinion of the Revenue Commissioners to the effect that the transaction is a tax avoidance transaction is void.

(6) (a) Where pursuant to subsections (2) and (4) the Revenue Commissioners form the opinion that a transaction is a tax avoidance transaction, they shall immediately on forming such an opinion give notice in writing of the opinion to any person from whom a tax advantage would be withdrawn or to whom a tax advantage would be denied or to whom relief from double taxation would be given if the opinion became final and conclusive, and the notice shall specify or describe –

(i) the transaction which in the opinion of the Revenue Commissioners is a tax avoidance transaction,

(ii) the tax advantage or part of the tax advantage, calculated by the Revenue Commissioners which would be withdrawn from or denied to the person to whom the notice is given,

(iii) the tax consequences of the transaction determined by the Revenue Commissioners in so far as they would refer to the person, and

(iv) the amount of any relief from double taxation calculated by the Revenue Commissioners which they would propose to give to the person in accordance with subsection (5) (c).

(b) Section 869 shall, with any necessary modifications, apply for the purposes of a notice given under this subsection or subsection (10) as if it were a notice given under the Income Tax Acts.

(7) Any person aggrieved by an opinion formed or, in so far as it refers to the person, a calculation or determination made by the Revenue Commissioners pursuant to subsection (4) may, by notice in writing given to the Revenue Commissioners within 30 days of the date of the notice of opinion, appeal to the Appeal Commissioners on the grounds and, notwithstanding any other provision of the Acts, only on the grounds that, having regard to all of the circumstances, including any fact or matter which was not known to the Revenue Commissioners when they formed their opinion or made their calculation or determination, and to this section—

(a) the transaction specified or described in the notice of opinion is not a tax avoidance transaction,

(b) the amount of the tax advantage or the part of the tax advantage, specified or described in the notice of opinion which would be withdrawn from or denied to the person is incorrect,

(c) the tax consequences specified or described in the notice of opinion, or such part of those consequences as shall be specified or described by the appellant in the notice of appeal, would not be just and reasonable in order to withdraw or to deny the tax advantage or part of the tax advantage specified or described in the notice of opinion, or

(d) the amount of relief from double taxation which the Revenue Commissioners propose to give to the person is insufficient or incorrect.

(8) The Appeal Commissioners shall hear and determine an appeal made to them under subsection (7) as if it were an appeal against an assessment to income tax and, subject to subsection (9), the provisions of the Income Tax Acts relating to the rehearing of an appeal and to the statement of a case for the opinion of the High Court on a point of law shall apply accordingly with any necessary modifications; but on the hearing or rehearing of the appeal—

(a) it shall not be lawful to enquire into any grounds of appeal other than those specified in subsection (7), and

(b) at the request of the appellants, 2 or more appeals made by 2 or more persons pursuant to the same opinion, calculation or determination formed or made by the Revenue Commissioners pursuant to subsection (4) may be heard or reheard together.

(9) (a) On the hearing of an appeal made under subsection (7), the Appeal Commissioners shall have regard to all matters to which the Revenue Commissioners may or are required to have regard under this section, and—

(i) in relation to an appeal made on the grounds referred to in subsection (7) (a), the Appeal Commissioners shall determine the appeal, in so far as it is made on those grounds, by ordering, if they or a majority of them—

(I)   consider that the transaction specified or described in the notice of opinion or any part of that transaction is a tax avoidance transaction, that the opinion or the opinion in so far as it relates to that part is to stand,

(II)   consider that, subject to such amendment or addition thereto as the Appeal Commissioners or the majority of them deem necessary and as they shall specify or describe, the transaction, or any part of it, specified or described in the notice of opinion, is a tax avoidance transaction, that the transaction or that part of it be so amended or added to and that, subject to the amendment or addition, the opinion or the opinion in so far as it relates to that part is to stand, or

(III)   do not so consider as referred to in clause (I) or (II), that the opinion is void,

(ii)   in relation to an appeal made on the grounds referred to in subsection (7) (b), they shall determine the appeal, in so far as it is made on those grounds, by ordering that the amount of the tax advantage or the part of the tax advantage specified or described in the notice of opinion be increased or reduced by such amount as they shall direct or that it shall stand,

(iii)   in relation to an appeal made on the grounds referred to in subsection (7) (c), they shall determine the appeal, in so far as it is made on those grounds, by ordering that the tax consequences specified or described in the notice of opinion shall be altered or added to in such manner as they shall direct or that they shall stand, or

(iv)   in relation to an appeal made on the grounds referred to in subsection (7) (d), they shall determine the appeal, in so far as it is made on those grounds, by ordering that the amount of the relief from double taxation specified or described in the notice of opinion shall be increased or reduced by such amount as they shall direct or that it shall stand.

(b)   This subsection shall, subject to any necessary modifications, apply to the rehearing of an appeal by a judge of the Circuit Court and, to the extent necessary, to the determination by the High Court of any question or questions of law arising on the statement of a case for the opinion of the High Court.

(10) The Revenue Commissioners may at any time amend, add to or withdraw any matter specified or described in a notice of opinion by giving notice (in this subsection referred to as "the notice of amendment") in writing of the amendment, addition or withdrawal to each and every person affected thereby, in so far as the person is so affected, and subsections (1) to (9) shall apply in all respects as if the notice of amendment were a notice of opinion and any matter

specified or described in the notice of amendment were specified or described in a notice of opinion; but no such amendment, addition or withdrawal may be made so as to set aside or alter any matter which has become final and conclusive on the determination of an appeal made with regard to that matter under subsection (7).

(11) Where pursuant to subsections (2) and (4) the Revenue Commissioners form the opinion that a transaction is a tax avoidance transaction and pursuant to that opinion notices are to be given under subsection (6) to 2 or more persons, any obligation on the Revenue Commissioners to maintain secrecy or any other restriction on the disclosure of information by the Revenue Commissioners shall not apply with respect to the giving of those notices or to the performance of any acts or the discharge of any functions authorised by this section to be performed or discharged by them or to the performance of any act or the discharge of any functions, including any act or function in relation to an appeal made under subsection (7), which is directly or indirectly related to the acts or functions so authorised.

(12) The Revenue Commissioners may nominate any of their officers to perform any acts and discharge any functions, including the forming of an opinion, authorised by this section to be performed or discharged by the Revenue Commissioners, and references in this section to the Revenue Commissioners shall with any necessary modifications be construed as including references to an officer so nominated.

(13) This section shall apply as respects any transaction where the whole or any part of the transaction is undertaken or arranged on or after the 25th day of January, 1989, and as respects any transaction undertaken or arranged wholly before that date in so far as it gives rise to, or would but for this section give rise to —

(a) a reduction, avoidance or deferral of any charge or assessment to tax, or part thereof, where the charge or assessment arises by virtue of any other transaction carried out wholly on or after a date, or

(b) a refund or a payment of an amount, or of an increase in an amount, of tax, or part thereof, refundable or otherwise payable to a person where that amount or increase in the amount would otherwise become first so refundable or otherwise payable to the person on a date,

which could not fall earlier than the 25th day of January, 1989.

Footnotes

1   Substituted for "Capital Acquisitions Tax Act, 1976" by s.119, CATCA, with effect from 21st February, 2003.

2   Substituted for "In this section –" by s.126(a)(i) FA 2006, with effect from 31st March, 2006.

3   Inserted by s.126(a)(ii), FA 2006, with effect from 31st March, 2006.

Commentary

A S.811, TCA, should be read in conjunction with s.811A, TCA, with which it is linked.

B See two articles on Anti-Avoidance by Derbhla Morgan and Denise Murphy at page 62 of the *Irish Tax Review* of March 2006 and at page 59 of the *Irish Tax Review* of May 2006.

Section 811A[1]

Transactions to avoid liability to tax: surcharge, interest and protective notification.

811A. (1) (a) In this section references to tax being payable shall, except where the context requires otherwise, include references to tax being payable by a person to withdraw from that person so much of a tax advantage as is a refund of, or a payment of, an amount of tax, or an increase in an amount of tax, refundable, or otherwise payable, to the person.

 (b) For the purposes of this section the date on which the opinion of the Revenue Commissioners that a transaction is a tax avoidance transaction becomes final and conclusive is—

  (i) where no appeal is made under section 811(7) against any matter or matters specified or described in the notice of that opinion, 31 days after the date of the notice of that opinion, or

  (ii) the date on which all appeals made under section 811(7) against any such matter or matters have been finally determined and none of the appeals has been so determined by an order directing that the opinion of the Revenue Commissioners to the effect that the transaction is a tax avoidance transaction is void.

 (c) This section shall be construed together with section 811 and shall have effect notwithstanding any of the provisions of section 811.

[(1A) Without prejudice to the generality of any provision of this section or section 811, sections 955(2)(a) and 956(1)(c), as construed together with section 950(2), shall not be construed as preventing an officer of the Revenue Commissioners from—

 (a) making any enquiry, or

 (b) taking any action,

at any time in connection with this section or section 811.

(1B) Where the Revenue Commissioners have received from, or on behalf of, a person, on or before the relevant date (within the meaning of subsection (3)(c)) a notification (referred to in subsection (3) and (6) as a "protective notification") of full details of a transaction, then the Revenue Commissioners shall not form the opinion that the transaction is a tax avoidance transaction pursuant to subsections

(2) and (4) of that section after the expiry of the period of 2 years commencing at —

(a)   the relevant date, or

(b)   if earlier, the date on which the notification was received by the Revenue Commissioners,

but this subsection shall not be construed as preventing an officer of the Revenue Commissioners from making any enquiry at any time in connection with this section or section 811.

(1C) Where the Revenue Commissioners have not received from, or on behalf of, a person, on or before the relevant date (within the meaning of subsection (3)(c)) a notification (referred to in subsection (3) and (6) as a "protective notification") of full details of the transaction, then section 811 shall apply as respects that transaction, if it is a transaction specified or described in a notice of opinion given by the Revenue Commissioners, as if the following clauses were substituted for clauses (I) and (II) of subsection (9)(a) (i):

"(I)   consider that there are grounds on which the transaction specified or described in the notice of opinion or any part of that transaction could reasonably be considered to be a tax avoidance transaction, that the opinion or the opinion in so far as it relates to that part is to stand,

(II)   consider that, subject to such amendment or addition thereto as the Appeal Commissioners or the majority of them deem necessary and as they shall specify or describe, there are grounds on which the transaction, or any part of it, specified or described in the notice of opinion, could reasonably be considered to be a tax avoidance transaction, that the transaction or that part of it be so amended or added to and that, subject to the amendment or addition, the opinion or the opinion in so far as it relates to that part is to stand, or",

and the provisions of section 811 shall be construed accordingly.][2]

(2)   Where, in accordance with adjustments made or acts done by the Revenue Commissioners under section 811(5), on foot of their opinion (as amended, or added to, on appeal where relevant) that a transaction is a tax avoidance transaction having become final and conclusive, an amount of tax is payable by a person that would not have been payable if the Revenue Commissioners had not formed the opinion concerned, then, subject to subsection (3) —

(a)   the person shall be liable to pay an amount (in this section referred to as the "surcharge") equal to [20 per cent][3] of the amount of that tax and the provisions of the Acts, including in particular section 811(5) and those provisions relating to the collection and recovery of that tax, shall apply to that surcharge, as if it were such tax, and

(b) for the purposes of liability to interest under the Acts on tax due and payable, the amount of tax, or parts of that amount, shall be deemed to be due and payable on the day or, as respects parts of that amount, days specified in the notice of opinion (as amended, or added to, on appeal where relevant) in accordance with section 811(6)(a)(iii) construed together with subsection (4)(a)of this section,

and the surcharge and interest shall be payable accordingly.

(3) (a) Subject to subsection (6), neither a surcharge nor interest shall be payable by a person in relation to a tax avoidance transaction finally and conclusively determined to be such a transaction if the Revenue Commissioners have received from, or on behalf of, that person, on or before the relevant date (within the meaning of paragraph (c)), notification (referred to in this subsection and subsection (6) as a "protective notification") of full details of that transaction.

(b) Where a person makes a protective notification, or a protective notification is made on a person's behalf, then the person shall be treated as making the protective notification—

(i) solely to prevent any possibility of [the application of subsection (1C) to the transaction concerned or][4] interest becoming payable by the person by virtue of subsection (2), and

(ii) wholly without prejudice as to whether any opinion that the transaction concerned was a tax avoidance transaction, if such an opinion were to be formed by the Revenue Commissioners, would be correct.

(c) Regardless of the type of tax concerned—

(i) where the whole or any part of the transaction, which is the subject of the protective notification, is undertaken or arranged on or after [19 February 2008][5], then the relevant date shall be—

(I) the date which is 90 days after the date on which the transaction commenced, or

(II) if it is later than the said 90 days, [19 May 2008][6],

(ii) where—

(I) the whole of the transaction is undertaken or arranged before [19 February 2008][5], and would give rise to, or would but for section 811 give rise to, a reduction, avoidance, or deferral of any charge or assessment to tax, or part thereof, and

(II) that charge or assessment would arise only by virtue of one or more other transactions carried out wholly on or after [19 February 2008][5]

then the relevant date shall be the date which is 90 days after the date on which the first of those other transactions commenced, or

(iii) where—

    (I) the whole of the transaction is undertaken or arranged before [19 February 2008][5], and would give rise to, or would but for section 811 give rise to, a refund or a payment of an amount, or of an increase in an amount of tax, or part thereof, refundable or otherwise payable to a person, and

    (II) that amount or increase in the amount would, but for section 811, become first so refundable or otherwise payable to the person on a date on or after [19 February 2008][5],

then the relevant date shall be the date which is 90 days after that date.

(d) Notwithstanding the receipt by the Revenue Commissioners of a protective notice, paragraph (a) shall not apply to any interest, payable in relation to a tax avoidance transaction finally and conclusively determined to be such a transaction, in respect of days on or after the date on which the opinion of the Revenue Commissioners in relation to that transaction becomes final and conclusive.

(4) (a) The determination of tax consequences, which would arise in respect of a transaction if the opinion of the Revenue Commissioners, that the transaction was a tax avoidance transaction, were to become final and conclusive, shall, for the purposes of charging interest, include the specification of—

(i) a date or dates, being a date or dates which is or are just and reasonable to ensure that tax is deemed to be due and payable not later than it would have been due and payable if the transaction had not been undertaken, disregarding any contention that another transaction would not have been undertaken or arranged to achieve the results, or any part of the results, achieved or intended to be achieved by the transaction, and

(ii) the date which, as respects such amount of tax as is due and payable by a person to recover from the person a refund of or a payment of tax, including an increase in tax refundable or otherwise payable, to the person, is the day on which the refund or payment was made, set off or accounted for, and the date or dates shall be specified for the purposes of this paragraph without regard to—

    (I) when an opinion of the Revenue Commissioners that the transaction concerned was a tax avoidance transaction was formed,

(II) the date on which any notice of that opinion was given, or

(III) the date on which the opinion (as amended, or added to, on appeal where relevant) became final and conclusive.

(b) Where the grounds of an appeal in relation to tax consequences refer to such a date or dates as are mentioned in paragraph (a), subsection (7) of section 811 shall apply, in that respect, as if the following paragraph were substituted for paragraph (c) of that subsection:

"(c) the tax consequences specified or described in the notice of opinion, or such part of those consequences as shall be specified or described by the appellant in the notice of appeal, would not be just and reasonable to ensure that tax is deemed to be payable on a date or dates in accordance with subsection (4)(a) of section 811A"

and the grounds of appeal referred to in section 811(8)(a) shall be construed accordingly.

(5) A surcharge payable by virtue of subsection (2)(a) shall be due and payable on the date that the opinion of the Revenue Commissioners that a transaction is a tax avoidance transaction becomes final and conclusive and interest shall be payable in respect of any delay in payment of the surcharge as if the surcharge were an amount of that tax by reference to an amount of which the surcharge was computed.

(6) (a) A protective notification shall –

(i) be delivered in such form as may be prescribed by the Revenue Commissioners and to such office of the Revenue Commissioners as –

(I) is specified in the prescribed form, or

(II) as may be identified, by reference to guidance in the prescribed form, as the office to which the notification concerned should be sent, and

(ii) contain –

(I) full details of the transaction which is the subject of the protective notification, including any part of that transaction that has not been undertaken before the protective notification is delivered,

(II) full reference to the provisions of the Acts that the person, by whom, or on whose behalf, the protective notification is delivered, considers to be relevant to the treatment of the transaction for tax purposes, and

(III) full details of how, in the opinion of the person, by whom, or on whose behalf, the protective notification is delivered, each provision, referred to in the protective notification in accordance with clause (II), applies, or does not apply, to the transaction.

(b) Without prejudice to the generality of paragraph (a), the specifying, under –

(i) section 19B of the Value-Added Tax Act 1972,

(ii) section 46A of the Capital Acquisitions Tax Consolidation Act 2003,

(iii) section 8 of the Stamp Duties Consolidation Act 1999, or

(iv) section 955(4) of this Act,

of a doubt as to the application of law to, or the treatment for tax purposes of, any matter to be contained in a return shall not be regarded as being, or being equivalent to, the delivery of a protective notification in relation to a transaction for [the purposes of subsections (1B) and (3)][7].

(c) Where the Revenue Commissioners form the opinion that a transaction is a tax avoidance transaction and believe that a protective notification in relation to the transaction has not been delivered by a person in accordance with subsection (6)(a) by the relevant date (within the meaning of subsection (3)(c)) then, in giving notice under section 811(6)(a) to the person of their opinion in relation to the transaction, they shall give notice that they believe that a protective notification has not been so delivered by the person and section 811 shall be construed, subject to any necessary modifications, as if –

(i) subsection (7) of that section included as grounds for appeal that a protective notification in relation to the transaction was so delivered by the person, and

(ii) subsection (9) of that section provided that an appeal were to be determined, in so far as it is made on those grounds, by ordering that a protective notification in relation to the transaction was so delivered or that a protective notification in relation to the transaction was not so delivered.

[(6A) **The Revenue Commissioners may nominate any of their officers to perform any acts and discharge any functions authorised by this section to be performed or discharged by the Revenue Commissioners, and references in this section to the Revenue Commissioners shall with any necessary modifications be construed as including references to an officer so nominated.**][9]

(7) This section shall apply –

(a) as respects any transaction where the whole or any part of the transaction is undertaken or arranged on or after [19 February 2008][8], and

(b) as respects any transaction, the whole of which was undertaken or arranged before that date, in so far as it gives rise to, or would but for section 811 give rise to—

   (i) a reduction, avoidance, or deferral of any charge or assessment to tax, or part thereof, where the charge or assessment arises only by virtue of another transaction or other transactions carried out wholly on or after [19 February 2008][8], or

   (ii) a refund or a payment of an amount, or of an increase in an amount of tax, or part thereof, refundable or otherwise payable to a person where, but for section 811, that amount or increase in the amount would become first so refundable or otherwise payable to the person on or after [19 February 2008][8].

Footnotes

1   Inserted by s.126(b), FA 2006, with effect from 31st March, 2006. S.811A, TCA, should be read in conjunction with s.811, TCA, with which it is linked.

2   Inserted by s.140(1)(a), FA 2008, which has application as shown in s.140(2), FA 2008, reproduced on page 1317.

3   Substituted for "10 per cent" by s.140(1)(b), FA 2008, which has application as shown in s.140(2), FA 2008, reproduced on page 1317.

4   Inserted by s.140(1)(c)(i), FA 2008, which has application as shown in s.140(2), FA 2008, reproduced on page 1317.

5   Substituted for "2 February 2006" by s.140(1)(c)(ii)(I), FA 2008, which has application as shown in s.140(2), FA 2008, reproduced on page 1317.

6   Substituted for "2 May 2006" by s.140(1)(c)(ii)(II), FA 2008, which has application as shown in s.140(2), FA 2008, reproduced on page 1317.

7   Substituted for "the purposes of subsection (3)" by s.140(1)(d), FA 2008, which has application as shown in s.140(2), FA 2008, reproduced on page 1317.

8   Substituted for "2 February 2006" by s.140(1)(e), FA 2008, which has application as shown in s.140(2), FA 2008, reproduced on page 1317.

9   Inserted by s.95, F(No.2)A, 2008, with effect from 24th December, 2008.

Commentary

A   See two articles on Anti-Avoidance by Derbhla Morgan and Denise Murphy at page 62 of the *Irish Tax Review* of March 2006 and at page 59 of the *Irish Tax Review* of May 2006.

B   See also s.46A, CATCA.

PART 34

Provisions Relating to the Residence of Individuals

Section 818

Interpretation (Part 34).

818. In this Part other than in section 825-

"the Acts" means—

(a) the Tax Acts,

(b) the Capital Gains Tax Acts, and

(c) the [Capital Acquisitions Tax Consolidation Act 2003,][1] and the enactments, amending or extending that Act,

and any instruments made thereunder;

["authorised officer" means an officer of the Revenue Commissioners;][2]

"present in the State", in relation to an individual, means the personal presence of the individual in the State;

"tax" means any tax payable in accordance with any provision of the Acts.

Footnotes

1   Substituted for "Capital Acquisitions Tax Act, 1976" by s.119, CATCA, with effect from 21st February, 2003.

2   The concluding words of the original definition, "authorised by them in writing for the purposes of this Part", deleted by s.135, FA 2008, with effect from 13th March, 2008.

Section 819

Residence.

819. (1) For the purposes of the Acts, an individual shall be resident in the State for a year of assessment if the individual is present in the State—

(a) at any one time or several times in the year of assessment for a period in the whole amounting to 183 days or more, or

(b) at any one time or several times—

(i) in the year of assessment, and

(ii) in the preceding year of assessment,

for a period (being a period comprising in the aggregate the number of days on which the individual is present in the State in the year of assessment and the number of days on which the individual was present in the State in the preceding year of assessment) in the aggregate amounting to 280 days or more.

(2) Notwithstanding subsection (1)(b), where for a year of assessment an individual is present in the State at any one time or several

times for a period in the aggregate amounting to not more than 30 days —

    (a)   the individual shall not be resident in the State for the year of assessment, and

    (b)   no account shall be taken of the period for the purposes of the aggregate mentioned in subsection (1)(b).

(3) (a)   Notwithstanding subsections (1) and (2), an individual —

        (i)   who is not resident in the State for a year of assessment, and

        (ii) to whom paragraph (b) applies,

       may at any time elect to be treated as resident in the State for that year and, where an individual so elects, the individual shall for the purposes of the Acts be deemed to be resident in the State for that year.

    (b)   This paragraph shall apply to an individual who satisfies an authorised officer that the individual is in the State —

        (i)   with the intention, and

        (ii) in such circumstances,

       that the individual will be resident in the State for the following year of assessment.

[(4) For the purposes of this section —

    (a)   as respects the year of assessment 2008 and previous years of assessment, an individual shall be deemed to be present in the State for a day if the individual is present in the State at the end of the day, and

    (b)   as respects the year of assessment 2009 and subsequent years of assessment, an individual shall be deemed to be present in the State for a day if the individual is present in the State at any time during that day.][1]

Footnote

1   As substituted by s.15 F(No.2)A, 2008 with effect as on and from 1st January, 2009.

Section 820

Ordinary residence.

820. (1) For the purposes of the Acts, an individual shall be ordinarily resident in the State for a year of assessment if the individual has been resident in the State for each of the 3 years of assessment preceding that year.

    (2) An individual ordinarily resident in the State shall not for the purposes of the Acts cease to be ordinarily resident in the State for

a year of assessment unless the individual has not been resident in the State in each of the 3 years of assessment preceding that year.

Section 822

Split year residence.

822. (1) For the purposes of a charge to tax on any income, profits or gains from an employment, where during a year of assessment (in this section referred to as "the relevant year") –

(a) (i) an individual who has not been resident in the State for the preceding year of assessment satisfies an authorised officer that the individual is in the State –

(I) with the intention, and

(II) in such circumstances,

that the individual will be resident in the State for the following year of assessment, or

(ii) an individual who is resident in the State satisfies an authorised officer that the individual is leaving the State, other than for a temporary purpose –

(I) with the intention, and

(II) in such circumstances,

that the individual will not be resident in the State for the following year of assessment,

and

(b) the individual would but for this section be resident in the State for the relevant year,

subsection (2) shall apply in relation to the individual.

(2) (a) An individual to whom paragraphs (a) (i) and (b) of subsection (1) apply shall be deemed to be resident in the State for the relevant year only from the date of his or her arrival in the State.

(b) An individual to whom paragraphs (a) (ii) and (b) of subsection (1) apply shall be deemed to be resident in the State for the relevant year only up to and including the date of his or her leaving the State.

(3) Where by virtue of this section an individual is resident in the State for part of a year of assessment, the Acts shall apply as if –

(a) income arising during that part of the year or, in a case to which section 71(3) applies, amounts received in the State during that part of the year were income arising or amounts received for a year of assessment in which the individual is resident in the State, and

(b)   income arising or, as the case may be, amounts received in the remaining part of the year were income arising or amounts received in a year of assessment in which the individual is not resident in the State.

Section 824

Appeals.

824. (1)   An individual aggrieved by a decision of an authorised officer on any question arising under the provisions of this Part which require an individual to satisfy an authorised officer on such a question may, by notice in writing to that effect given to the authorised officer within 2 months from the date on which notice of the decision is given to the individual, make an application to have the question heard and determined by the Appeal Commissioners.

       (2)   Where an application is made under subsection (1), the Appeal Commissioners shall hear and determine the question concerned in the like manner as an appeal made to them against an assessment, and the provisions of the Acts relating to such an appeal (including the provisions relating to the rehearing of an appeal and to the statement of a case for the opinion of the High Court on a point of law) shall apply accordingly with any necessary modifications.

Section 825

Residence treatment of donors of gifts to the State.

825. (1)   In this section—

       "the Acts" means—

       (a)   the Tax Acts,

       (b)   the Capital Gains Tax Acts, and

       (c)   the [Capital Acquisitions Tax Consolidation Act 2003;][1]

       "donor" means an individual who makes a gift to the State;

       "gift" means a gift of property to the State which, on acceptance of the gift by the Government pursuant to the State Property Act, 1954, becomes vested pursuant to that Act in a State authority within the meaning of that Act;

       "Irish tax" means any tax imposed by the Acts;

       "property" includes interests and rights of any description;

       "relevant date", in relation to an individual (being a donor or the spouse of a donor), means the date (not being earlier than the 1st day of September, 1974) on which the individual leaves the State for the purpose of residence (other than occasional residence) outside the State;

       "tax in that country" means any tax imposed in that country which is identical with or substantially similar to Irish tax;

"visits" means—

    (a)   in relation to a donor, visits by the donor to the State after the relevant date for the purpose of advising on the management of the property which is the subject of the gift, being visits that are in the aggregate less than 182 days in any year of assessment in which they are made, and

    (b)   in relation to the spouse of a donor, visits by that spouse when accompanying the donor on visits of the kind referred to in paragraph (a).

  (2) Where for any year of assessment a person (being a donor or the spouse of a donor) is resident in a country outside the State for the purposes of tax in that country and is chargeable to that tax without any limitation as to chargeability, then, notwithstanding anything to the contrary in the Tax Acts—

    (a)   as respects the year of assessment in which the relevant date occurs, that person shall not as from the relevant date be regarded as ordinarily resident in the State for the purposes of Irish tax, and

    (b)   as respects any subsequent year of assessment, in determining whether that person is resident or ordinarily resident in the State for the purposes of Irish tax, visits shall be disregarded.

Footnote

1   Substituted for "Capital Acquisitions Tax Act, 1976" by s.119, CATCA, with effect from 21st February, 2003.

PART 37

Administration

Section 858

Evidence of authorisation.

858. (1) In this section, except where the context otherwise requires—

"the Acts" means—

    (a)   (i)   the Customs Acts,

          (ii) the statutes relating to the duties of excise and to the management of those duties,

          (iii) the Tax Acts,

          (iv) the Capital Gains Tax Acts,

          (v)   the Value-Added Tax Act, 1972, and the enactments amending or extending that Act,

          (vi) the [Capital Acquisitions Tax Consolidation Act 2003,][1] and the enactments amending or extending that Act,

(vii) the statutes relating to stamp duty and to the management of that duty,

and any instruments made thereunder or under any other enactment and relating to tax, and

(b) the European Communities (Intrastat) Regulations, 1993 (S.I. No. 136 of 1993);

"authorised officer" means an officer of the Revenue Commissioners who is authorised, nominated or appointed under any provision of the Acts to exercise or perform any functions under any of the specified provisions, and "authorised" and "authorisation" shall be construed accordingly;

"functions" includes powers and duties;

"identity card", in relation to an authorised officer, means a card which is issued to the officer by the Revenue Commissioners and which contains —

(a) a statement to the effect that the officer —

   (i) is an officer of the Revenue Commissioners, and

   (ii) is an authorised officer for the purposes of the specified provisions,

(b) a photograph and signature of the officer,

(c) a hologram showing the logo of the Office of the Revenue Commissioners,

(d) the facsimile signature of a Revenue Commissioner, and

(e) particulars of the specified provisions under which the officer is authorised;

"specified provisions", in relation to an authorised officer, means either or both the provisions of the Acts under which the authorised officer —

(a) is authorised and which are specified on his or her identity card, and

(b) exercises or performs functions under the Customs Acts or any statutes relating to the duties of excise and to the management of those duties;

"tax" means any tax, duty, levy or charge under the care and management of the Revenue Commissioners.

(2) Where, in the exercise or performance of any functions under any of the specified provisions in relation to him or her, an authorised officer is requested to produce or show his or her authorisation for the purposes of that provision, the production by the authorised officer of his or her identity card —

(a) shall be taken as evidence of authorisation under that provision, and

(b) shall satisfy any obligation under that provision which requires the authorised officer to produce such authorisation on request.

(3) This section shall come into operation on such day as the Minister for Finance may appoint by order.[2]

Footnotes

1   Substituted for "Capital Acquisitions Tax Act, 1976" by s.119, CATCA, with effect from 21st February, 2003.

2   Into operation on 1st July, 1998 (S.I. No. 212 of 1998).

Section 859

Anonymity of authorised officers in relation to certain matters.

859. (1) In this section—

"authorised officer" means an officer of the Revenue Commissioners nominated by them to be a member of the staff of the body;

"the body" has the meaning assigned to it by section 58;

"proceedings" includes any hearing before the Appeal Commissioners (within the meaning of the Revenue Acts);

"the Revenue Acts" means—

(a)   the Customs Acts,

(b)   the statutes relating to the duties of excise and to the management of those duties,

(c)   the Tax Acts,

(d)   the Capital Gains Tax Acts,

(e)   the Value-Added Tax Act, 1972, and the enactments amending or extending that Act,

(f)   the [Capital Acquisitions Tax Consolidation Act 2003,][1] and the enactments amending or extending that Act,

(g)   the statutes relating to stamp duty and the management of that duty,

(h)   Chapter IV of Part 11 of the Finance Act, 1992, and

(i)   Part VI of the Finance Act, 1983,

and any instruments made thereunder or under any other enactment and relating to tax;

"tax" means any tax, duty, levy or charge under the care and management of the Revenue Commissioners.

(2) Notwithstanding any requirement made by or under any enactment or any other requirement in administrative and operational procedures, including internal procedures, all reasonable care shall be taken to ensure that the identity of an authorised officer shall not be revealed.

(3) In particular and without prejudice to the generality of subsection (2):

    (a) where, for the purposes of exercising or performing his or her powers or duties under the Revenue Acts in pursuance of the functions of the body, an authorised officer may apart from this section be required to produce or show any written authority or warrant of appointment under those Acts or otherwise to identify himself or herself, the authorised officer shall –

        (i) not be required to produce or show any such authority or warrant of appointment or to so identify himself or herself, for the purposes of exercising or performing his or her powers or duties under those Acts, and

        (ii) be accompanied by a member of the Garda Síochána who shall, on request by a person affected, identify himself or herself as a member of the Garda Síochána and shall state that he or she is accompanied by an authorised officer;

    (b) where, in pursuance of the functions of the body, an authorised officer exercises or performs in writing any of his or her powers or duties under the Revenue Acts or any provision of any other enactment, whenever passed, which relates to Revenue, such exercise or performance of his or her powers or duties shall be done in the name of the body and not in the name of the individual authorised officer involved, notwithstanding any provision to the contrary in any of those enactments;

    (c) in any proceedings arising out of the exercise or performance, in pursuance of the functions of the body, of powers or duties by an authorised officer, any documents relating to such proceedings shall not reveal the identity of any authorised officer, notwithstanding any requirements to the contrary in any provision, and in any proceedings the identity of such officer other than as an authorised officer shall not be revealed other than to the judge or the Appeal Commissioner, as the case may be, hearing the case;

    (d) where, in pursuance of the functions of the body, an authorised officer is required, in any proceedings, to give evidence and the judge or the Appeal Commissioner, as the case may be, is satisfied that there are reasonable grounds in the public interest to direct that evidence to be given by such authorised officer should be given in the hearing and not in the sight of any person, he or she may so direct.

Footnote
1   Substituted for "Capital Acquisitions Tax Act, 1976" by s.119, CATCA, with effect from 21st February, 2003.

Section 872

Use of information relating to other taxes and duties.

872. (1) Any information acquired, whether before or after the passing of this Act, in connection with any tax or duty under the care and management of the Revenue Commissioners may be used by them for any purpose connected with any other tax or duty under their care and management.

(2) ....

PART 38

Returns of Income and Gains, other Obligations and Returns, and Revenue Powers

CHAPTER 3
Other obligations and returns

Section 887

Use of electronic data processing.

887. (1) In this section—

"the Acts" means—

(a) the Tax Acts,

(b) the Capital Gains Tax Acts,

(c) the Value-Added Tax Act, 1972, and the enactments amending or extending that Act,

(d) the [Capital Acquisitions Tax Consolidation Act 2003,][1] and the enactments amending or extending that Act, and

(e) Part VI of the Finance Act, 1983,

and any instrument made under any of these enactments;

"record" means any document which a person is obliged by the Acts to keep, to issue or to produce for inspection, and any other written or printed material.

(2) For the purposes of the Acts, but subject to section 17 of the Value-Added Tax Act, 1972, a record may be stored, maintained, transmitted, reproduced or communicated, as the case may be, by any electronic, photographic or other process that—

(a) provides a reliable assurance as to the integrity of the record from the time when it was first generated in its final form by such electronic, photographic or other process,

(b) permits the record to be displayed in intelligible form and produced in an intelligible printed format,

(c) permits the record to be readily accessible for subsequent reference in accordance with paragraph (b), and

(d) conforms to the information technology and procedural requirements drawn up and published by the Revenue Commissioners in accordance with subsection (3).

(3) The Revenue Commissioners shall from time to time draw up and publish in Iris Oifigiúil the information technology and procedural requirements to which any electronic, photographic or other process used by a person for the storage, maintenance, transmission, reproduction and communication of any record shall conform.

(4) The authority conferred on the Revenue Commissioners by this section to draw up and publish requirements shall be construed as including the authority exercisable in a like manner to revoke and replace or to amend any such requirements.

(5) (a) Every person who preserves records by any electronic, photographic or other process, when required to do so by a notice in writing from the Revenue Commissioners, shall, within such period as is specified in the notice, not being less than 21 days from the date of service of the notice, supply to the Revenue Commissioners full particulars relating to the process used by that person, including full particulars relating to software (within the meaning of section 912).

(b) A person who fails or refuses to comply with a notice served on the person under paragraph (a) shall be liable to a penalty of [€3,000][2].

(6) (a) Subject to paragraph (b), where records are kept by a person (being a person who is obliged by the Acts to keep such records) by any electronic, photographic or other process which does not conform with the requirements referred to in paragraphs (a) to (d) of subsection (2), then the person shall be deemed to have failed to comply with that obligation and that person shall be liable to the same penalties as the person would be liable to if the person had failed to comply with any obligation under the Acts in relation to the keeping of records.

(b) Paragraph (a) shall not apply where the person referred to in that paragraph complies with any obligation under the Acts in relation to the keeping of records other than in accordance with the provisions of subsection (2).

(7) Where records are preserved by any electronic, photographic or other process, information contained in a document produced by any such process shall, subject to the rules of court, be admissible in evidence in any proceedings, whether civil or criminal, to the same extent as the records themselves.

(8) The Revenue Commissioners may nominate any of their officers to discharge any function authorised by this section to be discharged by the Revenue Commissioners.

Footnotes

1   Substituted for "Capital Acquisitions Tax Act, 1976" by s.119, CATCA, with effect from 21st February, 2003.

2   Substitued for "€1, 265" by s.98(1), and by para. 2(j) of Sch.5, of the F(No.2)A, 2008, and comes into effect after 24th December, 2008.

Section 896A[1]

Returns in relation to settlements and trusts.

896A.(1)   In this section —

"authorised officer" means an officer of the Revenue Commissioners authorised by them in writing to exercise the powers conferred on them by this section:

"settlement" and "settlor" have the same meanings respectively as in section 10.

(2)   Where any person, in the course of a trade or profession carried on by that person, has been concerned with the making of a settlement and knows or has reason to believe that, at the time of the making of the settlement —

(a)   the settlor was resident or ordinarily resident in the State, and

(b)   the trustees of the settlement were not resident in the State,

then that person shall, within the period specified in subsection (3), deliver to the appropriate inspector (within the meaning assigned by section 894(1)) a statement specifying —

(i)   the name and address of the settlor,

(ii)   the names and addresses of the persons who are the trustees of the settlement, and

(iii)   the date on which the settlement was made or created.

(3)   The statement referred to in subsection (2) shall be delivered —

(a)   in a case where the settlement is one made on or after the date of the passing of the Finance (No. 2) Act 2008, within 4 months of the date of the making of the settlement, or

(b)   in a case where the settlement is one made within the 5 year period prior to the passing of the Finance (No. 2) Act 2008, within 6 months of the date of the passing of the Act.

(4)   For the purposes of this section trustees of a settlement shall be regarded as not resident in the State unless the general administration of the settlement is ordinarily carried on in the State and the trustees or a majority of each class of trustees are for the time being resident in the State.

(5)   An authorised officer may by notice in writing require any person, whom the authorised officer has reason to belive has information relating to a settlement, to furnish to the authorised officer such

information within such time as the authorised officer may direct.

Footnote

1   Inserted by s.93, F(No. 2)A, 2008, with effect from 24th December, 2008.

CHAPTER 4
Revenue Powers

Section 900

Power to call for production of books, information, etc.

900. (1)   In this section and in section 901 −

"authorised officer" means an officer of the Revenue Commissioners authorised by them in writing to exercise the powers conferred by this section, or as the case may be, section 901;

"books, records or other documents" includes −

(a)   accounts (including balance sheets) relating to a trade or profession and where the accounts have been audited, a copy of the auditor's certificate,

(b)   books, accounts, rolls, registers, papers and other documents, whether −

(i)   comprised in bound volume, loose-leaf binders or other loose-leaf filing system, loose-leaf ledger sheets, pages, folios or cards, or

(ii)   kept on microfilm, magnetic tape or in any non-legible form (by the use of electronics or otherwise) which is capable of being reproduced in a legible form,

(c)   every electronic or other automatic means, if any, by which any such thing in non-legible form is so capable of being reproduced, and

(d)   documents in manuscript, documents which are typed, printed, stencilled or created by any other mechanical or partly mechanical process in use from time to time and documents which are produced by any photographic or photostatic process;

"judge" means a judge of the High Court;

"liability" in relation to a person, means any liability in relation to tax to which the person is or may be, or may have been, subject, or the amount of such liability;

"tax" means any tax, duty, levy or charge under the care and management of the Revenue Commissioners.

(2)   Subject to this section, an authorised officer may serve on a person a notice in writing, requiring the person, within such period as may

be specified in the notice, not being less than 21 days from the date of the service of the notice, to do either or both of the following, namely —

(a) to deliver to, or to make available for inspection by, the authorised officer such books, records or other documents as are in the person's possession, power or procurement and as contain, or may (in the authorised officer's opinion formed on reasonable grounds) contain, information relevant to a liability in relation to the person,

(b) to furnish to the authorised officer, in writing or otherwise, such information, explanations and particulars as the authorised officer may reasonably require, being information, explanations and particulars that are relevant to any such liability, and which are specified in the notice.

(3) A notice shall not be served on a person under subsection (2) unless the person has first been given a reasonable opportunity to deliver, or as the case may be, to make available to the authorised officer concerned the books, records or other documents in question, or to furnish the information, explanations and particulars in question.

[(4) Nothing in this section shall be construed as requiring any person to disclose to an authorised officer —

(a) information with respect to which a claim to legal professional privilege could be maintained in legal proceedings,

(b) information of a confidential medical nature, or

(c) professional advice of a confidential nature given to a client (other than advice given as part of a dishonet, fraudulent or criminal purpose).][1]

(5) Where, in compliance with the requirements of a notice served on a person under subsection (2), the person makes available for inspection by an authorised officer, books, records or other documents, the person shall afford the authorised officer reasonable assistance, including information, explanations and particulars, in relation to the use of all the electronic or other automatic means, if any, by which the books, records or other documents, in so far as they are in a non-legible form, are capable of being reproduced in a legible form, and any data equipment or any associated apparatus or material.

(6) Where, under subsection (2), a person makes books, records or other documents available for inspection by the authorised officer, the authorised officer may make extracts from or copies of all or any part of the books, records or other documents.

(7) A person who refuses or fails to comply with a notice served on the person under subsection (2) or fails to afford the assistance referred to in subsection (5) shall be liable to a penalty of **[€4,000][2]**.

Footnotes

1   As substituted by s.92(b), F(No. 2)A, 2008, with effect from 24th December, 2008.

2   Substituted for "€1,900" by s.98(1), and by para. 2(p) of Sch.5, of the F(No.2)A, 2008, and comes into effect after 24th December, 2008.

Section 901

Application to High Court: production of books, information, etc.

901. (1) An authorised officer may make an application to a judge for an order requiring a person, to do either or both of the following, namely—

(a) to deliver to the authorised officer, or to make available for inspection by the authorised officer, such books, records or other documents as are in the person's power, possession or procurement and as contain, or may (in the authorised officer's opinion formed on reasonable grounds) contain, information relevant to a liability in relation to the person,

(b) to furnish to the authorised officer such information, explanations and particulars as the authorised officer may reasonably require, being information, explanations and particulars that are relevant to any such liability,

and which are specified in the application.

(2) Where the judge, to whom an application is made under subsection (1), is satisfied that there are reasonable grounds for the application being made, that judge may, subject to such conditions as he or she may consider proper and specify in the order, make an order requiring the person to whom the application relates—

(a) to deliver to the authorised officer, or to make available for inspection by the authorised officer, such books, records or other documents, and

(b) to furnish to the authorised officer such information, explanations and particulars,

as may be specified in the order.

[(3) Nothing in this section shall be construed as requiring any person to disclose to an authorised officer—

(a) information with respect to which a claim to legal professional privilege could be maintained in legal proceedings,

(b) information of a confidential medical nature, or

(c) professional advice of a confidential nature given to a client (other than advice given as part of a dishonest, fraudulent or criminal purpose).][1]

(4) Where in compliance with an order made under subsection (2), a person makes available for inspection by an authorised officer,

books, records or other documents, the person shall afford the authorised officer reasonable assistance, including information, explanations and particulars, in relation to the use of all the electronic or other automatic means, if any, by which the books, records or other documents, in so far as they are in a non-legible form, are capable of being reproduced in a legible form, and any data equipment or any associated apparatus or material.

(5) Where in compliance with an order made under subsection (2), a person makes books, records or other documents available for inspection by the authorised officer, the authorised officer may make extracts from or copies of all or any part of the books, records or other documents.

Footnote

1   As substituted by s.92(c), F(No.2)A, 2008, with effect from 24th December, 2008.

Section 902

Information to be furnished by third party: request of an authorised officer.

902. (1) In this section and in section 902A –

"authorised officer" means an officer of the Revenue Commissioners authorised by them in writing to exercise the powers conferred by this section, or as the case may be, section 902A;

"books, records or other documents" and "liability", in relation to a person, have, respectively, the meaning assigned to them by section 900(1).

(2) Notwithstanding any obligation as to secrecy or other restriction upon disclosure of information imposed by or under statute or otherwise, and subject to this section, an authorised officer may for the purpose of enquiring into a liability in relation to a person (in this section referred to as "the taxpayer") serve on any other person (not being a financial institution within the meaning of section 906A) a notice in writing requiring that other person, within such period as may be specified in the notice, not being less than 30 days from the date of the service of the notice, to do either or both of the following, namely –

(a) to deliver to, or make available for inspection by, the authorised officer, such books, records or other documents as are in the other person's power, possession or procurement and as contain, or may (in the authorised officer's opinion formed on reasonable grounds) contain, information relevant to a liability in relation to the taxpayer,

(b) to furnish to the authorised officer, in writing or otherwise, such information, explanations and particulars as the authorised officer may reasonably require, being information, explanations and particulars that are relevant to any such liability,

and which are specified in the notice.

(3)   A notice shall not be served on a person under subsection (2) unless the authorised officer concerned has reasonable grounds to believe that the person is likely to have information relevant to the establishment of a liability in relation to the taxpayer.

(4)   The persons who may be treated as a taxpayer for the purposes of this section include a company which has been dissolved and an individual who has died.

(5)   A notice under subsection (2) shall name the taxpayer in relation to whose liability the authorised officer is enquiring.

(6)   Where an authorised officer serves a notice under subsection (2), a copy of such notice shall be given by the authorised officer to the taxpayer concerned.

(7)   Where, under subsection (2), a person has delivered any books, records or other documents and those books, records or other documents are retained by the authorised officer, the person shall, at all reasonable times and subject to such reasonable conditions as may be determined by the authorised officer, be entitled to inspect those books, records or other documents and to obtain copies of them.

(8)   Where, under subsection (2), a person makes books, records or other documents available for inspection by the authorised officer, the authorised officer may make extracts from or copies of all or any part of the books, records or other documents.

[(9)   Nothing in this section shall be construed as requiring any person to disclose to an authorised officer −

  (a)   information with respect to which a claim to legal professional privilege could be maintained in legal proceedings.

  (b)   information of a confidential medical nature, or

  (c)   professional advice of a confidential nature given to a client (other than advice given as part of a dishonest, fraudulent or criminal purpose).][1]

(10) Where, in compliance with the requirements of a notice under subsection (2), a person makes available for inspection by an authorised officer, books, records or other documents, the person shall afford the authorised officer reasonable assistance, including information, explanations and particulars, in relation to the use of all the electronic or other automatic means, if any, by which the books, records or other documents, in so far as they are in non-legible form, are capable of being reproduced in a legible form and any data equipment or any associated apparatus or material.

(11) A person who fails or refuses to comply with a notice served on the person under subsection (2) or to afford the assistance referred to in subsection (10) shall be liable to a penalty of **[€4,000]**[2], but nothing in section 1078 shall be construed as applying to such failure or refusal.

Footnotes

1   As substituted by s.92(d), F(No. 2)A, 2008, with effect from 24th December, 2008.

2   Substituted for "€1,900" by s.98(1), and by para. 2(q) of Sch. 5, of the F(No. 2)A, 2008, and has effect from 24th December, 2008.

Section 902A

Application to High Court: information from third party.

902A.(1)   In this section –

"the Acts" has the meaning assigned to it by section 1078(1),[1]

"judge" means a judge of the High Court;

"a taxpayer" means any person including a person whose identity is not known to the authorised officer, and a group or class of persons whose individual identities are not so known.

(2)   An authorised officer may make an application to a judge for an order requiring a person (other than a financial institution within the meaning of section 906A) to do either or both of the following, namely –

(a)   to deliver to the authorised officer, or to make available for inspection by the authorised officer, such books, records or other documents as are in the person's power, possession or procurement and as contain, or may (in the authorised officer's opinion formed on reasonable grounds) contain, information relevant to a liability in relation to a taxpayer,

(b)   to furnish to the authorised officer such information, explanations and particulars as the authorised officer may reasonably require, being information, explanations and particulars that are relevant to any such liability,

and which are specified in the application.

(3)   An authorised officer shall not make an application under subsection (2) without the consent in writing of a Revenue Commissioner, and without being satisfied –

(a)   that there are reasonable grounds for suspecting that the taxpayer, or, where the taxpayer is a group or class of persons, all or any one of those persons, may have failed or may fail to comply with any provision of the Acts,

(b)   that any such failure is likely to have led or to lead to serious prejudice to the proper assessment or collection of tax (having regard to the amount of a liability in relation to the taxpayer, or where the taxpayer is a group or class of persons, the amount of a liability in relation to all or any one of those persons, that arises or might arise from such failure), and

(c)   that the information –

(i)   which is likely to be contained in the books, records or other documents to which the application relates, or

(ii)   which is likely to arise from the information, explanations and particulars to which the application relates,

is relevant to the proper assessment or collection of tax.

(4)   Where the judge, to whom an application is made under subsection (2), is satisfied that there are reasonable grounds for the application being made, that judge may, subject to such conditions as he or she may consider proper and specify in the order, make an order requiring the person to whom the application relates —

(a)   to deliver to the authorised officer, or to make available for inspection by the authorised officer, such books, records or other documents, and

(b)   to furnish to the authorised officer such information, explanations and particulars,

as may be specified in the order.

(5)   The persons who may be treated as a taxpayer for the purposes of this section include a company which has been dissolved and an individual who has died.

[(6)   Nothing in this section shall be construed as requiring any person to disclose to an authorised officer —

(a)   information with respect to which a claim to legal professional privilege could be maintained in legal proceedings,

(b)   information of a confidential medical nature, or

(c)   professional advice of a confidential nature given to a client (other than advice given as part of a dishonest, fraudulent or criminal purpose).][2]

(6A) Where in compliance with an order made under subsection (4), a person makes available for inspection by an authorised officer, books, records or other documents, the person shall afford the authorised officer reasonable assistance, including information, explanations and particulars, in relation to the use of all the electronic or other automatic means, if any, by which the books, records or other documents, in so far as they are in a non-legible form, are capable of being reproduced in a legible form, and any data equipment or any associated apparatus or material.

(6B) Where in compliance with an order made under subsection (4), a person makes books, records or other documents available for inspection by the authorised officer, the authorised officer may make extracts from or copies of all or any part of the books, records or other documents.

(7) Every hearing of an application for an order under this section and of any appeal in connection with that application shall be held in camera.

Footnotes

1 S.1078(1) includes "the Capital Acquisitions Tax Consolidation Act 2003, and the enactments amending or extending that Act,".

2 As substituted by s.92(e), F(No. 2)A, 2008, with effect from 24th December, 2008.

Section 905

Inspection of documents and records.

905. (1) In this section—

"authorised officer" means an officer of the Revenue Commissioners authorised by them in writing to exercise the powers conferred by this section;

"property" means any asset relating to a tax liability;

"records" means any document or any other written or printed material in any form, and includes any information stored, maintained or preserved by means of any mechanical or electronic device, whether or not stored, maintained or preserved in a legible form—

(i) which relates to a business carried on by a person, or

(ii) which a person is obliged by any provision relating to tax to keep, retain, issue or produce for inspection or which may be inspected under any provision relating to tax;

"tax" means any tax, duty, levy or charge under the care and management of the Revenue Commissioners;

"tax liability" means any existing liability to tax or further liability to tax which may be established by an authorised officer following the exercise or performance of his or her powers or duties under this section.

(2) (a) An authorised officer may at all reasonable times enter any premises or place where the authorised officer has reason to believe that—

(i) any trade, profession or other activity, the profits or gains of which are chargeable to tax, is or has been carried on,

(ii) anything is or has been done in connection with any trade, profession or other activity the profits or gains of which are chargeable to tax,

(iii) any records relating to—

(I) any trade, profession, other source of profits or gains or chargeable gains,

(II) any tax liability, or

(III) any repayments of tax in regard to any person,

are or may be kept, or

(iv) any property is or has been located,

and the authorised officer may —

(A) require any person who is on those premises or in that place, other than a person who is there to purchase goods or to receive a service, to produce any records or property,

(B) if the authorised officer has reason to believe that any of the records or property which he or she has required to be produced to him or her under this subsection have not been produced, search on those premises or in that place for those records or property,

(C) examine any records or property and take copies of or extracts from any records,

(D) remove any records and retain them for a reasonable time for the purposes of their further examination or for the purposes of any legal proceedings instituted by an officer of the Revenue Commissioners or for the purposes of any criminal proceedings, and

(E) examine property listed in any records.

(b) An authorised officer may in the exercise or performance of his or her powers or duties under this section require any person whom he or she has reason to believe—

(i) is or was carrying on any trade, profession or other activity the profits or gains of which are chargeable to tax,

(ii) is or was liable to any tax, or

(iii) has information relating to any tax liability,

to give the authorised officer all reasonable assistance, including providing information and explanations or furnishing documents and making available for inspection property as required by the authorised officer in relation to any tax liability or any repayment of tax in regard to any person.

[(c) Nothing in this section shall be construed as requiring any person to disclose to an authorised officer—

(i) **information with respect to which a claim to legal professional privilege could be maintained in legal proceedings**

(ii) **information of a confidential medical nature, or**

       (iii) **professional advice of a confidential nature given to a client (other than advice given as part of a dishonest, fraudulent or criminal purpose).]**[5]

(d) ....

[(e) An authorised officer shall not, without the consent of the occupier, enter any premises, or that portion of any premises, which is occupied wholly and exclusively as a private residence, except on production by the officer of a warrant issued under subsection (2A).][2]

[(f) ....][3]

(2A)(a) In this subsection "the Acts" has the meaning assigned to it by section 1078(1).[1]

(b) Without prejudice to any power conferred by subsection (2), if a Judge of the District Court is satisfied by information on oath that there are reasonable grounds for suspecting—

    (i) that a person may have failed or may fail to comply with any provision of the Acts,

    (ii) that any such failure is likely to have led or to lead to serious prejudice to the proper assessment or collection of tax (having regard to the amount of any tax liability that arises or might arise from such failure),

    and

    (iii) that records, which are material to the proper assessment or collection of tax are likely to be kept or concealed at any premises or place,

the Judge may issue a search warrant.

(c) A search warrant issued under this subsection shall be expressed and shall operate to authorise an authorised officer accompanied by such other named officers of the Revenue Commissioners and such other named persons as the authorised officer considers necessary, at any time or times within one month of the date of issue of the warrant, to enter (if need be by force) the premises or other place named or specified in the warrant, to search such premises or other place, to examine anything found there, to inspect any records found there and, if there are reasonable grounds for suspecting that any records found there are material to the proper assessment or collection of tax, or that the records may be required for the purpose of any legal proceedings instituted by an officer of the Revenue Commissioners [......][4] remove such records and retain them for so long as they are reasonably required for the purpose aforesaid.

(3) A person who does not comply with any requirement of an authorised officer in the exercise or performance of the authorised

officer's powers or duties under this section shall be liable to a penalty of **[€4,000].**[6]

(4) An authorised officer when exercising or performing his or her powers or duties under this section shall on request show his or her authorisation for the purposes of this section.

Footnotes

1　S.1078(1) includes "the Capital Acquisitions Tax Consolidation Act 2003, and the enactments amending or extending that Act,".

2　As substituted by s.124(a)(i), FA 2007, with effect from 2nd April, 2007.

3　Deleted by s.124(a)(ii), FA 2007, with effect from 2nd April, 2007.

4　The words "or for the purpose of any criminal proceedings" deleted by s.124(b), FA 2007, with effect from 2nd April, 2007.

5　As substituted by s.92(f), F(No. 2)A, 2008, with effect from 24th December, 2008.

6　Substituted for "€1,265" by s.98(1), and by para. 2(t) of Sch. 5, of the F(No. 2)A, 2008, and comes into effort after 24th December, 2008.

Section 906

Authorised officers and Garda Síochána.

906. Where an authorised officer (within the meaning of section 903, 904 or 905, as the case may be) in accordance with section 903, 904 or 905 enters any premises or place, the authorised officer may be accompanied by a member or members of the Garda Síochána, and any such member may arrest without warrant any person who obstructs or interferes with the authorised officer in the exercise or performance of his or her powers or duties under any of those sections.

Section 906A

Information to be furnished by financial institutions.

906A.(1) In this section and in sections 907 and 908 —

"the Acts" has the meaning assigned to it by section 1078(1)[1];

"authorised officer" means an officer of the Revenue Commissioners authorised by them in writing to exercise the powers conferred by this section, or, as the case may be, section 907 or 908;

"books, records or other documents" includes —

(a) any records used in the business of a financial institution, or used in the transfer department of a financial institution acting as registrar of securities, whether —

　　(i) comprised in bound volume, loose-leaf binders or other loose-leaf filing system, loose-leaf ledger sheets, pages, folios or cards, or

　　(ii) kept on microfilm, magnetic tape or in any non-legible form (by the use of electronics or otherwise) which is capable of being reproduced in a legible form,

(b)   every electronic or other automatic means, if any, by which any such thing in non-legible form is so capable of being reproduced,

(c)   documents in manuscript, documents which are typed, printed, stencilled or created by any other mechanical or partly mechanical process in use from time to time and documents which are produced by any photographic or photostatic process,

and

(d)   correspondence and records of other communications between a financial institution and its customers;

"connected person" has the same meaning as in section 10; but an individual (other than in the capacity as a trustee of a settlement) shall be connected with another individual only if that other individual is the spouse of or a minor child of the first-mentioned individual;

"deposit" and "interest" have, respectively, the meaning assigned to them by section 256(1);

"financial institution" means−

[(a)   **a person who holds or has held a licence under section 9 of the Central Bank Act 1971, or a person who holds or has held a licence or other similar authorisation under the law of any other Member State of the European Communities which corresponds to a licence granted under that section,]²**

(b)   a person referred to in section 7(4) of the Central Bank Act, 1971, or

(c)   a credit institution (within the meaning of the European Communities (Licensing and Supervision of Credit Institutions) Regulations, 1992 (S.I. No. 395 of 1992)) which has been authorised by the Central Bank of Ireland to carry on business of a credit institution in accordance with the provisions of the supervisory enactments (within the meaning of those Regulations);

"liability" in relation to a person means any liability in relation to tax to which the person is or may be, or may have been, subject, or the amount of such liability;

"tax" means any tax, duty, levy or charge under the care and management of the Revenue Commissioners.

(2)   Notwithstanding any obligation as to secrecy or other restriction upon disclosure of information imposed by or under statute or otherwise, and subject to this section, an authorised officer may, for the purpose of enquiring into a liability in relation to a person (in this section referred to as the "taxpayer"), serve on a financial institution a notice in writing requiring the financial institution,

within such period as may be specified in the notice, not being less than 30 days from the date of the service of the notice, to do either or both of the following, namely –

(a)   to make available for inspection by the authorised officer such books, records or other documents as are in the financial institution's power, possession or procurement and as contain, or may (in the authorised officer's opinion formed on reasonable grounds) contain, information relevant to a liability in relation to the taxpayer,

(b)   to furnish to the authorised officer, in writing or otherwise, such information, explanations and particulars as the authorised officer may reasonably require, being information, explanations and particulars that are relevant to any such liability,

and which are specified in the notice.

(3)   Where, in compliance with the requirements of a notice under subsection (2), a financial institution makes available for inspection by an authorised officer, books, records or other documents, it shall afford the authorised officer reasonable assistance, including information, explanations and particulars, in relation to the use of all the electronic or other automatic means, if any, by which the books, records or other documents, in so far as they are in a non-legible form, are capable of being reproduced in a legible form and any data equipment or any associated apparatus or material.

(4)   An authorised officer shall not serve a notice on a financial institution under subsection (2) without the consent in writing of a Revenue Commissioner and without having reasonable grounds to believe that the financial institution is likely to have information relevant to a liability in relation to the taxpayer.

(5)   Without prejudice to the generality of subsection (2), the books, records or other documents which a financial institution may be required by notice under that subsection to deliver or to make available and the information, explanations and particulars which it may likewise be required to furnish, may include books, records or other documents and information, explanations and particulars relating to a person who is connected with the taxpayer.

(6)   The persons who may be treated as a taxpayer for the purposes of this section include a company which has been dissolved and an individual who has died.

(7)   A notice served under subsection (2) shall name the taxpayer in relation to whose liability the authorised officer is enquiring.

(8)   Where an authorised officer serves a notice under subsection (2), a copy of such notice shall be given by the authorised officer to the taxpayer concerned.

(9) Where, in compliance with a notice served under subsection (2), a financial institution makes books, records or other documents available for inspection by an authorised officer, the authorised officer may make extracts from or copies of all or any part of the books, records or other documents.

(10) A financial institution which fails or refuses to comply with a notice issued under subsection (2) or which fails or refuses to afford reasonable assistance to an authorised officer as required under subsection (3), shall be liable to a penalty of €19,045 and, if the failure or refusal to comply with such notice continues after the expiry of the period specified in the notice served under subsection (2), a further penalty of €2,535 for each day on which the failure or refusal continues.

Footnotes

1   S.1078(1) includes "the Capital Acquisitions Tax Consolidation Act 2003, and the enactments amending or extending that Act,".

2   As substituted by s.92(g), F(No. 2)A, 2008, with effect from 24th December, 2008.

Section 907

Application to Appeal Commissioners: information from financial institutions.

907. (1) In this section "a taxpayer" means any person including—

   (a) a person whose identity is not known to the authorised officer, and a group or class of persons whose individual identities are not so known, and

   (b) a person by or in respect of whom a declaration has been made under section 263(1) declaring that the person is beneficially entitled to all or part of the interest in relation to a deposit.

   (2) An authorised officer may, subject to this section, make an application to the Appeal Commissioners for their consent, under subsection (5), to the service by him or her of a notice on a financial institution requiring the financial institution to do either or both of the following, namely—

   (a) to make available for inspection by the authorised officer, such books, records or other documents as are in the financial institution's power, possession or procurement as contain, or may (in the authorised officer's opinion formed on reasonable grounds) contain, information relevant to a liability in relation to a taxpayer,

   (b) to furnish to the authorised officer such information, explanations and particulars as the authorised officer may reasonably require, being information, explanations and particulars that are relevant to any such liability,

   and which are specified in the application.

(3) An authorised officer shall not make an application under subsection (2) without the consent in writing of a Revenue Commissioner, and without being satisfied –

    (a) that there are reasonable grounds for suspecting that the taxpayer, or where the taxpayer is a group or class of persons, all or any one of those persons, may have failed or may fail to comply with any provision of the Acts,

    (b) that any such failure is likely to have led or to lead to serious prejudice to the proper assessment or collection of tax (having regard to the amount of a liability in relation to the taxpayer, or where the taxpayer is a group or class of persons, the amount of a liability in relation to all or any one of those persons, that arises or might arise from such failure), and

    (c) that the information –

        (i) which is likely to be contained in the books, records or other documents to which the application relates, or

        (ii) which is likely to arise from the information, explanations and particulars to which the application relates,

    is relevant to the proper assessment or collection of tax.

(4) Without prejudice to the generality of subsection (2), the authorised officer may make an application under that subsection to the Appeal Commissioners for their consent, under subsection (5), to the service by him or her of a notice on a financial institution in respect of the matters referred to in paragraphs (a) and (b) of subsection (2) in so far as they relate to a person who is connected with the taxpayer.

(5) Where the Appeal Commissioners determine that in all the circumstances there are reasonable grounds for the application being made, they may give their consent to the service by the authorised officer concerned of a notice on the financial institution, requiring the financial institution –

    (a) to make available for inspection by the authorised officer, such books, records or other documents, and

    (b) to furnish to the authorised officer such information, explanations and particulars,

    of the kind referred to in subsection (2) as may, with the Appeal Commissioners' consent, be specified in the notice.

(6) The persons who may be treated as a taxpayer for the purposes of this section include a company which has been dissolved and an individual who has died.

(7) Where the Appeal Commissioners have given their consent in accordance with this section, the authorised officer shall, as soon as practicable, but not later than 14 days from the time that such consent was given, serve a notice on the financial institution concerned and stating that –

(a) such consent has been given,

and

(b) the financial institution should, within a period of 30 days from the date of the service of the notice, comply with the requirements specified in the notice.

(7A) Where in compliance with the requirements of a notice served under subsection (7), a financial institution makes available for inspection by an authorised officer, books, records or other documents, the financial institution shall afford the authorised officer reasonable assistance, including information, explanations and particulars, in relation to the use of all the electronic or other automatic means, if any, by which the books, records or other documents, in so far as they are in a non-legible form, are capable of being reproduced in a legible form, and any data equipment or any associated apparatus or material.

(7B) Where in compliance with the requirements of a notice served under subsection (7), a financial institution makes books, records or other documents available for inspection by the authorised officer, the authorised officer may make extracts from or copies of all or any part of the books, records or other documents.

(8) (a) Subject to paragraph (b), an application by an authorised officer under subsection (2) shall, with any necessary modifications, be heard by the Appeal Commissioners as if it were an appeal against an assessment to income tax.

(b) Notwithstanding section 933(4), a determination by the Appeal Commissioners under this section shall be final and conclusive.

(9) A financial institution which fails to comply with a notice served on the financial institution by an authorised officer in accordance with this section shall be liable to a penalty of €19,045 and, if the failure continues after the expiry of the period specified in subsection (7)(b), a further penalty of €2,535 for each day on which the failure so continues.

Section 908

Application to High Court seeking order requiring information: financial institutions.

908. (1) In this section—

"judge" means a judge of the High Court;

"a taxpayer" means any person including—

(a) a person whose identity is not known to the authorised officer, and a group or class of persons whose individual identities are not so known, and

(b)   a person by or in respect of whom a declaration has been made under section 263(1) declaring that the person is beneficially entitled to all or part of the interest in relation to a deposit.

(2)   An authorised officer may, subject to this section, make an application to a judge for an order requiring a financial institution, to do either or both of the following, namely –

(a)   to make available for inspection by the authorised officer, such books, records or other documents as are in the financial institution's power, possession or procurement as contain, or may (in the authorised officer's opinion formed on reasonable grounds) contain information relevant to a liability in relation to a taxpayer,

(b)   to furnish to the authorised officer such information, explanations and particulars as the authorised officer may reasonably require, being information, explanations and particulars that are relevant to any such liability,

and which are specified in the application.

(3)   An authorised officer shall not make application under subsection (2) without the consent in writing of a Revenue Commissioner, and without being satisfied –

(a)   that there are reasonable grounds for suspecting that the taxpayer, or, where the taxpayer is a group or class of persons, all or any one of those persons, may have failed or may fail to comply with any provision of the Acts,

(b)   that any such failure is likely to have led or to lead to serious prejudice to the proper assessment or collection of tax (having regard to the amount of a liability in relation to the taxpayer, or where the taxpayer is a group or class of persons, the amount of a liability in relation to all or any one of them, that arises or might arise from such failure), and

(c)   that the information –

(i)   which is likely to be contained in the books, records or other documents to which the application relates, or

(ii)   which is likely to arise from the information, explanations and particulars to which the application relates,

is relevant to the proper assessment or collection of tax.

(4)   Without prejudice to the generality of subsection (2), the authorised officer may make an application under that subsection to the judge for an order in respect of the matters referred to in paragraphs (a) and (b) of that subsection in so far as they relate to a person who is connected with the taxpayer.

(5)   Where the judge, to whom an application is made under subsection (2), is satisfied that there are reasonable grounds for the application being made, the judge may, subject to such conditions as he or

she may consider proper and specify in the order, make an order requiring the financial institution—

(a) to make available for inspection by the authorised officer, such books, records or other documents, and

(b) to furnish to the authorised officer such information, explanations and particulars,

as may be specified in the order.

(6) The persons who may be treated as a taxpayer for the purposes of this section include a company which has been dissolved and an individual who has died.

(6A) Where in compliance with an order made under subsection (5), a financial institution makes available for inspection by an authorised officer, books, records or other documents, the financial institution shall afford the authorised officer reasonable assistance, including information, explanations and particulars, in relation to the use of all the electronic or other automatic means, if any, by which the books, records or other documents, in so far as they are in a non-legible form, are capable of being reproduced in a legible form, and any data equipment or any associated apparatus or material.

(6B) Where in compliance with an order made under subsection (5), a financial institution makes books, records or other documents available for inspection by the authorised officer, the authorised officer may make extracts from or copies of all or any part of the books, records or other documents.

(7) Every hearing of an application for an order under this section and of any appeal in connection with that application shall be held in camera.

(8) Where a judge makes an order under this section, he or she may also, on the application of the authorised officer concerned, make a further order prohibiting, for such period as the judge may consider proper and specify in the order, any transfer of, or any dealing with, without the consent of the judge, any assets or moneys of the person to whom the order relates that are in the custody of the financial institution at the time the order is made.

(9) (a) Where—

(i) a copy of any affidavit and exhibits grounding an application under subsection (2) or (8) and any order made under subsection (5) or (8) are to be made available to the taxpayer, or the taxpayer's solicitor or to the financial institution or the financial institution's solicitor, as the case may be, and

(ii) the judge is satisfied on the hearing of the application that there are reasonable grounds in the public interest that such copy of an affidavit, exhibits or order, as the case may be, should not include the name or address of the authorised officer,

such copy, or copies or order shall not include the name or address of the authorised officer.

(b) Where, on any application to the judge to vary or discharge an order made under this section, it is desired to cross-examine the deponent of any affidavit filed by or on behalf of the authorised officer and the judge is satisfied that there are reasonable grounds in the public interest to so order, the judge shall order either or both of the following—

(i) that the name and address of the authorised officer shall not be disclosed in court,

and

(ii) that such cross-examination shall only take place in the sight and hearing of the judge and in the hearing only of all other persons present at such cross-examination.

Section 908A

Revenue offence: power to obtain information from financial institutions.

908A.(1) In this section—

"the Acts" means the Waiver of Certain Tax, Interest and Penalties Act, 1993, together with the meaning assigned to it by section 1078(1)[1] and;

"authorised officer" means an officer of the Revenue Commissioners authorised by them in writing to exercise the powers conferred by this section;

"books, records or other documents" includes—

(a) any records used in the business of a financial institution, or used in the transfer department of a financial institution acting as registrar of securities, whether—

(i) comprised in bound volume, loose-leaf binders or other loose-leaf filing system, loose-leaf ledger sheets, pages, folios or cards, or

(ii) kept on microfilm, magnetic tape or in any non-legible form (by the use of electronics or otherwise) which is capable of being reproduced in a legible form, and

(b) documents in manuscript, documents which are typed, printed, stencilled or created by any other mechanical or partly mechanical process in use from time to time and documents which are produced by any photographic or photostatic process;

"judge" means a judge of the Circuit Court or of the District Court;

"financial institution" means—

[(a) **a person who holds or has held a licence under section 9 of the Central Bank Act 1971, or a person who holds or has held a licence or other similar authorisation under the law of any other Member State of the European Communities which corresponds to a licence granted under that section,]**[3]

(b) a person referred to in section 7(4) of the Central Bank Act, 1971, or

(c) a credit institution (within the meaning of the European Communities (Licensing and Supervision of Credit Institutions) Regulations, 1992 (S.I. No. 395 of 1992)) which has been authorised by the Central Bank of Ireland to carry on business of a credit institution in accordance with the provisions of the supervisory enactments (within the meaning of those Regulations);

"liability" in relation to a person means any liability in relation to tax to which the person is or may be, or may have been, subject, or the amount of such liability;

"offence" means an offence falling within any provision of the Acts;

"tax" means any tax, duty, levy or charge under the care and management of the Revenue Commissioners.

[(2) (a) In this subsection "documentation" includes information kept on microfilm, magnetic tape or in any non-legible form (by use of electronics or otherwise) which is capable of being reproduced in a permanent legible form.

(b) If, on application made by an authorised officer, with the consent in writing of a Revenue Commissioner, a judge is satisfied, on information given on oath by the authorised officer, that there are reasonable grounds for suspecting—

(i) that an offence, which would result (or but for its detection would have resulted) in serious prejudice to the proper assessment or collection of tax, is being, has been, or is about to be committed (having regard to the amount of a liability in relation to any person which might be, or might have been, evaded but for the detection of the relevant facts), and

(ii) that there is material in the possession of a financial institution specified in the application which is likely to be of substantial value (whether by itself or together with other material) to the investigation of the relevant facts,

the judge may make an order authorising the authorised officer to inspect and take copies of any entries in the books, records or other documents of the financial institution, and any documentation associated with or relating to an entry in such books, records or other documents, for the purposes of investigation of the relevant facts.][2]

(3) An offence the commission of which, if considered alone, would not be regarded as resulting in serious prejudice to the proper assessment or collection of tax for the purposes of this section may nevertheless be so regarded if there are reasonable grounds for suspecting that the commission of the offence forms part of a course of conduct which is, or but for its detection would be, likely to result in serious prejudice to the proper assessment or collection of tax.

(4) Subject to subsection (5), a copy of any entry in books, records or other documents of a financial institution shall in all legal proceedings be received as prima facie evidence of such an entry, and of the matters, transactions, and accounts therein recorded.

(5) A copy of an entry in the books, records or other documents of a financial institution shall not be received in evidence in legal proceedings unless it is further proved that—

(a) in the case where the copy sought to be received in evidence has been reproduced in a legible form directly by either mechanical or electronic means, or both such means, from a financial institution's books, records or other documents maintained in a non-legible form, it has been so reproduced;

(b) in the case where the copy sought to be received in evidence has been made (either directly or indirectly) from a copy to which paragraph (a) would apply—

(i) the copy sought to be so received has been examined with a copy so reproduced and is a correct copy, and

(ii) the copy so reproduced is a copy to which paragraph (a) would apply if it were sought to have it received in evidence,

and

(c) in any other case, the copy has been examined with the original entry and is correct.

(6) Proof of the matters to which subsection (5) relates shall be given—

(a) in respect of paragraph (a) or (b)(ii) of that subsection, by some person who has been in charge of the reproduction concerned, and

(b) in respect of paragraph (b)(i) of that subsection, by some person who has examined the copy with the reproduction concerned, and

    (c) in respect of paragraph (c) of that subsection, by some person who has examined the copy with the original entry concerned,

and may be given either orally or by an affidavit sworn before any commissioner or person authorised to take affidavits.

Footnotes

1   S.1078(1) includes "the Capital Acquisitions Tax Consolidation Act 2003, and the enactments amending or extending that Act,".

2   As substituted by s.88, FA 2004, with effect from 25th March, 2004.

3   As substituted by s.92(h), F(No. 2)A, 2008, with effect from 24th December, 2008.

Section 908B[1]

Application to High Court seeking order requiring information: associated institutions.

908B. (1) In this section—

"the Acts" has the meaning assigned to it by section 1078(1);[2]

"associated institution", in relation to a financial institution, means a person that—

    (a) is controlled by the financial institution (within the meaning of section 432), and

    (b) is not resident in the State;

"authorised officer" means an officer of the Revenue Commissioners authorised by them in writing to exercise the powers conferred by this section;

"books, records or other documents" includes—

    (a) any records used in the business of an associated institution, or used in the transfer department of an associated institution acting as registrar of securities, whether—

        (i) comprised in bound volume, loose-leaf binders or other loose-leaf filing system, loose-leaf ledger sheets, pages, folios or cards, or

        (ii) kept on microfilm, magnetic tape or in any non-legible form (by the use of electronics or otherwise) which is capable of being reproduced in a legible form,

    (b) every electronic or other automatic means, if any, by which any such thing in non-legible form is so capable of being reproduced,

    (c) documents in manuscript, documents which are typed, printed, stencilled or created by any other mechanical or partly mechanical process in use from time to time and documents which are produced by any photographic or photostatic process, and

    (d)   correspondence and records of other communications between an associated institution and its customers;

"financial institution" means—

[(a)   a person who holds or has held a licence under section 9 of the Central Bank Act 1971, or a person who holds or has held a licence or other similar authorisation under the law of any other Member State of the European Communities which corresponds to a licence granted under that section,][3]

    (b)   a person referred to in section 7(4) of the Central Bank Act 1971, or

    (c)   a credit institution (within the meaning of the European Communities (Licensing and Supervision of Credit Institutions) Regulations 1992 (S.I. No. 395 of 1992)) which has been authorised by the Central Bank and Financial Services Authority of Ireland to carry on business of a credit institution in accordance with the provisions of the supervisory enactments (within the meaning of those Regulations);

"judge" means a judge of the High Court;

"liability" in relation to a person means any liability in relation to tax which the person is or may be, or may have been, subject, or the amount of such liability;

"tax" means any tax, duty, levy or charge under the care and management of the Revenue Commissioners;

"a taxpayer" means any person including a person whose identity is not known to the authorised officer, and a group or class of persons whose individual identities are not so known.

  (2) An authorised officer may, subject to this section, make an application to a judge for an order requiring a financial institution to do either or both of the following, namely—

    (a)   to make available for inspection by the authorised officer, such books, records or other documents as are in the power, possession or procurement of an associated institution, in relation to the financial institution, as contain, or may (in the authorised officer's opinion formed on reasonable grounds) contain information relevant to a liability in relation to a taxpayer, or

    (b)   to furnish to the authorised officer such information, explanations and particulars held by, or available from, the financial institution or an associated institution, in relation to the financial institution, as the authorised officer may reasonably require, being information, explanations or particulars that are relevant to any such liability,

and which are specified in the application.

(3) An authorised officer shall not make an application under subsection (2) without the consent in writing of a Revenue Commissioner, and without being satisfied —

    (a) that there are reasonable grounds for suspecting that the taxpayer, or where the taxpayer is a group or class of persons, all or any one of those persons, may have failed or may fail to comply with any provision of the Acts,

    (b) that any such failure is likely to have led or to lead to serious prejudice to the proper assessment or collection of tax (having regard to the amount of a liability in relation to the taxpayer, or where the taxpayer is a group or class of persons, the amount of a liability, in relation to all or any one of them, that arises or might arise from such failure), and

    (c) that the information —

        (i) which is likely to be contained in the books, records or other documents to which the application relates, or

        (ii) which is likely to arise from the information, explanations and particulars to which the application relates,

    is relevant to the proper assessment or collection of tax.

(4) Where the judge, to whom an application is made under subsection (2), is satisfied that there are reasonable grounds for the application being made, then the judge may, subject to such conditions as he or she may consider proper and specify in the order, make an order requiring the financial institution —

    (a) to make available for inspection by the authorised officer, such books, records or other documents, and

    (b) to furnish to the authorised officer such information, explanations and particulars, as may be specified in the order.

(5) The persons who may be treated as a taxpayer for the purposes of this section include a company which has been dissolved and an individual who has died.

(6) Where in compliance with an order made under subsection (4) a financial institution makes available for inspection by an authorised officer, books, records or other documents, then the financial institution shall afford the authorised officer reasonable assistance, including information, explanations and particulars, in relation to the use of all the electronic or other automatic means, if any, by which the books, records or other documents, in so far as they are in a non-legible form, are capable of being reproduced in a legible form, and any data equipment or any associated apparatus or material.

(7) Where in compliance with an order made under subsection (4) a financial institution makes books, records or other documents available for inspection by the authorised officer, then the authorised

officer may make extracts from or copies of all or any part of the books, records or other documents.

(8) Every hearing of an application for an order under this section and of any appeal in connection with that application shall be held in camera.

Footnotes

1   As inserted by s.87, FA 2004, with effect from 25th March, 2004.

2   S.1078(1) includes "the Capital Acquisitions Tax Consolidation Act 2003, and the enactments amending or extending that Act,"

3   As substituted by by s.92(i), F(No. 2)A, 2008, with effect from 24th December, 2008.

Section 908C[1]

Search warrants.

908C. (1) In this section—

"the Acts" means the Waiver of Certain Tax, Interest and Penalties Act 1993 together with the meaning assigned to it in section 1078(1);[2]

"authorised officer" means an officer of the Revenue Commissioners authorised by them in writing to exercise the powers conferred by this section;

"commission", in relation to an offence, includes an attempt to commit the offence;

"computer" includes any electronic device capable of performing logical or arithmetical operations on data in accordance with a set of instructions;

"computer at the place which is being searched", includes any other computer, whether at that place or at any other place, which is lawfully accessible by means of that computer;

"information in non-legible form" means information which is kept (by electronic means or otherwise) on microfilm, microfiche, magnetic tape or disk or in any other non-legible form;

"material" means any books, documents, records or other things (including a computer);

"offence" means an offence under the Acts;

"place" includes any building (or part of a building), dwelling, vehicle, vessel, aircraft or hovercraft and any other place whatsoever;

"record" includes any information in non-legible form which is capable of being reproduced in a permanently legible form.

(2) If a judge of the District Court is satisfied by information given on oath by an authorised officer that there are reasonable grounds for suspecting—

(a)   that an offence is being, has been or is about to be committed, and

(b) (i)   that material which is likely to be of value (whether by itself or together with other information) to the investigation of the offence, or

      (ii)   that evidence of, or relating to the commission of, the offence, is to be found in any place,

the judge may issue a warrant for the search of that place, and of any thing and any persons, found there.

(3) A warrant issued under this section shall be expressed and shall operate to authorise the authorised officer, accompanied by such other named officers of the Revenue Commissioners and such other named persons as the authorised officer considers necessary —

(a)   to enter, at any time or times within one month from the date of issuing of the warrant (if necessary by the use of reasonable force), the place named in the warrant,

(b)   to search, or cause to be searched, that place and any thing and any persons, found there, but no person shall be searched except by a person of the same sex unless express or implied consent is given,

(c)   to require any person found there —

      (i)   to give his or her name, home address and occupation to the authorised officer, and

      (ii)   to produce to the authorised officer any material which is in the custody or possession of that person,

(d)   to examine, seize and retain (or cause to be examined, seized and retained) any material found there, or in the possession of a person present there at the time of the search, which the authorised officer reasonably believes —

      (i)   is likely to be of value (whether by itself or together with other information) to the investigation of the offence, or

      (ii)   to be evidence of, or relating to the commission of, the offence, and

(e)   to take any other steps which may appear to the authorised officer to be necessary for preserving any such material and preventing interference with it.

(4) The authority conferred by subsection (3)(d) to seize and retain (or to cause to be seized and retained) any material includes —

(a)   in the case of books, documents or records, authority to make and retain a copy of the books, documents or records, and

    (b) where necessary, authority to seize and, for as long as necessary, retain, any computer or other storage medium in which records are kept and to copy such records.

(5) An authorised officer acting under the authority of a warrant issued under this section may –

    (a) operate any computer at the place which is being searched or cause any such computer to be operated by a person accompanying the authorised officer, and

    (b) require any person at that place who appears to the authorised officer to be in a position to facilitate access to the information held in any such computer or which can be accessed by the use of that computer –

        (i) to give to the authorised officer any password necessary to operate it,

        (ii) otherwise to enable the authorised officer to examine the information accessible by the computer in a form in which the information is visible and legible, or

        (iii) to produce the information in a form in which it can be removed and in which it is, or can be made, visible and legible.

(6) A person who –

    (a) obstructs or attempts to obstruct the exercise of a right of entry and search conferred by virtue of a warrant issued under this section,

    (b) obstructs the exercise of a right so conferred to examine, seize and retain material,

    (c) fails to comply with a requirement under subsection (3)(c) or gives to the authorised officer a name, address or occupation that is false or misleading, or

    (d) fails to comply with a requirement under subsection (5)(b),

is guilty of an offence and is liable on summary conviction to a fine not exceeding **[€5,000]**[3] or imprisonment for a term not exceeding 6 months or to both the fine and the imprisonment.

(7) Where an authorised officer enters, or attempts to enter, any place in the execution of a warrant issued under subsection (2), the authorised officer may be accompanied by a member or members of the Garda Síochána, and any such member may arrest without warrant any person who is committing an offence under subsection (6) or whom the member suspects, with reasonable cause, of having done so.

(8) Any material which is seized under subsection (3) which is required for the purposes of any legal proceedings by an officer of the Revenue Commissioners or for the purpose of any criminal

proceedings, may be retained for so long as it is reasonably required for the purposes aforesaid.

Footnotes

1   This section was inserted by s.124(c), FA 2007, with effect from 2nd April, 2007.

2   S.1078(1) includes "the Capital Acquistions Tax Consolidation Act 2003, and the enactments amending or extending that Act,".

3   As substituted for "€3,000" by s.138(1)(b), FA 2008, as respects an offence committed on a day after 13th March, 2008.

Section 908D[1]

Order to produce evidential material.

908D. (1)   In this section—

"the Acts" means the Waiver of Certain Tax, Interest and Penalties Act 1993 together with the meaning assigned to it in section 1078(1);[2]

"authorised officer" means an officer of the Revenue Commissioners authorised by them in writing to exercise the powers conferred by this section;

"commission", in relation to an offence, includes an attempt to commit the offence;

"computer" includes any electronic device capable of performing logical or arithmetical operations on data in accordance with a set of instructions;

"information in non-legible form" means information which is kept (by electronic means or otherwise) on microfilm, microfiche, magnetic tape or disk or in any other non-legible form;

"material" means any books, documents, records or other things (including a computer);

"offence" means an offence under the Acts;

"record" includes any information in non-legible form which is capable of being reproduced in a permanently legible form.

(2)   If a judge of the District Court is satisfied by information given on oath by an authorised officer that there are reasonable grounds for suspecting—

(a)   that an offence is being, has been or is about to be committed, and

(b)   that material—

(i)   which is likely to be of value (whether by itself or together with other information) to the investigation of the offence, or

      (ii)   which constitutes evidence of, or relating to the commission of, the offence,

is in the possession or control of a person specified in the application,

the judge may order that the person shall—

(I)   produce the material to the authorised officer for the authorised officer to take away, or

(II) give the authorised officer access to it,

either immediately or within such period as the order may specify.

(3)   Where the material consists of or includes records contained in a computer, the order shall have effect as an order to produce the records, or to give access to them, in a form in which they are visible and legible and in which they can be taken away.

(4)   An order under this section—

    (a)   in so far as it may empower an authorised officer to take away books, documents or records, or to be given access to them, shall also have effect as an order empowering the authorised officer to take away a copy of the books, documents or, as the case may be, records (and for that purpose the authorised officer may, if necessary, make a copy of them),

    (b)   shall not confer any right to production of, or access to, any document subject to legal privilege, and

    (c)   shall have effect notwithstanding any other obligation as to secrecy or other restriction on disclosure of information imposed by statute or otherwise.

(5)   Any material taken away by an authorised officer under this section may be retained by the authorised officer for use as evidence in any criminal proceedings.

(6)   (a)   Information contained in books, documents or records which were produced to an authorised officer, or to which an authorised officer was given access, in accordance with an order under this section, shall be admissible in any criminal proceedings as evidence of any fact therein of which direct oral evidence would be admissible unless the information—

        (i)   is privileged from disclosure in such proceedings,

        (ii) was supplied by a person who would not be compellable to give evidence at the instance of the prosecution,

        (iii) was compiled for the purposes of, or in contemplation of, any—

           (I)   criminal investigation,

           (II) investigation or inquiry carried out pursuant to or under any enactment,

(III) civil or criminal proceedings, or

(IV) proceedings of a disciplinary nature, or unless the requirements of the provisions mentioned in paragraph (b) are not complied with.

(b) References in sections 7 (notice of documentary evidence to be served on accused), 8 (admission and weight of documentary evidence) and 9 (admissibility of evidence as to credibility of supplier of information) of the Criminal Evidence Act 1992 to a document or information contained in it shall be construed as including references to books, documents and records mentioned in paragraph (a) and the information contained in them, and those provisions shall have effect accordingly with any necessary modifications.

(7) A judge of the District Court may, on the application of an authorised officer, or of any person to whom an order under this section relates, vary or discharge the order.

(8) A person who without reasonable excuse fails or refuses to comply with an order under this section is guilty of an offence and liable on summary conviction to a fine not exceeding **[€5,000]**[3] or imprisonment for a term not exceeding 6 months or to both the fine and the imprisonment.

Footnotes

1   This section was inserted by s.124(c), FA 2007, with effect from 2nd April, 2007.

2   S.1078(1) includes "the Capital Acquistions Tax Consolidation Act 2003, and the enactments amending or extending that Act,".

3   As substituted for "€3,000" by s.138(1)(c), FA 2008, as respects an offence committed on a day after 13th March, 2008.

Section 910[1]

Power to obtain information from a Minister of the Government or public body.

910. (1) For the purposes of the assessment, charge, collection and recovery of any tax or duty placed under their care and management, the Revenue Commissioners may, by notice in writing, request any Minister of the Government or any body established by or under statute to provide them with such information in the possession of that Minister or body in relation to payments for any purposes made by that Minister or by that body, whether on that Minister's or that body's own behalf or on behalf of any other person, to such persons or classes of persons as the Revenue Commissioners may specify in the notice and a Minister of the Government or body of whom or of which such a request is made shall provide such information as may be so specified.

(2) The Revenue Commissioners may nominate any of their officers to perform any acts and discharge any functions authorised

by this section to be performed or discharged by the Revenue Commissioners.

[(3) Where information is to be provided to the Revenue Commissioners in accordance with subsection (1) it shall be provided, where the Revenue Commissioners so require, in an electronic format approved by them.]¹

Footnote

1   As inserted by s.123(c), FA 2007, with effect from 2nd April, 2007.

Section 912

Computer documents and records.

912. (1) In this section—

"the Acts" means—

(a)   the Customs Acts,

(b)   the statutes relating to the duties of excise and to the management of those duties,

(c)   the Tax Acts,

(d)   the Capital Gains Tax Acts,

(e)   the Value-Added Tax Act, 1972, and the enactments amending or extending that Act,

(f)   the [Capital Acquisitions Tax Consolidation Act 2003,]¹ and the enactments amending or extending that Act, and

(g)   Part VI of the Finance Act, 1983,

and any instruments made thereunder;

"data" means information in a form in which it can be processed;

"data equipment" means any electronic, photographic, magnetic, optical or other equipment for processing data;

"processing" means performing automatically logical or arithmetical operations on data, or the storing, maintenance, transmission, reproduction or communication of data;

"records" means documents which a person is obliged by any provision of the Acts to keep, issue or produce for inspection, and any other written or printed material;

"software" means any sequence of instructions used in conjunction with data equipment for the purpose of processing data or controlling the operation of the data equipment.

(2) Any provision under the Acts which—

(a)   requires a person to keep, retain, issue or produce any records or cause any records to be kept, retained, issued or produced, or

(b) permits an officer of the Revenue Commissioners –

(i) to inspect any records,

(ii) to enter premises and search for any records, or

(iii) to take extracts from or copies of or remove any records,

shall, where the records are processed by data equipment, apply to the data equipment together with any associated software, data, apparatus or material as it applies to the records.

(3) An officer of the Revenue Commissioners may in the exercise or performance of his or her powers or duties require –

(a) the person by or on whose behalf the data equipment is or has been used, or

(b) any person having charge of, or otherwise concerned with the operation of, the data equipment or any associated apparatus or material,

to afford him or her all reasonable assistance in relation to the exercise or performance of those powers or duties.

Footnote

1   Substituted for "Capital Acquisitions Tax Act, 1976" by s.119, CATCA, with effect from 21st February, 2003.

Section 912A[1]

Information for tax authorities in other territories.

912A.(1)   In this section -

"foreign tax" means a tax chargeable under the laws of a territory in relation to which arrangements (in this section referred to as "the arrangements") having the force of law by virtue of section 826 [or section 106 of the Capital Acqusitions Tax Consolidation Act 2003][2] apply;

"liability to foreign tax", in relation to a person, means any liability in relation to foreign tax to which the person is or may be, or may have been, subject, or the amount of any such liability.

(2) For the purposes of complying with provisions with respect to the exchange of information contained in the arrangements, sections 900, 901, 902, 902A, 906A, 907 and 908 shall, subject to subsection (3), have effect -

(a) as if references in those sections to tax included references to foreign tax, and

(b) as if references in those sections to liability, in relation to a person, included references to liability to foreign tax, in relation to a person.

(3) Where sections 902A, 907 and 908 have effect by virtue only of this section, they shall have effect as if -

    (a) there were substituted "a taxpayer means a person;" for the definition of "a taxpayer" in subsection (1) of each of those sections, and

    (b) the references in those sections to -

        (i) tax, were references to foreign tax, and

        (ii) any provision of the Acts, were references to any provision of the law of a territory in accordance with which foreign tax is charged or collected.

Footnotes

1   As inserted by s.38(b), FA 2003, which applies as on and from 1st January, 2003.

2   As inserted by s.82, FA 2004, with effect from 25th March, 2004.

CHAPTER 6

Electronic transmission of returns of income, profits, etc., and of other Revenue returns

Section 917D

Interpretation (Chapter 6).

917D. (1) In this Chapter—

"the Acts" means—

    (a) the statutes relating to the duties of excise and to the management of those duties,

    (b) the Tax Acts,

    (c) the Capital Gains Tax Acts,

    (d) the Value-Added Tax Act, 1972, and the enactments amending or extending that Act,

    (e) the [Capital Acquisitions Tax Consolidation Act 2003,][1] and the enactments amending or extending that Act, and

    (f) the [Stamp Duties Consolidation Act 1999,][3] and the enactments amending or extending that Act,

and any instruments made under any of the statutes and enactments referred to in paragraphs (a) to (f);

"approved person" shall be construed in accordance with section 917G;

"approved transmission" shall be construed in accordance with section 917H;

"authorised person" has the meaning assigned to it by **[section 917G(3)(a);]**[4]

"digital signature", in relation to a person, means an advanced electronic signature (within the meaning of the Electronic Commerce Act, 2000) provided to the person by the Revenue Commissioners solely for the purpose of making an electronic transmission of information which is required to be included in a return to which this Chapter applies and for no other purpose and a qualified certificate (within the meaning of that Act) provided to the person by the Revenue Commissioners or a person appointed in that behalf by the Revenue Commissioners;

["electronic identifier", in relation to a person, means -

(a)   the person's digital signature, or

(b)   such other means of electronic identification as may be specified or authorised by the Revenue Commissioners for the purposes of this Chapter;][2]

"hard copy", in relation to information held electronically, means a printed out version of that information;

"return" means any return, claim, application, notification, election, declaration, nomination, statement, list, registration, particulars or other information which a person is or may be required by the Acts to give to the Revenue Commissioners or any Revenue officer;

"revenue officer" means the Collector-General, an inspector or other officer of the Revenue Commissioners (including an inspector or other officer who is authorised under any provision of the Acts (however expressed) to receive a return or to require a return to be prepared and delivered);

"tax" means any income tax, corporation tax, capital gains tax, value-added tax, gift tax, inheritance tax, excise duty or stamp duty.

(2)   .....

(3)   Any references in this Chapter to the making of a return include references in any provision of the Acts to —

(a)   the preparing and delivering of a return;

(b)   the sending of a return;

(c)   the furnishing of a return or of particulars;

(d)   the delivering of a return;

(e)   the presentation of a return;

(f)   the rendering of a return;

(g)   the giving of particulars or of any information specified in any provision; and

(h)   any other means whereby a return is forwarded, however expressed.

Footnotes

1   Substituted for "Capital Acquisitions Tax Act, 1976" by s.119, CATCA, with effect from 21st February, 2003.

2   As inserted by s.22(a), FA 2005, with effect from 1st January, 2005, under s.150(8), FA 2005.

3   As substituted for "Stamp Act, 1891," by para. 1(q)(i), Sch.8, FA 2008, with effect as on and from 13th March, 2008.

4   As substituted for "section 917G(3)(b);" by para. 1(q)(ii), Sch.8, FA 2008, with effect as on from 13th March, 2008.

Section 917E

Application.

917E. This Chapter shall apply to a return if—

    (a)   the provision of the Acts under which the return is made is specified for the purpose of this Chapter by order[1] made by the Revenue Commissioners, and

    (b)   the return is required to be made after the day appointed by such order[1] in relation to returns to be made under the provision so specified.

Footnote

1   S.I. No. 443 of 2003 (see page 1375) appoints 28th September, 2003, as the day in relation to returns to be made under s.46, CATCA (other than subsections (3), (7), (13) and (15)).

Section 917EA[1]

Mandatory electronic filing and payment of tax.

917EA. (1) In this section -

    "electronic means" includes electrical, digital, magnetic, optical, electromagnetic, biometric, photonic means of transmission of data and other forms of related technology by means of which data is transmitted;

    "repayment of tax" includes any amount relating to tax which is to be paid or repaid by the Revenue Commissioners;

    "specified person" means any person, group of persons or class of persons specified in regulations made under this section for the purposes of either or both paragraphs (a) and (b) of subsection (3);

    "specified return" means a return specified in regulations made under this section;

    "specified tax liabilities" means liabilities to tax including interest on unpaid tax specified in regulations made under this section.

    (2)   Section 917D shall apply for the purposes of regulations made under this section in the same way as it applies for the purposes of this Chapter.

(3)   The Revenue Commissioners may make regulations -

(a)   requiring the delivery by specified persons of a specified return by electronic means where an order under section 917E has been made in respect of that return,

(b)   requiring the payment by electronic means of specified tax liabilities by specified persons, and

(c)   for the repayment of any tax specified in the regulations to be made by electronic means.

(4)   Regulations made under this section shall include provision for the exclusion of a person from the requirements of regulations made under this section where the Revenue Commissioners are satisfied that the person could not reasonably be expected to have the capacity to make a specified return or to pay the specified tax liabilities by electronic means, and allowing a person, aggrieved by a failure to exclude such person, to appeal that failure to the Appeal Commissioners.

(5)   Regulations made under this section may, in particular and without prejudice to the generality of subsection (3), include provision for -

(a)   the electronic means to be used to pay or repay tax,

(b)   the conditions to be complied with in relation to the electronic payment or repayment of tax,

(c)   determining the time when tax paid or repaid using electronic means is to be taken as having been paid or repaid,

(d)   the manner of proving, for any purpose, the time of payment or repayment of any tax paid or repaid using electronic means, including provision for the application of any conclusive or other presumptions,

(e)   notifying persons that they are specified persons, including the manner by which such notification may be made, and

(f)   such supplemental and incidental matters as appear to the Revenue Commissioners to be necessary.

(6)   The Revenue Commissioners may nominate any of their officers to perform any acts and discharge any functions authorised by regulation made under this section to be performed or discharged by the Revenue Commissioners.

(7)   Where a specified person -

(a)   makes a return which is a specified return for the purposes of regulations made under this section, or

(b)   makes a payment of tax which is specified tax liabilities for the purposes of regulations made under this section,

in a form other than that required by any such regulation, the specified person shall be liable to a penalty of €1,520 and, for the purposes of the recovery of a penalty under this subsection, section

1061 applies in the same manner as it applies for the purposes of the recovery of a penalty under any of the sections referred to in that section.

(8) Every regulation made under this section shall be laid before Dáil Éireann as soon as may be after it is made and, if a resolution annulling the regulation is passed by Dáil Éireann within the next 21 days on which Dáil Éireann has sat after the regulation is laid before it, the regulation shall be annulled accordingly but without prejudice to the validity of anything previously done under the regulation.

Footnote

1   As inserted by s.164(1)(a), FA 2003, with effect from such day as the Minister for Finance may appoint by order. S.I. No. 308 of 2008 appoints 28th July, 2008, as the effective day.

Section 917F

Electronic transmission of returns.

917F. (1) Notwithstanding any other provision of the Acts, the obligation of any person to make a return to which this Chapter applies shall be treated as fulfilled by that person if information is transmitted electronically in compliance with that obligation, but only if—

(a)   the transmission is made by an approved person or an authorised person,

(b)   the transmission is an approved transmission,

[(c)   the transmission bears the electronic identifier of that person, and][1]

(d)   the receipt of the transmission is acknowledged in accordance with section 917J.

(2) In subsection (1), the reference to the information which is required to be included in the return includes any requirement on a person to—

(a)   make any statement,

(b)   include any particulars, or

(c)   make or attach any claim.

(3) Where the obligation of any person to make a return to which this Chapter applies is treated as fulfilled in accordance with subsection (1) then, any provision of the Acts which—

(a)   requires that the return include or be accompanied by any description of declaration whatever by the person making the return, apart from a declaration of an amount,

(b)   requires that the return be signed or accompanied by a certificate,

   (c)   requires that the return be in writing,

   (d)   authorises the return to be signed by a person acting under the authority of the person obliged to make the return,

   (e)   authorises the Revenue Commissioners to prescribe the form of a return or which requires a return to be in or on any prescribed form, or

   (f)   for the purposes of any claim for exemption or for any allowance, deduction or repayment of tax under the Acts which is required to be made with the return, authorises the Revenue Commissioners to prescribe the form of a claim,

shall not apply.

(4) Where the obligation of any person to make a return to which this Chapter applies is treated as fulfilled in accordance with subsection (1) then, the time at which any requirement under the Acts to make a return is fulfilled shall be the day on which the receipt of the information referred to in that subsection is acknowledged in accordance with section 917J.

(5) Where an approved transmission is made by –

   (a)   an approved person on behalf of another person, or

   (b)   an authorised person on behalf of another person (not being the person who authorised that person),

a hard copy of the information shall be made and authenticated in accordance with section 917K.

(6) (a) Where the obligation of any person to make a return to which this Chapter applies is treated as fulfilled in accordance with subsection (1) then, any requirement that –

     (i)   the return or any claim which is to be made with or attached to the return should be accompanied by any document (in this subsection referred to as a "supporting document") other than the return or the claim, and

     (ii) the supporting document be delivered with the return or the claim,

    shall be treated as fulfilled by the person subject to the requirement if the person or the approved person referred to in subsection (1)(a) retains the document for inspection on request by a revenue officer.

  (b) Any person subject to the requirement referred to in paragraph (a) shall produce any supporting documents requested by a revenue officer within 30 days of that request.

(c)　The references in this subsection to a document include references to any accounts, certificate, evidence, receipts, reports or statements.

Footnote

1　As substituted by s.22(b), FA 2005, with effect from 1st January, 2005, under s.150(8), FA 2005.

Section 917G

Approved persons.

917G.(1)　A person shall be an approved person for the purposes of this Chapter if the person is approved by the Revenue Commissioners for the purposes of transmitting electronically information which is required to be included in a return to which this Chapter applies (in this section referred to as "the transmission") and complies with the condition specified in subsection (3)(a) in relation to authorised persons and the condition specified in subsection (3)(b) in relation to the making of transmissions and the use of [electronic identifiers][1].

(2)　A person seeking to be approved under this section shall make application in that behalf to the Revenue Commissioners by such means as the Revenue Commissioners may determine.

(3)　The conditions referred to in subsection (1) are that—

(a)　the person notifies the Revenue Commissioners in a manner to be determined by the Revenue Commissioners of the persons (each of whom is referred to in this section as an "authorised person"), in addition to the person, who are authorised to make the transmission, and

(b)　the person and each person who is an authorised person in relation to that person in making the transmission complies with the requirements referred to in subsections (2) and (3) of section 917H.

(4)　A person seeking to be approved under this section shall be given notice by the Revenue Commissioners of the grant or refusal by them of the approval and, in the case of a refusal, of the reason for the refusal.

(5)　An approval under this section may be withdrawn by the Revenue Commissioners by notice in writing or by such other means as the Revenue Commissioners may decide with effect from such date as may be specified in the notice.

(6)　(a)　A notice withdrawing an approval under the section shall state the grounds for the withdrawal.

(b) No approval under this section may be withdrawn unless an approved person or an authorised person has failed to comply with one or more of the requirements referred to in section 917H(2).

(7) A person who is refused approval under this section or whose approval under this section is withdrawn may appeal to the Appeal Commissioners against the refusal or withdrawal.

(8) The appeal under subsection (7) shall be made by notice to the Revenue Commissioners before the end of the period of 30 days beginning with the day on which notice of the refusal or withdrawal was given to the person.

(9) The Appeal Commissioners shall hear and determine an appeal made to them under subsection (7) as if it were an appeal against an assessment to income tax, and the provisions of the Tax Acts relating to appeals shall apply accordingly.

Footnote
1   Substituted for "digital signatures" by s.22(c), FA 2005, with effect from 1st January, 2005, under s.150(8), FA 2005.

Section 917H

Approved transmissions.

917H.(1) Where an approved person transmits electronically information which is required to be included in a return to which this Chapter applies the transmission shall not be an approved transmission unless it complies with the requirements of this section.

(2) The Revenue Commissioners shall publish and make known to each approved person and each authorised person any requirement for the time being determined by them as being applicable to –

(a) the manner in which information which is required to be included in a return to which this Chapter applies is to be transmitted electronically, and

(b) the use of a person's [electronic identifier][1].

(3) The requirements referred to in subsection (2) include –

(a) requirements as to the software or type of software to be used to make a transmission,

(b) the terms and conditions under which a person may make a transmission, and

(c) the terms and conditions under which a person may use that person's [electronic identifier][1].

[(4) For the purposes of subsection (3), the Revenue Commissioners may determine different terms and conditions in relation to different returns or categories of a return, different categories of persons and different returns or categories of a return made by different categories of persons.][2]

Footnotes

1   Substituted for "digital signature" by s.22(d)(i), FA 2005, with effect from 1st January, 2005, under s.150(8), FA 2005.

2.   As inserted by s.22(d)(ii), FA 2005, with effect from 1st January 2005, under s.150(8), FA 2005.

Section 917J

Acknowledgement of electronic transmissions.

917J. For the purposes of this Chapter, where an electronic transmission of information which is required to be included in a return to which this Chapter applies is received by the Revenue Commissioners, the Revenue Commissioners shall send an electronic acknowledgement of receipt of that transmission to the person from whom it was received.

Section 917K

Hard copies.

917K. (1) A hard copy shall be made in accordance with this subsection only if —

(a)   the hard copy is made under processes and procedures which are designed to ensure that the information contained in the hard copy shall only be the information transmitted or to be transmitted in accordance with section 917F(1),

(b)   the hard copy is in a form approved by the Revenue Commissioners which is appropriate to the information so transmitted, and

(c)   the hard copy is authenticated in accordance with subsection (2).

(2) For the purposes of this Chapter, a hard copy made in accordance with subsection (1) shall be authenticated only if the hard copy is signed by the person who would have been required to make the declaration, sign the return or furnish the certificate, as the case may be, but for paragraph (a), (b) or (d) of section 917F(3).

Section 917L

Exercise of powers.

917L. (1) This section shall apply where the obligation of any person to make a return to which this Chapter applies is treated as fulfilled in accordance with section 917F(1).

(2) Where this section applies the Revenue Commissioners and a revenue officer shall have all the powers and duties in relation to the information contained in the transmission as they or that officer would have had if the information had been contained in a return made by post.

(3) Where this section applies the person whose obligation to make a return to which this Chapter applies is treated as fulfilled in accordance with section 917F(1) shall have all the rights and duties in relation to the information contained in the transmission as the person would have had if that information had been contained in a return made by post.

Section 917M

Proceedings.

917M. (1) This section shall apply where the obligation of any person to make a return to which this Chapter applies is treated as fulfilled in accordance with section 917F(1).

(2) In this section, "proceedings" means civil and criminal proceedings, and includes proceedings before the Appeal Commissioners or any other tribunal having jurisdiction by virtue of any provision of the Acts.

(3) Where this section applies a hard copy certified by a revenue officer to be a true copy of the information transmitted electronically in accordance with section 917F(1) shall be treated for the purposes of the Acts as if the hard copy —

(a) were a return or, as the case may be, a claim made by post, and

(b) contained any declaration, certificate or signature required by the Acts on such a return or, as the case may be, such a claim.

(4) For the purposes of any proceedings under the Acts, unless a Judge or any other person before whom proceedings are taken determines at the time of the proceedings that it is unjust in the circumstances to apply this provision, any rule of law restricting the admissibility or use of hearsay evidence shall not apply to a representation contained in a document recording information which has been transmitted in accordance with section 917F(1) in so far as the representation is a representation as to—

(a) the information so transmitted,

(b)   the date on which, or the time at which, the information was so transmitted, or

(c)   the identity of the person by whom or on whose behalf the information was so transmitted.

Section 917N

Miscellaneous.

917N. The Revenue Commissioners may nominate any of their officers to perform any acts and discharge any functions authorised by this Chapter to be performed or discharged by the Revenue Commissioners.

PART 39
Assessments

CHAPTER 1
Income tax and corporation tax

Section 928

Transmission to Collector-General of particulars of sums to be collected.
928. **(1)** In this section—

"assessment" and "Revenue officer" have, respectively, the same meanings as in Chapter 1A of Part 42;

"tax" means income tax, corporation tax, capital gains tax, value-added tax, excise duty, stamp duty, gift tax and inheritance tax.

(2) After assessments to tax have been made, the inspectors or other Revenue officers shall transmit particulars of the sums to be collected to the Collector-General or to a Revenue officer nominated in writing under section 960B for collection.

(3) The entering by an inspector or other Revenue officer of details of assessment to tax and of the tax charged in such an assessment in an electronic, digital, magnetic, optical, electromagnetic, biometric, photonic, photographic or other record from which the Collector-General or a Revenue officer nominated in writing under section 960B may extract such details by electronic, digital, magnetic, optical, electromagnetic, biometric, photonic, photographic or other process shall constitute transmission of such details by the inspector or other Revenue officer to the Collector-General or to the Revenue officer nominated in writing under section 960B.

Footnote

1   Substituted entirely by s.97, and by para. 1(a) of Sch.4, of the F(No.2)A, 2008, which comes into effect and applies (para. 6 of that Sch.) as respects any tax that becomes due and payable after 1st March, 2009. Because of the definition of "assessment" in this section, it appears this section does not apply to the CATA.

PART 42
Collection and Recovery

CHAPTER 1A
Interpretation

Section 960A[1]

Interpretation.
960A.(1) In Chapters 1A, 1B and 1C, unless the contrary is expressly stated—

"Acts" means—

(a) the Tax Acts.

(b) the Capital Gains Tax Acts.

(c) the Value-Added Tax Act 1972, and the enactments amending and extending that Act.

(d) the statutes relating to the duties of excise and to the management of those duties and the enactments amending and extending those statutes.

(e) the Stamp Duties Consolidation Act 1999 and the enactments amending and extending that Act,

(f) the Capital Acquisitions Tax Consolidation Act 2003 and the enactments amending and extending that Act,

(g) Parts 18A and 18B (inserted by the Finance (No. 2) Act 2008),

and any instruments made under any of those Acts;

"assessment" means any assessment to tax made under any provision of the Acts, including any amended assessment, additional assessment, correcting assessment and any estimate made under section 990 or under Regulation 13 or 14 of the RCT Regulations and any estimate made under section 22 of the Value-Added Tax Act 1972;

"emoluments" has the same meaning as in section 983;

"income tax month" has the same meaning as in section 983;

"PAYE Regulations" means regulations made under section 986;

"RCT Regulations" means the Income Tax (Relevant Contracts) Regulations 2000 (S.I. No. 71 of 2000);

"Revenue officer" means any officer of the Revenue Commissioners;

"tax" means any income tax, corporation tax, capital gains tax, value-added tax, excise duty, stamp duty, gift tax, inheritance tax or any other levy or charge which is placed under the care and management of the Revenue Commissioners and includes—

(a) any interest, surcharge or penalty relating to any such tax, duty, levy or charge,

(b)   any clawback of a relief or an exemption relating to any such tax, duty, levy or charge, and

(c)   any sum which is required to be deducted or withheld by any person and paid or remitted to the Revenue Commissioners or the Collecter-General, as the case may be, under any provision of the Acts:

"tax due and payable" means tax due and payable under any provision of the Acts.

Footnote

1   This section was inserted by s.97, and by para. 1(b)(i) of Sch.4, of the F(No.2)A, 2008, and comes into force and applies (para.6 of that Sch.) as respects any tax that becomes due and payable after 1st March, 2009.

Section 960B[1]

Discharge of Collector-General's functions.

960B. **The Revenue Commissioners may nominate in writing any Revenue officer to perform any acts and to discharge any functions authorised by Chapters 1B and 1C to be performed or discharged by the Collector-General other than the acts and functions referred to in subsections (1) to (4) of section 960N, and references in this Part to "Collector-General" shall be read accordingly.**

Footnote

1   This section was inserted by s.97, and by para. 1(b)(i) of Sch.4, of the F(No.2)A, 2008, and comes into force and applies (para.6 of that Sch.) as respects any tax that becomes due and payable after 1st March, 2009.

CHAPTER 1B

Collection of tax, etc.

Section 960C[1]

Tax to be due and payable to Revenue Commissioners.

960C. **Tax due and payable under the Acts shall be due and payable to the Revenue Commissioners.**

Footnote

1   This section was inserted by s.97, and by para. 1(b)(i) of Sch.4, of the F(No.2A), 2008, and comes into force and applies (para. 6 of that Sch.) as respects any tax that becomes due and payable after 1st March, 2009.

Section 960D[1]

Tax to be debt due to Minister for Finance.

960D. Tax due and payable to the Revenue Commissioners shall be treated as a debt due to the Minister for Finance for the benefit of the Central Fund.

Footnote

1 This section was inserted by s.97, and by para. 1(b)(i) of Sch.4, of the F(No.2)A, 2008, and comes into force and applies (para. 6 of that Sch.) as respects any tax that becomes due and payable after 1st March, 2009.

Section 960E[1]

Collection of tax, issue of demands, etc.

960E. (1) Tax due and payable to the Revenue Commissioners by virtue of section 960C shall be paid to and collected by the Collector-General, including tax charged in all assessments to tax, particulars of which have been given to the Collector-General under section 928.

(2) The Collector-General shall demand payment of tax that is due and payable but remaining unpaid by the person from whom that tax is payable.

(3) Where tax is not paid in accordance with the demand referred to in subsection (2), the Collector-General shall collect and levy the tax that is due and payable but remaining unpaid by the person from whom that tax is payable.

(4) On payment of tax, the Collector-General may provide a receipt to the person concerned in respect of that payment and such receipt shall consist of whichever of the following the Collector-General considers appropriate, namely—

(a) a separate receipt in respect of each such payment, or

(b) a receipt for all such payments that have been made within the period specified in the receipt.

Footnote

1 This section was inserted by s.97, and by para. 1(b)(i) of Sch.4, of the F(No.2)A, 2008, and comes into force and applies (para.6 of that Sch.) as respects any tax that becomes due and payable after 1st March, 2009.

Section 960F[1]

Moneys received for capital acquisitions tax and stamp duties and not appropriated to be recoverable.

960F. (1) Any person who—

(a) having received a sum of money in respect of gift tax, inheritance tax or stamp duties, does not pay that sum to the Collector-General, and

    (b)   improperly withholds or detains such sum of money,

shall be accountable to the Revenue Commissioners for the payment of that sum to the extent of the amount so received by that person.

(2)   The sum of money referred to in subsection (1) shall be treated as a debt due to the Minister for Finance for the benefit of the Central Fund and section 960I shall apply to any such sum as if it were tax due and payable.

Footnote
1   This section was inserted by s.97, and by para. 1(b)(i) of Sch.4, of the F(No.2)A, 2008, and comes into force and applies (para.6 of that Sch.) as respects any tax that becomes due and payable after 1st March, 2009.

Section 960G[1]

Duty of taxpayer to identify liability against which payment to be set, etc.

960G. (1)   Subject to subsection (2), every person who makes a payment of tax to the Revenue Commissioners or to the Collector-General shall identify the liability to tax against which he or she wishes the payment to be set.

(2)   Where payment of tax is received by the Revenue Commissioners or the Collector-General and the payment is accompanied by a pay slip, a tax return, a tax demand or other document issued by the Revenue Commissioners or the Collector-General, the payment shall, unless the contrary intention is or has been clearly indicated, be treated as relating to the tax referred to in the document concerned.

(3)   Where a payment is received by the Revenue Commissioners or the Collector-General from a person and it cannot reasonably be determined by the Revenue Commissioners or the Collector-General from the instructions, if any, which accompanied the payment which liabilities the person wishes the payment to be set against, then the Revenue Commissioners or the Collector-General may set the payment against any liability due by the person under the Acts.

Footnote
1   This section was inserted by s.97, and by para. 1(b)(i) of Sch.4, of the F(No.2)A, 2008, and comes into force and applies (para.6 of that Sch.) as respects any tax that becomes due and payable after 1st March, 2009.

Section 960H[1]

Offset between taxes.

960H. (1) In this section—

"claim" means a claim that gives rise to either or both a repayment of tax and a payment of interest payable in respect of such a repayment and includes part of such a claim;

"liability" means any tax due and payable which is unpaid and includes any tax estimated to be due and payable;

"overpayment" means a payment or remittance (including part of such a payment or remittance) which is in excess of the amount of the liability against which it is credited.

(2) Where the Collector-General is satisfied that a person has not complied with the obligations imposed on the person in relation to either or both—

(a) the payment of tax that is due and payable, and

(b) the delivery of returns required to be made,

then the Collector-General may, in a case where a repayment is due to the person in respect of a claim or overpayment—

(i) where paragraph (a) applies, or where paragraphs (a) and (b) apply, instead of making the repayment, set the amount of the repayment against any liability, and

(ii) where paragraph (b) only applies, withhold making the repayment until such time as the returns required to be delivered have been delivered.

(3) (a) Where a person (referred to in this subsection as the "first-mentioned person") has assigned, transferred or sold a right to a claim or overpayment to another person (referred to in this subsection as the "second-mentioned person") and subsection (2)(a) applies, then the Collector-General shall, in a case where a repayment would have been due to the first-mentioned person in respect of the claim or overpayment if he or she had not assigned, transferred or sold his or her right to the claim or overpayment, instead of making the repayment ot the second-mentioned person, set that claim or over-payment against tax that is due and payable by that first-mentioned person.

(b) where the first-mentioned person and the second-mentioned person are connected persons within the meaning of section 10, then the balance, if any, of the repayment referred to in paragraph (a) shall be set against tax due and payable by the second-mentioned person.

(4) Where the Collector-General has set or withheld a repayment by virtue of subsection (2) or (3), then he or she shall give notice in writing to that effect to the person or persons concerned and,

where subsection (2)(ii) applies, interest shall not be payable under any provision of the Acts from the date of such notice in respect of any repayment so withheld.

(5) The Revenue Commissioners may make regulations for the purpose of giving effect to this section and, without prejudice to the generality of the foregoing, such regulations may provide for the order of priority of the liabilities to tax against which any claim or overpayment is to be set in accordance with subsection (2) or (3) or both.

(6) Every regulation made under this section is to be laid before Dáil Éireann as soon as may be after it is made and, if a resolution annulling the regulation is passed by Dáil Éireann within the next 21 days on which Dáil Éireann has sat after the regulation is laid before it, the regulation shall be annulled accordingly, but withourt prejudice to the validity of anything previously done under the regulation.

(7) The Taxes (Offset of Repayments) Regulations 2002 (S.I. No. 471 of 2002) shall have effect as if they were made under subsection (5) and had complied with subsection (6).

Footnote

1   This section was inserted by s.97, and by para. 1(b)(i) of Sch.4, of the F(No.2)A, 2008, and comes into force and applies (para.6 of that Sch.) as respects any tax that becomes due and payable after 1st March, 2009.

CHAPTER 1C
Recovery provisions, evidential rules, etc.

Section 960I

Recovery of tax by way of civil proceedings.

960I. (1)   Without prejudice to any other means by which payment of tax may be enforced, any tax due and payable or any balance of such tax may be sued for and recoverd by proceedings taken by the Collector-General in any court of competent jurisdiction.

(2) All or any of the amounts of tax due from any one person may be included in the same summons.

(3) The rules of court for the time being applicable to civil proceedings commenced by summary summons, in so far as they relate to the recovery of tax, shall apply to proceedings under this section.

(4) The acceptance of a part payment or a payment on account in respect of tax referred to in a summons shall not prejudice proceedings for the recovery of the balance of the tax due and the summons may be amended accordingly.

(5) (a) Proceedings under this section may be brought for the recovery of the total amount which an employer is liable, under Chapter 4 and the PAYE Regulations, to pay to the Collector-General for any income tax month without—

    (i) distinguishing the amounts for which the employer is liable to pay by reference to each employee, and

    (ii) specifying the employees in question.

(b) For the purposes of the proceedings referred to in paragraph (a), the total amount shall be one single cause of action or one matter of complaint.

(c) Nothing in this subsection shall prevent the bringing of separate proceedings for the recovery of each of the several amounts which the employer is liable to pay by reference to any income tax month and to the employer's several employees.

(6) For the purposes of subsection (5), any amount of tax—

(a) estimated under section 989, or

(b) estimated under section 990 or any balance of tax so estimated but remaining unpaid.

is deemed to be an amount of tax which any person paying emoluments was liable, uner Chapter 4 and the PAYE Regulations. to pay to the Collector-General.

Footnote

1   This section was inserted by s.97, and by para. 1(b)(i) of Sch.4, of the F(No.2)A, 2008, and comes into force and applies (para.6 of that Sch.) as respects any tax that becomes due and payable after 1st March, 2009.

Section 960J[1]

Evidential and procedural rules.

960J. (1) In proceedings for the recovery of tax, a certificate signed by the Collector-General to the effect that, before the proceedings were instituted, any one or more of the following matters occurred:

(a) the assessment to tax, if any, was duly made,

(b) the assessment, if any, has become final and conclusive,

(c) the tax or any specified part of the tax is due and outstanding,

(d) demand for the payment of the tax has been duly made,

shall be evidence until the contrary is proved of such of those matters that are so certified by the Collector-General.

(2) (a) Subsection (1) shall not apply in the case of tax to which Chapter 4 applies.

(b) In proceedings for the recovery of tax to which Chapter 4 applies, a certificate signed by the Collector-General that a stated amount of income tax under Schedule E is due and outstanding shall be evidence until the contrary is proved that the amount is so due and outstanding.

(3) In proceedings for the recovery of tax, a certificate purporting to be signed by the Collector-General certifying the matters or any of the matters referred to in subsection (1) or (2) may be tendered in evidence without proof and shall be deemed until the contrary is proved to have been duly signed by the person concerned.

(4) If a dispute relating to a certificate referred to in subsection (1), (2) or (3) arises during proceedings for the recovery of tax, the judge may adjourn the proceedings to allow the Collector-General or the Revenue officer concerned to attend and give oral evidence in the proceedings and for any register, file or other record relating to the tax to be produced and put in evidence in the proceedings.

Footnote
1   This section was inserted by s.97, and by para. 1(b)(i) of Sch.4, of the F(No.2)A, 2008, and comes into force and applies (para.6 of that Sch.) as respects any tax that becomes due and payable after 1st March, 2009.

Section 960K[1]

Judgments for recovery of tax.
960K.(1) In this section "judgment" includes any order or decree.

(2) Where, in any proceedings for the recovery of tax, judgment is given against a person and a sum of money is accepted from the person against whom the proceedings were brought on account or in part payment of the amount of which the judgment was given, then—

(a) such acceptance shall not prevent or prejudice the recovery under the judgment of the balance of that amount that remains unpaid,

(b) the judgment shall be capable of being executed and enforced in respect of the balance as fully in all respects and by the like means as if the balance were the amount for which the judgment was given,

(c) the law relating to the execution and enforcement of the judgment shall apply in respect of the balance accordingly, and

(d) a certificate signed by the Collector-General stating the amount of the balance shall, for the purposes of the enforcement and execution of the judgment, be evidence until the contrary is proved of the amount of the balance.

Footnote

1   This section was inserted by s.97, and by para. 1(b)(i) of Sch.4, of the F(No.2)A, 2008, which comes into force and applies (para.6 of that Sch.) as respects any tax that becomes due and payable after 1st March, 2009.

Section 960L

Recovery by sheriff or country registrar.

960L. (1)   Where any person does not pay any sum in respect of tax for which he or she is liable under the Acts, the Collector-General may issue a certificate to the county registrar or sheriff of the county in which the person resides or has a place of business certifying the amount due and outstanding and the person from whom that amount is payable.

(2)   (a)   For the purposes of this subsection –

"electronic" has the meaning assigned to it by the Electronic Commerce Act 2000 and an "electronic certificate" shall be construed accordingly;

"issued in non-paper format" includes issued in facsimile.

(b)   A certificate to be issued by the Collector-General under this section may –

(i)   be issued in an electronic or other format, and

(ii)   where the certificate is issued in a non-paper format, be reproduced in a paper format by the county registrar or sheriff or by persons authorised by the county registrar or sheriff to do so.

(c)   A certificate issued in a non-paper format in accordance with paragraph (b) shall –

(i)   constitute a valid certificate for the purposes of this section,

(ii)   be deemed to have been made by the Collector-General, and

(iii)   be deemed to have been issued on the date that the Collector-General caused the certificate to issue.

(d)   (i)   Where a certificate issued by the Collector-General is reproduced in a non-paper format in accordance with paragraph (b) (ii) and –

(I)   the reproduction contains, or there is appended to it, a note to the effect that it is a copy of the certificate so issued, and

(II) the note contains the signature of the county registrar or sheriff or of the person authorised under paragraph (b) (ii) and the date of such signing.

then the copy of the certificate with the note so signed and dated shall, for all purposes, have effect as if it was the certificate itself.

(ii) A signature or date in a note, on a copy of, or appended to, a certificate issued in a non-paper format by the Collector-General and reproduced in a paper format in accordance with paragraph (b)(ii) that—

(I) in respect of such signature, purports to be that of the county registrar or sheriff or of a person authorised to make a copy, shall be taken until the contrary is shown to be the signature of the county registrar or sheriff or of a person who at the material time was so authorised, and

(II) in respect of such date, shall be taken until be contrary is shown to have been duly dated.

(3) (a) Immediately on receipt of the certificate, the county registrar or sheriff shall proceed to levy the amount certified in the certificate to be in default by seizing all or any of the goods, animals or other chattels within his or her area of responsibility belonging to the defaulter.

(b) For the purposes of paragraph (a), the county registrar or sheriff shall (in addition to the rights, powers and duties conferred on him or her by this section) have all such rights, powers and duties as are for the time being vested in him or her by law in relation to the execution of a writ of *fieri facias* in so far as those rights, powers and duties are not inconsistent with the additional rights, powers and duties conferred on him or her by this section.

(4) A county registrar or sheriff executing a certificate under this section shall be entitled—

(a) if the sum certified in the certificate is in excess of €19,050, to charge and (where appropriate) to add to that sum and (in any case) to levy under the certificate such fees and expenses, calculated in accordance to the scales appointed by the Minister for Justice, Equality and Law Reform under section 14(1)(a) of the Enforcement of Court Orders Act 1926 and for the time being in force, as the county registrar or sheriff would be entitled so to charge or add and to levy if the certificate were an execution order, within the meaning of the Enforcement of Court Orders Act 1926 (in this section referred to as an "execution order") of the High Court.

(b)   if the sum referred to in the certificate to be in default exceeds €3,175 but does not exceed €19,050, to charge and (where appropriate) to add to that sum and (in any case) to levy under the certificate such fees and expenses, calculated according to the scales referred to in paragraph (a), as the county registrar or sheriff would be entitled so to charge or add and to levy if the certificate were an execution order of the Circuit Court, and

(c)   if the sum certified in the certificate to be in default does not exceed €3,175 and (where appropriate) to add to that sum and (in any case) to levy under the certificate such fees and expenses, calculated according to the scales referred to in paragraph (a), as the county registrar or sheriff would be entitled so to charge or add and to levy if the cetificate were an execution order of the District Court.

Footnote

1   This section was inserted by s.97, and by para. 1(b)(i) of Sch.4, of the F(No.2)A, 2008, and comes into force and applies (para.6 of that Sch.) as respects any tax that becomes due and payable after 1st March, 2009.

Section 960M[1]

Taking by Collector-General of proceedings in bankruptcy.

960M.(1) The Collector-General may in his or her own name apply for the grant of a bankruptcy summons under section 8 of the Bankruptcy Act 1988 or present a petition for adjudication under section 11 of that Act in respect of tax (except corporation tax) due and payable or any balance of such tax.

(2) Subject to this section the rules of court for the time being applicable and the enactments relating to bankruptcy shall apply to proceedings under this section.

Footnote

1   This section was inserted by s.97, and by para. 1(b)(i) of Sch.4, of the F(No.2)A, 2008, and comes into force and applies (para.6 of that Sch.) as respects any tax that becomes due and payable after 1st March, 2009.

Section 960N[1]

Continuance of pending proceedings and evidence in proceedings.

960N. (1) Where the Collector-General has instituted proceedings under section 960I(1) or 960M(1) for the recovery of tax or any balance of tax and, while such proceedings are pending, such Collector-General ceases for any reason to hold that office, the proceedings may be continued in the name of that Collector-General by any person (in this section referred to as the "successor") duly appointed to collect such tax in succession to that Collector-General or any subsequent Collector-General.

(2) In any case where subsection (1) applies, the successor shall inform the person or persons against whom the proceedings concerned are pending that those proceedings are being so continued and, on service of such notice, notwithstanding any rule of court, it shall not be necessary for the successor to obtain an order of court substituting him or her for the person who has instituted or continued proceedings.

(3) Any affidavit or oath to be made by a Collector-General for the purposes of the Judgment Mortgage (Ireland) Act 1850 or the Judgment Mortgage (Ireland) Act 1858 may be made by a successor.

(4) Where the Collector-General duly appointed to collect tax in succession to another Collector-General institutes or continues proceedings under section 960I(1) or 960M(1) for the recovery of tax or any balance of tax, then the person previously appointed as Collector-General shall for the purposes of the proceedings be deemed until the contrary is proved to have ceased to be the Collector-General appointed to collect the tax.

(5) Where a Revenue officer nominated in accordance with section 960B has instituted proceedings under section 960I(1) or 960M(1) for the recovery of tax or the balance of tax, and while such proceedings are pending, such officer dies or otherwise ceases for any reason to be a Revenue officer –

    (a) the right of such officer to continue proceedings shall cease and the right to continue proceedings shall vest in such other officer as may be nominated by Revenue Commissioners,

    (b) where such other officer is nominated he or she shall be entitled accordingly to be substituted as a party to the proceedings in the place of the first-mentioned officer, and

    (c) where an officer is so substituted, he or she shall give notice in writing of the substitution to the defendant.

(6) In proceedings under section 960I(1) or 960M(1) taken by a Revenue officer nominated in accordance with section 960B, a certificate signed by the Revenue Commissioners certifying the following facts –

    (a) that a person is an officer of the Revenue Commissioners,

    (b) that he or she has been nominated by them in accordance with section 960B, and

    (c) that he or she has been nominated by them in accordance with subsection (5)(a).

shall be evidence unless the contrary is proved of those facts.

(7) In proceedings under sections 960I(1) or 960M(1) taken by a Revenue officer nominated in accordance with section 960B, a certificate signed by the Revenue Commissioners certifying the following facts —

(a) that the plaintiff has ceased to be an officer of the Revenue Commissioners nominated by them in accordance with section 960B,

(b) that another person is a Revenue officer,

(c) that such other person has been nominated by them in accordance with section 960B, and

(d) that such other person has been nominated by them to take proceeding to recover tax.

shall be evidence until the contrary is proved of those facts.

Footnote

1   This section was inserted by s.97, and by para. 1(b)(i) of Sch. 4, of the F(No.2)A, 2008, and comes into force and applies (para. 6 of that Sch.) as respects any tax that becomes due and payable after 1st March, 2009.

CHAPTER 5
Miscellaneous Provisions

Section 1002

Deduction from payments due to defaulters of amounts due in relation to tax.

1002. (1) (a) In this section, except where the context otherwise requires —

"the Acts" means —

(i)   the Customs Acts,

(ii) the statutes relating to the duties of excise and to the management of those duties,

(iii) the Tax Acts,

[(iiia) Part 18A,][2]

(iv) the Capital Gains Tax Acts,

(v)   the Value-Added Tax Act, 1972, and the enactments amending or extending that Act,

(vi) the [Capital Acquisitions Tax Consolidation Act 2003,][1] and the enactments amending or extending that Act, and

(vii) the Stamp Act, 1891, and the enactments amending or extending that Act,

[(viii) Part 18B,][3]

and any instruments made thereunder;

"additional debt", in relation to a relevant person who has received a notice of attachment in respect of a taxpayer, means any amount which, at any time after the time of the receipt by the relevant person of the notice of attachment but before the end of the relevant period in relation to the notice, would be a debt due by the relevant person to the taxpayer if a notice of attachment were received by the relevant person at that time;

"debt", in relation to a notice of attachment given to a relevant person in respect of a taxpayer and in relation to that relevant person and taxpayer, means, subject to paragraphs (b) to (e), the amount or aggregate amount of any money which, at the time the notice of attachment is received by the relevant person, is due by the relevant person (whether on that person's own account or as an agent or trustee) to the taxpayer, irrespective of whether the taxpayer has applied for the payment (to the taxpayer or any other person) or for the withdrawal of all or part of the money;

"deposit" means a sum of money paid to a financial institution on terms under which it will be repaid with or without interest and either on demand or at a time or in circumstances agreed by or on behalf of the person making the payment and the financial institution to which it is made;

"emoluments" means anything assessable to income tax under Schedule E;

["financial institution" means—

(a) a person who holds or has held a licence under section 9 of the Central Bank Act 1971, or a person who holds or has held a licence or other similar authorisation under the law of any other Member State of the European Communities which corresponds to a licence granted under that section,

(b) a person referred to in section 7(4) of the Central Bank Act 1971,

(c) a credit institution (within the meaning of the European Communities (Licensing and Supervision of Credit Institutions) Regulations 1992 (S.I. No. 395 of 1992)) which has been authorised by the Central Bank and Financial Services Authority of Ireland to carry on business of a credit institution in accordance with the provisions of the supervisory enactments (within the meaning of those Regulations), or

(d) a branch of a financial institution which records deposits in its books as liabilities of the branch.][4]

"further return" means a return made by a relevant person under subsection (4);

"interest on unpaid tax", in relation to a specified amount specified in a notice of attachment, means interest that has accrued to the date on which the notice of attachment is given under any provision of the Acts providing for the charging of interest in respect of the unpaid tax, including interest on an undercharge of tax which is attributable to fraud or neglect, specified in the notice of attachment;

"notice of attachment" means a notice under subsection (2);

"notice of revocation" means a notice under subsection (10);

"penalty" means a monetary penalty imposed on a taxpayer under a provision of the Acts;

"relevant period", in relation to a notice of attachment, means, as respects the relevant person to whom the notice of attachment is given, the period commencing at the time at which the notice is received by the relevant person and ending on the earliest of—

(i) the date on which the relevant person completes the payment to the Revenue Commissioners out of the debt, or the aggregate of the debt and any additional debt, due by the relevant person to the taxpayer named in the notice, of an amount equal to the specified amount in relation to the taxpayer,

(ii) the date on which the relevant person receives a notice of revocation of the notice of attachment, and

(iii) where the relevant person or the taxpayer named in the notice—

  (I) is declared bankrupt, the date the relevant person or the taxpayer is so declared, or

  (II) is a company which commences to be wound up, the relevant date within the meaning of section 285 of the Companies Act, 1963, in relation to the winding up;

"relevant person", in relation to a taxpayer, means a person whom the Revenue Commissioners have reason to believe may have, at the time a notice of attachment is received by such person in respect of a taxpayer, a debt due to the taxpayer;

"return" means a return made by a relevant person under subsection (2) (a) (iii);

"specified amount" has the meaning assigned to it by subsection (2) (a) (ii);

"tax" means any tax, duty, levy or charge which in accordance with any provision of the Acts is placed under the care and management of the Revenue Commissioners;

"taxpayer" means a person who is liable to pay, remit or account for tax to the Revenue Commissioners under the Acts.

(b) Where a relevant person is a financial institution, any amount or aggregate amount of money, including interest on that money, which at the time the notice of attachment is received by the relevant person is a deposit held by the relevant person—

    (i) to the credit of the taxpayer for the taxpayer's sole benefit, or

    (ii) to the credit of the taxpayer and any other person or persons for their joint benefit,

shall be regarded as a debt due by the relevant person to the taxpayer at that time.

(c) Any amount of money due by the relevant person to the taxpayer as emoluments under a contract of service shall not be regarded as a debt due to the taxpayer.

(d) Where there is a dispute as to an amount of money which is due by the relevant person to the taxpayer, the amount in dispute shall be disregarded for the purposes of determining the amount of the debt.

(e) In the case referred to in paragraph (b), a deposit held by a relevant person which is a financial institution to the credit of the taxpayer and any other person or persons (in this paragraph referred to as "the other party or parties") for their joint benefit shall be deemed (unless evidence to the contrary is produced to the satisfaction of the relevant person within 10 days of the giving of the notices specified in subsection (2) (e)) to be held to the benefit of the taxpayer and the other party or parties to the deposit equally, and accordingly only the portion of the deposit so deemed shall be regarded as a debt due by the relevant person to the taxpayer at the time the notice of attachment is received by the relevant person and, where such evidence is produced within the specified time, only so much of the deposit as is shown to be held to the benefit of the taxpayer shall be regarded as a debt due by the relevant person to the taxpayer at that time.

(2) (a) Subject to subsection (3), where a taxpayer has made default whether before or after the passing of this Act in paying, remitting or accounting for any tax, interest on unpaid tax, or penalty to the Revenue Commissioners, the Revenue Commissioners may, if the taxpayer has not made good the default, give to a relevant person in relation to the taxpayer

a notice in writing (in this section referred to as "the notice of attachment") in which is entered –

(i) the taxpayer's name and address,

(ii) (I) the amount or aggregate amount, or

(II) in a case where more than one notice of attachment is given to a relevant person or relevant persons in respect of a taxpayer, a portion of the amount or aggregate amount,

of the taxes, interest on unpaid taxes and penalties in respect of which the taxpayer is in default at the time of the giving of the notice or notices of attachment (the amount, aggregate amount, or portion of the amount or aggregate amount, as the case may be, being referred to in this section as "the specified amount"), and

(iii) a direction to the relevant person –

(I) subject to paragraphs (b) and (c), to deliver to the Revenue Commissioners, within the period of 10 days from the time at which the notice of attachment is received by the relevant person, a return in writing specifying whether or not any debt is due by the relevant person to the taxpayer at the time the notice is received by the relevant person and, if any debt is so due, specifying the amount of the debt, and

(II) if the amount of any debt is so specified, to pay to the Revenue Commissioners within the period referred to in clause (I) a sum equal to the amount of the debt so specified.

(b) Where the amount of the debt due by the relevant person to the taxpayer is equal to or greater than the specified amount in relation to the taxpayer, the amount of the debt specified in the return shall be an amount equal to the specified amount.

(c) Where the relevant person is a financial institution and the debt due by the relevant person to the taxpayer is part of a deposit held to the credit of the taxpayer and any other person or persons to their joint benefit, the return shall be made within a period of 10 days from –

(i) the expiry of the period specified in the notices to be given under paragraph (e), or

(ii) the production of the evidence referred to in paragraph (e) (II).

(d) A relevant person to whom a notice of attachment has been given shall comply with the direction in the notice.

(e) Where a relevant person which is a financial institution is given a notice of attachment and the debt due by the relevant person to the taxpayer is part of a deposit held by the relevant person to the credit of the taxpayer and any other person or persons (in this paragraph referred to as "the other party or parties") for their joint benefit, the relevant person shall on receipt of the notice of attachment give to the taxpayer and the other party or parties to the deposit a notice in writing in which is entered –

(i) the taxpayer's name and address,

(ii) the name and address of the person to whom a notice under this paragraph is given,

(iii) the name and address of the relevant person, and

(iv) the specified amount,

and which states that –

(I) a notice of attachment under this section has been received in respect of the taxpayer,

(II) under this section a deposit is deemed (unless evidence to the contrary is produced to the satisfaction of the relevant person within 10 days of the giving of the notice under this paragraph) to be held to the benefit of the taxpayer and the other party or parties to the deposit equally, and

(III) unless such evidence is produced within the period specified in the notice given under this paragraph –

(A) a sum equal to the amount of the deposit so deemed to be held to the benefit of the taxpayer (and accordingly regarded as a debt due to the taxpayer by the relevant person) shall be paid to the Revenue Commissioners, where that amount is equal to or less than the specified amount, and

(B) where the amount of the deposit so deemed to be held to the benefit of the taxpayer (and accordingly regarded as a debt due to the taxpayer by the relevant person) is greater than the specified amount, a sum equal to the specified amount shall be paid to the Revenue Commissioners.

(3) An amount in respect of tax, interest on unpaid tax or a penalty, as respects which a taxpayer is in default as specified in subsection (2), shall not be entered in a notice of attachment unless –

(a) a period of 14 days has expired from the date on which such default commenced, and

(b) the Revenue Commissioners have given the taxpayer a notice in writing (whether or not the document containing the notice also contains other information being communicated by the Revenue Commissioners to the taxpayer), not later than 7 days before the date of the receipt by the relevant person or relevant persons concerned of a notice of attachment, stating that if the amount is not paid it may be specified in a notice or notices of attachment and recovered under this section from a relevant person or relevant persons in relation to the taxpayer.

(4) If, when a relevant person receives a notice of attachment, the amount of the debt due by the relevant person to the taxpayer named in the notice is less than the specified amount in relation to the taxpayer or no debt is so due and, at any time after the receipt of the notice and before the end of the relevant period in relation to the notice, an additional debt becomes due by the relevant person to the taxpayer, the relevant person shall within 10 days of that time —

(a) if the aggregate of the amount of any debt so due and the additional debt so due is equal to or less than the specified amount in relation to the taxpayer —

(i) deliver a further return to the Revenue Commissioners specifying the additional debt, and

(ii) pay to the Revenue Commissioners the amount of the additional debt,

and so on for each subsequent occasion during the relevant period in relation to the notice of attachment on which an additional debt becomes due by the relevant person to the taxpayer until —

(I) the aggregate amount of the debt and the additional debt or debts so due equals the specified amount in relation to the taxpayer, or

(II) paragraph (b) applies in relation to an additional debt, and

(b) if the aggregate amount of any debt and the additional debt or debts so due to the taxpayer is greater than the specified amount in relation to the taxpayer —

(i) deliver a further return to the Revenue Commissioners specifying such portion of the latest additional debt as when added to the aggregate of the debt and any earlier additional debts is equal to the specified amount in relation to the taxpayer, and

(ii) pay to the Revenue Commissioners that portion of the additional debt.

(5) Where a relevant person delivers, either fraudulently or negligently, an incorrect return or further return that purports to be a return or further return made in accordance with this section, the relevant person shall be deemed to be guilty of an offence under section 1078.

(6) (a) Where a notice of attachment has been given to a relevant person in respect of a taxpayer, the relevant person shall not, during the relevant period in relation to the notice, make any disbursements out of the debt, or out of any additional debt, due by the relevant person to the taxpayer except to the extent that any such disbursement –

    (i) will not reduce the debt or the aggregate of the debt and any additional debts so due to an amount that is less than the specified amount in relation to the taxpayer, or

    (ii) is made pursuant to an order of a court.

(b) For the purposes of this section, a disbursement made by a relevant person contrary to paragraph (a) shall be deemed not to reduce the amount of the debt or any additional debts due by the relevant person to the taxpayer.

(7) (a) Sections 1052 and 1054 shall apply to a failure by a relevant person to deliver a return required by a notice of attachment within the time specified in the notice or to deliver a further return within the time specified in subsection (4) as they apply to a failure to deliver a return referred to in section 1052.

(b) A certificate signed by an officer of the Revenue Commissioners which certifies that he or she has examined the relevant records and that it appears from those records that during a specified period a specified return was not received from a relevant person shall be evidence until the contrary is proved that the relevant person did not deliver the return during that period.

(c) A certificate certifying as provided by paragraph (b) and purporting to be signed by an officer of the Revenue Commissioners may be tendered in evidence without proof and shall be deemed until the contrary is proved to have been so signed.

(8) Where a relevant person to whom a notice of attachment in respect of a taxpayer has been given –

(a) delivers the return required to be delivered by that notice but fails to pay to the Revenue Commissioners within the time specified in the notice the amount specified in the return or any part of that amount, or

(b) delivers a further return under subsection (4) but fails to pay to the Revenue Commissioners within the time specified in that subsection the amount specified in the further return or any part of that amount, the amount specified in the return or further return or the part of that amount, as the case may be, which the relevant person has failed to pay to the Revenue Commissioners may, if the notice of attachment has not been revoked by a notice of revocation, be sued for and recovered by action or other appropriate proceedings at the suit of an officer of the Revenue Commissioners in any court of competent jurisdiction.

(9) Nothing in this section shall be construed as rendering any failure by a relevant person to make a return or further return required by this section, or to pay to the Revenue Commissioners the amount or amounts required by this section to be paid by the relevant person, liable to be treated as a failure to which section 1078 applies.

(10) (a) A notice of attachment given to a relevant person in respect of a taxpayer may be revoked by the Revenue Commissioners at any time by notice in writing given to the relevant person and shall be revoked forthwith if the taxpayer has paid the specified amount to the Revenue Commissioners.

(b) Where in pursuance of this section a relevant person pays any amount to the Revenue Commissioners out of a debt or an additional debt due by the relevant person to the taxpayer and, at the time of the receipt by the Revenue Commissioners of that amount, the taxpayer has paid to the Revenue Commissioners the amount or aggregate amount of the taxes, interest on unpaid taxes and penalties in respect of which the taxpayer is in default at the time of the giving of the notice or notices of attachment, the first-mentioned amount shall be refunded by the Revenue Commissioners forthwith to the taxpayer.

(11) Where a notice of attachment or a notice of revocation is given to a relevant person in relation to a taxpayer, a copy of such notice shall be given by the Revenue Commissioners to the taxpayer forthwith.

(12) (a) Where in pursuance of this section any amount is paid to the Revenue Commissioners by a relevant person, the relevant person shall forthwith give the taxpayer concerned a notice in writing specifying the payment, its amount and the reason for which it was made.

(b) On the receipt by the Revenue Commissioners of an amount paid in pursuance of this section, the Revenue Commissioners shall forthwith notify the taxpayer and the relevant person in writing of such receipt.

(13) Where in pursuance of this section a relevant person pays to the Revenue Commissioners the whole or part of the amount of a debt or an additional debt due by the relevant person to a taxpayer, or any portion of such an amount, the taxpayer shall allow such payment and the relevant person shall be acquitted and discharged of the amount of the payment as if it had been paid to the taxpayer.

(14) Where in pursuance of this section a relevant person is prohibited from making any disbursement out of a debt or an additional debt due to a taxpayer, no action shall lie against the relevant person in any court by reason of a failure to make any such disbursement.

(15) Any obligation on the Revenue Commissioners to maintain secrecy or any other restriction on the disclosure of information by the Revenue Commissioners shall not apply in relation to information contained in a notice of attachment.

(16) A notice of attachment in respect of a taxpayer shall not be given to a relevant person at a time when the relevant person or the taxpayer is an undischarged bankrupt or a company being wound up.

(17) The Revenue Commissioners may nominate any of their officers to perform any acts and discharge any functions authorised by this section to be performed or discharged by the Revenue Commissioners.

Footnotes

1   Substituted for "Capital Acquisitions Tax Act, 1976" by s.119, CATCA, with effect from 21st February, 2003.

2   Inserted by s.2(b), F(No. 2)A, 2008, with effect as on and from 1st January, 2009.

3   Inserted by s.3(1)(b), F(No. 2A)A, 2008, with effect as on and from 1st January, 2009.

4   As substituted by s.92(j), F(No. 2)A, 2008, with effect from 24th December, 2008.

Section 1003

Payment of tax by means of donation of heritage items.

1003. (1) (a)   In this section —

"the Acts" means —

(i)   the Tax Acts (other than Chapter 8 of Part 6, Chapter 2 of Part 18 and Chapter 4 of this Part),

(ii)   the Capital Gains Tax Acts, and

(iii)   the [Capital Acquisitions Tax Consolidation Act 2003,][1] and the enactments amending or extending that Act,

and any instruments made thereunder;

"approved body" means —

(i)   the National Archives,

(ii)   the National Gallery of Ireland,

(iii)   the National Library of Ireland,

(iv)   the National Museum of Ireland,

[(iva) the Crawford Art Gallery Cork Limited,][9]

(v)   the Irish Museum of Modem Art, or

(vi)   in relation to the offer of a gift of a particular item or collection of items, any other such body (being a body owned, or funded wholly or mainly, by the State or by any public or local authority) as may be approved, with the consent of the Minister for Finance, by the Minister for Arts, Heritage, Gaeltacht and the Islands for the purposes of this section;

"arrears of tax" means tax due and payable in accordance with any provision of the Acts (including any interest and penalties payable under any provision of the Acts in relation to such tax) —

(i)   in the case of income tax, corporation tax or capital gains tax, in respect of the relevant period, or

(ii)   in the case of gift tax or inheritance tax, before the commencement of the calendar year in which the relevant gift is made,

which has not been paid at the time a relevant gift is made;

"current liability" means —

(i)   in the case of income tax or capital gains tax, any liability to such tax arising in the year of assessment in which the relevant gift is made,

(ii)   in the case of corporation tax, any liability to such tax arising in the accounting period in which the relevant gift is made,

(iii) in the case of gift tax or inheritance tax, any liability to such tax which becomes due and payable in the calendar year in which the relevant gift is made;

"designated officer" means —

(i)   the member of the selection committee who represents the appropriate approved body on that committee where the approved body is so represented, or

(ii)   in any other case, a person nominated in that behalf by the Minister for Arts, Heritage, Gaeltacht and the Islands;

"heritage item" has the meaning assigned to it by subsection (2)(a);

"market value" has the meaning assigned to it by subsection (3);

"relevant gift" means a gift of a heritage item to an approved body in respect of which no consideration whatever (other than relief under this section) is received by the person making the gift, either directly or indirectly, from the approved body or otherwise;

"relevant period" means —

(i)   in the case of income tax and capital gains tax, any year of assessment preceding the year in which the relevant gift is made, and

(ii) in the case of corporation tax, any accounting period preceding the accounting period in which the relevant gift is made;

"selection committee" means a committee consisting of —

[(i) an officer of the Minister for Arts, Sport and Tourism, who shall act as Chairperson of the committee,

(ii) the Chief Executive of the Heritage Council,

(iii) the Director of the Arts Council,

(iv) the Director of the National Archives,

(v) the Director of the National Gallery of Ireland,

(vi) the Director of the National Library of Ireland,

[(iva) the Director of the Crawford Art Gallery Cork Limited,][10]

(vii) the Director of the National Museum of Ireland, and

(viii) the Director and Chief Executive of the Irish Museum of Modern Art,][2]

and includes any person duly acting in the capacity of any of those persons as a result of the person concerned being unable to fulfil his or her duties for any of the reasons set out in paragraph (b) (ii);

"tax" means income tax, corporation tax, capital gains tax, gift tax or inheritance tax, as the case may be, payable in accordance with any provision of the Acts;

"valuation date" means the date on which an application is made to the selection committee for a determination under subsection (2)(a).

(b) (i) The selection committee may act notwithstanding one or more vacancies among its members and may regulate its own procedure.

(ii) If and so long as a member of the selection committee is unable through illness, absence or other cause to fulfil his or her duties, a person nominated in that behalf by the member shall act as the member of the committee in the place of the member.

[(iii) For the purposes of making a decision in relation to an application made to it for a determination under subsection (2)(a), the selection committee shall not include the member of that committee who represents the approved body to which it is intended that the gift of the heritage item is to be made where that approved body is so represented but that member may participate in any discussion of the application by that committee prior to the making of the decision.][3]

(2) (a) In this section, "heritage item" means any kind of cultural item, including—

    (i) any archaeological item, archive, book, estate record, manuscript and painting, and

    (ii) any collection of cultural items and any collection of such items in their setting,

which, on application to the selection committee in writing in that behalf by a person who owns the item or collection of items, as the case may be, [is, subject to the provisions of paragraphs (aa) and (ab), determined by the selection committee,][4] to be an item or collection of items which is—

    (I) an outstanding example of the type of item involved, pre-eminent in its class, whose export from the State would constitute a diminution of the accumulated cultural heritage of Ireland or whose import into the State would constitute a significant enhancement of the accumulated cultural heritage of Ireland, and

    (II) suitable for acquisition by an approved body.

[(aa) In considering an application under paragraph (a), the selection committee shall—

    (i) consider such evidence as the person making the application submits to it, and

    (ii) seek and consider the opinion in writing in relation to the application of—

        (I) the approved body to which it is intended the gift is to be made, and

        (II) the Heritage Council, the Arts Council or such other person or body of persons as the committee considers to be appropriate in the circumstances.

(ab) Where an application under paragraph (a) is in respect of a collection of items, the selection committee shall not make a determination under that paragraph in relation to the collection unless, in addition to the making of a determination in relation to the collection as a whole, the selection committee is satisfied that, on the basis of its consideration of the application in accordance with paragraph (aa), it could make a determination in respect of at least one item comprised in the collection, if such were required.][5]

[(ac) Paragraph (ab) shall not apply in the case of a collection of items consisting wholly of archival material or manuscripts which was either—

    (i) created over time by one individual, family or organisation, or

      (ii)   was assembled by an individual family or organisation,

      and constitutes a collection of archival material or manuscripts where each item has been in such collection for a period of not less than 30 years and merits maintenance as a collection.][11]

(b)   On receipt of an application for a determination under paragraph (a), the selection committee shall request the Revenue Commissioners in writing to value the item or collection of items, as the case may be, in accordance with subsection (3).

(c)   The selection committee shall not make a determination under paragraph (a) where the market value of the item or collection of items, as the case may be, as determined by the Revenue Commissioners in accordance with subsection (3), at the valuation date—

    [(i)   is less than,

        (I)   subject to clause (II), €150,000, and

        (II) in the case of at least one item comprised in a collection of items, €50,000, or][6]

    (ii) exceeds an amount (which shall not be less than [€150,000][7]) determined by the formula—

$$€6,000,000 - M$$

where M is an amount (which may be nil) equal to the market value at the valuation date of the heritage item (if any) or the aggregate of the market values at the respective valuation dates of all the heritage items (if any), as the case may be, in respect of which a determination or determinations, as the case may be, under this subsection has been made by the selection committee in any one calendar year and not revoked in that year.

(d)   (i)   An item or collection of items shall cease to be a heritage item for the purposes of this section if—

        (I)   the item or collection of items is sold or otherwise disposed of to a person other than an approved body,

        (II) the owner of the item or collection of items notifies the selection committee in writing that it is not intended to make a gift of the item or collection of items to an approved body, or

        (III) the gift of the item or collection of items is not made to an approved body within the calendar year following the year in which the determination is made under paragraph (a).

    (ii) Where the selection committee becomes aware, at any time within the calendar year in which a determination under paragraph (a) is made in respect of an item or collection of items, that clause (I) or (II) of subparagraph (i) applies to the item or collection of items, the selection committee may revoke its determination with effect from that time.

[(2A)Notwithstanding subsection (2)(c), the selection committee may make a determination in respect of an item or collection of items, consisting wholly of archival material or manuscripts, and the market value limit in respect of any one item in such a collection at the valuation date as set out in subsection (2)(c)(i)(II) shall not apply.][12]

(3) [(a) For the purposes of this section, the market value of any item or collection of items (in this subsection referred to as "the property") shall, subject to paragraph (d), be estimated to be the lesser of —

(i) the price which, in the opinion of the Revenue Commissioners, the property would fetch if sold in the open market on the valuation date in such manner and subject to such conditions as might reasonably be calculated to obtain for the vendor the best price for the property, and

(ii) (I) the price which, in the opinion of the person making the gift of the property, the property would fetch on the valuation date if sold in the manner referred to in subparagraph (i), or

(II) at the election of that person, the amount paid for the property by that person.][8]

(b) The market value of the property shall be ascertained by the Revenue Commissioners in such manner and by such means as they think fit, and they may authorise a person to inspect the property and report to them the value of the property for the purposes of this section, and the person having custody or possession of the property shall permit the person so authorised to inspect the property at such reasonable times as the Revenue Commissioners consider necessary.

(c) Where the Revenue Commissioners require a valuation to be made by a person authorised by them, the cost of such valuation shall be defrayed by the Revenue Commissioners.

(d) Where the property is acquired at auction by the person making the gift, the market value of the property shall, for the purposes of this section, be deemed to include the auctioneer's fees in connection with the auction together with—

(i) any amount chargeable under the Value-Added Tax Act, 1972, by the auctioneer to the purchaser of the property in respect of those fees and in respect of which the purchaser is not entitled to any deduction or refund under that Act or any other enactment relating to value-added tax, or

(ii) in the case of an auction in a country other than the State, the amount chargeable to the purchaser of the property in respect of a tax chargeable under the law of that country which corresponds to value-added tax in the State and in relation to which the purchaser is not entitled to any deduction or refund.

(4) Where a relevant gift is made to an approved body –

(a) the designated officer of that body shall give a certificate to the person who made the relevant gift, in such form as the Revenue Commissioners may prescribe, certifying the receipt of that gift and the transfer of the ownership of the heritage item the subject of that gift to the approved body, and

(b) the designated officer shall transmit a duplicate of the certificate to the Revenue Commissioners.

(5) Subject to this section, where a person has made a relevant gift the person shall, on submission to the Revenue Commissioners of the certificate given to the person in accordance with subsection (4), be treated as having made on the date of such submission a payment on account of tax of **[an amount equal to 80 per cent of the market value]**[13] of the relevant gift on the valuation date.

(6) A payment on account of tax which is treated as having been made in accordance with subsection (5) shall be set in so far as possible against any liability to tax of the person who is treated as having made such a payment in the following order –

(a) firstly, against any arrears of tax due for payment by that person and against an arrear of tax for an earlier period in priority to a later period, and for this purpose the date on which an arrear of tax became due for payment shall determine whether it is for an earlier or later period, and

(b) only then, against any current liability of the person which the person nominates for that purpose,

and such set-off shall accordingly discharge a corresponding amount of that liability.

(7) To the extent that a payment on account of tax has not been set off in accordance with subsection (6), the balance remaining shall be set off against any future liability to tax of the person who is treated as having made the payment which that person nominates for that purpose.

(8) Where a person has power to sell any heritage item in order to raise money for the payment of gift tax or inheritance tax, such person shall have power to make a relevant gift of that heritage item in or towards satisfaction of that tax and, except as regards the nature of

the consideration and its receipt and application, any such relevant gift shall be subject to the same provisions and shall be treated for all purposes as a sale made in exercise of that power, and any conveyances or transfers made or purporting to be made to give effect to such a relevant gift shall apply accordingly.

(9) A person shall not be entitled to any refund of tax in respect of any payment on account of tax made in accordance with this section.

(10) Interest shall not be payable in respect of any overpayment of tax for any period which arises directly or indirectly by reason of the set-off against any liability for that period of a payment on account of tax made in accordance with this section.

(11) Where a person makes a relevant gift and in respect of that gift is treated as having made a payment on account of tax, the person concerned shall not be allowed relief under any other provision of the Acts in respect of that gift.

(12) (a) The Revenue Commissioners shall as respects each year compile a list of the titles (if any), descriptions and values of the heritage items (if any) in respect of which relief under this section has been given.

(b) Notwithstanding any obligation as to secrecy imposed on them by the Acts or the Official Secrets Act, 1963, the Revenue Commissioners shall include in their annual report to the Minister for Finance the list (if any) referred to in paragraph (a) for the year in respect of which the report is made.

Footnotes

1   Substituted for "Capital Acquisitions Act, 1976," by s.119, CATCA, with effect from 21st February, 2003.

2   As substituted by s.85(a)(i), FA 2004, as respects determinations made under s.1003(2)(a) on or after 25th March, 2004.

3   As inserted by s.85(a)(ii), FA 2004, as respects determinations made under s.1003(2)(a) on or after 25th March, 2004.

4   As substituted by s.85(b)(i), FA 2004, as respects determinations made under s.1003(2)(a) on or after 25th March, 2004.

5   As inserted by s.85(b)(ii), FA 2004, as respects determinations made under s.1003(2)(a) on or after 25th March, 2004.

6   As substituted by s.85(b)(iii)(I), FA 2004, as respects determinations made under s.1003(2)(a), on or after 25th March, 2004.

7   Substituted for "€100,000" by s.85(b)(iii)(II), FA 2004, as respects determinations made under s.1003(2)(a) on or after 25th March, 2004.

8   As substituted by s.121, FA 2006, as respects the year of assessment 2006 and subsequent years of assessment.

9   As inserted by s.125(a), FA 2007, with effect from 2nd April, 2007.

10 As inserted by s.125(b), FA 2007, with effect from 2nd April, 2007.

11 As inserted by s.131(a), FA 2008, with effect from 13th March, 2008.

12 As inserted by s.131(b), FA 2008, with effect from 13th March, 2008.

13 Substituted for "an amount equal to the market value" by s.94(1)(a), F(No. 2)A, 2008, as respects, under s.94(2)(a), any determination made by the selection committee on or after 1st January, 2009.

Section 1003A[1]

Payment of tax by means of donation of heritage property to an Irish heritage trust.

1003A. (1) In this section—

"the Acts" means—

(a) the Tax Acts (other than Chapter 8 of Part 6, Chapter 2 of Part 18 and Chapter 4 of this Part),

(b) the Capital Gains Tax Acts, and

(c) the Capital Acquisitions Tax Consolidation Act 2003, and the enactments amending or extending that Act,

and any instruments made thereunder;

"arrears of tax" means tax due and payable in accordance with any provision of the Acts (including any interest and penalties payable under any provision of the Acts in relation to such tax)—

(a) in the case of income tax, corporation tax or capital gains tax, in respect of the relevant period, or

(b) in the case of gift tax or inheritance tax, before the commencement of the calendar year in which the relevant gift is made,

which has not been paid at the time a relevant gift is made;

"contents of the building" means furnishings historically associated with the building and in respect of which the Minister is satisfied that they are important to establishing the historic or aesthetic context of the building;

"current liability' means—

(a) in the case of income tax or capital gains tax, any liability to such tax arising in the year of assessment in which the relevant gift is made,

(b) in the case of corporation tax, any liability to such tax arising in the accounting period in which the relevant gift is made,

(c) in the case of gift tax or inheritance tax, any liability to such tax which becomes due and payable in the calendar year in which the relevant gift is made;

"heritage property" has the meaning assigned to it by subsection (2)(a);

"market value" has the meaning assigned to it by subsection (3);

"Minister" means the Minister for the Environment, Heritage and Local Government;

"relevant gift" means a gift of heritage property to the Trust in respect of which no consideration whatever (other than relief under this section) is received by the person making the gift, either directly or indirectly, from the Trust or otherwise;

"'relevant period" means—

(a) in the case of income tax and capital gains tax, any year of assessment preceding the year in which the relevant gift is made, and

(b) in the case of corporation tax, any accounting period preceding the accounting period in which the relevant gift is made;

"tax" means income tax, corporation tax, capital gains tax, gift tax or inheritance tax, as the case may be, payable in accordance with any provision of the Acts;

"Trust" means the company designated for the purposes of this section by the order referred to in section 122(2) of the Finance Act 2006;[2]

"valuation date" means the date on which an application is made to the Minister for a determination under subsection (2)(a).

(2) (a) In this section "heritage property" means a building or a garden which, on application to the Minister in writing in that behalf by a person who owns the building or the garden is, subject to the provisions of paragraph (b), determined by the Minister to be a building or a garden which is—

(i) an outstanding example of the type of building or garden involved,

(ii) pre-eminent in its class,

(iii) intrinsically of significant scientific, historical, horticultural, national, architectural or aesthetic interest, and

(iv) suitable for acquisition by the Trust,

and, for the purposes of this section, a reference to "building" includes—

(I) any associated outbuilding, yard or land where the land is occupied or enjoyed with the building as part of its garden or designed landscape and contributes to the appreciation of the building in its setting, and

(II) the contents of the building.

(b) In considering an application under paragraph (a), the Minister shall consider such evidence as the person making the application submits to the Minister.

(c) On receipt of an application for a determination under paragraph (a), the Minister shall request the Revenue Commissioners in writing to value the heritage property in accordance with subsection (3).

(d) The Minister shall not make a determination under paragraph (a) where the market value of the property, as determined by the Revenue Commissioners in accordance with subsection (3), at the valuation date exceeds an amount determined by the formula —

$$[€8,000,000]^4 − M$$

where M is an amount (which may be nil) equal to the market value at the valuation date of the heritage property (if any) or the aggregate of the market values at the respective valuation dates of all the heritage properties (if any), as the case may be, in respect of which a determination or determinations, as the case may be, under this subsection has been made by the Minister in any one calendar year and not revoked in that year.

(e) (i) A property shall cease to be a heritage property for the purposes of this section if —

    (I) the property is sold or otherwise disposed of to a person other than the Trust,

    (II) the owner of the property notifies the Trust in writing that it is not intended to make a gift of the property to the Trust, or

    (III) the gift of the property is not made to the Trust within the calendar year following the year in which the determination is made under paragraph (a).

(ii) Where the Minister becomes aware, at any time within the calendar year in which a determination under paragraph (a) is made in respect of a property, that clause (I) or (II) of subparagraph (i) applies to the property, the Minister may revoke the determination with effect from that time.

(3) (a) For the purposes of this section, the market value of any property shall be estimated to be the lesser of —

(i) the price which, in the opinion of the Revenue Commissioners, the property would fetch if sold in the open market on the valuation date in such manner and subject to such conditions as might reasonably be calculated to obtain for the vendor the best price for the property, and

(ii) (I) the price which, in the opinion of the person making the gift of the property, the property would fetch on the valuation date if sold in the manner referred to in subparagraph (i), or

    (II) at the election of that person, the amount paid for the property by that person.

(b) The market value of the property shall be ascertained by the Revenue Commissioners in such manner and by such means as they think fit, and they may authorise a person to inspect the property and report to them the value of the property for the purposes of this section, and the person having custody or possession of the property shall permit the person so authorised to inspect the property at such reasonable times as the Revenue Commissioners consider necessary.

(c) Where the Revenue Commissioners require a valuation to be made by a person authorised by them, the cost of such valuation shall be defrayed by the Revenue Commissioners.

(4) Where a relevant gift is made to the Trust –

(a) the Trust shall give a certificate to the person who made the relevant gift, in such form as the Revenue Commissioners may prescribe, certifying the receipt of that gift and the transfer of the ownership of the heritage property the subject of that gift to the Trust, and

(b) the Trust shall transmit a duplicate of the certificate to the Revenue Commissioners.

(5) Subject to this section, where a person has made a relevant gift the person shall, on submission to the Revenue Commissioners of the certificate given to the person in accordance with subsection (4), be treated as having made on the date of such submission a payment on account of tax of **[an amount equal to 80 per cent of the market value]**[6] of the relevant gift on the valuation date.

(6) A payment on account of tax which is treated as having been made in accordance with subsection (5) shall be set in so far as possible against any liability to tax of the person who is treated as having made such a payment in the following order –

(a) firstly, against any arrears of tax due for payment by that person and against an arrear of tax for an earlier period in priority to a later period, and for this purpose the date on which an arrear of tax became due for payment shall determine whether it is for an earlier or later period, and

(b) only then, against any current liability of the person which the person nominates for that purpose,

and such set off shall accordingly discharge a corresponding amount of that liability.

(7) To the extent that a payment on account of tax has not been set off in accordance with subsection (6), the balance remaining shall be set off against any future liability to tax of the person who is treated as having made the payment which that person nominates for that purpose.

(8) Where a person has power to sell any heritage property in order to raise money for the payment of gift tax or inheritance tax, such person shall have power to make a relevant gift of that heritage property in or towards satisfaction of that tax and, except as regards the nature of the consideration and its receipt and application, any

such relevant gift shall be subject to the same provisions and shall be treated for all purposes as a sale made in exercise of that power, and any conveyances or transfers made or purporting to be made to give effect to such a relevant gift shall apply accordingly.

(9) A person shall not be entitled to any refund of tax in respect of any payment on account of tax made in accordance with this section.

(10) Interest shall not be payable in respect of any overpayment of tax for any period which arises directly or indirectly by reason of the set off against any liability for that period of a payment on account of tax made in accordance with this section.

(11) Where a person makes a relevant gift and in respect of that gift is treated as having made a payment on account of tax, the person concerned shall not be allowed relief under any other provision of the Acts in respect of that gift.

[(11A)(a) In the event that Fota House in County Cork is acquired by the Trust, either by way of a relevant gift under this section or otherwise, and the collection referred to in paragraph (b) is acquired by the Trust by way of gift, relief under this section shall, subject to paragraphs (c) and (d), be granted in respect of the collection on the basis that Fota House was acquired by the Trust by way of a relevant gift and the collection formed part of the contents of the building.

(b) The collection referred to in this paragraph (in this subsection referred to as the "collection") is a collection –

(i) of either or both Irish paintings and furniture which was displayed in Fota House in the period 1983 to 1990,

(ii) which is to be housed by the Trust in Fota House, and

(iii) in respect of which the Minister, after consulting with such person (if any) in the matter as the Minister may deem to be necessary, is satisfied that the collection is important to establishing the aesthetic context of Fota House.

(c) This subsection shall not apply unless the collection is gifted to the Trust before the end of [2008][5].

(d) Relief under this section, in respect of the market value of the collection as determined in accordance with subsection (3), shall, where this subsection applies, be granted to the person making the gift to the Trust of the collection, notwithstanding that that person is not the person from whom Fota House was acquired by the Trust.][3]

(12) (a) The Revenue Commissioners shall as respects each year compile a list of the titles (if any), descriptions and values of the heritage properties (if any) in respect of which relief under this section has been given.

(b) Notwithstanding any obligation as to secrecy imposed on them by the Acts or the Official Secrets Act 1963, the Revenue Commissioners shall include in their annual report to the Minister for Finance the list (if any) referred to in paragraph (a) for the year in respect of which the report is made.

Footnotes

1   This section was inserted by s.122(1), FA 2006, which section will come into operation on such day as the Minister for Finance may appoint by order. S.I. No. 520 of 2006 (see page 1381) appoints 5th October, 2006, as the date on which the section comes into operation.

2   Under s.122(2), FA 2006, the Minister for Finance shall designate by order the company (being a company incorporated under the Companies Acts) which is to be the Trust for the purposes of this section. S.I. No. 521 of 2006 (see page 1382) designates the Irish Heritage Trust Limited as the Trust.

3   As inserted by s.122(1), FA 2007, which applies only as stated in s.1003A(11A)(c) above.

4   "€10,000,000" substituted for "€6,000,000" by s.122(2), FA 2007, as respects the year of assessment 2007. "€8,000,000" substituted for "€10,000,000" by s.131(2), FA, 2008, as respects the year of assessment 2008.

5   "2008" substituted for "2007" by s.132(1), FA 2008.

6   Substituted for "an amount equal to the market value" by s.94(1)(b), F(No.2)A, 2008, as respects, under s.94(2)(b), any determination made by the Minister for the Environment, Heritage and Local Government on or after 1st January, 2009.

Section 1006

Poundage and certain other fees due to sheriffs or county registrars.

1006. (1)   In this section —

"the Acts" means —

(a)   the Tax Acts,

[(aa) Part 18A,][2]

(b)   the Capital Gains Tax Acts,

(c)   the Value-Added Tax Act, 1972, and the enactments amending or extending that Act,

(d)   the [Capital Acquisitions Tax Consolidation Act 2003,][1] and the enactments amending or extending that Act, and

(e)   Part VI of the Finance Act, 1983, and the enactments amending or extending that Part,

[(f)   Part 18B,][3]

and any instruments made thereunder;

"certificate" means a certificate issued under **[section 960L]**[4];

"county registrar" means a person appointed to be a county registrar under section 35 of the Court Officers Act, 1926;

"defaulter" means a person specified or certified in an execution order or certificate on whom a relevant amount specified or certified in the order or certificate is leviable;

"execution order" has the same meaning as in the Enforcement of Court Orders Act, 1926;

"fees" means the fees known as poundage fees payable under section 14 (1) of the Enforcement of Court Orders Act, 1926, and orders made under that section for services in or about the execution of an execution order directing or authorising the execution of an order of a court by the seizure and sale of a person's property or, as may be appropriate, the fees corresponding to those fees payable under **[section 960L]**[4] for the execution of a certificate;

"interest on unpaid tax" means interest which has accrued under any provision of the Acts providing for the charging of interest in respect of unpaid tax, including interest on an undercharge of tax which is attributable to fraud or neglect;

"relevant amount" means an amount of tax or interest on unpaid tax;

"tax" means any tax, duty, levy or charge which, in accordance with any provision of the Acts, is placed under the care and management of the Revenue Commissioners;

references, as respects an execution order, to a relevant amount include references to any amount of costs specified in the order.

(2) Where—

(a) an execution order or certificate specifying or certifying a defaulter and relating to a relevant amount is lodged with the appropriate sheriff or county registrar for execution,

(b) the sheriff or, as the case may be, the county registrar gives notice to the defaulter of the lodgment or of his or her intention to execute the execution order or certificate by seizure of the property of the defaulter to which it relates, or demands payment by the defaulter of the relevant amount, and

(c) the whole or part of the relevant amount is paid to the sheriff or, as the case may be, the county registrar or to the Collector-General, after the giving of that notice or the making of that demand,

then, for the purpose of the liability of the defaulter for the payment of fees and of the exercise of any rights or powers in relation to the collection of fees for the time being vested by law in sheriffs and county registrars—

(i) the sheriff or, as the case may be, the county registrar shall be deemed to have entered, in the execution of the execution order or certificate, into possession of the property referred to in paragraph (b), and

(ii) the payment mentioned in paragraph (c) shall be deemed to have been levied, in the execution of the execution order or certificate, by the sheriff or, as the case may be, the county registrar, and fees shall be payable by the defaulter to such sheriff or, as the case may be, country registrar accordingly in respect of the payment mentioned in paragraph (c).

Footnotes

1   Substituted for "Capital Acquisitions Tax Act, 1976" by s.119, CATCA, with effect from 21st February, 2003.

2   Inserted by s.2(c), F(No.2)A, 2008, with effect as on and from 1st January, 2009.

3   Inserted by s.3(1)(c), F(No.2)A, 2008, with effect as on and from 1st January, 2009.

4   Substituted for "section 962" by Part 2 of the Table to Sch. 4, F(No.2)A, 2008 and comes into force and applies (para. 6 of that Sch.) as respects any tax that becomes due and payable after 1st March, 2009.

Section 1006A

Offset between taxes.

1006A.   ....

Footnote

1   This section, amended as shown in the footnotes to s.1006A in the Second Part of this book, was applied to the CATCA with effect from 21st February, 2003, by s.119, CATCA. This section has been repealed by Part 1 of the Table to Sch. 4, F(No. 2)A, 2008, which repeal, under Part 6 of that Sch, applies as respects any tax that becomes due and payable after 1st March, 2009. See now s.960H, TCA, in page 268.

PART 47

Penalties, Revenue Offences, Interest on Overdue Tax and other Sanctions

CHAPTER 3A

Determination of Penalties and Recovery of Penalties

Section 1077A[1]

Interpretation (Chapter 3A).

1077A. In this Chapter—

"the Acts" means—

(a)   the Tax Acts,

(b)   the Capital Gains Tax Acts,

(c)   Parts 18A and 18B,

(d)   the Value-Added Tax Act 1972, and the enactments amending or extending that Act,

(e)   the Capital Acquisitions Tax Consolidation Act 2003, and the enactments amending or extending that Act,

(f)   the Stamp Duties Consolidation Act 1999, and the enactments amending or extending that Act,

(g) the statutes relating to the duties of excise and to the management of those duties,

and any instrument made thereunder and any instrument made under any other enactment relating to tax;

"relevant court" means the District Court, the Circuit Court or the High Court, as appropriate, by reference to the jurisdictional limits for civil matters laid down in the Courts of Justice Act 1924, as amended, and the Courts (Supplemental Provisions) Act 1961, as amended;

"Revenue officer" means an officer of the Revenue Commissioners;

"tax" means any tax, duty, levy or charge under the care and management of the Revenue Commissioners.

Footnote

1   Inserted by s.98(1) of, and by para. 1 of Sch. 5 to, the F(No.2)A, 2008, and comes into effect after 24th December, 2008.

Section 1077B[1]

Penalty notifications and determinations.

1077B. (1) In this section —

    (a)   in the absence of any agreement between a person and a Revenue officer that the person is liable to a penalty under the Acts, or

    (b)   following the failure by a person to pay a penalty the person has agreeed a liability to,

a Revenue officer is of the opinion that the person is liable to a penalty under the Acts, then that officer shall give notice in writing to the person and such notice shall identify —

    (i)   the provisions of the Acts under which the penalty arises,

    (ii)   the circumstances is which that person is liable to the penalty, and

    (iii)   the amount of the penalty to which that person is liable.

and include such other details as the Revenue officer considers necessary.

  (2) A Revenue officer may at any time amend an opinion that a person is liable to a penalty under the Acts and shall give due notice of such amended opinion in like manner to the notice referred to in subsection (1).

  (3) Where a person to whom a notice issued under subsection (1) or (2) does not, within 30 days after the date of such a notice —

    (a)   agree in writing with the opinion or amended opinion contained in such notice, and

    (b)   make a payment to the Revenue Commisioners of the amount of the penalty specified in such a notice.

then a Revenue officer may make an application to a relevant court for that court to determine whether –

    (i)   any action, inaction, omission or failure of, or

    (ii)   any claim, submission or delivery by,

the person in respect of whom the Revenue officer made the application gives rise to a liability to a penalty under the Acts on that person.

    (4)   A copy of any application to a relevant court for a determination under subsection (3) shall be issued to the person to whom the application relates.

    (5)   This section applies in respect of any act or omission giving rise to a liability to a penalty under the Acts whether arising before, on or after the passing of the Finance (No. 2) Act 2008 but shall not apply in respect of a penalty paid, or amounts paid in respect of a penalty, before the passing of that Act.

Footnote

1   Inserted by s.98(1) of, and by para. 1 of Sch. 5 to, the F(No. 2)A, 2008, and comes into effect after 24th December, 2008.

Section 1077C[1]

Recovery of penalties.

1077C. (1) Where a relevant court has made a determination that a person is liable to a penalty –

    (a)   that court shall also make an order as to the recovery of that penalty, and

    (b)   without prejudice to any other means of recovery, that penalty may be collected and recovered in like manner as an amount of tax.

    (2)   Where a person is liable to a penalty under the Acts, that penalty is due and payable from the date –

    (a)   it had been agreed in writing (or had been agreed in writing on the person's behalf) that the person is liable to that penalty,

    (b)   the Revenue Commissioners had agreed or undertaken to accept a specified sum of money in the circumstances mentioned in paragraph (c) or (d) of section 1086(2) from that [person,][2], or

    (c)   a relevant court has determined that the person is liable to that penalty.

(3)　This section applies in respect of any act or omission giving rise to a liability to a penalty under the Acts whether arising before, on or after the passing of the Finance (No. 2) Act 2008.

Footnotes

1　Inserted by s.98(1) of, and by para. 1 of Sch. 5 to, the F(No. 2) A, 2008, and comes into effect after 24th December, 2008.

2　Substituted for "individual" by s.30(2), FA 2009, and under s.30(5)(b), FA 2009, is deemed to have come into force and have taken effect as on and from 24th December, 2008.

Section 1077D

Proceedings against executor, administrator or estate.

1077D. (1) Where before an individual's death –

(a)　that individual had agreed in writing (or it had been agreed in writing on his or her behalf) that he or she was liable to a penalty under the Acts,

(b)　that individual had agreed in writing with an opinion or amended opinion of a Revenue officer that he or she was liable to a penalty under the Acts (or such opinion or amended opinion had been agreed in writing on his or her behalf),

(c)　the Revenue Commissioners had agreed or undertaken to accept a specified sum of money in the circumstances mentioned in paragraph (c) or (d) of section 1086(2) from that individual, or

(d)　a relevant court has determined that the individual was liable to a penalty under the Acts.

then the penalty shall be due and payable and, subject to subsection (2), any proceedings for the recovery of such penalty under the Acts which have been, or could have been, instituted against that individual may be continued or instituted against his or her executor, administrator or estate, as the case may be, and any penalty awarded in proceedings so continued or instituted shall be a debt due from and payable out of his or her estate.

(2)　Proceedings may not be instituted by virtue of subsection (1) against the executor or administrator of a person at a time when by virtue of subsection (2) of section 1048 that executor or administrator is not assessable and chargeable under that section in respect of tax on profits or gains which arose or accrued to the person before his or her death.

Footnote

1　Inserted by s.98(1) of, and by para. 1 of Sch. 5 to, the F(No. 2)A, 2008 and comes into effect after 24th December, 2008.

CHAPTER 4
Revenue Offences

Section 1078

Revenue offences.

1078. (1) In this Part—

"the Acts" means—

(a)   the Customs Acts,

(b)   the statutes relating to the duties of excise and to the management of those duties,

(c)   the Tax Acts,

[(ca) Part 18A,][9]

(d)   the Capital Gains Tax Acts,

(e)   the Value-Added Tax Act, 1972, and the enactments amending or extending that Act,

(f)   the [Capital Acquisitions Tax Consolidation Act 2003,][1] and the enactments amending or extending that Act,

(g)   the statutes relating to stamp duty and to the management of that duty, and

(h)   Part VI of the Finance Act, 1983,

[(i) Part 18B,][10]

and any instruments made thereunder and any instruments made under any other enactment and relating to tax;

"authorised officer" means an officer of the Revenue Commissioners authorised by them in writing to exercise any of the powers conferred by the Acts;

"tax" means any tax, duty, levy or charge under the care and management of the Revenue Commissioners.

[(1A) (a)   In this subsection—

"facilitating" means aiding, abetting, assisting, inciting or inducing;

"fraudulent evasion of tax by a person" means the person—

(a)   evading or attempting to evade any payment or deduction of tax required under the Acts to be paid by the person or, as the case may be, required under the Acts to be deducted from amounts due to the person, or

(b)   claiming or obtaining, or attempting to claim or obtain, relief or exemption from, or payment or repayment of, any tax, being relief, exemption, payment or repayment, to which the person is not entitled under the Acts, where, for those purposes, the person deceives, omits, conceals or uses any other dishonest means including –

   (i)   providing false, incomplete or misleading information, or

   (ii) failing to furnish information,

to the Revenue Commissioners or to any other person.

  (b) For the purposes of this subsection and subsection (5) a person (in this paragraph referred to as the "first-mentioned person") is reckless as to whether or not he or she is concerned in facilitating –

   (i)   the fraudulent evasion of tax by a person, being another person, or

   (ii) the commission of an offence under subsection (2) by a person, being another person,

if the first-mentioned person disregards a substantial risk that he or she is so concerned, and for those purposes "substantial risk" means a risk of such a nature and degree that, having regard to all the circumstances and the extent of the information available to the first-mentioned person, its disregard by that person involves culpability of a high degree.

  (c) A person shall, without prejudice to any other penalty to which the person may be liable, be guilty of an offence under this section if the person –

   (i)   is knowingly concerned in the fraudulent evasion of tax by the person or any other person,

   (ii) is knowingly concerned in, or is reckless as to whether or not the person is concerned in, facilitating –

     (I)   the fraudulent evasion of tax, or

     (II) the commission of an offence under subsection (2) (other than an offence under paragraph (b) of that subsection),

    by any other person, or

   (iii) is knowingly concerned in the fraudulent evasion or attempted fraudulent evasion of any prohibition or restriction on importation for the time being in force, or the removal of any goods from the State, in contravention of any provision of the Acts.][3]

[(1B) A person is guilty of an offence under this section if he or she, with the intention to deceive –

  (a) purports to be, or

  (b) makes any statement, or otherwise acts in a manner, that would lead another person to believe that he or she is,

an officer of the Revenue Commissioners.][8]

(2) A person shall, without prejudice to any other penalty to which the person may be liable, be guilty of an offence under this section if the person—

(a) knowingly or wilfully delivers any incorrect return, statement or accounts or knowingly or wilfully furnishes any incorrect information in connection with any tax,

(b) knowingly aids, abets, assists, incites or induces another person to make or deliver knowingly or wilfully any incorrect return, statement or accounts in connection with any tax,

(c) claims or obtains relief or exemption from, or repayment of, any tax, being a relief, exemption or repayment to which, to the person's knowledge, the person is not entitled,

(d) knowingly or wilfully issues or produces any incorrect invoice, receipt, instrument or other document in connection with any tax,

(e) (i) fails to make any deduction required to be made by the person under section 257(1),

(ii) fails, having made the deduction, to pay the sum deducted to the Collector-General within the time specified in that behalf in section 258(3), or

(iii) fails to pay to the Collector-General an amount on account of appropriate tax (within the meaning of Chapter 4 of Part 8) within the time specified in that behalf in section 258(4),

[(f) fails to pay to the Collector-General appropriate tax (within the meaning of section 739E) within the time specified in that behalf in section 739F,][4]

(g) fails without reasonable excuse to comply with any provision of the Acts requiring—

(i) the furnishing of a return of income, profits or gains, or of sources of income, profits or gains, for the purposes of any tax,

(ii) the furnishing of any other return, certificate, notification, particulars, or any statement or evidence, for the purposes of any tax,

(iii) the keeping or retention of books, records, accounts or other documents for the purposes of any tax, or

(iv) the production of books, records, accounts or other documents, when so requested, for the purposes of any tax,

(h) knowingly or wilfully, and within the time limits specified for their retention, destroys, defaces or conceals from an authorised officer—

    (i)   any documents, or

    (ii)   any other written or printed material in any form, including any information stored, maintained or preserved by means of any mechanical or electronic device, whether or not stored, maintained or preserved in a legible form, which a person is obliged by any provision of the Acts to keep, to issue or to produce for inspection,

(hh) knowingly or wilfully falsifies, conceals, destroys or otherwise disposes of, or causes or permits the falsification, concealment, destruction or disposal of, any books, records or other documents—

    (i)   which the person has been given the opportunity to deliver, or as the case may be, to make available in accordance with section 900(3), or

    (ii)   which the person has been required to deliver or, as the case may be, to make available in accordance with a notice served under section 900, 902, 906A or 907, or an order made under section 901, 902A or 908,

(i)   fails to remit any income tax payable pursuant to Chapter 4 of Part 42, and the regulations under that Chapter, or value-added tax within the time specified in that behalf in relation to income tax or value-added tax, as the case may be, [by the Acts,]⁵

[(ii) (i)   fails to deduct tax required to be deducted by the person under section 531(1), or

    (ii)   fails, having made that deduction, to pay the sum deducted to the Collector-General within the time specified in that behalf in section 531(3A),

    or]⁶

(j)   obstructs or interferes with any officer of the Revenue Commissioners, or any other person, in the exercise or performance of powers or duties under the Acts for the purposes of any tax.

(3)   A person convicted of an offence under this section shall be liable—

(a)   on summary conviction to a fine of [€5,000]² which may be mitigated to not less than one fourth part of such fine or, at the discretion of the court, to imprisonment for a term not exceeding 12 months or to both the fine and the imprisonment, or

(b)   on conviction on indictment, to a fine not exceeding €126,970 or, at the discretion of the court, to imprisonment for a term not exceeding 5 years or to both the fine and the imprisonment.

(3A) Where a person has been convicted of an offence referred to in subparagraph (i), (ii) or (iv) of subsection (2)(g), then, if an application is made, or caused to be made to the court in that regard, the court may make an order requiring the person concerned to comply with any provision of the Acts relating to the requirements specified in the said subparagraph (i), (ii) or (iv), as the case may be.

(3B) A person shall, without prejudice to any other penalty to which the person may be liable, be guilty of an offence under this section if the person fails or refuses to comply with an order referred to in subsection (3A) **[within a period of 30 days commencing on the day the order is made]**.

(4) Section 13 of the Criminal Procedure Act, 1967, shall apply in relation to an offence under this section as if, in place of the penalties specified in subsection (3) of that section, there were specified in that subsection the penalties provided for by subsection (3)(a), and the reference in subsection (2)(a) of section 13 of the Criminal Procedure Act, 1967, to the penalties provided for in subsection (3) of that section shall be construed and apply accordingly.

(5) Where an offence under this section is committed by a body corporate and the offence is shown [to have been committed with the consent or connivance of or to be attributable to any recklessness (as provided for by subsection (1A)(b)) on the part of][7] any person who, when the offence was committed, was a director, manager, secretary or other officer of the body corporate, or a member of the committee of management or other controlling authority of the body corporate, that person shall also be deemed to be guilty of the offence and may be proceeded against and punished accordingly.

(6) In any proceedings under this section, a return or statement delivered to an inspector or other officer of the Revenue Commissioners under any provision of the Acts and purporting to be signed by any person shall be deemed until the contrary is proved to have been so delivered and to have been signed by that person.

(7) Notwithstanding any other enactment, proceedings in respect of an offence under this section may be instituted within 10 years from the date of the commission of the offence or incurring of the penalty, as the case may be.

(8) Section 1 of the Probation of Offenders Act, 1907, shall not apply in relation to offences under this section.

(9) Sections 987(4) and 1052(4), subsections (3) and (7) of section 1053, **[subsections (9) and (17) of section 1077E,]**[12] and sections 1068 and 1069 **[, and section 27A(16) of the Value-Added Tax Act 1972,]**[13] shall, with any necessary modifications, apply for the purposes of this section as they apply for the purposes of those sections, including, in the case of such of those sections as are applied by the Capital Gains Tax Acts, the Corporation Tax Acts, or Part VI of the Finance Act, 1983, the purposes of those sections as so applied.

Footnotes

1   Substituted for "Capital Acquisitions Tax Act, 1976" by s.119, CATCA, with effect from 21st February, 2003.

2   "€3,000" substituted for "€1,900" by s.160, FA 2003, as respects an offence committed on or after 28th March, 2003. S. 138(1)(d), FA 2008, substituted "€5,000" for "€3,000" as respects an offence committed on a day after 13th March, 2008.

3   As inserted by s.142(a), FA 2005, with effect from 25th March, 2005.

4   As substituted by s.142(b)(i), FA 2005, with effect from 25th March, 2005.

5   As substituted for "by the Acts, or" by s.142(b)(ii), FA 2005, with effect from 25th March, 2005.

6   As inserted by s.142(b)(iii), FA 2005, with effect from 25th March, 2005.

7   Substituted for "to have been committed with the consent or connivance of" by s.142(c), FA 2005, with effect from 25th March, 2005.

8   As inserted by s.126, FA 2007, with effect from 2nd April, 2007

9   Inserted by s. 2(e), F(No.2)A, 2008, with effect as on and from 1st January, 2009.

10   Inserted by s. 3(1)(e), F(No.2)A, 2008, with effect as on and from 1st January, 2009.

11   Inserted by s. 92(k), F(No.2)A, 2008, with effect from 24th December, 2008.

12   Inserted by s. 98(1), and by para. 2(ar)(i) of Sch. 5, of the F(No.2)A, 2008, and comes into effect after 24th December, 2008.

13   Substituted for "and sections 26(6) and 27(7) of the Value-Added Tax Act, 1972," by s.98(1), and by para. 2(ar)(ii) of Sch. 5, of the F(No.2)A, 2008, and comes into effect after 24th December, 2008.

Section 1078A[1]

Concealing facts disclosed by documents.

1078A. (1)   Any person who -

    (a)   knows or suspects that an investigation by an officer of the Revenue Commissioners into an offence under the Acts or the Waiver of Certain Tax, Interest and Penalties Act 1993 is being, or is likely to be, carried out, and

    (b)   falsifies, conceals, destroys or otherwise disposes of material which the person knows or suspects is or would be relevant to the investigation or causes or permits its falsification, concealment, destruction or disposal,

is guilty of an offence.

  (2)   Where a person -

    (a)   falsifies, conceals, destroys or otherwise disposes of material, or

    (b)   causes or permits its falsification, concealment, destruction or disposal,

in such circumstances that it is reasonable to conclude that the person knew or suspected

    (i)   that an investigation by an officer of the Revenue Commissioners into an offence under the Acts or the Waiver of Certain Tax, Interest and Penalties Act 1993 was being, or was likely to be, carried out, and

(ii) that the material was or would be relevant to the investigation,

the person shall be taken, for the purposes of this section, to have so known or suspected, unless the court or the jury, as the case may be, is satisfied having regard to all the evidence that there is a reasonable doubt as to whether the person so knew or suspected.

(3) A person guilty of an offence under this section is liable -

(a) on summary conviction to a fine not exceeding **[€5,000]**[2], or at the discretion of the court, to imprisonment for a term not exceeding 6 months or to both the fine and the imprisonment, or

(b) on conviction on indictment, to a fine not exceeding €127,000 or, at the discretion of the court, to imprisonment for a term not exceeding 5 years or to both the fine and the imprisonment.

Footnotes

1   Inserted by s. 161, FA 2003, with effect from 28th March, 2003.

2   As substituted for "€3,000" by s.138(1)(e), FA 2008, as respects an offence committed on a day after 13th March, 2008.

Section 1078B[1]

Presumptions.

1078B. (1) In this section -

"return, statement or declaration" means any return, statement or declaration which a person is required to make under the Acts or the Waiver of Certain Tax, Interest and Penalties Act 1993.

(2) The presumptions specified in this section apply in any proceedings, whether civil or criminal, under any provision of the Acts or the Waiver of Certain Tax, Interest and Penalties Act 1993.

(3) Where a document purports to have been created by a person it shall be presumed, unless the contrary is shown, that the document was created by that person and that any statement contained therein, unless the document expressly attributes its making to some other person, was made by that person.

(4) Where a document purports to have been created by a person and addressed and sent to a second person, it shall be presumed, unless the contrary is shown, that the document was created and sent by the first person and received by the second person and that any statement contained therein -

(a) unless the document expressly attributes its making to some other person, was made by the first person, and

(b) came to the notice of the second person.

(5) Where a document is retrieved from an electronic storage and retrieval system, it shall be presumed unless the contrary is shown, that the author of the document is the person who ordinarily uses that electronic storage and retrieval system in the course of his or her business.

(6) Where an authorised officer in the exercise of his or her powers under subsection (2A) of section 905 **[or section (3) of section 908C]**[2] has removed records (within the meaning of that section) from any place, gives evidence in proceedings that to the best of the authorised officer's knowledge and belief, the records are the property of any person, the records shall be presumed unless the contrary is proved, to be the property of that person.

(7) Where in accordance with subsection (6) records are presumed in proceedings to be the property of a person and the authorised officer gives evidence that, to the best of the authorised officer's knowledge and belief, the records are records which relate to any trade, profession, or, as the case may be, other activity, carried on by that person, the records shall be presumed unless the contrary is proved, to be records which relate to that trade, profession, or, as the case may be, other activity, carried on by that person.

(8) In proceedings, a certificate signed by an inspector or other officer of the Revenue Commissioners certifying that a return, statement or declaration to which the certificate refers is in the possession of the Revenue Commissioners in such circumstances as to lead the officer to conclude that, to the best of his or her knowledge and belief it was delivered to an inspector or other officer of the Revenue Commissioners, it shall be presumed unless the contrary is proved, to be evidence that the said return, statement, or declaration was so delivered.

(9) In proceedings, a certificate, certifying the fact or facts referred to in subsection (8) and purporting to be signed as specified in that subsection, may be tendered in evidence without proof and shall be deemed until the contrary is proved to have been signed by a person holding, at the time of the signature, the office or position indicated in the certificate as the office or position of the person signing.

(10) References in this section to a document are references to a document in written, mechanical or electronic format and, for this purpose "written" includes any form of notation or code whether by hand or otherwise and regardless of the method by which, or the medium in or on which, the document concerned is recorded.

Footnotes

1   As inserted by s.161, FA 2003, with effect from 28th March, 2003.

2.   As inserted by s. 99, and by para.1(c), Sch. 6, of the F(No.2)A, 2008, and has effect as on and from 24th December, 2008

Section 1078C[1]

Provision of information to juries.

1078C. (1)   In a trial on indictment of an offence under the Acts or the Waiver of Certain Tax, Interest and Penalties Act 1993, the trial judge may order that copies of any or all of the following documents shall be given to the jury in any form that the judge considers appropriate:

(a)   any document admitted in evidence at the trial,

(b)   the transcript of the opening speeches of counsel,

(c)   any charts, diagrams, graphics, schedules or agreed summaries of evidence produced at the trial,

(d)   the transcript of the whole or any part of the evidence given at the trial,

(e)   the transcript of the closing speeches of counsel,

(f)   the transcript of the trial judge's charge to the jury,

(g)   any other document that in the opinion of the trial judge would be of assistance to the jury in its deliberations including, where appropriate, an affidavit by an accountant or other suitably qualified person, summarising, in a form which is likely to be comprehended by the jury, any transactions by the accused or other persons which are relevant to the offence.

(2)   If the prosecutor proposes to apply to the trial judge for an order that a document mentioned in subsection (1)(g) shall be given to the jury, the prosecutor shall give a copy of the document to the accused in advance of the trial and, on the hearing of the application, the trial judge shall take into account any representations made by or on behalf of the accused in relation to it.

(3)   Where the trial judge has made an order that an affidavit by an accountant or other person mentioned in subsection (1)(g) shall be given to the jury, the accountant, or as the case may be, the other person so mentioned -

(a)   shall be summoned by the prosecution to attend at the trial as an expert witness, and

(b)   may be required by the trial judge, in an appropriate case, to give evidence in regard to any relevant procedures or principles within his or her area of expertise.

Footnote
1   As inserted by s.161, FA 2003, with effect from 28th March, 2003.

Section 1079

Duties of relevant person in relation to certain revenue offences.

1079. (1)   In this section—

"the Acts" means—

(a) the Customs Acts,

(b) the statutes relating to the duties of excise and to the management of those duties,

(c) the Tax Acts,

[(ca)] Part 18A,]

(d) the Capital Gains Tax Acts,

(e) the Value-Added Tax Act, 1972, and the enactments amending or extending that Act,

(f) the [Capital Acquisitions Tax Consolidation Act 2003,][1] and the enactments amending or extending that Act,

(g) the statutes relating to stamp duty and to the management of that duty,

and any instruments made thereunder and any instruments made under any other enactment and relating to tax;

"appropriate officer" means any officer nominated by the Revenue Commissioners to be an appropriate officer for the purposes of this section;

"company" means any body corporate;

"relevant person", in relation to a company and subject to subsection (2), means a person who —

(a) (i) is an auditor to the company appointed in accordance with section 160 of the Companies Act, 1963 (as amended by the Companies Act, 1990), or

    (ii) in the case of an industrial and provident society or a friendly society, is a public auditor to the society for the purposes of the Industrial and Provident Societies Acts, 1893 to 1978, and the Friendly Societies Acts, 1896 to 1977,

or

(b) with a view to reward, assists or advises the company in the preparation or delivery of any information, declaration, return, records, accounts or other document which he or she knows will be or is likely to be used for any purpose of tax;

"relevant offence" means an offence committed by a company which consists of the company —

(a) knowingly or wilfully delivering any incorrect return, statement or accounts or knowingly or wilfully furnishing or causing to be furnished any incorrect information in connection with any tax,

(b) knowingly or wilfully claiming or obtaining relief or exemption from, or repayment of, any tax, being a relief, exemption or repayment to which there is no entitlement,

(c) knowingly or wilfully issuing or producing any incorrect invoice, receipt, instrument or other document in connection with any tax, or

(d) knowingly or wilfully failing to comply with any provision of the Acts requiring the furnishing of a return of income, profits or gains, or of sources of income, profits or gains, for the purposes of any tax, but an offence under this paragraph committed by a company shall not be a relevant offence if the company has made a return of income, profits or gains to the Revenue Commissioners in respect of an accounting period falling wholly or partly in the period of 3 years preceding the accounting period in respect of which the offence was committed;

"tax" means any tax, duty, levy or charge under the care and management of the Revenue Commissioners.

(2) For the purposes of paragraph (b) of the definition of "relevant person", a person who but for this subsection would be treated as a relevant person in relation to a company shall not be so treated if the person assists or advises the company solely in the person's capacity as an employee of the company, and a person shall be treated as assisting or advising the company in that capacity where the person's income from assisting or advising the company consists solely of emoluments to which Chapter 4 of Part 42 applies.

(3) If, having regard solely to information obtained in the course of examining the accounts of a company, or in the course of assisting or advising a company in the preparation or delivery of any information, declaration, return, records, accounts or other document for the purposes of tax, as the case may be, a person who is a relevant person in relation to the company becomes aware that the company has committed, or is in the course of committing, one or more relevant offences, the person shall, if the offence or offences are material—

(a) communicate particulars of the offence or offences in writing to the company without undue delay and request the company to—

(i) take such action as is necessary for the purposes of rectifying the matter, or

(ii) notify an appropriate officer of the offence or offences,

not later than 6 months after the time of communication, and

(b) (i) unless it is established to the person's satisfaction that the necessary action has been taken or notification made, as the case may be, under paragraph (a), cease to act as the auditor to the company or to assist or advise the company in such preparation or delivery as is specified in paragraph (b) of the definition of "relevant person", and

    (ii)   shall not so act, assist or advise before a time which is the earlier of—

        (I)   3 years after the time at which the particulars were communicated under paragraph (a), and

        (II)   the time at which it is established to the person's satisfaction that the necessary action has been taken or notification made, as the case may be, under paragraph (a).

(4)   Nothing in paragraph (b) of subsection (3) shall prevent a person from assisting or advising a company in preparing for, or conducting, legal proceedings, either civil or criminal, which are extant or pending at a time which is 6 months after the time of communication under paragraph (a) of that subsection.

(5)   Where a person, being in relation to a company a relevant person within the meaning of paragraph (a) of the definition of "relevant person", ceases under this section to act as auditor to the company, then, the person shall deliver—

    (a)   a notice in writing to the company stating that he or she is so resigning, and

    (b)   a copy of the notice to an appropriate officer not later than 14 days after he or she has delivered the notice to the company.

(6)   A person shall be guilty of an offence under this section if the person—

    (a)   fails to comply with subsection (3) or (5), or

    (b)   knowingly or wilfully makes a communication under subsection (3) which is incorrect.

(7)   Where a relevant person is convicted of an offence under this section, the person shall be liable—

    (a)   on summary conviction, to a fine of €1,265 which may be mitigated to not less than one-fourth part of such fine, or

    (b)   on conviction on indictment, to a fine not exceeding €6,345 or, at the discretion of the court, to imprisonment for a term not exceeding 2 years or to both the fine and the imprisonment.

(8)   Section 13 of the Criminal Procedure Act, 1967, shall apply in relation to this section as if, in place of the penalties specified in subsection (3) of that section, there were specified in that subsection the penalties provided for by subsection (7)(a), and the reference in subsection (2)(a) of section 13 of the Criminal Procedure Act, 1967, to the penalties provided for in subsection (3) of that section shall be construed and apply accordingly.

(9) Notwithstanding any other enactment, proceedings in respect of this section may be instituted within 6 years from the time at which a person is required under subsection (3) to communicate particulars of an offence or offences in writing to a company.

(10) It shall be a good defence in a prosecution for an offence under subsection (6)(a) in relation to a failure to comply with subsection (3) for an accused (being a person who is a relevant person in relation to a company) to show that he or she was in the ordinary scope of professional engagement assisting or advising the company in preparing for legal proceedings and would not have become aware that one or more relevant offences had been committed by the company if he or she had not been so assisting or advising.

(11) Where a person who is a relevant person takes any action required by subsection (3) or (5), no duty to which the person may be subject shall be regarded as having been contravened and no liability or action shall lie against the person in any court for having taken such action.

(12) The Revenue Commissioners may nominate an officer to be an appropriate officer for the purposes of this section, and the name of an officer so nominated and the address to which copies of notices under subsection (3) or (5) shall be delivered shall be published in *Iris Oifigiúil*.

(13) This section shall apply as respects a relevant offence committed by a company in respect of tax which is —

    (a) assessable by reference to accounting periods, for any accounting period beginning after the 30th day of June, 1995,

    (b) assessable by reference to years of assessment, for the year 1995-96 and subsequent years of assessment,

    (c) payable by reference to a taxable period, for a taxable period beginning after the 30th day of June, 1995,

    (d) chargeable on gifts or inheritances taken on or after the 30th day of June, 1995,

    (e) chargeable on instruments executed on or after the 30th day of June, 1995, or

    (f) payable in any other case, on or after the 30th day of June, 1995.

Footnotes

1   Substituted for "Capital Acquisitions Tax Act, 1976" by s.119, CATCA, with effect from 21st February, 2003.

2   Inserted by s.2(f), F(No. 2)A, 2008, with effect as on and from 1st January, 2009.

CHAPTER 6
Other Sanctions

Section 1086

Publication of names of tax defaulters.

1086. (1) In this section —

"the Acts" means —

(a) the Tax Acts,

(b) the Capital Gains Tax Acts,

(c) the Value-Added Tax Act, 1972, and the enactments amending or extending that Act,

(d) the [Capital Acquisitions Tax Consolidation Act 2003,][1] and the enactments amending or extending that Act,

(e) the Stamp Duties Consolidation Act, 1999, and the enactments amending or extending that Act,

(f) Part VI of the Finance Act, 1983,

(g) the Customs Acts,

(h) the statutes relating to the duties of excise and to the management of those duties,

and any instruments made thereunder;

"tax" means any tax, duty, levy or charge under the care and management of the Revenue Commissioners.

(2) The Revenue Commissioners shall, as respects each relevant period (being the period beginning on the 1st day of January, 1997, and ending on the 30th day of June, 1997, and each subsequent period of 3 months beginning with the period ending on the 30th day of September, 1997), compile a list of the names and addresses and the occupations or descriptions of every person —

(a) on whom a fine or other penalty was imposed [or determined][4] by a court under any of the Acts during that relevant period,

(b) on whom a fine or other penalty was otherwise imposed [or determined][4] by a court during that relevant period in respect of an act or omission by the person in relation to tax,

(c) in whose case the Revenue Commissioners, pursuant to an agreement made with the person in that relevant period, refrained from initiating proceedings for the recovery of any fine or penalty of the kind mentioned in paragraphs (a) and (b) and, in place of initiating such proceedings, accepted or undertook to accept a specified sum of money in settlement of any claim by the Revenue Commissioners in respect of any specified liability of the person under any of the Acts for —

(i) payment of any tax,

> (ii) except in the case of tax due by virtue of paragraphs (g) and (h) of the definition of "the Acts", payment of interest on that tax, and
>
> (iii) a fine or other monetary penalty in respect of that tax including penalties in respect of the failure to deliver any return, statement, declaration, list or other document in connection with the tax, or

(d) in whose case the Revenue Commissioners, having initiated proceedings for the recovery of any fine or penalty of the kind mentioned in paragraphs (a) and (b), and whether or not a fine or penalty of the kind mentioned in those paragraphs has been imposed **[or determined]**[4] by a court, accepted or undertook to accept, in that relevant period, a specified sum of money in settlement of any claim by the Revenue Commissioners in respect of any specified liability of the person under any of the Acts for —

> (i) payment of any tax,
>
> (ii) except in the case of tax due by virtue of paragraphs (g) and (h) of the definition of "the Acts", payment of interest on that tax, and
>
> (iii) a fine or other monetary penalty in respect of that tax including penalties in respect of the failure to deliver any return, statement, declaration, list or other document in connection with the tax.

[(2A) For the purposes of subsection (2), the reference to a specified sum in paragraphs (c) and (d) of that subsection includes a reference to a sum which is the full amount of the claim by the Revenue Commissioners in respect of the specified liability referred to in those paragraphs. Where the Revenue Commissioners accept or undertake to accept such a sum, being the full amount of their claim, then —

(a) they shall be deemed to have done so pursuant to an agreement, made with the person referred to in paragraph (c), whereby they refrained from initiating proceedings for the recovery of any fine or penalty of the kind mentioned in paragraph (a) and (b) of subsection (2), and

(b) that agreement shall be deemed to have been made in the relevant period in which the Revenue Commissioners accepted or undertook to accept that full amount.][5]

(3) Notwithstanding any obligation as to secrecy imposed on them by the Acts or the Official Secrets Act, 1963 —

(a) the Revenue Commissioners shall, before the expiration of 3 months from the end of each relevant period, cause each such list referred to in subsection (2) in relation to that period to be published in Iris Oifigiúil, and

(b)   the Revenue Commissioners may, at any time after each such list referred to in subsection (2) has been published as provided for in paragraph (a), cause any such list to be publicised or reproduced, or both, in whole or in part, in such manner, form or format as they consider appropriate.

(4)   Paragraphs (c) and (d) of subsection (2) shall not apply in relation to a person in whose case—

[(a)   **the Revenue Commissioners are satisfied that, before any investigation or inquiry had been started by them or by any of their officers into any matter occasioning a liability referred to in those paragraphs, the person had voluntarily furnished to them a qualifying disclosure (within the meaning of section 1077E, section 27A of the Value-Added Tax Act 1972 or section 134A of the Stamp Duties Consolidation Act 1999, as the case may be) in relation to and full particulars of that matter.]**[6]

(b)   section 72 of the Finance Act, 1988, or section 3 of the Waiver of Certain Tax, Interest and Penalties Act, 1993, applied,

(c)   the specified sum referred to in paragraph (c) or (d), as the case may be, of subsection (2) does not exceed €12,700, or

(d)   the amount of fine or other penalty included in the specified sum referred to in paragraph (c) or (d), as the case may be, of subsection (2) does not exceed 15 per cent of the amount of tax included in that specified sum.

[(4A)(a)   In this subsection—

"the consumer price index number" means the All Items Consumer Price Index Number compiled by the Central Statistics Office;

"the consumer price index number relevant to a year" means the consumer price index number at the mid-December before the commencement of that year expressed on the basis that the consumer price index at mid-December 2001 was 100;

"the Minister" means the Minister for Finance.

(b)   The Minister shall, in the year 2010 and in every fifth year thereafter, by order provide, in accordance with paragraph (c), an amount in lieu of the amount referred to in subsection (4)(c), or where such an order has been made previously, in lieu of the amount specified in the last order so made.

(c)   For the purposes of paragraph (b) the amount referred to in subsection (4)(c) or in the last previous order made under the said paragraph (b), as the case may be, shall be adjusted by—

(i)   multiplying that amount by the consumer price index number relevant to the year in which the adjustment is made and dividing the product by the consumer price index number relevant to the year in which the amount was previously provided for, and

      (ii)   rounding the resulting amount up to the next €1,000.

(d)   An order made under this subsection shall specify that the amount provided for by the order –

      (i)   takes effect from a specified date, being 1 January in the year in which the order is made, and

      (ii)   does not apply to any case in which the specified liability referred to in paragraphs (c) and (d) of subsection (2) includes tax, the liability in respect of which arose before, or which relates to periods which commenced before, that specified date.][3]

[(4B) Paragraphs (a) and (b) of subsection (2) shall not apply in relation to a person in whose case –

(a)   the amount of a penalty determined by a court does not exceed 15 per cent of, as appropriate –

      (i)   the amount of the difference referred to in subsection (11) or (12), as the case may be, of section 1077E,

      (ii)   the amount of the difference referred to in subsection (11) or (12), as the case may be, of section 27A of the Value-Added Tax Act 1972, or

      (iii)   the amount of the difference referred to in subsection (7), (8) or (9), as the case may be, of section 134A of the Stamp Duties Consolidation Act 1999,

(b)   the aggregate of the –

      (i)   the tax due in respect of which the penalty is computed,

      (ii)   except in the case of tax due by virtue of paragraphs (g) and (h) of the definition of "the Acts", interest on that tax, and

      (iii)   the penalty determined by a court,

      does not exceed €30,000, or

(c)   there has been a qualifying disclosure.][7]

(5)   Any list referred to in subsection (2) shall specify in respect of each person named in the list such particulars as the Revenue Commissioners think fit –

(a)   of the matter occasioning the fine or penalty of the kind referred to in subsection (2) imposed [or determined][8] on the person or, as the case may be, the liability of that kind to which the person was subject, and

(b)   of any interest, fine or other monetary penalty, and of any other penalty or sanction, to which that person was liable, or which was imposed **[or determined]**[8] on that person by a court, and which was occasioned by the matter referred to in paragraph (a).

(5A) Without prejudice to the generality of paragraph (a) of subsection (5), such particulars as are referred to in that paragraph may include—

    (a) in a case to which paragraph (a) or (b) of subsection (2) applies, a description, in such summary form as the Revenue Commissioners may think fit, of the act, omission or offence (which may also include the circumstances in which the act or omission arose or the offence was committed) in respect of which the fine or penalty referred to in those paragraphs was imposed **[or determined]**[9], and

    (b) in a case to which paragraph (c) or (d) of subsection (2) applies, a description, in such summary form as the Revenue Commissioners may think fit, of the matter occasioning the specified liability (which may also include the circumstances in which that liability arose) in respect of which the Revenue Commissioners accepted, or undertook to accept, a settlement, in accordance with those paragraphs.

Footnotes

1   Substituted for "Capital Acquisitions Tax Act, 1976" by s.119, CATCA, with effect from 21st February, 2003.

2   Substituted for "€12,700" by s.143(1)(a), FA 2005, but this substitution does not apply under s.143(2), FA 2005, where the specified liability referred to in s.1086(2)(c) and (d), TCA, includes tax, the liability in respect of which arose before, or which relates to periods which commenced before, 1st January, 2005.

3   As inserted by s.143(1)(b), FA, 2005, with effect from 25th March, 2005.

4   Inserted by s.98(1), and by para. 2(as)(i) of Sch. 5, of the F(No. 2)A, 2008, and applies as in s.98(2) of that Act (see page 1327) where the reference there to "subparagraph (ar)" should be to "subparagraph (as)". This reference has been corrected by s.30(4)(b), FA 2009, with effect as on and from 3rd June, 2009, under s.30(5)(e).

5   Substituted by s.98(1), and by para. 2(as)(ii) of Sch. 5, of the F(No. 2)A, 2008, and applies as in Footnote 4 above.

6   Substituted by s.98(1), and by para. 2(as)(iii) of Sch. 5, of the F(No. 2)A, 2008, and applies as in Footnote 4 above.

7   Inserted by s.98(1), and by para. 2(as)(iv) of Sch. 5, of the F(No. 2)A, 2008, and applies as in Footnote 4 above.

8   Inserted by s.98(1), and by para. 2(as)(v) of Sch. 5, of the F(No. 2)A, 2008, and applies as in Footnote 4 above.

9   Inserted by s.98(1), and by para. 2(as)(vi) of Sch. 5, of the F(No. 2)A, 2008, and applies as in Footnote 4 above.

PART 48

Miscellaneous and Supplemental

Section 1089

Status of interest on certain unpaid taxes and duties.
1089. (1) ....

(2) Interest payable under section 18 of the Wealth Tax Act, 1975, or [section 51 of Capital Acquisitions Tax Consolidation Act 2003,][1] shall not be allowed in computing any income, profits or losses for any of the purposes of the Tax Acts.[1]

Footnote

1   Substituted for "section 41 of the Capital Acquisitions Tax Act, 1976" by s.119, CATCA, with effect from 21st February, 2003.

Section 1093

Disclosure of information to Ombudsman.

1093. Any obligation to maintain secrecy or other restriction on the disclosure or production of information (including documents) obtained by or furnished to the Revenue Commissioners, or any person on their behalf, for taxation purposes, shall not apply to the disclosure or production of information (including documents) to the Ombudsman for the purposes of an examination or investigation by the Ombudsman under the Ombudsman Act, 1980, of any action (within the meaning of that Act) taken by or on behalf of the Revenue Commissioners, being such an action taken in the performance of administrative functions in respect of any tax or duty under the care and management of the Revenue Commissioners.

Section 1096B

Evidence of computer stored records in court proceedings etc.

1096B. (1) In this section –

"copy record" means any copy of an original record or a copy of that copy made in accordance with either of the methods referred to in subsection (2) and accompanied by the certificate referred to in subsection (4), which original record or copy of an original record is in the possession of the Revenue Commissioners;

"original record" means any document, record or record of an entry in a document or record or information stored by means of any storage equipment, whether or not in a legible form, made or stored by the Revenue Commissioners for the purposes of or in connection with tax, and which is in the possession of the Revenue Commissioners;

"provable record" means an original record or a copy record and, in the case of an original record or a copy record stored in any storage equipment, whether or not in a legible form, includes the production or reproduction of the record in a legible form;

"storage equipment" means any electronic, magnetic, mechanical, photographic, optical or other device used for storing information;

"tax" means any tax, duty, levy or charge under the care and management of the Revenue Commissioners.

(2) Where by reason of —

(a) the deterioration of,

(b) the inconvenience in storing, or

(c) the technical obsolescence in the manner of retaining or storing,

any original record or any copy record, the Revenue Commissioners may —

(i) make a legible copy of that record, or

(ii) store information concerning that record otherwise than in a legible form so that the information is capable of being used to make a legible copy of that record,

and, they may, thereupon destroy that original record or that copy record.

(3) The legible copy of —

(a) a record made, or

(b) the information concerning such record stored,

in accordance with subsection (2) shall be deemed to be an original record for the purposes of this section.

(4) In any proceedings a certificate signed by an officer of the Revenue Commissioners stating that a copy record has been made in accordance with the provisions of subsection (2) shall be evidence of the fact of the making of such a copy record and that it is a true copy, unless the contrary is shown.

(5) In any proceedings a document purporting to be a certificate signed by an officer of the Revenue Commissioners, referred to in subsection (4), shall for the purposes of this section be deemed to be such a certificate and to be so signed unless the contrary is shown.

(6) A provable record shall be admissible in evidence in any proceedings and shall be evidence of any fact stated in it or event recorded by it unless the contrary is shown, or unless the court is not satisfied as to the reliability of the system used to make or compile —

(a) in the case of an original record, that record, and

(b) in the case of a copy record, the original on which it was based.

(7) In any proceedings a certificate signed by an officer of the Revenue Commissioners, stating that a full and detailed search has been made for a record of any event in every place where such records are kept and that no such record has been found, shall be evidence that the event did not happen unless the contrary is shown or unless the court is not satisfied —

    (a)   as to the reliability of the system used to compile or make or keep such records,

    (b)   that, if the event had happened, a record would have been made of it, and

    (c)   that the system is such that the only reasonable explanation for the absence of such record is that the event did not happen.

(8)   For the purposes of this section, and subject to the direction and control of the Revenue Commissioners, any power, function or duty conferred or imposed on them may be exercised or performed on their behalf by an officer of the Revenue Commissioners.

SECOND PART

This Part relates to gifts and inheritances taken before 21st February, 2003, and contains capital acquisitions tax legislation, as amended and extended, in force immediately prior to that date.

However:

(i)   section 81 of the Finance Act 2004 extends section 55(3) of the Capital Acquisitions Tax Act, 1976, to include the Commissioners of Public Works in Ireland as a body to whom a sale of heritage objects does not result in a clawback of tax where the sale to such body occurs on or after 1st August, 1994, and

(ii)   section 145(6) of the Finance Act 2005 has repealed section 41 of the Capital Acquisitions Tax Act, 1976, with effect from 1st April, 2005, to the extent that such section 41 applies to interest chargeable or payable on gift tax and inheritance tax that has not been paid before that date, regardless of when that tax became due and payable.

In addition, as shown below at (vii), miscellaneous provisions of the Taxes Consolidation Act, 1997, apply to gift tax and inheritance tax, and amendments to these provisions, contained in the Finance Acts 2003, 2004, 2005, 2006, 2007 and 2008, may affect gifts and inheritances taken before 21st February, 2003.

For ease of reference, the legislation in this Part has been grouped under the following headings –

For Contents of this Part, see page xlv

SECOND PART

(I) GIFT / INHERITANCE TAX

For Contents of this Part, see page xlvi

CAPITAL ACQUISITIONS TAX ACT, 1976

Number 8 of 1976
(Enacted on 31st March, 1976)

PART I
Preliminary

Section 1

Short title.

1.   This Act may be cited as the Capital Acquisitions Tax Act, 1976.

Section 2

Interpretation.

2.   (1)   In this Act, unless the context otherwise requires —

"absolute interest", in relation to property, includes the interest of a person who has a general power of appointment over the property;

"accountable person" means a person who is accountable for the payment of tax by virtue of section 35;

"benefit" includes any estate, interest, income or right;

"child"[1] includes —

(a)   a stepchild;

(b)   a child adopted —

[(i)   under the Adoption Acts, 1952 to 1991;][2] or

[(ii)   under a foreign adoption which by virtue of section 2, 3, 4 or 5 of the Adoption Act, 1991, is deemed to have been effected by a valid adoption order within the meaning of section 1 of that Act;][3]

"Commissioners" means the Revenue Commissioners;

"date of the disposition" means —

(a)   in the case of a will, the date of the testator's death;

(b)   in the case of an intestacy or a partial intestacy, the date of death of the intestate;

(c)   in the case of a benefit under Part IX or section 56 of the Succession Act, 1965, the date of death of the relevant testator or other deceased person, and correspondingly in the case of an analogous benefit under the law of another territory;

(d) in the case of a disposition which consists of the failure to exercise a right or a power, the date of the latest time when the disponer could have exercised the right or the power if he were *sui juris* and not under any physical disability; and

(e) in any other case, the date on which the act (or where more than one act is involved, the last act) of the disponer was done by which he provided or bound himself to provide the property comprised in the disposition;

"date of the gift" means the date of the happening of the event upon which the donee, or any person in right of the donee or on his behalf, becomes beneficially entitled in possession to the benefit, and a reference to the time when a gift is taken shall be construed as a reference to the date of the gift;

"date of the inheritance" means –

(a) in the case where the successor or any person in right of the successor or on his behalf becomes entitled in possession to the benefit on the happening of any such event as is referred to in section 3 (2), the date of the event;

(b) in the case of a gift which becomes an inheritance by reason of its being taken under a disposition where the date of the disposition is within two years prior to the death of the disponer, the date which would have been the date of the gift if the entitlement were a gift; and

(c) in any other case, the date of the latest death which had to occur for the successor, or any person in right of the successor or on his behalf, to become beneficially entitled in possession to the benefit,

and a reference to the time when an inheritance is taken shall be construed as a reference to the date of the inheritance;

["discretionary trust" means any trust whereby, or by virtue or in consequence of which, property is held on trust to accumulate the income or part of the income of the property, or any trust whereby, or by virtue or in consequence of which, property (other than property to which for the time being a person is beneficially entitled for an interest in possession) is held on trust to apply, or with a power to apply, the income or capital or part of the income or capital of the property for the benefit of any person or persons or of any one or more of a number or of a class of persons whether at the discretion of trustees or any other person and notwithstanding that there may be a power to accumulate all or any part of the income;][4]

"disponer", in relation to a disposition, means the person who, for the purpose of the disposition, directly or indirectly provided the property comprised in the disposition, and in any case where more than one person provided the property each shall be deemed to be the disponer to the extent that he so provided the property; and for the purposes of this definition—

(a) the testator shall be the disponer in the case of a disposition referred to in paragraph (k) of the definition of "disposition";

(b) the intestate shall be the disponer in the case of a disposition referred to in paragraph (l) of that definition;

(c) the deceased person referred to in paragraph (m) of that definition shall be the disponer in the case of a disposition referred to in that paragraph; and

(d) a person who has made with any other person a reciprocal arrangement by which that other person provided property comprised in the disposition shall be deemed to have provided that property;

"disposition" includes—

(a) any act or omission by a person as a result of which the value of his estate immediately after such act or omission is less than it would be but for such act or omission;

(b) any trust, covenant, agreement or arrangement, whether made by a single operation or by associated operations;

(c) the creation of a debt or other right enforceable against the disponer personally or against any estate or interest he may have in property;

(d) the payment of money;

(e) the allotment of shares in a company;

(f) the grant or the creation of any benefit;

(g) the grant or the creation of any lease, mortgage, charge, licence, option, power, partnership or joint tenancy or other estate or interest in or over any property;

(h) the release, forfeiture, surrender or abandonment of any debt or benefit, or the failure to exercise a right; and, for the purpose of this paragraph, a debt or benefit shall be deemed to have been released when it has become unenforceable by action through lapse of time (save to the extent that it is recovered subsequent to its becoming so unenforceable);

(i) the exercise of a general power of appointment in favour of any person other than the holder of the power;

(j) a *donatio mortis causa*,

(k) a will or other testamentary disposition;

(l) an intestacy, whether total or partial;

(m) the payment of a share as a legal right under Part IX of the Succession Act, 1965, to a deceased person's spouse, or the making of provision for a widow or child of a deceased person under section 56 or section 117 of the Succession Act, 1965, or an analogous share or provision paid or made on the death of a deceased person to or for the benefit of any person under the law of another territory; and

(n) a resolution passed by a company which is deemed by subsection (3) to be a disposition;

"donee" means a person who takes a gift;

"entitled in possession" means having a present right to the enjoyment of property as opposed to having a future such right, and without prejudice to the generality of the foregoing a person shall also, for the purposes of this Act, be deemed to be entitled in possession to an interest or share in a partnership, joint tenancy or estate of a deceased person, in which he is a partner, joint tenant or beneficiary, as the case may be, but he shall not be deemed to be entitled in possession to an interest in expectancy until an event happens whereby this interest ceases to be an interest in expectancy;[11]

"general power of appointment" includes every power, right, or authority whether exercisable only by will or otherwise which would enable the holder thereof to appoint or dispose of property to whomsoever he thinks fit or to obtain such power, right or authority, but exclusive of any power exercisable solely in a fiduciary capacity under a disposition not made by himself, or exercisable by a tenant for life under the Settled Land Act, 1882, or as mortgagee;

"gift" means a gift which a person is by this Act deemed to take;

"inheritance" means an inheritance which a person is by this Act deemed to take;

"interest in expectancy" includes an estate in remainder or reversion and every other future interest, whether vested or contingent, but does not include a reversion expectant on the determination of a lease;

"limited interest" means—

(a) an interest (other than a leasehold interest) for the duration of a life or lives or for a period certain; or

(b) any other interest which is not an absolute interest;

"local authority" has the meaning assigned to it by section 2 (2) of the Local Government Act, 1941, and includes a body established under the Local Government Services (Corporate Bodies) Act, 1971;

"market value", in relation to property, means the market value thereof ascertained in accordance with sections 15, 16 and 17;

"minor child" means a child who has not attained the age of [18 years and is not or has not been married;][5]

"personal property" means any property other than real property;

"personal representative" means the executor or administrator for the time being of a deceased person and includes any person who takes possession of or intermeddles with the property of a deceased person and also includes any person having, in relation to the deceased person, under the law of another country, any functions corresponding to the functions, for administration purposes under the law of the State, of an executor or administrator;

"property" includes rights and interests of any description;

"real property" means real and chattel real property;

"regulations" means regulations made under section 71;

"relative" means a relative within the meaning of subsection (4);

"return" means such a return as is referred to in section 36;

["share" in relation to a company, includes any interest whatsoever in the company which is analogous to a share in the company, and "shareholder" shall be construed accordingly;][6]

"special power of appointment" means a power of appointment which is not a general power of appointment;

"successor" means a person who takes an inheritance;

"tax" means any tax chargeable under this Act;

"valuation date" has the meaning assigned to it by section 21;

["year of assessment" has the meaning assigned to it by section 2 of the Taxes Consolidation Act, 1997.][7]

(2) For the purpose of the definition of "general power of appointment" contained in subsection (1), a person shall be deemed to have a general power of appointment—

    (a) notwithstanding that he is not *sui juris* or is under a physical disability;

    (b) over money which he has a general power to charge on property; and

    (c) over property of which he is tenant in tail in possession.

(3) For the purpose of the definition of "disposition" contained in subsection (1), the passing by a company of a resolution which, by the extinguishment or alteration of the rights attaching to any share of the company, results, directly or indirectly, in the estate of any shareholder of the company being increased in value at the expense of the estate of any other shareholder, shall be deemed to be a disposition made by that other shareholder if he could have prevented the passing of the resolution by voting against it or otherwise; and in this subsection, "share" includes a debenture and loan stock and "shareholder" includes a debenture holder and a holder of loan stock.

(4) For the purposes of this Act, the following persons and no other person shall be relatives of another person, that is to say—

(a)   the spouse of that other person;

(b)   the father, mother, and any child, uncle or aunt of that other person;

(c)   any child (other than that other person), and any child of a child, of any person who is by virtue of paragraph (a) or (b) a relative of that other person; and

(d)   the spouse of a person who is by virtue of paragraph (b) or (c) a relative of that other person;

(e)   the grandparent of that other person.

(5)   For the purposes of this Act —

(a)   the relationship between a child, adopted in the manner referred to in paragraph (b) of the definition of "child" contained in subsection (1), and any other person, or between other persons, that would exist if such child had been born to the adoptor or adoptors in lawful wedlock, shall be deemed to exist between such child and that other person or between those other persons, and the relationship of any such child and any person that existed prior to his being so adopted shall be deemed to have ceased[10]; and

(b)   an illegitimate child who has not been —

(i)   legitimated; or

(ii)   adopted under —

(I)   the Adoption Acts, 1952 to [1988;][8] or

(II)   an adoption law other than the Adoption Acts, 1952 to [1988,][8] having the effect referred to in paragraph (b) (ii) of the definition of "child" contained in subsection (1),

shall be the child of his mother.

[(5A) For the purposes of this Act —

(a)   a reference to a person being resident in the State on a particular date shall be construed as a reference to that person being resident in the State in the year of assessment in which that date falls (but, for those purposes, the provisions of Part 34 of the Taxes Consolidation Act, 1997, relating to residence of individuals shall not be construed as requiring a year of assessment to have elapsed before a determination of whether or not a person is resident in the State on a date falling in that year may be made), and

(b)   a reference to a person being ordinarily resident in the State on a particular date shall be construed as a reference to that person being ordinarily resident in the State in the year of assessment in which that date falls.][9]

(6) In this Act, references to any enactment shall, unless the context otherwise requires, be construed as references to that enactment as amended or extended by any subsequent enactment.

(7) In this Act, a reference to a section or Schedule is a reference to a section of or Schedule to this Act unless it is indicated that reference to some other enactment is intended.

(8) In this Act, a reference to a subsection, paragraph or subparagraph is to the subsection, paragraph or subparagraph of the provision (including a Schedule) in which the reference occurs, unless it is indicated that reference to some other provision is intended.

Footnotes

1   See s.3, Status of Children Act, 1987 (reproduced on page 799) in relation to the marital status of parents. CAT is to be construed in accordance with this section under s.74, FA 1988, as respects gifts and inheritance taken on or after 14th January, 1988, and under s.8, TCA, with effect as on and from 6th April, 1997.

2   As amended by s.223, FA 1992, as respects gifts and inheritances taken on or after 30th May, 1991. Originally, in the CATA, this referred to the Adoption Acts, 1952 to 1974. As respects gifts and inheritances taken on or after 26th July, 1988, and before 30th May, 1991, this referred to the Adoption Acts, 1952 to 1988 (s.80(1)(a), FA 1989).

3   As amended by s.223, FA 1992, as respects gifts and inheritances taken on or after 30th May, 1991.

4   As extended by s.105, FA 1984, as respects gifts and inheritances taken on or after 23rd May, 1984.

5   As amended by s.112, FA 1986, as respects gifts and inheritances taken on or after 6th April, 1986.

6   See s.125 (1)(b), FA 1993, for an extended definition of "share" in relation to a private company as defined s.16(2), CATA.

7   As inserted with effect from 2nd June, 1995, by s.157, FA 1995, where the reference was to s.1, ITA. With effect from 6th April, 1997, the reference is to the corresponding provision in s.2, TCA.

8   As amended by s.80 (1)(b), FA 1989, as respects gifts and inheritances taken on or after 26th July, 1988. Strangely, there was no further amendment in s.223, FA 1992 – see note 2 above.

9   As inserted by s.137, FA 2000, as respects gifts and inheritances taken on or after 1st December, 1999.

10 In relation to gifts and inheritances taken on or after 30th March, 2001, s.59E, CATA, provides that, notwithstanding s.2(5)(a), an adopted child is also treated as a child of the natural father/mother.

11 However, s19(1)(b), CATA, deems a "farmer" to be beneficially entitled in possession to an interest in expectancy.

Commentary

A   See s.59D, CATA, in relation to gifts and inheritances taken on or after 6th December, 2000, by foster children.

B   As to the definition "entitled in possession", see *Pearson v IRC* [1981] AC 253.

C   As to the definition of "child" including a "stepchild", see Part 19.7 of the *Revenue CAT Manual* dealing with "lineal descendants" involving stepchildren.

D   As to adverse possession being a "disposition", see an article by Brendan Twohig at page 47 of the *Irish Tax Review* of May 2007.

Section 3

Meaning of "on a death".

3. (1) In this Act, "on a death" in relation to a person becoming beneficially entitled in possession, means –

  (a) on the death of a person or at a time ascertainable only by reference to the death of a person;

  (b) under a disposition where the date of the disposition is the date of the death of the disponer;

  (c) under a disposition where the date of the disposition is on or after the 1st day of April, 1975, and within two years prior to the death of the disponer; or

  (d) on the happening, after the cesser of an intervening life interest, of any such event as is referred to in subsection (2).

  (2) The events referred to in subsection (1) (d) are any of the following –

  (a) the determination or failure of any charge, estate, interest or trust;

  (b) the exercise of a special power of appointment;

  (c) in the case where a benefit was given under a disposition in such terms that the amount or value of the benefit could only be ascertained from time to time by the actual payment or application of property for the purpose of giving effect to the benefit, the making of any payment or the application of the property; or

  (d) any other event which, under a disposition, affects the right to property, or to the enjoyment thereof.

Cross-Reference

  1. S.3(2) is referred to in the definition of "date of the inheritance" in s.2(1), CATA.

PART II
Gift Tax

Section 4

Charge of gift tax.

4. A capital acquisitions tax, to be called gift tax and to be computed as hereinafter provided, shall, subject to this Act and the regulations thereunder, be charged, levied and paid upon the taxable value of every taxable gift taken by a donee, where the date of the gift is on or after the 28th day of February, 1974.

Section 5

Gift deemed to be taken.

5.   (1)   For the purposes of this Act, where, under or in consequence of any disposition, a person becomes beneficially entitled in possession, otherwise than on a death, to any benefit (whether or not the person becoming so entitled already has any interest in the property in which he takes such benefit), [otherwise than for full consideration in money or money's worth paid by him,][1] he shall be deemed to take a gift.

     (2)   A gift shall be deemed –

        (a)   to consist of the whole or the appropriate part, as the case may be, of the property in which the donee takes a benefit, or on which the benefit is charged or secured or on which the donee is entitled to have it charged or secured; and

        (b)   if the benefit is an annuity or other periodic payment which is not charged on or secured by any property and which the donee is not entitled to have so charged or secured, to consist of such sum as would, if invested on the date of the gift in the security of the Government which was issued last before that date for subscription in the State and is redeemable not less than 10 years after the date of issue, yield, on the basis of the current yield on the security, an annual income equivalent to the annual value of the annuity or of the other periodic payment receivable by the donee.

     (3)   For the purposes of section 6 (1)(c),[4] the sum referred to in subsection (2) (b) shall be deemed not to be situate in the State at the date of the gift.

     (4)   Where a person makes a disposition under which a relative of the person becomes beneficially entitled in possession to any benefit, the creation or disposition in favour of the person of an annuity or other interest limited to cease on the death, or at a time ascertainable only by reference to the death, of the person, shall not be treated for the purposes of this section as consideration for the grant of such benefit or of any part thereof.

     (5)   For the purposes of this Act, "appropriate part", in relation to property referred to in subsection (2), means that part of the entire property in which the benefit subsists, or on which the benefit is charged or secured, or on which the donee is entitled to have it so charged or secured, which bears the same proportion to the entire property as the gross annual value of the benefit bears to the gross annual value of the entire property, and the gift shall be deemed to consist of the appropriate part of each and every item of property comprised in the entire property.

     (6)   (a)   Where [. . . . .][2] a contract or agreement was entered into, under or as a consequence of which a person acquired the right, otherwise than for full

consideration in money or money's worth, to have a benefit transferred to him, or to another in his right or on his behalf, and an act or acts is or are done, on or after that date, in pursuance of, or in performance or satisfaction, whether in whole or in part, of such contract or agreement, then the gift or inheritance, as the case may be, taken by or in right or on behalf of that person, shall be deemed to have been taken, not when the right was acquired as aforesaid, but either –

(i) when the benefit was transferred to him or to another in his right or on his behalf; or

(ii) when he or another in his right or on his behalf became beneficially entitled in possession to the benefit.

whichever is the later.

(b) In this subsection, a reference to a contract or agreement does not include a reference to a contract or agreement –

(i) which is a complete grant, transfer, assignment or conveyance, or

(ii) which was enforceable by action [. . . . .]. [3]

Footnotes

1 In relation to shares in a private company, these words were deleted by s.121, FA 1993, with effect from 24th February, 1993, but were restored with retrospective effect by s.147, FA 1994, except as provided by the latter section.

2 The words ", before the 28th day of February, 1974," were deleted by s.99(a), FA 1982, as respects gifts and inheritances taken on or after 2nd June, 1982.

3 The words "prior to the 28th day of February, 1974" were deleted by s.99(b), FA 1982, as respects gifts and inheritances taken on or after 2nd June, 1982.

4 "section 6(1)(c)" should be "section 6(1)(d)".

Commentary

A As to "full consideration in money or money's worth paid by the disponer", see *AG v Boden* [1912] IKB 539 and *AG v Ralli* [1936] 15 ATC.

B As to successive interests in a trust fund received by the same beneficiary, see *Jacob v Revenue Commissioners* 3 ITR 104.

C See Part 19.18 of the *Revenue CAT Manual* in relation to Co-Directors and Business Partners Assurance. These are policies effected purely for commercial purposes and agreed between the individual shareholders/partners on an arms-length basis, without any intention of conferring a benefit. The approach to such policies, written in the form of own life in trust for others, is to treat the proceeds as exempt from gift tax on the basis of "full consideration".

Cross-References

1 The "sum" in s.5(2)(b) is also the "sum" for the purposes of s.28(1)(ii), CATA.

2 The definition of "appropriate part" in s.5(5) is also used in s.28(2), CATA, s.59C(1)(a), CATA, and para. 9(1), Part I, Second Sch., CATA.

Section 6

Taxable gift.

6.   [(1) In this Act "taxable gift" means –

   (a)   in the case of a gift, other than a gift taken under a discretionary trust, where the disponer is resident or ordinarily resident in the State at the date of the disposition under which the donee takes the gift, the whole of the gift;

   (b)   in the case of a gift taken under a discretionary trust where the disponer is resident or ordinarily resident in the State at the date of the disposition under which the donee takes the gift or at the date of the gift or was (in the case of a gift taken after the death of the disponer) so resident or ordinarily resident at the date of that death, the whole of the gift;

   (c)   in the case where the donee is resident or ordinarily resident in the State at the date of the gift, the whole of the gift; and

   (d)   in any other case, so much of the property of which the gift consists as is situate in the State at the date of the gift.][1]

   (2)   For the purposes of [subsection (1) (d)][3], a right to the proceeds of sale of property shall be deemed to be situate in the State to the extent that such property is unsold and situate in the State.

   [(3)   For the purposes of subsection (1), a person who is not domiciled in the State on a particular date shall be treated as not resident and not ordinarily resident in the State on that date unless –

   (a)   that date occurs on or after 1 December 2004,

   (b)   that person has been resident in the State for the 5 consecutive years of assessment immediately preceding the year of assessment in which that date falls, and

   (c)   that person is either resident or ordinarily resident in the State on that date.

   (4)   (a)   In this subsection –

      "company" means a private company within the meaning assigned to it by section 16 (2);

      "company controlled by the donee" has the same meaning as is assigned to "company controlled by the donee or successor" by section 16(3);

      "share" has the meaning assigned to it by section 16(2).

   (b)   For the purposes of subsection (1)(d), a proportion of the market value of any share in a private company incorporated outside the State which (after the taking of the gift) is a company controlled by the donee shall be deemed to be a sum situate in the State and shall be the amount determined by the following formula –

PART III

Inheritance Tax

Section 10

Charge of inheritance tax.

10. A capital acquisitions tax, to be called inheritance tax and to be computed as hereinafter provided, shall, subject to this Act and the regulations thereunder, be charged, levied and paid upon the taxable value of every taxable inheritance taken by a successor, where the date of the inheritance is on or after the 1st day of April, 1975.

Section 11

Inheritance deemed to be taken.

11. (1) For the purposes of this Act, where, under or in consequence of any disposition, a person becomes beneficially entitled in possession on a death to any benefit (whether or not the person becoming so entitled already has any interest in the property in which he takes such benefit), [otherwise than for full consideration in money or moneys worth paid by him,][1] he shall be deemed to take an inheritance.

(2) The provisions of subsections (2), (4) and (5) of section 5 shall apply, with any necessary modifications, in relation to an inheritance as they apply in relation to a gift.

(3) For the purposes of section 12 (1) (b)[2] the sum referred to in section 5 (2) (b) shall be deemed not to be situate in the State at the date of the inheritance.

Footnotes

1 In relation to shares in a private company, these words were deleted by s.123, FA 1993, with effect from 24th February, 1993, but were restored with retrospective effect by s.148, FA 1994, except as provided in the latter section.

2 "section 12(1)(b)" should be "section 12(1)(c)".

Commentary

A See Part 19.18 of the *Revenue CAT Manual* in relation to Co-Directors and Business Partners Assurance. These are policies effected purely for commercial purposes and agreed between the individual shareholders/partners on an arms-length basis, without any intention of conferring a benefit. The approach to such policies, written in the form of own life in trust for others, is to treat the proceeds as exempt from inheritance tax on the basis of "full consideration".

B As to "full consideration in money or money's worth paid by the disposer", see *AG v Boden* [1912] IKB 539 and *AG v Ralli* [1936] 15 ATC.

Section 12

Taxable inheritance.

12. (1) In this Act, "taxable inheritance" means —

[(a) in the case where the disponer is resident or ordinarily resident in the State at the date of the disposition under which the successor takes the inheritance, the whole of the inheritance;

(b) in the case where the successor (not being a successor in relation to a charge for tax arising by virtue of section 106 of the Finance Act, 1984, section 103 of the Finance Act, 1986, or section 110 of the Finance Act, 1993) is resident or ordinarily resident in the State at the date of the inheritance, the whole of the inheritance; and

(c) in any case, other than a case referred to in paragraph (a) or (b), where at the date of the inheritance —

(i) the whole of the property —

(I) which was to be appropriated to the inheritance; or

(II) out of which property was to be appropriated to the inheritance,

was situate in the State, the whole of the inheritance;

(ii) a part or proportion of the property —

(I) which was to be appropriated to the inheritance; or

(II) out of which property was to be appropriated to the inheritance,

was situate in the State, that part or proportion of the inheritance.][1]

(2) For the purposes of [subsection (1) (c)][2] —

(a) "property which was to be appropriated to the inheritance" and "property out of which property was to be appropriated to the inheritance" shall not include any property which was not applicable to satisfy the inheritance; and

(b) a right to the proceeds of sale of property shall be deemed to be situate in the State to the extent that such property is unsold and situate in the State.

[(3) For the purposes of subsection (1), a person who is not domiciled in the State on a particular date shall be treated as not resident and not ordinarily resident in the State on that date unless —

(a) that date occurs on or after 1 December 2004,

(b) that person has been resident in the State for the 5 consecutive years of assessment immediately preceding the year of assessment in which that date falls, and

(c)   that person is either resident or ordinarily resident in the State on that date.

(4) (a)   In this subsection –

"company" means a private company within the meaning of section 16(2);

"company controlled by the successor" has the same meaning as is assigned to "company controlled by the donee or successor" by section 16(3);

"share" has the meaning assigned to it by section 16(2).

(b)   For the purposes of subsection (1)(b)[4], a proportion of the market value of any share in a private company incorporated outside the State which (after the taking of the inheritance) is a company controlled by the successor shall be deemed to be a sum situate in the State and shall be the amount determined by the following formula –

$$A \times \frac{B}{C}$$

where –

A   is the market value of that share at the date of the inheritance ascertained under section 16,

B   is the market value of all property in the beneficial ownership of that company which is situate in the State at the date of the inheritance, and

C   is the total market value of all property in the beneficial ownership of that company at the date of the inheritance.

(c)   Paragraph (b) shall not apply in a case where the disponer was not domiciled in the State at the date of the disposition under which the successor takes the inheritance or where the share in question is actually situate in the State at the date of the inheritance.][3]

Footnotes

1   As substituted by s.139(1)(a), FA 2000, in relation to an inheritance taken on or after 1st December, 1999, save in relation to an inheritance taken under a disposition where the date of the disposition is before that date.

    Originally, s.12(1), CATA, provided that all the property in an inheritance was taxable where the disponer was domiciled in the State or where the proper law of the disposition was Irish. In the case of an inheritance taken on or after 17th June, 1993, and before 1st December, 1999, s.124, FA 1993, eliminated this universal inheritance tax charge based on the proper law of the disposition.

2   S.139(1)(b), FA 2000, substituted "subsection 1(c)" for "subsection 1(b)" in relation to an inheritance taken on or after 1st December, 1999, save in relation to an inheritance taken under a disposition where the date of the disposition is before that date.

3   As inserted by s.139(1)(c), FA 2000, in relation to an inheritance taken on or after 1st December, 1999, save in relation to an inheritance taken under a disposition where the date of the disposition is before that date.

4   "subsection (1)(b)" should be "subsection (1)(c)".

Commentary

A   The Appeal Commissioner decision (reference 25 AC 2000), dealing with a "taxable gift", is also relevant to a "taxable inheritance". Before that appeal was reheard in the Circuit Court, the taxpayer paid all the tax due.

B   See an article on the Scope of Capital Acquisitions Tax by Ann Williams in the *Irish Tax Review* of May 2001, page 269.

Section 13

Disclaimer.

13. (1) If—

    (a) (i)   a benefit under a will or an intestacy; or

        (ii) an entitlement to an interest in settled property,

        is disclaimed;

    (b) a claim—

        (i)   under a purported will in respect of which a grant of representation (within the meaning of the Succession Act, 1965) was not issued; or

        (ii) under an alleged intestacy where a will exists in respect of which such a grant was issued,

        is waived; or

    (c) a right under Part IX of the Succession Act, 1965, or any analogous right under the law of another territory, is renounced, disclaimed, elected against or lapses,

any liability to tax in respect of such benefit, entitlement, claim or right shall cease as if such benefit, entitlement, claim or right, as the case may be, had not existed.

(2) Notwithstanding anything contained in this Act—

    (a) a disclaimer of a benefit under a will or intestacy or of an entitlement to an interest in settled property;

    (b) the waiver of a claim—

        (i)   under a purported will in respect of which a grant of representation (within the meaning of the Succession Act, 1965) was not issued; or

        (ii) under an alleged intestacy where a will exists in respect of which such a grant issued; or

    (c) (i)   the renunciation or disclaimer of;

        (ii) the election against; or

        (iii) the lapse of,

a right under Part IX of the Succession Act, 1965, or any analogous right under the law of another territory,

shall not be a disposition for the purposes of this Act.

(3) Subsection (1) shall not have effect to the extent of the amount of any consideration in money or money's worth received for the disclaimer, renunciation, election or lapse or for the waiver of a claim; and the receipt of such consideration shall be deemed to be a gift or an inheritance, as the case may be, in respect of which no consideration was paid by the donee or successor and which was derived from the disponer who provided the property in relation to which the benefit, entitlement, claim or right, referred to in subsection (1), arose.

Commentary

A   Contrast s.142, UK Inheritance Tax Act, 1984.

B   As a general rule, a beneficiary may disclaim one of several separate legacies but a part of one legacy may not be disclaimed – see *Parnell v Boyd* [1896] 2 IR 571.

C   As to a disclaimer on intestacy, see s.72A, Succession Act, 1965, inserted by s.6, Family Law (Miscellaneous Provisions) Act, 1997, reproduced on page 678.

D   See Part 19.3 of the *Revenue CAT Manual* which deals with the Revenue practice where the State, as the ultimate intestate successor under s.73, Succession Act, 1965, waives its right in favour of a person.

E   See two articles on the Post Death Variation of Estates by Finola O'Hanlon and Anne Stephenson in the *Irish Tax Review* of May 2004 (page 232) and July 2004 (page 311).

F   See an article on disclaimers by Lorna Gallagher at page 78 of the *Irish Tax Review* of July 2007.

Section 14

Surviving joint tenant deemed to take an inheritance, etc.

14.   (1)   On the death of one of several persons who are beneficially and absolutely entitled in possession as joint tenants, the surviving joint tenant or surviving joint tenants shall be deemed to take an inheritance of the share of the deceased joint tenant, as successor or successors from the deceased joint tenant as disponer.

      (2)   The liability to inheritance tax in respect of an inheritance taken by persons as joint tenants shall be the same in all respects as if they took the inheritance as tenants in common in equal shares.

PART IV
Value of Property for Tax

Section 15

Market value of property.

15.   (1)   Subject to the provisions of this Act, the market value of any property for the purposes of this Act shall be estimated to be the price which, in the opinion of the Commissioners, such property would fetch if sold in the open market on the date on which the property is to be valued in such manner and subject to such conditions as might reasonably be calculated to obtain for the vendor the best price for the property.

(2) In estimating the market value of any property, the Commissioners shall not make any reduction in the estimate on account of the estimate being made on the assumption that the whole property is to be placed on the market at one and the same time.

(3) The market value of any property shall be ascertained by the Commissioners in such manner and by such means as they think fit, and they may authorise a person to inspect any property and report to them the value thereof for the purposes of this Act, and the person having the custody or possession of that property shall permit the person so authorised to inspect it at such reasonable times as the Commissioners consider necessary.

(4) Where the Commissioners require a valuation to be made by a person named by them, the costs of such valuation shall be defrayed by the Commissioners.

(5) Subject to the provisions of this Act, in estimating the price which unquoted shares or securities might be expected to fetch if sold in the open market, it shall be assumed that in that market there is available to any prospective purchaser of the shares or securities all the information which a prudent prospective purchaser might reasonably require if he were proposing to purchase them from a willing vendor by private treaty and at arm's length.

(6) In subsection (5), "unquoted shares or securities" means shares or securities which are not dealt in on a stock exchange.

Commentary

A   As to the valuation of unquoted shares, see *AG v Jameson* [1905] 2 IR 218 and *McNamee v Revenue Commissioners* [1954] IR 214.

B   See also *Ellesmere v CIR* [1918] 2 KB 735 and *Lynall v IRC* [1972] AC 680 in relation to the open-market value of property.

C   See a UK Special Commissioner case of *Williams, deceased, executors v IRC* [2003] SPC 392, referred to at page 284 of the *Irish Tax Review* of July 2004, which deals with a house owned by two tenants in common. It was held that the sum of the values of each of the half shares was less than the value of the whole.

D   See two articles on the Valuation of Shares by Denis Cremins in the *Irish Tax Review* of September 2006, page 60, and January 2007, page 55.

Section 16

Market value of certain shares in private trading companies.

16. [(1) (a) The market value of each share in a private company which (after the taking of the gift or of the inheritance) is, on the date of the gift or on the date of the inheritance, a company controlled by the donee or successor, shall be ascertained by the Commissioners, for the purposes of tax, as if, on the date on which the market value is to be ascertained, it formed an apportioned part of the market value of a group of shares in that company, such apportionment, as between shares of a particular class, to be by reference to nominal amount, and, as between different classes of shares, to have due regard to the rights attaching to each of the different classes.

(b) For the purpose of ascertaining the market value of a share in a private company in the manner described in paragraph (a), the benefit to any private company (in this paragraph referred to as "the first-mentioned company") by virtue of its ownership of an interest in shares in another private company (in this paragraph referred to as "the second-mentioned company"), shall, where each of the companies so connected is a company which (after the taking of the gift or of the inheritance) is, on the date of the gift or on the date of the inheritance, a company controlled by the donee or successor, be deemed to be—

   (i) such benefit as would be appropriate to the ownership of that interest if the second-mentioned company were under the control of the first-mentioned company in the same manner as (on the date on which the market value is to be ascertained) the second-mentioned company is under the control of the following, that is to say, the first-mentioned company, the donee or successor, the relatives of the donee or successor, nominees of the donee or successor, nominees of relatives of the donee or successor, and the trustees of a settlement whose objects include the donee or successor or relatives of the donee or successor, or

   (ii) the actual benefit appropriate to the ownership of that interest,

   whichever is the greater.][1]

(2) In this section—

["group of shares", in relation to a private company, means the aggregate of the shares in the company of the donee or successor, the relatives of the donee or successor, nominees of the donee or successor, nominees of relatives of the donee or successor, and the trustees of a settlement whose objects include the donee or successor or relatives of the donee or successor;][2]

"nominee" includes a person who may be required to exercise his voting power on the directions of, or who holds shares directly or indirectly on behalf of, another person;

["private company" means a body corporate (wherever incorporated) which—

(a) is under the control of not more than five persons, and

(b) is not a company which would fall within [section 431 of the Taxes Consolidation Act, 1997][3] if the words "private company" were substituted for the words "close company" in subsection [(3)][3] of that section, and if the words "if beneficially held by a company which is not a private company" were substituted for the words of paragraph (a) of subsection [(6)][3] of that section;][4]

["private trading company" means . . . .][5]

["share", in relation to a private company and in addition to the interpretation of "share" in section 2 (1), includes every debenture, or loan stock, issued otherwise than as part of a transaction which is wholly and exclusively a bona fide commercial transaction.][6]

(3) In this section, a reference to a company controlled by the donee or successor is a reference to a company that is under the control of any one or more of the following, that is to say, the donee or successor, the relatives of the donee or successor, nominees of the donee or successor, nominees of relatives of the donee or successor, and the trustees of a settlement whose objects include the donee or successor or relatives of the donee or successor; and for the purposes of this section, a company which is so controlled by the donee or successor shall be regarded as being itself a relative of the donee or successor.

(4) For the purposes of this section –

(a) a company shall be deemed to be under the control of not more than five persons if any five or fewer persons together exercise, or are able to exercise or are entitled to acquire control, whether direct or indirect, of the company; and for this purpose –

   (i) persons who are relatives of any other person together with that other person;

   (ii) persons who are nominees of any other person together with that other person;

   (iii) persons in partnership, and

   (iv) persons interested in any shares or obligations of the company which are subject to any trust or are part of the estate of a deceased person,

   shall respectively be treated as a single person; and

(b) a person shall be deemed to have control of a company at any time if –

   (i) he then had control of the powers of voting on all questions, or on any particular question, affecting the company as a whole, which, if exercised, would have yielded a majority of the votes capable of being exercised thereon, or could then have obtained such control by an exercise at that time of a power exercisable by him or at his direction or with his consent;

(ii) he then had the capacity, or could then by an exercise of a power exercisable by him or at his direction or with his consent obtain the capacity, to exercise or to control the exercise of any of the following powers, that is to say—

(I) the powers of a board of directors of the company;

(II) powers of a governing director of the company;

(III) power to nominate a majority of the directors of the company or a governing director thereof;

(IV) the power to veto the appointment of a director of the company,

or

(V) powers of a like nature;

(iii) he then had a right to receive, or the receipt of, more than one-half of the total amount of the dividends of the company, whether declared or not, and for the purposes of this subparagraph, "dividend" shall be deemed to include interest on any debentures of the company; or

(iv) he then had an interest in the shares of the company of an aggregate nominal value representing one-half or more of the aggregate nominal value of the shares of the company.

Footnotes

1   As substituted by s.125(1)(a), FA 1993, in relation to gifts and inheritances taken on or after 24th February, 1993.

2   As inserted by s.125(1)(b), FA 1993, in relation to gifts and inheritances taken on or after 24th February, 1993.

3   As amended by s.1100, TCA, with effect from 6th April, 1997. S.431, TCA, is reproduced on page 521.

4   As substituted by s.121, FA 1996, as respects gifts and inheritances taken on or after 28th March, 1996.

5   This definition, which was not amended, was repealed by s.125 (1)(b), FA1993, in relation to gifts and inheritances taken on or after 25th February, 1993.

6   As inserted by s.125(1)(b), FA 1993, in relation to gifts and inheritances taken on or after 24th February, 1993.

Commentary

A   See an article on Share Valuations by B. H. Giblin in the *Irish Tax Review* of July 2000, page 377.

B   The effect of s.16 is modified by s.127, FA 1993, for the purpose of the definition of "specified amount" in s.90(1), FA 1989, where the time of ascertainment of that amount is on or after 6th May, 1993.

C   See two articles on the Valuation of Shares by Denis Cremins in the *Irish Tax Review* of September 2006, page 60, and January 2007, page 55.

Cross-References

1   The definition of "group of shares" in s.16(2) is construed by s.107(a), FA 1984, in connection with the once-off discretionary trust tax, and by s.104(a), FA 1986, in connection with the annual discretionary trust tax.

2   The definition of "nominee" in s.16(2) is also used in para. 9(1), Part I, Second Sch, CATA.

3   The definition of "private company" in s.16(2) is also used in s.6(4), CATA, s.12(4), CATA, s.29(4), CATA, s.34(2), CATA, s.56(2)(a), CATA, s.59(4), CATA, para. 9(1), Part I, Second Sch., CATA, s.90(1), FA1989, s.121(2) and s.123(2), FA1993, and s.166(1), FA1995.

4   The definition of "share" in s.16(2) is also used in s.6(4), CATA, s.12(4), CATA, s.34(2), CATA, and s.121(2) and s.123(2), FA1993.

5   The definition of "company controlled by the donee or successor" in s.16(3) is also used in s.6(4), CATA, s.12(4), CATA, s.107(a), FA1984, s.104(a), FA1986, s.90(1), FA1989, s.127(1)(c), FA1994, and s.166(2), FA1995.

6   "Control of a company" within the meaning of s.16(4)(b) is also referred to in s.29(3), CATA, s.56(2)(a), CATA, para. 9(1), Part I, Second Sch, CATA, and s.129(3), FA1994.

Section 17

Market value of certain shares in private non-trading companies.

17.   . . . .[1]

Footnote

1   This section, which was not amended, was repealed by s.134, FA 1993, in relation to gifts and inheritances taken on or after 24th February, 1993.

Section 18

Taxable value of a taxable gift or taxable inheritance.

18.   (1)   In this section, "incumbrance-free value", in relation to a taxable gift or a taxable inheritance, means the market value at the valuation date of the property of which the taxable gift or taxable inheritance consists at that date, after deducting any liabilities, costs and expenses that are properly payable out of the taxable gift or taxable inheritance.

(2)   Subject to the provisions of this section (but save as provided in section 19), the taxable value of a taxable gift or a taxable inheritance (where the interest taken by the donee or successor is not a limited interest) shall be ascertained by deducting from the incumbrance-free value thereof the market value of any *bona fide* consideration in money or money's worth, paid by the donee or successor for the gift or inheritance, including —

(a)   any liability of the disponer which the donee or successor undertakes to discharge as his own personal liability; and

(b)   any other liability to which the gift or inheritance is subject under the terms of the disposition under which it is taken,

and the amount so ascertained shall be the taxable value:

Provided that no deduction shall be made under this subsection in respect of any liability which falls to be deducted in ascertaining the incumbrance-free value.

(3) Where a liability (other than a liability within the meaning of subsection (9)) for which a deduction may be made under the provisions of subsection (1) or (2) falls to be discharged after the time at which it falls to be taken into account as a deduction under either of those subsections, it shall be valued for the purpose of making such a deduction at its current market value at the time at which it falls to be so taken into account.

(4) The taxable value of a taxable gift or a taxable inheritance, where the interest taken by the donee or the successor is a limited interest, shall be ascertained as follows –

    (a) the value of the limited interest in a capital sum equal to the incumbrance-free value shall be ascertained in accordance with the Rules contained in the First Schedule; and

    (b) from the value ascertained in accordance with paragraph (a) a deduction shall be made in respect of the market value of any *bona fide* consideration in money or money's worth paid by the donee or the successor for the gift or the inheritance and the amount remaining after such deduction shall be the taxable value:

    Provided that no deduction shall be made under this paragraph in respect of any liability which falls to be deducted in ascertaining the incumbrance-free value.

(5) A deduction shall not be made under the provisions of this section –

    (a) in respect of any liability the payment of which is contingent on the happening of some future event:

    Provided that if the event on the happening of which the liability is contingent happens and the liability is paid, then, on a claim for relief being made to the Commissioners and subject to the other provisions of this section, a deduction shall be made in respect of the liability and such adjustment of tax as is appropriate shall be made; and such adjustment shall be made on the basis that the donee or successor had taken an interest in possession in the amount which falls to be deducted for the liability, for a period certain which was equal to the actual duration of the postponement of the payment of the liability;

    (b) in respect of any liability, costs or expenses in so far as the donee or successor has a right of reimbursement from any source, unless such reimbursement cannot be obtained;

    (c) in respect of any liability created by the donee or successor or any person claiming in right of the donee or successor or on his behalf;

(d)   in respect of tax, interest or penalties chargeable under this Act in respect of the gift or inheritance, or of the costs, expenses or interest incurred in raising or paying the same;

(e)   in respect of any liability in so far as such liability is an incumbrance on, or was created or incurred in acquiring, any property which is comprised in any gift or inheritance and which is exempt from tax under any provision of this Act or otherwise;

(f)   in the case of any gift or inheritance referred to in [section 6 (1) (d) or section 12 (1) (c)]¹ in respect of—

   (i)   any liability, costs or expenses due to a person resident outside the State (save in so far as such liability is required by contract to be paid in the State or is charged on the property which is situate in the State and which is comprised in the gift or inheritance); or

   (ii)   any liability, costs or expenses in so far as the same are charged on or secured by property which is comprised in the gift or inheritance and which is not situate in the State,

   save to the extent that all the property situate outside the State and comprised in the gift or inheritance is insufficient for the payment of the liability, costs or expenses;

(g)   for any tax in respect of which a credit is allowed under the provisions of section 66 or 67.

(6)   In the case of a gift or inheritance referred to in subsection (5) (f), any deduction to be made under subsection (2) or (4) (b) shall be restricted to the proportion of the consideration which bears the same proportion to the whole of the consideration as the taxable gift or taxable inheritance bears to the whole of the gift or the whole of the inheritance.

(7)   A deduction shall not be made under the provisions of this section—

(a)   more than once for the same liability, costs, expenses or consideration, in respect of all gifts and inheritances taken by the donee or successor from the disponer; or

(b)   for any liability, costs, expenses or consideration, a proportion of which falls to be allowed under the provisions of section 19 (2) (ii) or (iii) in respect of a gift or inheritance taken by the donee or successor from the disponer.

(8)   Where a taxable gift or a taxable inheritance is subject to a liability within the meaning of subsection (9), the deduction to be made in respect thereof under this section shall be an amount equal to the market value of the whole or the appropriate part, as the case may be, of the property, within the meaning of section 5 (5).

(9) For the purpose of subsection (8), "liability", in relation to a taxable gift or a taxable inheritance, means a liability which deprives the donee or successor, whether permanently or temporarily, of the use, enjoyment or income in whole or in part of the property, or of any part of the property, of which the taxable gift or taxable inheritance consists.

(10) Where —

    (a) *bona fide* consideration in money or money's worth has been paid by a person for the granting to him, by a disposition, of an interest in expectancy in property; and

    (b) at the coming into possession of the interest in expectancy, that person takes a gift or an inheritance of that property under that disposition,

the deduction to be made under subsection (2) or (4) (b) for consideration paid by that person shall be a sum equal to the same proportion of the taxable value of the taxable gift or taxable inheritance (as if no deduction had been made for such consideration) as the amount of the consideration so paid bore to the market value of the interest in expectancy at the date of the payment of the consideration.

(11) Any deduction, under the provisions of this section, in respect of a liability which is an incumbrance on any property shall so far as possible be made against that property.

Footnote

1   As substituted by s.216, FA 2001, in relation to gifts or inheritances taken on or after 1st December, 1999, save where the date of the disposition is before that date.

Commentary

A   S.12, CATA, has provisions for determining when an inheritance which consists of non-Irish property shall not be a taxable inheritance. According to Part 19.12 of the *Revenue CAT Manual*, the Revenue view has been upheld by the Appeal Commissioner and by the Circuit Court that, for the purposes of s.18(5)(e), CATA, this is an exemption of an inheritance.

B   As to a liability consisting of a claim for wages against an estate by a family member, see Part 19.1 of the *Revenue CAT Manual* which quotes two cases, *Jones v Padavatton* [1961] 1 WLR 328 and *Balfour v Balfour* [1919] 2KB 571. Such claims are disallowed.

C   See Part 19.5 of the *Revenue CAT Manual*. Where the worldwide property of a deceased person is taxable in the State under s.12, CATA, arrears of income tax, capital gains tax, etc., due to the British Revenue by the deceased person, are allowed as a liability of the deceased for CAT purposes, provided such tax is actually paid and whether or not the deceased person died possessed of assets in the UK.

D   See part 19.11 of the *Revenue CAT Manual*. Where it is shown, by evidence from the Inspector of Taxes, that a beneficiary of the estate of a person, dying on or after 6th April, 1985, was charged to income tax on income which accrued in relation to the deceased person's estate during the period between the date of death and the valuation date of the beneficiary's inheritance, that income is not taken into account in calculating the taxable value of the beneficiary's taxable inheritance. The proportion of any liabilities, costs and expenses which is payable out of the part of the estate represented by such increase will, if the figures justify apportionment, be disallowed accordingly.

Cross-Reference
1. "Liability" in s.18(9) is also dealt with in s.25(1), CATA, and s.28(1), CATA.

Section 19

Value of agricultural property.
19. (1) In this section—

["agricultural property" means agricultural land, pasture and woodland situate in the State and crops, trees and underwood growing on such land and also includes such farm buildings, farm houses and mansion houses (together with the lands occupied therewith) as are of a character appropriate to the property, and farm machinery, livestock and bloodstock thereon;][1]

["agricultural value" means the market value of agricultural property reduced by 90 per cent. of that value;][2]

"farmer", in relation to a donee or successor, means an individual who is domiciled.....[3] in the State and in respect of whom not less than [80 per cent][4] of the market value of the property to which [the individual][5] is beneficially entitled in possession is represented by the market value of property in the State which consists of [agricultural property,][6] and, for the purposes of this definition –

(a) no deduction shall be made from the market value of property for any debts or encumbrances, and

[(b) an individual shall be deemed to be beneficially entitled in possession to—

(i) an interest in expectancy, notwithstanding the definition of "entitled in possession" in section 2, and

(ii) property which is subject to a discretionary trust under or in consequence of a disposition made by the individual where the individual is an object of the trust.][7]

(2) Save as provided in subsection (7), in so far as any gift or inheritance consists of agricultural property –

(a) at the date of the gift or at the date of the inheritance; and

(b) at the valuation date,

and is taken by a donee or successor who is, on the valuation date and after taking the gift or inheritance, a farmer, the provisions of section 18 (other than subsection 7 (b) thereof) shall apply in relation to agricultural property as they apply in relation to other property subject to the following modifications –

    c)   in the case of an inheritance of land, 70% of the market value reduced by 35% of that market value or by £105,000, whichever is the lesser.

In relation to gifts and inheritances taken on or after 8th February, 1995, and before 23rd January, 1996, s.158 (1)(a), FA 1995, defined "agricultural value" as meaning –

    a)   in the case of farm machinery, livestock and bloodstock, 50% of the market value;

    b)   in the case of a gift of land, 50% of the market value reduced by 30% of that market value or by £90,000, whichever is the lesser;

    c)   in the case of an inheritance of land, 50% of the market value reduced by 15% of that market value or by £45,000, whichever is the lesser.

In relation to gifts or inheritances taken on or after 23rd January, 1996, and before 23rd January, 1997, s.122 (1)(a), FA 1996, defined "agricultural value" as the market value of land, and any farm machinery, livestock and bloodstock thereon, reduced by 75% of that market value, with the proviso that the relief available in respect of a gift of land would not be less than that available under s.158(1)(a), FA 1995.

3   The words "and ordinarily resident" were deleted by s.158(1)(b), FA 1995, in relation to a gift or inheritance where the valuation date is on or after 6th April, 1994.

4   S.114(b), FA 1991, substituted "80 per cent." for "75 per cent." as respects a gift or inheritance taken on or after 29th May, 1991.

5   S.141(1)(d), FA 1994, substituted "the individual" for "he", in relation to gifts and inheritances taken on or after 11th April, 1994.

6   S.141(1)(d), FA 1994, substituted "agricultural property" for "agricultural property, livestock, bloodstock and farm machinery" in relation to gifts and inheritances taken on or after 11th April, 1994.

7   In relation to gifts and inheritances taken on or after 10th February, 2000, s.140(1)(a), FA 2000, substantially re-states the definition of "farmer" with its existing amendments, but adds para. (b).

8   This subsection was repealed by s.122(1)(b), FA 1996, in relation to gifts and inheritances taken on or after 23rd January, 1996.

The subsection placed a limit on the total amount of the reductions in the market value of land available to the same donee or successor in respect of all taxable gifts of land taken by him on or after 28th February, 1969, and all taxable inheritances of land taken by him on or after 1st April, 1975, all from the same disponer.

Originally, in the CATA, the total amount of the reductions was limited to 50% of the market value of the land, or £100,000, whichever is the lesser.

As respects a gift or inheritance taken on or after 1st April, 1980 and before 2nd April, 1982, s.83, FA 1980, limited the total amount of the reductions to 50% of the market value of the land, or £150,000, whichever is the lesser.

As respects a gift taken on or after 1st April, 1982, and before 17th June, 1993, s.100, FA 1982, limited the total amount of the reductions to 50% of the market value of the land, or £200,000, whichever is the lesser. This section applied that limit to inheritances taken on after 1st April, 1982, and before 11th April, 1994.

As respects a gift taken on or after 17th June, 1993, and before 11th April, 1994, s.128, FA 1993, limited the total amount of the reductions to 50% of the market value of the land, or £250,000, whichever is the lesser.

In relation to gifts and inheritances taken on or after 11th April, 1994 and before 8th February, 1995, s.141(1)(c), FA 1994, provided that, in calculating the agricultural value of land, the amount deductible against the market value of the land should not exceed –

    a)   £150,000 in the case of a gift of land, and

    b)   £105,000 in the case of an inheritance of land,

in respect of the aggregate of all taxable gifts of land taken on or after 28th February, 1969, and all taxable inheritances of land taken on or after 1st April, 1976, all taken by the same donee or successor from the same disponer.

In relation to gifts and inheritances taken on or after 8th February, 1995, and before 23rd January, 1996, the figures of £150,000 and £105,000 at (a) and (b) of the preceding paragraph were amended to £90,000 and £45,000 respectively by s.158(1)(c), FA1995.

9   As substituted by s.141(1)(e), FA 1994, in relation to gifts and inheritances taken on or after 11th April, 1994.

10   Originally, in the CATA, "six years".

   In relation to gifts and inheritances taken on or after 23rd January, 1996, s.122(1)(c), FA 1996, substitutes "ten years" for "six years".

   Where the sale or compulsory acquisition which causes the agricultural value to cease to be applicable occurs on or after 10th January, 2000, "6 years" is substituted for "ten years" by s.140(1)(b), FA 2000.

11   A second proviso was added by s.122(1)(c), FA 1996, in relation to gifts and inheritances taken on or after 23rd January, 1996. This second proviso deals with a possible partial clawback if the sale or compulsory acquisition which causes the agricultural value to cease occurs between the relevant six and ten years. This second proviso was extended by s.134(1)(b), FA 1997, in relation to gifts and inheritances taken on or after 23rd January, 1997.

   The second proviso has been repealed by s.140(1)(b), FA 2000, which, with the amendment at footnote 9 above, re-states the present provisions of s.19(5), CATA, and has effect where the sale or compulsory acquisition which causes the agricultural value to cease to be applicable occurs on or after 10th January, 2000.

12   Inserted by s.158(1)(d), FA 1995, and has effect in relation to gifts and inheritances taken on or after 2nd June, 1995.

13   Substituted "4 years" for "1 year" by s.217, FA 2001, in relation to compulsory acquisitions made on or after 6th December, 2000, and before 25th March, 2002. Substituted "6 years" for "4 years" by s.116, FA 2002, in relation to compulsory acquisitions made on or after 25th March, 2002.

Commentary

A   See Part 19.13 of the *Revenue CAT Manual* citing a case where the owner of a dwelling house, a PAYE employee, inherited land situated three miles from the dwelling house. The Appeal Commissioners upheld a Revenue argument that the dwelling house was not "agricultural property" for the purpose of the "farmer test" as it was not of a character appropriate to the land.

B   See *Starke v IRC* [1995] STC 689 in relation to the definition of "agricultural property" contained in s.115(2), U.K. Inheritance Tax Act, 1984. There a 2.5 acre site, containing a substantial house and outbuildings, was held not to be "agricultural property".

C   See articles in relation to Agricultural Property Relief/Business Property Relief (dealing with both reliefs applying to agricultural property post FA 2000) by Brian Bohan in the *Irish Tax Review* of May 2000, page 279, and by Fergus McCarthy in the *Irish Tax Review* of July 2000, page 342.

D   See the Revenue Information Leaflet CAT5 in relation to agricultural relief.

E   See a discussion by Frank Carr at page 40 of the *Irish Tax Review* of March 2006 on a UK Land Tribunal case of *Lloyds TSB Private Banking plc., as personal representatives of Rosemary Antrobus, deceased v Inland Revenue* [2005] DET/47/2004. The issue involved the definition of a "farmhouse".

F   See a discussion by Frank Carr at page 25 of the *Irish Tax Review* of January 2007 on a UK Special Commissioners case of *McKenna, deceased, executors v Revenue Commissioners* [2006] SPC 565. The case decided that a listed medieval house attached to a farm did not qualify for agricultural relief.

G   As to a residence "being of a character appropriate to the property", see a Northern Ireland case of *John Sidney Higginson, deceased, executors v Commissioners of Inland Revenue* [2002] STC (SCD) 483.

Cross-References

1   The definition of "agricultural property" in s.19(1) is used in s.164(1), FA 1995, and in s.124(1), FA 1994.

2   The provisions of s.19(6) are applied to s.55, CATA, s.57, CATA and s.166, FA 1995.

Section 20

Contingencies affecting gifts or inheritances.

20. Where, under a disposition, a person becomes beneficially entitled in possession to any benefit and, under the terms of the disposition, the entitlement, or any part thereof, may cease upon the happening of a contingency (other than the revocation of the entitlement upon the exercise by the disponer of such a power as is referred to in section 30), the taxable value of any taxable gift or taxable inheritance taken by that person on becoming so entitled to that benefit shall be ascertained as if no part of the entitlement were so to cease; but, in the event and to the extent that the entitlement so ceases, the tax payable by that person shall, to that extent be adjusted (if, by so doing, a lesser amount of tax would be payable by him) on the basis that he had taken an interest in possession for a period certain which was equal to the actual duration of his beneficial entitlement in possession:

Provided that nothing in this section shall prejudice any charge for tax on the taking by such person of a substituted gift or inheritance on the happening of such a contingency.

Commentary

A   See Part 16 of the *Revenue Cat Manual*.

Section 21

Valuation date for tax purposes.

21. (1) Subject to the provisions of subsection (7), the valuation date of a taxable gift shall be the date of the gift.

(2) The valuation date of a taxable inheritance shall be the date of death of the deceased person on whose death the inheritance is taken if the successor or any person in right of the successor or on his behalf takes the inheritance –

(a) as a *donatio mortis causa,* or

(b) by reason of the failure to exercise a power of revocation.

(3) If a gift becomes an inheritance by reason of its being taken under a disposition where the date of the disposition is within two years prior to the death of the disponer, the valuation date thereof shall be determined as if it were a gift.

(4) The valuation date of a taxable inheritance, other than a taxable inheritance referred to in subsection (2) or (3), shall be the earliest date of the following –

(a) the earliest date on which a personal representative or trustee or the successor or any other person is entitled to retain the subject matter of the inheritance for the benefit of the successor or of any person in right of the successor or on his behalf;

(b) the date on which the subject matter of the inheritance is so retained; or

(c) the date of delivery, payment or other satisfaction or discharge of the subject matter of the inheritance to the successor or for his benefit or to or for the benefit of any person in right of the successor or on his behalf.

(5) If any part of a taxable inheritance referred to in subsection (4) may be retained, or is retained, delivered, paid or otherwise satisfied, whether by way of part payment, advancement, payment on account or in any manner whatsoever, before any other part or parts of such inheritance, the appropriate valuation date for each part of the inheritance shall be determined in accordance with that subsection as if each such part respectively were a separate inheritance.

(6) The Commissioners may give to an accountable person a notice in writing of the date determined by them to be the valuation date in respect of the whole or any part of an inheritance, and, subject to any decision on appeal pursuant to subsection (9), the date so determined shall be deemed to be the valuation date.

(7) If a taxable inheritance referred to in subsection (4) or (5) is disposed of, ceases or comes to an end before the valuation date referred to in those subsections in such circumstances as to give rise to a taxable gift, the valuation date in respect of such taxable gift shall be the same date as the valuation date of the taxable inheritance.

(8) Notwithstanding anything contained in this section, the Commissioners may, in case of doubt, with the agreement in writing of the accountable person or his agent, determine the valuation date of the whole or any part of any taxable inheritance and the valuation date so determined shall be substituted for the valuation date which would otherwise be applicable by virtue of this section.

(9) An appeal shall lie against any determination made by the Commissioners under subsection (6) and the provisions of section 52 shall apply, with any necessary modifications, in relation to an appeal under this subsection as they apply in relation to an appeal against an assessment of tax.

Commentary

A   As to the meaning of "retainer" see *Lord Advocate v Wotherspoon's Trustees* [1930] SLT 82.

B   As to s.21(5), see Part 19.2 of the *Revenue CAT Manual* dealing with the Revenue practice where advances are made out of a residuary estate.

C   See an article on the Valuation Date by Finola O'Hanlon at page 87 of the *Irish tax Review* of November 2008.

Cross-Reference

1   The provisions of s.21 are applied, with modifications, by s.107(b), FA 1984, to the once-off discretionary trust tax charge.

PART V

Provisions relating to Gifts and Inheritances

Section 22

Discretionary trusts.

22. Where a person becomes beneficially entitled in possession to any benefit —

(a) under a discretionary trust, other than a discretionary trust referred to in paragraph (b), otherwise than for full consideration in money or money's worth paid by him, he shall be deemed to have taken a gift;

(b) under a discretionary trust created —

    (i) by will at any time;

    (ii) by a disposition, where the date of the disposition is on or after the 1st day of April, 1975, and within two years prior to the death of the disponer; or

    (iii) by a disposition *inter vivos* and limited to come into operation on a death occurring before or after the passing of this Act,

otherwise than for full consideration in money or money's worth paid by him, he shall be deemed to have taken an inheritance.

Section 23

Dealings with future interests.

23. (1) Where a benefit, to which a person (in this section referred to as the remainderman) is entitled under a disposition, devolves, or is disposed of, either in whole or in part, before it has become an interest in possession so that, at the time when the benefit comes into possession, it is taken, either in whole or in part, by a person (in this section referred to as the transferee) other than the remainderman to whom it was limited by the disposition, then tax shall be payable, in respect of a gift or inheritance, as the case may be, of the remainderman in all respects as if, at that time, the remainderman had become beneficially entitled in possession to the full extent of the benefit limited to him under the disposition, and the transferee shall be the person primarily accountable for the payment of tax to the extent that the benefit is taken by him.

(2) The provisions of subsection (1) shall not prejudice any charge for tax in respect of any gift or inheritance affecting the same property or any part of it under any other disposition.

(3) In subsection (1), "benefit" includes the benefit of the cesser of a liability referred to in section 28.

Cross-References
1   The "remainderman" is s.23(1) is referred to in s.64(2)(b), CATA.
2   The "transferee" is s.23(1) is referred to in s.19(8), CATA, s.35, CATA, s.43(4), CATA, '
     s.59C(1A), CATA, and s.124(4), FA 1994.

Section 24

Release of limited interests, etc.

24.   (1)   Where an interest in property, which is limited by the disposition creating it to cease on an event, has come to an end (whether by another disposition, the taking of successive interests into one ownership, or by any means whatever other than the happening of another event on which the interest was limited by the first-mentioned disposition to cease) before the happening of such event, tax shall be payable under the first-mentioned disposition in all respects as if the event on which the interest was limited to cease under that disposition had happened immediately before the coming to an end of the interest.

       (2)   The provisions of subsection (1) shall not prejudice any charge for tax in respect of any gift or inheritance affecting the same property or any part of it under any disposition other than that first- mentioned in subsection (1).

       (3)   Notwithstanding anything contained in subsection (2), if –

              (a)   an interest in property which was limited to cease on an event was limited to the disponer by the disposition creating that interest; and

              (b)   on the coming to an end of that interest, the provisions of subsection (1) have effect in relation to a gift or inheritance which was taken by a donee or successor under that disposition and which consists of the property in which that interest subsisted, then –

              a further gift or inheritance taken by the same donee or successor under another disposition made by the same disponer (being the disposition by which that interest has come to an end) shall not be a taxable gift or a taxable inheritance in so far as it consists of the whole or any part of the same property.

       (4)   In this section, "event" includes –

              (a)   a death, and

              (b)   the expiration of a specified period.

Cross-Reference
1   "Event" in s.24(4) has the same meaning in s.25(3), CATA.

Section 25

‧ Settlement of an interest not in possession.

25. (1) Where any donee or successor takes a gift or an inheritance under a disposition made by himself then, if at the date of such disposition he was entitled to the property comprised in the disposition, either expectantly on the happening of an event, or subject to a liability within the meaning of section 18 (9), and such event happens or such liability ceases during the continuance of the disposition, tax shall be charged on the taxable value of the taxable gift or taxable inheritance which he would have taken on the happening of such event, or on the cesser of such liability, if no such disposition had been made.

(2) The provisions of subsection (1) shall not prejudice any charge for tax in respect of any gift or inheritance affecting the same property or any part of it under the said disposition.

(3) In this section, "event" has the same meaning as it has in section 24.

Section 26

Enlargement of interests.

26. (1) Where a person, having a limited interest in possession in property (in this section referred to as the first-mentioned interest), takes a further interest (in this section referred to as the second-mentioned interest) in the same property, as a taxable gift or a taxable inheritance, in consequence of which he becomes the absolute owner of the property, the taxable value of the taxable gift or taxable inheritance of the second-mentioned interest at the valuation date shall be reduced by the value at that date of the first-mentioned interest, taking such value to be the value, ascertained in accordance with the Rules contained in the First Schedule, of a limited interest which—

(a) is a limited interest in a capital sum equal to the value of the property;

(b) commences on that date; and

(c) is to continue for the unexpired balance of the term of the first-mentioned interest.

(2) For the purposes of subsection (1) (a), "value" means such amount as would be the incumbrance-free value, within the meaning of section 18 (1), if the limited interest were taken, at the date referred to in subsection (1), as a taxable gift or taxable inheritance.

(3) The provisions of this section shall not have effect where the second-mentioned interest is taken under the disposition under which the first-mentioned interest was created.

Section 27

Dispositions involving powers of appointment.

27. (1) Where, by virtue of or in consequence of the exercise of, or the failure to exercise, or the release of, a general power of appointment by any person having such a power, a person becomes beneficially entitled in possession to any benefit, then, for the purposes of this Act, the disposition shall be the exercise of, or the failure to exercise, or the release of, the power and not the disposition under which the power was created, and the person exercising, or failing to exercise, or releasing, the power shall be the disponer.

(2) Where, by virtue of or in consequence of the exercise of, or the failure to exercise, or the release of, a special power of appointment by any person having such a power, a person becomes beneficially entitled in possession to any benefit, then, for the purposes of this Act, the disposition shall be the disposition under which the power was created and the person who created the power shall be the disponer.

Section 28

Cesser of liabilities.

28. (1) The benefit of the cesser of —

(a) a liability within the meaning of section 18 (9); or

(b) any liability similar to that referred to in paragraph (a) to which the taking of a benefit which was a gift or inheritance was subject,

shall be deemed to be a gift or an inheritance, as the case may be, which shall be deemed —

(i) to the extent that the liability is charged on or secured by any property at the time of its cesser, to consist of the whole or the appropriate part, as the case may be, of that property; and

(ii) to the extent that the liability is not charged on or secured by any property at the time of its cesser, to consist of such sum as would, under the provisions of section 5 (2) (b), be the sum the annual income of which would be equal to the annual value of the liability.

(2) In this section, "appropriate part" has the meaning assigned to it by section 5 (5).

(3) For the purposes of sections 6 (1) (c) and 12 (1) (b)[1], the sum referred to in subparagraph (ii) of subsection (1) shall be deemed not to be situate in the State at the date of the gift or at the date of the inheritance.

Footnote
1   "sections 6(1)(c) and 12(1)(b)" should be "sections 6(1)(d) and 12(1)(c)".

Cross-Reference
1   A "benefit" in s.28(1) is also governed by s.23(1), CATA.

Section 29

Disposition enlarging value of property.

29. (1) In this section, "property" does not include any property to which a donee or successor became beneficially entitled in possession prior to the 28th day of February, 1969.

(2) Where the taking by any person of a beneficial interest in any property (hereinafter in this section referred to as additional property) under any disposition made by a disponer has the effect of increasing the value of any other property (hereinafter in this section referred to as original property) to which that person is beneficially entitled in possession, and which had been derived from the same disponer, the following provisions shall have effect—

(a) the increase in value so effected shall be deemed to be a gift or an inheritance, as the case may be, arising under that disposition and taken by that person, as donee or successor, from that disponer, at the time he took the beneficial interest in the additional property;

(b) the original property shall be treated as having been increased in value if the market value of that property at the time referred to in paragraph (a) would be greater if it was sold as part of an aggregate of the original property and the additional property rather than as a single item of property, and the increase in value for the purposes of this section shall be the amount by which the market value of the original property if sold at that time as part of such aggregate would be greater than the amount of the market value of that property if sold at that time as a single item of property;

(c) the additional property shall for the purpose of determining its market value be deemed to be part of an aggregate of the original property and the additional property; and

(d) the market value of any property which is to be valued as part of an aggregate of property shall be ascertained as being so much of the market value of such aggregate as may reasonably be ascribed to that part.

(3) For the purpose of this section, the donee or successor shall be deemed to be beneficially entitled in possession to any property notwithstanding that within five years prior to such a disposition

as is referred to in subsection (2) he has divested himself of such property, or any part thereof, otherwise than for full consideration in money or money's worth or has disposed of it to a company of which he is, at any time within that period of five years, deemed to have control within the meaning of section 16 (4) (b).

(4) In subsection (3), "company" means a private company within the meaning of section 16 (2).

Section 30

Gift subject to power of revocation.

30. Where, under any disposition, a person becomes beneficially entitled in possession to any benefit and, under the terms of the disposition, the disponer has reserved to himself the power to revoke the benefit, such person shall, for the purposes of this Act, be deemed not to be beneficially entitled in possession to the benefit unless and until the power of revocation is released by the disponer, or otherwise ceases to be exercisable.

Cross-Reference

1 A power of revocation in s.30 is not a "contingency" for the purposes of s.20, CATA.

Section 31

Free use of property, free loans, etc.

31. (1) A person shall be deemed to take a gift in each relevant period during the whole or part of which he is allowed to have the use, occupation or enjoyment of any property (to which property he is not beneficially entitled in possession) otherwise than for full consideration in money or money's worth.

(2) In subsections (1) and (4), "relevant period", in relation to any use, occupation or enjoyment of property, means the period from the 28th day of February, 1974, to the 31st day of December, 1974, and thereafter the period of twelve months ending on the 31st day of December in each year.

(3) A gift referred to in subsection (1) shall be deemed to consist of a sum equal to the difference between the amount of any consideration in money or money's worth, given by the person referred to in subsection (1) for such use, occupation or enjoyment, and the best price obtainable in the open market for such use, occupation or enjoyment.

(4) A gift referred to in subsection (1) shall be treated as being taken at the end of the relevant period or, if earlier, immediately prior

to the time when the use, occupation or enjoyment referred to in subsection (1) comes to an end.

(5) In any case where the use, occupation or enjoyment of property is allowed to a person, not being beneficially entitled in possession to that property, under a disposition—

(a) made by will;

(b) where the date of the disposition is on or after the 1st day of April, 1975 and within two years prior to the death of the disponer; or

(c) which is a disposition *inter vivos* and the use, occupation or enjoyment is had by that person after the cesser of another person's life interest,

subsections (1), (3) and (4) shall have effect in relation to that property as if a reference to an inheritance were substituted for the reference to a gift wherever it occurs in those subsections, and for the purpose of this subsection "relevant period" in subsections (1) and (4), in relation to the use, occupation or enjoyment of property, means the period of nine months ending on the 31st day of December, 1975, and thereafter the period of twelve months ending on the 31st day of December in any year.

(6) For the purposes of [sections 6 (1) (d) and 12 (1) (c)][1], the sum referred to in subsection (3) shall be deemed not to be situate in the State at the date of the gift or at the date of the inheritance.

Footnote
1 Substituted by para. 2(b), Sch. 6, FA 2002, for "sections 6(1)(c) and 12(1)(b)" in relation to gifts or inheritances taken on or after 1st December, 1999.

Commentary
A As to "best price" in s.31(3), see Part 19.14 of the *Revenue CAT Manual*.

Section 32

When interest in assurance policy becomes interest in possession.

32. (1) For the purposes of this Act, an interest in a policy of assurance upon human life shall be deemed to become an interest in possession when and only when, either—

(a) the policy matures; or

(b) prior to the maturing of the policy, the policy is surrendered to the insurer for a consideration in money or money's worth:

Provided that if, during the currency of the policy the insurer makes a payment of money or money's worth, in full or partial discharge of the policy, the interest shall be deemed to have come into possession to the extent of such payment.

(2) This section shall have effect in relation to a contract for a deferred annuity, and for the purposes of this section such a contract shall be deemed to mature on the date when the first instalment of the annuity falls due.

Commentary

A   See an article on Policies of Assurance and CAT by Brian Bohan in the *Irish Tax Review* of December 1990, page 263.

Section 33

Provisions to apply where section 98 of Succession Act, 1965, has effect.

33.   (1) If, on the death of a testator and by virtue of the provisions of section 98 of the Succession Act, 1965, or otherwise, a disposition takes effect as if a person, who had predeceased the testator, had survived the testator, the benefit taken by the estate of that person shall not be deemed to be an inheritance.

(2) Where a person survives a testator, and —

(a) such person becomes beneficially entitled, under a disposition made by a person who predeceased the testator, to any benefit in relation to any property devised or bequeathed by the testator; and

(b) section 33 of the Wills Act, 1837, or section 98 of the Succession Act, 1965, or any analogous provision of the law of another territory has effect in relation to the devise or bequest,

such person shall be deemed for the purposes of inheritance tax to derive the benefit from the testator, as disponer.

Section 34

Disposition by or to a company.

34.   [(1) For the purposes of this Act —

(a) consideration paid by, or a disposition made by, a company shall be deemed to be consideration, or a disposition (as the case may be) paid or made, and

(b) consideration, or a gift, or an inheritance taken by a company shall be deemed to be consideration, or a gift or an inheritance (as the case may be) taken,

by the beneficial owners of the shares in the company and the beneficial owners of the entitlements under any liability incurred by the company (otherwise than for the purposes of the business of the company, wholly and exclusively) in the same proportions as the specified amounts relating to their respective beneficial interests in the shares and entitlements bear to each other.

(ii) every trustee, guardian, committee, personal representative, agent or other person in whose care any property comprised in the gift or the income therefrom is placed at the date of the or at any time thereafter and every person in whom the property is vested after that date, other than a *bona fide* purchaser or mortgagee for full consideration in money or money's worth, or a person deriving title from or under such a purchaser or mortgagee;

(b)[1] in the case of an inheritance, every trustee, guardian, committee, personal representative, agent or other person in whose care any property comprised in the inheritance or the income therefrom is placed at the date of the inheritance or at any time thereafter and every person in whom the property is vested after that date, other than a *bona fide* purchaser or mortgagee for full consideration in money or money's worth, or a person deriving title from or under such a purchaser or mortgagee:

Provided that the disponer as such shall not be so accountable in the case where the date of the disposition was prior to the 28th day of February, 1974.

(3) No person referred to in subsection (2) (a) (ii) or (b) shall (unless he is a person who is also primarily accountable under subsection (1)) be liable for tax chargeable on any gift or inheritance to an amount in excess of—

(a) the market value of so much of the property of which the gift or inheritance consists; and

(b) so much of the income from such property,

which has been received by him, or which, but for his own neglect or default, would have been received by him or to which he is beneficially entitled in possession.

(4) A person who acts solely in the capacity of an agent shall not be liable for tax chargeable on a gift or inheritance to an amount in excess of the market value of so much of the property of which the gift or inheritance consists and of the income from such property which he held, or which came into his possession, at any time after the serving on him of the notice referred to in subsection (5).

(5) The Commissioners may serve on any person who acts solely in the capacity of agent in relation to any property comprised in a gift or an inheritance a notice in writing informing him of his liability under this section.

(6) The tax shall be recoverable from any one or more of—

(a) the accountable persons, and

(b) the personal representatives of any accountable persons who are dead, on whom the Commissioners have served notice in writing of the assessment of tax in exercise of the power conferred on them by section 39:

Provided that the liability of a personal representative under this subsection shall not exceed the amount for which the accountable person, of whom he is the personal representative, was liable.

(7) Any person referred to in subsection (2) (a) or (b) or in subsection (6) (b) who is authorised or required to pay, and pays, any tax in respect of any property comprised in a gift or in an inheritance may recover the amount paid by him in respect of tax from the person primarily accountable therefor [unless —

  (a) the latter person is the donee or successor referred to in paragraph (a) of subsection (1) and the interest taken by him is a limited interest, or

  (b) in the case referred to in paragraph (b) of the said subsection (1), the latter person is the transferee and the interest taken by the remainderman is a limited interest.][2]

(8) A person—

  (a) who is primarily accountable for the payment of tax; or

  (b) referred to in subsection (2) (a) or (b) or in subsection (6) (b) who is authorised or required to pay tax,

in respect of any property shall, for the purpose of paying the tax, or raising the amount of the tax when already paid, have power, whether the property is or is not vested in him, to raise the amount of such tax and any interest and expenses properly paid or incurred by him in respect thereof, by the sale or mortgage of, or a terminable charge on, that property or any part thereof.

(9) If a person, who is primarily accountable for the payment of tax in respect of a gift or inheritance (in this subsection and in subsection (11) referred to as the first gift or inheritance) derived from a disponer, has not paid the tax on the first gift or inheritance, the Commissioners may serve a notice in writing in accordance with subsection (11) on any person who is, by virtue of paragraph (a) (ii) or (b) of subsection (2), accountable for the payment of tax on any other gift or inheritance (referred to in subsections (10) and (11) as the second gift or inheritance) taken by the same donee or successor from the same disponer, and the person on whom the notice is served shall thereupon become accountable for the payment of tax in respect of the first gift or inheritance.

(10) The provisions of subsections (3), (4), (5), (6), (7) and (8) shall apply in relation to a person made accountable under subsection (9) as they apply in relation to a person referred to in paragraph (a) (ii) or (b) of subsection (2) and, for the purposes of this subsection—

  (a) references in subsections (3) and (4) to the property of which the gift or inheritance consists; and

(b)   the second and third references to property in subsection (8),

shall be construed as references to the property of which the second gift or inheritance consists, in so far as the last-mentioned property had not been duly paid out at the date of the service of the notice under subsection (9).

(11) A notice under subsection (9) shall refer expressly to the first and the second gift or inheritance, and shall inform the person on whom it is served of his accountability in respect of the first gift or inheritance.

(12) Every public officer having in his custody any rolls, books, records, papers, documents, or proceedings, the inspection whereof may tend to secure the tax, or to prove or lead to the discovery of any fraud or omission in relation to the tax, shall at all reasonable times permit any person thereto authorised by the Commissioners to inspect the rolls, books, records, papers, documents and proceedings, and to take notes and extracts as he may deem necessary.

Footnotes
1   S.35(2)(b) has been extended by s.81, FA 1989, to include the disponer, where the date of the disposition is on or after 1st May, 1989.
2.   As inserted by s.84, FA 1980, with retrospective effect to the enactment of the CATA.

Cross-References
1   S.35(7) or (8) do not derogate from the relief given under s.64, CATA.
2   See s.90(7), FA1989, as to the persons accountable for payment of tax under that section.
3   See s.107(c) and (d), FA1984, as to the persons accountable for payment of the once-off discretionary trust tax, and s.104(c) and (d), FA1986, as to the persons accountable for payment of the annual discretionary trust tax.

Section 36[1]

Delivery of returns.
36. (1)   In this section—

(a)   notwithstanding anything contained in sections 6 and 12—

(i)   a reference to a taxable gift is a reference to a taxable gift taken on or after the 28th day of February, 1974;

(ii)   a reference to a taxable inheritance is a reference to a taxable inheritance taken on or after the 1st day of April, 1975; and

[(iii) a reference, other than in subparagraph (i) or subsection (13) or (14), to a gift or a taxable gift includes a reference to an inheritance or a taxable inheritance, as the case may be; and][2]

(b)   a reference to a donee includes a reference to a successor.

(2) Any person who is primarily accountable for the payment of tax by virtue of section 35 (1), or by virtue of paragraph (c) of section 107 of the Finance Act, 1984, shall, within four months after the relevant date referred to in subsection (5)—

    (a) deliver to the Commissioners a full and true return of—

        (i) every gift in respect of which he is so primarily accountable;

        (ii) all the property comprised in such gift on the valuation date;

        (iii) an estimate of the market value of such property on the valuation date; and

        (iv) such particulars as may be relevant to the assessment of tax in respect of such gift;

    (b) notwithstanding the provisions of section 39, make on that return an assessment of such amount of tax as, to the best of his knowledge, information and belief, ought to be charged, levied and paid on that valuation date; and

    (c) duly pay the amount of such tax.

(3) The provisions of subsection (2) (c) shall be complied with—

    (a) where the tax due and payable in respect of any part of the gift is being paid by instalments under the provisions of section 43, by the due payment of—

        (i) an amount which includes any instalment of tax which has fallen due prior to or on the date of the assessment of the tax referred to in subsection (2) (b); and

        (ii) any further instalments of such tax on the due dates in accordance with that section;

    (b) where the tax due and payable is inheritance tax which is being wholly or partly paid by the transfer of securities to the Minister for Finance under the provisions of section 45, by—

        (i) delivering to the Commissioners with the return an application to pay all or part of the tax by such transfer;

        (ii) completing the transfer of the securities to the Minister for Finance within such time, not being less than 30 days, as may be specified by the Commissioners by notice in writing; and

        (iii) duly paying the excess, if any, of the amount of the tax referred to in subsection (2) (b), or in paragraph (a)(i), over the nominal face value of the securities tendered in payment of the tax in accordance with the provisions of subparagraph (i).

[(4) Subsection (2) applies to a charge for tax arising by reason of the provisions of section 106 of the Finance Act, 1984, and to any other gift where —

(a) the aggregate of the taxable values of all taxable gifts taken by the donee on or after [5 December 1991][6], which have the same group threshold (as defined in the Second Schedule) as that other gift, exceeds an amount which is 80 per cent of the threshold amount (as defined in the Second Schedule) which applies in the computation of tax on that aggregate; or

(b) the donee or, in a case to which section 23 (1) applies, the transferee (within the meaning of, and to the extent provided for by, that section) is required by notice in writing by the Commissioners to deliver a return,

and for the purposes of this subsection, a reference to a gift includes a reference to a part of a gift or to a part of a taxable gift, as the case may be.][3]

(5) For the purposes of this section, the relevant date shall be —

(a) the valuation date or the 1st day of September, 1989, whichever is the later; or

(b) where the donee or, in a case to which section 23 (1) applies, the transferee (within the meaning of, and to the extent provided for by, that section) is required by notice in writing by the Commissioners to deliver a return, the date of the notice.

(6) Any person who is accountable for the payment of tax by virtue of subsection (2) or (9) of section 35 shall, if he is required by notice in writing by the Commissioners to do so, comply with the provisions of paragraphs (a), (b) and (c) of subsection (2) of this section (as if he were a person primarily accountable for the payment of tax by virtue of section 35 (1)) within such time, not being less than 30 days, as may be specified in the notice.

(7) (a) Any accountable person shall, if he is so required by the Commissioners by notice in writing, deliver and verify to the Commissioners within such time, not being less than 30 days, as may be specified in the notice —

(i) a statement (where appropriate, on a form provided, or approved of, by them) of such particulars relating to any property; and

(ii) such evidence as they require,

as may, in their opinion, be relevant to the assessment of tax in respect of the gift.

(b) The Commissioners may authorise a person to inspect —

(i) any property comprised in a gift; or

> (ii) any books, records, accounts or other documents, in whatever form they are stored, maintained or preserved, relating to any property as may in their opinion be relevant to the assessment of tax in respect of a gift,

and the person having the custody or possession of that property, or of those books, records, accounts or documents, shall permit the person so authorised to make that inspection at such reasonable times as the Commissioners consider necessary.

(8) The Commissioners may by notice in writing require any accountable person to —

> (a) deliver to them within such time, not being less than 30 days, as may be specified in the notice, an additional return, if it appears to the Commissioners that a return made by that accountable person is defective in a material respect by reason of anything contained in or omitted from it;

> (b) notwithstanding the provisions of section 39, make on that additional return an assessment of such amended amount of tax as, to the best of his knowledge, information and belief, ought to be charged, levied and paid on the relevant gift; and

> (c) duly pay the outstanding tax, if any, for which he is accountable in respect of that gift;

and

> (i) the requirements of subparagraphs (ii), (iii) and (iv) of subsection (2) (a) shall apply to such additional return required by virtue of paragraph (a); and

> (ii) the provisions of subsection (3) shall, with any necessary modifications, apply to any payment required by virtue of paragraph (c).

(9) Where any accountable person who has delivered a return or an additional return is aware or becomes aware at any time that the return or additional return is defective in a material respect by reason of anything contained in or omitted from it, he shall, without application from the Commissioners and within three months of so becoming aware —

> (a) deliver to them an additional return;

> (b) notwithstanding the provisions of section 39, make on that additional return an assessment of such amended amount of tax as, to the best of his knowledge, information and belief, ought to be charged, levied and paid on the relevant gift; and

> (c) duly pay the outstanding tax, if any, for which he is accountable in respect of that gift;

and

(i)   the requirements of subparagraphs (ii), (iii) and (iv) of subsection (2) (a) shall apply to such additional return required by virtue of paragraph (a); and

(ii) the provisions of subsection (3) shall, with any necessary modifications, apply to any payment required by virtue of paragraph (c).

(10) Any amount of tax payable by an accountable person in respect of an assessment of tax made by him on a return delivered by him (other than an amount of that tax payable by the transfer of securities to the Minister for Finance under the provisions of section 45) shall accompany the return and be paid to the Accountant-General of the Commissioners.[8]

(11) Any assessment or payment of tax made under the provisions of this section shall include interest upon tax payable in accordance with the provisions of section 41.

[(12) The Commissioners may by notice in writing require any person to deliver to them within such time, not being less than 30 days, as may be specified in the notice, a full and true return showing details of every taxable gift (including the property comprised therein) taken by that person during the period specified in the notice or, as the case may be, indicating that that person has taken no taxable gift during that period.

(13) As respects a taxable gift to which this subsection applies, any accountable person who is a disponer shall within 4 months of the valuation date deliver to the Commissioners a full and true return —

(a)   of all the property comprised in such gift on the valuation date,

(b)   of an estimate of the market value of such property on the valuation date, and

(c)   of such particulars as may be relevant to the assessment of tax in respect of the gift.

(14) Subsection (13) applies to a taxable gift taken on or after the 11th day of February, 1999, in the case where —

[(a)   the taxable value of the taxable gift exceeds an amount which is 80 per cent of the group threshold (as defined in the Second Schedule) which applies in relation to that gift for the purposes of the computation of the tax on that gift,][5]

(b)   the taxable value of the taxable gift taken by the donee from the disponer increases the total taxable value of all taxable gifts and taxable inheritances taken on or after [5 December 1991][7], by the donee from the disponer from an amount less than or equal to the amount specified in paragraph (a) to an amount which exceeds the amount so specified, or

(c) the total taxable value of all taxable gifts and taxable inheritances taken on or after [5 December 1991][7], by the donee from the disponer exceeds the amount specified in paragraph (a) and the donee takes a further taxable gift from the disponer.

(15) Where, on or after the 11th day of February, 1999, under or in consequence of any disposition made by a person who is living and domiciled in the State at the date of the disposition, property becomes subject to a discretionary trust, the disponer shall within 4 months of the date of the disposition deliver to the Commissioners a full and true return of —

(a) the terms of the discretionary trust,

(b) the names and addresses of the trustees and objects of the discretionary trust, and

(c) an estimate of the market value at the date of the disposition of the property becoming subject to the discretionary trust.][4]

Footnotes

1 S.36(3), as originally enacted in the CATA, was substituted by s.42, FA 1978, which was deemed to come into operation on 31st March, 1976, and had effect in relation to gifts and inheritances taken before 2nd June, 1982.

S.36(3), as so amended, was in turn substituted by s.101, FA 1982, in relation to gifts and inheritances taken on or after 2nd June, 1982, and before 26th March, 1984.

S.36(3), as so amended, and s.36(4), as originally enacted in the CATA, were both substituted by a new s.36(3), contained in s.110(1), FA 1984, in relation to gifts and inheritances taken on or after 26th March, 1984, and before the valuation date or 1st September, 1989, whichever is later.

S.36 was substituted entirely by s.74, FA 1989, which came into operation on 24th May, 1989, and applied to valuation dates on or after 1st September, 1989. S.36, as so substituted, is reproduced here, with subsequent amendments.

2 As amended by s.200(a), FA 1999, with effect from 25th March, 1999.

3 Paragraphs (c) and (d) of subsection (4) were replaced by paragraphs (c), (d) and (e) by s.200(b), FA 1999, with effect from 25th March, 1999, up to 1st December, 1999.

Subsection (4), as so amended, was substituted as shown by s.141(1)(a), FA 2000, in relation to gifts and inheritances taken on or after 1st December, 1999.

4 As inserted by s.200(c), FA 1999, with effect from 25th March, 1999.

5 As substituted by s.141(1)(b), FA 2000, in relation to gifts and inheritances taken on or after 1st December, 1999

6 Substituted for "2 December 1988" by s.117(1)(a), FA 2002, in relation to gifts or inheritances taken on or after 5th December, 2001.

7 Substituted for "the 2nd day of December, 1988" by s.117(1)(b), FA 2002, in relation to gifts or inheritances taken on or after 5th December, 2001.

8 But see s.129, FA 1991.

Section 37

Signing of returns, etc.

37. (1) A return or an additional return required to be delivered under this Act shall be signed by the accountable person who delivers the return or the additional return and shall include a declaration by the person signing it that the return or additional return is, to the best of his knowledge, information and belief, correct and complete.

(2) The Commissioners may require a return or an additional return to be made on oath.

(3) The Commissioners may, if they so think fit, accept a return or an additional return under this Act that has not been signed in accordance with this section and such return or additional return shall be deemed to be duly delivered to the Commissioners under this Act.

[(4) (a) A return or additional return delivered under this Act shall—

(i) be made on a form provided, or approved of, by the Commissioners, or

(ii) except in a case to which subsection (2) relates but in a case where subsection (3) applies, be in a form approved of by the Commissioners and delivered by any electronic, photographic or other process approved of by them and in circumstances where the use of such process has been agreed by them and subject to such conditions as they may impose.

(b) An affidavit, additional affidavit, account or additional account, delivered under this Act, shall be made on a form provided, or approved of, by the Commissioners.][1]

(5) Any oath or affidavit to be made for the purposes of this Act may be made—

(a) before the Commissioners;

(b) before any officer or person authorised by the Commissioners in that behalf;

(c) before any Commissioner for Oaths or any Peace Commissioner or Notary Public in the State; or

(d) at any place outside the State, before any person duly authorised to administer oaths there.

Footnote

1   As substituted by s.82, FA 1989, with effect from 24th May, 1989.

Section 38

Affidavits and accounts.

38. (1) In this section, "Inland Revenue affidavit" has the meaning assigned to it by section 22 (1) (n) of the Finance Act, 1894.[1]

(2) The Inland Revenue affidavit required for an application for probate or letters of administration shall extend to the verification of a statement of the following particulars —

  (a) details of all property in respect of which the grant of probate or administration is required and, in the case of a deceased person who died domiciled in the State, details of all property, wheresoever situate the beneficial ownership of which, on his death, is affected —

    (i) by his will;

    (ii) by the rules for distribution on intestacy; or

    (iii) by Part IX or section 56 of the Succession Act, 1965;

  (b) details of any property which was the subject matter of a disposition inter vivos made by the deceased person where the date of the disposition was within two years prior to his death or of a donatio mortis causa;

  (c) details of the inheritances arising under the will or intestacy of the deceased person or under Part IX or section 56 of the Succession Act, 1965, or under the analogous law of another territory, together with a copy of any such will;

  (d) particulars of the inheritances (including the property comprised therein) other than those referred to in paragraphs (b) and (c), arising on the death of the deceased person;

  (e) the name and address of each person who takes an inheritance on the death of the deceased person and his relationship to the disponer; and

  (f) such other particulars as the Commissioners may require for the purposes of this Act.

(3) Where the interest of the deceased person was a limited interest and that person died on or after the 1st day of April, 1975, the trustee of the property in which the limited interest subsisted shall deliver an account which shall contain the following particulars —

  (a) details of each inheritance arising on the death of the deceased person under the disposition under which the limited interest of the deceased person arose, including the name and address of each person taking such inheritance and his relationship to the disponer; and

  (b) such other particulars as the Commissioners may require for the purposes of this Act.

(4)   If at any time it shall appear that any material error or omission was made in an affidavit or account referred to in this section, the persons liable to deliver an affidavit or account shall be liable to deliver an additional affidavit or an additional account, correcting the error or omission.

Footnote

1   Reproduced on page 654.

Section 39[1]

Assessment of tax.

39.   (1)   Assessments of tax under this Act shall be made by the Commissioners.

(2)   If at any time it appears that for any reason an assessment was incorrect, the Commissioners may make a correcting assessment, which shall be substituted for the first-mentioned assessment.

(3)   If at any time it appears that for any reason too little tax was assessed, the Commissioners may make an additional assessment.

(4)   The Commissioners may serve notice in writing of the assessment of tax on any accountable person or, at the request of an accountable person, on his agent, or on the personal representative of an accountable person if that person is dead.

(5)   Where the place of residence of the accountable person or of his personal representative is not known to the Commissioners they may publish in the *Iris Oifigiúil* a notice of the making of the assessment with such particulars thereof as they shall think proper and on the publication of the notice in the *Iris Oifigiúil* the accountable person or his personal representative, as the case may be, shall be deemed to have been served with the notice of the assessment on the date of such publication.

(6)   Any assessment, correcting assessment or additional assessment under this section may be made by the Commissioners from any return or additional return delivered under the provisions of section 36 or from any other information in the possession of the Commissioners or from any one or more of these sources.

[(7) The Commissioners, in making any assessment, correcting assessment or additional assessment, otherwise than from a return or an additional return which is satisfactory to them, shall make an assessment of such amount of tax as, to the best of their knowledge, information (including information received from a member of the Garda Síochána) and belief, ought to be charged, levied and paid.][2]

Footnotes

1   As to the application of this section, see s.75, FA 1989, which had effect from 24th May, 1989.

2.   S.39(7) was substituted, with effect from 30th July, 1996, by s.8, DCITPA, which contained a proviso which was deleted by s.24(4), CABA, with effect from 11th October, 1996.

Section 40

Computation of tax.

40.   The amount of tax payable shall be computed in accordance with the provisions of the Second Schedule.

PART VII

Payment and Recovery of Tax

Section 41[9]

Payment of tax and interest on tax.

41.   (1)   Tax shall be due and payable on the valuation date.

(2)   Simple interest at the rate of [0.0322 per cent per day or part of a day][1], without deduction of income tax, shall be payable upon the tax from the valuation date to the date of payment of the tax and shall be chargeable and recoverable in the same manner as if it were part of the tax.[2]

[(2A)Notwithstanding the provisions of subsection (2), interest shall not be payable upon the tax—

(a)   to the extent to which section 19(5)(a) applies, for the duration of the period from the valuation date to the date the agricultural value ceases to be applicable,

(b)   to the extent to which [subsection (3) or (4) of section 55][6] applies, for the duration of the period from the valuation date to the date the exemption ceases to apply,

(c)   to the extent to which section 135(2) of the Finance Act, 1994, applies, for the duration of the period from the valuation date to the date the reduction which would otherwise fall to be made under section 126 of that Act ceases to be applicable,

(d)   to the extent to which section 166(6) of the Finance Act, 1995, applies, for the duration of the period from the valuation date to the date the exemption ceases to apply,][3]

[(e)   to the extent to which subsection (5) or (6) of section 59C applies, for the duration of the period from the valuation date to the date the exemption ceases to apply.][7]

[(3) Notwithstanding the provisions of subsection (2), interest shall not be payable on tax which is paid within three months of the valuation date, and where tax and interest, if any, thereon is paid within thirty days of the date of assessment thereof, interest shall not run on that tax for the period of thirty days from the date of the assessment or any part of that period:

Provided that, in relation to an assessment of tax made by an accountable person on a return delivered by him, interest shall not be payable on tax which is paid within four months of the valuation date.][4]

(4) A payment on account of tax shall be applied —

(a) if there is interest due on tax at the date of the payment, to the discharge, so far as may be, of the interest so due; and

(b) if there is any balance of that payment remaining, to the discharge of so much tax as is equal to that balance.[5]

(5) Subject to the provisions of subsections (2), (3) and (4), payments on account may be made at any time, and when a payment on account is made, interest shall not be chargeable in respect of any period subsequent to the date of such payment on so much of the payment on account as is to be applied in discharge of the tax.

(6) In the case of a gift which becomes an inheritance by reason of its being taken under a disposition where the date of the disposition is within two years prior to the death of the disponer, the provisions of this section shall have effect as if the references to the valuation date in subsections (1), (2) and (3) were references to the date of death of the disponer.

(7) In the case of a gift or inheritance taken prior to the date of the passing of this Act, the provisions of this section shall have effect as if the references to the valuation date in subsections (1), (2) and (3) were references to the date of the passing of this Act, or to the valuation date, whichever is the later.

(8) Where the value of a limited interest falls to be ascertained in accordance with rule 8 of the First Schedule as if it were a series of absolute interests, this section shall have effect, in relation to each of those absolute interests, as if the references to the valuation date in subsections (1), (2) and (3) were references to the date of the taking of that absolute interest.

(9) All sums due under the provisions of this Act shall be paid to the Accountant-General of the Commissioners.[8]

Footnotes

1   The original rate of interest in the CATA was 1.5% per month, or part of a month. This rate was amended by s.43, FA 1978, to 1.25% with effect to interest accruing due after 5th July, 1978, and before 27th March, 1998. The rate of interest was further amended to 1% by s.133(4), FA 1998, as respects interest chargeable for any month, or any part of a month, commencing on or after 27th March, 1998, and before 1st September, 2002.

S.129(3)(a), FA 2002, amends the rate of interest to 0.0322 per cent per day, or part of a day, and applies to interest chargeable from 1st September, 2002.

2   See s.164, FA 1995, and s.129, FA 1996, in relation to interest on tax chargeable on agricultural and business assets.

3   As inserted by s.202, FA 1999, with effect where the event, which causes the exemption or reduction in question to cease, occurs on or after 11th February, 1999.

4   As substituted by s.76(1), FA 1989, with effect from 24th May, 1989.

5   See s.76(2), FA 1989, which has effect from 24th May, 1989.

6   Substituted for "section 55(4)" by s.118(1)(a), FA 2002, and applies where the event which causes the exemption to cease to be applicable occurs on or after 11th February, 1999.

7   As inserted by s.118(1)(c), FA 2002, and applies where the event, which causes the exemption to cease to be applicable, occurs on or after 1st December, 1999. As a consequence of this insertion, s.118(1)(c), FA 2002, also substituted a full-stop for a comma after "apply" in the previous line.

8   But see s.129, FA 1991, reproduced on page 846.

9   S.145(6), FA 2005, has repealed this section with effect from 1st April, 2005, to the extent that this section applies to interest chargeable or payable on gift tax and inheritance tax that has not been paid before that date, regardless of when that tax became due and payable. See Commentary B.

Commentary

A   See a Revenue Statement of Practice (SP-CAT/1/90) in relation to the postponement of payment of tax in exceptional circumstances. See also Part 17.3 of the *Revenue CAT Manual* regarding the registration of tax as a voluntary judgement mortgage.

B   See footnote 9 to this section. Since s.145(4), FA 2005, applies to the CATCA only, does it not follow that, in relation to tax chargeable under the CATA, interest is no longer payable?

Cross-Reference

1   See s.107(f), FA 1984, as to the modification of s.41 in relation to interest on the once-off discretionary trust tax, and s.104(f), FA 1986, as to the modification of s.41 in relation to interest on the annual discretionary trust tax.

Section 42

Set-off of gift tax paid in respect of an inheritance.

42.   Where an amount has been paid in respect of gift tax (or interest thereon) on a gift which, by reason of the death of the disponer within two years after the date of the disposition under which the gift was taken, becomes an inheritance in respect of which inheritance tax is payable, the amount so paid shall be treated as a payment on account of the inheritance tax.

Section 43

Payment of tax by instalments.

43.   (1)   Subject to the payment of interest in accordance with section 41 and save as hereinafter provided, the tax due and payable in respect of a

Section 46[1]

Overpayment of tax.

46. [(1) Where, on application to the Commissioners for relief under this section, it is proved to their satisfaction that an amount has been paid in excess of the liability for tax or for interest on tax, they shall give relief by way of repayment of the excess or otherwise as is reasonable and just; and any such repayment shall carry simple interest (not exceeding the amount of such excess) at the rate of [0.0161 per cent, or such other rate (if any) as stands prescribed by the Minister for Finance by regulations, for each day or part of a day][3] from the date on which the payment was made, and income tax shall not be deductible on payment of interest under this section and such interest shall not be reckoned in computing income for the purposes of the Tax Acts.

(2) Every regulation made under this section shall be laid before Dáil Éireann as soon as may be after it is made and if a resolution annulling the regulation is passed by Dáil Éireann within the next twenty-one days on which Dáil Éireann has sat after the regulation is laid before it, the regulation shall be annulled accordingly, but without prejudice to the validity of anything previously done thereunder.][2]

Footnotes

1   The provisions of the following sections should be noted in connection with the non-payment of interest on repayments of tax –

    (a) s.46(2), FA 1981;

    (b) s.61(2) and s.62(2), FA 1985;

    (c) s.116(3), FA 1991;

    (d) s.143(4), FA 1994;

    (e) s.1003(10), TCA, replacing s.176, FA 1995.

2   The original rate of interest in s.46 was 1.5% per month, or part of a month. In relation to interest repayable for any month, or any part of a month, commencing on or after 27th May, 1986, and before 1st August, 1990, s.109(1), FA 1986, provided a rate of 1% per month, or part of a month, by substituting s.46(1), as shown, and by inserting s.46(2), as shown.

    S.I. No. 176 of 1990 amended the rate of interest from 1% to 0.6% per month, or part of a month, with effect from 1st August, 1990, and before 27 March, 1998. See page 1374.

3   S.133(4), FA 1998, amended the rate of interest from 0.6% to 0.5% per month or part of a month as respects interest repayable for any month, or any part of a month, commencing on or after 27th March, 1998, and before 1st September, 2002.

    S.129(3)(b), FA 2002, substituted the rate of interest as shown and applies to interest repayable from 1st September, 2002.

Section 47

Tax to be a charge.

47. (1) Tax due and payable in respect of a taxable gift or a taxable inheritance shall, subject to the provisions of this section, be and remain a charge on the property (other than money or negotiable instruments) of which the taxable gift or taxable inheritance consists at the valuation date and the tax shall have priority over all charges and interests created by the donee or successor or any person claiming in right of the donee or successor or on his behalf:

Provided that where any settled property comprised in any taxable gift or taxable inheritance shall be subject to any power of sale, exchange, or partition, exercisable with the consent of the donee or successor, or by the donee or successor with the consent of another person, the donee or successor shall not be precluded by the charge of tax on his taxable gift or taxable inheritance from consenting to the exercise of such power, or exercising any power with proper consent, as the case may be; and where any such power is exercised, the tax shall be charged upon the property acquired, in substitution for charging it on the property previously comprised in the gift or inheritance, and upon all moneys arising from the exercise of any such power, and upon all investments of such moneys.

(2) Property comprised in a taxable gift or taxable inheritance shall not, as against a *bona fide* purchaser or mortgagee for full consideration in money or money's worth, or a person deriving title from or under such a purchaser or mortgagee, remain charged with or liable to the payment of tax after the expiration of twelve years from the date of the gift or the date of the inheritance.

(3) Tax shall not be a charge on property under subsection (1) as against a *bona fide* purchaser or mortgagee of such property for full consideration in money or money's worth without notice, or a person deriving title from or under such a purchaser or mortgage.

Commentary

A   See Part 4.4 of the *Revenue CAT Manual* in relation to the issue of a letter of clearance from inheritance tax, where there is a sale in course of administration before the valuation date, and the charge for tax applies to the proceeds of sale.

Cross-Reference

1   The priority of the charge in s.47(1) is qualified by s.64(2)(d) and (f), CATA.

Section 48

Receipts and certificates.

48. (1) When any amount in respect of tax is paid, the Commissioners shall give a receipt for the payment.

(2) The Commissioners shall, on application to them by a person who has paid the tax in respect of any property comprised in any taxable gift or taxable inheritance, give to the person a certificate, in such form as they think fit, of the amount of the tax paid by him in respect of that property.

[(3) The Commissioners shall, on application to them by a person who is an accountable person in respect of any of the property of which a taxable gift or taxable inheritance consists, if they are satisfied that the tax charged on the property in respect of the taxable gift or taxable inheritance has been or will be paid, or that there is no tax so charged, give a certificate to the person, in such form as they think fit, to that effect.

(3A) Where a person who is an accountable person in respect of the property of which a taxable gift or taxable inheritance consists has—

    (a) delivered to the Commissioners, a full and true return of all the property comprised in the gift or inheritance on the valuation date and such particulars as may be relevant to the assessment of tax in respect of the gift or inheritance,

    (b) made on that return an assessment of such amount of tax as, to the best of that person's knowledge, information and belief, ought to be charged, levied and paid, and

    (c) duly paid the amount of such tax (if any),

the Commissioners may give a certificate to the person, in such form as they think fit, to the effect that the tax charged on the property in respect of the taxable gift or taxable inheritance has been paid or that there is no tax so charged.

(4) A certificate referred to in subsection (3) or (3A) shall discharge the property from liability for tax (if any) in respect of the gift or inheritance, to the extent specified in the certificate, but shall not discharge the property from tax in case of fraud or failure to disclose material facts and, in any case, shall not affect the tax payable in respect of any other property or the extent to which tax is recoverable from any accountable person or from the personal representatives of any accountable person:

Provided that a certificate purporting to be a discharge of the whole tax payable in respect of any property included in the certificate in respect of a gift or inheritance shall exonerate from liability for such tax a *bona fide* purchaser or mortgagee for full consideration in money or money's worth without notice of such fraud or failure and a person deriving title from or under such a purchaser or mortgagee.][1]

[(5) Subject to the provisions of subsection (6), where tax is chargeable on the taxable value of a taxable gift or taxable inheritance and —

   (a) application is made to the Commissioners by any person (in this section referred to as "the applicant") —

      (i) who is a person accountable, but not primarily accountable, for the payment of the whole or part of the tax, or

      (ii) who is the personal representative of any person referred to in subparagraph (i),

   and

   (b) the applicant —

      (i) delivers to the Commissioners a full and true return of all the property comprised in the gift or inheritance and such particulars as may be relevant to the assessment of tax in respect of the gift or inheritance, and

      (ii) makes on that return an assessment of such amount of tax as, to the best of that person's knowledge, information and belief, ought to be charged, levied and paid,

the Commissioners may, upon payment of the tax assessed by the applicant, give a certificate to the applicant which shall discharge the applicant from any other claim for tax in respect of the gift or inheritance.][2]

[(6) A certificate by the Commissioners under subsection (5) shall not discharge the applicant in the case of fraud or failure to disclose material facts within his own knowledge and shall not affect any further tax that may be payable by the applicant if any further property is afterwards shown to have been comprised in the taxable gift or taxable inheritance to which the certificate relates and in respect of which further property the applicant is liable for the tax.][3]

(7) . . . .[4]

Footnotes

1   As substituted by s.142(a), FA 2000, with effect from 23rd March, 2000.

2   With effect from 23rd March, 2000, substituting by s.142(a), FA 2000, the subsection (5) inserted by s.113, FA 1984, the latter section having respect to gifts and inheritances taken on or after 2nd June, 1982, and before 23rd March, 2000.

3   As inserted by s.113, FA 1984, with respect to gifts and inheritances taken on or after 2nd June, 1982.

4   This subsection, inserted by s.113, FA 1984, with respect to gifts and inheritances taken on or after 2nd June, 1982, was deleted by s.142(b), FA 2000, with effect from 23rd March, 2000.

Commentary

A   See Part 4.4 of the *Revenue CAT Manual* in relation to the issue of a letter of clearance from inheritance tax, where there is a sale in course of administration before the valuation date, and the charge for tax applies to the proceeds of sale.

Section 49

Recovery of tax and penalties.

49. (1) Any sum due and payable in respect of tax or interest thereon and any penalty incurred in connection with tax or interest thereon shall be deemed to be a debt due by the accountable person or, if he is dead, by his personal representative, to the Minister for Finance for the benefit of the Central Fund and shall be payable to the Commissioners and may (without prejudice to any other mode of recovery thereof) be sued for and recovered by action, or other appropriate proceeding, at the suit of the Attorney-General or the Minister for Finance or the Commissioners in any court of competent jurisdiction, notwithstanding anything to the contrary contained in the Inland Revenue Regulation Act, 1890.

(2) Any person who, having received any sum of money as or for any tax, interest, or penalty under this Act, does not apply the money to the due payment of the tax, interest or penalty, and improperly withholds or detains the same, shall be accountable for the payment of the tax, interest or penalty to the extent of the amount so received by him and the same shall be a debt due by him to the Minister for Finance for the benefit of the Central Fund and shall be recoverable in like manner as a debt under subsection (1).

(3) If any accountable person is liable under section 36 to deliver to the Commissioners a return or an additional return and makes default in so doing, the Attorney-General or the Minister for Finance or the Commissioners may sue by action or other appropriate proceeding in the Circuit Court for an order directing the person so making default to deliver such return or additional return or to show cause to the contrary; and the Circuit Court may by order direct such accountable person to deliver such return or additional return within such time as may be specified in the order.

(4) Whenever property is subject to a charge by virtue of section 47, the Attorney-General or the Minister for Finance or the Commissioners may sue by action or other appropriate proceeding in any court of competent jurisdiction for, and the court may make, an order directing the owner of the property to pay the tax with which the property is charged.

Section 50

Evidence in proceedings for recovery of tax.

50. The provisions of section 39 of the Finance Act, 1926,[1] shall apply in any proceedings in the Circuit Court or the District Court for or in relation to the recovery of the tax.

Footnote

1   Reproduced on page 657.

PART VIII
Appeals

Section 51

Appeals regarding value of real property.

51. (1) If a person is aggrieved by the decision of the Commissioners as to the market value of any real property, he may appeal against the decision in the manner prescribed by section 33 of the Finance (1909-10) Act, 1910[1], and the provisions as to appeals under that section of that Act shall apply accordingly with any necessary modifications.

[(2) The particulars of any transfer or lease which are presented to or obtained by the Commissioners under section 107 of the Finance Act, 1994, shall, in any appeal under this section, be received as prima facie evidence of all matters and things stated in such particulars.][2]

Footnote
1   Reproduced on page 655.
2   As inserted by s.203, FA 1999, with effect from 25th March, 1999.

Section 52

Appeals in other cases.

52. (1) In this section —

"Appeal Commissioners" has the meaning assigned to it by [section 850 of the Taxes Consolidation Act, 1997;][1]

"appellant" means a person who appeals to the Appeal Commissioners under subsection (2) of this section.

(2) Subject to the other provisions of this Act, a person who is called upon by the Commissioners to pay an assessment of tax in respect of any property and who is aggrieved by the assessment may, in accordance with the provisions of this section, appeal to the Appeal Commissioners against the assessment and the appeal shall be heard and determined by the Appeal Commissioners whose determination shall be final and conclusive unless the appeal is required to be reheard by a judge of the Circuit Court or a case is required to be stated in relation to it for the opinion of the High Court on a point of law.

(3) An appeal shall not lie under this section in relation to the market value of real property.

(4) A person who intends to appeal under this section against an assessment shall, within 30 days after the date of the assessment, give notice in writing to the Commissioners of his intention to appeal against the assessment.

(5) (a) Subject to the provisions of this section, the provisions of the Income Tax Acts relating to –

    (i) the appointment of times and places for the hearing of appeals;

    (ii) the giving of notice to each person who has given notice of appeal of the time and place appointed for the hearing of his appeal;

    (iii) the determination of an appeal by agreement between the appellant and an officer appointed by the Commissioners in that behalf;

    (iv) the determination of an appeal by the appellant giving notice of his intention not to proceed with the appeal;

    (v) the hearing and determination of an appeal by the Appeal Commissioners, including the hearing and determination of an appeal by one Appeal Commissioner;

    [(va) the publication of reports of determinations of the Appeal Commissioners;][2]

    (vi) the determination of an appeal through the neglect or refusal of a person who has given notice of appeal to attend before the Appeal Commissioners at the time and place appointed;

    (vii) the extension of the time for giving notice of appeal and the readmission of appeals by the Appeal Commissioners and the provisions which apply where action by way of court proceedings has been taken;

    (viii) the rehearing of an appeal by a judge of the Circuit Court and the statement of a case for the opinion of the High Court on a point of law;

    (ix) the payment of tax in accordance with the determination of the Appeal Commissioners notwithstanding that an appeal is required to be reheard by a judge of the Circuit Court or that a case for the opinion of the High Court on a point of law has been required to be stated or is pending;

    (x) the procedures for appeal,

    [(xi) the refusal of an application for an appeal hearing,][3] shall, with any necessary modifications, apply to an appeal under this section as if the appeal were an appeal against an assessment to income tax.

(b) The Commissioners shall, subject to their giving notice in writing in that behalf to the appellant within ten days after the determination of an appeal by the Appeal Commissioners, have the same right as the appellant to have the appeal reheard by a judge of the Circuit Court.

(c) The rehearing of an appeal under this section by a judge of the Circuit Court shall be by a judge of the Circuit Court in whose circuit the appellant or one of the appellants resides or (in the case of a body corporate) has its principal place of business:

Provided that—

(i) in any case where no appellant is resident in or (in the case of a body corporate) has a place of business in the State; or

(ii) in any case where there is a doubt or a dispute as to the circuit,

the appeal shall be reheard by a judge of the Circuit Court assigned to the Dublin Circuit.

(6) (a) Where a notice or other document which is required or authorised to be served by this section falls to be served on a body corporate, such notice shall be served on the secretary or other officer of the body corporate.

(b) Any notice or other document which is required or authorised by this section to be served by the Commissioners or by an appellant may be served by post and in the case of a notice or other document addressed to the Commissioners, shall be sent to the Secretaries, Revenue Commissioners, Dublin Castle, Dublin 2.

(c) Any notice or other document which is required or authorised to be served by the Commissioners on an appellant under this section may be sent to the solicitor, accountant or other agent of the appellant and a notice thus served shall be deemed to have been served on the appellant unless the appellant proves to the satisfaction of the Appeal Commissioners, or the Circuit Court, as the case may be, that he had, before the notice or other document was served, withdrawn the authority of such solicitor, accountant or other agent to act on his behalf.

[(7) *Prima facie* evidence of any notice given under this section by the Commissioners or by an officer of the Commissioners may be given in any proceedings by the production of a document purporting—

(a) to be a copy of the notice, or

(b) if the details specified in the notice are contained in an electronic, photographic or other record maintained by the Commissioners, to reproduce those details in so far as they relate to the said notice,

and it shall not be necessary to prove the official position of the person by whom the notice purports to be given or, if it is signed, the signature, or that the person signing and giving it was authorised to do so.][4]

(8) (a) The Commissioners may serve notice in writing, referring expressly to this subsection, on any person whom they have reason to believe to be accountable for the payment of tax, of any decision they have made which is relevant to such tax.

(b) Any person who is informed of a decision in accordance with paragraph (a) may appeal to the Appeal Commissioners against the decision.

(c) The Appeal Commissioners shall hear and determine an appeal to them under this subsection as if it were an appeal to them against an assessment to tax, and the provisions of this section relating to an appeal or to the rehearing of an appeal or to the statement of a case for the opinion of the High Court on a point of law shall, with any necessary modifications, apply accordingly.

Footnotes

1   As amended by s.1100, TCA, with effect from 6th April, 1997.

2   As inserted by s.134(3), FA 1998, and applying to appeals determined by the Appeal Commissioners after 27th March, 1998.

3   As inserted by s.159, FA 1995, with effect from 2nd June, 1995.

4   As substituted by s.119, FA 2002, which has effect in relation to evidence of any notice given by the Revenue Commissioners or by an officer of the Revenue Commissioners in any proceedings on or after 25th March, 2002.

Cross-Reference

1   An appeal under s.52 may also be made against a "determination" under s.21(6), CATA, against a "decision" under s.56(3), CATA, against the imposition of a surcharge under s.79(3), FA1989, against an "opinion" under s.811(7), TCA, against a "failure" under s.917EA(4), TCA, and against a "refusal" under s.917G(7), TCA.

Section 52A[1]

Conditions before appeal may be made.

[52A. No appeal shall lie under section 51 or 52 until such time as the person aggrieved by the decision or assessment (as the case may be) complies with section 36(2) in respect of the gift or inheritance in relation to which the decision or assessment is made, as if there were no time-limit for complying with section 36(2) and that person were a person primarily accountable for the payment of tax by virtue of section 35(1) and required by notice in writing by the Commissioners to deliver a return.]

Footnote
1   As inserted by s.129, FA 1998, in relation to gifts or inheritances taken on or after 12th February, 1998.

PART IX
Exemptions

Section 53

Exemption of small gifts.

53.   (1)   The first [€1,270][1] of the total taxable value of all taxable gifts taken by a donee from any one disponer in any relevant period shall be exempt from tax and shall not be taken into account in computing tax.

(2)   In the case of a gift which becomes an inheritance by reason of its being taken under a disposition where the date of the disposition is within two years prior to the death of the disponer, the same relief shall be granted in respect thereof under subsection (1) as if it were a gift.

(3)   . . . . . . [2]

(4)   In this section, "relevant period" means the period commencing on the 28th day of February, 1969, and ending on the 31st day of December, 1969, and thereafter the period of twelve months ending on the 31st day of December in each year.

Footnotes
1   The original amount in the CATA was £250. This amount was amended to £500 by s.44, FA 1978, as respects relevant periods ending on or after 31st December, 1978, up to and including 31st December, 1998.

The amount was further amended to £1,000 by s.204, FA 1999, as respects relevant periods ending after 31st December, 1998.

S.240(2)(g) and Part 5 of the Fifth Sch., FA2001, substitute "€1,270" for "£1,000" as respects gifts or inheritances taken on or after 1st January, 2002.

2   This subsection, which was not amended, was repealed by s.110(2), FA 1984, in relation to gifts and inheritances taken on or after 26th March, 1984.

computing tax, to the extent that the Commissioners are satisfied that it was brought into the State solely for public exhibition, cleaning or restoration.][6]

Footnotes

1   The section was applied to a house or garden by s.39, FA 1978, where the date of the gift or the date of the inheritance is on or after 5th July, 1978.

A similar exemption was applied by s.166, FA 1995, to objects, houses or gardens owned by a private company, in relation to gifts and inheritances taken on or after 12th April, 1995.

2   The words "from the same disponer" were deleted by s.110(4), FA 1984, in relation to gifts and inheritances taken on or after 26th March, 1984.

3   As substituted by s.160(1)(a), FA 1995, in relation to gifts and inheritances taken on or after 12th April, 1995.

4   As substituted by s.160(1)(b), FA 1995, in relation to gifts or inheritances taken on or after 12th April, 1995.

5   Words inserted by s.144(1), FA 2000, in relation to gifts and inheritances taken on or after 10th February, 2000.

6   As inserted by s.218, FA2001, in relation to inheritances taken on or after 26th January, 2001.

7   As inserted by s.81, FA 2004, as respects sales on or after 1st August, 1994.

Commentary

A   See the Revenue Information Leaflet CAT8 in relation to this section.

B   See an article on the Favourable Treatment of Heritage Objects by Anne Corrigan and Marie Griffin in the *Irish Tax Review* of March 2002, page 179.

Section 56

Payments relating to retirement, etc.

56.   (1)   Subject to the provisions of subsection (2), any payment to an employee or former employee by, or out of funds provided by, his employer or any other person, *bona fide* by way of retirement benefit, redundancy payment or pension shall not be a gift or an inheritance.

(2)   Subsection (1) shall not have effect in relation to a payment referred to in that subsection, and any such payment shall be deemed to be a gift or an inheritance where –

(a)   (i)   the employee is a relative of the employer or other disponer; or

(ii)   the employer is a private company within the meaning of section 16 (2), and of which private company the employee is deemed to have control within the meaning of that section:

(b)   the payment is not made under a scheme (relating to superannuation, retirement or redundancy) approved by the Commissioners under the Income Tax Acts; and

(c)   the Commissioners decide that in the circumstances of the case the payment is excessive.

(3) The Commissioners shall serve on an accountable person a notice in writing of their decision referred to in subsection (2) and the accountable person concerned may appeal against such decision and section 52 shall apply with any necessary modifications in relation to such appeal as it applies in relation to an appeal against an assessment of tax.

(4) Any benefit taken by a person other than the person in respect of whose service the benefit arises, under the provisions of any superannuation fund, or under any superannuation scheme, established solely or mainly for persons employed in a profession, trade, undertaking or employment, and their dependants, shall (whether or not any person had a right enforceable at law to the benefit) be deemed to be a gift or an inheritance, as the case may be, derived under a disposition made by the person in respect of whose service the benefit arises and not by any other person.

(5) In this section —

"superannuation scheme" includes any arrangement in connection with employment for the provision of a benefit on or in connection with the retirement or death of an employee;

"employment" includes employment as a director of a body corporate and cognate words shall be construed accordingly.

Cross-Reference
1   A benefit under s.56(4) is excluded from the exemption given by s.54(3), CATA.

Section 57

Exemption of certain securities.
57. (1) In this section —

"security" means any security, stock, share, debenture, debenture stock, certificate of charge or other form of security issued, whether before or after the passing of this Act, and which by virtue of any enactment or by virtue of the exercise of any power conferred by any enactment is exempt from taxation when in the beneficial ownership of a person neither domiciled nor ordinarily resident in the State;

["unit trust scheme" means an authorised unit trust scheme within the meaning of the Unit Trusts Act, 1990, whose deed expressing the trusts of the scheme restricts the property subject to those trusts to securities.][1]

[(2) Securities, or units (within the meaning of the Unit Trusts Act, [1990][3]) of a unit trust scheme, comprised in a gift or an inheritance taken on or after the 14th day of April, 1978, shall be exempt from tax (and shall not be taken into account in computing tax on any gift or inheritance taken by the donee or successor [...................][4]) if, but only if, it is shown to the satisfaction of the Commissioners that —

[(a) the securities or units were comprised in the disposition continuously for a period of six years immediately before the date of the gift or the date of the inheritance, and any period immediately before the date of the disposition during which the securities or units were continuously in the beneficial ownership of the disponer shall be deemed, for the purpose of this paragraph, to be a period or part of a period immediately before the date of the gift or the date of the inheritance during which they were continuously comprised in the disposition;][6]

(b) the securities or units were comprised in the gift or inheritance—

(i) at the date of the gift or the date of the inheritance; and

(ii) at the valuation date; and

(c) the donee or successor is at the date of the gift or the date of the inheritance neither domiciled nor ordinarily resident in the State,

and the provisions of section 19 (6) shall apply, for the purposes of this subsection, as they apply in relation to agricultural property.

(3) Subsection (2) (a) shall not apply in a case where the disponer was neither domiciled nor ordinarily resident in the State at the date of the disposition [. . . . .][5]][2]

Footnotes

1   As substituted by s.121(1)(a), FA 1991, in relation to gifts and inheritances taken on or after 26th December, 1990.

2   As substituted by s.40, FA 1978, in relation to securities or units where the date of the gift or the date of the inheritance is on or after 14th April, 1978.

3   As substituted by s.121(1)(b), FA 1991, in relation to gifts and inheritances taken on or after 26th December, 1990.

4   The words, "from the same disponer", were deleted by s.110(5), FA 1984, in relation to gifts and inheritances taken on or after 26th March, 1984.

5   The words ", or at the date of the gift or the date of the inheritance" were deleted by s.135, FA 1997, in relation to securities or units where the date of the gift or the date of the inheritance is on or after 26th March, 1997, and the securities or units came into the beneficial ownership of the disponer on or after 26th March, 1997, or became subject to the disposition on or after 26th March, 1997, without having been previously in the beneficial ownership of the disponer.

6   Subsection (2)(a) substituted by s.219, FA2001, where the date of the gift/inheritance is on or after 15th February, 2001, and the securities or units (a) come into the beneficial ownership of the disponer on or after that date, or (b) become subject to the disposition on or after that date without having been previously in the beneficial ownership of the disponer.

Commentary

A   See Part 19.19 of the *Revenue CAT Manual*. Where s.57 securities are held in a unit trust which is being wound up but certain of the securities are not sold but are distributed in specie to the unit-holders, then provided all other conditions laid down by s.57 are fulfilled, and the direct ownership of the securities commences at the instant the ownership of the units by the unit-holders ceases, the period of time unit-holders held the units will be treated as aggregable with the period they directly hold the securities.

Section 58

Exemption of certain receipts.

58. (1) The following shall not be gifts or inheritances —

    (a) the receipt by a person of any sum *bona fide* by way of compensation or damages for any wrong or injury suffered by him in his person, property, reputation or means of livelihood;

    (b) the receipt by a person of any sum *bona fide* by way of compensation or damages for any wrong or injury resulting in the death of any other person;

    (c) the receipt by a person of any sum *bona fide* by way of winnings from betting (including pool betting) or from any lottery, sweepstake or game with prizes;

    (d) any benefit arising out of —

        (i) the payment to the Official Assignee in Bankruptcy of money which has been provided by, or which represents property provided by, friends of a bankrupt; or

        (ii) a remission or abatement of debts by the creditors of a bankrupt,

    to enable the bankrupt to fulfil an offer of composition after bankruptcy in accordance with the provisions of section 149 of the Irish Bankrupt and Insolvent Act, 1857; and

    (e) any benefit arising out of —

        (i) the payment to the Official Assignee in Bankruptcy of money which has been provided by, or which represents property provided by, friends of an arranging debtor; or

        (ii) a remission or abatement of debts by the creditors of an arranging debtor,

    to enable the debtor to carry out the terms of a proposal made by him under section 345 of the Irish Bankrupt and Insolvent Act, 1857, which has been accepted by his creditors and approved and confirmed by the High Court.

  (2) Notwithstanding anything contained in this Act, the receipt in the lifetime of the disponer of money or money's worth —

    (a) by —

        (i) the spouse or child of the disponer; or

        (ii) a person in relation to whom the disponer stands *in loco parentis*,

    for support, maintenance or education; or

(b) by a person who is in relation to the disponer a dependent relative under [section 466 of the Taxes Consolidation Act, 1997][1] for support or maintenance,

shall not be a gift or an inheritance, where the provision of such support, maintenance or education, or such support or maintenance —

(i) is such as would be part of the normal expenditure of a person in the circumstances of the disponer; and

(ii) is reasonable having regard to the financial circumstances of the disponer.

[(3) (a) The receipt by an incapacitated individual of the whole or any part of trust funds which are held on a qualifying trust, or of the income therefrom, shall not be a gift or an inheritance.

(b) In this subsection "incapacitated individual", "trust funds" and "qualifying trust" have the meanings assigned to them, respectively, by section 189A (inserted by the Finance Act, 1999) of the Taxes Consolidation Act, 1997.

(c) This subsection shall apply in relation to gifts or inheritances taken on or after the 6th day of April, 1997.][2]

[(4) The receipt by a minor child of the disponer of money or money's worth for support, maintenance or education, at a time when the disponer and the other parent of that minor child are dead, shall not be a gift or an inheritance where the provision of such support, maintenance or education —

(a) is such as would be part of the normal expenditure of a person in the circumstances of the disponer immediately prior to the death of the disponer; and

(b) is reasonable having regard to the financial circumstances of the disponer immediately prior to the death of the disponer.][3]

Footnotes

1   As amended by s.1110, TCA, with effect from 6th April, 1997.

2   As inserted by s.205, FA 1999. See s.189A, TCA, (inserted by s.12, FA 1999) on page 1006 for definitions.

3   As inserted by s.152(1), FA 2000, in relation to gifts and inheritances taken on or after 23rd March, 2000.

Commentary

A   As to s.58(2) and (4), see *Bennett v Inland Revenue Commissioners* [1995] STC 54 in relation to s.21, UK Inheritance Tax Act, 1984, and "normal expenditure out of income".

Section 59

Exemption where disposition was made by the donee or successor.

59. (1) Tax shall not be chargeable upon a gift or an inheritance taken by the donee or successor under a disposition made by himself.

(2) Where, at the date of the gift, two companies are associated in the manner described in subsection (3), a gift taken by one of them under a disposition made by the other shall be deemed to be a gift to which subsection (1) applies.

(3) For the purposes of subsection (2), two companies shall be regarded as associated if—

(a) one company would be beneficially entitled to not less than 90 per cent. of any assets of the other company available for distribution to the owners of its shares and entitlements of the kind referred to in section 34 (1) on a winding up; or

(b) a third company would be beneficially entitled to not less than 90 per cent. of any assets of each of them available as in paragraph (a).

(4) In this section, "company" means a body corporate (wherever incorporated), other than a private company within the meaning of section 16 (2).

Section 59A[1]

Exemption relating to qualifying expenses of incapacitated persons.

59A. (1) A gift or inheritance which is taken exclusively for the purpose of discharging qualifying expenses of an individual who is permanently incapacitated by reason of physical or mental infirmity shall, to the extent that the Commissioners are satisfied that it has been or will be applied to such purpose, be exempt from tax and shall not be taken into account in computing tax.

(2) In this section "qualifying expenses" means expenses relating to medical care including the cost of maintenance in connection with such medical care.

Footnote

1   Inserted by s.123, FA 1996, in relation to gifts or inheritances taken on or after 28th March, 1996.

Section 59B[1]

Exemption relating to retirement benefits.

59B. (1) The whole or any part of a retirement fund which is comprised in an inheritance which is taken upon the death of a disponer dying on or after the date of the passing of the Finance Act, 1999, shall be exempt from tax in relation to that inheritance and in relation to a charge for tax arising on that death by virtue of section 110 of

(a)　before the dwelling-house is sold or disposed of, and

(b)　before the death of the donee or successor,

the condition specified in paragraph (c) of subsection (2) has not been complied with unless that non-compliance occurs in consequence of the donee or successor requiring long-term medical care in a hospital, nursing home or convalescent home, or in consequence of any condition imposed by the employer of the donee or successor requiring the donee or successor to reside elsewhere.

(7)　Where a dwelling-house exempted from tax by virtue of subsection (2) (hereafter in this section referred to as the "first-mentioned dwelling-house") is replaced within the relevant period by another dwelling-house, the condition specified in paragraph (c) of subsection (2) shall be treated as satisfied if the donee or successor has occupied as his or her only or main residence the first-mentioned dwelling-house, that other dwelling-house and any dwelling-house which has within the relevant period directly or indirectly replaced that other dwelling-house for periods which together comprised at least 6 years falling within the period of 7 years commencing on the date of the gift or the date of the inheritance.

(8)　Any period of absence which would satisfy the condition specified in paragraph (c) of subsection (2) in relation to the first-mentioned dwelling-house shall, if it occurs in relation to any dwelling-house which has directly or indirectly replaced that dwelling-house, likewise satisfy the said condition as it has effect by virtue of subsection (7).

(9)　Subsection (5) shall not apply to a case falling within subsection (7), but the extent of the exemption under this section in such a case shall, where the donee or successor had not attained the age of 55 years at the date of the gift or at the date of the inheritance, not exceed what it would have been had the replacement of one dwelling-house by another referred to in subsection (7), or any one or more of such replacements, taken place immediately prior to that date.

Footnotes

1　As inserted by s.151(1), FA 2000, in relation to gifts and inheritances taken on or after 1st December, 1999. It replaces the relief in respect of certain dwellings given by s.117, FA 1991, which section is now repealed by s.153(1), FA 2000, in relation to gifts and inheritances taken on or after 1st December, 1999.

Originally, s.117, FA 1991, which applied to inheritances taken on or after 30th January, 1991, gave relief from inheritance tax to certain brothers and sisters of the disponer by reducing the market value of a house by 50%, or £50,000, whichever is the lesser.

S.144, FA 1994, in relation to inheritances taken on or after 11th April, 1994, increased the reduction to 60%, or £60,000, whichever is the lesser, for certain brothers and sisters.

S.138, FA 1997, in relation to inheritances taken on or after 10th May, 1997, increased the reduction to 60%, or £80,000, whichever is the lesser, for certain brothers and sisters.

S.126, FA 1998, in relation to inheritances taken on or after 3rd December, 1997, and prior to 1st December, 1999, increased the reduction to 80%, or £150,000, whichever is the lesser, and extended the potential beneficiaries to include certain grandparents, grandchildren, nephews and nieces.

2   As inserted by s.220, FA2001, in relation to a gift or inheritance taken on or after 1st December, 1999.

Commentary

A   See an article in relation to s.59C by Ann Williams in the *Irish Tax Review* of January 2001, page 13.

B   See page 32, Issue 40, of the *Revenue Tax Briefing* of June 2000, in relation to a partial clawback where a replacement dwelling-house is involved.

C   See the Revenue Information Leaflet CAT10 in relation to gift/inheritance tax exemption for dwelling-house.

D   See an Irish Circuit Court case, *Paul Danaher v The Revenue Commissioners* [2005] No. 8RA, which decided that a house was not replaced property to qualify for the relief.

E   In relation to s.59C(2)(b), see Part 19.15 of the *Revenue CAT Manual* what refers to a Circuit Court decision that a beneficiary, who inherited two houses, did not qualify for relief.

Section 59D[1]

Gifts and inheritances taken by foster children.

59D. (1)   In this section—

"the appropriate period" means periods which together comprised at least 5 years falling within the 18 years immediately following the birth of the donee or successor.

(2)   Where, on a claim being made to them in that behalf in relation to a gift or inheritance taken on or after 6 December 2000, the Commissioners are, subject to subsection (3), satisfied—

(a)   where the inheritance is taken by a successor on the date of death of the disponer, that the successor had, prior to the date of the inheritance, been placed in the foster care of the disponer under the Child Care (Placement of Children in Foster Care) Regulations, 1995 (S.I. No. 260 of 1995), or the Child Care (Placement of Children with Relatives) Regulations, 1995 (S.I. No. 261 of 1995), or

(b)   that throughout the appropriate period the donee or successor—

(i)   has resided with the disponer, and

(ii)   was under the care of and maintained by the disponer at the disponer's own expense,

then, subject to subsection (3), for the purpose of computing the tax payable on that gift or inheritance, that donee or successor shall be deemed to bear to that disponer the relationship of a child.

(3)   Relief under subsection (2) shall not apply where the claim for such relief is based on the uncorroborated testimony of one witness.

Footnote
1   As inserted by s.221, FA 2001.

Section 59E[1]

Gifts and inheritances taken by adopted children from natural parent.

59E. Where, on a claim being made to them in that behalf in relation to a gift or inheritance taken on or after the date.of the passing of the Finance Act, 2001, the Commissioners are satisfied that—

(a) the donee or successor had at the date of the gift or the date of the inheritance been adopted in the manner referred to in paragraph (b) of the definition of "child" contained in section 2(1), and

(b) the disponer is the natural mother or the natural father of the donee or successor,

then, notwithstanding section 2(5)(a), for the purpose of computing the tax payable on that gift or inheritance, that donee or successor shall be deemed to bear to that disponer the relationship of a child.

Footnote

1   As inserted by s.222, FA 2001, in relation to a gift or inheritance taken on or after 30th March, 2001.

PART X

Miscellaneous

Section 60

Certificates for probate.

60. (1) Where an Inland Revenue affidavit has been delivered to the Commissioners and they are satisfied —

(a) that an adequate payment on account of inheritance tax in respect of the property passing under the deceased person's will or intestacy or Part IX or section 56 of the Succession Act, 1965, has been made; or

(b) that the payment of inheritance tax in respect of such property may be deferred for the time being,

they shall certify in writing—

(i) that the Inland Revenue affidavit was delivered to them; and

(ii) (I) that a payment referred to in paragraph (a) has been made; or

(II) that the payment referred to in paragraph (b) has been deferred for the time being,

as the case may be.

(2) In this section "Inland Revenue affidavit" has the meaning referred to in section 38 (1).

(3) If, in the opinion of the Commissioners, the payment of inheritance tax in respect of the property passing under the deceased person's will or intestacy or Part IX or section 56 of the Succession Act, 1965, cannot be deferred for the time being without serious risk of such tax not being recovered, they may refuse to issue the certificate referred to in subsection (1) until the tax has been paid, or until such payment as is referred to in paragraph (a) of that subsection has been made.

(4) The certificate required by section 30 of the Customs and Inland Revenue Act, 1881,[1] to be made by the proper officer of the court, shall not be made until a certificate of the Commissioners issued under subsection (1) has been produced to such officer and shall (instead of showing that the affidavit, if liable to stamp duty, has been duly stamped) show that the Commissioners have issued a certificate under subsection (1) and shall state the substance of the certificate so issued by the Commissioners.

(5) The form of certificate required to be given by the proper officer of the court under section 30 of the Customs and Inland Revenue Act, 1881,[1] may be prescribed by rule of court in such manner as may be necessary for giving effect to this Act.

(6) This section shall apply only where the deceased person dies on or after the 1st day of April, 1975.

Footnote
1   Reproduced on page 651.

Section 61

Payment of money standing in names of two or more persons.

61. (1) Where, either before or after the passing of this Act, a sum of money exceeding [€31,750][3] is lodged or deposited (otherwise than on a current account) in the State with a banker, in the joint names of two or more persons, and one of such persons (in this section referred to as the deceased) dies on or after the 1st day of April, 1975, the banker shall not pay such money or any part thereof to the survivor or all or any of the survivors of such persons, or to any other person, unless or until there is furnished to such banker a certificate by the Commissioners certifying that there is no outstanding claim for inheritance tax in connection with the death of the deceased in respect of such money or any part thereof or a consent in writing by the Commissioners to such payment pending the ascertainment and payment of such tax.

(2) Notwithstanding anything contained in this Act, tax chargeable on the death of the deceased shall be deemed for the purposes of this section to become due on the day of the death of the deceased.

(3) A banker who, after the passing of this Act, pays money in contravention of this section shall be liable to a penalty of [€1,265]⁴.

(4) Where a penalty is demanded of a banker under this section, the onus of proving that such certificate or such consent as is mentioned in this section was furnished to such banker before he paid such money shall lie on such banker.

(5) Where a penalty is demanded of a banker under this section, it shall be a good defence to prove that, at the time when such banker paid such money, he had reasonable ground for believing that none of the persons in whose joint names such money was lodged or deposited with him was dead.

(6) Section 33 of the Finance Act, 1935,¹ shall not have effect in any case where the death of a person, referred to in that section as the deceased, occurs on or after the 1st day of April, 1975.

(7) In this section —

"banker" means a person who carries on banking business in the State and includes a friendly society, an industrial and provident society, a building society, the Post Office Savings Bank, a trustee savings bank, [...............,]⁵ and any person with whom money is lodged or deposited:

"pay" includes transfer in the books of a banker and any dealings whatsoever with any moneys which were lodged or deposited in the name of a person who died after the time of the lodgment or deposit and any other person or persons;

"current account" means an account which is customarily operated upon by means of a cheque or banker's order;

"banking business" has the meaning assigned to it by section 2 of the Central Bank Act, 1971;

references to moneys lodged or deposited include references to shares of a building society, friendly society or industrial and provident society.

[(8) This section shall not apply or have effect where the sum of money referred to in subsection (1) is lodged or deposited in the joint names of two persons, one of whom dies on or after the 30th day of January, 1985, and is at the time of his death the spouse of that other person.]²

Footnotes

1   Reproduced on page 664.

2   As inserted by s.110, FA 1986.

3   "£25,000" substituted for "£5,000" by s.223(a), FA 2001, as respects persons dying on or

> after 26th January, 2001, and prior to 1st January, 2002. S.223(b), FA 2001, substituted "€31,750" for "£25,000" as respects persons dying on or after 1st January, 2002.

4   S.240(2)(k) and Part 5 of the Fifth Sch., FA 2001, substituted "€1,270" for "£1,000" for any act or omission which takes place or begins on or after 1st January, 2002.

5   The words, "the Industrial Credit Company Limited," were deleted by s.7(1), ICC Bank Act, 2000, with effect from 12th February, 2001, under S.I. No. 46 of 2001. The words, "the Agricultural Credit Corporation Limited" were deleted by s.12(1), ACC Bank Act, 2001, with effect from 28th February, 2002, under S.I. No 69 of 2002.

Section 62

Court to provide for payment of tax.

62.   Where any suit is pending in any court for the administration of any property chargeable with tax under this Act, such court shall provide, out of any such property which may be in the possession or control of the court, for the payment to the Commissioners of any of the tax or the interest thereon which remains unpaid.

Section 63

Penalties.

63.   [(1) (a) Any person who contravenes or fails to comply with any requirement or provision under section 36 shall be liable to a penalty of [€2,535][6].

        (b) Where the contravention or failure referred to in paragraph (a) continues after judgment has been given by the court before which proceedings for the penalty have been commenced, the person concerned shall be liable to a further penalty of [€30][7] for each day on which the contravention or failure so continues.][1]

    (2) Where, under, or for the purposes of, any of the provisions of this Act, a person is authorised to inspect any property for the purpose of reporting to the Commissioners the market value thereof and the person having custody or possession of that property prevents such inspection or obstructs the person so authorised in the performance of his functions in relation to the inspection, the person so having custody or possession shall be liable to a penalty of [€1,265].[2]

    (3) Where an accountable person fraudulently or negligently –

        (a) delivers any incorrect return or additional return;

        (b) makes or furnishes any incorrect statement, declaration, evidence or valuation in connection with any property comprised in any disposition;

        (c) makes or furnishes any incorrect statement, declaration, evidence or valuation in connection with any claim for any allowance, deduction, exemption or relief; or

(d)   makes or furnishes any incorrect statement, declaration, evidence or valuation in connection with any other matter,

on the basis of which the amount of tax assessable in respect of a taxable gift or taxable inheritance would be less than it would have been if the correct return, additional return, statement, declaration, evidence or valuation had been delivered, made or furnished, he shall be liable to a penalty of —

(i)   [€6,345];[3] and

(ii)   the amount, or in the case of fraud, twice the amount, of the difference specified in subsection (5).

(4)   Where any such return, additional return, statement, declaration, evidence or valuation as is mentioned in subsection (3) was delivered, made or furnished neither fraudulently nor negligently by a person and it comes to his notice that it was incorrect, then, unless the error is remedied without unreasonable delay, such matter shall be treated, for the purposes of this section, as having been negligently done by him.

(5)   The difference referred to in subsection (3) is the difference between —

(a)   the amount of tax payable in respect of the taxable gift or taxable inheritance to which the return, additional return, statement, declaration, evidence or valuation relates; and

(b)   the amount which would have been the amount so payable if the return, additional return, statement, declaration, evidence or valuation as made or submitted had been correct.

(6)   For the purpose of subsection (3), where anything referred to in that subsection is delivered, made or furnished on behalf of a person, it shall be deemed to have been delivered, made or furnished by that person unless he proves that it was done without his knowledge or consent.

(7)   Any person who assists in or induces the delivery, making or furnishing for any purposes of the tax of any return, additional return, statement, declaration, evidence or valuation which he knows to be incorrect shall be liable to a penalty of [€1,265].[4]

(8)   The provisions of this section shall not affect any criminal proceedings.

(9)   Subject to the provisions of this section, [sections 987(4), 1061, 1062, 1063, 1064, 1065, 1066 and 1068 of the Taxes Consolidation Act, 1997][5], shall, with any necessary modifications, apply to a penalty under this Act as if the penalty were a penalty under the Income Tax Acts.

Footnotes

1   As substituted by s.77(a), FA 1989, with effect from 24th May, 1989.

2   "£1,000" substituted for "£500" by s.77(b), FA 1989, with effect from 24th May, 1989.

     S.240(2)(k) and Part 5 of the Fifth Sch., FA 2001, substituted "€1,265" for "£1,000" for any act or omission which takes place on or after 1st January, 2002.

3   "£5,000" substituted for "£1,000" by s.77(c), FA 1989, with effect from 24th May, 1989.

     S.240(2)(k) and Part 5 of the Fifth Sch, FA 2001, substituted "€6,345" for "£5,000" for any act or omission which takes place on or after 1st January, 2002.

4   "£1,000" substituted for "£250" by s.77(d), FA 1989, with effect from 24th May, 1989.

     S240(2)(k) and Part 5 of the Fifth Sch., FA 2001, substituted "€1,265" for "£1,000" for any act or omission which takes place on or after 1st January, 2002.

5   As amended by s.1100, TCA, with effect from 6th April, 1997.

6   S.240(2)(k) and Part 5 of the Fifth Sch., FA2001, substituted"€2,535" for "£2,000" for any act or omission which takes place on or after 1st January, 2002.

7   S.240(2)(k) and Part 5 of the Fifth Sch., FA2001, substituted "€30" for "£25" for any act or omission which takes place on or after 1st January, 2002.

Commentary

A   See an article on interest and penalties at page 3, Issue 55, of the *Revenue Tax Briefing* of April 2004.

Section 64

Liability to tax in respect of certain sales and mortgages.

64.   (1)   In this section —

"death duties" has the meaning assigned to it by section 30 of the Finance Act, 1971,[1] and

"purchaser or mortgagee" includes a person deriving title from or under a purchaser or mortgagee in the case of such a sale or mortgage as is referred to in this section.

(2)   Where an interest in expectancy has, prior to the 1st day of April, 1975, been *bona fide* sold or mortgaged for full consideration in money or money's worth, and that interest comes into possession on a death occurring on or after that date, the following provisions shall have effect, that is to say —

(a)   the purchaser or mortgagee shall not be liable in respect of inheritance tax on the inheritance referred to in paragraph (b) for an amount greater than that referred to in paragraph (c);

(b)   the inheritance referred to in paragraph (a) is the inheritance of property in which the interest so sold or mortgaged subsists and which arises in respect of the interest of the remainderman referred to in section 23 so coming into possession;

(c)   the amount referred to in paragraph (a) shall be the amount that would then have been payable by the purchaser or mortgagee in respect of death duties on the property in which the interest subsists as property passing under the same disposition as that under which the said inheritance is taken, if the property, on so coming into possession, had been chargeable to death duties—

(i)   under the law in force; and

(ii)   at the rate or rates having effect,

at the date of the sale or mortgage;

(d)   where such an interest is so mortgaged, any amount of inheritance tax payable in respect of the inheritance referred to in paragraph (b), and from the payment of which the mortgagee is relieved under this section, shall, notwithstanding the priority referred to in section 47 (1), rank, in relation to property charged with such tax under that section, as a charge subsequent to the mortgage;

(e)   any person, other than the purchaser or mortgagee, who is accountable for the payment of so much of the inheritance tax as is not the liability of the purchaser or mortgagee by virtue of the relief given by this section, shall not be liable for the payment of any amount in respect thereof in excess of the amount which is available to him for such payment by reason of there being, at the time when the interest comes into possession, other property, or an equity of redemption, or both, subject to the same trusts, under the disposition referred to in paragraph (c), as the property in which the interest in expectancy subsists; and

(f)   nothing in section 35 (7) or (8) or section 47 (1) shall be construed as derogating from the relief given by this section to a purchaser or mortgagee.

Footnote
1   Reproduced on page 679.

Section 65

References in deeds and wills, etc. to death duties.

65.   In so far as a provision in a document refers (in whatever terms) to any death duty to arise on any death occurring on or after the 1st day of April, 1975, it shall have effect, as far as may be, as if the reference included a reference to inheritance tax—

(a)   if that document was executed prior to the passing of this Act, and the reference is to legacy duty and succession duty or either of them;

(b)   if that document was so executed, and the reference is to estate duty, and it may reasonably be inferred from all the circumstances (including any similarity of the incidence of inheritance tax to that of estate duty) that the inclusion of the reference to inheritance tax would be just; and

(c) whether the document was executed prior to or after the passing of this Act, if the reference is to death duties, without referring to any particular death duty.

Section 66

Arrangements for relief from double taxation.

66. (1) If the Government by order declare that arrangements specified in the order have been made with the government of any territory outside the State in relation to affording relief from double taxation in respect of gift tax or inheritance tax payable under the laws of the State and any tax imposed under the laws of that territory which is of a similar character or is chargeable by reference to death or to gifts *inter vivos* and that it is expedient that those arrangements should have the force of law, the arrangements shall, notwithstanding anything in any enactment, have the force of law.

(2) Any arrangements to which the force of law is given under this section may include provision for relief from tax charged before the making of the arrangements and provisions as to property which is not itself subject to double tax, and the provisions of this section shall have effect accordingly.

(3) For the purposes of subsection (1), arrangements made with the head of a foreign state shall be regarded as made with the government thereof.

(4) Where any arrangements have the force of law by virtue of this section, the obligation as to secrecy imposed by any enactment shall not prevent the Commissioners from disclosing to any authorised officer of the government with which the arrangements are made such information as is required to be disclosed under the arrangements.

(5) (a) Any order made under this section may be revoked by a subsequent order and any such revoking order may contain such transitional provisions as appear to the Government to be necessary or expedient.

(b) Where an order is proposed to be made under this section, a draft thereof shall be laid before Dáil Éireann and the order shall not be made until a resolution approving of the draft has been passed by Dáil Éireann.

Commentary

A   Two such "arrangements" have been made, (i) with the USA, the provisions of s.10, FA 1950, being treated as applicable to US Federal Estate Tax, and to Irish inheritance tax (not gift tax) and probate tax (see page 517), and (ii) with the UK in relation to UK inheritance tax, and to Irish gift tax, inheritance tax and probate tax (see page 524).

Probate tax was abolished by s.225, FA 2001, in relation to persons dying on or after 6th December, 2000.

B   See an article on CAT and Double Taxation Relief by Ann Williams in the *Irish Tax Review* of September 2000, page 437.

Section 67

Other relief from double taxation.

67.   (1)   (a)   In this section—

"foreign tax" means any tax which is chargeable under the laws of any territory outside the State and is of a character similar to estate duty, gift tax or inheritance tax;

"event" means—

(i)   a death; or

(ii)   any other event,

by reference to which the date of the gift or the date of the inheritance is determined.

(b)   For the purposes of this section, a reference to property situate in a territory outside the State is a reference to property situate in that territory at the date of the gift or the date of the inheritance, as the case may be, or to property representing such property.

(2)   Where the Commissioners are satisfied that a taxable gift or taxable inheritance, taken under a disposition by a donee or successor on the happening of any event, is reduced by the payment of foreign tax which is chargeable in connection with the same event under the same disposition in respect of property which is situate in the territory outside the State in which that foreign tax is chargeable, they shall allow a credit in respect of that foreign tax against the gift tax or inheritance tax payable by that donee or successor on that taxable gift or taxable inheritance; but such credit shall not exceed—

(a)   the amount of the gift tax or inheritance tax payable in respect of the same property by reason of such property being comprised in any taxable gift or taxable inheritance taken under that disposition on the happening of that event; or

(b)   the amount of that foreign tax,

whichever is the lesser.

(3)   The provisions of this section shall be subject to any arrangement to which the force of law is given under section 66, and, if any such arrangement provides for the allowance of the amount of a tax payable in a territory outside the State as a credit against gift tax or inheritance tax, the provisions of the arrangement shall apply in relation to the tax payable in that territory in lieu of the provisions of subsection (2).

(4)   . . . .[1]

(5) Where the foreign tax in respect of property comprised in a taxable gift or a taxable inheritance taken under a disposition on the happening of an event is, under the terms of the disposition, directed to be paid out of a taxable gift or a taxable inheritance (taken under that disposition on the happening of the same event) other than the taxable gift or taxable inheritance out of which it would be payable in the absence of such a direction, then, for the purposes of subsection (2), the taxable gift or taxable inheritance out of which the foreign tax would be payable in the absence of such a direction, and no other taxable gift or taxable inheritance, shall be treated as reduced by the payment of the foreign tax.

Footnote

1   This subsection, which was not amended, was repealed by s.54(3), FA 1977, in relation to gifts and inheritances taken on or after 1st June, 1977.

Section 68

Tax, in relation to certain legislation.

68. (1) Inheritance tax shall not be a duty or a death duty for the purposes of section 9 of the Succession Act, 1965, but it shall be a death duty for the purposes of —

    (a) section 34 (3) of that Act;

    (b) the definition of pecuniary legacy in section 3 (1) of that Act; and

    (c) paragraph 8 of Part II of the First Schedule to that Act.

(2) Section 72 of the Registration of Title Act, 1964, shall apply as if gift tax and inheritance tax were therein mentioned as well as estate duty and succession duty.

Section 69

Extension of certain Acts.

69. (1) Section 1 of [the Provisional Collection of Taxes Act, 1927][1], is hereby amended by the insertion of "and gift tax and inheritance tax" before "but no other tax or duty".

(2) Section 39 of the Inland Revenue Regulation Act, 1890, is hereby amended by the insertion of "gift tax and inheritance tax," before "stamp duties".

Footnote

1   Reproduced on page 658.

Section 70

Delivery, service and evidence of notices and forms, etc.

70. (1) Any notice which under this Act is authorised or required to be given by the Commissioners may be served by post.

(2) A notice or form which is to be served on a person may be either delivered to him or left at his usual or last known place of abode.

[(3) *Prima facie* evidence of any notice given under this Act by the Commissioners or by an officer of the Commissioners may be given in any proceedings by the production of a document purporting—

(a) to be a copy of that notice, or

(b) if the details specified in that notice are contained in an electronic, photographic or other record maintained by the Commissioners, to reproduce those details in so far as they relate to that notice,

and it shall not be necessary to prove the official position of the person by whom the notice purports to be given or, if it is signed, the signature, or that the person signing and giving it was authorised to do so.]¹

(4) In any case where a time limit is specified by or under this Act, other than Part VIII hereof, for the doing of any act required by or under this Act, other than Part VIII thereof, to be done by any person other than the Commissioners, the Commissioners may, in their discretion, extend such time limit.

Footnote
1   As substituted by s.120, FA 2002, which has effect in relation to evidence of any notice given by the Revenue Commissioners or by any officer of the Revenue Commissioners in any proceedings on or after 25th March, 2002.

Section 71

Regulations.

71. (1) The Commissioners shall make such regulations as seem to them to be necessary for the purpose of giving effect to this Act and of enabling them to discharge their functions thereunder.

(2) Every regulation made under this section shall be laid before Dáil Éireann as soon as may be after it is made and, if a resolution annulling the regulation is passed by Dáil Éireann within the next twenty-one days on which Dáil Éireann has sat after the regulation is laid before it, the regulation shall be annulled accordingly, but without prejudice to the validity of anything previously done thereunder.

Section 72

Care and management.

72. (1) Tax is hereby placed under the care and management of the Commissioners.

(2) Subject to the direction and control of the Commissioners, any power, function or duty conferred or imposed on the Commissioners by this Act may be exercised or performed on their behalf by an officer of the Commissioners.

FIRST SCHEDULE

Valuation Of Limited Interests

PART I

Rules relating to the valuation of limited interests utilising Tables A and B in Parts II and III of this Schedule

1. The value of an interest for a single life in a capital sum shall be that sum multiplied by the factor, contained in column 3 or 4 respectively of Table A, which is appropriate to the age and sex of the person in respect of the duration of whose life the interest is to be valued.

2. The value of an interest in a capital sum for the joint continuance of two lives shall be the value of an interest in that sum for the older life, ascertained in accordance with rule 1, multiplied by the joint factor in column 2 of Table A which is appropriate to the younger life.

3. The value of an interest in a capital sum for the joint continuance of three or more lives shall be the value of an interest in that sum for the joint continuance of the two oldest of those lives, ascertained in accordance with rule 2, multiplied by the joint factor of the youngest of those lives.

4. The value of an interest in a capital sum for the longer of two lives shall be ascertained by deducting from the total of the values of an interest in that sum for each of those lives, ascertained in accordance with rule 1, the value of an interest in the capital sum for the joint continuance of the same two lives, ascertained in accordance with rule 2.

5. Where an interest is given for the longest of more than two lives, it shall be valued, in accordance with rule 4, as if it were for the longer of the two youngest of those lives.

6. The value of an interest in a capital sum for a period certain shall be the aggregate of—

   (a) the value of the capital sum, multiplied by the factor in Table B which is appropriate to the number of whole years in that period (or zero if that period is less than a whole year); and

   (b) where the period is not an integral number of years, a fraction (of which the numerator is the number of days in excess of the number of whole years, if any, in that period and the denominator is 365) of the difference between—

(i)   the value of an interest in the capital sum for one year longer than the number of whole years, if any, in the period; and

(ii) the value ascertained under the provisions of paragraph (a) (or zero, where so provided in the said paragraph).

7.   In the case of a limited interest where the interest is for a life or lives, but is guaranteed for a period certain, the value shall be the higher of—

(a) the value of an interest for such life or lives, ascertained in accordance with the appropriate rule in this part of this Schedule; and

(b) the value of an interest for the period certain, ascertained in accordance with rule 6.

8.   The value of a limited interest for which the other rules in this Part of this Schedule provide no method of valuing shall be ascertained as if the interest taken were a series of absolute interests in the property applied in satisfaction of the interest from time to time, taken as separate gifts or inheritances, as the case may be.

PART II
Table A

1	2	3	4
Years of age	Joint factor	Value of an interest in a capital of [€1][1] for a male life aged as in column 1	Value of an interest in a capital of [€1][1] for a female life aged as in column 1
0	.99	.9519	.9624
1	.99	.9767	.9817
2	.99	.9767	.9819
3	.99	.9762	.9817
4	.99	.9753	.9811
5	.99	.9742	.9805
6	.99	.9730	.9797
7	.99	.9717	.9787
8	.99	.9703	.9777
9	.99	.9688	.9765
10	.99	.9671	.9753
11	.98	.9653	.9740
12	.98	.9634	.9726
13	.98	.9614	.9710
14	.98	.9592	.9693

1	2	3	4
Years of age	Joint factor	Value of an interest in a capital of [€1][1] for a male life aged as in column 1	Value of an interest in a capital of [€1][1] for a female life aged as in column 1
15	.98	.9569	.9676
16	.98	.9546	.9657
17	.98	.9522	.9638
18	.98	.9497	.9617
19	.98	.9471	.9596
20	.97	.9444	.9572
21	.97	.9416	.9547
22	.97	.9387	.9521
23	.97	.9356	.9493
24	.97	.9323	.9464
25	.97	.9288	.9432
26	.97	.9250	.9399
27	.97	.9209	.9364
28	.97	.9165	.9328
29	.97	.9119	.9289
30	.96	.9068	.9248
31	.96	.9015	.9205
32	.96	.8958	.9159
33	.96	.8899	.9111
34	.96	.8836	.9059
35	.96	.8770	.9005
36	.96	.8699	.8947
37	.96	.8626	.8886
38	.95	.8549	.8821
39	.95	.8469	.8753
40	.95	.8384	.8683
41	.95	.8296	.8610
42	.95	.8204	.8534
43	.95	.8107	.8454
44	.94	.8005	.8370
45	.94	.7897	.8283
46	.94	.7783	.8192
47	.94	.7663	.8096
48	.93	.7541	.7997
49	.93	.7415	.7896
50	.92	.7287	.7791
51	.91	.7156	.7683

1	2	3	4
Years of age	Joint factor	Value of an interest in a capital of [€1][1] for a male life aged as in column 1	Value of an interest in a capital of [€1][1] for a female life aged as in column 1
52	.90	.7024	.7572
53	.89	.6887	.7456
54	.89	.6745	.7335
55	.88	.6598	.7206
56	.88	.6445	.7069
57	.88	.6288	.6926
58	.87	.6129	.6778
59	.86	.5969	.6628
60	.86	.5809	.6475
61	.86	.5650	.6320
62	.86	.5492	.6162
63	.85	.5332	.6000
64	.85	.5171	.5830
65	.85	.5007	.5650
66	.85	.4841	.5462
67	.84	.4673	.5266
68	.84	.4506	.5070
69	.84	.4339	.4873
70	.83	.4173	.4679
71	.83	.4009	.4488
72	.82	.3846	.4301
73	.82	.3683	.4114
74	.81	.3519	.3928
75	.80	.3352	.3743
76	.79	.3181	.3559
77	.78	.3009	.3377
78	.76	.2838	.3198
79	.74	.2671	.3023
80	.72	.2509	.2855
81	.71	.2353	.2693
82	.70	.2203	.2538
83	.69	.2057	.2387
84	.68	.1916	.2242
85	.67	.1783	.2104
86	.66	.1657	.1973
87	.65	.1537	.1849
88	.64	.1423	.1730

1	2	3	4
Years of age	Joint factor	Value of an interest in a capital of [€1][1] for a male life aged as in column 1	Value of an interest in a capital of [€1][1] for a female life aged as in column 1
89	.62	.1315	.1616
90	.60	.1212	.1509
91	.58	.1116	.1407
92	.56	.1025	.1310
93	.54	.0939	.1218
94	.52	.0858	.1132
95	.50	.0781	.1050
96	.49	.0710	.0972
97	.48	.0642	.0898
98	.47	.0578	.0828
99	.45	.0517	.0762
100 or over	.43	.0458	.0698

PART III

Table B

(Column 2 shows the value of an interest in a capital of [€1][1] for the number of years shown in column 1).

1	2	1	2
Number of years	Value	Number of years	Value
1	.0654	18	.7032
2	.1265	19	.7225
3	.1836	20	.7405
4	.2370	21	.7574
5	.2869	22	.7731
6	.3335	23	.7878
7	.3770	24	.8015
8	.4177	25	.8144
9	.4557	26	.8263
10	.4913	27	.8375
11	.5245	28	.8480
12	.5555	29	.8578
13	.5845	30	.8669
14	.6116	31	.8754
15	.6369	32	.8834
16	.6605	33	.8908
17	.6826	34	.8978

1 Number of years	2 Value	1 Number of years	2 Value
35	.9043	43	.9555
36	.9100	44	.9620
37	.9165	45	.9685
38	.9230	46	.9750
39	.9295	47	.9815
40	.9360	48	.9880
41	.9425	49	.9945
42	.9490	50 and over	1.0000

Footnote

1   S.240(2)(l)(viii) and Part 5 of the Fifth Sch., FA 2001, substituted "€1" for "£1" as respects the computation of tax on gifts and inheritance taken on or after 1st January, 2002.

SECOND SCHEDULE [1]

Computation of Tax

PART I

Preliminary

[1.   In this Schedule—

"group threshold", in relation to a taxable gift or a taxable inheritance taken on a particular day, means—

(a)   [€381,000][13], where—

    (i)   the donee or successor is on that day the child, or minor child of a deceased child, of the disponer, or

    [(ii)   the successor is on that day a parent of the disponer and—

        (I)   the interest taken is not a limited interest, and

        (II)   the inheritance is taken on the death of the disponer;][3]

(b)   [€38,100][13], where the donee or successor is on that day, a lineal ancestor, a lineal descendant (other than a child, or a minor child of a deceased child), a brother, a sister, or a child of a brother or of a sister of the disponer;

(c)   [€19,050][13], where the donee or successor (who is not a spouse of the disponer) does not, on that day, stand to the disponer in a relationship referred to in subparagraph (a) or (b);

"the consumer price index number", in relation to a year, means the All Items Consumer Price Index Number for that year as compiled by the Central Statistics Office and expressed on the basis that the consumer price index number at mid-November 1996 is 100;

"Table" means the Table contained in Part II of this Schedule;

"threshold amount" in relation to the computation of tax on any aggregate of taxable values under paragraph 3, means the group threshold that applies in relation to all of the taxable gifts and taxable inheritances included in that aggregate but, in computing under this Schedule the tax chargeable on a taxable gift or taxable inheritance taken after 31 December 2000, that group threshold shall, for the purposes of this definition, be multiplied by the figure, rounded to the nearest third decimal place, determined by dividing by 104.8 the consumer price index number for the year immediately preceding the year in which that taxable gift or taxable inheritance is taken.

2.   In the Table "Value" means the appropriate aggregate referred to in paragraph 3.

3.   The tax chargeable on the taxable value of a taxable gift or a taxable inheritance (hereafter in this Schedule referred to as the first-mentioned gift or inheritance) taken by a donee or successor shall be of an amount equal to the amount by which the tax computed on aggregate A exceeds the tax computed on aggregate B, where—

     (a)   aggregate A is the aggregate of the following:

         (i)   the taxable value of the first-mentioned gift or inheritance, and

         (ii)   the taxable value of each and every taxable gift and taxable inheritance taken previously by the said donee or successor on or after [5 December 1991,][14], which has the same group threshold as the first-mentioned gift or inheritance,

     (b)   aggregate B is the aggregate of the taxable values of all such taxable gifts and taxable inheritances so previously taken which have the same group threshold as the first-mentioned gift or inheritance, and

     (c)   the tax on an aggregate is computed at the rate or rates of tax applicable under the Table to that aggregate:

         Provided that—

         (i)   in a case where no such taxable gift or taxable inheritance was so previously taken, the amount of the tax computed on aggregate B shall be deemed to be nil, and

         (ii)   the amount of an aggregate that comprises only a single taxable value shall be equal to that value.

4.   In the Table any rate of tax shown in the second column is that applicable to such portion of the value (within the meaning of paragraph 2) as is shown in the first column.

5.   For the purposes of this Schedule, all gifts and inheritances which have the same group threshold and which are taken by a donee or successor on the same day shall count as one, and to ascertain the amount of tax payable on one such gift or inheritance of several so taken on the same day, the amount of tax computed under this Schedule as being payable

on the total of such gifts and inheritances so taken on that day shall be apportioned rateably, according to the taxable values of the several taxable gifts and taxable inheritances so taken on that day.][2]

6.   . . . . [4]

7.   . . . . [5]

8.   Where any donee or successor is, at the date of the gift or at the date of the inheritance, the surviving spouse of a deceased person who, at the time of his death, was of nearer relationship than such donee or successor to the disponer, then such donee or successor shall, in the computation of the tax payable on such taxable gift or taxable inheritance, be deemed to bear to the disponer the relationship of that deceased person.

[9.   (1)   In this paragraph –

["company" means a private company which, for the relevant period –

(a)   is a private company controlled by the disponer and of which the disponer is a director, and

(b)   is not a private non-trading company;][7]

"control", in relation to a company, shall be construed in accordance with section 16 (4) (b);

["investment income", in relation to a private company, means income which, if the company were an individual, would not be earned income within the meaning of section 3 of the Taxes Consolidation Act, 1997];[8]

"nominee" has the same meaning as it has in section 16;

["private company" has the meaning assigned to it by section 16 (2);

"private company controlled by the disponer" means a private company that is under the control of any one or more of the following, that is to say –

(a)   the disponer,

(b)   nominees of the disponer,

(c)   the trustees of a settlement made by the disponer;

"private non-trading company" means a private company –

(a)   whose income (if any) in the twelve months preceding the date at which a share therein is to be valued consisted wholly or mainly of investment income; and

(b)   whose property, on the date referred to in paragraph (a), consisted wholly or mainly of property from which investment income is derived;][9]

"relevant period" means –

    (a)   the period of five years ending on the date of the disposition; or

    (b)   where, at the date of the disposition,

        (i)   an interest in possession in—

            (I)   the property referred to in subparagraph (2) (a), or

            (II) the shares referred to in subparagraph (2) (b),

            as the case may be, is limited to the disponer under the disposition, and

        (ii) such property is not, or such shares are not, property consisting of the appropriate part of property, within the meaning of section 5 (5), on which is charged or secured an annuity or other annual right limited to cease on the death of the disponer,

        the period of five years ending on the coming to an end of that interest,

subject, in relation to work, to the exclusion of reasonable periods of annual or sick leave from that period of five years.

  (2)   For the purpose of computing the tax payable on a gift or inheritance, the donee or successor shall be deemed to bear to the disponer the relationship of a child in any case where the donee or successor is a child of a brother, or a child of a sister, of the disponer and either—

    (a)   the donee or successor has worked substantially on a full-time basis for the disponer for the relevant period in carrying on, or in assisting in carrying on, the trade, business or profession of the disponer, and the gift or inheritance consists of property which was used in connection with that business, trade or profession; or

    (b)   the donee or successor has worked substantially on a full-time basis for a company for the relevant period in carrying on, or in assisting in carrying on, the trade, business or profession of the company, and the gift or inheritance consists of shares in that company.

  (3)   Without prejudice to the generality of subparagraph (2), a donee or successor shall not be deemed to be working substantially on a full-time basis for a disponer or a company unless—

    (a)   where the gift or inheritance consists of property which was used in connection with the business, trade or profession of the disponer, the donee or successor works—

        (i)   more than 24 hours a week for the disponer, at a place where that business, trade or profession, is carried on; or

        (ii) more than 15 hours a week for the disponer, at a place where that business, trade or profession is carried on, and such business, trade or profession is carried on exclusively by the disponer, any spouse of the disponer, and the donee or successor;

or

(b) where the gift or inheritance consists of shares in the company, the donee or successor works—

(i) more than 24 hours a week for the company, at a place where the business, trade or profession of the company is carried on; or

(ii) more than 15 hours a week for the company, at a place where the business, trade or profession of the company is carried on, and such business, trade or profession is carried on exclusively by the disponer, any spouse of the disponer, and the donee or successor.

(4) The provisions of this paragraph shall not apply to a gift or inheritance taken by a donee or successor under a discretionary trust.][6]

[10. (a) In this paragraph "specified disposition" means a disposition—

(i) the date of which is a date prior to the 1st day of April, 1975,

(ii) in relation to which the disponer is a grandparent of the donee or successor, and

(iii) in which the marriage of the parents of the donee or successor was, at the date of the disposition, expressed to be the consideration.

(b) Where, on the cesser of a limited interest to which a parent of the donee or successor was entitled in possession, the donee or successor takes a gift or an inheritance under a specified disposition, then, for the purpose of computing the tax payable on the gift or inheritance, the donee or successor shall be deemed to bear to the disponer the relationship of a child.][10]

[11. For the purposes of this Schedule, a reference to a gift or an inheritance, or to a taxable gift or a taxable inheritance, includes a reference to a part of a gift or an inheritance, or to a part of a taxable gift or a taxable inheritance, as the case may be.][11]

PART II
Table[12]

Portion of Value	Rate of tax
	Per cent
The threshold amount	Nil
The balance	20

Footnotes

1. Since originally enacted, the CATA has been extensively amended in relation to the computation of tax.

    In relation to gifts and inheritances taken prior to 2nd June, 1982, tax was charged on gifts and inheritances taken by any one donee/successor from the same disponer. Four Tables of Rates of Tax applied, depending on the relationship of the donee/successor to the disponer, with tax-free thresholds respectively of £150,000 (Table I), £15,000 (Table II), £10,000 (Table III), and £5,000 (Table IV).

    S.41, FA 1978, in relation to gifts and inheritances taken on or after 1st April, 1978, and prior to 2nd June, 1982, effectively increased the tax-free thresholds in Tables II, III and IV to £30,000, £20,000 and £10,000 respectively, while preserving the remainder of the four Tables and the method of computing tax.

    In relation to gifts and inheritances taken on or after 2nd June, 1982, and prior to 26th March, 1984, s.102, FA 1982, introduced aggregation of taxable gifts/inheritances to which the same appropriate Table applied, while preserving the existing four amended Tables. This was accomplished (i) by substituting paras. 3, 4 and 7 in Part I of the Second Schedule, (ii) by inserting a new para. 11 and (iii) by the insertion of "or disponers" after "disponer" in each place where it occurred in para. 1 or in Part II.

    In relation to gifts and inheritances taken on or after 26th March, 1984, and prior to 1st December, 1999, s.111, FA 1984, introduced aggregation of all taxable gifts/inheritances taken by the same donee/successor from any disponer on or after 2nd June, 1982 (on or after 2nd December, 1988, in relation to gifts and inheritances taken on or after 2nd December, 1998 – s.201, FA 1999). This was accomplished by substituting, in Part I of the Second Schedule, new paras. 1, 2, 3, 5 and 7 for the existing paras. 1 to 5 and 7, and by substituting in Part II, for the existing four Tables of Rates of Tax, a new single Table as follows –

Portion of Value	Rate of tax
	Per cent
The threshold amount	Nil
The next £10,000	20
The next £40,000	30
The next £50,000	35
The next £50,000	40
The next £50,000	45
The balance	55

In computing the tax chargeable on the taxable value of a taxable gift or a taxable inheritance taken on or after 1st January, 1990, and prior to 11th April, 1994, the "threshold amount", as defined in s.111, FA 1984, is indexed in accordance with s.128, FA 1990. The resultant indexation factor applicable in each calendar year is -

1990	1.04
1991	1.076
1992	1.109
1993	1.145
1994, prior to 11th April, 1994	1.16

In relation to gifts and inheritances taken on or after 30th January, 1991, and prior to 11th April, 1994, the 45% and 55% bands of tax in that single Table of Rates of Tax were deleted by s.115, FA 1991, resulting in the maximum rate of tax being 40% for that period.

In relation to gifts and inheritances taken on or after 11th April, 1994, and prior to 1st December, 1999, s.142, FA 1994, substituted a new single Table of Rates of Tax as follows–

Portion of Value	Rate of tax
	Per cent
The threshold amount	Nil
The next £10,000	20
The next £30,000	30
The balance	40

In computing the tax chargeable on the taxable value of a taxable gift or a taxable inheritance taken on or after 11th April, 1994, and prior to 1st December, 1999, the "class threshold", as defined in s.111, FA 1984, is indexed in accordance with s.145, FA 1994. This produced the following results in relation to the class thresholds of £150,000(a), £20,000(b) and £10,000(c) –

Calendar Year	Indexation Factor	Class Threshold (£)	
1994, on or after 11th April 1994	1.16	174,000	(a)
		23,200	(b)
		11,600	(c)
1995	1.188	178,200	(a)
		23,760	(b)
		11,880	(c)
1996	1.217	182,550	(a)
		24,340	(b)
		12,170	(c)
1997	1.237	185,550	(a)
		24,740	(b)
		12,370	(c)
1998	1.256	188,400	(a)
		25,120	(b)
		12,560	(c)
1999, prior to 1st December 1999	1.286	192,900	(a)
		25,720	(b)
		12,860	(c)

For the avoidance of doubt, s.136, FA 1997, declared that para. 3 of the First Part of the Second Schedule (inserted by s.111, FA 1984) is deemed always to have effect as if a new para. 3 contained in s.136 were substituted therefor. However, the new para. 3 does not apply to a gift or inheritance in relation to which the old para. 3 was the subject of a determination of the Appeal Commissioners made before 1st May, 1999, under s.52, CATA.

In relation to gifts and inheritances taken on or after 1st December, 1999, and prior to 21st February, 2003, s.145(1)(a), FA 2000, substituted new paragraphs 1 to 5, as now shown, for the then existing paragraphs 1 to 7, as amended. The effect of the substituted paragraphs is –

(i)   to set out three groups of donees/successors (depending on their relationship to the disponer) to whom the same "group threshold" applies, the group thresholds being originally £300,000(a), £30,000(b) and £15,000(c), but converted from 1st January, 2002, to €381,000(a), €38,100(b) and €19,050(c),

(ii)   to provide for indexation of each group threshold after 31st December, 2000 (see below),

(iii)   to provide that the taxable value of prior gifts/inheritances taken by the same donee/successor on or after 2nd December, 1988, (on or after 5th December, 1991, in relation to gifts and inheritances taken on or after 5th December, 2001 – s.121, FA 2002,) to which the same group threshold applies, are aggregated with the taxable value of the current gift/inheritance to determine the amount of tax on the current gift/inheritance,

(iv)   after a "threshold amount" on which the tax is nil, to provide a single 20% rate of tax, replacing the existing multiple structure, and

(vi)   to eliminate the 25% reduction in the rate of tax for gifts as opposed to inheritances.

Indexation produced the following results in relation to the group thresholds of £300,000(a), £30,000(b) and £15,000(c) -

Calendar Year	Indexation Factor	Class Threshold	
2001	1.056	£316,800	(a)
		£31,680	(b)
		£15,840	(c)
2002	1.108	€422,148	(a)
		€42,215	(b)
		€21,108	(c)
2003, prior to 21st February 2003	1.158	€441,198	(a)
		€44,120	(b)
		€22,060	(c)

2   As substituted by s.145(1)(a), FA 2000, in relation to gifts and inheritances taken on or after 1st December, 1999.

3   Incorporating from 1st December, 1999, the provisions of s.116, FA 1991, which is repealed from that date by s.153(1), FA 2000.

4   Para. 6, providing for the 25% reduction in the rate of tax for gifts as opposed to inheritances, no longer applies in relation to gifts taken on or after 1st December, 1999.

5   Para. 7 no longer applies in relation to gifts and inheritances taken on or after 1st December, 1999. Its provisions, dealing with all gifts and inheritances taken by a donee/successor on the same day, are now in para. 5.

6   As substituted by s.83, FA 1989, as respects gifts and inheritances taken on or after 1st May, 1989.

7   As substituted by s.130(a), FA 1993, as respects gifts and inheritances taken on or after 24th February, 1993.

8   As inserted by s.130(c), FA 1993, as respects gifts and inheritances taken on or after 24th February, 1993. The reference there, to "section 2 of the Income Tax Act 1967" is, since 6th April, 1997, now amended by s.1100, TCA, to "section 3 of the Taxes Consolidation Act, 1997".

9   As inserted as respects gifts and inheritances taken on or after 24th February, 1993, by s.130(d), FA 1993. From that date, the definition of "company controlled by the disponer" was deleted by s.130(b), FA 1993.

10   As inserted by s.46, FA 1981, with retrospective effect.

11   As inserted by s.102(1)(a), FA 1982, in relation to gifts and inheritances taken on or after 2nd June, 1982.

12   As substituted by s.145(1)(b), FA 2000, in relation to gifts and inheritances taken on or after 1st December, 1999.

13   S.240(2)(l)(viii) and Part 5 of the Fifth Sch., FA2001, substituted "€381,000", "€38,100" and "€19,050" respectively for "£300,000", "£30,000" and "£15,000" as respects the computation of tax on gifts and inheritances taken on or after 1st January, 2002.

14   As substituted for "2 December 1988" by s.121, FA 2002, in relation to gifts and inheritances taken on or after 5th December, 2001.

Commentary

A   As to the definition of "child" in s.2, CATA, including a "stepchild", see Part 19.17 of the *Revenue CAT Manual* dealing with "lineal descendants" involving stepchildren.

B   With regard to para.8 of Part I of the Second Schedule, Part 19.10 of the *Revenue CAT Manual* provides that this paragraph applies to a surviving spouse even if the surviving spouse has re-married before the date of the gift or inheritance.

C   See s.59D, CATA, in relation to gifts and inheritances taken on or after 6th December, 2000, by foster children.

D   With regard to para.9 of Part I of the Second Schedule, see a Circuit Court decision in *A.E. v Revenue Commissioners* [1984] ILRM 301, in relation to a niece working on a farm.

FINANCE ACT, 1978

Number 21 of 1978
(Enacted on 5th July, 1978)

PART VI
Capital Acquisitions Tax

Section 39

Extension of section 55 (exemption of certain objects) of Capital Acquisitions Tax Act, 1976.

39. (1) Section 55 of the Capital Acquisitions Tax Act, 1976, shall apply, as it applies to the objects specified therein, to a house or garden that is situated in the State and is not held for the purposes of trading and —

  (a) which, on a claim being made to the Commissioners, appears to them to be of national, scientific, historic or artistic interest,

  (b) in respect of which reasonable facilities for viewing were allowed to members of the public from the date of the passing of this Act to the date of the gift or the date of the inheritance, or during the three years immediately before the date of the gift or the date of the inheritance, and

  (c) in respect of which reasonable facilities for viewing are allowed to members of the public,

  with the modification that the reference in subsection (4) of that section to subsection (1) (b) or (c) of that section shall be construed as a reference to paragraph (c) of this subsection and with any other necessary modifications.

  [(1A) Without prejudice to the generality of subsection (1), the provision of facilities for the viewing by members of the public of a house or garden shall not be regarded as reasonable in relation to any year, which is the year 1997 or any subsequent year and which is taken into account for the purposes of paragraphs (b) and (c) of subsection (1), unless —

  (a) Bord Fáilte Éireann (hereinafter in this section referred to as "the Board") has, as regards the year 1997, on or before the 1st day of July, 1997, and, as regards any subsequent year, on or before the 1st day of January in that year, been provided with particulars of —

    (i) the name, if any, and address of the house or garden, and

    (ii) the days and times during the year when access to the house or garden is afforded to the public and the price, if any, payable for such access, and

    (b) in the opinion of the Commissioners—

        (i) subject to such temporary closure necessary for the purpose of the repair, maintenance or restoration of the house or garden as is reasonable, access to the house or garden is afforded for not less than 60 days (including not less than 40 days during the period commencing on the 1st day of May and ending on the 30th day of September [of which not less than 10 of the days during that period shall fall on a Saturday or a Sunday or both][1]) in that year;

        (ii) on each day on which access to the house or garden is afforded, the access is afforded in a reasonable manner and at reasonable times for a period, or periods in the aggregate, of not less than four hours;

        (iii) access to the whole or to a substantial part of the house or garden is afforded at the same time; and

        (iv) the price, if any, paid by members of the public in return for that access is reasonable in amount and does not operate to preclude members of the public from seeking access to the house or garden.][2]

  (2) This section shall apply where the date of the gift or the date of the inheritance is on or after the date of the passing of this Act.

Footnotes

1   As inserted by s.146(1), FA 2000, in relation to gifts and inheritances taken on or after 10th February, 2000, and as respects the year 2001 and subsequent years.

2   As inserted, in relation to gifts and inheritances taken on or after 1st February, 1987, by s.137, FA 1997, which also revoked, with effect from 1st January, 1997, the Capital Acquisitions Tax (Heritage Houses and Gardens) Regulations, 1987 (S.I. No. 28 of 1987). These Regulations are reproduced on page 1373.

Commentary

A   See the Revenue Information Leaflet CAT8 in relation to this section.

B   See an article on the Favourable Treatment of Heritage Objects by Anne Corrigan and Marie Griffin in the *Irish Tax Review* of March 2002, page 179.

FINANCE ACT, 1982

Number 14 of 1982
(Enacted on 17th July, 1982)

PART V
Capital Acquisitions Tax

Section 98

Exemption of certain benefits.
98. Where a gift or an inheritance is taken, by direction of the disponer, free of tax on or after the date of the passing of this Act, the benefit taken shall be deemed to include the amount of tax chargeable on such gift or inheritance but not the amount of tax chargeable on such tax.

Commentary

A   See Part 14 of the *Revenue CAT Manual*.

FINANCE ACT, 1985

Number 10 of 1985
(Enacted on 30th May, 1985)

PART V
Capital Acquisitions Tax

Section 59

Exemption for spouses.

59. (1) Notwithstanding the provisions of [the Capital Acquisitions Tax Act, 1976], an inheritance taken by a successor, who is at the date of the inheritance the spouse of the disponer, shall be exempt from tax and shall not be taken into account in computing tax.

(2) This section shall have effect in relation to an inheritance taken on or after the 30th day of January, 1985.

Commentary

A   This exemption does not apply to a common-law spouse, who is treated as a stranger to the disponer. However, according to Part 19.9 of the *Revenue CAT Manual*, the hardship provisions of s.44, CATA, may apply where the financial position of surviving common-law spouses and their children is particularly difficult.

B   See Part 19.8 of the *Revenue CAT Manual*. In cases where there is an interval between the death of the disponer and the taking of an inheritance from the disponer by the disponer's spouse, the surviving spouse is still regarded as being the disponer's spouse at the date of the inheritance even if the surviving spouse has then re-married.

Section 61

Relief from double aggregation.

61. (1) Property in respect of which tax is chargeable more than once on the same event shall not be included more than once in relation to that event in any aggregate referred to in the Second Schedule to [the Capital Acquisitions Tax Act, 1976].

(2) Paragraph 7 of Part I of the said Second Schedule shall not have effect in ascertaining the tax payable in respect of property which is chargeable to tax as being taken more than once on the same day.

(3) This section shall have effect in relation to gifts and inheritances taken on or after the 2nd day of June, 1982.

(4) Notwithstanding the provisions of section 46 of [the Capital Acquisitions Tax Act, 1976], interest shall not be payable on any repayment of tax which arises by virtue of this section where such tax was paid prior to the date of the passing of this Act.

Section 63

Allowance for capital gains tax[1] on the same event.

63. (1) Where gift tax or inheritance tax is charged in respect of property on an event happening on or after the 30th day of January, 1985, and the same event constitutes for capital gains tax purposes a disposal of an asset (being the same property or any part of the same property), the capital gains tax, if any, chargeable on the disposal shall not be deducted in ascertaining the taxable value for the purposes of the gift tax or inheritance tax but, in so far as it has been paid, shall be deducted from the net gift tax or inheritance tax as a credit against [the same:

Provided that, in relation to each asset, or to a part of each asset, so disposed of, the amount deducted shall be the lesser of—

(a) an amount equal to the amount of the capital gains tax attributable to such asset, or to the part of such asset, or

(b) an amount equal to the amount of the gift tax or inheritance tax attributable to the property which is that asset, or that part of that asset.][2]

(2) For the purposes of any computation of the amount of capital gains tax to be deducted under this section, any necessary apportionments shall be made of any reliefs or expenditure and the method of apportionment adopted shall be such method as appears to the Commissioners, or on appeal to the Appeal Commissioners, to be just and reasonable.

Footnotes

1 Under s.730GB, TCA, inserted by s.70(1)(f), FA 2001, which applies as on and from 1st January, 2001, capital gains tax includes "appropriate tax" payable as a result of the death of a person.

Under s.739G(5), TCA, inserted by s.74(1)(e)(ii), FA2001, which is deemed to have applied on or after 1st April, 2001, capital gains tax includes "appropriate tax" payable as a result of a death of a person.

Under s.747E(5), TCA, inserted by s.72(1), FA 2001, which is deemed to have applied on and from 1st January, 2001, capital gains tax includes tax payable under s.747E(1), TCA.

2 As substituted by s.66(1), FA 1988, which applies where gift or inheritance tax is charged in respect of property on an event happening on or after 6th April, 1988.

Commentary

A See Part 13 of the *Revenue CAT Manual*.

B See Part 19.4 of the *Revenue CAT Manual*. Where there is a disposition of a house charged with a mortgage, or subject to partial consideration, the entire of the capital gains tax attributable to the disposal (being a disposal of the whole house) is deductible from the entire of the CAT attributable to the disposition (being a disposition of the entire house).

C See Part 19.17 of the *Revenue CAT Manual* confirming that Revenue will allow a temporary credit for capital gains tax until such time as it is paid.

FINANCE ACT, 1989

Number 10 of 1989
(Enacted on 24th May, 1989)

PART V
Capital Acquisitions Tax

CHAPTER II
Arrangements with regard to Returns and Assessments

Section 75

Application of section 39 (assessment of tax) of [the Capital Acquisitions Tax Act, 1976].

75. Nothing in section 36 of [the Capital Acquisitions Tax Act, 1976,] shall preclude the Commissioners from making an assessment of tax, a correcting assessment of tax, or an additional assessment of tax, under the provisions of section 39 of that Act.

Section 76

Amendment of section 41 (payment of tax and interest on tax) of [the Capital Acquisitions Tax Act, 1976].

76. (1) ....

(2) A payment by an accountable person of tax shall be treated as a payment on account of tax for the purposes of section 41 of [the Capital Acquisitions Tax Act, 1976], notwithstanding that the payment may be conditional or that the assessment of tax is incorrect.

Section 79

Surcharge for undervaluation of property.

79. (1) Where−

    (a) an accountable person delivers a return, and

    (b) the estimate of the market value of any asset comprised in a gift or inheritance and included in that return, when expressed as a percentage of the ascertained value of that asset, is within any of the percentages specified in column (1) of the Table to this section,

    then the amount of tax attributable to the property which is that asset shall be increased by a sum (hereafter in this section referred to as the "surcharge") equal to the corresponding percentage, set out in column (2) of that Table opposite the relevant percentages in the said column (1), of that amount of tax.

(2) Interest shall be payable under the provisions of section 41 of [the Capital Acquisitions Tax Act, 1976,] upon any surcharge as if the surcharge were tax, and the surcharge and any interest thereon shall be chargeable and recoverable as if the surcharge and that interest were part of the tax.

(3) Any person aggrieved by the imposition on him of a surcharge under this section in respect of any asset may, within 30 days of the notification to him of the amount of such surcharge, appeal to the Appeal Commissioners against the imposition of such surcharge on the grounds, and only on the grounds, that, having regard to all the circumstances, there were sufficient grounds on which he might reasonably have based his estimate of the market value of the asset.

(4) The Appeal Commissioners shall hear and determine an appeal to them under subsection (3) as if it were an appeal to them against an assessment to tax, and the provisions of section 52 of [the Capital Acquisitions Tax Act, 1976,] relating to an appeal or to the rehearing of an appeal or to the statement of a case for the opinion of the High Court on a point of law shall, with any necessary modifications, apply accordingly.

(5) In this section "ascertained value" means the market value subject to the right of appeal under section 51 or section 52 of [the Capital Acquisitions Tax Act, 1976].

TABLE

Estimate of the market value of the asset in the return, expressed as a percentage of the ascertained value of that asset (1)	Surcharge (2)
Equal to or greater than 0 per cent. but less than 40 per cent.	30 per cent.
Equal to or greater than 40 per cent. but less than 50 per cent.	20 per cent.
Equal to or greater than 50 per cent. but less than 67 per cent.	10 per cent.

CHAPTER III
Miscellaneous

Section 81

Extension of section 35 (accountable persons) of [the Capital Acquisitions Tax Act, 1976].

81. (1) In the case of an inheritance taken on or before the date of death of the disponer, the disponer shall also be a person accountable for the payment of any amount of the tax for which the persons referred to in section 35 (1) of [the Capital Acquisitions Tax Act, 1976,] are made primarily accountable, and, subject to subsection (2), [the Capital Acquisitions Tax Act, 1976,] shall have effect as if such disponer were a person referred to in section 35 (2) (b) of that Act:

Provided that the disponer as such shall not be so accountable in the case where the date of the disposition was prior to the 1st day of May, 1989.

(2) The provisions of subsections (3) and (9) of section 35 of [the Capital Acquisitions Tax Act, 1976,] shall not apply to a disponer who is accountable for the payment of tax under subsection (1).

Section 85

Exemption of specified collective investment undertakings.

85. [(1) In this section—

"investment undertaking" has the meaning assigned to it by section 739B of the Taxes Consolidation Act, 1997;

"specified collective investment undertaking" has the meaning assigned to it by section 734 of the Taxes Consolidation Act, 1997;

"unit", in relation to an investment undertaking, has the meaning assigned to it by section 739B of the Taxes Consolidation Act, 1997;

"unit", in relation to a specified collective investment undertaking, has the meaning assigned to it by section 734 of the Taxes Consolidation Act, 1997.

(2) Where any unit of an investment undertaking or of a specified collective investment undertaking is comprised in a gift or an inheritance, then such unit—

(a) shall be exempt from tax, and

(b) shall not be taken into account in computing tax on any gift or inheritance taken by the donee or successor,

if, but only if, it is shown to the satisfaction of the Commissioners that—

(i) the unit is comprised in the gift or inheritance—

(I)   at the date of the gift or at the date of the inheritance, and

(II) at the valuation date,

(ii) at the date of the disposition, the disponer is neither domiciled nor ordinarily resident in the State, and

(iii)[1] at the date of the gift or at the date of the inheritance, the donee or successor is neither domiciled nor ordinarily resident in the State.][2]

(3)   This section shall have effect as respects gifts and inheritances taken on or after the date of the passing of this Act.

Footnotes

1   S.85(2)(iii) does not apply to probate tax – see s.119, FA 1993.

2   As substituted by s.224(1), FA 2001. As to the treatment and coming into effect of this substitution, see s.224, FA 2001, at page 1049.

PART VI
Anti-Avoidance

Section 90

Arrangements reducing value of company shares.

90.   (1)   In this section—

"arrangement" includes—

(a)   any act or omission by a person or by the trustees of a disposition;

(b)   any act or omission by any person having an interest in shares in a company;

(c)   the passing by any company of a resolution; or

(d)   any combination of acts, omissions or resolutions referred to in paragraphs (a), (b) and (c);

"company" means a private company within the meaning assigned by section 16(2) of [the Capital Acquisitions Tax Act, 1976];

"company controlled by a donee or successor" has the same meaning as is assigned to "company controlled by the donee or the successor" by section 16 of [the Capital Acquisitions Tax Act, 1976];

"event" includes—

(a)   a death; and

(b)   the expiration of a specified period;

"the Principal Act" means the Capital Acquisitions Tax Act, 1976;

"related shares" means the shares in a company, the market value of which shares is increased by any arrangement;

"related trust" has the meaning assigned to it by subsections (2) and (4);

"specified amount"[1] means an amount equal to the difference between—

(a) the market value of shares in a company immediately before an arrangement is made, and ascertained under the provisions of section 16. . . . . . .[2] of [the Capital Acquisitions Tax Act, 1976,] as if each share were a share in a company controlled by a donee or successor; and

(b) the market value of those shares, or of property representing those shares, immediately after the arrangement is made, and ascertained under the provisions of section 15 of [the Capital Acquisitions Tax Act, 1976],

and such specified amount shall be deemed to be situate where the company is incorporated.

(2) Where—

(a) a person has an absolute interest in possession in shares in a company;

and

(b) any arrangement results in the market value of those shares, or of property representing those shares, immediately after that arrangement is made, being less than it would be but for that arrangement,

then, tax shall be payable in all respects as if a specified amount which relates to that arrangement were a benefit taken, immediately after that arrangement is made, from that person, as disponer, by—

(i) the beneficial owners of the related shares in that company; and

(ii) so far as the related shares in that company are held in trust (in this section referred to as the "related trust") and have no ascertainable beneficial owners, by the disponer in relation to that related trust as if, immediately after that arrangement is made, that disponer was the absolute beneficial owner of those related shares,

in the same proportions as the market value of the related shares, which are beneficially owned by them or are deemed to be so beneficially owned, is increased by that arrangement.

(3) Where—

(a) an interest in property is limited by the disposition creating it to cease on an event;

(b) immediately before the making of an arrangement to which paragraph (c) relates, the property includes shares in a company; and

(c) the arrangement results in the market value of those shares, or of property representing those shares, immediately after that arrangement is made, being less than it would be but for that arrangement,

then, tax shall be payable under that disposition in all respects –

(i) where the interest in property is an interest in possession, as if such property included a specified amount which relates to that arrangement;

(ii) where the interest in property is not an interest in possession, as if it were an interest in possession and such property included a specified amount which relates to that arrangement; and

(iii) as if the event on which the interest was limited to cease under that disposition had happened, to the extent of the specified amount, immediately before that arrangement is made.

(4) Where –

(a) shares in a company are, immediately before the making of an arrangement to which paragraph (b) relates, subject to a discretionary trust under or in consequence of any disposition; and

(b) the arrangement results in those shares, or property representing those shares, remaining subject to that discretionary trust but, immediately after that arrangement is made, the market value of those shares, or of property representing those shares, is less than it would be but for that arrangement,

then, tax shall be payable under that disposition in all respects as if a specified amount, which relates to that arrangement, were a benefit taken immediately after that arrangement is made –

(i) by the beneficial owners of the related shares in that company; and

(ii) so far as the related shares in that company are held in trust (in this section referred to as the "related trust") and have no ascertainable beneficial owners, by the disponer in relation to that related trust as if, immediately after that arrangement is made, that disponer was the absolute beneficial owner of those related shares,

in the same proportions as the market value of the related shares, which are beneficially owned by them or are deemed to be so beneficially owned, is increased by that arrangement.

(5) The provisions of subsections (2), (3) and (4) shall not prejudice any charge for tax in respect of any gift or inheritance taken under any

disposition on or after the making of an arrangement referred to in those subsections and comprising shares in a company, or property representing such shares.

(6) Where shares in a company, which are held in trust under a disposition made by any disponer, are related shares by reason of any arrangement referred to in this section, any gift or inheritance taken under the disposition on or after the arrangement is made and comprising those related shares, or property representing those related shares, shall be deemed to be taken from that disponer.

(7) In relation to the tax due and payable in respect of any gift or inheritance taken under the provisions of paragraph (ii) of subsection (2) or paragraph (ii) of subsection (4), and notwithstanding the provisions of [the Capital Acquisitions Tax Act, 1976,]—

    (a) the disponer in relation to the related trust shall not be a person primarily accountable for the payment of such tax; and

    (b) a person who is a trustee of the related trust concerned for the time being at the date of the gift or at the date of the inheritance, or at any date subsequent thereto, shall be so primarily accountable.

(8) A person who is accountable for the payment of tax in respect of any specified amount, or part of a specified amount, taken as a gift or an inheritance under this section shall, for the purpose of paying the tax, or raising the amount of the tax when already paid, have power, whether the related shares are or are not vested in him, to raise the amount of such tax and any interest and expenses properly paid or incurred by him in respect thereof, by the sale or mortgage of, or a terminable charge on, the related shares in the relevant company.

(9) Tax due and payable in respect of a taxable gift or a taxable inheritance taken under this section shall be and remain a charge on the related shares in the relevant company.

(10) Where related shares are subject to a discretionary trust immediately after an arrangement is made in accordance with the provisions of this section, the amount by which the market value of such shares is increased by such arrangement shall be property for the purposes of a charge for tax arising by reason of the provisions of section 106 of the Finance Act, 1984.

(11) This section shall apply only as respects a gift or an inheritance taken as a result of an arrangement which is made on or after the 25th day of January, 1989.

[(12) Where, immediately after and as a result of an arrangement, shares in a company have been redeemed, the redeemed shares shall, for the purpose of the references to property representing shares in subsection (1) and subsection (2), (3) or (4), except a reference in relation to which the redeemed shares are actually represented by property, be deemed, immediately after the arrangement, to be represented by property, and the market value of the property so deemed to represent the redeemed shares shall be deemed to be nil.]³

Footnotes

1   The definition of "specified amount" is construed by s.127, FA 1993, where the time referred to in paragraph (a) of that definition is on or after 6th May, 1993.

2   S126(1)(a), FA 1993, deleted "or 17" where the time referred to in paragraph (a) of the definition of "specified amount" is on or after 24th February, 1993.

3   As inserted by s.126(1)(b), FA 1993, where the arrangement referred to in s.90(12) above is made on or after 6th May, 1993.

FINANCE ACT, 1990

Number 10 of 1990
(Enacted on 30th May, 1990)

PART VI

Capital Acquisitions Tax

Section 127

Exemption for spouses (gifts).

127. (1) Notwithstanding the provisions of [the Capital Acquisitions Tax Act, 1976], a gift taken by a donee, who is at the date of the gift the spouse of the disponer, shall be exempt from tax and shall not be taken into account in computing tax.

(2) This section shall have effect in relation to a gift taken on or after the 31st day of January, 1990.

Commentary

A   This exemption does not apply to a common-law spouse, who is treated as a stranger to the disponer. However, according to Part 19.9 of the *Revenue CAT Manual*, the hardship provisions of s.44, CATA, may apply where the financial position of surviving common-law spouses and their children is particularly difficult.

Section 128

Amendment of Second Schedule to [the Capital Acquisitions Tax Act, 1976].
128. . . . .[1]

Footnote

1   The original s.128(1), FA 1990, in respect of gifts and inheritances taken on or after 1st January, 1990, and prior to 11th April, 1994, effectively indexed, in accordance with "the consumer price index number", the "threshold amount" in para. 1 of Part I of the Second Schedule to the CATA (inserted by s.111, FA 1984, in relation to gifts and inheritances taken on or after 26th March, 1984, and before 1st December, 1999).

S.145, FA 1994, in respect of gifts and inheritances taken on or after 11th April, 1994, and prior to 1st December, 1999, effectively substituted indexation of the "class threshold" (for indexation of the "threshold amount") contained in that para. 1 of Part I of the Second Schedule to the CATA.

In relation to gifts and inheritances taken on or after 1st December, 1999, indexation provisions are currently contained in the definition of "threshold amount" in para. 1 of Part I of the Second Schedule to the CATA (inserted by s.145(1), FA 2000). Accordingly, s.128, FA 1990 (as so amended) is no longer relevant and is repealed by s.153(a), FA 2000, in respect of gifts and inheritances taken on or after 1st December, 1999.

FINANCE ACT, 1991

Number 13 of 1991
(Enacted on 29th May, 1991)

PART VI

Capital Acquisitions Tax and Death Duties

Section 116

Inheritances taken by parents.

116. . . . .[1]

Footnote

1   This section applied the "class threshold of £150,000" to a taxable inheritance taken absolutely on or after 2nd June, 1982, and prior to 1st December, 1999, by a parent of the disponer on the death of the disponer. "Class threshold of £150,000" means the class threshold of £150,000 in the definition of "class threshold" contained in para. 1 (inserted by s.111, FA 1984) of the Second Schedule to the CATA.

This section is now repealed by s.153(1), FA 2000, in relation to inheritances taken on or after 1st December, 1999, since a similar provision, in relation to inheritances taken on or after that date, is now included in the definition of "group threshold" contained in para. 1(a)(ii) of Part I of the Second Schedule to the CATA (inserted by s.145(1), FA 2000).

Section 117

Reduction in estimated market value of certain dwellings.

117. . . . .[1]

Footnote

1   Originally, s.117, FA 1991, which applied to inheritances taken on or after 30th January, 1991, gave relief from inheritance tax to certain brothers and sisters of the disponer by reducing the market value of a house by 50%, or £50,000, whichever is the lesser.

S.144, FA 1994, in relation to inheritances taken on or after 11th April, 1994, increased the reduction to 60%, or £60,000, whichever is the lesser, in relation to brothers and sisters.

S.138, FA 1997, in relation to inheritances taken on or after 10th May, 1997, increased the reduction to 60%, or £80,000, whichever is the lesser, for certain brothers and sisters.

S.126, FA 1998, in relation to inheritances taken on or after 3rd December, 1997, and prior to 1st December, 1999, increased the reduction to 80%, or £150,000, whichever is the lesser, and extended the potential beneficiaries to include certain grandparents, grandchildren, nephews and nieces.

S.117, FA 1991, has now been repealed by s.153(1) FA 2000, in relation to gifts and inheritances taken on or after 1st December, 1999. It has been replaced by s.59C, CATA (inserted by s.151, FA 2000) which gives an exemption from gift tax and inheritance tax for certain dwellings, irrespective of the relationship of the donee/successor, and applies to gifts and inheritances taken on or after 1st December, 1999.

Section 127

Construction of certain references in section 16 of [the Capital Acquisitions Tax Act, 1976,] for purposes of "specified amount" in section 90 of Finance Act, 1989.

127. (1) For the purpose of paragraph (a) of the definition of "specified amount" in subsection (1) of section 90 of the Finance Act, 1989, section 16 of [the Capital Acquisitions Tax Act, 1976,] shall have effect as if —

(a)   the references therein to the donee or successor were references to the person who, for the purposes of section 90 of the Finance Act, 1989, is the disponer of the specified amount,

(b)   the references therein to the time at which a company is controlled were references to the time referred to in the said paragraph, and

(c)   the shares referred to in the said paragraph were, at the time referred to therein, the absolute property of the aforesaid disponer.

(2) This section shall apply where the time referred to in paragraph (a) of the definition of "specified amount" in subsection (1) of section 90 of the Finance Act, 1989, is on or after the 6th day of May, 1993.

Section 133

Exemption of certain policies of assurance.

133. [(1) In this section —

"assurance company" has the meaning assigned to it by section 706 of the Taxes Consolidation Act, 1997;

"new policy" means a contract entered into by an assurance company which is a policy of assurance on the life of any person issued on or after 1 January 2001;

"old policy" means a contract entered into by an assurance company in the course of carrying on a foreign life assurance business within the meaning of section 451 of the Taxes Consolidation Act, 1997, and issued on or after 1 December 1992 and before 1 January 2001.][1]

(2) Where any interest in a [new policy or in an old policy][2] is comprised in a gift or an inheritance, then any such interest —

(a)   shall be exempt from tax, and

(b)   shall not be taken into account in computing tax on any gift or inheritance taken by a donee or successor, if, but only if, it is shown to the satisfaction of the Commissioners that—

(i) such interest is comprised in the gift or inheritance at the date of the gift or at the date of the inheritance;

[(ii) at the date of the disposition, the disponer is neither domiciled nor ordinarily resident in the State;][3]

(iii) at the date of the gift or at the date of the inheritance, the donee or successor is neither domiciled nor ordinarily resident in the State.[4]

[(3) Where—

(a) an interest in a new policy or in an old policy, as the case may be, which is comprised in a gift or inheritance came into the beneficial ownership of the disponer or became subject to the disposition prior to 15 February 2001, and

(b) the conditions at subparagraphs (i) and (iii) of subsection (2) are complied with,

then that subsection shall apply to that interest in a new policy or in an old policy, as the case may be, if, at the date of the disposition, the proper law of the disposition was not the law of the State.][5]

Footnotes

1   As substituted by s.122(a), FA 2002, which was enacted on 25th March, 2002.

     The original s.133(1) referred to "s.36 FA 1988", but this reference was amended to "s.451, TCA", by s.1100, TCA, with effect from 6th April, 1997.

2   Substituted for "policy" by s.122(b) FA 2002, which was enacted on 25th March, 2002.

3   As substituted by s.226(1), FA2001, which has effect in relation to a policy comprised in a gift/inheritance where the date of the gift/inheritance is on or after 15th February, 2001, and the policy (a) comes into the beneficial ownership of the disponer on or after that date, or (b) become subject to the disposition on or after that date without having been previously in the beneficial ownership of the disponer.

4   S.133(2)(iii) does not apply to probate tax – see s.119, FA 1993.

5   As substituted by s.122(c), FA 2002, which was enacted on 25th March, 2002.

FINANCE ACT, 1994

Number 13 of 1994
(Enacted on 23rd May, 1994)

PART VI

Capital Acquisitions Tax

CHAPTER II

Miscellaneous

Section 146

Certificate relating to registration of title based on possession.

146. (1) After the passing of this Act a person shall not be registered as owner of property in a register of ownership maintained under the Act of 1964 on foot of an application made to the Registrar on or after the 11th day of April, 1994, which is —

(a) based on possession, and

(b) made under the Rules of 1972, or any other rule made for carrying into effect the objects of the Act of 1964,

unless the applicant produces to the Registrar a certificate issued by the Commissioners to the effect that the Commissioners are satisfied —

(i) that the property did not become charged with gift tax or inheritance tax during the relevant period, or

(ii) that any charge for gift tax or inheritance tax to which the property became subject during that period has been discharged, or will (to the extent that it has not been discharged) be discharged within a time considered by the Commissioners to be reasonable.

(2) In the case of an application for registration in relation to which a solicitor's certificate is produced for the purpose of rule 19 (3), 19 (4) or 35 of the Rules of 1972, the Registrar may accept that the application is not based on possession if the solicitor makes to the Registrar a declaration in writing to that effect.

(3) Where, on application to them by the applicant for registration, the Commissioners are satisfied that they may issue a certificate for the purpose of subsection (1), they shall issue a certificate for that purpose, and the certificate and the application therefor shall be on a form provided by the Commissioners.

(4) A certificate issued by the Commissioners for the purpose of subsection (1) shall be in such terms and subject to such

qualifications as the Commissioners think fit, and shall not be a certificate for any other purpose.

[(4A) In subsection (1), the reference to a certificate issued by the Commissioners shall be construed as including a reference to a certificate to which subsection (4B) relates, and the provisions of subsection (1) shall be construed accordingly.

(4B) (a) A certificate to which this subsection relates is a certificate by the solicitor for the applicant for registration in which it is certified, on a form provided by the Commissioners, that the solicitor –

    (i) is satisfied –

      (I) in a case where the applicant is a statutory authority within the definition of "statutory authority" contained in section 3(1) of the Act of 1964, that the market value of the relevant property at the time of the application does not exceed [€127,000]¹, or

      (II) in any other case, that –

        (A) the area of the relevant property does not exceed five hectares, and

        (B) the market value of the relevant property at the time of the application does not exceed [€19,050]²,

    and

    (ii) having investigated the title to the relevant property, has no reason to believe that the relevant particulars, in so far as relating to the relevant property at any time during the relevant period, are particulars which related at that time to significant other real property, that is to say, real property which, if combined with the relevant property for the purposes of subparagraph (i), would cause a limit which applies to the relevant property by virtue of that subparagraph to be exceeded.

(b) In this subsection –

"the relevant particulars" means the particulars of title to the relevant property which are required to be produced to the Registrar for the purposes of paragraph 2 of Form 5 of the Schedule of Forms referred to in the definition of "Forms" contained in rule 2 (1) of the Rules of 1972;

"the relevant property" means the property in respect of which the application for registration is being made.

(4C) Notwithstanding the provisions of subsection (4B), a certificate by the solicitor for the applicant for registration shall be a certificate to which subsection (4B) relates if it certifies, on a form provided by the Commissioners, that the solicitor is satisfied that –

(a) the area of the property in respect of which the application for registration is being made does not exceed 500 square metres,

(b) the market value of the said property at the time of the application does not exceed [€2,540]³, and

(c) the application is not part of a series of related applications covering a single piece of property the total area of which exceeds 500 square metres or the market value of which at the time of the application exceeds [€2,540]³.]⁴

(5) In this section —

"the Act of 1964" means the Registration of Title Act, 1964;

"the Registrar" means the Registrar of Titles;

"relevant period", in relation to a person's application to be registered as owner of property, means the period commencing on the 28th day of February, 1974, and ending on the date as of which the registration was made:

Provided that —

(a) where the certificate referred to in subsection (1) is a certificate for a period ending prior to the date of the registration, the period covered by the certificate shall be deemed to be the relevant period if, at the time of the registration, the Registrar had no reason to believe that a death relevant to the application for registration occurred after the expiration of the period covered by the certificate, and

(b) where the registration of the person (if any) who, at the date of that application, was the registered owner of the property had been made as of a date after the 28th day of February, 1974, the relevant period shall commence on the date as of which that registration was made;

"the Rules of 1972" means the Land Registration Rules, 1972 (S.I. No. 230 of 1972).

Footnotes

1 S.240(2)(g) and Part 5 of the Fifth Sch., FA 2001, substituted "€127,000" for "£100,000" as respects applications for registration made on or after 1st January, 2002.

2 S.240(2)(g) and Part 5 of the Fifth Sch, FA 2001, substituted "€19,050" for "£15,000" as respects applications for registration made on or after 1st January, 2002.

3 S.240(2)(g) and Part 5 of the Fifth Sch, FA 2001, substituted "€2,540" for "£2,000" as respects applications for registration made on or after 1st January, 2002.

4 As inserted by s.128, FA1996, with effect from 15th May, 1996.

Section 147

Provision relating to section 5 (gift deemed to be taken) of [the Capital Acquisitions Tax Act, 1976,] and section 121 of Finance Act, 1993.

147. Without prejudice to the meaning of section 5 of [the Capital Acquisitions Tax Act, 1976,] as enacted, that section shall have effect and be deemed always to have had effect as if the provisions of section 121 of the Finance Act, 1993, had not been enacted, except where the consideration referred to in the said section 5, being consideration in relation to a disposition, could not reasonably be regarded (taking into account the disposer's position prior to the disposition) as representing full consideration to the disposer for having made such a disposition.

Section 148

Provision relating to section 11 (inheritance deemed to be taken) of [the Capital Acquisitions Tax Act, 1976,] and section 123 of Finance Act, 1993.

148. Without prejudice to the meaning of section 11 of [the Capital Acquisitions Tax Act, 1976,] as enacted, that section shall have effect and be deemed always to have had effect as if the provisions of section 123 of the Finance Act, 1993, had not been enacted, except where the consideration referred to in the said section 11, being consideration in relation to a disposition, could not reasonably be regarded (taking into account the disposer's position prior to the disposition) as representing full consideration to the disposer for having made such a disposition.

FINANCE ACT, 1995

Number 8 of 1995
(Enacted on 2nd June, 1995)

PART VI
Capital Acquisitions Tax

Section 164

Payment of tax on certain assets by instalments.

164. (1)   In this section—

"agricultural property" has the meaning assigned to it by section 19 of [the Capital Acquisitions Tax Act, 1976] (as amended by the Finance Act, 1994);

"relevant business property" has the same meaning as it has in section 127 of the Finance Act, 1994, other than shares in or securities of a company (being shares or securities quoted on a recognised stock exchange) and without regard to sections 128 and 134 (3) of that Act.

(2)   Where the whole or part of the tax which is due and payable in respect of a taxable gift or taxable inheritance is attributable to either or both agricultural property and relevant business property—

[(a)   section 43 of [the Capital Acquisitions Tax Act, 1976,] shall apply to that whole or part of the tax notwithstanding subsection (3) or (4) of that section:

Provided that where all or any part of that agricultural property or relevant business property, or any property which directly or indirectly replaces such property, is sold or compulsorily acquired and, by virtue of subsection (5) of section 19 of [the Capital Acquisitions Tax Act, 1976,] or section 135 of the Finance Act, 1994, that sale or compulsory acquisition causes the taxable value of such a taxable gift or taxable inheritance to be increased, or would cause such increase if subsection (2) of section 19 of [the Capital Acquisitions Tax Act, 1976,] or section 126 of the Finance Act, 1994, applied, all unpaid instalments referable to the property sold or compulsorily acquired shall, unless the interest of the donee or successor is a limited interest, be paid on completion of that sale or compulsory acquisition and, if not so paid, shall be tax in arrear, and][1]

(b)   notwithstanding subsection (2) of section 41 of [the Capital Acquisitions Tax Act, 1976,] the rate at which interest is payable upon that whole or part of the tax shall be 0.75 per cent., or such other rate (if any) as stands prescribed by the Minister for Finance by regulations, for each month or part of a month instead of at the rate specified in that section and that section shall have effect as regards that whole or part of the tax as if the rate so payable were substituted for the rate specified in that section:

Provided that the rate at which interest is payable upon any overdue instalment of that whole or part of the tax, or upon such part of the tax as would represent any such overdue instalment if that whole or part of the tax were being paid by instalments, shall continue to be at the rate specified in section 41 of [the Capital Acquisitions Tax Act, 1976,].

[(2A) For the purposes of this section reference to an overdue instalment in the proviso to paragraph (b) of subsection (2) is a reference to an instalment which is overdue for the purposes of section 43 (as it applies to this section) of [the Capital Acquisitions Tax Act, 1976,] or for the purposes of the proviso to paragraph (a) of the said subsection (2).][2]

(3) For the purposes of this section the value of a business or of an interest in a business shall be taken to be its net value ascertained in accordance with section 132 of the Finance Act, 1994.

(4) This section shall have effect in relation to gifts and inheritances taken on or after the 8th day of February, 1995, but shall not have effect in relation to an inheritance taken by a relevant trust by virtue of section 110 (1) of the Finance Act, 1993, or to an inheritance taken by a discretionary trust by virtue of section 106 (1) of the Finance Act, 1984, or section 103 (1) of the Finance Act, 1986.

(5) Every regulation made under this section shall be laid before Dáil Éireann as soon as may be after it is made and, if a resolution annulling the regulation is passed by Dáil Éireann within the next twenty-one days on which Dáil Éireann has sat after the regulation is laid before it, the regulation shall be annulled accordingly, but without prejudice to the validity of anything previously done thereunder.

Footnotes

1   As substituted by s.129(1)(a), FA 1996, retrospectively in relation to gifts or inheritances taken on or after 8th February, 1995.

2.   As inserted by s.129(1)(b), FA 1996, retrospectively in relation to gifts or inheritances taken on or after 8th February, 1995.

Section 165

Exemption of certain inheritances taken by parents.

165. Notwithstanding the provisions of [the Capital Acquisitions Tax Act, 1976], an inheritance taken on or after the 12th day of April, 1995, by a person from a disponer shall, where—

(a) that person is a parent of that disponer, and

(b) the date of the inheritance is the date of death of that disponer,

be exempt from tax and shall not be taken into account in computing tax if and only if that disponer took a non-exempt gift or inheritance from either or both of that disponer's parents within the period of 5 years immediately prior to the date of death of that disponer.

Section 166

Heritage property of companies.

166. (1) In this section—

"relevant heritage property" means any one or more of the following—

(a) objects to which section 55 of [the Capital Acquisitions Tax Act, 1976,] applies;

(b) a house or garden referred to in section 39 of the Finance Act, 1978;

"private company" has the meaning assigned to it by section 16 of [the Capital Acquisitions Tax Act, 1976];

"subsidiary" has the meaning assigned to it by section 155 of the Companies Act, 1963.

(2) Where a gift or inheritance consists in whole or in part—

(a) at the date of the gift or at the date of the inheritance, and

(b) at the valuation date,

of one or more shares in a private company which (after the taking of the gift or inheritance) is, on the date of the gift or on the date of the inheritance, a company controlled by the donee or successor within the meaning of section 16 of [the Capital Acquisitions Act, 1976], then each such share shall, to the extent that its market value for tax purposes is, at the valuation date, attributable to relevant heritage property, be exempt from tax and the value thereof shall to that extent not be taken into account in computing tax on any gift or inheritance taken by that person unless the exemption ceases to apply under the provisions of subsection (5) or (6):

Provided that that relevant heritage property was in the beneficial ownership of the company on the 12th day of April, 1995, or in the beneficial ownership on that date of another company which was on that date a subsidiary of the first-mentioned company.

(3) The provisions of section 19 (6) of [the Capital Acquisitions Tax Act, 1976,] shall apply, for the purposes of subsection (2), as they apply in relation to agricultural property.

(4) Where in relation to a gift or inheritance —

(a) a part of a share in a private company is exempt from tax by virtue of subsection (2), and

(b) such share is relevant business property within the meaning of Chapter I of Part VI of the Finance Act, 1994,

then the relevant heritage property to which the market value of such share is partly attributable shall be left out of account in determining for the purposes of that Chapter what part of the taxable value of that gift or inheritance is attributable to such share, but the amount of the reduction (if any) which would but for subsection (2) fall to be made under that Chapter in respect of such share shall not otherwise be restricted notwithstanding subsection (2).

(5) If a share in a private company which is exempted in whole or in part from tax by virtue of subsection (2) is sold within 6 years after the valuation date, and before the death of the donee or successor, the exemption referred to in subsection (2) shall, subject to subsection (7), cease to apply to such share.

(6) Where the whole or part of the market value of a share in a private company which is comprised in a gift or inheritance is on the valuation date attributable to an item of relevant heritage property and —

(a) that item of relevant heritage property is sold within 6 years after the valuation date, and before the death of the donee or successor, or

(b) at any time after the valuation date and —

(i) before the sale of such share or such item of relevant heritage property,

(ii) before the death of the donee or successor, and

(iii) before such share or such item of relevant heritage property forms part of the property comprised in a subsequent gift or inheritance in respect of which gift or inheritance an absolute interest is taken by a person other than the spouse of that donee or successor

there has been a breach of any condition specified in subsection (1) (b) or (c) of section 55 of [the Capital Acquisitions Tax Act, 1976,] or in section 39 (1) (c) of the Finance Act, 1978,

then the exemption referred to in subsection (2) shall, subject to subsection (7), cease to apply to such share to the extent that that market value is attributable to such item of relevant heritage property.

(7) Notwithstanding subsections (5) and (6), the exemption referred to in subsection (2) shall continue to apply if the sale of the share referred to in subsection (5), or the sale of the item of relevant heritage property referred to in subsection (6), is a sale by private treaty to the National Gallery of Ireland, the National Museum of Science and Art or any other similar national institution, any university in the State or any constituent college thereof, a local authority or the Friends of the National Collections of Ireland.

(8) This section shall have effect in relation to gifts and inheritances taken on or after the 12th day of April, 1995.

Commentary

A   See the Revenue Information Leaflet CAT8 in relation to this section.

B   See an article on the Favourable Treatment of Heritage Objects by Anne Corrigan and Marie Griffin in the *Irish Tax Review* of March 2002, page 179.

FINANCE ACT, 1997

Number 22 of 1997
(Enacted on 10th May, 1997)

PART VI
Capital Acquisitions Tax

Section 142[1]

Exemption of certain transfers from capital acquisitions tax following the dissolution of a marriage.

142. (1) Notwithstanding the provisions of [the Capital Acquisitions Tax Act, 1976], a gift or inheritance (within the meaning, in each case, of that Act) taken by virtue or in consequence of an order to which this subsection applies by a spouse who was a party to the marriage concerned shall be exempt from any capital acquisitions tax under that Act and shall not be taken into account in computing such a tax.

(2) Subsection (1) applies—

(a) to a relief order or an order under section 25 of the Family Law Act, 1995, made following the dissolution of a marriage, or

(b) to a maintenance pending relief order made following the granting of leave under section 23 (3) of the Family Law Act, 1995, to a spouse whose marriage has been dissolved,

(c) to an order referred to in section 41 (a) of the Family Law Act, 1995, or an order under section 42 (1) of that Act made in addition to or instead of an order under section 41 (a) of that Act, in favour of a spouse whose marriage has been dissolved,[
. . . .][2]

(d) to an order under Part III of the Family Law (Divorce) Act, [1996, and][2]

[(e) to an order or other determination to like effect, which is analogous to an order referred to in paragraph (a), (b), (c) or (d), of a court under the law of another territory made under or in consequence of the dissolution of a marriage, being a dissolution that is entitled to be recognised as valid in the State.][2]

(3) Section 51 of the Family Law Act, 1995, and section 34 of the Family Law (Divorce) Act, 1996, are hereby repealed.

Footnotes

1   This section has effect from 10th May, 1997. It re-enacts the provisions of s.51, Family Law Act, 1995 (which came into force on 1st August, 1996 – see page 925) and of s.34, Family Law (Divorce) Act, 1996 (which was enacted on 27th November, 1996 – see page 938), both of which sections 51 and 34 are now repealed by this section.

2   Under s.149(1), FA 2000, in relation to an order or other determination to like effect made on or after 10th February, 2000,

    (i)   the word "and" is deleted at the end of subsection (2)(c),

    (ii) the words "1996, and" are substituted for "1996." at the end of subsection 2(d), and

    (iii) subsection 2(e) is inserted.

FINANCE ACT, 2001

Number 7 of 2001
(Enacted on 30th March, 2001)

PART 6
Capital Acquisitions Tax

Section 224

Amendment of section 85 (exemption of specified collective investment undertakings) of Finance Act, 1989.

224. (1)[1] ......

    (2) In relation to any unit of an investment undertaking comprised in a gift or an inheritance, section 85(2)(ii) (inserted by subsection (1)) of the Finance Act, 1989, shall, notwithstanding that the disponer was domiciled or ordinarily resident in the State at the date of the disposition, be treated as satisfied where —

        (a) the proper law of the disposition was not the law of the State at the date of the disposition, and

        (b) the unit came into the beneficial ownership of the disponer or became subject to the disposition prior to 15 February 2001.

    (3) This section shall have effect in relation to units of an investment undertaking comprised in a gift or an inheritance where the date of the gift or the date of the inheritance is on or after 1 April 2000.

    (4) This section shall have effect in relation to units of a specified collective investment undertaking comprised in a gift or an inheritance where the date of the gift or the date of the inheritance is on or after 15 February 2001 and the units —

        (a) come into the beneficial ownership of the disponer on or after 15 February 2001, or

        (b) become subject to the disposition on or after that date without having been previously in the beneficial ownership of the disponer.

Footnote

1   This subsection substituted s.85(1) and (2), FA 1989 – see page 442.

FINANCE ACT 200...

Number 4, 2001

Operation: 30th May, 2001

PART 6

Capital Acquisitions Tax

Section 2.4

Amend section 88 (exemption of specified collective investments) of the Taxation of Finance Act, 1990.

(1)

(2) In relation to any gift of an investment under China companies... in a gift or an inheritance Section 871(b), inserted by subsection (1) of the Finance Act, 1999, shall notwithstanding that the disponer is domiciled or ordinarily resident in the State at the date of the disposition, be treated as situate where—

(a) the property or the disposition was not that by of the State at the date of the disposition, and

(b) the remittance into the residence ownership risk from the disponer or becomes subject to the disposition on each 18 February 2001.

(7) This section shall have effect in relation to units that an investment undertaking company, unit or an inheritance where the date of the gift or the date of the inheritance is on or after 18 April 2000.

(8) This section ... shall have effect in relation to units of a specified collective investment undertaking company or a gift or an inheritance where the date of the gift or the date of the inheritance is on or after 18 February 2001 and before...

(a) come into the beneficial ownership of the disponer on or before 18 February 2001, or

(b) become subject to the disposition prior to that date without having been previously in the beneficial ownership of the disponer.

Footnote

The subsection amended 88(1) and 2001 Finance Act Page 172.

466

SECOND PART

(II) ONCE-OFF DISCRETIONARY TRUST TAX

For Contents of this Part, see page li

FINANCE ACT, 1984

Number 9 of 1984
(Enacted on 23rd May, 1984)

PART V
Capital Acquisitions Tax

CHAPTER I
Discretionary Trusts

Section 104

Interpretation (Part V).
104. In this Part—

"the Principal Act" means the Capital Acquisitions Tax Act, 1976;

"object", in relation to a discretionary trust, means a person for whose benefit the income or capital, or any part of the income or capital, of the trust property is applied, or may be applied;

"principal objects", in relation to a discretionary trust, means such objects, if any, of the trust for the time being as are—

(a)   the spouse of the disponer,

(b)   the children of the disponer, or

(c)   the children of a child of the disponer where such child predeceased the disponer.

Commentary

A   See an article on discretionary trust tax by Eamon O'Connor in the *Irish Tax Review* of November 1997, page 561.

Section 105

Amendment of section 2 (interpretation) of [the Capital Acquisitions Tax Act, 1976].
105. Section 2 (1) of [the Capital Acquisitions Tax Act, 1976,] is hereby amended by the insertion, in the definition of "discretionary trust" after "property is held on trust" of—

"to accumulate the income or part of the income of the property, or any trust whereby, or by virtue or in consequence of which, property (other than property to which for the time being a person is beneficially entitled for an interest in possession) is held on trust", and the said definition, as so amended, is set out in the Table to this section.

TABLE

"discretionary trust" means any trust whereby, or by virtue or in consequence of which, property is held on trust to accumulate the income or part of the income of the property, or any trust whereby, or by virtue or in consequence of which, property (other than property to which for the time being a person is beneficially entitled for an interest in possession) is held on trust to apply, or with a power to apply, the income or capital or part of the income or capital of the property for the benefit of any person or persons or of any one or more of a number or of a class of persons whether at the discretion of trustees or any other person and notwithstanding that there may be a power to accumulate all or any part of the income;

Section 106

Acquisitions by discretionary trusts.

106. (1) Where, on or after the 25th day of January, 1984, under or in consequence of any disposition, property becomes subject to a discretionary trust (which expression has in this Part the meaning assigned to it by [the Capital Acquisitions Act, 1976,] as amended by section 105) . . . .,[1] the trust shall be deemed, on —

(a) the date on which that property becomes or became subject to the discretionary trust;

(b) the date of death of the disponer; or

(c) where there are principal objects of the trust, the date on which there ceases to be a principal object of the trust who is under the age of [21][2] years,

whichever date is the latest, to become or to have become beneficially entitled in possession to an absolute interest in so much, if any, of that property or of property representing that property and of accumulations of income thereof or of property representing those accumulations as remains subject to the discretionary trust on that latest date, and to take or to have taken an inheritance accordingly as if the trust, and the trustees as such for the time being of the trust, were together a person for the purposes of [the Capital Acquisitions Tax Act, 1976], and that latest date shall be the date of the inheritance.

(2) Property which, under or in consequence of any disposition, was subject to a discretionary trust on the 25th day of January, 1984, shall, for the purposes of subsection (1), be deemed to have become subject to the trust on that date.

[(2A) Property which, under or in consequence of any disposition, is subject to a discretionary trust on the 31st day of January, 1993, shall, for the purposes of subsection (1), be deemed to become subject to the trust on that date.]³

(3) For the purposes of this section –

(a) an interest in expectancy shall not be property until an event happens whereby the interest ceases to be an interest in expectancy or is represented by property which is not an interest in expectancy;

(b) an interest in a policy of assurance upon human life shall not be property until, and then only to the extent that, the interest becomes an interest in possession under the provisions of section 32 of [the Capital Acquisitions Tax Act, 1976,] or is represented by property which is not an interest in expectancy.

(4) Where, apart from this subsection, property or property representing such property would be chargeable under this section with tax more than once under the same disposition, such property shall be so chargeable with tax once only, that is to say, on the earliest occasion on which such property becomes so chargeable with tax.

Footnotes

1   Words "otherwise than for full consideration in money or money's worth paid by the trustee of the trust" were deleted by s.64, FA 1985, with retrospective effect.

2   "21" substituted for "25" by s.224(1)(a), FA 1992, in relation to property becoming subject to a discretionary trust on or after 31st January, 1993.

3   As inserted by s.224(1)(b), FA 1992.

Commentary

A   See an Irish High Court case, *Revenue Commissioners v Executors and Trustees of the will of Jeannie Hammett Irvine, deceased* [2005] No. 172 R which decided that the bequest of the residue of an estate to a discretionary trust does not become subject to the trust until the residue is ascertained. This case is discussed by Paraic Madigan at page 70 of the *Irish Tax Review* of September 2007.

Cross-Reference

1   See s.90(10), FA 1989, which extends to "related shares" the charge for tax arising under s.106.

Section 107

Application of [the Capital Acquisitions Tax Act, 1976].

107. In relation to a charge for tax arising by reason of the provisions of section 106 –

[(a) a reference in section 16 of [the Capital Acquisitions Tax Act, 1976,] to a company controlled by the successor and the definition in that section of "group of shares" shall be construed as if (for the purpose of that reference) the list of persons contained in subsection (3) of that section and (for the purpose of that definition) the list of persons contained in that definition included the following, that is to say, the trustees of the discretionary trust, the living objects of the discretionary trust, the relatives of those objects, nominees of those trustees or of those objects or of the relatives of those objects, and the trustees of a settlement whose objects include the living objects of the discretionary trust or relatives of those living objects;][1]

(b) section 21 of [the Capital Acquisitions Tax Act, 1976,] shall apply, with the modification that the valuation date of the taxable inheritance shall be—

    (i)   the date of the inheritance, or

    (ii) the valuation date ascertained in accordance with that section,

whichever is the later, and with any other necessary modifications;

(c) a person who is a trustee of the discretionary trust concerned for the time being at the date of the inheritance or at any date subsequent thereto shall be a person primarily accountable for the payment of the tax;

(d) an object of the discretionary trust concerned to whom or for whose benefit any of the property subject to the trust is applied or appointed shall also be accountable for the payment of tax the charge in respect of which has arisen prior to the date of the application or appointment of the property to him or for his benefit, and [the Capital Acquisitions Tax Act, 1976,] shall have effect, in its application to that charge for tax, as if that object of the discretionary trust were a person referred to in section 35 (2) of [the Capital Acquisitions Tax Act, 1976];

(e) . . . .[2]

(f) the provisions of section 41 of [the Capital Acquisitions Tax Act, 1976,] shall have effect, in the application of [the Capital Acquisitions Tax Act, 1976,] to any such charge for tax as aforesaid arising before the date of the passing of this Act, as if the references to the valuation date in subsections (1), (2) and (3) of that section were references to the date of the passing of this Act, or to the valuation date, whichever is the later; and

[(g) sections 35 (1), 40, 45 and 57 of, and the Second Schedule to, [the Capital Acquisitions Tax Act, 1976,] shall not apply.][3]

Footnotes

1   As substituted by s.131, FA 1993, in relation to an inheritance taken on or after 24th February, 1993.

2   Paragraph (e) deleted by s.78(a), FA 1989, with effect from 24th May, 1989.

3   As substituted by s.78(b), FA 1989, with effect from 24th May, 1989.

Section 108

Exemptions.

108. (1) Section 106 shall not apply or have effect in relation to a discretionary trust which is shown to the satisfaction of the Commissioners to have been created exclusively –

   (a) for public or charitable purposes in the State or Northern Ireland;

   (b) for the purposes of –

   (i) any scheme for the provision of superannuation benefits on retirement established by or under any enactment or by or under an instrument made under any enactment, or

   (ii) any sponsored superannuation scheme within the meaning of [subsection (1) of section 783 of the Taxes Consolidation Tax Act, 1997,][1] or a trust scheme or part of a trust scheme approved by the Commissioners under that section or section [785][2] of that Act;[3]

   (c) for the purposes of a registered unit trust scheme within the meaning of the Unit Trusts Act, 1972;

   (d) (i) for the benefit of one or more named individuals, and

   (ii) for the reason that such individual, or all such individuals, is or are, because of age or improvidence, or of physical, mental or legal incapacity, incapable of managing his or their affairs; or

   (e) for the purpose of providing for the upkeep of a house or garden referred to in section 39 of the Finance Act, 1978.

[(2) Section 106 shall not apply or have effect –

   (a) in relation to a discretionary trust in respect of the property subject to or becoming subject to the trust which, on the termination of the trust, is comprised in a gift or an inheritance taken by the State; or

   (b) in respect of an inheritance which, apart from this subsection, would be deemed, by the combined effect of section 31 of [the Capital Acquisitions Tax Act, 1976,] and section 106, to be taken by a discretionary trust.][4]

Footnotes

1   As substituted for "subsection 9 of section 235 of the Income Tax Act, 1967" by s.1100, TCA, with effect from 6th April, 1997.

2   As substituted for "235A" by s.1100, TCA, with effect from 6th April, 1997.

3   S.108(1)(b)(ii) restricted by s.129, FA 1990, in relation to a once-off discretionary trust tax charge, or an annual 1% discretionary trust tax charge, arising on or after 5th April, 1990. See page 475.

4   As inserted with retrospective effect by s.65, FA 1985.

Section 109

Computation of tax.

109. The tax chargeable on the taxable value of a taxable inheritance which is charged to tax by reason of the provisions of section 106 shall be computed at the rate of [six per cent.][1] of such taxable value.

Footnote

1   Substituted for "three per cent." in relation to an inheritance deemed to be taken by a discretionary trust on or after 11th April, 1994, by s.143, FA 1994, which also provides for the restoration of the 6% rate of tax. See page 476.

FINANCE ACT, 1990

Number 10 of 1990
(Enacted on 30th May, 1990)

PART VI
Capital Acquisitions Tax

Section 129

Application of section 108 (exemptions) of Finance Act, 1984.

129. (1) For the purposes of section 108 (b) (ii) of the Finance Act, 1984, a sponsored superannuation scheme within the meaning of [subsection (1) of section 783 of the Taxes Consolidation Act, 1997],[1] shall not include a scheme or arrangement which relates to matters other than service in particular offices or employments.

(2) This section shall have effect in relation to a charge for tax which, apart from section 108 (b) (ii) of the Finance Act, 1984, arises on or after the 5th day of April, 1990, under the provisions of section 106 of the said Act of 1984 or of section 103 of the Finance Act, 1986.

Footnote

1 Substituted for "subsection 9 of section 235 of the Income Tax Act, 1967" by s.1100, TCA, with effect from 6th April, 1997.

FINANCE ACT, 1994

Number 13 of 1994
(Enacted on 23rd May, 1994)

PART VI
Capital Acquisitions Tax

CHAPTER II
Miscellaneous

Section 143

Computation of tax.

143. (1) In this section—

"earlier relevant inheritance" means a relevant inheritance deemed to be taken on the date of death of the disponer;

"later relevant inheritance" means a relevant inheritance which, after the date of death of the disponer, is deemed to be taken by a discretionary trust by virtue of there ceasing to be a principal object of that trust who is under the age of 21 years;

"relevant inheritance" means an inheritance which, by virtue of section 106 (1) of the Finance Act, 1984, is, on or after the 11th day of April, 1994, deemed to be taken by a discretionary trust;

["settled relevant inheritance" means a relevant inheritance taken on the death of a life tenant;][1]

["relevant period" means—

(a) in relation to an earlier relevant inheritance, the period of 5 years commencing on the date of death of the disponer,

(b) in relation to a settled relevant inheritance, the period of 5 years commencing on the date of death of the life tenant concerned, and

(c) in relation to a later relevant inheritance, the period of 5 years commencing on the latest date on which a later relevant inheritance was deemed to be taken from the disponer;][2]

"the appropriate trust", in relation to a relevant inheritance, means the trust by which that inheritance was deemed to be taken.

(2) Section 109 of the Finance Act, 1984, is hereby amended by the substitution of "six per cent." for "three per cent.":

[Provided that where in the case of each and every earlier relevant inheritance, each and every settled relevant inheritance or each and every later relevant inheritance, as the case may be, taken from one and the same disponer, one or more objects of the appropriate trust became beneficially entitled in possession before the expiration of the relevant period to an absolute interest in the entire of the property of which that inheritance consisted on and at all times after the date of that inheritance (other than property which ceased to be subject to the terms of the appropriate trust by virtue of a sale or exchange of an absolute interest in that property for full consideration in money or money's worth), then, in relation to all such earlier relevant inheritances, all such settled relevant inheritances or all such later relevant inheritances, as the case may be, this section shall cease to apply and tax shall be computed accordingly in accordance with the provisions of the said section 109 as if this section had not been enacted.][3]

(3) Where two or more persons are together beneficially entitled in possession to an absolute interest in property, those persons shall not, by reason only that together they are beneficially so entitled in possession, be regarded for the purposes of subsection (2) as beneficially so entitled in possession.

(4) Notwithstanding the provisions of section 46 of [the Capital Acquisitions Tax Act, 1976], interest shall not be payable on any repayment of tax which arises by virtue of the provisions of this section.

Footnotes

1   Definition inserted by s.229(1)(a)(i), FA 2001, as respects relevant inheritances taken on or after 26th January, 2001.

2   Definition substituted by s.229(1)(a)(ii), FA 2001, as respects relevant inheritances taken on or after 26th January, 2001.

3   Proviso substituted by s.229(1)(b), FA 2001, as respects relevant inheritances taken on or after 26th January, 2001.

SECOND PART

(III) ANNUAL DISCRETIONARY TRUST TAX

For Contents of this Part, see page li

FINANCE ACT, 1986

Number 13 of 1986
(Enacted on 27th May, 1986)

PART V

Capital Acquisitions Tax

CHAPTER I
Discretionary Trusts

Section 102

Interpretation (Part V).
102. In this Part —

"the Principal Act" means the Capital Acquisitions Tax Act, 1976;

"chargeable date", in relation to any year, means the 5th day of April in that year;

"chargeable discretionary trust" means a discretionary trust in relation to which —

(a) the disponer is dead, and

(b) none of the principal objects of the trust, if any, is under the age of [21][1] years;

"object" and "principal objects", in relation to a discretionary trust, have the meanings respectively assigned to them by section 104 of the Finance Act, 1984.

Footnote
1   "21" substituted for "25" by s.225(1), FA 1992, in relation to any chargeable date occurring on or after 5th April, 1994.

Commentary
A   See an article on discretionary trust tax by Eamon O'Connor in the *Irish Tax Review* of November 1997, page 561.

Section 103

Annual acquisitions by discretionary trusts.
103. (1) Where, in any year commencing with the year 1986, under or in consequence of any disposition, property is subject to a chargeable discretionary trust on the chargeable date, the trust shall be deemed on each such date to become beneficially entitled in possession to an absolute interest in that property, and to take on each such date an inheritance accordingly as if the trust, and the trustees as such for the time being of the trust, were together a person for the

purposes of [the Capital Acquisitions Tax Act, 1976], and each such chargeable date shall be the date of such inheritance.

(2) (a) Where –

    (i) under or in consequence of any disposition, property was subject to a discretionary trust prior to a chargeable date,

    (ii) that property is not on that chargeable date subject to that discretionary trust (being on that date a chargeable discretionary trust) because such property is on that date property to which for the time being a person is beneficially entitled for an interest in possession, and

    (iii) on that chargeable date that property is property which is limited to become subject again to that chargeable discretionary trust, or will do so by the exercise of a power of revocation,

that property shall be deemed to be subject to that chargeable discretionary trust on that chargeable date if that interest in possession is an interest which is revocable or which is limited to cease on an event other than –

    (I) the death of that person, or

    (II) the expiration of a specified period, where that interest is taken by that person under a power of appointment contained in that disposition and is, at the time of the appointment thereof, an interest for a period certain of five years or more.

(b) In this subsection, "property" includes property representing such property.

(3) For the purposes of this section –

(a) an interest in expectancy shall not be property until an event happens whereby the interest ceases to be an interest in expectancy or is represented by property which is not an interest in expectancy;

(b) an interest in a policy of assurance upon human life shall not be property until, and then only to the extent that, the interest becomes an interest in possession under the provisions of section 32 of [the Capital Acquisitions Tax Act, 1976,] or is represented by property which is not an interest in expectancy.

(4) This section shall not apply or have effect in relation to property which is subject to a chargeable discretionary trust on a chargeable date if that property or property representing that property is subject to a charge for tax arising under or in consequence of the same disposition by reason of the provisions of section 106 of the

Finance Act, 1984, on that same date or within the year prior to that date.

Commentary

A   See an Irish High Court case, *Revenue Commissioners v Executors and Trustees of the will of Jeannie Hammett Irvine, deceased [2005]* No. 172 R which decided that the bequest of the residue of an estate to a discretionary trust does not become subject to the trust until the residue is ascertained. This case is discussed by Paraic Madigan at page 70 of the *Irish Tax Review* of September 2007.

Section 104

Application of [the Capital Acquisitions Tax Act, 1976].

104. In relation to a charge for tax arising by reason of the provisions of section 103-

[(a) a reference in section 16 of [the Capital Acquisitions Act, 1976,] to a company controlled by the successor and the definition in that section of "group of shares" shall be construed as if (for the purpose of that reference) the list of persons contained in subsection (3) of that section and (for the purpose of that definition) the list of persons contained in that definition included the following, that is to say, the trustees of the discretionary trust, the living objects of the discretionary trust, the relatives of those objects, nominees of those trustees or of those objects or of the relatives of those objects, and the trustees of a settlement whose objects include the living objects of the discretionary trust or relatives of those living objects;][1]

(b) (i) subject to the provisions of subparagraph (ii), the valuation date of the taxable inheritance shall be the relevant chargeable date;

     (ii) where—

         (I) a charge for tax arises on a particular date by reason of the provisions of section 106 of the Finance Act, 1984, giving rise to a taxable inheritance (in this subparagraph called the first taxable inheritance),

        (II) on a later date, a charge for tax arises under or in consequence of the same disposition by reason of the provisions of section 103 giving rise to a taxable inheritance (in this subparagraph called the second taxable inheritance) comprising the same property or property representing that property, and

       (III) the valuation date of the first taxable inheritance is a date after the chargeable date of the second taxable inheritance,

the valuation date of the second taxable inheritance shall be the same date as the valuation date of the first taxable inheritance;

(c) a person who is a trustee of the discretionary trust concerned for the time being at the date of the inheritance or at any date subsequent thereto shall be a person primarily accountable for the payment of the tax;

(d) an object of the discretionary trust concerned to whom or for whose benefit any of the property subject to the trust is applied or appointed shall also be accountable for the payment of tax the charge in respect of which has arisen prior to the date of the application or appointment of the property to him or for his benefit, and [the Capital Acquisitions Tax Act, 1976,] shall have effect, in its application to that charge for tax, as if that object of the discretionary trust were a person referred to in section 35 (2) of [the Capital Acquisitions Tax Act, 1976];

(e) any person who is primarily accountable for the payment of tax by virtue of paragraph (c) shall, within three months after the valuation date or the date of passing of this Act, whichever is the later –

  (i) deliver to the Commissioners a full and true return –

    (I) of every inheritance in respect of which he is so primarily accountable;

    (II) of all the property comprised in such inheritance; and

    (III) of an estimate of the market value of such property;

  (ii) notwithstanding the provisions of [the Capital Acquisitions Tax Act, 1976], make an assessment of such amount of tax as, to the best of his knowledge, information and belief, ought to be charged, levied and paid on that valuation date; and

  (iii) pay the amount of such tax to the Accountant-General of the Commissioners;[2]

(f) the provisions of section 41 of [the Capital Acquisitions Tax Act, 1976,] shall have effect, in the application of [the Capital Acquisitions Tax Act, 1976,] to any such charge for tax as aforesaid arising before the date of the passing of this Act, as if the references to the valuation date in subsections (1), (2) and (3) of that section were references to the date of the passing of this Act, or to the valuation date, whichever is the later;

  and

(g) section 21, subsection (1) of section 35, subsections (2), (3), (4) and (5) of section 36 and sections 40, 43, 45 and 57 of, and the Second Schedule to, [the Capital Acquisitions Tax Act, 1976,] shall not apply.

Footnotes

1   As substituted by s.132, FA 1993, in relation to an inheritance taken on or after 24th February, 1993.

2   But see s.129, FA 1991.

Section 105

Exemptions.

105. Section 103 shall not apply or have effect in relation to a discretionary trust referred to in section 108 of the Finance Act, 1984, or in respect of the property or the inheritance referred to in section 65 of the Finance Act, 1985.

Section 106

Computation of tax.

106. The tax chargeable on the taxable value of a taxable inheritance which is charged to tax by reason of the provisions of section 103 shall be computed at the rate of one per cent. of such taxable value.

Section 107

Values agreed.

107. (1) Where—

    (a) under or in consequence of any disposition, a charge for tax arises by reason of the provisions of section 103 on a chargeable date (in this section called the first chargeable date),

    (b) an accountable person has furnished all the information necessary to enable the Commissioners to ascertain the market value of—

        (i) real property, or

        (ii) shares which are not dealt in on a stock exchange,

    comprised in the taxable inheritance so taken on the valuation date of that taxable inheritance,

    (c) pursuant to an application in writing to the Commissioners on that behalf, the market value of such property on that valuation date is agreed on between that person and the Commissioners,

    (d) under or in consequence of the same disposition, a charge for tax arises by reason of the provisions of section 103 on either or both of the two chargeable dates in the years next following the year in which the first chargeable date occurs (in this section called the subsequent chargeable dates), and

    (e) the same property at subparagraph (i) or (ii) of paragraph (b) is comprised in the taxable inheritances so taken on the subsequent chargeable dates,

the value so agreed on shall be treated for the purposes of this Part as the market value of such property on that valuation date and on the valuation dates of the taxable inheritances so taken on the subsequent chargeable dates.

(2) Notwithstanding the provisions of subsection (1), the market value so agreed shall not be binding—

    (a) in any case where there is failure to disclose material facts in relation to any part of the property comprised in the taxable inheritances taken on the first chargeable date or on the subsequent chargeable dates, or

    (b) where, at any time after the first chargeable date and before the third of those chargeable dates—

        (i) in the case of real property, there is any alteration in the tenure under which the property is held or let, or

        (ii) in the case of shares, there is any alteration in the capital or the ownership of the capital of the company concerned or of the rights of the shareholders inter se, or

    (c) where, at any time after the first chargeable date and before the third of those chargeable dates—

        (i) in the case of real property, there is any change whatever, whether affecting that or any other property, which would materially increase or decrease the market value over and above any increase or decrease which might normally be expected if such a change had not occurred, or

        (ii) in the case of shares, there has been any material change in the assets of the company or in their market value over and above any such change which might normally be expected,

and in such cases the market value of the real property, or of the shares, may be ascertained again by the Commissioners for each of the relevant valuation dates:

Provided that, in the case of any change referred to in paragraph (c), the market value may be ascertained again by the Commissioners only at the request of the person primarily accountable for the payment of the tax arising by reason of the provisions of section 103 on that relevant valuation date.

(3) Any agreement made under this section shall be binding only on the persons who as such are accountable for the payment of the tax arising by reason of the provisions of section 103 on the first chargeable date and on the subsequent chargeable dates.

Section 108

Penalty.
108. Any person who contravenes or fails to comply with any requirement under paragraph (e) of section 104 shall be liable to a penalty of—

(a) [€1,265]¹, or

(b) twice the amount of tax payable in respect of the taxable inheritance to which the return relates,

whichever is the lesser.

Footnote

1   s.240(2)(k) and Part 5 of the Fifth Sch., FA 2001, substituted "€1,265" for "£1,000" for any act or omission which takes place on or after 1st January, 2001.

SECOND PART

(IV) TAX PAID WITH INSURANCE POLICIES

For Contents of this Part, see page li

FINANCE ACT, 1985

Number 10 of 1985
(Enacted on 30th May, 1985)

PART V
Capital Acquisitions Tax

Section 60[1]

Relief in respect of certain policies of insurance.

60. (1) In this section –

"qualifying insurance policy" means a policy of insurance –

(a) which is in a form approved by the Commissioners for the purposes of this section;

(b) in respect of which annual premiums are paid by the insured during his life; and

(c) which is expressly effected under this section for the purpose of paying relevant tax;

"relevant tax"[2] means inheritance tax payable in respect of an inheritance (excluding, in computation of such tax, an interest in a qualifying insurance policy) taken under a disposition made by the insured, where the inheritance is taken on or after the date of death of the insured and not later than one year after that death.

[(1A)In this section "insured" means an individual or, in relation to a qualifying insurance policy where –

(a) the insured is an individual and the spouse of that individual at the date the policy is effected;

(b) annual premiums are paid by either or both of them during their joint lives, and by the survivor of them during the life of such survivor; and

(c) the proceeds of the policy are payable on the death of such survivor, or on the simultaneous deaths of both such spouses,

means –

(i) where the proceeds of the policy are so payable on the death of such survivor, that survivor, and the proceeds of the policy shall be deemed to have been provided by such survivor, as disponer; or

(ii) where the proceeds of the policy are so payable on the simultaneous deaths of both such spouses, each of the spouses, and each such spouse shall be deemed to have provided the proceeds of the policy –

(I)   to the extent that such proceeds are applied in paying the relevant tax of the insured who is that spouse, and

(II)   where the proceeds of the policy are not applied in paying relevant tax, to the extent that the proceeds not so applied are comprised in an inheritance taken under a disposition made by that spouse.][3]

(2) (a) An interest in a qualifying insurance policy which is comprised in an inheritance taken under a disposition made by the insured shall, to the extent that the proceeds thereof are applied in paying relevant tax, be exempt from tax in relation to that inheritance and shall not be taken into account in computing tax.

     (b) An interest in a qualifying insurance policy which is comprised in an inheritance taken under a disposition made by the insured shall, to the extent that the proceeds thereof are not applied in paying relevant tax, and notwithstanding the provisions of [the Capital Acquisitions Tax Act, 1976], be deemed to be taken on a day immediately after –

        (i)   the date of death of the insured; or

        (ii) the latest date (if any) on which an inheritance is taken in respect of which that relevant tax is payable,

        whichever is the later.

(3) . . . .[4]

Footnotes

1   S.60 took effect from 30th May, 1985.

2   The definition of "relevant tax" has been extended by –

     (i)   s.130, FA 1990, with effect from 30th May, 1990;

     (ii) s.118, FA 1991, with effect from 29th May, 1991;

     (iii) s.124, FA 1996, in relation to inheritances taken on or after 28th March, 1996.

3   As inserted by s.84, FA 1989, with effect from 24th May, 1989.

4   This subsection, which denied a deduction for income tax purposes in respect of premiums payable on a "qualifying insurance policy", was deleted by s.4, FA 1992, for 1992-93 and later years.

Commentary

A   See the Revenue Statement of Practice (SP-CAT/1/04) which sets out Revenue guidelines in relation to s.60 and s.119 policies.

B   See an article on Section 60 Life Assurance Policies by John Caslin in the *Irish Tax Review* of May 1991, page 406.

C   See articles, on different types of Section 60 policies, by John Crowe in the *Irish Tax Review* of November 1996, page 385, and by Owen Morton in the *Irish Tax Review* of July 1998, page 436.

D   See Part 15 of the *Revenue CAT Manual* in relation to these policies.

FINANCE ACT, 1990

Number 10 of 1990
(Enacted on 30th May, 1990)

PART VI
Capital Acquisitions Tax

Section 130[1]

Application of section 60 (relief in respect of certain policies of insurance) of Finance Act, 1985.

130. For the purposes of section 60 of the Finance Act, 1985, "relevant tax" shall be deemed to include inheritance tax payable in respect of an inheritance taken under a disposition made by the spouse of the insured —

    (a) where the inheritance is taken on the date of death of the insured, or

    (b) where the inheritance is taken only in the event of the insured not surviving the spouse by a period of up to 31 days,

and the relevant qualifying insurance policy is –

    (i) a policy of insurance within the meaning of paragraphs (a), (b) and (c) of subsection (1A) of that section (inserted by section 84 of the Finance Act, 1989), or

    (ii) a policy of insurance where the insured is an individual and the proceeds of the policy are payable only on the contingency of the insured surviving that spouse.

Footnote

1   This section has effect from 30th May, 1990.

FINANCE ACT, 1991

Number 13 of 1991
(Enacted on 29th May, 1991)

PART VI

Capital Acquisitions Tax and Death Duties

Section 118[1]

Application of section 60 (relief in respect of certain policies of insurance) of Finance Act, 1985.

118. For the purposes of section 60 of the Finance Act, 1985, "relevant tax" shall be deemed to include inheritance tax payable in respect of an inheritance taken . . . .[2] on the date of death of the insured.

Footnotes

1   This section came into effect on 29th May, 1991

2   The words "under a disposition made by the spouse of the insured where the inheritance is taken" were deleted by s.124, FA 1996, in relation to inheritances taken on or after 28th March, 1996.

Section 119[1]

Relief in respect of certain policies of insurance relating to tax payable on gifts.

119. (1)   In this section—

"appointed date" means—

(a)   a date occurring not earlier than 8 years after the date on which a relevant insurance policy is effected, or

(b)   a date on which the proceeds of a relevant insurance policy become payable either on the critical illness or the death of the insured, or one of the insured in a case to which paragraph (b) of the definition of "insured" relates, being a date prior to the date to which paragraph (a) of this definition relates;

"insured" means—

(a)   where the insured is an individual, that individual, or

(b)   where the insured is an individual and the spouse of that individual at the date the policy is effected, that individual and the spouse of that individual, jointly or separately, or the survivor of them, as the case may be;

"relevant insurance policy" means a policy of insurance—

(a)   which is in a form approved by the Commissioners for the purposes of this section,

(b)   in respect of which annual premiums are paid by the insured,

(c)   the proceeds of which are payable on the appointed date, and

(d)   which is expressly effected under this section for the purpose of paying relevant tax;

"relevant tax" means gift tax or inheritance tax, payable in connection with an inter vivos disposition made by the insured within one year after the appointed date, excluding gift tax or inheritance tax payable on an appointment out of an inter vivos discretionary trust set up by the insured.

(2)   The proceeds of a relevant insurance policy shall, to the extent that such proceeds are used to pay relevant tax, be exempt from tax and shall not be taken into account in computing such tax.

(3)   Subject to the provisions of section 54 of [the Capital Acquisitions Tax Act, 1976,] and section 127 of the Finance Act, 1990, where the insured makes an inter vivos disposition of the proceeds, or any part of the proceeds, of a relevant insurance policy other than in paying relevant tax, such proceeds shall not be exempt from tax.

(4)   A relevant insurance policy shall be a qualifying insurance policy for the purposes of section 60 of the Finance Act, 1985, where the proceeds of such relevant insurance policy become payable on the death of the insured or one of the insured in a case to which paragraph (b) of the definition of "insured" relates:

Provided that such relevant insurance policy would have been a qualifying insurance policy if it had been expressly effected under that section.

(5)   A qualifying insurance policy for the purposes of section 60 of the Finance Act, 1985, shall be a relevant insurance policy where the proceeds of such qualifying insurance policy are used to pay relevant tax arising under an inter vivos disposition made by the insured within one year after the appointed date.

(6)   .... [2]

Footnotes

1   S.119 took effect from 29th May, 1991.

2   This subsection, which denied a deduction for income tax purposes in respect of premiums payable on a "relevant insurance policy", was deleted by s.4, FA 1992, for 1992-93 and later years.

Commentary

A   See the Revenue Statement of Practice (SP-CAT/1/04) which sets out Revenue guidelines in relation to s.60 and s.119 policies.

B   See Part 15 of the *Revenue CAT Manual* in relation to these policies.

SECOND PART

(V) BUSINESS RELIEF

For Contents of this Part, see page lii

subsidiaries and any subsidiary of such an associated company are members of a group.

[(4) In this Chapter any reference to a donee or successor shall be construed as including a reference to the transferee referred to in section 23 (1) of [the Capital Acquisitions Tax Act, 1976].][1]

Footnote

1   As inserted by s.227(1), FA 2001, in relation to gifts or inheritances taken on or after 11th April, 1994.

Commentary

A   Part 12 of the *Revenue CAT Manual* deals with business relief.

B   See the Revenue Information leaflet CAT4 in relation to business relief.

C   According to Appendix I to Part 12 of the *Revenue CAT Manual*, business relief may be claimed for shares and securities quoted on the Unlisted Securities Market (USM) on the basis that they are "unquoted" within the meaning of that definition.

D   According to Appendix I to Part 12 of the *Revenue CAT Manual*, "securities" may be treated as including any debt which is either charged on property or is evidenced by a document under seal. Debts such as debentures and loan notes, even if described as "unsecured", may therefore rank as "securities".

E   See articles on business relief by Kieran Twomey in the *Irish Tax Review* of July 1994, page 979, by Jim Muddiman in the *Irish Tax Review* of March 1997, page 169, and by John Quinlan in the *Irish Tax Review* of March 1998, page 194.

Section 125

Application (Chapter I).

125. The provisions of this Chapter shall have effect in relation to gifts and inheritances taken on or after the 11th day of April, 1994, but those provisions shall not have effect in relation to an inheritance taken by a relevant trust by virtue of section 110 (1) of the Finance Act, 1993, or to an inheritance taken by a discretionary trust by virtue of section 106 (1) of the Finance Act, 1984, or section 103 (1) of the Finance Act, 1986.

Section 126

Business relief.

[126. (1)   Where the whole or part of the taxable value of any taxable gift or taxable inheritance is attributable to the value of any relevant business property, the whole or that part of the taxable value shall, subject to the other provisions of this Chapter, be treated as being reduced by 90 per cent.][1]

Footnote

1   When introduced, business relief consisted of a reduction in taxable value of 50% of the first £250,000 of taxable value, plus 25% of any balance.

In relation to gifts or inheritances taken on or after 8th February, 1995, and before 23rd January, 1996, the reduction was amended to 50% of all taxable value by s.161, FA 1995.

In relation to gifts or inheritances taken on or after 23rd January, 1996, and before 23rd January, 1997, the reduction was amended to 75% of all taxable value by s.124, FA 1996.

In relation to gifts or inheritances taken on or after 23rd January, 1997, the reduction was amended to 90% of all taxable value by s.139, FA 1997.

Commentary

A   As to the calculation of business relief, see Part 12.6 of the *Revenue CAT Manual.*

B   See Taxfax (Irish Taxation Institute) dated 31st May, 1996, confirming a Revenue concession which applies only where a sole-trader business or partnership interest, and other property, are comprised in the one acquisition, and not where company shares and other property are so comprised. Liabilities affecting the business should be deducted from the value of the business property, but other liabilities and consideration should, as far as possible, be deducted from the value of the other property (see page 1 of the Revenue form I.T.5 for use where business relief is claimed).

Section 127

Relevant business property.

127. (1) In this Chapter and subject to the following provisions of this section and to sections 128, 130 and 134 (3) "relevant business property" means, in relation to a gift or inheritance, any one or more of the following, that is to say:

(a)   property consisting of a business or interest in a business;

(b)   unquoted shares in or securities of a company [whether incorporated in the State or otherwise][1] to which paragraph (c) does not relate, and which on the valuation date (either by themselves alone or together with other shares or securities in that company in the absolute beneficial ownership of the donee or successor on that date) give control of powers of voting on all questions affecting the company as a whole which if exercised would yield more than 25 per cent. of the votes capable of being exercised thereon;

[(c)   unquoted shares in or securities of a company [whether incorporated in the State or otherwise][1] which is, on the valuation date (after the taking of the gift or inheritance), a company controlled by the donee or successor within the meaning of section 16 of [the Capital Acquisitions Tax Act, 1976];][2]

(d)   unquoted shares in or securities of a company [whether incorporated in the State or otherwise][1] which do not fall within paragraph (b) or (c) and which on the valuation date (either by themselves alone or together with other shares or securities in that company in the absolute beneficial ownership of the donee or successor on that date) have an aggregate nominal value which represents 10 per cent. or more of the aggregate nominal value of the entire share capital and securities of the company:

Provided that the donee or successor has been a full-time working officer or employee of the company, or if that company is a member of a group, of one or more companies which are members of the group, throughout the period of 5 years ending on the date of the gift or inheritance;

(e) ....[3] any land or building, machinery or plant which, immediately before the gift or inheritance was used wholly or mainly for the purposes of a business carried on by a company of which the disponer then had control or by a partnership of which the disponer then was a partner and for the purposes of this paragraph a person shall be deemed to have control of a company at any time if he then had control of powers of voting on all questions affecting the company as a whole which if exercised would have yielded a majority of the votes capable of being exercised thereon;

(f) quoted shares in or securities of a company which, but for the fact that they are quoted, would be shares or securities to which paragraph (b), (c) or (d) would relate:

Provided that such shares or securities, or other shares in or securities of the same company which are represented by those shares or securities, were in the beneficial ownership of the disponer immediately prior to the disposition and were unquoted at the date of the commencement of that beneficial ownership or at the date of the passing of this Act, whichever is the later date.

(2) Where a company has shares or securities of any class giving powers of voting limited to either or both —

(a) the question of winding-up the company, and

(b) any question primarily affecting shares or securities of that class,

the reference in subsection (1) to all questions affecting the company as a whole shall have effect as a reference to all such questions except any in relation to which those powers are capable of being exercised.

(3) .....[4]

(4) A business or interest in a business, or shares in or securities of a company, shall not be relevant business property if the business or, as the case may be, the business carried on by the company consists wholly or mainly of one or more of the following, that is to say, dealing in currencies, securities, stocks or shares, land or buildings, or making or holding investments.

(5) Subsection (4) shall not apply to shares in or securities of a company if the business of the company consists wholly or mainly in being a holding company of one or more companies whose business does not fall within that subsection.

[(6) Any land, building, machinery or plant used wholly or mainly for the purposes of a business carried on as mentioned in subsection (1) (e) shall not be relevant business property in relation to a gift or inheritance, unless the disponer's interest in the business is, or shares in or securities of the company carrying on the business immediately before the gift or inheritance are, relevant business property in relation to the gift or inheritance or in relation to a simultaneous gift or inheritance taken by the same donee or successor.

(7) The references to a disponer in subsections (1) (e) and (6) shall include a reference to a person in whom the land, building, machinery or plant concerned is vested for a beneficial interest in possession immediately before the gift or inheritance.

(8) Where shares or securities are vested in the trustees of a settlement, any powers of voting which they give to the trustees of the settlement shall, for the purposes of subsection (1) (e), be deemed to be given to the person beneficially entitled in possession to the shares or securities except in a case where no individual is so entitled.][5]

Footnotes

1   Substituted for "incorporated in the State" by s.228(1)(a), FA 2001, in relation to gifts or inheritances taken on or after 15th February, 2001.

2   As substituted by s.126, FA 1996, in relation to gifts or inheritances taken on or after 28th March, 1996.

3   The words "in so far as situate in the State," deleted by s.228(1)(b), FA 2001, in relation to gifts or inheritances taken on or after 15th February, 2001.

4   S.127(3) deleted by s.228(1)(c), FA 2001, in relation to gifts or inheritances on or after 15th February, 2001.

5   S.127(6) substituted, and s.127(7) and s.127(8) inserted, by s.140, FA 1997, in relation to gifts and inheritances taken on or after 26th March, 1997.

Commentary

A   See the Revenue Information Leaflet CAT4 in relation to what is "relevant business property".

B   See Part 12.5, and Appendix II to Part 12, of the *Revenue CAT Manual* in relation to the interpretation of "relevant business property".

C   In Appendix II to Part 12 of the *Revenue CAT Manual,* see a query dated 12th August, 1994, and the Revenue reply, in relation to the operation of s.127(4).

D   In Appendix II to Part 12 of the *Revenue CAT Manual,* see a query dated 22nd November, 1994, and the Revenue reply, in relation to the operation of s.127(4) and (5).

E   In Appendix II to Part 12 of the *Revenue CAT Manual,* see a query dated 28th March, 1995, and the Revenue reply, in relation to multiple holding companies and s.127(4) and (5). Business relief is available for a holding company (Company A) which owns (say) 100% of the shares of a second holding company (Company B) which in turn owns (say) 100% of the shares of a trading company (Company C). It is also understood that Revenue agree that business relief is available where more than two holding companies (Companies C and D) are involved.

F   In Appendix II to Part 12 of the *Revenue CAT Manual,* see a query dated 21st April, 1995, and the Revenue reply, in relation to s.127(4) and property developers who deal in land.

G   In Appendix II to Part 12 of the *Revenue CAT Manual,* see a query dated 1st July, 1997, and the Revenue reply, in relation to s.127(4) and forested land owned by a company.

H   In Appendix II to Part 12 of the *Revenue CAT Manual,* see a query dated 15th August, 1997, and the Revenue reply, in relation to s.127(4).

I   As to the operation of a caravan park, see page 420 of the *Irish Tax Review* of September 1997 which refers to a UK Special Commissioners case of *Powell and Another v IRC* [1997] STC (SCD) 181 (where business relief was not granted) and page 573 of the *Irish Tax Review* of November 1999 which refers to a U.K. Special Commissioners case of *Furniss v IRC* [1999] SpC 202, STC(SCD) 232 (where business relief was granted). A further case involving a caravan park (where relief was not granted) is *Weston v IRC* [1999] SpC 222, STC(SCD) 321, referred to at page 227 of the *Irish Tax Review* of May 2000 and at page 135 of the *Irish Tax Review* of March 2001. Again, the matter was considered by the UK Special Commissioners in the case of *Stedman, deceased* – see page 427 of the *Irish Tax Review* of November 2002. The *Stedman* case *(IRC v George and Another, executors of Stedman, deceased* [2004] STC 147), is discussed by Frank Carr at page 232 of the *Irish Tax Review* of May 2003, and at page 111 of the *Irish Tax Review* of March 2004.

According to page 240 of the *Irish Tax Review* of May 2002, the Minister for Finance (Charles McCreevy) stated at the Select Committee stage of the Finance Bill, 2002 – "Revenue's approach is to look at the type of letting activity which takes place at caravan sites, that is, how much of the letting relates to the provision of furnished caravans owned by the business and how much involves letting of pitched sites. As a general guideline, where the operator's own caravans account for at least half of the total number of lettings, the caravan park is likely to qualify for business relief. Parks where the letting of pitched sites predominates will not qualify for the relief as the business primarily involves an exploitation of an interest in land."

See page 15, Issue 55, of the *Revenue Tax Briefing* which now clarifies the Revenue position on "caravan sites" contained at Part 12.5 of the *Revenue CAT Manual*.

J   See page 224 of the *Irish Tax Review* of May 2000 which refers to a UK Special Commissioner case of *Beckman v IRC* [2000] SpC 226. This case decided that business relief did not apply to the capital account of a retired partner who had died before the amount of the capital account was paid, since on retirement the capital account had become merely a debt.

K   See articles in relation to Agricultural Property Relief/Business Property Relief (dealing with both reliefs applying to agricultural property post FA 2000) by Brian Bohan in the *Irish Tax Review* of May 2000, page 279, and by Fergus McCarthy in the *Irish Tax Review* of July 2000, page 342.

L   See *Hardcastle v CIR* [2000] SpC 259, which held that Lloyds underwriting activities constituted a business consisting of the net funds held by Lloyds at a deceased person's death, but that money owing to Lloyds on open account (that is, amounts owed on account for which a result had not been notified before the death) was not a liability incurred for the purposes of the business.

M   See an article *Hertford v CIR* [2004] SpC 444, at page 23 of the *Irish Tax Review* of January 2005. The UK Special Commissioner accepted that a heritage house, 78% of which was open to the fee-paying public, was a business. He also held that the remaining 22% was not an excepted asset (see s.134, FA 1994).

N   See a discussion by Frank Carr at page 40 of the *Irish Tax Review* of March 2006 on a UK Special Commissioners case of *Clark and Another v Revenue* [2005] STC (SCD) 823. The issue involved the shares in a private company which rented out some properties and managed others, while retaining a substantial labour force to refurbish etc. the properties.

O   See a discussion by Frank Carr at page 22 of the *Irish Tax Review* of January 2007 on a UK Special Commissioners case of *Phillips, deceased, executors v Revenue Commissioners* [2006] SPC 555. The case involved the shares of a private company whose business consisted wholly or mainly of lending money to related family companies. Business relief was refused.

P   See *Nelson Dance Family Settlement, trustees v Commissioners for Revenue and Customs* [2008] SpC 682, which decided that a transfer of business assets, rather than the business itself, qualified for business relief.

Q   See *Piercy, deceased, executors v Commissioners for Revenue and Customs* [2008] SpC 687, as to whether shares in a company were shares in a company "whose business consisted wholly are mainly… in making or holdings investments" (no exemption) or whether the company was a property development company whose holdings of land ranked as stock (exemption).

Cross-Reference

1   The definition of "relevant business property" in s.127 is used, with modifications, in s.164(1), FA 1995.

Section 128

Minimum period of ownership.

128. In relation to a gift or an inheritance, property shall not be relevant business property unless it was comprised in the disposition continuously –

(a) in the case of an inheritance, which is taken on the date of death of the disponer, for a period of two years immediately prior to the date of the inheritance, or

(b) in any other case, for a period of five years immediately prior to the date of the gift or inheritance,

and any period immediately before the date of the disposition during which the property was continuously in the beneficial ownership of the disponer, or of the spouse of the disponer, shall be deemed, for the purposes of this Chapter, to be a period or part of a period immediately before the date of the gift or inheritance during which it was continuously comprised in the disposition.

Commentary

A   See the Revenue Information Leaflet CAT4, and Part 12.5, and appendix II to Part 12, of the *Revenue CAT Manual,* in relation to this section.

B   In appendix II to Part 12 of the *Revenue CAT Manual,* see a query dated 4th July, 1994, and the Revenue reply, which involves the operation of s.128(b). The query concerns a gift by a private trading company, owned 100% by a husband and wife, of shares in its 100% owned subsidiary private trading company to children of those parents, and involves s.34, CATA.

Section 129

Replacements.

129. (1) Property shall be treated as complying with section 128 if –

(a) the property replaced other property and the said property, that other property and any property directly or indirectly replaced by that other property were comprised in the disposition for periods which together comprised –

(i)   in a case referred to at paragraph (a) of section 128, at least two years falling within the three years immediately preceding the date of the inheritance, or

(ii) in a case referred to at paragraph (b) of section 128, at least five years falling within the six years immediately preceding the date of the gift or inheritance, and

Section 133

Value of certain shares and securities.

133. (1) Where a company is a member of a group and the business of any other company which is a member of the group falls within section 127 (4), then, unless that business consists wholly or mainly in the holding of land or buildings wholly or mainly occupied by members of the group whose business does not fall within section 127 (4), the value of shares in or securities of the company shall be taken for the purposes of this Chapter to be what it would be if that other company were not a member of the group.

(2) (a) In this subsection "shares" include securities and "shares in a company" include other shares in the same company which are represented by those shares.

(b) Where unquoted shares in a company which is a member of a group are comprised in a gift or inheritance and shares in another company which is also a member of the group are quoted on the valuation date, the value of the first-mentioned shares shall be taken, for the purpose of this Chapter, to be what it would be if that other company were not a member of the group, unless those unquoted shares were in the beneficial ownership of the disponer immediately prior to the disposition and, those quoted shares were—

(i) unquoted[1] at some time prior to the gift or inheritance when they were in the beneficial ownership of the disponer or a member of that group, while being a member of such group, or

(ii) at the date of the passing of this Act,

whichever is the later date.

Footnote

1   The word "unquoted" should have been included in the previous line.

Commentary

A   See Part 12.5 of the *Revenue CAT Manual* regarding the operation of this section.

B   In Appendix II to Part 12 of the *Revenue CAT Manual*, see a query dated 12th August, 1994, and the Revenue reply, in relation to (i) interest-free loans between companies of a group resulting in some companies of the group being dormant, and (ii) a company in a group owning property from which other companies in the group trade.

Section 134

Exclusion of value of excepted assets.

134. [(1) In determining for the purposes of this Chapter what part of the taxable value of a gift or inheritance is attributable to the value of relevant business property, so much of the last-mentioned value as is attributable to —

(a) any excepted assets within the meaning of subsection (2), or

(b) any excluded property within the meaning of subsection (7),

shall be left out of account.

(2) An asset shall be an excepted asset in relation to any relevant business property if it was not used wholly or mainly for the purposes of the business concerned throughout the whole or the last two years of the relevant period, but where the business concerned is carried on by a company which is a member of a group, the use of an asset for the purposes of a business carried on by another company which at the time of the use and immediately prior to the gift or inheritance was also a member of that group shall be treated as use for the purposes of the business concerned, unless that other company's membership of the group falls to be disregarded under section 133:

Provided that the use of an asset for the purposes of a business to which section 127(4) relates shall not be treated as use for the purposes of the business concerned.]¹

(3) Subsection (2) shall not apply in relation to an asset which is relevant business property by virtue only of section 127 (1) (e), and an asset shall not be relevant business property by virtue only of that provision unless either —

(a) it was used in the manner referred to in that provision —

   (i) in the case where the disponer's interest in the business or the shares in or securities of the company carrying on the business are comprised in an inheritance taken on the date of death of the disponer, throughout the two years immediately preceding the date of the inheritance, or

   (ii) in any other case, throughout the five years immediately preceding the date of the gift or inheritance,

or

(b) it replaced another asset so used and it and the other asset and any asset directly or indirectly replaced by that other asset were so used for periods which together comprised —

   (i) in the case referred to at paragraph (a) (i), at least two years falling within the three years immediately preceding the date of the inheritance, or

   (ii) in any other case, at least five years falling within the six years immediately preceding the date of the gift or inheritance;

but where section 131 applies paragraphs (a) and (b) shall be deemed to be complied with if the asset, or that asset and the asset or assets replaced by it, was or were so used throughout the period between the earlier and the subsequent benefit mentioned in that section, or throughout the part of that period during which it or they were in the beneficial ownership of the disponer or the disponer's spouse.

(4) Where part but not the whole of any land or building is used exclusively for the purposes of any business and the land or building would, but for this subsection, be an excepted asset, or, as the case may be, prevented by subsection (3) from being relevant business property, the part so used and the remainder shall for the purposes of this section be treated as separate assets, and the value of the part so used shall (if it would otherwise be less) be taken to be such proportion of the value of the whole as may be just.

(5) For the purposes of this section the relevant period, in relation to any asset, shall be the period immediately preceding the gift or inheritance during which the asset or, if the relevant business property is an interest in a business, a corresponding interest in the asset, was comprised in the disposition (within the meaning of section 128) or, if the business concerned is that of a company, was beneficially owned by that company or any other company which immediately before the gift or inheritance was a member of the same group.

(6) For the purposes of this section an asset shall be deemed not to have been used wholly or mainly for the purposes of the business concerned at any time when it was used wholly or mainly for the personal benefit of the disponer or of a relative of the disponer.

[(7) Where, in relation to a gift or an inheritance —

(a) relevant business property consisting of shares in or securities of a company are comprised in the gift or inheritance on the valuation date, and

(b) property consisting of a business, or interest in a business, not falling within section 127(4) (hereinafter in this section referred to as "company business property") is on that date beneficially owned by that company or, where that company is a holding company of one or more companies within the same group, by any company within that group,

that company business property shall, for the purposes of subsection (1), be excluded property in relation to those shares or securities unless it would, apart from section 127(3), have been relevant business property if —

(i) it had been the subject matter of that gift or inheritance, and

(ii) it had been comprised in the disposition for the periods during which it was in the beneficial ownership of that first-mentioned company or of any member of that group, while being such a member, or actually comprised in the disposition.

(8) In ascertaining whether or not company business property complies with paragraphs (i) and (ii) of subsection (7), the provisions of

section 129 shall, with any necessary modifications, apply to that company business property as to a case to which subsection (1) of section 129 relates.][2]

Footnotes

1   As substituted by s.148(1)(a), FA 2000, in relation to gifts and inheritances taken on or after 10th February, 2000.

     The original s.134, FA 1994, was amended by s.162, FA 1995, in relation to gifts and inheritances taken on or after 12th April, 1995, and prior to 10th February, 2000, by the insertion of a proviso to s.134(1) and by the insertion of a substituted proviso to s.134(2).

2   As substituted retrospectively for s.134(7) by s.128, FA 1998, in relation to gifts and inheritances taken on or after 11th April, 1994.

Commentary

A   See the Revenue Information Leaflet CAT4 in relation to this section. It should be noted, however, that in relation to gifts and inheritances taken on or after 10th February, 2000, agricultural property may qualify for business relief.

B   See Part 12.5, and Appendix II to Part 12, of the *Revenue CAT Manual* in relation to the interpretation of this section. It should be noted, however, that in relation to gifts and inheritances taken on or after 10th February, 2000, agricultural property may qualify for business relief.

C   In Appendix II to Part 12 of the *Revenue CAT Manual*, see a query dated 12th August, 1994, and the Revenue reply, in relation to (i) interest-free loans between companies of a group resulting in some companies of the group being dormant, and (ii) a company in a group owning property from which other companies in the group trade.

D   In Appendix II to Part 12 of the *Revenue CAT Manual,* see a query dated 15th August, 1997, and the Revenue reply, in relation to s.134(2).

E   With regard to s.134(2) and cash balances held by a trading company, see page 344 of the *Irish Tax Review* of July 1998 which refers to a case of *Barclays Bank v IRC* [1998] ST1 738 heard before the U.K. Special Commissioners.

F   See Commentary M to s.127, FA 1994.

Section 135

Withdrawal of relief.

135. [(1) In this section "relevant period", in relation to relevant business property comprised in a gift or inheritance, means the period of 6 years commencing on the date of the gift or inheritance.][1]

(2) The reduction which would fall to be made under section 126 in respect of relevant business property comprised in a gift or inheritance shall cease to be applicable if and to the extent that the property, or any property which directly or indirectly replaces it—

    (a)   would not be relevant business property (apart from section 128 and the provisos to paragraphs (d) and (f) of subsection (1) of section 127 and other than by reason of bankruptcy or a bona fide winding-up on grounds of insolvency) in relation to a notional gift of such property taken by the same donee or successor from the same disponer at any time within the relevant period, unless it would be relevant business property (apart from section 128 and the provisos to paragraphs (d) and (f) of subsection (1) of section 127) in relation to another such notional gift taken within a year after the first-mentioned notional gift;

(b)   is sold, redeemed or compulsorily acquired within the relevant period and is not replaced, within a year of the sale, redemption or compulsory acquisition, by other property (other than quoted shares or securities or unquoted shares or securities to which section 133 (2) (b) relates) which would be relevant business property (apart from section 128 and the proviso to section 127 (1) (d)) in relation to a notional gift of that other property taken by the same donee or successor from the same disponer on the date of the replacement,

and tax shall be chargeable in respect of the gift or inheritance as if the property were not relevant business property:

[Provided that—

(i)   any land, building, machinery or plant which are comprised in the gift or inheritance and which qualify as relevant business property by virtue of section 127 (1) (e) shall, together with any similar property which has replaced such property, continue to be relevant business property for the purposes of this section for so long as they are used for the purposes of the business concerned,][2]

[(ii) this section shall not have effect where the donee or successor dies before the event which would otherwise cause the reduction to cease to be applicable.][3]

(iii)   . . . .[4]

Footnotes

1   As substituted by s.148(1)(b)(i), FA 2000, which has effect where the event which causes the reduction to cease to be applicable occurs on or after 10th February, 2000.

The original s.135(1), which had a clawback period of six years, was amended by s.163(1)(a), FA 1995, in relation to gifts and inheritances taken on or after 12th April, 1995. S.127(1)(a), FA 1996, extended the clawback period of six years to ten years in relation to gifts and inheritances taken on or after 23rd January 1996.

The current s.134(1) shown here restores the clawback period of six years.

2   This is the original sole proviso, re-stated by s.163(1)(b), FA 1995, as proviso (i).

3   This proviso (ii) was inserted by s.163(1)(b), FA 1995, in relation to gifts and inheritances taken on or after 12th April, 1995. It is re-stated in s.148(1)(b)(ii), FA 2000, which has effect where the event which causes the reduction to cease to be applicable occurs on or after 10th February, 2000.

4   Proviso (iii) was inserted by s.127(1)(b), FA 1996, in relation to gifts and inheritances taken on or after 23rd January, 1996, and is repealed by s.148(1)(b)(ii), FA 2000 with effect where the event which causes the reduction to cease to be applicable occurs on or after 10th February, 2000.

With an amendment contained in s.141, FA 1997, and applicable to gifts and inheritances taken on or after 23rd January, 1997, proviso (iii) provided a partial clawback of business relief where the event which caused the reduction to cease to be applicable occurs between the sixth and tenth years.

Commentary

A   See Part 12.7, and Appendix II to Part 12, of the *Revenue CAT Manual* in relation to the interpretation of this section.

B   See the Revenue Information Leaflet CAT4 in relation to this section.

Section 135A[1]

Avoidance of double relief.

135A. Where the whole or part of the taxable value of any taxable gift or taxable inheritance is attributable to agricultural property to which subsection (2) of section 19 of [the Capital Acquisitions Tax Act, 1976,] applies, such whole or part of the taxable value shall not be reduced under this Chapter.

Footnote

1   As inserted by s.148(1)(c), FA 2000, in relation to gifts and inheritances taken on or after 10th February, 2000.

SECOND PART

(iv) DOUBLE TAXATION CONVENTIONS

For Contents of this Part, see page lii

FINANCE ACT, 1950

Number 18 of 1950
(Enacted on 5th July, 1950)

PART III
Death Duties

Section 10

Confirmation of Convention set forth in First Schedule.

10. (1) The convention set forth in the First Schedule to this Act and concluded on the 13th day of September, 1949, between the Government and the Government of the United States of America (in this section referred to as the Convention) is hereby confirmed and shall have the force of law.

(2) Subsection (4) of section 7 of the Finance Act, 1894[1] (which provides for relief in respect of duty payable in a foreign country) shall not have effect in relation to estate tax chargeable under the laws of the United States of America to which the provisions of the Convention apply.

Footnote
1 Reproduced on page 653.

Commentary
A   The Convention is treated as applying to Irish inheritance tax (not gift tax) and to probate tax. It does not apply to any death taxes imposed by individual U.S.A. States.

B   See an article on CAT and Double Taxation Relief by Ann Williams in the *Irish Tax Review* of September 2000, page 437.

FIRST SCHEDULE

Convention between Ireland and the United States of America.

Convention between the Government of Ireland and the Government of the United States of America for the avoidance of double taxation and the prevention of fiscal evasion with respect to taxes on the estates of deceased persons.

The Government of Ireland and the Government of the United States of America,

Desiring to conclude a Convention for the avoidance of double taxation and the prevention of fiscal evasion with respect to taxes on estates of deceased persons,

---

Have appointed for that purpose as their Plenipotentiaries:

> The Government of Ireland:
> Patrick McGilligan, Minister for Finance;
> Sean MacBride, Minister for External Affairs;

and

> The Government of the United States of America:
> George A Garrett, Envoy Extraordinary and Minister Plenipotentiary of the United States of America at Dublin;

Who, having exhibited their respective full powers, found in good and due form, have agreed as follows:-

ARTICLE I

(1)   The taxes which are the subject of the present Convention are:

(a) In the United States of America, the Federal estate tax, and

(b) In Ireland, the estate duty imposed in that territory.

(2)   The present Convention shall also apply to any other taxes of a substantially similar character imposed by either Contracting Party subsequently to the date of signature of the present Convention.

ARTICLE II

(1)   In the present Convention, unless the context otherwise requires:

(a) The term "United States" means the United States of America, and when used in a geographical sense means the States, the Territories of Alaska and of Hawaii, and the District of Columbia.

(b) The term "Ireland" means the Republic of Ireland.

(c) The term "territory" when used in relation to one or the other Contracting Party means the United States or Ireland, as the context requires.

(d) The term "tax" means the estate duty imposed in Ireland or the United States Federal estate tax, as the context requires.

(2)   In the application of the provisions of the present Convention by one of the Contracting Parties, any term not otherwise defined shall, unless the context otherwise requires, have the meaning which it has under the laws of that Contracting Party relating to the taxes which are the subject of the present Convention.

ARTICLE III

(1)   For the purposes of the present Convention, the question whether a decedent was domiciled in any part of the territory of one of the

Contracting Parties at the time of his death shall be determined in accordance with the law in force in that territory.

(2)   Where a person dies domiciled in any part of the territory of one Contracting Party, the situs of any rights or interests, legal or equitable, in or over any of the following classes of property which for the purposes of tax form part of the estate of such person or pass on his death, shall, for the purposes of the imposition of tax and for the purposes of the credit to be allowed under Article V, be determined exclusively in accordance with the following rules, but in cases not within such rules the situs of any such rights or interests shall be determined for those purposes in accordance with the law relating to tax in force in the territory of the other Contracting Party:

(a) Immovable property shall be deemed to be situated at the place where such property is located;

(b) Tangible movable property (other than such property for which specific provision is hereinafter made) and bank or currency notes, other forms of currency recognised as legal tender in the place of issue, negotiable bills of exchange and negotiable promissory notes, shall be deemed to be situated at the place where such property, notes, currency or documents are located at the time of death, or, if in transitu, at the place of destination;

(c) Debts, secured or unsecured, other than the forms of indebtedness for which specific provision is made herein, shall be deemed to be situate at the place where the decedent was domiciled at the time of death;

(d) Shares or stock in a corporation other than a municipal or governmental corporation (including shares or stock held by a nominee where the beneficial ownership is evidenced by scrip certificates or otherwise) shall be deemed to be situated at the place in or under the law of which such corporation was created or organised; but, if such corporation was created or organised under the laws of the United Kingdom of Great Britain and Northern Ireland or under the laws of Northern Ireland, and if the shares or stock of such corporation when registered on a branch register of such corporation kept in Ireland are deemed under the laws of the United Kingdom or of Northern Ireland and of Ireland to be assets situated in Ireland, such shares or stock shall be deemed to be assets situated in Ireland;

(e) Moneys payable under a policy of assurance or insurance on the life of the decedent shall be deemed to be situated at the place where the decedent was domiciled at the time of death;

(f) Ships and aircraft and shares thereof shall be deemed to be situated at the place of registration or documentation of the ship or aircraft;

(g) Goodwill as a trade, business or professional asset shall be deemed to be situated at the place where the trade, business or profession to which it pertains is carried on;

present Convention. No information shall be exchanged which would disclose any trade secret or trade process.

(2)   As used in this Article, the Term "taxation authorities" means, in the case of the United States, the Commissioner of Internal Revenue or his authorised representative; in the case or Ireland, the Revenue Commissioners or their authorised representative.

ARTICLE VIII

(1)   The present Convention shall be ratified and the instruments of ratification shall be exchanged at Washington, District of Columbia, as soon as possible.

(2)   The present Convention shall come into force on the date of exchange of ratifications and shall be effective only as to

   (a)   the estates of persons dying on or after such date; and

   (b)   the estate of any person dying before such date and after the last day of the calendar year immediately preceding such date whose personal representative elects, in such manner as may be prescribed, that the provisions of the present Convention shall be applied to such estate.

ARTICLE IX

(1)   The present Convention shall remain in force for not less than three years after the date of its coming into force.

(2)   If not less than six months before the expiration of such period of three years, neither of the Contracting Parties shall have given to the other Contracting Party, through diplomatic channels, written notice of its intention to terminate the present Convention, the Convention shall remain in force after such period of three years until either of the Contracting Parties shall have given written notice of such intention, in which event the present Convention shall not be effective as to the estates of persons dying on or after the date (not being earlier than the sixtieth day after the date of such notice) specified in such notice, or, if no date is specified, on or after the sixtieth day after the date of such notice.

IN WITNESS WHEREOF the above-named Plenipotentiaries have signed the present Convention and have affixed thereto their seals.

Done at Dublin, in duplicate, this 13th day of September, 1949.

For the Government of Ireland:
(Signed)
PATRICK McGILLIGAN

SEAN MacBRIDE

For the Government of the United States of America:
(Signed)
GEORGE A GARRETT.

S. I. No. 279 of 1978

Convention between Ireland and the United Kingdom.

DOUBLE TAXATION RELIEF (TAXES ON ESTATES OF DECEASED PERSONS AND INHERITANCES AND ON GIFTS) (UNITED KINGDOM) ORDER, 1978

WHEREAS it is enacted by section 66 (1) of the Capital Acquisitions Tax Act. 1976 (No. 8 of 1976), that if the Government by order declare that arrangements specified in the order have been made with the government of any territory outside the State in relation to affording relief from double taxation in respect of gift tax or inheritance tax payable under the laws of the State and any tax imposed under the laws of that territory which is of a similar character or is chargeable by reference to death or to gifts *inter vivos* and that it is expedient that those arrangements should have the force of law, the arrangements shall, notwithstanding anything in any enactment, have the force of law:

AND WHEREAS it is further enacted by section 66(5) of that Act that, where such an order is proposed to be made, a draft thereof shall be laid before Dáil Eireann and the order shall not be made until a resolution approving of the draft has been passed by Dáil Eireann:

AND WHEREAS a draft of this Order has been laid before Dáil Eireann and a resolution approving of the draft has been passed by Dáil Eireann:

NOW, the Government, in exercise of the powers conferred on them by section 66 of the Capital Acquisitions Tax Act, 1976, hereby order as follows:

1. This Order may be cited as the Double Taxation Relief (Taxes on Estates of Deceased Persons and Inheritances and on Gifts) (United Kingdom) Order, 1978.

2. It is hereby declared –

   (a) that the arrangements specified in the Convention set out in the Schedule to this Order have been made with the Government of the United Kingdom in relation to affording relief from double taxation in respect of gift tax and inheritance tax payable under the laws of the State and any tax imposed under the laws of the United Kingdom which is of a similar character, and

   (b) that it is expedient that those arrangements should have the force of law.

SCHEDULE

CONVENTION BETWEEN THE GOVERNMENT OF IRELAND AND THE GOVERNMENT OF THE UNITED KINGDOM FOR THE AVOIDANCE OF DOUBLE TAXATION AND THE PREVENTION OF FISCAL EVASION WITH RESPECT TO TAXES ON ESTATES OF DECEASED PERSONS AND INHERITANCES AND ON GIFTS

The Government of Ireland and the Government of the United Kingdom;
Desiring to conclude a Convention for the avoidance of double taxation and the prevention of fiscal evasion with respect to taxes on estates of deceased persons and inheritances and on gifts;
Have agreed as follows:

ARTICLE 1

Scope
This Convention shall apply to any person who is within the scope of a tax which is the subject of this Convention, and to any property by reference to which there is a charge to such a tax.

ARTICLE 2

Taxes Covered
(1)   The taxes which are the subject of this Convention are:

   (a)   in Ireland

      (i)   the gift tax, and

      (ii)   the inheritance tax;

   (b)   in the United Kingdom, the capital transfer tax.

(2)   This Convention shall also apply to any identical or substantially similar taxes which are imposed by either Contracting State after the date of signature of this Convention in addition to, or in place of, the existing taxes.

ARTICLE 3

General definitions
(1)   In this Convention, unless the context otherwise requires:

   (a)   the term "nationals" means:

      (i)   in relation to Ireland, all citizens of Ireland and all legal persons, associations or other entities deriving their status as such from the law in force in Ireland;

      (ii)   in relation to the United Kingdom, citizens of the United Kingdom and Colonies, British subjects under Section 2 of the British Nationality Act 1948 whose notices given under that

Section have been acknowledged before the date of signature of this Convention, British subjects by virtue of Section 13 (1) or Section 16 of the British Nationality Act 1948 or Section 1 of the British Nationality Act 1965, and British protected persons within the meaning of the British Nationality Act 1948; and all legal persons, associations or other entities deriving their status as such from the law in force in the United Kingdom;

(b) the term "tax" means the gift tax or the inheritance tax imposed in Ireland or the capital transfer tax imposed in the United Kingdom, as the context requires;

(c) the term "a Contracting State" and "the other Contracting State" mean Ireland or the United Kingdom, as the context requires;

(d) the term "person" includes an individual, a company and any other body of persons;

(e) the term "company" means any body corporate or any entity which is treated as a body corporate for tax purposes;

(f) the term "competent authority" means, in the case of the United Kingdom, the Commissioners of Inland Revenue or their authorised representative, and in the case of Ireland, the Revenue Commissioners or their authorised representative;

(g) the term "event" includes a death.

(2) As regards the application of this Convention by a Contracting State any term not otherwise defined shall, unless the context otherwise requires, have the meaning which it has under the law of that Contracting State relating to the taxes which are the subject of this Convention.

ARTICLE 4

Fiscal domicile

(1) For the purposes of this Convention, the question whether a person is, or was at any material time, domiciled in a Contracting State shall be determined by whether he is, or was at that time, domiciled in that Contracting State in accordance with the law of that Contracting State or is or was treated as so domiciled for the purposes of a tax which is the subject of this Convention.

(2) Where by reason of the provisions of paragraph (1) a person is, or was at any material time, domiciled in both Contracting States, then this question shall be determined in accordance with the following rules:

(a) he shall be deemed to be domiciled in the Contracting State in which he has, or had at the material time, a permanent home available to him. If he has or had a permanent home available to him in both Contracting States, the domicile shall be deemed to be in the Contracting State with which his personal and economic relations are, or were at the material time, closer (centre of vital interests);

(b) if the Contracting State in which he has or had his centre of vital interests cannot be determined, or if he has not or had not a permanent home available to him in either Contracting State, the domicile shall be deemed to be in the Contracting State in which he has, or had at the material time, an habitual abode;

(c) if he has or had an habitual abode in both Contracting States or in neither of them, the domicile shall be deemed to be in the Contracting State of which he is, or was at the material time, a national;

(d) if he is or was a national of both Contracting States or of neither of them, the competent authorities of the Contracting States shall settle the question by mutual agreement.

ARTICLE 5

Taxing rights

(1) Subject to the following provisions of this Convention, each Contracting State shall retain the right to tax which it would have under its own law apart from this Convention.

(2) For the purposes of paragraph (2) of Article 6 and paragraph (2) of Article 8, the Contracting State with subsidiary taxing rights shall be determined as follows:

(a) in relation to property other than property comprised in a settlement, where a person's domicile has been determined under paragraph (2) of Article 4, that Contracting State shall be the Contracting State in which the person is or was, by virtue of that paragraph, not domiciled;

(b) in relation to property comprised in a settlement:

(i) where the proper law of the settlement as regards that property at the time when the settlement was made was the law of Ireland and the settlor's domicile at the time when the settlement was made has been determined under paragraph (1) of Article 4 as being in the United Kingdom, then that Contracting State shall be the United Kingdom;

(ii) where the proper law of the settlement as regards that property at the time when the settlement was made was not the law of Ireland and the settlor's domicile at that time has been determined under paragraph (1) of Article 4 as being in the United Kingdom but under its own law Ireland would impose tax on property outside its territory because at some later time either the proper law of the settlement as regards that property was the law of Ireland or the settlor's domicile has been determined under the said paragraph as being in Ireland, then that Contracting State shall be Ireland;

(iii) subject to paragraph (ii) of this subparagraph, where the proper law of the settlement as regards that property at the time when the settlement was made was not the law of Ireland and the settler's domicile at that time has been determined under paragraph (2) of Article 4, then that contracting state in which the settler was, by virtue of that pargraph, not domiciled at that time.

(3)   In subparagraph (a) of paragraph (2) of this Article, the term "person" means, in Ireland the disponer, and in the United Kingdom the transferor.

(4)   In paragraph (2) of this Article, "settlement" has the meaning which it has under the law of the United Kingdom relating to capital transfer tax and for the purposes of that paragraph a settlement is made when property first becomes comprised in it.

ARTICLE 6

Situs

(1)   For the purposes of this Convention, the situs of any property shall be determined by each Contracting State under its own law, except that, where part of the value by reference to which tax is imposed in the United Kingdom is represented by a liability to tax which is satisfied out of property situated outside the United Kingdom, then that part of the value shall be deemed to be attributable to that property.

(2)   If the situs of any property as determined by one Contracting State under paragraph (1) of this Article is not the same as that so determined by the other Contracting State, and the credit to be allowed under Article 8 is thereby affected, then the question shall be determined exclusively under the law of the Contracting State which, by virtue of paragraph (2) of Article 5, has subsidiary taxing rights or, if there is no such Contracting State, shall be determined by mutual agreement.

ARTICLE 7

Deduction of debts

In determining the amount on which tax is to be computed, permitted deductions shall be allowed under the law in force in the Contracting State in which the tax is imposed.

ARTICLE 8

Elimination of double taxation

(1)   Where a Contracting State imposes tax on an event by reference to any property which is not situated in that Contracting State but is situated in the other Contracting State, the former Contracting State shall allow against so much of its tax (as otherwise computed) as is attributable to that property a credit (not exceeding the amount of tax so attributable)

equal to so much of the tax imposed in the other Contracting State on the same event as is attributable to such property.

(2) Where both Contracting States impose tax on an event by reference to any property which is not situated in either Contracting State but is situated in a third territory, the Contracting State which, by virtue of paragraph (2) of Article 5, has subsidiary taxing rights shall allow against so much of its tax (as otherwise computed) as is attributable to that property a credit (not exceeding the amount of tax so attributable) equal to so much of the tax imposed in the other Contracting State on the same event as is attributable to such property.

(3) Any credit to be allowed in Ireland under this Article in relation to gifts or inheritances shall be allowed only so as to relieve the tax imposed in Ireland on the gift or inheritance which is reduced by the payment of the tax in respect of which that credit is to be allowed; and a gift which in the United Kingdom is a chargeable transfer shall be treated as reduced by the amount of tax imposed in the United Kingdom on that gift and borne by the transferor.

(4) For the purposes of this Article:

(a) the tax attributable to any property imposed in a Contracting State is tax as reduced by the amount of any credit allowed by that Contracting State in respect of tax attributable to that property imposed in a territory other than a Contracting State;

(b) tax is imposed in a Contracting State or a territory if it is chargeable under the law of that Contracting State or territory and duly paid; and

(c) property includes property representing property.

ARTICLE 9

Time limit

Any claim for a credit or for a repayment of tax founded on the provisions of this Convention shall be made within six years from the date of the event in respect of which the claim was made.

ARTICLE 10

Non-discrimination

(1) The nationals of a Contracting State shall not be subjected in the other Contracting State to any taxation or any requirement connected therewith which is other or more burdensome that the taxation and connected requirements to which nationals of that Contracting State in the same circumstances are or may be subjected.

(2) The taxation on a permanent establishment which an enterprise of a Contracting State has in the other Contracting State shall not be less

favourably levied in that other Contracting State than the taxation levied on enterprises of that other Contracting State carrying on the same activities.

(3) Enterprises of a Contracting State, the capital of which is wholly or partly owned or controlled, directly or indirectly, by one or more residents of the other Contracting State, shall not be subjected in the first-mentioned Contracting State to any taxation or any requirement connected therewith which is other or more burdensome that the taxation and connected requirements to which other similar enterprises of that first-mentioned Contracting State are or may be subjected.

(4) Nothing contained in this Article shall be construed as obliging either Contracting State to grant to individuals not domiciled in that Contracting State, any of the personal allowances, relief, and reductions for tax purposes which are granted to individuals so domiciled.

(5) In this Article the term "taxation" means taxes covered by this Convention.

ARTICLE 11

Mutual agreement procedure

(1) Where a person considers that the actions of one or both of the Contracting States result or will result for him in taxation not in accordance with the provisions of this Convention, he may, irrespective of the remedies provided by the domestic laws of those Contracting States, present his case to the competent authority of either Contracting State.

(2) The competent authority shall endeavour, if the objection appears to it to be justified and if it is not itself able to arrive at a satisfactory solution, to resolve the case by mutual agreement with the competent authority of the other Contracting State, with a view to the avoidance of taxation which is not in accordance with the provisions of this Convention.

(3) The competent authorities of the Contracting States shall endeavour to resolve by mutual agreement any difficulties or doubts arising as to the interpretation or application of this Convention.

(4) The competent authorities of the Contracting States may communicate with each other directly for the purpose of reaching an agreement in the sense of the preceding paragraphs.

ARTICLE 12

Exchange of information

(1) The competent authorities of the Contracting States shall exchange such information as is necessary for carrying out the provisions of this

Convention and the domestic laws of the Contracting States concerning taxes covered by this Convention in so far as the taxation thereunder is in accordance with this Convention. Any information so exchanged shall be treated as secret and shall not be disclosed to any persons other than persons (including a Court or administrative body) concerned with the assessment or collection of, or prosecution in respect of, or the determination of appeals in relation to, the taxes which are the subject of this Convention.

(2) In no case shall the provisions of paragraph (1) be construed so as to impose on the competent authority of either Contracting State the obligation:

(a) to carry out administrative measures at variance with the laws or administrative practice prevailing in either Contracting State;

(b) to supply particulars which are not obtainable under the laws or in the normal course of the administration of that or of the other Contracting State;

(c) to supply information which would disclose any trade, business, industrial, commercial or professional secret or trade process, or information, the disclosure of which would be contrary to public policy.

ARTICLE 13

Diplomatic and consular officials

Nothing in this Convention shall affect the fiscal privileges of diplomatic or consular officials under the general rules of international law or under the provisions of special agreements.

ARTICLE 14

Entry into force

This Convention shall enter into force on the exchange of Notes confirming that the necessary steps have been taken to give it the force of law in Ireland and in the United Kingdom and shall thereupon have effect:

(a) In Ireland:

(i) in respect of gift tax, from 28 February 1974;

(ii) in respect of inheritance tax, from 1 April 1975;

(b) In the United Kingdom:

(i) in respect of capital transfer tax other than capital transfer tax on a death, from 27 March 1974;

(ii) in respect of capital transfer tax on a death, from 13 March 1975.

ARTICLE 25

Termination

This Convention shall remain in force until terminated by one of the Contracting States. Either Contracting State may terminate the Convention, through the diplomatic channel, by giving notice of termination at least six months before the end of any calendar year after the year in which this Convention shall cease to have effect at the end of the calendar year in which the notice is given but shall continue to apply in respect of persons permanent to which ... arises before the end of the calendar year.

In witness thereof the undersigned, duly authorised thereto ... have this Convention have signed this Convention.

Done in two originals at London this 5th day of December 1985.

SECOND PART

TAXES CONSOLIDATION ACT, 1997

For Contents for this Part see page iii

TAXES CONSOLIDATION ACT, 1997

Number 39 of 1997
(Enacted on 30th November, 1997)

PART I
Interpretation

Section 7[1]

Application to certain taxing statutes of Age of Majority Act, 1985.

7. (1) Notwithstanding subsection (4) of [section 2 of the Age of Majority Act, 1985][2] (in this section referred to as "the Act of 1985"), subsections (2) and (3) of that section shall, subject to subsection (2), apply for the purposes of the Income Tax Acts and any other statutory provision (within the meaning of the Act of 1985) dealing with the imposition, repeal, remission, alteration or regulation of any tax or other duty under the care and management of the Revenue Commissioners, and accordingly section 2 (4)(b)(vii) of the Act of 1985 shall cease to apply.

    (2) Nothing in subsection (1) shall affect a claimant's entitlement to a deduction under section 462 or 465.

Footnotes

1   This section replaced, with effect from 6th April, 1997, s.112, FA 1986.

2   Reproduced on page 782.

Section 8[1]

Construction of certain taxing statutes in accordance with Status of Children Act, 1987.

8. (1) In this section, "the Acts" means-

    (a) the Tax Acts,

    (b) the Capital Gains Tax Acts,

    (c) the Capital Acquisitions Tax Act, 1976, and the enactments amending or extending that Act, and

    (d) the statutes relating to stamp duty,

    and any instruments made thereunder.

    (2) Notwithstanding any provision of the Acts or the dates on which they were passed, in deducing any relationship between persons for the purposes of the Acts, the Acts shall be construed in accordance with [section 3 of the Status of Children Act, 1987][2].

535

Footnotes

1   This section replaced, with effect from 6th April, 1997, s.74, FA 1988.

2   Reproduced on page 799.

PART 6

Company Distributions, Tax Credits, Franked Investment Income and Advance Corporation Tax

CHAPTER 9

Taxation of acquisition by a company of its own shares

Section 176[1]

Purchase of unquoted shares by issuing company or its subsidiary.

176. (1) Notwithstanding Chapter 2 of this Part, references in the Tax Acts to distributions of a company, other than any such references in sections 440 and 441, shall be construed so as not to include references to a payment made by a company on the redemption, repayment or purchase of its own shares if the company is an unquoted trading company or the unquoted holding company of a trading group and either–

    (a) (i) the redemption, repayment or purchase–

          (I) is made wholly or mainly for the purpose of benefiting a trade carried on by the company or by any of its 51 per cent subsidiaries, and

          (II) does not form part of a scheme or arrangement the main purpose or one of the main purposes of which is to enable the owner of the shares to participate in the profits of the company or of any of its 51 per cent subsidiaries without receiving a dividend,

        and

      (ii) the conditions specified in sections 177 to 181, in so far as applicable, are satisfied in relation to the owner of the shares, or

    (b) the person to whom the payment is made–

      (i) applies the whole or substantially the whole of the payment (apart from any sum applied in discharging that person's liability to capital gains tax, if any, in respect of the redemption, repayment or purchase) to discharging–

          (I) within 4 months of the valuation date (within the meaning of section 21 of the Capital Acquisitions

Tax Act, 1976) of a taxable inheritance of the company's shares taken by that person, a liability to inheritance tax in respect of that inheritance, or

(II) within one week of the day on which the payment is made, a debt incurred by that person for the purpose of discharging that liability to inheritance tax,

and

(ii) could not without undue hardship have otherwise discharged that liability to inheritance tax and, where appropriate, the debt so incurred.

(2) Where subsection (1) would apply to a payment made by a company which is a subsidiary (within the meaning of section 155 of the Companies Act, 1963) of another company on the acquisition of shares of the other company if for the purposes of the Tax Acts other than this subsection –

(a) the payment were to be treated as a payment by the other company on the purchase of its own shares, and

(b) the acquisition by the subsidiary of the shares were to be treated as a purchase by the other company of its own shares,

then, notwithstanding Chapter 2 of this Part, references in the Tax Acts to distributions of a company, other than references in sections 440 and 441, shall be construed so as not to include references to the payment made by the subsidiary.

Footnote

1   This section replaced, with effect from 6th April, 1997, s.61, FA 1991.

Commentary

A   See an article on s.176(1)(b) by Tony Fitzpatrick in the *Irish Tax Review* of September 1991, page 543.

PART 13
Close Companies

CHAPTER 1
Interpretation and General

Section 431[1]

Certain companies with quoted shares not to be close companies.

431. (1) In this section, "share" includes "stock".

(2) For the purposes of this section-

    (a) a person shall be a principal member of a company-

        (i) if such person possesses a percentage of the voting power in the company of more than 5 per cent and, where there are more than 5 such persons, if such person is one of the 5 persons who possess the greatest percentages, or

        (ii) if (because 2 or more persons possess equal percentages of the voting power in the company) there are no such 5 persons, such person is one of the 6 or more persons (so as to include those 2 or more who possess equal percentages) who possess the greatest percentages,

    (b) a principal member's holding shall consist of the shares which carry the voting power possessed by the principal member, and

    (c) in determining the voting power which a person possesses, there shall be attributed to such person any voting power which for the purposes of section 432 would be attributed to such person under subsection (5) or (6) of that section.

(3) Subject to this section, a company shall not be treated as being at any time a close company if-

    (a) shares in the company carrying not less than 35 per cent of the voting power in the company (not being shares entitled to a fixed rate of dividend, whether with or without a further right to participate in profits) have been allotted unconditionally to, or acquired unconditionally by, and are at that time beneficially held by, the public, and

    (b) any such shares have within the preceding 12 months been the subject of dealings on a recognised stock exchange, and the shares have within those 12 months been quoted in the official list of a recognised stock exchange.

(4) Subsection (3) shall not apply to a company at any time when the total percentage of the voting power in the company possessed by all of the company's principal members exceeds 85 per cent.

(5) For the purposes of subsection (3), shares in a company shall be deemed to be beneficially held by the public only if the shares-

    (a) are within subsection (6), and

    (b) are not within the exceptions in subsection (7),

and the reference to shares which have been allotted unconditionally to, or acquired unconditionally by, the public shall be construed accordingly.

(6) Shares are within this subsection (as being beneficially held by the public) if the shares-

    (a) are beneficially held by a company resident in the State which is not a close company, or by a company not so resident which would not be a close company if it were so resident,

  (b) are held on trust for an exempt approved scheme (within the meaning of Chapter 1 of Part 30), or

  (c) are not comprised in a principal member's holding.

 (7) (a) Shares shall be deemed not to be held by the public if the shares are held-

   (i) by any director, or associate of a director, of the company,

   (ii) by any company under the control of any such director or associate, or of 2 or more persons each of whom is such a director or associate,

   (iii) by an associated company of the company, or

   (iv) as part of any fund the capital or income of which is applicable or applied wholly or mainly for the benefit of, or of the dependants of, the employees or directors, or past employees or directors, of the company, or of any company within subparagraph (ii) or (iii).

  (b) References in this subsection to shares held by any person include references to any shares the rights or powers attached to which could for the purposes of section 432 be attributed to that person under subsection (5) of that section.

Footnote

1 This section replaced, with effect from 6th April, 1997, s.95, Corporation Tax Act, 1976. It provides a definition of "private company" in s.16(2), CATA, and s.27(1), CATCA.

PART 26
Life Assurance Companies

CHAPTER 5
Policyholders — New Basis

Section 730GB[1]

Capital acquisitions tax: set-off.

730GB. Where on the death of a person, an assurance company is liable to account for appropriate tax (within the meaning of section 730F(1)) in connection with a gain arising on a chargeable event in relation to a life policy, the amount of such tax, in so far as it does not exceed the amount of appropriate tax to which the assurance company would be liable if that tax was calculated in accordance with section 730F(1)(a), shall be treated as an amount of capital gains tax paid for the purposes of section 63 of the Finance Act 1985.

(5) (a) Where the opinion of the Revenue Commissioners that a transaction is a tax avoidance transaction becomes final and conclusive, they may, notwithstanding any other provision of the Acts, make all such adjustments and do all such acts as are just and reasonable (in so far as those adjustments and acts have been specified or described in a notice of opinion given under subsection (6) and subject to the manner in which any appeal made under subsection (7) against any matter specified or described in the notice of opinion has been finally determined, including any adjustments and acts not so specified or described in the notice of opinion but which form part of a final determination of any such appeal) in order that the tax advantage resulting from a tax avoidance transaction shall be withdrawn from or denied to any person concerned.

(b) Subject to but without prejudice to the generality of paragraph (a), the Revenue Commissioners may –

  (i) allow or disallow in whole or in part any deduction or other amount which is relevant in computing tax payable, or any part of such deduction or other amount,

  (ii) allocate or deny to any person any deduction, loss, abatement, relief, allowance. exemption, income or other amount, or any part thereof, or

  (iii) recharacterize for tax purposes the nature of any payment or other amount.

(c) Where the Revenue Commissioners make any adjustment or do any act for the purposes of paragraph (a), they shall afford relief from any double taxation which they consider would but for this paragraph arise by virtue of any adjustment made or act done by them pursuant to paragraphs (a) and (b).

(d) Notwithstanding any other provision of the Acts, where –

  (i) pursuant to subsection (4) (c), the Revenue Commissioners determine the tax consequences which they consider would arise in respect of a transaction if their opinion that the transaction is a tax avoidance transaction were to become final and conclusive, and

  (ii) pursuant to that determination, they specify or describe in a notice of opinion any adjustment or act which they consider would be, or be part of, those tax consequences,

  then, in so far as any right of appeal lay under subsection (7) against any such adjustment or act so specified or described, no right or further right of appeal shall lie under the Acts against that adjustment or act when it is made or done in accordance with this subsection, or against any adjustment or act so made or done that is not so specified or described in the notice of opinion but which forms part of the final determination of any appeal made under subsection (7) against any matter specified or described in the notice of opinion.

(e) For the purposes of this subsection, an opinion of the Revenue Commissioners that a transaction is a tax avoidance transaction shall be final and conclusive –

(i) if within the time limited no appeal is made under subsection (7) against any matter or matters specified or described in a notice or notices of opinion given pursuant to that opinion, or

(ii) as and when all appeals made under subsection (7) against any such matter or matters have been finally determined and none of the appeals has been so determined by an order directing that the opinion of the Revenue Commissioners to the effect that the transaction is a tax avoidance transaction is void.

(6) (a) Where pursuant to subsections (2) and (4) the Revenue Commissioners form the opinion that a transaction is a tax avoidance transaction, they shall immediately on forming such an opinion give notice in writing of the opinion to any person from whom a tax advantage would be withdrawn or to whom a tax advantage would be denied or to whom relief from double taxation would be given if the opinion became final and conclusive, and the notice shall specify or describe –

(i) the transaction which in the opinion of the Revenue Commissioners is a tax avoidance transaction,

(ii) the tax advantage or part of the tax advantage, calculated by the Revenue Commissioners which would be withdrawn from or denied to the person to whom the notice is given,

(iii) the tax consequences of the transaction determined by the Revenue Commissioners in so far as they would refer to the person, and

(iv) the amount of any relief from double taxation calculated by the Revenue Commissioners which they would propose to give to the person in accordance with subsection (5) (c).

(b) Section 869 shall, with any necessary modifications, apply for the purposes of a notice given under this subsection or subsection (10) as if it were a notice given under the Income Tax Acts.

(7) Any person aggrieved by an opinion formed or, in so far as it refers to the person, a calculation or determination made by the Revenue Commissioners pursuant to subsection (4) may, by notice in writing given to the Revenue Commissioners within 30 days of the date of the notice of opinion, appeal to the Appeal Commissioners on

the grounds and, notwithstanding any other provision of the Acts, only on the grounds that, having regard to all of the circumstances, including any fact or matter which was not known to the Revenue Commissioners when they formed their opinion or made their calculation or determination, and to this section—

(a) the transaction specified or described in the notice of opinion is not a tax avoidance transaction,

(b) the amount of the tax advantage or the part of the tax advantage, specified or described in the notice of opinion which would be withdrawn from or denied to the person is incorrect,

(c) the tax consequences specified or described in the notice of opinion, or such part of those consequences as shall be specified or described by the appellant in the notice of appeal, would not be just and reasonable in order to withdraw or to deny the tax advantage or part of the tax advantage specified or described in the notice of opinion, or

(d) the amount of relief from double taxation which the Revenue Commissioners propose to give to the person is insufficient or incorrect.

(8) The Appeal Commissioners shall hear and determine an appeal made to them under subsection (7) as if it were an appeal against an assessment to income tax and, subject to subsection (9), the provisions of the Income Tax Acts relating to the rehearing of an appeal and to the statement of a case for the opinion of the High Court on a point of law shall apply accordingly with any necessary modifications; but on the hearing or rehearing of the appeal—

(a) it shall not be lawful to enquire into any grounds of appeal other than those specified in subsection (7), and

(b) at the request of the appellants, 2 or more appeals made by 2 or more persons pursuant to the same opinion, calculation or determination formed or made by the Revenue Commissioners pursuant to subsection (4) may be heard or reheard together.

(9) (a) On the hearing of an appeal made under subsection (7), the Appeal Commissioners shall have regard to all matters to which the Revenue Commissioners may or are required to have regard under this section, and—

(i) in relation to an appeal made on the grounds referred to in subsection (7) (a), the Appeal Commissioners shall determine the appeal, in so far as it is made on those grounds, by ordering, if they or a majority of them—

(I) consider that the transaction specified or described in the notice of opinion or any part of that transaction is a tax avoidance transaction, that the opinion or the opinion in so far as it relates to that part is to stand,

        (II) consider that, subject to such amendment or addition thereto as the Appeal Commissioners or the majority of them deem necessary and as they shall specify or describe, the transaction, or any part of it, specified or described in the notice of opinion, is a tax avoidance transaction, that the transaction or that part of it be so amended or added to and that, subject to the amendment or addition, the opinion or the opinion in so far as it relates to that part is to stand, or

        (III) do not so consider as referred to in clause (I) or (II), that the opinion is void,

    (ii) in relation to an appeal made on the grounds referred to in subsection (7) (b), they shall determine the appeal, in so far as it is made on those grounds, by ordering that the amount of the tax advantage or the part of the tax advantage specified or described in the notice of opinion be increased or reduced by such amount as they shall direct or that it shall stand,

    (iii) in relation to an appeal made on the grounds referred to in subsection (7) (c), they shall determine the appeal, in so far as it is made on those grounds, by ordering that the tax consequences specified or described in the notice of opinion shall be altered or added to in such manner as they shall direct or that they shall stand, or

    (iv) in relation to an appeal made on the grounds referred to in subsection (7) (d), they shall determine the appeal, in so far as it is made on those grounds, by ordering that the amount of the relief from double taxation specified or described in the notice of opinion shall be increased or reduced by such amount as they shall direct or that it shall stand.

  (b) This subsection shall, subject to any necessary modifications, apply to the rehearing of an appeal by a judge of the Circuit Court and, to the extent necessary, to the determination by the High Court of any question or questions of law arising on the statement of a case for the opinion of the High Court.

(10) The Revenue Commissioners may at any time amend, add to or withdraw any matter specified or described in a notice of opinion by giving notice (in this subsection referred to as "the notice of amendment") in writing of the amendment, addition or withdrawal to each and every person affected thereby, in so far as the person is so affected, and subsections (1) to (9) shall apply in all respects as if the notice of amendment were a notice of opinion and any matter specified or described in the notice of amendment were specified or described in a notice of opinion; but no such amendment, addition or withdrawal may be made so as to set aside or alter any matter

(a) the individual shall not be resident in the State for the year of assessment, and

(b) no account shall be taken of the period for the purposes of the aggregate mentioned in subsection (1)(b).

(3) (a) Notwithstanding subsections (1) and (2), an individual –

(i) who is not resident in the State for a year of assessment, and

(ii) to whom paragraph (b) applies,

may at any time elect to be treated as resident in the State for that year and, where an individual so elects, the individual shall for the purposes of the Acts be deemed to be resident in the State for that year.

(b) This paragraph shall apply to an individual who satisfies an authorised officer that the individual is in the State –

(i) with the intention, and

(ii) in such circumstances,

that the individual will be resident in the State for the following year of assessment.

[(4) For the purposes of this section –

(a) as respects the year of assessment 2008 and previous years of assessment, an individual shall be deemed to be present in the State for a day if the individual is present in the State at the end of the day, and

(b) as respects the year of assessment 2009 and subsequent years of assessment, an individual shall be deemed to be present in the State for a day if the individual is present in the State at any time during the day.][2]

Footnotes

1   This section replaced, with effect from 6th April, 1997, s.150, FA 1994.
2   As substituted by s.15, F(No. 2)A, 2008, with effect as on and from 1st January, 2009.

Section 820[1]

Ordinary residence.

820. (1) For the purposes of the Acts, an individual shall be ordinarily resident in the State for a year of assessment if the individual has been resident in the State for each of the 3 years of assessment preceding that year.

(2) An individual ordinarily resident in the State shall not for the purposes of the Acts cease to be ordinarily resident in the State for a year of assessment unless the individual has not been resident in the State in each of the 3 years of assessment preceding that year.

Footnote
1   This section replaced, with effect from 6th April, 1997, s.151, FA 1994.

Section 822[1]

Split year residence.

822. (1) For the purposes of a charge to tax on any income, profits or gains from an employment, where during a year of assessment (in this section referred to as "the relevant year") –

  (a) (i)   an individual who has not been resident in the State for the preceding year of assessment satisfies an authorised officer that the individual is in the State –

    (I)   with the intention, and

    (II) in such circumstances,

    that the individual will be resident in the State for the following year of assessment, or

  (ii) an individual who is resident in the State satisfies an authorised officer that the individual is leaving the State, other than for a temporary purpose –

    (I)   with the intention, and

    (II) in such circumstances,

    that the individual will not be resident in the State for the following year of assessment,

  and

  (b) the individual would but for this section be resident in the State for the relevant year,

  subsection (2) shall apply in relation to the individual.

  (2) (a) An individual to whom paragraphs (a) (i) and (b) of subsection (1) apply shall be deemed to be resident in the State for the relevant year only from the date of his or her arrival in the State.

  (b) An individual to whom paragraphs (a) (ii) and (b) of subsection (1) apply shall be deemed to be resident in the State for the relevant year only up to and including the date of his or her leaving the State.

  (3) Where by virtue of this section an individual is resident in the State for part of a year of assessment, the Acts shall apply as if –

  (a) income arising during that part of the year or, in a case to which section 71(3) applies, amounts received in the State during that part of the year were income arising or amounts received for a year of assessment in which the individual is resident in the State, and

      (b)   income arising or, as the case may be, amounts received in the remaining part of the year were income arising or amounts received in a year of assessment in which the individual is not resident in the State.

Footnote

1   This section replaced, with effect from 6th April, 1997, s.153, FA 1994.

Section 824[1]

Appeals.

824. (1) An individual aggrieved by a decision of an authorised officer on any question arising under the provisions of this [Part][2] which require an individual to satisfy an authorised officer on such a question may, by notice in writing to that effect given to the authorised officer within 2 months from the date on which notice of the decision is given to the individual, make an application to have the question heard and determined by the Appeal Commissioners.

  (2) Where an application is made under subsection (1), the Appeal Commissioners shall hear and determine the question concerned in the like manner as an appeal made to them against an assessment, and the provisions of the Acts relating to such an appeal (including the provisions relating to the rehearing of an appeal and to the statement of a case for the opinion of the High Court on a point of law) shall apply accordingly with any necessary modifications.

Footnote

1   This section replaced, with effect from 6th April, 1997, s.156, FA 1994.

2   "Part" substituted for "Chapter" by s.160, FA 2000, with effect as on and from 23rd March, 2000.

Section 825[1]

Residence treatment of donors of gifts to the State.

825. (1) In this section—

"the Acts" means—

  (a) the Tax Acts,

  (b) the Capital Gains Tax Acts, and

  (c) the Capital Acquisitions Tax Act, 1976;

"donor" means an individual who makes a gift to the State;

"gift" means a gift of property to the State which, on acceptance of the gift by the Government pursuant to the State Property Act, 1954, becomes vested pursuant to that Act in a State authority within the meaning of that Act;

"Irish tax" means any tax imposed by the Acts;

"property" includes interests and rights of any description;

"relevant date", in relation to an individual (being a donor or the spouse of a donor), means the date (not being earlier than the 1st day of September, 1974) on which the individual leaves the State for the purpose of residence (other than occasional residence) outside the State;

"tax in that country" means any tax imposed in that country which is identical with or substantially similar to Irish tax;

"visits" means—

    (a)   in relation to a donor, visits by the donor to the State after the relevant date for the purpose of advising on the management of the property which is the subject of the gift, being visits that are in the aggregate less than 182 days in any year of assessment in which they are made, and

    (b)   in relation to the spouse of a donor, visits by that spouse when accompanying the donor on visits of the kind referred to in paragraph (a).

(2)   Where for any year of assessment a person (being a donor or the spouse of a donor) is resident in a country outside the State for the purposes of tax in that country and is chargeable to that tax without any limitation as to chargeability, then, notwithstanding anything to the contrary in the Tax Acts—

    (a)   as respects the year of assessment in which the relevant date occurs, that person shall not as from the relevant date be regarded as ordinarily resident in the State for the purposes of Irish tax, and

    (b)   as respects any subsequent year of assessment, in determining whether that person is resident or ordinarily resident in the State for the purposes of Irish tax, visits shall be disregarded.

Footnote

1   This section replaced, with effect from 6th April, 1997, s.53, FA 1974.

PART 37
Administration

Section 858[1]

Evidence of authorisation.

858.   (1)   In this section, except where the context otherwise requires—

"the Acts" means—

    (a)   (i)   the Customs Acts,

        (ii)   the statutes relating to the duties of excise and to the management of those duties,

    (iii) the Tax Acts,

    (iv) the Capital Gains Tax Acts,

    (v) the Value-Added Tax Act, 1972, and the enactments amending or extending that Act,

    (vi) the Capital Acquisitions Tax Act, 1976, and the enactments amending or extending that Act,

    (vii) the statutes relating to stamp duty and to the management of that duty,

and any instruments made thereunder or under any other enactment and relating to tax, and

(b)   the European Communities (Intrastat) Regulations, 1993 (S.I. No. 136 of 1993);

"authorised officer" means an officer of the Revenue Commissioners who is authorised, nominated or appointed under any provision of the Acts to exercise or perform any functions under any of the specified provisions, and "authorised" and "authorisation" shall be construed accordingly;

"functions" includes powers and duties;

"identity card", in relation to an authorised officer, means a card which is issued to the officer by the Revenue Commissioners and which contains—

(a)   a statement to the effect that the officer—

    (i) is an officer of the Revenue Commissioners, and

    (ii) is an authorised officer for the purposes of the specified provisions,

(b)   a photograph and signature of the officer,

(c)   a hologram showing the logo of the Office of the Revenue Commissioners,

(d)   the facsimile signature of a Revenue Commissioner, and

(e)   particulars of the specified provisions under which the officer is authorised;

"specified provisions", in relation to an authorised officer, means either or both the provisions of the Acts under which the authorised officer—

(a)   is authorised and which are specified on his or her identity card, and

(b)   exercises or performs functions under the Customs Acts or any statutes relating to the duties of excise and to the management of those duties;

"tax" means any tax, duty, levy or charge under the care and management of the Revenue Commissioners.

(2) Where, in the exercise or performance of any functions under any of the specified provisions in relation to him or her, an authorised officer is requested to produce or show his or her authorisation for the purposes of that provision, the production by the authorised officer of his or her identity card –

    (a) shall be taken as evidence of authorisation under that provision, and

    (b) shall satisfy any obligation under that provision which requires the authorised officer to produce such authorisation on request.

(3) This section shall come into operation on such day as the Minister for Finance may appoint by order.[2]

Footnotes

1   This section replaced, with effect from 6th April, 1997, s.159, FA 1997.

2   Into operation on 1st July, 1998 (S.I. No. 212 of 1998).

Section 859[1]

Anonymity of authorised officers in relation to certain matters.

859. (1) In this section –

"authorised officer" means an officer of the Revenue Commissioners nominated by them to be a member of the staff of the body;

"the body" has the meaning assigned to it by section 58;

"proceedings" includes any hearing before the Appeal Commissioners (within the meaning of the Revenue Acts);

"the Revenue Acts" means –

    (a) the Customs Acts,

    (b) the statutes relating to the duties of excise and to the management of those duties,

    (c) the Tax Acts,

    (d) the Capital Gains Tax Acts,

    (e) the Value-Added Tax Act, 1972, and the enactments amending or extending that Act,

    (f) the Capital Acquisitions Tax Act, 1976, and the enactments amending or extending that Act,

    (g) the statutes relating to stamp duty and the management of that duty,

    (h) Chapter IV of Part 11 of the Finance Act, 1992, and

    (i) Part VI of the Finance Act, 1983,

and any instruments made thereunder or under any other enactment and relating to tax;

"tax" means any tax, duty, levy or charge under the care and management of the Revenue Commissioners.

(2) Notwithstanding any requirement made by or under any enactment or any other requirement in administrative and operational procedures, including internal procedures, all reasonable care shall be taken to ensure that the identity of an authorised officer shall not be revealed.

(3) In particular and without prejudice to the generality of subsection (2):

    (a) where, for the purposes of exercising or performing his or her powers or duties under the Revenue Acts in pursuance of the functions of the body, an authorised officer may apart from this section be required to produce or show any written authority or warrant of appointment under those Acts or otherwise to identify himself or herself, the authorised officer shall—

        (i) not be required to produce or show any such authority or warrant of appointment or to so identify himself or herself, for the purposes of exercising or performing his or her powers or duties under those Acts, and

        (ii) be accompanied by a member of the Garda Síochána who shall, on request by a person affected, identify himself or herself as a member of the Garda Síochána and shall state that he or she is accompanied by an authorised officer;

    (b) where, in pursuance of the functions of the body, an authorised officer exercises or performs in writing any of his or her powers or duties under the Revenue Acts or any provision of any other enactment, whenever passed, which relates to Revenue, such exercise or performance of his or her powers or duties shall be done in the name of the body and not in the name of the individual authorised officer involved, notwithstanding any provision to the contrary in any of those enactments;

    (c) in any proceedings arising out of the exercise or performance, in pursuance of the functions of the body, of powers or duties by an authorised officer, any documents relating to such proceedings shall not reveal the identity of any authorised officer, notwithstanding any requirements to the contrary in any provision, and in any proceedings the identity of such officer other than as an authorised officer shall not be revealed other than to the judge or the Appeal Commissioner, as the case may be, hearing the case;

    (d) where, in pursuance of the functions of the body, an authorised officer is required, in any proceedings, to give evidence and the judge or the Appeal Commissioner, as the case may be, is satisfied that there are reasonable grounds in the public interest to direct that evidence to be given by such authorised officer should be given in the hearing and not in the sight of any person, he or she may so direct.

Footnote

1   This section replaced, with effect from 6th April, 1997, s.19A, FA 1983, as amended.

Section 872[1]

Use of information relating to other taxes and duties.

872. (1)   Any information acquired, whether before or after the passing of this Act, in connection with any tax or duty under the care and management of the Revenue Commissioners may be used by them for any purpose connected with any other tax or duty under their care and management.

(2)   ....

Footnote

1   This section replaced, with effect from 6th April, 1997, s.34(2), FA 1928.

PART 38

Returns of Income and Gains, other Obligations and Returns, and Revenue Powers

CHAPTER 3

Other obligations and returns

Section 887[1]

Use of electronic data processing.

887. (1)   In this section—

"the Acts" means—

(a)   the Tax Acts,

(b)   the Capital Gains Tax Acts,

(c)   the Value-Added Tax Act, 1972, and the enactments amending or extending that Act,

(d)   the Capital Acquisitions Tax Act, 1976, and the enactments amending or extending that Act, and

(e)   Part VI of the Finance Act, 1983,

and any instrument made under any of these enactments;

"record" means any document which a person is obliged by the Acts to keep, to issue or to produce for inspection, and any other written or printed material.

(2) For the purposes of the Acts, but subject to section 17 of the Value-Added Tax Act, 1972, a record may be stored, maintained, transmitted, reproduced or communicated, as the case may be, by any electronic, photographic or other process that –

(a) provides a reliable assurance as to the integrity of the record from the time when it was first generated in its final form by such electronic, photographic or other process,

(b) permits the record to be displayed in intelligible form and produced in an intelligible printed format,

(c) permits the record to be readily accessible for subsequent reference in accordance with paragraph (b), and

(d) conforms to the information technology and procedural requirements drawn up and published by the Revenue Commissioners in accordance with subsection (3).

(3) The Revenue Commissioners shall from time to time draw up and publish in Iris Oifigiúil the information technology and procedural requirements to which any electronic, photographic or other process used by a person for the storage, maintenance, transmission, reproduction and communication of any record shall conform.

(4) The authority conferred on the Revenue Commissioners by this section to draw up and publish requirements shall be construed as including the authority exercisable in a like manner to revoke and replace or to amend any such requirements.

(5) (a) Every person who preserves records by any electronic, photographic or other process, when required to do so by a notice in writing from the Revenue Commissioners, shall, within such period as is specified in the notice, not being less than 21 days from the date of service of the notice, supply to the Revenue Commissioners full particulars relating to the process used by that person, including full particulars relating to software (within the meaning of section 912).

(b) A person who fails or refuses to comply with a notice served on the person under paragraph (a) shall be liable to a penalty of [€3,000]².

(6) (a) Subject to paragraph (b), where records are kept by a person (being a person who is obliged by the Acts to keep such records) by any electronic, photographic or other process which does not conform with the requirements referred to in paragraphs (a) to (d) of subsection (2), then the person shall be deemed to have failed to comply with that obligation and that person shall be liable to the same penalties as the person would be

liable to if the person had failed to comply with any obligation under the Acts in relation to the keeping of records.

(b) Paragraph (a) shall not apply where the person referred to in that paragraph complies with any obligation under the Acts in relation to the keeping of records other than in accordance with the provisions of subsection (2).

(7) Where records are preserved by any electronic, photographic or other process, information contained in a document produced by any such process shall, subject to the rules of court, be admissible in evidence in any proceedings, whether civil or criminal, to the same extent as the records themselves.

(8) The Revenue Commissioners may nominate any of their officers to discharge any function authorised by this section to be discharged by the Revenue Commissioners.

Footnotes

1   S.887 replaced, with effect from 6th April, 1997, s.113(1),(2) and (3), FA 1986, as amended. S.887 was entirely substituted by s.232(1)(a), FA 2001, with effect from 30th March, 2001.

2   "£1,000" substituted for "€1,265" from 1st January, 2002, by s.232(3), FA 2001. "€3,000" was substituted for "€1,265" by s.98(1), and by para. 1(f) of Part 2 of Sch. 5, to the F(No. 2)A, 2008, and comes into effect after 24th December, 2008.

Section 896A[1]

Returns in relation to settlements and trusts.
896A.(1)   In this section —

"authorised officer" means an officer of the Revenue Commissioners authorised by them in writing to exercise the powers conferred on them by this section:

"settlement and settlor" have the same meanings respectively as in section 10.

(2) Where any person, in the course of a trade or profession carried on by that person, has been concerned with the making of a settlement and knows or has reason to believe that, at the time of the making of the settlement —

(a) the settlor was resident or ordinarily resident in the State, and

(b) the trustees of the settlement were not resident in the State,

then that person shall, within the period specified in subsection (3), deliver to the appropriate inspector (within the meaning assigned by section 894(1)) a statement specifying —

(i) the name and address of the settlor,

(ii) the names and addresses of the persons who are the trustees of the settlement, and

(iii) the date on which the settlement was made or created.

(3) The statement referred to in subsection (2) shall be delivered —

    (a) in a case where the settlement is one made on or after the date of the passing of the Finance (No. 2) Act 2008, within 4 months of the date of the making of the settlement, or

    (b) in a case where the settlement is one made within the 5 year period prior to the passing of the Finance (No. 2) Act 2008, within 6 months of the date of the passing of the Act.

(4) For the purposes of this section trustees of a settlement shall be regarded as not resident in the State unless the general administration of the settlement is ordinarily carried on in the State and the trustees or a majority of each class of trustees are for the time being resident in the State.

(5) An authorised officer may by notice in writing require any person, whom the authorised officer has reason to believe has information relating to a settlement, to furnish to the authorised officer such information within such time as the authorised officer may direct.

Footnotes

1   Inserted by s.93, F (No. 2) A, 2008, with effect from 24th December, 2008.

CHAPTER 4
Revenue Powers

Section 900[1]

Power to call for production of books, information, etc.

900. **(1)** In this section and in section 901 —

"authorised officer" means an officer of the Revenue Commissioners authorised by them in writing to exercise the powers conferred by this section, or as the case may be, section 901;

"books, records or other documents" includes —

    (a) accounts (including balance sheets) relating to a trade or profession and where the accounts have been audited, a copy of the auditor's certificate,

    (b) books, accounts, rolls, registers, papers and other documents, whether —

        (i) comprised in bound volume, loose-leaf binders or other loose-leaf filing system, loose-leaf ledger sheets, pages, folios or cards, or

        (ii) kept on microfilm, magnetic tape or in any non-legible form (by the use of electronics or otherwise) which is capable of being reproduced in a legible form,

    (c) every electronic or other automatic means, if any, by which any such thing in non-legible form is so capable of being reproduced, and

    (d) documents in manuscript, documents which are typed, printed, stencilled or created by any other mechanical or partly mechanical process in use from time to time and documents which are produced by any photographic or photostatic process;

"judge" means a judge of the High Court;

"liability" in relation to a person, means any liability in relation to tax to which the person is or may be, or may have been, subject, or the amount of such liability;

"tax" means any tax, duty, levy or charge under the care and management of the Revenue Commissioners.

(2) Subject to this section, an authorised officer may serve on a person a notice in writing, requiring the person, within such period as may be specified in the notice, not being less than 21 days from the date of the service of the notice, to do either or both of the following, namely –

    (a) to deliver to, or to make available for inspection by, the authorised officer such books, records or other documents as are in the person's possession, power or procurement and as contain, or may (in the authorised officer's opinion formed on reasonable grounds) contain, information relevant to a liability in relation to the person,

    (b) to furnish to the authorised officer, in writing or otherwise, such information, explanations and particulars as the authorised officer may reasonably require, being information, explanations and particulars that are relevant to any such liability, and which are specified in the notice.

(3) A notice shall not be served on a person under subsection (2) unless the person has first been given a reasonable opportunity to deliver, or as the case may be, to make available to the authorised officer concerned the books, records or other documents in question, or to furnish the information, explanations and particulars in question.

[(4) **Nothing in this section shall be construed as requiring any person to disclose to an authorised officer –**

    (a) **information with respect to which a claim to legal professional privilege could be maintained in legal proceedings,**

    (b) **information of a confidential medical nature, or**

    (c) **professional advice of a confidential nature given to a client (other than advice given as part of a dishonest, fraudulent or criminal purpose).]**[3]

Section 902[1]

Information to be furnished by third party: request of an authorised officer.

902. (1) In this section and in section 902A –

"authorised officer" means an officer of the Revenue Commissioners authorised by them in writing to exercise the powers conferred by this section, or as the case may be, section 902A;

"books, records or other documents" and "liability", in relation to a person, have, respectively, the meaning assigned to them by section 900(1).

(2) Notwithstanding any obligation as to secrecy or other restriction upon disclosure of information imposed by or under statute or otherwise, and subject to this section, an authorised officer may for the purpose of enquiring into a liability in relation to a person (in this section referred to as "the taxpayer") serve on any other person (not being a financial institution within the meaning of section 906A) a notice in writing requiring that other person, within such period as may be specified in the notice, not being less than 30 days from the date of the service of the notice, to do either or both of the following, namely –

(a) to deliver to, or make available for inspection by, the authorised officer, such books, records or other documents as are in the other person's power, possession or procurement and as contain, or may (in the authorised officer's opinion formed on reasonable grounds) contain, information relevant to a liability in relation to the taxpayer,

(b) to furnish to the authorised officer, in writing or otherwise, such information, explanations and particulars as the authorised officer may reasonably require, being information, explanations and particulars that are relevant to any such liability,

and which are specified in the notice.

(3) A notice shall not be served on a person under subsection (2) unless the authorised officer concerned has reasonable grounds to believe that the person is likely to have information relevant to the establishment of a liability in relation to the taxpayer.

(4) The persons who may be treated as a taxpayer for the purposes of this section include a company which has been dissolved and an individual who has died.

(5) A notice under subsection (2) shall name the taxpayer in relation to whose liability the authorised officer is enquiring.

(6) Where an authorised officer serves a notice under subsection (2), a copy of such notice shall be given by the authorised officer to the taxpayer concerned.

(7) Where, under subsection (2), a person has delivered any books, records or other documents and those books, records or other documents are retained by the authorised officer, the person shall, at all reasonable times and subject to such reasonable conditions as may be determined by the authorised officer, be entitled to inspect those books, records or other documents and to obtain copies of them.

(8) Where, under subsection (2), a person makes books, records or other documents available for inspection by the authorised officer, the authorised officer may make extracts from or copies of all or any part of the books, records or other documents.

[(9) Nothing in this section shall be construed as requiring any person to disclose to an authorised officer —

(a) information with respect to which a claim to legal professional privilege could be maintained in legal proceedings,

(b) information of a confidential medical nature, or

(c) professional advice of a confidential nature given to a client (other than advice given as part of a dishonest, fraudulent or criminal purpose).][3]

(10) Where, in compliance with the requirements of a notice under subsection (2), a person makes available for inspection by an authorised officer, books, records or other documents, the person shall afford the authorised officer reasonable assistance, including information, explanations and particulars, in relation to the use of all the electronic or other automatic means, if any, by which the books, records or other documents, in so far as they are in non-legible form, are capable of being reproduced in a legible form and any data equipment or any associated apparatus or material.

(11) A person who fails or refuses to comply with a notice served on the person under subsection (2) or to afford the assistance referred to in subsection (10) shall be liable to a penalty of **[€4,000][2]**, but nothing in section 1078 shall be construed as applying to such failure or refusal.

Footnotes

1   S.902, as enacted, did not apply to CAT. The present section, which was substituted by s.207(c), FA 1999, does apply to CAT and has effect from 25th March, 1999.

2.   S.240(2)(k) and Part 1 of the Fifth Sch., FA 2001, substituted "€1,900" for "£1,500" for any act or omission which takes place on or after 1st January, 2002. "€4,000" substituted for "€1,900" by s.98(1), and by para. 1(q) of Part 2 of Sch. 5, of the F(No. 2)A, 2008, and comes into effect after 24th December, 2008.

3.   As substituted by s.92(d), F(No. 2)A, 2008, with effect from 24th December, 2008.

Section 902A[1]

Application to High Court: information from third party.

902A.(1)   In this section –

"the Acts" has the meaning assigned to it by section 1078(1),[2]

"judge" means a judge of the High Court;

"a taxpayer" means any person including a person whose identity is not known to the authorised officer, and a group or class of persons whose individual identities are not so known.

(2)   An authorised officer may make an application to a judge for an order requiring a person (other than a financial institution within the meaning of section 906A) to do either or both of the following, namely –

(a)   to deliver to the authorised officer, or to make available for inspection by the authorised officer, such books, records or other documents as are in the person's power, possession or procurement and as contain, or may (in the authorised officer's opinion formed on reasonable grounds) contain, information relevant to a liability in relation to a taxpayer,

(b)   to furnish to the authorised officer such information, explanations and particulars as the authorised officer may reasonably require, being information, explanations and particulars that are relevant to any such liability,

and which are specified in the application.

(3)   An authorised officer shall not make an application under subsection (2) without the consent in writing of a Revenue Commissioner, and without being satisfied –

(a)   that there are reasonable grounds for suspecting that the taxpayer, or, where the taxpayer is a group or class of persons, all or any one of those persons, may have failed or may fail to comply with any provision of the Acts,

(b)   that any such failure is likely to have led or to lead to serious prejudice to the proper assessment or collection of tax (having regard to the amount of a liability in relation to the taxpayer, or where the taxpayer is a group or class of persons, the amount of a liability in relation to all or any one of those persons, that arises or might arise from such failure), and

(c)   that the information –

(i)   which is likely to be contained in the books, records or other documents to which the application relates, or

(ii)   which is likely to arise from the information, explanations and particulars to which the application relates,

is relevant to the proper assessment or collection of tax.

(4) Where the judge, to whom an application is made under subsection (2), is satisfied that there are reasonable grounds for the application being made, that judge may, subject to such conditions as he or she may consider proper and specify in the order, make an order requiring the person to whom the application relates −

   (a) to deliver to the authorised officer, or to make available for inspection by the authorised officer, such books, records or other documents, and

   (b) to furnish to the authorised officer such information, explanations and particulars,

   as may be specified in the order.

(5) The persons who may be treated as a taxpayer for the purposes of this section include a company which has been dissolved and an individual who has died.

[(6) Nothing in this section shall be construed as requiring any person to disclose to an authorised officer −

   (a) information with respect to which a claim to legal professional privilege could be maintained in legal proceedings,

   (b) information of a confidential medical nature, or

   (c) professional advice of a confidential nature given to a client (other than advice given as part of a dishonest, fraudulent or criminal purpose.][4]

[(6A) Where in compliance with an order made under subsection (4), a person makes available for inspection by an authorised officer, books, records or other documents, the person shall afford the authorised officer reasonable assistance, including information, explanations and particulars, in relation to the use of all the electronic or other automatic means, if any, by which the books, records or other documents, in so far as they are in a non-legible form, are capable of being reproduced in a legible form, and any data equipment or any associated apparatus or material.

(6B) Where in compliance with an order made under subsection (4), a person makes books, records or other documents available for inspection by the authorised officer, the authorised officer may make extracts from or copies of all or any part of the books, records or other documents.][3]

(7) Every hearing of an application for an order under this section and of any appeal in connection with that application shall be held in camera.

Footnotes

1   This section was inserted by s.207(d), FA 1999, with effect from 25th March, 1999.

2   S.1078(1), before 21st February, 2003, includes "the Capital Acquisitions Tax Act, 1976, and the enactments amending or extending that Act,".

3   As inserted by s.132(b), FA 2002, with effect from 25th March, 2002.

4   As substituted by s.92(e), F(No. 2)A, 2008, with effect from 24th December, 2008.

Section 905[1]

Inspection of documents and records.

905. (1) In this section—

"authorised officer" means an officer of the Revenue Commissioners authorised by them in writing to exercise the powers conferred by this section;

"property" means any asset relating to a tax liability;

["records" means any document or any other written or printed material in any form, and includes any information stored, maintained or preserved by means of any mechanical or electronic device, whether or not stored, maintained or preserved in a legible form—

(i) which relates to a business carried on by a person, or

(ii) which a person is obliged by any provision relating to tax to keep, retain, issue or produce for inspection or which may be inspected under any provision relating to tax;][2]

"tax" means any tax, duty, levy or charge under the care and management of the Revenue Commissioners;

"tax liability" means any existing liability to tax or further liability to tax which may be established by an authorised officer following the exercise or performance of his or her powers or duties under this section.

(2) (a) An authorised officer may at all reasonable times enter any premises or place where the authorised officer has reason to believe that—

(i) any trade, profession or other activity, the profits or gains of which are chargeable to tax, is or has been carried on,

(ii) anything is or has been done in connection with any trade, profession or other activity the profits or gains of which are chargeable to tax,

(iii) any records relating to—

(I) any trade, profession, other source of profits or gains or chargeable gains,

(II) any tax liability, or

(III) any repayments of tax in regard to any person,

are or may be kept, or

(iv) any property is or has been located,

and the authorised officer may—

(A) require any person who is on those premises or in that place, other than a person who is there to purchase goods or to receive a service, to produce any records or property,

(B) if the authorised officer has reason to believe that any of the records or property which he or she has required to be produced to him or her under this subsection have not been produced, search on those premises or in that place for those records or property,

(C) examine any records or property and take copies of or extracts from any records,

(D) remove any records and retain them for a reasonable time for the purposes of their further examination or for the purposes of any legal proceedings instituted by an officer of the Revenue Commissioners or for the purposes of any criminal proceedings, and

(E) examine property listed in any records.

(b) An authorised officer may in the exercise or performance of his or her powers or duties under this section require any person whom he or she has reason to believe –

(i) is or was carrying on any trade, profession or other activity the profits or gains of which are chargeable to tax,

(ii) is or was liable to any tax, or

(iii) has information relating to any tax liability,

to give the authorised officer all reasonable assistance, including providing information and explanations or furnishing documents and making available for inspection property as required by the authorised officer in relation to any tax liability or any repayment of tax in regard to any person.

[(c) **Nothing in this section shall be construed as requiring any person to disclose to an authorised officer –**

(i) **information with respect to which a claim to legal professional privilege could be maintained in legal proceedings,**

(ii) **information of a confidential medical nature, or**

(iii) **professional advice of a confidential nature given to a client (other than advice given as part of a dishonest, fraudulent or criminal purpose).][10]**

(d) . . . .[3]

[(e) An authorised officer shall not, without the consent of the occupier, enter any premises, or that portion of any premises, which is occupied wholly and exclusively as a private residence, except on production by the officer of a warrant issued under subsection (2A).][4]

[(f) . . . .][5]

    (b)   every electronic or other automatic means, if any, by which any such thing in non-legible form is so capable of being reproduced,

    (c)   documents in manuscript, documents which are typed, printed, stencilled or created by any other mechanical or partly mechanical process in use from time to time and documents which are produced by any photographic or photostatic process,

    and

    (d)   correspondence and records of other communications between a financial institution and its customers;

"connected person" has the same meaning as in section 10; but an individual (other than in the capacity as a trustee of a settlement) shall be connected with another individual only if that other individual is the spouse of or a minor child of the first-mentioned individual;

"deposit" and "interest" have, respectively, the meaning assigned to them by section 256(1);

["financial institution" means—

[(a)   a person who holds or has held a licence under section 9 of the Central Bank Act 1971, or a person who holds or has held a licence or other similar authorisation under the law of any other Member State of the European Communities which corresponds to a licence granted under that section.][5]

    (b)   a person referred to in section 7(4) of the Central Bank Act, 1971, or

    (c)   a credit institution (within the meaning of the European Communities (Licensing and Supervision of Credit Institutions) Regulations, 1992 (S.I. No. 395 of 1992)) which has been authorised by the Central Bank of Ireland to carry on business of a credit institution in accordance with the provisions of the supervisory enactments (within the meaning of those Regulations);][3]

"liability" in relation to a person means any liability in relation to tax to which the person is or may be, or may have been, subject, or the amount of such liability;

"tax" means any tax, duty, levy or charge under the care and management of the Revenue Commissioners.

  (2) Notwithstanding any obligation as to secrecy or other restriction upon disclosure of information imposed by or under statute or otherwise, and subject to this section, an authorised officer may, for the purpose of enquiring into a liability in relation to a person (in this section referred to as the "taxpayer"), serve on a financial institution a notice in writing requiring the financial institution, within such period as may be specified in the notice, not being less

than 30 days from the date of the service of the notice, to do either or both of the following, namely —

(a) to make available for inspection by the authorised officer such books, records or other documents as are in the financial institution's power, possession or procurement and as contain, or may (in the authorised officer's opinion formed on reasonable grounds) contain, information relevant to a liability in relation to the taxpayer,

(b) to furnish to the authorised officer, in writing or otherwise, such information, explanations and particulars as the authorised officer may reasonably require, being information, explanations and particulars that are relevant to any such liability,

and which are specified in the notice.

(3) Where, in compliance with the requirements of a notice under subsection (2), a financial institution makes available for inspection by an authorised officer, books, records or other documents, it shall afford the authorised officer reasonable assistance, including information, explanations and particulars, in relation to the use of all the electronic or other automatic means, if any, by which the books, records or other documents, in so far as they are in a non-legible form, are capable of being reproduced in a legible form and any data equipment or any associated apparatus or material.

(4) An authorised officer shall not serve a notice on a financial institution under subsection (2) without the consent in writing of a Revenue Commissioner and without having reasonable grounds to believe that the financial institution is likely to have information relevant to a liability in relation to the taxpayer.

(5) Without prejudice to the generality of subsection (2), the books, records or other documents which a financial institution may be required by notice under that subsection to deliver or to make available and the information, explanations and particulars which it may likewise be required to furnish, may include books, records or other documents and information, explanations and particulars relating to a person who is connected with the taxpayer.

(6) The persons who may be treated as a taxpayer for the purposes of this section include a company which has been dissolved and an individual who has died.

(7) A notice served under subsection (2) shall name the taxpayer in relation to whose liability the authorised officer is enquiring.

(8) Where an authorised officer serves a notice under subsection (2), a copy of such notice shall be given by the authorised officer to the taxpayer concerned.

(9) Where, in compliance with a notice served under subsection (2), a financial institution makes books, records or other documents available for inspection by an authorised officer, the authorised officer may make extracts from or copies of all or any part of the books, records or other documents.

(10) A financial institution which fails or refuses to comply with a notice issued under subsection (2) or which fails or refuses to afford reasonable assistance to an authorised officer as required under subsection (3), shall be liable to a penalty of [€19,045][4] and, if the failure or refusal to comply with such notice continues after the expiry of the period specified in the notice served under subsection (2), a further penalty of [€2,535][4] for each day on which the failure or refusal continues.

Footnotes

1   This section was inserted by s.207(g), FA 1999, with effect from 25th March, 1999.

2   S.1078(1) includes, before 21st February, 2003, "the Capital Acquisitions Tax Act, 1976, and the enactments amending or extending that Act,".

3   As substituted by s.68(c), FA 2000, with effect from 23rd March, 2000.

4.   S.240(2)(k) and Part I of the Fifth Sch., FA 2001, substituted "€19,045" and "€2,535" respectively for "£15,000" and "£2,000" for any act or omission which takes place on or after 1st January, 2002.

5.   As substituted by s.92(g), F(No. 2)A, 2008, with effect from 24th December, 2008.

Section 907[1]

Application to Appeal Commissioners: information from financial institutions.

907. (1) In this section "a taxpayer" means any person including —

(a) a person whose identity is not known to the authorised officer, and a group or class of persons whose individual identities are not so known, and

(b) a person by or in respect of whom a declaration has been made under section 263(1) declaring that the person is beneficially entitled to all or part of the interest in relation to a deposit.

(2) An authorised officer may, subject to this section, make an application to the Appeal Commissioners for their consent, under subsection (5), to the service by him or her of a notice on a financial institution requiring the financial institution to do either or both of the following, namely —

(a) to make available for inspection by the authorised officer, such books, records or other documents as are in the financial institution's power, possession or procurement as contain, or may (in the authorised officer's opinion formed on reasonable grounds) contain, information relevant to a liability in relation to a taxpayer,

(b) to furnish to the authorised officer such information, explanations and particulars as the authorised officer may reasonably require, being information, explanations and particulars that are relevant to any such liability,

and which are specified in the application.

(3) An authorised officer shall not make an application under subsection (2) without the consent in writing of a Revenue Commissioner, and without being satisfied —

(a) that there are reasonable grounds for suspecting that the taxpayer, or where the taxpayer is a group or class of persons, all or any one of those persons, may have failed or may fail to comply with any provision of the Acts,

(b) that any such failure is likely to have led or to lead to serious prejudice to the proper assessment or collection of tax (having regard to the amount of a liability in relation to the taxpayer, or where the taxpayer is a group or class of persons, the amount of a liability in relation to all or any one of those persons, that arises or might arise from such failure), and

(c) that the information —

(i) which is likely to be contained in the books, records or other documents to which the application relates, or

(ii) which is likely to arise from the information, explanations and particulars to which the application relates,

is relevant to the proper assessment or collection of tax.

(4) Without prejudice to the generality of subsection (2), the authorised officer may make an application under that subsection to the Appeal Commissioners for their consent, under subsection (5), to the service by him or her of a notice on a financial institution in respect of the matters referred to in paragraphs (a) and (b) of subsection (2) in so far as they relate to a person who is connected with the taxpayer.

(5) Where the Appeal Commissioners determine that in all the circumstances there are reasonable grounds for the application being made, they may give their consent to the service by the authorised officer concerned of a notice on the financial institution, requiring the financial institution —

(a) to make available for inspection by the authorised officer, such books, records or other documents, and

(b) to furnish to the authorised officer such information, explanations and particulars,

of the kind referred to in subsection (2) as may, with the Appeal Commissioners' consent, be specified in the notice.

(6) The persons who may be treated as a taxpayer for the purposes of this section include a company which has been dissolved and an individual who has died.

(7) Where the Appeal Commissioners have given their consent in accordance with this section, the authorised officer shall, as soon as practicable, but not later than 14 days from the time that such consent was given, serve a notice on the financial institution concerned and stating that—

(a) such consent has been given,

and

(b) the financial institution should, within a period of 30 days from the date of the service of the notice, comply with the requirements specified in the notice.

[(7A) Where in compliance with the requirements of a notice served under subsection (7), a financial institution makes available for inspection by an authorised officer, books, records or other documents, the financial institution shall afford the authorised officer reasonable assistance, including information, explanations and particulars, in relation to the use of all the electronic or other automatic means, if any, by which the books, records or other documents, in so far as they are in a non-legible form, are capable of being reproduced in a legible form, and any data equipment or any associated apparatus or material.

(7B) Where in compliance with the requirements of a notice served under subsection (7), a financial institution makes books, records or other documents available for inspection by the authorised officer, the authorised officer may make extracts from or copies of all or any part of the books, records or other documents.]²

(8) (a) Subject to paragraph (b), an application by an authorised officer under subsection (2) shall, with any necessary modifications, be heard by the Appeal Commissioners as if it were an appeal against an assessment to income tax.

(b) Notwithstanding section 933(4), a determination by the Appeal Commissioners under this section shall be final and conclusive.

(9) A financial institution which fails to comply with a notice served on the financial institution by an authorised officer in accordance with this section shall be liable to a penalty of [€19,045]³ and, if the failure continues after the expiry of the period specified in subsection (7) (b), a further penalty of [€2,535]³ for each day on which the failure so continues.

Footnotes

1   S.907, as enacted, did not apply to CAT. The present section, which was substituted by s.207(h), FA 1999, does apply to CAT and has effect from 25th March, 1999.

2   As inserted by s.132(e), FA 2002, with effect from 25th March, 2002.

3   S.240(2)(k) and Part I of the Fifth Sch., FA 2001, substituted "€19,045" and "€2,535" respectively for "£15,000" and "£2,000" for any act or omission which takes place on or after 1st January, 2002.

Section 908[1]

Application to High Court seeking order requiring information: financial institutions.

908. (1) In this section—

"judge" means a judge of the High Court;

"a taxpayer" means any person including—

(a) a person whose identity is not known to the authorised officer, and a group or class of persons whose individual identities are not so known, and

(b) a person by or in respect of whom a declaration has been made under section 263(1) declaring that the person is beneficially entitled to all or part of the interest in relation to a deposit.

(2) An authorised officer may, subject to this section, make an application to a judge for an order requiring a financial institution, to do either or both of the following, namely—

(a) to make available for inspection by the authorised officer, such books, records or other documents as are in the financial institution's power, possession or procurement as contain, or may (in the authorised officer's opinion formed on reasonable grounds) contain information relevant to a liability in relation to a taxpayer,

(b) to furnish to the authorised officer such information, explanations and particulars as the authorised officer may reasonably require, being information, explanations and particulars that are relevant to any such liability,

and which are specified in the application.

(3) An authorised officer shall not make application under subsection (2) without the consent in writing of a Revenue Commissioner, and without being satisfied—

(a) that there are reasonable grounds for suspecting that the taxpayer, or, where the taxpayer is a group or class of persons, all or any one of those persons, may have failed or may fail to comply with any provision of the Acts,

(b) that any such failure is likely to have led or to lead to serious prejudice to the proper assessment or collection of tax (having regard to the amount of a liability in relation to the taxpayer, or where the taxpayer is a group or class of persons, the amount of a liability in relation to all or any one of them, that arises or might arise from such failure), and

(c) that the information—

(i) which is likely to be contained in the books, records or other documents to which the application relates, or

(ii) which is likely to arise from the information, explanations and particulars to which the application relates,

is relevant to the proper assessment or collection of tax.

(4) Without prejudice to the generality of subsection (2), the authorised officer may make an application under that subsection to the judge for an order in respect of the matters referred to in paragraphs (a) and (b) of that subsection in so far as they relate to a person who is connected with the taxpayer.

(5) Where the judge, to whom an application is made under subsection (2), is satisfied that there are reasonable grounds for the application being made, the judge may, subject to such conditions as he or she may consider proper and specify in the order, make an order requiring the financial institution—

(a) to make available for inspection by the authorised officer, such books, records or other documents, and

(b) to furnish to the authorised officer such information, explanations and particulars,

as may be specified in the order.

(6) The persons who may be treated as a taxpayer for the purposes of this section include a company which has been dissolved and an individual who has died.

[(6A) Where in compliance with an order made under subsection (5), a financial institution makes available for inspection by an authorised officer, books, records or other documents, the financial institution shall afford the authorised officer reasonable assistance, including information, explanations and particulars, in relation to the use of all the electronic or other automatic means, if any, by which the books, records or other documents, in so far as they are in a non-legible form, are capable of being reproduced in a legible form, and any data equipment or any associated apparatus or material.

(6B) Where in compliance with an order made under subsection (5), a financial institution makes books, records or other documents available for inspection by the authorised officer, the authorised officer may make extracts from or copies of all or any part of the books, records or other documents.][2]

(7) Every hearing of an application for an order under this section and of any appeal in connection with that application shall be held in camera.

(8) Where a judge makes an order under this section, he or she may also, on the application of the authorised officer concerned, make a further order prohibiting, for such period as the judge may consider proper and specify in the order, any transfer of, or any dealing with, without the consent of the judge, any assets or moneys of the person to whom the order relates that are in the custody of the financial institution at the time the order is made.

(9) (a) Where—

    (i) a copy of any affidavit and exhibits grounding an application under subsection (2) or (8) and any order made under subsection (5) or (8) are to be made available to the taxpayer, or the taxpayer's solicitor or to the financial institution or the financial institution's solicitor, as the case may be, and

    (ii) the judge is satisfied on the hearing of the application that there are reasonable grounds in the public interest that such copy of an affidavit, exhibits or order, as the case may be, should not include the name or address of the authorised officer,

such copy, or copies or order shall not include the name or address of the authorised officer.

(b) Where, on any application to the judge to vary or discharge an order made under this section, it is desired to cross-examine the deponent of any affidavit filed by or on behalf of the authorised officer and the judge is satisfied that there are reasonable grounds in the public interest to so order, the judge shall order either or both of the following—

    (i) that the name and address of the authorised officer shall not be disclosed in court,

and

    (ii) that such cross-examination shall only take place in the sight and hearing of the judge and in the hearing only of all other persons present at such cross-examination.

Footnotes

1   S.908, as enacted, did not apply to CAT. The present section, which was substituted by s.207(i), FA 1999, does apply to CAT and has effect from 25th March, 1999.

2   As inserted by s.132(f), FA 2002, with effect from 25th March, 2002.

Section 908A[1]

Revenue offence: power to obtain information from financial institutions.

908A.(1)   In this section—

["the Acts" means the Waiver of Certain Tax, Interest and Penalties Act, 1993, together with the meaning assigned to it by section 1078(1) and;][2]

"authorised officer" means an officer of the Revenue Commissioners authorised by them in writing to exercise the powers conferred by this section;

"books, records or other documents" includes—

    (a)   any records used in the business of a financial institution, or used in the transfer department of a financial institution acting as registrar of securities, whether –

        (i)   comprised in bound volume, loose-leaf binders or other loose-leaf filing system, loose-leaf ledger sheets, pages, folios or cards, or

        (ii) kept on microfilm, magnetic tape or in any non-legible form (by the use of electronics or otherwise) which is capable of being reproduced in a legible form, and

    (b)   documents in manuscript, documents which are typed, printed, stencilled or created by any other mechanical or partly mechanical process in use from time to time and documents which are produced by any photographic or photostatic process;

"judge" means a judge of the Circuit Court or of the District Court;

["financial institution" means –

[(a)   a person who holds or has held a licence under section 9 of the Central Bank Act 1971, or a person who holds or has held a licence or other similar authorisartion under the law of any other Member State of the European Communities which corresponds to a licence granted under that section.][6]

    (b)   a person referred to in section 7(4) of the Central Bank Act, 1971, or

    (c)   a credit institution (within the meaning of the European Communities (Licensing and Supervision of Credit Institutions) Regulations, 1992 (S.I. No. 395 of 1992)) which has been authorised by the Central Bank of Ireland to carry on business of a credit institution in accordance with the provisions of the supervisory enactments (within the meaning of those Regulations);][3]

"liability" in relation to a person means any liability in relation to tax to which the person is or may be, or may have been, subject, or the amount of such liability;

["offence" means an offence falling within any provision of the Acts;][4]

"tax" means any tax, duty, levy or charge under the care and management of the Revenue Commissioners.

  [(2) (a)   In this subsection "documentation" includes information kept on microfilm, magnetic tape or in any non-legible form (by use of electronics or otherwise) which is capable of being reproduced in a permanent legible form.

      (b)   If, on application made by an authorised officer, with the consent in writing of a Revenue Commissioner, a judge is satisfied, on information given on oath by the authorised officer, that there are reasonable grounds for suspecting—

(i) that an offence, which would result (or but for its detection would have resulted) in serious prejudice to the proper assessment or collection of tax, is being, has been, or is about to be committed (having regard to the amount of a liability in relation to any person which might be, or might have been, evaded but for the detection of the relevant facts), and

(ii) that there is material in the possession of a financial institution specified in the application which is likely to be of substantial value (whether by itself or together with other material) to the investigation of the relevant facts,

the judge may make an order authorising the authorised officer to inspect and take copies of any entries in the books, records or other documents of the financial institution, and any documentation associated with or relating to an entry in such books, records or other documents, for the purposes of investigation of the relevant facts.]⁵

(3) An offence the commission of which, if considered alone, would not be regarded as resulting in serious prejudice to the proper assessment or collection of tax for the purposes of this section may nevertheless be so regarded if there are reasonable grounds for suspecting that the commission of the offence forms part of a course of conduct which is, or but for its detection would be, likely to result in serious prejudice to the proper assessment or collection of tax.

(4) Subject to subsection (5), a copy of any entry in books, records or other documents of a financial institution shall in all legal proceedings be received as prima facie evidence of such an entry, and of the matters, transactions, and accounts therein recorded.

(5) A copy of an entry in the books, records or other documents of a financial institution shall not be received in evidence in legal proceedings unless it is further proved that—

(a) in the case where the copy sought to be received in evidence has been reproduced in a legible form directly by either mechanical or electronic means, or both such means, from a financial institution's books, records or other documents maintained in a non-legible form, it has been so reproduced;

(b) in the case where the copy sought to be received in evidence has been made (either directly or indirectly) from a copy to which paragraph (a) would apply—

(i) the copy sought to be so received has been examined with a copy so reproduced and is a correct copy, and

        (ii)   the copy so reproduced is a copy to which paragraph (a) would apply if it were sought to have it received in evidence,

and

   (c)   in any other case, the copy has been examined with the original entry and is correct.

(6)   Proof of the matters to which subsection (5) relates shall be given—

   (a)   in respect of paragraph (a) or (b)(ii) of that subsection, by some person who has been in charge of the reproduction concerned, and

   (b)   in respect of paragraph (b)(i) of that subsection, by some person who has examined the copy with the reproduction concerned, and

   (c)   in respect of paragraph (c) of that subsection, by some person who has examined the copy with the original entry concerned,

and may be given either orally or by an affidavit sworn before any commissioner or person authorised to take affidavits.

Footnotes

1   This section was inserted by s.207(j), FA 1999, with effect from 25th March, 1999.

2   As inserted by s.132(g)(i)(I), FA 2002, with effect from 25th March, 2002. S.1078(1) includes, before 21st February, 2003, "the Capital Acquisitions Tax Act, 1976, and the enactments amending or extending that Act,".

3   As substituted by s.68(c), FA 2000, with effect from 23rd March, 2000.

4   As substituted by s.132(g)(i)(II), FA 2002, with effect from 25th March, 2002.

5   Substituted by s.68(d), FA 2000, with effect from 23rd March, 2000. Substituted by s.132(g)(ii), FA 2002, with effect from 25th March, 2002. As substituted by s.88, FA 2004, with effect from 25th March, 2004.

6   As substituted by s.92(h), F(No.2)A, 2008, with effect from 24th December, 2008.

Section 908B[1]

Application to High Court seeking order requiring information: associated institutions.

908B. (1)   In this section—

"the Acts" has the meaning assigned to it by section 1078(1);[2]

"associated institution", in relation to a financial institution, means a person that—

   (a)   is controlled by the financial institution (within the meaning of section 432), and

   (b)   is not resident in the State;

"authorised officer" means an officer of the Revenue Commissioners authorised by them in writing to exercise the powers conferred by this section;

"books, records or other documents" includes –

(a) any records used in the business of an associated institution, or used in the transfer department of an associated institution acting as registrar of securities, whether –

    (i) comprised in bound volume, loose-leaf binders or other loose-leaf filing system, loose-leaf ledger sheets, pages, folios or cards, or

    (ii) kept on microfilm, magnetic tape or in any non-legible form (by the use of electronics or otherwise) which is capable of being reproduced in a legible form,

(b) every electronic or other automatic means, if any, by which any such thing in non-legible form is so capable of being reproduced,

(c) documents in manuscript, documents which are typed, printed, stencilled or created by any other mechanical or partly mechanical process in use from time to time and documents which are produced by any photographic or photostatic process, and

(d) correspondence and records of other communications between an associated institution and its customers;

"financial institution" means –

[(a) a person who holds or has held a licence under section 9 of the Central Bank Act 1971, or a person who holds or has held a licence or other similar authorisation under the law of any other Member State of the European Communities which corresponds to a licence granted under that section,][3]

(b) a person referred to in section 7(4) of the Central Bank Act 1971, or

(c) a credit institution (within the meaning of the European Communities (Licensing and Supervision of Credit Institutions) Regulations 1992 (S.I. No. 395 of 1992)) which has been authorised by the Central Bank and Financial Services Authority of Ireland to carry on business of a credit institution in accordance with the provisions of the supervisory enactments (within the meaning of those Regulations);

"judge" means a judge of the High Court;

"liability" in relation to a person means any liability in relation to tax which the person is or may be, or may have been, subject, or the amount of such liability;

"commission", in relation to an offence, includes an attempt to commit the offence;

"computer" includes any electronic device capable of performing logical or arithmetical operations on data in accordance with a set of instructions;

"computer at the place which is being searched", includes any other computer, whether at that place or at any other place, which is lawfully accessible by means of that computer;

"information in non-legible form" means information which is kept (by electronic means or otherwise) on microfilm, microfiche, magnetic tape or disk or in any other non-legible form;

"material" means any books, documents, records or other things (including a computer);

"offence" means an offence under the Acts;

"place" includes any building (or part of a building), dwelling, vehicle, vessel, aircraft or hovercraft and any other place whatsoever;

"record" includes any information in non-legible form which is capable of being reproduced in a permanently legible form.

(2) If a judge of the District Court is satisfied by information given on oath by an authorised officer that there are reasonable grounds for suspecting —

    (a)   that an offence is being, has been or is about to be committed, and

    (b) (i) that material which is likely to be of value (whether by itself or together with other information) to the investigation of the offence, or

        (ii) that evidence of, or relating to the commission of, the offence,

is to be found in any place,

the judge may issue a warrant for the search of that place, and of any thing and any persons, found there.

(3) A warrant issued under this section shall be expressed and shall operate to authorise the authorised officer, accompanied by such other named officers of the Revenue Commissioners and such other named persons as the authorised officer considers necessary —

    (a)   to enter, at any time or times within one month from the date of issuing of the warrant (if necessary by the use of reasonable force), the place named in the warrant,

    (b)   to search, or cause to be searched, that place and any thing and any persons, found there, but no person shall be searched except by a person of the same sex unless express or implied consent is given,

(c)   to require any person found there—

   (i)   to give his or her name, home address and occupation to the authorised officer, and

   (ii)   to produce to the authorised officer any material which is in the custody or possession of that person,

(d)   to examine, seize and retain (or cause to be examined, seized and retained) any material found there, or in the possession of a person present there at the time of the search, which the authorised officer reasonably believes—

   (i)   is likely to be of value (whether by itself or together with other information) to the investigation of the offence, or

   (ii)   to be evidence of, or relating to the commission of, the offence, and

(e)   to take any other steps which may appear to the authorised officer to be necessary for preserving any such material and preventing interference with it.

(4)   The authority conferred by subsection (3)(d) to seize and retain (or to cause to be seized and retained) any material includes—

(a)   in the case of books, documents or records, authority to make and retain a copy of the books, documents or records, and

(b)   where necessary, authority to seize and, for as long as necessary, retain, any computer or other storage medium in which records are kept and to copy such records.

(5)   An authorised officer acting under the authority of a warrant issued under this section may—

(a)   operate any computer at the place which is being searched or cause any such computer to be operated by a person accompanying the authorised officer, and

(b)   require any person at that place who appears to the authorised officer to be in a position to facilitate access to the information held in any such computer or which can be accessed by the use of that computer—

   (i)   to give to the authorised officer any password necessary to operate it,

   (ii)   otherwise to enable the authorised officer to examine the information accessible by the computer in a form in which the information is visible and legible, or

   (iii)   to produce the information in a form in which it can be removed and in which it is, or can be made, visible and legible.

(6) A person who—

    (a) obstructs or attempts to obstruct the exercise of a right of entry and search conferred by virtue of a warrant issued under this section,

    (b) obstructs the exercise of a right so conferred to examine, seize and retain material,

    (c) fails to comply with a requirement under subsection (3)(c) or gives to the authorised officer a name, address or occupation that is false or misleading, or

    (d) fails to comply with a requirement under subsection (5)(b),

is guilty of an offence and is liable on summary conviction to a fine not exceeding [€5,000][3] or imprisonment for a term not exceeding 6 months or to both the fine and the imprisonment.

(7) Where an authorised officer enters, or attempts to enter, any place in the execution of a warrant issued under subsection (2), the authorised officer may be accompanied by a member or members of the Garda Síochána, and any such member may arrest without warrant any person who is committing an offence under subsection (6) or whom the member suspects, with reasonable cause, of having done so.

(8) Any material which is seized under subsection (3) which is required for the purposes of any legal proceedings by an officer of the Revenue Commissioners or for the purpose of any criminal proceedings, may be retained for so long as it is reasonably required for the purposes aforesaid.

Footnotes

1   This section was inserted by s.124(c), FA 2007, with effect from 2nd April, 2007.

2   S.1078(1) includes, before 21st February, 2003, "the Capital Acquistions Tax Act, 1976, and the enactments amending or extending that Act,".

3   As substituted for "€3,000" by s.138(1)(b), FA 2008, as respects an offence committed on a day after 13th March, 2008.

Section 908D[1]

Order to produce evidential material.

908D. (1) In this section—

"the Acts" means the Waiver of Certain Tax, Interest and Penalties Act 1993 together with the meaning assigned to it in section 1078(1);[2]

"authorised officer" means an officer of the Revenue Commissioners authorised by them in writing to exercise the powers conferred by this section;

"commission", in relation to an offence, includes an attempt to commit the offence;

"computer" includes any electronic device capable of performing logical or arithmetical operations on data in accordance with a set of instructions;

"information in non-legible form" means information which is kept (by electronic means or otherwise) on microfilm, microfiche, magnetic tape or disk or in any other non-legible form;

"material" means any books, documents, records or other things (including a computer);

"offence" means an offence under the Acts;

"record" includes any information in non-legible form which is capable of being reproduced in a permanently legible form.

(2) If a judge of the District Court is satisfied by information given on oath by an authorised officer that there are reasonable grounds for suspecting—

(a) that an offence is being, has been or is about to be committed, and

(b) that material—

(i)   which is likely to be of value (whether by itself or together with other information) to the investigation of the offence, or

(ii) which constitutes evidence of, or relating to the commission of, the offence,

is in the possession or control of a person specified in the application,

the judge may order that the person shall—

(I)   produce the material to the authorised officer for the authorised officer to take away, or

(II) give the authorised officer access to it,

either immediately or within such period as the order may specify.

(3) Where the material consists of or includes records contained in a computer, the order shall have effect as an order to produce the records, or to give access to them, in a form in which they are visible and legible and in which they can be taken away.

(4) An order under this section—

(a) in so far as it may empower an authorised officer to take away books, documents or records, or to be given access to them, shall also have effect as an order empowering the authorised officer to take away a copy of the books, documents or, as the case may be, records (and for that purpose the authorised officer may, if necessary, make a copy of them),

(b) shall not confer any right to production of, or access to, any document subject to legal privilege, and

  (e) the Value-Added Tax Act, 1972, and the enactments amending or extending that Act,

  (f) the Capital Acquisitions Tax Act, 1976, and the enactments amending or extending that Act, and

  (g) Part V1 of the Finance Act, 1983,

and any instruments made thereunder;

"data" means information in a form in which it can be processed;

"data equipment" means any electronic, photographic, magnetic, optical or other equipment for processing data;

"processing" means performing automatically logical or arithmetical operations on data, or the storing, maintenance, transmission, reproduction or communication of data;

"records" means documents which a person is obliged by any provision of the Acts to keep, issue or produce for inspection, and any other written or printed material;

"software" means any sequence of instructions used in conjunction with data equipment for the purpose of processing data or controlling the operation of the data equipment.

 (2) Any provision under the Acts which —

  (a) requires a person to keep, retain, issue or produce any records or cause any records to be kept, retained, issued or produced, or

  (b) permits an officer of the Revenue Commissioners —

   (i) to inspect any records,

   (ii) to enter premises and search for any records, or

   (iii) to take extracts from or copies of or remove any records,

shall, where the records are processed by data equipment, apply to the data equipment together with any associated software, data, apparatus or material as it applies to the records.

 (3) An officer of the Revenue Commissioners may in the exercise or performance of his or her powers or duties require —

  (a) the person by or on whose behalf the data equipment is or has been used, or

  (b) any person having charge of, or otherwise concerned with the operation of, the data equipment or any associated apparatus or material,

to afford him or her all reasonable assistance in relation to the exercise or performance of those powers or duties.

Footnotes

1 This section replaced, with effect from 6th April, 1997, s.237, FA 1992.

CHAPTER 6

Electronic transmission of returns of income, profits, etc., and of other Revenue returns

Section 917D[1]

Interpretation (Chapter 6).
917D. (1) In this Chapter –

"the Acts" means –

(a) the statutes relating to the duties of excise and to the management of those duties,

(b) the Tax Acts,

(c) the Capital Gains Tax Acts,

(d) the Value-Added Tax Act, 1972, and the enactments amending or extending that Act,

(e) the Capital Acquisitions Tax Act, 1976, and the enactments amending or extending that Act, and

(f) the [Stamp Duties Consolidation Act 1999,][2] and the enactments amending or extending that Act,

and any instruments made under any of the statutes and enactments referred to in paragraphs (a) to (f);

"approved person" shall be construed in accordance with section 917G;

"approved transmission" shall be construed in accordance with section 917H;

"authorised person" has the meaning assigned to it by [section 917G(3)(a);][3]

["digital signature", in relation to a person, means an advanced electronic signature (within the meaning of the Electronic Commerce Act, 2000) provided to the person by the Revenue Commissioners solely for the purpose of making an electronic transmission of information which is required to be included in a return to which this Chapter applies and for no other purpose and a qualified certificate (within the meaning of that Act) provided to the person by the Revenue Commissioners or a person appointed in that behalf by the Revenue Commissioners;][4]

"electronic identifier", in relation to a person, means -

(a) the person's digital signature, or

(b) such other means of electronic identification as may be specified or authorised by the Revenue Commissioners for the purposes of this Chapter;][5]

"hard copy", in relation to information held electronically, means a printed out version of that information;

["return" means any return, claim, application, notification, election, declaration, nomination, statement, list, registration, particulars or other information which a person is or may be required by the Acts to give to the Revenue Commissioners or any Revenue officer;][6]

"revenue officer" means the Collector-General, an inspector or other officer of the Revenue Commissioners (including an inspector or other officer who is authorised under any provision of the Acts (however expressed) to receive a return or to require a return to be prepared and delivered);

"tax" means any income tax, corporation tax, capital gains tax, value-added tax, gift tax, inheritance tax, excise duty or stamp duty.

(2) .....[7]

(3) Any references in this Chapter to the making of a return include references in any provision of the Acts to—

    (a)   the preparing and delivering of a return;

    (b)   the sending of a return;

    (c)   the furnishing of a return or of particulars;

    (d)   the delivering of a return;

    (e)   the presentation of a return;

    (f)   the rendering of a return;

    (g)   the giving of particulars or of any information specified in any provision; and

    (h)   any other means whereby a return is forwarded, however expressed.

Footnotes

1   This section was inserted by s.209, FA 1999, with effect from 25th March, 1999.

2   As substituted for "Stamp Act, 1891," by para.1(q)(i), Sch. 8, FA 2008, with effect as on and from 13th March, 2008

3   As substituted for "section 917G(3)(b)" by para. 1(q)(ii), Sch. 8, FA 2008, with effect as on and from 13th March, 2008

4   As substituted by s.235(a)(i)(I), FA 2001, with effect from 15th February, 2001.

5   As inserted by s.22(a), FA 2005, with effect from 1st January, 2005, under s.150(8), FA 2005.

6   As substituted by s.235(a)(i)(II), FA 2001, with effect from 15th February, 2001.

7   Deleted by s.235(a)(iii), FA 2001, with effect from 15th February, 2001.

Section 917E[1]

Application.

917E. This Chapter shall apply to a return if—

   (a) the provision of the Acts under which the return is made is specified for the purpose of this Chapter by order[2] made by the Revenue Commissioners, and

   (b) the return is required to be made after the day appointed by such order[2] in relation to returns to be made under the provision so specified.

Footnotes

  1   This section was inserted by s.209, FA 1999, with effect from 25th March, 1999.

  2   S.I. No. 443 of 2003 (see page 1375) does not apply to the CATA.

Section 917EA[1]

Mandatory electronic filing and payment of tax.

917EA. (1) In this section -

       "electronic means" includes electrical, digital, magnetic, optical, electromagnetic, biometric, photonic means of transmission of data and other forms of related technology by means of which data is transmitted;

       "repayment of tax" includes any amount relating to tax which is to be paid or repaid by the Revenue Commissioners;

       "specified person" means any person, group of persons or class of persons specified in regulations made under this section for the purposes of either or both paragraphs (a) and (b) of subsection (3);

       "specified return" means a return specified in regulations made under this section;

       "specified tax liabilities" means liabilities to tax including interest on unpaid tax specified in regulations made under this section.

  (2) Section 917D shall apply for the purposes of regulations made under this section in the same way as it applies for the purposes of this Chapter.

  (3) The Revenue Commissioners may make regulations -

     (a) requiring the delivery by specified persons of a specified return by electronic means where an order under section 917E has been made in respect of that return,

     (b) requiring the payment by electronic means of specified tax liabilities by specified persons, and

     (c) for the repayment of any tax specified in the regulations to be made by electronic means.

(4) Regulations made under this section shall include provision for the exclusion of a person from the requirements of regulations made under this section where the Revenue Commissioners are satisfied that the person could not reasonably be expected to have the capacity to make a specified return or to pay the specified tax liabilities by electronic means, and allowing a person, aggrieved by a failure to exclude such person, to appeal that failure to the Appeal Commissioners.

(5) Regulations made under this section may, in particular and without prejudice to the generality of subsection (3), include provision for -

    (a) the electronic means to be used to pay or repay tax,

    (b) the conditions to be complied with in relation to the electronic payment or repayment of tax,

    (c) determining the time when tax paid or repaid using electronic means is to be taken as having been paid or repaid,

    (d) the manner of proving, for any purpose, the time of payment or repayment of any tax paid or repaid using electronic means, including provision for the application of any conclusive or other presumptions,

    (e) notifying persons that they are specified persons, including the manner by which such notification may be made, and

    (f) such supplemental and incidental matters as appear to the Revenue Commissioners to be necessary.

(6) The Revenue Commissioners may nominate any of their officers to perform any acts and discharge any functions authorised by regulation made under this section to be performed or discharged by the Revenue Commissioners.

(7) Where a specified person -

    (a) makes a return which is a specified return for the purposes of regulations made under this section, or

    (b) makes a payment of tax which is specified tax liabilities for the purposes of regulations made under this section,

in a form other than that required by any such regulation, the specified person shall be liable to a penalty of €1,520 and, for the purposes of the recovery of a penalty under this subsection, section 1061 applies in the same manner as it applies for the purposes of the recovery of a penalty under any of the sections referred to in that section.

(8) Every regulation made under this section shall be laid before Dáil Éireann as soon as may be after it is made and, if a resolution annulling the regulation is passed by Dáil Éireann within the next 21 days on which Dáil Éireann has sat after the regulation is laid before it, the regulation shall be annulled accordingly but without prejudice to the validity of anything previously done under the regulation.

Footnote

1   As inserted by s.164(1)(a), FA 2003, with effect from such day as the Minister for Finance may appoint by order. S.I. No. 308 of 2008 appoints 28th July, 2008, as the effective day.

Section 917F[1]

Electronic transmission of returns.

917F. (1)   Notwithstanding any other provision of the Acts, the obligation of any person to make a return to which this Chapter applies shall be treated as fulfilled by that person if information is transmitted electronically in compliance with that obligation, but only if –

    (a)   the transmission is made by an approved person or an authorised person,

    (b)   the transmission is an approved transmission,

    [(c)   the transmission bears the electronic identifier of that person, and][2]

    (d)   the receipt of the transmission is acknowledged in accordance with section 917J.

  (2)   In subsection (1), the reference to the information which is required to be included in the return includes any requirement on a person to –

    (a)   make any statement,

    (b)   include any particulars, or

    (c)   make or attach any claim.

  (3)   Where the obligation of any person to make a return to which this Chapter applies is treated as fulfilled in accordance with subsection (1) then, any provision of the Acts which –

    (a)   requires that the return include or be accompanied by any description of declaration whatever by the person making the return, apart from a declaration of an amount,

    (b)   requires that the return be signed or accompanied by a certificate,

    (c)   requires that the return be in writing,

    (d)   authorises the return to be signed by a person acting under the authority of the person obliged to make the return,

    (e)   authorises the Revenue Commissioners to prescribe the form of a return or which requires a return to be in or on any prescribed form, or

    (f)   for the purposes of any claim for exemption or for any allowance, deduction or repayment of tax under the Acts which is required to be made with the return, authorises the Revenue Commissioners to prescribe the form of a claim,

shall not apply.

Footnotes

1   This section was inserted by s.209, FA 1999, with effect from 25th March, 1999.

2   Words substituted for "complies with the provisions of this section and, in particular, with the conditions specified in subsection (3)" by s.235(c)(i), FA 2001, with effect from 15th February, 2001. In that substitution, the words "electronic identifiers" were substituted for "digital signatures" by s.22(c), FA 2005, the latter substitution with effect from 1st January, 2005, under s.150(8), FA 2005.

3   Words substituted for "in writing or by such other means as may be approved by the Revenue Commissioners" by s.235(c)(ii), FA 2001, with effect from 15th February, 2001.

4   As substituted by s.235(c)(iii), FA 2001, with effect from 15th February, 2001.

Section 917H[1]

Approved transmissions.

917H. (1) Where an approved person transmits electronically information which is required to be included in a return to which this Chapter applies the transmission shall not be an approved transmission unless it complies with the requirements of this section.

[(2) The Revenue Commissioners shall publish and make known to each approved person and each authorised person any requirement for the time being determined by them as being applicable to –

(a) the manner in which information which is required to be included in a return to which this Chapter applies is to be transmitted electronically, and

(b) the use of a person's [electronic identifier][2].

(3) The requirements referred to in subsection (2) include –

(a) requirements as to the software or type of software to be used to make a transmission,

(b) the terms and conditions under which a person may make a transmission, and

(c) the terms and conditions under which a person may use that person's digital signature.][3]

[(4) For the purposes of subsection (3), the Revenue Commissioners may determine different terms and conditions in relation to different returns or categories of a return, different categories of persons and different returns or categories of a return made by different categories of persons.][4]

Footnotes

1   This section was inserted by s.209, FA 1999, with effect from 25th March, 1999.

2   Substituted for "digital signature" by s.22(d)(i), FA 2005, with effect from 1st January, 2005, under s.150(8), FA 2005.

3   As substituted by s.235(d), FA 2001, with effect from 15th February, 2001.

4   As inserted by s.22(d)(ii), FA 2005, with effect from 1st January, 2005, under s.150(8), FA 2005.

Section 917I[1]

Digital signatures.

917I. (1) .....

Footnote
1   This section was inserted by s.209, FA 1999, with effect from 25th March, 1999, and was
        deleted by s.235(e), FA 2001, with effect from 15th February, 2001.

Section 917J[1]

Acknowledgement of electronic transmissions.

917J. For the purposes of this Chapter, where an electronic transmission of information which is required to be included in a return to which this Chapter applies is received by the Revenue Commissioners, the Revenue Commissioners shall send an electronic acknowledgement of receipt of that transmission to the person from whom it was received.

Footnote
1   This section was inserted by s.209, FA 1999, with effect from 25th March, 1999.

Section 917K[1]

Hard copies.

917K.(1)   A hard copy shall be made in accordance with this subsection only if—

   (a)   the hard copy is made under processes and procedures which are designed to ensure that the information contained in the hard copy shall only be the information [transmitted or to be transmitted][2] in accordance with section 917F(1),

   (b)   the hard copy is in a form approved by the Revenue Commissioners which is appropriate to the information so transmitted, and

   (c)   the hard copy is authenticated in accordance with subsection (2).

   (2)   For the purposes of this Chapter, a hard copy made in accordance with subsection (1) shall be authenticated only if the hard copy is signed by the person who would have been required to make the declaration, sign the return or furnish the certificate, as the case may be, but for paragraph (a), (b) or (d) of section 917F(3).

Footnotes
1   This section was inserted by s.209, FA 1999, with effect from 25th March, 1999.

2   Words substituted for "to be transmitted" by s.235(f), FA 2001, with effect from 15th
        February 2001.

Section 917L[1]

Exercise of powers.

917L. (1) This section shall apply where the obligation of any person to make a return to which this Chapter applies is treated as fulfilled in accordance with section 917F(1).

(2) Where this section applies the Revenue Commissioners and a revenue officer shall have all the powers and duties in relation to the information contained in the transmission as they or that officer would have had if the information had been contained in a return made by post.

(3) Where this section applies the person whose obligation to make a return to which this Chapter applies is treated as fulfilled in accordance with section 917F(1) shall have all the rights and duties in relation to the information contained in the transmission as the person would have had if that information had been contained in a return made by post.

Footnote

1   This section was inserted by s.209, FA 1999, with effect from 25th March, 1999.

Section 917M[1]

Proceedings.

917M.(1) This section shall apply where the obligation of any person to make a return to which this Chapter applies is treated as fulfilled in accordance with section 917F(1).

(2) In this section, "proceedings" means civil and criminal proceedings, and includes proceedings before the Appeal Commissioners or any other tribunal having jurisdiction by virtue of any provision of the Acts.

(3) Where this section applies a hard copy certified by a revenue officer to be a true copy of the information transmitted electronically in accordance with section 917F(1) shall be treated [for the purposes of the Acts][2] as if the hard copy –

(a) were a return or, as the case may be, a claim made by post, and

(b) contained any declaration, certificate or signature required by the Acts on such a return or, as the case may be, such a claim.

(4) For the purposes of any proceedings under the Acts, unless a Judge or any other person before whom proceedings are taken determines at the time of the proceedings that it is unjust in the circumstances to apply this provision, any rule of law restricting the admissibility or use of hearsay evidence shall not apply to a representation contained in a document recording information which has been transmitted in accordance with section 917F(1) in so far as the representation is a representation as to–

(a) the information so transmitted,

(b) the date on which, or the time at which, the information was so transmitted, or

(c) the identity of the person by whom or on whose behalf the information was so transmitted.

Footnotes
1   This section was inserted by s.209, FA 1999, with effect from 25th March, 1999.
2   Words substituted for "for the purposes of any proceedings in relation to which the certificate is given" by s.235(g), FA 2001, with effect from 15th February, 2001.

Section 917N[1]

Miscellaneous.
917N. The Revenue Commissioners may nominate any of their officers to perform any acts and discharge any functions authorised by this Chapter to be performed or discharged by the Revenue Commissioners.

Footnote
1   This section was inserted by s.209, FA 1999, with effect from 25th March, 1999.

PART 42
Collection and Recovery

CHAPTER 5
Miscellaneous Provisions

Section 1002[1]

Deduction from payments due to defaulters of amounts due in relation to tax.
1002. (1) (a) In this section, except where the context otherwise requires −
"the Acts" means −

(i)   the Customs Acts,

(ii)   the statutes relating to the duties of excise and to the management of those duties,

[(iiia) Part 18A,][3]

(iii) the Tax Acts,

(iv)   the Capital Gains Tax Acts,

(v)   the Value-Added Tax Act, 1972, and the enactments amending or extending that Act,

(vi)   the Capital Acquisitions Tax Act, 1976, and the enactments amending or extending that Act, and

(vii) the Stamp Act, 1891, and the enactments amending or extending that Act,

[(viii) Part 18B,]⁴

and any instruments made thereunder;

"additional debt", in relation to a relevant person who has received a notice of attachment in respect of a taxpayer, means any amount which, at any time after the time of the receipt by the relevant person of the notice of attachment but before the end of the relevant period in relation to the notice, would be a debt due by the relevant person to the taxpayer if a notice of attachment were received by the relevant person at that time;

"debt", in relation to a notice of attachment given to a relevant person in respect of a taxpayer and in relation to that relevant person and taxpayer, means, subject to paragraphs (b) to (e), the amount or aggregate amount of any money which, at the time the notice of attachment is received by the relevant person, is due by the relevant person (whether on that person's own account or as an agent or trustee) to the taxpayer, irrespective of whether the taxpayer has applied for the payment (to the taxpayer or any other person) or for the withdrawal of all or part of the money;

"deposit" means a sum of money paid to a financial institution on terms under which it will be repaid with or without interest and either on demand or at a time or in circumstances agreed by or on behalf of the person making the payment and the financial institution to which it is made;

"emoluments" means anything assessable to income tax under Schedule E;

["financial institution" means —

(a) a person who holds or has held a licence under section 9 of the Central Bank Act 1971, or a person who holds or has held a licence or other similar authorisation under the law of any other Member State of the European Communities which corresponds to a licence granted under that section,

(b) a person referred to in section 7(4) of the Central Bank Act 1971,

(c) a credit institution (within the meaning of the European Communities (Licensing and Supervision of Credit Institutions) Regulations 1992 (S.I. No. 395 of 1992)) which has been authorised by the Central Bank and Financial Services Authority of Ireland to carry on business of a credit institution in accordance with the provisions of the supervisory enactments (within the meaning of those Regulations), or

(d) a branch of a financial institution which records deposits in its books as liabilities of the branch;][5]

"further return" means a return made by a relevant person under subsection (4);

"interest on unpaid tax", in relation to a specified amount specified in a notice of attachment, means interest that has accrued to the date on which the notice of attachment is given under any provision of the Acts providing for the charging of interest in respect of the unpaid tax, including interest on an undercharge of tax which is attributable to fraud or neglect, specified in the notice of attachment;

"notice of attachment" means a notice under subsection (2);

"notice of revocation" means a notice under subsection (10);

"penalty" means a monetary penalty imposed on a taxpayer under a provision of the Acts;

"relevant period", in relation to a notice of attachment, means, as respects the relevant person to whom the notice of attachment is given, the period commencing at the time at which the notice is received by the relevant person and ending on the earliest of –

(i) the date on which the relevant person completes the payment to the Revenue Commissioners out of the debt, or the aggregate of the debt and any additional debt, due by the relevant person to the taxpayer named in the notice, of an amount equal to the specified amount in relation to the taxpayer,

(ii) the date on which the relevant person receives a notice of revocation of the notice of attachment, and

(iii) where the relevant person or the taxpayer named in the notice –

(I) is declared bankrupt, the date the relevant person or the taxpayer is so declared, or

(II) is a company which commences to be wound up, the relevant date within the meaning of section 285 of the Companies Act, 1963, in relation to the winding up;

"relevant person", in relation to a taxpayer, means a person whom the Revenue Commissioners have reason to believe may have, at the time a notice of attachment is received by such person in respect of a taxpayer, a debt due to the taxpayer;

"return" means a return made by a relevant person under subsection (2) (a) (iii);

"specified amount" has the meaning assigned to it by subsection (2) (a) (ii);

"tax" means any tax, duty, levy or charge which in accordance with any provision of the Acts is placed under the care and management of the Revenue Commissioners;

"taxpayer" means a person who is liable to pay, remit or account for tax to the Revenue Commissioners under the Acts.

(b) Where a relevant person is a financial institution, any amount or aggregate amount of money, including interest on that money, which at the time the notice of attachment is received by the relevant person is a deposit held by the relevant person—

(i) to the credit of the taxpayer for the taxpayer's sole benefit, or

(ii) to the credit of the taxpayer and any other person or persons for their joint benefit,

shall be regarded as a debt due by the relevant person to the taxpayer at that time.

(c) Any amount of money due by the relevant person to the taxpayer as emoluments under a contract of service shall not be regarded as a debt due to the taxpayer.

(d) Where there is a dispute as to an amount of money which is due by the relevant person to the taxpayer, the amount in dispute shall be disregarded for the purposes of determining the amount of the debt.

(e) In the case referred to in paragraph (b), a deposit held by a relevant person which is a financial institution to the credit of the taxpayer and any other person or persons (in this paragraph referred to as "the other party or parties") for their joint benefit shall be deemed (unless evidence to the contrary is produced to the satisfaction of the relevant person within 10 days of the giving of the notices specified in subsection (2) (e)) to be held to the benefit of the taxpayer and the other party or parties to the deposit equally, and accordingly only the portion of the deposit so deemed shall be regarded as a debt due by the relevant person to the taxpayer at the time the notice of attachment is received by the relevant person and, where such evidence is produced within the specified time, only so much of the deposit as is shown to be held to the benefit of the taxpayer shall be regarded as a debt due by the relevant person to the taxpayer at that time.

(2) (a) Subject to subsection (3), where a taxpayer has made default whether before or after the passing of this Act in paying, remitting or accounting for any tax, interest on unpaid tax, or penalty to the Revenue Commissioners, the Revenue Commissioners may, if the taxpayer has not made good the

default, give to a relevant person in relation to the taxpayer a notice in writing (in this section referred to as "the notice of attachment") in which is entered –

    (i)   the taxpayer's name and address,

    (ii) (I)   the amount or aggregate amount, or

          (II) in a case where more than one notice of attachment is given to a relevant person or relevant persons in respect of a taxpayer, a portion of the amount or aggregate amount,

of the taxes, interest on unpaid taxes and penalties in respect of which the taxpayer is in default at the time of the giving of the notice or notices of attachment (the amount, aggregate amount, or portion of the amount or aggregate amount, as the case may be, being referred to in this section as "the specified amount"), and

    (iii) a direction to the relevant person –

          (I)   subject to paragraphs (b) and (c), to deliver to the Revenue Commissioners, within the period of 10 days from the time at which the notice of attachment is received by the relevant person, a return in writing specifying whether or not any debt is due by the relevant person to the taxpayer at the time the notice is received by the relevant person and, if any debt is so due, specifying the amount of the debt, and

          (II) if the amount of any debt is so specified, to pay to the Revenue Commissioners within the period referred to in clause (I) a sum equal to the amount of the debt so specified.

(b)   Where the amount of the debt due by the relevant person to the taxpayer is equal to or greater than the specified amount in relation to the taxpayer, the amount of the debt specified in the return shall be an amount equal to the specified amount.

(c)   Where the relevant person is a financial institution and the debt due by the relevant person to the taxpayer is part of a deposit held to the credit of the taxpayer and any other person or persons to their joint benefit, the return shall be made within a period of 10 days from –

    (i)   the expiry of the period specified in the notices to be given under paragraph (e), or

    (ii) the production of the evidence referred to in paragraph (e) (II).

(d)   A relevant person to whom a notice of attachment has been given shall comply with the direction in the notice.

(e)   Where a relevant person which is a financial institution is given a notice of attachment and the debt due by the relevant person to the taxpayer is part of a deposit held by the relevant person to the credit of the taxpayer and any other person or persons (in this paragraph referred to as "the other party or parties") for their joint benefit, the relevant person shall on receipt of the notice of attachment give to the taxpayer and the other party or parties to the deposit a notice in writing in which is entered –

    (i)   the taxpayer's name and address,

    (iii) the name and address of the person to whom a notice under this paragraph is given,

    (iii) the name and address of the relevant person, and

    (iv) the specified amount,

and which states that –

    (I)   a notice of attachment under this section has been received in respect of the taxpayer,

    (II)   under this section a deposit is deemed (unless evidence to the contrary is produced to the satisfaction of the relevant person within 10 days of the giving of the notice under this paragraph) to be held to the benefit of the taxpayer and the other party or parties to the deposit equally, and

    (III) unless such evidence is produced within the period specified in the notice given under this paragraph –

        (A)   a sum equal to the amount of the deposit so deemed to be held to the benefit of the taxpayer (and accordingly regarded as a debt due to the taxpayer by the relevant person) shall be paid to the Revenue Commissioners, where that amount is equal to or less than the specified amount, and

        (B)   where the amount of the deposit so deemed to be held to the benefit of the taxpayer (and accordingly regarded as a debt due to the taxpayer by the relevant person) is greater than the specified amount, a sum equal to the specified amount shall be paid to the Revenue Commissioners.

(3)   An amount in respect of tax, interest on unpaid tax or a penalty, as respects which a taxpayer is in default as specified in subsection (2), shall not be entered in a notice of attachment unless –

    (a)   a period of [14 days]² has expired from the date on which such default commenced, and

    (b)   the Revenue Commissioners have given the taxpayer a notice in writing (whether or not the document containing the notice also contains other information being communicated by the

Revenue Commissioners to the taxpayer), not later than 7 days before the date of the receipt by the relevant person or relevant persons concerned of a notice of attachment, stating that if the amount is not paid it may be specified in a notice or notices of attachment and recovered under this section from a relevant person or relevant persons in relation to the taxpayer.

(4) If, when a relevant person receives a notice of attachment, the amount of the debt due by the relevant person to the taxpayer named in the notice is less than the specified amount in relation to the taxpayer or no debt is so due and, at any time after the receipt of the notice and before the end of the relevant period in relation to the notice, an additional debt becomes due by the relevant person to the taxpayer, the relevant person shall within 10 days of that time—

    (a) if the aggregate of the amount of any debt so due and the additional debt so due is equal to or less than the specified amount in relation to the taxpayer—

        (i) deliver a further return to the Revenue Commissioners specifying the additional debt, and

        (ii) pay to the Revenue Commissioners the amount of the additional debt,

    and so on for each subsequent occasion during the relevant period in relation to the notice of attachment on which an additional debt becomes due by the relevant person to the taxpayer until—

        (I) the aggregate amount of the debt and the additional debt or debts so due equals the specified amount in relation to the taxpayer, or

        (II) paragraph (b) applies in relation to an additional debt, and

    (b) if the aggregate amount of any debt and the additional debt or debts so due to the taxpayer is greater than the specified amount in relation to the taxpayer—

        (i) deliver a further return to the Revenue Commissioners specifying such portion of the latest additional debt as when added to the aggregate of the debt and any earlier additional debts is equal to the specified amount in relation to the taxpayer, and

        (ii) pay to the Revenue Commissioners that portion of the additional debt.

(5) Where a relevant person delivers, either fraudulently or negligently, an incorrect return or further return that purports to be a return or further return made in accordance with this section, the relevant person shall be deemed to be guilty of an offence under section 1078.

(6) (a) Where a notice of attachment has been given to a relevant person in respect of a taxpayer, the relevant person shall not, during the relevant period in relation to the notice, make any disbursements out of the debt, or out of any additional debt, due by the relevant person to the taxpayer except to the extent that any such disbursement—

      (i) will not reduce the debt or the aggregate of the debt and any additional debts so due to an amount that is less than the specified amount in relation to the taxpayer, or

      (ii) is made pursuant to an order of a court.

  (b) For the purposes of this section, a disbursement made by a relevant person contrary to paragraph (a) shall be deemed not to reduce the amount of the debt or any additional debts due by the relevant person to the taxpayer.

(7) (a) Sections 1052 and 1054 shall apply to a failure by a relevant person to deliver a return required by a notice of attachment within the time specified in the notice or to deliver a further return within the time specified in subsection (4) as they apply to a failure to deliver a return referred to in section 1052.

  (b) A certificate signed by an officer of the Revenue Commissioners which certifies that he or she has examined the relevant records and that it appears from those records that during a specified period a specified return was not received from a relevant person shall be evidence until the contrary is proved that the relevant person did not deliver the return during that period.

  (c) A certificate certifying as provided by paragraph (b) and purporting to be signed by an officer of the Revenue Commissioners may be tendered in evidence without proof and shall be deemed until the contrary is proved to have been so signed.

(8) Where a relevant person to whom a notice of attachment in respect of a taxpayer has been given—

  (a) delivers the return required to be delivered by that notice but fails to pay to the Revenue Commissioners within the time specified in the notice the amount specified in the return or any part of that amount, or

  (b) delivers a further return under subsection (4) but fails to pay to the Revenue Commissioners within the time specified in that subsection the amount specified in the further return or any part of that amount,

the amount specified in the return or further return or the part of that amount, as the case may be, which the relevant person has failed to pay to the Revenue Commissioners may, if the notice of attachment has not been revoked by a notice of revocation, be sued for and recovered by action or other appropriate proceedings at the suit of an officer of the Revenue Commissioners in any court of competent jurisdiction.

(9) Nothing in this section shall be construed as rendering any failure by a relevant person to make a return or further return required by this section, or to pay to the Revenue Commissioners the amount or amounts required by this section to be paid by the relevant person, liable to be treated as a failure to which section 1078 applies.

(10) (a) A notice of attachment given to a relevant person in respect of a taxpayer may be revoked by the Revenue Commissioners at any time by notice in writing given to the relevant person and shall be revoked forthwith if the taxpayer has paid the specified amount to the Revenue Commissioners.

(b) Where in pursuance of this section a relevant person pays any amount to the Revenue Commissioners out of a debt or an additional debt due by the relevant person to the taxpayer and, at the time of the receipt by the Revenue Commissioners of that amount, the taxpayer has paid to the Revenue Commissioners the amount or aggregate amount of the taxes, interest on unpaid taxes and penalties in respect of which the taxpayer is in default at the time of the giving of the notice or notices of attachment, the first-mentioned amount shall be refunded by the Revenue Commissioners forthwith to the taxpayer.

(11) Where a notice of attachment or a notice of revocation is given to a relevant person in relation to a taxpayer, a copy of such notice shall be given by the Revenue Commissioners to the taxpayer forthwith.

(12) (a) Where in pursuance of this section any amount is paid to the Revenue Commissioners by a relevant person, the relevant person shall forthwith give the taxpayer concerned a notice in writing specifying the payment, its amount and the reason for which it was made.

(b) On the receipt by the Revenue Commissioners of an amount paid in pursuance of this section, the Revenue Commissioners shall forthwith notify the taxpayer and the relevant person in writing of such receipt.

(13) Where in pursuance of this section a relevant person pays to the Revenue Commissioners the whole or part of the amount of a debt or an additional debt due by the relevant person to a taxpayer, or any portion of such an amount, the taxpayer shall allow such payment and the relevant person shall be acquitted and discharged of the amount of the payment as if it had been paid to the taxpayer.

(14) Where in pursuance of this section a relevant person is prohibited from making any disbursement out of a debt or an additional debt due to a taxpayer, no action shall lie against the relevant person in any court by reason of a failure to make any such disbursement.

(ii) in the case of corporation tax, any accounting period preceding the accounting period in which the relevant gift is made;

"selection committee" means a committee consisting of –

[(i) an officer of the Minister for Arts, Sport and Tourism, who shall act as Chairperson of the committee,

(ii) the Chief Executive of the Heritage Council,

(iii) the Director of the Arts Council,

(iv) the Director of the National Archives,

(v) the Director of the National Gallery of Ireland,

(vi) the Director of the National Library of Ireland,

[(iva) the Director of the Crawford Art Gallery Cork Limited,][3]

(vii) the Director of the National Museum of Ireland, and

(viii) the Director and Chief Executive of the Irish Museum of Modern Art,][4]

and includes any person duly acting in the capacity of any of those persons as a result of the person concerned being unable to fulfil his or her duties for any of the reasons set out in paragraph (b) (ii);

"tax" means income tax, corporation tax, capital gains tax, gift tax or inheritance tax, as the case may be, payable in accordance with any provision of the Acts;

"valuation date" means the date on which an application is made to the selection committee for a determination under subsection (2) (a).

(b) (i) The selection committee may act notwithstanding one or more vacancies among its members and may regulate its own procedure.

(ii) If and so long as a member of the selection committee is unable through illness, absence or other cause to fulfil his or her duties, a person nominated in that behalf by the member shall act as the member of the committee in the place of the member.

[(iii) For the purposes of making a decision in relation to an application made to it for a determination under subsection (2)(a), the selection committee shall not include the member of that committee who represents the approved body to which it is intended that the gift of the heritage item is to be made where that approved body is so represented but that member may participate in any discussion of the application by that committee prior to the making of the decision.][5]

(2) (a) In this section, "heritage item" means any kind of cultural item, including—

   (i) any archaeological item, archive, book, estate record, manuscript and painting, and

   (ii) any collection of cultural items and any collection of such items in their setting,

   which, on application to the selection committee in writing in that behalf by a person who owns the item or collection of items, as the case may be, [is, subject to the provisions of paragraphs (aa) and (ab), determined by the selection committee,][6] to be an item or collection of items which is—

   (I) an outstanding example of the type of item involved, pre-eminent in its class, whose export from the State would constitute a diminution of the accumulated cultural heritage of Ireland [or whose import into the State would constitute a significant enhancement of the accumulated cultural heritage of Ireland][7], and

   (II) suitable for acquisition by an approved body.

[(aa) In considering an application under paragraph (a), the selection committee shall—

   (i) consider such evidence as the person making the application submits to it, and

   (ii) seek and consider the opinion in writing in relation to the application of—

      (I) the approved body to which it is intended the gift is to be made, and

      (II) the Heritage Council, the Arts Council or such other person or body of persons as the committee considers to be appropriate in the circumstances.

(ab) Where an application under paragraph (a) is in respect of a collection of items, the selection committee shall not make a determination under that paragraph in relation to the collection unless, in addition to the making of a determination in relation to the collection as a whole, the selection committee is satisfied that, on the basis of its consideration of the application in accordance with paragraph (aa), it could make a determination in respect of at least one item comprised in the collection, if such were required.][8]

[(ac) Paragraph (ab) shall not apply in the case of a collection of items, consisting wholly of archival material or manuscripts, which was either—

   (i) created over time by one individual family or organisation, or

(ii)   was assembled by an individual, family or organisation,

and constitutes a collection of archival material or manuscripts where each item has been in such collection for a period of not less than 30 years and merits maintenance as a collection.][9]

(b)   On receipt of an application for a determination under paragraph (a), the selection committee shall request the Revenue Commissioners in writing to value the item or collection of items, as the case may be, in accordance with subsection (3).

(c)   The selection committee shall not make a determination under paragraph (a) where the market value of the item or collection of items, as the case may be, as determined by the Revenue Commissioners in accordance with subsection (3), at the valuation date—

[(i)   is less than,

(I)   subject to clause (II), €150,000, and

(II)   in the case of at least one item comprised in a collection of items, €50,000, or][10]

(ii)   exceeds an amount (which shall not be less than [€150,000][11]) determined by the formula—

$$€6,000,000^{12} - M$$

where M is an amount (which may be nil) equal to the market value at the valuation date of the heritage item (if any) or the aggregate of the market values at the respective valuation dates of all the heritage items (if any), as the case may be, in respect of which a determination or determinations, as the case may be, under this subsection has been made by the selection committee in any one calendar year and not revoked in that year.

(d)   (i)   An item or collection of items shall cease to be a heritage item for the purposes of this section if—

(I)   the item or collection of items is sold or otherwise disposed of to a person other than an approved body,

(II)   the owner of the item or collection of items notifies the selection committee in writing that it is not intended to make a gift of the item or collection of items to an approved body, or

(III)   the gift of the item or collection of items is not made to an approved body within the calendar year following the year in which the determination is made under paragraph (a).

(ii)   Where the selection committee becomes aware, at any time within the calendar year in which a determination under paragraph (a) is made in respect of an item or collection of items, that clause (I) or (II) of subparagraph (i) applies to the item or collection of items, the selection committee may revoke its determination with effect from that time.

[(2A)Notwithstanding subsection (2)(c), the selection committee may make a determination in respect of an item or collection of items, consisting wholly of archival material or manuscripts, and the market value limit in respect of any one item in such a collection at the valuation date as set out in subsection (2)(c)(i)(II) shall not apply.]¹³

(3) [(a) For the purposes of this section, the market value of any item or collection of items (in this subsection referred to as "the property") shall, subject to paragraph (d), be estimated to be the lesser of —

      (i)   the price which, in the opinion of the Revenue Commissioners, the property would fetch if sold in the open market on the valuation date in such manner and subject to such conditions as might reasonably be calculated to obtain for the vendor the best price for the property, and

      (ii) (I) the price which, in the opinion of the person making the gift of the property, the property would fetch on the valuation date if sold in the manner referred to in subparagraph (i), or

          (II) at the election of that person, the amount paid for the property by that person.]¹⁴

  (b) The market value of the property shall be ascertained by the Revenue Commissioners in such manner and by such means as they think fit, and they may authorise a person to inspect the property and report to them the value of the property for the purposes of this section, and the person having custody or possession of the property shall permit the person so authorised to inspect the property at such reasonable times as the Revenue Commissioners consider necessary.

  (c) Where the Revenue Commissioners require a valuation to be made by a person authorised by them, the cost of such valuation shall be defrayed by the Revenue Commissioners.

  [(d) Where the property is acquired at auction by the person making the gift, the market value of the property shall, for the purposes of this section, be deemed to include the auctioneer's fees in connection with the auction together with —

      (i)   any amount chargeable under the Value-Added Tax Act, 1972, by the auctioneer to the purchaser of the property in respect of those fees and in respect of which the purchaser is not entitled to any deduction or refund under that Act or any other enactment relating to value-added tax, or

(ii)   in the case of an auction in a country other than the State, the amount chargeable to the purchaser of the property in respect of a tax chargeable under the law of that country which corresponds to value-added tax in the State and in relation to which the purchaser is not entitled to any deduction or refund.][15]

(4) Where a relevant gift is made to an approved body —

    (a)   the designated officer of that body shall give a certificate to the person who made the relevant gift, in such form as the Revenue Commissioners may prescribe, certifying the receipt of that gift and the transfer of the ownership of the heritage item the subject of that gift to the approved body, and

    (b)   the designated officer shall transmit a duplicate of the certificate to the Revenue Commissioners.

(5) Subject to this section, where a person has made a relevant gift the person shall, on submission to the Revenue Commissioners of the certificate given to the person in accordance with subsection (4), be treated as having made on the date of such submission a payment on account of tax of **[an amount equal to 80 per cent of the market value]**[16] of the relevant gift on the valuation date.

(6) A payment on account of tax which is treated as having been made in accordance with subsection (5) shall be set in so far as possible against any liability to tax of the person who is treated as having made such a payment in the following order —

    (a)   firstly, against any arrears of tax due for payment by that person and against an arrear of tax for an earlier period in priority to a later period, and for this purpose the date on which an arrear of tax became due for payment shall determine whether it is for an earlier or later period, and

    (b)   only then, against any current liability of the person which the person nominates for that purpose,

and such set-off shall accordingly discharge a corresponding amount of that liability.

(7) To the extent that a payment on account of tax has not been set off in accordance with subsection (6), the balance remaining shall be set off against any future liability to tax of the person who is treated as having made the payment which that person nominates for that purpose.

(8) Where a person has power to sell any heritage item in order to raise money for the payment of gift tax or inheritance tax, such person shall have power to make a relevant gift of that heritage item in or towards satisfaction of that tax and, except as regards the nature of the consideration and its receipt and application, any such relevant gift shall be subject to the same provisions and shall be treated for all purposes as a sale made in exercise of that power, and any

conveyances or transfers made or purporting to be made to give effect to such a relevant gift shall apply accordingly.

(9) A person shall not be entitled to any refund of tax in respect of any payment on account of tax made in accordance with this section.

(10) Interest shall not be payable in respect of any overpayment of tax for any period which arises directly or indirectly by reason of the set-off against any liability for that period of a payment on account of tax made in accordance with this section.

(11) Where a person makes a relevant gift and in respect of that gift is treated as having made a payment on account of tax, the person concerned shall not be allowed relief under any other provision of the Acts in respect of that gift.

(12) (a) The Revenue Commissioners shall as respects each year compile a list of the titles (if any), descriptions and values of the heritage items (if any) in respect of which relief under this section has been given.

(b) Notwithstanding any obligation as to secrecy imposed on them by the Acts or the Official Secrets Act, 1963, the Revenue Commissioners shall include in their annual report to the Minister for Finance the list (if any) referred to in paragraph (a) for the year in respect of which the report is made.

Footnotes

1   This section replaced, with effect from 6th April, 1997, s.176, FA 1995, as amended.

2   As inserted by s.125(a), FA 2007, with effect from 2nd April, 2007.

3   As inserted by s.125(b), FA 2007, with effect from 2nd April, 2007.

4   As substituted by s.85(a)(i), FA 2004, as respects determinations made under s.1003(2)(a) on or after 25th March, 2004.

5   As inserted by s.85(a)(ii), FA 2004, as respects determinations made under s.1003(2)(a) on or after 25th March, 2004.

6   As substituted by s.85(b)(i), FA 2004, as respects determinations made under s.1003(2)(a) on or after 25th March, 2004.

7   As inserted by s.124(a), FA 2002, with effect from 25th March, 2002.

8   As inserted by s.85(b)(ii), FA 2004, as respects determinations made under s.1003(2)(a) on or after 25th March, 2004.

9   As inserted by s.131(a), FA 2008, with effect from 13th March, 2008.

10   S.1003(2)(c)(i) originally read "is less than £75,000, or". S.240(2)(a) and Part I of the Fifth Sch., FA 2001, substituted "€95,250" for "£75,000" as respects the year of assessment 2002 and subsequent years of assessment. S.124(b)(i), FA 2002, substituted "€100,000" for "€95,250" with effect from 25th March, 2002. The present s.1003(2)(c)(i) was substituted by s.85(b)(iii)(I), FA 2004, as respects determinations made under s.1003(2)(a) on or after 25th March, 2004.

11   Orginally "£75,000". S.240(2)(a) and Part I of the Fifth Sch., FA 2001, substituted "£95,250" for "£75,000" as respects the year of assessment 2002 and subsequent years of assessment. S.124(b)(i), FA 2002, substituted "€100,000" for "€95,250" with effect from 25th March, 2002. S.85(b)(iii)(II) substituted "€150,000" for "€100,000" as respects determinations made under s.1003(2)(a) on or after 25th March, 2004.

12   Substituted "£3,000,000" for "£750,000" by s.161, FA 2000, with effect from 23rd March, 2000, as respects the calendar year 2000, and subsequent calendar years. S.240(2)(a) and Part I of the Fifth Sch., FA 2001, substituted "€3,810,000" for "£3,000,000" as respects the year of assessment 2002 and subsequent years of assessment. S.124(b)(ii), FA 2002, substituted "€6,000,000" for "€3,810,000" with effect from 25th March, 2002.

13   As inserted by s.131(b), FA 2008, with effect from 13th March, 2008.

14   As substituted by s.121, FA 2006, as respects the year of assessment 2006 and subsequent years of assessment. The original s.1003(3)(a) had already been amended by substituting "shall, subject to paragraph (d), be estimated" for "shall be estimated" by s.124(c), FA 2002, with effect from 25th March, 2002.

15   As inserted by s.124(d), FA 2002, with effect from 25th March, 2002.

16   Substituted for "an amount equal to the market value" by s.94(1)(a), F(No. 2)A, 2008, as respects, under s.94(2)(a), any determination made by the selection commitee on or after 1st January, 2009.

Section 1006¹

Poundage and certain other fees due to sheriffs or county registrars.

1006. (1)   In this section—

"the Acts" means—

(a)   the Tax Acts,

[(aa) Part 18A,]²

(b)   the Capital Gains Tax Acts,

(c)   the Value-Added Tax Act, 1972, and the enactments amending or extending that Act,

(d)   the Capital Acquisitions Tax Act, 1976, and the enactments amending or extending that Act, and

(e)   Part VI of the Finance Act, 1983, and the enactments amending or extending that Part,

[(f) Part 18B,]³

and any instruments made thereunder;

"certificate" means a certificate issued under section 962;

"county registrar" means a person appointed to be a county registrar under section 35 of the Court Officers Act, 1926;

"defaulter" means a person specified or certified in an execution order or certificate on whom a relevant amount specified or certified in the order or certificate is leviable;

"execution order" has the same meaning as in the Enforcement of Court Orders Act, 1926;

"fees" means the fees known as poundage fees payable under section 14 (1) of the Enforcement of Court Orders Act, 1926, and orders made under that section for services in or about the execution of an execution order directing or authorising the execution of an order of a court by the seizure and sale of a person's property or, as may be appropriate, the fees corresponding to those fees payable under section 962 for the execution of a certificate;

"interest on unpaid tax" means interest which has accrued under any provision of the Acts providing for the charging of interest in respect of unpaid tax, including interest on an undercharge of tax which is attributable to fraud or neglect;

"relevant amount" means an amount of tax or interest on unpaid tax;

"tax" means any tax, duty, levy or charge which, in accordance with any provision of the Acts, is placed under the care and management of the Revenue Commissioners;

references, as respects an execution order, to a relevant amount include references to any amount of costs specified in the order.

(2) Where —

    (a) an execution order or certificate specifying or certifying a defaulter and relating to a relevant amount is lodged with the appropriate sheriff or county registrar for execution,

    (b) the sheriff or, as the case may be, the county registrar gives notice to the defaulter of the lodgment or of his or her intention to execute the execution order or certificate by seizure of the property of the defaulter to which it relates, or demands payment by the defaulter of the relevant amount, and

    (c) the whole or part of the relevant amount is paid to the sheriff or, as the case may be, the county registrar or to the Collector-General, after the giving of that notice or the making of that demand,

then, for the purpose of the liability of the defaulter for the payment of fees and of the exercise of any rights or powers in relation to the collection of fees for the time being vested by law in sheriffs and county registrars —

    (i) the sheriff or, as the case may be, the county registrar shall be deemed to have entered, in the execution of the execution order or certificate, into possession of the property referred to in paragraph (b), and

    (ii) the payment mentioned in paragraph (c) shall be deemed to have been levied, in the execution of the execution order or certificate, by the sheriff or, as the case may be, the county registrar,

and fees shall be payable by the defaulter to such sheriff or, as the case may be, country registrar accordingly in respect of the payment mentioned in paragraph (c).

Footnotes

1   This section replaced, with effect from 6th April, 1997, s.71, FA 1988.
2   Inserted by s.2(c), F(No. 2)A, 2008, with effect as on and from 1st January, 2009.
3   Inserted by s.3(1)(c), F(No. 2)A, 2008, with effect as on and from 1st January, 2009.

Section 1006A[1]

Offset between taxes.

1006A.(1) In this section—

"Acts" mean—

(a)   the Tax Acts,

[(aa) Part 18A,][7]

(b)   the Capital Gains Tax Acts,

(c)   the Value-Added Tax Act, 1972, and the enactments amending or extending that Act,

(d)   the statutes relating to the duties of excise and to the management of those duties,

(e)   the Capital Acquisitions Tax Act, 1976, and the enactments amending or extending that Act,

(f)   the Stamp Duties Consolidation Act, 1999,

(g)   Part VI of the Finance Act, 1983, and the enactments amending or extending that Part,

(h)   Chapter IV of Part II of the Finance Act, 1992,

[(i) Part 18B,][8]

and any instrument made thereunder;

["claim" means a claim that gives rise to either or both a repayment of tax and a payment of interest payable in respect of such a repayment under any of the Acts and includes part of such a claim;][2]

["liability" means any tax due or estimated to be due under the Acts for any period or in respect of any event, as may be appropriate in the circumstances, and includes any interest due under the Acts in respect of that tax;][3]

"overpayment" means a payment or remittance under the Acts (including part of such a payment or remittance) which is in excess of the amount of the liability against which it is credited;

["tax" means any tax, duty, levy or other charge under any of the Acts.][4]

[(2) Notwithstanding any other provision of the Acts, where the Revenue Commissioners are satisfied that a person has not complied with the obligations imposed on the person by the Acts, in relation to either or both—

(a)   the payment of a liability required to be paid, and

(b)   the delivery of returns required to be made,

they may, in a case where a repayment is due to the person in respect of a claim or overpayment—

(i)   where paragraph (a) applies, or where paragraphs (a) and (b) apply, instead of making the repayment set the amount of the claim or overpayment against any liability due under the Acts, and.

(ii) where paragraph (b) only applies, withhold making the repayment until such time as the returns required to be delivered have been delivered.

(2A) Where the Revenue Commissioners have set or withheld a repayment by virtue of subsection (2), they shall give notice in writing to that effect to the person concerned and, where subsection (2)(ii) applies, interest shall not be payable under any provision of the Acts from the date of such notice in respect of any repayment so withheld.][5]

(3) The Revenue Commissioners shall make regulations for the purpose of giving effect to this section and, without prejudice to the generality of the foregoing, such regulations shall provide for the order of priority of liabilities due under the Acts against which any claim or overpayment is to be set in accordance with subsection (2).

(4) Every regulation made under this section shall be laid before Dáil Éireann as soon as may be after it is made and, if a resolution annulling the regulation is passed by Dáil Éireann within the next 21 days on which Dáil Éireann has sat after the regulation is laid before it, the regulation shall be annulled accordingly, but without prejudice to the validity of anything previously done thereunder.

[(5) Any act to be performed or function to be discharged (other than the making of regulations) by the Revenue Commissioners which is authorised by this section may be performed or discharged by any of their officers acting under their authority.][6]

Footnotes

1   This section was inserted by s.164, FA 2000, with effect from 23rd March, 2000.

2   As substituted by s.125(a)(i)(I), FA 2002, with effect from 25th March, 2002.

3   The original definition of "liability" was extended by s.239(a), FA 2001, with effect from 30th March, 2001, and the extended definition was substituted by s.125(a)(i)(II), FA 2002, with effect from 25th March, 2002.

4   As inserted by s.125(a)(i)(IV), FA 2002, with effect from 25th March, 2002.

5   As substituted for subsection (2) by s.239(b), FA 2001, with effect from 30th March, 2001.

6   As inserted by s.125(a)(ii), FA 2002, with effect from 25th March, 2002.

7   Inserted by s.2(d), F(No. 2)A, 2008, with effect as on and from 1st January, 2009.

8   Inserted by s.3(1)(d), F(No. 2)A, 2008, with effect as on and from 1st January, 2009.

PART 47
Penalties, Revenue Offences, Interest on Overdue Tax and other Sanctions

CHAPTER 4
Revenue Offences

Section 1078[1]

Revenue offences.

1078. (1) In this Part—

"the Acts" means—

(a) the Customs Acts,

(b) the statutes relating to the duties of excise and to the management of those duties,

(c) the Tax Acts,

[(ca) Part 18A,][14]

(d) the Capital Gains Tax Acts,

(e) the Value-Added Tax Act, 1972, and the enactments amending or extending that Act,

(f) the Capital Acquisitions Tax Act, 1976, and the enactments amending or extending that Act,

(g) the statutes relating to stamp duty and to the management of that duty, and

(h) Part VI of the Finance Act, 1983,

[(i) Part 18B,][15]

and any instruments made thereunder and any instruments made under any other enactment and relating to tax;

"authorised officer" means an officer of the Revenue Commissioners authorised by them in writing to exercise any of the powers conferred by the Acts;

"tax" means any tax, duty, levy or charge under the care and management of the Revenue Commissioners.

[(1A)(a) In this subsection—

"facilitating" means aiding, abetting, assisting, inciting or inducing;

"fraudulent evasion of tax by a person" means the person—

(a) evading or attempting to evade any payment or deduction of tax required under the Acts to be paid by the person or, as the case may be, required under the Acts to be deducted from amounts due to the person, or

(b)   claiming or obtaining, or attempting to claim or obtain, relief or exemption from, or payment or repayment of, any tax, being relief, exemption, payment or repayment, to which the person is not entitled under the Acts,

where, for those purposes, the person deceives, omits, conceals or uses any other dishonest means including –

(i)   providing false, incomplete or misleading information, or

(ii)   failing to furnish information,

to the Revenue Commissioners or to any other person.

(b)   For the purposes of this subsection and subsection (5) a person (in this paragraph referred to as the "first-mentioned person") is reckless as to whether or not he or she is concerned in facilitating –

(i)   the fraudulent evasion of tax by a person, being another person, or

(ii)   the commission of an offence under subsection (2) by a person, being another person,

if the first-mentioned person disregards a substantial risk that he or she is so concerned, and for those purposes "substantial risk" means a risk of such a nature and degree that, having regard to all the circumstances and the extent of the information available to the first-mentioned person, its disregard by that person involves culpability of a high degree.

(c)   A person shall, without prejudice to any other penalty to which the person may be liable, be guilty of an offence under this section if the person –

(i)   is knowingly concerned in the fraudulent evasion of tax by the person or any other person,

(ii)   is knowingly concerned in, or is reckless as to whether or not the person is concerned in, facilitating –

(I)   the fraudulent evasion of tax, or

(II)   the commission of an offence under subsection (2) (other than an offence under paragraph (b) of that subsection),

by any other person, or

(iii)   is knowingly concerned in the fraudulent evasion or attempted fraudulent evasion of any prohibition or restriction on importation for the time being in force, or the removal of any goods from the State, in contravention of any provision of the Acts.][2]

[(1B)A person is guilty of an offence under this section if he or she, with the intention to deceive –

(a) purports to be, or

(b) makes any statement, or otherwise acts in a manner, that would lead another person to believe that he or she is,

an officer of the Revenue Commissioners.]³

(2) A person shall, without prejudice to any other penalty to which the person may be liable, be guilty of an offence under this section if the person—

(a) knowingly or wilfully delivers any incorrect return, statement or accounts or knowingly or wilfully furnishes any incorrect information in connection with any tax,

(b) knowingly aids, abets, assists, incites or induces another person to make or deliver knowingly or wilfully any incorrect return, statement or accounts in connection with any tax,

(c) claims or obtains relief or exemption from, or repayment of, any tax, being a relief, exemption or repayment to which, to the person's knowledge, the person is not entitled,

(d) knowingly or wilfully issues or produces any incorrect invoice, receipt, instrument or other document in connection with any tax,

(e) (i) fails to make any deduction required to be made by the person under section 257(1),

(ii) fails, having made the deduction, to pay the sum deducted to the Collector-General within the time specified in that behalf in section 258(3), or

(iii) fails to pay to the Collector-General an amount on account of appropriate tax (within the meaning of Chapter 4 of Part 8) within the time specified in that behalf in section 258(4),

[(f) fails to pay to the Collector-General appropriate tax (within the meaning of section 739E) within the time specified in that behalf in section 739F,]⁴

(g) [fails without reasonable excuse]⁵ to comply with any provision of the Acts requiring—

(i) the furnishing of a return of income, profits or gains, or of sources of income, profits or gains, for the purposes of any tax,

(ii) the furnishing of any other return, certificate, notification, particulars, or any statement or evidence, for the purposes of any tax,

(iii) the keeping or retention of books, records, accounts or other documents for the purposes of any tax, or

(iv) the production of books, records, accounts or other documents, when so requested, for the purposes of any tax,

(h) knowingly or wilfully, and within the time limits specified for their retention, destroys, defaces or conceals from an authorised officer –

    (i) any documents, or

    (ii) any other written or printed material in any form, including any information stored, maintained or preserved by means of any mechanical or electronic device, whether or not stored, maintained or preserved in a legible form, which a person is obliged by any provision of the Acts to keep, to issue or to produce for inspection,

[(hh) knowingly or wilfully falsifies, conceals, destroys or otherwise disposes of, or causes or permits the falsification, concealment, destruction or disposal of, any books, records or other documents –

    (i) which the person has been given the opportunity to deliver, or as the case may be, to make available in accordance with section 900(3), or

    (ii) which the person has been required to deliver or, as the case may be, to make available in accordance with a notice served under section 900, 902, 906A or 907, or an order made under section 901, 902A or 908,][6]

(i) fails to remit any income tax payable pursuant to Chapter 4 of Part 42, and the regulations under that Chapter, or value-added tax within the time specified in that behalf in relation to income tax or value-added tax, as the case may be, [by the Acts,][7]

[(ii) (i) fails to deduct tax required to be deducted by the person under section 531(1), or

    (ii) fails, having made that deduction, to pay the sum deducted to the Collector-General within the time specified in that behalf in section 531(3A),

or][8]

(j) obstructs or interferes with any officer of the Revenue Commissioners, or any other person, in the exercise or performance of powers or duties under the Acts for the purposes of any tax.

(3) A person convicted of an offence under this section shall be liable –

(a) on summary conviction to a fine of [€5,000][9] which may be mitigated to not less than one fourth part of such fine or, at the discretion of the court, to imprisonment for a term not exceeding 12 months or to both the fine and the imprisonment, or

(b) on conviction on indictment, to a fine not exceeding [€126,970][10] or, at the discretion of the court, to imprisonment for a term not exceeding 5 years or to both the fine and the imprisonment.

[(3A)Where a person has been convicted of an offence referred to in subparagraph (i), (ii) or (iv) of subsection (2)(g), then, if an application is made, or caused to be made to the court in that regard, the court may make an order requiring the person concerned to comply with any provision of the Acts relating to the requirements specified in the said subparagraph (i), (ii) or (iv), as the case may be.][11]

[(3B) A person shall, without prejudice to any other penalty to which the person may be liable, be guilty of an offence under this section if the person fails or refuses to comply with an order referred to in subsection (3A) **[within a period of 30 days commencing on the day the order is made][16].][12]**

(4) Section 13 of the Criminal Procedure Act, 1967, shall apply in relation to an offence under this section as if, in place of the penalties specified in subsection (3) of that section, there were specified in that subsection the penalties provided for by subsection (3)(a), and the reference in subsection (2)(a) of section 13 of the Criminal Procedure Act, 1967, to the penalties provided for in subsection (3) of that section shall be construed and apply accordingly.

(5) Where an offence under this section is committed by a body corporate and the offence is shown [to have been committed with the consent or connivance of or to be attributable to any recklessness (as provided by subsection (1A)(b) on the part of][13] any person who, when the offence was committed, was a director, manager, secretary or other officer of the body corporate, or a member of the committee of management or other controlling authority of the body corporate, that person shall also be deemed to be guilty of the offence and may be proceeded against and punished accordingly.

(6) In any proceedings under this section, a return or statement delivered to an inspector or other officer of the Revenue Commissioners under any provision of the Acts and purporting to be signed by any person shall be deemed until the contrary is proved to have been so delivered and to have been signed by that person.

(7) Notwithstanding any other enactment, proceedings in respect of an offence under this section may be instituted within 10 years from the date of the commission of the offence or incurring of the penalty, as the case may be.

(8) Section 1 of the Probation of Offenders Act, 1907, shall not apply in relation to offences under this section.

(9) Sections 987(4) and 1052(4), subsections (3) and (7) of section 1053, **[subsections (9) and (17) of section 1077E,][17]** and sections 1068 and 1069 **[, and section 27(A)(16) of the Value-Added Tax Act 1972,][18]** shall, with any necessary modifications, apply for the purposes

of this section as they apply for the purposes of those sections, including, in the case of such of those sections as are applied by the Capital Gains Tax Acts, the Corporation Tax Acts, or Part VI of the Finance Act, 1983, the purposes of those sections as so applied.

Footnotes

1   This section replaced, with effect from 6th April, 1997, s.94, FA 1983, as amended.

2   As inserted by s.142(a), FA 2005, with effect from 25th March, 2005.

3   As inserted by s.126, FA 2007, with effect from 2nd April, 2007.

4   As substituted by s.142(b)(i), FA 2005, with effect from 25th March, 2005.

5   Substituted for "knowingly or wilfully fails" by s.133(a), FA 2002, with effect from 25th March, 2002.

6   Inserted by s.211(a), FA 1999, with effect from 25th March, 1999.

7   Substituted for "by the Acts, or" by s.142(b)(ii), FA 2005, with effect from 25th March, 2005.

8   As inserted by s.142(b)(iii), FA 2005, with effect from 25th March, 2005.

9   S.233(1), FA 2001, substituted "£1,500" for "£1,000", with effect from 30th March, 2001. S.233(2), FA 2001, substituted "€1,900" for "£1,500" from 1st January, 2002. S.160, FA 2003, substituted "€3,000" for "€1,900" as respects an offence committed on or after 28th March, 2003. Section 138(1)(d), FA 2008, substituted "€5,000" for "€3,000" as respects an offence committed on a day after 13th March, 2008.

10   S.211(b), FA 1999, substituted "£100,000" for "£10,000" with effect from 25th March, 1999. S.240(2)(k) and Part I of the Fifth Sch., FA 2001, substituted "€126,970" for "£100,000" for any act or omission which takes place on or after 1st January, 2002.

11   As inserted by s.211(c), FA 1999, with effect from 25th March, 1999.

12   As inserted by s.132(b), FA 2002, with effect from 25th March, 2002.

13   Substituted for "to have been committed with the consent or connivance of" by s.142(c), FA 2005, with effect from 25th March, 2005.

14   Inserted by s.2(e), F(No. 2)A, 2008, with effect as on and from 1st January, 2009.

15   Inserted by s.3(1)(e), F(No. 2)A, 2008, with effect as on and from 1st January, 2009.

16   As inserted by s.92(k), F(No. 2)A, 2008, with effect from 24th December, 2008.

17   Inserted by s.98(1), and by para. 1(ar)(i) of Part 2 of Sch. 5, of the F (No. 2) A, 2008, and comes into effect after 24th December, 2008.

18   Substituted for "and sections 26(6) and 27(7) of the Value-Added Tax Act, 1972," by s.98(1), and by para. 1(ar)(ii) of Part 2 of Sch. 5, of the F(No. 2)A, 2008, and comes into effect after 24th December, 2008.

Section 1078A[1]

Concealing facts disclosed by documents.

1078A. (1) Any person who –

     (a)   knows or suspects that an investigation by an officer of the Revenue Commissioners into an offence under the Acts or the Waiver of Certain Tax, Interest and Penalties Act 1993 is being, or is likely to be, carried out, and

     (b)   falsifies, conceals, destroys or otherwise disposes of material which the person knows or suspects is or would be relevant to the investigation or causes or permits its falsification, concealment, destruction or disposal,

     is guilty of an offence.

(2) Where a person -

    (a) falsifies, conceals, destroys or otherwise disposes of material, or

    (b) causes or permits its falsification, concealment, destruction or disposal,

in such circumstances that it is reasonable to conclude that the person knew or suspected

    (i) that an investigation by an officer of the Revenue Commissioners into an offence under the Acts or the Waiver of Certain Tax, Interest and Penalties Act 1993 was being, or was likely to be, carried out, and

    (ii) that the material was or would be relevant to the investigation,

the person shall be taken, for the purposes of this section, to have so known or suspected, unless the court or the jury, as the case may be, is satisfied having regard to all the evidence that there is a reasonable doubt as to whether the person so knew or suspected.

(3) A person guilty of an offence under this section is liable -

    (a) on summary conviction to a fine not exceeding [€5,000][2], or at the discretion of the court, to imprisonment for a term not exceeding 6 months or to both the fine and the imprisonment, or

    (b) on conviction on indictment, to a fine not exceeding €127,000 or, at the discretion of the court, to imprisonment for a term not exceeding 5 years or to both the fine and the imprisonment.

Footnotes

1   As inserted by s.161, FA 2003, with effect from 28th March, 2003.

2   As substituted for "€3,000" by s.138(1)(e), FA 2008, as respects an offence committed on a day after 13th March, 2008.

Section 1078B[1]

Presumptions.

1078B.(1) In this section -

"return, statement or declaration" means any return, statement or declaration which a person is required to make under the Acts or the Waiver of Certain Tax, Interest and Penalties Act 1993.

(2) The presumptions specified in this section apply in any proceedings, whether civil or criminal, under any provision of the Acts or the Waiver of Certain Tax, Interest and Penalties Act 1993.

(3) Where a document purports to have been created by a person it shall be presumed, unless the contrary is shown, that the document was created by that person and that any statement contained therein,

unless the document expressly attributes its making to some other person, was made by that person.

(4) Where a document purports to have been created by a person and addressed and sent to a second person, it shall be presumed, unless the contrary is shown, that the document was created and sent by the first person and received by the second person and that any statement contained therein -

(a) unless the document expressly attributes its making to some other person, was made by the first person, and

(b) came to the notice of the second person.

(5) Where a document is retrieved from an electronic storage and retrieval system, it shall be presumed unless the contrary is shown, that the author of the document is the person who ordinarily uses that electronic storage and retrieval system in the course of his or her business.

(6) Where an authorised officer in the exercise of his or her powers under subsection (2A) of section 905 **[or section (3) of section 908C]**[2] has removed records (within the meaning of that section) from any place, gives evidence in proceedings that to the best of the authorised officer's knowledge and belief, the records are the property of any person, the records shall be presumed unless the contrary is proved, to be the property of that person.

(7) Where in accordance with subsection (6) records are presumed in proceedings to be the property of a person and the authorised officer gives evidence that, to the best of the authorised officer's knowledge and belief, the records are records which relate to any trade, profession, or, as the case may be, other activity, carried on by that person, the records shall be presumed unless the contrary is proved, to be records which relate to that trade, profession, or, as the case may be, other activity, carried on by that person.

(8) In proceedings, a certificate signed by an inspector or other officer of the Revenue Commissioners certifying that a return, statement or declaration to which the certificate refers is in the possession of the Revenue Commissioners in such circumstances as to lead the officer to conclude that, to the best of his or her knowledge and belief it was delivered to an inspector or other officer of the Revenue Commissioners, it shall be presumed unless the contrary is proved, to be evidence that the said return, statement, or declaration was so delivered.

(9) In proceedings, a certificate, certifying the fact or facts referred to in subsection (8) and purporting to be signed as specified in that subsection, may be tendered in evidence without proof and shall be deemed until the contrary is proved to have been signed by a person holding, at the time of the signature, the office or position indicated in the certificate as the office or position of the person signing.

(10) References in this section to a document are references to a document in written, mechanical or electronic format and, for this purpose "written" includes any form of notation or code whether by hand or otherwise and regardless of the method by which, or the medium in or on which, the document concerned is recorded.

Footnotes
1   As inserted by s.161, FA 2003, with effect from 28th March, 2003.
2   As inserted by s.99, and by para. 1(c), Sch. 6, of the F(No. 2)A, 2008, and has effect as on and from 24th December, 2008.

Section 1078C[1]

Provision of information to juries.

1078C. (1) In a trial on indictment of an offence under the Acts or the Waiver of Certain Tax, Interest and Penalties Act 1993, the trial judge may order that copies of any or all of the following documents shall be given to the jury in any form that the judge considers appropriate:

(a)   any document admitted in evidence at the trial,

(b)   the transcript of the opening speeches of counsel,

(c)   any charts, diagrams, graphics, schedules or agreed summaries of evidence produced at the trial,

(d)   the transcript of the whole or any part of the evidence given at the trial,

(e)   the transcript of the closing speeches of counsel,

(f)   the transcript of the trial judge's charge to the jury,

(g)   any other document that in the opinion of the trial judge would be of assistance to the jury in its deliberations including, where appropriate, an affidavit by an accountant or other suitably qualified person, summarising, in a form which is likely to be comprehended by the jury, any transactions by the accused or other persons which are relevant to the offence.

(2) If the prosecutor proposes to apply to the trial judge for an order that a document mentioned in subsection (1)(g) shall be given to the jury, the prosecutor shall give a copy of the document to the accused in advance of the trial and, on the hearing of the application, the trial judge shall take into account any representations made by or on behalf of the accused in relation to it.

(3) Where the trial judge has made an order that an affidavit by an accountant or other person mentioned in subsection (1)(g) shall be given to the jury, the accountant, or as the case may be, the other person so mentioned -

(a)   shall be summoned by the prosecution to attend at the trial as an expert witness, and

(b) may be required by the trial judge, in an appropriate case, to give evidence in regard to any relevant procedures or principles within his or her area of expertise.

Footnote

1   As inserted by s.161, FA 2003, with effect from 28th March, 2003.

Section 1079[1]

Duties of relevant person in relation to certain revenue offences.

1079. (1)   In this section —

"the Acts" means —

(a)   the Customs Acts,

(b)   the statutes relating to the duties of excise and to the management of those duties,

(c)   the Tax Acts,

[(ca) Part 18A,][3]

(d)   the Capital Gains Tax Acts,

(e)   the Value-Added Tax Act, 1972, and the enactments amending or extending that Act,

(f)   the Capital Acquisitions Tax Act, 1976, and the enactments amending or extending that Act,

(g)   the statutes relating to stamp duty and to the management of that duty,

and any instruments made thereunder and any instruments made under any other enactment and relating to tax;

"appropriate officer" means any officer nominated by the Revenue Commissioners to be an appropriate officer for the purposes of this section;

"company" means any body corporate;

"relevant person", in relation to a company and subject to subsection (2), means a person who —

(a)   (i)   is an auditor to the company appointed in accordance with section 160 of the Companies Act, 1963 (as amended by the Companies Act, 1990), or

(ii) in the case of an industrial and provident society or a friendly society, is a public auditor to the society for the purposes of the Industrial and Provident Societies Acts, 1893 to 1978, and the Friendly Societies Acts, 1896 to 1977,

or

(b)   with a view to reward, assists or advises the company in the preparation or delivery of any information, declaration, return, records, accounts or other document which he or she knows will be or is likely to be used for any purpose of tax;

"relevant offence" means an offence committed by a company which consists of the company –

(a)   knowingly or wilfully delivering any incorrect return, statement or accounts or knowingly or wilfully furnishing or causing to be furnished any incorrect information in connection with any tax,

(b)   knowingly or wilfully claiming or obtaining relief or exemption from, or repayment of, any tax, being a relief, exemption or repayment to which there is no entitlement,

(c)   knowingly or wilfully issuing or producing any incorrect invoice, receipt, instrument or other document in connection with any tax, or

(d)   knowingly or wilfully failing to comply with any provision of the Acts requiring the furnishing of a return of income, profits or gains, or of sources of income, profits or gains, for the purposes of any tax, but an offence under this paragraph committed by a company shall not be a relevant offence if the company has made a return of income, profits or gains to the Revenue Commissioners in respect of an accounting period falling wholly or partly in the period of 3 years preceding the accounting period in respect of which the offence was committed;

"tax" means any tax, duty, levy or charge under the care and management of the Revenue Commissioners.

(2)   For the purposes of paragraph (b) of the definition of "relevant person", a person who but for this subsection would be treated as a relevant person in relation to a company shall not be so treated if the person assists or advises the company solely in the person's capacity as an employee of the company, and a person shall be treated as assisting or advising the company in that capacity where the person's income from assisting or advising the company consists solely of emoluments to which Chapter 4 of Part 42 applies.

(3)   If, having regard solely to information obtained in the course of examining the accounts of a company, or in the course of assisting or advising a company in the preparation or delivery of any information, declaration, return, records, accounts or other document for the purposes of tax, as the case may be, a person who is a relevant person in relation to the company becomes aware that the company has committed, or is in the course of committing, one or more relevant offences, the person shall, if the offence or offences are material –

    (a)   communicate particulars of the offence or offences in writing to the company without undue delay and request the company to—

        (i)   take such action as is necessary for the purposes of rectifying the matter, or

        (ii) notify an appropriate officer of the offence or offences,

        not later than 6 months after the time of communication, and

    (b)   (i)   unless it is established to the person's satisfaction that the necessary action has been taken or notification made, as the case may be, under paragraph (a), cease to act as the auditor to the company or to assist or advise the company in such preparation or delivery as is specified in paragraph (b) of the definition of "relevant person", and

        (ii) shall not so act, assist or advise before a time which is the earlier of—

           (I)   3 years after the time at which the particulars were communicated under paragraph (a), and

           (II) the time at which it is established to the person's satisfaction that the necessary action has been taken or notification made, as the case may be, under paragraph (a).

(4)   Nothing in paragraph (b) of subsection (3) shall prevent a person from assisting or advising a company in preparing for, or conducting, legal proceedings, either civil or criminal, which are extant or pending at a time which is 6 months after the time of communication under paragraph (a) of that subsection.

(5)   Where a person, being in relation to a company a relevant person within the meaning of paragraph (a) of the definition of "relevant person", ceases under this section to act as auditor to the company, then, the person shall deliver—

    (a)   a notice in writing to the company stating that he or she is so resigning, and

    (b)   a copy of the notice to an appropriate officer not later than 14 days after he or she has delivered the notice to the company.

(6)   A person shall be guilty of an offence under this section if the person—

    (a)   fails to comply with subsection (3) or (5), or

    (b)   knowingly or wilfully makes a communication under subsection (3) which is incorrect.

(7)   Where a relevant person is convicted of an offence under this section, the person shall be liable—

(a)   on summary conviction, to a fine of [€1,265]² which may be mitigated to not less than one-fourth part of such fine, or

(b)   on conviction on indictment, to a fine not exceeding [€6,345]² or, at the discretion of the court, to imprisonment for a term not exceeding 2 years or to both the fine and the imprisonment.

(8) Section 13 of the Criminal Procedure Act, 1967, shall apply in relation to this section as if, in place of the penalties specified in subsection (3) of that section, there were specified in that subsection the penalties provided for by subsection (7)(a), and the reference in subsection (2)(a) of section 13 of the Criminal Procedure Act, 1967, to the penalties provided for in subsection (3) of that section shall be construed and apply accordingly.

(9) Notwithstanding any other enactment, proceedings in respect of this section may be instituted within 6 years from the time at which a person is required under subsection (3) to communicate particulars of an offence or offences in writing to a company.

(10) It shall be a good defence in a prosecution for an offence under subsection (6) (a) in relation to a failure to comply with subsection (3) for an accused (being a person who is a relevant person in relation to a company) to show that he or she was in the ordinary scope of professional engagement assisting or advising the company in preparing for legal proceedings and would not have become aware that one or more relevant offences had been committed by the company if he or she had not been so assisting or advising.

(11) Where a person who is a relevant person takes any action required by subsection (3) or (5), no duty to which the person may be subject shall be regarded as having been contravened and no liability or action shall lie against the person in any court for having taken such action.

(12) The Revenue Commissioners may nominate an officer to be an appropriate officer for the purposes of this section, and the name of an officer so nominated and the address to which copies of notices under subsection (3) or (5) shall be delivered shall be published in *Iris Oifigiúil*.

(13) This section shall apply as respects a relevant offence committed by a company in respect of tax which is —

(a)   assessable by reference to accounting periods, for any accounting period beginning after the 30th day of June, 1995,

(b)   assessable by reference to years of assessment, for the year 1995-96 and subsequent years of assessment,

(c)   payable by reference to a taxable period, for a taxable period beginning after the 30th day of June, 1995,

(d)   chargeable on gifts or inheritances taken on or after the 30th day of June, 1995,

(e)   chargeable on instruments executed on or after the 30th day of June, 1995, or

(f)   payable in any other case, on or after the 30th day of June, 1995.

Footnotes

1   This section replaced, with effect from 6th April, 1997, s.172, FA 1995.

2   S.240(2)(k) and Part I of the Fifth Sch., FA 2001, substituted "€1,265" and "€6,345" respectively for "£1,000" and "£5,000" for any act or omission which takes place on or after 1st January, 2001.

3   Inserted by s.2(f), F(No. 2)A, 2008, with effect as on and from 1st January, 2009.

CHAPTER 6
Other Sanctions

Section 1086[1]

Publication of names of tax defaulters.

1086. (1) In this section—

"the Acts" means—

(a)   the Tax Acts,

(b)   the Capital Gains Tax Acts,

(c)   the Value-Added Tax Act, 1972, and the enactments amending or extending that Act,

(d)   the Capital Acquisitions Tax Act, 1976, and the enactments amending or extending that Act,

[(e)   the Stamp Duties Consolidation Act, 1999, and the enactments amending or extending that Act,][2]

(f)   Part VI of the Finance Act, 1983,

[(g)   the Customs Acts,

(h)   the statutes relating to the duties of excise and to the management of those duties,][3]

and any instruments made thereunder;

["tax" means any tax, duty, levy or charge under the care and management of the Revenue Commissioners.][4]

(2) The Revenue Commissioners shall, as respects each relevant period (being the period beginning on the 1st day of January, 1997, and ending on the 30th day of June, 1997, and each subsequent period of 3 months beginning with the period ending on the 30th day of September, 1997), compile a list of the names and addresses and the occupations or descriptions of every person—

(a) on whom a fine or other penalty was imposed **[or determined]**[19] by a court under any of the Acts during that relevant period,

(b) on whom a fine or other penalty was otherwise imposed **[or determined]**[19] by a court during that relevant period in respect of an act or omission by the person in relation to [tax,][5]

(c) in whose case the Revenue Commissioners, pursuant to an agreement made with the person in that relevant period, refrained from initiating proceedings for the recovery of any fine or penalty of the kind mentioned in paragraphs (a) and (b) and, in place of initiating such proceedings, accepted or undertook to accept a specified sum of money in settlement of any claim by the Revenue Commissioners in respect of any specified liability of the person under any of the Acts for —

   (i) payment of any tax,

   [(ii) except in the case of tax due by virtue of paragraphs (g) and (h) of the definition of "the Acts", payment of interest on that tax, and

   (iii) a fine or other monetary penalty in respect of that tax including penalties in respect of the failure to deliver any return, statement, declaration, list or other document in connection with the tax, or][6]

[(d) in whose case the Revenue Commissioners, having initiated proceedings for the recovery of any fine or penalty of the kind mentioned in paragraphs (a) and (b), and whether or not a fine or penalty of the kind mentioned in those paragraphs has been imposed **[or determined]**[19] by a court, accepted or undertook to accept, in that relevant period, a specified sum of money in settlement of any claim by the Revenue Commissioners in respect of any specified liability of the person under any of the Acts for —

   (i) payment of any tax,

   [(ii) except in the case of tax due by virtue of paragraphs (g) and (h) of the definition of "the Acts", payment of interest on that tax, and

   (iii) a fine or other monetary penalty in respect of that tax including penalties in respect of the failure to deliver any return, statement, declaration, list or other document in connection with the tax.][7]

[(2A) For the purposes of subsection (2), the reference to a specified sum in paragraphs (c) and (d) of that subsection includes a reference to a sum which is the full amount of the claim by the Revenue Commissioners in respect of the specified liability referred to in those paragraphs. Where the Revenue Commissioners accept or undertake to accept such a sum, being the amount of their claim, then —

    (a) **they shall be deemed to have done so pursuant to an agreement, made with the person referred to in paragraph (c), whereby they refrained from initiating proceedings for the recovery of any fine or penalty of the kind mentioned in paragraphs (a) and (b) of subsection (2), and**

    (b) **that agreement shall be deemed to have been made in the relevant period in which the Revenue Commissioners accepted or undertook to accept that full amount.]**[8]

(3) Notwithstanding any obligation as to secrecy imposed on them by the Acts or the Official Secrets Act, 1963 –

    (a) the Revenue Commissioners shall, before the expiration of 3 months from the end of each relevant period, cause each such list referred to in subsection (2) in relation to that period to be published in *Iris Oifigiúil*, and

    [(b) the Revenue Commissioners may, at any time after each such list referred to in subsection (2) has been published as provided for in paragraph (a), cause any such list to be publicised or reproduced, or both, in whole or in part, in such manner, form or format as they consider appropriate.][9]

(4) [Paragraphs (c) and (d)][10] of subsection (2) shall not apply in relation to a person in whose case –

    [(a) **the Revenue Commissioners are satisfied that, before any investigation or inquiry had been started by them or by any of their officers into any matter occasioning a liability referred to in those paragraphs, the person had voluntarily furnished to them a qualifying disclosure (within the meaning of section 1077E, section 27A of the Value-Added Tax Act 1972 or section 134A of the Stamp Duties Consolidation Act 1999, as the case may be) in relation to and full particulars of that matter.]**[20]

    (b) section 72 of the Finance Act, 1988, or section 3 of the Waiver of Certain Tax, Interest and Penalties Act, 1993, applied, [.....][12]

    (c) the specified sum referred to in [paragraph (c) or (d), as the case may be,][13] of subsection (2) does not exceed [€30,000][14], [or][15].

    [(d) the amount of fine or other penalty included in the specified sum referred to in paragraph (c) or (d), as the case may be, of subsection (2) does not exceed 15 per cent of the amount of tax included in that specified sum.][16]

[(4A)(a) In this subsection –

    "the consumer price index number" means the All Items Consumer Price Index Number compiled by the Central Statistics Office;

"the consumer price index number relevant to a year" means the consumer price index number at the mid-December before the commencement of that year expressed on the basis that the consumer price index at mid-December 2001 was 100;

"the Minister" means the Minister for Finance.

(b) The Minister shall, in the year 2010 and in every fifth year thereafter, by order provide, in accordance with paragraph (c), an amount in lieu of the amount referred to in subsection (4)(c), or where such an order has been made previously, in lieu of the amount specified in the last order so made.

(c) For the purposes of paragraph (b) the amount referred to in subsection (4)(c) or in the last previous order made under the said paragraph (b), as the case may be, shall be adjusted by —

(i) multiplying that amount by the consumer price index number relevant to the year in which the adjustment is made and dividing the product by the consumer price index number relevant to the year in which the amount was previously provided for, and

(ii) rounding the resulting amount up to the next €1,000.

(d) An order made under this subsection shall specify that the amount provided for by the order —

(i) takes effect from a specified date, being 1 January in the year in which the order is made, and

(ii) does not apply to any case in which the specified liability referred to in paragraphs (c) and (d) of subsection (2) includes tax, the liability in respect of which arose before, or which relates to periods which commenced before, that specified date.][17]

[(4B)Paragraphs (a) and (b) of subsection (2) shall not apply in relation to a person in whose case—

(a) the amount of a penalty determined by a court does not exceed 15 per cent of, as appropriate—

(i) the amount of the difference referred to in subsection (11) or (12), as the case may be, of section 1077E,

(ii) the amount of the difference referred to in subsection (11) or (12), as the case may be, of section 27A of the Value-Added Tax Act 1972, or

(iii) the amount of the difference referred to in subsection (7), (8) or (9), as the case may be, of section 134A of the Stamp Duties Consolidation Act 1999,

(b) the aggregate of the—

(i) the tax due in respect of which the penalty is computed,

      (ii) **except in the case of tax due by virtue of paragraphs (g) and (h) of the definition of "the Acts", interest on that tax, and**

      (iii) **the penalty determined by a court, does not exceed €30,000, or**

  (c) **there has been a qualifying disclosure.]²¹**

(5) Any list referred to in subsection (2) shall specify in respect of each person named in the list such particulars as the Revenue Commissioners think fit—

  (a) of the matter occasioning the fine or penalty of the kind referred to in subsection (2) imposed **[or determined]²²** on the person or, as the case may be, the liability of that kind to which the person was subject, and

  (b) of any interest, fine or other monetary penalty, and of any other penalty or sanction, to which that person was liable, or which was imposed **[or determined]²²** on that person by a court, and which was occasioned by the matter referred to in paragraph (a).

[(5A) Without prejudice to the generality of paragraph (a) of subsection (5), such particulars as are referred to in that paragraph may include—

  (a) in a case to which paragraph (a) or (b) of subsection (2) applies, a description, in such summary form as the Revenue Commissioners may think fit, of the act, omission or offence (which may also include the circumstances in which the act or omission arose or the offence was committed) in respect of which the fine or penalty referred to in those paragraphs was imposed, **[or determined]²³** and

  (b) in a case to which paragraph (c) or (d) of subsection (2) applies, a description, in such summary form as the Revenue Commissioners may think fit, of the matter occasioning the specified liability (which may also include the circumstances in which that liability arose) in respect of which the Revenue Commissioners accepted, or undertook to accept, a settlement, in accordance with those paragraphs.]¹⁸

Footnotes

1   This section replaced, with effect from 6th April, 1997, s.23, FA 1983, as amended.

2   As substituted by s.126(1)(a)(ii)(I), FA 2002, as respects fines or penalties imposed by a court, or a specified sum accepted by the Revenue Commissioners, on or after 25th March, 2002.

3   As inserted by s.126(1)(a)(i)(II), FA 2002, which applies as in Footnote 2.

4   As substituted by s.126(1)(a)(ii), FA 2002, which applies as in Footnote 2.

5   Substituted by s.162(1)(a)(i), FA 2000, for "tax, or" as respects fines or other penalties, referred to in s.1086(2)(a) and (b), imposed by a court on or after 23rd March, 2000.

6   As substituted by s.126(1)(b)(i) FA 2002, which applies as in Footnote 2.

7   As inserted by s.162(1)(b), FA 2000, as respect specified sums, referred to in s.1086(2)
    (c) and (d), which the Revenue Commissioners accepted, or undertook to accept, on or
    after 23rd March, 2000, in settlement of a specified liability. Subparagraphs (ii) and (iii)
    were substituted by s.126(1)(b)(ii), FA 2002, which apply as in Footnote 2.

8   Inserted by s.162(1)(c), FA 2000, with effect from 23rd March, 2000. As substituted
    by s.98(1), and by para. 2(as)(ii) of Sch. 5, of the F(No. 2)A, 2008, and applies as in
    Footnote 19 below.

9   As substituted by s.126(1)(c), FA 2002, which applies as in Footnote 2.

10 Substituted by s.162(1)(c)(i), FA 2000, for "Paragraph (c)" with effect from 23rd March,
    2000.

11 As substituted by s.126(d)(i), FA 2002, which applies as in Footnote 2.

12 The word "or" deleted by s.126(d)(ii), FA 2002, which applies as in Footnote 2.

13 Substituted by s.162(1)(c)(ii), FA 2000, for "paragraph (c)" with effect from 23rd March,
    2000.

14 S.240(2)(i) and Part I of the Fifth Sch., FA 2001, substituted "€12,700" for "£10,000" as
    respects specified sums such as are referred to in s.1086(2)(c) and (d), TCA, which the
    Revenue Commissioners accept, or undertake to accept, on or after 1st January, 2002.

    S.143(1)(a), FA 2005, substituted "€30,000" for "€12,700" but this latter substitution does
    not apply under s.143(2), FA 2005, where the specified liability referred to in s.1086(2)(c)
    and (d), TCA, includes tax, the liability in respect of which arose before, or which relates
    to periods which commenced before, 1st January, 2005.

15 The word "or" inserted by s.126(d)(iii), FA 2002, which applies as in Footnote 2.

16 As inserted by s.126(d)(iv), FA 2002, which applies as in Footnote 2.

17 As inserted by s.143(1)(b), FA 2005, with effect from 25th March, 2005.

18 As inserted by s.162(1)(d), FA 2000, with effect from 23rd March, 2000.

19 As inserted by s.98(1), and by para. 2(as)(i) of Sch. 5, of the F(No. 2)A, 2008, and applies
    as in s.98(2) of that Act (see page 1327) where the reference there to "subparagraph (ar)"
    should be to "subparagraph (as)". This reference has been corrected by s.30(4)(b), FA
    2009, with effect as on and from 3rd June, 2009, under s.30(5)(e) of that Act.

20 As substituted by s.98(1), and by para. 2(as)(iii) of Sch. 5, of the F(No. 2)A, 2008, and
    applies as in Footnote 19 above.

21 As inserted by s.98(1), and by para. 2(as)(iv) of Sch. 5, of the F(No. 2)A, 2008, and applies
    as in Footnote 19 above.

22 As inserted by s.98(1), and by para. 2(as)(v) of Sch. 5, of the F(No. 2)A, 2008, and applies
    as in Footnote 19 above.

23 As inserted by s.98(1), and by para. 2(as)(vi) of Sch. 5, of the F(No. 2)A, 2008, and applies
    as in Footnote 19 above.

PART 48
Miscellaneous and Supplemental

Section 1089[1]

Status of interest on certain unpaid taxes and duties.
1089. (1) ....

(2) Interest payable under section 18 of the Wealth Tax Act, 1975, or section 41 of the Capital Acquisitions Tax Act, 1976, shall not be allowed in computing any income, profits or losses for any of the purposes of the Tax Acts.[1]

Footnote
1   S.1089(2) replaces, with effect from 6th April, 1997, s.29, FA 1976.

Section 1093[1]

Disclosure of information to Ombudsman.
1093. Any obligation to maintain secrecy or other restriction on the disclosure or production of information (including documents) obtained by or furnished to the Revenue Commissioners, or any person on their behalf, for taxation purposes, shall not apply to the disclosure or production of information (including documents) to the Ombudsman for the purposes of an examination or investigation by the Ombudsman under the Ombudsman Act, 1980, of any action (within the meaning of that Act) taken by or on behalf of the Revenue Commissioners, being such an action taken in the performance of administrative functions in respect of any tax or duty under the care and management of the Revenue Commissioners.

Footnote
1   This section replaces, with effect from 6th April, 1997, s.52, FA 1981.

Section 1096B[1]

Evidence of computer stored records in court proceedings etc.
1096B. (1) In this section –

"copy record" means any copy of an original record or a copy of that copy made in accordance with either of the methods referred to in subsection (2) and accompanied by the certificate referred to in subsection (4), which original record or copy of an original record is in the possession of the Revenue Commissioners;

"original record" means any document, record or record of an entry in a document or record or information stored by means of any storage equipment, whether or not in a legible form, made or stored by the Revenue Commissioners for the purposes of or in connection with tax, and which is in the possession of the Revenue Commissioners;

"provable record" means an original record or a copy record and, in the case of an original record or a copy record stored in any storage equipment, whether or not in a legible form, includes the production or reproduction of the record in a legible form;

"storage equipment" means any electronic, magnetic, mechanical, photographic, optical or other device used for storing information;

"tax" means any tax, duty, levy or charge under the care and management of the Revenue Commissioners.

(2) Where by reason of —

   (a) the deterioration of,

   (b) the inconvenience in storing, or

   (c) the technical obsolescence in the manner of retaining or storing,

   any original record or any copy record, the Revenue Commissioners may —

   (i) make a legible copy of that record, or

   (ii) store information concerning that record otherwise than in a legible form so that the information is capable of being used to make a legible copy of that record,

   and, they may, thereupon destroy that original record or that copy record.

(3) The legible copy of —

   (a) a record made, or

   (b) the information concerning such record stored,

   in accordance with subsection (2) shall be deemed to be an original record for the purposes of this section.

(4) In any proceedings a certificate signed by an officer of the Revenue Commissioners stating that a copy record has been made in accordance with the provisions of subsection (2) shall be evidence of the fact of the making of such a copy record and that it is a true copy, unless the contrary is shown.

(5) In any proceedings a document purporting to be a certificate signed by an officer of the Revenue Commissioners, referred to in subsection (4), shall for the purposes of this section be deemed to be such a certificate and to be so signed unless the contrary is shown.

(6) A provable record shall be admissible in evidence in any proceedings and shall be evidence of any fact stated in it or event recorded by it unless the contrary is shown, or unless the court is not satisfied as to the reliability of the system used to make or compile —

   (a) in the case of an original record, that record, and

    (b)   in the case of a copy record, the original on which it was based.

(7) In any proceedings a certificate signed by an officer of the Revenue Commissioners, stating that a full and detailed search has been made for a record of any event in every place where such records are kept and that no such record has been found, shall be evidence that the event did not happen unless the contrary is shown or unless the court is not satisfied –

    (a)   as to the reliability of the system used to compile or make or keep such records,

    (b)   that, if the event had happened, a record would have been made of it, and

    (c)   that the system is such that the only reasonable explanation for the absence of such record is that the event did not happen.

(8) For the purposes of this section, and subject to the direction and control of the Revenue Commissioners, any power, function or duty conferred or imposed on them may be exercised or performed on their behalf by an officer of the Revenue Commissioners.

Footnote

1   As inserted by s.135, FA 2002, with effect from 25th March, 2002.

THIRD PART

This Part contains, in order of enactment, Acts, Rules, Regulations and Orders dealing directly or indirectly with capital acquisitions tax. It includes the Capital Acquisitions Tax Act, 1976, the Capital Acquisitions Tax Consolidation Act 2003, and other legislation up to and including the Finance (No. 2) Act 2008, which was enacted on 24th December, 2008. The Finance Act 2009 has no effect on this Part. These Acts, Rules, Regulations and Orders are as enacted and before subsequent amendments, save in relation to a small number of pre-CAT enactments, which are in their final form.

For Contents of this Part, see page lv

CUSTOMS AND INLAND REVENUE ACT, 1880

43 Vict., c. 14

(Enacted on 24th March, 1880)

PART III

Stamps

Section 10[1]

Account to accompany affidavit on application for probate or letters of administration.

10. (1) Together with the affidavit to be required and received from the person applying for a probate or letters of administration in England,[2] ... there shall be delivered an account of the particulars of the personal estate for or in respect of which the probate or letters of administration is or are granted, and of the estimated value of such particulars.

(2) The account so delivered shall be transmitted to the Commissioners of Inland Revenue, together with the documents mentioned in section ninety-three of the Court of Probate Act, 1857.

(3) A like account shall be annexed to the affidavit to be required and received from the person applying for a probate or letters of administration in Ireland.

(4) Every account to be delivered in pursuance of this section shall be in accordance with such form as may be prescribed by the[3] ... Treasury.

Footnotes

1 This section is part of the definition of "Inland Revenue affidavit" – see s. 38(1), CATA, and s.48(1), CATCA, both of which sections quote s.22(1)(n), FA 1894.

2 Words omitted repealed by the Statute Law Revision Act, 1893.

3 Words omitted repealed by the Statute Law Revision Act, 1894.

CUSTOMS AND INLAND REVENUE ACT, 1881

44 and 45 Vict., c. 12

(Enacted on 3rd June, 1881)

PART III
Stamps

Section 29[1]

As to forms of affidavit.

29. The affidavit to be required or received from any person applying for probate or letters of administration in England or Ireland shall extend to the verification of the account of the estate and effects, or to the verification of such account and the schedule of debts and funeral expenses, as the case may be, and shall be in accordance with such forms as may be prescribed by the ...[2] Treasury; and the Commissioners of Inland Revenue shall provide forms of affidavit stamped to denote the duties payable under this Act.

Section 30[3]

Probate or letters of administration to bear a certificate in lieu of stamp duty.

30. No probate or letters of administration shall be granted by the Probate, Divorce, and Admiralty Division of the High Court of Justice in England, or by the Probate and Matrimonial Division of the High Court of Justice in Ireland, unless the same bear a certificate in writing under the hand of the proper officer of the court, showing that the affidavit for the Commissioners of Ireland Revenue has been delivered, and that such affidavit, if liable to stamp duty, was duly stamped, and stating the amount of the gross value of the estate and effects as shown by the account.

Section 32[1]

Provision for payment of further duty.

32. If at any time it shall be discovered that the personal estate and effects of the deceased were at the time of the grant of probate or letters of administration of greater value than the value mentioned in the certificate, or that any deduction for debts or funeral expenses was made erroneously, the person acting in the administration of such estate and effects shall, within six months after the discovery, deliver a further affidavit with an account to the Commissioners of Inland Revenue, duly stamped for the amount which, with the duty (if any) previously paid on an affidavit in respect of such estate and effects, shall be sufficient to cover the duty chargeable according to the true value thereof, and shall at the same time pay to the said Commissioners interest upon such amount at the rate of five pounds per centum per annum from the date of the grant, or from such subsequent date as the said Commissioners may in the circumstances think proper.

The Commissioners of Inland Revenue, upon the receipt of such affidavit duly stamped as aforesaid, shall cause a certificate to be written by an authorised officer on the probate or letters of administration setting forth the true value of the estate and effects as then ascertained, or, as the case may be, the corrected amount of deduction, and such certificate shall be substituted for, and have the same force and effect as, the certificate of the officer of the court.

Footnotes

1   Sections 29 and 32 are part of the definition of "Inland Revenue affidavit" – see s. 38(1), CATA, and s.48(1), CATCA, both of which sections quote s.22(1)(n), FA 1894.

2   Words omitted repealed by the Statute Law Revision Act, 1893.

3   Section 30 is referred to in s. 60(4), CATA, and s.108(4), CATCA.

FINANCE ACT, 1894

57 and 58 Vict., c. 30
(Enacted on 31st July, 1894)

PART I
Estate Duty

Section 7

Value of property.

7.   (1)   . . . .

(4)   Where any property passing on the death of deceased is situate in a foreign country, and the Commissioners are satisfied that by reason of such death any duty is payable in that foreign country in respect of that property, they shall make an allowance of the amount of that duty from the value of the property[1].

Section 10[2]

Appeal from Commissioners.

10.   (1)   . . . .

(2)   No appeal shall be allowed from any order, direction, determination, or decision of the High Court in any appeal under this section except with the leave of the High Court or Court of Appeal.

(3)   The costs of the appeal shall be in the discretion of the Court, and the Court, where it appears to the Court just, may order the Commissioners to pay on any excess of duty repaid by them interest at the rate of three[3] per cent. per annum for such period as it appears to the Court just.

(4)   Provided that the High Court, if satisfied that it would impose hardship to require the appellant, as a condition of an appeal, to pay the whole or, as the case may be, any part of the duty claimed by the Commissioners or of such portion of it as is then payable by him, may allow an appeal to be brought on payment of no duty, or of such part only of the duty as to the Court seems reasonable, and on security to the satisfaction of the Court being given for the duty, or so much of the duty as is not so paid, but in such case the Court may order interest at the rate of three[3] per cent. per annum to be paid on the unpaid duty so far as it becomes payable under the decision of the Court.

Section 13

Powers to accept composition for death duties.

13. (1) ....

(3) In this section the expression "death duties" means the Estate duty under this Act, the duties mentioned in the First Schedule to this Act and the legacy and succession duties, and the duty payable on any representation or inventory under any Act in force before the Customs and Inland Revenue Act, 1881.[4]

Section 22

Definitions.

22. (1) ....

(n) The expression "Inland Revenue affidavit" means an affidavit made under the enactments specified in the Second Schedule to this Act with the account and schedule annexed thereto:[5]

SECOND SCHEDULE
Acts referred to[6]

Session and Chapter	Title or Short Title	Section referred to
56 Geo. 3, c. 56	The Probate Duty (Ireland) Act, 1816.	Section one hundred and seventeen.
43 Vict., c. 14	The Customs and Inland Revenue Act, 1880.	Section ten.
44 & 45 Vict., c. 12	The Customs and Inland Revenue Act, 1881.	Sections twenty-nine and thirty-two.

Footnotes

1   Restricted by s. 10(2), FA 1950.

2   This section is referred to in s.33(4), Finance (1909-10) Act, 1910, reproduced on page 656.

3   Extended to nine per cent. by s.32(3), FA 1971.

4   Section 13(3), with s. 30, FA 1971 (see page 679), provides the definition of "death duties" in s. 64(1), CATA, and s.111(1), CATCA.

5   Section 22(1)(n) and the Second Schedule provide the definition of "Inland Revenue affidavit" in s. 38(1), CATA, and s.48(1), CATCA.

6   Reproduced on pages 649, 650 and 651.

FINANCE (1909-10) ACT, 1910

10 Edw. 7, c. 8

(Enacted on 29 April, 1910)

PART I

Duties on Land Values.

Section 33[1]

Appeals to referees.

33. (1) Except as expressly provided in this Part of this Act, any person aggrieved may appeal within such time and in such manner as may be provided by rules made under this section against the first or any subsequent determination by the Commissioners of the total value or site value of any land; or against the amount of any assessment of duty under this Part of this Act; or against a refusal of the Commissioners to make any allowance or to make the allowance claimed, where the Commissioners have power to make such an allowance under this Part of this Act; or against any apportionment of the value of land or of duty or any assessment or apportionment of the consideration on any transfer or lease made by the Commissioners under this Part of this Act; or against the determination of any other matter which the Commissioners are to determine or may determine under this Part of this Act:

Provided that-

    (a) an appeal shall not lie against a provisional valuation made by the Commissioners of the total or site value of any land except on the part of a person who has made an objection to the provisional valuation in accordance with this Act;

    and

    (b) the original total value and the original site value and the site value as ascertained under any subsequent valuation shall be questioned only by means of an appeal against the determination by the Commissioners of that value where there is an appeal under this Act, and shall not be questioned in any case on an appeal against an assessment of duty.

(2) An appeal under this section shall be referred to such one of the panel of referees appointed under this Part of this Act as may be selected in manner provided by rules under this section, and the decision of the referee to whom the matter is so referred shall be given in the form provided by rules under this section and shall, subject to appeal to the Court under this section, be final.

(3) The referee shall determine any matter referred to him in consultation with the Commissioners and the appellant, or any persons nominated by the Commissioners and the appellant respectively

PROVISIONAL COLLECTION OF TAXES ACT, 1927

Number 7 of 1927
(Enacted on 19th March, 1927)

Section 1

Definition.

1.   In this Act –

the expression "Committee on Finance" means the Committee on Finance of Dáil Éireann when and so long as such Committee is a committee of the whole House;

[the expression "new tax" when used in relation to a resolution under this Act means a tax which was not in force immediately before the date on which the resolution is expressed to take effect or, where no such date is expressed, the passing of the resolution by Dáil Éireann;][1]

the expression "permanent tax" means a tax which was last imposed or renewed without any limit of time being fixed for its duration;

the expression "temporary tax" means a tax which was last imposed or renewed for a limited period only;

the expression "normal expiration" when used in relation to a temporary tax means the end of the limited period for which the tax was last imposed or renewed;

the word "tax" includes duties of customs, duties of excise, income tax, [...][2] [...][3] [and value added tax][4] [and capital gains tax][5] [...][6] [and corporation tax][7] [...][8] [and residential property tax][9] [and stamp duties][10] **[and parking levy][18]** [and gift tax and inheritance tax][8] but no other tax or duty.

Section 2

Certain resolutions to have statutory effect.

2.   Whenever a resolution (in this Act referred to as a resolution under this Act) is passed by [Dáil Éireann][11] resolving –

(a)   that a new tax specified in the resolution be imposed, or

(b)   that a specified permanent tax in force [immediately before the date on which the resolution is expressed to take effect or, where no such date is expressed, the passing of the resolution by Dáil Éireann][12] be increased, reduced, or otherwise varied, or be abolished, or

(c)   that a specified temporary tax in force [immediately before the date on which the resolution is expressed to take effect or, where no such date is expressed, the passing of the resolution of Dáil Éireann][12] be renewed (whether at the same or a different rate and whether with or without modification) as from the date of its normal expiration or from an earlier date or be discontinued on a date prior to the date of its normal expiration,

and the resolution contains a declaration that it is expedient in the public interest that the resolution should have statutory effect under the provisions of this Act, the resolution shall, subject to the provisions of this Act, have statutory effect as if contained in an Act of the Oireachtas.

Section 3

Application of general taxing enactments.

3.   (1)   Whenever a new tax is imposed by a resolution under this Act and such resolution describes the tax as a duty of customs or as a duty of excise or as an income tax [...][2], the enactments which immediately before the end of the previous financial year were in force in relation to customs duties generally, or excise duties generally, or income tax generally [...][2] (as the case may require) shall, subject to the provisions of this Act, apply to and have full force and effect in respect of such new tax so long as the resolution continues to have statutory effect.

    (2)   Whenever a permanent tax is increased, reduced, or otherwise varied by a resolution under this Act, all enactments which were in force with respect to that tax [immediately before the date on which the resolution is expressed to take effect or, where no such date is expressed, the passing of the resolution by Dáil Éireann][12] shall, so long as the resolution continues to have statutory effect and subject to the provisions of this Act, have full force and effect with respect to the tax as so increased, reduced, or otherwise varied.

    (3)   Whenever a temporary tax is renewed (whether at the same or a different rate and whether with or without modification) by a resolution under this Act, all enactments which were in force with respect to that tax [immediately before the date on which the resolution is expressed to take effect or, where no such date is expressed, the passing of the resolution by Dáil Éireann][12] shall, so long as the resolution continues to have statutory effect and subject to the provisions of this Act, have full force and effect with respect to the tax as renewed by the resolution.

Section 4 [13]

Duration of statutory effect of resolution.

4.   A resolution under this Act shall cease to have statutory effect upon the happening of whichever of the following events first occurs, that is to say:

    [(a)   subject to section 4A of this Act, if a Bill containing provisions to the same effect (with or without modifications) as the resolution is not read a second time by Dáil Éireann –

(i) where Dáil Éireann is in recess on any day between the eighty-second and the eighty-fourth day after the resolution is passed by Dáil Éireann, within the next five sitting days of the resumption of Dáil Éireann after that recess,

(ii) in any other case, within the next eighty-four days after the resolution is passed by Dáil Éireann,][14]

(b) if those provisions of the said Bill are rejected by Dáil Éireann during the passage of the Bill through the Oireachtas;

(c) the coming into operation of an Act of the Oireachtas containing provisions to the same effect (with or without modification) as the resolution;

(d) [subject to section 4A of this Act][15] the expiration of a period of four months from that date on which the resolution is expressed to take effect or, where no such date is expressed, from the passing of the resolution by Dáil Éireann.

Section 4A[16]

Effect of dissolution of Dáil Éireann.

4A. Where Dáil Éireann, having passed a resolution under this Act, has been dissolved on the date the resolution was so passed or within four months of that date, then the period of dissolution shall be disregarded for the purposes of calculating any period to which paragraph (a) or (d) of section 4 of this Act relates.

Section 5

Repayment of certain payments and deductions.

5. (1) Whenever a resolution under this Act ceases to have statutory effect by reason of the happening of any event other than the coming into operation of an Act of the Oireachtas containing provisions to the same effect (with or without modification) as the resolution, all moneys paid in pursuance of the resolution shall be repaid or made good and every deduction made in pursuance of the resolution shall be deemed to be an unauthorised deduction.

(2) [...][17]

(3) Whenever an Act of the Oireachtas comes into operation containing provisions to the same effect with modifications as a resolution under this Act and such resolution ceases by virtue of such coming into operation to have statutory effect, all moneys paid in pursuance of such resolution which would not be payable under such Act shall be repaid or made good and every deduction made in pursuance of such resolution which would not be authorised by such Act shall be deemed to be an unauthorised deduction.

Section 6

Certain payments and deductions deemed to be legal.

6. (1) Any payment or deduction on account of a temporary tax to which this section applies made within two months after the expiration of such tax in respect of a period or event occurring after such expiration shall, if such payment or deduction would have been a legal payment or deduction if the tax had not expired, be deemed to be a legal payment or deduction subject to the conditions that -

(a) if a resolution under this Act renewing the tax (with or without modification) is not passed by the Committee on Finance within two months after the expiration of the tax, the amount of such payment or deduction shall be repaid or made good on the expiration of such two months, and

(b) if (such resolution having been so passed) an Act of the Oireachtas renewing the tax (with or without modification) does not come into operation when or before such resolution ceases to have statutory effect, the amount of such payment or deduction shall be repaid or made good on such cesser, and

(c) if (such Act having been so passed) the tax is renewed by such Act with such modifications that the whole or some portion of such payment or deduction is not a legal payment or deduction under such Act, the whole or such portion (as the case may be) of such payment or deduction shall be repaid or made good on the coming into operation of such Act.

(2) This section applies only to a temporary tax which was last imposed or renewed for a limited period not exceeding eighteen months and was in force immediately before the end of the financial year next preceding the financial year in which the payment or deduction under this section is made.

Section 7

Repeal.

7. The Provisional Collection of Taxes Act, 1913, is hereby repealed.

Section 8

Short title.

8. This Act may be cited as the Provisional Collection of Taxes Act, 1927.

Footnotes

1   As substituted by s.139(a), FA 2002.

2   Deleted by s.86, FA 1974.

3   Deleted by s.41, Value-Added Tax Act, 1972.

4   Deleted by s.38, Value-Added Tax Act, 1972.

5   As inserted by s.50, Capital Gains Tax Act, 1975.

6 Deleted by s.38, FA 1978.

7 As inserted by s.6, Corporation Tax Act, 1976.

8 The words "and gift tax and inheritance tax" inserted by s.69(1), CATA, but, with effect from 21st February, 2003, deleted by s.118(1), CATCA, and re-inserted by s.115(1), CATCA.

9 As inserted by s.114, FA 1983.

10 As inserted by s.100, FA 1986.

11 As substituted by s.85, FA 1974.

12 As substituted by s.139(b), FA 2002.

13 Section substituted by s.2, Appropriation Act, 1991.

14 As substituted by s.2, Appropriation Act, 1991.

15 As inserted by s.2, Appropriation Act, 1991.

16 As substituted by s.250, FA 1992.

17 Deleted by s.85, FA 1974.

18 As inserted by s 3(2), F(No. 2)A, 2008, with effect as on and from 1st January, 2009.

FINANCE ACT, 1928

Number 11 of 1928
(Enacted on 17th July, 1928)

PART V

Miscellaneous and General

Section 34

Care and management of taxes and duties.

34.   (1)   . . . .

      (2)   Any information acquired, whether before or after the passing of this Act, by the Revenue Commissioners in connection with any tax or duty under their care and management may be used by them for any purpose connected with any other tax or duty under their care and management.[1]

Footnote

1   S.34(2) replaced by s.872(1), TCA, with effect as on and from 6th April, 1997.

FINANCE ACT, 1935

Number 28 of 1935
(Enacted on 30th July, 1935)

PART III
Death Duties

Section 33[1]

Payment of money standing in names of two or more persons.

33. (1) Where, either before or after the passing of this Act, a sum of money exceeding one thousand pounds is lodged or deposited (otherwise than on a current account) in Saorstát Eireann with a banker in the joint names of two or more persons, and one of such persons (in this section referred to as the deceased) dies after the passing of this Act, such banker shall not pay such money or any part thereof to the survivor or all or any of the survivors of such person or to any other person unless or until there is furnished to such banker a certificate by the Revenue Commissioners (acting by any of such Commissioners or by any of their officers) certifying that there is no outstanding claim for duty in connection with the death of the deceased in respect of such money or any part thereof or a consent in writing by the Revenue Commissioners (acting as aforesaid) to such payment pending the ascertainment and discharge of such duty.

(2) Notwithstanding anything contained in subsection (7) of section 6 of the Finance Act, 1894, duty leviable and payable on the death of the deceased shall be deemed for the purposes of this section to become due on the day of the death of the deceased.

[(3) Every banker who shall pay any money in contravention of this section shall be guilty of an offence under this section and shall be liable on summary conviction thereof to an excise penalty of five hundred pounds.][2]

(4) Where a banker is charged with an offence under this section, the onus of proving that such certificate or such consent as is mentioned in this section was furnished to such banker before he made the payment which is alleged to constitute such offence shall lie on such banker.

(5) Where a banker is charged with an offence under this section, it shall be a good defence to such charge to prove that, at the time when such banker made the payment of money which is alleged to constitute such offence, he had reasonable ground for believing that none of the persons in whose joint names such money was lodged or deposited with him was dead.

(6) In this section—

"banker" means a person who carries on banking business in the State and includes a friendly society, an industrial and provident society, a building society, the Post Office Savings Bank, a trustee savings bank, [...............,][3] the Agricultural Credit Corporation Limited, and any person with whom money is lodged or deposited;

"pay" includes transfer in the books of a banker and any dealings whatsoever with any moneys which were lodged or deposited in the name of a person who died after the time of the lodgment or deposit and any other person or persons;

"current account" means an account which is customarily operated upon by means of cheque or banker's order;

"banking business" has the meaning assigned to it by section 2 of the Central Bank Act, 1971;

references to moneys lodged or deposited include references to shares of a building society, friendly society or industrial and provident society.

Footnotes

1   This section is as amended by s.16, FA 1937, s. 17, FA 1952, s.36, FA 1963 and s. 61, FA 1973. It is referred to in s. 61(6), CATA.

2   Repealed by s.53, FA 1971, but s.42(5), FA 1971, provided an alternative penalty of £1,000.

3   The words "the Industrial Credit Company, Limited," were deleted by s.7(1), ICC Bank Act, 2000, with effect from 12th February 2001, under S.I. No. 46 of 2001.

FINANCE ACT, 1950

Number 18 of 1950
(Enacted on 5th July, 1950)

PART III
Death Duties

Section 10

Confirmation of Convention set forth in First Schedule.

10.   (1)   The convention set forth in the First Schedule to this Act and concluded on the 13th day of September, 1949, between the Government and the Government of the United States of America (in this section referred to as the Convention) is hereby confirmed and shall have the force of law.

        (2)   Subsection (4) of section 7 of the Finance Act, 1894[1] (which provides for relief in respect of duty payable in a foreign country) shall not have effect in relation to estate tax chargeable under the laws of the United States of America to which the provisions of the Convention apply.

Footnote

1   Reproduced on page 653.

FIRST SCHEDULE
Convention between the Government of Ireland and the Government of the United States of America for the avoidance of Double Taxation and the Prevention of Fiscal Evasion with respect to taxes on the estates of deceased persons.

The Government of Ireland and the Government of the United States of America,

Desiring to conclude a Convention for the avoidance of double taxation and the prevention of fiscal evasion with respect to taxes on estates of deceased persons,

Have appointed for that purpose as their Plenipotentiaries:

     The Government of Ireland:
     Patrick McGilligan, Minister for Finance;
     Sean MacBride, Minister for External Affairs;

and

     The Government of the United States of America:
     George A Garrett, Envoy Extraordinary and Minister Plenipotentiary of the United States of America at Dublin;

Who, having exhibited their respective full powers, found in good and due form, have agreed as follows:-

ARTICLE I

(1)   The taxes which are the subject of the present Convention are:

(a)   In the United States of America, the Federal estate tax, and

(b)   In Ireland, the estate duty imposed in that territory.

(2)   The present Convention shall also apply to any other taxes of a substantially similar character imposed by either Contracting Party subsequently to the date of signature of the present Convention.

ARTICLE II

(1)   In the present Convention, unless the context otherwise requires:

(a)   The term "United States" means the United States of America, and when used in a geographical sense means the States, the Territories of Alaska and of Hawaii, and the District of Columbia.

(b)   The term "Ireland" means the Republic of Ireland.

(c)   The term "territory" when used in relation to one or the other Contracting Party means the United States or Ireland, as the context requires.

(d)   The term "tax" means the estate duty imposed in Ireland or the United States Federal estate tax, as the context requires.

(2)   In the application of the provisions of the present Convention by one of the Contracting Parties, any term not otherwise defined shall, unless the context otherwise requires, have the meaning which it has under the laws of that Contracting Party relating to the taxes which are the subject of the present Convention.

ARTICLE III

(1)   For the purposes of the present Convention, the question whether a decedent was domiciled in any part of the territory of one of the Contracting Parties at the time of his death shall be determined in accordance with the law in force in that territory.

(2)   Where a person dies domiciled in any part of the territory of one Contracting Party, the situs of any rights or interests, legal or equitable, in or over any of the following classes of property which for the purposes of tax form part of the estate of such person or pass on his death, shall, for the purposes of the imposition of tax and for the purposes of the credit to be allowed under Article V, be determined exclusively in accordance with the following rules, but in cases not within such rules the situs of any such rights or interests shall be determined for those purposes in accordance with the law relating to tax in force in the territory of the other Contracting Party:

(a)   Immovable property shall be deemed to be situated at the place where such property is located;

(4) For the purposes of this Article, the amount of tax of a Contracting Party attributable to any property shall be ascertained after taking into account any credit, allowance or relief, or any remission or reduction of tax, otherwise than in respect of tax payable in the territory of the other Contracting Party; and if, in respect of property situated outside the territories of both parties, a Contracting Party allows against its tax a credit for tax payable in the country where the property is situated, that credit shall be taken into account in ascertaining, for the purposes of paragraph (2) of this Article, the amount of the tax of that Party attributable to the property.

ARTICLE VI

(1) Any claim for a credit or for a refund of tax founded on the provisions of the present Convention shall be made within six years from the date of the death of the decedent in respect of whose estate the claim is made, or, in the case of a reversionary interest where payment of tax is deferred until on or after the date on which the interest falls into possession, within six years from that date.

(2) Any such refund shall be made without payment of interest on the amount so refunded, save to the extent to which interest was paid on the amount so refunded when the tax was paid.

ARTICLE VII

(1) The taxation authorities of the Contracting Parties shall exchange such information (being information available under the respective taxation laws of the Contracting Parties) as is necessary for carrying out the provisions of the present Convention or for the prevention of fraud or the administration of statutory provisions against legal avoidance in relation to the taxes which are the subject of the present Convention. Any information so exchanged shall be treated as secret and shall not be disclosed to any person other than those concerned with the assessment and collection of the taxes which are the subject of the present Convention. No information shall be exchanged which would disclose any trade secret or trade process.

(2) As used in this Article, the Term "taxation authorities" means, in the case of the United States, the Commissioner of Internal Revenue. or his authorised representative; in the case or Ireland, the Revenue Commissioners or their authorised representative.

ARTICLE VIII

(1) The present Convention shall be ratified and the instruments of ratification shall be exchanged at Washington, District of Columbia, as soon as possible.

(2) The present Convention shall come into force on the date of exchange of ratifications and shall be effective only as to

(a) the estates of persons dying on or after such date; and

(b) the estate of any person dying before such date and after the last day of the calendar year immediately preceding such date whose personal representative elects, in such manner as may be prescribed, that the provisions of the present Convention shall be applied to such estate.

ARTICLE IX

(1) The present Convention shall remain in force for not less than three years after the date of its coming into force.

(2) If not less than six months before the expiration of such period of three years, neither of the Contracting Parties shall have given to the other Contracting Party, through diplomatic channels, written notice of its intention to terminate the present Convention, the Convention shall remain in force after such period of three years until either of the Contracting Parties shall have given written notice of such intention, in which event the present Convention shall not be effective as to the estates of persons dying on or after the date (not being earlier than the sixtieth day after the date of such notice) specified in such notice, or, if no date is specified, on or after the sixtieth day after the date of such notice.

IN WITNESS WHEREOF the above-named Plenipotentiaries have signed the present Convention and have affixed thereto their seals.

Done at Dublin, in duplicate, this 13th day of September, 1949.

For the Government of Ireland:
(Signed)
PATRICK McGILLIGAN

SEAN MacBRIDE

For the Government of the United States of America:
(Signed)
GEORGE A GARRETT.

FINANCE ACT, 1951

Number 15 of 1951
(Enacted on 11th July, 1951)

PART III
Death Duties

Section 12[1]

Operation of certain exemptions.

12. (1) In this section "exemption to which this section applies" means –

    (a) an exemption from taxation by virtue of a condition for such exemption under section 47 of the Finance (No. 2) Act, 1915, or that section as amended, adapted or amended and adapted,

    (b) an exemption from taxation under section 63 of the Finance Act, 1916, or that section as amended, adapted or amended and adapted,

    (c) an exemption from taxation by virtue of a condition for such exemption under subsection (1) of section 21 of the Finance Act, 1923 (No. 21 of 1923), or that subsection as adapted, or

    (d) an exemption from taxation under subsection (1) of section 37 of the Finance Act, 1929 (No. 32 of 1929), or that subsection as adapted.

(2) An exemption to which this section applies, so far as relates to duties leviable on or with reference to a death (whether a death which occurs at any time after the passing of this Act or a death which occurred at any time after the passing of the Act referred to in subsection (1) of this section in relation to the exemption and before the passing of this Act), shall be or be taken to have been such as to operate by reference to persons in whose beneficial ownership the relevant securities are or were immediately before, not after, the death.

Footnote

1   This section has been included in the book at the request of the Revenue Commissioners but its relevance to CAT is not apparent to the Editor, particularly in view of s.81, CATCA, and s.57, CATA.

FINANCE ACT, 1954

Number 22 of 1954
(Enacted on 13th July, 1954)

PART IV
Death Duties

Section 22[1]

Discharge of death duties by transfer of securities.

22. (1) In this section—

"the Minister" means the Minister for Finance;

"the Account" means such account as is prescribed pursuant to subsection (4) of this section.

(2) This section applies to the following securities:

    (a) the 4½% National Loan, 1973/78;

    (b) any security which—

        (i) after the passing of this Act is created and issued by the Minister on terms that, subject to specified conditions, it will be accepted in payment of any death duty, and

        (ii) is charged on the Central Fund.

(3) For the purposes of this section—

    (a) the value at the date of transfer of any security transferred to the Account shall be the nominal face value with the addition of any interest accrued due at the date of the transfer but then remaining unpaid, after deducting any interest which may be receivable by the transferor after that date, and

    (b) interest on any such security shall be deemed to accrue from day to day.

(4) A person from whom any sum is due on account of any death duty may, subject to the relevant regulations under this section, pay the sum or any part thereof by means of a transfer, to such account of the Minister as is prescribed by the regulations, of so much of any security to which this section applies as is equal in value at the date of the transfer to the sum or part, and the transfer shall be accepted by the Revenue Commissioners as a cash payment to them of the sum or part.

(5) The Minister may make regulations prescribing the conditions under which any security to which this section applies shall be accepted in payment of any death duty.[2]

(6) Securities transferred to the Account may be held therein or sold, cancelled or otherwise dealt with as the Minister directs.

(7) The Minister shall pay out of the Account to the Revenue Commissioners the values at the dates of transfer of all securities transferred to the Account.

(8) Sums paid by way of interest on or redemption of securities held in the Account and sums derived from sales of or other dealings with such securities shall be paid into the Account.

(9) Sums paid into the Account shall be applied in or towards meeting payments which the Minister is required by this section to make to the Revenue Commissioners out of the Account, and any balance shall, as and when the Minister directs, be paid into the Exchequer in repayment of moneys advanced to the Account from the Central Fund or the growing produce thereof, and, if the balance is in excess of the sum required for repaying moneys advanced from the Central Fund or the growing produce thereof, the excess amount shall be disposed of for the benefit of the Exchequer in such manner as the Minister directs.

(10) There shall be issued out of the Central Fund or the growing produce thereof to the Account such sums as may be required to meet any payments under this section by the Minister to the Revenue Commissioners out of the Account which are not met under subsection (9) of this section, and so much of the sums issued as is not authorised by this section to be met by borrowing by the Minister shall be charged on the Central Fund and the growing produce thereof.

(11) For the purpose, of providing, wholly or partly, for so much of the issues authorised by this section to be made out of the Central Fund or the growing produce thereof as is equal to the price at which the relevant security was issued for public subscription, the Minister may borrow from any person any sum or sums, and for the purpose of such borrowing he may create and issue securities bearing such rates of interest and subject to such conditions as to repayment, redemption or any other matter as he thinks fit, and he shall pay any moneys so borrowed into the Exchequer.

(12) The principal of and interest on any securities issued under subsection (11) of this section and the expenses incurred in connection with the issue of such securities shall be charged on and payable out of the Central Fund or the growing produce thereof.

(13) (a) Where stock of the 4½ per cent. National Loan, 1973/78, has been accepted by the Revenue Commissioners in payment of death duties pursuant to the Prospectus of that Loan and has been transferred to them before the passing of this Act, the stock shall be deemed to have been a cash payment to them of a sum equal to the value of the stock at the date of the transfer, such value being the nominal face value of the stock with the addition of any interest accrued due (on the basis of interest accruing from day to day) at the date of the transfer but then remaining unpaid, after deducting any interest which may be receivable by the transferor after that date.

(b) As soon as may be after the passing of this Act, the Revenue Commissioners shall, as respects any stock so transferred and held by them, transfer the stock to such account as is prescribed by the regulations under this section relating to the 4½ per cent. National Loan, 1973/78, and shall pay into that account any interestn which has been paid to them on the stock, but the payment to be made under subsection (7) of this section in relation to the stock shall be the value referred to in paragraph (a)[1] of this subsection.

Footnotes

1   This section is referred to in s. 45, CATA, and s.56, CATCA.

2   See S.I. No. 309 of 1967 for regulations made under s.22(5) above in connection with 6½% Exchequer Stock, 2000/05. These are reproduced on page 1362. At the date of publication of this book, this Stock was the last security available to pay inheritance tax and was redeemed on 27th June, 2000.

PART VI[1]
Miscellaneous and General
Section 29

Repeals.

29. Each enactment specified in column (2) of the Third Schedule to this Act is hereby repealed to the extent specified in column (3) of the said Schedule as on and from the date mentioned in column (4) of the said Schedule.

Section 30

Care and management of taxes and duties.

30. All taxes and duties imposed by this Act are hereby placed under the care and management of the Revenue Commissioners.

Section 31

Short title, construction and commencement.

31. (1) This Act may be cited as the Finance Act, 1954.

(2) Part I of this Act shall be construed together with the Income Tax Acts.

(3) Part II of this Act, so far as it relates to duties of customs, shall be construed together with the Customs Acts and, so far as it relates to the duties of excise, be construed together with the Statutes which relate to the duties of excise and the management of those duties.

(4) Part V of this Act shall be construed together with the Stamp Act, 1891, and the enactments amending or extending that Act.

(5) Part I of this Act shall, save as is otherwise expressly provided therein, be deemed to come into force on and shall take effect as on and from the 6th day of April, 1954.

Footnote

1   Part VI has been included in the book at the request of te Revenue Commissioners but its relevance to CAT is not apparent to the Editor.

PROPERTY VALUES (ARBITRATIONS AND APPEALS) ACT, 1960

Number 45 of 1960
(Enacted on 21st December, 1960)

Section 1

Interpretation.
1.   In this Act—

"the Act of 1910" means the Finance (1909-10) Act, 1910;

"the Act of 1919" means the Acquisition of Land (Assessment of Compensation) Act, 1919;

"the Act of 1945" means the Arterial Drainage Act, 1945;

"the Reference Committee" means the Reference Committee established by section 1 of the Act of 1919 as amended by the Acquisition of Land (Reference Committee) Act, 1925.[1]

Footnote
1   The Reference Committee consists of the Chief Justice, the President of the High Court and the Chairman of the Surveyors' Institution (Irish Branch).

Section 2

Property arbitrators.
2.   (1)   The Reference Committee may appoint one or more persons having special knowledge of the valuation of land or having such other qualifications as the Reference Committee considers suitable to be an arbitrator or arbitrators for the purposes of Part I of the Act of 1910, the Act of 1919 and the Act of 1945 and a person so appointed shall be known, and is referred to in this Act, as a property arbitrator.

      (2)   A property arbitrator shall hold office on such terms and conditions, other than those provided for under subsection (3) of this section, as the Reference Committee may from time to time determine with the approval of the Minister for Finance.

      (3)   A property arbitrator shall be paid, out of moneys provided by the Oireachtas, such remuneration and allowances for expenses as the Minister for Finance may from time to time determine.

      (4)   Where, immediately before the date of the passing of this Act, a person holds office as a member of the panel of official arbitrators under the Act of 1919 and is in receipt of an annual salary in respect of such office, that person shall be deemed to have been appointed under this section on such date to be a property arbitrator for the purposes of Part 1 of the Act of 1910, the Act of 1919 and the

Act of 1945 and to hold office on terms and conditions (including terms and conditions relating to remuneration and allowances for expenses) not less favourable than those on which he held office as a member of the panel aforesaid.

Section 3

Arbitrators for the purpose of section 33 of Act of 1910.[1]

3.   (1)   An appeal under section 33 of the Act of 1910 shall be referred to a property arbitrator who shall be nominated by the Reference Committee for the purposes of such reference in accordance with rules made by the Reference Committee under this section and, accordingly —

     (a)   so much of subsection (2) of the said section 33 as provides for the reference of an appeal thereunder to such one of a panel of referees appointed under Part 1 of the Act of 1910 as may be selected in manner provided by rules under the said section 33 shall cease to have effect, and

     (b)   references in the said section 33 to a referee selected under that section shall be construed as references to a property arbitrator nominated under this section and the reference in the said section 33 to the Reference Committee established under that section shall be construed as a reference to the Reference Committee.

    (2)   Where, in an appeal under the said section 33, the value of any minerals is relevant to the determination of the property arbitrator, the appellant and the Revenue Commissioners may each, in addition to the persons, if any, nominated under subsection (3) of the said section 33, nominate one person having experience in the valuation of minerals to consult the property arbitrator and, in determining the appeal, the property arbitrator shall consult any person nominated under this subsection.

Footnote

1   Reproduced on page 655. S.33, F(1909-10)A, 1910, is referred to in s.51(1), CATA, and in s.66(1), CATCA.

SUCCESSION ACT, 1965

Number 27 of 1965
(Enacted on 22nd December, 1965)

PART VI

Distribution on Intestacy

Section 72A[1]

Distribution of disclaimed estate.

72A. Where the estate, or part of the estate, as to which a person dies intestate is disclaimed after the passing of the Family Law (Miscellaneous Provisions) Act, 1997 (otherwise than under section 73 of this Act), the estate or part, as the case may be, shall be distributed in accordance with this Part –

    (a) as if the person disclaiming had died immediately before the death of the intestate, and

    (b) if that person is not the spouse or a direct lineal ancestor of the intestate, as if that person had died without leaving issue.

Footnote

1   This section was inserted by s.6, Family Law (Miscellaneous Provisions) Act, 1997, which was enacted on 5th May, 1997.

Commentary

A   As to disclaimers, see s.13, CATA, and s.12, CATCA

FINANCE ACT, 1971

Number 23 of 1971
(Enacted on 28th July, 1971)

PART III
Death Duties

Section 30[1]

"Death Duties".

30. In this Act and in every other enactment for the time being in force (whether passed or made before or after the passing of this Act), unless the contrary intention appears, "death duties" has, and in the case of enactments for the time being in force that were passed or made before the passing of this Act, shall be deemed always to have had the same meaning as in section 13 (3) of the Finance Act, 1894.[2]

Footnotes

1   This section is referred to in s. 64(1), CATA, and s.111(1), CATCA.

2   Reproduced on page 654.

CAPITAL ACQUISITIONS TAX ACT, 1976

Number 8 of 1976
(Enacted on 31st March, 1976)

PART I
Preliminary

Section 1

Short title.
1.   This Act may be cited as the Capital Acquisitions Tax Act, 1976.

Section 2

Interpretation.
2.   (1)   In this Act, unless the context otherwise requires –

"absolute interest", in relation to property, includes the interest of a person who has a general power of appointment over the property;

"accountable person" means a person who is accountable for the payment of tax by virtue of section 35;

"benefit" includes any estate, interest, income or right;

"child" includes –

(a)   a stepchild;

(b)   a child adopted –

(i)   under the Adoption Acts, 1952 to 1974; or

(ii)   under an adoption law, other than the Adoption Acts, 1952 to 1974, being an adoption that has, in the place where the law applies, substantially the same effect in relation to property rights (including the law of succession) as an adoption under the Adoption Acts, 1952 to 1974, has in the State in relation to such rights;

"Commissioners" means the Revenue Commissioners;

"date of the disposition" means –

(a)   in the case of a will, the date of the testator's death;

(b)   in the case of an intestacy or a partial intestacy, the date of death of the intestate;

(c)   in the case of a benefit under Part IX or section 56 of the Succession Act, 1965, the date of death of the relevant testator or other deceased person, and correspondingly in the case of an analogous benefit under the law of another territory;

(d)   in the case of a disposition which consists of the failure to exercise a right or a power, the date of the latest time when the disposer could have exercised the right or the power if he were *sui juris* and not under any physical disability; and

(e) in any other case, the date on which the act (or where more than one act is involved, the last act) of the disposer was done by which he provided or bound himself to provide the property comprised in the disposition;

"date of the gift" means the date of the happening of the event upon which the donee, or any person in right of the donee or on his behalf, becomes beneficially entitled in possession to the benefit, and a reference to the time when a gift is taken shall be construed as a reference to the date of the gift;

"date of the inheritance" means —

(a) in the case where the successor or any person in right of the successor or on his behalf becomes entitled in possession to the benefit on the happening of any such event as is referred to in section 3 (2), the date of the event;

(b) in the case of a gift which becomes an inheritance by reason of its being taken under a disposition where the date of the disposition is within two years prior to the death of the disposer, the date which would have been the date of the gift if the entitlement were a gift; and

(c) in any other case, the date of the latest death which had to occur for the successor, or any person in right of the successor or on his behalf, to become beneficially entitled in possession to the benefit,

and a reference to the time when an inheritance is taken shall be construed as a reference to the date of the inheritance;

"discretionary trust" means any trust whereby, or by virtue or in consequence of which, property is held on trust to apply, or with a power to apply, the income or capital or part of the income or capital of the property for the benefit of any person or persons or of any one or more of a number or of a class of persons whether at the discretion of trustees or any other person and notwithstanding that there may be a power to accumulate all or any part of the income;

"disposer", in relation to a disposition, means the person who, for the purpose of the disposition, directly or indirectly provided the property comprised in the disposition, and in any case where more than one person provided the property each shall be deemed to be the disposer to the extent that he so provided the property; and for the purposes of this definition —

(a) the testator shall be the disposer in the case of a disposition referred to in paragraph (k) of the definition of "disposition";

(b) the intestate shall be the disposer in the case of a disposition referred to in paragraph (l) of that definition;

(c)   the deceased person referred to in paragraph (m) of that definition shall be the disponer in the case of a disposition referred to in that paragraph; and

(d)   a person who has made with any other person a reciprocal arrangement by which that other person provided property comprised in the disposition shall be deemed to have provided that property;

"disposition" includes—

(a)   any act or omission by a person as a result of which the value of his estate immediately after such act or omission is less than it would be but for such act or omission;

(b)   any trust, covenant, agreement or arrangement, whether made by a single operation or by associated operations;

(c)   the creation of a debt or other right enforceable against the disponer personally or against any estate or interest he may have in property;

(d)   the payment of money;

(e)   the allotment of shares in a company;

(f)   the grant or the creation of any benefit;

(g)   the grant or the creation of any lease, mortgage, charge, licence, option, power, partnership or joint tenancy or other estate or interest in or over any property;

(h)   the release, forfeiture, surrender or abandonment of any debt or benefit, or the failure to exercise a right; and, for the purpose of this paragraph, a debt or benefit shall be deemed to have been released when it has become unenforceable by action through lapse of time (save to the extent that it is recovered subsequent to its becoming so unenforceable);

(i)   the exercise of a general power of appointment in favour of any person other than the holder of the power;

(j)   a donatio mortis causa,

(k)   a will or other testamentary disposition;

(l)   an intestacy, whether total or partial;

(m)   the payment of a share as a legal right under Part IX of the Succession Act, 1965, to a deceased person's spouse, or the making of provision for a widow or child of a deceased person under section 56 or section 117 of the Succession Act, 1965, or an analogous share or provision paid or made on the death of a deceased person to or for the benefit of any person under the law of another territory; and

(n)   a resolution passed by a company which is deemed by subsection (3) to be a disposition;

"donee" means a person who takes a gift;

"entitled in possession" means having a present right to the enjoyment of property as opposed to having a future such right, and without prejudice to the generality of the foregoing a person shall also, for the purposes of this Act, be deemed to be entitled in possession to an interest or share in a partnership, joint tenancy or estate of a deceased person, in which he is a partner, joint tenant or beneficiary, as the case may be, but he shall not be deemed to be entitled in possession to an interest in expectancy until an event happens whereby this interest ceases to be an interest in expectancy;

"general power of appointment" includes every power, right, or authority whether exercisable only by will or otherwise which would enable the holder thereof to appoint or dispose of property to whomsoever he thinks fit or to obtain such power, right or authority, but exclusive of any power exercisable solely in a fiduciary capacity under a disposition not made by himself, or exercisable by a tenant for life under the Settled Land Act, 1882, or as mortgagee;

"gift" means a gift which a person is by this Act deemed to take;

"inheritance" means an inheritance which a person is by this Act deemed to take;

"interest in expectancy" includes an estate in remainder or reversion and every other future interest, whether vested or contingent, but does not include a reversion expectant on the determination of a lease;

"limited interest" means —

(a)   an interest (other than a leasehold interest) for the duration of a life or lives or for a period certain; or

(b)   any other interest which is not an absolute interest;

"local authority" has the meaning assigned to it by section 2 (2) of the Local Government Act, 1941, and includes a body established under the Local Government Services (Corporate Bodies) Act, 1971;

"market value", in relation to property, means the market value thereof ascertained in accordance with sections 15, 16 and 17;

"minor child" means a child who has not attained the age of 21 years;

"personal property" means any property other than real property;

"personal representative" means the executor or administrator for the time being of a deceased person and includes any person who takes possession of or intermeddles with the property of a deceased person and also includes any person having, in relation to the deceased person, under the law of another country, any functions corresponding to the functions, for administration purposes under the law of the State, of an executor or administrator;

"property" includes rights and interests of any description;

"real property" means real and chattel real property;

"regulations" means regulations made under section 71;

"relative" means a relative within the meaning of subsection (4);

"return" means such a return as is referred to in section 36;

"share" in relation to a company, includes any interest whatsoever in the company which is analogous to a share in the company, and "shareholder" shall be construed accordingly;

"special power of appointment" means a power of appointment which is not a general power of appointment;

"successor" means a person who takes an inheritance;

"tax" means any tax chargeable under this Act;

"valuation date" has the meaning assigned to it by section 21.

(2) For the purpose of the definition of "general power of appointment" contained in subsection (1), a person shall be deemed to have a general power of appointment—

    (a) notwithstanding that he is not sui juris or is under a physical disability;

    (b) over money which he has a general power to charge on property; and

    (c) over property of which he is tenant in tail in possession.

(3) For the purpose of the definition of " disposition " contained in subsection (1), the passing by a company of a resolution which, by the extinguishment or alteration of the rights attaching to any share of the company, results, directly or indirectly, in the estate of any shareholder of the company being increased in value at the expense of the estate of any other shareholder, shall be deemed to be a disposition made by that other shareholder if he could have prevented the passing of the resolution by voting against it or otherwise; and in this subsection, "share" includes a debenture and loan stock and "shareholder" includes a debenture holder and a holder of loan stock.

(4) For the purposes of this Act, the following persons and no other person shall be relatives of another person, that is to say—

    (a) the spouse of that other person;

    (b) the father, mother, and any child, uncle or aunt of that other person;

    (c) any child (other than that other person), and any child of a child, of any person who is by virtue of paragraph (a) or (b) a relative of that other person; and

    (d) the spouse of a person who is by virtue of paragraph (b) or (c) a relative of that other person;

    (e) the grandparent of that other person.

(5) For the purposes of this Act—

    (a) the relationship between a child, adopted in the manner referred to in paragraph (b) of the definition of "child" contained in subsection (1), and any other person, or between other persons, that would exist if such child had been born to the adoptor or adoptors in lawful wedlock, shall be deemed to exist between such child and that other person or between those other persons, and the relationship of any such child and any person that existed prior to his being so adopted shall be deemed to have ceased; and

    (b) an illegitimate child who has not been—

        (i) legitimated; or

        (ii) adopted under—

            (I) the Adoption Acts, 1952 to 1974; or

            (II) an adoption law other than the Adoption Acts, 1952 to 1974, having the effect referred to in paragraph (b) (ii) of the definition of "child" contained in subsection (1),

    shall be the child of his mother.

(6) In this Act, references to any enactment shall, unless the context otherwise requires, be construed as references to that enactment as amended or extended by any subsequent enactment.

(7) In this Act, a reference to a section or Schedule is a reference to a section of or Schedule to this Act unless it is indicated that reference to some other enactment is intended.

(8) In this Act, a reference to a subsection, paragraph or subparagraph is to the subsection, paragraph or subparagraph of the provision (including a Schedule) in which the reference occurs, unless it is indicated that reference to some other provision is intended.

Section 3

Meaning of "on a death".

3. (1) In this Act, "on a death" in relation to a person becoming beneficially entitled in possession, means—

    (a) on the death of a person or at a time ascertainable only by reference to the death of a person;

    (b) under a disposition where the date of the disposition is the date of the death of the disponer;

    (c) under a disposition where the date of the disposition is on or after the 1st day of April, 1975, and within two years prior to the death of the disponer; or

    (d) on the happening, after the cesser of an intervening life interest, of any such event as is referred to in subsection (2).

(2)   The events referred to in subsection (1) (d) are any of the following—

(a)   the determination or failure of any charge, estate, interest or trust;

(b)   the exercise of a special power of appointment;

(c)   in the case where a benefit was given under a disposition in such terms that the amount or value of the benefit could only be ascertained from time to time by the actual payment or application of property for the purpose of giving effect to the benefit, the making of any payment or the application of the property; or

(d)   any other event which, under a disposition, affects the right to property, or to the enjoyment thereof.

PART II
Gift Tax

Section 4

Charge of gift tax.

4.   A capital acquisitions tax, to be called gift tax and to be computed as hereinafter provided, shall, subject to this Act and the regulations thereunder, be charged, levied and paid upon the taxable value of every taxable gift taken by a donee, where the date of the gift is on or after the 28th day of February, 1974.

Section 5

Gift deemed to be taken.

5.   (1)   For the purposes of this Act, where, under or in consequence of any disposition, a person becomes beneficially entitled in possession, otherwise than on a death, to any benefit (whether or not the person becoming so entitled already has any interest in the property in which he takes such benefit), otherwise than for full consideration in money or money's worth paid by him, he shall be deemed to take a gift.

(2)   A gift shall be deemed—

(a)   to consist of the whole or the appropriate part, as the case may be, of the property in which the donee takes a benefit, or on which the benefit is charged or secured or on which the donee is entitled to have it charged or secured; and

(b)   if the benefit is an annuity or other periodic payment which is not charged on or secured by any property and which the donee is not entitled to have so charged or secured, to consist of such sum as would, if invested on the date of the gift in the security of the Government which was issued last before that date for subscription in the State and is redeemable not less than 10 years after the date of issue, yield, on the basis of the current yield on the security, an annual income equivalent to the annual value of the annuity or of the other periodic payment receivable by the donee.

(3) For the purposes of section 6 (1) (c), the sum referred to in subsection (2) (b) shall be deemed not to be situate in the State at the date of the gift.

(4) Where a person makes a disposition under which a relative of the person becomes beneficially entitled in possession to any benefit, the creation or disposition in favour of the person of an annuity or other interest limited to cease on the death, or at a time ascertainable only by reference to the death, of the person, shall not be treated for the purposes of this section as consideration for the grant of such benefit or of any part thereof.

(5) For the purposes of this Act, "appropriate part", in relation to property referred to in subsection (2), means that part of the entire property in which the benefit subsists, or on which the benefit is charged or secured, or on which the donee is entitled to have it so charged or secured, which bears the same proportion to the entire property as the gross annual value of the benefit bears to the gross annual value of the entire property, and the gift shall be deemed to consist of the appropriate part of each and every item of property comprised in the entire property.

(6) (a) Where, before the 28th day of February, 1974, a contract or agreement was entered into, under or as a consequence of which a person acquired the right, otherwise than for full consideration in money or money's worth, to have a benefit transferred to him, or to another in his right or on his behalf, and an act or acts is or are done, on or after that date, in pursuance of, or in performance or satisfaction, whether in whole or in part, of such contract or agreement, then the gift or inheritance, as the case may be, taken by or in right or on behalf of that person, shall be deemed to have been taken, not when the right was acquired as aforesaid, but either –

    (i) when the benefit was transferred to him or to another in his right or on his behalf; or

    (ii) when he or another in his right or on his behalf became beneficially entitled in possession to the benefit.

whichever is the later.

(b) In this subsection, a reference to a contract or agreement does not include a reference to a contract or agreement –

    (i) which is a complete grant, transfer, assignment or conveyance, or

    (ii) which was enforceable by action prior to the 28th day of February, 1974.

Section 6

Taxable gift.

6.   (1)   In this Act, "taxable gift" means —

    (a)   in the case of a gift, other than a gift taken under a discretionary trust, where —

        (i)   the disponer is domiciled in the State at the date of the disposition under which the donee takes the gift; or

        (ii)   the proper law of the disposition under which the donee takes the gift is, at the date of the disposition, the law of the State,

    the whole of the gift;

    (b)   in the case of a gift taken under a discretionary trust where —

        (i)   the disponer is domiciled in the State at the date of the gift or was (in the case of a gift taken after his death) so domiciled at the time of his death; or

        (ii)   the proper law of the discretionary trust at the date of the gift is the law of the State,

    the whole of the gift; and

    (c)   in any other case, so much of the property of which the gift consists as is situate in the State at the date of the gift.

(2)   For the purposes of subsection (1) (c), a right to the proceeds of sale of property shall be deemed to be situate in the State to the extent that such property is unsold and situate in the State.

(3)   Notwithstanding anything contained in subsection (1), no part of the property of which a gift consists shall be a taxable gift where —

    (a)   the gift is taken prior to the 1st day of April, 1975; and

    (b)   the disponer in relation to the gift dies prior to that date.

Section 7

Liability to gift tax in respect of gift taken by joint tenants.

7.   The liability to gift tax in respect of a gift taken by persons as joint tenants shall be the same in all respects as if they took the gift as tenants in common in equal shares.

Section 8

Disponer in certain connected dispositions.

8.   (1)   Where a donee takes a gift under a disposition made by a disponer (in this section referred to as the original disponer) and, within the period commencing three years before and ending three years after the date of that gift, the donee makes a disposition under which a second donee takes a gift and whether or not the second donee makes a disposition within the same period under which a third donee takes a gift, and so on, each donee shall be deemed to take a gift

from the original disponer (and not from the immediate disponer under whose disposition the gift was taken); and a gift so deemed to be taken shall be deemed to be an inheritance (and not a gift) taken by the donee, as successor, from the original disponer if—

(a) the original disponer dies within two years after the date of the disposition made by him , and

(b) the date of the disposition was on or after the 1st day of April, 1975.

(2) This section shall not apply in the case of any disposition (in this subsection referred to as the first-mentioned disposition) in so far as no other disposition, which was connected in the manner described in subsection (1) with such first-mentioned disposition, was made with a view to enabling or facilitating the making of the first mentioned- disposition or the recoupment in any manner of the cost thereof.

Section 9

Aggregable gifts.

9. Any gift taken by a donee on or after the 28th day of February, 1969, and before the 28th day of February, 1974, so far as it is a taxable gift, shall, for the purpose of computing tax—

(a) on any taxable gift taken by that donee from the same disponer on or after the 28th day of February, 1974; and

(b) on any taxable inheritance taken by that donee, as successor, from the same disponer on or after the 1st day of April, 1975,

be aggregated with the latter taxable gift or taxable inheritance in accordance with the provisions of the Second Schedule.

PART III
Inheritance Tax

Section 10

Charge of inheritance tax.

10. A capital acquisitions tax, to be called inheritance tax and to be computed as hereinafter provided, shall, subject to this Act and the regulations thereunder, be charged, levied and paid upon the taxable value of every taxable inheritance taken by a successor, where the date of the inheritance is on or after the 1st day of April, 1975.

Section 11

Inheritance deemed to be taken.

11. (1) For the purposes of this Act, where, under or in consequence of any disposition, a person becomes beneficially entitled in possession

on a death to any benefit (whether or not the person becoming so entitled already has any interest in the property in which he takes such benefit), otherwise than for full consideration in money or moneys worth paid by him, he shall be deemed to take an inheritance.

(2) The provisions of subsections (2), (4) and (5) of section 5 shall apply, with any necessary modifications, in relation to an inheritance as they apply in relation to a gift.

(3) For the purposes of section 12 (1) (b) the sum referred to in section 5 (2) (b) shall be deemed not to be situate in the State at the date of the inheritance.

Section 12

Taxable inheritance.

12. (1) In this Act, "taxable inheritance" means—

    (a) in the case where—

        (i) the disponer is domiciled in the State at the date of the disposition under which the successor takes the inheritance; or

        (ii) the proper law of the disposition under which the successor takes the inheritance is, at the date of the disposition, the law of the State,

    the whole of the inheritance; and

    (b) in any case, other than the case referred to in paragraph (a), where, at the date of the inheritance—

        (i) the whole of the property—

            (I) which was to be appropriated to the inheritance; or

            (II) out of which property was to be appropriated to the inheritance,

    was situate in the State, the whole of the inheritance;

        (ii) a part or proportion of the property—

            (I) which was to be appropriated to the inheritance; or

            (II) out of which property was to be appropriated to the inheritance,

    was situate in the State, that part or proportion of the inheritance.

(2) For the purposes of subsection (1) (b)—

    (a) "property which was to be appropriated to the inheritance" and "property out of which property was to be appropriated to the inheritance" shall not include any property which was not applicable to satisfy the inheritance; and

(b) a right to the proceeds of sale of property shall be deemed to be situate in the State to the extent that such property is unsold and situate in the State.

Section 13

Disclaimer.

13. (1) If—

    (a) (i) a benefit under a will or an intestacy; or

        (ii) an entitlement to an interest in settled property,

      is disclaimed;

    (b) a claim—

        (i) under a purported will in respect of which a grant of representation (within the meaning of the Succession Act, 1965) was not issued; or

        (ii) under an alleged intestacy where a will exists in respect of which such a grant was issued,

      is waived; or

    (c) a right under Part IX of the Succession Act, 1965, or any analogous right under the law of another territory, is renounced, disclaimed, elected against or lapses,

any liability to tax in respect of such benefit, entitlement, claim or right shall cease as if such benefit, entitlement, claim or right, as the case may be, had not existed.

  (2) Notwithstanding anything contained in this Act—

    (a) a disclaimer of a benefit under a will or intestacy or of an entitlement to an interest in settled property;

    (b) the waiver of a claim—

        (i) under a purported will in respect of which a grant of representation (within the meaning of the Succession Act, 1965) was not issued; or

        (ii) under an alleged intestacy where a will exists in respect of which such a grant issued; or

    (c) (i) the renunciation or disclaimer of;

        (ii) the election against; or

        (iii) the lapse of,

      a right under Part IX of the Succession Act, 1965, or any analogous right under the law of another territory,

shall not be a disposition for the purposes of this Act.

  (3) Subsection (1) shall not have effect to the extent of the amount of any consideration in money or money's worth received for the

disclaimer, renunciation, election or lapse or for the waiver of a claim; and the receipt of such consideration shall be deemed to be a gift or an inheritance, as the case may be, in respect of which no consideration was paid by the donee or successor and which was derived from the disponer who provided the property in relation to which the benefit, entitlement, claim or right, referred to in subsection (1), arose.

Section 14

Surviving joint tenant deemed to take an inheritance, etc.

14. (1) On the death of one of several persons who are beneficially and absolutely entitled in possession as joint tenants, the surviving joint tenant or surviving joint tenants shall be deemed to take an inheritance of the share of the deceased joint tenant, as successor or successors from the deceased joint tenant as disponer.

(2) The liability to inheritance tax in respect of an inheritance taken by persons as joint tenants shall be the same in all respects as if they took the inheritance as tenants in common in equal shares.

PART IV
Value of Property for Tax

Section 15

Market value of property.

15. (1) Subject to the provisions of this Act, the market value of any property for the purposes of this Act shall be estimated to be the price which, in the opinion of the Commissioners, such property would fetch if sold in the open market on the date on which the property is to be valued in such manner and subject to such conditions as might reasonably be calculated to obtain for the vendor the best price for the property.

(2) In estimating the market value of any property, the Commissioners shall not make any reduction in the estimate on account of the estimate being made on the assumption that the whole property is to be placed on the market at one and the same time.

(3) The market value of any property shall be ascertained by the Commissioners in such manner and by such means as they think fit, and they may authorise a person to inspect any property and report to them the value thereof for the purposes of this Act, and the person having the custody or possession of that property shall permit the person so authorised to inspect it at such reasonable times as the Commissioners consider necessary.

(4) Where the Commissioners require a valuation to be made by a person named by them, the costs of such valuation shall be defrayed by the Commissioners.

(5) Subject to the provisions of this Act, in estimating the price which unquoted shares or securities might be expected to fetch if sold in the open market, it shall be assumed that in that market there is available to any prospective purchaser of the shares or securities all the information which a prudent prospective purchaser might reasonably require if he were proposing to purchase them from a willing vendor by private treaty and at arm's length.

(6) In subsection (5), "unquoted shares or securities" means shares or securities which are not dealt in on a stock exchange.

Section 16

Market value of certain shares in private trading companies.

16. (1) The market value of each share in a private trading company which (after the taking of the gift or of the inheritance) is, on the date of the gift or on the date of the inheritance, a company controlled by the donee or the successor, shall be ascertained by the Commissioners, for the purposes of tax, as if it formed part of a group of shares sufficient in number to give the owner of the group control of the company.

(2) In this section —

"nominee" includes a person who may be required to exercise his voting power on the directions of, or who holds shares directly or indirectly on behalf of, another person;

"private company" means a body corporate (wherever incorporated) —

(a) in which the number of shareholders (excluding employees who are not directors of the company and any shareholder who is such as nominee of a beneficial owner of shares) is not more than fifty;

(b) which has not issued any of its shares as a result of a public invitation to subscribe for shares; and

(c) which is under the control of not more than five persons;

"private trading company" means a private company which is not a private non-trading company within the meaning of section 17.

(3) In this section, a reference to a company controlled by the donee or successor is a reference to a company that is under the control of any one or more of the following, that is to say, the donee or successor, the relatives of the donee or successor, nominees of the donee or successor, nominees of relatives of the donee or successor, and the trustees of a settlement whose objects include the donee or successor or relatives of the donee or successor; and for the purposes of this section, a company which is so controlled by the donee or successor shall be regarded as being itself a relative of the donee or successor.

(4) For the purposes of this section —

(a) a company shall be deemed to be under the control of not more than five persons if any five or fewer persons together exercise, or are able to exercise or are entitled to acquire control, whether direct or indirect, of the company; and for this purpose —

(i) persons who are relatives of any other person together with that other person;

(ii) persons who are nominees of any other person together with that other person;

(iii) persons in partnership, and

(iv) persons interested in any shares or obligations of the company which are subject to any trust or are part of the estate of a deceased person,

shall respectively be treated as a single person; and

(b) a person shall be deemed to have control of a company at any time if —

(i) he then had control of the powers of voting on all questions, or on any particular question, affecting the company as a whole, which, if exercised, would have yielded a majority of the votes capable of being exercised thereon, or could then have obtained such control by an exercise at that time of a power exercisable by him or at his direction or with his consent;

(ii) he then had the capacity, or could then by an exercise of a power exercisable by him or at his direction or with his consent obtain the capacity, to exercise or to control the exercise of any of the following powers, that is to say —

(I) the powers of a board of directors of the company;

(II) powers of a governing director of the company;

(III) power to nominate a majority of the directors of the company or a governing director thereof;

(IV) the power to veto the appointment of a director of the company,

or

(V) powers of a like nature;

(iii) he then had a right to receive, or the receipt of, more than one-half of the total amount of the dividends of the company, whether declared or not, and for the purposes of this subparagraph, "dividend" shall be deemed to include interest on any debentures of the company; or

(iv) he then had an interest in the shares of the company of an aggregate nominal value representing one-half or more of the aggregate nominal value of the shares of the company.

Section 17

Market value of certain shares in private non-trading companies.

17. (1) The market value of each share in a private non-trading company which (after the taking of the gift or of the inheritance) is, on the date of the gift or on the date of the inheritance, a company controlled by the donee or the successor, shall for the purposes of this Act, be such sum as would have been payable in respect of the share to the owner thereof if the company had been voluntarily wound up and all the assets realised on the date at which the share is to be valued.

(2) In this section —

"investment income", in relation to a private company, means income which, if the company were an individual, would not be earned income within the meaning of section 2 of the Income Tax Act, 1967;

"private company" and "company controlled by the donee or the successor" have the meanings assigned to them by section 16;

"private non-trading company" means a private company —

(a) whose income (if any) in the twelve months preceding the date at which a share therein is to be valued consisted wholly or mainly of investment income, and

(b) whose property, on the date referred to in paragraph (a), consisted wholly or mainly of property from which investment income is derived.

(3) Where the assets of such a private non-trading company as is referred to in subsection (1) include a share in another such private non-trading company (hereinafter referred to as the latter company), the market value of such share shall be ascertained on the basis that the latter company is voluntarily wound up and its assets realised on the date on which the share is to be valued.

(4) In determining the market value of the share referred to in subsection (1) or (3), no allowance shall be made for the costs of winding up any company or of realising its assets.

(5) In ascertaining, for the purposes of subsection (1) or (3) the amount which the assets of a company would realise, the assets shall be deemed to realise the amount of their market value as at the date at which the share referred to in subsection (1) or (3) is to be valued.

Section 18

Taxable value of a taxable gift or taxable inheritance.

18. (1) In this section, "incumbrance-free value", in relation to a taxable gift or a taxable inheritance, means the market value at the valuation date of the property of which the taxable gift or taxable inheritance consists at that date, after deducting any liabilities, costs and expenses that are properly payable out of the taxable gift or taxable inheritance.

(2) Subject to the provisions of this section (but save as provided in section 19), the taxable value of a taxable gift or a taxable inheritance (where the interest taken by the donee or successor is not a limited interest) shall be ascertained by deducting from the incumbrance-free value thereof the market value of any bona fide consideration in money or money's worth, paid by the donee or successor for the gift or inheritance, including—

  (a) any liability of the disponer which the donee or successor undertakes to discharge as his own personal liability; and

  (b) any other liability to which the gift or inheritance is subject under the terms of the disposition under which it is taken,

  and the amount so ascertained shall be the taxable value:

  Provided that no deduction shall be made under this subsection in respect of any liability which falls to be deducted in ascertaining the incumbrance-free value.

(3) Where a liability (other than a liability within the meaning of subsection (9)) for which a deduction may be made under the provisions of subsection (1) or (2) falls to be discharged after the time at which it falls to be taken into account as a deduction under either of those subsections, it shall be valued for the purpose of making such a deduction at its current market value at the time at which it falls to be so taken into account.

(4) The taxable value of a taxable gift or a taxable inheritance, where the interest taken by the donee or the successor is a limited interest, shall be ascertained as follows—

  (a) the value of the limited interest in a capital sum equal to the incumbrance-free value shall be ascertained in accordance with the Rules contained in the First Schedule; and

  (b) from the value ascertained in accordance with paragraph (a) a deduction shall be made in respect of the market value of any bona fide consideration in money or money's worth paid by the donee or the successor for the gift or the inheritance and the amount remaining after such deduction shall be the taxable value:

  Provided that no deduction shall be made under this paragraph in respect of any liability which falls to be deducted in ascertaining the incumbrance-free value.

(5) A deduction shall not be made under the provisions of this section —

(a) in respect of any liability the payment of which is contingent on the happening of some future event:

Provided that if the event on the happening of which the liability is contingent happens and the liability is paid, then, on a claim for relief being made to the Commissioners and subject to the other provisions of this section, a deduction shall be made in respect of the liability and such adjustment of tax as is appropriate shall be made; and such adjustment shall be made on the basis that the donee or successor had taken an interest in possession in the amount which falls to be deducted for the liability, for a period certain which was equal to the actual duration of the postponement of the payment of the liability;

(b) in respect of any liability, costs or expenses in so far as the donee or successor has a right of reimbursement from any source, unless such reimbursement cannot be obtained;

(c) in respect of any liability created by the donee or successor or any person claiming in right of the donee or successor or on his behalf;

(d) in respect of tax, interest or penalties chargeable under this Act in respect of the gift or inheritance, or of the costs, expenses or interest incurred in raising or paying the same;

(e) in respect of any liability in so far as such liability is an incumbrance on, or was created or incurred in acquiring, any property which is comprised in any gift or inheritance and which is exempt from tax under any provision of this Act or otherwise;

(f) in the case of any gift or inheritance referred to in section 6 (1) (c) or section 12 (1) (b) in respect of —

(i) any liability, costs or expenses due to a person resident outside the State (save in so far as such liability is required by contract to be paid in the State or is charged on the property which is situate in the State and which is comprised in the gift or inheritance); or

(ii) any liability, costs or expenses in so far as the same are charged on or secured by property which is comprised in the gift or inheritance and which is not situate in the State,

save to the extent that all the property situate outside the State and comprised in the gift or inheritance is insufficient for the payment of the liability, costs or expenses;

(g) for any tax in respect of which a credit is allowed under the provisions of section 66 or 67.

(6) In the case of a gift or inheritance referred to in subsection (5) (f), any deduction to be made under subsection (2) or (4) (b) shall be restricted to the proportion of the consideration which bears the same proportion to the whole of the consideration as the taxable gift or taxable inheritance bears to the whole of the gift or the whole of the inheritance.

(7) A deduction shall not be made under the provisions of this section —

    (a) more than once for the same liability, costs, expenses or consideration, in respect of all gifts and inheritances taken by the donee or successor from the disponer; or

    (b) for any liability, costs, expenses or consideration, a proportion of which falls to be allowed under the provisions of section 19 (2) (ii) or (iii) in respect of a gift or inheritance taken by the donee or successor from the disponer.

(8) Where a taxable gift or a taxable inheritance is subject to a liability within the meaning of subsection (9), the deduction to be made in respect thereof under this section shall be an amount equal to the market value of the whole or the appropriate part, as the case may be, of the property, within the meaning of section 5 (5).

(9) For the purpose of subsection (8), "liability", in relation to a taxable gift or a taxable inheritance, means a liability which deprives the donee or successor, whether permanently or temporarily, of the use, enjoyment or income in whole or in part of the property, or of any part of the property, of which the taxable gift or taxable inheritance consists.

(10) Where —

    (a) bona fide consideration in money or money's worth has been paid by a person for the granting to him, by a disposition, of an interest in expectancy in property; and

    (b) at the coming into possession of the interest in expectancy, that person takes a gift or an inheritance of that property under that disposition,

the deduction to be made under subsection (2) or (4) (b) for consideration paid by that person shall be a sum equal to the same proportion of the taxable value of the taxable gift or taxable inheritance (as if no deduction had been made for such consideration) as the amount of the consideration so paid bore to the market value of the interest in expectancy at the date of the payment of the consideration.

(11) Any deduction, under the provisions of this section, in respect of a liability which is an incumbrance on any property shall so far as possible be made against that property.

Section 19

Value of agricultural property.

19. (1) In this section —

"agricultural property" means agricultural land, pasture and woodland situate in the State and crops, trees and underwood growing on such land and also includes such farm buildings, farm houses and mansion houses (together with the lands occupied therewith) as are of a character appropriate to the property,

"agricultural value" means the market value of agricultural property reduced by 50 per cent. of that value, or by a sum of £100,000, whichever is the lesser;

"farmer" in relation to a donee or successor, means an individual who is domiciled and ordinarily resident in the State and in respect of whom not less than 75 per cent. of the market value of the property to which he is beneficially entitled in possession is represented by the market value of property in the State which consists of agricultural property, livestock, bloodstock and farm machinery, and, for the purposes of this definition, no deduction shall be made from the market value of property for any debts or incumbrances.

(2) Save as provided in subsection (7), in so far as any gift or inheritance consists of agricultural property —

(a) at the date of the gift or at the date of the inheritance; and

(b) at the valuation date,

and is taken by a donee or successor who is, on the valuation date and after taking the gift or inheritance, a farmer, the provisions of section 18 (other than subsection 7 (b) thereof) shall apply in relation to agricultural property as they apply in relation to other property subject to the following modifications —

(i) in subsection (1) of that section, the reference to market value shall be construed as a reference to agricultural value;

(ii) where a deduction is to be made for any liability, costs or expenses, in accordance with subsection (1) of that section, only a proportion of such liability, costs or expenses shall be deducted and that proportion shall be the proportion that the agricultural value of the agricultural property bears to the market value of that property; and

(iii) where a deduction is to be made for any consideration under subsection (2) or (4) (b) of that section, only a proportion of such consideration shall be deducted and that proportion shall be the proportion that the agricultural value of the agricultural property bears to the market value of that property.

(3) Where a taxable gift or a taxable inheritance is taken by a donee or successor subject to the condition that the whole or part thereof will be invested in agricultural property and such condition is complied with within two years after the date of the gift or the date of the inheritance, then the gift or inheritance shall be deemed, for the purposes of this section, to have consisted –

(a) at the date of the gift or at the date of the inheritance; and

(b) at the valuation date,

of agricultural property to the extent to which the gift or inheritance is subject to such condition and has been so invested.

(4) In relation to the deduction, in respect of agricultural property, of 50 per cent. of its market value, or £100,000, whichever is the lesser, the total amount deductible in ascertaining the agricultural value shall not exceed £100,000, in respect of the aggregate of –

(a) all taxable gifts taken on or after the 28th day of February, 1969; and

(b) all taxable inheritances taken on or after the 1st day of April, 1975,

which consist in whole or in part of agricultural property, taken by the same person, as donee or successor, from the same disponer.

(5) (a) The agricultural value shall cease to be applicable to real property which is agricultural property if and to the extent that the property –

(i) is sold or compulsorily acquired within the period of six years after the date of the gift or the date of the inheritance; and

(ii) is not replaced, within a year of the sale or compulsory acquisition, by other agricultural property,

and tax shall be chargeable in respect of the gift or inheritance as if the property were not agricultural property :

Provided that this paragraph shall not have effect where the donee or successor dies before the property is sold or compulsorily acquired.

(b) If an arrangement is made, in the administration of property subject to a disposition, for the appropriation of property in or towards the satisfaction of a benefit under the disposition, such arrangement shall be deemed not to be a sale or a compulsory acquisition for the purposes of paragraph (a).

(6) For the purposes of subsection (2), if, in the administration of property subject to a disposition, property is appropriated in or towards the satisfaction of a benefit in respect of which a person is deemed to take a gift or an inheritance under the disposition, the property so appropriated, if it was subject to the disposition at the

date of the gift or at the date of the inheritance, shall be deemed to have been comprised in that gift or inheritance at the date of the gift or at the date of the inheritance.

(7) The provisions of subsection (2) shall have effect in relation to agricultural property which consists of trees or underwood as if the words "and is taken by a donee or successor who is, on the valuation date and after taking the gift or inheritance, a farmer," were omitted therefrom.

(8) In this section, other than in subsection (4), any reference to a donee or successor shall include a reference to the transferee referred to in section 23 (1).

Section 20

Contingencies affecting gifts or inheritances.

20. Where, under a disposition, a person becomes beneficially entitled in possession to any benefit and, under the terms of the disposition, the entitlement, or any part thereof, may cease upon the happening of a contingency (other than the revocation of the entitlement upon the exercise by the disponer of such a power as is referred to in section 30), the taxable value of any taxable gift or taxable inheritance taken by that person on becoming so entitled to that benefit shall be ascertained as if no part of the entitlement were so to cease; but, in the event and to the extent that the entitlement so ceases, the tax payable by that person shall, to that extent be adjusted (if, by so doing, a lesser amount of tax would be payable by him) on the basis that he had taken an interest in possession for a period certain which was equal to the actual duration of his beneficial entitlement in possession:

Provided that nothing in this section shall prejudice any charge for tax on the taking by such person of a substituted gift or inheritance on the happening of such a contingency.

Section 21

Valuation date for tax purposes.

21. (1) Subject to the provisions of subsection (7), the valuation date of a taxable gift shall be the date of the gift.

(2) The valuation date of a taxable inheritance shall be the date of death of the deceased person on whose death the inheritance is taken if the successor or any person in right of the successor or on his behalf takes the inheritance—

(a) as a donatio mortis causa, or

(b) by reason of the failure to exercise a power of revocation.

(3) If a gift becomes an inheritance by reason of its being taken under a disposition where the date of the disposition is within two years

prior to the death of the disponer, the valuation date thereof shall be determined as if it were a gift.

(4) The valuation date of a taxable inheritance, other than a taxable inheritance referred to in subsection (2) or (3), shall be the earliest date of the following –

    (a) the earliest date on which a personal representative or trustee or the successor or any other person is entitled to retain the subject matter of the inheritance for the benefit of the successor or of any person in right of the successor or on his behalf;

    (b) the date on which the subject matter of the inheritance is so retained; or

    (c) the date of delivery, payment or other satisfaction or discharge of the subject matter of the inheritance to the successor or for his benefit or to or for the benefit of any person in right of the successor or on his behalf.

(5) If any part of a taxable inheritance referred to in subsection (4) may be retained, or is retained, delivered, paid or otherwise satisfied, whether by way of part payment, advancement, payment on account or in any manner whatsoever, before any other part or parts of such inheritance, the appropriate valuation date for each part of the inheritance shall be determined in accordance with that subsection as if each such part respectively were a separate inheritance.

(6) The Commissioners may give to an accountable person a notice in writing of the date determined by them to be the valuation date in respect of the whole or any part of an inheritance, and, subject to any decision on appeal pursuant to subsection (9), the date so determined shall be deemed to be the valuation date.

(7) If a taxable inheritance referred to in subsection (4) or (5) is disposed of, ceases or comes to an end before the valuation date referred to in those subsections in such circumstances as to give rise to a taxable gift, the valuation date in respect of such taxable gift shall be the same date as the valuation date of the taxable inheritance.

(8) Notwithstanding anything contained in this section, the Commissioners may, in case of doubt, with the agreement in writing of the accountable person or his agent, determine the valuation date of the whole or any part of any taxable inheritance and the valuation date so determined shall be substituted for the valuation date which would otherwise be applicable by virtue of this section.

(9) An appeal shall lie against any determination made by the Commissioners under subsection (6) and the provisions of section 52 shall apply, with any necessary modifications, in relation to an appeal under this subsection as they apply in relation to an appeal against an assessment of tax.

PART V

Provisions relating to Gifts and Inheritances

Section 22

Discretionary trusts.

22. Where a person becomes beneficially entitled in possession to any benefit –

    (a) under a discretionary trust, other than a discretionary trust referred to in paragraph (b), otherwise than for full consideration in money or money's worth paid by him, he shall be deemed to have taken a gift;

    (b) under a discretionary trust created –

        (i) by will at any time;

        (ii) by a disposition, where the date of the disposition is on or after the 1st day of April, 1975, and within two years prior to the death of the disponer; or

        (iii) by a disposition inter vivos and limited to come into operation on a death occurring before or after the passing of this Act,

    otherwise than for full consideration in money or money's worth paid by him, he shall be deemed to have taken an inheritance.

Section 23

Dealings with future interests.

23. (1) Where a benefit, to which a person (in this section referred to as the remainderman) is entitled under a disposition, devolves, or is disposed of, either in whole or in part, before it has become an interest in possession so that, at the time when the benefit comes into possession, it is taken, either in whole or in part, by a person (in this section referred to as the transferee) other than the remainderman to whom it was limited by the disposition, then tax shall be payable, in respect of a gift or inheritance, as the case may be, of the remainderman in all respects as if, at that time, the remainderman had become beneficially entitled in possession to the full extent of the benefit limited to him under the disposition, and the transferee shall be the person primarily accountable for the payment of tax to the extent that the benefit is taken by him.

    (2) The provisions of subsection (1) shall not prejudice any charge for tax in respect of any gift or inheritance affecting the same property or any part of it under any other disposition.

    (3) In subsection (1), " benefit " includes the benefit of the cesser of a liability referred to in section 28.

Section 24

Release of limited interests, etc.

24. (1) Where an interest in property, which is limited by the disposition creating it to cease on an event, has come to an end (whether by another disposition, the taking of successive interests into one ownership, or by any means whatever other than the happening of another event on which the interest was limited by the first-mentioned disposition to cease) before the happening of such event, tax shall be payable under the first-mentioned disposition in all respects as if the event on which the interest was limited to cease under that disposition had happened immediately before the coming to an end of the interest.

(2) The provisions of subsection (1) shall not prejudice any charge for tax in respect of any gift or inheritance affecting the same property or any part of it under any disposition other than that first mentioned in subsection (1).

(3) Notwithstanding anything contained in subsection (2), if —

(a) an interest in property which was limited to cease on an event was limited to the disponer by the disposition creating that interest; and

(b) on the coming to an end of that interest, the provisions of subsection (1) have effect in relation to a gift or inheritance which was taken by a donee or successor under that disposition and which consists of the property in which that interest subsisted, then —

a further gift or inheritance taken by the same donee or successor under another disposition made by the same disponer (being the disposition by which that interest has come to an end) shall not be a taxable gift or a taxable inheritance in so far as it consists of the whole or any part of the same property.

(4) In this section, "event" includes —

(a) a death, and

(b) the expiration of a specified period.

Section 25

Settlement of an interest not in possession.

25. (1) Where any donee or successor takes a gift or an inheritance under a disposition made by himself then, if at the date of such disposition he was entitled to the property comprised in the disposition, either expectantly on the happening of an event, or subject to a liability within the meaning of section 18 (9), and such event happens or such liability ceases during the continuance of the disposition, tax shall be charged on the taxable value of the taxable gift or taxable inheritance which he would have taken on the happening of such event, or on the cesser of such liability, if no such disposition had been made.

(2) The provisions of subsection (1) shall not prejudice any charge for tax in respect of any gift or inheritance affecting the same property or any part of it under the said disposition.

(3) In this section, "event" has the same meaning as it has in section 24.

Section 26

Enlargement of interests.

26. (1) Where a person, having a limited interest in possession in property (in this section referred to as the first-mentioned interest), takes a further interest (in this section referred to as the second-mentioned interest) in the same property, as a taxable gift or a taxable inheritance, in consequence of which he becomes the absolute owner of the property, the taxable value of the taxable gift or taxable inheritance of the second-mentioned interest at the valuation date shall be reduced by the value at that date of the first-mentioned interest, taking such value to be the value, ascertained in accordance with the Rules contained in the First Schedule, of a limited interest which—

    (a) is a limited interest in a capital sum equal to the value of the property;

    (b) commences on that date; and

    (c) is to continue for the unexpired balance of the term of the first-mentioned interest.

(2) For the purposes of subsection (1) (a), "value" means such amount as would be the incumbrance-free value, within the meaning of section 18 (1), if the limited interest were taken, at the date referred to in subsection (1), as a taxable gift or taxable inheritance.

(3) The provisions of this section shall not have effect where the second-mentioned interest is taken under the disposition under which the first-mentioned interest was created.

Section 27

Dispositions involving powers of appointment.

27. (1) Where, by virtue of or in consequence of the exercise of, or the failure to exercise, or the release of, a general power of appointment by any person having such a power, a person becomes beneficially entitled in possession to any benefit, then, for the purposes of this Act, the disposition shall be the exercise of, or the failure to exercise, or the release of, the power and not the disposition under which the power was created, and the person exercising, or failing to exercise, or releasing, the power shall be the disponer.

(2) Where, by virtue of or in consequence of the exercise of, or the failure to exercise, or the release of, a special power of appointment by any person having such a power, a person becomes beneficially entitled in possession to any benefit, then, for the purposes of this Act, the disposition shall be the disposition under which the power was created and the person who created the power shall be the disponer.

Section 28

Cesser of liabilities.

28. (1) The benefit of the cesser of —

   (a) a liability within the meaning of section 18 (9); or

   (b) any liability similar to that referred to in paragraph (a) to which the taking of a benefit which was a gift or inheritance was subject,

   shall be deemed to be a gift or an inheritance, as the case may be, which shall be deemed —

   (i)   to the extent that the liability is charged on or secured by any property at the time of its cesser, to consist of the whole or the appropriate part, as the case may be, of that property; and

   (ii) to the extent that the liability is not charged on or secured by any property at the time of its cesser, to consist of such sum as would, under the provisions of section 5 (2) (b), be the sum the annual income of which would be equal to the annual value of the liability.

(2) In this section, "appropriate part" has the meaning assigned to it by section 5 (5).

(3) For the purposes of sections 6 (1) (c) and 12 (1) (b), the sum referred to in subparagraph (ii) of subsection (1) shall be deemed not to be situate in the State at the date of the gift or at the date of the inheritance.

Section 29

Disposition enlarging value of property.

29. (1) In this section, "property" does not include any property to which a donee or successor became beneficially entitled in possession prior to the 28th day of February, 1969.

(2) Where the taking by any person of a beneficial interest in any property (hereinafter in this section referred to as additional property) under any disposition made by a disponer has the effect of increasing the value of any other property (hereinafter in this section referred to as original property) to which that person is beneficially entitled in

possession, and which had been derived from the same disponer, the following provisions shall have effect—

(a) the increase in value so effected shall be deemed to be a gift or an inheritance, as the case may be, arising under that disposition and taken by that person, as donee or successor, from that disponer, at the time he took the beneficial interest in the additional property;

(b) the original property shall be treated as having been increased in value if the market value of that property at the time referred to in paragraph (a) would be greater if it was sold as part of an aggregate of the original property and the additional property rather than as a single item of property, and the increase in value for the purposes of this section shall be the amount by which the market value of the original property if sold at that time as part of such aggregate would be greater than the amount of the market value of that property if sold at that time as a single item of property;

(c) the additional property shall for the purpose of determining its market value be deemed to be part of an aggregate of the original property and the additional property; and

(d) the market value of any property which is to be valued as part of an aggregate of property shall be ascertained as being so much of the market value of such aggregate as may reasonably be ascribed to that part.

(3) For the purpose of this section, the donee or successor shall be deemed to be beneficially entitled in possession to any property notwithstanding that within five years prior to such a disposition as is referred to in subsection (2) he has divested himself of such property, or any part thereof, otherwise than for full consideration in money or money's worth or has disposed of it to a company of which he is, at any time within that period of five years, deemed to have control within the meaning of section 16 (4) (b).

(4) In subsection (3), "company" means a private company within the meaning of section 16 (2).

Section 30

Gift subject to power of revocation.

30. Where, under any disposition, a person becomes beneficially entitled in possession to any benefit and, under the terms of the disposition, the disponer has reserved to himself the power to revoke the benefit, such person shall, for the purposes of this Act, be deemed not to be beneficially entitled in possession to the benefit unless and until the power of revocation is released by the disponer, or otherwise ceases to be exercisable.

Section 31

Free use of property, free loans, etc.

31. (1) A person shall be deemed to take a gift in each relevant period during the whole or part of which he is allowed to have the use, occupation or enjoyment of any property (to which property he is not beneficially entitled in possession) otherwise than for full consideration in money or money's worth.

(2) In subsections (1) and (4), "relevant period", in relation to any use, occupation or enjoyment of property, means the period from the 28th day of February, 1974, to the 31st day of December, 1974, and thereafter the period of twelve months ending on the 31st day of December in each year.

(3) A gift referred to in subsection (1) shall be deemed to consist of a sum equal to the difference between the amount of any consideration in money or money's worth, given by the person referred to in subsection (1) for such use, occupation or enjoyment, and the best price obtainable in the open market for such use, occupation or enjoyment.

(4) A gift referred to in subsection (1) shall be treated as being taken at the end of the relevant period or, if earlier, immediately prior to the time when the use, occupation or enjoyment referred to in subsection (1) comes to an end.

(5) In any case where the use, occupation or enjoyment of property is allowed to a person, not being beneficially entitled in possession to that property, under a disposition—

(a) made by will;

(b) where the date of the disposition is on or after the 1st day of April, 1975 and within two years prior to the death of the disponer; or

(c) which is a disposition inter vivos and the use, occupation or enjoyment is had by that person after the cesser of another person's life interest,

subsections (1), (3) and (4) shall have effect in relation to that property as if a reference to an inheritance were substituted for the reference to a gift wherever it occurs in those subsections, and for the purpose of this subsection "relevant period" in subsections (1) and (4), in relation to the use, occupation or enjoyment of property, means the period of nine months ending on the 31st day of December, 1975, and thereafter the period of twelve months ending on the 31st day of December in any year.

(6) For the purposes of sections 6 (1) (c) and 12 (1) (b), the sum referred to in subsection (3) shall be deemed not to be situate in the State at the date of the gift or at the date of the inheritance.

Section 32

When interest in assurance policy becomes interest in possession.

32. (1) For the purposes of this Act, an interest in a policy of assurance upon human life shall be deemed to become an interest in possession when and only when, either —

    (a) the policy matures; or

    (b) prior to the maturing of the policy, the policy is surrendered to the insurer for a consideration in money or money's worth:

Provided that if, during the currency of the policy the insurer makes a payment of money or money's worth, in full or partial discharge of the policy, the interest shall be deemed to have come into possession to the extent of such payment.

    (2) This section shall have effect in relation to a contract for a deferred annuity, and for the purposes of this section such a contract shall be deemed to mature on the date when the first instalment of the annuity falls due.

Section 33

Provisions to apply where section 98 of Succession Act, 1965, has effect.

33. (1) If, on the death of a testator and by virtue of the provisions of section 98 of the Succession Act, 1965, or otherwise, a disposition takes effect as if a person, who had predeceased the testator, had survived the testator, the benefit taken by the estate of that person shall not be deemed to be an inheritance.

    (2) Where a person survives a testator, and —

    (a) such person becomes beneficially entitled, under a disposition made by a person who predeceased the testator, to any benefit in relation to any property devised or bequeathed by the testator; and

    (b) section 33 of the Wills Act, 1837, or section 98 of the Succession Act, 1965, or any analogous provision of the law of another territory has effect in relation to the devise or bequest,

such person shall be deemed for the purposes of inheritance tax to derive the benefit from the testator, as disponer.

Section 34

Disposition by or to a company.

34. (1) For the purposes of this Act —

    (a) consideration paid by, or a disposition made by, a company shall be deemed to be consideration, or a disposition, as the case may be, paid or made; and

(b) consideration, or a gift, or an inheritance taken by a company shall be deemed to be consideration, or a gift or an inheritance, as the case may be, taken,

by the beneficial owners of the shares in the company and the beneficial owners of the entitlements under any liability incurred by the company (otherwise than for the purposes of the business of the company, wholly and exclusively) in the same proportions as the amounts which would be payable to them if the company were wound up voluntarily and its assets were realised on the date of the payment, disposition, gift or inheritance, as the case may be, would bear to each other (the amount of any realisation being ascertained for this purpose in accordance with section 17 as if the date of the payment, disposition, gift or inheritance were the date of such realisation).

(2) In this section, "company" means a private company within the meaning of section 16 (2).

(3) For the purposes of subsection (1) all acts, omissions and receipts of the company shall be deemed to be those of the beneficial owners of the shares and entitlements, referred to in subsection (1), in the company, in the proportions mentioned in that subsection.

(4) Where the beneficial owner of any shares in a company or of any entitlement of the kind referred to in subsection (1), is itself a company, the beneficial owners of the shares and entitlements, referred to in subsection (1), in the latter company, shall be deemed to be the beneficial owners of the latter company's shares and entitlements in the former company, in the proportions in which they are the beneficial owners of the shares and entitlements in the latter company.

(5) So far as the shares and entitlements referred to in subsection (1) are held in trust and have no ascertainable beneficial owners, consideration paid, or a disposition made, by the company shall be deemed to be paid or made by the disponer who made the disposition under which the shares and entitlements are so held in trust.

PART VI
Returns and Assessments

Section 35

Accountable persons.

35. (1) The person primarily accountable for the payment of tax shall be—

(a) save as provided in paragraph (b), the donee or successor, as the case may be; and

(6) Any person who is accountable for the payment of tax by virtue of subsection (2) or (9) of section 35 shall, if he is required by notice in writing by the Commissioners to do so, deliver a return to the Commissioners within such time, not being less than 30 days, as may be specified in the notice.

(7) Any accountable person shall, if he is so required by the Commissioners by notice in writing, deliver and verify to the Commissioners within such time, not being less than 30 days, as may be specified in the notice, a statement of such particulars together with such evidence as they require relating to any property, as may be relevant to the assessment of tax in respect of the gift.

(8) The Commissioners may by notice in writing require any accountable person to deliver to them within such time, not being less than 30 days, as may be specified in the notice, an additional return, if it appears to the Commissioners that a return made by that accountable person is defective in a material respect by reason of anything contained in or omitted from it.

(9) Where any accountable person who has delivered a return or an additional return is aware or becomes aware at any time that the return or additional return is defective in a material respect by reason of anything contained in or omitted from it, he shall, without application from the Commissioners and within three months of so becoming aware, deliver to them an additional return.

Section 37

Signing of returns, etc.

37. (1) A return or an additional return required to be delivered under this Act shall be signed by the accountable person who delivers the return or the additional return and shall include a declaration by the person signing it that the return or additional return is, to the best of his knowledge, information and belief, correct and complete.

(2) The Commissioners may require a return or an additional return to be made on oath.

(3) The Commissioners may, if they so think fit, accept a return or an additional return under this Act that has not been signed in accordance with this section and such return or additional return shall be deemed to be duly delivered to the Commissioners under this Act.

(4) A return, additional return, affidavit, additional affidavit, account or additional account, delivered under this Act, shall be made on a form provided by the Commissioners.

(5) Any oath or affidavit to be made for the purposes of this Act may be made —

(a) before the Commissioners;

(b)   before any officer or person authorised by the Commissioners in that behalf;

(c)   before any Commissioner for Oaths or any Peace Commissioner or Notary Public in the State; or

(d)   at any place outside the State, before any person duly authorised to administer oaths there.

Section 38

Affidavits and accounts.

38.   (1)   In this section, "Inland Revenue affidavit" has the meaning assigned to it by section 22 (1) (n) of the Finance Act, 1894.[1]

(2)   The Inland Revenue affidavit required for an application for probate or letters of administration shall extend to the verification of a statement of the following particulars –

(a)   details of all property in respect of which the grant of probate or administration is required and, in the case of a deceased person who died domiciled in the State, details of all property, wheresoever situate the beneficial ownership of which, on his death, is affected –

(i)   by his will;

(ii)   by the rules for distribution on intestacy; or

(iii)   by Part IX or section 56 of the Succession Act, 1965;

(b)   details of any property which was the subject matter of a disposition inter vivos made by the deceased person where the date of the disposition was within two years prior to his death or of a donatio mortis causa;

(c)   details of the inheritances arising under the will or intestacy of the deceased person or under Part IX or section 56 of the Succession Act, 1965, or under the analogous law of another territory, together with a copy of any such will;

(d)   particulars of the inheritances (including the property comprised therein) other than those referred to in paragraphs (b) and (c), arising on the death of the deceased person;

(e)   the name and address of each person who takes an inheritance on the death of the deceased person and his relationship to the disponer; and

(f)   such other particulars as the Commissioners may require for the purposes of this Act.

(3)   Where the interest of the deceased person was a limited interest and that person died on or after the 1st day of April, 1975, the trustee of the property in which the limited interest subsisted shall deliver an account which shall contain the following particulars –

(a) details of each inheritance arising on the death of the deceased person under the disposition under which the limited interest of the deceased person arose, including the name and address of each person taking such inheritance and his relationship to the disponer; and

(b) such other particulars as the Commissioners may require for the purposes of this Act.

(4) If at any time it shall appear that any material error or omission was made in an affidavit or account referred to in this section, the persons liable to deliver an affidavit or account shall be liable to deliver an additional affidavit or an additional account, correcting the error or omission.

Footnote

1   Reproduced on page 654.

Section 39

Assessment of tax.

39. (1) Assessments of tax under this Act shall be made by the Commissioners.

(2) If at any time it appears that for any reason an assessment was incorrect, the Commissioners may make a correcting assessment, which shall be substituted for the first-mentioned assessment.

(3) If at any time it appears that for any reason too little tax was assessed, the Commissioners may make an additional assessment.

(4) The Commissioners may serve notice in writing of the assessment of tax on any accountable person or, at the request of an accountable person, on his agent, or on the personal representative of an accountable person if that person is dead.

(5) Where the place of residence of the accountable person or of his personal representative is not known to the Commissioners they may publish in the Iris Oifigiúil a notice of the making of the assessment with such particulars thereof as they shall think proper and on the publication of the notice in the Iris Oifigiúil the accountable person or his personal representative, as the case may be, shall be deemed to have been served with the notice of the assessment on the date of such publication.

(6) Any assessment, correcting assessment or additional assessment under this section may be made by the Commissioners from any return or additional return delivered under the provisions of section 36 or from any other information in the possession of the Commissioners or from any one or more of these sources.

(7) The Commissioners, in making any assessment, correcting assessment or additional assessment, otherwise than from a return or an additional return which is satisfactory to them, shall make an assessment of such amount of tax as, to the best of their knowledge, information and belief, ought to be charged, levied and paid.

Section 40

Computation of tax.

40. The amount of tax payable shall be computed in accordance with the provisions of the Second Schedule.

PART VII

Payment and Recovery of Tax.

Section 41

Payment of tax and interest on tax.

41. (1) Tax shall be due and payable on the valuation date.

(2) Simple interest at the rate of one and one-half per cent. per month or part of a month, without deduction of income tax, shall be payable upon the tax from the valuation date to the date of payment of the tax and shall be chargeable and recoverable in the same manner as if it were part of the tax.

(3) Notwithstanding the provisions of subsection (2), interest shall not be payable on tax which is paid within three months of the valuation date, and where tax and interest, if any, thereon is paid within thirty days of the date of assessment thereof, interest shall not run on that tax for the period of thirty days from the date of the assessment or any part of that period.

(4) A payment on account of tax shall be applied —

(a) if there is interest due on tax at the date of the payment, to the discharge, so far as may be, of the interest so due; and

(b) if there is any balance of that payment remaining, to the discharge of so much tax as is equal to that balance.

(5) Subject to the provisions of subsections (2), (3) and (4), payments on account may be made at any time, and when a payment on account is made, interest shall not be chargeable in respect of any period subsequent to the date of such payment on so much of the payment on account as is to be applied in discharge of the tax.

(6) In the case of a gift which becomes an inheritance by reason of its being taken under a disposition where the date of the disposition is within two years prior to the death of the disponer, the provisions of this section shall have effect as if the references to the valuation

date in subsections (1), (2) and (3) were references to the date of death of the disponer.

(7) In the case of a gift or inheritance taken prior to the date of the passing of this Act, the provisions of this section shall have effect as if the references to the valuation date in subsections (1), (2) and (3) were references to the date of the passing of this Act, or to the valuation date, whichever is the later.

(8) Where the value of a limited interest falls to be ascertained in accordance with rule 8 of the First Schedule as if it were a series of absolute interests, this section shall have effect, in relation to each of those absolute interests, as if the references to the valuation date in subsections (1), (2) and (3) were references to the date of the taking of that absolute interest.

(9) All sums due under the provisions of this Act shall be paid to the Accountant-General of the Commissioners.

Section 42

Set-off of gift tax paid in respect of an inheritance.

42. Where an amount has been paid in respect of gift tax (or interest thereon) on a gift which, by reason of the death of the disponer within two years after the date of the disposition under which the gift was taken, becomes an inheritance in respect of which inheritance tax is payable, the amount so paid shall be treated as a payment on account of the inheritance tax.

Section 43

Payment of tax by instalments.

43. (1) Subject to the payment of interest in accordance with section 41 and save as hereinafter provided, the tax due and payable in respect of a taxable gift or a taxable inheritance may, at the option of the person delivering the return or additional return, be paid by five equal yearly instalments, the first of which shall be due at the expiration of twelve months from the date on which the tax became due and payable and the interest on the unpaid tax shall be added to each instalment and shall be paid at the same time as such instalment.

(2) An instalment not due may be paid at any time before it falls due.

(3) In any case where and to the extent that the property of which the taxable gift or taxable inheritance consists is sold or compulsorily acquired, all unpaid instalments shall, unless the interest of the donee or successor is a limited interest, be paid on completion of the sale or compulsory acquisition and, if not so paid, shall be tax in arrear.

(4) This section shall not apply in any case where and to the extent to which a taxable gift or a taxable inheritance consists of personal property

in which the donee, or the successor, or the transferee referred to in section 23 (1), as the case may be, takes an absolute interest.

(5) In any case where the interest taken by a donee or a successor is an interest limited to cease on his death, and his death occurs before all the instalments of the tax in respect of the taxable gift or taxable inheritance would have fallen due if such tax were being paid by instalments, any instalment of such tax which would not have fallen due prior to the date of the death of that donee or successor shall cease to be payable, and the payment, if made, of any such last-mentioned instalment shall be treated as an overpayment of tax for the purposes of section 46.

Section 44

Postponement, remission and compounding of tax.

44. (1) Where the Commissioners are satisfied that tax leviable in respect of any gift or inheritance cannot without excessive hardship be raised at once, they may allow payment to be postponed for such period, to such extent and on such terms (including the waiver of interest) as they think fit.

(2) If, after the expiration of the relevant period immediately following the date on which any tax became due and payable, the tax or any part thereof remains unpaid, the Commissioners may, if they think fit, remit the payment of any interest accruing after such expiration on the unpaid tax; and in this subsection, "relevant period" means the period at the end of which the interest, on an amount payable in respect of tax would, at the rate from time to time chargeable during that period in respect of interest on tax, equal the amount of such tax.

(3) If, after the expiration of twenty years from the date on which any tax became due and payable, the tax or any part thereof remains unpaid, the Commissioners may, if they think fit, remit the payment of such tax or any part thereof and all or any interest thereon.

(4) Where, in the opinion of the Commissioners, the complication of circumstances affecting a gift or inheritance or the value thereof or the assessment or recovery of tax thereon are such as to justify them in doing so, they may compound the tax payable on the gift or inheritance upon such terms as they shall think fit, and may give a discharge to the person or persons accountable for the tax upon payment of the tax according to such composition.

Section 45

Payment of inheritance tax by transfer of securities.

45. The provisions of section 22 of the Finance Act, 1954,[1] (which relates to the payment of death duties by the transfer of securities to the Minister for Finance) and the regulations made thereunder shall apply, with any

necessary modifications, to the payment of inheritance tax by the transfer of securities to the Minister for Finance, as they apply to the payment of death duties by the transfer of securities to the Minister for Finance.

Footnote

1   Reproduced on page 673.

Section 46

Overpayment of tax.

46.   Where, on application to the Commissioners for relief under this section, it is proved to their satisfaction that an amount has been paid in excess of the liability for tax or for interest on tax, they shall give relief by way of repayment of the excess or otherwise as is reasonable and just; and any such repayment shall carry simple interest (not exceeding the amount of such excess), without deduction of income tax, from the date on which the payment was made, at the same rate as that at which the tax would from time to time have carried interest if it were due and such payment had not been made.

Section 47

Tax to be a charge.

47.   (1)   Tax due and payable in respect of a taxable gift or a taxable inheritance shall, subject to the provisions of this section, be and remain a charge on the property (other than money or negotiable instruments) of which the taxable gift or taxable inheritance consists at the valuation date and the tax shall have priority over all charges and interests created by the donee or successor or any person claiming in right of the donee or successor or on his behalf:

Provided that where any settled property comprised in any taxable gift or taxable inheritance shall be subject to any power of sale, exchange, or partition, exercisable with the consent of the donee or successor, or by the donee or successor with the consent of another person, the donee or successor shall not be precluded by the charge of tax on his taxable gift or taxable inheritance from consenting to the exercise of such power, or exercising any power with proper consent, as the case may be; and where any such power is exercised, the tax shall be charged upon the property acquired, in substitution for charging it on the property previously comprised in the gift or inheritance, and upon all moneys arising from the exercise of any such power, and upon all investments of such moneys.

(2)   Property comprised in a taxable gift or taxable inheritance shall not, as against a bona fide purchaser or mortgagee for full consideration in money or money's worth, or a person deriving title from or under such a purchaser or mortgagee, remain charged with or liable to the payment of tax after the expiration of twelve years from the date of the gift or the date of the inheritance.

(3) Tax shall not be a charge on property under subsection (1) as against a bona fide purchaser or mortgagee of such property for full consideration in money or money's worth without notice, or a person deriving title from or under such a purchaser or mortgagee.

Section 48

Receipts and certificates.

48. (1) When any amount in respect of tax is paid, the Commissioners shall give a receipt for the payment.

(2) The Commissioners shall, on application to them by a person who has paid the tax in respect of any property comprised in any taxable gift or taxable inheritance, give to the person a certificate, in such form as they think fit, of the amount of the tax paid by him in respect of that property.

(3) The Commissioners shall, on application to them by a person who is an accountable person in respect of any of the property of which a taxable gift or taxable inheritance consists, if they are satisfied that the tax charged on the property in respect of the taxable gift or taxable inheritance has been or will be paid, or that there is no tax so charged, give a certificate to the person, in such form as they think fit, to that effect, which shall discharge the property from liability for tax (if any) in respect of the gift or inheritance, to the extent specified in the certificate.

(4) A certificate referred to in subsection (3) shall not discharge the property from tax in case of fraud or failure to disclose material facts and, in any case, shall not affect the tax payable in respect of any other property:

Provided that a certificate purporting to be a discharge of the whole tax payable in respect of any property included in the certificate in respect of a gift or inheritance shall exonerate from liability for such tax a bona fide purchaser or mortgagee for full consideration in money or money's worth without notice of such fraud or failure and a person deriving title from or under such a purchaser or mortgagee.

Section 49

Recovery of tax and penalties.

49. (1) Any sum due and payable in respect of tax or interest thereon and any penalty incurred in connection with tax or interest thereon shall be deemed to be a debt due by the accountable person or, if he is dead, by his personal representative, to the Minister for Finance for the benefit of the Central Fund and shall be payable to the Commissioners and may (without prejudice to any other mode of recovery thereof) be sued for and recovered by action, or other appropriate proceeding, at the suit of the Attorney-General or the Minister for Finance or the Commissioners in any court of competent jurisdiction, notwithstanding anything to the contrary contained in the Inland Revenue Regulation Act, 1890.

(2) Any person who, having received any sum of money as or for any tax, interest, or penalty under this Act, does not apply the money to the due payment of the tax, interest or penalty, and improperly withholds or detains the same, shall be accountable for the payment of the tax, interest or penalty to the extent of the amount so received by him and the same shall be a debt due by him to the Minister for Finance for the benefit of the Central Fund and shall be recoverable in like manner as a debt under subsection (1).

(3) If any accountable person is liable under section 36 to deliver to the Commissioners a return or an additional return and makes default in so doing, the Attorney-General or the Minister for Finance or the Commissioners may sue by action or other appropriate proceeding in the Circuit Court for an order directing the person so making default to deliver such return or additional return or to show cause to the contrary; and the Circuit Court may by order direct such accountable person to deliver such return or additional return within such time as may be specified in the order.

(4) Whenever property is subject to a charge by virtue of section 47, the Attorney-General or the Minister for Finance or the Commissioners may sue by action or other appropriate proceeding in any court of competent jurisdiction for, and the court may make, an order directing the owner of the property to pay the tax with which the property is charged.

Section 50

Evidence in proceedings for recovery of tax.

50. The provisions of section 39 of the Finance Act, 1926,[1] shall apply in any proceedings in the Circuit Court or the District Court for or in relation to the recovery of the tax.

Footnote

1   Reproduced on page 657.

PART VIII
Appeals

Section 51

Appeals regarding value of real property.

51. If a person is aggrieved by the decision of the Commissioners as to the market value of any real property, he may appeal against the decision in the manner prescribed by section 33 of the Finance (1909-10) Act,

1910[1], and the provisions as to appeals under that section of that Act shall apply accordingly with any necessary modifications.

Footnote
1   Reproduced on page 655.

Section 52

Appeals in other cases.

52.   (1)   In this section—

"Appeal Commissioners" has the meaning assigned to it by section 156 of the Income Tax Act, 1967;

"appellant" means a person who appeals to the Appeal Commissioners under subsection (2) of this section.

(2)   Subject to the other provisions of this Act, a person who is called upon by the Commissioners to pay an assessment of tax in respect of any property and who is aggrieved by the assessment may, in accordance with the provisions of this section, appeal to the Appeal Commissioners against the assessment and the appeal shall be heard and determined by the Appeal Commissioners whose determination shall be final and conclusive unless the appeal is required to be reheard by a judge of the Circuit Court or a case is required to be stated in relation to it for the opinion of the High Court on a point of law.

(3)   An appeal shall not lie under this section in relation to the market value of real property.

(4)   A person who intends to appeal under this section against an assessment shall, within 30 days after the date of the assessment, give notice in writing to the Commissioners of his intention to appeal against the assessment.

(5)   (a)   Subject to the provisions of this section, the provisions of the Income Tax Acts relating to—

(i)   the appointment of times and places for the hearing of appeals;

(ii)   the giving of notice to each person who has given notice of appeal of the time and place appointed for the hearing of his appeal;

(iii)   the determination of an appeal by agreement between the appellant and an officer appointed by the Commissioners in that behalf;

(iv)   the determination of an appeal by the appellant giving notice of his intention not to proceed with the appeal;

(v) the hearing and determination of an appeal by the Appeal Commissioners, including the hearing and determination of an appeal by one Appeal Commissioner;

(vi) the determination of an appeal through the neglect or refusal of a person who has given notice of appeal to attend before the Appeal Commissioners at the time and place appointed;

(vii) the extension of the time for giving notice of appeal and the readmission of appeals by the Appeal Commissioners and the provisions which apply where action by way of court proceedings has been taken;

(viii) the rehearing of an appeal by a judge of the Circuit Court and the statement of a case for the opinion of the High Court on a point of law;

(ix) the payment of tax in accordance with the determination of the Appeal Commissioners notwithstanding that an appeal is required to be reheard by a judge of the Circuit Court or that a case for the opinion of the High Court on a point of law has been required to be stated or is pending;

(x) the procedures for appeal,

shall, with any necessary modifications, apply to an appeal under this section as if the appeal were an appeal against an assessment to income tax.

(b) The Commissioners shall, subject to their giving notice in writing in that behalf to the appellant within ten days after the determination of an appeal by the Appeal Commissioners, have the same right as the appellant to have the appeal reheard by a judge of the Circuit Court.

(c) The rehearing of an appeal under this section by a judge of the Circuit Court shall be by a judge of the Circuit Court in whose circuit the appellant or one of the appellants resides or (in the case of a body corporate) has its principal place of business:

Provided that—

(i) in any case where no appellant is resident in or (in the case of a body corporate) has a place of business in the State; or

(ii) in any case where there is a doubt or a dispute as to the circuit,

the appeal shall be reheard by a judge of the Circuit Court assigned to the Dublin Circuit.

(6) (a) Where a notice or other document which is required or authorised to be served by this section falls to be served on a

body corporate, such notice shall be served on the secretary or other officer of the body corporate.

(b) Any notice or other document which is required or authorised by this section to be served by the Commissioners or by an appellant may be served by post and in the case of a notice or other document addressed to the Commissioners, shall be sent to the Secretaries, Revenue Commissioners, Dublin Castle, Dublin 2.

(c) Any notice or other document which is required or authorised to be served by the Commissioners on an appellant under this section may be sent to the solicitor, accountant or other agent of the appellant and a notice thus served shall be deemed to have been served on the appellant unless the appellant proves to the satisfaction of the Appeal Commissioners, or the Circuit Court, as the case may be, that he had, before the notice or other document was served, withdrawn the authority of such solicitor, accountant or other agent to act on his behalf.

(7) Prima facie evidence of any notice given under this section by the Commissioners or by an officer of the Commissioners may be given in any proceedings by production of a document purporting to be a copy of the notice and it shall not be necessary to prove the official position of the person by whom the notice purports to be given or, if it is signed, the signature, or that the person signing and giving it was authorised so to do.

(8) (a) The Commissioners may serve notice in writing, referring expressly to this subsection, on any person whom they have reason to believe to be accountable for the payment of tax, of any decision they have made which is relevant to such tax.

(b) Any person who is informed of a decision in accordance with paragraph (a) may appeal to the Appeal Commissioners against the decision.

(c) The Appeal Commissioners shall hear and determine an appeal to them under this subsection as if it were an appeal to them against an assessment to tax, and the provisions of this section relating to an appeal or to the rehearing of an appeal or to the statement of a case for the opinion of the High Court on a point of law shall, with any necessary modifications, apply accordingly.

PART IX
Exemptions

Section 53

Exemption of small gifts.
53. (1) The first £250 of the total taxable value of all taxable gifts taken by a donee from any one disponer in any relevant period shall be

exempt from tax and shall not be taken into account in computing tax.

(2) In the case of a gift which becomes an inheritance by reason of its being taken under a disposition where the date of the disposition is within two years prior to the death of the disposer, the same relief shall be granted in respect thereof under subsection (1) as if it were a gift.

(3) The first £250 of the total aggregate value of all aggregable gifts (within the meaning of paragraph 1 of Part I of the Second Schedule) which are taken by the donee from any one disponer in any relevant period shall not be taken into account in computing tax.

(4) In this section, "relevant period" means the period commencing on the 28th day of February, 1969, and ending on the 31st day of December, 1969, and thereafter the period of twelve months ending on the 31st day of December in each year.

Section 54

Provisions relating to charities, etc.

54. (1) Any benefit taken by a person for public or charitable purposes shall, for the purposes of sections 5 (1) and 11 (1), be deemed to be taken beneficially by a person who is other than a donee or successor referred to in Table I, II or III of Part II of the Second Schedule.

(2) A gift or an inheritance which is taken for public or charitable purposes shall, to the extent that the Commissioners are satisfied that it has been or will be applied to public or charitable purposes in the State or Northern Ireland, be exempt from tax and shall not be taken into account in computing tax.

(3) Save as provided in section 56 (4), a gift or inheritance which a person takes on becoming entitled to any benefit on the application to public or charitable purposes of property (including moneys provided by the Oireachtas or a local authority) held for such purposes shall be exempt from tax and shall not be taken into account in computing tax.

Section 55

Exemption of certain objects.

55. (1) This section applies to the following objects, that is to say, any pictures, prints, books, manuscripts, works of art, jewellery, scientific collections or other things not held for the purposes of trading —

(a) which, on a claim being made to the Commissioners, appear to them to be of national, scientific, historic or artistic interest;

"unit trust scheme" means a unit trust scheme registered in the register established by the Unit Trusts Act, 1972, whose deed expressing the trusts of the scheme restricts the property subject to those trusts to securities.

(2) Any security, or units (within the meaning of the Unit Trusts Act, 1972) of a unit trust scheme, comprised in a gift or an inheritance shall be exempt from tax (and shall not be taken into account in computing tax on any gift or inheritance taken by the donee or successor from the same disponer) if and only if –

(a) the security or units was or were comprised in the gift or inheritance –

(i) at the date of the gift or at the date of the inheritance; and

(ii) at the valuation date; and

(b) the donee or successor is at the date of the gift or at the date of the inheritance neither domiciled nor ordinarily resident in the State and the provisions of section 19 (6) shall apply, for the purposes of this subsection, as they apply in relation to agricultural property:

Provided that if a security or units or any part thereof comprised –

(a) in a gift; or

(b) in a gift which becomes an inheritance by reason that it was taken under a disposition where the date of the disposition was within two years prior to the death of the disponer,

is within one year after the valuation date sold or exchanged, or is converted (otherwise than into another security or other units respectively, which, during that period of one year, are not sold or exchanged), the donee or successor shall be deemed to have taken from the disponer a gift or an inheritance, as the case may be, consisting of a sum equal to the market value at the valuation date of the security or units or of the part thereof that has been sold, exchanged or converted.

(3) For the purposes of sections 6 (1) (c) and 12 (1) (b), the sum referred to in the proviso to subsection (2) shall be deemed to be situate in the State at the date of the gift or at the date of the inheritance, as the case may be, if the security or units (or the part thereof) so sold, exchanged or converted had at that date been situate in the State and not otherwise.

Section 58

Exemption of certain receipts.

58. (1) The following shall not be gifts or inheritances –

(a) the receipt by a person of any sum bona fide by way of compensation or damages for any wrong or injury suffered by him in his person, property, reputation or means of livelihood;

(b) the receipt by a person of any sum bona fide by way of compensation or damages for any wrong or injury resulting in the death of any other person;

(c) the receipt by a person of any sum bona fide by way of winnings from betting (including pool betting) or from any lottery, sweepstake or game with prizes;

(d) any benefit arising out of —

(i) the payment to the Official Assignee in Bankruptcy of money which has been provided by, or which represents property provided by, friends of a bankrupt; or

(ii) a remission or abatement of debts by the creditors of a bankrupt,

to enable the bankrupt to fulfil an offer of composition after bankruptcy in accordance with the provisions of section 149 of the Irish Bankrupt and Insolvent Act, 1857; and

(e) any benefit arising out of —

(i) the payment to the Official Assignee in Bankruptcy of money which has been provided by, or which represents property provided by, friends of an arranging debtor; or

(ii) a remission or abatement of debts by the creditors of an arranging debtor,

to enable the debtor to carry out the terms of a proposal made by him under section 345 of the Irish Bankrupt and Insolvent Act, 1857, which has been accepted by his creditors and approved and confirmed by the High Court.

(2) Notwithstanding anything contained in this Act, the receipt in the lifetime of the disponer of money or money's worth —

(a) by —

(i) the spouse or child of the disponer; or

(ii) a person in relation to whom the disponer stands in loco parentis,

for support, maintenance or education; or

(b) by a person who is in relation to the disponer a dependent relative under section 142 of the Income Tax Act, 1967, for support or maintenance,

shall not be a gift or an inheritance, where the provision of such support, maintenance or education, or such support or maintenance —

(i) is such as would be part of the normal expenditure of a person in the circumstances of the disponer; and

(ii) is reasonable having regard to the financial circumstances of the disponer.

Section 59

Exemption where disposition was made by the donee or successor.

59. (1) Tax shall not be chargeable upon a gift or an inheritance taken by the donee or successor under a disposition made by himself.

   (2) Where, at the date of the gift, two companies are associated in the manner described in subsection (3), a gift taken by one of them under a disposition made by the other shall be deemed to be a gift to which subsection (1) applies.

   (3) For the purposes of subsection (2), two companies shall be regarded as associated if —

      (a) one company would be beneficially entitled to not less than 90 per cent. of any assets of the other company available for distribution to the owners of its shares and entitlements of the kind referred to in section 34 (1) on a winding up; or

      (b) a third company would be beneficially entitled to not less than 90 per cent. of any assets of each of them available as in paragraph (a).

   (4) In this section, "company" means a body corporate (wherever incorporated), other than a private company within the meaning of section 16 (2).

PART X
Miscellaneous

Section 60

Certificates for probate.

60. (1) Where an Inland Revenue affidavit has been delivered to the Commissioners and they are satisfied —

      (a) that an adequate payment on account of inheritance tax in respect of the property passing under the deceased person's will or intestacy or Part IX or section 56 of the Succession Act, 1965, has been made; or

      (b) that the payment of inheritance tax in respect of such property may be deferred for the time being,

   they shall certify in writing —

      (i) that the Inland Revenue affidavit was delivered to them; and

      (ii) (I) that a payment referred to in paragraph (a) has been made; or

          (II) that the payment referred to in paragraph (b) has been deferred for the time being,

   as the case may be.

(2) In this section "Inland Revenue affidavit" has the meaning referred to in section 38 (1).

(3) If, in the opinion of the Commissioners, the payment of inheritance tax in respect of the property passing under the deceased person's will or intestacy or Part IX or section 56 of the Succession Act, 1965, cannot be deferred for the time being without serious risk of such tax not being recovered, they may refuse to issue the certificate referred to in subsection (1) until the tax has been paid, or until such payment as is referred to in paragraph (a) of that subsection has been made.

(4) The certificate required by section 30 of the Customs and Inland Revenue Act, 1881,[1] to be made by the proper officer of the court, shall not be made until a certificate of the Commissioners issued under subsection (1) has been produced to such officer and shall (instead of showing that the affidavit, if liable to stamp duty, has been duly stamped) show that the Commissioners have issued a certificate under subsection (1) and shall state the substance of the certificate so issued by the Commissioners.

(5) The form of certificate required to be given by the proper officer of the court under section 30 of the Customs and Inland Revenue Act, 1881,[1] may be prescribed by rule of court in such manner as may be necessary for giving effect to this Act.

(6) This section shall apply only where the deceased person dies on or after the 1st day of April, 1975.

Footnote
1   Reproduced on page 651.

Section 61

Payment of money standing in names of two or more persons.

61. (1) Where, either before or after the passing of this Act, a sum of money exceeding £5,000 is lodged or deposited (otherwise than on a current account) in the State with a banker, in the joint names of two or more persons, and one of such persons (in this section referred to as the deceased) dies on or after the 1st day of April, 1975, the banker shall not pay such money or any part thereof to the survivor or all or any of the survivors of such persons, or to any other person, unless or until there is furnished to such banker a certificate by the Commissioners certifying that there is no outstanding claim for inheritance tax in connection with the death of the deceased in respect of such money or any part thereof or a consent in writing by the Commissioners to such payment pending the ascertainment and payment of such tax.

(2) Notwithstanding anything contained in this Act, tax chargeable on the death of the deceased shall be deemed for the purposes of this section to become due on the day of the death of the deceased.

(3) A banker who, after the passing of this Act, pays money in contravention of this section shall be liable to a penalty of £1,000.

(4) Where a penalty is demanded of a banker under this section, the onus of proving that such certificate or such consent as is mentioned in this section was furnished to such banker before he paid such money shall lie on such banker.

(5) Where a penalty is demanded of a banker under this section, it shall be a good defence to prove that, at the time when such banker paid such money, he had reasonable ground for believing that none of the persons in whose joint names such money was lodged or deposited with him was dead.

(6) Section 33 of the Finance Act, 1935,[1] shall not have effect in any case where the death of a person, referred to in that section as the deceased, occurs on or after the 1st day of April, 1975.

(7) In this section—

"banker" means a person who carries on banking business in the State and includes a friendly society, an industrial and provident society, a building society, the Post Office Savings Bank, a trustee savings bank, the Industrial Credit Company Limited, the Agricultural Credit Corporation Limited and any person with whom money is lodged or deposited:

"pay" includes transfer in the books of a banker and any dealings whatsoever with any moneys which were lodged or deposited in the name of a person who died after the time of the lodgment or deposit and any other person or persons;

"current account" means an account which is customarily operated upon by means of a cheque or banker's order;

"banking business" has the meaning assigned to it by section 2 of the Central Bank Act, 1971;

references to moneys lodged or deposited include references to shares of a building society, friendly society or industrial and provident society.

Footnote
1   Reproduced on page 664.

Section 62

Court to provide for payment of tax.
62.   Where any suit is pending in any court for the administration of any property chargeable with tax under this Act, such court shall provide,

out of any such property which may be in the possession or control of the court, for the payment to the Commissioners of any of the tax or the interest thereon which remains unpaid.

Section 63

Penalties.

63. (1) (a) Any person who contravenes or fails to comply with—

    (i)   any requirement under section 36 (6), (7) or (8); or

    (ii) the provisions of section 36 (2) or (9)

    shall be liable to a penalty of £500.

  (b) Where the contravention or failure referred to in paragraph (a) continues after judgment has been given by the court before which proceedings for the penalty have been commenced, the person concerned shall be liable to a further penalty of £25 for each day on which the contravention or failure so continues.

(2) Where, under, or for the purposes of, any of the provisions of this Act, a person is authorised to inspect any property for the purpose of reporting to the Commissioners the market value thereof and the person having custody or possession of that property prevents such inspection or obstructs the person so authorised in the performance of his functions in relation to the inspection, the person so having custody or possession shall be liable to a penalty of £500.

(3) Where an accountable person fraudulently or negligently—

  (a) delivers any incorrect return or additional return;

  (b) makes or furnishes any incorrect statement, declaration, evidence or valuation in connection with any property comprised in any disposition;

  (c) makes or furnishes any incorrect statement, declaration, evidence or valuation in connection with any claim for any allowance, deduction, exemption or relief; or

  (d) makes or furnishes any incorrect statement, declaration, evidence or valuation in connection with any other matter,

on the basis of which the amount of tax assessable in respect of a taxable gift or taxable inheritance would be less than it would have been if the correct return, additional return, statement, declaration, evidence or valuation had been delivered, made or furnished, he shall be liable to a penalty of—

    (i)   £1,000; and

    (ii) the amount, or in the case of fraud, twice the amount, of the difference specified in subsection (5).

(4) Where any such return, additional return, statement, declaration, evidence or valuation as is mentioned in subsection (3) was

delivered, made or furnished neither fraudulently nor negligently by a person and it comes to his notice that it was incorrect, then, unless the error is remedied without unreasonable delay, such matter shall be treated, for the purposes of this section, as having been negligently done by him.

(5) The difference referred to in subsection (3) is the difference between—

    (a) the amount of tax payable in respect of the taxable gift or taxable inheritance to which the return, additional return, statement, declaration, evidence or valuation relates; and

    (b) the amount which would have been the amount so payable if the return, additional return, statement, declaration, evidence or valuation as made or submitted had been correct.

(6) For the purpose of subsection (3), where anything referred to in that subsection is delivered, made or furnished on behalf of a person, it shall be deemed to have been delivered, made or furnished by that person unless he proves that it was done without his knowledge or consent.

(7) Any person who assists in or induces the delivery, making or furnishing for any purposes of the tax of any return, additional return, statement, declaration, evidence or valuation which he knows to be incorrect shall be liable to a penalty of £250.

(8) The provisions of this section shall not affect any criminal proceedings.

(9) Subject to the provisions of this section, sections 128 (4), 507, 508, 510, 511, 512, 517 and 518 of the Income Tax Act, 1967, shall, with any necessary modifications, apply to a penalty under this Act as if the penalty were a penalty under the Income Tax Acts.

Section 64

Liability to tax in respect of certain sales and mortgages.

64.   (1)   In this section—

"death duties" has the meaning assigned to it by section 30 of the Finance Act, 1971,[1] and

"purchaser or mortgagee" includes a person deriving title from or under a purchaser or mortgagee in the case of such a sale or mortgage as is referred to in this section.

(2) Where an interest in expectancy has, prior to the 1st day of April, 1975, been bona fide sold or mortgaged for full consideration in money or money's worth, and that interest comes into possession on a death occurring on or after that date, the following provisions shall have effect, that is to say—

(a) the purchaser or mortgagee shall not be liable in respect of inheritance tax on the inheritance referred to in paragraph (b) for an amount greater than that referred to in paragraph (c);

(b) the inheritance referred to in paragraph (a) is the inheritance of property in which the interest so sold or mortgaged subsists and which arises in respect of the interest of the remainderman referred to in section 23 so coming into possession;

(c) the amount referred to in paragraph (a) shall be the amount that would then have been payable by the purchaser or mortgagee in respect of death duties on the property in which the interest subsists as property passing under the same disposition as that under which the said inheritance is taken, if the property, on so coming into possession, had been chargeable to death duties —

(i) under the law in force; and

(ii) at the rate or rates having effect,

at the date of the sale or mortgage;

(d) where such an interest is so mortgaged, any amount of inheritance tax payable in respect of the inheritance referred to in paragraph (b), and from the payment of which the mortgagee is relieved under this section, shall, notwithstanding the priority referred to in section 47 (1), rank, in relation to property charged with such tax under that section, as a charge subsequent to the mortgage;

(e) any person, other than the purchaser or mortgagee, who is accountable for the payment of so much of the inheritance tax as is not the liability of the purchaser or mortgagee by virtue of the relief given by this section, shall not be liable for the payment of any amount in respect thereof in excess of the amount which is available to him for such payment by reason of there being, at the time when the interest comes into possession, other property, or an equity of redemption, or both, subject to the same trusts, under the disposition referred to in paragraph (c), as the property in which the interest in expectancy subsists; and

(f) nothing in section 35 (7) or (8) or section 47 (1) shall be construed as derogating from the relief given by this section to a purchaser or mortgagee.

Footnote
1   Reproduced on page 679.

Section 65

References in deeds and wills, etc. to death duties.

65. In so far as a provision in a document refers (in whatever terms) to any death duty to arise on any death occurring on or after the 1st day of April, 1975, it shall have effect, as far as may be, as if the reference included a reference to inheritance tax —

  (a) if that document was executed prior to the passing of this Act, and the reference is to legacy duty and succession duty or either of them;

  (b) if that document was so executed, and the reference is to estate duty, and it may reasonably be inferred from all the circumstances (including any similarity of the incidence of inheritance tax to that of estate duty) that the inclusion of the reference to inheritance tax would be just; and

  (c) whether the document was executed prior to or after the passing of this Act, if the reference is to death duties, without referring to any particular death duty.

Section 66

Arrangements for relief from double taxation.

66. (1) If the Government by order declare that arrangements specified in the order have been made with the government of any territory outside the State in relation to affording relief from double taxation in respect of gift tax or inheritance tax payable under the laws of the State and any tax imposed under the laws of that territory which is of a similar character or is chargeable by reference to death or to gifts inter vivos and that it is expedient that those arrangements should have the force of law, the arrangements shall, notwithstanding anything in any enactment, have the force of law.

  (2) Any arrangements to which the force of law is given under this section may include provision for relief from tax charged before the making of the arrangements and provisions as to property which is not itself subject to double tax, and the provisions of this section shall have effect accordingly.

  (3) For the purposes of subsection (1), arrangements made with the head of a foreign state shall be regarded as made with the government thereof.

  (4) Where any arrangements have the force of law by virtue of this section, the obligation as to secrecy imposed by any enactment shall not prevent the Commissioners from disclosing to any authorised officer of the government with which the arrangements are made such information as is required to be disclosed under the arrangements.

  (5) (a) Any order made under this section may be revoked by a subsequent order and any such revoking order may contain

such transitional provisions as appear to the Government to be necessary or expedient.

(b) Where an order is proposed to be made under this section, a draft thereof shall be laid before Dáil Éireann and the order shall not be made until a resolution approving of the draft has been passed by Dáil Éireann.

Section 67

Other relief from double taxation.

67. (1) (a) In this section —

"foreign tax" means any tax which is chargeable under the laws of any territory outside the State and is of a character similar to estate duty, gift tax or inheritance tax;

"event" means —

(i) a death; or

(ii) any other event,

by reference to which the date of the gift or the date of the inheritance is determined.

(b) For the purposes of this section, a reference to property situate in a territory outside the State is a reference to property situate in that territory at the date of the gift or the date of the inheritance, as the case may be, or to property representing such property.

(2) Where the Commissioners are satisfied that a taxable gift or taxable inheritance, taken under a disposition by a donee or successor on the happening of any event, is reduced by the payment of foreign tax which is chargeable in connection with the same event under the same disposition in respect of property which is situate in the territory outside the State in which that foreign tax is chargeable, they shall allow a credit in respect of that foreign tax against the gift tax or inheritance tax payable by that donee or successor on that taxable gift or taxable inheritance; but such credit shall not exceed —

(a) the amount of the gift tax or inheritance tax payable in respect of the same property by reason of such property being comprised in any taxable gift or taxable inheritance taken under that disposition on the happening of that event; or

(b) the amount of that foreign tax,

whichever is the lesser.

(3) The provisions of this section shall be subject to any arrangement to which the force of law is given under section 66, and, if any such arrangement provides for the allowance of the amount of a tax payable in a territory outside the State as a credit against gift tax

or inheritance tax, the provisions of the arrangement shall apply in relation to the tax payable in that territory in lieu of the provisions of subsection (2).

(4) If the amount of tax payable in respect of a taxable gift or taxable inheritance would be less by making a deduction (in ascertaining the taxable value of the taxable gift or taxable inheritance) of the amount of the foreign tax to which the taxable gift or taxable inheritance is subject than by making the allowance of a credit—

    (a) under subsection (2); or

    (b) under any arrangement to which the force of law is given under section 66,

such deduction shall be made notwithstanding the provisions of section 18 (5) (b), and no such credit shall be allowed.

(5) Where the foreign tax in respect of property comprised in a taxable gift or a taxable inheritance taken under a disposition on the happening of an event is, under the terms of the disposition, directed to be paid out of a taxable gift or a taxable inheritance (taken under that disposition on the happening of the same event) other than the taxable gift or taxable inheritance out of which it would be payable in the absence of such a direction, then, for the purposes of subsection (2), the taxable gift or taxable inheritance out of which the foreign tax would be payable in the absence of such a direction, and no other taxable gift or taxable inheritance, shall be treated as reduced by the payment of the foreign tax.

Section 68

Tax, in relation to certain legislation.

68. (1) Inheritance tax shall not be a duty or a death duty for the purposes of section 9 of the Succession Act, 1965, but it shall be a death duty for the purposes of—

    (a) section 34 (3) of that Act;

    (b) the definition of pecuniary legacy in section 3 (1) of that Act; and

    (c) paragraph 8 of Part 11 of the First Schedule to that Act.

(2) Section 72 of the Registration of Title Act, 1964, shall apply as if gift tax and inheritance tax were therein mentioned as well as estate duty and succession duty.

Section 69

Extension of certain Acts.

69. (1) Section 1 of the Provisional Collection of Taxes Act, 1927[1], is hereby amended by the insertion of "and gift tax and inheritance tax" before "but no other tax or duty".

(2) Section 39 of the Inland Revenue Regulation Act, 1890, is hereby amended by the insertion of "gift tax and inheritance tax," before "stamp duties".

Footnote

1   Reproduced on page 658.

Section 70

Delivery, service and evidence of notices and forms, etc.

70.   (1)   Any notice which under this Act is authorised or required to be given by the Commissioners may be served by post.

      (2)   A notice or form which is to be served on a person may be either delivered to him or left at his usual or last known place of abode.

      (3)   Prima facie evidence of any notice given under this Act by the Commissioners or any officer of the Commissioners may be given in any proceedings by production of a document purporting to be a copy of the notice, and it shall not be necessary to prove the official position of the person by whom the notice purports to be given or, if it is signed, the signature, or that the person signing and giving it was authorised so to do.

      (4)   In any case where a time limit is specified by or under this Act, other than Part VIII hereof, for the doing of any act required by or under this Act, other than Part VIII thereof, to be done by any person other than the Commissioners, the Commissioners may, in their discretion, extend such time limit.

Section 71

Regulations.

71.   (1)   The Commissioners shall make such regulations as seem to them to be necessary for the purpose of giving effect to this Act and of enabling them to discharge their functions thereunder.

      (2)   Every regulation made under this section shall be laid before Dáil Éireann as soon as may be after it is made and, if a resolution annulling the regulation is passed by Dáil Éireann within the next twenty-one days on which Dáil Éireann has sat after the regulation is laid before it, the regulation shall be annulled accordingly, but without prejudice to the validity of anything previously done thereunder.

Section 72

Care and management.

72.   (1)   Tax is hereby placed under the care and management of the Commissioners.

(2) Subject to the direction and control of the Commissioners, any power, function or duty conferred or imposed on the Commissioners by this Act may be exercised or performed on their behalf by an officer of the Commissioners.

FIRST SCHEDULE
Valuation of Limited Interests

PART I

Rules relating to the valuation of limited interests utilising Tables A and B in Parts II and III of this Schedule

1. The value of an interest for a single life in a capital sum shall be that sum multiplied by the factor, contained in column 3 or 4 respectively of Table A, which is appropriate to the age and sex of the person in respect of the duration of whose life the interest is to be valued.
2. The value of an interest in a capital sum for the joint continuance of two lives shall be the value of an interest in that sum for the older life, ascertained in accordance with rule 1, multiplied by the joint factor in column 2 of Table A which is appropriate to the younger life.
3. The value of an interest in a capital sum for the joint continuance of three or more lives shall be the value of an interest in that sum for the joint continuance of the two oldest of those lives, ascertained in accordance with rule 2, multiplied by the joint factor of the youngest of those lives.
4. The value of an interest in a capital sum for the longer of two lives shall be ascertained by deducting from the total of the values of an interest in that sum for each of those lives, ascertained in accordance with rule 1, the value of an interest in the capital sum for the joint continuance of the same two lives, ascertained in accordance with rule 2.
5. Where an interest is given for the longest of more than two lives, it shall be valued, in accordance with rule 4, as if it were for the longer of the two youngest of those lives.
6. The value of an interest in a capital sum for a period certain shall be the aggregate of —
   (a) the value of the capital sum, multiplied by the factor in Table B which is appropriate to the number of whole years in that period (or zero if that period is less than a whole year); and
   (b) where the period is not an integral number of years, a fraction (of which the numerator is the number of days in excess of the number of whole years, if any, in that period and the denominator is 365) of the difference between —
      (i) the value of an interest in the capital sum for one year longer than the number of whole years, if any, in the period; and
      (ii) the value ascertained under the provisions of paragraph (a) (or zero, where so provided in the said paragraph).

7. In the case of a limited interest where the interest is for a life or lives, but is guaranteed for a period certain, the value shall be the higher of —

    (a) the value of an interest for such life or lives, ascertained in accordance with the appropriate rule in this part of this Schedule; and

    (b) the value of an interest for the period certain, ascertained in accordance with rule 6.

8. The value of a limited interest for which the other rules in this Part of this Schedule provide no method of valuing shall be ascertained as if the interest taken were a series of absolute interests in the property applied in satisfaction of the interest from time to time, taken as separate gifts or inheritances, as the case may be.

PART II

Table A

1	2	3	4
Years of age	Joint factor	Value of an interest in a capital of £1 for a male life aged as in column 1	Value of an interest in a capital of £1 for a female life aged as in column 1
0	.99	.9519	.9624
1	.99	.9767	.9817
2	.99	.9767	.9819
3	.99	.9762	.9817
4	.99	.9753	.9811
5	.99	.9742	.9805
6	.99	.9730	.9797
7	.99	.9717	.9787
8	.99	.9703	.9777
9	.99	.9688	.9765
10	.99	.9671	.9753
11	.98	.9653	.9740
12	.98	.9634	.9726
13	.98	.9614	.9710
14	.98	.9592	.9693
15	.98	.9569	.9676
16	.98	.9546	.9657
17	.98	.9522	.9638
18	.98	.9497	.9617
19	.98	.9471	.9596
20	.97	.9444	.9572
21	.97	.9416	.9547
22	.97	.9387	.9521
23	.97	.9356	.9493

1	2	3	4
Years of age	Joint factor	Value of an interest in a capital of £1 for a male life aged as in column 1	Value of an interest in a capital of £1 for a female life aged as in column 1
24	.97	.9323	.9464
25	.97	.9288	.9432
26	.97	.9250	.9399
27	.97	.9209	.9364
28	.97	.9165	.9328
29	.97	.9119	.9289
30	.96	.9068	.9248
31	.96	.9015	.9205
32	.96	.8958	.9159
33	.96	.8899	.9111
34	.96	.8836	.9059
35	.96	.8770	.9005
36	.96	.8699	.8947
37	.96	.8626	.8886
38	.95	.8549	.8821
39	.95	.8469	.8753
40	.95	.8384	.8683
41	.95	.8296	.8610
42	.95	.8204	.8534
43	.95	.8107	.8454
44	.94	.8005	.8370
45	.94	.7897	.8283
46	.94	.7783	.8192
47	.94	.7663	.8096
48	.93	.7541	.7997
49	.93	.7415	.7896
50	.92	.7287	.7791
51	.91	.7156	.7683
52	.90	.7024	.7572
53	.89	.6887	.7456
54	.89	.6745	.7335
55	.88	.6598	.7206
56	.88	.6445	.7069
57	.88	.6288	.6926
58	.87	.6129	.6778
59	.86	.5969	.6628
60	.86	.5809	.6475
61	.86	.5650	.6320
62	.86	.5492	.6162

1	2	3	4
Years of age	Joint factor	Value of an interest in a capital of £1 for a male life aged as in column 1	Value of an interest in a capital of £1 for a female life aged as in column 1
63	.85	.5332	.6000
64	.85	.5171	.5830
65	.85	.5007	.5650
66	.85	.4841	.5462
67	.84	.4673	.5266
68	.84	.4506	.5070
69	.84	.4339	.4873
70	.83	.4173	.4679
71	.83	.4009	.4488
72	.82	.3846	.4301
73	.82	.3683	.4114
74	.81	.3519	.3928
75	.80	.3352	.3743
76	.79	.3181	.3559
78	.76	.2838	.3198
78	.76	.2838	.3198
79	.74	.2671	.3023
80	.72	.2509	.2855
81	.71	.2353	.2693
82	.70	.2203	.2538
83	.69	.2057	.2387
84	.68	.1916	.2242
85	.67	.1783	.2104
86	.66	.1657	.1973
87	.65	.1537	.1849
88	.64	.1423	.1730
89	.62	.1315	.1616
90	.60	.1212	.1509
91	.58	.1116	.1407
92	.56	.1025	.1310
93	.54	.0939	.1218
94	.52	.0858	.1132
95	.50	.0781	.1050
96	.49	.0710	.0972
97	.48	.0642	.0898
98	.47	.0578	.0828
99	.45	.0517	.0762
100 or over	.43	.0458	.0698

PART III

Table B

(Column 2 shows the value of an interest in a capital of £1 for the number of years shown in column 1).

1 Number of years	2 Value	1 Number of years	2 Value
1	.0654	26	.8263
2	.1265	27	.8375
3	.1836	28	.8480
4	.2370	29	.8578
5	.2869	30	.8669
6	.3335	31	.8754
7	.3770	32	.8834
8	.4177	33	.8908
9	.4557	34	.8978
10	.4913	35	.9043
11	.5245	36	.9100
12	.5555	37	.9165
13	.5845	38	.9230
14	.6116	39	.9295
15	.6369	40	.9360
16	.6605	41	.9425
17	.6826	42	.9490
18	.7032	43	.9555
19	.7225	44	.9620
20	.7405	45	.9685
21	.7574	46	.9750
22	.7731	47	.9815
23	.7878	48	.9880
24	.8015	49	.9945
25	.8144	50 and over	1.0000

SECOND SCHEDULE
Computation of Tax

PART I
Preliminary

1. In this Schedule —

    "aggregable gift" means a gift taken by a donee on or after the 28th day of February, 1969, and before the 28th day of February, 1974, which, so far as it is a taxable gift, is by virtue of section 9 to be aggregated with any later taxable gift or taxable inheritance for the purpose mentioned in that section;

    "aggregable value " means the taxable value of an aggregable gift;

    "appropriate Table", in relation to a donee or successor who, at the date of the gift or at the date of the inheritance, in respect of which gift or inheritance the tax is being computed, is —

    (a) the spouse, child, or minor child of a deceased child, of the disponer, means Table I;

    (b) a lineal ancestor or a lineal descendant (other than a child, or a minor child of a deceased child) of the disponer, means Table II;

    (c) a brother or sister, or a child of a brother or of a sister, of the disponer, means Table III;

    (d) a donee or successor who does not stand to the disponer in a relationship referred to in subparagraph (a), (b) or (c), means Table IV;

    contained in Part II of this Schedule.

2. In each Table contained in Part II of this Schedule, "value" means —

    (a) in the case referred to in paragraph 3, the taxable value referred to in that paragraph;

    (b) in the case referred to in paragraph 4, the aggregate referred to in that paragraph.

3. Subject to the provisions of paragraph 6, the tax chargeable on the taxable value of a taxable gift or a taxable inheritance, in the case where the donee or successor has taken no other taxable gift or taxable inheritance or aggregable gift from the same disponer, shall be computed at the rate or rates of tax applicable to that taxable value under the appropriate Table.

4. Subject to the provisions of paragraph 6, the tax chargeable on the taxable value of a taxable gift or a taxable inheritance, in the case where the donee or successor has previously taken one or more taxable gifts on or after the 28th day of February, 1974, or taxable inheritances on or after the 1st day of April, 1975, or aggregable gifts, from the same

disponer, shall be computed at the rate or rates of tax applicable under the appropriate Table to such part of the aggregate of—

(a) that taxable value;

(b) the taxable values of all such previous taxable gifts and taxable inheritances (if any); and

(c) the aggregable values of all such aggregable gifts (if any),

as is the highest part of that aggregate and is equal to that taxable value.

5. In each Table contained in Part II of this Schedule, any rate of tax shown in the third column is that applicable to such portion of the value (within the meaning of paragraph 2) as exceeds the lower limit shown in the first column but does not exceed the upper limit (if any) shown in the second column.

6. The tax chargeable on the taxable value of a taxable gift shall be 75 per cent. of the amount of tax computed in accordance with this Schedule.

7. For the purposes of this Schedule, all gifts and inheritances taken by a donee or successor from one disponer on the same day shall count as one, and to ascertain the amount of tax payable on one gift or inheritance of several taken on the same day, the amount of tax computed under this Schedule as being payable on the gifts or inheritances taken on that day shall be apportioned rateably, according to the taxable values of the several taxable gifts and taxable inheritances taken on the one day.

8. Where any donee or successor is, at the date of the gift or at the date of the inheritance, the surviving spouse of a deceased person who, at the time of his death, was of nearer relationship than such donee or successor to the disponer, then such donee or successor shall, in the computation of the tax payable on such taxable gift or taxable inheritance, be deemed to bear to the disponer the relationship of that deceased person.

9. In any case where—

(a) the donee or successor is a nephew or niece of the disponer who has worked substantially on a full-time basis for the period of 5 years ending on the date of the gift or the date of the inheritance in carrying on, or assisting in the carrying on of, the trade, business or profession or the work of or connected with the office or employment of the disponer; and

(b) the gift or inheritance consists of property which was used in connection with such trade, business, profession, office or employment or of shares in a company owning such property,

then, for the purpose of computing the tax payable on the gift or inheritance, the donee or successor shall be deemed to bear to the disponer the relationship of a child.

PART II

Table I

Applicable where the donee or successor is the spouse, child, or minor child of a deceased child, of the disponer.

Portion of value		Rate of tax
Lower Limit £	Upper Limit £	Per cent
0	150,000	Nil
150,000	200,000	25
200,000	250,000	30
250,000	300,000	35
300,000	350,000	40
350,000	400,000	45
400,000	—	50

Table II

Applicable where the donee or successor is a lineal ancestor or a lineal descendant (other than a child, or a minor child of a deceased child) of the disponer.

Portion of value		Rate of tax
Lower Limit £	Upper Limit £	Per cent
0	15,000	Nil
15,000	18,000	5
18,000	23,000	7
23,000	33,000	10
33,000	43,000	13
43,000	53,000	16
53,000	63,000	19
63,000	73,000	22
73,000	88,000	25
88,000	103,000	28
103,000	118,000	31
118,000	133,000	34
133,000	148,000	37
148,000	163,000	40
163,000	178,000	43

Portion of value		Rate of tax
Lower Limit £	Upper Limit £	Per cent
178,000	193,000	46
193,000	208,000	49
208,000	–	50

Table III

Applicable where the donee or successor is a brother or a sister, or a child of a brother or of a sister, of the disponer.

Portion of value		Rate of tax
Lower Limit £	Upper Limit £	Per cent
0	10,000	Nil
10,000	13,000	10
13,000	18,000	12
18,000	28,000	15
28,000	38,000	19
38,000	48,000	23
48,000	58,000	27
58,000	68,000	31
68,000	83,000	35
83,000	98,000	40
98,000	113,000	45
113,000	–	50

Table IV

Applicable where the donee or successor does not stand to the disponer in a relationship referred to in Table I, II or III of this Part of this Schedule.

Portion of value		Rate of tax
Lower Limit £	Upper Limit £	Per cent
0	5,000	Nil
5,000	8,000	20
8,000	13,000	22
13,000	23,000	25
23,000	33,000	30

Portion of value		Rate of tax
Lower Limit £	Upper Limit £	Per cent
33,000	43,000	35
43,000	53,000	40
53,000	63,000	45
63,000	78,000	50
78,000	93,000	55
93,000	—	60

FINANCE ACT, 1976

Number 16 of 1976
(Enacted on 27th May, 1976)

———

PART I – Chapter VI

Income Tax, Sur-Tax, Corporation Profits Tax, Corporation Tax and Capital Gains Tax

Section 29[1]

Interest on unpaid wealth tax and capital acquisitions tax.

29.   Interest payable under section 18 of the Wealth Tax Act, 1975, or section 41 of the Capital Acquisitions Tax Act, 1976, shall not be allowed in computing any income, profits or losses for any of the purposes of the Tax Acts or of any of the enactments relating to corporation profits tax.

Footnote

1.   Substituted, with effect from 6th April, 1997, by s.1089(2), TCA.

Section 34

Inspection of documents and records.

34.   (1)   In this section—

"an authorised officer" means an inspector or other officer of the Revenue Commissioners authorised by them to exercise the powers conferred by this section;

"trade" means any trade or business (other than banking business within the meaning of the Central Bank Act, 1971).

(2)   An authorised officer may at all reasonable times enter any premises or place where any trade is carried on or anything is done in connection with the trade and—

(a)   may require the owner or manager of the premises or place or any person on the premises or in that place who is employed by the person carrying on the trade to produce any books, records, accounts or other documents relating to the trade and may remove and retain any such books, records, accounts or other documents for such period as may be reasonable for their examination,

(b)   may examine any such books, records, accounts or other documents and may take copies of or extracts from the books, records, accounts or other documents,

(c) may examine any property listed in any balance sheets, stock sheets or other such statements,

(d) may require the owner or manager of the premises or place or any person on the premises or in that place, who is employed by the person carrying on the trade, to give to the inspector or authorised officer all reasonable assistance.

(3) A person shall not wilfully obstruct or delay an authorised officer in the exercise of his powers under this section.

(4) A person who contravenes subsection (3) or does not comply with a requirement of an authorised officer under this section shall be liable to a penalty of £500.

(5) When exercising any powers conferred by this section, an authorised officer shall, if so requested by any person affected, produce to that person a certificate of the Revenue Commissioners stating that he is authorised to exercise the powers so conferred.

Footnote

1   This section was substituted by s.232, FA 1992, (enacted on 28th May, 1992) and was in turn substituted by s.905, TCA, with effect from 6th April, 1997.

FINANCE ACT, 1977

Number 18 of 1977
(Enacted on 1st June, 1977)

PART V
Miscellaneous

Section 53

Residence treatment of donors of gifts to the State.

53. (1) In this section —

"the Acts" means —

(a) the Tax Acts,

(b) the Capital Gains Tax Act, 1975,

(c) the Wealth Tax Act, 1975, and

(d) the Capital Acquisitions Tax Act, 1976;

"donor" means an individual who makes a gift to the State;

"gift" means a gift of property to the State which, upon acceptance of the gift by the Government pursuant to the State Property Act, 1954, becomes vested, pursuant to that Act, in a State authority within the meaning of that Act;

"Irish tax" means any tax imposed by the Acts;

"property" includes interests and rights of any description;

"relevant date", in relation to an individual (being a donor or spouse of a donor), means the date (being a date not earlier than the 1st day of September, 1974) on which he leaves the State for the purpose of residence (other than occasional residence) outside the State;

"tax in that country" means any tax imposed in that country which is identical with or substantially similar to Irish tax;

"visits" means —

(a) in relation to a donor, visits by him to the State after the relevant date for the purpose of advising on the management of the property which is the subject of the gift, being visits that are, in the aggregate, less than 182 days in any year of assessment in which they are made, and

(b) in relation to the spouse of a donor, visits by the said spouse when accompanying the donor on visits of the kind referred to in paragraph (a).

(2) Where, for any year of assessment, a person (being a donor or the spouse of a donor) is resident in a country outside the State for the purposes of tax in that country and is chargeable to that tax without

any limitation as to chargeability, then, notwithstanding anything to the contrary in the Tax Acts—

(a)   as respects the year of assessment in which the relevant date occurs, that person shall not, as from the relevant date, be regarded as ordinarily resident in the State for the purposes of Irish tax, and

(b)   as respects any subsequent year of assessment, in determining whether that person is resident or ordinarily resident in the State for the purposes of Irish tax, visits shall be disregarded.

Section 54

Repeals.

54.   (1) ....

(3) (a)   The enactment mentioned in column (2) of Part IV of the Second Schedule to this Act is hereby repealed to the extent specified in column (3) of that Part in relation to a gift or inheritance in respect of which the date of the gift or the date of the inheritance, as the case may be, is on or after the date of the passing of this Act.

(b)   In paragraph (a) "gift", "inheritance", "date of the gift" and "date of the inheritance" have the meanings assigned to them by section 2 of the Capital Acquisitions Tax Act, 1976.

SECOND SCHEDULE
Enactments Repealed

PART IV

Number and Year (1)	Short title (2)	Extent of Repeal (3)
No. 8 of 1976	Capital Acquisitions Tax Act, 1976	Section 67(4)

FINANCE ACT, 1978

Number 21 of 1978
(Enacted on 5th July, 1978)

PART VI

Capital Acquisitions Tax

Section 39

Extension of section 55 (exemption of certain objects) of Capital Acquisitions Tax Act, 1976.

39. (1) Section 55 of the Capital Acquisitions Tax Act, 1976, shall apply, as it applies to the objects specified therein, to a house or garden that is situated in the State and is not held for the purposes of trading and—

    (a) which, on a claim being made to the Commissioners, appears to them to be of national, scientific, historic or artistic interest,

    (b) in respect of which reasonable facilities for viewing were allowed to members of the public from the date of the passing of this Act to the date of the gift or the date of the inheritance, or during the three years immediately before the date of the gift or the date of the inheritance, and

    (c) in respect of which reasonable facilities for viewing are allowed to members of the public,

with the modification that the reference in subsection (4) of that section to subsection (1) (b) or (c) of that section shall be construed as a reference to paragraph (c) of this subsection and with any other necessary modifications.

(2) This section shall apply where the date of the gift or the date of the inheritance is on or after the date of the passing of this Act.

Section 40

Amendment of section 57 (exemption of certain securities) of Capital Acquisitions Tax Act, 1976.

40. (1) Section 57 of the Capital Acquisitions Tax Act, 1976, is hereby amended by the substitution for subsections (2) and (3) of the following subsections:

    "(2) Securities, or units (within the meaning of the Unit Trusts Act, 1972) of a unit trust scheme, comprised in a gift or an inheritance taken on or after the 14th day of April, 1978, shall be exempt from tax (and shall not be taken into account in computing tax on any gift or inheritance taken by the donee or successor from the same disponer) if, but only if, it is shown to the satisfaction of the Commissioners that—

(a) the securities or units were comprised in the disposition continuously for a period from the date aforesaid to the date of the gift or the date of the inheritance, or continuously for a period of three years immediately before the date of the gift or the date of the inheritance, and any period immediately before the date of the disposition during which the securities or units were continuously in the beneficial ownership of the disponer shall be deemed, for the purposes of this paragraph, to be a period or part of a period immediately before the date of the gift or the date of the inheritance during which they were continuously comprised in the disposition;

(b) the securities or units were comprised in the gift or inheritance—

(i) at the date of the gift or the date of the inheritance; and

(ii) at the valuation date; and

(c) the donee or successor is at the date of the gift or the date of the inheritance neither domiciled nor ordinarily resident in the State,

and the provisions of section 19 (6) shall apply, for the purposes of this subsection, as they apply in relation to agricultural property.

(3) Subsection (2) (a) shall not apply in a case where the disponer was neither domiciled nor ordinarily resident in the State at the date of the disposition, or at the date of the gift or the date of the inheritance.".

(2) This section shall have and be deemed to have had effect only in relation to securities or units comprised in a gift or an inheritance where the date of the gift or the date of the inheritance is on or after the 14th day of April, 1978.

Section 41

Alteration of rates of tax.

41. The Second Schedule to the Capital Acquisitions Tax Act, 1976, is hereby amended, as respects taxable gifts and taxable inheritances taken on or after the 1st day of April, 1978, by the substitution of the Part set out in the Third Schedule to this Act for Part II.

Section 42

Amendment of section 36 (delivery of returns) of Capital Acquisitions Tax Act, 1976.

42. (1) Section 36 of the Capital Acquisitions Tax Act, 1976, is hereby amended by the substitution for subsection (3) of the following subsection —

"(3) Subsection (2) applies to a gift where —

    (a) the taxable value of such gift, so far as it is a taxable gift, exceeds an amount which is 80 per cent. of the lowest value upon which, at the date of such gift, tax becomes chargeable in respect of a gift taken by the donee of such gift from the disponer thereof,

    (b) the taxable value of such gift, so far as it is a taxable gift, falls to be aggregated with previous gifts taken by the donee of such gift from the disponer thereof and thereby increases the total taxable value of all taxable gifts taken by such donee from such disponer from an amount which is less than or equal to the amount specified in paragraph (a) to an amount which exceeds the amount so specified,

    (c) the taxable value of such gift, so far as it is a taxable gift, falls to be aggregated with previous gifts taken by the donee of such gift from the disponer thereof and thereby increases the total taxable value of all taxable gifts taken by such donee from such disponer from an amount which is greater than the amount specified in paragraph (a), or

    (d) the donee is required by notice in writing by the Commissioners to deliver a return.".

    (2) Subsection (1) of this section shall be deemed to have come into operation on the 31st day of March, 1976.

Section 43

Amendment of section 41 (payment of tax and interest on tax) of Capital Acquisitions Tax Act, 1976.

43. Section 41 (2) of the Capital Acquisitions Tax Act, 1976, shall have effect, in its application to interest accruing due after the date of the passing of this Act, as if "1.25 per cent." were substituted for "one and one-half per cent."

Section 44

Amendment of section 53 (exemption of small gifts) of Capital Acquisitions Tax Act, 1976.

44. Section 53 (1) of the Capital Acquisitions Tax Act, 1976, shall have effect, as respects relevant periods ending on or after the 31st day of December, 1978, as if "£500" were substituted for "£250".

THIRD SCHEDULE
Rates of Capital Acquisitions Tax

"PART II
Table I

Applicable where the donee or successor is the spouse, child, or minor child of a deceased child of the disponer

Portion of value		Rate of tax
Lower Limit £	Upper Limit £	Per cent
0	150,000	Nil
150,000	200,000	25
200,000	250,000	30
250,000	300,000	35
300,000	350,000	40
350,000	400,000	45
400,000	–	50

Table II

Applicable where the donee or successor is a lineal ancestor or a lineal descendant (other than a child, or a minor child of a deceased child) of the disponer.

Portion of value		Rate of tax
Lower Limit £	Upper Limit £	Per cent
0	30,000	Nil
30,000	33,000	5
33,000	38,000	7
38,000	48,000	10
48,000	58,000	13

Portion of value		Rate of tax
Lower Limit £	Upper Limit £	Per cent
58,000	68,000	16
68,000	78,000	19
78,000	88,000	22
88,000	103,000	25
103,000	118,000	28
118,000	133,000	31
133,000	148,000	34
148,000	163,000	37
163,000	178,000	40
178,000	193,000	43
193,000	208,000	46
208,000	223,000	49
223,000	–	50

Table III

Applicable where the donee or successor is a brother or a sister, or a child of a brother or of a sister, of the disponer.

Portion of value		Rate of tax
Lower Limit £	Upper Limit £	Per cent
0	20,000	Nil
20,000	23,000	10
23,000	28,000	12
28,000	38,000	15
38,000	48,000	19
48,000	58,000	23
58,000	68,000	27
68,000	78,000	31
78,000	93,000	35
93,000	108,000	40
108,000	123,000	45
123,000	–	50

Table IV

Applicable where the donee or successor does not stand to the disponer in a relationship referred to in Table I, II or III of this Part of this Schedule.

Portion of value		Rate of tax
Lower Limit £	Upper Limit £	Per cent
0	10,000	Nil
10,000	13,000	20
13,000	18,000	22
18,000	28,000	25
28,000	38,000	30
38,000	48,000	35
48,000	58,000	40
58,000	68,000	45
68,000	83,000	50
83,000	98,000	55
98,000	—	60

"

FINANCE ACT, 1980

Number 14 of 1980
(Enacted on 25th June, 1980)

PART IV
Capital Acquisitions Tax

Section 83

Amendment of section 19 of Capital Acquisitions Tax Act, 1976.

83.   Section 19 of the Capital Acquisitions Tax Act, 1976, shall, as respects a gift or inheritance taken on or after the 1st day of April, 1980, have effect as if "£150,000" were substituted for "£100,000" in each place where it occurs.

Section 84

Amendment of section 35 of Capital Acquisitions Tax Act, 1976.

84.   Section 35 of the Capital Acquisitions Tax Act, 1976, shall, as respects a gift taken on or after the 28th day of February, 1974, or an inheritance taken on or after the 1st day of April, 1975, have effect as if after "therefor" in subsection (7) there were inserted "unless—

(a)   the latter person is the donee or successor referred to in paragraph (a) of subsection (1) and the interest taken by him is a limited interest, or

(b)   in the case referred to in paragraph (b) of the said subsection (1), the latter person is the transferee and the interest taken by the remainderman is a limited interest".

FINANCE ACT, 1981

Number 16 of 1981
(Enacted on 28th May, 1981)

PART IV
Capital Acquisitions Tax

Section 46

Relief in respect of certain marriage settlements.

46. (1) Part I of the Second Schedule to the Capital Acquisitions Tax Act, 1976, is hereby amended by the insertion after paragraph 9 of the following paragraph:

"10. (a) In this paragraph 'specified disposition' means a disposition—

(i) the date of which is a date prior to the 1st day of April, 1975,

(ii) in relation to which the disponer is a grandparent of the donee or successor, and

(iii) in which the marriage of the parents of the donee or successor was, at the date of the disposition, expressed to be the consideration.

(b) Where, on the cesser of a limited interest to which a parent of the donee or successor was entitled in possession, the donee or successor takes a gift or an inheritance under a specified disposition, then, for the purpose of computing the tax payable on the gift or inheritance, the donee or successor shall be deemed to bear to the disponer the relationship of a child.".

(2) Notwithstanding the provisions of section 46 of the Capital Acquisitions Tax Act, 1976, interest shall not be payable on any repayment of tax which arises by virtue of this section where such tax was paid prior to the date of the passing of this Act.

Part VI
Miscellaneous

Section 52

Disclosure of information to the Ombudsman.

52. Any obligation to maintain secrecy or other restriction upon the disclosure or production of information (including documents) obtained by or furnished to the Revenue Commissioners, or any person on their behalf, for taxation purposes, shall not apply to the disclosure or production of information (including documents) to the Ombudsman for the purposes of an examination or investigation by the Ombudsman, under the Ombudsman Act, 1980, of any action (within the meaning of the Ombudsman Act, 1980) taken by or on behalf of the Revenue Commissioners, being such an action taken in the performance of administrative functions in respect of any tax or duty under the care and management of the Revenue Commissioners.

FINANCE ACT, 1982

Number 14 of 1982

(Enacted on 17th July, 1982)

PART V

Capital Acquisitions Tax

Section 97

Interpretation (Part V).

97. In this Part "the Principal Act" means the Capital Acquisitions Tax Act, 1976.

Section 98

Exemption of certain benefits.

98. Where a gift or an inheritance is taken, by direction of the disponer, free of tax on or after the date of the passing of this Act, the benefit taken shall be deemed to include the amount of tax chargeable on such gift or inheritance but not the amount of tax chargeable on such tax.

Section 99

Amendment of section 5 (gift deemed to be taken) of [the Capital Acquisitions Tax Act, 1976].

99. Section 5 (6) of [the Capital Acquisitions Tax Act, 1976,] shall, as respects a gift or inheritance deemed to be taken on or after the 2nd day of June, 1982, have effect as if —

(a) in paragraph (a), ", before the 28th day of February, 1974," were deleted, and

(b) in paragraph (b), "prior to the 28th day of February, 1974" were deleted.

Section 100

Amendment of section 19 (value of agricultural property) of [the Capital Acquisitions Tax Act, 1976].

100. Section 19 of the [the Capital Acquisitions Tax Act, 1976,] shall, as respects a gift or inheritance taken on after the 1st day of April, 1982, have effect as if "£200,000" were substituted for "£150,000" (inserted by the Finance Act, 1980) in each place where it occurs.

Section 101

Amendment of section 36 (delivery of returns) of [the Capital Acquisitions Tax Act, 1976].

101. (1) Section 36 of the [the Capital Acquisitions Tax Act, 1976,] is hereby amended by the substitution of the following subsection for subsection (3) (inserted by the Finance Act, 1978) –

"(3) Subsection (2) applies to a gift where –

(a) the taxable value of such gift, so far as it is a taxable gift, exceeds an amount which is 80 per cent of the lowest value upon which, at the date of such gift, tax becomes chargeable in respect of a gift taken by the donee of such gift from the disponer thereof,

(b) the taxable value of such gift, so far as it is a taxable gift, falls to be aggregated with gifts taken by the donee of such gift, either on or before the date of such gift, from any disponer and thereby increases the total taxable value of all taxable gifts so aggregated taken by such donee from any disponer from an amount which is less than or equal to the amount specified in paragraph (a) to an amount which exceeds the amount so specified,

(c) the taxable value of such gift, so far as it is a taxable gift, falls to be aggregated with gifts taken by the donee of such gift, either on or before the date of such gift, from any disponer and thereby increases the total taxable value of all taxable gifts so aggregated taken by such donee from any disponer from an amount which is greater than the amount specified in paragraph (a), or

(d) the donee is required by notice in writing by the Commissioners to deliver a return,

and for the purposes of this subsection, a reference to a gift or to a taxable gift includes a reference to a part of a gift or to a part of a taxable gift, as the case may be."

(2) This section shall have effect in relation to gifts taken on or after the 2nd day of June, 1982.

Section 102

Amendment of Second Schedule to [the Capital Acquisitions Tax Act, 1976].

102. (1) The Second Schedule to the [the Capital Acquisitions Tax Act, 1976,] is hereby amended –

(a) in Part I –

(i) by the substitution of the following paragraphs for paragraphs 3, 4 and 7:

"3. Subject to the provisions of paragraph 6, the tax chargeable on the taxable value of a taxable gift or a taxable inheritance, in the case where the donee or successor has taken no other taxable gift or taxable inheritance on or after the 2nd day of June, 1982, to which the same appropriate Table applied, shall be computed at the rate or rates of tax applicable to that taxable value under that appropriate Table.

4. Subject to the provisions of paragraph 6, the tax chargeable on the taxable value of a taxable gift or a taxable inheritance, in the case where the donee or successor has previously taken one or more taxable gifts or taxable inheritances on or after the 2nd day of June, 1982, to which the same appropriate Table applied, shall be computed at the rate or rates of tax applicable under that appropriate Table to such part of the aggregate of —

    (a) that taxable value; and

    (b) the taxable values of all such previous taxable gifts and taxable inheritances,

    as is the highest part of that aggregate and is equal to that taxable value.

7. For the purposes of this Schedule, all gifts and inheritances taken by a donee or successor from one disponer, or several disponers, on the same day shall count as one where the same appropriate Table applies to all such gifts and inheritances, and to ascertain the amount of tax payable on one gift or inheritance of several so taken on the same day, the amount of tax computed under this Schedule as being payable on all such gifts or inheritances taken on that day, and counted as one, shall be apportioned rateably, according to the taxable values of the several taxable gifts and taxable inheritances so taken on the same day.",
    and

(ii) by the insertion after paragraph 10 (inserted by the Finance Act, 1981) of the following paragraph:

"11. For the purposes of this Schedule, a reference to a gift or an inheritance, or to a taxable gift or a taxable inheritance, includes a reference to a part of a gift or an inheritance, or to a part of a taxable gift or a taxable inheritance, as the case may be.",
and

(b) in paragraph 1 of Part I and in Part II, by the insertion of "or disponers" after "disponer", in each place where it occurs.

(2) This section shall have effect in relation to gifts and inheritances taken on or after the 2nd day of June, 1982.

FINANCE ACT, 1983

Number 15 of 1983
(Enacted on 8th June, 1983)

PART I – CHAPTER IV
Anti-avoidance and Anti-evasion

Section 23

Publication of names of tax defaulters.

23. (1) In this section "the Acts" means —

    (a) the Tax Acts,

    (b) the Capital Gains Tax Acts,

    (c) the Value-Added Tax Act, 1972, and the enactments amending or extending that Act,

    (d) the Capital Acquisitions Tax Act, 1976, and the enactments amending or extending that Act,

    (e) the statutes relating to stamp duty and to the management of that duty, and

    (f) Part VI,

and any instruments made thereunder.

(2) The Revenue Commissioners shall, as respects each year (being the year 1984 or a subsequent year), compile a list of the names and addresses and the occupations or descriptions of every person —

    (a) upon whom a fine or other penalty was imposed by a court under any of the Acts during that year,

    (b) upon whom a fine or other penalty was otherwise imposed by a court during that year in respect of an act or omission by the person in relation to tax, or

    (c) in whose case the Revenue Commissioners, pursuant to an agreement made with the person in that year, refrained from initiating proceedings for recovery of any fine or penalty of the kind mentioned in paragraphs (a) and (b) and, in lieu of initiating such proceedings, accepted, or undertook to accept, a specified sum of money in settlement of any claim by the Revenue Commissioners in respect of any specified liability of the person under any of the Acts for —

    (i) payment of any tax,

    (ii) payment of interest thereon, and

    (iii) a fine or other monetary penalty in respect thereof.

(3) Notwithstanding any obligation as to secrecy imposed on them by the Acts or the Official Secrets Act, 1963 –

    (a) the Revenue Commissioners shall include in their annual report to the Minister for Finance, commencing with the report for the year 1984, the list referred to in subsection (2) for the year in respect of which the report is made, and

    (b) the Revenue Commissioners may, at any time, cause any such list as is referred to in subsection (2) to be published in Iris Oifigiúil.

(4) Paragraph (c) of subsection (2) does not apply in relation to a person in whose case –

    (a) the Revenue Commissioners are satisfied that, before any investigation or inquiry had been commenced by them or by any of their officers into any matter occasioning a liability referred to in the said paragraph of the person, the person had voluntarily furnished to them complete information in relation to and full particulars of the said matter, or

    (b) the specified sum referred to in the said paragraph (c) does not exceed £10,000 or was paid on or before the 31st day of December, 1983.

(5) Any such list as is referred to in subsection (2) shall specify in respect of each person named in the list such particulars as the Revenue Commissioners think fit –

    (a) of the matter occasioning the fine or penalty of the kind referred to in subsection (2) imposed on the person or, as the case may be, the liability of that kind to which the person was subject, and

    (b) of any interest, fine or other monetary penalty, and of any other penalty or sanction, to which that person was liable, or which was imposed on him by a court, and which was occasioned by the said matter.

(6) In this section "tax" means income tax, capital gains tax, corporation tax, value-added tax, gift tax, inheritance tax, residential property tax and stamp duty.

PART V

Revenue Offences

Section 94

Revenue offences.

94. (1) In this Part –

    "the Acts" means –

    (a) the Customs Acts,

(b) the statutes relating to the duties of excise and to the management of those duties,

(c) the Tax Acts,

(d) the Capital Gains Tax Acts,

(e) the Value-Added Tax Act, 1972, and the enactments amending or extending that Act,

(f) the Capital Acquisitions Tax Act, 1976, and the enactments amending or extending that Act,

(g) the statutes relating to stamp duty and to the management of that duty, and

(h) Part VI,

and any instruments made thereunder and any instruments made under any other enactment and relating to tax;

"tax" means any tax, duty, levy or charge under the care and management of the Revenue Commissioners.

(2) A person shall, without prejudice to any other penalty to which he may be liable, be guilty of an offence under this section if, after the date of the passing of this Act, he —

(a) knowingly or wilfully delivers any incorrect return, statement or accounts or knowingly or wilfully furnishes any incorrect information in connection with any tax,

(b) knowingly aids, abets, assists, incites or induces another person to make or deliver knowingly or wilfully any incorrect return, statement or accounts in connection with any tax,

(c) claims or obtains relief or exemption from, or repayment of, any tax, being a relief, exemption or repayment to which, to his knowledge, he is not entitled,

(d) knowingly or wilfully issues or produces any incorrect invoice, receipt, instrument or other document in connection with any tax,

(e) knowingly or wilfully fails to comply with any provision of the Acts requiring —

(i) the furnishing of a return of income, profits or gains, or of sources of income, profits or gains, for the purposes of any tax,

(ii) the furnishing of any other return, certificate, notification, particulars, or any statement or evidence, for the purposes of any tax,

(iii) the keeping or retention of books, records, accounts or other documents for the purposes of any tax, or

        (iv) the production of books, records, accounts or other documents, when so requested, for the purposes of any tax,

    (f) fails to remit any income tax payable pursuant to Chapter IV of Part V of the Income Tax Act, 1967, and the regulations thereunder, or section 7 of the Finance Act, 1968, and the said regulations, or value-added tax within the time specified in that behalf in relation to income tax or value-added tax, as the case may be, by the Acts, or

    (g) obstructs or interferes with any officer of the Revenue Commissioners, or any other person, in the exercise or performance of powers or duties under the Acts for the purposes of any tax.

(3) A person guilty of an offence under this section shall be liable –

    (a) on summary conviction, to a fine not exceeding £1,000 or, at the discretion of the court, to imprisonment for a term not exceeding 12 months or to both the fine and the imprisonment, or

    (b) on conviction on indictment, to a fine not exceeding £10,000 or, at the discretion of the court, to imprisonment for a term not exceeding 5 years or to both the fine and the imprisonment.

(4) Section 13 of the Criminal Procedure Act, 1967, shall apply in relation to an offence under this section as if, in lieu of the penalties specified in subsection (3) of the said section 13, there were specified therein the penalties provided for by subsection (3) (a) of this section, and the reference in subsection (2) (a) of the said section 13 to the penalties provided for in the said subsection (3) shall be construed and have effect accordingly.

(5) Where an offence under this section is committed by a body corporate and the offence is shown to have been committed with the consent or connivance of any person who, when the offence was committed, was a director, manager, secretary or other officer of the body corporate, or a member of the committee of management or other controlling authority of the body corporate, that person shall also be deemed to be guilty of the offence and may be proceeded against and punished accordingly.

(6) In any proceedings under this section, a return or statement delivered to an inspector or other officer of the Revenue Commissioners under any provision of the Acts and purporting to be signed by any person shall be deemed, until the contrary is proved, to have been so delivered, and to have been signed, by that person.

(7) Notwithstanding the provisions of any other enactment, proceedings in respect of an offence under this section may be instituted within 10 years from the date of the commission of the offence or incurring of the penalty (as the case may be).

(8) Section 1 of the Probation of Offenders Act, 1907, shall not apply in relation to offences under this section.

(9) The provisions of sections 128 (4), 500 (4), 501 (3), 502 (3), 506 and 507 of the Income Tax Act, 1967, and sections 26 (6) and 27 (7) of the Value-Added Tax Act, 1972, shall, with any necessary modifications, apply for the purposes of this section as they apply for the purposes of those provisions, including, in the case of such of those provisions as were applied by the Capital Gains Tax Act, 1975, the Corporation Tax Act, 1976, or Part VI, the purposes of those provisions as so applied.

FINANCE ACT, 1984

Number 9 of 1984
(Enacted on 23rd May, 1984)

PART V

Capital Acquisitions Tax

CHAPTER I

Discretionary Trusts

Section 104

Interpretation (Part V).
104. In this Part—

"the Principal Act" means the Capital Acquisitions Tax Act, 1976;

"object", in relation to a discretionary trust, means a person for whose benefit the income or capital, or any part of the income or capital, of the trust property is applied, or may be applied;

"principal objects", in relation to a discretionary trust, means such objects, if any, of the trust for the time being as are—

(a) the spouse of the disponer,

(b) the children of the disponer, or

(c) the children of a child of the disponer where such child predeceased the disponer.

Section 105

Amendment of section 2 (interpretation) of [the Capital Acquisitions Tax Act, 1976].
105. Section 2 (1) of the [the Capital Acquisitions Tax Act, 1976,] is hereby amended by the insertion, in the definition of "discretionary trust" after "property is held on trust" of—

"to accumulate the income or part of the income of the property, or any trust whereby, or by virtue or in consequence of which, property (other than property to which for the time being a person is beneficially entitled for an interest in possession) is held on trust",

and the said definition, as so amended, is set out in the Table to this section.

TABLE

"discretionary trust" means any trust whereby, or by virtue or in consequence of which, property is held on trust to accumulate the income or part of the income of the property, or any trust whereby, or by virtue or in consequence of which, property (other than property to which for the time being a person is beneficially entitled for an interest in possession) is held on trust to apply, or with a power to apply, the income or capital or part of the income or capital of the property for the benefit of any person or persons or of any one or more of a number or of a class of persons whether at the discretion of trustees or any other person and notwithstanding that there may be a power to accumulate all or any part of the income;

Section 106

Acquisitions by discretionary trusts.

106. (1) Where, on or after the 25th day of January, 1984, under or in consequence of any disposition, property becomes subject to a discretionary trust (which expression has in this Part the meaning assigned to it by [the Capital Acquisitions Tax Act, 1976,] as amended by section 105) otherwise than for full consideration in money or money's worth paid by the trustees of the trust, the trust shall be deemed, on—

(a) the date on which that property becomes or became subject to the discretionary trust;

(b) the date of death of the disponer; or

(c) where there are principal objects of the trust, the date on which there ceases to be a principal object of the trust who is under the age of 25 years,

whichever date is the latest, to become or to have become beneficially entitled in possession to an absolute interest in so much, if any, of that property or of property representing that property and of accumulations of income thereof or of property representing those accumulations as remains subject to the discretionary trust on that latest date, and to take or to have taken an inheritance accordingly as if the trust, and the trustees as such for the time being of the trust, were together a person for the purposes of [the Capital Acquisitions Tax Act, 1976], and that latest date shall be the date of the inheritance.

(2) Property which, under or in consequence of any disposition, was subject to a discretionary trust on the 25th day of January, 1984, shall, for the purposes of subsection (1), be deemed to have become subject to the trust on that date.

(3) For the purposes of this section—

(a) an interest in expectancy shall not be property until an event happens whereby the interest ceases to be an interest in expectancy or is represented by property which is not an interest in expectancy;

(b) an interest in a policy of assurance upon human life shall not be property until, and then only to the extent that, the interest becomes an interest in possession under the provisions of section 32 of [the Capital Acquisitions Tax Act, 1976,] or is represented by property which is not an interest in expectancy.

(4) Where, apart from this subsection, property or property representing such property would be chargeable under this section with tax more than once under the same disposition, such property shall be so chargeable with tax once only, that is to say, on the earliest occasion on which such property becomes so chargeable with tax.

Section 107

Application of [the Capital Acquisitions Tax Act, 1976].

107. In relation to a charge for tax arising by reason of the provisions of section 106 —

(a) a reference in section 16 of [the Capital Acquisitions Tax Act, 1976,] to a company controlled by the successor shall be construed as including a reference to a company that is under the control of any one or more of the following, that is to say, the trustees of the discretionary trust, the living objects of the discretionary trust, the relatives of those objects, and nominees of those trustees or of those objects or of the relatives of those objects;

(b) section 21 of [the Capital Acquisitions Tax Act, 1976,] shall apply, with the modification that the valuation date of the taxable inheritance shall be —

(i) the date of the inheritance, or

(ii) the valuation date ascertained in accordance with that section,

whichever is the later, and with any other necessary modifications;

(c) a person who is a trustee of the discretionary trust concerned for the time being at the date of the inheritance or at any date subsequent thereto shall be a person primarily accountable for the payment of the tax;

(d) an object of the discretionary trust concerned to whom or for whose benefit any of the property subject to the trust is applied or appointed shall also be accountable for the payment of tax the charge in respect of which has arisen prior to the date of the application or appointment of the property to him or for his benefit, and [the Capital Acquisitions Tax Act, 1976,] shall have effect, in its application to that charge for tax, as if that object of the discretionary trust were a person referred to in section 35 (2) of [the Capital Acquisitions Tax Act, 1976];

(e) any person who is primarily accountable for the payment of tax by virtue of paragraph (c) shall, within three months after the valuation date or the date of the passing of this Act, whichever is the later, deliver to the Commissioners a full and true return –

    (i) of every inheritance in respect of which he is so primarily accountable;

    (ii) of all the property comprised in such inheritance; and

    (iii) of an estimate of the market value of such property;

(f) the provisions of section 41 of [the Capital Acquisitions Tax Act, 1976,] shall have effect, in the application of [the Capital Acquisitions Tax Act, 1976,] to any such charge for tax as aforesaid arising before the date of the passing of this Act, as if the references to the valuation date in subsections (1), (2) and (3) of that section were references to the date of the passing of this Act, or to the valuation date, whichever is the later; and

(g) section 35 (1), subsections (2), (3), (4) and (5) of section 36 and sections 40, 45 and 57 of, and the Second Schedule to, [the Capital Acquisitions Tax Act, 1976,] shall not apply.

Section 108

Exemptions.

108. Section 106 shall not apply or have effect in relation to a discretionary trust which is shown to the satisfaction of the Commissioners to have been created exclusively –

(a) for public or charitable purposes in the State or Northern Ireland;

(b) for the purposes of –

    (i) any scheme for the provision of superannuation benefits on retirement established by or under any enactment or by or under an instrument made under any enactment, or

    (ii) any sponsored superannuation scheme within the meaning of subsection (9) of section 235 of the Income Tax Act, 1967, or a trust scheme or part of a trust scheme approved by the Commissioners under that section or section 235A of that Act;

(c) for the purposes of a registered unit trust scheme within the meaning of the Unit Trusts Act, 1972;

(d) (i) for the benefit of one or more named individuals, and

    (ii) for the reason that such individual, or all such individuals, is or are, because of age or improvidence, or of physical, mental or legal incapacity, incapable of managing his or their affairs; or

(e) for the purpose of providing for the upkeep of a house or garden referred to in section 39 of the Finance Act, 1978.

Section 109

Computation of tax.

109. The tax chargeable on the taxable value of a taxable inheritance which is charged to tax by reason of the provisions of section 106 shall be computed at the rate of three per cent. of such taxable value.

CHAPTER II
Revised Computation

Section 110

Amendment of certain sections of [the Capital Acquisitions Tax Act, 1976].

110. (1) Section 36 of [the Capital Acquisitions Tax Act, 1976,] is hereby amended by the substitution of the following subsection for subsections (3) and (4):

"(3) Subsection (2) applies to a gift where—

(a) the aggregate of the taxable values of all taxable gifts taken by the donee on or after the 2nd day of June, 1982, exceeds an amount which is 80 per cent. of the threshold amount (as defined in the Second Schedule) which applies in the computation of the tax on that aggregate, or

(b) the donee is required by notice in writing by the Commissioners to deliver a return.".

(2) Sections 9 and 53 (3) of [the Capital Acquisitions Tax Act, 1976,] shall not apply or have effect.

(3) Section 54 of [the Capital Acquisitions Tax Act, 1976,] is hereby amended by the substitution of the following subsection for subsection (1):

"(1) Where any person takes a benefit for public or charitable purposes he

shall be deemed—

(a) for the purposes of sections 5 (1) and 11 (1), to have taken that benefit beneficially, and

(b) for the purposes of the Second Schedule, to have taken a gift or an inheritance accordingly to which the class threshold of £10,000 applies.".

(4) Section 55 of [the Capital Acquisitions Tax Act, 1976] (as extended by the Finance Act, 1978) is hereby amended by the deletion of "from the same disponer" in subsection (2) (a).

(5) Section 57 of [the Capital Acquisitions Tax Act, 1976] (as amended by the Finance Act, 1978) is hereby amended by the deletion of "from the same disponer" in subsection (2).

Section 111

Amendment of Second Schedule to [the Capital Acquisitions Tax Act, 1976].

111. The Second Schedule to [the Capital Acquisitions Tax Act, 1976,] is hereby amended —

(a) in Part I, by the substitution of the following paragraphs for paragraphs 1 to 5 and 7:

"1. In this Schedule —

'class threshold', in relation to a taxable gift or a taxable inheritance taken on a particular day, means —

(a) £150,000, where the donee or successor is on that day the spouse, child, or minor child of a deceased child, of the disponer;

(b) £20,000, where the donee or successor is, on that day, a lineal ancestor, a lineal descendant (other than a child, or a minor child of a deceased child), a brother, a sister, or a child of a brother or of a sister, of the disponer;

(c) £10,000, where the donee or successor does not, on that day, stand to the disponer in a relationship referred to in subparagraph (a) or (b);

'revised class threshold', in relation to a taxable gift or a taxable inheritance included in any aggregate of taxable values under the provisions of paragraph 3, means —

(a) the class threshold that applies to that taxable gift or taxable inheritance, or

(b) the total of the taxable values of all the taxable gifts and taxable inheritances to which that class threshold applies and which are included in that aggregate,

whichever is the lesser:

Provided that where the revised class threshold so ascertained is less than the smallest of the class thresholds that apply in relation to all of the taxable gifts and taxable inheritances included in that aggregate, the revised class threshold shall be that smallest class threshold;

'Table' means the Table contained in Part II of this Schedule;

'threshold amount', in relation to the computation of tax on any aggregate of taxable values under the provisions of paragraph 3, means the greatest of the revised class thresholds that apply in relation to all of the taxable gifts and taxable inheritances included in that aggregate.

2.   In the Table 'value' means the appropriate aggregate referred to in paragraph 3.

3.   Subject to the provisions of paragraph 6, the tax chargeable on the taxable value of a taxable gift or a taxable inheritance taken by a donee or successor shall be of an amount equal to the amount by which the tax, computed at the rate or rates of tax applicable under the Table, on the aggregate of —

(a)   that taxable value; and

(b)   the taxable values of all taxable gifts and taxable inheritances (if any) taken previously by that donee or successor on or after the 2nd day of June, 1982,

exceeds the tax, computed at the rate or rates of tax applicable under the Table, on the aggregate of the taxable values of all taxable gifts and taxable inheritances so previously taken (if any):

Provided that the tax so chargeable on the taxable value of a taxable gift or a taxable inheritance shall not be greater than an amount equal to the tax computed at the rate or rates applicable under the Table to such part of the aggregate of the values referred to in subparagraphs (a) and (b) as is the highest part of that aggregate and is equal to that taxable value.

5.   In the Table any rate of tax shown in the second column is that applicable to such portion of the value (within the meaning of paragraph 2) as is shown in the first column.

7.   For the purposes of this Schedule, all gifts and inheritances taken by a donee or successor on the same day shall (except for the purposes of the determination of the threshold amount) count as one, and to ascertain the amount of tax payable on one gift or inheritance of several taken on the same day, the amount of tax computed under this Schedule as being payable on the total of the gifts and inheritances taken on that day shall be apportioned rateably, according to the taxable values of the several taxable gifts and taxable inheritances taken on that day.".

(b) in Part II, by the substitution of the following Table for Tables I to IV:

TABLE

Portion of Value	Rate of tax
	Per cent.
The threshold amount	Nil
The next £10,000	20
The next £40,000	30
The next £50,000	35
The next £50,000	40
The next £50,000	45
The balance	55

".

Section 112

Application of Chapter II.

112. This Chapter shall have effect in relation to gifts and inheritances taken on or after the 26th day of March, 1984.

CHAPTER III

Certificate of Discharge

Section 113

Extension of section 48 (receipts and certificates) of [the Capital Acquisitions Tax Act, 1976].

113. Section 48 of [the Capital Acquisitions Tax Act, 1976,] is hereby amended, with respect to gifts and inheritances taken on or after the 2nd day of June, 1982, by the insertion after subsection (4) of the following subsections:

"(5) Subject to the provisions of subsection (6), where tax is chargeable on the taxable value of a taxable gift or taxable inheritance and —

    (a) after the expiration of two years from the valuation date of such taxable gift or taxable inheritance, application is made to the Commissioners by any person (in this section referred to as the applicant) —

        (i) who is a person accountable, but not primarily accountable, for the payment of the whole or part of the tax, or

(ii)   who is the personal representative of any person referred to in subparagraph (i),

and

(b)   the applicant delivers to the Commissioners a full statement of all the property comprised in the taxable gift or taxable inheritance and of such particulars as may be relevant to the assessment of the tax, together with such evidence as they require relating to such property or particulars,

the Commissioners may determine the amount of the tax that is recoverable from the applicant, and on payment of the tax so determined, the Commissioners shall give a certificate of their determination, in such form as they think fit, which shall discharge the applicant from any further claim for tax in respect of the taxable gift or taxable inheritance.

(6)   A certificate by the Commissioners under subsection (5) shall not discharge the applicant in the case of fraud or failure to disclose material facts within his own knowledge and shall not affect any further tax that may be payable by the applicant if any further property is afterwards shown to have been comprised in the taxable gift or taxable inheritance to which the certificate relates and in respect of which further property the applicant is liable for the tax.

(7)   The Commissioners may, if they think fit, entertain any application made for the purpose of subsection (5) at whatever time the application is made and, as respects any application so entertained, the provisions of that subsection shall have effect notwithstanding that the application is made before the lapse of the two years mentioned in that subsection.".

AGE OF MAJORITY ACT, 1985

Number 2 of 1985
(Enacted on 12th February, 1985)

Section 2[1]

Reduction of age of majority.

2. (1) Where a person has not attained the age of twenty-one years prior to the commencement of this Act, he shall, subject to section 4, attain full age –

   (a) on such commencement if he has attained the age of eighteen years or is or has been married, or

   (b) after such commencement when he attains the age of eighteen years or, in case he marries before attaining that age, upon his marriage.

   (2) Subsection (1) applies for the purposes of any rule of law and, in the absence of a definition or of any indication of a contrary intention, for the construction of "age of majority", "full age", "infancy", "infant", "minor", "minority" and of other cognate words and expressions in –

   (a) any statutory provision passed or made before, on or after the commencement of this Act, and

   (b) any deed, will, court order or other instrument (not being a statutory provision) made on or after such commencement.

   (3) Where there is, in any statutory provision passed or made before the commencement of this Act, a reference to the age of twenty-one years, such provision shall, subject to subsection (4), be construed and have effect as if the reference therein were a reference to full age.

   (4) (a) This section does not affect the construction of any reference to the age of twenty-one years, or of any word or expression to which subsection (2) relates, in any statutory provision to which this subsection applies.

   (b) This subsection applies to –

   (i) the Marriages (Ireland) Act, 1844,

   (ii) the Marriage Law (Ireland) Amendment Act, 1863,

   (iii) the Matrimonial Causes and Marriage Law (Ireland) Amendment Act, 1870,

   (iv) the Marriages Act, 1972,

   (v) the Adoption Acts, 1952 to 1976,

   (vi) the Social Welfare Acts, 1981 to 1984,

(vii) the Income Tax Acts and any other statutory provision dealing with the imposition, repeal, remission, alteration or regulation of any tax or other duty under the care and management of the Revenue Commissioners,

(viii) any provision of the Illegitimate Children (Affiliation Orders) Act, 1930, the Guardianship of Infants Act, 1964, or the Family Law (Maintenance of Spouses and Children) Act, 1976, that provides for payments to be made for maintenance or support of children up to the age of twenty-one years,

(ix) any statutory provision that provides for the payment of a pension or other allowance for children up to the age of twenty-one years, and

(x) any statutory provision relating to prisons, to Saint Patrick's Institution or to any other place for the custody of persons.

Footnote

1   This section should be read in conjunction with s.112, FA 1986, and s.7, TCA.

FINANCE ACT, 1985

Number 10 of 1985
(Enacted on 30th May, 1985)

PART V

Capital Acquisitions Tax

Section 58

Interpretation (Part V).

58. In this Part "the Principal Act" means the Capital Acquisitions Tax Act, 1976.

Section 59

Exemption for spouses.

59. (1) Notwithstanding the provisions of [the Capital Acquisitions Tax Act, 1976], an inheritance taken by a successor, who is at the date of the inheritance the spouse of the disponer, shall be exempt from tax and shall not be taken into account in computing tax.

(2) This section shall have effect in relation to an inheritance taken on or after the 30th day of January, 1985.

Section 60

Relief in respect of certain policies of insurance.

60. (1) In this section—

"qualifying insurance policy" means a policy of insurance—

(a) which is in a form approved by the Commissioners for the purposes of this section;

(b) in respect of which annual premiums are paid by the insured during his life; and

(c) which is expressly effected under this section for the purpose of paying relevant tax;

"relevant tax" means inheritance tax payable in respect of an inheritance (excluding, in computation of such tax, an interest in a qualifying insurance policy) taken under a disposition made by the insured, where the inheritance is taken on or after the date of death of the insured and not later than one year after that death.

(2) (a) An interest in a qualifying insurance policy which is comprised in an inheritance taken under a disposition made by the insured shall, to the extent that the proceeds thereof are applied in

paying relevant tax, be exempt from tax in relation to that inheritance and shall not be taken into account in computing tax.

(b)   An interest in a qualifying insurance policy which is comprised in an inheritance taken under a disposition made by the insured shall, to the extent that the proceeds thereof are not applied in paying relevant tax, and notwithstanding the provisions of [the Capital Acquisitions Tax Act, 1976], be deemed to be taken on a day immediately after—

(i)   the date of death of the insured; or

(ii)   the latest date (if any) on which an inheritance is taken in respect of which that relevant tax is payable,

whichever is the later.

(3) Section 143 of the Income Tax Act, 1967, is hereby amended by the substitution, in subsection (5), of the following paragraphs for paragraph (b) —

"(b)   be given in respect of premiums or payments payable during the period of deferment in respect of a policy of deferred assurance; or

(c)   be given for the year 1985-86 and subsequent years of assessment in respect of premiums payable in respect of a qualifying insurance policy within the meaning of section 60 of the Finance Act, 1985:".

Section 61

Relief from double aggregation.

61.   (1) Property in respect of which tax is chargeable more than once on the same event shall not be included more than once in relation to that event in any aggregate referred to in the Second Schedule to [the Capital Acquisitions Tax Act, 1976].

(2) Paragraph 7 of Part I of the said Second Schedule shall not have effect in ascertaining the tax payable in respect of property which is chargeable to tax as being taken more than once on the same day.

(3) This section shall have effect in relation to gifts and inheritances taken on or after the 2nd day of June, 1982.

(4) Notwithstanding the provisions of section 46 of [the Capital Acquisitions Tax Act, 1976], interest shall not be payable on any repayment of tax which arises by virtue of this section where such tax was paid prior to the date of the passing of this Act.

Section 62

Allowance for prior tax on the same event.

62. (1) [The Capital Acquisitions Tax Act, 1976,] shall have effect, and shall be deemed always to have had effect, as if the following section were inserted after section 34 of that Act:

"34A. Where tax is charged more than once in respect of the same property on the same event, the net tax payable which is earlier in priority shall not be deducted in ascertaining the taxable value for the purposes of the tax which is later in priority, but shall be deducted from the tax which is later in priority as a credit against the same, up to the net amount of the same.".

(2) Notwithstanding the provisions of section 46 of [the Capital Acquisitions Tax Act, 1976], interest shall not be payable on any repayment of tax which arises by virtue of this section where such tax was paid prior to the date of the passing of this Act.

Section 63

Allowance for capital gains tax on the same event.

63. (1) Where gift tax or inheritance tax is charged in respect of property on an event happening on or after the 30th day of January, 1985, and the same event constitutes for capital gains tax purposes a disposal of an asset (being the same property or any part of the same property), the capital gains tax, if any, chargeable on the disposal shall not be deducted in ascertaining the taxable value for the purposes of the gift tax or inheritance tax but, in so far as it has been paid, shall be deducted from the net gift tax or inheritance tax as a credit against the same, up to the net amount of the same.

(2) For the purposes of any computation of the amount of capital gains tax to be deducted under this section, any necessary apportionments shall be made of any reliefs or expenditure and the method of apportionment adopted shall be such method as appears to the Commissioners, or on appeal to the Appeal Commissioners, to be just and reasonable.

Section 64

Amendment of section 106 (acquisitions by discretionary trusts) of Finance Act, 1984.

64. Section 106 (1) of the Finance Act, 1984, shall have effect, and shall be deemed always to have had effect, as if "otherwise than for full consideration in money or money's worth paid by the trustees of the trust" were deleted.

Section 65

Amendment of section 108 (exemptions) of Finance Act, 1984.

65. Section 108 of the Finance Act, 1984, shall have effect, and shall be deemed always to have had effect, as if the following subsection were added thereto:

"(2) Section 106 shall not apply or have effect—

    (a)   in relation to a discretionary trust in respect of the property subject to or becoming subject to the trust which, on the termination of the trust, is comprised in a gift or an inheritance taken by the State; or

    (b)   in respect of an inheritance which, apart from this subsection, would be deemed, by the combined effect of section 31 of [the Capital Acquisitions Tax Act, 1976,] and section 106, to be taken by a discretionary trust.".

FINANCE ACT, 1986

Number 13 of 1986
(Enacted on 27th May, 1986)

PART I – CHAPTER IV
Interest Payments by Certain Deposit Takers

Section 40

Penalties.
40. (1) ....

(2) Section 94 (2) of the Finance Act, 1983, is hereby amended by the insertion after paragraph (d) of the following paragraph:

"(dd)(i) fails to make any deduction required to be made by him under section 32 (1) of the Finance Act, 1986,

(ii) fails, having made the deduction, to pay the sum deducted to the Collector-General within the time specified in that behalf in section 33 (3) of that Act, or

(iii) fails to pay to the Collector-General an amount on account of appropriate tax (within the meaning of Chapter IV of Part I of that Act) within the time specified in that behalf in section 33 (4) of that Act,".

PART V
Capital Acquisitions Tax

CHAPTER I
Discretionary Trusts

Section 102

Interpretation (Part V).
102. In this Part—

"the Principal Act" means the Capital Acquisitions Tax Act, 1976;

"chargeable date", in relation to any year, means the 5th day of April in that year;

"chargeable discretionary trust" means a discretionary trust in relation to which—

(a) the disponer is dead, and

(b) none of the principal objects of the trust, if any, is under the age of 25 years;

"object" and "principal objects", in relation to a discretionary trust, have the meanings respectively assigned to them by section 104 of the Finance Act, 1984.

Section 103

Annual acquisitions by discretionary trusts.

103. (1) Where, in any year commencing with the year 1986, under or in consequence of any disposition, property is subject to a chargeable discretionary trust on the chargeable date, the trust shall be deemed on each such date to become beneficially entitled in possession to an absolute interest in that property, and to take on each such date an inheritance accordingly as if the trust, and the trustees as such for the time being of the trust, were together a person for the purposes of [the Capital Acquisitions Tax Act, 1976], and each such chargeable date shall be the date of such inheritance.

(2) (a) Where—

(i) under or in consequence of any disposition, property was subject to a discretionary trust prior to a chargeable date,

(ii) that property is not on that chargeable date subject to that discretionary trust (being on that date a chargeable discretionary trust) because such property is on that date property to which for the time being a person is beneficially entitled for an interest in possession, and

(iii) on that chargeable date that property is property which is limited to become subject again to that chargeable discretionary trust, or will do so by the exercise of a power of revocation,

that property shall be deemed to be subject to that chargeable discretionary trust on that chargeable date if that interest in possession is an interest which is revocable or which is limited to cease on an event other than—

(I) the death of that person, or

(II) the expiration of a specified period, where that interest is taken by that person under a power of appointment contained in that disposition and is, at the time of the appointment thereof, an interest for a period certain of five years or more.

(b) In this subsection, "property" includes property representing such property.

(3) For the purposes of this section—

(a) an interest in expectancy shall not be property until an event happens whereby the interest ceases to be an interest in expectancy or is represented by property which is not an interest in expectancy;

(b) an interest in a policy of assurance upon human life shall not be property until, and then only to the extent that, the interest becomes an interest in possession under the provisions of section 32 of [the Capital Acquisitions Tax Act, 1976,] or is represented by property which is not an interest in expectancy.

(4) This section shall not apply or have effect in relation to property which is subject to a chargeable discretionary trust on a chargeable date if that property or property representing that property is subject to a charge for tax arising under or in consequence of the same disposition by reason of the provisions of section 106 of the Finance Act, 1984, on that same date or within the year prior to that date.

Section 104

Application of [the Capital Acquisitions Tax Act, 1976].

104. In relation to a charge for tax arising by reason of the provisions of section 103-

(a) a reference in section 16 of [the Capital Acquisitions Tax Act, 1976,] to a company controlled by the successor shall be construed as including a reference to a company that is under the control of any one or more of the following, that is to say, the trustees of the discretionary trust, the living objects of the discretionary trust, the relatives of those objects, and nominees of those trustees or of those objects or of the relatives of those objects;

(b) (i) subject to the provisions of subparagraph (ii), the valuation date of the taxable inheritance shall be the relevant chargeable date;

(ii) where—

(I) a charge for tax arises on a particular date by reason of the provisions of section 106 of the Finance Act, 1984, giving rise to a taxable inheritance (in this subparagraph called the first taxable inheritance),

(II) on a later date, a charge for tax arises under or in consequence of the same disposition by reason of the provisions of section 103 giving rise to a taxable inheritance (in this subparagraph called the second taxable inheritance) comprising the same property or property representing that property, and

(III) the valuation date of the first taxable inheritance is a date after the chargeable date of the second taxable inheritance, the valuation date of the second taxable inheritance shall be the same date as the valuation date of the first taxable inheritance;

(c) a person who is a trustee of the discretionary trust concerned for the time being at the date of the inheritance or at any date subsequent thereto shall be a person primarily accountable for the payment of the tax;

(d) an object of the discretionary trust concerned to whom or for whose benefit any of the property subject to the trust is applied or appointed shall also be accountable for the payment of tax the charge in respect of which has arisen prior to the date of the application or appointment of the property to him or for his benefit, and [the Capital Acquisitions Tax Act, 1976,] shall have effect, in its application to that charge for tax, as if that object of the discretionary trust were a person referred to in section 35 (2) of [the Capital Acquisitions Tax Act, 1976];

(e) any person who is primarily accountable for the payment of tax by virtue of paragraph (c) shall, within three months after the valuation date or the date of the passing of this Act, whichever is the later —

(i) deliver to the Commissioners a full and true return —

(I) of every inheritance in respect of which he is so primarily accountable;

(II) of all the property comprised in such inheritance; and

(III) of an estimate of the market value of such property;

(ii) notwithstanding the provisions of [the Capital Acquisitions Tax Act, 1976], make an assessment of such amount of tax as, to the best of his knowledge, information and belief, ought to be charged, levied and paid on that valuation date; and

(iii) pay the amount of such tax to the Accountant-General of the Commissioners;

(f) the provisions of section 41 of [the Capital Acquisitions Tax Act, 1976,] shall have effect, in the application of [the Capital Acquisitions Tax Act, 1976,] to any such charge for tax as aforesaid arising before the date of the passing of this Act, as if the references to the valuation date in subsections (1), (2) and (3) of that section were references to the date of the passing of this Act, or to the valuation date, whichever is the later;

and

(g) section 21, subsection (1) of section 35, subsections (2), (3), (4) and (5) of section 36 and sections 40, 43, 45 and 57 of, and the Second Schedule to, [the Capital Acquisitions Tax Act, 1976,] shall not apply.

Section 105

Exemptions.

105. Section 103 shall not apply or have effect in relation to a discretionary trust referred to in section 108 of the Finance Act, 1984, or in respect of the property or the inheritance referred to in section 65 of the Finance Act, 1985.

Section 106

Computation of tax.

106. The tax chargeable on the taxable value of a taxable inheritance which is charged to tax by reason of the provisions of section 103 shall be computed at the rate of one per cent. of such taxable value.

Section 107

Values agreed.

107. (1) Where—

   (a) under or in consequence of any disposition, a charge for tax arises by reason of the provisions of section 103 on a chargeable date (in this section called the first chargeable date),

   (b) an accountable person has furnished all the information necessary to enable the Commissioners to ascertain the market value of—

   (i) real property, or

   (ii) shares which are not dealt in on a stock exchange,

   comprised in the taxable inheritance so taken on the valuation date of that taxable inheritance,

   (c) pursuant to an application in writing to the Commissioners on that behalf, the market value of such property on that valuation date is agreed on between that person and the Commissioners,

   (d) under or in consequence of the same disposition, a charge for tax arises by reason of the provisions of section 103 on either or both of the two chargeable dates in the years next following the year in which the first chargeable date occurs (in this section called the subsequent chargeable dates), and

   (e) the same property at subparagraph (i) or (ii) of paragraph (b) is comprised in the taxable inheritances so taken on the subsequent chargeable dates,

   the value so agreed on shall be treated for the purposes of this Part as market value of such property on that valuation date and on the valuation dates of the taxable inheritances so taken on the subsequent chargeable dates.

(2) Notwithstanding the provisions of subsection (1), the market value so agreed shall not be binding—

    (a) in any case where there is failure to disclose material facts in relation to any part of the property comprised in the taxable inheritances taken on the first chargeable date or on the subsequent chargeable dates, or

    (b) where, at any time after the first chargeable date and before the third of those chargeable dates—

        (i) in the case of real property, there is any alteration in the tenure under which the property is held or let, or

        (ii) in the case of shares, there is any alteration in the capital or the ownership of the capital of the company concerned or of the rights of the shareholders inter se, or

    (c) where, at any time after the first chargeable date and before the third of those chargeable dates—

        (i) in the case of real property, there is any change whatever, whether affecting that or any other property, which would materially increase or decrease the market value over and above any increase or decrease which might normally be expected if such a change had not occurred, or

        (ii) in the case of shares, there has been any material change in the assets of the company or in their market value over and above any such change which might normally be expected,

    and in such cases the market value of the real property, or of the shares, may be ascertained again by the Commissioners for each of the relevant valuation dates:

    Provided that, in the case of any change referred to in paragraph (c), the market value may be ascertained again by the Commissioners only at the request of the person primarily accountable for the payment of the tax arising by reason of the provisions of section 103 on that relevant valuation date.

(3) Any agreement made under this section shall be binding only on the persons who as such are accountable for the payment of the tax arising by reason of the provisions of section 103 on the first chargeable date and on the subsequent chargeable dates.

Section 108

Penalty.

108. Any person who contravenes or fails to comply with any requirement under paragraph (e) of section 104 shall be liable to a penalty of—

    (a) £1,000, or

(b) twice the amount of tax payable in respect of the taxable inheritance to which the return relates,

whichever is the lesser.

CHAPTER II
General

Section 109

Amendment of section 46 (overpayment of tax) of [the Capital Acquisitions Tax Act, 1976].

109. (1) Section 46 of [the Capital Acquisitions Tax Act, 1976,] is hereby amended—

   (a) by the substitution of "at the rate of one per cent., or such other rate (if any) as stands prescribed by the Minister for Finance by regulations, for each month or part of a month from the date on which the payment was made, and income tax shall not be deductible on payment of interest under this section and such interest shall not be reckoned in computing income for the purposes of the Tax Acts" for ", without deduction of income tax, from the date on which the payment was made, at the same rate as that at which the tax would from time to time have carried interest if it were due and such payment had not been made", and

   (b) by the insertion of the following subsection:

   "(2) Every regulation made under this section shall be laid before Dáil Éireann as soon as may be after it is made and, if a resolution annulling the regulation is passed by Dáil Éireann within the next twenty-one days on which Dáil Éireann has sat after the regulation is laid before it, the regulation shall he annulled accordingly, but without prejudice to the validity of anything previously done thereunder.",

and the said section 46, as so amended, is set out in the Table to this subsection.

TABLE

46. (1) Where, on application to the Commissioners for relief under this section, it is proved to their satisfaction that an amount has been paid in excess of the liability for tax or for interest on tax, they shall give relief by way of repayment of the excess or otherwise as is reasonable and just; and any such repayment shall carry simple interest (not exceeding the amount of such excess) at the rate of one per cent., or such other rate (if any) as stands prescribed by the Minister for Finance by regulations, for each month or part of a month from the date on which the payment was made, and income tax shall not be deductible on payment of interest under this section and such interest shall not be reckoned in computing income for the purposes of the Tax Acts.

    (2) Every regulation made under this section shall be laid before Dáil Éireann as soon as may be after it is made and if a resolution annulling the regulation is passed by Dáil Éireann within the next twenty-one days on which Dáil Éireann has sat after the regulation is laid before it, the regulation shall be annulled accordingly, but without prejudice to the validity of anything previously done thereunder.

(2) This section shall apply and have effect in relation to interest payable under the said section 46 for any month, or any part of a month, commencing on or after the date of the passing of this Act.

Section 110

Amendment of section 61 (payment of money standing in names of two or more persons) of [the Capital Acquisitions Tax Act, 1976].

110. Section 61 of [the Capital Acquisitions Tax Act, 1976,] is hereby amended by the insertion after subsection (7) of the following subsection:

"(8) This section shall not apply or have effect where the sum of money referred to in subsection (1) is lodged or deposited in the joint names of two persons, one of whom dies on or after the 30th day of January, 1985, and is at the time of his death the spouse of that other person.".

PART VI

Miscellaneous

Section 112

Application of Age of Majority Act, 1985.

112. (1) Notwithstanding the provisions of subsection (4) of [section 2 of the Age of Majority Act, 1985],[1] subsections (2) and (3) of the said section 2 shall, subject to subsection (2), apply and have effect for the purposes of the Income Tax Acts and any other statutory provision (within the meaning of the said Act) dealing with the imposition, repeal, remission, alteration or regulation of any tax or other duty under the care and management of the Revenue Commissioners and accordingly subparagraph (vii) of paragraph (b) of the said subsection (4) shall cease to have effect.

(2) Nothing in subsection (1) shall affect a claimant's entitlement to a deduction under section 138A (inserted by the Finance Act, 1985) or section 141 (inserted by this Act) of the Income Tax Act, 1967.

(3) This section shall be deemed to have come into force and shall take effect as on and from the 6th day of April, 1986, and so far as it relates to gift tax or inheritance tax shall have effect in relation to gifts and inheritances taken on or after that date.

Footnote

1   Reproduced on page 782. S.112 was replaced by s.7, TCA.

Section 113

Use of electronic data processing.

113. (1) In this section —

"the Acts" means —

(a) the Tax Acts,

(b) the Capital Gains Tax Acts,

(c) section 24 of the Value-Added Tax Act, 1972,

(d) the Capital Acquisitions Tax Act, 1976, and the enactments amending or extending that Act, and

(e) Part VI of the Finance Act, 1983,

and any instruments made thereunder;

"records" means documents which a person is obliged by any provision of the Acts to keep, to issue or to produce for inspection, and any other written or printed material;

"tax" means income tax, corporation tax, capital gains tax, value-added tax or residential property tax, as the case may be.

(2) Subject to the agreement of the Revenue Commissioners, records may be stored, maintained, transmitted, reproduced or communicated, as the case may be, by any electronic, photographic or other process approved of by the Revenue Commissioners, and in circumstances where the use of such process has been agreed by them and subject to such conditions as they may impose.

(3) Where, in pursuance of subsection (2), records are preserved by electronic, photographic or other process, a statement contained in a document produced by any such process shall, subject to the rules of court, be admissible in evidence in any proceedings, whether civil or criminal, to the same extent as the records themselves.

(4) . . . .[1]

Footnote

1   This and subsequent subsections do not relate to CAT.

FINANCE ACT, 1987

Number 10 of 1987
(Enacted on 9th July, 1987)

Part V
Capital Acquisitions Tax

Section 50

Amendment of section 54 (provisions relating to charities, etc.) of Capital Acquisitions Tax Act, 1976.

50. (1) Section 54 of the Capital Acquisitions Tax Act, 1976, is hereby amended by the substitution of the following subsection for subsection (2):

"(2) A gift or an inheritance which is taken for public or charitable purposes shall be exempt from tax, and shall not be taken into account in computing tax, to the extent that the Commissioners are satisfied that it has been, or will be, applied to purposes which, in accordance with the law of the State, are public or charitable.".

(2) This section shall apply where the date of the gift or the date of the inheritance is on or after the date of the passing of this Act.

STATUS OF CHILDREN ACT, 1987

Number 26 of 1987
(Enacted on 14th December, 1987)

Section 3[1]

Marital status of parents to be of no effect on relationships.

3.　(1)　In deducing any relationship for the purposes of this Act or of any Act of the Oireachtas passed after the commencement of this section, the relationship between every person and his father and mother (or either of them) shall, unless the contrary intention appears, be determined irrespective of whether his father and mother are or have been married to each other, and all other relationships shall be determined accordingly.

　　(2)　(a)　An adopted person shall, for the purposes of subsection (1) of this section, be deemed from the date of the adoption to be the child of the adopter or adopters and not the child of any other person or persons.

　　　　(b)　In this subsection "adopted person" means a person who has been adopted under the Adoption Acts, 1952 to 1976, or, where the person has been adopted outside the State, whose adoption is recognised by virtue of the law for the time being in force in the State.

Footnote

1　This section should be read in conjunction with s.74, FA 1988, and s.8, TCA.

FINANCE ACT, 1988

Number 12 of 1988
(Enacted on 25th May, 1988)

Part V
Capital Acquisitions Tax

Section 66

Amendment of section 63 (allowance for capital gains tax on the same event) of Finance Act, 1985.

66. (1) Section 63 (1) of the Finance Act, 1985, is hereby amended by the substitution for "the same, up to the net amount of the same" of –
"the same:

Provided that, in relation to each asset, or to a part of each asset, so disposed of, the amount deducted shall be the lesser of –

   (a)   an amount equal to the amount of the capital gains tax attributable to such asset, or to the part of such asset, or

   (b)   an amount equal to the amount of the gift tax or inheritance tax attributable to the property which is that asset, or that part of that asset",

and the said subsection 63 (1), as so amended, is set out in the Table to this section.

   (2)   This section shall apply where gift tax or inheritance tax is charged in respect of property on an event happening on or after the 6th day of April, 1988.

TABLE

63.   (1)   Where gift tax or inheritance tax is charged in respect of property on an event happening on or after the 30th day of January, 1985, and the same event constitutes for capital gains tax purposes a disposal of an asset (being the same property or any part of the same property), the capital gains tax, if any, chargeable on the disposal shall not be deducted in ascertaining the taxable value for the purposes of the gift tax or inheritance tax but, in so far as it has been paid, shall be deducted from the net gift tax or inheritance tax as a credit against the same: Provided that, in relation to each asset, or to a part of each asset, so disposed of, the amount deducted shall be the lesser of –

> (a) an amount equal to the amount of the capital gains tax attributable to such asset, or to the part of such asset, or
>
> (b) an amount equal to the amount of the gift tax or inheritance tax attributable to the property which is that asset, or that part of that asset.

PART VI
Miscellaneous

Section 71

Poundage and certain other fees.

71. (1) (a) In this section—

"the Acts" means—

(a) the Tax Acts,

(b) the Capital Gains Tax Acts,

(c) the Value-Added Tax Act, 1972, and the enactments amending or extending that Act,

(d) the Capital Acquisitions Tax Act, 1976, and the enactments amending or extending that Act, and

(e) Part VI of the Finance Act, 1983, and the enactments amending or extending that Part,

and any instruments made thereunder;

"certificate" means a certificate issued under section 485 of the Income Tax Act, 1967;

"county registrar" means a person appointed to be a county registrar under section 35 of the Court Officers Act, 1926;

"defaulter" means a person specified or certified in an execution order or certificate upon whom a relevant amount specified or certified in the order or certificate is leviable;

"execution order" has the same meaning as in the Enforcement of Court Orders Act, 1926;

"fees" means the fees known as poundage fees payable under section 14 (1) of the Enforcement of Court Orders Act, 1926, and orders made thereunder for services in or about the execution of an execution order directing or authorising the execution of an order of a court by the seizure and sale of a person's property or, as may be appropriate, the fees, corresponding to the fees aforesaid, payable under section 485 of the Income Tax Act, 1967, for the execution of a certificate;

"interest on unpaid tax" means interest that has accrued under any provision of the Acts providing for the charging of interest in respect of unpaid tax including interest on an undercharge of tax which is attributable to fraud or neglect;

"relevant amount" means an amount of tax or interest on unpaid tax;

"tax" means any tax, duty, levy or charge which, in accordance with any provision of the Acts, is placed under the care and management of the Revenue Commissioners.

(b) References, as respects an execution order, to a relevant amount include references to any amount of costs specified in the order.

(2) (a) Where—

(i) an execution order or certificate specifying or certifying a defaulter and relating to a relevant amount is lodged, whether before or after the passing of this Act, with the appropriate sheriff or county registrar for execution,

(ii) the sheriff or, as the case may be, the county registrar gives notice to the defaulter of the lodgement or of his intention to execute the execution order or certificate by seizure of the property of the defaulter to which it relates, or demands payment by the defaulter of the relevant amount, and

(iii) the whole or part of the relevant amount is paid to the sheriff or, as the case may be, the county registrar or to the Collector-General, after the giving of the notice or the making of the demand, aforesaid,

then, for the purpose of the liability of the defaulter for the payment of fees and of the exercise of any rights or powers in relation to the collection of fees for the time being vested by law in sheriffs and county registrars—

(I) the sheriff or, as the case may be, the county registrar shall be deemed to have entered, in the execution of the execution order or certificate, into possession of the property aforesaid, and

(II) the payment mentioned in subparagraph (iii) shall be deemed to have been levied, in the execution of the execution order or certificate, by the sheriff or, as the case may be, the county registrar,

and fees shall be payable by the defaulter to such sheriff or, as the case may be, the county registrar accordingly in respect of the payment mentioned in subparagraph (iii).

(b) Paragraph (a) shall, with any necessary modifications, apply also in a case in which such a notice or demand as is mentioned in subparagraph (ii) of that paragraph was given or made before the passing of this Act if the fees concerned were paid to the sheriff or county registrar concerned before such passing.

Section 73

Deduction from payments due to defaulters of amounts due in relation to tax.

73. (1) (a) This section shall apply and have effect as on and from the 1st day of October, 1988.

(b) In this section, except where the context otherwise requires —

"the Acts" means —

(i) the Tax Acts,

(ii) the Capital Gains Tax Acts, and

(iii) the Value Added Tax Act, 1972, and the enactments amending or extending that Act,

and any instruments made thereunder;

"additional debt" means, in relation to a relevant person who has received a notice of attachment in respect of a taxpayer, any amount which, at any time after the time of the receipt by the relevant person of the notice of attachment but before the end of the relevant period in relation to the notice, would be a debt due by him to the taxpayer if a notice of attachment were received by him at that time;

"debt" means, in relation to a notice of attachment given to a relevant person in respect of a taxpayer and in relation to the said relevant person and tax payer, the amount or aggregate amount of any money which, at the time the notice of attachment is received by the relevant person, is due by the relevant person (whether on his own account, or as an agent or trustee) to the taxpayer, irrespective of whether the taxpayer has applied for the payment (to himself or any other person) or for the withdrawal of all or part of the money:

Provided that —

(i) where a relevant person is a financial institution, any amount or aggregate amount of money, including interest thereon, which at that time is a deposit held by the relevant person to the credit of the taxpayer for his sole benefit, shall be regarded as a debt due by the relevant person to the taxpayer at that time,

(ii) any amount of money due by the relevant person to the taxpayer as emoluments under a contract of service shall not be so regarded, and

(iii) where there is a dispute as to an amount of money which is due by the relevant person to the taxpayer, the amount in dispute shall be disregarded for the purposes of determining the amount of the debt;

"deposit" means a sum of money paid to a financial institution on terms under which it will be repaid with or without interest and either on demand or at a time or in circumstances agreed by or on behalf of the person making the payment and the person to whom it is made;

"emoluments" means anything assessable to income tax under Schedule E;

"financial institution" means a holder of a licence issued under section 9 of the Central Bank Act, 1971, or a person referred to in section 7 (4) of that Act and includes a branch of a financial institution that records deposits in its books as liabilities of the branch;

"further return" means a return made by a relevant person under subsection (4);

"interest on unpaid tax" means, in relation to a specified amount specified in a notice of attachment, interest, that has accrued to the date on which them notice of attachment is given, under any provision of the Acts providing for the charging of interest in respect of unpaid tax including interest on an under charge of tax which is attributable to fraud or neglect;

"notice of attachment" means a notice under subsection (2);

"notice of revocation" means a notice under subsection (10);

"penalty" means a monetary penalty imposed on a taxpayer under a provision of the Acts;

"relevant period", in relation to a notice of attachment, means, as respects the relevant person to whom the notice of attachment is given, the period commencing at the time at which the notice is received by the relevant person and ending on —

(i) the date on which he completes the payment to the Revenue Commissioners out of the debt, or the aggregate of the debt and any additional debt, due by him to the taxpayer named in the notice, of an amount equal to the specified amount in relation to the taxpayer,

(ii) the date on which he receives a notice of revocation of the notice of attachment, or

(iii) where he or the taxpayer named in the notice is —

(I) declared bankrupt, the date he or the taxpayer is so declared, or

(II) a company which commences to be wound up, the "relevant date" within the meaning of section 285 of the Companies Act, 1963, in relation to the winding up,

whichever is the earliest;

"relevant person" means, in relation to a taxpayer, a person in respect of whom the Revenue Commissioners have reason to believe that he may have, at the time a notice of attachment is received by him in respect of a taxpayer, a debt due to the taxpayer;

"return" means a return made by a relevant person under subsection (2) (a) (iii);

"specified amount" has the meaning assigned to it by subsection (2) (a) (ii);

"tax" means any tax, duty, levy or charge which, in accordance with any provision of the Acts, is placed under the care and management of the Revenue Commissioners;

"taxpayer" means a person who is liable to pay, remit or account for tax to the Revenue Commissioners under the Acts.

(2) (a) Subject to subsection (3), where a taxpayer has made default, whether before or after the passing of this Act, in paying, remitting, or accounting for, any tax, interest on unpaid tax, or penalty to the Revenue Commissioners, the Revenue Commissioners may, if the taxpayer has not made good the default, give to a relevant person in relation to the taxpayer a notice in writing (in this section referred to as "the notice of attachment") in which is entered –

(i) the taxpayer's name and address,

(ii) the amount or aggregate amount (in this section referred to as "the specified amount") of the taxes, interest on unpaid taxes and penalties in respect of which the taxpayer is in default at the time of the giving of the notice of attachment, and

(iii) a direction to the relevant person –

(I) to deliver to the Revenue Commissioners, within the period of 10 days from the time at which the notice of attachment is received by him, a return in writing specifying whether or not any debt is due by him to the taxpayer at the time the notice is received by him, and if any debt is so due, specifying the amount of the debt:

Provided that where the amount of the debt due by the relevant person to the taxpayer is equal to or greater than the specified amount in relation to the taxpayer, the amount of the debt specified in the return shall be an amount equal to the specified amount,

and

    (II)   if the amount of any debt is so specified to pay to the Revenue Commissioners within the period aforesaid a sum equal to the amount of the debt so specified.

(b)   A relevant person to whom a notice of attachment has been given shall comply with the direction in the notice.

(3)   An amount in respect of tax, interest on unpaid tax or a penalty, as respects which a taxpayer is in default as specified in subsection (2) shall not be entered in a notice of attachment unless –

(a)   a period of one month has expired from the date on which such default commenced, and

(b)   the Revenue Commissioners have given the taxpayer a notice in writing (whether or not the document containing the notice also contains other information being communicated by the Revenue Commissioners to the taxpayer), not later than 10 days before the date of the receipt by the relevant person concerned of the notice of attachment, stating that, if the amount is not paid, it may be specified in a notice of attachment and recovered under this section from a relevant person in relation to the taxpayer.

(4)   If, when a relevant person receives a notice of attachment, the amount of the debt due by him to the taxpayer named in the notice is less than the specified amount in relation to the taxpayer or no debt is so due and, at any time thereafter before the end of the relevant period in relation to the notice, an additional debt becomes due by the relevant person to the taxpayer, the relevant person shall, within 10 days of that time –

(a)   if the aggregate of the amount of any debt so due and the additional debt so due is equal to or less than the specified amount in relation to the taxpayer –

    (i)   deliver a further return to the Revenue Commissioners specifying the additional debt, and

    (ii)   pay to the Revenue Commissioners the amount of the additional debt,

and so on for each subsequent occasion during the relevant period in relation to the notice of attachment on which an additional debt becomes due by the relevant person to the taxpayer until the aggregate amount of the debt and the additional debt or debts so due equals the specified amount in relation to the taxpayer or the provisions of paragraph (b) apply in relation to an additional debt, and

(b) if the aggregate amount of any debt and the additional debt or debts so due to the taxpayer is greater than the specified amount in relation to the taxpayer—

    (i) deliver a further return to the Revenue Commissioners specifying such portion of the latest additional debt as when added to the aggregate of the debt and any earlier additional debts is equal to the specified amount in relation to the taxpayer, and

    (ii) pay to the Revenue Commissioners the said portion of the additional debt.

(5) Where a relevant person delivers, either fraudulently or negligently, an incorrect return or further return that purports to be a return or further return made in accordance with this section, he shall be deemed to be guilty of an offence under section 94 of the Finance Act, 1983.

(6) (a) Where a notice of attachment has been given to a relevant person in respect of a taxpayer, the relevant person shall not, during the relevant period in relation to the notice, make any disbursements out of the debt, or any additional debt, due by him to the taxpayer save to the extent that any such disbursement—

    (i) will not reduce the debt or the aggregate of the debt and any additional debts so due to an amount that is less than the specified amount in relation to the taxpayer, or

    (ii) is made pursuant to an order of a court.

(b) For the purposes of this section, a disbursement made by a relevant person contrary to paragraph (a) shall be deemed not to reduce the amount of the debt or any additional debts due by him to the taxpayer.

(7) (a) Sections 500 and 503 of the Income Tax Act, 1967, shall apply to a failure by a relevant person to deliver a return required by a notice of attachment within the time specified in the notice or to deliver a further return within the time specified in subsection (4) as they apply to a failure to deliver a return referred to in the said section 500 and Schedule 15 to the said Act is hereby amended by the insertion in Column 1 of "Finance Act, 1988, paragraph (a) (iii) (I) of subsection (2) and paragraphs (a) (i) and (b) (i) of subsection (4) of section 73".

(b) A certificate signed by an officer of the Revenue Commissioners which certifies that he has examined the relevant records and that it appears from them that, during a specified period, a specified return was not received from a relevant person shall be evidence until the contrary is proved that the relevant person did not deliver the return during that period and a certificate certifying as provided by this paragraph and purporting to be signed by an officer of the Revenue Commissioners may be tendered in evidence without proof and shall be deemed until the contrary is proved to have been so signed.

(8) Where a relevant person to whom a notice of attachment in respect of a taxpayer has been given —

    (a)   delivers the return required to be delivered by the said notice but fails to pay to the Revenue Commissioners, within the time specified in the notice, the amount specified in the return or any part of that amount, or

    (b)   delivers a further return under subsection (4) but fails to pay to the Revenue Commissioners, within the time specified in the said subsection (4), the amount specified in the further return or any part of that amount,

the amount specified in the return or further return, or the part of that amount, as the case may be, which he has failed to pay to the Revenue Commissioners may, if the notice of attachment has not been revoked by a notice of revocation, be sued for and recovered by action, or other appropriate proceedings, at the suit of an officer of the Revenue Commissioners in any court of competent jurisdiction.

(9) Nothing in this section shall be construed as rendering any failure by a relevant person to make a return or further return required by this section, or pay to the Revenue Commissioners the amount or amounts required by this section to be paid by him, liable to be treated as a failure to which section 94 of the Finance Act, 1983, applies.

(10) (a)   A notice of attachment given to a relevant person in respect of a taxpayer may be revoked by the Revenue Commissioners, at any time, by notice in writing given to the relevant person and shall be revoked forthwith if the taxpayer has paid the specified amount to the Revenue Commissioners.

    (b)   Where, in pursuance of this section, a relevant person pays any amount to the Revenue Commissioners out of a debt or an additional debt due by him to the taxpayer and, at the time of the receipt by the Revenue Commissioners of the said amount, the taxpayer has paid the specified amount to the Revenue Commissioners, the first-mentioned amount shall be refunded by the Revenue Commissioners forthwith to the taxpayer.

(11) If a notice of attachment or a notice of revocation is given to a relevant person in relation to a taxpayer a copy thereof shall be given by the Revenue Commissioners to the taxpayer forthwith.

(12) (a)   If, in pursuance of this section, any amount is paid to the Revenue Commissioners by a relevant person, the relevant person shall forthwith give the taxpayer concerned a notice in

writing specifying the payment, its amount and the reason for which it was made.

(b) On the receipt by the Revenue Commissioners of an amount paid in pursuance of this section, the Revenue Commissioners shall forthwith notify the taxpayer and the relevant person in writing of such receipt.

(13) If, in pursuance of this section, a relevant person pays to the Revenue Commissioners the whole or part of the amount of a debt, or an additional debt, due by him to a taxpayer, or any portion of such an amount, the taxpayer shall allow such payment and the relevant person shall be acquitted and discharged of the amount of the payment as if it had been paid to the taxpayer.

(14) If, in pursuance of this section, a relevant person is prohibited from making any disbursement out of a debt, or an additional debt, due to a taxpayer, no action shall lie against the relevant person in any court by reason of a failure to make any such disbursement.

(15) Any obligation on the Revenue Commissioners to maintain secrecy or any other restriction upon the disclosure of information by the Revenue Commissioners shall not apply in relation to information contained in a notice of attachment.

(16) A notice of attachment in respect of a taxpayer shall not be given to a relevant person at a time when the relevant person or the taxpayer is an undischarged bankrupt or a company being wound up.

(17) Where the Revenue Commissioners have given a notice of attachment to a relevant person in respect of a taxpayer, they shall not, during the relevant period in relation to the notice, give a notice of attachment in respect of the taxpayer to any other relevant person.

(18) The Revenue Commissioners may nominate any of their officers to perform any acts and discharge any functions authorised by this section to be performed or discharged by the Revenue Commissioners.

Section 74

Construction of certain Acts in accordance with Status of Children Act, 1987.

74. (1) In this section "the Acts" means—

(i) the Tax Acts,

(ii) the Capital Gains Tax Acts,

(iii) the Capital Acquisitions Tax Act, 1976, and the enactments amending or extending that Act, and

(iv) the statutes relating to stamp duty,

and any instruments made thereunder.

(2) Notwithstanding any provision of the Acts or the dates on which they were passed, in deducing any relationship between persons for

the purposes of the Acts, the Acts shall be construed in accordance with [section 3 of the Status of Children Act, 1987].[1]

(3) This section shall have effect—

    (i)   in relation to the Tax Acts, as respects the year 1987-88 and subsequent years of assessment or accounting periods ending on or after the 14th day of January, 1988, as the case may be,

    (ii) in relation to the Capital Gains Tax Acts, as respects disposals made on or after the 14th day of January, 1988,

    (iii) in relation to the Capital Acquisitions Tax Act, 1976, as respects gifts and inheritances taken on or after the 14th day of January, 1988, and

    (iv) in relation to the statutes relating to stamp duties, as respects any instrument executed on or after the 14th day of January, 1988.

Footnote
1   Reproduced on page 799.

FINANCE ACT, 1989

Number 10 of 1989
(Enacted on 24th May, 1989)

PART V
Capital Acquisitions Tax

CHAPTER I
General

Section 73

Interpretation (Part V).

73. In this Part "the Principal Act" means the Capital Acquisitions Tax Act, 1976.

CHAPTER II
Arrangements with regard to Returns and Assessments

Section 74

Delivery of returns.

74. [The Capital Acquisitions Tax Act, 1976,] is hereby amended by the substitution for section 36 of the following section—

"36. (1) In this section—

    (a) notwithstanding anything contained in sections 6 and 12—

        (i) a reference to a taxable gift is a reference to a taxable gift taken on or after the 28th day of February, 1974;

        (ii) a reference to a taxable inheritance is a reference to a taxable inheritance taken on or after the 1st day of April, 1975; and

        (iii) a reference, other than in subparagraph (i), to a gift or a taxable gift includes a reference to an inheritance or a taxable inheritance, as the case may be; and

    (b) a reference to a donee includes a reference to a successor.

    (2) Any person who is primarily accountable for the payment of tax by virtue of section 35 (1), or by virtue of paragraph (c) of section 107 of the Finance Act, 1984, shall, within four months after the relevant date referred to in subsection (5)—

    (a) deliver to the Commissioners a full and true return of—

        (i)   every gift in respect of which he is so primarily accountable;

        (ii)   all the property comprised in such gift on the valuation date;

        (iii) an estimate of the market value of such property on the valuation date; and

        (iv) such particulars as may be relevant to the assessment of tax in respect of such gift;

    (b)   notwithstanding the provisions of section 39, make on that return an assessment of such amount of tax as, to the best of his knowledge, information and belief, ought to be charged, levied and paid on that valuation date; and

    (c)   duly pay the amount of such tax.

  (3)   The provisions of subsection (2) (c) shall be complied with –

    (a)   where the tax due and payable in respect of any part of the gift is being paid by instalments under the provisions of section 43, by the due payment of –

        (i)   an amount which includes any instalment of tax which has fallen due prior to or on the date of the assessment of the tax referred to in subsection (2) (b); and

        (ii)   any further instalments of such tax on the due dates in accordance with that section;

    (b)   where the tax due and payable is inheritance tax which is being wholly or partly paid by the transfer of securities to the Minister for Finance under the provisions of section 45, by –

        (i)   delivering to the Commissioners with the return an application to pay all or part of the tax by such transfer;

        (ii)   completing the transfer of the securities to the Minister for Finance within such time, not being less than 30 days, as may be specified by the Commissioners by notice in writing; and

        (iii) duly paying the excess, if any, of the amount of the tax referred to in subsection (2) (b), or in paragraph (a)(i), over the nominal face value of the securities tendered in payment of the tax in accordance with the provisions of subparagraph (i).

  (4)   Subsection (2) applies to a charge for tax arising by reason of the provisions of section 106 of the Finance Act, 1984, and to any other gift where –

(a)   so far as it is a taxable gift taken before the 2nd day of June, 1982—

    (i)   the taxable value of such gift exceeds an amount which is 80 per cent. of the lowest value upon which, at the date of such gift, tax becomes chargeable in respect of a gift taken by the donee of such gift from the disponer thereof;

    (ii)   the taxable value of such gift falls to be aggregated with previous gifts taken by the donee of such gift from the disponer thereof and thereby increases the total taxable value of all taxable gifts so aggregated taken by such donee from such disponer from an amount which is less than or equal to the amount specified in subparagraph (i) to an amount which exceeds the amount so specified; or

    (iii)   the taxable value of such gift falls to be aggregated with previous gifts taken by the donee of such gift from the disponer thereof and thereby increases the total taxable value of all taxable gifts so aggregated taken by such donee from such disponer from an amount which is greater than the amount specified in subparagraph (i);

and, in this paragraph—

    (I)   any reference to the total taxable value of all taxable gifts includes a reference to the total aggregable value of all aggregable gifts;

    (II)   'aggregable gift' and 'aggregable value' have the meanings assigned to them by paragraph 1 of Part I of the Second Schedule;

(b)   so far as it is a taxable gift taken on or after the 2nd day of June, 1982, and before the 26th day of March, 1984—

    (i)   the taxable value of such gift exceeds an amount which is 80 per cent. of the lowest value upon which, at the date of such gift, tax becomes chargeable in respect of a gift taken by the donee of such gift from the disponer thereof;

    (ii)   the taxable value of such gift falls to be aggregated with gifts taken by the donee of such gift, either on or before the date of such gift, from any disponer and thereby increases the total taxable value of all taxable gifts so aggregated taken by such donee from any disponer from an amount which is less than or equal to the amount specified in subparagraph (i) to an amount which exceeds the amount so specified; or

(iii) the taxable value of such gift falls to be aggregated with gifts taken by the donee of such gift, either on or before the date of such gift, from any disponer and thereby increases the total taxable value of all taxable gifts so aggregated taken by such donee from any disponer from an amount which is greater than the amount specified in subparagraph (i);

(c) so far as it is a taxable gift taken on or after the 26th day of March, 1984, the aggregate of the taxable values of all taxable gifts taken by the donee on or after the 2nd day of June, 1982, exceeds an amount which is 80 per cent. of the threshold amount (as defined in the Second Schedule) which applies in the computation of the tax on that aggregate; or

(d) the donee or, in a case to which section 23 (1) applies, the transferee (within the meaning of, and to the extent provided for by, that section) is required by notice in writing by the Commissioners to deliver a return,

and, for the purposes of this subsection, a reference to a gift or a taxable gift includes a reference to a part of a gift or to a part of a taxable gift, as the case may be.

(5) For the purposes of this section, the relevant date shall be –

(a) the valuation date or the 1st day of September, 1989, whichever is the later; or

(b) where the donee or, in a case to which section 23 (1) applies, the transferee (within the meaning of, and to the extent provided for by, that section) is required by notice in writing by the Commissioners to deliver a return, the date of the notice.

(6) Any person who is accountable for the payment of tax by virtue of subsection (2) or (9) of section 35 shall, if he is required by notice in writing by the Commissioners to do so, comply with the provisions of paragraphs (a), (b) and (c) of subsection (2) of this section (as if he were a person primarily accountable for the payment of tax by virtue of section 35 (1)) within such time, not being less than 30 days, as may be specified in the notice.

(7) (a) Any accountable person shall, if he is so required by the Commissioners by notice in writing, deliver and verify to the Commissioners within such time, not being less than 30 days, as may be specified in the notice –

(i) a statement (where appropriate, on a form provided, or approved of, by them) of such particulars relating to any property; and

(ii)   such evidence as they require,

as may, in their opinion, be relevant to the assessment of tax in respect of the gift.

(b)   The Commissioners may authorise a person to inspect—

(i)   any property comprised in a gift; or

(ii)   any books, records, accounts or other documents, in whatever form they are stored, maintained or preserved, relating to any property as may in their opinion be relevant to the assessment of tax in respect of a gift,

and the person having the custody or possession of that property, or of those books, records, accounts or documents, shall permit the person so authorised to make that inspection at such reasonable times as the Commissioners consider necessary.

(8)   The Commissioners may by notice in writing require any accountable person to—

(a)   deliver to them within such time, not being less than 30 days, as may be specified in the notice, an additional return, if it appears to the Commissioners that a return made by that accountable person is defective in a material respect by reason of anything contained in or omitted from it;

(b)   notwithstanding the provisions of section 39, make on that additional return an assessment of such amended amount of tax as, to the best of his knowledge, information and belief, ought to be charged, levied and paid on the relevant gift; and

(c)   duly pay the outstanding tax, if any, for which he is accountable in respect of that gift;

and

(i)   the requirements of subparagraphs (ii), (iii) and (iv) of subsection (2) (a) shall apply to such additional return required by virtue of paragraph (a); and

(ii)   the provisions of subsection (3) shall, with any necessary modifications, apply to any payment required by virtue of paragraph (c).

(9)   Where any accountable person who has delivered a return or an additional return is aware or becomes aware at any time that the return or additional return is defective in a material respect by reason of anything contained in or omitted from it, he shall, without application from the

Commissioners and within three months of so becoming aware —

(a) deliver to them an additional return;

(b) notwithstanding the provisions of section 39, make on that additional return an assessment of such amended amount of tax as, to the best of his knowledge, information and belief, ought to be charged, levied and paid on the relevant gift; and

(c) duly pay the outstanding tax, if any, for which he is accountable in respect of that gift;

and

(i) the requirements of subparagraphs (ii), (iii) and (iv) of subsection (2) (a) shall apply to such additional return required by virtue of paragraph (a); and

(ii) the provisions of subsection (3) shall, with any necessary modifications, apply to any payment required by virtue of paragraph (c).

(10) Any amount of tax payable by an accountable person in respect of an assessment of tax made by him on a return delivered by him (other than an amount of that tax payable by the transfer of securities to the Minister for Finance under the provisions of section 45) shall accompany the return and be paid to the Accountant-General of the Commissioners.

(11) Any assessment or payment of tax made under the provisions of this section shall include interest upon tax payable in accordance with the provisions of section 41.".

Section 75

Application of section 39 (assessment of tax) of [the Capital Acquisitions Tax Act, 1976].

75. Nothing in section 36 of [the Capital Acquisitions Tax Act, 1976,] shall preclude the Commissioners from making an assessment of tax, a correcting assessment of tax, or an additional assessment of tax, under the provisions of section 39 of that Act.

Section 76

Amendment of section 41 (payment of tax and interest on tax) of [the Capital Acquisitions Tax Act, 1976].

76. (1) Section 41 of [the Capital Acquisitions Tax Act, 1976,] is hereby amended by the substitution for subsection (3) of the following subsection:

"(3) Notwithstanding the provisions of subsection (2), interest shall not be payable on tax which is paid within three months of the valuation date, and where tax and interest, if any, thereon is paid within thirty days of the date of assessment thereof, interest shall not run on that tax for the period of thirty days from the date of the assessment or any part of that period:

Provided that, in relation to an assessment of tax made by an accountable person on a return delivered by him, interest shall not be payable on tax which is paid within four months of the valuation date.".

(2) A payment by an accountable person of tax shall be treated as a payment on account of tax for the purposes of section 41 of [the Capital Acquisitions Tax Act, 1976], notwithstanding that the payment may be conditional or that the assessment of tax is incorrect.

Section 77

Amendment of section 63 (penalties) of [the Capital Acquisitions Tax Act, 1976].

77. Section 63 of [the Capital Acquisitions Tax Act, 1976] is hereby amended —

(a) by the substitution for subsection (1) of the following subsection:

"(1) (a) Any person who contravenes or fails to comply with any requirement or provision under section 36 shall be liable to a penalty of £2,000.

(b) Where the contravention or failure referred to in paragraph (a) continues after judgment has been given by the court before which proceedings for the penalty have been commenced, the person concerned shall be liable to a further penalty of £25 for each day on which the contravention or failure so continues.",

(b) by the substitution for "£500" of "£1,000" in subsection (2),

(c) by the substitution for "£1,000" of "£5,000" in subsection (3), and

(d) by the substitution for "£250" of "£1,000" in subsection (7).

Section 78

Amendment of section 107 (application of [the Capital Acquisitions Tax Act, 1976]) of Finance Act, 1984.

78. Section 107 of the Finance Act, 1984, is hereby amended —

(a) by the deletion of paragraph (e), and

(b) by the substitution for paragraph (g) of the following paragraph:

"(g) sections 35 (1), 40, 45 and 57 of, and the Second Schedule to, [the Capital Acquisitions Act, 1976,] shall not apply.".

Section 79

Surcharge for undervaluation of property.

79. (1) Where—

    (a) an accountable person delivers a return, and

    (b) the estimate of the market value of any asset comprised in a gift or inheritance and included in that return, when expressed as a percentage of the ascertained value of that asset, is within any of the percentages specified in column (1) of the Table to this section,

    then the amount of tax attributable to the property which is that asset shall be increased by a sum (hereafter in this section referred to as the "surcharge") equal to the corresponding percentage, set out in column (2) of that Table opposite the relevant percentages in the said column (1), of that amount of tax.

(2) Interest shall be payable under the provisions of section 41 of [the Capital Acquisitions Tax Act, 1976,] upon any surcharge as if the surcharge were tax, and the surcharge and any interest thereon shall be chargeable and recoverable as if the surcharge and that interest were part of the tax.

(3) Any person aggrieved by the imposition on him of a surcharge under this section in respect of any asset may, within 30 days of the notification to him of the amount of such surcharge, appeal to the Appeal Commissioners against the imposition of such surcharge on the grounds, and only on the grounds, that, having regard to all the circumstances, there were sufficient grounds on which he might reasonably have based his estimate of the market value of the asset.

(4) The Appeal Commissioners shall hear and determine an appeal to them under subsection (3) as if it were an appeal to them against an assessment to tax, and the provisions of section 52 of [the Capital Acquisitions Tax Act, 1976,] relating to an appeal or to the rehearing of an appeal or to the statement of a case for the opinion of the High Court on a point of law shall, with any necessary modifications, apply accordingly.

(5) In this section "ascertained value" means the market value subject to the right of appeal under section 51 or section 52 of the [the Capital Acquisitions Tax Act, 1976].

TABLE

Estimate of the market value of the asset in the return, expressed as a percentage of the ascertained value of that asset (1)	Surcharge (2)
Equal to or greater than 0 per cent. but less than 40 per cent.	30 per cent.
Equal to or greater than 40 per cent. but less than 50 per cent.	20 per cent.
Equal to or greater than 50 per cent. but less than 67 per cent.	10 per cent.

CHAPTER III
Miscellaneous

Section 80

Amendment of section 2 (interpretation) of [the Capital Acquisitions Tax Act, 1976].

80. (1) Section 2 of [the Capital Acquisitions Tax Act, 1976,] is hereby amended—

   (a) in the definition of "child" in subsection (1), by the substitution for "the Adoption Acts, 1952 to 1974" of "the Adoption Acts, 1952 to 1988" in each place where it occurs, and

   (b) in subsection (5), by the substitution for "the Adoption Acts, 1952 to 1974" of "the Adoption Acts, 1952 to 1988" in both places where it occurs.

   (2) This section shall have effect as respects gifts and inheritances taken on or after the 26th day of July, 1988.

Section 81

Extension of section 35 (accountable persons) of [the Capital Acquisitions Tax Act, 1976].

81. (1) In the case of an inheritance taken on or before the date of death of the disponer, the disponer shall also be a person accountable for the payment of any amount of the tax for which the persons referred to in section 35 (1) of [the Capital Acquisitions Tax Act, 1976,] are made primarily accountable, and, subject to subsection (2), [the Capital Acquisitions Tax Act, 1976,] shall have effect as if such disponer were a person referred to in section 35 (2) (b) of that Act:

   Provided that the disponer as such shall not be so accountable in the case where the date of the disposition was prior to the 1st day of May, 1989.

(2) The provisions of subsections (3) and (9) of section 35 of [the Capital Acquisitions Tax Act, 1976,] shall not apply to a disponer who is accountable for the payment of tax under subsection (1).

Section 82

Amendment of section 37 (signing of returns, etc.) of [the Capital Acquisitions Tax Act, 1976].

82. Section 37 of [the Capital Acquisitions Tax Act, 1976,] is hereby amended by the substitution for subsection (4) of the following subsection:

"(4) (a) A return or additional return delivered under this Act shall—

(i) be made on a form provided, or approved of, by the Commissioners, or

(ii) except in a case to which subsection (2) relates but in a case where subsection (3) applies, be in a form approved of by the Commissioners and delivered by any electronic, photographic or other process approved of by them and in circumstances where the use of such process has been agreed by them and subject to such conditions as they may impose.

(b) An affidavit, additional affidavit, account or additional account, delivered under this Act, shall be made on a form provided, or approved of, by the Commissioners. ".

Section 83

Amendment of Second Schedule to [the Capital Acquisitions Tax Act, 1976].

83. (1) Part I of the Second Schedule to [the Capital Acquisitions Tax Act, 1976,] is hereby amended by the substitution for paragraph 9 of the following paragraph:

"9. (1) In this paragraph—

'company' means a company which—

(a) is a private trading company within the meaning assigned by section 16 (2); and

(b) for the relevant period, is such a company—

(i) controlled by the disponer; and

(ii) where the disponer is a director thereof;

'company controlled by the disponer' means a company that is under the control of any one or more of the following, that is to say—

(a) the disponer,

(b) nominees of the disponer,

(c) the trustees of a settlement made by the disponer;

'control', in relation to a company, shall be construed in accordance with section 16 (4) (b);

'nominee' has the same meaning as it has in section 16;

'relevant period' means—

(a) the period of five years ending on the date of the disposition; or

(b) where, at the date of the disposition,

    (i) an interest in possession in—

        (I) the property referred to in subparagraph (2) (a), or

        (II) the shares referred to in subparagraph (2) (b),

        as the case may be, is limited to the disponer under the disposition, and

    (ii) such property is not, or such shares are not, property consisting of the appropriate part of property, within the meaning of section 5 (5), on which is charged or secured an annuity or other annual right limited to cease on the death of the disponer,

    the period of five years ending on the coming to an end of that interest,

subject, in relation to work, to the exclusion of reasonable periods of annual or sick leave from that period of five years.

(2) For the purpose of computing the tax payable on a gift or inheritance, the donee or successor shall be deemed to bear to the disponer the relationship of a child in any case where the donee or successor is a child of a brother, or a child of a sister, of the disponer and either—

(a) the donee or successor has worked substantially on a full-time basis for the disponer for the relevant period in carrying on, or in assisting in carrying on, the trade, business or profession of the disponer, and the gift or inheritance consists of property which was used in connection with that business, trade or profession; or

(b) the donee or successor has worked substantially on a full-time basis for a company for the relevant period in carrying on, or in assisting in carrying on, the trade, business or profession of the company, and the gift or inheritance consists of shares in that company.

(3) Without prejudice to the generality of subparagraph (2), a donee or successor shall not be deemed to be working substantially on a full-time basis for a disponer or a company unless—

(a) where the gift or inheritance consists of property which was used in connection with the business, trade or profession of the disponer, the donee or successor works—

(i) more than 24 hours a week for the disponer, at a place where that business, trade or profession, is carried on; or

(ii) more than 15 hours a week for the disponer, at a place where that business, trade or profession is carried on, and such business, trade or profession is carried on exclusively by the disponer, any spouse of the disponer, and the donee or successor;

or

(b) where the gift or inheritance consists of shares in the company, the donee or successor works—

(i) more than 24 hours a week for the company, at a place where the business, trade or profession of the company is carried on; or

(ii) more than 15 hours a week for the company, at a place where the business, trade or profession of the company is carried on, and such business, trade or profession is carried on exclusively by the disponer, any spouse of the disponer, and the donee or successor.

(4) The provisions of this paragraph shall not apply to a gift or inheritance taken by a donee or successor under a discretionary trust.".

(2) This section shall have effect as respects gifts and inheritances taken on or after the 1st day of May, 1989.

Section 84

Amendment of section 60 (relief in respect of certain policies of insurance) of Finance Act, 1985.

84. Section 60 of the Finance Act, 1985, is hereby amended by the insertion of the following subsection after subsection (1):

"(1A) In this section 'insured' means an individual or, in relation to a qualifying insurance policy where—

    (a)   the insured is an individual and the spouse of that individual at the date the policy is effected;

    (b)   annual premiums are paid by either or both of them during their joint lives, and by the survivor of them during the life of such survivor; and

    (c)   the proceeds of the policy are payable on the death of such survivor, or on the simultaneous deaths of both such spouses,

means —

    (i)   where the proceeds of the policy are so payable on the death of such survivor, that survivor, and the proceeds of the policy shall be deemed to have been provided by such survivor, as disponer; or

    (ii)   where the proceeds of the policy are so payable on the simultaneous deaths of both such spouses, each of the spouses, and each such spouse shall be deemed to have provided the proceeds of the policy —

        (I)   to the extent that such proceeds are applied in paying the relevant tax of the insured who is that spouse, and

        (II)   where the proceeds of the policy are not applied in paying relevant tax, to the extent that the proceeds not so applied are comprised in an inheritance taken under a disposition made by that spouse."

Section 85

Exemption of specified collective investment undertakings.

85.   (1)   In this section "specified collective investment undertaking" and "unit" have, respectively, the same meanings as they have in section 18.

    (2)   Where any unit of a specified collective investment undertaking is comprised in a gift or an inheritance, then such unit —

        (a)   shall be exempt from tax, and

        (b)   shall not be taken into account in computing tax on any gift or inheritance taken by the donee or successor,

if, but only if, it is shown to the satisfaction of the Commissioners that —

    (i)   the unit is comprised in the gift or inheritance —

        (I)   at the date of the gift or at the date of the inheritance; and

        (II)   at the valuation date;

    (ii) at the date of the disposition –

        (I) the disponer is neither domiciled nor ordinarily resident in the State; or

        (II) the proper law of the disposition is not the law of the State;

    and

    (iii) at the date of the gift or at the date of the inheritance, the donee or successor is neither domiciled nor ordinarily resident in the State.

  (3) This section shall have effect as respects gifts and inheritances taken on or after the date of the passing of this Act.

PART VI
Anti-Avoidance

Section 86

Transactions to avoid liability to tax.

86. (1) (a) In this section –

    "the Acts" means –

    (i) the Tax Acts,

    (ii) the Capital Gains Tax Acts,

    (iii) the Value-Added Tax Act, 1972, and the enactments amending or extending that Act,

    (iv) the Capital Acquisitions Tax Act, 1976, and the enactments amending or extending that Act,

    (v) Part VI of the Finance Act, 1983, and the enactments amending or extending that Part, and

    (vi) the statutes relating to stamp duty,

    and any instrument made thereunder;

    "business" means any trade, profession or vocation;

    "notice of opinion" means a notice given by the Revenue Commissioners under the provisions of subsection (6);

    "tax" means any tax, duty, levy or charge which, in accordance with the provisions of the Acts, is placed under the care and management of the Revenue Commissioners and any interest, penalty or other amount payable pursuant to those provisions;

"tax advantage" means—

(i)   a reduction, avoidance or deferral of any charge or assessment to tax, including any potential or prospective charge or assessment, or

(ii)   a refund of or a payment of an amount of tax, or an increase in an amount of tax, refundable or otherwise payable to a person, including any potential or prospective amount so refundable or payable,

arising out of, or by reason of, a transaction, including a transaction where another transaction would not have been undertaken or arranged to achieve the results, or any part of the results, achieved or intended to be achieved by the transaction;

"tax avoidance transaction" has the meaning assigned to it by subsection (2);

"tax consequences" means, in relation to a tax avoidance transaction, such adjustments and acts as may be made and done by the Revenue Commissioners pursuant to subsection (5) in order to withdraw or deny the tax advantage resulting from the tax avoidance transaction;

"transaction" means—

(i)   any transaction, action, course of action, course of conduct, scheme, plan or proposal, and

(ii)   any agreement, arrangement, understanding, promise or undertaking, whether express or implied and whether or not enforceable or intended to be enforceable by legal proceedings, and

(iii)   any series of or combination of the circumstances referred to in paragraphs (i) and (ii) ,

whether entered into or arranged by one person or by two or more persons—

(I)   whether acting in concert or not, or

(II)   whether or not entered into or arranged wholly or partly outside the State, or

(III)   whether or not entered into or arranged as part of a larger transaction or in conjunction with any other transaction or transactions.

(b)   In subsections (2) and (3), for the purposes of the hearing or rehearing under subsection (8) of an appeal made under subsection (7) or for the purposes of the determination of a question of law arising on the statement of a case for the opinion of the High Court, the references to the Revenue Commissioners shall, subject to any necessary modifications, be construed as references to the Appeal Commissioners or to a judge of the Circuit Court or, to the extent necessary, to a judge of the High Court, as appropriate.

(2) For the purposes of this section and subject to subsection (3), a transaction is a "tax avoidance transaction" if, having regard to any one or more of the following, that is to say—

(a) the results of the transaction,

(b) its use as a means of achieving those results, and

(c) any other means by which the results or any part of the results could have been achieved,

the Revenue Commissioners form the opinion that—

(i) it gives rise to, or, but for this section, would give rise to, a tax advantage, and

(ii) the transaction was not undertaken or arranged primarily for purposes other than to give rise to a tax advantage,

and references in this section to the Revenue Commissioners forming an opinion that a transaction is a tax avoidance transaction shall be construed as references to them forming an opinion with regard to the transaction in accordance with the provisions of this subsection.

(3) Without prejudice to the generality of the provisions of subsection (2), in forming an opinion in accordance with that subsection and subsection (4), as to whether or not a transaction is a tax avoidance transaction, the Revenue Commissioners shall not regard the transaction as being a tax avoidance transaction if they are satisfied that—

(a) notwithstanding that the purpose or purposes of the transaction could have been achieved by some other transaction which would have given rise to a greater amount of tax being payable by the person, the transaction—

(i) was undertaken or arranged by a person with a view, directly or indirectly, to the realisation of profits in the course of the business activities of a business carried on by the person, and

(ii) was not undertaken or arranged primarily to give rise to a tax advantage,

or

(b) the transaction was undertaken or arranged for the purpose of obtaining the benefit of any relief, allowance or other abatement provided by any provision of the Acts and that transaction would not result directly or indirectly in a misuse of the provision or an abuse of the provision having regard to the purposes for which it was provided:

Provided that, in forming an opinion as aforesaid in relation to any transaction, the Revenue Commissioner shall have regard to –

(I)   the form of that transaction,

(II) the substance of that transaction,

(III) the substance of any other transaction or transactions which that transaction may reasonably be regarded as being directly or indirectly related to or connected with, and

(IV) the final outcome and result of that transaction and any combination of those other transactions which are so related or connected.n

(4) Subject to the provisions of this section, the Revenue Commissioners, as respect any transaction, may, at any time –

(a)   form the opinion that the transaction is a tax avoidance transaction,

(b)   calculate the tax advantage which they consider arises, or which, but for this section, would arise, from the transaction,

(c)   determine the tax consequences which they consider would arise in respect of the transaction if their opinion were to become final and conclusive in accordance with subsection (5) (e), and

(d)   calculate the amount of any relief from double taxation which they would propose to give to any person in accordance with the provisions of subsection (5) (c).

(5) (a) Where the opinion of the Revenue Commissioners that a transaction is a tax avoidance transaction becomes final and conclusive they may, notwithstanding any other provision of the Acts, make all such adjustments and do all such acts as are just and reasonable (in so far as those adjustments and acts have been specified or described in a notice of opinion given under subsection (6) and subject to the manner in which any appeal made under subsection (7) against any matter specified or described in the notice of opinion has been finally determined, including any adjustments and acts not so specified or described in the notice of opinion but which form part of a final determination of any appeal as aforesaid) in order that the tax advantage resulting from a tax avoidance transaction shall be withdrawn from or denied to any person concerned.

(b)   Subject to, but without prejudice to the generality of paragraph (a), the Revenue Commissioners may –

(i)   allow or disallow, in whole or in part, any deduction or other amount which is relevant in computing tax payable, or any part thereof,

(ii) allocate or deny to any person any deduction, loss, abatement, relief, allowance, exemption, income or other amount, or any part thereof, or

(iii) recharacterize for tax purposes the nature of any payment or other amount.

(c) Where the Revenue Commissioners make any adjustment or do any act for the purposes of paragraph (a), they shall afford relief from any double taxation which they consider would, but for this paragraph, arise by virtue of any adjustment made or act done by them pursuant to the foregoing provisions of this subsection.

(d) Notwithstanding any other provision of the Acts, where –

(i) pursuant to subsection (4)(c), the Revenue Commissioners determine the tax consequences which they consider would arise in respect of a transaction if their opinion, that the transaction is a tax avoidance transaction, were to become final and conclusive, and

(ii) pursuant to that determination, they specify or describe in a notice of opinion any adjustment or act which they consider would be, or be part of, the said tax consequences,

then, in so far as any right of appeal lay under subsection (7) against any such adjustment or act so specified or described, no right or further right of appeal shall lie under the Acts against that adjustment or act when it is made or done in accordance with the provisions of this subsection or against any adjustment or act so made or done that is not so specified or described in the notice of opinion but which forms part of the final determination of any appeal made under the said subsection (7) against any matter specified or described in the notice of opinion.

(e) For the purposes of this subsection an opinion of the Revenue Commissioners that a transaction is a tax avoidance transaction shall be final and conclusive –

(i) if, within the time limited, no appeal is made under subsection (7) against any matter or matters specified or described in a notice or notices of opinion given pursuant to that opinion, or

(ii) as and when all appeals made under the said subsection (7) against any such matter or matters have been finally determined and none of the appeals has been so determined by an order directing that the opinion of the Revenue Commissioners to the effect that the transaction is a tax avoidance transaction is void.

(6) (a) Where, pursuant to subsections (2) and (4), the Revenue Commissioners form the opinion that a transaction is a tax avoidance transaction, they shall immediately thereupon give notice in writing of the opinion to any person from whom a tax advantage would be withdrawn or to whom a tax advantage would be denied or to whom relief from double taxation would be given, if the opinion became final and conclusive, and the notice shall specify or describe—

    (i) the transaction which in the opinion of the Revenue Commissioners is a tax avoidance transaction,

    (ii) the tax advantage, or part thereof, calculated by the Revenue Commissioners which would be withdrawn from or denied to the person to whom the notice is given,

    (iii) the tax consequences of the transaction determined by the Revenue Commissioners, in so far as they would refer to the person, and

    (iv) the amount of any relief from double taxation calculated by the Revenue Commissioners which they would propose to give to the person in accordance with subsection (5) (c).

(b) Section 542 of the Income Tax Act, 1967, shall, with any necessary modifications, apply for the purposes of a notice given under this subsection, or subsection (10), as if it were a notice given under that Act.

(7) Any person aggrieved by an opinion formed or, in so far as it refers to the person, a calculation or determination made by the Revenue Commissioners pursuant to subsection (4) may, by notice in writing given to the Revenue Commissioners within 30 days of the date of the notice of opinion, appeal to the Appeal Commissioners on the grounds and, notwithstanding any other provision of the Acts, only on the grounds that, having regard to all of the circumstances, including any fact or matter which was not known to the Revenue Commissioners when they formed their opinion or made their calculation or determination, and to the provisions of this section—

(a) the transaction specified or described in the notice of opinion is not a tax avoidance transaction, or

(b) the amount of the tax advantage, or the part thereof, specified or described in the notice of opinion which would be withdrawn from or denied to the person is incorrect, or

(c) the tax consequences specified or described in the notice of opinion, or such part thereof as shall be specified or described by the appellant in the notice of appeal, would not be just and reasonable in order to withdraw or to deny the tax advantage, or part thereof, specified or described in the notice of opinion, or

(d) the amount of relief from double taxation which the Revenue Commissioners propose to give to the person is insufficient or incorrect.

(8) The Appeal Commissioners shall hear and determine an appeal made to them under subsection (7) as if it were an appeal against an assessment to income tax and, subject to subsection (9), all the provisions of the Income Tax Act, 1967, relating to the rehearing of an appeal and the statement of a case for the opinion of the High Court on a point of law shall apply accordingly with any necessary modifications:

Provided that on the hearing or rehearing of the appeal—

(a) it shall not be lawful to go into any grounds of appeal other than those specified in subsection (7), and

(b) at the request of the appellants, two or more appeals made by two or more persons pursuant to the same opinion, calculation or determination formed or made by the Revenue Commissioners pursuant to subsection (4) may be heard or reheard together.

(9) (a) On the hearing of an appeal made under subsection (7) the Appeal Commissioners shall have regard to all matters to which the Revenue Commissioners may or are required to have regard under the provisions of this section and—

(i) in relation to an appeal made on the grounds referred to in paragraph (a) of subsection (7), they shall determine the appeal, in so far as it is made on those grounds, by ordering, if they, or a majority of them—

(I) consider that the transaction specified or described in the notice of opinion, or any part of that transaction, is a tax avoidance transaction, that the opinion, or the opinion in so far as it relates to that part, is to stand good, or

(II) consider that, subject to such amendment or addition thereto as the Appeal Commissioners, or the said majority of them, deem necessary and as they shall specify or describe the transaction, or any part of it, specified or described in the notice of opinion, is a tax avoidance transaction, that the transaction, or that part of it, be so amended or added to and that, subject to the amendment or addition, the opinion, or the opinion in so far as it relates to that part, is to stand good, or

(III) do not so consider as referred to in clause (I) or (II), that the opinion is void,

or

(ii) in relation to an appeal made on the grounds referred to in paragraph (b) of subsection (7), they shall determine the appeal, in so far as it is made on those grounds, by ordering that the amount of the tax advantage, or the part thereof, specified or described in the notice of opinion be increased or reduced by such amount as they shall direct or that it shall stand good,

or

(iii) in relation to an appeal made on the grounds referred to in paragraph (c) of subsection (7), they shall determine the appeal, in so far as it is made on those grounds, by ordering that the tax consequences specified or described in the notice of opinion shall be altered or added to in such manner as they shall direct or that they shall stand good,

or

(iv) in relation to an appeal made on the grounds referred to in paragraph (d) of subsection (7), they shall determine the appeal, in so far as it is made on those grounds, by ordering that the amount of the relief from double taxation specified or described in the notice of opinion shall be increased or reduced by such amount as they shall direct or that it shall stand good.

(b) The provisions of this subsection shall, subject to any necessary modifications, apply to the rehearing of an appeal by a judge of the Circuit Court and, to the extent necessary, to the determination by the High Court of any question or questions of law arising on the statement of a case for the opinion of the High Court.

(10) The Revenue Commissioners may, at any time, amend, add to or withdraw any matter specified or described in a notice of opinion by giving notice (hereafter in this subsection referred to as the "notice of amendment") in writing of the amendment, addition or withdrawal to each and every person affected thereby, in so far as the person is so affected, and the foregoing provisions of this section shall apply in all respects as if the notice of amendment were a notice of opinion and any matter specified or described in the notice of amendment were specified or described in a notice of opinion:

Provided that no such amendment, addition or withdrawal may be made so as to set aside or alter any matter which has become final and conclusive on the determination of an appeal made with regard to that matter under subsection (7).

(11) Where pursuant to subsections (2) and (4), the Revenue Commissioners form the opinion that a transaction is a tax avoidance transaction and, pursuant to that opinion, notices are to be given under subsection (6) to two or more persons, any obligation on the Revenue Commissioners to maintain secrecy or any other restriction upon the disclosure of information by the Revenue Commissioners shall not apply with respect to the giving of the notices as aforesaid or to the performance of any acts or the discharge of any functions authorised by this section to be performed or discharged by them or to the performance of any act or the discharge of any functions, including any act or function in relation to an appeal made under subsection (7), which is directly or indirectly related to the acts or functions so authorised.

(12) The Revenue Commissioners may nominate any of their officers to perform any acts and discharge any functions, including the forming of an opinion, authorised by this section to be performed or discharged by the Revenue Commissioners and references in this section to the Revenue Commissioners shall, with any necessary modifications, be construed as including references to an officer so nominated.

(13) This section shall apply as respects any transaction where the whole or any part of the transaction is undertaken or arranged on or after the 25th day of January, 1989, and as respects any transaction undertaken or arranged wholly before that date in so far as it gives rise to, or would, but for this section, give rise to —

    (a) a reduction, avoidance or deferral of any charge or assessment to tax, or part thereof, where the charge or assessment arises by virtue of any other transaction carried out wholly on or after a date, or

    (b) a refund or a payment of an amount, or of an increase in an amount, of tax, or part thereof, refundable or otherwise payable to a person where that amount, or increase in the amount, would otherwise become first so refundable or otherwise payable to the person on a date,

which could not fall earlier than the said 25th day of January, 1989, as the case may be.

Section 90

Arrangements reducing value of company shares.

90. (1) In this section —

"arrangement" includes —

(a) any act or omission by a person or by the trustees of a disposition;

(b) any act or omission by any person having an interest in shares in a company;

(c) the passing by any company of a resolution; or

(d) any combination of acts, omissions or resolutions referred to in paragraphs (a), (b) and (c);

"company" means a private company within the meaning assigned by section 16(2) of [the Capital Acquisitions Tax Act, 1976];

"company controlled by a donee or successor" has the same meaning as is assigned to "company controlled by the donee or the successor" by section 16 of [the Capital Acquisitions Tax Act, 1976];

"event" includes —

(a) a death; and

(b) the expiration of a specified period;

"the Principal Act" means the Capital Acquisitions Tax Act, 1976;

"related shares" means the shares in a company, the market value of which shares is increased by any arrangement;

"related trust" has the meaning assigned to it by subsections (2) and (4);

"specified amount" means an amount equal to the difference between —

(a) the market value of shares in a company immediately before an arrangement is made, and ascertained under the provisions of section 16 or 17 of [the Capital Acquisitions Tax Act, 1976,] as if each share were a share in a company controlled by a donee or successor; and

(b) the market value of those shares, or of property representing those shares, immediately after the arrangement is made, and ascertained under the provisions of section 15 of [the Capital Acquisitions Tax Act, 1976],

and such specified amount shall be deemed to be situate where the company is incorporated.

(2) Where —

(a) a person has an absolute interest in possession in shares in a company;

and

(b)   any arrangement results in the market value of those shares, or of property representing those shares, immediately after that arrangement is made, being less than it would be but for that arrangement,

then, tax shall be payable in all respects as if a specified amount which relates to that arrangement were a benefit taken, immediately after that arrangement is made, from that person, as disponer, by—

(i)   the beneficial owners of the related shares in that company; and

(ii)   so far as the related shares in that company are held in trust (in this section referred to as the "related trust") and have no ascertainable beneficial owners, by the disponer in relation to that related trust as if, immediately after that arrangement is made, that disponer was the absolute beneficial owner of those related shares,

in the same proportions as the market value of the related shares, which are beneficially owned by them or are deemed to be so beneficially owned, is increased by that arrangement.

(3) Where—

(a)   an interest in property is limited by the disposition creating it to cease on an event;

(b)   immediately before the making of an arrangement to which paragraph (c) relates, the property includes shares in a company; and

(c)   the arrangement results in the market value of those shares, or of property representing those shares, immediately after that arrangement is made, being less than it would be but for that arrangement,

then, tax shall be payable under that disposition in all respects—

(i)   where the interest in property is an interest in possession, as if such property included a specified amount which relates to that arrangement;

(ii)   where the interest in property is not an interest in possession, as if it were an interest in possession and such property included a specified amount which relates to that arrangement; and

(iii)   as if the event on which the interest was limited to cease under that disposition had happened, to the extent of the specified amount, immediately before that arrangement is made.

(4) Where—

(a)   shares in a company are, immediately before the making of an arrangement to which paragraph (b) relates, subject to a discretionary trust under or in consequence of any disposition; and

(b) the arrangement results in those shares, or property representing those shares, remaining subject to that discretionary trust but, immediately after that arrangement is made, the market value of those shares, or of property representing those shares, is less than it would be but for that arrangement,

then, tax shall be payable under that disposition in all respects as if a specified amount, which relates to that arrangement, were a benefit taken immediately after that arrangement is made –

(i) by the beneficial owners of the related shares in that company; and

(ii) so far as the related shares in that company are held in trust (in this section referred to as the "related trust") and have no ascertainable beneficial owners, by the disponer in relation to that related trust as if, immediately after that arrangement is made, that disponer was the absolute beneficial owner of those related shares,

in the same proportions as the market value of the related shares, which are beneficially owned by them or are deemed to be so beneficially owned, is increased by that arrangement.

(5) The provisions of subsections (2), (3) and (4) shall not prejudice any charge for tax in respect of any gift or inheritance taken under any disposition on or after the making of an arrangement referred to in those subsections and comprising shares in a company, or property representing such shares.

(6) Where shares in a company, which are held in trust under a disposition made by any disponer, are related shares by reason of any arrangement referred to in this section, any gift or inheritance taken under the disposition on or after the arrangement is made and comprising those related shares, or property representing those related shares, shall be deemed to be taken from that disponer.

(7) In relation to the tax due and payable in respect of any gift or inheritance taken under the provisions of paragraph (ii) of subsection (2) or paragraph (ii) of subsection (4), and notwithstanding the provisions of [the Capital Acquisitions Tax Act, 1976] –

(a) the disponer in relation to the related trust shall not be a person primarily accountable for the payment of such tax; and

(b) a person who is a trustee of the related trust concerned for the time being at the date of the gift or at the date of the inheritance, or at any date subsequent thereto, shall be so primarily accountable.

(8) A person who is accountable for the payment of tax in respect of any specified amount, or part of a specified amount, taken as a gift or an inheritance under this section shall, for the purpose of paying the tax, or raising the amount of the tax when already paid, have

power, whether the related shares are or are not vested in him, to raise the amount of such tax and any interest and expenses properly paid or incurred by him in respect thereof, by the sale or mortgage of, or a terminable charge on, the related shares in the relevant company.

(9) Tax due and payable in respect of a taxable gift or a taxable inheritance taken under this section shall be and remain a charge on the related shares in the relevant company.

(10) Where related shares are subject to a discretionary trust immediately after an arrangement is made in accordance with the provisions of this section, the amount by which the market value of such shares is increased by such arrangement shall be property for the purposes of a charge for tax arising by reason of the provisions of section 106 of the Finance Act, 1984.

(11) This section shall apply only as respects a gift or an inheritance taken as a result of an arrangement which is made on or after the 25th day of January, 1989.

FIRST SCHEDULE
Accounting for and Payment of Tax Deducted from Relevant Payments and Undistributed Relevant Income

Penalties

3. (1) ....

(2) Section 94 (2) of the Finance Act, 1983, is hereby amended by the insertion after paragraph (dd) (inserted by the Finance Act, 1986) of the following paragraph:

"(ddd) (i) fails to make any deduction required to be made by him under section 18 (5) of the Finance Act, 1989, or

(ii) fails, having made the deduction, to pay the sum deducted to the Collector-General within the time specified in paragraph 1 (3) of the First Schedule to that Act.".

FINANCE ACT, 1990

Number 10 of 1990
(Enacted on 30th May, 1990)

PART VI
Capital Acquisitions Tax

Section 126

Interpretation (Part VI).

126. In this Part "the Principal Act" means the Capital Acquisitions Tax Act, 1976.

Section 127

Exemption for spouses (gifts).

127. (1) Notwithstanding the provisions of [the Capital Acquisitions Tax Act, 1976], a gift taken by a donee, who is at the date of the gift the spouse of the disponer, shall be exempt from tax and shall not be taken into account in computing tax.

(2) This section shall have effect in relation to a gift taken on or after the 31st day of January, 1990.

Section 128

Amendment of Second Schedule to [the Capital Acquisitions Tax Act, 1976].

128. (1) In computing in accordance with the provisions of the Second Schedule to [the Capital Acquisitions Tax Act, 1976,] the tax chargeable on the taxable value of a taxable gift or a taxable inheritance taken by a donee or successor on or after the 1st day of January, 1990, the threshold amount in relation to the computation of tax on any relevant aggregate of taxable values under the provisions of paragraph 3 of Part I of that Schedule (inserted by section 111 of the Finance Act, 1984) shall be adjusted by multiplying each such threshold amount by the figure, rounded to the nearest third decimal place, determined by dividing by 133.5 the consumer price index number for the year immediately preceding the year in which that taxable gift or taxable inheritance is taken:

Provided that, where the tax so computed on the taxable value of that taxable gift or that taxable inheritance is a minus amount, that tax shall be nil.

(2) In this section "the consumer price index number" means the All Items Consumer Price Index Number for a year as compiled by the Central Statistics Office and expressed on the basis that the consumer price index number at mid-November, 1982, is 100.

Section 129

Application of section 108 (exemptions) of Finance Act, 1984.

129. (1) For the purposes of section 108 (b) (ii) of the Finance Act, 1984, a sponsored superannuation scheme within the meaning of subsection (9) of section 235 of the Income Tax Act, 1967, shall not include a scheme or arrangement which relates to matters other than service in particular offices or employments.

(2) This section shall have effect in relation to a charge for tax which, apart from section 108 (b) (ii) of the Finance Act, 1984, arises on or after the 5th day of April, 1990, under the provisions of section 106 of the said Act of 1984 or of section 103 of the Finance Act, 1986.

Section 130

Application of section 60 (relief in respect of certain policies of insurance) of Finance Act, 1985.

130. For the purposes of section 60 of the Finance Act, 1985, "relevant tax" shall be deemed to include inheritance tax payable in respect of an inheritance taken under a disposition made by the spouse of the insured —

(a) where the inheritance is taken on the date of death of the insured, or

(b) where the inheritance is taken only in the event of the insured not surviving the spouse by a period of up to 31 days,

and the relevant qualifying insurance policy is –

(i) a policy of insurance within the meaning of paragraphs (a), (b) and (c) of subsection (1A) of that section (inserted by section 84 of the Finance Act, 1989), or

(ii) a policy of insurance where the insured is an individual and the proceeds of the policy are payable only on the contingency of the insured surviving that spouse.

FINANCE ACT, 1991

Number 13 of 1991
(Enacted on 29th May, 1991)

PART I – CHAPTER VIII
Taxation of Acquisition by a Company of its Own Shares

Section 61

Purchase of unquoted shares by issuing company or its subsidiary.

61. (1) Notwithstanding any provision of Part IX of the Act of 1976, references in the Tax Acts to distributions of a company, other than any such references in sections 101 and 162 of the Act of 1976, shall be construed so as not to include references to a payment made on or after the relevant day by a company on the redemption, repayment or purchase of its own shares if the company is an unquoted trading company or the unquoted holding company of a trading group and either –

    (a) (i) the redemption, repayment or purchase –

          (I) is made wholly or mainly for the purpose of benefiting a trade carried on by the company or by any of its 51 per cent. subsidiaries, and

          (II) does not form part of a scheme or arrangement the main purpose or one of the main purposes of which is to enable the owner of the shares to participate in the profits of the company or of any of its 51 per cent. subsidiaries without receiving a dividend,

        and

        (ii) the conditions specified in sections 62 to 66, so far as applicable, are satisfied in relation to the owner of the shares, or

    (b) the person to whom the payment is made –

        (i) applies the whole, or substantially the whole, of the payment (apart from any sum applied in discharging his liability to capital gains tax, if any, in respect of the redemption, repayment or purchase) to discharging,

          (I) within 4 months of the valuation date of a taxable inheritance of the company's shares taken by him, a liability to inheritance tax in respect of that inheritance, or

(II) within one week of the day on which the payment is made, a debt incurred by him for the purpose of discharging the said liability to inheritance tax,

and

(ii) could not, without undue hardship, have otherwise discharged that liability to inheritance tax and, where appropriate, the debt so incurred.

(2) Where subsection (1) would apply to a payment, made on or after the relevant day by a company which is a subsidiary (within the meaning of section 155 of the Companies Act, 1963) of another company on the acquisition of shares of the other company, if, for all the purposes of the Tax Acts other than this subsection—

(a) the payment were to be treated as a payment by the other company on the purchase of its own shares, and

(b) the acquisition by the subsidiary of the shares were to be treated as a purchase by the other company of its own shares,

then, notwithstanding any provision of Part IX of the Act of 1976, references in the Tax Acts to distributions of a company, other than references in sections 101 and 162 of the Act of 1976, shall be construed so as not to include references to the payment made by the subsidiary.

(3) In subsection (1) (b) (i) "valuation date" has the meaning assigned to it by section 21 of the Capital Acquisitions Tax Act, 1976.

PART VI

Capital Acquisitions Tax and Death Duties

Section 113

Interpretation (Part VI).
113. In this Part "the Principal Act" means the Capital Acquisitions Tax Act, 1976.

Section 114

Amendment of section 19 (value of agricultural property) of [the Capital Acquisitions Tax Act, 1976].
114. Subsection (1) of section 19 of [the Capital Acquisitions Tax Act, 1976,] shall—

(a) as respects a gift or inheritance taken on or after the 30th day of January, 1991, have effect as if "55 per cent." were substituted for "50 per cent." in the definition of "agricultural value", and

(b) as respects a gift or inheritance taken on or after the passing of this Act, have effect as if "80 per cent." were substituted for "75 per cent." in the definition of "farmer".

Section 115

Amendment of Second Schedule to [the Capital Acquisitions Tax Act, 1976].

115. (1) The Second Schedule to [the Capital Acquisitions Tax Act, 1976] (as amended by section 111 of the Finance Act, 1984) is hereby amended by the substitution of the following Part for Part II:

"PART II

Table

Portion of Value	Rate of tax
	Per cent.
The threshold amount	Nil
The next £10,000	20
The next £40,000	30
The next £50,000	35
The balance	40

"

(2) This section shall have effect in relation to gifts and inheritances taken on or after the 30th day of January, 1991.

Section 116

Inheritances taken by parents.

116. (1) In this section "class threshold of £150,000" means the class threshold of £150,000 in the definition of "class threshold" contained in paragraph 1 (inserted by section 111 of the Finance Act, 1984) of the Second Schedule to [the Capital Acquisitions Tax Act, 1976].

(2) Subject to subsection (3), the class threshold of £150,000 shall apply, and be deemed always to have applied, in relation to a taxable inheritance taken on or after the 2nd day of June, 1982, by a parent of the disponer where—

(a) the interest taken by the successor is not a limited interest, and

(b) the inheritance is taken on the date of death of the disponer.

(3) Notwithstanding the provisions of section 46 of [the Capital Acquisitions Tax Act, 1976], interest shall not be payable on any repayment of tax which arises by virtue of this section where such tax was paid prior to the date of the passing of this Act.

Section 117

Reduction in estimated market value of certain dwellings.

117. (1) In so far as an inheritance consists of a house or the appropriate part of a house —

(a) at the date of the inheritance, and

(b) at the valuation date,

and is taken by a successor who, at the date of the inheritance —

(i) is a brother or sister of the disponer,

(ii) has attained the age of 55 years,

(iii) has resided in the house with the disponer continuously for a period of not less than 5 years ending on the date of the inheritance, and

(iv) is not beneficially entitled in possession to any other house or the appropriate part of any other house,

the estimated market value of the house or the appropriate part of the house shall, notwithstanding anything to the contrary in section 15 of [the Capital Acquisitions Tax Act, 1976], be reduced by 50 per cent. or £50,000, whichever is the lesser:

Provided that where the house or the appropriate part of the house comprised in the inheritance referred to in subsection (1) is agricultural property within the meaning of subsection (1) of section 19 of [the Capital Acquisitions Tax Act, 1976,] and the successor is a farmer within the meaning of that subsection, the provisions of this section shall not apply.

(2) Where a house, or the appropriate part of a house to which subsection (1) relates was not in the beneficial ownership of the disponer for the period of 5 years ending on the date of the inheritance, that period of 5 years shall be deemed to include any period, immediately prior to the date on which the disponer acquired such beneficial ownership, during which the successor was residing continuously with the disponer in any other house, or the appropriate part of any other house, of the disponer.

(3) In this section —

"appropriate part", in relation to a house, has the meaning assigned to it in relation to property by subsection (5) of section 5 of [the Capital Acquisitions Tax Act, 1976];

"house" means a building, or a part of a building, used by the disponer as his main or only dwelling together with its garden or grounds of an ornamental nature.

(4) This section shall have effect in relation to inheritances taken on or after the 30th day of January, 1991.

Section 118

Application of section 60 (relief in respect of certain policies of insurance) of Finance Act, 1985.

118. For the purposes of section 60 of the Finance Act, 1985, "relevant tax" shall be deemed to include inheritance tax payable in respect of an inheritance taken under a disposition made by the spouse of the insured where the inheritance is taken on the date of death of the insured.

Section 119

Relief in respect of certain policies of insurance relating to tax payable on gifts.

119. (1) In this section—

"appointed date" means—

  (a) a date occurring not earlier than 8 years after the date on which a relevant insurance policy is effected, or

  (b) a date on which the proceeds of a relevant insurance policy become payable either on the critical illness or the death of the insured, or one of the insured in a case to which paragraph (b) of the definition of "insured" relates, being a date prior to the date to which paragraph (a) of this definition relates;

"insured" means—

  (a) where the insured is an individual, that individual, or

  (b) where the insured is an individual and the spouse of that individual at the date the policy is effected, that individual and the spouse of that individual, jointly or separately, or the survivor of them, as the case may be;

"relevant insurance policy" means a policy of insurance—

  (a) which is in a form approved by the Commissioners for the purposes of this section,

  (b) in respect of which annual premiums are paid by the insured,

  (c) the proceeds of which are payable on the appointed date, and

  (d) which is expressly effected under this section for the purpose of paying relevant tax;

"relevant tax" means gift tax or inheritance tax, payable in connection with an inter vivos disposition made by the insured within one year after the appointed date, excluding gift tax or inheritance tax payable on an appointment out of an inter vivos discretionary trust set up by the insured.

(2) The proceeds of a relevant insurance policy shall, to the extent that such proceeds are used to pay relevant tax, be exempt from tax and shall not be taken into account in computing such tax.

(3) Subject to the provisions of section 54 of [the Capital Acquisitions Tax Act, 1976,] and section 127 of the Finance Act, 1990, where the insured makes an inter vivos disposition of the proceeds, or any part of the proceeds, of a relevant insurance policy other than in paying relevant tax, such proceeds shall not be exempt from tax.

(4) A relevant insurance policy shall be a qualifying insurance policy for the purposes of section 60 of the Finance Act, 1985, where the proceeds of such relevant insurance policy become payable on the death of the insured or one of the insured in a case to which paragraph (b) of the definition of "insured" relates:

Provided that such relevant insurance policy would have been a qualifying insurance policy if it had been expressly effected under that section.

(5) A qualifying insurance policy for the purposes of section 60 of the Finance Act, 1985, shall be a relevant insurance policy where the proceeds of such qualifying insurance policy are used to pay relevant tax arising under an inter vivos disposition made by the insured within one year after the appointed date.

(6) Section 143 of the Income Tax Act, 1967 (as amended by section 60 of the Finance Act, 1985) is hereby amended by the addition to subsection (5) of the following paragraph after paragraph (c):

"(d) be given for the year 1991-92 and subsequent years of assessment in respect of premiums payable in respect of a relevant insurance policy within the meaning of section 119 of the Finance Act, 1991.".

Section 120

Capital acquisitions tax, waiver in respect of certain interest payable, etc.

120. (1) In this section "donee" includes a successor and a reference to a gift or a taxable gift includes a reference to an inheritance or a taxable inheritance, as the case may be, and a reference to gift tax includes a reference to inheritance tax.

(2) Where in respect of a gift taken on or before the 30th day of January, 1991 –

(a) gift tax is due and payable by a donee on any date on or before the 30th day of September, 1991, and

(b) in the period beginning on the 30th day of January, 1991, and ending on the 30th day of September, 1991, a return is delivered and gift tax is assessed in respect of the gift in accordance with the provisions of section 36 (inserted by section 74 of the Finance Act, 1989) of [the Capital Acquisitions Tax Act, 1976,] or section 104 of the Finance Act, 1986, and

(c) such gift tax is paid on or before the 30th day of September, 1991, interest payable on such gift tax up to the 30th day of April, 1991, shall be waived and penalties, if incurred, shall not be collected.

(3) For the purposes of subsection (2) where —

    (a) gift tax assessed on a taxable gift is being paid by instalments, or

    (b) a payment on account of gift tax has been made,

sums paid in discharge of earlier instalments or as a payment on account of tax shall, notwithstanding the provisions of subsection (4) of section 41 of [the Capital Acquisitions Tax Act, 1976], be applied or reapplied towards the discharge of tax in the first instance:

Provided that where the sum so paid is in excess of the sum to be so applied or reapplied, the excess shall not be repaid.

(4) This section shall not apply in relation to a gift —

    (a) where gift tax is due and payable by the donee concerned in respect of any other gift taken by him, unless such gift tax is paid on or before the 30th day of September, 1991,

    (b) where any capital gains tax is due and payable in respect of a disposal of the property comprised in the gift concerned, unless such capital gains tax and penalties (together with all interest due in respect of that tax) is paid at the same time or prior to the date of payment of the gift tax on that gift.

(5) Where additional gift tax becomes due and payable as a result of a revaluation of property included in a self assessed return, which was delivered on or after the 30th day of January, 1991, interest payable on such additional gift tax shall not be waived.

(6) (a) A fine or other penalty imposed by a court in connection with a gift shall not be waived.

    (b) Interest on gift tax, which has been ordered to be paid by a court, shall not be waived.

Section 121

Amendment of section 57 (exemption of certain securities) of Capital Acquisitions Tax Act, 1976.

121. (1) Section 57 of [the Capital Acquisitions Tax Act, 1976,] is hereby amended —

    (a) in subsection (1) by the substitution of the following definition for the definition of unit trust scheme:

"'unit trust scheme' means an authorised unit trust scheme within the meaning of the Unit Trusts Act, 1990, whose deed expressing the trusts of the scheme restricts the property subject to those trusts to securities.",

and

(b) in subsection (2) (as amended by section 40 of the Finance Act, 1978) by the substitution for "Unit Trusts Act, 1972" of "Unit Trusts Act, 1990".

(2) This section shall have effect in relation to gifts and inheritances taken on or after the 26th day of December, 1990.

PART VII
Miscellaneous

Section 129

Application of certain income tax provisions in relation to the collection and recovery of capital acquisitions tax, etc.

129. (1) In this section—

"the Collector" means the Collector-General appointed under section 162 of the Income Tax Act, 1967;

"the Commissioners" means the Revenue Commissioners;

"functions" includes powers and duties;

"the Principal Act" means the Capital Acquisitions Tax Act, 1976;

"tax" means any tax chargeable under the provisions of [the Capital Acquisitions Tax Act, 1976].

(2) Notwithstanding anything in [the Capital Acquisitions Tax Act, 1976], all sums due under the provisions of that Act shall be paid to the Collector or to such person as may be nominated under the provisions of this section.[1]

(3) Section 187 of the Income Tax Act, 1967, shall, with any necessary modifications, apply in relation to an assessment of tax, a correcting assessment of tax, or an additional assessment of tax as it applies in relation to assessments to income tax.

(4) The Collector shall collect and levy the tax from time to time charged in all assessments, correcting assessments and additional assessments of which particulars have been transmitted to him under subsection (3).

(5) All the provisions of the Income Tax Acts relating to the collection and recovery of income tax shall, subject to any necessary modifications, apply in relation to tax as they apply in relation to income tax chargeable under Schedule D.

(6) (a) The Revenue Commissioners may nominate persons to exercise on behalf of the Collector any or all of the functions conferred upon him by this section and, accordingly, those functions, as well as being exercisable by the Collector, shall also be exercisable on his behalf by persons so nominated.

(b) A person shall not be nominated under this subsection unless he is an officer or employee of the Commissioners.

(7) This section shall apply and have effect as on and from the 1st day of October, 1991.

Footnote

1   This provision affects s.41(9), CATA.

Section 130

Amendment of section 73 (deduction from payments due to defaulters of amounts due in relation to tax) of Finance Act, 1988.

130. (1) Section 73 of the Finance Act, 1988, is hereby amended in subsection (1) by the substitution of the following definition for the definition of "the Acts":

"'the Acts' means —

(i)   the Tax Acts,

(ii)   the Capital Gains Tax Acts,

(iii) the Value-Added Tax Act, 1972, and the enactments amending or extending that Act,

(iv) the Capital Acquisitions Tax Act, 1976, and the enactments amending or extending that Act, and

(v)   the Stamp Act, 1891, and the enactments amending or extending that Act,

and any instruments made thereunder;".

(2) This section shall apply and have effect as on and from the 1st day of October, 1991.

FINANCE ACT, 1992

Number 9 of 1992
(Enacted on 28th May, 1992)

PART VI
Capital Acquisitions Tax

Section 222

Interpretation (Part VI).
222. In this Part "the Principal Act" means the Capital Acquisitions Tax Act, 1976.

Section 223

Amendment of section 2 (interpretation) of [the Capital Acquisitions Tax Act, 1976].
223. (1) Section 2 of [the Capital Acquisitions Tax Act, 1976] (as amended by the Finance Act, 1989) is hereby amended by the substitution of the following for the interpretation of the word "child" in subsection (1):

"'child' includes

    (a)   a stepchild;

    (b)   a child adopted —

        (i)   under the Adoption Acts, 1952 to 1991; or

        (ii) under a foreign adoption which by virtue of section 2, 3, 4 or 5 of the Adoption Act, 1991, is deemed to have been effected by a valid adoption order within the meaning of section 1 of that Act;".

    (2)   This section shall have effect in relation to gifts and inheritances taken on or after the 30th day of May, 1991.

Section 224

Amendment of section 106 (acquisitions by discretionary trusts) of Finance Act, 1984.
224. (1) Section 106 of the Finance Act, 1984, is hereby amended —

    (a)   in subsection (1) (as amended by the Finance Act, 1985), by the substitution of "21 years" for "25 years" in paragraph (c), and

    (b)   by the insertion after subsection (2) of the following subsection —

"(2A) Property which, under or in consequence of any disposition, is subject to a discretionary trust on the 31st day of January, 1993, shall, for the purposes of subsection (1), be deemed to become subject to the trust on that date.".

(2) Subsection (1)(a) shall have effect in relation to property which becomes subject to a discretionary trust on or after the 31st day of January, 1993.

Section 225

Amendment of section 102 (interpretation (Part V)) of Finance Act, 1986.

225. (1) The definition of "chargeable discretionary trust" in section 102 of the Finance Act, 1986, is hereby amended by the substitution of "21 years" for "25 years" in paragraph (b).

(2) This section shall have effect in relation to any chargeable date occurring on or after the 5th day of April, 1994.

PART VII
Anti-Avoidance and Anti-Evasion

Section 232

Inspection of documents and records.

232. Chapter VI of Part I of the Finance Act, 1976, is hereby amended by the substitution of the following section for section 34:

"34. (1) In this section—

'authorised officer' means an officer of the Revenue Commissioners authorised by them in writing to exercise the powers conferred by this section;

'property' means any asset relating to a tax liability;

'records' means any document, or any other written or printed material in any form including any information stored, maintained or preserved by means of any mechanical or electronic device, whether or not stored, maintained or preserved in a legible form, which a person is obliged by any provision relating to tax to keep, to retain, to issue, to produce for inspection or which may be inspected under any provision relating to tax;

'tax' means any tax, duty, levy or charge under the care and management of the Revenue Commissioners;

'tax liability' means any existing liability to tax or further liability to tax which may be established by an authorised officer following the exercise or performance of his powers or duties under this section.

(2) (a) An authorised officer may at all reasonable times enter any premises or place where he has reason to believe that —

   (i) any trade or profession or other activity, the profits or gains of which are chargeable to tax, is or has been carried on,

   (ii) anything is or has been done in connection with any trade, profession or other activity the profits or gains of which are chargeable to tax,

   (iii) any records relating to —

      (I) any trade, profession, other source of profits or gains or chargeable gains,

      (II) any tax liability, or

      (III) any repayments of tax in regard to any person

   are or may be kept, or

   (iv) any property is or has been located,

   and may

   (A) require any person who is on those premises or in that place, other than a person who is there to purchase goods or to receive a service, to produce any records or property,

   (B) if he has reason to believe that any of the records or property which he has required to be produced to him under the provisions of this subsection have not been produced, search on those premises or in that place for those records or property,

   (C) examine any records or property and take copies of or extracts from any records,

   (D) remove any records and retain them for a reasonable time for the purposes of their further examination or for the purposes of any legal proceedings instituted by an officer of the Revenue Commissioners, or for the purposes of any criminal proceedings, and

   (E) examine property listed in any records.

(b) An authorised officer may, in the exercise or performance of his powers or duties under this section, require any person, whom he has reason to believe —

   (i) is or was carrying on any trade, profession or other activity the profits or gains of which are chargeable to tax,

(ii)   is or was liable to any tax, or

(iii) has information relating to any tax liability,

to give the authorised officer all reasonable assistance including providing information and explanations or furnishing documents and making available for inspection property as required by the authorised officer in relation to any tax liability or any repayment of tax in regard to any person.

(c)   Nothing in this subsection shall be construed as requiring any person carrying on a profession, or any person employed by any person carrying on a profession, to produce to an authorised officer any documents relating to a client, other than such documents—

(i)   as pertain to the payment of fees to the person carrying on the profession or to other financial transactions of the person carrying on the profession,

(ii)   as are otherwise material to the tax liability of the person carrying on the profession, or

(iii) as are already required to be provided following a request issued under the provisions of section 16 (inserted by section 101 of the Finance Act, 1991) of the Stamp Act, 1891,

and, in particular, he shall not be required to disclose any information or professional advice of a confidential nature given to a client.

(d)   This subsection shall not apply to any premises or place where a banking business, within the meaning of the Central Bank Act, 1971, is carried on or to any person, or an employee of any person, carrying on such a business.

(e)   (i)   An authorised officer shall not, without the consent of the occupier, enter any premises, or that portion of any premises, which is occupied wholly and exclusively as a private residence, except on production by such officer of a warrant issued by a Judge of the District Court expressly authorising the authorised officer to so enter.

(ii)   A Judge of the District Court may issue a warrant under subparagraph (i), if satisfied by information on oath that it is proper for him to do so for the purposes of this section.

(3)   A person who does not comply with any requirement of an authorised officer in the exercise or performance of his powers or duties under this section shall be liable to a penalty of £1,000.

(4)   An authorised officer, when exercising or performing his powers or duties under this section, shall on request show his authorisation for the purposes of this section.".

Section 236

Authorised officers and Garda Síochána.

236. Where an authorised officer (within the meaning of section 127A (inserted by this Act) of the Income Tax Act, 1967, section 17A (as so inserted) of the Finance Act, 1970, or section 34 (as so inserted) of the Finance Act, 1976, as the case may be) in accordance with the said section 127A, 17A or 34 enters any premises or place, he may be accompanied by a member or members of the Garda Síochána and any such member may arrest without warrant any person who obstructs or interferes with the authorised officer in the exercise or performance of his powers or duties under any of the said sections.

Section 237

Inspection of computer documents and records.

237. (1) In this section—

"the Acts" means—

(a)   the Customs Acts,

(b)   the statutes relating to the duties of excise and to the management of those duties,

(c)   the Tax Acts,

(d)   the Capital Gains Tax Acts,

(e)   the Value-Added Tax Act, 1972, and the enactments amending or extending that Act,

(f)   the Capital Acquisitions Tax Act, 1976, and the enactments amending or extending that Act, and

(g)   Part VI of the Finance Act, 1983,

and any instruments made thereunder;

"data" means information in a form in which it can be processed;

"data equipment" means any electronic, photographic, magnetic, optical or other equipment for processing data;

"processing" means performing automatically logical or arithmetical operations on data, or the storing, maintenance, transmission, reproduction or communication of data;

"records" means documents which a person is obliged by any provision of the Acts to keep, to issue or to produce for inspection, and any other written or printed material;

"software" means any sequence of instructions used in conjunction with data equipment for the purpose of processing data or controlling the operation of the data equipment.

(2) Any provision under the Acts which —

    (a) requires a person to keep, retain, issue or produce any records or cause any records to be kept, retained, issued or produced, or

    (b) permits an officer of the Revenue Commissioners —

        (i) to inspect any records,

        (iii) to enter premises and search for any records, or

        (iii) to take extracts from or copies of or remove any records,

shall, where the records are processed by data equipment, apply to the data equipment together with any associated software, data, apparatus or material as it applies to the records.

(3) An officer of the Revenue Commissioners may, in the exercise or performance of his powers or duties, require —

    (a) the person by or on whose behalf the data equipment is or has been used, or

    (b) any person having charge of, or otherwise concerned with the operation of, the data equipment or any associated apparatus or material,

to afford him all reasonable assistance in relation thereto.

Section 240

Amendment of section 23 (publication of names of defaulters) of Finance Act, 1983.

240. As respects the year 1992 and subsequent years, section 23 of the Finance Act, 1983, is hereby amended —

    (a) in subsection (2), by the insertion of "or any part of a year as they see fit" after "as respects each year", and

    (b) in subsection (3), by the insertion in paragraph (a) of "or lists" after "the list",

and the said subsection (2) and the said paragraph (a), as so amended, are set out in the Table to this section.

TABLE

> (2) The Revenue Commissioners shall, as respects each year or any part of a year as they see fit (being the year 1984 or a subsequent year), compile a list of names and addresses and the occupations or descriptions of every person—
>
> (a) upon whom a fine or other penalty was imposed by a court under any of the Acts during that year,
>
> (b) upon whom a fine or other penalty was otherwise imposed by a court during that year in respect of an act or omission by the person in relation to tax, or
>
> (c) in whose case the Revenue Commissioners, pursuant to an agreement made with the person in that year, refrained from initiating proceedings for recovery of any fine or penalty of the kind mentioned in paragraphs (a) and (b) and, in lieu of initiating such proceedings, accepted, or undertook to accept, a specified sum of money in settlement of any claim by the Revenue Commissioners in respect of any specified liability of the person under any of the Acts for-
>
> (i) payment of any tax,
>
> (ii) payment of interest thereon, and
>
> (iii) a fine or other monetary penalty in respect thereof.
>
> (a) the Revenue Commissioners shall include in their annual report to the Minister for Finance, commencing with the report for the year 1984, the list or lists referred to in subsection (2) for the year in respect of which the report is made, and

Section 241

Amendment of section 73 (deduction from payments due to defaulters of amounts due in relation to tax) of Finance Act, 1988.

241. Section 73 of the Finance Act, 1988, is hereby amended—

(a) in subsection (1) (b)-

(i) by the substitution of the following definition for the definition of "the Acts":

"'the Acts' means—

(i) the Customs Acts,

(iii) the statutes relating to the duties of excise and to the management of those duties,

(iii) the Tax Acts,

(iv) the Capital Gains Tax Acts,

(v) the Value-Added Tax Act, 1972, and the enactments amending or extending that Act,

    (vi) the Capital Acquisitions Tax Act, 1976, and the enactments amending or extending that Act, and

    (vii) the Stamp Act, 1891, and the enactments amending or extending that Act,

and any instrument made thereunder;",

  (ii) by the substitution of the following subparagraph for subparagraph (i) of the proviso to the definition of "debt":

    "(i) where a relevant person is a financial institution, any amount or aggregate amount of money, including interest thereon, which at that time is a deposit held by the relevant person —

      (I) to the credit of the taxpayer for his sole benefit, or

      (II) to the credit of the taxpayer and any other person or persons for their joint benefit,

    shall be regarded as a debt due by the relevant person to the taxpayer at that time,",

  (iii) by the insertion of the following additional proviso after the proviso to the definition of "debt":

"Provided also that, in the case of paragraph (i) of the preceding proviso, a deposit held by a relevant person which is a financial institution to the credit of the taxpayer and any other person or persons (hereafter referred to in this proviso as 'the other party or parties') for their joint benefit shall be deemed (unless evidence to the contrary is produced to the satisfaction of the relevant person within 10 days of the giving of the notices specified in paragraph (c) of subsection (2)) to be held to the benefit of the taxpayer and the other party or parties to the deposit equally and, accordingly, only the portion thereof so deemed shall be regarded as a debt due by the relevant person to the taxpayer at that time and where such evidence is produced within the specified time only so much of the deposit as is shown to be held to the benefit of the taxpayer shall be regarded as a debt due by the relevant person to the taxpayer at that time;",

and

  (iv) by the substitution of the following definition for the definition of "interest on unpaid tax":

"'interest on unpaid tax', in relation to a specified amount specified in a notice of attachment, means interest, that has accrued to the date on which the notice of attachment is given, under any provision of the Acts providing for the charging of interest in respect of the unpaid tax, including interest on an undercharge of tax which is attributable to fraud or neglect, specified in the notice of attachment;",

(b) in subsection 2 –

(i) by the substitution of the following subparagraph for subparagraph (ii) of paragraph (a):

"(ii) (I) the amount or aggregate amount, or

(II) in a case where more than one notice of attachment is given to a relevant person or relevant persons in respect of a taxpayer, a portion of the amount or aggregate amount,

of the taxes, interest on unpaid taxes and penalties in respect of which the taxpayer is in default at the time of the giving of the notice or notices of attachment (the said amount, aggregate amount, or portion of the amount or aggregate amount, as the case may be, being referred to in this section as 'the specified amount'),",

(ii) by the insertion of the following additional proviso after the proviso to subparagraph (iii) (I) of paragraph (a):

"Provided also that where the relevant person is a financial institution and the debt due by the relevant person to the taxpayer is part of a deposit held to the credit of the taxpayer and any other person or persons to their joint benefit the said return shall be made within a period of 10 days from –

(A) the expiry of the period specified in the notices to be given under paragraph (c), or

(B) the production of the evidence referred to in paragraph (c) (II).",

and

(iii) by the insertion of the following paragraph after paragraph (b):

"(c) Where a relevant person which is a financial institution is given a notice of attachment and the debt due by the relevant person to the taxpayer is part of a deposit held by the relevant person to the credit of the taxpayer and any other person or persons (hereafter in this paragraph referred to as 'the other party or parties') for their joint benefit, the relevant person shall, on receipt of the notice of attachment, give to the taxpayer and the other party or parties to the deposit a notice in writing in which is entered –

(i) the taxpayer's name and address,

(ii) the name and address of the person to whom a notice under this paragraph is given,

(iii) the name and address of the relevant person, and

(iv) the specified amount,

and which states that —

(I) a notice of attachment under this section has been received in respect of the taxpayer,

(II) under this section, a deposit is deemed (unless evidence to the contrary is produced to the satisfaction of the relevant person within 10 days of the giving of the notice under this paragraph) to be held to the benefit of the taxpayer and the other party or parties to the deposit equally, and

(III) unless such evidence is produced within the period specified in the notice given under this paragraph, a sum equal to the amount of the deposit so deemed to be held to the benefit of the taxpayer, and, accordingly, regarded as a debt due to the taxpayer by the relevant person, shall be paid to the Revenue Commissioners where that amount is equal to or less than the specified amount and where that amount is greater than the specified amount an amount equal to the specified amount shall be paid to the Revenue Commissioners.",

(c) in subsection (3), by the substitution of the following paragraph for paragraph (b):

"(b) the Revenue Commissioners have given the taxpayer a notice in writing (whether or not the document containing the notice also contains other information being communicated by the Revenue Commissioners to the taxpayer), not later than 7 days before the date of the receipt by the relevant person or relevant persons concerned of a notice of attachment, stating that, if the amount is not paid, it may be specified in a notice or notices of attachment and recovered under this section from a relevant person or relevant persons in relation to the taxpayer.",

(d) in subsection (10), by the substitution in paragraph (b) of "amount or aggregate amount of the taxes, interest on unpaid taxes and penalties in respect of which the taxpayer is in default at the time of the giving of the notice or notices of attachment" for "specified amount", and the said paragraph (b), as so amended, is set out in the Table to this section,

and

(e)   by the deletion of subsection (17).

TABLE

> (b)   Where, in pursuance of this section, a relevant person pays any amount to the Revenue Commissioners out of a debt due by him to the taxpayer and, at the time of the receipt by the Revenue Commissioners of the said amount, the taxpayer has paid the amount or aggregate amount of the taxes, interest on unpaid taxes and penalties in respect of which the taxpayer is in default at the time of the giving of the notice or notices of attachment to the Revenue Commissioners, the first-mentioned amount shall be refunded by the Revenue Commissioners forthwith to the taxpayer.

Section 243

Amendment of section 94 (revenue offences) of Finance Act, 1983.

243.   Section 94 of the Finance Act, 1983, is hereby amended —

(a)   in subsection 1 —

(i)   by the insertion of the following definition after the definition of "the Acts":

"'an authorised officer' means an officer of the Revenue Commissioners authorised by them in writing to exercise any of the powers conferred by the Acts;",

and

(ii)   by the insertion of the following paragraph after paragraph (e):

"(ee) knowingly or wilfully, and within the time limits specified for their retention, destroys, defaces, or conceals from an authorised officer —

(i)   any documents, or

(ii)   any other written or printed material in any form, including any information stored, maintained or preserved by means of any mechanical or electronic device, whether or not stored, maintained or preserved in a legible form, which a person is obliged by any provision of the Acts to keep, to issue or to produce for inspection.",

and

(b)   in subsection (3), by the substitution of the following paragraph for paragraph (a):

"(a) on summary conviction to a fine of £1,000 which may be mitigated to not less than one fourth part thereof or, at the discretion of the court, to imprisonment for a term not exceeding 12 months or to both the fine and the imprisonment, or".

FINANCE ACT, 1993

Number 13 of 1993
(Enacted on 17th June, 1993)

PART VI

Capital Acquisitions Tax

CHAPTER I

Taxation of Assets passing on Inheritance (Probate Tax)

Section 109

Interpretation (Chapter I).

109. (1) In this Chapter, except where the context otherwise requires—

"the Act of 1965" means the Succession Act, 1965;

"the consumer price index number" means the All Items Consumer Price Index Number for a year as compiled by the Central Statistics Office and expressed on the basis that the consumer price index number at mid-November, 1989, is 100;

"the deceased", in relation to the disposition referred to in section 110 (1), means the disponer;

"dependent child", in relation to the deceased, means a child who at the time of the deceased's death—

(a) was living and had not attained the age of 18 years, or

(b) was receiving full-time education or instruction at any university, college, school or other educational establishment and was under the age of 21 years or, if over the age of 21 years, was receiving such full-time education or instruction continuously since before attaining the age of 21 years;

"dependent relative", in relation to the deceased, has the meaning assigned to it by subsection (9A) (a) (inserted by the Finance Act, 1979) of section 25 of the Capital Gains Tax Act, 1975;

"the dwelling-house" means—

(a) a dwelling-house, or part of a dwelling-house, which was occupied by the deceased as his only or principal place of residence, at the date of his death,

(b) the curtilage of the dwelling-house which the deceased had for his own use and enjoyment with that dwelling-house up to an area (exclusive of the site of the dwelling-house) of one acre, and

(c) furniture and household effects being the normal contents of the dwelling-house:

Provided that—

(i) in the case of a dwelling-house, part of which was used mainly for the purpose of a trade, business, profession or vocation or was let, this definition shall not apply to the part so used or let, and

(ii) in a case where more than one dwelling-house is included in the estate of the deceased, and more than one such dwelling-house is used equally as a place of residence this definition shall apply only to one dwelling-house so used;

"the estate of the deceased" means the real and personal estate of the deceased as defined by section 10 (4) of the Act of 1965;

"the net market value of the dwelling-house" means the market value of the dwelling-house at the date of death of the deceased or, if less, that market value less the market value at that date of any sum which is charged or secured on the dwelling-house by the will, or other testamentary disposition, of the deceased and which is comprised in the share of an object of the relevant trust in the estate of the deceased, other than the share of a person whose place of normal residence was at that date the dwelling-house and who was on that date a dependent child or dependent relative of the deceased;

"object", in relation to a relevant trust, means a person entitled to a share in the estate of the deceased (otherwise than as a creditor);

"occupied", in relation to a dwelling-house or part of a dwelling-house, means having the use thereof, whether actually used or not;

"the Principal Act" means the Capital Acquisitions Tax Act, 1976;

"relevant threshold" means £10,000 multiplied by the figure, rounded to the nearest third decimal place, determined by dividing by 108.2 the consumer price index number for the year immediately preceding the year in which the death of the deceased occurred;

"relevant trust" means

(a) any trust under which, by virtue of the provisions of section 10 (3) of the Act of 1965, the executors of a deceased person hold the estate of the deceased as trustees for the persons by law entitled thereto, or

(b) any trust of which, by virtue of section 110 (3), the President of the High Court is deemed to be a trustee;

"share", in relation to the estate of the deceased, includes any share or interest, whether arising—

(a) under a will or other testamentary disposition, or

(b) on intestacy, or

(c) as a legal right under section 111 of the Act of 1965, or

(d)   as the subject of an order under section 117 (as amended by the Status of Children Act, 1987) of the Act of 1965. or

(e)   in accordance with the law of another country,

and includes also the right to the entire of the estate of the deceased.

(2)   A reference in this Act or in any Act of the Oireachtas passed after the passing of this Act to probate tax shall, unless the contrary intention appears, be construed as a reference to the tax chargeable on the taxable value of a taxable inheritance which is charged to tax by virtue of section 110.

Section 110

Acquisitions by relevant trusts.

110. (1)   Where, under or in consequence of any disposition, property becomes subject to a relevant trust on the death of a person dying after the date of the passing of this Act (in this section referred to as "the disponer") the trust shall be deemed on the date of death of the disponer to become beneficially entitled in possession to an absolute interest in that property and to take an inheritance accordingly as if the trust, and the trustees as such for the time being of the trust, were together a person for the purposes of [the Capital Acquisitions Tax Act, 1976,] and that date shall be the date of the inheritance.

(2)   The provisions of subsection (1) shall not prejudice any charge for tax in respect of any inheritance affecting the same property or any part of it taken under the disposition referred to in subsection (1) —

(a)   by an object of the relevant trust referred to in subsection (1), or

(b)   by a discretionary trust by virtue of section 106 (1) of the Finance Act, 1984,

and any such inheritance shall, except for the purposes of subsections (3) and (4) of section 55 of [the Capital Acquisitions Tax Act, 1976], be deemed to be taken after the inheritance referred to in subsection (1).

(3)   Where, under the provisions of section 13 of the Act of 1965, the estate of a deceased person vests on the date of death of the deceased in the President of the High Court, then, for the purpose of subsection (1), the President of the High Court shall be deemed to hold that estate as a trustee in trust for the persons by law entitled thereto, and the estate of the deceased shall be deemed to be property which became subject to that trust on that date.

(4)   The provisions of sections 10 and 13 of the Act of 1965, shall, for the purposes of subsection (1), be deemed to apply irrespective

of the domicile of the deceased or the locality of the estate of the deceased.

Section 111

Application of [the Capital Acquisitions Tax Act, 1976].

111. In relation to a charge for tax arising by virtue of section 110 –

(a) the valuation date of the taxable inheritance shall be the date of the inheritance;

(b) a reference in section 16 of [the Capital Acquisitions Tax Act, 1976] (as amended by the Finance Act, 1993) to a company controlled by the successor and the definition in that section of "group of shares" shall be construed as if (for the purpose of that reference) the list of persons contained in subsection (3) of that section and (for the purpose of that definition) the list of persons contained in that definition included the following persons, that is to say, the trustees of the relevant trust, the relatives of the deceased, the nominees of those trustees or of those relatives, and the trustees of a settlement whose objects include the relatives of the deceased;

(c) a person who is a personal representative of the deceased shall be a person primarily accountable for the payment of the tax;

(d) every person entitled for an interest in possession to a share in the estate of the deceased, and every person to whom or for whose benefit any of the property subject to the relevant trust is applied or appointed, shall also be accountable for the payment of the tax and [the Capital Acquisitions Tax Act, 1976,] shall have effect, in its application to that charge for tax, as if each of those persons were a person referred to in section 35 (2) of [the Capital Acquisitions Tax Act, 1976];

(e) where the total taxable value referred to in paragraph (a) of the proviso to section 113 exceeds the relevant threshold, section 36 (2) of [the Capital Acquisitions Tax Act, 1976] (inserted by the Finance Act, 1989) shall have effect, in the application of [the Capital Acquisitions Tax Act, 1976,] to any such charge for tax as aforesaid, as if –

(i) the reference in that subsection to four months were construed as a reference to nine months, and

(ii) the reference in that subsection to a person primarily accountable for the payment of tax were construed as including a reference to a person primarily accountable by virtue of paragraph (c) of this section;

(f) sections 19, 21, 35 (1), 36 (4) and 40, subsections (1) to (3) of section 41, and section 43 of, and the Second Schedule to, [the Capital Acquisitions Tax Act, 1976,] shall not apply;

(g) section 18 of [the Capital Acquisitions Tax Act, 1976,] shall have effect, in the application of [the Capital Acquisitions Tax Act, 1976,] to any such charge for tax as aforesaid, as if —

    (i) liabilities, costs or expenses incurred after the death of the deceased, other than reasonable funeral expenses, were not an allowable deduction,

    (ii) any bona fide consideration paid prior to the death of the deceased by an object of the relevant trust, in return for a share in the estate of the deceased, were consideration paid by the relevant trust on the date on which it was paid by the object, and

    (iii) where the property which is exempt from such tax is the dwelling-house, or a part thereof, the restriction on the deduction of any liability referred to in subsection (5) (e) of the said section 18 did not apply;

(h) section 60 of [the Capital Acquisitions Tax Act, 1976,] shall apply with the modification that, notwithstanding subsection (3) of that section, the Commissioners may refuse to issue the certificate referred to in subsection (1) of that section —

    (i) in a case where the tax is being wholly or partly paid by the transfer of securities to the Minister for Finance under the provisions of section 45 of [the Capital Acquisitions Tax Act, 1976], until such security as they think fit has been given for the completion of the transfer of the securities to the Minister for Finance, or

    (ii) in a case where payment of such tax has been postponed under the provisions of section 44 (1) of [the Capital Acquisitions Tax Act, 1976], or under section 118, until such tax as has not been so postponed has been paid together with the interest, if any, thereon, or

    (iii) in any other case, until the tax has been paid together with the interest, if any, thereon;

(i) section 2 (a) of section 57 of [the Capital Acquisitions Tax Act, 1976] (inserted by the Finance Act, 1978) shall not apply and subsection (2) (c) of that section shall be construed as if the reference therein to the donee or successor were a reference to the deceased;

(j) subsection (6) of section 36 of [the Capital Acquisitions Tax Act, 1976] (inserted by the Finance Act, 1989) shall have effect, in the application of [the Capital Acquisitions Tax Act, 1976,] to any such charge for tax as aforesaid, as if the reference in that subsection to a person primarily accountable for the payment of tax by virtue of section 35 (1) were a reference to a person primarily accountable by virtue of paragraph (c) of this section;

(k) section 55 of [the Capital Acquisitions Tax Act, 1976,] shall be construed as if the reference in subsection (4) of that section to the successor were a reference to the person who would be the successor for the purpose of that subsection if this Chapter had not been enacted; and

(l) section 63 of [the Capital Acquisitions Tax Act, 1976] (as amended by the Finance Act, 1989) shall have effect, in the application of [the Capital Acquisitions Tax Act, 1976] to any such charge for tax as aforesaid, as if —

(i) £1,000 were substituted for £5,000 in subsection (3) of that section,

(ii) £400 were substituted for £2,000 in subsection (1) (a) of that section,

(iii) £200 were substituted for £1,000 in subsections (2) and (7) of that section, and

(iv) £5 were substituted for £25 in subsection (1) (b) of that section.

Section 112

Exemptions.
112. The following property shall be exempt from tax (and shall not be taken into account in computing tax) in relation to a charge for tax arising by virtue of section 110 —

(a) any right to receive any benefit —

(i) under —

(A) any sponsored superannuation scheme within the meaning of section 235 (9) of the Income Tax Act, 1967, but excluding any scheme or arrangement which relates to matters other than service in particular offices or employments, or

(B) a trust scheme or part of a trust scheme approved under the said section 235 or section 235A of the said Act;

or

(ii) under any scheme for the provision of superannuation benefits on retirement established by or under any enactment; or

(iii) under a contract approved by the Commissioners for the purposes of granting relief for the purposes of section 236 of the Income Tax Act, 1967, in respect of the premiums payable in respect thereof;

(b) property given by the will of the deceased for public or charitable purposes to the extent that the Commissioners are satisfied that it has been, or will be, applied to purposes which, in accordance with the law of the State, are public or charitable;

(c) the dwelling-house, in a case where the deceased is survived by his spouse;

(d) in the case where the deceased is not survived by his spouse, the dwelling-house comprised in an inheritance which, on the date of death of the deceased, is taken under the will or other testamentary disposition or under the intestacy of the deceased, by a person who was on that date a dependent child of the deceased or a dependent relative of the deceased and whose place of normal residence was at that date the dwelling-house:

Provided that—

(i) the total income from all sources of that dependent child or that dependent relative, for income tax purposes, in the year of assessment ending on the 5th day of April next before that date, did not exceed the "specified amount" referred to in subsection (1A) of section 142 of the Income Tax Act, 1967,

(ii) the amount of the exemption shall (subject, with any necessary modifications, to the provisions of section 18 (4) (a) of [the Capital Acquisitions Tax Act, 1976,] in the case of a limited interest, and to the provisions of section 20 of that Act in the case of a contingency) be the whole or, as the case may be, the appropriate part (within the meaning of section 5 (5) of [the Capital Acquisitions Tax Act, 1976]) of the net market value of the dwelling-house, and

(iii) the amount of the exemption shall not be reduced by virtue of the provisions of section 20 of [the Capital Acquisitions Tax Act, 1976,] where an entitlement ceasing within the meaning of that section ceases because of an enlargement of that entitlement.

Section 113

Computation of tax.

113. The tax chargeable on the taxable value of a taxable inheritance which is charged to tax by virtue of section 110 shall be computed at the rate of two per cent. of such taxable value:

Provided that—

(a) where the total taxable value on which tax is chargeable by virtue of section 110 on the death of the deceased does not exceed the relevant threshold, that tax shall be nil, and

(b) where that total taxable value exceeds the relevant threshold, that tax shall not exceed the amount by which that total taxable value exceeds the relevant threshold.

Section 114

Relief in respect of quick succession.

114. Where by virtue of section 110 tax is payable in respect of any property on the death of one party to a marriage, then a charge to tax shall not arise by virtue of that section in respect of that property, or in respect of any property representing that property, on the death of the other party to the marriage within—

(a) one year after the death of the first-mentioned party, or

(b) 5 years after the death of the first-mentioned party, if that other party is survived by a dependent child of that other party.

Section 115

Incidence.

115. In relation to a charge for tax arising by virtue of section 110, property which, at the date of death of the deceased, represents any share in the estate of the deceased, shall, save to the extent that it is exempt from or not chargeable to such tax, bear its due proportion of such tax, and any dispute as to the proportion of tax to be borne by any such property, or by property representing any such property, may be determined upon application by any person interested in manner directed by rules of court, either by the High Court, or, where the amount in dispute is less than £15,000, by the Circuit Court in whose circuit the person recovering the same resides, or the property in respect of which the tax is paid is situate.

Section 116

Payment of tax.

116. (1) The person applying for probate or letters of administration of the estate of the deceased shall—

(a) notwithstanding the provisions of section 36 (inserted by the Finance Act, 1989) or section 39 of [the Capital Acquisitions Tax Act, 1976], make, on a form provided by the Commissioners, an assessment of the tax arising on the death of the deceased by virtue of section 110, and that assessment shall include the interest, if any, payable on the tax in accordance with paragraph (b) of section 117, and shall be of such amount as to the best of the said person's knowledge, information and belief, ought to be charged, levied and paid, and the form on which the assessment is made shall accompany the Inland Revenue Affidavit which is required to be delivered to the Commissioners, and

(b) on delivering the Inland Revenue Affidavit to the Commissioners, duly pay the amount of such tax and interest, and the Inland Revenue Affidavit and the form on which the assessment is made shall together, for the purpose of section 36 (2) of [the Capital Acquisitions Tax Act, 1976], be deemed, in relation to the tax arising by virtue of section 110, to be a return delivered by a person primarily accountable.

(2) The provisions of section 36 (3) (b) of [the Capital Acquisitions Tax Act, 1976] (inserted by the Finance Act, 1989) shall, with any necessary modifications, apply to any payment required by virtue of this section.

Section 117

Interest on tax.

117. In relation to a charge for tax arising by virtue of section 110—

(a) the tax shall be due and payable on the valuation date;

(b) simple interest to the date of payment of the tax shall, from the first day after the expiration of the period of 9 months commencing on the valuation date, be payable upon the tax at the rate of one and one-quarter per cent. per month or part of a month, without deduction of Income Tax, and shall be chargeable and recoverable in the same manner as if it were part of the tax;

(c) notwithstanding the provisions of paragraph (a), where, during the said period of 9 months, a payment is made on foot of the tax, the tax due at the time of the payment shall be discounted by an amount appropriate to the payment, such discount being calculated on tax at a rate per cent. equal to one and one-quarter per cent. multiplied by the number of months in the period from the date of payment to the date of the expiration of the said period of 9 months, and for this purpose a month shall include a part of a month:

Provided that insofar as the payment is repaid by the Commissioners in accordance with the provisions of section 46 of [the Capital Acquisitions Tax Act, 1976], no discount shall be appropriate to the payment;

(d) notwithstanding the provisions of paragraph (b), the interest payable upon the tax shall not exceed the amount of the tax.

Section 118

Postponement of tax.

118. Where the Commissioners are satisfied that there are insufficient liquid assets comprised in the estate of the deceased to meet any tax arising by virtue of section 110, they may allow payment to be postponed for such period, to such extent and on such terms as they think fit.

Section 119

Application of section 85 of Finance Act, 1989, and section 133 of Finance Act, 1993.

119. In relation to a charge for tax arising by virtue of section 110, section 85 (2) (b) (iii) of the Finance Act, 1989, and section 133 (2) (b) (iii) shall not apply.

CHAPTER II
Miscellaneous Amendments, etc.

Section 120

Interpretation (Chapter II).

120. In this Chapter "the Principal Act" means the Capital Acquisitions Tax Act, 1976.

Section 121

Amendment of section 5 (gift deemed to be taken) of [the Capital Acquisitions Tax Act, 1976].

121. (1) Where, on or after the 24th day of February, 1993, a person becomes beneficially entitled in possession to a benefit, and the property in which the benefit is taken consists wholly or partly of shares in a private company, section 5 of [the Capital Acquisitions Tax Act, 1976,] shall have effect as if "otherwise than for full consideration in money or money's worth paid by him" were deleted in subsection (1) thereof.

(2) In subsection (1) the expression "shares in a private company" shall be construed by reference to the meanings that "share" (as amended by this Act) and "private company" have, respectively, in section 16 of [the Capital Acquisitions Tax Act, 1976].

Section 122

Amendment of section 6 (taxable gift) of [the Capital Acquisitions Tax Act, 1976].

122. (1) Section 6 of [the Capital Acquisitions Tax Act, 1976,] is hereby amended by the substitution of the following subsection for subsection (1):

"(1) In this Act 'taxable gift' means—

(a) in the case of a gift, other than a gift taken under a discretionary trust, where the disponer is domiciled in the State at the date of the disposition under which the donee takes the gift, the whole of the gift;

(b) in the case of a gift taken under a discretionary trust where the disponer is domiciled in the State at the date

of the disposition under which the donee takes the gift
or at the date of the gift or was (in the case of a gift taken
after his death) so domiciled at the time of his death, the
whole of the gift; and

(c)   in any other case, so much of the property of which the
gift consists as is situate in the State at the date of the
gift.".

(2)   This section shall have effect in relation to a gift taken on or after
the date of the passing of this Act.

Section 123

Amendment of section 11 (inheritance deemed to be taken) of [the Capital
Acquisitions Tax Act, 1976].

123. (1)   Where, on or after the 24th day of February, 1993, a person becomes
beneficially entitled in possession to a benefit, and the property in
which the benefit is taken consists wholly or partly of shares in a
private company, section 11 of [the Capital Acquisitions Tax Act,
1976,] shall have effect as if "otherwise than for full consideration in
money or money's worth paid by him" were deleted in subsection
(1) thereof.

(2)   In subsection (1) the expression "shares in a private company"
shall be construed by reference to the meanings that "share" (as
amended by this Act) and "private company" have, respectively, in
section 16 of [the Capital Acquisitions Tax Act, 1976].

Section 124

Amendment of section 12 (taxable inheritance) of [the Capital Acquisitions
Tax Act, 1976].

124. (1)   Section 12 of [the Capital Acquisitions Tax Act, 1976,] is hereby
amended by the substitution of the following paragraph for
paragraph (a) of subsection (1):

"(a)   in the case where the disponer is domiciled in the State at the
date of the disposition under which the successor takes the
inheritance, the whole of the inheritance; and".

(2)   This section shall have effect in relation to an inheritance taken on
or after the date of the passing of this Act.

Section 125

Amendment of section 16 (market value of certain shares) of [the Capital Acquisitions Tax Act, 1976].

125. (1) Section 16 of [the Capital Acquisitions Tax Act, 1976,] is hereby amended —

    (a) by the substitution of the following subsection for subsection (1):

        "(1) (a) The market value of each share in a private company which (after the taking of the gift or of the inheritance) is, on the date of the gift or on the date of the inheritance, a company controlled by the donee or successor, shall be ascertained by the Commissioners, for the purposes of tax, as if, on the date on which the market value is to be ascertained, it formed an apportioned part of the market value of a group of shares in that company, such apportionment, as between shares of a particular class, to be by reference to nominal amount, and, as between different classes of shares, to have due regard to the rights attaching to each of the different classes.

        (b) For the purpose of ascertaining the market value of a share in a private company in the manner described in paragraph (a), the benefit to any private company (in this paragraph referred to as 'the first-mentioned company') by virtue of its ownership of an interest in shares in another private company (in this paragraph referred to as 'the second-mentioned company'), shall, where each of the companies so connected is a company which (after the taking of the gift or of the inheritance) is, on the date of the gift or on the date of the inheritance, a company controlled by the donee or successor, be deemed to be —

            (i) such benefit as would be appropriate to the ownership of that interest if the second-mentioned company were under the control of the first-mentioned company in the same manner as (on the date on which the market value is to be ascertained) the second-mentioned company is under the control of the following, that is to say, the first-mentioned company, the donee or successor, the relatives of the donee or successor, nominees of the donee or successor, nominees of relatives of the donee or successor, and the trustees of a settlement whose objects include the donee or successor or relatives of the donee or successor, or

        (ii)   the actual benefit appropriate to the ownership of that interest,

whichever is the greater.",

and

(b)   in subsection (2) –

    (i)   by the insertion of the following definition before the definition of "nominee":

      "'group of shares', in relation to a private company, means the aggregate of the shares in the company of the donee or successor, the relatives of the donee or successor, nominees of the donee or successor, nominees of relatives of the donee or successor, and the trustees of a settlement whose objects include the donee or successor or relatives of the donee or successor;",

   (ii) by the deletion of the definition of "private trading company", and

  (iii) by the insertion of the following definition after the definition of "private company":

      "'share', in relation to a private company and in addition to the interpretation of 'share' in section 2 (1), includes every debenture, or loan stock, issued otherwise than as part of a transaction which is wholly and exclusively a bona fide commercial transaction.".

(2) This section shall have effect in relation to gifts or inheritances taken on or after the 24th day of February, 1993.

Section 126

Amendment of section 90 (arrangements reducing value of company shares) of Finance Act, 1989.

126. (1) Section 90 of the Finance Act, 1989, is hereby amended –

(a)   in subsection (1), by the deletion of "or 17" in paragraph (a) of the definition of "specified amount", and

(b)   by the insertion after subsection (11) of the following subsection:

    "(12)Where, immediately after and as a result of an arrangement, shares in a company have been redeemed, the redeemed shares shall, for the purpose of the references to property representing shares in subsection (1) and subsection (2), (3) or (4), except a reference in relation to which the redeemed shares are actually represented by property, be deemed, immediately after the arrangement, to be represented by property, and the market value of the property so deemed to represent the redeemed shares shall be deemed to be nil.".

(2) This section shall apply where—

  (a) as respects subsection (1) (a), the time referred to in paragraph (a) of the definition of "specified amount" is on or after the 24th day of February, 1993, and

  (b) as respects subsection (1) (b), the arrangement to which the said subsection relates is made on or after the 6th day of May, 1993.

Section 127

Construction of certain references in section 16 of [the Capital Acquisitions Tax Act, 1976,] for purposes of "specified amount" in section 90 of Finance Act, 1989.

127. (1) For the purpose of paragraph (a) of the definition of "specified amount" in subsection (1) of section 90 of the Finance Act, 1989, section 16 of [the Capital Acquisitions Tax Act, 1976,] shall have effect as if—

  (a) the references therein to the donee or successor were references to the person who, for the purposes of section 90 of the Finance Act, 1989, is the disponer of the specified amount,

  (b) the references therein to the time at which a company is controlled were references to the time referred to in the said paragraph, and

  (c) the shares referred to in the said paragraph were, at the time referred to therein, the absolute property of the aforesaid disponer.

(2) This section shall apply where the time referred to in paragraph (a) of the definition of "specified amount" in subsection (1) of section 90 of the Finance Act, 1989, is on or after the 6th day of May, 1993.

Section 128

Amendment of section 19 (value of agricultural property) of [the Capital Acquisitions Tax Act, 1976].

128. Section 19 of [the Capital Acquisitions Tax Act, 1976,] shall, in so far as it relates to a gift taken on or after the passing of this Act, be construed as if —

  (a) in the definition of "agricultural value" the reference to 55 per cent. (inserted by the Finance Act, 1991) were a reference to 75 per cent., and

  (b) the references to £200,000 (inserted by the Finance Act, 1982) were references to £250,000.

Section 129

Amendment of section 34 (disposition by or to a company) of [the Capital Acquisitions Tax Act, 1976].

129. (1) Section 34 of [the Capital Acquisitions Tax Act, 1976,] is hereby amended by the substitution of the following subsections for subsections (1) and (2):

"(1) For the purposes of this Act –

(a) consideration paid by, or a disposition made by, a company shall be deemed to be consideration, or a disposition (as the case may be) paid or made, and

(b) consideration, or a gift, or an inheritance taken by a company shall be deemed to be consideration, or a gift or an inheritance (as the case may be) taken,

by the beneficial owners of the shares in the company and the beneficial owners of the entitlements under any liability incurred by the company (otherwise than for the purposes of the business of the company, wholly and exclusively) in the same proportions as the specified amounts relating to their respective beneficial interests in the shares and entitlements bear to each other.

(2) In this section –

'company' means a private company within the meaning of section 16 (2);

'market value' means –

(a) in the case of a person's beneficial interest in shares and entitlements, the market value of that interest on the date of the payment, disposition, gift or inheritance, as the case may be, ascertained by reference to the market value on that date of the shares and entitlements in which the interest subsists, and

(b) in the case of a share in which a beneficial interest subsists, the market value of that share ascertained in the manner described in section 16 as if, on the date on which the market value is to be ascertained, it formed an apportioned part of the market value of a group of shares consisting of all the shares in the company issued and outstanding at that date;

'share' has the same meaning as it has in section 16 (as amended by the Finance Act, 1993);

'specified amount', in relation to a person's beneficial interest in shares and entitlements, means –

(a) in the case of consideration paid, or a disposition made, by the company, a nil amount or, if greater, the amount by which the market value of the beneficial interest was decreased as a result of the payment of the consideration or the making of the disposition, and

    (b) in the case of consideration, or a gift, or an inheritance taken by the company, a nil amount or, if greater, the amount by which the market value of the beneficial interest was increased as a result of the taking of the consideration, gift or inheritance.".

(2) This section shall apply where the date of the payment, disposition, gift, or inheritance, to which subsection (1) relates, is on or after the 24th day of February, 1993.

Section 130

Amendment of Second Schedule (computation of tax) to [the Capital Acquisitions Tax Act, 1976].

130. As respects gifts or inheritances taken on or after the 24th day of February, 1993, paragraph 9 (inserted by the Finance Act, 1989) of Part 1 of the Second Schedule to [the Capital Acquisitions Tax Act, 1976,] is hereby amended —

  (a) by the substitution of the following definition for the definition of "company":

"'company' means a private company which, for the relevant period —

    (a) is a private company controlled by the disponer and of which the disponer is a director, and

    (b) is not a private non-trading company;",

  (b) by the deletion of the definition of "company controlled by the disponer",

  (c) by the insertion of the following definition after the definition of "control":

"'investment income', in relation to a private company, means income which, if the company were an individual, would not be earned income within the meaning of section 2 of the Income Tax Act, 1967;",

and

  (d) by the insertion of the following definitions after the definition of "nominee":

"'private company' has the meaning assigned to it by section 16 (2);

'private company controlled by the disponer' means a private company that is under the control of any one or more of the following, that is to say —

    (a) the disponer,

    (b) nominees of the disponer,

(c)   the trustees of a settlement made by the disponer;

'private non-trading company' means a private company—

(a)   whose income (if any) in the twelve months preceding the date at which a share therein is to be valued consisted wholly or mainly of investment income; and

(b)   whose property, on the date referred to in paragraph (a), consisted wholly or mainly of property from which investment income is derived;".

Section 131

Amendment of section 107 (application of [the Capital Acquisitions Tax Act, 1976]) of Finance Act, 1984.

131. (1)   Section 107 of the Finance Act, 1984, is hereby amended by the substitution of the following paragraph for paragraph (a):

"(a)   a reference in section 16 of [the Capital Acquisitions Tax Act, 1976,] to a company controlled by the successor and the definition in that section of 'group of shares' shall be construed as if (for the purpose of that reference) the list of persons contained in subsection (3) of that section and (for the purpose of that definition) the list of persons contained in that definition included the following, that is to say, the trustees of the discretionary trust, the living objects of the discretionary trust, the relatives of those objects, nominees of those trustees or of those objects or of the relatives of those objects, and the trustees of a settlement whose objects include the living objects of the discretionary trust or relatives of those living objects;".

(2)   This section shall have effect in relation to an inheritance taken on or after the 24th day of February, 1993.

Section 132

Amendment of section 104 (application of [the Capital Acquisitions Tax Act, 1976]) of Finance Act, 1986.

132. (1)   Section 104 of the Finance Act, 1986, is hereby amended by the substitution of the following paragraph for paragraph (a):

"(a)   a reference in section 16 of [the Capital Acquisitions Tax Act, 1976,] to a company controlled by the successor and the definition in that section of 'group of shares' shall be construed as if (for the purpose of that reference) the list of persons contained in subsection (3) of that section and (for the purpose of that definition) the list of persons contained in that definition included the following, that is to say, the trustees of the discretionary trust, the living objects of the discretionary trust, the relatives of those objects, nominees of those trustees or of those objects or of the relatives of those objects, and the trustees of a settlement whose objects include the living objects of the discretionary trust or relatives of those living objects;".

(2) This section shall have effect in relation to an inheritance taken on or after the 24th day of February, 1993.

Section 133

Exemption of certain policies of assurance.

133. (1) In this section "policy" means a contract entered into by a company in the course of carrying on a foreign life assurance business within the meaning of section 36 of the Finance Act, 1988.

(2) Where any interest in a policy is comprised in a gift or an inheritance, then any such interest —

(a) shall be exempt from tax, and

(b) shall not be taken into account in computing tax on any gift or inheritance taken by a donee or successor,

if, but only if, it is shown to the satisfaction of the Commissioners that —

(i) such interest is comprised in the gift or inheritance at the date of the gift or at the date of the inheritance;

(ii) at the date of the disposition —

(I) the disponer is neither domiciled nor ordinarily resident in the State, or

(II) the proper law of the disposition is not the law of the State;

(iii) at the date of the gift or at the date of the inheritance, the donee or successor is neither domiciled nor ordinarily resident in the State.

(3) This section shall apply to any interest in a policy issued on or after the 1st day of December, 1992.

Section 134

Repeal, etc. (Chapter II).

134. (1) Section 17 of [the Capital Acquisitions Tax Act, 1976,] is hereby repealed.

(2) This section shall have effect in relation to gifts or inheritances taken on or after the 24th day of February, 1993.

WAIVER OF CERTAIN TAX, INTEREST AND PENALTIES ACT, 1993

Number 24 of 1993
(Enacted on 14th July, 1993)

Section 3

Waiver of certain interest and penalties in respect of certain tax.

3. (1) (a) In this section—

"the Acts" means—

(i) the Acts within the meaning of section 2,

(ii) Chapter IV of Part V of the Income Tax Act, 1967,

(iii) section 17 of the Finance Act, 1970,

(iv) the Corporation Tax Acts,

(v) Part V of the Finance Act, 1920, and the enactments amending or extending that Part,

(vi) the Value-Added Tax Act, 1972, and the enactments amending or extending that Act,

(vii) the Capital Acquisitions Tax Act, 1976, and the enactments amending or extending that Act,

(viii) the Stamp Act, 1891, and the enactments amending or extending that Act, and

(ix) Part VI of the Finance Act, 1983, and the enactments amending or extending that Part,

and any instruments made thereunder;

"the due date" means, in relation to an amount of tax, the date on which a person becomes liable to interest under any of the specified provisions in respect of the late payment of that tax;

"tax" means any tax, duty, levy or contributions payable in accordance with any provision of the Acts.

(b) The reference in subsection (2) to an amount of tax due and payable shall, in a case where tax is assessed or estimated in an assessment or estimate against which an appeal has been made, be construed as a reference to the amount of tax which becomes due and payable on the determination of the appeal (within the meaning of section 550 (2A) (c) of the Income Tax Act, 1967) or, pending such determination, the tax as assessed or estimated.

(2) This section applies to a person who had not paid or remitted before the due date an amount of tax (in this Act referred to as "arrears of

tax") due and payable by him, or chargeable, in accordance with any provision of the Acts in respect of or during the relevant period.

(3) Where a person to whom this section applies has unpaid arrears of tax on the passing of this Act, he shall on or before the 14th day of January, 1994, and subject to the provisions of subsection (6), pay or remit those arrears of tax.

(4) Notwithstanding any other provision of the Acts but subject to the provisions of subsection (5) and section 4, where a person has paid or remitted, on or before the 14th day of January, 1994, his arrears of tax —

    (a) any amount of relevant interest to which the person may be liable in relation to arrears of tax and which is unpaid at the date of the payment or remittance referred to in subsection (3) shall be waived,

    (b) any amount of relevant interest in relation to arrears of tax which is paid by the person on or after the 26th day of May, 1993, shall be refunded to him, and

    (c) proceedings shall not be initiated or continued for the recovery of any fine or penalty to which the person may be liable under any of the specified provisions in relation to arrears of tax, nor shall the Revenue Commissioners seek or demand from the person payment of any sum in lieu of such fine or penalty.

(5) This section shall not apply to any interest, fine or other penalty that —

    (a) in the case of a fine or other penalty, is imposed by a court under any of the Acts,

    (b) in the case of interest, is ordered by a court in any proceedings for the recovery of tax or interest to be paid by a person, or

    (c) in any case, is included in a specified sum such as is referred to in subsection (2) (c) of section 23 of the Finance Act, 1983, where the full amount of the specified sum was not paid on or before the 25th day of May, 1993.

(6) (a) Where a payment or remittance in accordance with the provisions of subsection (3) is made by an individual who also remits a settlement amount, then, without prejudice to the amount of that payment or remittance, so much of that payment or remittance as is referable to value-added tax may be remitted to the Chief Special Collector.

    (b) Where, in accordance with paragraph (a), an individual makes a remittance to the Chief Special Collector, the individual by whom the remittance is made shall on the earlier of —

        (i) the date of payment, or

        (ii) a date within the specified period,

give a declaration in writing to the Chief Special Collector which—

    (I)   is made and signed by the individual,

    (II) is in a form prescribed by the Revenue Commissioners and approved of by the Minister, and

    (III) contains, in relation to that individual, a full and true statement of the amount of value-added tax comprised in the arrears of tax.

(c)   On receipt by him of the declaration referred to in paragraph (b) and the remittance referred to in paragraph (a), the Chief Special Collector shall give to the individual by whom the remittance is made—

    (i)   a certificate, in a form prescribed by the Revenue Commissioners and approved of by the Minister, stating, in relation to that individual—

        (I)   his name and address, and

        (II) the amount of the said remittance, and

    (ii) evidence, in a form prescribed by the Revenue Commissioners and approved of by the Minister, that such a certificate has been given.

(7)   Section 23 (4) of the Finance Act, 1983, is hereby amended by the substitution of the following paragraph for paragraph (aa) (inserted by section 72 of the Finance Act, 1988):

"(aa) the provisions of section 72 of the Finance Act, 1988, or section 3 of the Waiver of Certain Tax, Interest and Penalties Act, 1993, apply, or".

FINANCE ACT, 1994

Number 13 of 1994
(Enacted on 23rd May, 1994)

PART VI
Capital Acquisitions Tax

CHAPTER I
Business Relief

Section 124

Interpretation (Chapter I).

124.   (1)   In this Chapter —

"agricultural property" has the meaning assigned to it by section 19 of [the Capital Acquisitions Tax Act, 1976] (as amended by the Finance Act, 1994);

"associated company" has the meaning assigned to it by section 16 (1) (b) of the Companies (Amendment) Act, 1986;

"business" includes a business carried on in the exercise of a profession or vocation, but does not include a business carried on otherwise than for gain;

"excepted asset" shall be construed in accordance with section 134;

"full-time working officer or employee", in relation to one or more companies, means any officer or employee who devotes substantially the whole of his time to the service of that company, or those companies taken together, in a managerial or technical capacity;

"holding company" and "subsidiary" have the meanings assigned to them, respectively, by section 155 of the Companies Act, 1963;

"the Principal Act" means the Capital Acquisitions Tax Act, 1976;

"quoted", in relation to any shares or securities, means quoted on a recognised stock exchange and "unquoted", in relation to any shares or securities, means not so quoted;

"relevant business property" shall be construed in accordance with section 127.

(2)   In this Chapter a reference to a gift shall be construed as a reference to a taxable gift and a reference to an inheritance shall be construed as a reference to a taxable inheritance.

(3)   For the purposes of this Chapter a company and all its subsidiaries and any associated company of that company or of any of those

subsidiaries and any subsidiary of such an associated company are members of a group.

Section 125

Application (Chapter I).

125. The provisions of this Chapter shall have effect in relation to gifts and inheritances taken on or after the 11th day of April, 1994, but those provisions shall not have effect in relation to an inheritance taken by a relevant trust by virtue of section 110 (1) of the Finance Act, 1993, or to an inheritance taken by a discretionary trust by virtue of section 106 (1) of the Finance Act, 1984, or section 103 (1) of the Finance Act, 1986.

Section 126

Business relief.

126. (1) Where the whole or part of the taxable value of any gift or inheritance is attributable to the value of any relevant business property, the whole or that part of the taxable value shall, subject to the other provisions of this Chapter, be treated as being reduced —

(a) by 25 per cent., and

(b) by a further 25 per cent. or £62,500, whichever is the lesser.

(2) In relation to the deduction referred to at paragraph (b) of subsection (1), the total amount deductible under that paragraph shall not exceed £62,500, in respect of the aggregate of all gifts and inheritances, which consist in whole or in part of relevant business property, taken on or after the 11th day of April, 1994, by the same person, as donee or successor.

Section 127

Relevant business property.

127. (1) In this Chapter and subject to the following provisions of this section and to sections 128, 130 and 134 (3) "relevant business property" means, in relation to a gift or inheritance, any one or more of the following, that is to say:

(a) property consisting of a business or interest in a business;

(b) unquoted shares in or securities of a company incorporated in the State to which paragraph (c) does not relate, and which on the valuation date (either by themselves alone or together with other shares or securities in that company in the absolute beneficial ownership of the donee or successor on that date) give control of powers of voting on all questions affecting the company as a whole which if exercised would yield more than 25 per cent. of the votes capable of being exercised thereon;

(c) unquoted shares in or securities of a company incorporated in the State which on the valuation date (either by themselves alone or together with other shares or securities in that company in the absolute beneficial ownership of the donee or successor on that date) have an aggregate nominal value which represents 10 per cent. or more of the aggregate nominal value of the entire share capital and securities of the company, if but only if the company (after the taking of the gift or inheritance) is on that date a company controlled by the donee or successor within the meaning of section 16 of [the Capital Acquisitions Tax Act, 1976];

(d) unquoted shares in or securities of a company incorporated in the State which do not fall within paragraph (b) or (c) and which on the valuation date (either by themselves alone or together with other shares or securities in that company in the absolute beneficial ownership of the donee or successor on that date) have an aggregate nominal value which represents 10 per cent. or more of the aggregate nominal value of the entire share capital and securities of the company:

Provided that the donee or successor has been a full-time working officer or employee of the company, or if that company is a member of a group, of one or more companies which are members of the group, throughout the period of 5 years ending on the date of the gift or inheritance;

(e) in so far as is situated in the State, any land or building, machinery or plant which, immediately before the gift or inheritance was used wholly or mainly for the purposes of a business carried on by a company of which the disponer then had control or by a partnership of which the disponer then was a partner and for the purposes of this paragraph a person shall be deemed to have control of a company at any time if he then had control of powers of voting on all questions affecting the company as a whole which if exercised would have yielded a majority of the votes capable of being exercised thereon;

(f) quoted shares in or securities of a company which, but for the fact that they are quoted, would be shares or securities to which paragraph (b), (c) or (d) would relate:

Provided that such shares or securities, or other shares in or securities of the same company which are represented by those shares or securities, were in the beneficial ownership of the disponer immediately prior to the disposition and were unquoted at the date of the commencement of that beneficial ownership or at the date of the passing of this Act, whichever is the later date.

(2) Where a company has shares or securities of any class giving powers of voting limited to either or both —

    (a) the question of winding-up the company, and

    (b) any question primarily affecting shares or securities of that class,

the reference in subsection (1) to all questions affecting the company as a whole shall have effect as a reference to all such questions except any in relation to which those powers are capable of being exercised.

(3) A business or interest in a business, or shares in or securities of a company, shall not be relevant business property in relation to a gift or inheritance if, on the date of the gift or inheritance, the business or, as the case may be, the business carried on by the company was wholly or mainly carried on outside the State, and where the business concerned was carried on by a holding company, the business of that holding company shall be treated as having been carried on wholly or mainly outside the State on that date if that business and the business carried on by any subsidiary of that holding company were, taken as a whole, carried on wholly or mainly outside the State.

(4) A business or interest in a business, or shares in or securities of a company, shall not be relevant business property if the business or, as the case may be, the business carried on by the company consists wholly or mainly of one or more of the following, that is to say, dealing in currencies, securities, stocks or shares, land or buildings, or making or holding investments.

(5) Subsection (4) shall not apply to shares in or securities of a company if the business of the company consists wholly or mainly in being a holding company of one or more companies whose business does not fall within that subsection.

(6) Any land, building, machinery or plant in the beneficial ownership of the disponer and used wholly or mainly for the purposes of a business carried on as mentioned in subsection (1) (e) shall not be relevant business property in relation to a gift or inheritance taken by a donee or successor, unless the disponer's interest in the business is, or shares in or securities of the company carrying on the business immediately before the gift or inheritance are, relevant business property in relation to that gift or inheritance or in relation to a simultaneous gift or inheritance taken by that donee or successor from the same disponer.

Section 128

Minimum period of ownership.

128. In relation to a gift or an inheritance, property shall not be relevant business property unless it was comprised in the disposition continuously —

(a) in the case of an inheritance, which is taken on the date of death of the disponer, for a period of two years immediately prior to the date of the inheritance, or

(b) in any other case, for a period of five years immediately prior to the date of the gift or inheritance,

and any period immediately before the date of the disposition during which the property was continuously in the beneficial ownership of the disponer, or of the spouse of the disponer, shall be deemed, for the purposes of this Chapter, to be a period or part of a period immediately before the date of the gift or inheritance during which it was continuously comprised in the disposition.

Section 129

Replacements.

129. (1) Property shall be treated as complying with section 128 if —

(a) the property replaced other property and the said property, that other property and any property directly or indirectly replaced by that other property were comprised in the disposition for periods which together comprised —

(i) in a case referred to at paragraph (a) of section 128, at least two years falling within the three years immediately preceding the date of the inheritance, or

(ii) in a case referred to at paragraph (b) of section 128, at least five years falling within the six years immediately preceding the date of the gift or inheritance, and

(b) any other property concerned was such that, had the gift or inheritance been taken immediately before it was replaced, it would, apart from section 128, have been relevant business property in relation to the gift or inheritance.

(2) In a case to which subsection (1) relates, relief under this Chapter shall not exceed what it would have been had the replacement or any one or more of the replacements not been made.

(3) For the purposes of subsection (2) changes resulting from the formation, alteration or dissolution of a partnership, or from the acquisition of a business by a company controlled (within the meaning of section 16 of [the Capital Acquisitions Tax Act, 1976]) by the former owner of the business, shall be disregarded.

Section 130

Succession.

130. For the purposes of sections 128 and 129, where a disponer became beneficially entitled to any property on the death of another person the disponer shall be deemed to have been beneficially entitled to it from the date of that death.

Section 131

Successive benefits.

131. (1) Where —

(a) a gift or inheritance (in this section referred to as "the earlier benefit") was eligible for relief under this Chapter or would have been so eligible if such relief had been capable of being given in respect of gifts and inheritances taken at that time, and

(b) the whole or part of the property which, in relation to the earlier benefit was relevant business property became, through the earlier benefit, the property of the person or of the spouse of the person who is the disponer in relation to a subsequent gift or inheritance (in this section referred to as "the subsequent benefit"), and

(c) that property, or part, or any property directly or indirectly replacing it, would, apart from section 128, have been relevant business property in relation to the subsequent benefit, and

(d) the subsequent benefit is an inheritance taken on the death of the disponer,

then the property which would have been relevant business property but for section 128 shall be relevant business property notwithstanding that section.

(2) Where the property which, by virtue of subsection (1), is relevant business property replaced the property or part referred to in subsection (1) (c), relief under this Chapter shall not exceed what it would have been had the replacement or any one or more of the replacements not been made, and section 129 (3) shall apply with the necessary modifications for the purposes of this subsection.

(3) Where, in relation to the earlier benefit, the amount of the taxable value of the gift or inheritance which was attributable to the property or part referred to in subsection (1) (c) was part only of its value, a like part only of the value which, apart from this subsection, would fall to be reduced under this Chapter by virtue of this section shall be so reduced.

Section 132

Value of business.

132. For the purposes of this Chapter —

(a) the value of a business or of an interest in a business shall be taken to be its net value;

(b) subject to paragraph (c), the net value of a business shall be taken to be the market value of the assets used in the business (including goodwill) reduced by the aggregate market value of any liabilities incurred for the purposes of the business;

(c) in ascertaining the net value of an interest in a business, no regard shall be had to assets or liabilities other than those by reference to which the net value of the entire business would fall to be ascertained.

Section 133

Value of certain shares and securities.

133. (1) Where a company is a member of a group and the business of any other company which is a member of the group falls within section 127 (4), then, unless that business consists wholly or mainly in the holding of land or buildings wholly or mainly occupied by members of the group whose business does not fall within section 127 (4), the value of shares in or securities of the company shall be taken for the purposes of this Chapter to be what it would be if that other company were not a member of the group.

(2) (a) In this subsection "shares" include securities and "shares in a company" include other shares in the same company which are represented by those shares.

(b) Where unquoted shares in a company which is a member of a group are comprised in a gift or inheritance and shares in another company which is also a member of the group are quoted on the valuation date, the value of the first-mentioned shares shall be taken, for the purpose of this Chapter, to be what it would be if that other company were not a member of the group, unless those unquoted shares were in the beneficial ownership of the disponer immediately prior to the disposition and those quoted shares were —

(i) unquoted[1] at some time prior to the gift or inheritance when they were in the beneficial ownership of the disponer or a member of that group, while being a member of such group, or

(ii) at the date of the passing of this Act,

whichever is the later date.

Footnote

1   The word "unquoted" should have been included in the previous line.

Section 134

Exclusion of value of excepted assets.

134. (1) In determining for the purposes of this Chapter what part of the taxable value of a gift or inheritance is attributable to the value of relevant business property, so much of the last-mentioned value as is attributable to —

(a) agricultural property,

(b) any excepted assets within the meaning of subsection (2), or

(c) any excluded property within the meaning of subsection (7),

shall be left out of account.

(2) An asset shall be an excepted asset in relation to any relevant business property if it was not used wholly or mainly for the purposes of the business concerned throughout the whole or the last two years of the relevant period, but where the business concerned is carried on by a company which is a member of a group, the use of an asset for the purposes of a business carried on by another company which at the time of the use and immediately prior to the gift or inheritance was also a member of that group shall be treated as use for the purposes of the business concerned, unless that other company's membership of the group falls to be disregarded under section 133:

Provided that the use of an asset for the purposes of farming (within the meaning of section 13 of the Finance Act, 1974) or for the purposes of a business to which section 127 (4) relates shall not be treated as use for the purposes of the business concerned.

(3) Subsection (2) shall not apply in relation to an asset which is relevant business property by virtue only of section 127 (1) (e), and an asset shall not be relevant business property by virtue only of that provision unless either —

(a) it was used in the manner referred to in that provision —

(i) in the case where the disponer's interest in the business or the shares in or securities of the company carrying on the business are comprised in an inheritance taken on the date of death of the disponer, throughout the two years immediately preceding the date of the inheritance, or

(ii) in any other case, throughout the five years immediately preceding the date of the gift or inheritance,

or

(b) it replaced another asset so used and it and the other asset and any asset directly or indirectly replaced by that other asset were so used for periods which together comprised —

(i) in the case referred to at paragraph (a) (i), at least two years falling within the three years immediately preceding the date of the inheritance, or

(ii) in any other case, at least five years falling within the six years immediately preceding the date of the gift or inheritance;

but where section 131 applies paragraphs (a) and (b) shall be deemed to be complied with if the asset, or that asset and the asset or assets replaced by it, was or were so used throughout the period between the earlier and the subsequent benefit mentioned in that section, or throughout the part of that period during which it or they were in the beneficial ownership of the disponer or the disponer's spouse.

(4) Where part but not the whole of any land or building is used exclusively for the purposes of any business and the land or building would, but for this subsection, be an excepted asset, or, as the case may be, prevented by subsection (3) from being relevant business property, the part so used and the remainder shall for the purposes of this section be treated as separate assets, and the value of the part so used shall (if it would otherwise be less) be taken to be such proportion of the value of the whole as may be just.

(5) For the purposes of this section the relevant period, in relation to any asset, shall be the period immediately preceding the gift or inheritance during which the asset or, if the relevant business property is an interest in a business, a corresponding interest in the asset, was comprised in the disposition (within the meaning of section 128) or, if the business concerned is that of a company, was beneficially owned by that company or any other company which immediately before the gift or inheritance was a member of the same group.

(6) For the purposes of this section an asset shall be deemed not to have been used wholly or mainly for the purposes of the business concerned at any time when it was used wholly or mainly for the personal benefit of the disponer or of a relative of the disponer.

(7) Where, in relation to a gift or an inheritance—

(a) relevant business property consisting of shares in or securities of a company are comprised in the gift or inheritance on the valuation date, and

(b) property consisting of a business, or interest in a business, not falling within section 127 (4) (hereinafter in this section referred to as "company business property") is on that date beneficially owned by that company or, where that company is a holding company of one or more companies within the same group, by any company within that group,

that company business property shall, for the purposes of subsection (1), be excluded property in relation to those shares or securities unless it would have been relevant business property if—

(i) it had been the subject matter of that gift or inheritance, and

    (ii)   it and any other company business property directly or indirectly replaced by it had been comprised in the disposition for the periods during which they were in the beneficial ownership of any member of that group, while being such a member, or actually comprised in the disposition,

and shares in or securities of a company which replace, or which are replaced by, other such shares or company business property shall be treated as company business property for the purposes of this section if the company was the beneficial owner of the company business property and a member of that group at the time of the replacement:

Provided that where, by virtue of the provisions of this subsection, company business property would have been excluded property but for the conditions of paragraphs (i) and (ii) having been complied with, the provisions of subsection (2) of section 129 shall, with any necessary modifications, apply to that company business property as to a case to which subsection (1) of section 129 relates.

Section 135

Withdrawal of relief.

135. (1)   In this section "relevant period", in relation to relevant business property comprised in a gift or inheritance, means the period of six years after the valuation date or the period between the date of the gift or inheritance and the date of a subsequent gift or inheritance consisting of the same property or of property representing that property, whichever is the lesser period.

(2)   The reduction which would fall to be made under section 126 in respect of relevant business property comprised in a gift or inheritance shall cease to be applicable if and to the extent that the property, or any property which directly or indirectly replaces it—

    (a)   would not be relevant business property (apart from section 128 and the provisos to paragraphs (d) and (f) of subsection (1) of section 127 and other than by reason of bankruptcy or a bona fide winding-up on grounds of insolvency) in relation to a notional gift of such property taken by the same donee or successor from the same disponer at any time within the relevant period, unless it would be relevant business property (apart from section 128 and the provisos to paragraphs (d) and (f) of subsection (1) of section 127) in relation to another such notional gift taken within a year after the first-mentioned notional gift;

    (b)   is sold, redeemed or compulsorily acquired within the relevant period and is not replaced, within a year of the sale, redemption or compulsory acquisition, by other property (other than quoted shares or securities or unquoted shares or securities to which section 133 (2) (b) relates) which would be relevant business property (apart from section 128 and the proviso to section 127 (1) (d)) in relation to a notional gift of that other property taken by the same donee or successor from the same disponer on the date of the replacement,

and tax shall be chargeable in respect of the gift or inheritance as if the property were not relevant business property:

Provided that any land, building, machinery or plant which are comprised in the gift or inheritance and which qualify as relevant business property by virtue of section 127 (1) (e) shall, together with any similar property which has replaced such property, continue to be relevant business property for the purposes of this section for so long as they are used for the purposes of the business concerned.

CHAPTER II
Miscellaneous

Section 136

Interpretation (Chapter II).

136. In this Chapter "the Principal Act" means the Capital Acquisitions Tax Act, 1976.

Section 137

Amendment of section 109 (interpretation) of Finance Act, 1993.

137. (1) Section 109 of the Finance Act, 1993, is hereby amended by the insertion of the following definitions after the definition of "the Act of 1965":

"'agricultural property' has the same meaning as it has in section 19 (as amended by the Finance Act, 1994) of [the Capital Acquisitions Tax Act, 1976,] but excluding farm machinery, livestock and bloodstock;

'agricultural value' means the market value of agricultural property reduced by 30 per cent. of that value;".

(2) This section shall have effect in relation to persons dying after the 17th day of June, 1993.

Section 138

Amendment of section 111 (application of [the Capital Acquisitions Tax Act, 1976]) of Finance Act, 1993.

138. (1) Section 111 of the Finance Act, 1993, is hereby amended –

    (a)   by the deletion of "and" in subparagraph (ii) of paragraph (g) and by the insertion after that subparagraph of the following subparagraph:

        "(iia) in so far as the inheritance consists of agricultural property, the reference to market value in subsection (1) of the said section 18 were a reference to agricultural value, and",

    (b)   by the insertion of the following proviso to subparagraph (iii) of paragraph (g)of that section –

        "Provided that nothing in this subparagraph shall have effect so as to reduce the tax which would but for this subparagraph be borne by property which at the date of death of the deceased represented the share in the estate of the deceased of a person who was not on that date a dependent child or a dependent relative of the deceased;".

    (2)   Paragraph (a) of subsection (1) shall have effect in relation to persons dying after the 17th day of June, 1993.

Section 139

Amendment of section 112 (exemptions) of Finance Act, 1993.

139. (1) Section 112 of the Finance Act, 1993, is hereby amended –

    (a)   by the deletion of paragraph (c) of that section, and

    (b)   by the substitution of the following paragraph for paragraph (d) of that section:

        "(d) the dwelling-house comprised in an inheritance which, on the date of death of the deceased, is taken under the will or other testamentary disposition or under the intestacy of the deceased, by a person who was on that date a dependent child of the deceased or a dependent relative of the deceased and whose place of normal residence was on that date the dwelling-house:

        Provided that –

        (i)   the total income from all sources of that dependent child or that dependent relative, for income tax purposes, in the year of assessment ending on the 5th day of April next before that date, did not exceed the 'specified amount' referred to in subsection (1A) of section 142 of the Income Tax Act, 1967,

(ii) the amount of the exemption shall (subject, with any necessary modifications, to the provisions of section 18(4) (a) of [the Capital Acquisitions Tax Act, 1976,] in the case of a limited interest, and to the provisions of section 20 of that Act in the case of a contingency) be the whole or, as the case may be, the appropriate part (within the meaning of section 5 (5) of [the Capital Acquisitions Tax Act, 1976]) of the net market value of the dwelling- house, and

(iii) the amount of the exemption shall not be reduced by virtue of the provisions of section 20 of [the Capital Acquisitions Tax Act, 1976,] where an entitlement ceasing within the meaning of that section ceases because of an enlargement of that entitlement.".

(2) This section shall have effect in relation to persons dying on or after the date of the passing of this Act.

Section 140

Abatement and postponement of tax.

140. (1) Chapter I of Part VI of the Finance Act, 1993, is hereby amended by the insertion after section 115 of the following section—

"115A. (1) Where the spouse of a deceased survives the deceased, probate tax chargeable by virtue of section 110 which is borne by property which, at the date of death of the deceased, represents the share of that spouse in the estate of the deceased, shall be abated to a nil amount:

Provided that—

(a) where the same property represents more than one person's share in the estate of the deceased and that spouse's interest in that property at that date is not a limited interest to which paragraph (b) relates, only a proportion of the probate tax borne by that property shall be abated to a nil amount and that proportion shall be the proportion which the value of that interest at that date bears to the total value of the property at that date, and for this purpose the value of that interest at that date shall not include the value of any interest in expectancy created by the will or other testamentary disposition of the deceased;

(b) where a limited interest to which that spouse became beneficially entitled in possession on that date was created by the will or other testamentary disposition of the deceased, probate tax borne by the property in which that limited interest subsisted on that date shall not be abated to a nil amount, but, notwithstanding section 117 (a), that tax shall not become due and payable until the date of the cesser of that limited interest and every person who (on the cesser of that limited interest) takes an inheritance which consists of all or part of the property in which that limited interest subsisted immediately prior to that cesser (hereinafter in this proviso referred to as 'the said property') and every trustee or other person in whose care the said property or the income therefrom is placed at the date of that cesser and every person in whom the said property is vested after that date, other than a bona fide purchaser or mortgagee for full consideration in money or money's worth, or a person deriving title from or under such a purchaser or mortgagee shall, notwithstanding any other provision to the contrary, be the only persons accountable for the payment of that tax and that tax shall be a charge on the said property in all respects as if the date of the inheritance in respect of which that tax is chargeable were the date of such cesser and the said property were property of which, for the purpose of section 47 of [the Capital Acquisitions Tax Act, 1976], that inheritance consisted at that date;

(c) if consideration in money or money's worth is paid to that spouse on the coming to an end of the limited interest referred to in paragraph (b) of this proviso before the event on which that interest was limited to cease, an appropriate proportion of the probate tax borne by the said property shall be abated to a nil amount and that proportion shall be the proportion which the value of that consideration bears to the value of the said property at the date of the cesser.

(2) Where the spouse of a deceased survives the deceased, probate tax chargeable by virtue of section 110 which is borne by the dwelling-house, or by any part thereof, shall, notwithstanding subsection (1) and section 117 (a), not become due and payable until the date of death of that spouse and, notwithstanding any provision to the contrary, the only persons who shall be accountable for that tax shall be the following, that is to say −

(a) any person who takes an inheritance under the will or other testamentary disposition of the deceased which consists in whole or in part of the dwelling-house, or part thereof, or which consists of property which represents that dwelling-house or part; and

(b) any trustee in whom the property comprised in any such inheritance is vested at the date of death of that spouse or at any time thereafter and any other person in whom the property comprised in any such inheritance becomes vested for a beneficial interest in possession at any time thereafter, other than a bona fide purchaser or mortgagee for full consideration in money or money's worth, or a person deriving title from or under such a purchaser or mortgagee.

(3) Where the date upon which tax becomes due and payable is postponed by virtue of subsection (1) (b) or subsection (2), then, notwithstanding paragraph (b) of section 117, interest upon that tax shall not be payable in respect of the period commencing on the valuation date and ending 9 months after the date on which that tax actually becomes due and payable.".

(2) This section shall have effect in relation to persons dying after the 17th day of June, 1993.

Section 141

Amendment of section 19 (value of agricultural property) of [the Capital Acquisitions Tax Act, 1976].

141. (1) Section 19 of [the Capital Acquisitions Tax Act, 1976,] is hereby amended—

(a) by the substitution of the following definition for the definition of "agricultural property":

"'agricultural property' means agricultural land, pasture and woodland situate in the State and crops, trees and underwood growing on such land and also includes such farm buildings, farm houses and mansion houses (together with the lands occupied therewith) as are of a character appropriate to the property, and farm machinery, livestock and bloodstock thereon;",

(b) by the substitution of the following definition for the definition of "agricultural value":

"'agricultural value' means—

(a) in the case of farm machinery, livestock and bloodstock, 75 per cent. of the market value of such property,

(b) in the case of a gift of agricultural property, other than farm machinery, livestock and bloodstock, 70 per cent. of the market value of the agricultural property comprised in the gift reduced by 50 per cent. of that market value or by a sum of £150,000, whichever is the lesser, and

(c) in the case of an inheritance of agricultural property, other than farm machinery, livestock and bloodstock, 70 per cent. of the market value of the agricultural property comprised in the inheritance reduced by 35 per cent. of that market value or by a sum of £105,000, whichever is the lesser;",

(c) by the substitution of the following subsection for subsection (4):

"(4) In relation to the deduction, in respect of agricultural property, of —

(a) in the case of a gift, 50 per cent. of its market value, or £150,000, whichever is the lesser, and

(b) in the case of an inheritance, 35 per cent. of its market value, or £105,000, whichever is the lesser,

the amount deductible shall not exceed £150,000 in the case of a gift and £105,000 in the case of an inheritance, in respect of the aggregate of —

(i) all taxable gifts taken on or after the 28th day of February, 1969, and

(ii) all taxable inheritances taken on or after the 1st day of April, 1975, which consist in whole or in part of agricultural property, taken by the same person, as donee or successor, from the same disponer.",

(d) by the substitution of the following definition for the definition of "farmer":

"'farmer', in relation to a donee or successor, means an individual who is domiciled and ordinarily resident in the State and in respect of whom not less than 80 per cent. of the market value of the property to which the individual is beneficially entitled in possession is represented by the market value of property in the State which consists of agricultural property, and, for the purposes of this definition, no deduction shall be made from the market value of property for any debts or incumbrances.",

and

(e) in subsection (5), by the substitution of the following paragraph for paragraph (a):

"(a) The agricultural value shall cease to be applicable to agricultural property, other than crops, trees or underwood, if and to the extent that such property, or any agricultural property which directly or indirectly replaces such property —

(i)   is sold or compulsorily acquired within the period of six years after the date of the gift or the date of the inheritance; and

(ii)   is not replaced, within a year of the sale or compulsory acquisition, by other agricultural property,

and tax shall be chargeable in respect of the gift or inheritance as if the property were not agricultural property:

Provided that this paragraph shall not have effect where the donee or successor dies before the property is sold or compulsorily acquired.".

(2)   This section shall have effect in relation to gifts or inheritances taken on or after the 11th day of April, 1994.

Section 142

Amendment of Second Schedule (computation of tax) to [the Capital Acquisitions Tax Act, 1976].

142.   (1)   The Second Schedule to [the Capital Acquisitions Tax Act, 1976,] is hereby amended by the substitution of the following Part for Part II (inserted by section 115 of the Finance Act, 1991):

"PART II

TABLE

Portion of Value	Rate of tax
	Per cent.
The threshold amount	Nil
The next £10,000	20
The next £30,000	30
The balance	40

".

(2)   This section shall have effect in relation to gifts and inheritances taken on or after the 11th day of April, 1994.

Section 143

Computation of tax.

143. (1) In this section—

"earlier relevant inheritance" means a relevant inheritance deemed to be taken on the date of death of the disponer;

"later relevant inheritance" means a relevant inheritance which, after the date of death of the disponer, is deemed to be taken by a discretionary trust by virtue of there ceasing to be a principal object of that trust who is under the age of 21 years;

"relevant inheritance" means an inheritance which, by virtue of section 106 (1) of the Finance Act, 1984, is, on or after the 11th day of April, 1994, deemed to be taken by a discretionary trust;

"the relevant period" means—

(a) in relation to an earlier relevant inheritance, the period of five years commencing on the date of death of the disponer, and

(b) in relation to a later relevant inheritance, the period of five years commencing on the latest date on which a later relevant inheritance was deemed to be taken from the disponer;

"the appropriate trust", in relation to a relevant inheritance, means the trust by which that inheritance was deemed to be taken.

(2) Section 109 of the Finance Act, 1984, is hereby amended by the substitution of "six per cent." for "three per cent.":

Provided that where, in the case of each and every earlier relevant inheritance or each and every later relevant inheritance, as the case may be, taken from one and the same disponer, one or more objects of the appropriate trust became beneficially entitled in possession before the expiration of the relevant period to an absolute interest in the entire of the property of which that inheritance consisted on and at all times after the date of that inheritance (other than property which ceased to be subject to the terms of the appropriate trust by virtue of a sale or exchange of an absolute interest in that property for full consideration in money or money's worth), then, in relation to all such earlier relevant inheritances or all such later relevant inheritances, as the case may be, this section shall cease to apply and tax shall be computed accordingly in accordance with the provisions of the said section 109 as if this section had not been enacted.

(3) Where two or more persons are together beneficially entitled in possession to an absolute interest in property, those persons shall not, by reason only that together they are beneficially so entitled in possession, be regarded for the purposes of subsection (2) as beneficially so entitled in possession.

(4) Notwithstanding the provisions of section 46 of [the Capital Acquisitions Tax Act, 1976], interest shall not be payable on any

repayment of tax which arises by virtue of the provisions of this section.

Section 144

Amendment of section 117 (reduction in estimated value of certain dwellings) of Finance Act, 1991.

144. (1) Section 117 of the Finance Act, 1991, is hereby amended by the substitution in subsection (1) of "60 per cent." for "50 per cent." and "£60,000" for "£50,000".

(2) This section shall have effect in relation to inheritances taken on or after the 11th day of April, 1994.

Section 145

Amendment of section 128 (amendment of Second Schedule (computation of tax) to [the Capital Acquisitions Tax Act, 1976]) of Finance Act, 1990.

145. Section 128 of the Finance Act, 1990, is hereby amended by the substitution of the following subsection for subsection (1) (including the proviso thereto):

"(1) In computing in accordance with the provisions of the Second Schedule to [the Capital Acquisitions Tax Act, 1976,] the tax chargeable on the taxable value of a taxable gift or a taxable inheritance taken by a donee or successor on or after 11th day of April, 1994, the class threshold, as defined in paragraph 1 (inserted by section 111 of the Finance Act, 1984) of Part I of that Schedule, in respect of each taxable gift or taxable inheritance included in any aggregate of taxable values referred to in paragraph 3 (inserted by the said section 111) of Part I shall be adjusted by multiplying each such class threshold by the figure, rounded to the nearest third decimal place, determined by dividing by 133.5 the consumer price index number for the year immediately preceding the year in which that taxable gift or taxable inheritance is taken, and the references to the class threshold (including the reference to the class thresholds) in the definition of 'revised class threshold' and the proviso thereto in the said paragraph 1 shall be construed accordingly.".

Section 146

Certificate relating to registration of title based on possession.

146. (1) After the passing of this Act a person shall not be registered as owner of property in a register of ownership maintained under the Act of 1964 on foot of an application made to the Registrar on or after the 11th day of April, 1994, which is —

(a) based on possession, and

(b) made under the Rules of 1972, or any other rule made for carrying into effect the objects of the Act of 1964, unless the applicant produces to the Registrar a certificate issued by the Commissioners to the effect that the Commissioners are satisfied—

(i) that the property did not become charged with gift tax or inheritance tax during the relevant period, or

(ii) that any charge for gift tax or inheritance tax to which the property became subject during that period has been discharged, or will (to the extent that it has not been discharged) be discharged within a time considered by the Commissioners to be reasonable.

(2) In the case of an application for registration in relation to which a solicitor's certificate is produced for the purpose of rule 19 (3), 19 (4) or 35 of the Rules of 1972, the Registrar may accept that the application is not based on possession if the solicitor makes to the Registrar a declaration in writing to that effect.

(3) Where, on application to them by the applicant for registration, the Commissioners are satisfied that they may issue a certificate for the purpose of subsection (1), they shall issue a certificate for that purpose, and the certificate and the application therefor shall be on a form provided by the Commissioners.

(4) A certificate issued by the Commissioners for the purpose of subsection (1) shall be in such terms and subject to such qualifications as the Commissioners think fit, and shall not be a certificate for any other purpose.

(5) In this section—

"the Act of 1964" means the Registration of Title Act, 1964;

"the Registrar" means the Registrar of Titles;

"relevant period", in relation to a person's application to be registered as owner of property, means the period commencing on the 28th day of February, 1974, and ending on the date as of which the registration was made:

Provided that—

(a) where the certificate referred to in subsection (1) is a certificate for a period ending prior to the date of the registration, the period covered by the certificate shall be deemed to be the relevant period if, at the time of the registration, the Registrar had no reason to believe that a death relevant to the application for registration occurred after the expiration of the period covered by the certificate, and

(b) where the registration of the person (if any) who, at the date of that application, was the registered owner of the property had been made as of a date after the 28th day of February, 1974, the relevant period shall commence on the date as of which that registration was made;

"the Rules of 1972" means the Land Registration Rules, 1972 (S.I. No. 230 of 1972).

Section 147

Provision relating to section 5 (gift deemed to be taken) of [the Capital Acquisitions Tax Act, 1976,] and section 121 of Finance Act, 1993.

147. Without prejudice to the meaning of section 5 of [the Capital Acquisitions Tax Act, 1976,] as enacted, that section shall have effect and be deemed always to have had effect as if the provisions of section 121 of the Finance Act, 1993, had not been enacted, except where the consideration referred to in the said section 5, being consideration in relation to a disposition, could not reasonably be regarded (taking into account the disponer's position prior to the disposition) as representing full consideration to the disponer for having made such a disposition.

Section 148

Provision relating to section 11 (inheritance deemed to be taken) of [the Capital Acquisitions Tax Act, 1976,] and section 123 of Finance Act, 1993.

148. Without prejudice to the meaning of section 11 of [the Capital Acquisitions Tax Act, 1976,] as enacted, that section shall have effect and be deemed always to have had effect as if the provisions of section 123 of the Finance Act, 1993, had not been enacted, except where the consideration referred to in the said section 11, being consideration in relation to a disposition, could not reasonably be regarded (taking into account the disponer's position prior to the disposition) as representing full consideration to the disponer for having made such a disposition.

PART VII
Miscellaneous

CHAPTER I
Provisions Relating to Residence of Individuals

Section 149

Interpretation (Chapter I).

149. In this Part—

"the Acts" means—

(a) the Income Tax Acts,

(b) the Corporation Tax Acts,

(c) the Capital Gains Tax Acts, and

(d) the Capital Acquisitions Tax Act, 1976, and the enactments amending or extending that Act, and any instrument made thereunder;

"authorised officer" means an officer of the Revenue Commissioners authorised by them in writing for the purposes of this Chapter;

"present in the State", in relation to an individual, means the personal presence of the individual in the State;

"tax" means any tax payable in accordance with any provision of the Acts.

Section 150

Residence.

150. (1) For the purposes of the Acts, an individual is resident in the State for a year of assessment if the individual is present in the State—

    (a) at any one time or several times in the year of assessment for a period in the whole amounting to 183 days or more, or

    (b) at any one time or several times—

        (i) in the year of assessment, and

        (ii) in the preceding year of assessment,

for a period (being a period comprising in the aggregate the number of days on which the individual is present in the State in the year of assessment and the number of days on which the individual was present in the State in the preceding year of assessment) in the whole amounting to 280 days or more:

Provided that, notwithstanding paragraph (b), where for a year of assessment an individual is present in the State at any one time or several times for a period in the whole amounting to not more than 30 days—

    (a) the individual shall not be resident in the State for the year of assessment, and

    (b) no account shall be taken of the period for the purposes of the aggregate mentioned in paragraph (b).

  (2) (a) Notwithstanding subsection (1), an individual—

        (i) who is not resident in the State for a year of assessment, and

        (ii) to whom paragraph (b) applies,

may, at any time, elect to be treated as resident in the State for that year and, where an individual so elects, the individual shall, for the purposes of the Acts, be deemed to be resident in the State for that year.

    (b) This paragraph applies to an individual who satisfies an authorised officer that the individual is in the State—

        (i) with the intention, and

   (ii) in such circumstances,

   that the individual will be resident in the State for the following year of assessment.

 (3) For the purposes of this section, an individual shall be deemed to be present in the State for a day if the individual is present in the State at the end of the day.

Section 151

Ordinary residence.

151. (1) For the purposes of the Acts, an individual is ordinarily resident in the State for a year of assessment if the individual has been resident in the State for each of the 3 years of assessment preceding that year.

 (2) An individual who is ordinarily resident in the State shall not, for the purposes of the Acts, cease to be ordinarily resident in the State for a year of assessment unless the individual has not been resident in the State in each of the 3 years of assessment preceding that year.

Section 153

Split year residence.

153. (1) For the purposes of a charge to tax on any income, profits or gains from an employment, where, during a year of assessment ("the relevant year")—

  (a) (i) an individual who has not been resident in the State for the preceding year of assessment, satisfies an authorised officer that the individual is in the State—

    (I) with the intention, and

    (II) in such circumstances,

    that the individual will be resident in the State for the following year of assessment, or

  (ii) an individual who is resident in the State, satisfies an authorised officer that the individual is leaving the State, other than for a temporary purpose,

    (I) with the intention, and

    (II) in such circumstances,

    that the individual will not be resident in the State for the following year of assessment,

  and

  (b) the individual would, but for the provisions of this section, be resident in the State for the relevant year,

  subsection (2) shall apply in relation to the individual.

(2) (a) An individual to whom paragraphs (a) (i) and (b) of subsection (1) apply, shall be deemed to be resident in the State for the relevant year only from the date of his or her arrival in the State.

(b) An individual to whom paragraphs (a) (ii) and (b) of subsection (1) apply, shall be deemed to be resident in the State for the relevant year only up to and including the date of his or her leaving the State.

(3) Where, by virtue of this section, an individual is resident in the State for part of a year of assessment, all the provisions of the Acts shall apply as if —

(a) income arising during that part of the year or, in a case to which the provisions of section 76 (3) of the Income Tax Act, 1967, apply, amounts received in the State during that part of the year, were income arising or amounts received for a year of assessment in which the individual is resident in the State, and

(b) income arising or, as the case may be, amounts received in the remaining part of the year, were income arising or amounts received in a year of assessment in which the individual is not resident in the State.

Section 156

Appeals.

156. (1) An individual who is aggrieved by the decision of an authorised officer on any question arising under those provisions of this Chapter which require an individual to satisfy an authorised officer on such a question may, by notice in writing to that effect given to the authorised officer within two months from the date on which notice of the decision is given to the individual, make an application to have the question heard and determined by the Appeal Commissioners.

(2) Where an application is made under subsection (1), the Appeal Commissioners shall hear and determine the question concerned in like manner as an appeal made to them against an assessment and all the provisions of the Acts relating to such an appeal (including the provisions relating to the rehearing of an appeal and to the statement of a case for the opinion of the High Court on a point of law) shall apply accordingly with any necessary modifications.

Section 158

Commencement (Chapter I).

158. (1) Subject to subsection (2), this Chapter shall apply as respects the year 1994-95 and subsequent years of assessment.

(2) Where in any case an individual –

 (a) was resident in the State for the year of assessment 1991-92 but not resident in the State for the years of assessment 1992-93 and 1993-94, or

 (b) was resident in the State for the year of assessment 1992-93 but not resident in the State for the year of assessment 1993-94, or

 (c) was resident in the State for the year of assessment 1993-94 and would not, but for section 150, be resident in the State in the year of assessment 1994-95, or

 (d) left the State in the years of assessment 1992-93 or 1993-94 for the purpose of commencing a period of ordinary residence outside the State and did not recommence ordinary residence in the State prior to the end of the year of assessment 1993-94,

section 150 and section 157, in so far as it relates to the repeal of section 4 of the Finance Act, 1987, shall apply as respects the year 1995-96 and subsequent years of assessment in that case.

FINANCE ACT, 1995

Number 8 of 1995
(Enacted on 2nd June, 1995)

PART VI
Capital Acquisitions Tax

Section 156

Interpretation (Part VI).
156. In this Part "the Principal Act" means the Capital Acquisitions Tax Act, 1976.

Section 157

Amendment of section 2 (interpretation) of [the Capital Acquisitions Tax Act, 1976].
157. Subsection (1) of section 2 of [the Capital Acquisitions Tax Act, 1976,] is hereby amended by the insertion of the following definition after the definition of "valuation date":

"'year of assessment' has the meaning assigned to it by section 1 of the Income Tax Act, 1967.".

Section 158

Amendment of section 19 (value of agricultural property) of [the Capital Acquisitions Tax Act, 1976].
158. (1) Section 19 of [the Capital Acquisitions Tax Act, 1976,] is hereby amended—

    (a) in the definition of "agricultural value" in subsection (1) (inserted by the Finance Act, 1994)—

        (i) by the substitution of "50 per cent." for "75 per cent." in paragraph (a),

        (ii) by the substitution of "50 per cent." for "70 per cent.", "30 per cent." for "50 per cent." and "£90,000" for "£150,000" in paragraph (b), and

        (iii) by the substitution of "50 per cent." for "70 per cent.", "15 per cent." for "35 per cent." and "£45,000" for "£105,000" in paragraph (c),

    and the said definition, as so amended, is set out in the Table to this section,

    (b) in the definition of "farmer" in subsection (1), by the deletion of "and ordinarily resident",

    (c)   by the substitution, in subsection (4) (inserted by the Finance Act, 1994), of "30 per cent." for "50 per cent.", £90,000" for "£150,000" in both places where it occurs, "15 per cent." for "35 per cent." and "£45,000" for "£105,000" in both places where it occurs, and the said subsection, as so amended, is set out in the Table to this section, and

    (d)   by the insertion after paragraph (b) of subsection (5) of the following paragraph:

       "(c) The agricultural value in relation to a gift or inheritance referred to in subsection (2) shall cease to be applicable to agricultural property, other than crops, trees or underwood, if the donee or successor is not resident in the State for any of the three years of assessment immediately following the year of assessment in which the valuation date falls.".

  (2) Paragraphs (a) and (c) of subsection (1) shall have effect in relation to gifts or inheritances taken on or after the 8th day of February, 1995, paragraph (b) shall have effect in relation to a gift or inheritance where the valuation date in relation to that gift or inheritance is on or after the 6th day of April, 1994, and paragraph (d) shall have effect in relation to gifts and inheritances taken on or after the date of the passing of this Act.

TABLE

"agricultural value" means —	
(a)	in the case of farm machinery, livestock and bloodstock, 50 per cent. of the market value of such property,
(b)	in the case of a gift of agricultural property, other than farm machinery, livestock and bloodstock, 50 per cent. of the market value of the agricultural property comprised in the gift reduced by 30 per cent. of that market value or by a sum of £90,000, whichever is the lesser, and
(c)	in the case of an inheritance of agricultural property, other than farm machinery, livestock and bloodstock 50 per cent. of the market value of the agricultural property comprised in the inheritance reduced by 15 per cent. of that market value or by a sum of £45,000, whichever is the lesser;
(4)	In relation to the deduction, in respect of agricultural property, of —
(a)	in the case of a gift, 30 per cent. of its market value, or £90,000, whichever is the lesser, and
(b)	in the case of an inheritance, 15 per cent. of its market value, or £45,000, whichever is the lesser,

> the amount deductible shall not exceed £90,000 in the case of a
> gift and £45,000 in the case of an inheritance, in respect of the
> aggregate of —
>
> (i)   all taxable gifts taken on or after the 28th day of February, 1969,
> and
>
> (ii)   all taxable inheritances taken on or after the 1st day of April,
> 1975, which consist in whole or in part of agricultural property,
> taken by the same person, as donee or successor, from the same
> disponer.

Section 159

Amendment of section 52 (appeals in other cases) of [the Capital Acquisitions
Tax Act, 1976].

159. Paragraph (a) of subsection (5) of section 52 of [the Capital Acquisitions
Tax Act, 1976,] is hereby amended by the insertion of the following
subparagraph after subparagraph (x):

"(xi) the refusal of an application for an appeal hearing,".

Section 160

Amendment of section 55 (exemption of certain objects) of [the Capital
Acquisitions Tax Act, 1976].

160. (1) Section 55 of [the Capital Acquisitions Tax Act, 1976,] is hereby
amended —

(a) by the substitution of the following subsection for
subsection (3):

"(3) If an object exempted from tax by virtue of subsection
(2) is sold within 6 years after the valuation date,
and before the death of the donee or successor, the
exemption referred to in subsection (2) shall cease to
apply to such object:

Provided that, if the sale of such object is a sale by private
treaty to the National Gallery of Ireland, the National
Museum of Science and Art or any other similar national
institution, any university in the State or any constituent
college thereof, a local authority or the Friends of the
National Collections of Ireland, the exemption referred
to in subsection (2) shall continue to apply.",

and

(b) by the substitution of the following subsection for
subsection (4):

"(4) The exemption referred to in subsection (2) shall cease
to apply to an object, if at any time after the valuation
date and —

(a) before the sale of the object,

(b) before the death of the donee or successor, and

(c) before such object again forms part of the property comprised in a gift or an inheritance in respect of which gift or inheritance an absolute interest is taken by a person other than the spouse of that donee or successor,

there has been a breach of any condition specified in paragraph (b) or (c) of subsection (1).".

(2) This section shall have effect in relation to gifts or inheritances taken on or after the 12th day of April, 1995.

Section 161

Business relief.

161. (1) The Finance Act, 1994, is hereby amended by the substitution of the following section for section 126:

"126. Where the whole or part of the taxable value of any taxable gift or taxable inheritance is attributable to the value of any relevant business property, the whole or that part of the taxable value shall, subject to the other provisions of this Chapter, be treated as being reduced by 50 per cent.".

(2) This section shall have effect in relation to gifts or inheritances taken on or after the 8th day of February, 1995.

Section 162

Amendment of section 134 (exclusion of value of excepted assets) of Finance Act, 1994.

162. (1) Section 134 of the Finance Act, 1994, is hereby amended —

(a) by the addition of the following proviso to subsection (1):

"Provided that so much of the last-mentioned value as is attributable to agricultural property in the beneficial ownership of a company shall not fall to be left out of account unless it would fall to be left out of account by virtue of paragraph (b) or (c) of this subsection.",

and

(b) by the substitution of the following proviso for the proviso to subsection (2):

"Provided that—

(a) the use of an asset for the purposes of a business to which section 127 (4) relates, and

(b) where the business concerned is not carried on by a company, the use of an asset for the purposes of farming (within the meaning of section 13 of the Finance Act, 1974),

shall not be treated as use for the purposes of the business concerned.".

(2) This section shall have effect in relation to gifts or inheritances taken on or after the 12th day of April, 1995.

Section 163

Amendment of section 135 (withdrawal of relief) of Finance Act, 1994.

163. (1) Section 135 of the Finance Act, 1994, is hereby amended —

(a) by the substitution, in subsection (1), of "commencing on the valuation date." for "after the valuation date or the period between the date of the gift or inheritance and the date of a subsequent gift or inheritance consisting of the same property or of property representing that property, whichever is the lesser period.", and

(b) by the substitution of the following proviso for the proviso to subsection (2):

"Provided that —

(i) any land, building, machinery or plant which are comprised in the gift or inheritance and which qualify as relevant business property by virtue of section 127 (1) (e) shall, together with any similar property which has replaced such property, continue to be relevant business property for the purposes of this section for so long as they are used for the purposes of the business concerned, and

(ii) this section shall not have effect where the donee or successor dies before the event which would otherwise cause the reduction to cease to be applicable.".

(2) This section shall have effect in relation to gifts or inheritances taken on or after the 12th day of April, 1995.

Section 164

Payment of tax on certain assets by instalments.

164. (1) In this section —

"agricultural property" has the meaning assigned to it by section 19 of [the Capital Acquisitions Tax Act, 1976] (as amended by the Finance Act, 1994);

"relevant business property" has the same meaning as it has in section 127 of the Finance Act, 1994, other than shares in or securities of a company (being shares or securities quoted on a recognised stock exchange) and without regard to sections 128 and 134 (3) of that Act.

(2) Where the whole or part of the tax which is due and payable in respect of a taxable gift or taxable inheritance is attributable to either or both agricultural property and relevant business property —

(a) section 43 of [the Capital Acquisitions Tax Act, 1976,] shall apply to that whole or part of the tax notwithstanding subsection (4) of that section, and

(b) notwithstanding subsection (2) of section 41 of [the Capital Acquisitions Tax Act, 1976,] the rate at which interest is payable upon that whole or part of the tax shall be 0.75 per cent., or such other rate (if any) as stands prescribed by the Minister for Finance by regulations, for each month or part of a month instead of at the rate specified in that section and that section shall have effect as regards that whole or part of the tax as if the rate so payable were substituted for the rate specified in that section:

Provided that the rate at which interest is payable upon any overdue instalment of that whole or part of the tax, or upon such part of the tax as would represent any such overdue instalment if that whole or part of the tax were being paid by instalments, shall continue to be at the rate specified in section 41 of [the Capital Acquisitions Tax Act, 1976].

(3) For the purposes of this section the value of a business or of an interest in a business shall be taken to be its net value ascertained in accordance with section 132 of the Finance Act, 1994.

(4) This section shall have effect in relation to gifts and inheritances taken on or after the 8th day of February, 1995, but shall not have effect in relation to an inheritance taken by a relevant trust by virtue of section 110 (1) of the Finance Act, 1993, or to an inheritance taken by a discretionary trust by virtue of section 106 (1) of the Finance Act, 1984, or section 103 (1) of the Finance Act, 1986.

(5) Every regulation made under this section shall be laid before Dáil Éireann as soon as may be after it is made and, if a resolution annulling the regulation is passed by Dáil Éireann within the next twenty-one days on which Dáil Éireann has sat after the regulation is laid before it, the regulation shall be annulled accordingly, but without prejudice to the validity of anything previously done thereunder.

Section 165

Exemption of certain inheritances taken by parents.

165. Notwithstanding the provisions of [the Capital Acquisitions Tax Act, 1976], an inheritance taken on or after the 12th day of April, 1995, by a person from a disponer shall, where –

(a) that person is a parent of that disponer, and

(b) the date of the inheritance is the date of death of that disponer,

be exempt from tax and shall not be taken into account in computing tax if and only if that disponer took a non-exempt gift or inheritance from either or both of that disponer's parents within the period of 5 years immediately prior to the date of death of that disponer.

Section 166

Heritage property of companies.

166. (1) In this section –

"relevant heritage property" means any one or more of the following –

(a) objects to which section 55 of [the Capital Acquisitions Tax Act, 1976,] applies;

(b) a house or garden referred to in section 39 of the Finance Act, 1978;

"private company" has the meaning assigned to it by section 16 of [the Capital Acquisitions Tax Act, 1976];

"subsidiary" has the meaning assigned to it by section 155 of the Companies Act, 1963.

(2) Where a gift or inheritance consists in whole or in part –

(a) at the date of the gift or at the date of the inheritance, and

(b) at the valuation date,

of one or more shares in a private company which (after the taking of the gift or inheritance) is, on the date of the gift or on the date of the inheritance, a company controlled by the donee or successor within the meaning of section 16 of [the Capital Acquisitions Tax Act, 1976], then each such share shall, to the extent that its market value for tax purposes is, at the valuation date, attributable to relevant heritage property, be exempt from tax and the value thereof shall to that extent not be taken into account in computing tax on any gift or inheritance taken by that person unless the exemption ceases to apply under the provisions of subsection (5) or (6):

Provided that that relevant heritage property was in the beneficial ownership of the company on the 12th day of April, 1995, or in the beneficial ownership on that date of another company which was on that date a subsidiary of the first-mentioned company.

(3) The provisions of section 19 (6) of [the Capital Acquisitions Tax Act, 1976,] shall apply, for the purposes of subsection (2), as they apply in relation to agricultural property.

(4) Where in relation to a gift or inheritance —

   (a) a part of a share in a private company is exempt from tax by virtue of subsection (2), and

   (b) such share is relevant business property within the meaning of Chapter I of Part VI of the Finance Act, 1994,

   then the relevant heritage property to which the market value of such share is partly attributable shall be left out of account in determining for the purposes of that Chapter what part of the taxable value of that gift or inheritance is attributable to such share, but the amount of the reduction (if any) which would but for subsection (2) fall to be made under that Chapter in respect of such share shall not otherwise be restricted notwithstanding subsection (2).

(5) If a share in a private company which is exempted in whole or in part from tax by virtue of subsection (2) is sold within 6 years after the valuation date, and before the death of the donee or successor, the exemption referred to in subsection (2) shall, subject to subsection (7), cease to apply to such share.

(6) Where the whole or part of the market value of a share in a private company which is comprised in a gift or inheritance is on the valuation date attributable to an item of relevant heritage property and —

   (a) that item of relevant heritage property is sold within 6 years after the valuation date, and before the death of the donee or successor, or

   (b) at any time after the valuation date and —

      (i) before the sale of such share or such item of relevant heritage property,

      (ii) before the death of the donee or successor, and

      (iii) before such share or such item of relevant heritage property forms part of the property comprised in a subsequent gift or inheritance in respect of which gift or inheritance an absolute interest is taken by a per son other than the spouse of that donee or successor

   there has been a breach of any condition specified in subsection (1) (b) or (c) of section 55 of [the Capital Acquisitions Tax Act, 1976,] or in section 39 (1) (c) of the Finance Act, 1978,

   then the exemption referred to in subsection (2) shall, subject to subsection (7), cease to apply to such share to the extent that that market value is attributable to such item of relevant heritage property.

(7) Notwithstanding subsections (5) and (6), the exemption referred to in subsection (2) shall continue to apply if the sale of the share referred to in subsection (5), or the sale of the item of relevant heritage property referred to in subsection (6), is a sale by private treaty to the National Gallery of Ireland, the National Museum of Science and Art or any other similar national institution, any university in the State or any constituent college thereof, a local authority or the Friends of the National Collections of Ireland.

(8) This section shall have effect in relation to gifts and inheritances taken on or after the 12th day of April, 1995.

PART VII
Miscellaneous

CHAPTER II
General

Section 172

Duties of a relevant person in relation to certain revenue offences.

172. (1) In this section—

"the Acts" means—

(a) the Customs Acts,

(b) the statutes relating to the duties of excise and to the management of those duties,

(c) the Tax Acts,

(d) the Capital Gains Tax Acts,

(e) the Value-Added Tax Act, 1972, and the enactments amending or extending that Act,

(f) the Capital Acquisitions Tax Act, 1976, and the enactments amending or extending that Act,

(g) the statutes relating to stamp duty and to the management of that duty,

and any instruments made thereunder and any instruments made under any other enactment and relating to tax;

"appropriate officer" means any officer nominated by the Revenue Commissioners to be an appropriate officer for the purposes of this section;

"company" means any body corporate;

"relevant person", in relation to a company, means a person who—

(a) (i) is an auditor to the company appointed in accordance with section 160 of the Companies Act, 1963 (as amended by the Companies Act, 1990), or

    (ii) in the case of an industrial and provident society or a friendly society, is a public auditor to the society for the purposes of the Industrial and Provident Societies Acts, 1893 to 1978, and the Friendly Societies Acts, 1896 to 1977,

or

(b) with a view to reward assists or advises the company in the preparation or delivery of any information, declaration, return, records, accounts or other document which he or she knows will be, or is likely to be, used for any purpose of tax:

Provided that a person who would, but for this proviso, be treated as a relevant person in relation to a company shall not be so treated if the person assists or advises the company solely in the person's capacity as an employee of the said company, and a person shall be treated as assisting or advising the company in that capacity where the person's income from assisting or advising the company consists solely of emoluments to which Chapter IV of Part V of the Income Tax Act, 1967, applies;

"relevant offence" means an offence committed by a company which consists of the company —

(a) knowingly or wilfully delivering any incorrect return, statement or accounts or knowingly or wilfully furnishing or causing to be furnished any incorrect information in connection with any tax,

(b) knowingly or wilfully claiming or obtaining relief or exemption from, or repayment of, any tax, being a relief, exemption or repayment to which there is no entitlement,

(c) knowingly or wilfully issuing or producing any incorrect invoice, receipt, instrument or other document in connection with any tax,

(d) knowingly or wilfully failing to comply with any provision of the Acts requiring the furnishing of a return of income, profits or gains, or of sources of income, profits or gains, for the purposes of any tax:

Provided that an offence under this paragraph committed by a company shall not be a relevant offence if the company has made a return of income, profits or gains to the Revenue Commissioners in respect of an accounting period falling wholly or partly into the period of 3 years immediately preceding the accounting period in respect of which the offence was committed;

"tax" means tax, duty, levy or charge under the care and management of the Revenue Commissioners.

(2) If, having regard solely to information obtained in the course of examining the accounts of a company, or in the course of assisting or advising a company in the preparation or delivery of any information, declaration, return, records, accounts or other document for the purposes of tax, as the case may be, a person who is a relevant person in relation to the company becomes aware that the company has committed, or is in the course of committing, one or more relevant offences, the person shall, if the offence or offences are material –

    (a) communicate particulars of the offence or offences in writing to the company without undue delay and request the company to –

        (i) take such action as is necessary for the purposes of rectifying the matter, or

        (ii) notify an appropriate officer of the offence or offences,

        not later than 6 months after the time of communication, and

    (b) (i) unless it is established to the person's satisfaction that the necessary action has been taken or notification made, as the case may be, under paragraph (a), cease to act as the auditor to the company or to assist or advise the company in such preparation or delivery as is specified in paragraph (b) of the definition of relevant person, and

        (ii) shall not so act, assist or advise before a time which is –

            (I) 3 years after the time at which the particulars were communicated under paragraph (a), or

            (II) the time at which it is established to the person's satisfaction that the necessary action has been taken or notification made, as the case may be, under paragraph (a),

        whichever is the earlier:

Provided that nothing in this paragraph shall prevent a person from assisting or advising a company in preparing for, or conducting, legal proceedings, either civil or criminal, which are extant or pending at a time which is 6 months after the time of communication under paragraph (a).

(3) Where a person, being in relation to a company a relevant person within the meaning of paragraph (a) of the definition of relevant person, ceases under the provisions of this section to act as auditor to the company, then the person shall deliver –

    (a) a notice in writing to the company stating that he or she is so resigning, and

     (b)   a copy of the notice to an appropriate officer not later than 14 days after he or she has delivered the notice to the company.

(4) A person shall be guilty of an offence under this section if the person—

     (a)   fails to comply with subsection (2) or (3), or

     (b)   knowingly or wilfully makes a communication under subsection (2) which is incorrect.

(5) Where a relevant person is found guilty of an offence under this section the person shall be liable—

     (a)   on summary conviction to a fine of £1,000 which may be mitigated to not less than one-fourth part thereof, or

     (b)   on conviction on indictment, to a fine not exceeding £5,000 or, at the discretion of the court, to imprisonment for a term not exceeding 2 years or to both the fine and the imprisonment.

(6) Section 13 of the Criminal Procedure Act, 1967, shall apply in relation to this section as if, in lieu of the penalties specified in subsection (3) of the said section 13, there were specified therein the penalties provided for by subsection (5) (a) of this section, and the reference in subsection (2) (a) of the said section 13 to the penalties provided for in the said subsection (3) shall be construed and have effect accordingly.

(7) Notwithstanding the provisions of any other enactment, proceedings in respect of this section may be instituted within 6 years from the time at which a person is required under subsection (2) to communicate particulars of an offence or offences in writing to a company.

(8) It shall be a good defence in a prosecution for an offence under subsection (4) (a) in relation to a failure to comply with subsection (2) for an accused (being a person who is a relevant person in relation to a company) to show that he or she was, in the ordinary scope of professional engagement, assisting or advising the company in preparing for legal proceedings and would not have become aware that one or more relevant offences had been committed by the company if he or she had not been so assisting or advising.

(9) If a person who is a relevant person takes any action required by subsection (2) or (3), no duty to which the person may be subject shall be regarded as contravened and no liability or action shall lie against the person in any court for so doing.

(10) The Revenue Commissioners may nominate an officer to be an appropriate officer for the purposes of this section and the name of an officer so nominated and the address to which copies of notices under subsection (2) or (3) shall be delivered shall be published in the Iris Oifigiúil.

(11) This section shall have effect as respects a relevant offence committed by a company in respect of tax which is —

(a) assessable by reference to accounting periods, for any accounting period beginning after the 30th day of June, 1995,

(b) assessable by reference to years of assessment, for the year of assessment 1995-96 and subsequent years,

(c) payable by reference to a taxable period, for a taxable period beginning after the 30th day of June, 1995,

(d) chargeable on gifts or inheritances taken on or after the 30th day of June, 1995,

(e) chargeable on instruments executed on or after the 30th day of June, 1995, or

(f) payable in any other case, on or after the 30th day of June, 1995.

Section 175

Power to obtain information.

175. (1) For the purposes of the assessment, charge, collection and recovery of any tax or duty placed under their care and management, the Revenue Commissioners may, by notice in writing, request any Minister of the Government to provide them with such information in the possession of the Minister in relation to payments for any purposes made by the Minister, whether on his own behalf or on behalf of any other person, to such persons or classes of persons as the Revenue Commissioners may specify in the notice and a Minister so requested shall provide such information as may be specified.

(2) The Revenue Commissioners may nominate any of their officers to perform any acts and discharge any functions authorised by this section to be performed or discharged by the Revenue Commissioners.

Section 176

Relief for donations of heritage items.

176. (1) (a) In this section —

"the Acts" means —

(i) the Tax Acts (other than Chapter IV of Part V of the Income Tax Act, 1967, section 17 of the Finance Act, 1970, and Chapter VII of Part I of the Finance Act, 1983),

(ii) the Capital Gains Tax Acts, and

(iii) the Capital Acquisitions Tax Act, 1976, and the enactments amending or extending that Act, and any instrument made thereunder;

"approved body" means—

(i)   the National Archives,

(ii)   the National Gallery of Ireland,

(iii) the National Library of Ireland,

(iv) the National Museum of Ireland,

(v)   the Irish Museum of Modern Art, or

(vi) in relation to the offer of a gift of a particular item or collection of items, any other such body (being a body owned, or funded wholly or mainly, by the State or by any public or local authority) as may be approved, with the consent of the Minister for Finance, by the Minister for Arts, Culture and the Gaeltacht for the purposes of this section;

"arrears of tax" means tax due and payable in accordance with any provision of the Acts (including any interest and penalties payable under any provision of the Acts in relation to such tax)—

(i)   in the case of income tax, corporation tax or capital gains tax, in respect of the relevant period, or

(ii)   in the case of gift tax or inheritance tax, prior to the commencement of the calendar year in which the relevant gift is made,

which has not been paid at the time a relevant gift is made,

"current liability" means—

(i)   in the case of income tax or capital gains tax, any liability to such tax arising in the year of assessment in which the relevant gift is made, or

(ii)   in the case of corporation tax, any liability to such tax arising in the accounting period in which the relevant gift is made, or

(iii) in the case of gift tax or inheritance tax, any liability to such tax which becomes due and payable in the calendar year in which the relevant gift is made;

"designated officer" means—

(i)   the member of the selection committee who represents the appropriate approved body on that committee where the approved body is so represented, or

(ii)   in any other case, a person nominated in that behalf by the Minister for Arts, Culture and the Gaeltacht;

"heritage item" has the meaning assigned to it by subsection (2) (a);

"market value" has the meaning assigned to it by subsection (3);

"relevant gift" means a gift of a heritage item to an approved body which is made on or after the date of the passing of this Act and in respect of which no consideration whatsoever (other than relief under this section) is received by the person making the gift, either directly or indirectly, from the approved body or otherwise;

"relevant period" means—

(i)   in the case of income tax and capital gains tax, any year of assessment preceding the year in which the relevant gift is made, and

(ii)   in the case of corporation tax, any accounting period preceding the accounting period in which the relevant gift is made;

"selection committee" means a committee consisting of the Chairperson of the Heritage Council, the Director of the Arts Council, the Director of the National Archives, the Director of the National Gallery of Ireland, the Director of the National Library of Ireland, the Director of the National Museum of Ireland and the Director of the Irish Museum of Modern Art and includes any person duly acting in the capacity of any of the foregoing as a result of the member concerned being unable to fulfil his or her duties for any of the reasons set out in paragraph (b) (ii);

"tax" means income tax, corporation tax, capital gains tax, gift tax or inheritance tax, as the case may be, payable in accordance with any provision of the Acts;

"valuation date" means the date on which an application is made, to the selection committee, for a determination under subsection (2) (a).

(b) (i)   The selection committee may act notwithstanding one or more vacancies among its members and may regulate its own procedure.

      (ii)   If and so long as a member of the selection committee is unable through illness, absence or other cause to fulfil his or her duties, a person nominated in that behalf by the member shall act as the member of the committee in the place of the member.

(2) (a) In this section "heritage item" means any kind of cultural item including—

(i) any archaeological item, archive, book, estate record, manuscript and painting, and

(ii) any collection of cultural items and any collection thereof in their setting,

which, on application to the selection committee in writing in that behalf by a person who owns the item or collection of items (as the case may be) is determined by the selection committee, after consideration of any evidence in relation to the matter which the person submits to the committee and after such consultation (if any) as may seem to the committee to be necessary with such person or body of persons as in the opinion of the committee may be of assistance to them, to be an item or collection of items—

(I) which is an outstanding example of the type of item involved, pre-eminent in its class, whose export from the State would constitute a diminution of the accumulated cultural heritage of Ireland, and

(II) suitable for acquisition by an approved body.

(b) On receipt of an application for a determination under paragraph (a) the selection committee shall request the Revenue Commissioners in writing to value the item or collection of items, as the case may be, in accordance with the provisions of subsection (3).

(c) The selection committee shall not make a determination under paragraph (a) where the market value of the item or collection of items (as the case may be), as determined by the Revenue Commissioners in accordance with subsection (3), at the valuation date—

(i) is less than £75,000, or

(ii) exceeds an amount (which shall not be less than £75,000) determined by the formula—

$$£500,000 - M$$

where M is an amount (which may be nil) equal to the market value at the valuation date of the heritage item (if any) or the aggregate of the market values at the respective valuation dates of all the heritage items (if any), as the case may be, in respect of which a determination or determinations, as the case may be, under this subsection has been made by the selection committee in any one calendar year and not revoked in that year.

(d) (i) An item or collection of items shall cease to be a heritage item for the purposes of this section if the item or collection of items—

(I)   is sold or otherwise disposed of to a person other than an approved body, or

(II)   the owner thereof notifies the selection committee in writing that it is not intended to make a gift thereof to an approved body, or

(III)   the gift of the item or collection of items is not made to an approved body within the calendar year following the year in which the determination is made under paragraph (a).

(ii)   Where the selection committee becomes aware, at any time within the calendar year in which a determination under paragraph (a) is made in respect of an item or collection of items, that clause (I) or (II) of subparagraph (i) applies to the item or collection of items the selection committee may revoke its determination with effect from that time.

(3) (a)   For the purposes of this section, the market value of any item or collection of items (hereafter in this subsection referred to as "the property") shall be estimated to be the price which, in the opinion of the Revenue Commissioners, the property would fetch if sold in the open market on the valuation date in such manner and subject to such conditions as might reasonably be calculated to obtain for the vendor the best price for the property.

     (b)   The market value of the property shall be ascertained by the Revenue Commissioners in such manner and by such means as they think fit, and they may authorise a person to inspect the property and report to them the value thereof for the purposes of this section, and the person having custody or possession of the property shall permit the person so authorised to inspect the property at such reasonable times as the Revenue Commissioners consider necessary.

     (c)   Where the Revenue Commissioners require a valuation to be made by a person authorised by them, the cost of such valuation shall be defrayed by the Revenue Commissioners.

(4)   Where a relevant gift is made to an approved body –

     (a)   the designated officer of that body shall give a certificate to the person who made the relevant gift, in such form as the Revenue Commissioners may prescribe, certifying the receipt of that gift and the transfer of the ownership of the heritage item the subject of that gift to the approved body, and

     (b)   the designated officer shall transmit a duplicate of the certificate to the Revenue Commissioners.

(5)   Subject to the provisions of this section, where a person has made a relevant gift the person shall, on submission to the Revenue

Commissioners of the certificate given to the person in accordance with subsection (4), be treated as having made on the date of such submission a payment on account of tax of an amount equal to the market value of the relevant gift on the valuation date.

(6) A payment on account of tax which is treated as having been made in accordance with the provisions of subsection (5) shall be set, so far as possible, against any liability to tax of the person who is treated as having made such a payment in the following order—

    (a) firstly, against any arrears of tax due for payment by that person and against an arrear of tax for an earlier period in priority to a later period and, for this purpose, the date on which an arrear of tax became due for payment shall determine whether it is for an earlier or later period, and

    (b) then, and only then, against any current liability of the person which the person nominates for that purpose,

and such set-off shall accordingly discharge a corresponding amount of that liability.

(7) Where and to the extent that a payment on account of tax has not been set off in accordance with the provisions of subsection (6), the balance remaining shall be set off against any future liability to tax of the person who is treated as having made the payment which that person nominates for that purpose.

(8) Where a person has power to sell any heritage item in order to raise money for the payment of gift tax or inheritance tax, such person shall have power to make a relevant gift of that heritage item in or towards satisfaction of that tax and, except as regards the nature of the consideration and its receipt and application, any such relevant gift shall be subject to the same provisions and shall be treated for all purposes as a sale made in exercise of that power and any conveyances or transfers made or purporting to be made to give effect to such a relevant gift shall have effect accordingly.

(9) A person shall not be entitled to any refund of tax in respect of any payment on account of tax made in accordance with the provisions of this section.

(10) Interest shall not be payable in respect of any overpayment of tax for any period which arises directly or indirectly due to the set-off against any liability for that period of a payment on account of tax made in accordance with the provisions of this section.

(11) Where a person makes a relevant gift and in respect of that gift is treated as having made a payment on account of tax the person concerned shall not be allowed relief under any other provision of the Acts in respect of that gift.

(12) (a) The Revenue Commissioners shall, as respects each year (being the calendar year 1995 and subsequent calendar years), compile a list of the names (if any), descriptions and values of

the heritage items (if any) in respect of which relief under this section has been given.

(b) Notwithstanding any obligation as to secrecy imposed on them by the Acts or the Official Secrets Act, 1963, the Revenue Commissioners shall include in their annual report to the Minister for Finance, commencing with the report for the year 1995, the list (if any) referred to in paragraph (a) for the year in respect of which the report is made.

FAMILY LAW ACT, 1995

Number 26 of 1995
(Enacted on 2nd October, 1995 – into force on 1st August, 1996)

PART VI
Miscellaneous

Section 51

Exemption of certain transfers from capital acquisitions tax.

51. (1) Notwithstanding the provisions of the Capital Acquisitions Tax Act, 1976, a gift or inheritance (within the meaning, in each case, of that Act) taken by virtue or in consequence of an order to which this subsection applies by a spouse who was a party to the marriage concerned shall be exempt from any capital acquisitions tax under that Act and shall not be taken into account in computing such a tax.

(2) Subsection (1) applies to—

   (a) a relief order or an order under section 25 made following the dissolution of a marriage,

   (b) a maintenance pending relief order made following the granting of leave under section 23 (3) to a spouse whose marriage has been dissolved, and

   (c) an order referred to in section 41 (a), or an order under section 42 (1) made in addition to or instead of an order under section 41 (a), in favour of a spouse whose marriage has been dissolved.

Section 53

Abatement and postponement of probate tax on property the subject of an order under section 25.

53. Subsection (1) of section 115A of the Finance Act, 1993 (which was inserted by the Finance Act, 1994, and provides for the abatement or postponement of probate tax payable by a surviving spouse)—

   (a) shall apply to a spouse in whose favour an order has been made under section 25 as it applies to a spouse referred to in the said section 115A, and

   (b) shall apply to property or an interest in property the subject of such an order as it applies to the share of a spouse referred to in the said section 115A in the estate of a deceased referred to in that section or the interest of such a spouse in property referred to in that section,

with any necessary modifications.

FINANCE ACT, 1996

Number 9 of 1996
(Enacted on 15th May, 1996)

PART V
Capital Acquisitions Tax

Section 120

Interpretation (Part V).
120. In this Part "the Principal Act" means the Capital Acquisitions Tax Act, 1976.

Section 121

Amendment of section 16 (market value of certain shares in private trading companies) of [the Capital Acquisitions Tax Act, 1976].
121. As respects gifts and inheritances taken on or after the 28th day of March, 1996, section 16 of [the Capital Acquisitions Tax Act, 1976,] is hereby amended in subsection (2) by the substitution of the following definition for the definition of "private company":

"'private company' means a body corporate (wherever incorporated) which—

(a) is under the control of not more than five persons, and

(b) is not a company which would fall within section 95 of the Corporation Tax Act, 1976, if the words 'private company' were substituted for the words 'close company' in subsection (1) of that section, and if the words 'if beneficially held by a company which is not a private company' were substituted for the words of paragraph (a) of subsection (4) of that section.".

Section 122

Amendment of section 19 (value of agricultural property) of [the Capital Acquisitions Tax Act, 1976].
122. (1) Section 19 of [the Capital Acquisitions Tax Act, 1976,] is hereby amended—

(a) by the substitution of the following definition for the definition of "agricultural value" in subsection (1) (inserted by the Finance Act, 1994):

"'agricultural value' means the market value of agricultural property reduced by 75 per cent. of that value:

Provided that the agricultural value of agricultural property, other than farm machinery, livestock and bloodstock, comprised in a gift shall not be greater than it would have been if section 122 of the Finance Act, 1996, had not been enacted;",

(b) by the deletion of subsection (4) (inserted by the Finance Act, 1994),

and

(c) in paragraph (a) (inserted by the Finance Act, 1994) of subsection (5) —

(i) by the substitution of "ten years" for "six years" in subparagraph (i),

(ii) by the substitution of the following proviso for the proviso to that paragraph:

"Provided that—

(I) this paragraph shall not have effect, where the donee or successor dies before the property is sold or compulsorily acquired;

(II) where the event which causes the agricultural value to cease to be applicable occurs after the expiration of the period of six years commencing on the date of the gift or the date of the inheritance, the tax chargeable in respect of the gift or inheritance shall not be greater than it would have been if section 122 of the Finance Act, 1996, had not been enacted.".

(2) This section shall have effect in relation to gifts or inheritances taken on or after the 23rd day of January, 1996.

Section 123

Exemption relating to qualifying expenses of incapacitated persons.

123. (1) [The Capital Acquisitions Tax Act, 1976,] is hereby amended by the insertion of the following section after section 59:

"59A (1) A gift or inheritance which is taken exclusively for the purpose of discharging qualifying expenses of an individual who is permanently incapacitated by reason of physical or mental infirmity shall, to the extent that the Commissioners are satisfied that it has been or will be applied to such purpose, be exempt from tax and shall not be taken into account in computing tax.

(2) In this section 'qualifying expenses' means expenses relating to medical care including the cost of maintenance in connection with such medical care.".

(2) This section shall have effect in relation to gifts or inheritances taken on or after the 28th day of March, 1996.

Section 124

Amendment of section 118 (application of section 60 (relief in respect of certain policies of insurance) of Finance Act, 1985) of Finance Act, 1991.

124. (1) Section 118 of the Finance Act, 1991, is hereby amended by the deletion of "under a disposition made by the spouse of the insured where the inheritance is taken".

(2) This section shall apply to inheritances taken on or after the 28th day of March, 1996.

Section 125

Amendment of section 126 (business relief) of Finance Act, 1994.

125. (1) Section 126 (inserted by the Finance Act, 1995) of the Finance Act, 1994, is hereby amended by the substitution of "75 per cent." for "50 per cent.".

(2) This section shall have effect in relation to gifts or inheritances taken on or after the 23rd day of January, 1996.

Section 126

Amendment of section 127 (relevant business property) of Finance Act, 1994.

126. (1) Section 127 of the Finance Act, 1994, is hereby amended by the substitution of the following paragraph for paragraph (c) of subsection (1):

"(c) unquoted shares in or securities of a company incorporated in the State which is, on the valuation date (after the taking of the gift or inheritance), a company controlled by the donee or successor within the meaning of section 16 of [the Capital Acquisitions Tax Act, 1976];".

(2) This section shall have effect in relation to gifts or inheritances taken on or after the 28th day of March, 1996.

Section 127

Amendment of section 135 (withdrawal of relief) of Finance Act, 1994.

127. (1) Section 135 of the Finance Act, 1994, is hereby amended —

(a) by the substitution of "ten years" for "six years" in subsection (1) (as amended by the Finance Act, 1995), and

(b) by the substitution of the following proviso for the proviso (inserted by the Finance Act, 1995) to subsection (2):

"Provided that —

(i) any land, building, machinery or plant which are comprised in the gift or inheritance and which qualify as relevant business property by virtue of section 127 (1) (e) shall, together with any similar property which has replaced such property, continue to be relevant business property for the purposes of this section for so long as they are used for the purposes of the business concerned,

(ii) this section shall not have effect where the donee or successor dies before the event which would otherwise cause the reduction to cease to be applicable,

(iv) where the event which causes the reduction to cease to be applicable occurs after the expiration of the period of six years commencing on the valuation date, then only one-third of that reduction shall cease to be applicable.".

(2) This section shall apply to gifts or inheritances taken on or after the 23rd day of January, 1996.

Section 128

Amendment of section 146 (certificate relating to registration of title based on possession) of Finance Act, 1994.

128. Section 146 of the Finance Act, 1994, is hereby amended by the insertion of the following subsections after subsection (4):

"(4A) In subsection (1), the reference to a certificate issued by the Commissioners shall be construed as including a reference to a certificate to which subsection (4B) relates, and the provisions of subsection (1) shall be construed accordingly.

(4B) (a) A certificate to which this subsection relates is a certificate by the solicitor for the applicant for registration in which it is certified, on a form provided by the Commissioners, that the solicitor —

(i) is satisfied —

(I) in a case where the applicant is a statutory authority within the definition of 'statutory authority' contained in section 3(1) of the Act of 1964, that the market value of the relevant property at the time of the application does not exceed £100,000, or

(II) in any other case, that —

(A) the area of the relevant property does not exceed five hectares, and

(B) the market value of the relevant property at the time of the application does not exceed £15,000,

and

(ii) having investigated the title to the relevant property, has no reason to believe that the relevant particulars, in so far as relating to the relevant property at any time during the relevant period, are particulars which related at that time to significant other real property, that is to say, real property which, if combined with the relevant property for the purposes of subparagraph (i), would cause a limit which applies to the relevant property by virtue of that subparagraph to be exceeded.

(b)   In this subsection—

'the relevant particulars' means the particulars of title to the relevant property which are required to be produced to the Registrar for the purposes of paragraph 2 of Form 5 of the Schedule of Forms referred to in the definition of 'Forms' contained in rule 2 (1) of the Rules of 1972;

'the relevant property' means the property in respect of which the application for registration is being made.

(4C) Notwithstanding the provisions of subsection (4B), a certificate by the solicitor for the applicant for registration shall be a certificate to which subsection (4B) relates if it certifies, on a form provided by the Commissioners, that the solicitor is satisfied that—

(a)   the area of the property in respect of which the application for registration is being made does not exceed 500 square metres,

(b)   the market value of the said property at the time of the application does not exceed £2,000, and

(c)   the application is not part of a series of related applications covering a single piece of property the total area of which exceeds 500 square metres or the market value of which at the time of the application exceeds £2,000.".

Section 129

Amendment of section 164 (payment of tax on certain assets by instalments) of Finance Act, 1995.

129. (1)   Section 164 of the Finance Act, 1995, is hereby amended—

(a)   by the substitution of the following paragraph for paragraph (a) of subsection (2):

"(a) section 43 of [the Capital Acquisitions Tax Act, 1976,] shall apply to that whole or part of the tax notwithstanding subsection (3) or (4) of that section:

Provided that where all or any part of that agricultural property or relevant business property, or any property which directly or indirectly replaces such property, is sold or compulsorily acquired and, by virtue of subsection (5) of section 19 of [the Capital Acquisitions Tax Act, 1976,] or section 135 of the Finance Act, 1994, that sale or compulsory acquisition causes the taxable value of such a taxable gift or taxable inheritance to be increased, or would cause such increase if subsection (2) of section 19 of [the Capital Acquisitions Tax Act, 1976,] or section 126 of the Finance Act, 1994, applied, all unpaid instalments referable to the property sold or compulsorily acquired shall, unless the interest of the donee or successor is a limited interest, be paid on completion of that sale or compulsory acquisition and, if not so paid, shall be tax in arrear, and",

and

(b) by the insertion of the following subsection after subsection (2):

"(2A) For the purposes of this section reference to an overdue instalment in the proviso to paragraph (b) of subsection (2) is a reference to an instalment which is overdue for the purposes of section 43 (as it applies to this section) of [the Capital Acquisitions Tax Act, 1976,] or for the purposes of the proviso to paragraph (a) of the said subsection (2).".

(2) This section shall apply in relation to gifts or inheritances taken on or after the 8th day of February, 1995.

PART VI
Miscellaneous Pre-Consolidation Provisions

CHAPTER I
Income Tax, Corporation Tax and Capital Gains Tax

Section 132

Pre-consolidation amendments and repeals.

132. (1) The enactments specified in Part I of the Fifth Schedule shall have effect subject to the amendments specified in that Schedule, being amendments designed to facilitate, or otherwise desirable in connection with, the consolidation of the Tax Acts and the Capital Gains Tax Acts.

(2) ....

PART VII
Miscellaneous

Section 139

Amendment of section 176 (relief for donations of heritage items) of Finance Act, 1995.

139. As respects each year (being the calendar year 1996 and subsequent calendar years) section 176 of the Finance Act, 1995, is hereby amended, in subsection (2), by the substitution in subparagraph (ii) of paragraph (c) of "£750,000" for "£500,000", and the said subparagraph (ii), as so amended, is set out in the Table to this section.

TABLE

(ii)   exceeds an amount (which shall not be less than £75,000) determined by the formula—

$$£750,000 - M$$

where M is an amount (which may be nil) equal to the market value at the valuation date of the heritage item (if any) or the aggregate of the market values at the respective valuation dates of all the heritage items (if any), as the case may be, in respect of which a determination or determinations, as the case may be, under this subsection has been made by the selection committee in any one calendar year and not revoked in that year.

FIFTH SCHEDULE
PART I
Pre-Consolidation Amendments

13.   The Finance Act, 1983, is hereby amended in accordance with the following provisions of this paragraph.

(1)   . . . .

(2)   In section 94 (2), after paragraph (e), there shall be inserted the following:

"(ee) knowingly or wilfully, and within the time limits specified for their retention, destroys, defaces, or conceals from an authorised officer—

(i)   any documents, or

(ii)   any other written or printed material in any form, including any information stored, maintained or preserved by means of any mechanical or electronic device, whether or not stored, maintained or preserved in a legible form, which a person is obliged by any provision of the Acts to keep, to issue or to produce for inspection,".

DISCLOSURE OF CERTAIN INFORMATION FOR TAXATION AND OTHER PURPOSES ACT, 1996

Number 25 of 1996
(Enacted on 30th July, 1996)

Section 8

Amendment of section 39 (assessment of tax) of Capital Acquisitions Tax Act, 1976.

8. Section 39 of the Capital Acquisitions Tax Act, 1976, is hereby amended by the substitution of the following subsection for subsection (7):

"(7) The Commissioners, in making any assessment, correcting assessment or additional assessment, otherwise than from a return or an additional return which is satisfactory to them, shall make an assessment of such amount of tax as, to the best of their knowledge, information (including information received from a member of the Garda Síochána) and belief, ought to be charged, levied and paid:

Provided that, where an assessment raised under this section is based, in whole or in part, or directly or indirectly, on information received from a member of the Garda Síochána, the said member's source of the said information shall not, without the express permission in writing of a member of the Garda Síochána not below the rank of Chief Superintendent, be revealed in any correspondence or communication in relation to the assessment or on the hearing or rehearing of an appeal against the assessment.".

Section 12

Anonymity.

12. The Finance Act, 1983, is hereby amended by the insertion of the following section after section 19:

"19A. (1) In this section—

'authorised officer' means an officer of the Revenue Commissioners nominated by them to be a member of the staff of the body;

'the body' has the same meaning as in section 19;

'proceedings' includes any hearing before the Appeal Commissioners (within the meaning of the Revenue Acts);

'the Revenue Acts' means the Acts within the meaning of section 94 of this Act together with Chapter IV of Part II of the Finance Act, 1992, and any instruments made thereunder and any instruments made under any other enactment and relating to tax;

'tax' means any tax, duty, levy or charge under the care and management of the Revenue Commissioners.

(2) Notwithstanding any requirement made by or under any enactment or any other requirement in administrative and operational procedures, including internal procedures, all reasonable care shall be taken to ensure that the identity of an authorised officer shall not be revealed.

(3) In particular and without prejudice to the generality of subsection (2) –

    (a) when exercising or performing his or her powers or duties under the Revenue Acts in pursuance of the functions of the body, an authorised officer shall –

        (i) not be required to produce or show any written authority or warrant of appointment under the Revenue Acts when exercising or performing his or her powers or duties under those Acts, notwithstanding any provision to the contrary in any of those Acts, and

        (ii) be accompanied by a member of the Garda Síochána who shall, on request, by a person affected identify himself or herself as a member of the Garda Síochána and shall state that he or she is accompanied by an authorised officer,

    (b) where, in pursuance of the functions of the body, an authorised officer exercises or performs in writing any of his or her powers or duties under the Revenue Acts or any provisions of any other enactment, whenever passed, which relate to Revenue, such exercise or performance of his or her powers or duties shall be done in the name of the body and not in the name of the individual authorised officer involved, notwithstanding any provision to the contrary in any of those enactments,

    (c) in any proceedings arising out of the exercise or performance, in pursuance of the functions of the body, of powers or duties by an authorised officer, any documents relating to such proceedings shall not reveal the identity of any authorised officer, notwithstanding any requirements in any provision to the contrary, and in any proceedings the identity of such officer other than as an authorised officer shall not be revealed other than to the judge or the Appeal Commissioner, as the case may be, hearing the case,

    (d) where, in pursuance of the functions of the body, an authorised officer is required, in any proceedings, to give evidence and the judge or the Appeal Commissioner, as the case may be, is satisfied that there are reasonable grounds in the public interest to direct that evidence to be given by such authorised officer should be given in the hearing and not in the sight of any person, he or she may so direct.".

CRIMINAL ASSETS BUREAU ACT, 1996

Number 31 of 1996
(Enacted on 11th October, 1996)

Section 23

Amendment of section 19A (anonymity) of Finance Act, 1983.

23. Section 19A (inserted by the Disclosure of Certain Information for Taxation and Other Purposes Act, 1996) of the Finance Act, 1983, is hereby amended in subsection (3), by the substitution of the following for paragraph (a):

"(a) where, for the purposes of exercising or performing his or her powers or duties under the Revenue Acts in pursuance of the functions of the body, an authorised officer may, apart from this section, be required to produce or show any written authority or warrant of appointment under those Acts or otherwise to identify himself or herself, the authorised officer shall —

(i) not be required to produce or show any such authority or warrant of appointment or to so identify himself or herself, for the purposes of exercising or performing his or her powers or duties under those Acts, and

(ii) be accompanied by a member of the Garda Síochána who shall, on request, by a person affected identify himself or herself as a member of the Garda Síochána and shall state that he or she is accompanied by an authorised officer,".

Section 24

Amendment of certain taxation provisions.

24. (1) . . . .

(4) The proviso to subsection (7) (as amended by the Disclosure of Certain Information for Taxation and Other Purposes Act, 1996) of section 39 of the Capital Acquisitions Tax Act, 1976, is hereby deleted.

FAMILY LAW (DIVORCE) ACT, 1996

Number 33 of 1996
(Enacted on 27th November, 1996)

Section 34

Exemption of certain transfers from capital acquisitions tax.

34. Notwithstanding the provisions of the Capital Acquisitions Tax Act, 1976, a gift or inheritance (within the meaning, in each case, of that Act) taken by virtue or in consequence of an order under Part III by a spouse who was a party to the marriage concerned shall be exempt from any capital acquisitions tax under that Act and shall not be taken into account in computing such a tax.

Section 36

Abatement and postponement of probate tax on property the subject of an order under section 18.

36. Subsection (1) of section 115A of the Finance Act, 1993 (which was inserted by the Finance Act, 1994, and provides for the abatement or postponement of probate tax payable by a surviving spouse) −

(a) shall apply to a spouse in whose favour an order has been made under section 18 as it applies to a spouse referred to in the said section 115A, and

(b) shall apply to property or an interest in property the subject of such an order as it applies to the share of a spouse referred to in the said section 115A in the estate of a deceased referred to in that section or the interest of such a spouse in property referred to in that section,

with any necessary modifications.

FINANCE ACT, 1997

Number 22 of 1997
(Enacted on 10th May, 1997)

PART VI
Capital Acquisitions Tax

Section 133

Interpretation (Part VI).

133. In this Part "the Principal Act" means the Capital Acquisitions Tax Act, 1976.

Section 134

Amendment of section 19 (value of agricultural property) of [the Capital Acquisitions Tax Act, 1976].

134. (1) Section 19 of [the Capital Acquisitions Tax Act, 1976,] is hereby amended—

   (a) by the substitution of the following definition for the definition of "agricultural value" in subsection (1) (inserted by the Finance Act, 1996):

   "'agricultural value' means the market value of agricultural property reduced by 90 per cent. of that value;",

   (b) in paragraph (II) of the proviso (inserted by the Finance Act, 1996) to paragraph (a) (inserted by the Finance Act, 1994) of subsection (5), by the insertion of "or section 134 of the Finance Act, 1997," after "Finance Act, 1996,".

   (2) This section shall have effect in relation to gifts or inheritances taken on or after the 23rd day of January, 1997.

Section 135

Amendment of section 57 (exemption of certain securities) of [the Capital Acquisitions Tax Act, 1976].

135. (1) Subsection (3) of section 57 of [the Capital Acquisitions Tax Act, 1976,] is hereby amended by the substitution of "disposition" for "disposition, or at the date of the gift or the date of the inheritance".

   (2) This section shall have effect in relation to securities or units comprised in a gift or an inheritance where the date of the gift or the date of the inheritance is on or after the 26th day of March, 1997, and the securities or units come into the beneficial ownership of the disponer on or after the 26th day of March, 1997, or become

subject to the disposition on or after that date without having been previously in the beneficial ownership of the disponer.

Section 136

Second Schedule (computation of tax) to [the Capital Acquisitions Tax Act, 1976], declaratory provision.

136. (1) For the avoidance of doubt it is hereby declared that paragraph 3 (inserted by the Finance Act, 1984) of the Second Schedule to [the Capital Acquisitions Tax Act, 1976,] shall have effect and be deemed always to have had effect as if the following paragraph were substituted therefor:

"3. Subject to the provisions of paragraph 6, the tax chargeable on the taxable value of a taxable gift or a taxable inheritance taken by a donee or successor shall be of an amount equal to the amount by which the tax computed on aggregate A exceeds the tax computed on aggregate B, where—

(a) aggregate A is the aggregate of the following:

(i) the said taxable value, and

(ii) the taxable value of each and every taxable gift and taxable inheritance taken previously by the said donee or successor on or after the 2nd day of June, 1982,

(b) aggregate B is the aggregate of the taxable values of all taxable gifts and taxable inheritances so previously taken, and

(c) the tax on an aggregate is computed at the rate or rates of tax applicable under the Table to that aggregate:

Provided that—

(i) in a case where no taxable gift or taxable inheritance was so previously taken, the amount of the tax computed on aggregate B shall be deemed to be nil,

(ii) in every other case, the amount of the tax chargeable shall not exceed the amount which would be chargeable if the threshold amount which applies to aggregate A were deemed, irrespective of the definition of 'threshold amount', to be also the threshold amount which applies to aggregate B, and

(iii) the amount of an aggregate that comprises only a single taxable value shall be equal to that value.".

(2) Subsection (1) shall not apply to a gift or inheritance in relation to which paragraph 3 of the Second Schedule to [the Capital

Acquisitions Tax Act, 1976,] was the subject of a determination of the Appeal Commissioners, being a determination made before the 1st day of May, 1997, under section 52 of [the Capital Acquisitions Tax Act, 1976].

Section 137

Amendment of section 39 (extension of section 55 (exemption of certain objects) of Capital Acquisitions Tax Act, 1976) of Finance Act, 1978.

137. (1) Section 39 of the Finance Act, 1978, is hereby amended by the insertion of the following subsection after subsection (1):

"(1A) Without prejudice to the generality of subsection (1), the provision of facilities for the viewing by members of the public of a house or garden shall not be regarded as reasonable in relation to any year, which is the year 1997 or any subsequent year and which is taken into account for the purposes of paragraphs (b) and (c) of subsection (1), unless—

(a) Bord Fáilte Éireann (hereinafter in this section referred to as 'the Board') has, as regards the year 1997, on or before the 1st day of July, 1997, and, as regards any subsequent year, on or before the 1st day of January in that year, been provided with particulars of—

(i) the name, if any, and address of the house or garden, and

(ii) the days and times during the year when access to the house or garden is afforded to the public and the price, if any, payable for such access, and

(b) in the opinion of the Commissioners—

(i) subject to such temporary closure necessary for the purpose of the repair, maintenance or restoration of the house or garden as is reasonable, access to the house or garden is afforded for not less than 60 days (including not less than 40 days during the period commencing on the 1st day of May and ending on the 30th day of September) in that year;

(ii) on each day on which access to the house or garden is afforded, the access is afforded in a reasonable manner and at reasonable times for a period, or periods in the aggregate, of not less than four hours;

(iii) access to the whole or to a substantial part of the house or garden is afforded at the same time; and

(iv) the price, if any, paid by members of the public in return for that access is reasonable in amount and does not operate to preclude members of the public from seeking access to the house or garden.".

(2) The Capital Acquisitions Tax (Heritage Houses and Gardens) Regulations, 1987 (S.I. No. 28 of 1987), shall be deemed to have been revoked with effect from the 1st day of January, 1997.

(3) This section shall have effect in relation to gifts and inheritances taken on or after the 1st day of February, 1987.

Section 138

Amendment of section 117 (reduction of market value of certain dwellings) of Finance Act, 1991.

138. (1) Section 117 of the Finance Act, 1991 (as amended by section 144 of the Finance Act, 1994), is hereby amended by the substitution in subsection (1) of "£80,000" for "£60,000".

(2) This section shall have effect in relation to inheritances taken on or after the date of the passing of this Act.

Section 139

Amendment of section 126 (business relief) of Finance Act, 1994.

139. (1) Section 126 (inserted by the Finance Act, 1995) of the Finance Act, 1994, is hereby amended by the substitution of "90 per cent." for "75 per cent." (inserted by the Finance Act, 1996).

(2) This section shall have effect in relation to gifts or inheritances taken on or after the 23rd day of January, 1997.

Section 140

Amendment of section 127 (relevant business property) of Finance Act, 1994.

140. (1) Section 127 of the Finance Act, 1994, is hereby amended by the substitution of the following subsections for subsection (6):

"(6) Any land, building, machinery or plant used wholly or mainly for the purposes of a business carried on as mentioned in subsection (1) (e) shall not be relevant business property in relation to a gift or inheritance, unless the disponer's interest in the business is, or shares in or securities of the company carrying on the business immediately before the gift or inheritance are, relevant business property in relation to the gift or inheritance or in relation to a simultaneous gift or inheritance taken by the same donee or successor.

(7) The references to a disponer in subsections (1) (e) and (6) shall include a reference to a person in whom the land, building, machinery or plant concerned is vested for a beneficial interest in possession immediately before the gift or inheritance.

(8) Where shares or securities are vested in the trustees of a settlement, any powers of voting which they give to the

trustees of the settlement shall, for the purposes of subsection (1) (e), be deemed to be given to the person beneficially entitled in possession to the shares or securities except in a case where no individual is so entitled.".

(2) This section shall have effect in relation to gifts and inheritances taken on or after the 26th day of March, 1997.

Section 141

Amendment of section 135 (withdrawal of relief) of Finance Act, 1994.

141. (1) Section 135 of the Finance Act, 1994, is hereby amended, in subparagraph (iii) of the proviso (inserted by the Finance Act, 1996) to subsection (2), by the substitution of "four-ninths" for "one-third".

(2) This section shall have effect in relation to gifts or inheritances taken on or after the 23rd day of January, 1997.

Section 142

Exemption of certain transfers from capital acquisitions tax following the dissolution of a marriage.

142. (1) Notwithstanding the provisions of [the Capital Acquisitions Tax Act, 1976], a gift or inheritance (within the meaning, in each case, of that Act) taken by virtue or in consequence of an order to which this subsection applies by a spouse who was a party to the marriage concerned shall be exempt from any capital acquisitions tax under that Act and shall not be taken into account in computing such a tax.

(2) Subsection (1) applies —

(a) to a relief order or an order under section 25 of the Family Law Act, 1995, made following the dissolution of a marriage, or

(b) to a maintenance pending relief order made following the granting of leave under section 23 (3) of the Family Law Act, 1995, to a spouse whose marriage has been dissolved,

(c) to an order referred to in section 41 (a) of the Family Law Act, 1995, or an order under section 42 (1) of that Act made in addition to or instead of an order under section 41 (a) of that Act, in favour of a spouse whose marriage has been dissolved, and

(d) to an order under Part III of the Family Law (Divorce) Act, 1996.

(3) Section 51 of the Family Law Act, 1995, and section 34 of the Family Law (Divorce) Act, 1996, are hereby repealed.

Section 143

Abatement and postponement of probate tax on certain property.

143. (1) Subsection (1) of section 115A of the Finance Act, 1993 (which was inserted by the Finance Act, 1994, and provides for the abatement or postponement of probate tax payable by a surviving spouse) —

    (a) shall apply to a spouse in whose favour an order has been made —

        (i) under section 25 of the Family Law Act, 1995, or

        (ii) under section 18 of the Family Law (Divorce) Act, 1996,

    as it applies to a spouse referred to in the said section 115A, and

    (b) shall apply to property or an interest in property the subject of such an order as it applies to the share of a spouse referred to in the said section 115A in the estate of a deceased referred to in that section or the interest of such a spouse in property referred to in that section,

with any necessary modifications.

    (2) Section 53 of the Family Law Act, 1995, and section 36 of the Family Law (Divorce) Act, 1996, are hereby repealed.

PART VIII
Miscellaneous

Section 158

Amendment of section 23 (publication of names of defaulters) of Finance Act, 1983.

158. As respects the year 1997 and subsequent years, section 23 of the Finance Act, 1983, is hereby amended —

    (a) by the substitution of the following subsection for subsection (2):

    "(2) The Revenue Commissioners shall, as respects each relevant period (being the period beginning on the 1st day of January, 1997, and ending on the 30th day of June, 1997, and each subsequent period of three months beginning with the period ending on the 30th day of September, 1997), compile a list of names and addresses and the occupations or descriptions of every person —

        (a) upon whom a fine or other penalty was imposed by a court under any of the Acts during that relevant period,

        (b) upon whom a fine or other penalty was otherwise imposed by a court during that relevant period in respect of an act or omission by the person in relation to tax, or

(c) in whose case the Revenue Commissioners, pursuant to an agreement made with the person in that relevant period, refrained from initiating proceedings for recovery of any fine or penalty of the kind mentioned in paragraphs (a) and (b) and, in lieu of initiating such proceedings, accepted, or undertook to accept, a specified sum of money in settlement of any claim by the Revenue Commissioners in respect of any specified liability of the person under any of the Acts for—

(i) payment of any tax,

(ii) payment of interest thereon, and

(iii) a fine or other monetary penalty in respect thereof.",

and

(b) by the substitution of the following subsection for subsection (3):

"(3) Notwithstanding any obligation as to secrecy imposed on them by the Acts or the Official Secrets Act, 1963—

(a) the Revenue Commissioners shall, before the expiration of three months from the end of each relevant period, cause each such list referred to in subsection (2) in relation to that period to be published in Iris Oifigiúil, and

(b) the Revenue Commissioners may, at any time, cause any such list referred to in subsection (2) to be publicised in such manner as they shall consider appropriate.".

Section 159

Evidence of authorisation.

159. (1) In this section, except where the context otherwise requires—

"the Acts" means—

(a) (i) the Customs Acts,

(ii) the statutes relating to the duties of excise and to the management of those duties,

(iii) the Tax Acts,

(iv) the Capital Gains Tax Acts,

(v) the Value-Added Tax Act, 1972, and the enactments amending or extending that Act,

(vi) the Capital Acquisitions Tax Act, 1976, and the enactments amending or extending that Act,

(vii) the statutes relating to stamp duty and to the management of that duty, and any instruments made thereunder or under any other enactment and relating to tax, and

(b) the European Communities (Intrastat) Regulations, 1993 (S.I. No. 136 of 1993);

"authorised officer" means an officer of the Revenue Commissioners who is authorised, nominated or appointed under any provision of the Acts, to exercise or perform any functions under any of the specified provisions, and "authorised" and "authorisation" shall be construed accordingly;

"functions" includes powers and duties;

"identity card", in relation to an authorised officer, means a card which is issued to the officer by the Revenue Commissioners and which contains –

(a) a statement to the effect that the officer –

    (i) is an officer of the Revenue Commissioners, and

    (ii) is an authorised officer for the purposes of the specified provisions,

(b) a photograph and signature of the officer,

(c) a hologram showing the logo of the Office of the Revenue Commissioners,

(d) the facsimile signature of a Revenue Commissioner, and

(e) particulars of the specified provisions under which the officer is authorised;

"specified provisions", in relation to an authorised officer, means either or both the provisions of the Acts under which the authorised officer –

(a) is authorised and which are specified on his or her identity card, and

(b) exercises or performs functions under the Customs Acts or any statutes relating to the duties of excise and to the management of those duties;

"tax" means any tax, duty, levy, charge under the care and management of the Revenue Commissioners.

(2) Where, in the exercise or performance of any functions under any of the specified provisions in relation to him or her, an authorised officer is requested to produce or show his or her authorisation for the purposes of that provision, the production by the authorised officer of his or her identity card –

(a) shall be taken as evidence of authorisation under that provision, and

(b) shall satisfy any obligation under that provision which requires the authorised officer to produce such authorisation on request.

(3) This section shall come into operation on such day as the Minister for Finance may appoint by order.[1]

Footnote

1   S.159 never took effect, as no order was made under s.159(3).

TAXES CONSOLIDATION ACT, 1997

Number 39 of 1997
(Enacted on 30th November, 1997)

PART I
Interpretation

Section 7

Application to certain taxing statutes of Age of Majority Act, 1985.

7. (1) Notwithstanding subsection (4) of section 2 of the Age of Majority Act, 1985[1] (in this section referred to as "the Act of 1985"), subsections (2) and (3) of that section shall, subject to subsection (2), apply for the purposes of the Income Tax Acts and any other statutory provision (within the meaning of the Act of 1985) dealing with the imposition, repeal, remission, alteration or regulation of any tax or other duty under the care and management of the Revenue Commissioners, and accordingly section 2 (4)(b)(vii) of the Act of 1985 shall cease to apply.

(2) Nothing in subsection (1) shall affect a claimant's entitlement to a deduction under section 462 or 465.

Footnote
1   Reproduced on page 782.

Section 8

Construction of certain taxing statutes in accordance with Status of Children Act, 1987.

8. (1) In this section, "the Acts" means-

(a) the Tax Acts,

(b) the Capital Gains Tax Acts,

(c) the Capital Acquisitions Tax Act, 1976, and the enactments amending or extending that Act, and

(d) the statutes relating to stamp duty,

and any instruments made thereunder.

(2) Notwithstanding any provision of the Acts or the dates on which they were passed, in deducing any relationship between persons for the purposes of the Acts, the Acts shall be construed in accordance with section 3 of the Status of Children Act, 1987[1].

Footnote
1   Reproduced on page 799.

PART 6

Company Distributions, Tax Credits, Franked Investment Income and Advance Corporation Tax

CHAPTER 9
Taxation of acquisition by a company of its own shares

Section 176

Purchase of unquoted shares by issuing company or its subsidiary.

176. (1) Notwithstanding Chapter 2 of this Part, references in the Tax Acts to distributions of a company, other than any such references in sections 440 and 441, shall be construed so as not to include references to a payment made by a company on the redemption, repayment or purchase of its own shares if the company is an unquoted trading company or the unquoted holding company of a trading group and either—

    (a) (i) the redemption, repayment or purchase—

        (I) is made wholly or mainly for the purpose of benefiting a trade carried on by the company or by any of its 51 per cent subsidiaries, and

        (II) does not form part of a scheme or arrangement the main purpose or one of the main purposes of which is to enable the owner of the shares to participate in the profits of the company or of any of its 51 per cent subsidiaries without receiving a dividend,

      and

      (ii) the conditions specified in sections 177 to 181, in so far as applicable, are satisfied in relation to the owner of the shares, or

    (b) the person to whom the payment is made—

      (i) applies the whole or substantially the whole of the payment (apart from any sum applied in discharging that person's liability to capital gains tax, if any, in respect of the redemption, repayment or purchase) to discharging—

        (I) within 4 months of the valuation date (within the meaning of section 21 of the Capital Acquisitions Tax Act, 1976) of a taxable inheritance of the company's shares taken by that person, a liability to inheritance tax in respect of that inheritance, or

        (II) within one week of the day on which the payment is made, a debt incurred by that person for the purpose of discharging that liability to inheritance tax,

and

   (ii) could not without undue hardship have otherwise discharged that liability to inheritance tax and, where appropriate, the debt so incurred.

(2) Where subsection (1) would apply to a payment made by a company which is a subsidiary (within the meaning of section 155 of the Companies Act, 1963) of another company on the acquisition of shares of the other company if for the purposes of the Tax Acts other than this subsection —

   (a) the payment were to be treated as a payment by the other company on the purchase of its own shares, and

   (b) the acquisition by the subsidiary of the shares were to be treated as a purchase by the other company of its own shares,

then, notwithstanding Chapter 2 of this Part, references in the Tax Acts to distributions of a company, other than references in sections 440 and 441, shall be construed so as not to include references to the payment made by the subsidiary.

PART 13
Close Companies

CHAPTER 1
Interpretation and General

Section 431

Certain companies with quoted shares not to be close companies.

431. (1) In this section, "share" includes "stock".

(2) For the purposes of this section-

   (a) a person shall be a principal member of a company-

      (i) if such person possesses a percentage of the voting power in the company of more than 5 per cent and, where there are more than 5 such persons, if such person is one of the 5 persons who possess the greatest percentages, or

      (ii) if (because 2 or more persons possess equal percentages of the voting power in the company) there are no such 5 persons, such person is one of the 6 or more persons (so as to include those 2 or more who possess equal percentages) who possess the greatest percentages,

   (b) a principal member's holding shall consist of the shares which carry the voting power possessed by the principal member, and

(c) in determining the voting power which a person possesses, there shall be attributed to such person any voting power which for the purposes of section 432 would be attributed to such person under subsection (5) or (6) of that section.

(3) Subject to this section, a company shall not be treated as being at any time a close company if-

(a) shares in the company carrying not less than 35 per cent of the voting power in the company (not being shares entitled to a fixed rate of dividend, whether with or without a further right to participate in profits) have been allotted unconditionally to, or acquired unconditionally by, and are at that time beneficially held by, the public, and

(b) any such shares have within the preceding 12 months been the subject of dealings on a recognised stock exchange, and the shares have within those 12 months been quoted in the official list of a recognised stock exchange.

(4) Subsection (3) shall not apply to a company at any time when the total percentage of the voting power in the company possessed by all of the company's principal members exceeds 85 per cent.

(5) For the purposes of subsection (3), shares in a company shall be deemed to be beneficially held by the public only if the shares-

(a) are within subsection (6), and

(b) are not within the exceptions in subsection (7),

and the reference to shares which have been allotted unconditionally to, or acquired unconditionally by, the public shall be construed accordingly.

(6) Shares are within this subsection (as being beneficially held by the public) if the shares-

(a) are beneficially held by a company resident in the State which is not a close company, or by a company not so resident which would not be a close company if it were so resident,

(b) are held on trust for an exempt approved scheme (within the meaning of Chapter 1 of Part 30), or

(c) are not comprised in a principal member's holding.

(7) (a) Shares shall be deemed not to be held by the public if the shares are held-

(i) by any director, or associate of a director, of the company,

(ii) by any company under the control of any such director or associate, or of 2 or more persons each of whom is such a director or associate,

(iii) by an associated company of the company, or

(iv) as part of any fund the capital or income of which is applicable or applied wholly or mainly for the benefit of, or of the dependants of, the employees or directors, or past employees or directors, of the company, or of any company within subparagraph (ii) or (iii).

(b) References in this subsection to shares held by any person include references to any shares the rights or powers attached to which could for the purposes of section 432 be attributed to that person under subsection (5) of that section.

PART 33
Anti-Avoidance

CHAPTER 2
Miscellaneous

Section 811

Transactions to avoid liability to tax.

811. (1) (a)   In this section—

"the Acts" means—

(i)   the Tax Acts,

(ii)   the Capital Gains Tax Acts,

(iii)   the Value-Added Tax Act, 1972, and the enactments amending or extending that Act,

(iv)   the Capital Acquisitions Tax Act, 1976, and the enactments amending or extending that Act,

(v)   Part VI of the Finance Act, 1983, and the enactments amending or extending that Part, and

(vi)   the statutes relating to stamp duty,

and any instruments made thereunder;

"business" means any trade, profession or vocation;

"notice of opinion" means a notice given by the Revenue Commissioners under subsection (6);

"tax" means any tax, duty, levy or charge which in accordance with the Acts is placed under the care and management of the Revenue Commissioners and any interest, penalty or other amount payable pursuant to the Acts;

"tax advantage" means—

(i) a reduction, avoidance or deferral of any charge or assessment to tax, including any potential or prospective charge or assessment, or

(ii) a refund of or a payment of an amount of tax, or an increase in an amount of tax, refundable or otherwise payable to a person, including any potential or prospective amount so refundable or payable,

arising out of or by reason of a transaction, including a transaction where another transaction would not have been undertaken or arranged to achieve the results, or any part of the results, achieved or intended to be achieved by the transaction;

"tax avoidance transaction" has the meaning assigned to it by subsection (2);

"tax consequences", in relation to a tax avoidance transaction, means such adjustments and acts as may be made and done by the Revenue Commissioners pursuant to subsection (5) in order to withdraw or deny the tax advantage resulting from the tax avoidance transaction;

"transaction" means—

(i) any transaction, action, course of action, course of conduct, scheme, plan or proposal,

(ii) any agreement, arrangement, understanding, promise or undertaking, whether express or implied and whether or not enforceable or intended to be enforceable by legal proceedings, and

(iii) any series of or combination of the circumstances referred to in paragraphs (i) and (ii),

whether entered into or arranged by one person or by 2 or more persons—

(I) whether acting in concert or not,

(II) whether or not entered into or arranged wholly or partly outside the State, or

(III) whether or not entered into or arranged as part of a larger transaction or in conjunction with any other transaction or transactions.

(b) In subsections (2) and (3), for the purposes of the hearing or rehearing under subsection (8) of an appeal made under subsection (7) or for the purposes of the determination of a question of law arising on the statement of a case for the opinion of the High Court, the references to the Revenue Commissioners shall, subject to any necessary modifications, be construed as references to the Appeal Commissioners or to a judge of the Circuit Court or, to the extent necessary, to a judge of the High Court, as appropriate.

(2) For the purposes of this section and subject to subsection (3), a transaction shall be a "tax avoidance transaction" if having regard to any one or more of the following—

(a) the results of the transaction,

(b) its use as a means of achieving those results, and

(c) any other means by which the results or any part of the results could have been achieved,

the Revenue Commissioners form the opinion that—

(i) the transaction gives rise to, or but for this section would give rise to, a tax advantage, and

(ii) the transaction was not undertaken or arranged primarily for purposes other than to give rise to a tax advantage,

and references in this section to the Revenue Commissioners forming an opinion that a transaction is a tax avoidance transaction shall be construed as references to the Revenue Commissioners forming an opinion with regard to the transaction in accordance with this subsection.

(3) (a) Without prejudice to the generality of subsection (2), in forming an opinion in accordance with that subsection and subsection (4) as to whether or not a transaction is a tax avoidance transaction, the Revenue Commissioners shall not regard the transaction as being a tax avoidance transaction if they are satisfied that—

(i) notwithstanding that the purpose or purposes of the transaction could have been achieved by some other transaction which would have given rise to a greater amount of tax being payable by the person, the transaction—

(I) was undertaken or arranged by a person with a view, directly or indirectly, to the realisation of profits in the course of the business activities of a business carried on by the person, and

(II) was not undertaken or arranged primarily to give rise to a tax advantage,

or

(ii) the transaction was undertaken or arranged for the purpose of obtaining the benefit of any relief, allowance or other abatement provided by any provision of the Acts and that the transaction would not result directly or indirectly in a misuse of the provision or an abuse of the provision having regard to the purposes for which it was provided.

(b) In forming an opinion referred to in paragraph (a) in relation to any transaction, the Revenue Commissioners shall have regard to —

    (i) the form of that transaction,

    (ii) the substance of that transaction,

    (iii) the substance of any other transaction or transactions which that transaction may reasonably be regarded as being directly or indirectly related to or connected with, and

    (iv) the final outcome and result of that transaction and any combination of those other transactions which are so related or connected.

(4) Subject to this section, the Revenue Commissioners as respects any transaction may at any time —

    (a) form the opinion that the transaction is a tax avoidance transaction,

    (b) calculate the tax advantage which they consider arises, or which but for this section would arise, from the transaction,

    (c) determine the tax consequences which they consider would arise in respect of the transaction if their opinion were to become final and conclusive in accordance with subsection (5) (e), and

    (d) calculate the amount of any relief from double taxation which they would propose to give to any person in accordance with subsection (5) (c).

(5) (a) Where the opinion of the Revenue Commissioners that a transaction is a tax avoidance transaction becomes final and conclusive, they may, notwithstanding any other provision of the Acts, make all such adjustments and do all such acts as are just and reasonable (in so far as those adjustments and acts have been specified or described in a notice of opinion given under subsection (6) and subject to the manner in which any appeal made under subsection (7) against any matter specified or described in the notice of opinion has been finally determined, including any adjustments and acts not so specified or described in the notice of opinion but which form part of a final determination of any such appeal) in order that the tax advantage resulting from a tax avoidance transaction shall be withdrawn from or denied to any person concerned.

    (b) Subject to but without prejudice to the generality of paragraph (a), the Revenue Commissioners may —

    (i)   allow or disallow in whole or in part any deduction or other amount which is relevant in computing tax payable, or any part of such deduction or other amount,

    (ii) allocate or deny to any person any deduction, loss, abatement, relief, allowance. exemption, income or other amount, or any part thereof, or

    (iii) recharacterize for tax purposes the nature of any payment or other amount.

(c)   Where the Revenue Commissioners make any adjustment or do any act for the purposes of paragraph (a), they shall afford relief from any double taxation which they consider would but for this paragraph arise by virtue of any adjustment made or act done by them pursuant to paragraphs (a) and (b).

(d)   Notwithstanding any other provision of the Acts, where –

    (i)   pursuant to subsection (4) (c), the Revenue Commissioners determine the tax consequences which they consider would arise in respect of a transaction if their opinion that the transaction is a tax avoidance transaction were to become final and conclusive, and

    (ii) pursuant to that determination, they specify or describe in a notice of opinion any adjustment or act which they consider would be, or be part of, those tax consequences,

then, in so far as any right of appeal lay under subsection (7) against any such adjustment or act so specified or described, no right or further right of appeal shall lie under the Acts against that adjustment or act when it is made or done in accordance with this subsection, or against any adjustment or act so made or done that is not so specified or described in the notice of opinion but which forms part of the final determination of any appeal made under subsection (7) against any matter specified or described in the notice of opinion.

(e)   For the purposes of this subsection, an opinion of the Revenue Commissioners that a transaction is a tax avoidance transaction shall be final and conclusive –

    (i)   if within the time limited no appeal is made under subsection (7) against any matter or matters specified or described in a notice or notices of opinion given pursuant to that opinion, or

    (ii) as and when all appeals made under subsection (7) against any such matter or matters have been finally determined and none of the appeals has been so determined by an order directing that the opinion of the

Revenue Commissioners to the effect that the transaction is a tax avoidance transaction is void.

(6) (a) Where pursuant to subsections (2) and (4) the Revenue Commissioners form the opinion that a transaction is a tax avoidance transaction, they shall immediately on forming such an opinion give notice in writing of the opinion to any person from whom a tax advantage would be withdrawn or to whom a tax advantage would be denied or to whom relief from double taxation would be given if the opinion became final and conclusive, and the notice shall specify or describe —

(i) the transaction which in the opinion of the Revenue Commissioners is a tax avoidance transaction,

(ii) the tax advantage or part of the tax advantage, calculated by the Revenue Commissioners which would be withdrawn from or denied to the person to whom the notice is given,

(iii) the tax consequences of the transaction determined by the Revenue Commissioners in so far as they would refer to the person, and

(iv) the amount of any relief from double taxation calculated by the Revenue Commissioners which they would propose to give to the person in accordance with subsection (5) (c).

(b) Section 869 shall, with any necessary modifications, apply for the purposes of a notice given under this subsection or subsection (10) as if it were a notice given under the Income Tax Acts.

(7) Any person aggrieved by an opinion formed or, in so far as it refers to the person, a calculation or determination made by the Revenue Commissioners pursuant to subsection (4) may, by notice in writing given to the Revenue Commissioners within 30 days of the date of the notice of opinion, appeal to the Appeal Commissioners on the grounds and, notwithstanding any other provision of the Acts, only on the grounds that, having regard to all of the circumstances, including any fact or matter which was not known to the Revenue Commissioners when they formed their opinion or made their calculation or determination, and to this section —

(a) the transaction specified or described in the notice of opinion is not a tax avoidance transaction,

(b) the amount of the tax advantage or the part of the tax advantage, specified or described in the notice of opinion which would be withdrawn from or denied to the person is incorrect,

(c) the tax consequences specified or described in the notice of opinion, or such part of those consequences as shall be specified or described by the appellant in the notice of appeal, would not be just and reasonable in order to withdraw or to deny the tax advantage or part of the tax advantage specified or described in the notice of opinion, or

(d) the amount of relief from double taxation which the Revenue Commissioners propose to give to the person is insufficient or incorrect.

(8) The Appeal Commissioners shall hear and determine an appeal made to them under subsection (7) as if it were an appeal against an assessment to income tax and, subject to subsection (9), the provisions of the Income Tax Acts relating to the rehearing of an appeal and to the statement of a case for the opinion of the High Court on a point of law shall apply accordingly with any necessary modifications; but on the hearing or rehearing of the appeal—

(a) it shall not be lawful to enquire into any grounds of appeal other than those specified in subsection (7), and

(b) at the request of the appellants, 2 or more appeals made by 2 or more persons pursuant to the same opinion, calculation or determination formed or made by the Revenue Commissioners pursuant to subsection (4) may be heard or reheard together.

(9) (a) On the hearing of an appeal made under subsection (7), the Appeal Commissioners shall have regard to all matters to which the Revenue Commissioners may or are required to have regard under this section, and—

(i) in relation to an appeal made on the grounds referred to in subsection (7) (a), the Appeal Commissioners shall determine the appeal, in so far as it is made on those grounds, by ordering, if they or a majority of them—

(I) consider that the transaction specified or described in the notice of opinion or any part of that transaction is a tax avoidance transaction, that the opinion or the opinion in so far as it relates to that part is to stand,

(II) consider that, subject to such amendment or addition thereto as the Appeal Commissioners or the majority of them deem necessary and as they shall specify or describe, the transaction, or any part of it, specified or described in the notice of opinion, is a tax avoidance transaction, that the transaction or that part of it be so amended or added to and that, subject to the amendment or addition, the opinion or the opinion in so far as it relates to that part is to stand, or

(III) do not so consider as referred to in clause (I) or (II), that the opinion is void,

(ii) in relation to an appeal made on the grounds referred to in subsection (7) (b), they shall determine the appeal, in so far as it is made on those grounds, by ordering that the amount of the tax advantage or the part of the tax advantage specified or described in the notice of opinion be increased or reduced by such amount as they shall direct or that it shall stand,

(iii) in relation to an appeal made on the grounds referred to in subsection (7) (c), they shall determine the appeal, in so far as it is made on those grounds, by ordering that the tax consequences specified or described in the notice of opinion shall be altered or added to in such manner as they shall direct or that they shall stand, or

(iv) in relation to an appeal made on the grounds referred to in subsection (7) (d), they shall determine the appeal, in so far as it is made on those grounds, by ordering that the amount of the relief from double taxation specified or described in the notice of opinion shall be increased or reduced by such amount as they shall direct or that it shall stand.

(b) This subsection shall, subject to any necessary modifications, apply to the rehearing of an appeal by a judge of the Circuit Court and, to the extent necessary, to the determination by the High Court of any question or questions of law arising on the statement of a case for the opinion of the High Court.

(10) The Revenue Commissioners may at any time amend, add to or withdraw any matter specified or described in a notice of opinion by giving notice (in this subsection referred to as "the notice of amendment") in writing of the amendment, addition or withdrawal to each and every person affected thereby, in so far as the person is so affected, and subsections (1) to (9) shall apply in all respects as if the notice of amendment were a notice of opinion and any matter specified or described in the notice of amendment were specified or described in a notice of opinion; but no such amendment, addition or withdrawal may be made so as to set aside or alter any matter which has become final and conclusive on the determination of an appeal made with regard to that matter under subsection (7).

(11) Where pursuant to subsections (2) and (4) the Revenue Commissioners form the opinion that a transaction is a tax avoidance transaction and pursuant to that opinion notices are to be given under subsection (6) to 2 or more persons, any obligation on the Revenue Commissioners to maintain secrecy or any other restriction on the disclosure of information by the Revenue Commissioners shall not apply with respect to the giving of those notices or to the performance of any acts or the discharge of any

functions authorised by this section to be performed or discharged by them or to the performance of any act or the discharge of any functions, including any act or function in relation to an appeal made under subsection (7), which is directly or indirectly related to the acts or functions so authorised.

(12) The Revenue Commissioners may nominate any of their officers to perform any acts and discharge any functions, including the forming of an opinion, authorised by this section to be performed or discharged by the Revenue Commissioners, and references in this section to the Revenue Commissioners shall with any necessary modifications be construed as including references to an officer so nominated.

(13) This section shall apply as respects any transaction where the whole or any part of the transaction is undertaken or arranged on or after the 25th day of January, 1989, and as respects any transaction undertaken or arranged wholly before that date in so far as it gives rise to, or would but for this section give rise to —

   (a) a reduction, avoidance or deferral of any charge or assessment to tax, or part thereof, where the charge or assessment arises by virtue of any other transaction carried out wholly on or after a date, or

   (b) a refund or a payment of an amount, or of an increase in an amount, of tax, or part thereof, refundable or otherwise payable to a person where that amount or increase in the amount would otherwise become first so refundable or otherwise payable to the person on a date,

which could not fall earlier than the 25th day of January, 1989.

PART 34
Provisions Relating to the Residence of Individuals

Section 818

Interpretation (Part 34).

818. In this Part other than in section 825-

"the Acts" means —

(a) the Tax Acts,

(b) the Capital Gains Tax Acts, and

(c) the Capital Acquisitions Tax Act, 1976, and the enactments, amending or extending that Act,

and any instruments made thereunder;

"authorised officer" means an officer of the Revenue Commissioners authorised by them in writing for the purposes of this Part;

"present in the State", in relation to an individual, means the personal presence of the individual in the State;

"tax" means any tax payable in accordance with any provision of the Acts.

Section 819

Residence.

819. (1) For the purposes of the Acts, an individual shall be resident in the State for a year of assessment if the individual is present in the State —

    (a) at any one time or several times in the year of assessment for a period in the whole amounting to 183 days or more, or

    (b) at any one time or several times —

        (i) in the year of assessment, and

        (ii) in the preceding year of assessment,

for a period (being a period comprising in the aggregate the number of days on which the individual is present in the State in the year of assessment and the number of days on which the individual was present in the State in the preceding year of assessment) in the aggregate amounting to 280 days or more.

(2) Notwithstanding subsection (1)(b), where for a year of assessment an individual is present in the State at any one time or several times for a period in the aggregate amounting to not more than 30 days —

    (a) the individual shall not be resident in the State for the year of assessment, and

    (b) no account shall be taken of the period for the purposes of the aggregate mentioned in subsection (1)(b).

(3) (a) Notwithstanding subsections (1) and (2), an individual —

        (i) who is not resident in the State for a year of assessment, and

        (ii) to whom paragraph (b) applies,

may at any time elect to be treated as resident in the State for that year and, where an individual so elects, the individual shall for the purposes of the Acts be deemed to be resident in the State for that year.

    (b) This paragraph shall apply to an individual who satisfies an authorised officer that the individual is in the State —

        (i) with the intention, and

        (ii) in such circumstances,

that the individual will be resident in the State for the following year of assessment.

(4) For the purposes of this section, an individual shall be deemed to be present in the State for a day if the individual is present in the State at the end of the day.

Section 820

Ordinary residence.

820. (1) For the purposes of the Acts, an individual shall be ordinarily resident in the State for a year of assessment if the individual has been resident in the State for each of the 3 years of assessment preceding that year.

(2) An individual ordinarily resident in the State shall not for the purposes of the Acts cease to be ordinarily resident in the State for a year of assessment unless the individual has not been resident in the State in each of the 3 years of assessment preceding that year.

Section 822

Split year residence.

822. (1) For the purposes of a charge to tax on any income, profits or gains from an employment, where during a year of assessment (in this section referred to as "the relevant year") —

    (a) (i) an individual who has not been resident in the State for the preceding year of assessment satisfies an authorised officer that the individual is in the State —

        (I) with the intention, and

        (II) in such circumstances,

      that the individual will be resident in the State for the following year of assessment, or

      (ii) an individual who is resident in the State satisfies an authorised officer that the individual is leaving the State, other than for a temporary purpose —

        (I) with the intention, and

        (II) in such circumstances,

      that the individual will not be resident in the State for the following year of assessment,

      and

    (b) the individual would but for this section be resident in the State for the relevant year,

subsection (2) shall apply in relation to the individual.

(2) (a) An individual to whom paragraphs (a) (i) and (b) of subsection (1) apply shall be deemed to be resident in the State for the relevant year only from the date of his or her arrival in the State.

(b) An individual to whom paragraphs (a) (ii) and (b) of subsection (1) apply shall be deemed to be resident in the State for the relevant year only up to and including the date of his or her leaving the State.

(3) Where by virtue of this section an individual is resident in the State for part of a year of assessment, the Acts shall apply as if –

(a) income arising during that part of the year or, in a case to which section 71(3) applies, amounts received in the State during that part of the year were income arising or amounts received for a year of assessment in which the individual is resident in the State, and

(b) income arising or, as the case may be, amounts received in the remaining part of the year were income arising or amounts received in a year of assessment in which the individual is not resident in the State.

Section 824

Appeals.
824. (1) An individual aggrieved by a decision of an authorised officer on any question arising under the provisions of this Chapter which require an individual to satisfy an authorised officer on such a question may, by notice in writing to that effect given to the authorised officer within 2 months from the date on which notice of the decision is given to the individual, make an application to have the question heard and determined by the Appeal Commissioners.

(2) Where an application is made under subsection (1), the Appeal Commissioners shall hear and determine the question concerned in the like manner as an appeal made to them against an assessment, and the provisions of the Acts relating to such an appeal (including the provisions relating to the rehearing of an appeal and to the statement of a case for the opinion of the High Court on a point of law) shall apply accordingly with any necessary modifications.

Section 825

Residence treatment of donors of gifts to the State.
825. (1) In this section –

"the Acts" means –

(a) the Tax Acts,

(b) the Capital Gains Tax Acts, and

(c)   the Capital Acquisitions Tax Act, 1976;

"donor" means an individual who makes a gift to the State;

"gift" means a gift of property to the State which, on acceptance of the gift by the Government pursuant to the State Property Act, 1954, becomes vested pursuant to that Act in a State authority within the meaning of that Act;

"Irish tax" means any tax imposed by the Acts;

"property" includes interests and rights of any description;

"relevant date", in relation to an individual (being a donor or the spouse of a donor), means the date (not being earlier than the 1st day of September, 1974) on which the individual leaves the State for the purpose of residence (other than occasional residence) outside the State;

"tax in that country" means any tax imposed in that country which is identical with or substantially similar to Irish tax;

"visits" means —

(a)   in relation to a donor, visits by the donor to the State after the relevant date for the purpose of advising on the management of the property which is the subject of the gift, being visits that are in the aggregate less than 182 days in any year of assessment in which they are made, and

(b)   in relation to the spouse of a donor, visits by that spouse when accompanying the donor on visits of the kind referred to in paragraph (a).

(2) Where for any year of assessment a person (being a donor or the spouse of a donor) is resident in a country outside the State for the purposes of tax in that country and is chargeable to that tax without any limitation as to chargeability, then, notwithstanding anything to the contrary in the Tax Acts —

(a)   as respects the year of assessment in which the relevant date occurs, that person shall not as from the relevant date be regarded as ordinarily resident in the State for the purposes of Irish tax, and

(b)   as respects any subsequent year of assessment, in determining whether that person is resident or ordinarily resident in the State for the purposes of Irish tax, visits shall be disregarded.

PART 37

Administration

Section 858

Evidence of authorisation.

858. (1) In this section, except where the context otherwise requires —

"the Acts" means —

(a) (i) the Customs Acts,

(ii) the statutes relating to the duties of excise and to the management of those duties,

(iii) the Tax Acts,

(iv) the Capital Gains Tax Acts,

(v) the Value-Added Tax Act, 1972, and the enactments amending or extending that Act,

(vi) the Capital Acquisitions Tax Act, 1976, and the enactments amending or extending that Act,

(vii) the statutes relating to stamp duty and to the management of that duty,

and any instruments made thereunder or under any other enactment and relating to tax, and

(b) the European Communities (Intrastat) Regulations, 1993 (S.I. No. 136 of 1993);

"authorised officer" means an officer of the Revenue Commissioners who is authorised, nominated or appointed under any provision of the Acts to exercise or perform any functions under any of the specified provisions, and "authorised" and "authorisation" shall be construed accordingly;

"functions" includes powers and duties;

"identity card", in relation to an authorised officer, means a card which is issued to the officer by the Revenue Commissioners and which contains —

(a) a statement to the effect that the officer —

(i) is an officer of the Revenue Commissioners, and

(ii) is an authorised officer for the purposes of the specified provisions,

(b) a photograph and signature of the officer,

(c) a hologram showing the logo of the Office of the Revenue Commissioners,

(d) the facsimile signature of a Revenue Commissioner, and

(e)   particulars of the specified provisions under which the officer is authorised;

"specified provisions", in relation to an authorised officer, means either or both the provisions of the Acts under which the authorised officer –

(a)   is authorised and which are specified on his or her identity card, and

(b)   exercises or performs functions under the Customs Acts or any statutes relating to the duties of excise and to the management of those duties;

"tax" means any tax, duty, levy or charge under the care and management of the Revenue Commissioners.

(2)   Where, in the exercise or performance of any functions under any of the specified provisions in relation to him or her, an authorised officer is requested to produce or show his or her authorisation for the purposes of that provision, the production by the authorised officer of his or her identity card –

(a)   shall be taken as evidence of authorisation under that provision, and

(b)   shall satisfy any obligation under that provision which requires the authorised officer to produce such authorisation on request.

(3)   This section shall come into operation on such day as the Minister for Finance may appoint by order.[1]

Footnote

1   Into operation on 1st July, 1998 (S.I. No. 212 of 1998).

Section 859

Anonymity of authorised officers in relation to certain matters.

859.   (1)   In this section –

"authorised officer" means an officer of the Revenue Commissioners nominated by them to be a member of the staff of the body;

"the body" has the meaning assigned to it by section 58;

"proceedings" includes any hearing before the Appeal Commissioners (within the meaning of the Revenue Acts);

"the Revenue Acts" means –

(a)   the Customs Acts,

(b)   the statutes relating to the duties of excise and to the management of those duties,

(c)   the Tax Acts,

(d)   the Capital Gains Tax Acts,

(e) the Value-Added Tax Act, 1972, and the enactments amending or extending that Act,

(f) the Capital Acquisitions Tax Act, 1976, and the enactments amending or extending that Act,

(g) the statutes relating to stamp duty and the management of that duty,

(h) Chapter IV of Part 11 of the Finance Act, 1992, and

(i) Part VI of the Finance Act, 1983,

and any instruments made thereunder or under any other enactment and relating to tax;

"tax" means any tax, duty, levy or charge under the care and management of the Revenue Commissioners.

(2) Notwithstanding any requirement made by or under any enactment or any other requirement in administrative and operational procedures, including internal procedures, all reasonable care shall be taken to ensure that the identity of an authorised officer shall not be revealed.

(3) In particular and without prejudice to the generality of subsection (2):

(a) where, for the purposes of exercising or performing his or her powers or duties under the Revenue Acts in pursuance of the functions of the body, an authorised officer may apart from this section be required to produce or show any written authority or warrant of appointment under those Acts or otherwise to identify himself or herself, the authorised officer shall—

(i) not be required to produce or show any such authority or warrant of appointment or to so identify himself or herself, for the purposes of exercising or performing his or her powers or duties under those Acts, and

(ii) be accompanied by a member of the Garda Síochána who shall, on request by a person affected, identify himself or herself as a member of the Garda Síochána and shall state that he or she is accompanied by an authorised officer;

(b) where, in pursuance of the functions of the body, an authorised officer exercises or performs in writing any of his or her powers or duties under the Revenue Acts or any provision of any other enactment, whenever passed, which relates to Revenue, such exercise or performance of his or her powers or duties shall be done in the name of the body and not in the name of the individual authorised officer involved, notwithstanding any provision to the contrary in any of those enactments;

(c) in any proceedings arising out of the exercise or performance, in pursuance of the functions of the body, of powers or duties by an authorised officer, any documents relating to such proceedings shall not reveal the identity of any authorised officer, notwithstanding any requirements to the contrary in any provision, and in any proceedings the identity of such officer other than as an authorised officer shall not be revealed other than to the judge or the Appeal Commissioner, as the case may be, hearing the case;

(d) where, in pursuance of the functions of the body, an authorised officer is required, in any proceedings, to give evidence and the judge or the Appeal Commissioner, as the case may be, is satisfied that there are reasonable grounds in the public interest to direct that evidence to be given by such authorised officer should be given in the hearing and not in the sight of any person, he or she may so direct.

Section 872

Use of information relating to other taxes and duties.

872. (1) Any information acquired, whether before or after the passing of this Act, in connection with any tax or duty under the care and management of the Revenue Commissioners may be used by them for any purpose connected with any other tax or duty under their care and management.

(2) The Revenue Commissioners or any of their officers may, for any purpose in connection with the assessment and collection of income tax, corporation tax or capital gains tax, make use of or produce in evidence any returns, correspondence, schedules, accounts, statements or other documents or information to which the Revenue Commissioners or any of their officers have or has had or may have lawful access for the purposes of the Acts relating to any tax, duty, levy or charge under the care and management of the Revenue Commissioners.

PART 38
Returns of Income and Gains, other Obligations and Returns, and Revenue Powers

CHAPTER 3
Other obligations and returns

Section 887

Use of electronic data processing.

887. (1) In this section—

"the Acts" means—

(a) the Tax Acts,

(b) the Capital Gains Tax Acts,

(c) the Value-Added Tax Act, 1972,

(d) the Capital Acquisitions Tax Act, 1976, and the enactments amending or extending that Act, and

(e) Part VI of the Finance Act, 1983,

and any instruments made thereunder;

"records" means documents which a person is obliged by the Acts to keep, to issue or to produce for inspection, and any other written or printed material.

(2) For the purposes of the Acts and subject to the agreement of the Revenue Commissioners, records may be stored, maintained, transmitted, reproduced or communicated, as the case may be, by any electronic, photographic or other process approved of by the Revenue Commissioners, and in circumstances where the use of such process has been agreed by the Revenue Commissioners and subject to such conditions as they may impose.

(4) Where in accordance with subsection (2) records are preserved by electronic, photographic or other process, a statement contained in a document produced by any such process shall, subject to the rules of court, be admissible in evidence in any proceedings, whether civil or criminal, to the same extent as the records themselves.

CHAPTER 4
Revenue Powers

Section 905

Inspection of documents and records.

905. (1) In this section—

"authorised officer" means an officer of the Revenue Commissioners authorised by them in writing to exercise the powers conferred by this section;

"property" means any asset relating to a tax liability;

"records" means any document or any other written or printed material in any form, including any information stored, maintained or preserved by means of any mechanical or electronic device, whether or not stored, maintained or preserved in a legible form, which a person is obliged by any provision relating to tax to keep, retain, issue or produce for inspection or which may be inspected under any provision relating to tax;

"tax" means any tax, duty, levy or charge under the care and management of the Revenue Commissioners;

"tax liability" means any existing liability to tax or further liability to tax which may be established by an authorised officer following the exercise or performance of his or her powers or duties under this section.

(2) (a) An authorised officer may at all reasonable times enter any premises or place where the authorised officer has reason to believe that—

    (i) any trade, profession or other activity, the profits or gains of which are chargeable to tax, is or has been carried on,

    (ii) anything is or has been done in connection with any trade, profession or other activity the profits or gains of which are chargeable to tax,

    (iii) any records relating to—

        (I) any trade, profession, other source of profits or gains or chargeable gains,

        (II) any tax liability, or

        (III) any repayments of tax in regard to any person,

    are or may be kept, or

    (iv) any property is or has been located,

and the authorised officer may—

    (A) require any person who is on those premises or in that place, other than a person who is there to purchase goods or to receive a service, to produce any records or property,

    (B) if the authorised officer has reason to believe that any of the records or property which he or she has required to be produced to him or her under this subsection have not been produced, search on those premises or in that place for those records or property,

    (C) examine any records or property and take copies of or extracts from any records,

(D) remove any records and retain them for a reasonable time for the purposes of their further examination or for the purposes of any legal proceedings instituted by an officer of the Revenue Commissioners or for the purposes of any criminal proceedings, and

(E) examine property listed in any records.

(b) An authorised officer may in the exercise or performance of his or her powers or duties under this section require any person whom he or she has reason to believe—

(i) is or was carrying on any trade, profession or other activity the profits or gains of which are chargeable to tax,

(ii) is or was liable to any tax, or

(iii) has information relating to any tax liability,

to give the authorised officer all reasonable assistance, including providing information and explanations or furnishing documents and making available for inspection property as required by the authorised officer in relation to any tax liability or any repayment of tax in regard to any person.

(c) Nothing in this subsection shall be construed as requiring any person carrying on a profession, or any person employed by any person carrying on a profession, to produce to an authorised officer any documents relating to a client, other than such documents—

(i) as pertain to the payment of fees to the person carrying on the profession or to other financial transactions of the person carrying on the profession,

(ii) as are otherwise material to the tax liability of the person carrying on the profession, or

(iii) as are already required to be provided following a request issued under section 16 of the Stamp Act, 1891,

and in particular that person shall not be required to disclose any information or professional advice of a confidential nature given to a client.

(d) This subsection shall not apply to any premises or place where a banking business (within the meaning of the Central Bank Act, 1971) is carried on or to any person or an employee of any person carrying on such a business.

(e) An authorised officer shall not, without the consent of the occupier, enter any premises, or that portion of any premises, which is occupied wholly and exclusively as a private residence, except on production by such officer of a warrant issued by a Judge of the District Court expressly authorising the authorised officer to so enter.

(f) A Judge of the District Court may issue a warrant under paragraph (e) if satisfied by information on oath that it is proper to do so for the purposes of this section.

(3) A person who does not comply with any requirement of an authorised officer in the exercise or performance of the authorised officer's powers or duties under this section shall be liable to a penalty of £1,000.

(4) An authorised officer when exercising or performing his or her powers or duties under this section shall on request show his or her authorisation for the purposes of this section.

Section 906

Authorised officers and Garda Síochána.

906. Where an authorised officer (within the meaning of section 903, 904 or 905, as the case may be) in accordance with section 903, 904 or 905 enters any premises or place, the authorised officer may be accompanied by a member or members of the Garda Síochána, and any such member may arrest without warrant any person who obstructs or interferes with the authorised officer in the exercise or performance of his or her powers or duties under any of those sections.

Section 910

Power to obtain information from Minister of the Government.

910. (1) For the purposes of the assessment, charge, collection and recovery of any tax or duty placed under their care and management, the Revenue Commissioners may, by notice in writing, request any Minister of the Government to provide them with such information in the possession of that Minister in relation to payments for any purposes made by that Minister, whether on that Minister's own behalf or on behalf of any other person, to such persons or classes of persons as the Revenue Commissioners may specify in the notice and a Minister so requested shall provide such information as may be specified.

(2) The Revenue Commissioners may nominate any of their officers to perform any acts and discharge any functions authorised by this section to be performed or discharged by the Revenue Commissioners.

Section 912

Computer documents and records.

912. (1) In this section –

"the Acts" means –

(a) the Customs Acts,

(b) the statutes relating to the duties of excise and to the management of those duties,

(c) the Tax Acts,

(d) the Capital Gains Tax Acts,

(e) the Value-Added Tax Act, 1972, and the enactments amending or extending that Act,

(f) the Capital Acquisitions Tax Act, 1976, and the enactments amending or extending that Act, and

(g) Part V1 of the Finance Act, 1983,

and any instruments made thereunder;

"data" means information in a form in which it can be processed;

"data equipment" means any electronic, photographic, magnetic, optical or other equipment for processing data;

"processing" means performing automatically logical or arithmetical operations on data, or the storing, maintenance, transmission, reproduction or communication of data;

"records" means documents which a person is obliged by any provision of the Acts to keep, issue or produce for inspection, and any other written or printed material;

"software" means any sequence of instructions used in conjunction with data equipment for the purpose of processing data or controlling the operation of the data equipment.

(2) Any provision under the Acts which –

(a) requires a person to keep, retain, issue or produce any records or cause any records to be kept, retained, issued or produced, or

(b) permits an officer of the Revenue Commissioners –

(i) to inspect any records,

(ii) to enter premises and search for any records, or

(iii) to take extracts from or copies of or remove any records,

shall, where the records are processed by data equipment, apply to the data equipment together with any associated software, data, apparatus or material as it applies to the records.

(3) An officer of the Revenue Commissioners may in the exercise or performance of his or her powers or duties require –

(a) the person by or on whose behalf the data equipment is or has been used, or

(b) any person having charge of, or otherwise concerned with the operation of, the data equipment or any associated apparatus or material,

to afford him or her all reasonable assistance in relation to the exercise or performance of those powers or duties.

PART 42

Collection and Recovery

CHAPTER 5

Miscellaneous Provisions

Section 1002

Deduction from payments due to defaulters of amounts due in relation to tax.

1002. (1) (a)   In this section, except where the context otherwise requires—

"the Acts" means—

(i)   the Customs Acts,

(ii)   the statutes relating to the duties of excise and to the management of those duties,

(iii)   the Tax Acts,

(iv)   the Capital Gains Tax Acts,

(v)   the Value-Added Tax Act, 1972, and the enactments amending or extending that Act,

(vi)   the Capital Acquisitions Tax Act, 1976, and the enactments amending or extending that Act, and

(vii)   the Stamp Act, 1891, and the enactments amending or extending that Act,

and any instruments made thereunder;

"additional debt", in relation to a relevant person who has received a notice of attachment in respect of a taxpayer, means any amount which, at any time after the time of the receipt by the relevant person of the notice of attachment but before the end of the relevant period in relation to the notice, would be a debt due by the relevant person to the taxpayer if a notice of attachment were received by the relevant person at that time;

"debt", in relation to a notice of attachment given to a relevant person in respect of a taxpayer and in relation to that relevant person and taxpayer, means, subject to paragraphs (b) to (e), the amount or aggregate amount of any money which, at the time the notice of attachment is received by the relevant person, is due by the relevant person (whether on that person's own account or as an agent or trustee) to the taxpayer, irrespective of whether the taxpayer has applied for the payment (to the taxpayer or any other person) or for the withdrawal of all or part of the money;

"deposit" means a sum of money paid to a financial institution on terms under which it will be repaid with or without interest and either on demand or at a time or in circumstances agreed by or on behalf of the person making the payment and the financial institution to which it is made;

"emoluments" means anything assessable to income tax under Schedule E;

"financial institution" means a holder of a licence issued under section 9 of the Central Bank Act, 1971, or a person referred to in section 7(4) of that Act, and includes a branch of a financial institution which records deposits in its books as liabilities of the branch;

"further return" means a return made by a relevant person under subsection (4);

"interest on unpaid tax", in relation to a specified amount specified in a notice of attachment, means interest that has accrued to the date on which the notice of attachment is given under any provision of the Acts providing for the charging of interest in respect of the unpaid tax, including interest on an undercharge of tax which is attributable to fraud or neglect, specified in the notice of attachment;

"notice of attachment" means a notice under subsection (2);

"notice of revocation" means a notice under subsection (10);

"penalty" means a monetary penalty imposed on a taxpayer under a provision of the Acts;

"relevant period", in relation to a notice of attachment, means, as respects the relevant person to whom the notice of attachment is given, the period commencing at the time at which the notice is received by the relevant person and ending on the earliest of —

(i)   the date on which the relevant person completes the payment to the Revenue Commissioners out of the debt, or the aggregate of the debt and any additional debt, due by the relevant person to the taxpayer named in the notice, of an amount equal to the specified amount in relation to the taxpayer,

(ii) the date on which the relevant person receives a notice of revocation of the notice of attachment, and

(iii) where the relevant person or the taxpayer named in the notice –

(I) is declared bankrupt, the date the relevant person or the taxpayer is so declared, or

(II) is a company which commences to be wound up, the relevant date within the meaning of section 285 of the Companies Act, 1963, in relation to the winding up;

"relevant person", in relation to a taxpayer, means a person whom the Revenue Commissioners have reason to believe may have, at the time a notice of attachment is received by such person in respect of a taxpayer, a debt due to the taxpayer;

"return" means a return made by a relevant person under subsection (2) (a) (iii);

"specified amount" has the meaning assigned to it by subsection (2) (a) (ii);

"tax" means any tax, duty, levy or charge which in accordance with any provision of the Acts is placed under the care and management of the Revenue Commissioners;

"taxpayer" means a person who is liable to pay, remit or account for tax to the Revenue Commissioners under the Acts.

(b) Where a relevant person is a financial institution, any amount or aggregate amount of money, including interest on that money, which at the time the notice of attachment is received by the relevant person is a deposit held by the relevant person –

(i) to the credit of the taxpayer for the taxpayer's sole benefit, or

(ii) to the credit of the taxpayer and any other person or persons for their joint benefit,

shall be regarded as a debt due by the relevant person to the taxpayer at that time.

(c) Any amount of money due by the relevant person to the taxpayer as emoluments under a contract of service shall not be regarded as a debt due to the taxpayer.

(d) Where there is a dispute as to an amount of money which is due by the relevant person to the taxpayer, the amount in dispute shall be disregarded for the purposes of determining the amount of the debt.

(e) In the case referred to in paragraph (b), a deposit held by a relevant person which is a financial institution to the credit of the taxpayer and any other person or persons (in this paragraph referred to as "the other party or parties") for their joint benefit shall be deemed (unless evidence to the contrary is produced to the satisfaction of the relevant person within 10 days of the giving of the notices specified in subsection (2) (e)) to be held to the benefit of the taxpayer and the other party or parties to the deposit equally, and accordingly only the portion of the deposit so deemed shall be regarded as a debt due by the relevant person to the taxpayer at the time the notice of attachment is received by the relevant person and, where such evidence is produced within the specified time, only so much of the deposit as is shown to be held to the benefit of the taxpayer shall be regarded as a debt due by the relevant person to the taxpayer at that time.

(2) (a) Subject to subsection (3), where a taxpayer has made default whether before or after the passing of this Act in paying, remitting or accounting for any tax, interest on unpaid tax, or penalty to the Revenue Commissioners, the Revenue Commissioners may, if the taxpayer has not made good the default, give to a relevant person in relation to the taxpayer a notice in writing (in this section referred to as "the notice of attachment") in which is entered—

(i) the taxpayer's name and address,

(ii) (I) the amount or aggregate amount, or

(II) in a case where more than one notice of attachment is given to a relevant person or relevant persons in respect of a taxpayer, a portion of the amount or aggregate amount,

of the taxes, interest on unpaid taxes and penalties in respect of which the taxpayer is in default at the time of the giving of the notice or notices of attachment (the amount, aggregate amount, or portion of the amount or aggregate amount, as the case may be, being referred to in this section as "the specified amount"), and

(iii) a direction to the relevant person—

(I) subject to paragraphs (b) and (c), to deliver to the Revenue Commissioners, within the period of 10 days from the time at which the notice of attachment is received by the relevant person, a return in writing specifying whether or not any debt is due by the relevant person to the taxpayer at the time the notice is received by the relevant person and, if any debt is so due, specifying the amount of the debt, and

    (II) if the amount of any debt is so specified, to pay to the Revenue Commissioners within the period referred to in clause (I) a sum equal to the amount of the debt so specified.

(b) Where the amount of the debt due by the relevant person to the taxpayer is equal to or greater than the specified amount in relation to the taxpayer, the amount of the debt specified in the return shall be an amount equal to the specified amount.

(c) Where the relevant person is a financial institution and the debt due by the relevant person to the taxpayer is part of a deposit held to the credit of the taxpayer and any other person or persons to their joint benefit, the return shall be made within a period of 10 days from—

    (i) the expiry of the period specified in the notices to be given under paragraph (e), or

    (ii) the production of the evidence referred to in paragraph (e) (II).

(d) A relevant person to whom a notice of attachment has been given shall comply with the direction in the notice.

(e) Where a relevant person which is a financial institution is given a notice of attachment and the debt due by the relevant person to the taxpayer is part of a deposit held by the relevant person to the credit of the taxpayer and any other person or persons (in this paragraph referred to as "the other party or parties") for their joint benefit, the relevant person shall on receipt of the notice of attachment give to the taxpayer and the other party or parties to the deposit a notice in writing in which is entered—

    (i) the taxpayer's name and address,

    (ii) the name and address of the person to whom a notice under this paragraph is given,

    (iii) the name and address of the relevant person, and

    (iv) the specified amount,

and which states that—

    (I) a notice of attachment under this section has been received in respect of the taxpayer,

    (II) under this section a deposit is deemed (unless evidence to the contrary is produced to the satisfaction of the relevant person within 10 days of the giving of the notice under this paragraph) to be held to the benefit of the taxpayer and the other party or parties to the deposit equally, and

    (III) unless such evidence is produced within the period specified in the notice given under this paragraph—

        (A) a sum equal to the amount of the deposit so deemed to be held to the benefit of the taxpayer (and accordingly regarded as a debt due to the taxpayer by the relevant person) shall be paid to the Revenue Commissioners, where that amount is equal to or less than the specified amount, and

        (B) where the amount of the deposit so deemed to be held to the benefit of the taxpayer (and accordingly regarded as a debt due to the taxpayer by the relevant person) is greater than the specified amount, a sum equal to the specified amount shall be paid to the Revenue Commissioners.

(3) An amount in respect of tax, interest on unpaid tax or a penalty, as respects which a taxpayer is in default as specified in subsection (2), shall not be entered in a notice of attachment unless—

    (a) a period of one month has expired from the date on which such default commenced, and

    (b) the Revenue Commissioners have given the taxpayer a notice in writing (whether or not the document containing the notice also contains other information being communicated by the Revenue Commissioners to the taxpayer), not later than 7 days before the date of the receipt by the relevant person or relevant persons concerned of a notice of attachment, stating that if the amount is not paid it may be specified in a notice or notices of attachment and recovered under this section from a relevant person or relevant persons in relation to the taxpayer.

(4) If, when a relevant person receives a notice of attachment, the amount of the debt due by the relevant person to the taxpayer named in the notice is less than the specified amount in relation to the taxpayer or no debt is so due and, at any time after the receipt of the notice and before the end of the relevant period in relation to the notice, an additional debt becomes due by the relevant person to the taxpayer, the relevant person shall within 10 days of that time—

    (a) if the aggregate of the amount of any debt so due and the additional debt so due is equal to or less than the specified amount in relation to the taxpayer—

        (i) deliver a further return to the Revenue Commissioners specifying the additional debt, and

        (ii) pay to the Revenue Commissioners the amount of the additional debt, and so on for each subsequent occasion during the relevant period in relation to the notice of attachment on which an additional debt becomes due by the relevant person to the taxpayer until —

    (I)   the aggregate amount of the debt and the additional debt or debts so due equals the specified amount in relation to the taxpayer, or

    (II) paragraph (b) applies in relation to an additional debt, and

  (b) if the aggregate amount of any debt and the additional debt or debts so due to the taxpayer is greater than the specified amount in relation to the taxpayer —

    (i)   deliver a further return to the Revenue Commissioners specifying such portion of the latest additional debt as when added to the aggregate of the debt and any earlier additional debts is equal to the specified amount in relation to the taxpayer, and

    (ii) pay to the Revenue Commissioners that portion of the additional debt.

(5) Where a relevant person delivers, either fraudulently or negligently, an incorrect return or further return that purports to be a return or further return made in accordance with this section, the relevant person shall be deemed to be guilty of an offence under section 1078.

(6) (a) Where a notice of attachment has been given to a relevant person in respect of a taxpayer, the relevant person shall not, during the relevant period in relation to the notice, make any disbursements out of the debt, or out of any additional debt, due by the relevant person to the taxpayer except to the extent that any such disbursement —

    (i)   will not reduce the debt or the aggregate of the debt and any additional debts so due to an amount that is less than the specified amount in relation to the taxpayer, or

    (ii) is made pursuant to an order of a court.

  (b) For the purposes of this section, a disbursement made by a relevant person contrary to paragraph (a) shall be deemed not to reduce the amount of the debt or any additional debts due by the relevant person to the taxpayer.

(7) (a) Sections 1052 and 1054 shall apply to a failure by a relevant person to deliver a return required by a notice of attachment within the time specified in the notice or to deliver a further return within the time specified in subsection (4) as they apply to a failure to deliver a return referred to in section 1052.

(b)   A certificate signed by an officer of the Revenue Commissioners which certifies that he or she has examined the relevant records and that it appears from those records that during a specified period a specified return was not received from a relevant person shall be evidence until the contrary is proved that the relevant person did not deliver the return during that period.

(c)   A certificate certifying as provided by paragraph (b) and purporting to be signed by an officer of the Revenue Commissioners may be tendered in evidence without proof and shall be deemed until the contrary is proved to have been so signed.

(8)   Where a relevant person to whom a notice of attachment in respect of a taxpayer has been given—

(a)   delivers the return required to be delivered by that notice but fails to pay to the Revenue Commissioners within the time specified in the notice the amount specified in the return or any part of that amount, or

(b)   delivers a further return under subsection (4) but fails to pay to the Revenue Commissioners within the time specified in that subsection the amount specified in the further return or any part of that amount,

the amount specified in the return or further return or the part of that amount, as the case may be, which the relevant person has failed to pay to the Revenue Commissioners may, if the notice of attachment has not been revoked by a notice of revocation, be sued for and recovered by action or other appropriate proceedings at the suit of an officer of the Revenue Commissioners in any court of competent jurisdiction.

(9)   Nothing in this section shall be construed as rendering any failure by a relevant person to make a return or further return required by this section, or to pay to the Revenue Commissioners the amount or amounts required by this section to be paid by the relevant person, liable to be treated as a failure to which section 1078 applies.

(10)(a)   A notice of attachment given to a relevant person in respect of a taxpayer may be revoked by the Revenue Commissioners at any time by notice in writing given to the relevant person and shall be revoked forthwith if the taxpayer has paid the specified amount to the Revenue Commissioners.

(b)   Where in pursuance of this section a relevant person pays any amount to the Revenue Commissioners out of a debt or an additional debt due by the relevant person to the taxpayer and, at the time of the receipt by the Revenue Commissioners of that amount, the taxpayer has paid to the Revenue Commissioners the amount or aggregate amount of the taxes, interest on unpaid taxes and penalties in respect of which the taxpayer is in default at the time of the giving of the notice or notices of attachment, the first-mentioned amount shall be refunded by the Revenue Commissioners forthwith to the taxpayer.

(11) Where a notice of attachment or a notice of revocation is given to a relevant person in relation to a taxpayer, a copy of such notice shall be given by the Revenue Commissioners to the taxpayer forthwith.

(12) (a) Where in pursuance of this section any amount is paid to the Revenue Commissioners by a relevant person, the relevant person shall forthwith give the taxpayer concerned a notice in writing specifying the payment, its amount and the reason for which it was made.

(b) On the receipt by the Revenue Commissioners of an amount paid in pursuance of this section, the Revenue Commissioners shall forthwith notify the taxpayer and the relevant person in writing of such receipt.

(13) Where in pursuance of this section a relevant person pays to the Revenue Commissioners the whole or part of the amount of a debt or an additional debt due by the relevant person to a taxpayer, or any portion of such an amount, the taxpayer shall allow such payment and the relevant person shall be acquitted and discharged of the amount of the payment as if it had been paid to the taxpayer.

(14) Where in pursuance of this section a relevant person is prohibited from making any disbursement out of a debt or an additional debt due to a taxpayer, no action shall lie against the relevant person in any court by reason of a failure to make any such disbursement.

(15) Any obligation on the Revenue Commissioners to maintain secrecy or any other restriction on the disclosure of information by the Revenue Commissioners shall not apply in relation to information contained in a notice of attachment.

(16) A notice of attachment in respect of a taxpayer shall not be given to a relevant person at a time when the relevant person or the taxpayer is an undischarged bankrupt or a company being wound up.

(17) The Revenue Commissioners may nominate any of their officers to perform any acts and discharge any functions authorised by this section to be performed or discharged by the Revenue Commissioners.

Section 1003

Payment of tax by means of donation of heritage items.

1003. (1) (a) In this section –

"the Acts" means –

(i) the Tax Acts (other than Chapter 8 of Part 6, Chapter 2 of Part 18 and Chapter 4 of this Part),

(ii)   the Capital Gains Tax Acts, and

(iii) the Capital Acquisitions Tax Act, 1976, and the enactments amending or extending that Act,

and any instruments made thereunder;

"approved body" means—

(i)   the National Archives,

(ii)   the National Gallery of Ireland,

(iii) the National Library of Ireland,

(iv)   the National Museum of Ireland,

(v)   the Irish Museum of Modern Art, or

(vi)   in relation to the offer of a gift of a particular item or collection of items, any other such body (being a body owned, or funded wholly or mainly, by the State or by any public or local authority) as may be approved, with the consent of the Minister for Finance, by the Minister for Arts, Heritage, Gaeltacht and the Islands for the purposes of this section;

"arrears of tax" means tax due and payable in accordance with any provision of the Acts (including any interest and penalties payable under any provision of the Acts in relation to such tax)—

(i)   in the case of income tax, corporation tax or capital gains tax, in respect of the relevant period, or

(ii)   in the case of gift tax or inheritance tax, before the commencement of the calendar year in which the relevant gift is made,

which has not been paid at the time a relevant gift is made;

"current liability" means—

(i)   in the case of income tax or capital gains tax, any liability to such tax arising in the year of assessment in which the relevant gift is made,

(ii)   in the case of corporation tax, any liability to such tax arising in the accounting period in which the relevant gift is made,

(iii) in the case of gift tax or inheritance tax, any liability to such tax which becomes due and payable in the calendar year in which the relevant gift is made;

"designated officer" means—

(i)   the member of the selection committee who represents the appropriate approved body on that committee where the approved body is so represented, or

      (ii)   in any other case, a person nominated in that behalf by the Minister for Arts, Heritage, Gaeltacht and the Islands;

"heritage item" has the meaning assigned to it by subsection (2) (a);

"market value" has the meaning assigned to it by subsection (3);

"relevant gift" means a gift of a heritage item to an approved body in respect of which no consideration whatever (other than relief under this section) is received by the person making the gift, either directly or indirectly, from the approved body or otherwise;

"relevant period" means —

      (i)   in the case of income tax and capital gains tax, any year of assessment preceding the year in which the relevant gift is made, and

      (ii)   in the case of corporation tax, any accounting period preceding the accounting period in which the relevant gift is made;

"selection committee" means a committee consisting of —

      (i)   the Chairperson of the Heritage Council,

      (ii)   the Director of the Arts Council,

      (iii)   the Director of the National Archives,

      (iv)   the Director of the National Gallery of Ireland,

      (v)   the Director of the National Library of Ireland,

      (vi)   the Director of the National Museum of Ireland, and

      (vii)   the Director of the Irish Museum of Modern Art,

and includes any person duly acting in the capacity of any of those persons as a result of the person concerned being unable to fulfil his or her duties for any of the reasons set out in paragraph (b) (ii);

"tax" means income tax, corporation tax, capital gains tax, gift tax or inheritance tax, as the case may be, payable in accordance with any provision of the Acts;

"valuation date" means the date on which an application is made to the selection committee for a determination under subsection (2) (a).

  (b)   (i)   The selection committee may act notwithstanding one or more vacancies among its members and may regulate its own procedure.

        (ii)   If and so long as a member of the selection committee is unable through illness, absence or other cause to fulfil his or her duties, a person nominated in that behalf by the member shall act as the member of the committee in the place of the member.

(2) (a) In this section, "heritage item" means any kind of cultural item, including —

(i) any archaeological item, archive, book, estate record, manuscript and painting, and

(ii) any collection of cultural items and any collection of such items in their setting,

which, on application to the selection committee in writing in that behalf by a person who owns the item or collection of items, as the case may be, is determined by the selection committee, after consideration of any evidence in relation to the matter which the person submits to the committee and after such consultation (if any) as may seem to the committee to be necessary with such person or body of persons as in the opinion of the committee may be of assistance to them, to be an item or collection of items which is —

(I) an outstanding example of the type of item involved, pre-eminent in its class, whose export from the State would constitute a diminution of the accumulated cultural heritage of Ireland, and

(II) suitable for acquisition by an approved body.

(b) On receipt of an application for a determination under paragraph (a), the selection committee shall request the Revenue Commissioners in writing to value the item or collection of items, as the case may be, in accordance with subsection (3).

(c) The selection committee shall not make a determination under paragraph (a) where the market value of the item or collection of items, as the case may be, as determined by the Revenue Commissioners in accordance with subsection (3), at the valuation date —

(i) is less than £75,000, or

(ii) exceeds an amount (which shall not be less than £75,000) determined by the formula —

$$£750,000 - M$$

where M is an amount (which may be nil) equal to the market value at the valuation date of the heritage item (if any) or the aggregate of the market values at the respective valuation dates of all the heritage items (if any), as the case may be, in respect of which a determination or determinations, as the case may be, under this subsection has been made by the selection committee in any one calendar year and not revoked in that year.

   (d) (i) An item or collection of items shall cease to be a heritage item for the purposes of this section if –

       (I) the item or collection of items is sold or otherwise disposed of to a person other than an approved body,

       (II) the owner of the item or collection of items notifies the selection committee in writing that it is not intended to make a gift of the item or collection of items to an approved body, or

       (III) the gift of the item or collection of items is not made to an approved body within the calendar year following the year in which the determination is made under paragraph (a).

     (ii) Where the selection committee becomes aware, at any time within the calendar year in which a determination under paragraph (a) is made in respect of an item or collection of items, that clause (I) or (II) of subparagraph (i) applies to the item or collection of items, the selection committee may revoke its determination with effect from that time.

  (3) (a) For the purposes of this section, the market value of any item or collection of items (in this subsection referred to as "the property") shall be estimated to be the price which in the opinion of the Revenue Commissioners the property would fetch if sold in the open market on the valuation date in such manner and subject to such conditions as might reasonably be calculated to obtain for the vendor the best price for the property.

    (b) The market value of the property shall be ascertained by the Revenue Commissioners in such manner and by such means as they think fit, and they may authorise a person to inspect the property and report to them the value of the property for the purposes of this section, and the person having custody or possession of the property shall permit the person so authorised to inspect the property at such reasonable times as the Revenue Commissioners consider necessary.

    (c) Where the Revenue Commissioners require a valuation to be made by a person authorised by them, the cost of such valuation shall be defrayed by the Revenue Commissioners.

  (4) Where a relevant gift is made to an approved body –

    (a) the designated officer of that body shall give a certificate to the person who made the relevant gift, in such form as the Revenue Commissioners may prescribe, certifying the receipt of that gift and the transfer of the ownership of the heritage item the subject of that gift to the approved body, and

(b) the designated officer shall transmit a duplicate of the certificate to the Revenue Commissioners.

(5) Subject to this section, where a person has made a relevant gift the person shall, on submission to the Revenue Commissioners of the certificate given to the person in accordance with subsection (4), be treated as having made on the date of such submission a payment on account of tax of an amount equal to the market value of the relevant gift on the valuation date.

(6) A payment on account of tax which is treated as having been made in accordance with subsection (5) shall be set in so far as possible against any liability to tax of the person who is treated as having made such a payment in the following order —

(a) firstly, against any arrears of tax due for payment by that person and against an arrear of tax for an earlier period in priority to a later period, and for this purpose the date on which an arrear of tax became due for payment shall determine whether it is for an earlier or later period, and

(b) only then, against any current liability of the person which the person nominates for that purpose,

and such set-off shall accordingly discharge a corresponding amount of that liability.

(7) To the extent that a payment on account of tax has not been set off in accordance with subsection (6), the balance remaining shall be set off against any future liability to tax of the person who is treated as having made the payment which that person nominates for that purpose.

(8) Where a person has power to sell any heritage item in order to raise money for the payment of gift tax or inheritance tax, such person shall have power to make a relevant gift of that heritage item in or towards satisfaction of that tax and, except as regards the nature of the consideration and its receipt and application, any such relevant gift shall be subject to the same provisions and shall be treated for all purposes as a sale made in exercise of that power, and any conveyances or transfers made or purporting to be made to give effect to such a relevant gift shall apply accordingly.

(9) A person shall not be entitled to any refund of tax in respect of any payment on account of tax made in accordance with this section.

(10) Interest shall not be payable in respect of any overpayment of tax for any period which arises directly or indirectly by reason of the set-off against any liability for that period of a payment on account of tax made in accordance with this section.

(11) Where a person makes a relevant gift and in respect of that gift is treated as having made a payment on account of tax, the person

concerned shall not be allowed relief under any other provision of the Acts in respect of that gift.

(12) (a) The Revenue Commissioners shall as respects each year compile a list of the titles (if any), descriptions and values of the heritage items (if any) in respect of which relief under this section has been given.

(b) Notwithstanding any obligation as to secrecy imposed on them by the Acts or the Official Secrets Act, 1963, the Revenue Commissioners shall include in their annual report to the Minister for Finance the list (if any) referred to in paragraph (a) for the year in respect of which the report is made.

Section 1006

Poundage and certain other fees due to sheriffs or county registrars.
1006. (1) In this section –

"the Acts" means –

(a) the Tax Acts,

(b) the Capital Gains Tax Acts,

(c) the Value-Added Tax Act, 1972, and the enactments amending or extending that Act,

(d) the Capital Acquisitions Tax Act, 1976, and the enactments amending or extending that Act, and

(e) Part VI of the Finance Act, 1983, and the enactments amending or extending that Part,

and any instruments made thereunder;

"certificate" means a certificate issued under section 962;

"county registrar" means a person appointed to be a county registrar under section 35 of the Court Officers Act, 1926;

"defaulter" means a person specified or certified in an execution order or certificate on whom a relevant amount specified or certified in the order or certificate is leviable;

"execution order" has the same meaning as in the Enforcement of Court Orders Act, 1926;

"fees" means the fees known as poundage fees payable under section 14 (1) of the Enforcement of Court Orders Act, 1926, and orders made under that section for services in or about the execution of an execution order directing or authorising the execution of an order of a court by the seizure and sale of a person's property or, as may be appropriate, the fees corresponding to those fees payable under section 962 for the execution of a certificate;

"interest on unpaid tax" means interest which has accrued under any provision of the Acts providing for the charging of interest in respect of unpaid tax, including interest on an undercharge of tax which is attributable to fraud or neglect;

"relevant amount" means an amount of tax or interest on unpaid tax;

"tax" means any tax, duty, levy or charge which, in accordance with any provision of the Acts, is placed under the care and management of the Revenue Commissioners;

references, as respects an execution order, to a relevant amount include references to any amount of costs specified in the order.

(2) Where—

    (a) an execution order or certificate specifying or certifying a defaulter and relating to a relevant amount is lodged with the appropriate sheriff or county registrar for execution,

    (b) the sheriff or, as the case may be, the county registrar gives notice to the defaulter of the lodgment or of his or her intention to execute the execution order or certificate by seizure of the property of the defaulter to which it relates, or demands payment by the defaulter of the relevant amount, and

    (c) the whole or part of the relevant amount is paid to the sheriff or, as the case may be, the county registrar or to the Collector-General, after the giving of that notice or the making of that demand,

then, for the purpose of the liability of the defaulter for the payment of fees and of the exercise of any rights or powers in relation to the collection of fees for the time being vested by law in sheriffs and county registrars—

    (i) the sheriff or, as the case may be, the county registrar shall be deemed to have entered, in the execution of the execution order or certificate, into possession of the property referred to in paragraph (b), and

    (ii) the payment mentioned in paragraph (c) shall be deemed to have been levied, in the execution of the execution order or certificate, by the sheriff or, as the case may be, the county registrar,

and fees shall be payable by the defaulter to such sheriff or, as the case may be, country registrar accordingly in respect of the payment mentioned in paragraph (c).

PART 47
Penalties, Revenue Offences, Interest on Overdue Tax and other Sanctions

CHAPTER 4
Revenue Offences

Section 1078

Revenue offences.

1078. (1) In this Part—

"the Acts" means—

(a) the Customs Acts,

(b) the statutes relating to the duties of excise and to the management of those duties,

(c) the Tax Acts,

(d) the Capital Gains Tax Acts,

(e) the Value-Added Tax Act, 1972, and the enactments amending or extending that Act,

(f) the Capital Acquisitions Tax Act, 1976, and the enactments amending or extending that Act,

(g) the statutes relating to stamp duty and to the management of that duty, and

(h) Part VI of the Finance Act, 1983,

and any instruments made thereunder and any instruments made under any other enactment and relating to tax;

"authorised officer" means an officer of the Revenue Commissioners authorised by them in writing to exercise any of the powers conferred by the Acts;

"tax" means any tax, duty, levy or charge under the care and management of the Revenue Commissioners.

(2) A person shall, without prejudice to any other penalty to which the person may be liable, be guilty of an offence under this section if the person—

(a) knowingly or wilfully delivers any incorrect return, statement or accounts or knowingly or wilfully furnishes any incorrect information in connection with any tax,

(b) knowingly aids, abets, assists, incites or induces another person to make or deliver knowingly or wilfully any incorrect return, statement or accounts in connection with any tax,

(c) claims or obtains relief or exemption from, or repayment of, any tax, being a relief, exemption or repayment to which, to the person's knowledge, the person is not entitled,

(d) knowingly or wilfully issues or produces any incorrect invoice, receipt, instrument or other document in connection with any tax,

(e) (i) fails to make any deduction required to be made by the person under section 257(1),

    (ii) fails, having made the deduction, to pay the sum deducted to the Collector-General within the time specified in that behalf in section 258(3), or

    (iii) fails to pay to the Collector-General an amount on account of appropriate tax (within the meaning of Chapter 4 of Part 8) within the time specified in that behalf in section 258(4),

(f) (i) fails to make any deduction required to be made by the person under section 734(5), or

    (ii) fails, having made the deduction, to pay the sum deducted to the Collector-General within the time specified in paragraph 1(3) of Schedule 18,

(g) knowingly or wilfully fails to comply with any provision of the Acts requiring—

    (i) the furnishing of a return of income, profits or gains, or of sources of income, profits or gains, for the purposes of any tax,

    (ii) the furnishing of any other return, certificate, notification, particulars, or any statement or evidence, for the purposes of any tax,

    (iii) the keeping or retention of books, records, accounts or other documents for the purposes of any tax, or

    (iv) the production of books, records, accounts or other documents, when so requested, for the purposes of any tax,

(h) knowingly or wilfully, and within the time limits specified for their retention, destroys, defaces or conceals from an authorised officer—

    (i) any documents, or

    (ii) any other written or printed material in any form, including any information stored, maintained or preserved by means of any mechanical or electronic device, whether or not stored, maintained or preserved in a legible form, which a person is obliged by any provision of the Acts to keep, to issue or to produce for inspection,

(i) fails to remit any income tax payable pursuant to Chapter 4 of Part 42, and the regulations under that Chapter, or value-added tax within the time specified in that behalf in relation to income tax or value-added tax, as the case may be, by the Acts, or

(j) obstructs or interferes with any officer of the Revenue Commissioners, or any other person, in the exercise or performance of powers or duties under the Acts for the purposes of any tax.

(3) A person convicted of an offence under this section shall be liable—

(a) on summary conviction to a fine of £1,000 which may be mitigated to not less than one fourth part of such fine or, at the discretion of the court, to imprisonment for a term not exceeding 12 months or to both the fine and the imprisonment, or

(b) on conviction on indictment, to a fine not exceeding £10,000 or, at the discretion of the court, to imprisonment for a term not exceeding 5 years or to both the fine and the imprisonment.

(4) Section 13 of the Criminal Procedure Act, 1967, shall apply in relation to an offence under this section as if, in place of the penalties specified in subsection (3) of that section, there were specified in that subsection the penalties provided for by subsection (3)(a), and the reference in subsection (2)(a) of section 13 of the Criminal Procedure Act, 1967, to the penalties provided for in subsection (3) of that section shall be construed and apply accordingly.

(5) Where an offence under this section is committed by a body corporate and the offence is shown to have been committed with the consent or connivance of any person who, when the offence was committed, was a director, manager, secretary or other officer of the body corporate, or a member of the committee of management or other controlling authority of the body corporate, that person shall also be deemed to be guilty of the offence and may be proceeded against and punished accordingly.

(6) In any proceedings under this section, a return or statement delivered to an inspector or other officer of the Revenue Commissioners under any provision of the Acts and purporting to be signed by any person shall be deemed until the contrary is proved to have been so delivered and to have been signed by that person.

(7) Notwithstanding any other enactment, proceedings in respect of an offence under this section may be instituted within 10 years from the date of the commission of the offence or incurring of the penalty, as the case may be.

(8) Section 1 of the Probation of Offenders Act, 1907, shall not apply in relation to offences under this section.

(9) Sections 987(4) and 1052(4), subsections (3) and (7) of section 1053, and sections 1068 and 1069 and sections 26(6) and 27(7) of the Value-Added Tax Act, 1972, shall, with any necessary modifications, apply for the purposes of this section as they apply for the purposes of those sections, including, in the case of such of those sections as are applied by the Capital Gains Tax Acts, the Corporation Tax Acts, or Part VI of the Finance Act, 1983, the purposes of those sections as so applied.

Section 1079

Duties of relevant person in relation to certain revenue offences.

1079. (1) In this section—

"the Acts" means—

(a) the Customs Acts,

(b) the statutes relating to the duties of excise and to the management of those duties,

(c) the Tax Acts,

(d) the Capital Gains Tax Acts,

(e) the Value-Added Tax Act, 1972, and the enactments amending or extending that Act,

(f) the Capital Acquisitions Tax Act, 1976, and the enactments amending or extending that Act,

(g) the statutes relating to stamp duty and to the management of that duty,

and any instruments made thereunder and any instruments made under any other enactment and relating to tax;

"appropriate officer" means any officer nominated by the Revenue Commissioners to be an appropriate officer for the purposes of this section;

"company" means any body corporate;

"relevant person", in relation to a company and subject to subsection (2), means a person who—

(a) (i) is an auditor to the company appointed in accordance with section 160 of the Companies Act, 1963 (as amended by the Companies Act, 1990), or

(ii) in the case of an industrial and provident society or a friendly society, is a public auditor to the society for the purposes of the Industrial and Provident Societies Acts, 1893 to 1978, and the Friendly Societies Acts, 1896 to 1977,

or

(b) with a view to reward, assists or advises the company in the preparation or delivery of any information, declaration, return, records, accounts or other document which he or she knows will be or is likely to be used for any purpose of tax;

"relevant offence" means an offence committed by a company which consists of the company –

(a) knowingly or wilfully delivering any incorrect return, statement or accounts or knowingly or wilfully furnishing or causing to be furnished any incorrect information in connection with any tax,

(b) knowingly or wilfully claiming or obtaining relief or exemption from, or repayment of, any tax, being a relief, exemption or repayment to which there is no entitlement,

(c) knowingly or wilfully issuing or producing any incorrect invoice, receipt, instrument or other document in connection with any tax, or

(d) knowingly or wilfully failing to comply with any provision of the Acts requiring the furnishing of a return of income, profits or gains, or of sources of income, profits or gains, for the purposes of any tax, but an offence under this paragraph committed by a company shall not be a relevant offence if the company has made a return of income, profits or gains to the Revenue Commissioners in respect of an accounting period falling wholly or partly in the period of 3 years preceding the accounting period in respect of which the offence was committed;

"tax" means any tax, duty, levy or charge under the care and management of the Revenue Commissioners.

(2) For the purposes of paragraph (b) of the definition of "relevant person", a person who but for this subsection would be treated as a relevant person in relation to a company shall not be so treated if the person assists or advises the company solely in the person's capacity as an employee of the company, and a person shall be treated as assisting or advising the company in that capacity where the person's income from assisting or advising the company consists solely of emoluments to which Chapter 4 of Part 42 applies.

(3) If, having regard solely to information obtained in the course of examining the accounts of a company, or in the course of assisting or advising a company in the preparation or delivery of any information, declaration, return, records, accounts or other document for the purposes of tax, as the case may be, a person who is a relevant person in relation to the company becomes aware that

the company has committed, or is in the course of committing, one or more relevant offences, the person shall, if the offence or offences are material –

    (a) communicate particulars of the offence or offences in writing to the company without undue delay and request the company to –

        (i) take such action as is necessary for the purposes of rectifying the matter, or

        (ii) notify an appropriate officer of the offence or offences,

    not later than 6 months after the time of communication, and

    (b) (i) unless it is established to the person's satisfaction that the necessary action has been taken or notification made, as the case may be, under paragraph (a), cease to act as the auditor to the company or to assist or advise the company in such preparation or delivery as is specified in paragraph (b) of the definition of "relevant person", and

        (ii) shall not so act, assist or advise before a time which is the earlier of –

            (I) 3 years after the time at which the particulars were communicated under paragraph (a), and

            (II) the time at which it is established to the person's satisfaction that the necessary action has been taken or notification made, as the case may be, under paragraph (a).

(4) Nothing in paragraph (b) of subsection (3) shall prevent a person from assisting or advising a company in preparing for, or conducting, legal proceedings, either civil or criminal, which are extant or pending at a time which is 6 months after the time of communication under paragraph (a) of that subsection.

(5) Where a person, being in relation to a company a relevant person within the meaning of paragraph (a) of the definition of "relevant person", ceases under this section to act as auditor to the company, then, the person shall deliver –

    (a) a notice in writing to the company stating that he or she is so resigning, and

    (b) a copy of the notice to an appropriate officer not later than 14 days after he or she has delivered the notice to the company.

(6) A person shall be guilty of an offence under this section if the person –

    (a) fails to comply with subsection (3) or (5), or

    (b) knowingly or wilfully makes a communication under subsection (3) which is incorrect.

(7) Where a relevant person is convicted of an offence under this section, the person shall be liable –

    (a)   on summary conviction, to a fine of £1,000 which may be mitigated to not less than one-fourth part of such fine, or

    (b)   on conviction on indictment, to a fine not exceeding £5,000 or, at the discretion of the court, to imprisonment for a term not exceeding 2 years or to both the fine and the imprisonment.

(8) Section 13 of the Criminal Procedure Act, 1967, shall apply in relation to this section as if, in place of the penalties specified in subsection (3) of that section, there were specified in that subsection the penalties provided for by subsection (7)(a), and the reference in subsection (2)(a) of section 13 of the Criminal Procedure Act, 1967, to the penalties provided for in subsection (3) of that section shall be construed and apply accordingly.

(9) Notwithstanding any other enactment, proceedings in respect of this section may be instituted within 6 years from the time at which a person is required under subsection (3) to communicate particulars of an offence or offences in writing to a company.

(10) It shall be a good defence in a prosecution for an offence under subsection (6) (a) in relation to a failure to comply with subsection (3) for an accused (being a person who is a relevant person in relation to a company) to show that he or she was in the ordinary scope of professional engagement assisting or advising the company in preparing for legal proceedings and would not have become aware that one or more relevant offences had been committed by the company if he or she had not been so assisting or advising.

(11) Where a person who is a relevant person takes any action required by subsection (3) or (5), no duty to which the person may be subject shall be regarded as having been contravened and no liability or action shall lie against the person in any court for having taken such action.

(12) The Revenue Commissioners may nominate an officer to be an appropriate officer for the purposes of this section, and the name of an officer so nominated and the address to which copies of notices under subsection (3) or (5) shall be delivered shall be published in Iris Oifigiúil.

(13) This section shall apply as respects a relevant offence committed by a company in respect of tax which is –

    (a)   assessable by reference to accounting periods, for any accounting period beginning after the 30th day of June, 1995,

    (b)   assessable by reference to years of assessment, for the year 1995-96 and subsequent years of assessment,

    (c)   payable by reference to a taxable period, for a taxable period beginning after the 30th day of June, 1995,

(d) chargeable on gifts or inheritances taken on or after the 30th day of June, 1995,

(e) chargeable on instruments executed on or after the 30th day of June, 1995, or

(f) payable in any other case, on or after the 30th day of June, 1995.

CHAPTER 6
Other sanctions

Section 1086

Publication of names of tax defaulters.

1086. (1) In this section —

"the Acts" means —

(a) the Tax Acts,

(b) the Capital Gains Tax Acts,

(c) the Value-Added Tax Act, 1972, and the enactments amending or extending that Act,

(d) the Capital Acquisitions Tax Act, 1976, and the enactments amending or extending that Act,

(e) the statutes relating to stamp duty and to the management of that duty, and

(f) Part VI of the Finance Act, 1983,

and any instruments made thereunder;

"tax" means income tax, capital gains tax, corporation tax, value-added tax, gift tax, inheritance tax, residential property tax and stamp duty.

(2) The Revenue Commissioners shall, as respects each relevant period (being the period beginning on the 1st day of January, 1997, and ending on the 30th day of June, 1997, and each subsequent period of 3 months beginning with the period ending on the 30th day of September, 1997), compile a list of the names and addresses and the occupations or descriptions of every person —

(a) on whom a fine or other penalty was imposed by a court under any of the Acts during that relevant period,

(b) on whom a fine or other penalty was otherwise imposed by a court during that relevant period in respect of an act or omission by the person in relation to tax, or

(c) in whose case the Revenue Commissioners, pursuant to an agreement made with the person in that relevant period, refrained from initiating proceedings for the recovery of any fine or penalty of the kind mentioned in paragraphs (a) and (b) and, in place of initiating such proceedings, accepted or undertook to accept a specified sum of money in settlement of any claim by the Revenue Commissioners in respect of any specified liability of the person under any of the Acts for—

(i)   payment of any tax,

(ii)   payment of interest on that tax, and

(iii) a fine or other monetary penalty in respect of that tax.

(3) Notwithstanding any obligation as to secrecy imposed on them by the Acts or the Official Secrets Act, 1963—

   (a)   the Revenue Commissioners shall, before the expiration of 3 months from the end of each relevant period, cause each such list referred to in subsection (2) in relation to that period to be published in Iris Oifigiúil, and

   (b)   the Revenue Commissioners may at any time cause any such list referred to in subsection (2) to be publicised in such manner as they shall consider appropriate.

(4) Paragraph (c) of subsection (2) shall not apply in relation to a person in whose case—

   (a)   the Revenue Commissioners are satisfied that, before any investigation or inquiry had been commenced by them or by any of their officers into any matter occasioning a liability referred to in that paragraph of the person, the person had voluntarily furnished to them complete information in relation to and full particulars of that matter,

   (b)   section 72 of the Finance Act, 1988, or section 3 of the Waiver of Certain Tax, Interest and Penalties Act, 1993, applied, or

   (c)   the specified sum referred to in paragraph (c) of subsection (2) does not exceed £10,000.

(5) Any list referred to in subsection (2) shall specify in respect of each person named in the list such particulars as the Revenue Commissioners think fit—

   (a)   of the matter occasioning the fine or penalty of the kind referred to in subsection (2) imposed on the person or, as the case may be, the liability of that kind to which the person was subject, and

   (b)   of any interest, fine or other monetary penalty, and of any other penalty or sanction, to which that person was liable, or which was imposed on that person by a court, and which was occasioned by the matter referred to in paragraph (a).

PART 48
Miscellaneous and Supplemental

Section 1089

Status of interest on certain unpaid taxes and duties.
1089. (1) ....

    (2) Interest payable under section 18 of the Wealth Tax Act, 1975, or section 41 of the Capital Acquisitions Tax Act, 1976, shall not be allowed in computing any income, profits or losses for any of the purposes of the Tax Acts.

Section 1093

Disclosure of information to Ombudsman.
1093. Any obligation to maintain secrecy or other restriction on the disclosure or production of information (including documents) obtained by or furnished to the Revenue Commissioners, or any person on their behalf, for taxation purposes, shall not apply to the disclosure or production of information (including documents) to the Ombudsman for the purposes of an examination or investigation by the Ombudsman under the Ombudsman Act, 1980, of any action (within the meaning of that Act) taken by or on behalf of the Revenue Commissioners, being such an action taken in the performance of administrative functions in respect of any tax or duty under the care and management of the Revenue Commissioners.

PART 49
Commencement, Repeals, Transitional Provisions, Etc.

Section 1100

Consequential amendments to other enactments.
1100. Schedule 31, which provides for amendments to other enactments consequential on the passing of this Act, shall apply for the purposes of this Act.

SCHEDULE 31

Consequential Amendments

In the enactments specified in Column (1) of the following Table for the words set out or referred to in Column (2) there shall be substituted the words set out in the corresponding entry in Column (3).

Enactment amended (1)	Words to be replaced (2)	Words to be substituted (3)
The Capital Acquisitions Tax Act, 1976:		
section 16 (2), in the definition of "private company"	section 95 of the Corporation Tax Act, 1976	section 431 of the Taxes Consolidation Act, 1997
	subsection (1)	subsection (3)
	subsection (4)	subsection (6)
section 52 (1), in the definition of "Appeal Commissioners"	section 156 of the Income Tax Act, 1967	section 850 of the Taxes Consolidation Act, 1997
section 58 (2) (b)	section 142 of the Income Tax Act, 1967	section 466 of the Taxes Consolidation Act, 1997
section 63 (9)	sections 128 (4), 507, 508, 510, 511, 512, 517, and 518 of the Income Tax Act, 1967	sections 987 (4), 1061, 1062, 1063, 1064, 1065, 1066 and 1068 of the Taxes Consolidation Act, 1997
Second Schedule, Part I, paragraph 9, in the definition of "investment income"	section 2 of the Income Tax Act, 1967	section 3 of the Taxes Consolidation Act, 1997
The Finance Act 1984:		
Section 108 (i) (b) (ii)	subsection (9) of section 235 of the Income Tax Act, 1967	subsection (1) of section 783 of the Taxes Consolidation Act, 1997
	section 235 A	section 785

Enactment amended (1)	Words to be replaced (2)	Words to be substituted (3)
The Finance Act, 1990:		
section 129 (1)	subsection (9) of section 235 of the Income Tax Act, 1967	subsection (1) of section 783 of the Taxes Consolidation Act, 1997
The Finance Act, 1991:		
section 129 (1) in the definition of "the Collector"	section 162 of the Income Tax Act, 1967	section 851 of the Taxes Consolidation Act, 1997
section 129 (3)	section 187 of the Income Tax Act, 1967	sections 928 (1) and 964 (2) of the Taxes Consolidation Act, 1997
The Finance Act, 1993:		
section 109 (1), in the definition of "dependent relative"	subsection (9A) (inserted by the Finance Act, 1979) of section 25 of the Capital Gains Tax Act, 1975	subsection (11) of section 604 of the Taxes Consolidation Act, 1997
section 112 (a) (i) (A)	section 235 (9) of the Income Tax Act, 1967	section 783 (1) of the Taxes Consolidation Act, 1997
section 112 (a) (i) (B)	section 235 or section 235A	section 784 or section 785
section 112 (a) (iii)	section 236 of the Income Tax Act, 1967	section 787 of the Taxes Consolidation Act, 1997
section 112 (d), proviso (i)	subsection (1A) of section 142 of the Income Tax Act, 1967	subsection (1) of section 466 of the Taxes Consolidation Act, 1997
section 133 (1)	section 36 of the Finance Act, 1988	section 451 of the Taxes Consolidation Act, 1997

FINANCE ACT, 1998

Number 3 of 1998
(Enacted on 27th March, 1998)

PART 5
Capital Acquisitions Tax

Section 126

Amendment of section 117 (reduction in estimated market value of certain dwellings) of Finance Act, 1991.

126. (1) The Finance Act, 1991, is hereby amended by the substitution of the following section for section 117:

> "117. (1) Insofar as an inheritance consists of a house or the appropriate part of a house—
>
> > (a) at the date of the inheritance, and
> >
> > (b) at the valuation date,
>
> and is taken by a successor who, at the date of the inheritance, is a lineal ancestor, a lineal descendant (other than a child, or a minor child of a deceased child), a brother or a sister, or a child of a brother or of a sister, of the disponer, and
>
> > (i) has resided continuously with the disponer in the house or, where that house has directly or indirectly replaced other property, in that house and in that other property, for periods which together comprised—
> >
> > > (I) in the case where the successor is a brother or a sister of the disponer and has, at the date of the inheritance, attained the age of 55 years, the 5 years immediately preceding the date of the inheritance, and
> > >
> > > (II) in any other case, the 10 years immediately preceding the date of the inheritance, and
> >
> > (ii) is not beneficially entitled in possession to any other house or the appropriate part of any other house,
>
> the estimated market value of the house or the appropriate part of the house shall, notwithstanding anything to the contrary in section 15 of [the Capital Acquisitions Tax Act, 1976], be reduced by 80 per cent or £150,000, whichever is the lesser:

Provided that where the house or the appropriate part of the house comprised in the inheritance is, on both of those dates, agricultural property within the meaning of section 19(1) of [the Capital Acquisitions Tax Act, 1976,] and the successor is, at the valuation date and after taking the inheritance, a farmer within the meaning of that section, the provisions of this section shall not apply.

(2) In this section—

'appropriate part', in relation to a house, has the meaning assigned to it in relation to property by subsection (5) of section 5 of [the Capital Acquisitions Tax Act, 1976];

'house' means a building, or a part of a building used by the disponer as his main or only dwelling together with its garden or grounds of an ornamental nature.".

(2) This section shall have effect in relation to inheritances taken on or after the 3rd day of December, 1997.

Section 127

Amendment of section 117 (interest on tax) of Finance Act, 1993.

127. (1) Section 117 of the Finance Act, 1993, is hereby amended—

    (a) in paragraph (b), by the substitution of "one per cent" for "one and one-quarter per cent.", and

    (b) in paragraph (c), by the substitution of "one per cent" for "one and one-quarter per cent.".

(2) This section shall have effect in relation to probate tax due before, on or after the date of the passing of this Act where the period in respect of which interest is to be charged, or a discount falls to be made, commences on or after that date.

Section 128

Amendment of section 134 (exclusion of value of excepted assets) of Finance Act, 1994.

128. Section 134 of the Finance Act, 1994, shall have effect and be deemed always to have had effect as if the following subsections were substituted for subsection (7):

"(7) Where, in relation to a gift or an inheritance—

    (a) relevant business property consisting of shares in or securities of a company are comprised in the gift or inheritance on the valuation date, and

    (b) property consisting of a business, or interest in a business, not falling within section 127(4) (hereinafter in this section referred to as 'company business property') is on that date beneficially owned by that company or, where that company is a holding company of one or more companies within the same group, by any company within that group,

that company business property shall, for the purposes of subsection (1), be excluded property in relation to those shares or securities unless it would, apart from section 127(3), have been relevant business property if —

    (i)   it had been the subject matter of that gift or inheritance, and

    (ii) it had been comprised in the disposition for the periods during which it was in the beneficial ownership of that first-mentioned company or of any member of that group, while being such a member, or actually comprised in the disposition.

(8) In ascertaining whether or not company business property complies with paragraphs (i) and (ii) of subsection (7), the provisions of section 129 shall, with any necessary modifications, apply to that company business property as to a case to which subsection (1) of section 129 relates.''.

Section 129

Conditions before appeal may be made.

129. (1) The Capital Acquisitions Tax Act, 1976, is hereby amended by the insertion of the following section after section 52 of that Act:

"52A. No appeal shall lie under section 51 or 52 until such time as the person aggrieved by the decision or assessment (as the case may be) complies with section 36(2) in respect of the gift or inheritance in relation to which the decision or assessment is made, as if there were no time-limit for complying with section 36(2) and that person were a person primarily accountable for the payment of tax by virtue of section 35(1) and required by notice in writing by the Commissioners to deliver a return.''.

(2) This section shall have effect in relation to gifts or inheritances taken on or after the 12th day of February, 1998.

PART 6
Miscellaneous

Section 133

Interest on unpaid or overpaid taxes.

133. (1) ....

(4) The Capital Acquisitions Tax Act, 1976, is hereby amended –

    (a) in section 41(2), as construed by reference to section 43 of the Finance Act, 1978, by the substitution of "1 per cent" for "1.25 per cent.", and

    (b) in section 46(1), notwithstanding Regulation 3 of the Payment of Interest on Overpaid Tax Regulations, 1990, by the substitution of "0.5 per cent" for "one per cent.".

(6) This section shall apply as respects interest chargeable or payable under –

    (i) ....

    (iii) sections 41 and 46 of the Capital Acquisitions Tax Act, 1976,

for any month, or any part of a month, commencing on or after the date of the passing of this Act, in respect of an amount due to be paid or remitted or an amount due to be repaid or retained, as the case may be, whether before, on or after that date in accordance with those provisions.

Section 134

Appeals.
134. (1) ....

(3) Section 52(5) of the Capital Acquisitions Tax Act, 1976, is hereby amended by the insertion, in paragraph (a), of the following subparagraph after subparagraph (v):

"(va) the publication of reports of determinations of the Appeal Commissioners;".

(4) This section shall apply to appeals determined by the Appeal Commissioners after the date of the passing of this Act.

FINANCE ACT, 1999

Number 2 of 1999
(Enacted on 25th March, 1999)

PART I
Income Tax, Corporation Tax and Capital Gains Tax

CHAPTER II
Income Tax

Section 12

Treatment of income arising as a result of certain public subscriptions raised on behalf of incapacitated individuals.

12. [The Taxes Consolidation Act, 1997,] is hereby amended—

(a) in Chapter 1 of Part 7 by the insertion of the following section after section 189:

"Special trusts for permanently incapacitated individuals.

189A.[1] (1) In this section —

'incapacitated individual' means an individual who is permanently and totally incapacitated, by reason of mental or physical infirmity, from being able to maintain himself or herself;

'public subscriptions' means subscriptions, in the form of money or other property, raised, following an appeal made in that behalf to members of the public, for the benefit of one or more incapacitated individual or individuals, whose identity or identities is or are known to the persons making the subscriptions, being subscriptions that meet either of the following conditions, namely—

(a) the total amount of the subscriptions does not exceed £300,000,

or

(b) no amount of the subscriptions, at any time on or after the specified return date for the chargeable period for which exemption is first claimed under either subsection (2) or (3), constitutes a subscription made by any one person that is greater than 30 per cent of the total amount of the subscriptions;

'qualifying trust' means a trust established by deed in respect of which it is shown to the satisfaction of the inspector or, on appeal, to the Appeal Commissioners, that—

(a) the trust has been established exclusively for the benefit of one or more specified incapacitated individual or individuals, for whose benefit public subscriptions, within the meaning of this section, have been raised,

(b) the trust requires that—

(i) the trust funds be applied for the benefit of that individual or those individuals, as the case may be, at the discretion of the trustees of the trust, and

(ii) in the event of the death of that individual or those individuals, as the case may be, the undistributed part of the trust funds be applied for charitable purposes or be appointed in favour of the trustees of charitable bodies,

and

(c) none of the trustees of the trust is connected (within the meaning of section 10) with that individual or any of those individuals, as the case may be;

. . . .

'trust funds' means, in relation to a qualifying trust—

(a) public subscriptions, raised for the benefit of the incapacitated individual or individuals, the subject or subjects of the trust, and

(b) all moneys and other property derived directly or indirectly from such public subscriptions.

(2) . . . .''

Footnote

1   This section contains definitions used in s.58, CATA, and s.82, CATCA.

PART 6
Capital Acquisitions Tax

Section 199

Interpretation (Part 6).

199. In this Part "the Principal Act" means the "Capital Acquisitions Tax Act, 1976".

Section 200

Amendment of section 36 (delivery of returns) of [the Capital Acquisitions Tax Act, 1976].

200. Section 36 of [the Capital Acquisitions Tax Act, 1976,] is hereby amended—

(a) in paragraph (a) of subsection (1) by the substitution of the following subparagraph for subparagraph (iii):

"(iii) a reference, other than in subparagraph (i) or subsection (13) or (14), to a gift or a taxable gift includes a reference to an inheritance or a taxable inheritance, as the case may be; and",

(b) in subsection (4) by the substitution of the following paragraphs for paragraphs (c) and (d):

"(c) so far as it is a taxable gift taken on or after the 26th day of March, 1984, and before the 2nd day of December, 1998, the aggregate of the taxable values of all taxable gifts taken by the donee on or after the 2nd day of June, 1982, exceeds an amount which is 80 per cent of the threshold amount (as defined in the Second Schedule) which applies in the computation of the tax on that aggregate; or

(d) so far as it is a taxable gift taken on or after the 2nd day of December, 1998, the aggregate of the taxable values of all taxable gifts taken by the donee on or after the 2nd day of December, 1988, exceeds an amount which is 80 per cent of the threshold amount (as defined in the Second Schedule) which applies in the computation of the tax on that aggregate; or

(e) the donee or, in a case to which section 23(1) applies, the transferee (within the meaning of, and to the extent provided for by, that section) is required by notice in writing by the Commissioners to deliver a return",

and

(c) by the insertion of the following subsections after subsection (11):

"(12) The Commissioners may by notice in writing require any person to deliver to them within such time, not being less than 30 days, as may be specified in the notice, a full and true return showing details of every taxable gift (including the property comprised therein) taken by that person during the period specified in the notice or, as the case may be, indicating that that person has taken no taxable gift during that period.

(13) As respects a taxable gift to which this subsection applies, any accountable person who is a disponer shall within 4 months of the valuation date deliver to the Commissioners a full and true return—

(a) of all the property comprised in such gift on the valuation date,

(b)   of an estimate of the market value of such property on the valuation date, and

(c)   of such particulars as may be relevant to the assessment of tax in respect of the gift.

(14) Subsection (13) applies to a taxable gift taken on or after the 11th day of February, 1999, in the case where—

(a)   the taxable value of the taxable gift exceeds an amount which is 80 per cent of the class threshold (as defined in the Second Schedule) which applies in relation to that gift for the purposes of the computation of the tax on that gift,

(b)   the taxable value of the taxable gift taken by the donee from the disponer increases the total taxable value of all taxable gifts and taxable inheritances taken on or after the 2nd day of December, 1988, by the donee from the disponer from an amount less than or equal to the amount specified in paragraph (a) to an amount which exceeds the amount so specified, or

(c)   the total taxable value of all taxable gifts and taxable inheritances taken on or after the 2nd day of December, 1988, by the donee from the disponer exceeds the amount specified in paragraph (a) and the donee takes a further taxable gift from the disponer.

(15) Where, on or after the 11th day of February, 1999, under or in consequence of any disposition made by a person who is living and domiciled in the State at the date of the disposition, property becomes subject to a discretionary trust, the disponer shall within 4 months of the date of the disposition deliver to the Commissioners a full and true return of—

(a)   the terms of the discretionary trust,

(b)   the names and addresses of the trustees and objects of the discretionary trust, and

(c)   an estimate of the market value at the date of the disposition of the property becoming subject to the discretionary trust.".

Section 201

Amendment of Second Schedule (computation of tax) to [the Capital Acquisitions Tax Act, 1976].

201. (1) The Second Schedule to [the Capital Acquisitions Tax Act, 1976,] is hereby amended in paragraph 3(a)(ii) (inserted by the Finance Act, 1997) by the substitution of "2nd day of December, 1988" for "2nd day of June, 1982".

(2) This section shall have effect in relation to gifts or inheritances taken on or after the 2nd day of December, 1998.

Section 202

Amendment of section 41 (payment of tax and interest on tax) of [the Capital Acquisitions Tax Act, 1976].

202. (1) Section 41 of [the Capital Acquisitions Tax Act, 1976,] is hereby amended by the insertion of the following subsection after subsection (2):

"(2A) Notwithstanding the provisions of subsection (2), interest shall not be payable upon the tax —

(a) to the extent to which section 19(5)(a) applies, for the duration of the period from the valuation date to the date the agricultural value ceases to be applicable,

(b) to the extent to which section 55(4) applies, for the duration of the period from the valuation date to the date the exemption ceases to apply,

(c) to the extent to which section 135(2) of the Finance Act, 1994, applies, for the duration of the period from the valuation date to the date the reduction which would otherwise fall to be made under section 126 of that Act ceases to be applicable,

(d) to the extent to which section 166(6) of the Finance Act, 1995, applies, for the duration of the period from the valuation date to the date the exemption ceases to apply.".

(2) This section shall have effect where the event which causes the exemption or reduction in question to cease to be applicable occurs on or after the 11th day of February, 1999.

Section 203

Amendment of section 51 (appeals regarding value of real property) of [the Capital Acquisitions Tax Act, 1976].

203. Section 51 of [the Capital Acquisitions Tax Act, 1976,] is hereby amended by the insertion of the following subsection:

"(2) The particulars of any transfer or lease which are presented to or obtained by the Commissioners under section 107 of the Finance Act, 1994, shall, in any appeal under this section, be received as prima facie evidence of all matters and things stated in such particulars.".

Section 204

Amendment of section 53 (exemption of small gifts) of [the Capital Acquisitions Tax Act, 1976].

204. Section 53(1) of [the Capital Acquisitions Tax Act, 1976,] shall have effect, as respects relevant periods ending after the 31st day of December, 1998, as if "£1,000" were substituted for "£500" (provided for by section 44 of the Finance Act, 1978).

Section 205

Amendment of section 58 (exemption of certain receipts) of [the Capital Acquisitions Tax Act, 1976].

205. Section 58 of [the Capital Acquisitions Tax Act, 1976,] is hereby amended by the insertion of the following subsection after subsection (2):

"(3) (a) The receipt by an incapacitated individual of the whole or any part of trust funds which are held on a qualifying trust, or of the income therefrom, shall not be a gift or an inheritance.

(b) In this subsection 'incapacitated individual', 'trust funds' and 'qualifying trust' have the meanings assigned to them, respectively, by section 189A (inserted by the Finance Act, 1999) of the Taxes Consolidation Act, 1997.[1]

(c) This subsection shall apply in relation to gifts or inheritances taken on or after the 6th day of April, 1997.".

Footnote
1   Reproduced on page 1006.

Section 206

Exemption relating to retirement benefits.

206. [The Capital Acquisitions Tax Act, 1976,] is hereby amended by the insertion of the following section after section 59A:

"59B. (1) The whole or any part of a retirement fund which is comprised in an inheritance which is taken upon the death of a disponer dying on or after the date of the passing of the Finance Act, 1999, shall be exempt from tax in relation to that inheritance and in relation to a charge for tax arising on that death by virtue of section 110 of the Finance Act, 1993, and the value thereof shall not be taken into account in computing tax, where—

(a) the disposition under which the inheritance is taken is the will or intestacy of the disponer, and

(b) the successor is a child of the disponer and had attained 21 years of age at the date of that disposition.

(b)   as are otherwise material to the liability in relation to the person carrying on the profession,

and in particular that person shall not be required to disclose any information or professional advice of a confidential nature given to a client.

(5)   Where, in compliance with the requirements of a notice served on a person under subsection (2), the person makes available for inspection by an authorised officer, books, records or other documents, the person shall afford the authorised officer reasonable assistance, including information, explanations and particulars, in relation to the use of all the electronic or other automatic means, if any, by which the books, records or other documents, in so far as they are in a non-legible form, are capable of being reproduced in a legible form, and any data equipment or any associated apparatus or material.

(6)   Where, under subsection (2), a person makes books, records or other documents available for inspection by the authorised officer, the authorised officer may make extracts from or copies of all or any part of the books, records or other documents.

(7)   A person who refuses or fails to comply with a notice served on the person under subsection (2) or fails to afford the assistance referred to in subsection (5) shall be liable to a penalty of £1,500.",

(b)   by the substitution for section 901 of the following section:

"Application to High Court: production of books, information, etc.

901.   (1)   An authorised officer may make an application to a judge for an order requiring a person, to do either or both of the following, namely –

(a)   to deliver to the authorised officer, or to make available for inspection by the authorised officer, such books, records or other documents as are in the person's power, possession or procurement and as contain, or may (in the authorised officer's opinion formed on reasonable grounds) contain, information relevant to a liability in relation to the person,

(b)   to furnish to the authorised officer such information, explanations and particulars as the authorised officer may reasonably require, being information, explanations and particulars that are relevant to any such liability,

and which are specified in the application.

(2)   Where the judge, to whom an application is made under subsection (1), is satisfied that there are reasonable grounds for the application being made, that judge may, subject to such conditions as he or she may consider proper and specify in the order, make an order requiring the person to whom the application relates –

      (a)   to deliver to the authorised officer, or to make available for inspection by the authorised officer, such books, records or other documents, and

      (b)   to furnish to the authorised officer such information, explanations and particulars,

   as may be specified in the order.

  (3)   Nothing in this section shall oblige a person who is carrying on a profession to furnish any information, explanations or particulars relating to a client to an authorised officer, or to deliver to, or make available for inspection by, an authorised officer any books, records or other documents relating to the client, without the consent of the client, other than such —

      (a)   as pertain to the payment of fees to the person carrying on the profession or to other financial transactions of the person carrying on the profession,

      or

      (b)   as are otherwise material to the liability in relation to the person carrying on the profession,

   and in particular that person shall not be required to disclose any information or professional advice of a confidential nature given to the client.",

   (c)   by the substitution for section 902 of the following section:

"Information to be furnished by third party: request of an authorised officer.

902. (1)   In this section and in section 902A —

   'authorised officer' means an officer of the Revenue Commissioners authorised by them in writing to exercise the powers conferred by this section, or as the case may be, section 902A;

   'books, records or other documents' and 'liability', in relation to a person, have, respectively, the meaning assigned to them by section 900(1).

  (2)   Notwithstanding any obligation as to secrecy or other restriction upon disclosure of information imposed by or under statute or otherwise, and subject to this section, an authorised officer may for the purpose of enquiring into a liability in relation to a person (in this section referred to as 'the taxpayer') serve on any other person (not being a financial institution within the meaning of section 906A) a notice in writing requiring that other person, within such period as may be specified in the notice, not being less than 30 days from the date of the service of the notice, to do either or both of the following, namely —

      (a)   to deliver to, or make available for inspection by, the authorised officer, such books, records or other documents as are in the other person's power, possession or procurement and as contain, or may (in the authorised officer's opinion formed on reasonable grounds) contain, information relevant to a liability in relation to the taxpayer,

(b) to furnish to the authorised officer, in writing or otherwise, such information, explanations and particulars as the authorised officer may reasonably require, being information, explanations and particulars that are relevant to any such liability,

and which are specified in the notice.

(3) A notice shall not be served on a person under subsection (2) unless the authorised officer concerned has reasonable grounds to believe that the person is likely to have information relevant to the establishment of a liability in relation to the taxpayer.

(4) The persons who may be treated as a taxpayer for the purposes of this section include a company which has been dissolved and an individual who has died.

(5) A notice under subsection (2) shall name the taxpayer in relation to whose liability the authorised officer is enquiring.

(6) Where an authorised officer serves a notice under subsection (2), a copy of such notice shall be given by the authorised officer to the taxpayer concerned.

(7) Where, under subsection (2), a person has delivered any books, records or other documents and those books, records or other documents are retained by the authorised officer, the person shall, at all reasonable times and subject to such reasonable conditions as may be determined by the authorised officer, be entitled to inspect those books, records or other documents and to obtain copies of them.

(8) Where, under subsection (2), a person makes books, records or other documents available for inspection by the authorised officer, the authorised officer may make extracts from or copies of all or any part of the books, records or other documents.

(9) Nothing in this section shall be construed as requiring any person carrying on a profession, and on whom a notice is served under subsection (2), to furnish any information, explanations and particulars relating to a client to an authorised officer or to deliver to, or make available for inspection by, an authorised officer any books, records or other documents relating to a client, other than such —

(a) as pertain to the payment of fees or other financial transactions, or

(b) as are otherwise material to a liability in relation to the client,

and in particular such person shall not be required to disclose any information or professional advice of a confidential nature.

(10) Where, in compliance with the requirements of a notice under subsection (2), a person makes available for inspection by an authorised officer, books, records or other documents, the person shall afford the authorised officer reasonable assistance, including information, explanations and particulars, in relation to the use of all the electronic or other automatic means, if any, by which the books, records or other documents, in so far as they are in non-legible form, are capable of being reproduced in a legible form and any data equipment or any associated apparatus or material.

(11) A person who fails or refuses to comply with a notice served on the person under subsection (2) or to afford the assistance referred to in subsection (10) shall be liable to a penalty of £1,500, but nothing in section 1078 shall be construed as applying to such failure or refusal.",

(d) by the insertion after section 902 of the following section:

"Application to High Court: information from third party.

902A. (1) In this section —

'the Acts' has the meaning assigned to it by section 1078(1);

'judge' means a judge of the High Court;

'a taxpayer' means any person including a person whose identity is not known to the authorised officer, and a group or class of persons whose individual identities are not so known.

(2) An authorised officer may make an application to a judge for an order requiring a person (other than a financial institution within the meaning of section 906A) to do either or both of the following, namely —

(a) to deliver to the authorised officer, or to make available for inspection by the authorised officer, such books, records or other documents as are in the person's power, possession or procurement and as contain, or may (in the authorised officer's opinion formed on reasonable grounds) contain, information relevant to a liability in relation to a taxpayer,

(b) to furnish to the authorised officer such information, explanations and particulars as the authorised officer may reasonably require, being information, explanations and particulars that are relevant to any such liability,

and which are specified in the application.

(3) An authorised officer shall not make an application under subsection (2) without the consent in writing of a Revenue Commissioner, and without being satisfied —

(a) that there are reasonable grounds for suspecting that the taxpayer, or, where the taxpayer is a group or class of persons, all or any one of those persons, may have failed or may fail to comply with any provision of the Acts,

    (b)   that any such failure is likely to have led or to lead to serious prejudice to the proper assessment or collection of tax (having regard to the amount of a liability in relation to the taxpayer, or where the taxpayer is a group or class of persons, the amount of a liability in relation to all or any one of those persons, that arises or might arise from such failure), and

    (c)   that the information—

        (i)   which is likely to be contained in the books, records or other documents to which the application relates, or

        (ii)   which is likely to arise from the information, explanations and particulars to which the application relates,

    is relevant to the proper assessment or collection of tax.

(4)   Where the judge, to whom an application is made under subsection (2), is satisfied that there are reasonable grounds for the application being made, that judge may, subject to such conditions as he or she may consider proper and specify in the order, make an order requiring the person to whom the application relates—

    (a)   to deliver to the authorised officer, or to make available for inspection by the authorised officer, such books, records or other documents, and

    (b)   to furnish to the authorised officer such information, explanations and particulars,

    as may be specified in the order.

(5)   The persons who may be treated as a taxpayer for the purposes of this section include a company which has been dissolved and an individual who has died.

(6)   Nothing in this section shall oblige any person carrying on a profession to furnish any information, explanations or particulars relating to a client to an authorised officer, or to deliver to, or make available for inspection by, an authorised officer any books, records or other documents relating to a client, without the client's consent, other than such—

    (a)   as pertain to the payment of fees or other financial transactions, or

    (b)   as are otherwise material to a liability in relation to the client,

    and in particular such person shall not be required to disclose any information or professional advice of a confidential nature.

(7)   Every hearing of an application for an order under this section and of any appeal in connection with that application shall be held in camera.",

    (e)   ......

    (f)   in section 905—

    (i)   in subsection (2) by the deletion of paragraph (d), and

    (ii) by the insertion after subsection (2) of the following subsection:

"(2A) (a) In this subsection 'the Acts' has the meaning assigned to it by section 1078(1).

(b) Without prejudice to any power conferred by subsection (2), if a Judge of the District Court is satisfied by information on oath that there are reasonable grounds for suspecting—

(i) that a person may have failed or may fail to comply with any provision of the Acts,

(ii) that any such failure is likely to have led or to lead to serious prejudice to the proper assessment or collection of tax (having regard to the amount of any tax liability that arises or might arise from such failure),

and

(iii) that records, which are material to the proper assessment or collection of tax are likely to be kept or concealed at any premises or place,

the Judge may issue a search warrant.

(c) A search warrant issued under this subsection shall be expressed and shall operate to authorise an authorised officer accompanied by such other named officers of the Revenue Commissioners and such other named persons as the authorised officer considers necessary, at any time or times within one month of the date of issue of the warrant, to enter (if need be by force) the premises or other place named or specified in the warrant, to search such premises or other place, to examine anything found there, to inspect any records found there and, if there are reasonable grounds for suspecting that any records found there are material to the proper assessment or collection of tax, or that the records may

required by notice under that subsection to deliver or to make available and the information, explanations and particulars which it may likewise be required to furnish, may include books, records or other documents and information, explanations and particulars relating to a person who is connected with the taxpayer.

(6) The persons who may be treated as a taxpayer for the purposes of this section include a company which has been dissolved and an individual who has died.

(7) A notice served under subsection (2) shall name the taxpayer in relation to whose liability the authorised officer is enquiring.

(8) Where an authorised officer serves a notice under subsection (2), a copy of such notice shall be given by the authorised officer to the taxpayer concerned.

(9) Where, in compliance with a notice served under subsection (2), a financial institution makes books, records or other documents available for inspection by an authorised officer, the authorised officer may make extracts from or copies of all or any part of the books, records or other documents.

(10) A financial institution which fails or refuses to comply with a notice issued under subsection (2) or which fails or refuses to afford reasonable assistance to an authorised officer as required under subsection (3), shall be liable to a penalty of £15,000 and, if the failure or refusal to comply with such notice continues after the expiry of the period specified in the notice served under subsection (2), a further penalty of £2,000 for each day on which the failure or refusal continues.",

(h) by the substitution for section 907 of the following section:

"Application to Appeal Commissioners: information from financial institutions.

907. (1) In this section 'a taxpayer' means any person including —

(a) a person whose identity is not known to the authorised officer, and a group or class of persons whose individual identities are not so known, and

(b) a person by or in respect of whom a declaration has been made under section 263(1) declaring that the person is beneficially entitled to all or part of the interest in relation to a deposit.

(2) An authorised officer may, subject to this section, make an application to the Appeal Commissioners for their consent, under subsection (5), to the service by him or her of a notice on a financial institution requiring the financial institution to do either or both of the following, namely —

(a) to make available for inspection by the authorised officer, such books, records or other documents as are in the financial institution's power, possession or procurement as contain, or may (in the authorised officer's opinion formed on reasonable grounds) contain, information relevant to a liability in relation to a taxpayer,

(b) to furnish to the authorised officer such information, explanations and particulars as the authorised officer may reasonably require, being information, explanations and particulars that are relevant to any such liability,

and which are specified in the application.

(3) An authorised officer shall not make an application under subsection (2) without the consent in writing of a Revenue Commissioner, and without being satisfied —

(a) that there are reasonable grounds for suspecting that the taxpayer, or where the taxpayer is a group or class of persons, all or any one of those persons, may have failed or may fail to comply with any provision of the Acts,

(b) that any such failure is likely to have led or to lead to serious prejudice to the proper assessment or collection of tax (having regard to the amount of a liability in relation to the taxpayer, or where the taxpayer is a group or class of persons, the amount of a liability in relation to all or any one of those persons, that arises or might arise from such failure), and

(c) that the information —

   (i) which is likely to be contained in the books, records or other documents to which the application relates, or

   (ii) which is likely to arise from the information, explanations and particulars to which the application relates,

   is relevant to the proper assessment or collection of tax.

(4) Without prejudice to the generality of subsection (2), the authorised officer may make an application under that subsection to the Appeal Commissioners for their consent, under subsection (5), to the service by him or her of a notice on a financial institution in respect of the matters referred to in paragraphs (a) and (b) of subsection (2) in so far as they relate to a person who is connected with the taxpayer.

(5) Where the Appeal Commissioners determine that in all the circumstances there are reasonable grounds for the application being made, they may give their consent to the service by the authorised officer concerned of a notice on the financial institution, requiring the financial institution —

(a) to make available for inspection by the authorised officer, such books, records or other documents, and

(b) to furnish to the authorised officer such information, explanations and particulars,

of the kind referred to in subsection (2) as may, with the Appeal Commissioners' consent, be specified in the notice.

(6) The persons who may be treated as a taxpayer for the purposes of this section include a company which has been dissolved and an individual who has died.

(7) Where the Appeal Commissioners have given their consent in accordance with this section, the authorised officer shall, as soon as practicable, but not later than 14 days from the time that such consent was given, serve a notice on the financial institution concerned and stating that—

    (a) such consent has been given,

    and

    (b) the financial institution should, within a period of 30 days from the date of the service of the notice, comply with the requirements specified in the notice.

(8) (a) Subject to paragraph (b), an application by an authorised officer under subsection (2) shall, with any necessary modifications, be heard by the Appeal Commissioners as if it were an appeal against an assessment to income tax.

    (b) Notwithstanding section 933(4), a determination by the Appeal Commissioners under this section shall be final and conclusive.

(9) A financial institution which fails to comply with a notice served on the financial institution by an authorised officer in accordance with this section shall be liable to a penalty of £15,000 and, if the failure continues after the expiry of the period specified in subsection (7)(b), a further penalty of £2,000 for each day on which the failure so continues.",

    (i) by the substitution for section 908 of the following section:

"Application to High Court seeking order requiring information: financial institutions.

908. (1) In this section—

    'judge' means a judge of the High Court;

    'a taxpayer' means any person including—

    (a) a person whose identity is not known to the authorised officer, and a group or class of persons whose individual identities are not so known, and

    (b) a person by or in respect of whom a declaration has been made under section 263(1) declaring that the person is beneficially entitled to all or part of the interest in relation to a deposit.

(2) An authorised officer may, subject to this section, make an application to a judge for an order requiring a financial institution, to do either or both of the following, namely—

    (a) to make available for inspection by the authorised officer, such books, records or other documents as are in the financial institution's power, possession or procurement as contain, or may (in the authorised officer's opinion formed on reasonable grounds) contain information relevant to a liability in relation to a taxpayer,

(b) to furnish to the authorised officer such information, explanations and particulars as the authorised officer may reasonably require, being information, explanations and particulars that are relevant to any such liability,

and which are specified in the application.

(3) An authorised officer shall not make application under subsection (2) without the consent in writing of a Revenue Commissioner, and without being satisfied —

(a) that there are reasonable grounds for suspecting that the taxpayer, or, where the taxpayer is a group or class of persons, all or any one of those persons, may have failed or may fail to comply with any provision of the Acts,

(b) that any such failure is likely to have led or to lead to serious prejudice to the proper assessment or collection of tax (having regard to the amount of a liability in relation to the taxpayer, or where the taxpayer is a group or class of persons, the amount of a liability in relation to all or any one of them, that arises or might arise from such failure), and

(c) that the information —

(i) which is likely to be contained in the books, records or other documents to which the application relates, or

(ii) which is likely to arise from the information, explanations and particulars to which the application relates,

is relevant to the proper assessment or collection of tax.

(4) Without prejudice to the generality of subsection (2), the authorised officer may make an application under that subsection to the judge for an order in respect of the matters referred to in paragraphs (a) and (b) of that subsection in so far as they relate to a person who is connected with the taxpayer.

(5) Where the judge, to whom an application is made under subsection (2), is satisfied that there are reasonable grounds for the application being made, the judge may, subject to such conditions as he or she may consider proper and specify in the order, make an order requiring the financial institution —

(a) to make available for inspection by the authorised officer, such books, records or other documents, and

(b) to furnish to the authorised officer such information, explanations and particulars,

as may be specified in the order.

(6) The persons who may be treated as a taxpayer for the purposes of this section include a company which has been dissolved and an individual who has died.

(7) Every hearing of an application for an order under this section and of any appeal in connection with that application shall be held in camera.

(8) Where a judge makes an order under this section, he or she may also, on the application of the authorised officer concerned, make a further order prohibiting, for such period as the judge may consider proper and specify in the order, any transfer of, or any dealing with, without the consent of the judge, any assets or moneys of the person to whom the order relates that are in the custody of the financial institution at the time the order is made.

(9) (a) Where —

    (i) a copy of any affidavit and exhibits grounding an application under subsection (2) or (8) and any order made under subsection (5) or (8) are to be made available to the taxpayer, or the taxpayer's solicitor or to the financial institution or the financial institution's solicitor, as the case may be, and

    (ii) the judge is satisfied on the hearing of the application that there are reasonable grounds in the public interest that such copy of an affidavit, exhibits or order, as the case may be, should not include the name or address of the authorised officer,

such copy, or copies or order shall not include the name or address of the authorised officer.

(b) Where, on any application to the judge to vary or discharge an order made under this section, it is desired to cross-examine the deponent of any affidavit filed by or on behalf of the authorised officer and the judge is satisfied that there are reasonable grounds in the public interest to so order, the judge shall order either or both of the following —

    (i) that the name and address of the authorised officer shall not be disclosed in court,

    and

    (ii) that such cross-examination shall only take place in the sight and hearing of the judge and in the hearing only of all other persons present at such cross-examination.",

(j) by the insertion after section 908 of the following section:

"Revenue offence: power to obtain information from financial institutions.
908A.(1) In this section —

> 'authorised officer' means an officer of the Revenue Commissioners authorised by them in writing to exercise the powers conferred by this section;

> 'books, records or other documents' includes —

>> (a) any records used in the business of a financial institution, or used in the transfer department of a financial institution acting as registrar of securities, whether —

>>> (i) comprised in bound volume, loose-leaf binders or other loose-leaf filing system, loose-leaf ledger sheets, pages, folios or cards, or

>>> (ii) kept on microfilm, magnetic tape or in any non-legible form (by the use of electronics or otherwise) which is capable of being reproduced in a legible form, and

>> (b) documents in manuscript, documents which are typed, printed, stencilled or created by any other mechanical or partly mechanical process in use from time to time and documents which are produced by any photographic or photostatic process;

> 'judge' means a judge of the Circuit Court or of the District Court;

> 'financial institution' means —

>> (a) a person who holds or has held a licence under section 9 of the Central Bank Act, 1971, and

>> (b) a person referred to in section 7(4) of that Act;

> 'liability' in relation to a person means any liability in relation to tax to which the person is or may be, or may have been, subject, or the amount of such liability;

> 'offence' means an offence falling within section 1078(2);

> 'tax' means any tax, duty, levy or charge under the care and management of the Revenue Commissioners.

> (2) If, on application made by an authorised officer, with the consent in writing of a Revenue Commissioner, a judge is satisfied, on information given on oath by the authorised officer, that there are reasonable grounds for suspecting —

>> (a) that an offence which would result in serious prejudice to the proper assessment or collection of tax is being, has been or is about to be committed (having regard to the amount of a liability in relation to any person which might be evaded but for the detection of the offence), and

>> (b) that there is material in the possession of a financial institution specified in the application which is likely to be of substantial

(c)   the Capital Gains Tax Acts,

(d)   the Value-Added Tax Act, 1972, and the enactments amending or extending that Act,

(e)   the Capital Acquisitions Tax Act, 1976, and the enactments amending or extending that Act, and

(f)   the Stamp Act, 1891, and the enactments amending or extending that Act,

and any instruments made under any of the statutes and enactments referred to in paragraphs (a) to (f);

'approved person' shall be construed in accordance with section 917G;

'approved transmission' shall be construed in accordance with section 917H;

'authorised person' has the meaning assigned to it by section 917G(3)(b);

'digital signature' has the meaning assigned to it by section 917I;

'hard copy', in relation to information held electronically, means a printed out version of that information;

'return' means any return which is required –

(a)   to be made under section 172F, 172K, 172L, 258 or 525,

(b)   to be prepared and delivered under section 894, 895, 895 (as modified by section 896) or 951,

(c)   by any provision of the Acts (however expressed), to be prepared and delivered under a notice from the Revenue Commissioners or, as the case may be, a revenue officer requiring such a return to be prepared and delivered,

(d)   to be sent under Regulation 35 of the Income Tax (Employments) Regulations, 1960 (S.I. No. 28 of 1960),

(e)   to be sent under Regulation 21 of the Income Tax (Construction Contracts) Regulations, 1971 (S.I. No. 7 of 1971),

(f)   to be furnished under section 19 of the Value-Added Tax Act, 1972,

(g)   to be delivered under subsection (2) or (9) of section 36 of the Capital Acquisitions Tax Act, 1976,

(h)   to be delivered under section 36(8) of the Capital Acquisitions Tax Act, 1976,

(i)   to be presented under the Stamp Act, 1891, and the enactments amending or extending that Act, and

(j)   to be made under any of the statutes relating to the duties of excise and to the management of those duties;

'revenue officer' means the Collector-General, an inspector or other officer of the Revenue Commissioners (including an inspector or other officer who is authorised under any provision of the Acts (however expressed) to receive a return or to require a return to be prepared and delivered);

'tax' means any income tax, corporation tax, capital gains tax, value-added tax, gift tax, inheritance tax, excise duty or stamp duty.

(2) Any references in this Chapter to a return include references in any provision of the Acts to a statement, particulars, evidence or any other means whereby information is required or given, however expressed.

(3) Any references in this Chapter to the making of a return include references in any provision of the Acts to —

    (a) the preparing and delivering of a return;

    (b) the sending of a return;

    (c) the furnishing of a return or of particulars;

    (d) the delivering of a return;

    (e) the presentation of a return;

    (f) the rendering of a return;

    (g) the giving of particulars or of any information specified in any provision; and

    (h) any other means whereby a return is forwarded, however expressed.

Application.
917E. This Chapter shall apply to a return if —

    (a) the provision of the Acts under which the return is made is specified for the purpose of this Chapter by order made by the Revenue Commissioners, and

    (b) the return is required to be made after the day appointed by such order in relation to returns to be made under the provision so specified.

Electronic transmission of returns.
917F. (1) Notwithstanding any other provision of the Acts, the obligation of any person to make a return to which this Chapter applies shall be treated as fulfilled by that person if information is transmitted electronically in compliance with that obligation, but only if —

    (a) the transmission is made by an approved person or an authorised person,

    (b) the transmission is an approved transmission,

    (c) the transmission bears the approved person's digital signature or such other means of electronic identification as may be specified or authorised by the Revenue Commissioners, and

    (d)   the receipt of the transmission is acknowledged in accordance with section 917J.

(2) In subsection (1), the reference to the information which is required to be included in the return includes any requirement on a person to—

    (a)   make any statement,

    (b)   include any particulars, or

    (c)   make or attach any claim.

(3) Where the obligation of any person to make a return to which this Chapter applies is treated as fulfilled in accordance with subsection (1) then, any provision of the Acts which—

    (a)   requires that the return include or be accompanied by any description of declaration whatever by the person making the return, apart from a declaration of an amount,

    (b)   requires that the return be signed or accompanied by a certificate,

    (c)   requires that the return be in writing,

    (d)   authorises the return to be signed by a person acting under the authority of the person obliged to make the return,

    (e)   authorises the Revenue Commissioners to prescribe the form of a return or which requires a return to be in or on any prescribed form, or

    (f)   for the purposes of any claim for exemption or for any allowance, deduction or repayment of tax under the Acts which is required to be made with the return, authorises the Revenue Commissioners to prescribe the form of a claim,

shall not apply.

(4) Where the obligation of any person to make a return to which this Chapter applies is treated as fulfilled in accordance with subsection (1) then, the time at which any requirement under the Acts to make a return is fulfilled shall be the day on which the receipt of the information referred to in that subsection is acknowledged in accordance with section 917J.

(5) Where the obligation of any person to make a return to which this Chapter applies is treated as fulfilled in accordance with subsection (1), then, in a case where the transmission is made by—

    (a)   an approved person on behalf of another person, or

    (b)   an authorised person on behalf of another person (not being the person who authorised that authorised person),

a hard copy of the information to be transmitted shall be made and authenticated in accordance with section 917K.

(6) (a) Where the obligation of any person to make a return to which this Chapter applies is treated as fulfilled in accordance with subsection (1) then, any requirement that—

(i) the return or any claim which is to be made with or attached to the return should be accompanied by any document (in this subsection referred to as a 'supporting document') other than the return or the claim, and

(ii) the supporting document be delivered with the return or the claim,

shall be treated as fulfilled by the person subject to the requirement if the person or the approved person referred to in subsection (1)(a) retains the document for inspection on request by a revenue officer.

(b) Any person subject to the requirement referred to in paragraph (a) shall produce any supporting documents requested by a revenue officer within 30 days of that request.

(c) The references in this subsection to a document include references to any accounts, certificate, evidence, receipts, reports or statements.

Approved persons.

917G.(1) A person shall be an approved person for the purposes of this Chapter if the person is approved by the Revenue Commissioners for the purposes of transmitting electronically information which is required to be included in a return to which this Chapter applies (in this section referred to as 'the transmission') and complies with the provisions of this section and, in particular, with the conditions specified in subsection (3).

(2) A person seeking to be approved under this section shall make application in that behalf to the Revenue Commissioners in writing or by such other means as may be approved of by the Revenue Commissioners for the purposes of this section.

(3) The conditions referred to in subsection (1) are that—

(a) the applicant for approval under this section signs an undertaking to comply with the requirements referred to in section 917H(2), and

(b) the applicant signs an undertaking to permit, in addition to the applicant, only individuals duly authorised in writing by the applicant (each of whom is referred to in this section as an 'authorised person') to make a transmission.

(4) A person seeking to be approved under this section shall be given notice by the Revenue Commissioners of the grant or refusal by them of the approval and, in the case of a refusal, of the reason for the refusal.

(5) An approval under this section may be withdrawn by the Revenue Commissioners by notice in writing or by such other means as the

Revenue Commissioners may decide with effect from such date as may be specified in the notice.

(6) (a) A notice withdrawing an approval under the section shall state the grounds for the withdrawal.

(b) No approval under this section may be withdrawn unless an approved person or an authorised person has failed to comply with one or more of the requirements referred to in section 917H(2).

(7) A person who is refused approval under this section or whose approval under this section is withdrawn may appeal to the Appeal Commissioners against the refusal or withdrawal.

(8) The appeal under subsection (7) shall be made by notice to the Revenue Commissioners before the end of the period of 30 days beginning with the day on which notice of the refusal or withdrawal was given to the person.

(9) The Appeal Commissioners shall hear and determine an appeal made to them under subsection (7) as if it were an appeal against an assessment to income tax, and the provisions of the Tax Acts relating to appeals shall apply accordingly.

Approved transmissions.

917H. (1) Where an approved person transmits electronically information which is required to be included in a return to which this Chapter applies the transmission shall not be an approved transmission unless it complies with the requirements of this section.

(2) The Revenue Commissioners shall notify an approved person of any requirements for the time being determined by them as being applicable to that person with respect to the manner in which information which is required to be included in a return to which this Chapter applies is to be transmitted electronically.

(3) The requirements referred to in subsection (2) include, in particular, requirements as to the software or type of software to be used to make a transmission.

Digital signatures.

917I. (1) In this section—

'asymmetric cryptosystem' means an algorithm or series of algorithms which provide a secure key pair;

'digital signature' means the transformation of a message by an approved person or an authorised person using an approved asymmetric cryptosystem such that the Revenue Commissioners having possession of the message and the public key in respect of that approved person can accurately determine—

(a) whether the transformation was created using the private key which corresponds to that public key, and

(b) whether the message has been altered since the transformation was made;

'key pair' means a private key and its corresponding public key in an asymmetric cryptosystem such that the public key verifies a digital signature that the private key creates;

'private key' means the key of a key pair used by an approved person to create a digital signature;

'public key' means the key of a key pair used by the Revenue Commissioners to verify a digital signature;

'message' means the information referred to in section 917F(1).

(2) This section shall apply solely for the purposes of affixing an electronic signature to an electronic transmission of information which is required to be included in a return to which this Chapter applies and for no other purpose.

(3) The Revenue Commissioners, or a person or persons appointed in that behalf by the Revenue Commissioners, (in this section referred to as the 'certification authority') shall assign to each approved person a unique key pair.

(4) The certification authority shall ensure that it uses an accurate and reliable system to create a key pair.

(5) The certification authority shall ensure that an approved person is issued with the private key component of that person's key pair in a secure manner and subject to such conditions as it considers necessary to ensure that the key is not misused.

(6) A private key shall be used by an approved person or an authorised person solely for the purposes of affixing the digital signature referred to in section 917F(1)(c).

Acknowledgement of electronic transmissions.

917J. For the purposes of this Chapter, where an electronic transmission of information which is required to be included in a return to which this Chapter applies is received by the Revenue Commissioners, the Revenue Commissioners shall send an electronic acknowledgement of receipt of that transmission to the person from whom it was received.

Hard copies.

917K.(1) A hard copy shall be made in accordance with this subsection only if –

(a) the hard copy is made under processes and procedures which are designed to ensure that the information contained in the hard copy shall only be the information to be transmitted in accordance with section 917F(1),

(b) the hard copy is in a form approved by the Revenue Commissioners which is appropriate to the information so transmitted, and

(c) the hard copy is authenticated in accordance with subsection (2).

(2) For the purposes of this Chapter, a hard copy made in accordance with subsection (1) shall be authenticated only if the hard copy is

FINANCE ACT, 2000

Number 3 of 2000
(Enacted on 23rd March, 2000)

PART I
Income Tax, Corporation Tax and Capital Gains Tax

CHAPTER 4
Income Tax, Corporation Tax and Capital Gains Tax

Section 68

Amendment of Chapter 4 (revenue powers) of Part 38 of [the Taxes Consolidation Act, 1997].

68. [The Taxes Consolidation Act, 1997,] is amended in Chapter 4 of Part 38 –

    (a) .....

    (c) in sections 906A(1) and 908A(1), by the substitution for the definition of "financial institution" of the following:

        " 'financial institution' means –

            (a) a person who holds or has held a licence under section 9 of the Central Bank Act, 1971,

            (b) a person referred to in section 7(4) of the Central Bank Act, 1971, or

            (c) a credit institution (within the meaning of the European Communities (Licensing and Supervision of Credit Institutions) Regulations, 1992 (S.I. No. 395 of 1992)) which has been authorised by the Central Bank of Ireland to carry on business of a credit institution in accordance with the provisions of the supervisory enactments (within the meaning of those Regulations);",

    and

    (d) in section 908A by the substitution for subsection (2) of the following:

        "(2) (a) In this subsection 'documentation' includes information kept on microfilm, magnetic tape or in any non-legible form (by use of electronics or otherwise) which is capable of being reproduced in a permanent legible form.

            (b) If, on application made by an authorised officer, with the consent in writing of a Revenue Commissioner, a judge is satisfied, on information given on oath by the authorised officer, that there are reasonable grounds for suspecting—

(i) that an offence which would result in serious prejudice to the proper assessment or collection of tax is being, has been or is about to be committed (having regard to the amount of a liability in relation to any person which might be evaded but for the detection of the relevant facts), and

(ii) that there is material in the possession of a financial institution specified in the application which is likely to be of substantial value (whether by itself or together with other material) to the investigation of the relevant facts,

the judge may make an order authorising the authorised officer to inspect and take copies of any entries in the books, records or other documents of the financial institution, or of any documentation associated with or relating to an entry in such books, records or other documents, for the purposes of investigation of the relevant facts.".

PART 6
Capital Acquisitions Tax

Section 136

Interpretation (Part 6).

136. In this Part "Principal Act" means the Capital Acquisitions Tax Act, 1976.

Section 137

Amendment of section 2 (interpretation) of [the Capital Acquisitions Tax Act, 1976].

137. (1) Section 2 of [the Capital Acquisitions Tax Act, 1976,] is amended by the insertion after subsection (5) of the following subsection:

"(5A) For the purposes of this Act—

(a) a reference to a person being resident in the State on a particular date shall be construed as a reference to that person being resident in the State in the year of assessment in which that date falls (but, for those purposes, the provisions of Part 34 of the Taxes Consolidation Act, 1997, relating to residence of individuals shall not be construed as requiring a year of assessment to have elapsed before a determination of whether or not a person is resident in the State on a date falling in that year may be made), and

(b) a reference to a person being ordinarily resident in the State on a particular date shall be construed as a reference to that person being ordinarily resident in the State in the year of assessment in which that date falls.".

(2) This section shall have effect in relation to gifts or inheritances taken on or after 1 December 1999.

Section 138

Amendment of section 6 (taxable gift) of [the Capital Acquisitions Tax Act, 1976].

138. (1) Section 6 of [the Capital Acquisitions Tax Act, 1976,] is amended by –

(a) the substitution of the following subsection for subsection (1):

"(1) In this Act 'taxable gift' means –

(a) in the case of a gift, other than a gift taken under a discretionary trust, where the disponer is resident or ordinarily resident in the State at the date of the disposition under which the donee takes the gift, the whole of the gift;

(b) in the case of a gift taken under a discretionary trust where the disponer is resident or ordinarily resident in the State at the date of the disposition under which the donee takes the gift or at the date of the gift or was (in the case of a gift taken after the death of the disponer) so resident or ordinarily resident at the date of that death, the whole of the gift;

(c) in the case where the donee is resident or ordinarily resident in the State at the date of the gift, the whole of the gift; and

(d) in any other case, so much of the property of which the gift consists as is situate in the State at the date of the gift.",

(b) the substitution of the following subsections for subsection (3):

"(3) For the purposes of subsection (1), a person who is not domiciled in the State on a particular date shall be treated as not resident and not ordinarily resident in the State on that date unless –

   (a)   that date occurs on or after 1 December 2004,

   (b)   that person has been resident in the State for the 5 consecutive years of assessment immediately preceding the year of assessment in which that date falls, and

   (c)   that person is either resident or ordinarily resident in the State on that date.

(4) (a) In this subsection—

'company' means a private company within the meaning assigned to it by section 16 (2);

'company controlled by the donee' has the same meaning as is assigned to 'company controlled by the donee or successor' by section 16(3);

'share' has the meaning assigned to it by section 16(2).

  (b) For the purposes of subsection (1)(d), a proportion of the market value of any share in a private company incorporated outside the State which (after the taking of the gift) is a company controlled by the donee shall be deemed to be a sum situate in the State and shall be the amount determined by the following formula—

$$A \times \frac{B}{C}$$

where—

A   is the market value of that share at the date of the gift ascertained under section 16,

B   is the market value of all property in the beneficial ownership of that company which is situate in the State at the date of the gift, and

C   is the total market value of all property in the beneficial ownership of that company at the date of the gift.

  (c) Paragraph (b) shall not apply in a case where the disponer was domiciled outside the State at all times up to and including the date of the gift or, in the case of a gift taken after the death of the disponer, up to and including the date of that death or where the share in question is actually situate in the State at the date of the gift.''.

(2) Subject to subsection (3), this section shall have effect in relation to gifts taken on or after 1 December 1999.

(3) Notwithstanding subsection (2), this section shall not have effect in relation to a gift taken under a disposition where the date of the disposition is before 1 December 1999.

Section 139

Amendment of section 12 (taxable inheritance) of [the Capital Acquisitions Tax Act, 1976].

139. (1) Section 12 of [the Capital Acquisitions Tax Act, 1976,] is amended by —

    (a) the substitution of the following subsection for subsection (1):

        ''(1) In this Act, 'taxable inheritance' means —

            (a) in the case where the disponer is resident or ordinarily resident in the State at the date of the disposition under which the successor takes the inheritance, the whole of the inheritance;

            (b) in the case where the successor (not being a successor in relation to a charge for tax arising by virtue of section 106 of the Finance Act, 1984, section 103 of the Finance Act, 1986, or section 110 of the Finance Act, 1993) is resident or ordinarily resident in the State at the date of the inheritance, the whole of the inheritance; and

            (c) in any case, other than a case referred to in paragraph (a) or (b), where at the date of the inheritance —

                (i) the whole of the property —

                    (I) which was to be appropriated to the inheritance; or

                    (II) out of which property was to be appropriated to the inheritance,

                  was situate in the State, the whole of the inheritance;

                (ii) a part or proportion of the property —

                    (I) which was to be appropriated to the inheritance; or

                    (II) out of which property was to be appropriated to the inheritance,

                  was situate in the State, that part or proportion of the inheritance.'',

    (b) in subsection (2), by the substitution of ''subsection (1)(c)'' for ''subsection (1)(b)'',

    (c)   the insertion of the following subsections after subsection (2):

"(3) For the purposes of subsection (1), a person who is not domiciled in the State on a particular date shall be treated as not resident and not ordinarily resident in the State on that date unless —

    (a)   that date occurs on or after 1 December 2004,

    (b)   that person has been resident in the State for the 5 consecutive years of assessment immediately preceding the year of assessment in which that date falls, and

    (c)   that person is either resident or ordinarily resident in the State on that date.

(4)   (a) In this subsection —

    'company' means a private company within the meaning of section 16(2);

    'company controlled by the successor' has the same meaning as is assigned to 'company controlled by the donee or successor' by section 16(3);

    'share' has the meaning assigned to it by section 16(2).

    (b) For the purposes of subsection (1)(b), a proportion of the market value of any share in a private company incorporated outside the State which (after the taking of the inheritance) is a company controlled by the successor shall be deemed to be a sum situate in the State and shall be the amount determined by the following formula —

$$A \times \frac{B}{C}$$

where —

    A   is the market value of that share at the date of the inheritance ascertained under section 16,

    B   is the market value of all property in the beneficial ownership of that company which is situate in the State at the date of the inheritance, and

    C   is the total market value of all property in the beneficial ownership of that company at the date of the inheritance.

    (c) Paragraph (b) shall not apply in a case where the disponer was not domiciled in the State at the date of the disposition under which the successor takes the inheritance or where the share in question is actually situate in the State at the date of the inheritance.".

(2) Subject to subsection (3), this section shall have effect in relation to inheritances taken on or after 1 December 1999.

(3) Notwithstanding subsection (2), this section shall not have effect in relation to an inheritance taken under a disposition where the date of the disposition is before 1 December 1999.

Section 140

Amendment of section 19 (value of agricultural property) of [the Capital Acquisitions Tax Act, 1976].

140. (1) Section 19 of [the Capital Acquisitions Tax Act, 1976,] is amended—

    (a) by the substitution of the following definition for the definition of "farmer" in subsection (1):

    "'farmer', in relation to a donee or successor, means an individual who is domiciled in the State and in respect of whom not less than 80 per cent of the market value of the property to which the individual is beneficially entitled in possession is represented by the market value of property in the State which consists of agricultural property, and, for the purposes of this definition—

    (a) no deduction shall be made from the market value of property for any debts or encumbrances,

    and

    (b) an individual shall be deemed to be beneficially entitled in possession to—

    (i) an interest in expectancy, notwithstanding the definition of 'entitled in possession' in section 2, and

    (ii) property which is subject to a discretionary trust under or in consequence of a disposition made by the individual where the individual is an object of the trust.".

    (b) in subsection (5), by the substitution of the following paragraph for paragraph (a):

    "(a) The agricultural value shall cease to be applicable to agricultural property, other than crops, trees or underwood, if and to the extent that such property, or any agricultural property which directly or indirectly replaces such property—

(i)   is sold or compulsorily acquired within the period of 6 years after the date of the gift or the date of the inheritance; and

(ii) is not replaced, within a year of the sale or compulsory acquisition, by other agricultural property,

and tax shall be chargeable in respect of the gift or inheritance as if the property were not agricultural property:

Provided that this paragraph shall not have effect where the donee or successor dies before the property is sold or compulsorily acquired.".

(2) Paragraph (a) of subsection (1) shall have effect in relation to gifts or inheritances taken on or after 10 February 2000, and paragraph (b) of subsection (1) shall have effect where the sale or compulsory acquisition which causes the agricultural value to cease to be applicable occurs on or after 10 February 2000.

Section 141

Amendment of section 36 (delivery of returns) of [the Capital Acquisitions Tax Act, 1976].

141. (1) Section 36 of [the Capital Acquisitions Tax Act, 1976,] is amended —

(a) by the substitution of the following subsection for subsection (4):

"(4) Subsection (2) applies to a charge for tax arising by reason of the provisions of section 106 of the Finance Act, 1984, and to any other gift where —

(a) the aggregate of the taxable values of all taxable gifts taken by the donee on or after 2 December 1988, which have the same group threshold (as defined in the Second Schedule) as that other gift, exceeds an amount which is 80 per cent of the threshold amount (as defined in the Second Schedule) which applies in the computation of tax on that aggregate; or

(b) the donee or, in a case to which section 23 (1) applies, the transferee (within the meaning of, and to the extent provided for by, that section) is required by notice in writing by the Commissioners to deliver a return,

and for the purposes of this subsection, a reference to a gift includes a reference to a part of a gift or to a part of a taxable gift, as the case may be.",

  (b) by the substitution of the following paragraph for paragraph (a) of subsection (14):

    "(a) the taxable value of the taxable gift exceeds an amount which is 80 per cent of the group threshold (as defined in the Second Schedule) which applies in relation to that gift for the purposes of the computation of the tax on that gift.".

 (2) This section shall have effect in relation to gifts or inheritances taken on or after 1 December 1999.

Section 142

Amendment of section 48 (receipts and certificates) of [the Capital Acquisitions Tax Act, 1976].

142. Section 48 of [the Capital Acquisitions Tax Act, 1976,] is amended by —

  (a) the substitution of the following subsections for subsections (3), (4) and (5):

    "(3) The Commissioners shall, on application to them by a person who is an accountable person in respect of any of the property of which a taxable gift or taxable inheritance consists, if they are satisfied that the tax charged on the property in respect of the taxable gift or taxable inheritance has been or will be paid, or that there is no tax so charged, give a certificate to the person, in such form as they think fit, to that effect.

    (3A) Where a person who is an accountable person in respect of the property of which a taxable gift or taxable inheritance consists has —

      (a) delivered to the Commissioners, a full and true return of all the property comprised in the gift or inheritance on the valuation date and such particulars as may be relevant to the assessment of tax in respect of the gift or inheritance,

      (b) made on that return an assessment of such amount of tax as, to the best of that person's knowledge, information and belief, ought to be charged, levied and paid, and

      (c) duly paid the amount of such tax (if any),

    the Commissioners may give a certificate to the person, in such form as they think fit, to the effect that the tax charged on the property in respect of the taxable gift or taxable inheritance has been paid or that there is no tax so charged.

    (4) A certificate referred to in subsection (3) or (3A) shall discharge the property from liability for tax (if any) in respect of the gift or inheritance, to the extent specified in the certificate, but shall not discharge the property from tax in case of fraud or failure to disclose material facts and, in any case, shall not affect the

tax payable in respect of any other property or the extent to which tax is recoverable from any accountable person or from the personal representatives of any accountable person:

Provided that a certificate purporting to be a discharge of the whole tax payable in respect of any property included in the certificate in respect of a gift or inheritance shall exonerate from liability for such tax a bona fide purchaser or mortgagee for full consideration in money or money's worth without notice of such fraud or failure and a person deriving title from or under such a purchaser or mortgagee.

(5) Subject to the provisions of subsection (6), where tax is chargeable on the taxable value of a taxable gift or taxable inheritance and—

    (a) application is made to the Commissioners by any person (in this section referred to as 'the applicant')—

        (i) who is a person accountable, but not primarily accountable, for the payment of the whole or part of the tax, or

        (ii) who is the personal representative of any person referred to in subparagraph (i),

    and

    (b) the applicant—

        (i) delivers to the Commissioners a full and true return of all the property comprised in the gift or inheritance and such particulars as may be relevant to the assessment of tax in respect of the gift or inheritance, and

        (ii) makes on that return an assessment of such amount of tax as, to the best of that person's knowledge, information and belief, ought to be charged, levied and paid,

    the Commissioners may, upon payment of the tax assessed by the applicant, give a certificate to the applicant which shall discharge the applicant from any other claim for tax in respect of the gift or inheritance.",

and

(b) the deletion of subsection (7).

Section 143

Amendment of section 54 (provisions relating to charities, etc.) of [the Capital Acquisitions Tax Act, 1976].

143. (1) Section 54 of [the Capital Acquisitions Tax Act, 1976,] is amended by the substitution of the following subsection for subsection (1):

"(1) Where any person takes a benefit for public or charitable purposes that person shall be deemed –

(a) for the purposes of sections 5(1) and 11(1), to have taken that benefit beneficially, and

(b) for the purposes of the Second Schedule, to have taken a gift or an inheritance accordingly to which the group threshold of £15,000 applies.".

(2) This section shall have effect in relation to gifts or inheritances taken on or after 1 December 1999.

Section 144

Amendment of section 55 (exemption of certain objects) of [the Capital Acquisitions Tax Act, 1976].

144. (1) Section 55 of [the Capital Acquisitions Tax Act, 1976,] is amended by the substitution of the following subsection for subsection (4):

"(4) The exemption referred to in subsection (2) shall cease to apply to an object, if at any time after the valuation date and –

(a) before the sale of the object,

(b) before the death of the donee or successor, and

(c) before such object again forms part of the property comprised in a gift or an inheritance (other than an inheritance arising by virtue of section 103 of the Finance Act, 1986) in respect of which gift or inheritance an absolute interest is taken by a person other than the spouse of that donee or successor,

there has been a breach of any condition specified in paragraph (b) or (c) of subsection (1).".

(2) This section shall have effect in relation to gifts or inheritances taken on or after 10 February 2000.

Section 145

Amendment of Second Schedule to [the Capital Acquisitions Tax Act, 1976].

145. (1) The Second Schedule to [the Capital Acquisitions Tax Act, 1976,] is amended –

(a) in Part I, by the substitution of the following paragraphs for paragraphs 1 to 7:

"1. In this Schedule –

'group threshold', in relation to a taxable gift or a taxable inheritance taken on a particular day, means –

(a)   £300,000, where—

   (i)   the donee or successor is on that day the child, or minor child of a deceased child, of the disponer, or

   (ii) the successor is on that day a parent of the disponer and—

      (I) the interest taken is not a limited interest, and

      (II) the inheritance is taken on the death of the disponer;

(b)   £30,000, where the donee or successor is on that day, a lineal ancestor, a lineal descendant (other than a child, or a minor child of a deceased child), a brother, a sister, or a child of a brother or of a sister of the disponer;

(c)   £15,000, where the donee or successor (who is not a spouse of the disponer) does not, on that day, stand to the disponer in a relationship referred to in subparagraph (a) or (b);

'the consumer price index number', in relation to a year, means the All Items Consumer Price Index Number for that year as compiled by the Central Statistics Office and expressed on the basis that the consumer price index number at mid-November 1996 is 100;

'Table' means the Table contained in Part II of this Schedule;

'threshold amount' in relation to the computation of tax on any aggregate of taxable values under paragraph 3, means the group threshold that applies in relation to all of the taxable gifts and taxable inheritances included in that aggregate but, in computing under this Schedule the tax chargeable on a taxable gift or taxable inheritance taken after 31 December 2000, that group threshold shall, for the purposes of this definition, be multiplied by the figure, rounded to the nearest third decimal place, determined by dividing by 104.8 the consumer price index number for the year immediately preceding the year in which that taxable gift or taxable inheritance is taken.

2.   In the Table 'Value' means the appropriate aggregate referred to in paragraph 3.

3.   The tax chargeable on the taxable value of a taxable gift or a taxable inheritance (hereafter in this Schedule referred to as the first mentioned gift or inheritance) taken by a

donee or successor shall be of an amount equal to the amount by which the tax computed on aggregate A exceeds the tax computed on aggregate B, where—

(a) aggregate A is the aggregate of the following:

(i) the taxable value of the first-mentioned gift or inheritance, and

(ii) the taxable value of each and every taxable gift and taxable inheritance taken previously by the said donee or successor on or after 2 December 1988, which has the same group threshold as the first-mentioned gift or inheritance,

(b) aggregate B is the aggregate of the taxable values of all such taxable gifts and taxable inheritances so previously taken which have the same group threshold as the first-mentioned gift or inheritance, and

(c) the tax on an aggregate is computed at the rate or rates of tax applicable under the Table to that aggregate:

Provided that—

(i) in a case where no such taxable gift or taxable inheritance was so previously taken, the amount of the tax computed on aggregate B shall be deemed to be nil,

and

(ii) the amount of an aggregate that comprises only a single taxable value shall be equal to that value.

4. In the Table any rate of tax shown in the second column is that applicable to such portion of the value (within the meaning of paragraph 2) as is shown in the first column.

5. For the purposes of this Schedule, all gifts and inheritances which have the same group threshold and which are taken by a donee or successor on the same day shall count as one, and to ascertain the amount of tax payable on one such gift or inheritance of several so taken on the same day, the amount of tax computed under this Schedule as being payable on the total of such gifts and inheritances so taken on that day shall be apportioned rateably, according to the taxable values of the several taxable gifts and taxable inheritances so taken on that day.".

(b) by the substitution of the following Part for Part II:

"PART II

TABLE

Portion of Value	Rate of tax
	Per cent
The threshold amount	Nil
The balance	20

".

(2) This section shall have effect in relation to gifts or inheritances taken on or after 1 December 1999.

Section 146

Amendment of section 39 (extension of section 55 (exemption of certain objects) of Capital Acquisitions Tax Act, 1976) of Finance Act, 1978.

146. (1) As respects the year 2001 and subsequent years, section 39 of the Finance Act, 1978, is amended in subsection (1A)(b) by the insertion in subparagraph (i) after "September" of "of which not less than 10 of the days during that period shall fall on a Saturday or a Sunday or both".

(2) This section shall apply to gifts and inheritances taken on or after 10 February 2000.

Section 147

Amendment of section 109 (interpretation) of Finance Act, 1993.

147. (1) Section 109 of the Finance Act, 1993, is amended –

(a) by the substitution in the definition of "the consumer price index number" of "mid-November 1996" for "mid-November, 1989", and

(b) by the substitution of the following definition for the definition of "relevant threshold":

" 'relevant threshold' means –

(a) £40,000, where the death of the deceased occurred on or before 31 December 2000, and

(b) in any other case, £40,000 multiplied by the figure, rounded up to the nearest third decimal place, determined by dividing by 104.8 the consumer price index number for the year immediately preceding the year in which the death of the deceased occurred;".

(2) This section shall apply and have effect in relation to persons dying on or after 1 December 1999.

Section 148

Amendment of Chapter 1 (business relief) of Part VI of Finance Act, 1994.

148. (1) Part VI of the Finance Act, 1994, is amended in Chapter 1—

> (a) in section 134, by the substitution of the following subsections for subsections (1) and (2):
>
> > "(1) In determining for the purposes of this Chapter what part of the taxable value of a gift or inheritance is attributable to the value of relevant business property, so much of the last-mentioned value as is attributable to—
> >
> > (a) any excepted assets within the meaning of subsection (2), or
> >
> > (b) any excluded property within the meaning of subsection (7),
> >
> > shall be left out of account.
> >
> > (2) An asset shall be an excepted asset in relation to any relevant business property if it was not used wholly or mainly for the purposes of the business concerned throughout the whole or the last two years of the relevant period, but where the business concerned is carried on by a company which is a member of a group, the use of an asset for the purposes of a business carried on by another company which at the time of the use and immediately prior to the gift or inheritance was also a member of that group shall be treated as use for the purposes of the business concerned, unless that other company's membership of the group falls to be disregarded under section 133:
> >
> > Provided that the use of an asset for the purposes of a business to which section 127(4) relates shall not be treated as use for the purposes of the business concerned.",
>
> (b) in section 135—
>
> > (i) by the substitution of the following subsection for subsection (1):
> >
> > > "(1) In this section 'relevant period', in relation to relevant business property comprised in a gift or inheritance, means the period of 6 years commencing on the date of the gift or inheritance.",
> >
> > and
> >
> > (ii) by the substitution of the following paragraph for paragraphs (ii) and (iii) of the proviso (inserted by the Finance Act, 1996) to subsection (2):
> >
> > > "(ii) this section shall not have effect where the donee or successor dies before the event which would

otherwise cause the reduction to cease to be applicable.'',

and

(c)   by the insertion of the following section after section 135:

''Avoidance of double relief

135A. Where the whole or part of the taxable value of any taxable gift or taxable inheritance is attributable to agricultural property to which subsection (2) of section 19 of [the Capital Acquisitions Tax Act, 1976,] applies, such whole or part of the taxable value shall not be reduced under this Chapter.''.

(2)   Paragraphs (a) and (c) of subsection (1) shall have effect in relation to gifts or inheritances taken on or after 10 February 2000 and paragraph (b) of subsection (1) shall have effect where the event which causes the reduction to cease to be applicable occurs on or after 10 February 2000.

Section 149

Amendment of section 142 (exemption of certain transfers from capital acquisitions tax following the dissolution of a marriage) of Finance Act, 1997.

149.   (1)   Section 142 of the Finance Act, 1997, is amended in subsection (2):

(a)   by the deletion of ''and'' in paragraph (c),

(b)   by the substitution in paragraph (d) of ''1996, and'' for ''1996.'', and

(c)   by the insertion of the following paragraph after paragraph (d):

''(e)   to an order or other determination to like effect, which is analogous to an order referred to in paragraph (a), (b), (c) or (d), of a court under the law of another territory made under or in consequence of the dissolution of a marriage, being a dissolution that is entitled to be recognised as valid in the State.''.

(2)   This section shall apply to an order or other determination to like effect where the order or the determination is made on or after 10 February 2000.

Section 150

Amendment of section 143 (abatement and postponement of probate tax on certain property) of Finance Act, 1997.

150.   (1)   Section 143 of the Finance Act, 1997, is amended in subsection (1):

(a)   by the deletion in subparagraph (i) of paragraph (a) of ''or'',

(b) by the substitution in subparagraph (ii) of paragraph (a) of "1996, or" for "1996,", and

(c) by the insertion of the following subparagraph after subparagraph (ii):

"(iii) to an order or other determination to like effect, which is analogous to an order referred to in subparagraph (i) or (ii), of a court under the law of another territory made under or in consequence of the dissolution of a marriage, being a dissolution that is entitled to be recognised as valid in the State.".

(2) This section shall apply to an order or other determination to like effect where the order or the determination is made on or after 10 February 2000.

Section 151

Exemption relating to certain dwellings.

151. (1) [The Capital Acquisitions Tax Act, 1976,] is amended by the insertion of the following section after section 59B:

"59C.(1) In this section—

'dwelling-house' means—

(a) a building or part (including an appropriate part within the meaning of subsection (5) of section 5) of a building which was used or was suitable for use as a dwelling, and

(b) the curtilage of the dwelling-house up to an area (exclusive of the site of the dwelling-house) of one acre but if the area of the curtilage (exclusive of the site of the dwelling-house) exceeds one acre then the part which comes within this definition is the part which, if the remainder were separately occupied, would be the most suitable for occupation and enjoyment with the dwelling-house;

'relevant period', in relation to a dwelling-house comprised in a gift or inheritance, means the period of 6 years commencing on the date of the gift or the date of the inheritance.

(2) Subject to subsections (3), (4), (5) and (6), a dwelling-house comprised in a gift or inheritance which is taken by a donee or successor who—

(a) has continuously occupied as his or her only or main residence—

(i)   that dwelling-house throughout the period of 3 years immediately preceding the date of the gift or the date of the inheritance, or

(ii)   where that dwelling-house has directly or indirectly replaced other property, that dwelling-house and that other property for periods which together comprised at least 3 years falling within the period of 4 years immediately preceding the date of the gift or the date of the inheritance,

(b)   is not, at the date of the gift or at the date of the inheritance, beneficially entitled to any other dwelling-house or to any interest in any other dwelling-house, and

(c)   continues to occupy that dwelling-house as his or her only or main residence throughout the relevant period,

shall be exempt from tax in relation to that gift or inheritance, and the value thereof shall not be taken into account in computing tax on any gift or inheritance taken by that person unless the exemption ceases to apply under subsection (5) or (6).

(3)   The condition in paragraph (c) of subsection (2) shall not apply where the donee or successor has attained the age of 55 years at the date of the gift or at the date of the inheritance.

(4)   For the purpose of paragraph (c) of subsection (2), the donee or successor shall be deemed to occupy the dwelling-house concerned as his or her only or main residence throughout any period of absence during which he or she worked in an employment or office all the duties of which were performed outside the State.

(5)   If a dwelling-house exempted from tax by virtue of subsection (2) is sold or disposed of, either in whole or in part, within the relevant period, and before the death of the donee or successor (not being a donee or successor who had attained the age of 55 years at the date of the gift or inheritance), the exemption referred to in that subsection shall cease to apply to such dwelling-house unless the sale or disposal occurs in consequence of the donee or successor requiring long-term medical care in a hospital, nursing home or convalescent home.

(6) The exemption referred to in subsection (2) shall cease to apply to a dwelling-house, if at any time during the relevant period and—

    (a) before the dwelling-house is sold or disposed of, and

    (b) before the death of the donee or successor,

the condition specified in paragraph (c) of subsection (2) has not been complied with unless that non-compliance occurs in consequence of the donee or successor requiring long-term medical care in a hospital, nursing home or convalescent home, or in consequence of any condition imposed by the employer of the donee or successor requiring the donee or successor to reside elsewhere.

(7) Where a dwelling-house exempted from tax by virtue of subsection (2) (hereafter in this section referred to as the 'first-mentioned dwelling-house') is replaced within the relevant period by another dwelling-house, the condition specified in paragraph (c) of subsection (2) shall be treated as satisfied if the donee or successor has occupied as his or her only or main residence the first-mentioned dwelling-house, that other dwelling-house and any dwelling-house which has within the relevant period directly or indirectly replaced that other dwelling-house for periods which together comprised at least 6 years falling within the period of 7 years commencing on the date of the gift or the date of the inheritance.

(8) Any period of absence which would satisfy the condition specified in paragraph (c) of subsection (2) in relation to the first-mentioned dwelling-house shall, if it occurs in relation to any dwelling-house which has directly or indirectly replaced that dwelling-house, likewise satisfy the said condition as it has effect by virtue of subsection (7).

(9) Subsection (5) shall not apply to a case falling within subsection (7), but the extent of the exemption under this section in such a case shall, where the donee or successor had not attained the age of 55 years at the date of the gift or at the date of the inheritance, not exceed what it would have been had the replacement of one dwelling-house by another referred to in subsection (7), or any one or more of such replacements, taken place immediately prior to that date.''.

(2) This section shall have effect in relation to gifts or inheritances taken on or after 1 December 1999.

Section 152

Amendment of section 58 (exemption of certain receipts) of [the Capital Acquisitions Tax Act, 1976].

152. (1) Section 58 of [the Capital Acquisitions Tax Act, 1976,] is amended by the insertion after subsection (3) of the following subsection:

"(4) The receipt by a minor child of the disponer of money or money's worth for support, maintenance or education, at a time when the disponer and the other parent of that minor child are dead, shall not be a gift or an inheritance where the provision of such support, maintenance or education—

(a) is such as would be part of the normal expenditure of a person in the circumstances of the disponer immediately prior to the death of the disponer; and

(b) is reasonable having regard to the financial circumstances of the disponer immediately prior to the death of the disponer.".

(2) This section shall have effect in relation to gifts or inheritances taken on or after the date of the passing of this Act.

Section 153

Repeals, etc.

153. (1) Section 128 of the Finance Act, 1990, and sections 116 and 117 of the Finance Act, 1991, are repealed.

(2) This section shall have effect in relation to gifts or inheritances taken on or after 1 December 1999.

PART 7
Miscellaneous

Section 160

Amendment of section 824 (appeals) of [the Taxes Consolidation Act, 1997].

160. Section 824 of [the Taxes Consolidation Act, 1997,] is amended in subsection (1) by the substitution of "Part" for "Chapter".

Section 161

Amendment of section 1003 (payment of tax by means of donation of heritage items) of [the Taxes Consolidation Act, 1997].

161. As respects each year (being the calendar year 2000 and subsequent calendar years) section 1003 of [the Taxes Consolidation Act, 1997,] is amended in subsection (2)(c) by the substitution in subparagraph (ii) of "£3,000,000" for "£750,000", and that subparagraph, as so amended, is set out in the Table to this section.

TABLE

(ii) exceeds an amount (which shall not be less than £75,000) determined by the formula—

$$£3,000,000 - M$$

where M is an amount (which may be nil) equal to the market value of the heritage item (if any) or the aggregate of the market values at the respective valuation dates of all the heritage items (if any), as the case may be, in respect of which a determination or determinations, as the case may be, under this subsection has been made by the selection committee in any one calendar year and not revoked in that year.

Section 162

Amendment of section 1086 (publication of names of tax defaulters) of [the Taxes Consolidation Act, 1997].

162. (1) Section 1086 of [the Taxes Consolidation Act, 1997,] is amended—

    (a) in subsection (2)—

        (i) by the substitution in paragraph (b) of "tax," for "tax, or" and the substitution in paragraph (c)(iii) of "tax, or" for "tax.", and

        (ii) by the insertion after paragraph (c) of the following:

        "(d) in whose case the Revenue Commissioners, having initiated proceedings for the recovery of any fine or penalty of the kind mentioned in paragraphs (a) and (b), and whether or not a fine or penalty of the kind mentioned in those paragraphs has been imposed by a court, accepted or undertook to accept, in that relevant period, a specified sum of money in settlement of any claim by the Revenue Commissioners in respect of any specified liability of the person under any of the Acts for—

            (i) payment of any tax,

            (ii) payment of interest on that tax, and

            (iii) a fine or other monetary penalty in respect of that tax.",

    (b) by the insertion after subsection (2) of the following:

        "(2A) For the purposes of subsection (2), the reference to a specified sum in paragraphs (c) and (d) of that subsection includes a reference to a sum which is the full amount of the claim by the Revenue Commissioners in respect of the specified liability referred to in those paragraphs.",

    (c) in subsection (4)—

        (i) by the substitution of "Paragraphs (c) and (d)" for "Paragraph (c)", and

(ii) by the substitution, in paragraph (c) of "paragraph (c) or (d), as the case may be," for "paragraph (c)",

and

(d) by the insertion after subsection (5) of the following:

"(5A) Without prejudice to the generality of paragraph (a) of subsection (5), such particulars as are referred to in that paragraph may include—

(a) in a case to which paragraph (a) or (b) of subsection (2) applies, a description, in such summary form as the Revenue Commissioners may think fit, of the act, omission or offence (which may also include the circumstances in which the act or omission arose or the offence was committed) in respect of which the fine or penalty referred to in those paragraphs was imposed, and

(b) in a case to which paragraph (c) or (d) of subsection (2) applies, a description, in such summary form as the Revenue Commissioners may think fit, of the matter occasioning the specified liability (which may also include the circumstances in which that liability arose) in respect of which the Revenue Commissioners accepted, or undertook to accept, a settlement, in accordance with those paragraphs.".

(2) This section shall apply—

(a) as respects fines or other penalties, as are referred to in paragraphs (a) and (b) of section 1086(2), which are imposed by a court, and

(b) as respects specified sums, as are referred to in paragraphs (c) and (d) of section 1086(2), which the Revenue Commissioners accepted, or undertook to accept, in settlement of a specified liability,

on or after the passing of this Act.

Section 164

Amendment of Chapter 5 (miscellaneous provisions) of Part 42 (collection and recovery) of [the Taxes Consolidation Act, 1997].

164. Part 42 of [the Taxes Consolidation Act, 1997,] is amended in Chapter 5 by the insertion after section 1006 of the following:

"Offset between taxes.

1006A. (1) In this section—

'Acts' mean—

(a) the Tax Acts,

(b) the Capital Gains Tax Acts,

(c) the Value-Added Tax Act, 1972, and the enactments amending or extending that Act,

(d) the statutes relating to the duties of excise and to the management of those duties,

(e) the Capital Acquisitions Tax Act, 1976, and the enactments amending or extending that Act,

(f) the Stamp Duties Consolidation Act, 1999,

(g) Part VI of the Finance Act, 1983, and the enactments amending or extending that Part,

(h) Chapter IV of Part II of the Finance Act, 1992,

and any instrument made thereunder;

'claim' means a claim that gives rise to a repayment of tax under any of the Acts and includes part of such a claim;

'liability' means any tax, duty, levy or other charge due or estimated to be due under the Acts for a taxable period, income tax month, income tax year, chargeable period or chargeable event, as appropriate;

'overpayment' means a payment or remittance under the Acts (including part of such a payment or remittance) which is in excess of the amount of the liability against which it is credited.

(2) Notwithstanding any other provision of the Acts, where the Revenue Commissioners are satisfied that a person has not complied with all the obligations imposed on the person by the Acts, in relation to –

(a) the payment of a liability required to be paid, and

(b) the delivery of returns required to be made,

they may instead of making a repayment to the person in respect of any claim or overpayment made by the person set the amount of the claim or overpayment against any liability due under the Acts.

(3) The Revenue Commissioners shall make regulations for the purpose of giving effect to this section and, without prejudice to the generality of the foregoing, such regulations shall provide for the order of priority of liabilities due under the Acts against which any claim or overpayment is to be set in accordance with subsection (2).

(4) Every regulation made under this section shall be laid before Dáil Éireann as soon as may be after it is made and, if a

resolution annulling the regulation is passed by Dáil Éireann within the next 21 days on which Dáil Éireann has sat after the regulation is laid before it, the regulation shall be annulled accordingly, but without prejudice to the validity of anything previously done thereunder.".

FINANCE ACT, 2001

Number 7 of 2001
(Enacted on 30th March, 2001)

PART I

Income Tax, Corporation Tax and Capital Gains Tax

CHAPTER 3

Income Tax, Corporation Tax and Capital Gains Tax

Section 70

Amendment of Chapter 5 (policyholders – new basis) of Part 26 of [the Taxes Consolidation Act, 1997].

70. (1) Chapter 5 of Part 26 of [the Taxes Consolidation Act, 1997,] is amended –

(a) .....

(f) by the insertion after section 730G of the following:

.....

"Capital acquisitions tax: set-off.

730GB. Where appropriate tax is payable as a result of the death of a person, the amount of such tax, in so far as it has been paid, shall be treated as an amount of capital gains tax paid for the purposes of section 63 of the Finance Act, 1985.''.

(2) [Subsection (1) shall]¹

(a) .....

(b) as respects paragraphs..... (f), apply as on and from 1 January 2001.

Footnote

1   Substituted for "This section shall" by para. 5(b), Sch.6, FA 2002, with effect as on and from 30th March, 2001.

PART 6

Capital Acquisitions Tax

Section 215

Interpretation (Part 6).

215. In this Part "Principal Act" means the Capital Acquistions Tax Act, 1976.

Section 216

Amendment of section 18 (taxable value of a taxable gift or taxable inheritance) of [the Capital Acquisitions Tax Act, 1976].

216. (1) Section 18 of [the Capital Acquisitions Tax Act, 1976,] is amended in subsection (5)(f) by the substitution of "section 6(1)(d) or 12(1) (c)" for "section 6(1)(c) or section 12(1)(b)".

(2) Subject to subsection (3), this section shall have effect in relation to gifts or inheritances taken on or after 1 December 1999.

(3) Notwithstanding subsection (2), this section shall not have effect in relation to gifts or inheritances taken under a disposition where the date of the disposition is before 1 December 1999.

Section 217

Amendment of section 19 (value of agricultural property) of [the Capital Acquisitions Tax Act, 1976].

217. (1) Section 19 of [the Capital Acquisitions Tax Act, 1976,] is amended by the substitution in subparagraph (ii) of subsection (5)(a) of "or within 4 years of the compulsory acquisition" for "or compulsory acquisition".

(2) Subsection (1) shall have effect in relation to compulsory acquisitions made on or after 6 December 2000.

Section 218

Amendment of section 55 (exemption of certain objects) of [the Capital Acquisitions Tax Act, 1976].

218. (1) Section 55 of [the Capital Acquisitions Tax Act, 1976,] is amended by the insertion of the following subsection after subsection (4):

"(5) Any work of art normally kept outside the State which is comprised in an inheritance which is charged to tax by virtue of section 12(1)(c) shall be exempt from tax and shall not be taken into account in computing tax, to the extent that the Commissioners are satisfied that it was brought into the State solely for public exhibition, cleaning or restoration.".

(2) This section shall have effect in relation to inheritances taken on or after 26 January 2001.

Section 219

Amendment of section 57 (exemption of certain securities) of [the Capital Acquisitions Tax Act, 1976].

219. (1) Section 57 of [the Capital Acquisitions Tax Act, 1976,] is amended by the substitution in subsection (2) of the following for paragraph (a):

"(a) the securities or units were comprised in the disposition continuously for a period of six years immediately before the date of the gift or the date of the inheritance, and any period immediately before the date of the disposition during which the securities or units were continuously in the beneficial ownership of the disponer shall be deemed, for the purpose of this paragraph, to be a period or part of a period immediately before the date of the gift or the date of the inheritance during which they were continuously comprised in the disposition;".

(2) This section shall have effect in relation to securities or units comprised in a gift or an inheritance where the date of the gift or the date of the inheritance is on or after 15 February 2001 and the securities or units —

(a) come into the beneficial ownership of the disponer on or after 15 February 2001, or

(b) become subject to the disposition on or after that date without having been previously in the beneficial ownership of the disponer.

Section 220

Amendment of section 59C (exemption relating to certain dwellings) of [the Capital Acquisitions Tax Act, 1976].

220. (1) Section 59C of [the Capital Acquisitions Tax Act, 1976,] is amended by the insertion of the following after subsection (1):

"(1A) In this section any reference to a donee or successor shall be construed as including a reference to the transferee referred to in section 23(1).".

(2) This section shall have effect in relation to a gift or inheritance taken on or after 1 December 1999.

Section 221

Gifts and inheritances taken by foster children.

221. [The Capital Acquisitions Tax Act, 1976,] is amended by the insertion of the following section after section 59C:

"59D. (1) In this section —

'the appropriate period' means periods which together comprised at least 5 years falling within the 18 years immediately following the birth of the donee or successor.

(2) Where, on a claim being made to them in that behalf in relation to a gift or inheritance taken on or after 6 December 2000, the Commissioners are, subject to subsection (3), satisfied —

(a) where the inheritance is taken by a successor on the date of death of the disponer, that the successor had, prior to the date of the inheritance, been placed in the foster care of the disponer under the Child Care (Placement of Children in Foster Care) Regulations, 1995 (S.I. No. 260 of 1995), or the Child Care (Placement of Children with Relatives) Regulations, 1995 (S.I. No. 261 of 1995), or

(b) that throughout the appropriate period the donee or successor—

(i) has resided with the disponer, and

(ii) was under the care of and maintained by the disponer at the disponer's own expense,

then, subject to subsection (3), for the purpose of computing the tax payable on that gift or inheritance, that donee or successor shall be deemed to bear to that disponer the relationship of a child.

(3) Relief under subsection (2) shall not apply where the claim for such relief is based on the uncorroborated testimony of one witness.".

Section 222

Gifts and inheritances taken by adopted children from natural parent.

222. [The Capital Acquisitions Tax Act, 1976,] is amended by the insertion of the following section after section 59D (inserted by the Finance Act, 2001):

"59E. Where, on a claim being made to them in that behalf in relation to a gift or inheritance taken on or after the date of the passing of the Finance Act, 2001, the Commissioners are satisfied that—

(a) the donee or successor had at the date of the gift or the date of the inheritance been adopted in the manner referred to in paragraph (b) of the definition of 'child' contained in section 2(1), and

(b) the disponer is the natural mother or the natural father of the donee or successor,

then, notwithstanding section 2(5)(a), for the purpose of computing the tax payable on that gift or inheritance, that donee or successor shall be deemed to bear to that disponer the relationship of a child.".

Section 223

Amendment of section 61 (payment of money standing in names of two or more persons) of [the Capital Acquisitions Tax Act, 1976].

223. Section 61 of [the Capital Acquisitions Tax Act, 1976,] is amended in subsection (1)—

(a) as respects persons dying on or after 26 January 2001 and prior to 1 January 2002, by the substitution of "£25,000" for "£5,000", and

(b) as respects persons dying on or after 1 January 2002, by the substitution of "€31,750" for "£5,000".

Section 224

Amendment of section 85 (exemption of specified collective investment undertakings) of Finance Act, 1989.

224. (1) Section 85 of the Finance Act, 1989, is amended by the substitution of the following for subsections (1) and (2):

"(1) In this section—

'investment undertaking' has the meaning assigned to it by section 739B of the Taxes Consolidation Act, 1997;

'specified collective investment undertaking' has the meaning assigned to it by section 734 of the Taxes Consolidation Act, 1997;

'unit', in relation to an investment undertaking, has the meaning assigned to it by section 739B of the Taxes Consolidation Act, 1997;

'unit', in relation to a specified collective investment undertaking, has the meaning assigned to it by section 734 of the Taxes Consolidation Act, 1997.

(2) Where any unit of an investment undertaking or of a specified collective investment undertaking is comprised in a gift or an inheritance, then such unit—

(a) shall be exempt from tax, and

(b) shall not be taken into account in computing tax on any gift or inheritance taken by the donee or successor,

if, but only if, it is shown to the satisfaction of the Commissioners that—

(i) the unit is comprised in the gift or inheritance—

(I) at the date of the gift or at the date of the inheritance, and

(II) at the valuation date,

(ii) at the date of the disposition, the disponer is neither domiciled nor ordinarily resident in the State, and

(iii) at the date of the gift or at the date of the inheritance, the donee or successor is neither domiciled nor ordinarily resident in the State.".

(2) In relation to any unit of an investment undertaking comprised in a gift or an inheritance, section 85(2)(ii) (inserted by subsection (1)) of the Finance Act, 1989, shall, notwithstanding that the disponer was domiciled or ordinarily resident in the State at the date of the disposition, be treated as satisfied where—

    (a) the proper law of the disposition was not the law of the State at the date of the disposition, and

    (b) the unit came into the beneficial ownership of the disponer or became subject to the disposition prior to 15 February 2001.

(3) This section shall have effect in relation to units of an investment undertaking comprised in a gift or an inheritance where the date of the gift or the date of the inheritance is on or after 1 April 2000.

(4) This section shall have effect in relation to units of a specified collective investment undertaking comprised in a gift or an inheritance where the date of the gift or the date of the inheritance is on or after 15 February 2001 and the units—

    (a) come into the beneficial ownership of the disponer on or after 15 February 2001, or

    (b) become subject to the disposition on or after that date without having been previously in the beneficial ownership of the disponer.

Section 225

Abolition of probate tax.

225. (1) Chapter I (which relates to the taxation of assets passing on inheritance) of Part VI of the Finance Act, 1993, is repealed.

(2) Sections 137, 138, 139 and 140 of the Finance Act, 1994, section 143 of the Finance Act, 1997, section 127 of the Finance Act, 1998, and sections 147 and 150 of the Finance Act, 2000, are repealed.

(3) Subsections (1) and (2) shall have effect in relation to probate tax which would but for this section first become due and payable on or after 6 December 2000.

Section 226

Amendment of section 133 (exemption of certain policies of assurance) of Finance Act, 1993.

226. (1) Section 133 of the Finance Act, 1993, is amended by the substitution in subsection (2)(b) of the following for subparagraph (ii):

"(ii) at the date of the disposition, the disponer is neither domiciled nor ordinarily resident in the State;".

(2) This section shall have effect in relation to a policy comprised in a gift or an inheritance where the date of the gift or the date of the inheritance is on or after 15 February 2001 and the policy—

(a) comes into the beneficial ownership of the disponer on or after 15 February 2001, or

(b) becomes subject to the disposition on or after that date without having been previously in the beneficial ownership of the disponer.

Section 227

Amendment of section 124 (interpretation (Chapter 1)) of Finance Act, 1994.

227. (1) Section 124 of the Finance Act, 1994, is amended by the insertion of the following after subsection (3):

"(4) In this Chapter any reference to a donee or successor shall be construed as including a reference to the transferee referred to in section 23 (1) of [the Capital Acquisitions Tax Act, 1976.]".

(2) This section shall have effect in relation to gifts or inheritances taken on or after 11 April 1994.

Section 228

Amendment of section 127 (relevant business property) of Finance Act, 1994.

228. (1) Section 127 of the Finance Act, 1994, is amended –

(a) by the substitution of "whether incorporated in the State or otherwise" for "incorporated in the State" in each place where it occurs,

(b) by the deletion of "in so far as situated in the State," in paragraph (e) of subsection (1), and

(c) by the deletion of subsection (3).

(2) This section shall have effect in relation to gifts or inheritances taken on or after 15 February 2001.

Section 229

Amendment of provisions relating to the taxation of discretionary trusts.

229. (1) Section 143 of the Finance Act, 1994, is amended –

(a) in subsection (1) –

(i) by the insertion of the following definition after the definition of "relevant inheritance":

"'settled relevant inheritance' means a relevant inheritance taken on the death of a life tenant;",

(ii) by the substitution of the following definition for the definition of "the relevant period":

" 'relevant period' means –

(a) in relation to an earlier relevant inheritance, the period of 5 years commencing on the date of death of the disponer,

        (b)   in relation to a settled relevant inheritance, the period of 5 years commencing on the date of death of the life tenant concerned, and

        (c)   in relation to a later relevant inheritance, the period of 5 years commencing on the latest date on which a later relevant inheritance was deemed to be taken from the disponer;'',

and

(b)   in subsection (2) by the substitution of the following for the proviso to subsection (2):

"Provided that where in the case of each and every earlier relevant inheritance, each and every settled relevant inheritance or each and every later relevant inheritance, as the case may be, taken from one and the same disponer, one or more objects of the appropriate trust became beneficially entitled in possession before the expiration of the relevant period to an absolute interest in the entire of the property of which that inheritance consisted on and at all times after the date of that inheritance (other than property which ceased to be subject to the terms of the appropriate trust by virtue of a sale or exchange of an absolute interest in that property for full consideration in money or money's worth), then, in relation to all such earlier relevant inheritances, all such settled relevant inheritances or all such later relevant inheritances, as the case may be, this section shall cease to apply and tax shall be computed accordingly in accordance with the provisions of the said section 109 as if this section had not been enacted.''.

(2)   This section shall have effect as respects relevant inheritances taken on or after 26 January 2001.

PART 8

Miscellaneous

Section 232

Amendment of Chapter 3 (other obligations and returns) of Part 38 of [the Taxes Consolidation Act, 1997].

232. (1) Chapter 3 of Part 38 of [the Taxes Consolidation Act, 1997,] is amended—

(a) by the substitution for section 887 of the following:

"Use of electronic data processing.

887. (1) In this section—

'the Acts' means—

(a) the Tax Acts,

(b) the Capital Gains Tax Acts,

(c) the Value-Added Tax Act, 1972, and the enactments amending or extending that Act,

(d) the Capital Acquisitions Tax Act, 1976, and the enactments amending or extending that Act, and

(e) Part VI of the Finance Act, 1983,

and any instrument made under any of these enactments;

'record' means any document which a person is obliged by the Acts to keep, to issue or to produce for inspection, and any other written or printed material.

(2) For the purposes of the Acts, but subject to section 17 of the Value-Added Tax Act, 1972, a record may be stored, maintained, transmitted, reproduced or communicated, as the case may be, by any electronic, photographic or other process that—

(a) provides a reliable assurance as to the integrity of the record from the time when it was first generated in its final form by such electronic, photographic or other process,

(b) permits the record to be displayed in intelligible form and produced in an intelligible printed format,

(c) permits the record to be readily accessible for subsequent reference in accordance with paragraph (b), and

(d) conforms to the information technology and procedural requirements drawn up and published by the Revenue Commissioners in accordance with subsection (3).

(3) The Revenue Commissioners shall from time to time draw up and publish in Iris Oifigiúil the information technology and procedural requirements to which any electronic, photographic or other process used by a person for the storage, maintenance, transmission, reproduction and communication of any record shall conform.

(4) The authority conferred on the Revenue Commissioners by this section to draw up and publish requirements shall be construed as including the authority exercisable in a like manner to revoke and replace or to amend any such requirements.

(5) (a) Every person who preserves records by any electronic, photographic or other process, when required to do so by a notice in writing from the Revenue Commissioners, shall, within such period as is specified in the notice, not being less than 21 days from the date of service of the notice, supply to the Revenue Commissioners full particulars relating to the process used by that person, including full particulars relating to software (within the meaning of section 912).

(b) A person who fails or refuses to comply with a notice served on the person under paragraph (a) shall be liable to a penalty of £1,000.

(6) (a) Subject to paragraph (b), where records are kept by a person (being a person who is obliged by the Acts to keep such records) by any electronic, photographic or other process which does not conform with the requirements referred to in paragraphs (a) to (d) of subsection (2), then the person shall be deemed to have failed to comply with that obligation and that person shall be liable to the same penalties as the person would be liable to if the person had failed to comply with any obligation under the Acts in relation to the keeping of records.

(b) Paragraph (a) shall not apply where the person referred to in that paragraph complies with any obligation under the Acts in relation to the

                  keeping of records other than in accordance
                  with the provisions of subsection (2).

    (7)   Where records are preserved by any electronic, photographic or other process, information contained in a document produced by any such process shall, subject to the rules of court, be admissible in evidence in any proceedings, whether civil or criminal, to the same extent as the records themselves.

    (8)   The Revenue Commissioners may nominate any of their officers to discharge any function authorised by this section to be discharged by the Revenue Commissioners.'',

  (b) .....

(2) ....

(3) (a) [The Taxes Consolidaton Act, 1997,] is amended—

      (i)   in section 887 (substituted by subsection (1)(a)) by the substitution in subsection (5)(b) for "£1,000" of "€1,265", and

      (ii) .....

  (b) This subsection shall apply as on and from 1 January 2002.

Section 233

Amendment of section 1078 (revenue offences) of [the Taxes Consolidation Act, 1997].

233. (1) Section 1078(3) of [the Taxes Consolidation Act, 1997,] is amended by the substitution in paragraph (a) of "£1,500" for "£1,000".

    (2) (a) Section 1078(3) of [the Taxes Consolidation Act, 1997,] is amended by the substitution in paragraph (a) of "€1,900" for "£1,500".

        (b) This subsection shall apply as on and from 1 January 2002.

Section 235

Amendment of Chapter 6 (electronic transmission of returns of income, profits, etc., and of other Revenue returns) of Part 38 of [the Taxes Consolidation Act, 1997].

235. Chapter 6 of Part 38 of [the Taxes Consolidation Act, 1997,] is amended with effect from 15 February 2001—

  (a) in section 917D(1)—

    (i) by the substitution—

      (I) for the definition of "digital signature" of the following:

        " 'digital signature', in relation to a person, means an advanced electronic signature (within the meaning of the

Electronic Commerce Act, 2000) provided to the person by the Revenue Commissioners solely for the purpose of making an electronic transmission of information which is required to be included in a return to which this Chapter applies and for no other purpose and a qualified certificate (within the meaning of that Act) provided to the person by the Revenue Commissioners or a person appointed in that behalf by the Revenue Commissioners;",

(II) for the definition of "return" of the following:

"'return' means any return, claim, application, notification, election, declaration, nomination, statement, list, registration, particulars or other information which a person is or may be required by the Acts to give to the Revenue Commissioners or any Revenue officer;",

and

(ii) by the deletion of subsection (2);

(b) in section 917F –

(i) by the substitution in paragraph (c) of subsection (1) for "the approved person's digital signature" of "the approved person's or the authorised person's digital signature", and

(ii) by the substitution for subsection (5) of the following:

"(5) Where an approved transmission is made by –

(a) an approved person on behalf of another person, or

(b) an authorised person on behalf of another person (not being the person who authorised that person),

a hard copy of the information shall be made and authenticated in accordance with section 917K.";

(c) in section 917G –

(i) by the substitution in subsection (1) for "complies with the provisions of this section and, in particular, with the conditions specified in subsection (3)" of "complies with the condition specified in subsection (3)(a) in relation to authorised persons and the condition specified in subsection (3)(b) in relation to the making of transmissions and the use of digital signatures",

(ii) by the substitution in subsection (2) for "in writing or by such other means as may be approved by the Revenue Commissioners" of "by such means as the Revenue Commissioners may determine", and

(iii) by the substitution for subsection (3) of the following:

"(3) The conditions referred to in subsection (1) are that –

(a) the person notifies the Revenue Commissioners in a manner to be determined by the Revenue

Commissioners of the persons (each of whom is referred to in this section as an 'authorised person'), in addition to the person, who are authorised to make the transmission, and

(b) the person and each person who is an authorised person in relation to that person in making the transmission complies with the requirements referred to in subsections (2) and (3) of section 917H.";

(d) by the substitution in section 917H for subsections (2) and (3) of the following:

"(2) The Revenue Commissioners shall publish and make known to each approved person and each authorised person any requirement for the time being determined by them as being applicable to —

(a) the manner in which information which is required to be included in a return to which this Chapter applies is to be transmitted electronically, and

(b) the use of a person's digital signature.

(3) The requirements referred to in subsection (2) include —

(a) requirements as to the software or type of software to be used to make a transmission,

(b) the terms and conditions under which a person may make a transmission, and

(c) the terms and conditions under which a person may use that person's digital signature.";

(e) by the deletion of section 917I;

(f) in section 917K(1)(a) by the substitution for "to be transmitted" of "transmitted or to be transmitted", and

(g) in section 917M(3) by the substitution for "for the purposes of any proceedings in relation to which the certificate is given" of "for the purposes of the Acts".

Section 238

Amendment of section 1002 (deduction from payments due to defaulters of amounts due in relation to tax) of [the Taxes Consolidation Act, 1997].

238. Section 1002 of [the Taxes Consolidation Act, 1997,] is amended, in paragraph (a) of subsection (3), by the substitution for "one month" of "14 days", and the said paragraph (a), as so amended, is set out in the Table to this section.

TABLE

(a)   a period of 14 days has expired from the date on which such default commenced, and

Section 239

Amendment of section 1006A (offset between taxes) of [the Taxes Consolidation Act, 1997].

239. Section 1006A of [the Taxes Consolidation Act, 1997,] is amended—

(a)   in subsection (1) in the definition of "liability" by the insertion after "as appropriate" of ", and includes any interest due under the Acts in relation to such tax, duty, levy or other charge", and

(b)   by the substitution of the following for subsection (2):

"(2)   Notwithstanding any other provision of the Acts, where the Revenue Commissioners are satisfied that a person has not complied with the obligations imposed on the person by the Acts, in relation to either or both—

(a)   the payment of a liability required to be paid, and

(b)   the delivery of returns required to be made,

they may, in a case where a repayment is due to the person in respect of a claim or overpayment—

(i)   where paragraph (a) applies, or where paragraphs (a) and (b) apply, instead of making the repayment set the amount of the claim or overpayment against any liability due under the Acts, and.

(ii)   where paragraph (b) only applies, withhold making the repayment until such time as the returns required to be delivered have been delivered.

(2A)   Where the Revenue Commissioners have set or withheld a repayment by virtue of subsection (2), they shall give notice in writing to that effect to the person concerned and, where subsection (2)(ii) applies, interest shall not be payable under any provision of the Acts from the date of such notice in respect of any repayment so withheld.".

Section 240

Amendments of enactments consequent on changeover to Euro.

240.   (1)   (a)   Subject to subsection (2), in each provision specified in column (1) of Schedule 5 for the words or amount set out in column (2) of that Schedule at that entry there shall be substituted the words or amount set out at the corresponding entry in column (3) of that Schedule.

(b)   Where words are or an amount is mentioned more than once in a provision specified in column (1) of Schedule 5, then the substitution provided for by paragraph (a) shall apply as respects those words or that amount to each mention of those words or that amount in that provision.

(2)   Subsection (1) shall apply —

(a)   .....

(g)   to the extent that the amendments relate to capital acquisitions tax and related matters, other than the amendments relating to such matters referred to in subparagraphs (viii) and (ix) of paragraph (l), as respects gifts or inheritances taken on or after 1 January 2002,

(h)   .....

(k)   to the extent that the enactment amended imposes any fine, forfeiture, penalty or punishment for any act or omission, as respects any act or omission which takes place or begins on or after 1 January 2002,

and

(l)   to the extent that —

(i)   .....

(viii) the First and Second Schedule to the Capital Acquisitions Tax Act, 1976 and section 54(1)(b) of that Act are amended, as respects the computation of tax on gifts and inheritances taken on or after 1 January 2002,

(ix) sections 146(4B)(a)(i)(I), 146(4B)(a)(i)(II)(B), 146 (4C)(b) and 146(4C)(c) of the Finance Act, 1994 are amended, as respects applications for registration made on or after 1 January 2002,

SCHEDULE 5

Amendment of Enactments Consequent on Changeover to Euro

PART 5
Capital Acquisitions Tax and related matters

Enactment amended	Amount or words to be replaced	Amount or words to be inserted
(1)	(2)	(3)
Capital Acquisitions Tax Act, 1976 (No. 8 of 1976) (as amended):		
section 53(1)	£1,000	€1,270
section 54(1)(b)	£15,000	€19,050
section 61(3)	£1,000	€1,265
section 63(1)(a)	£2,000	€2,535
section 63(1)(b)	£25	€30
section 63(2)	£1,000	€1,265
section 63(3)(i)	£5,000	€6,345
section 63(7)	£1,000	€1,265
FIRST SCHEDULE, PART II, TABLE A	£1	€1
FIRST SCHEDULE, PART III, TABLE B	£1	€1
SECOND SCHEDULE, PART I, paragraph 1(a)	£300,000	€381,000
SECOND SCHEDULE, PART I, paragraph 1(b)	£30,000	€38,100
SECOND SCHEDULE, PART I, paragraph 1(c)	£15,000	€19,050
Finance Act, 1986 (No. 13 of 1986):		
section 108(a)	£1,000	€1,265
Finance Act, 1993 (No. 13 of 1993):		
section 111(l)(i)	£1,000	€1,265
section 111(l)(i)	£5,000	€6,345

Enactment amended (1)	Amount or words to be replaced (2)	Amount or words to be inserted (3)
section 111(l)(ii)	£400	€505
section 111(l)(ii)	£2,000	€2,535
section 111(l)(iii)	£200	€250
section 111(l)(iii)	£1,000	€1,265
section 111(l)(iv)	£5	€6
section 111(l)(iv)	£25	€30
Finance Act, 1994 (No. 13 of 1994)(as amended):		
section 146(4B)(a)(i)(I)	£100,000	€127,000
section 146(4B)(a)(i)(II)(B)	£15,000	€19,050
section 146(4C)(b)	£2,000	€2,540
section 146(4C)(c)	£2,000	€2,540

FINANCE ACT, 2002

Number 5 of 2002
(Enacted on 25th March, 2002)

PART 5

Capital Acquisitions Tax

Section 115

Interpretation (Part 5).
115. In this Part "Principal Act" means the Capital Acquisitions Tax Act, 1976.

Section 116

Amendment of section 19 (value of agricultural property) of [the Capital Acquisitions Tax Act, 1976].
116. (1) Section 19 of [the Capital Acquisitions Tax Act, 1976,] is amended in subparagraph (ii) of subsection (5)(a) by substituting "6 years" for "4 years" (inserted by the Finance Act, 2001).

(2) Subsection (1) has effect in relation to compulsory acquisitions made on or after the passing of this Act.

Section 117

Amendment of section 36 (delivery of returns) of [the Capital Acquisitions Tax Act, 1976].
117. (1) Section 36 of [the Capital Acquisitions Tax Act, 1976,] is amended—

(a) in paragraph (a) of subsection (4) by substituting "5 December 1991" for "2 December 1988", and

(b) in paragraphs (b) and (c) of subsection (14) by substituting "5 December 1991" for "the 2nd day of December, 1988".

(2) This section has effect in relation to gifts or inheritances taken on or after 5 December 2001.

Section 118

Amendment of section 41 (payment of tax and interest on tax) of [the Capital Acquisitions Tax Act, 1976].
118. (1) Section 41 of [the Capital Acquisitions Tax Act, 1976,] is amended in subsection (2A)—

(a) by substituting in paragraph (b) "subsection (3) or (4) of section 55" for "section 55(4)",

    (b) by substituting in paragraph (d) "to apply," for "to apply.", and

    (c) by inserting the following after paragraph (d):

       "(e) to the extent to which subsection (5) or (6) of section 59C applies, for the duration of the period from the valuation date to the date the exemption ceases to apply.".

(2) (a) Paragraph (a) of subsection (1) applies where the event which causes the exemption to cease to be applicable occurs on or after 11 February 1999.

    (b) Paragraph (c) of subsection (1) applies where the event which causes the exemption to cease to be applicable occurs on or after 1 December 1999.

Section 119

Amendment of section 52 (appeals in other cases) of [the Capital Acquisitions Tax Act, 1976].

119. (1) Section 52 of [the Capital Acquisitions Tax Act, 1976,] is amended by substituting the following for subsection (7):

    "(7) Prima facie evidence of any notice given under this section by the Commissioners or by an officer of the Commissioners may be given in any proceedings by the production of a document purporting—

      (a) to be a copy of the notice, or

      (b) if the details specified in the notice are contained in an electronic, photographic or other record maintained by the Commissioners, to reproduce those details in so far as they relate to the said notice,

and it shall not be necessary to prove the official position of the person by whom the notice purports to be given or, if it is signed, the signature, or that the person signing and giving it was authorised to do so.".

(2) This section has effect in relation to evidence of any notice given by the Commissioners or by an officer of the Commissioners in any proceedings on or after the passing of this Act.

Section 120

Amendment of section 70 (delivery, service and evidence of notices and forms, etc.) of [the Capital Acquisitions Tax Act, 1976].

120. (1) Section 70 of [the Capital Acquisitions Tax Act, 1976,] is amended by substituting the following for subsection (3):

    "(3) Prima facie evidence of any notice given under this Act by the Commissioners or by an officer of the Commissioners may be given in any proceedings by the production of a document purporting—

(a) to be a copy of that notice, or

(b) if the details specified in that notice are contained in an electronic, photographic or other record maintained by the Commissioners, to reproduce those details in so far as they relate to that notice,

and it shall not be necessary to prove the official position of the person by whom the notice purports to be given or, if it is signed, the signature, or that the person signing and giving it was authorised to do so.''.

(2) This section has effect in relation to evidence of any notice given by the Commmissioners or by an officer of the Commissioners in any proceedings on or after the passing of this Act.

Section 121

Amendment of Second Schedule (computation of tax) to [the Capital Acquisitions Tax Act, 1976].

121. (1) The Second Schedule to [the Capital Acquisitions Tax Act, 1976,] is amended in paragraph 3(a)(ii) by substituting "5 December 1991" for "2 December 1988".

(2) This section has effect in relation to gifts or inheritances taken on or after 5 December 2001.

Section 122

Amendment of section 133 (exemption of certain policies of assurance) of Finance Act, 1993.

122. (1) Section 133 of the Finance Act, 1993, is amended—

(a) by substituting the following for subsection (1):

"(1) In this section—

'assurance company' has the meaning assigned to it by section 706 of the Taxes Consolidation Act, 1997;

'new policy' means a contract entered into by an assurance company which is a policy of assurance on the life of any person issued on or after 1 January 2001;

'old policy' means a contract entered into by an assurance company in the course of carrying on a foreign life assurance business within the meaning of section 451 of the Taxes Consolidation Act, 1997, and issued on or after 1 December 1992 and before 1 January 2001.",

(b) in subsection (2) by substituting "new policy or in an old policy" for "policy", and

(c)   by substituting the following for subsection (3):

"(3) Where—

(a)   an interest in a new policy or in an old policy, as the case may be, which is comprised in a gift or inheritance came into the beneficial ownership of the disponer or became subject to the disposition prior to 15 February 2001, and

(b)   the conditions at subparagraphs (i) and (iii) of subsection (2) are complied with,

then that subsection shall apply to that interest in a new policy or in an old policy, as the case may be, if, at the date of the disposition, the proper law of the disposition was not the law of the State.".

PART 6

Miscellaneous

Section 124

Amendment of section 1003 (payment of tax by means of donation of heritage items) of [the Taxes Consolidation Act, 1997].

124.   Section 1003 of [the Taxes Consolidation Act, 1997,] is amended—

(a)   in subsection (2)(a)(I) by inserting the following after "cultural heritage of Ireland":

"or whose import into the State would constitute a significant enhancement of the accumulated cultural heritage of Ireland",

(b)   in subsection (2)(c)—

(i)   by substituting "€100,000" for "€95,250" in both places where it occurs, and

(ii)   by substituting "€6,000,000" for "€3,810,000",

(c)   in subsection (3)(a) by substituting "shall, subject to paragraph (d), be estimated" for "shall be estimated", and

(d)   by inserting the following after subsection (3)(c):

"(d) Where the property is acquired at auction by the person making the gift, the market value of the property shall, for the purposes of this section, be deemed to include the auctioneer's fees in connection with the auction together with—

(i)   any amount chargeable under the Value-Added Tax Act, 1972, by the auctioneer to the purchaser of the property in respect of those fees and in respect of which the purchaser is not entitled to any deduction or refund under that Act or any other enactment relating to value-added tax, or

    (ii)   in the case of an auction in a country other than the State, the amount chargeable to the purchaser of the property in respect of a tax chargeable under the law of that country which corresponds to value-added tax in the State and in relation to which the purchaser is not entitled to any deduction or refund.".

Section 125

Amendment of Chapter 5 (miscellaneous provisions) of Part 42 of [the Taxes Consolidation Act, 1997].

125. Chapter 5 of Part 42 of [the Taxes Consolidation Act, 1997,] is amended—

  (a) in section 1006A (inserted by the Finance Act, 2000)—

     (i)   in subection (1)—

        (I)   by substituting the following for the definition of "claim":

           " 'claim' means a claim that gives rise to either or both a repayment of tax and a payment of interest payable in respect of such a repayment under any of the Acts and includes part of such a claim;",

        (II) by substituting the following for the definition of "liability":

           " 'liability' means any tax due or estimated to be due under the Acts for any period or in respect of any event, as may be appropriate in the circumstances, and includes any interest due under the Acts in respect of that tax;",

       (III) by substituting "credited;" for "credited." in the definition of "overpayment", and

      (IV) by the insertion of the following after the definition of "overpayment":

           " 'tax' means any tax, duty, levy or other charge under any of the Acts.",

     and

    (ii) by inserting the following after subsection (4):

       "(5) Any act to be performed or function to be discharged (other than the making of regulations) by the Revenue Commissioners which is authorised by this section may be performed or discharged by any of their officers acting under their authority.",

  and

  (b) ....

Section 126

Amendment of section 1086 (publication of names of tax defaulters) of [the Taxes Consolidation Act, 1997].

126. (1) Section 1086 of [the Taxes Consolidation Act, 1997,] is amended –

    (a) in subsection (1) –

        (i) in the definition of "the Acts" –

            (I) by substituting the following for paragraph (e):

                "(e) the Stamp Duties Consolidation Act, 1999, and the enactments amending or extending that Act", and

            (II) by inserting the following after paragraph (f):

                "(g) the Customs Acts,

                (h) the statutes relating to the duties of excise and to the management of those duties,",

        and

        (ii) by substituting the following for the definition of "tax":

            " 'tax' means any tax, duty, levy or charge under the care and management of the Revenue Commissioners. ",

    (b) in subsection (2) –

        (i) in paragraph (c), by substituting the following for sub-paragraphs (ii) and (iii):

            "(ii) except in the case of tax due by virtue of paragraphs (g) and (h) of the definition of 'the Acts', payment of interest on that tax, and

            (iii) a fine or other monetary penalty in respect of that tax including penalties in respect of the failure to deliver any return, statement, declaration, list or other document in connection with the tax, or",

        and

        (ii) in paragraph (d), by substituting the following for subparagraphs (ii) and (iii):

            "(ii) except in the case of tax due by virtue of paragraphs (g) and (h) of the definition of 'the Acts', payment of interest on that tax, and

            (iii) a fine or other monetary penalty in respect of that tax including penalties in respect of the failure to deliver any return, statement, declaration, list or other document in connection with the tax.",

    (c) in subsection (3), by substituting the following for paragraph (b):

"(b) the Revenue Commissioners may, at any time after each such list referred to in subsection (2) has been published as provided for in paragraph (a), cause any such list to be publicised or reproduced, or both, in whole or in part, in such manner, form or format as they consider appropriate.",

and

(d) in subsection (4) –

   (i) in paragraph (a), by substituting "those paragraphs" for "that paragraph",

   (ii) in paragraph (b), by substituting "applied," for "applied, or",

   (iii) in paragraph (c), by substituting "€12,700, or" for "€12,700.", and

   (iv) by inserting the following after paragraph (c):

     "(d) the amount of fine or other penalty included in the specified sum referred to in paragraph (c) or (d), as the case may be, of subsection (2) does not exceed 15 per cent of the amount of tax included in that specified sum.".

(2) This section applies –

(a) as respects fines or other penalties, as are referred to in paragraphs (a) and (b) of section 1086(2), which are imposed by a court, and

(b) as respects specified sums, as are referred to in paragraphs (c) and (d) of section 1086(2), which the Revenue Commissioners accepted, or undertook to accept, in settlement of a specified liability,

on or after the passing of this Act.

Section 129

Interest on unpaid and overpaid tax.

129. (1) ....

(3) The Capital Acquisitions Tax Act, 1976, is amended –

(a) in section 41(2), by substituting "0.0322 per cent per day or part of a day" for "1 per cent per month or part of a month", and

(b) in section 46(1), by substituting "0.0161 per cent, or such other rate (if any) as stands prescribed by the Minister for Finance by regulations, for each day or part of a day" for "0.5 per cent, or such other rate (if any) as stands prescribed by the

Minister for Finance by regulations, for each month or part of a month''.

(4)   ....

(5)   Section 117 of the Finance Act, 1993, is amended in paragraph (b) by substituting ''0.0322 per cent per day or part of a day'' for ''one per cent per month or part of a month''.

(6)   ....

(7)   This section applies from 1 September 2002 to interest chargeable or payable under the provisions mentioned in subsections (1) to (6) in respect of an amount due to be paid or remitted or an amount to be repaid or retained, as the case may be, whether before, on or after that date in accordance with those provisions.

Section 132

Amendment of Chapter 4 (revenue powers) of Part 38 of [the Taxes Consolidation Act, 1997].

132. Chapter 4 of Part 38 of [the Taxes Consolidation Act, 1997,] is amended —

(a) in section 901 by inserting the following after subsection (3):

''(4) Where in compliance with an order made under subsection (2), a person makes available for inspection by an authorised officer, books, records or other documents, the person shall afford the authorised officer reasonable assistance, including information, explanations and particulars, in relation to the use of all the electronic or other automatic means, if any, by which the books, records or other documents, in so far as they are in a non-legible form, are capable of being reproduced in a legible form, and any data equipment or any associated apparatus or material.

(5)   Where in compliance with an order made under subsection (2), a person makes books, records or other documents available for inspection by the authorised officer, the authorised officer may make extracts from or copies of all or any part of the books, records or other documents.'',

(b) in section 902A by inserting the following after subsection (6):

''(6A) Where in compliance with an order made under subsection (4), a person makes available for inspection by an authorised officer, books, records or other documents, the person shall afford the authorised officer reasonable assistance, including information, explanations and particulars, in relation to the use of all the electronic or other automatic means, if any, by which the books, records or other documents, in so far as they are in a non-legible form, are capable of being reproduced in a legible form, and any data equipment or any associated apparatus or material.

(6B) Where in compliance with an order made under subsection (4), a person makes books, records or other documents available for inspection by the authorised officer, the authorised officer may make extracts from or copies of all or any part of the books, records or other documents.",

(c) ....

(d) in section 905(1) by substituting the following for the definition of "records":

" 'records' means any document or any other written or printed material in any form, and includes any information stored, maintained or preserved by means of any mechanical or electronic device, whether or not stored, maintained or preserved in a legible form—

(i) which relates to a business carried on by a person, or

(ii) which a person is obliged by any provision relating to tax to keep, retain, issue or produce for inspection or which may be inspected under any provision relating to tax;",

(e) in section 907 by inserting the following after subsection (7):

"(7A) Where in compliance with the requirements of a notice served under subsection (7), a financial institution makes available for inspection by an authorised officer, books, records or other documents, the financial institution shall afford the authorised officer reasonable assistance, including information, explanations and particulars, in relation to the use of all the electronic or other automatic means, if any, by which the books, records or other documents, in so far as they are in a non-legible form, are capable of being reproduced in a legible form, and any data equipment or any associated apparatus or material.

(7B) Where in compliance with the requirements of a notice served under subsection (7), a financial institution makes books, records or other documents available for inspection by the authorised officer, the authorised officer may make extracts from or copies of all or any part of the books, records or other documents.",

(f) in section 908 by inserting the following after subsection (6):

"(6A) Where in compliance with an order made under subsection (5), a financial institution makes available for inspection by an authorised officer, books, records or other documents, the financial institution shall afford the authorised officer reasonable assistance, including information, explanations and particulars, in relation to the use of all the electronic or other automatic means, if any, by which the books, records or other documents, in so far as they are in a non-legible form, are capable of being reproduced in a legible form, and any data equipment or any associated apparatus or material.

(6B) Where in compliance with an order made under subsection (5), a financial institution makes books, records or other documents available for inspection by the authorised officer, the authorised officer may make extracts from or copies of all or any part of the books, records or other documents.",

and

(g) in section 908A –

    (i) in subsection (1) –

        (I) by inserting the following before the definition of "authorised officer":

" 'the Acts' means the Waiver of Certain Tax, Interest and Penalties Act, 1993, together with the meaning assigned to it by section 1078(1) and;",

and

        (II) by substituting the following for the definition of "offence":

" 'offence' means an offence falling within any provision of the Acts;",

and

    (ii) by substituting the following for subsection (2):

"(2) If, on application made by an authorised officer, with the consent in writing of a Revenue Commissioner, a judge is satisfied, on information given on oath by the authorised officer, that there are reasonable grounds for suspecting –

    (a) that an offence, which would result (or but for its detection would have resulted) in serious prejudice to the proper assessment and collection of tax, is being, has been, or is or was about to be, committed (having regard to the amount of a liability in relation to any person which might be, or might have been, evaded but for the detection of the relevant facts),

and

    (b) that there is material in possession of a financial institution specified in the application which is

> > likely to be of substantial value (whether by itself or together with other material) to the investigation of the relevant facts,

> the judge may make an order authorising the authorised officer to inspect and take copies of any entries in the books, records or other documents of the financial institution for the purposes of investigation of the offence.".

Section 133

Amendment of section 1078 (revenue offences) of [the Taxes Consolidation Act, 1997].

133. Section 1078 of [the Taxes Consolidation Act, 1997,] is amended –

(a) in subsection (2)(g) by substituting "fails without reasonable excuse" for "knowingly or wilfully fails", and

(b) by inserting the following after subsection (3A):

> "(3B) A person shall, without prejudice to any other penalty to which the person may be liable, be guilty of an offence under this section if the person fails or refuses to comply with an order referred to in subsection (3A).".

Section 135

Amendment of Part 48 (miscellaneous and supplemental) of [the Taxes Consolidation Act, 1997].

135. Part 48 of the [the Taxes Consolidation Act, 1997,] is amended by inserting the following after section 1096A:

"Evidence of computer stored records in court proceedings etc.

1096B. (1) In this section –

> 'copy record' means any copy of an original record or a copy of that copy made in accordance with either of the methods referred to in subsection (2) and accompanied by the certificate referred to in subsection (4), which original record or copy of an original record is in the possession of the Revenue Commissioners;

> 'original record' means any document, record or record of an entry in a document or record or information stored by means of any storage equipment, whether or not in a legible form, made or stored by the Revenue Commissioners for the purposes of or in connection with tax, and which is in the possession of the Revenue Commissioners;

> 'provable record' means an original record or a copy record and, in the case of an original record or a copy record stored in any storage equipment, whether or not in a legible form,

includes the production or reproduction of the record in a legible form;

'storage equipment' means any electronic, magnetic, mechanical, photographic, optical or other device used for storing information;

'tax' means any tax, duty, levy or charge under the care and management of the Revenue Commissioners.

(2) Where by reason of –

   (a) the deterioration of,

   (b) the inconvenience in storing, or

   (c) the technical obsolescence in the manner of retaining or storing,

   any original record or any copy record, the Revenue Commissioners may –

   (i)   make a legible copy of that record, or

   (ii) store information concerning that record otherwise than in a legible form so that the information is capable of being used to make a legible copy of that record,

   and, they may, thereupon destroy that original record or that copy record.

(3) The legible copy of –

   (a) a record made, or

   (b) the information concerning such record stored,

   in accordance with subsection (2) shall be deemed to be an original record for the purposes of this section.

(4) In any proceedings a certificate signed by an officer of the Revenue Commissioners stating that a copy record has been made in accordance with the provisions of subsection (2) shall be evidence of the fact of the making of such a copy record and that it is a true copy, unless the contrary is shown.

(5) In any proceedings a document purporting to be a certificate signed by an officer of the Revenue Commissioners, referred to in subsection (4), shall for the purposes of this section be deemed to be such a certificate and to be so signed unless the contrary is shown.

(6) A provable record shall be admissible in evidence in any proceedings and shall be evidence of any fact stated in it or event recorded by it unless the contrary is shown, or

unless the court is not satisfied as to the reliability of the system used to make or compile –

(a) in the case of an original record, that record, and

(b) in the case of a copy record, the original on which it was based.

(7) In any proceedings a certificate signed by an officer of the Revenue Commissioners, stating that a full and detailed search has been made for a record of any event in every place where such records are kept and that no such record has been found, shall be evidence that the event did not happen unless the contrary is shown or unless the court is not satisfied –

(a) as to the reliability of the system used to compile or make or keep such records,

(b) that, if the event had happened, a record would have been made of it, and

(c) that the system is such that the only reasonable explanation for the absence of such record is that the event did not happen.

(8) For the purposes of this section, and subject to the direction and control of the Revenue Commissioners, any power, function or duty conferred or imposed on them may be exercised or performed on their behalf by an officer of the Revenue Commissioners.".

Section 138

Miscellaneous technical amendments in relation to tax.

138. The enactments specified in Schedule 6 are amended to the extent and in the manner specified in that Schedule.

Section 139

Amendment of Provisional Collection of Taxes Act, 1927.

139. The Provisional Collection of Taxes Act, 1927, is amended –

(a) in section 1, by substituting the following for the definition of "new tax":

"the expression 'new tax' when used in relation to a resolution under this Act means a tax which was not in force immediately before the date on which the resolution is expressed to take effect or, where no such date is expressed, the passing of the resolution by Dáil Éireann;'',

and

CAPITAL ACQUISITIONS TAX CONSOLIDATION
ACT 2003

Number 1 of 2003
(Enacted on 21st February 2003)

PART 1

Preliminary

Section 1

Short title.

1. This Act may be cited as the Capital Acquisitions Tax Consolidation Act 2003.

Section 2

[S.2, CATA, as amended]

General interpretation.

2. (1) In this Act, unless the context otherwise requires —

"absolute interest", in relation to property, includes the interest of a person who has a general power of appointment over the property;

"accountable person" means a person who is accountable for the payment of tax by virtue of section 45;

"benefit" includes any estate, interest, income or right;

"child" includes —

(a) a stepchild;

(b) a child adopted —

   (i) under the Adoption Acts 1952 to 1998, or

   (ii) under a foreign adoption which by virtue of section 2, 3, 4 or 5 of the Adoption Act 1991, is deemed to have been effected by a valid adoption order within the meaning of section 1 of that Act;

"Collector" means the Collector-General appointed under section 851 of the Taxes Consolidation Act 1997;

"Commissioners" means the Revenue Commissioners; "date of the disposition" means —

(a) in the case of a will, the date of the testator's death,

(b) in the case of an intestacy or a partial intestacy, the date of death of the intestate,

(c) in the case of a benefit under Part IX or section 56 of the

Succession Act 1965, the date of death of the relevant testator or other deceased person, and correspondingly in the case of an analogous benefit under the law of another territory,

(d) in the case of a disposition which consists of the failure to exercise a right or a power, the date of the latest time when the disponer could have exercised the right or the power if that disponer were sui juris and not under any physical disability, and

(e) in any other case, the date on which the act (or where more than one act is involved, the last act) of the disponer was done by which that disponer provided or bound that disponer to provide the property comprised in the disposition;

"date of the gift" means the date of the happening of the event on which the donee, or any person in right of the donee or on that donee's behalf, becomes beneficially entitled in possession to the benefit, and a reference to the time when a gift is taken is construed as a reference to the date of the gift;

"date of the inheritance" means —

(a) in the case where the successor or any person in right of the successor or on that successor's behalf becomes entitled in possession to the benefit on the happening of any such event as is referred to in section 3(2), the date of the event,

(b) in the case of a gift which becomes an inheritance by reason of its being taken under a disposition where the date of the disposition is within 2 years prior to the death of the disponer, the date which would have been the date of the gift if the entitlement were a gift, and

(c) in any other case, the date of the latest death which had to occur for the successor, or any person in right of the successor or on that successor's behalf, to become beneficially entitled in possession to the benefit,

and a reference to the time when an inheritance is taken is construed as a reference to the date of the inheritance;

"discretionary trust" means any trust whereby, or by virtue or in consequence of which —

(a) property is held on trust to accumulate the income or part of the income of the property, or

(b) property (other than property to which for the time being a person is beneficially entitled for an interest in possession) is held on trust to apply, or with a power to apply, the income or capital or part of the income or capital of the property for the benefit of any person or persons or of any one or more of a number or of a class of persons whether at the discretion of trustees or any other person and notwithstanding that there may be a power to accumulate all or any part of the income;

"disponer", in relation to a disposition, means the person who, for the purpose of the disposition, directly or indirectly provided the property comprised in the disposition, and in any case where more than one person provided the property each is deemed to be the disponer to the extent that that disponer so provided the property; and for the purposes of this definition—

(a) the testator is the disponer in the case of a disposition referred to in paragraph (k) of the definition of "disposition",

(b) the intestate is the disponer in the case of a disposition referred to in paragraph (l) of that definition,

(c) the deceased person referred to in paragraph (m) of that definition is the disponer in the case of a disposition referred to in that paragraph, and

(d) a person who has made with any other person a reciprocal arrangement by which that other person provided property comprised in the disposition is deemed to have provided that property;

"disposition" includes—

(a) any act or omission by a person as a result of which the value of that person's estate immediately after the act or omission is less than it would be but for the act or omission,

(b) any trust, covenant, agreement or arrangement, whether made by a single operation or by associated operations,

(c) the creation of a debt or other right enforceable against the disponer personally or against any estate or interest that disponer may have in property,

(d) the payment of money,

(e) the allotment of shares in a company,

(f) the grant or the creation of any benefit,

(g) the grant or the creation of any lease, mortgage, charge, licence, option, power, partnership or joint tenancy or other estate or interest in or over any property,

(h) the release, forfeiture, surrender or abandonment of any debt or benefit, or the failure to exercise a right, and, for the purpose of this paragraph, a debt or benefit is deemed to have been released when it has become unenforceable by action through lapse of time (except to the extent that it is recovered subsequent to its becoming so unenforceable),

(i) the exercise of a general power of appointment in favour of any person other than the holder of the power,

(j) a donatio mortis causa,

(k) a will or other testamentary disposition,

(l) an intestacy, whether total or partial,

(m) the payment of a share as a legal right under Part IX of the Succession Act 1965, to a deceased person's spouse, or the making of provision for a widow or child of a deceased person under section 56 or section 117 of the Succession Act 1965, or an analogous share or provision paid or made on the death of a deceased person to or for the benefit of any person under the law of another territory, and

(n) a resolution passed by a company which is deemed by subsection (3) to be a disposition;

"donee" means a person who takes a gift;

"entitled in possession" means having a present right to the enjoyment of property as opposed to having a future such right, and without prejudice to the generality of the foregoing a person is also, for the purposes of this Act, deemed to be entitled in possession to an interest or share in a partnership, joint tenancy or estate of a deceased person, in which that person is a partner, joint tenant or beneficiary, as the case may be, but that person is not deemed to be entitled in possession to an interest in expectancy until an event happens whereby this interest ceases to be an interest in expectancy;

"general power of appointment" includes every power, right, or authority whether exercisable only by will or otherwise which would enable the holder of such power, right, or authority to appoint or dispose of property to whoever the holder thinks fit or to obtain such power, right or authority, but exclusive of any power exercisable solely in a fiduciary capacity under a disposition not made by the holder, or exercisable by a tenant for life under the Settled Land Act 1882, or as mortgagee;

"gift" means a gift which a person is by this Act deemed to take;

"inheritance" means an inheritance which a person is by this Act deemed to take;

"interest in expectancy" includes an estate in remainder or reversion and every other future interest, whether vested or contingent, but does not include a reversion expectant on the determination of a lease;

"limited interest" means—

(a) an interest (other than a leasehold interest) for the duration of a life or lives or for a period certain, or

(b) any other interest which is not an absolute interest;

"local authority" has the meaning assigned to it by section 2(1) of the Local Government Act 2001 and includes a body established under the Local Government Services (Corporate Bodies) Act 1971;

"market value", in relation to property, means the market value of that property ascertained in accordance with sections 26 and 27;

"minor child" means a child who has not attained the age of 18 years and is not and has not been married;

"personal property" means any property other than real property;

"personal representative" means the executor or administrator for the time being of a deceased person and includes—

(a) any person who takes possession of or intermeddles with the property of a deceased person,

(b) any person having, in relation to the deceased person, under the law of another country, any functions corresponding to the functions, for administration purposes under the law of the State, of an executor or administrator;

"property" includes rights and interests of any description;

"real property" means real and chattel real property;

"regulations" means regulations made under section 116;

"relative" means a relative within the meaning of subsection (4);

"return" means such a return as is referred to in section 46;

"share", in relation to a company, includes any interest whatever in the company which is analogous to a share in the company, and

"shareholder" shall be construed accordingly;

"special power of appointment" means a power of appointment which is not a general power of appointment;

"successor" means a person who takes an inheritance;

"tax" means any tax chargeable under this Act;

"valuation date" has the meaning assigned to it by section 30;

"year of assessment" has the meaning assigned to it by section 2 of the Taxes Consolidation Act 1997.

(2) For the purpose of the definition of "general power of appointment" contained in subsection (1), a person is deemed to have a general power of appointment—

(a) notwithstanding that the person is not sui juris or is under a physical disability,

(b) over money which the person has a general power to charge on property, and

(c) over property of which the person is tenant in tail in possession.

(3) For the purpose of the definition of "disposition" contained in subsection (1), the passing by a company of a resolution which, by the extinguishment or alteration of the rights attaching to any share of the company, results, directly or indirectly, in the estate of any shareholder of the company being increased in value at the expense of the estate of any other shareholder, is deemed to be a disposition made by that other shareholder if that other shareholder could have prevented the passing of the resolution by voting against it

or otherwise; and in this subsection, "share" includes a debenture and loan stock and "shareholder" includes a debenture holder and a holder of loan stock.

(4) For the purposes of this Act, the following persons and no other person are relatives of another person, that is —

    (a) the spouse of that other person,

    (b) the father, mother, and any child, uncle or aunt of that other person,

    (c) any child (other than that other person), and any child of a child, of any person who is by virtue of paragraph (a) or (b) a relative of that other person, and

    (d) the spouse of a person who is by virtue of paragraph (b) or (c) a relative of that other person,

    (e) the grandparent of that other person.

(5) For the purposes of this Act, the relationship between a child, adopted in the manner referred to in paragraph (b) of the definition of "child" contained in subsection (1), and any other person, or between other persons, that would exist if such child had been born to the adoptor or adoptors in lawful wedlock, is deemed to exist between such child and that other person or between those other persons, and the relationship of any such child and any person that existed prior to that child being so adopted is deemed to have ceased.

(6) For the purposes of this Act —

    (a) a reference to a person being resident in the State on a particular date is construed as a reference to that person being resident in the State in the year of assessment in which that date falls (but, for those purposes, the provisions of Part 34 of the Taxes Consolidation Act 1997, relating to residence of individuals is not construed as requiring a year of assessment to have elapsed before a determination of whether or not a person is resident in the State on a date falling in that year may be made), and

    (b) a reference to a person being ordinarily resident in the State on a particular date is construed as a reference to that person being ordinarily resident in the State in the year of assessment in which that date falls.

(7) In this Act, references to any enactment are, unless the context otherwise requires, construed as references to that enactment as amended or extended by any subsequent enactment.

(8) In this Act, a reference to a Part, Chapter, section or Schedule is a reference to a Part, Chapter, section of, or Schedule to, this Act, unless it is indicated that reference to some other enactment is intended.

(9) In this Act, a reference to a subsection, paragraph, subparagraph, clause or subclause is to the subsection, paragraph, subparagraph,

clause or subclause of the provision (including a Schedule) in which the reference occurs, unless it is indicated that reference to some other provision is intended.

Section 3

[S.3, CATA]

Meaning of "on a death".

3. (1) In this Act, "on a death", in relation to a person becoming beneficially entitled in possession, means—

(a) on the death of a person or at a time ascertainable only by reference to the death of a person,

(b) under a disposition where the date of the disposition is the date of the death of the disponer,

(c) under a disposition where the date of the disposition is on or after 1 April 1975 and within 2 years prior to the death of the disponer, or

(d) on the happening, after the cesser of an intervening life interest, of any such event as is referred to in subsection (2).

(2) The events referred to in subsection (1)(d) are any of the following—

(a) the determination or failure of any charge, estate, interest or trust,

(b) the exercise of a special power of appointment,

(c) in the case where a benefit was given under a disposition in such terms that the amount or value of the benefit could only be ascertained from time to time by the actual payment or application of property for the purpose of giving effect to the benefit, the making of any payment or the application of the property, or

(d) any other event which, under a disposition, affects the right to property, or to the enjoyment of that property.

PART 2
Gift Tax

Section 4
[S.4, CATA - part]

Charge of gift tax.

4. A capital acquisitions tax, to be called gift tax and to be computed in accordance with this Act, shall, subject to this Act and any regulations made under the Act, be charged, levied and paid on the taxable value of every taxable gift taken by a donee.

Section 5
[S.5, CATA, as amended, s.121, FA 1993, and s.147, FA 1994]

Gift deemed to be taken.

5. (1) For the purposes of this Act, a person is deemed to take a gift, where, under or in consequence of any disposition, a person becomes beneficially entitled in possession, otherwise than on a death, to any benefit (whether or not the person becoming so entitled already has any interest in the property in which such person takes such benefit), otherwise than for full consideration in money or money's worth paid by such person.

    (2) A gift is deemed—

        (a) to consist of the whole or the appropriate part, as the case may be, of the property in which the donee takes a benefit, or on which the benefit is charged or secured or on which the donee is entitled to have it charged or secured, and

        (b) if the benefit is an annuity or other periodic payment which is not charged on or secured by any property and which the donee is not entitled to have so charged or secured, to consist of such sum as would, if invested on the date of the gift in the security of the Government which was issued last before that date for subscription in the State and is redeemable not less than 10 years after the date of issue, yield, on the basis of the current yield on the security, an annual income equivalent to the annual value of the annuity or of the other periodic payment receivable by the donee.

    (3) For the purposes of section 6(1)(c) and 6(2)(d), the sum referred to in subsection (2)(b) is deemed not to be situate in the State at the date of the gift.

    (4) Where a person makes a disposition under which a relative of the person becomes beneficially entitled in possession to any benefit, the creation or disposition in favour of the person of an annuity or other interest limited to cease on the death, or at a time ascertainable only

by reference to the death, of the person, shall not be treated for the purposes of this section as consideration for the grant of such benefit or of any part of such benefit.

(5) For the purposes of this Act, "appropriate part", in relation to property referred to in subsection (2), means that part of the entire property in which the benefit subsists, or on which the benefit is charged or secured, or on which the donee is entitled to have it so charged or secured, which bears the same proportion to the entire property as the gross annual value of the benefit bears to the gross annual value of the entire property, and the gift shall be deemed to consist of the appropriate part of each and every item of property comprised in the entire property.

(6) (a) Where a contract or agreement was entered into, under or as a consequence of which a person acquired the right, otherwise than for full consideration in money or money's worth, to have a benefit transferred to that person, or to another in that person's right or on that person's behalf, and an act or acts is or are done, on or after that date, in pursuance of, or in performance or satisfaction, whether in whole or in part, of such contract or agreement, then the gift or inheritance, as the case may be, taken by or in right or on behalf of that person, is deemed to have been taken, not when the right was acquired, but either –

   (i) when the benefit was transferred to that person or to another in that person's right or on that person's behalf, or

   (ii) when that person or another in that person's right or on that person's behalf became beneficially entitled in possession to the benefit,

   whichever is the later

(b) In this subsection, a reference to a contract or agreement does not include a reference to a contract or agreement –

   (i) which is a complete grant, transfer, assignment or conveyance, or

   (ii) which was enforceable by action.

(7) (a) In paragraph (b), the expression "shares in a private company" shall be construed by reference to the meanings that "share" and "private company" have, respectively, in section 27.

(b) Where a person becomes beneficially entitled in possession to a benefit, and the property in which the benefit is taken consists wholly or partly of shares in a private company and where the consideration referred to in subsection (1), being consideration in relation to a disposition, could not reasonably be regarded (taking into account the disponer's position prior to the disposition) as representing full consideration to the disponer for having made such a disposition, subsection (1) is deemed to apply as if "otherwise than for full consideration in money or money's worth paid by such person" were deleted in that subsection.

Section 6

[S.6, CATA, as amended]

Taxable gift.

6. (1) In relation to a gift taken under a disposition, where the date of the disposition is before 1 December 1999, "taxable gift" in this Act means—

(a) in the case of a gift, other than a gift taken under a discretionary trust, where the disponer is domiciled in the State at the date of the disposition under which the donee takes the gift, the whole of the gift,

(b) in the case of a gift taken under a discretionary trust where the disponer is domiciled in the State at the date of the disposition under which the donee takes the gift or at the date of the gift or was (in the case of a gift taken after that donee's death) so domiciled at the time of that donee's death, the whole of the gift, and

(c) in any other case, so much of the property of which the gift consists as is situate in the State at the date of the gift.

(2) In relation to a gift taken under a disposition, where the date of the disposition is on or after 1 December 1999, "taxable gift" in this Act means—

(a) in the case of a gift, other than a gift taken under a discretionary trust, where the disponer is resident or ordinarily resident in the State at the date of the disposition under which the donee takes the gift, the whole of the gift,

(b) in the case of a gift taken under a discretionary trust where the disponer is resident or ordinarily resident in the State at the date of the disposition under which the donee takes the gift or at the date of the gift or was (in the case of a gift taken after the death of the disponer) so resident or ordinarily resident at the date of that death, the whole of the gift,

(c) in the case where the donee is resident or ordinarily resident in the State at the date of the gift, the whole of the gift, and

(d) in any other case, so much of the property of which the gift consists as is situate in the State at the date of the gift.

(3) For the purposes of subsections (1)(c) and (2)(d), a right to the proceeds of sale of property is deemed to be situate in the State to the extent that such property is unsold and situate in the State.

(4) For the purposes of subsection (2), a person who is not domiciled in the State on a particular date is treated as not resident and not ordinarily resident in the State on that date unless—

(a) that date occurs on or after 1 December 2004,

(b) that person has been resident in the State for the 5 consecutive years of assessment immediately preceding the year of assessment in which that date falls, and

(c) that person is either resident or ordinarily resident in the State on that date.

(5) (a) In this subsection—

"company" and "share" have the same meaning as they have in section 27;

"company controlled by the donee" has the same meaning as is assigned to "company controlled by the donee or successor" by section 27.

(b) For the purposes of subsection (2)(d), a proportion of the market value of any share in a private company incorporated outside the State which (after the taking of the gift) is a company controlled by the donee is deemed to be a sum situate in the State and is the amount determined by the following formula—

$$A \times \frac{B}{C}$$

where

A is the market value of that share at the date of the gift ascertained under section 27,

B is the market value of all property in the beneficial ownership of that company which is situate in the State at the date of the gift, and

C is the total market value of all property in the beneficial ownership of that company at the date of the gift.

(c) Paragraph (b) shall not apply in a case where the disponer was domiciled outside the State at all times up to and including the date of the gift or, in the case of a gift taken after the death of the disponer, up to and including the date of that death or where the share in question is actually situate in the State at the date of the gift.

Section 7

[S.7, CATA]

Liability to gift tax in respect of gift taken by joint tenants.

7. The liability to gift tax in respect of a gift taken by persons as joint tenants is the same in all respects as if they took the gift as tenants in common in equal shares.

Section 8

[S.8, CATA]

Disponer in certain connected dispositions.

8. (1) Where a donee takes a gift under a disposition made by a disponer (in this section referred to as the original disponer) and, within the period commencing 3 years before and ending 3 years after the date of that gift, the donee makes a disposition under which a second donee takes a gift and whether or not the second donee makes a disposition within the same period under which a third donee takes a gift, and so on, each donee is deemed to take a gift from the original disponer (and not from the immediate disponer under whose disposition the gift was taken); and a gift so deemed to be taken is deemed to be an inheritance (and not a gift) taken by the donee, as successor, from the original disponer if —

    (a) the original disponer dies within 2 years after the date of the disposition made by that original disponer, and

    (b) the date of the disposition was on or after 1 April 1975.

    (2) This section shall not apply in the case of any disposition (in this subsection referred to as the first-mentioned disposition) in so far as no other disposition, which was connected in the manner described in subsection (1) with such first-mentioned disposition, was made with a view to enabling or facilitating the making of the first-mentioned disposition or the recoupment in any manner of the cost of such first-mentioned disposition.

PART 3

Inheritance Tax

CHAPTER 1
General

Section 9

[S.10, CATA – part]

Charge of inheritance tax.

9. A capital acquisitions tax, to be called inheritance tax and to be computed in accordance with this Act, shall, subject to this Act and any regulations made under the Act, be charged, levied and paid on the taxable value of every taxable inheritance taken by a successor.

Section 10

[S.11, CATA, as amended, s.123, FA 1993, and s.148, FA 1994]

Inheritance deemed to be taken.

10. (1) For the purposes of this Act a person is deemed to take an inheritance, where, under or in consequence of any disposition, a person becomes beneficially entitled in possession on a death to any benefit (whether or not the person becoming so entitled already has any interest in the property in which such person takes such benefit), otherwise than for full consideration in money or money's worth paid by such person.

(2) Subsections (2), (4) and (5) of section 5 shall apply, with any necessary modifications, in relation to an inheritance as they apply in relation to a gift.

(3) For the purposes of section 11(1)(b) and 11(2)(c), the sum referred to in section 5(2)(b) is deemed not to be situate in the State at the date of the inheritance.

(4) (a) In paragraph (b), the expression "shares in a private company" is construed by reference to the meanings that "share" and "private company" have, respectively, in section 27.

(b) Where a person becomes beneficially entitled in possession to a benefit, and the property in which the benefit is taken consists wholly or partly of shares in a private company and where the consideration referred to in subsection (1), being consideration in relation to a disposition, could not reasonably be regarded (taking into account the disponer's position prior to the disposition) as representing full consideration to the disponer for having made such a disposition, subsection (1) is deemed to apply as if "otherwise than for full consideration in money or money's worth paid by such person" were deleted in that subsection.

Section 11

[S.12, CATA, as amended]

Taxable inheritance.

11. (1) In relation to an inheritance taken under a disposition, where the date of the disposition is before 1 December 1999, "taxable inheritance" in this Act means –

(a) in the case where the disponer is domiciled in the State at the date of the disposition under which the successor takes the inheritance, the whole of the inheritance, and

(b) in any case, other than the case referred to in paragraph (a), where, at the date of the inheritance –

(i) the whole of the property –

(I) which was to be appropriated to the inheritance, or

>> (II) out of which property was to be appropriated to the inheritance,
>>
>> was situate in the State, the whole of the inheritance;
>
> (ii) a part or proportion of the property—
>
>> (I) which was to be appropriated to the inheritance, or
>>
>> (II) out of which property was to be appropriated to the inheritance,
>>
>> was situate in the State, that part or proportion of the inheritance.

(2) In relation to an inheritance taken under a disposition, where the date of the disposition is on or after 1 December 1999, "taxable inheritance" in the Act means—

  (a) in the case where the disponer is resident or ordinarily resident in the State at the date of the disposition under which the successor takes the inheritance, the whole of the inheritance,

  (b) in the case where the successor (not being a successor in relation to a charge for tax arising by virtue of sections 15(1) and 20(1)) is resident or ordinarily resident in the State at the date of the inheritance, the whole of the inheritance, and.

  (c) in any case, other than a case referred to in paragraph (a) or (b), where at the date of the inheritance—

  (i) the whole of the property—

>> (I) which was to be appropriated to the inheritance, or
>>
>> (II) out of which property was to be appropriated to the inheritance,
>>
>> was situate in the State, the whole of the inheritance;

  (ii) a part or proportion of the property—

>> (I) which was to be appropriated to the inheritance, or
>>
>> (II) out of which property was to be appropriated to the inheritance,
>>
>> was situate in the State, that part or proportion of the inheritance.

(3) For the purposes of subsections (1)(b) and (2)(c)—

  (a) "property which was to be appropriated to the inheritance" and "property out of which property was to be appropriated to the inheritance" shall not include any property which was not applicable to satisfy the inheritance, and

  (b) a right to the proceeds of sale of property is deemed to be situate in the State to the extent that such property is unsold and situate in the State.

(4) For the purposes of subsection (2), a person who is not domiciled in the State on a particular date is treated as not resident and not ordinarily resident in the State on that date unless –

    (a) that date occurs on or after 1 December 2004,

    (b) that person has been resident in the State for the 5 consecutive years of assessment immediately preceding the year of assessment in which that date falls, and

    (c) that person is either resident or ordinarily resident in the State on that date.

(5) (a) In this subsection –

"company" and "share" have the same meaning as they have in section 27;

"company controlled by the donee" has the same meaning as is assigned to "company controlled by the donee or successor" by section 27.

    (b) For the purposes of subsection (2)(c), a proportion of the market value of any share in a private company incorporated outside the State which (after the taking of the inheritance) is a company controlled by the successor is deemed to be a sum situate in the State and is the amount determined by the following formula –

$$A \times \frac{B}{C}$$

where

    A is the market value of that share at the date of the inheritance ascertained under section 27,

    B is the market value of all property in the beneficial ownership of that company which is situate in the State at the date of the inheritance, and

    C is the total market value of all property in the beneficial ownership of that company at the date of the inheritance.

    (c) Paragraph (b) shall not apply in a case where the disponer was not domiciled in the State at the date of the disposition under which the successor takes the inheritance or where the share in question is actually situate in the State at the date of the inheritance.

Section 12

[S.13, CATA]

Disclaimer.

12. (1) If −

(a) (i) a benefit under a will or an intestacy, or

(ii) an entitlement to an interest in settled property,

is disclaimed;

(b) a claim −

(i) under a purported will in respect of which a grant of representation (within the meaning of the Succession Act 1965) was not issued, or

(ii) under an alleged intestacy where a will exists in respect of which such a grant was issued,

is waived; or

(c) a right under Part IX of the Succession Act 1965, or any analogous right under the law of another territory, is renounced, disclaimed, elected against or lapses,

any liability to tax in respect of such benefit, entitlement, claim or right shall cease as if such benefit, entitlement, claim or right, as the case may be, had not existed.

(2) Notwithstanding anything contained in this Act −

(a) a disclaimer of a benefit under a will or intestacy or of an entitlement to an interest in settled property;

(b) the waiver of a claim −

(i) under a purported will in respect of which a grant of representation (within the meaning of the Succession Act 1965) was not issued, or

(ii) under an alleged intestacy where a will exists in respect of which such a grant issued; or

(c) (i) the renunciation or disclaimer of,

(ii) the election against, or

(iii) the lapse of,

a right under Part IX of the Succession Act 1965, or any analogous right under the law of another territory,

is not a disposition for the purposes of this Act.

(3) Subsection (1) shall not apply to the extent of the amount of any consideration in money or money's worth received for the disclaimer, renunciation, election or lapse or for the waiver of a claim; and the receipt of such consideration is deemed to be a gift or an inheritance,

as the case may be, in respect of which no consideration was paid by the donee or successor and which was derived from the disponer who provided the property in relation to which the benefit, entitlement, claim or right referred to in subsection (1), arose.

Section 13

[S.14, CATA]

Surviving joint tenant deemed to take an inheritance, etc.

13. (1) On the death of one of several persons who are beneficially and absolutely entitled in possession as joint tenants, the surviving joint tenant or surviving joint tenants is or are deemed to take an inheritance of the share of the deceased joint tenant, as successor or successors from the deceased joint tenant as disponer.

(2) The liability to inheritance tax in respect of an inheritance taken by persons as joint tenants is the same in all respects as if they took the inheritance as tenants in common in equal shares.

CHAPTER 2

Initial Levy on Discretionary Trusts

Section 14

[S.104, FA 1984]

Interpretation (Chapter 2).

14. In this Chapter —

"object", in relation to a discretionary trust, means a person for whose benefit the income or capital, or any part of the income or capital, of the trust property is applied, or may be applied;

"principal objects", in relation to a discretionary trust, means such objects, if any, of the trust for the time being as are —

(a) the spouse of the disponer,

(b) the children of the disponer, or

(c) the children of a child of the disponer where such child predeceased the disponer.

Section 15

[S.106, FA 1984, as amended]

Acquisitions by discretionary trusts.

15. (1) Where, on or after 25 January 1984, under or in consequence of any disposition, property becomes subject to a discretionary trust, the trust is deemed, on —

(a) the date on which that property becomes or became subject to the discretionary trust,

(b) the date of death of the disponer, or

(c) where there are principal objects of the trust, the date on which there ceases to be a principal object of the trust who is—

    (i) under the age of 25 years, where the property became subject to the trust on or after 25 January 1984 and before 31 January 1993, or

    (ii) under the age of 21 years, where the property becomes or became subject to the trust on or after 31 January 1993,

whichever date is the latest, to become or to have become beneficially entitled in possession to an absolute interest in so much, if any, of that property or of property representing that property and of accumulations of income of that property or of property representing those accumulations as remains subject to the discretionary trust on that latest date, and to take or to have taken an inheritance accordingly as if the trust, and the trustees as such for the time being of the trust, were together a person for the purposes of this Act, and that latest date shall be the date of the inheritance.

(2) Property which, under or in consequence of any disposition, was subject to a discretionary trust on 25 January 1984 is, for the purposes of subsection (1), deemed to have become subject to the trust on that date.

(3) Property which, under or in consequence of any disposition, was subject to a discretionary trust on 31 January 1993 is, for the purposes of subsection (1), deemed to have become subject to the trust on that date.

(4) For the purposes of this section—

(a) an interest in expectancy is not property until an event happens whereby the interest ceases to be an interest in expectancy or is represented by property which is not an interest in expectancy,

(b) an interest in a policy of assurance on human life is not property until, and then only to the extent that, the interest becomes an interest in possession under section 41 or is represented by property which is not an interest in expectancy.

(5) Where, apart from this subsection, property or property representing such property would be chargeable under this section, or under this section and the corresponding provisions of the repealed enactments, with tax more than once under the same disposition, such property is so chargeable with tax once only, that is, on the earliest occasion on which such property would become so chargeable with tax.

Section 16

[S.107, FA 1984, as amended]

Application of this Act.

16. In relation to a charge for tax arising by reason of section 15 —

(a) a reference in section 27 to a company controlled by the successor and the definition in that section of "group of shares" is construed as if (for the purpose of that reference) the list of persons contained in subsection (3) of that section and (for the purpose of that definition) the list of persons contained in that definition included the following, that is, the trustees of the discretionary trust, the living objects of the discretionary trust, the relatives of those objects, nominees of those trustees or of those objects or of the relatives of those objects, and the trustees of a settlement whose objects include the living objects of the discretionary trust or relatives of those living objects,

(b) section 30 shall apply, with the modification that the valuation date of the taxable inheritance is —

(i) the date of the inheritance, or

(ii) the valuation date ascertained in accordance with that section,

whichever is the later, and with any other necessary modifications;

(c) a person who is a trustee of the discretionary trust concerned for the time being at the date of the inheritance or at any date subsequent to that date is a person primarily accountable for the payment of the tax;

(d) an object of the discretionary trust concerned to whom or for whose benefit any of the property subject to the trust is applied or appointed is also accountable for the payment of tax the charge in respect of which has arisen prior to the date of the application or appointment of the property to that person or for that person's benefit, and this Act shall apply, in its application to that charge for tax, as if that object of the discretionary trust were a person referred to in section 45(2); and

(e) section 45(1), sections 50, 56 and 81 and Schedule 2 shall not apply.

Section 17

[S.108, FA 1984, as amended, and s.129, FA 1990]

Exemptions.

17. (1) Section 15 shall not apply in relation to a discretionary trust which is shown to the satisfaction of the Commissioners to have been created exclusively —

(a) for public or charitable purposes in the State or Northern Ireland,

   (b) for the purposes of —

      (i) any scheme for the provision of superannuation benefits on retirement established by or under any enactment or by or under an instrument made under any enactment, or

      (ii) any sponsored superannuation scheme within the meaning of subsection (1) of section 783 of the Taxes Consolidation Act 1997 or a trust scheme or part of a trust scheme approved by the Commissioners under that section or section 785 of that Act, but shall not include a scheme or arrangement which relates to matters other than service in particular offices or employments;

   (c) for the purposes of a registered unit trust scheme within the meaning of the Unit Trusts Act 1990;

   (d) (i) for the benefit of one or more named individuals, and

      (ii) for the reason that such individual, or all such individuals, is or are, because of age or improvidence, or of physical, mental or legal incapacity, incapable of managing that individual or those individuals' affairs;

     or

   (e) for the purpose of providing for the upkeep of a house or garden referred to in section 77(6).

  (2) Section 15 shall not apply —

   (a) in relation to a discretionary trust in respect of the property subject to or becoming subject to the trust which, on the termination of the trust, is comprised in a gift or an inheritance taken by the State, or

   (b) in respect of an inheritance which, apart from this subsection, would be deemed, by the combined effect of section 15 and section 40, to be taken by a discretionary trust.

Section 18

[S.109, FA 1984, as amended, and s.143, FA 1994, as amended]

Computation of tax.

18. (1) In this section —

"earlier relevant inheritance" means a relevant inheritance deemed to be taken on the date of death of the disponer;

"later relevant inheritance" means a relevant inheritance which, after the date of death of the disponer, is deemed to be taken by a discretionary trust by virtue of there ceasing to be a principal object of that trust who is under the age of 21 years;

"relevant inheritance" means an inheritance which, by virtue of section 15(1), is deemed to be taken by a discretionary trust;

"relevant period" means —

(a) in relation to an earlier relevant inheritance, the period of 5 years commencing on the date of death of the disponer,

(b) in relation to a settled relevant inheritance, the period of 5 years commencing on the date of death of the life tenant concerned, and

(c) in relation to a later relevant inheritance, the period of 5 years commencing on the latest date on which a later relevant inheritance was deemed to be taken from the disponer;

"settled relevant inheritance" means a relevant inheritance taken on the death of a life tenant;.

"the appropriate trust", in relation to a relevant inheritance, means the trust by which that inheritance was deemed to be taken.

(2) Subject to subsection (3), the tax chargeable on the taxable value of a taxable inheritance which is charged to tax by reason of section 15 is computed at the rate of 6 per cent of such taxable value.

(3) Where, in the case of each earlier relevant inheritance, each settled relevant inheritance or each later relevant inheritance, as the case may be, taken from the same disponer, one or more objects of the appropriate trust became beneficially entitled in possession before the expiration of the relevant period to an absolute interest in the entire of the property of which that inheritance consisted on and at all times after the date of that inheritance (other than property which ceased to be subject to the terms of the appropriate trust by virtue of a sale or exchange of an absolute interest in that property for full consideration in money or money's worth), then, in relation to all such earlier relevant inheritances, all such settled relevant inheritances or all such later relevant inheritances, as the case may be, the tax so chargeable is computed at the rate of 3 per cent.

(4) Where 2 or more persons are together beneficially entitled in possession to an absolute interest in property, those persons shall not, by reason only that together they are beneficially so entitled in possession, be regarded for the purposes of subsection (3) as beneficially so entitled in possession.

(5) Notwithstanding section 57, interest shall not be payable on any repayment of tax which arises by virtue of subsection (3).

CHAPTER 3

Annual Levy on Discretionary Trusts

Section 19

[S.102, FA 1986, as amended]

Interpretation (Chapter 3).

19. In this Chapter—

"chargeable date", in relation to any year, means 5 April in that year;

"chargeable discretionary trust" means a discretionary trust in relation to which—

(a) the disponer is dead, and

(b) none of the principal objects of the trust, if any, is under the age of 21 years;

"object" and "principal objects", in relation to a discretionary trust, have the meanings respectively assigned to them by section 14.

Section 20

[S.103, FA 1986]

Annual acquisitions by discretionary trusts.

20. (1) Where, in any year commencing with the year 2003, under or in consequence of any disposition, property is subject to a chargeable discretionary trust on the chargeable date, the trust is deemed on each such date to become beneficially entitled in possession to an absolute interest in that property, and to take on each such date an inheritance accordingly as if the trust, and the trustees as such for the time being of the trust, were together a person for the purposes of this Act, and each such chargeable date shall be the date of such inheritance.

(2) (a) In this subsection, "property" includes property representing such property.

(b) Where—

(i) under or in consequence of any disposition, property was subject to a discretionary trust prior to a chargeable date,

(ii) that property is not on that chargeable date subject to that discretionary trust (being on that date a chargeable discretionary trust) because such property is on that date property to which for the time being a person is beneficially entitled for an interest in possession, and

(iii) on that chargeable date that property is property which is limited to become subject again to that chargeable discretionary trust, or will do so by the exercise of a power of revocation, that property is deemed to be subject to that chargeable discretionary trust on that chargeable date if that interest in possession is an interest which is revocable or which is limited to cease on an event other than —

(I)   the death of that person, or

(II) the expiration of a specified period, where that interest is taken by that person under a power of appointment contained in that disposition and is, at the time of the appointment of that interest, an interest for a period certain of 5 years or more.

(3)   For the purposes of this section —

(a)   an interest in expectancy is not property until an event happens whereby the interest ceases to be an interest in expectancy or is represented by property which is not an interest in expectancy;

(b)   an interest in a policy of assurance on human life is not property until, and then only to the extent that, the interest becomes an interest in possession under the provisions of section 41 or is represented by property which is not an interest in expectancy.

(4)   This section shall not apply in relation to property which is subject to a chargeable discretionary trust on a chargeable date if that property or property representing that property is subject to a charge for tax arising under or in consequence of the same disposition by reason of section 15, or that provision of the repealed enactments which corresponds with section 15, on that same date or within the year prior to that date.

Section 21

[S.104, FA 1986, as amended]

Application of this Act.

21. In relation to a charge for tax arising by reason of section 20 —

(a)   a reference in section 27 to a company controlled by the successor and the definition in that section of "group of shares" is construed as if (for the purpose of that reference) the list of persons contained in subsection (3) of that section and (for the purpose of that definition) the list of persons contained in that definition included the following, that is, the trustees of the discretionary trust, the living objects of the discretionary trust, the relatives of those objects, nominees of those trustees or of those objects or of the relatives of those objects, and the trustees of a settlement whose objects include the living objects of the discretionary trust or relatives of those living objects;

(b)   (i) subject to the provisions of subparagraph (ii), the valuation date of the taxable inheritance is the relevant chargeable date;

(ii) where—

   (I) a charge for tax arises on a particular date by reason of section 15, or that provision of the repealed enactments which corresponds with section 15, giving rise to a taxable inheritance (in this subparagraph called the first taxable inheritance),

   (II) on a later date, a charge for tax arises under or in consequence of the same disposition by reason of section 20 giving rise to a taxable inheritance (in this subparagraph called the second taxable inheritance) comprising the same property or property representing that property, and

   (III) the valuation date of the first taxable inheritance is a date after the chargeable date of the second taxable inheritance,

   the valuation date of the second taxable inheritance is the same date as the valuation date of the first taxable inheritance;

(c) a person who is a trustee of the discretionary trust concerned for the time being at the date of the inheritance or at any date subsequent to that date is a person primarily accountable for the payment of the tax;

(d) an object of the discretionary trust concerned to whom or for whose benefit any of the property subject to the trust is applied or appointed is also accountable for the payment of tax the charge in respect of which has arisen prior to the date of the application or appointment of the property to that object or for that object's benefit, and this Act shall apply, in its application to that charge for tax, as if that object of the discretionary trust were a person referred to in section 45(2);

(e) any person who is primarily accountable for the payment of tax by virtue of paragraph (c) shall, within 3 months after the valuation date—

   (i) deliver to the Commissioners a full and true return—

      (I) of every inheritance in respect of which that person is so primarily accountable,

      (II) of all the property comprised in such inheritance, and

      (III) of an estimate of the market value of such property;

   (ii) notwithstanding any other provision of this Act, make an assessment of such amount of tax as, to the best of that person's knowledge, information and belief, ought to be charged, levied and paid on that valuation date; and

   (iii) pay the amount of such tax to the Collector;

   and

(f) section 30, section 45(1), section 46(2), (3), (4) and (5) and sections 50, 54, 56 and 81 and Schedule 2 shall not apply.

Section 22

[S.105, FA 1986]

Exemptions.

22. Section 20 shall not apply in relation to a discretionary trust referred to in section 17(1) or in respect of the property or the inheritance referred to in section 17(2).

Section 23

[S.106, FA 1986]

Computation of tax.

23. The tax chargeable on the taxable value of a taxable inheritance which is charged to tax by reason of section 20 is computed at the rate of one per cent of that taxable value.

Section 24

[S.107, FA 1986]

Values agreed.

24. (1)   Where—

(a) under or in consequence of any disposition, a charge for tax arises by reason of section 20 on a chargeable date (in this section called the first chargeable date),

(b) an accountable person has furnished all the information necessary to enable the Commissioners to ascertain the market value of—

(i)   real property, or

(ii) shares which are not dealt in on a stock exchange,

comprised in the taxable inheritance so taken on the valuation date of that taxable inheritance,

(c) pursuant to an application in writing to the Commissioners on that behalf, the market value of such property on that valuation date is agreed on between that person and the Commissioners,

(d) under or in consequence of the same disposition, a charge for tax arises by reason of section 20 on either or both of the 2 chargeable dates in the years next following the year in which the first chargeable date occurs (in this section called the subsequent chargeable dates), and

(e) the same property at subparagraph (i) or (ii) of paragraph (b) is comprised in the taxable inheritances so taken on the subsequent chargeable dates,

the value so agreed on is treated for the purposes of this Chapter as the market value of such property on that valuation date and on the valuation dates of the taxable inheritances so taken on the subsequent chargeable dates.

(2) Notwithstanding subsection (1), the market value so agreed is not binding—

(a) in any case where there is failure to disclose material facts in relation to any part of the property comprised in the taxable inheritances taken on the first chargeable date or on the subsequent chargeable dates, or

(b) where, at any time after the first chargeable date and before the third of those chargeable dates—

(i) in the case of real property, there is any alteration in the tenure under which the property is held or let, or

(ii) in the case of shares, there is any alteration in the capital or the ownership of the capital of the company concerned or of the rights of the shareholders inter se,

or

(c) where, at any time after the first chargeable date and before the third of those chargeable dates—

(i) in the case of real property, there is any change whatever, whether affecting that or any other property, which would materially increase or decrease the market value over and above any increase or decrease which might normally be expected if such a change had not occurred, or

(ii) in the case of shares, there has been any material change in the assets of the company or in their market value over and above any such change which might normally be expected,

and in such cases the market value of the real property, or of the shares, may be ascertained again by the Commissioners for each of the relevant valuation dates, but in the case of any change referred to in paragraph (c), the market value may be ascertained again by the Commissioners only at the request of the person primarily accountable for the payment of the tax arising by reason of section 20 on that relevant valuation date.

(3) Any agreement made under this section shall be binding only on the persons who as such are accountable for the payment of the tax arising by reason of section 20 on the first chargeable date and on the subsequent chargeable dates.

Section 25

[S.108, FA 1986]

Penalty.

25. Any person who contravenes or fails to comply with any requirement under paragraph (e) of section 21 is liable to a penalty of—

(a) €1,265, or

(b) twice the amount of tax payable in respect of the taxable inheritance to which the return relates,

whichever is the lesser.

PART 4

Value of Property for Tax

Section 26

[S.15, CATA]

Market value of property.

26. (1) In subsection (6), "unquoted shares or securities" means shares or securities which are not dealt in on a stock exchange.

(2) Subject to this Act, the market value of any property for the purposes of this Act is estimated to be the price which, in the opinion of the Commissioners, such property would fetch if sold in the open market on the date on which the property is to be valued in such manner and subject to such conditions as might reasonably be calculated to obtain for the vendor the best price for the property.

(3) In estimating the market value of any property, the Commissioners shall not make any reduction in the estimate on account of the estimate being made on the assumption that the whole property is to be placed on the market at one and the same time.

(4) The market value of any property shall be ascertained by the Commissioners in such manner and by such means as they think fit, and they may authorise a person to inspect any property and report to them the value of such property for the purposes of this Act, and the person having the custody or possession of that property shall permit the person so authorised to inspect it at such reasonable times as the Commissioners consider necessary.

(5) Where the Commissioners require a valuation to be made by a person named by them, the costs of such valuation shall be defrayed by the Commissioners.

(6) Subject to this Act, in estimating the price which unquoted shares or securities might be expected to fetch if sold in the open market, it shall be assumed that in that market there is available to any prospective purchaser of the shares or securities all the information

which a prudent prospective purchaser might reasonably require if that prudent prospective purchaser were proposing to purchase them from a willing vendor by private treaty and at arm's length.

Section 27

[S.16, CATA, as amended]

Market value of certain shares in private companies.

27. (1) In this section —

"group of shares", in relation to a private company, means the aggregate of the shares in the company of the donee or successor, the relatives of the donee or successor, nominees of the donee or successor, nominees of relatives of the donee or successor, and the trustees of a settlement whose objects include the donee or successor or relatives of the donee or successor;

"nominee" includes a person who may be required to exercise that person's voting power on the directions of, or who holds shares directly or indirectly on behalf of, another person;

"private company" means a body corporate (wherever incorporated) which —

(a) is under the control of not more than five persons, and

(b) is not a company which would fall within section 431 of the Taxes Consolidation Act 1997 if the words "private company" were substituted for the words "close company" in subsection (3) of that section, and if the words "are beneficially held by a company which is not a private company" were substituted for the words of paragraph (a) of subsection (6) of that section;

"share", in relation to a private company and in addition to the interpretation of "share" in section 2(1), includes every debenture, or loan stock, issued otherwise than as part of a transaction which is wholly and exclusively a bona fide commercial transaction.

(2) (a) The market value of each share in a private company which (after the taking of the gift or of the inheritance) is, on the date of the gift or on the date of the inheritance, a company controlled by the donee or successor, shall be ascertained by the Commissioners, for the purposes of tax, as if, on the date on which the market value is to be ascertained, it formed an apportioned part of the market value of a group of shares in that company, such apportionment, as between shares of a particular class, to be by reference to nominal amount, and, as between different classes of shares, to have due regard to the rights attaching to each of the different classes.

(b) For the purpose of ascertaining the market value of a share in a private company in the manner described in paragraph (a), the benefit to any private company (in this paragraph referred to as "the first-mentioned company") by virtue of its ownership of an interest in shares in another private company (in this paragraph referred to as "the second-mentioned company") is, where each of the companies so connected is a company which (after the taking of the gift or of the inheritance) is, on the date of the gift or on the date of the inheritance, a company controlled by the donee or successor, deemed to be —

    (i) such benefit as would be appropriate to the ownership of that interest if the second-mentioned company were under the control of the first-mentioned company in the same manner as (on the date on which the market value is to be ascertained) the second-mentioned company is under the control of the following, that is, the first-mentioned company, the donee or successor, the relatives of the donee or successor, nominees of the donee or successor, nominees of relatives of the donee or successor, and the trustees of a settlement whose objects include the donee or successor or relatives of the donee or successor, or

    (ii) the actual benefit appropriate to the ownership of that interest,

whichever is the greater.

(3) In this section, a reference to a company controlled by the donee or successor is a reference to a company that is under the control of any one or more of the following, that is, the donee or successor, the relatives of the donee or successor, nominees of the donee or successor, nominees of relatives of the donee or successor, and the trustees of a settlement whose objects include the donee or successor or relatives of the donee or successor; and for the purposes of this section, a company which is so controlled by the donee or successor shall be regarded as being itself a relative of the donee or successor.

(4) For the purposes of this section —

    (a) a company is deemed to be under the control of not more than 5 persons if any 5 or fewer persons together exercise, or are able to exercise, or are entitled to acquire control, whether direct or indirect, of the company and for this purpose —

        (i) persons who are relatives of any other person together with that other person,

        (ii) persons who are nominees of any other person together with that other person,

        (iii) persons in partnership, and

        (iv) persons interested in any shares or obligations of the company which are subject to any trust or are part of the estate of a deceased person,

shall respectively be treated as a single person, and

(b) a person is deemed to have control of a company at any time if —

  (i) that person then had control of the powers of voting on all questions, or on any particular question, affecting the company as a whole, which, if exercised, would have yielded a majority of the votes capable of being exercised on such questions or question, or could then have obtained such control by an exercise at that time of a power exercisable by that person or at that person's direction or with that person's consent,

  (ii) that person then had the capacity, or could then by an exercise of a power exercisable by that person or at that person's direction or with that person's consent obtain the capacity, to exercise or to control the exercise of any of the following powers, that is:

    (I) the powers of a board of directors of the company,

    (II) powers of a governing director of the company,

    (III) power to nominate a majority of the directors of the company or a governing director of the company,

    (IV) the power to veto the appointment of a director of the company, or

    (V) powers of a like nature;

  (iii) that person then had a right to receive, or the receipt of, more than one-half of the total amount of the dividends of the company, whether declared or not, and for the purposes of this subparagraph, "dividend" is deemed to include interest on any debentures of the company, or

  (iv) that person then had an interest in the shares of the company of an aggregate nominal value representing one-half or more of the aggregate nominal value of the shares of the company.

Section 28

[S.18, CATA, as amended]

Taxable value of a taxable gift or inheritance.

28. (1) In this section, "incumbrance-free value", in relation to a taxable gift or a taxable inheritance, means the market value at the valuation date of the property of which the taxable gift or taxable inheritance consists at that date, after deducting any liabilities, costs and expenses that are properly payable out of the taxable gift or taxable inheritance.

(2) Subject to this section (but except where provided in section 89), the taxable value of a taxable gift or a taxable inheritance (where the interest taken by the donee or successor is not a limited interest) is

ascertained by deducting from the incumbrance-free value of such a taxable gift or a taxable inheritance the market value of any bona fide consideration in money or money's worth, paid by the donee or successor for the gift or inheritance, including −

(a) any liability of the disponer which the donee or successor undertakes to discharge as that disponer's own personal liability, and

(b) any other liability to which the gift or inheritance is subject under the terms of the disposition under which it is taken,

and the amount so ascertained is the taxable value, but no deduction shall be made under this subsection in respect of any liability which is to be deducted in ascertaining the incumbrance-free value.

(3) Where a liability (other than a liability within the meaning of subsection (9)) for which a deduction may be made under subsection (1) or (2) is to be discharged after the time when it is to be taken into account as a deduction under either of those subsections, it is valued for the purpose of making such a deduction at its current market value at the time when it is to be so taken into account.

(4) The taxable value of a taxable gift or a taxable inheritance, where the interest taken by the donee or the successor is a limited interest, is ascertained as follows −

(a) the value of the limited interest in a capital sum equal to the incumbrance-free value is ascertained in accordance with the Rules contained in Schedule 1, and

(b) from the value ascertained in accordance with paragraph (a) a deduction is made in respect of the market value of any bona fide consideration in money or money's worth paid by the donee or the successor for the gift or the inheritance and the amount remaining after such deduction is the taxable value, but no deduction is made under this paragraph in respect of any liability which is to be deducted in ascertaining the incumbrance-free value.

(5) A deduction shall not be made under this section −

(a) in respect of any liability the payment of which is contingent on the happening of some future event, but if the event on the happening of which the liability is contingent happens and the liability is paid, then, on a claim for relief being made to the Commissioners and subject to the other provisions of this section, a deduction is made in respect of the liability and such adjustment of tax as is appropriate is made; and such adjustment is made on the basis that the donee or successor had taken an interest in possession in the amount which is to be deducted for the liability, for a period certain which was equal to the actual duration of the postponement of the payment of the liability,

(b) in respect of any liability, costs or expenses in so far as the donee or successor has a right of reimbursement from any source, unless such reimbursement can not be obtained,

(c) in respect of any liability created by the donee or successor or any person claiming in right of the donee or successor or on that donee or successor's behalf,

(d) in respect of tax, interest or penalties chargeable under this Act in respect of the gift or inheritance, or of the costs, expenses or interest incurred in raising or paying the same,

(e) in respect of any liability in so far as such liability is an incumbrance on, or was created or incurred in acquiring, any property which is comprised in any gift or inheritance and which is exempt from tax under any provision of this Act or otherwise,

(f) in the case of any gift or inheritance referred to in section 6(1)(c), 6(2)(d), 11(1)(b) or 11(2)(c) in respect of —

   (i) any liability, costs or expenses due to a person resident outside the State (except in so far as such liability is required by contract to be paid in the State or is charged on the property which is situate in the State and which is comprised in the gift or inheritance), or

   (ii) any liability, costs or expenses in so far as the same are charged on or secured by property which is comprised in the gift or inheritance and which is not situate in the State,

except to the extent that all the property situate outside the State and comprised in the gift or inheritance is insufficient for the payment of the liability, costs or expenses,

(g) for any tax in respect of which a credit is allowed under section 106 or 107.

(6) In the case of a gift or inheritance referred to in subsection (5)(f), any deduction to be made under subsection (2) or (4)(b) is restricted to the proportion of the consideration which bears the same proportion to the whole of the consideration as the taxable gift or taxable inheritance bears to the whole of the gift or the whole of the inheritance.

(7) A deduction shall not be made under this section —

(a) more than once for the same liability, costs, expenses or consideration, in respect of all gifts and inheritances taken by the donee or successor from the disponer, or.

(b) for any liability, costs, expenses or consideration, a proportion of which is to be allowed under section 89(2)(ii) or (iii) in respect of a gift or inheritance taken by the donee or successor from the disponer.

(8) Where a taxable gift or a taxable inheritance is subject to a liability within the meaning of subsection (9), the deduction to be made in

respect of that liability under this section shall be an amount equal to the market value of the whole or the appropriate part, as the case may be, of the property, within the meaning of section 5(5).

(9) For the purpose of subsection (8), "liability", in relation to a taxable gift or a taxable inheritance, means a liability which deprives the donee or successor, whether permanently or temporarily, of the use, enjoyment or income in whole or in part of the property, or of any part of the property, of which the taxable gift or taxable inheritance consists.

(10) Where—

    (a) bona fide consideration in money or money's worth has been paid by a person for the granting to that person, by a disposition, of an interest in expectancy in property, and

    (b) at the coming into possession of the interest in expectancy, that person takes a gift or an inheritance of that property under that disposition,

the deduction to be made under subsection (2) or (4)(b) for consideration paid by that person is a sum equal to the same proportion of the taxable value of the taxable gift or taxable inheritance (as if no deduction had been made for such consideration) as the amount of the consideration so paid bore to the market value of the interest in expectancy at the date of the payment of the consideration.

(11) Any deduction, under this section, in respect of a liability which is an incumbrance on any property, is, so far as possible, made against that property.

Section 29

[S.20, CATA]

Contingencies affecting gifts or inheritances.

29. (1) Where, under a disposition, a person becomes beneficially entitled in possession to any benefit and, under the terms of the disposition, the entitlement, or any part of the entitlement, may cease on the happening of a contingency (other than the revocation of the entitlement on the exercise by the disponer of such a power as is referred to in section 39), the taxable value of any taxable gift or taxable inheritance taken by that person on becoming so entitled to that benefit is ascertained as if no part of the entitlement were so to cease; but, in the event and to the extent that the entitlement so ceases, the tax payable by that person is, to that extent, adjusted (if, by so doing, a lesser amount of tax would be payable by such person) on the basis that such person had taken an interest in possession for a period certain which was equal to the actual duration of such person's beneficial entitlement in possession.

(2) Nothing in this section shall prejudice any charge for tax on the taking by such person of a substituted gift or inheritance on the happening of such a contingency.

Section 30

[S.21, CATA]

Valuation date for tax purposes.

30. (1) Subject to subsection (7), the valuation date of a taxable gift is the date of the gift.

(2) The valuation date of a taxable inheritance is the date of death of the deceased person on whose death the inheritance is taken if the successor or any person in right of the successor or on that successor's behalf takes the inheritance—

    (a) as a donatio mortis causa, or

    (b) by reason of the failure to exercise a power of revocation.

(3) If a gift becomes an inheritance by reason of its being taken under a disposition where the date of the disposition is within 2 years prior to the death of the disponer, the valuation date of the inheritance is determined as if it were a gift.

(4) The valuation date of a taxable inheritance, other than a taxable inheritance referred to in subsection (2) or (3), is the earliest date of the following:

    (a) the earliest date on which a personal representative or trustee or the successor or any other person is entitled to retain the subject matter of the inheritance for the benefit of the successor or of any person in right of the successor or on that successor's behalf,

    (b) the date on which the subject matter of the inheritance is so retained, or

    (c) the date of delivery, payment or other satisfaction or discharge of the subject matter of the inheritance to the successor or for that successor's benefit or to or for the benefit of any person in right of the successor or on that successor's behalf.

(5) If any part of a taxable inheritance referred to in subsection (4) may be retained, or is retained, delivered, paid or otherwise satisfied, whether by means of part payment, advancement, payment on account or in any manner whatever, before any other part or parts of such inheritance, the appropriate valuation date for each part of the inheritance is determined in accordance with that subsection as if each such part respectively were a separate inheritance.

(6) The Commissioners may give to an accountable person a notice in writing of the date determined by them to be the valuation date in respect of the whole or any part of an inheritance, and, subject to any decision on appeal pursuant to subsection (9), the date so determined is deemed to be the valuation date.

(7) If a taxable inheritance referred to in subsection (4) or (5) is disposed of, ceases or comes to an end before the valuation date referred to in those subsections in such circumstances as to give rise to a taxable

gift, the valuation date in respect of such taxable gift is the same date as the valuation date of the taxable inheritance.

(8) Notwithstanding anything contained in this section, the Commissioners may, in case of doubt, with the agreement in writing of the accountable person or that person's agent, determine the valuation date of the whole or any part of any taxable inheritance and the valuation date so determined is substituted for the valuation date which would otherwise be applicable by virtue of this section.

(9) An appeal shall lie against any determination made by the Commissioners under subsection (6) and section 67 shall apply, with any necessary modifications, in relation to an appeal under this subsection as it applies in relation to an appeal against an assessment of tax.

PART 5
Provisions Relating to Gifts and Inheritances

Section 31

[S.22, CATA]

Distributions from discretionary trusts.

31. Where a person becomes beneficially entitled in possession to any benefit—

(a) under a discretionary trust, other than a discretionary trust referred to in paragraph (b), otherwise than for full consideration in money or money's worth paid by the person, that person is deemed to have taken a gift,

(b) under a discretionary trust created—

(i) by will at any time,

(ii) by a disposition, where the date of the disposition is on or after 1 April 1975 and within 2 years prior to the death of the disponer, or

(iii) by a disposition inter vivos and limited to come into operation on a death occurring before, on or after the passing of this Act,

otherwise than for full consideration in money or money's worth paid by the person, that person is deemed to have taken an inheritance.

Section 32

[S.23, CATA]

Dealings with future interests.

32. (1)   In subsection (2), "benefit" includes the benefit of the cesser of a liability referred to in section 37.

(2)   Where a benefit, to which a person (in this section referred to as the remainderman) is entitled under a disposition, devolves, or is disposed of, either in whole or in part, before it has become an interest in possession so that, at the time when the benefit comes into possession, it is taken, either in whole or in part, by a person (in this section referred to as the transferee) other than the remainderman to whom it was limited by the disposition, then tax is payable, in respect of a gift or inheritance, as the case may be, of the remainderman in all respects as if, at that time, the remainderman had become beneficially entitled in possession to the full extent of the benefit limited to that remainderman under the disposition, and the transferee is the person primarily accountable for the payment of tax to the extent that the benefit is taken by that transferee.

(3)   Subsection (2) shall not prejudice any charge for tax in respect of any gift or inheritance affecting the same property or any part of it under any other disposition.

Section 33

[S.24, CATA]

Release of limited interests, etc.

33.   (1)   In this section, "event" includes —

(a)   a death, and

(b)   the expiration of a specified period.

(2)   Where an interest in property, which is limited by the disposition creating it to cease on an event, has come to an end (whether by another disposition, the taking of successive interests into one ownership, or by any means whatever other than the happening of another event on which the interest was limited by the first-mentioned disposition to cease) before the happening of such event, tax is payable under the first-mentioned disposition in all respects as if the event on which the interest was limited to cease under that disposition had happened immediately before the coming to an end of the interest.

(3)   Subsection (2) shall not prejudice any charge for tax in respect of any gift or inheritance affecting the same property or any part of it under any disposition other than that first mentioned in subsection (2).

(4)   Notwithstanding anything contained in subsection (3), if —

(a) an interest in property which was limited to cease on an event was limited to the disponer by the disposition creating that interest, and

(b) on the coming to an end of that interest, subsection (2) has effect in relation to a gift or inheritance which was taken by a donee or successor under that disposition and which consists of the property in which that interest subsisted, then—

a further gift or inheritance taken by the same donee or successor under another disposition made by the same disponer (being the disposition by which that interest has come to an end) is not a taxable gift or a taxable inheritance in so far as it consists of the whole or any part of the same property.

Section 34
[S.25, CATA]

Settlement of an interest not in possession.

34. (1) In this section, "event" has the same meaning as it has in section 33(1).

(2) Where any donee or successor takes a gift or an inheritance under a disposition made by such donee or successor then, if at the date of such disposition such donee or successor was entitled to the property comprised in the disposition, either expectantly on the happening of an event, or subject to a liability within the meaning of section 28(9), and such event happens or such liability ceases during the continuance of the disposition, tax is charged on the taxable value of the taxable gift or taxable inheritance which such donee or successor would have taken on the happening of such event, or on the cesser of such liability, if no such disposition had been made.

(3) Subsection (2) shall not prejudice any charge for tax in respect of any gift or inheritance affecting the same property or any part of it under the disposition referred to in that subsection.

Section 35
[S.26, CATA]

Enlargement of interests.

35. (1) Where a person, having a limited interest in possession in property (in this section referred to as the first-mentioned interest), takes a further interest (in this section referred to as the second-mentioned interest) in the same property, as a taxable gift or a taxable inheritance, in consequence of which that person becomes the absolute owner of the property, the taxable value of the taxable gift or taxable inheritance of the second-mentioned interest at the valuation date is reduced by the value at that date of the first-mentioned interest, taking such value to be the value, ascertained in accordance with the Rules contained in Schedule 1, of a limited interest which—

(a) is a limited interest in a capital sum equal to the value of the property,

(b) commences on that date, and

(c) is to continue for the unexpired balance of the term of the first-mentioned interest.

(2) For the purposes of subsection (1)(a), "value" means such amount as would be the incumbrance-free value, within the meaning of section 28(1), if the limited interest were taken, at the date referred to in subsection (1), as a taxable gift or taxable inheritance.

(3) This section shall not apply where the second-mentioned interest is taken under the disposition under which the first-mentioned interest was created.

Section 36

[S.27, CATA]

Dispositions involving powers of appointment.

36. (1) Where, by virtue of or in consequence of the exercise of, or the failure to exercise, or the release of, a general power of appointment by any person having such a power, a person becomes beneficially entitled in possession to any benefit, then, for the purposes of this Act, the disposition is the exercise of, or the failure to exercise, or the release of, the power and not the disposition under which the power was created, and the person exercising, or failing to exercise, or releasing, the power is the disponer.

(2) Where, by virtue of or in consequence of the exercise of, or the failure to exercise, or the release of, a special power of appointment by any person having such a power, a person becomes beneficially entitled in possession to any benefit, then, for the purposes of this Act, the disposition is the disposition under which the power was created and the person who created the power is the disponer.

Section 37

[S.28, CATA]

Cesser of liabilities.

37. (1) In this section, "appropriate part" has the meaning assigned to it by section 5(5).

(2) The benefit of the cesser of —

(a) a liability within the meaning of section 28(9),or

(b) any liability similar to that referred to in paragraph (a) to which the taking of a benefit which was a gift or inheritance was subject,

is deemed to be a gift or an inheritance, as the case may be, which is deemed —

(i) to the extent that the liability is charged on or secured by any property at the time of its cesser, to consist of the whole or the appropriate part, as the case may be, of that property, and

(ii) to the extent that the liability is not charged on or secured by any property at the time of its cesser, to consist of such sum as would, under section 5(2)(b), be the sum the annual income of which would be equal to the annual value of the liability.

(3) For the purposes of sections 6(1)(c), 6(2)(d), 11(1)(b) and 11(2)(c), the sum referred to in subparagraph (ii) of subsection (2) is deemed not to be situate in the State at the date of the gift or at the date of the inheritance.

Section 38

[S.29, CATA]

Disposition enlarging value of property.

38. (1) In subsection (4), "company" means a private company within the meaning of section 27.

(2) In this section, "property" does not include any property to which a donee or successor became beneficially entitled in possession prior to 28 February 1969.

(3) Where the taking by any person of a beneficial interest in any property (in this section referred to as additional property) under any disposition made by a disponer has the effect of increasing the value of any other property (in this section referred to as original property) to which that person is beneficially entitled in possession, and which had been derived from the same disponer, the following provisions shall apply —

(a) the increase in value so effected is deemed to be a gift or an inheritance, as the case may be, arising under that disposition and taken by that person, as donee or successor, from that disponer, at the time that donee or successor took the beneficial interest in the additional property,

(b) the original property is treated as having been increased in value if the market value of that property at the time referred to in paragraph (a) would be greater if it was sold as part of an aggregate of the original property and the additional property rather than as a single item of property, and the increase in value for the purposes of this section is the amount by which the market value of the original property if sold at that time as part of such aggregate would be greater than the amount of the market value of that property if sold at that time as a single item of property,

(c) the additional property is, for the purpose of determining its market value, deemed to be part of an aggregate of the original property and the additional property, and

(d) the market value of any property which is to be valued as part of an aggregate of property is ascertained as being so much of the market value of such aggregate as may reasonably be ascribed to that part.

(4) For the purpose of this section, the donee or successor is deemed to be beneficially entitled in possession to any property notwithstanding that within 5 years prior to such a disposition as is referred to in subsection (3) that donee or successor has divested such donee or successor of such property, or any part of such property, otherwise than for full consideration in money or money's worth or has disposed of it to a company of which such donee or successor is, at any time within that period of 5 years, deemed to have control within the meaning of section 27(4)(b).

Section 39

[S.30, CATA]

Gift subject to power of revocation.

39. Where, under any disposition, a person becomes beneficially entitled in possession to any benefit and, under the terms of the disposition, the disponer has reserved to such disponer the power to revoke the benefit, such person is, for the purposes of this Act,. deemed not to be beneficially entitled in possession to the benefit unless and until the power of revocation is released by the disponer, or otherwise ceases to be exercisable.

Section 40

[S.31, CATA]

Free use of property, free loans, etc.

40. (1) In subsections (2) and (4), "relevant period", in relation to any use, occupation or enjoyment of property, means the period of 12 months ending on 31 December in each year.

(2) A person is deemed to take a gift in each relevant period during the whole or part of which that person is allowed to have the use, occupation or enjoyment of any property (to which property that person is not beneficially entitled in possession) otherwise than for full consideration in money or money's worth.

(3) A gift referred to in subsection (2) is deemed to consist of a sum equal to the difference between the amount of any consideration in money or money's worth, given by the person referred to in subsection (2) for such use, occupation or enjoyment, and the best price obtainable in the open market for such use, occupation or enjoyment.

(4) A gift referred to in subsection (2) is treated as being taken at the end of the relevant period or, if earlier, immediately prior to the time when the use, occupation or enjoyment referred to in subsection (2) comes to an end.

(5) In any case where the use, occupation or enjoyment of property is allowed to a person, not being beneficially entitled in possession to that property, under a disposition—

(a) made by will,

(b) here the date of the disposition is on or after 1 April 1975 and within 2 years prior to the death of the disposer, or

(c) which is a disposition inter vivos and the use, occupation or enjoyment is had by that person after the cesser of another person's life interest,

subsections (2), (3) and (4) shall apply in relation to that property as if a reference to an inheritance were substituted for the reference to a gift wherever it occurs in those subsections, and for the purpose of this subsection "relevant period" in subsections (2) and (4), in relation to the use, occupation or enjoyment of property, means the period of 12 months ending on 31 December in any year.

(6) For the purposes of sections 6(1)(c), 6(2)(d), 11(1)(b) and 11(2)(c), the sum referred to in subsection (3) is deemed not to be situate in the State at the date of the gift or at the date of the inheritance.

Section 41

[S.32, CATA]

When interest in assurance policy becomes interest in possession.

41. (1) For the purposes of this Act, an interest in a policy of assurance on human life is deemed to become an interest in possession when either—

(a) the policy matures, or

(b) prior to the maturing of the policy, the policy is surrendered to the insurer for a consideration in money or money's worth, but if during the currency of the policy the insurer makes a payment of money or money's worth, in full or partial discharge of the policy, the interest is deemed to have come into possession to the extent of such payment.

(2) This section has effect in relation to a contract for a deferred annuity, and for the purposes of this section such a contract is deemed to mature on the date when the first instalment of the annuity is due.

Section 42

[S.33, CATA]

Provisions to apply where section 98 of Succession Act 1965 has effect.

42. (1) If, on the death of a testator and by virtue of section 98 of the Succession Act 1965, or otherwise, a disposition takes effect as if a person, who had predeceased the testator, had survived the testator, the benefit taken by the estate of that person is not deemed to be an inheritance.

(2) Where a person survives a testator, and—

(a) such person becomes beneficially entitled, under a disposition made by a person who predeceased the testator, to any benefit in relation to any property devised or bequeathed by the testator, and

(b) section 33 of the Wills Act 1837, or section 98 of the Succession Act 1965, or any analogous provision of the law of another territory has effect in relation to the devise or bequest,

such person is deemed for the purposes of inheritance tax to derive the benefit from the testator, as disponer.

Section 43

[S.34, CATA, as amended]

Disposition by or to a company.

43. (1) In this section—

"company" means a private company within the meaning of section 27;

"market value" means—

(a) in the case of a person's beneficial interest in shares and entitlements, the market value of that interest on the date of the payment, disposition, gift or inheritance, as the case may be, ascertained by reference to the market value on that date of the shares and entitlements in which the interest subsists, and

(b) in the case of a share in which a beneficial interest subsists, the market value of that share ascertained in the manner described in section 27 as if, on the date on which the market value is to be ascertained, it formed an apportioned part of the market value of a group of shares consisting of all the shares in the company issued and outstanding at that date;

"share" has the same meaning as it has in section 27;

"specified amount", in relation to a person's beneficial interest in shares and entitlements, means—

(a) in the case of consideration paid, or a disposition made, by the company, a nil amount or, if greater, the amount by which the market value of the beneficial interest was decreased as a result of the payment of the consideration or the making of the disposition, and

(b) in the case of consideration, or a gift, or an inheritance taken by the company, a nil amount or, if greater, the amount by which the market value of the beneficial interest was increased as a result of the taking of the consideration, gift or inheritance.

(2) For the purposes of this Act—

(a) consideration paid by, or a disposition made by, a company is deemed to be consideration, or a disposition, as the case may be, paid or made, and

(b) consideration, or a gift, or an inheritance taken by a company is deemed to be consideration, or a gift or an inheritance, as the case may be, taken,

by the beneficial owners of the shares in the company and the beneficial owners of the entitlements under any liability incurred by the company (otherwise than for the purposes of the business of the company, wholly and exclusively) in the same proportions as the specified amounts relating to their respective beneficial interests in the shares and entitlements bear to each other.

(3) For the purposes of subsection (2) all acts, omissions and receipts of the company are deemed to be those of the beneficial owners of the shares and entitlements, referred to in subsection (2), in the company, in the proportions mentioned in that subsection.

(4) Where the beneficial owner of any shares in a company or of any entitlement of the kind referred to in subsection (2), is itself a company, the beneficial owners of the shares and entitlements, referred to in subsection (2), in the latter company, are deemed to be the beneficial owners of the latter company's shares and entitlements in the former

company, in the proportions in which they are the beneficial owners of the shares and entitlements in the latter company.

(5) So far as the shares and entitlements referred to in subsection (2) are held in trust and have no ascertainable beneficial owners, consideration paid, or a disposition made, by the company are deemed to be paid or made by the disponer who made the disposition under which the shares and entitlements are so held in trust.

Section 44

[S.90, FA 1989, as amended, and s.127, FA 1993].

Arrangements reducing value of company shares.

44. (1) In this section—

"arrangement" means an arrangement which is made on or after 25 January 1989, and includes—

(a) any act or omission by a person or by the trustees of a disposition,

(b) any act or omission by any person having an interest in shares in a company,

(c) the passing by any company of a resolution, or

(d) any combination of acts, omissions or resolutions referred to in paragraphs (a), (b) and (c);

"company" means a private company within the meaning of section 27;

"event" includes—

(a) a death, and

(b) the expiration of a specified period;

"related shares" means the shares in a company, the market value of which shares is increased by any arrangement;

"related trust" has the meaning assigned to it by subsections (3) and (5);

"specified amount" means an amount equal to the difference between—

(a) the market value of shares in a company immediately before an arrangement is made, and ascertained under section 27 as if each share were a share in a company controlled at that time by the disponer concerned and that share was the absolute property of that disponer at that time, and

(b) the market value of those shares, or of property representing those shares, immediately after the arrangement is made, and ascertained under section 26,

and such specified amount is deemed to be situate where the company is incorporated.

(2) In this section, a reference to a company controlled by the disponer concerned is a reference to a company that is under the control of any one or more of the following, that is, that disponer, the relatives of that disponer, nominees of relatives of that disponer, and the trustees of a settlement whose objects include that disponer or relatives of that disponer, and for the purposes of this section, a company which is so controlled by that disponer is regarded as being itself a relative of that disponer.

(3) Where—

(a) a person has an absolute interest in possession in shares in a company, and

(b) any arrangement results in the market value of those shares, or of property representing those shares, immediately after that arrangement is made, being less than it would be but for that arrangement,

then, tax is payable in all respects as if a specified amount which relates to that arrangement were a benefit taken, immediately after that arrangement is made, from that person, as disponer, by—

(i) the beneficial owners of the related shares in that company, and

(ii) so far as the related shares in that company are held in trust (in this section referred to as the "related trust") and have no ascertainable beneficial owners, by the disponer in relation to that related trust as if, immediately after that arrangement is made, that disponer was the absolute beneficial owner of those related shares,

in the same proportions as the market value of the related shares, which are beneficially owned by them or are deemed to be so beneficially owned, is increased by that arrangement.

(4) Where—

(a) an interest in property is limited by the disposition creating it to cease on an event,

(b) immediately before the making of an arrangement to which paragraph (c) relates, the property includes shares in a company, and

(c) the arrangement results in the market value of those shares, or of property representing those shares, immediately after that arrangement is made, being less than it would be but for that arrangement,

then, tax is payable under that disposition in all respects—

(i) where the interest in property is an interest in possession, as if such property included a specified amount which relates to that arrangement,

(ii) where the interest in property is not an interest in possession, as if it were an interest in possession and such property included a specified amount which relates to that arrangement, and

(iii) as if the event on which the interest was limited to cease under that disposition had happened, to the extent of the specified amount, immediately before that arrangement is made.

(5) Where—

(a) shares in a company are, immediately before the making of an arrangement to which paragraph (b) relates, subject to a discretionary trust under or in consequence of any disposition, and

(b) the arrangement results in those shares, or property representing those shares, remaining subject to that discretionary trust but, immediately after that arrangement is made, the market value of those shares, or of property representing those shares, is less than it would be but for that arrangement,

then, tax shall be payable under that disposition in all respects as if a specified amount, which relates to that arrangement, were a benefit taken immediately after that arrangement is made—

(i) by the beneficial owners of the related shares in that company, and

(ii) so far as the related shares in that company are held in trust (in this section referred to as the "related trust") and have no ascertainable beneficial owners, by the disponer in relation to that related trust as if, immediately after that arrangement is made, that disponer was the absolute beneficial owner of those related shares,

in the same proportions as the market value of the related shares, which are beneficially owned by them or are deemed to be so beneficially owned, is increased by that arrangement.

(6) Subsections (3), (4) and (5) shall not prejudice any charge for tax in respect of any gift or inheritance taken under any disposition on or after the making of an arrangement referred to in those subsections and comprising shares in a company, or property representing such shares.

(7) Where shares in a company, which are held in trust under a disposition made by any disponer, are related shares by reason of any arrangement referred to in this section, any gift or inheritance taken under the disposition on or after the arrangement is made and comprising those related shares, or property representing those related shares, are deemed to be taken from that disponer.

(8) In relation to the tax due and payable in respect of any gift or inheritance taken under paragraph (ii) of subsection (3) or paragraph (ii) of subsection (5), and notwithstanding any other provision of this Act—

      (a) the disponer in relation to the related trust is not a person primarily accountable for the payment of such tax, and

      (b) a person who is a trustee of the related trust concerned for the time being at the date of the gift or at the date of the inheritance, or at any date subsequent to that date, is so primarily accountable.

(9) A person who is accountable for the payment of tax in respect of any specified amount, or part of a specified amount, taken as a gift or an inheritance under this section shall, for the purpose of paying the tax, or raising the amount of the tax when already paid, have power, whether the related shares are or are not vested in that person, to raise the amount of such tax and any interest and expenses properly paid or incurred by that person in respect of such tax, by the sale or mortgage of, or a terminable charge on, the related shares in the relevant company.

(10) Tax due and payable in respect of a taxable gift or a taxable inheritance taken under this section shall be and remain a charge on the related shares in the relevant company.

(11) Where related shares are subject to a discretionary trust immediately after an arrangement is made in accordance with the provisions of this section, the amount by which the market value of such shares is increased by such arrangement is property for the purposes of a charge for tax arising by reason of section 15.

(12) Where, immediately after and as a result of an arrangement, shares in a company have been redeemed, the redeemed shares are, for the purpose of the references to property representing shares in subsection (1) and subsection (3), (4) or (5), except a reference in relation to which the redeemed shares are actually represented by property, deemed, immediately after the arrangement, being an arrangement made on or after 6 May 1993, to be represented by property, and the market value of the property so deemed to represent the redeemed shares is deemed to be nil.

PART 6
Returns and Assessments

Section 45

[S.35, CATA, as amended, and s.81, FA 1989]

Accountable persons.

45. (1) The person primarily accountable for the payment of tax shall be –

      (a) except where provided in paragraph (b), the donee or successor, as the case may be, and

      (b) in the case referred to in section 32(2), the transferee referred to in that subsection, to the extent referred to in that subsection.

(2) Subject to subsections (3) and (4), the following persons shall also be accountable for the payment of any amount of the tax for which the persons referred to in subsection (1) are made primarily accountable —

(a) in the case of a gift —

(i) the disponer (other than a disponer in relation to a disposition where the date of the disposition was prior to 28 February 1974), and

(ii) every trustee, guardian, committee, personal representative, agent or other person in whose care any property comprised in the gift or the income from such property is placed at the date of the gift or at any time after that date and every person in whom the property is vested after that date, other than a bona fide purchaser or mortgagee for full consideration in money or money's worth, or a person deriving title from or under such a purchaser or mortgagee,

(b) (i) in the case of an inheritance, taken on or before the death of the disponer, the disponer (other than a disponer in relation to a disposition, where the date of the disposition was prior to 1 May 1989), and

(ii) in the case of any other inheritance, every trustee, guardian, committee, personal representative, agent or other person in whose care any property comprised in the inheritance or the income from such property is placed at the date of the inheritance or at any time after that date and every person in whom the property is vested after that date, other than a bona fide purchaser or mortgagee for full consideration in money or money's worth, or a person deriving title from or under such a purchaser or mortgagee.

(3) No person referred to in subsection (2)(a)(ii) or (b)(ii) is (unless that person is a person who is also primarily accountable under subsection (1)) liable for tax chargeable on any gift or inheritance to an amount in excess of —

(a) the market value of so much of the property of which the gift or inheritance consists, and

(b) so much of the income from such property,

which has been received by that person, or which, but for that person's own neglect or default, would have been received by that person or to which that person is beneficially entitled in possession.

(4) A person who acts solely in the capacity of an agent is not liable for tax chargeable on a gift or inheritance to an amount in excess of the market value of so much of the property of which the gift or inheritance consists and of the income from such property which that person held, or which came into that person's possession, at

any time after the serving on that person of the notice referred to in subsection (5).

(5) The Commissioners may serve on any person who acts solely in the capacity of agent in relation to any property comprised in a gift or an inheritance a notice in writing informing that person of that person's liability under this section.

(6) The tax shall be recoverable from any one or more of —

   (a) the accountable persons, and

   (b) the personal representatives of any accountable persons who are dead,

on whom the Commissioners have served notice in writing of the assessment of tax in exercise of the power conferred on them by section 49, but the liability of a personal representative under this subsection shall not exceed the amount for which the accountable person, of whom that person is the personal representative, was liable.

(7) Any person referred to in subsection (2)(a) or (b) or in subsection (6)(b) who is authorised or required to pay, and pays, any tax in respect of any property comprised in a gift or in an inheritance may recover the amount paid by that person in respect of tax from the person primarily accountable for that tax unless —

   (a) the latter person is the donee or successor referred to in paragraph (a) of subsection (1) and the interest taken by that latter person is a limited interest, or

   (b) in the case referred to in paragraph (b) of subsection (1), the latter person is the transferee and the interest taken by the remainderman is a limited interest.

(8) A person —

   (a) who is primarily accountable for the payment of tax, or

   (b) referred to in subsection (2)(a) or (b) or in subsection (6)(b) who is authorised or required to pay tax,

in respect of any property shall, for the purpose of paying the tax, or raising the amount of the tax when already paid, have power, whether the property is or is not vested in that person, to raise the amount of such tax and any interest and expenses properly paid or incurred by that person in respect thereof, by the sale or mortgage of, or a terminable charge on, that property or any part of that property.

(9) If a person, who is primarily accountable for the payment of tax in respect of a gift or inheritance (in this subsection and in subsection (11) referred to as the first gift or inheritance) derived from a disponer, has not paid the tax on the first gift or inheritance, the Commissioners may serve a notice in writing in accordance with subsection (11)

on any person who is, by virtue of paragraph (a)(ii) or (b)(ii) of subsection (2), accountable for the payment of tax on any other gift or inheritance (referred to in subsections (10) and (11) as the second gift or inheritance) taken by the same donee or successor from the same disponer, and the person on whom the notice is served shall at that time become accountable for the payment of tax in respect of the first gift or inheritance.

(10) Subsections (3), (4), (5), (6), (7) and (8) shall apply in relation to a person made accountable under subsection (9) as they apply in relation to a person referred to in paragraph (a)(ii) or (b) of subsection (2) and, for the purposes of this subsection—

(a) references in subsections (3) and (4) to the property of which the gift or inheritance consists, and

(b) the second and third references to property in subsection (8),

shall be construed as references to the property of which the second gift or inheritance consists, in so far as the last-mentioned property had not been duly paid out at the date of the service of the notice under subsection (9).

(11) A notice under subsection (9) shall refer expressly to the first and the second gift or inheritance, and shall inform the person on whom it is served of that person's accountability in respect of the first gift or inheritance.

(12) Every public officer having in such person's custody any rolls, books, records, papers, documents, or proceedings, the inspection of which may tend to secure the tax, or to prove or lead to the discovery of any fraud or omission in relation to the tax, shall at all reasonable times permit any person authorised by the Commissioners to inspect the rolls, books, records, papers, documents and proceedings, and to take notes and extracts as that person may deem necessary.

Section 46

[S.36, CATA, as amended]

Delivery of returns.

46. (1) In this section—

(a) notwithstanding anything contained in sections 6 and 11 a reference, other than in subsection (13) or (14), to a gift or a taxable gift includes a reference to an inheritance or a taxable inheritance, as the case may be, and

(b) a reference to a donee includes a reference to a successor.

(2) Subject to paragraph (e) of section 21, any person who is primarily accountable for the payment of tax by virtue of section 45(1), or by virtue of paragraph (c) of section 16 shall, within 4 months after the relevant date referred to in subsection (5)—

    (a) deliver to the Commissioners a full and true return of —

       (i) every gift in respect of which that person is so primarily accountable,

      (ii) all the property comprised in such gift on the valuation date,

    (iii) an estimate of the market value of such property on the valuation date, and

    (iv) such particulars as may be relevant to the assessment of tax in respect of such gift;

    (b) notwithstanding section 49, make on that return an assessment of such amount of tax as, to the best of that person's knowledge, information and belief, ought to be charged, levied and paid on that valuation date, and

    (c) duly pay the amount of such tax.

(3) Subsection (2)(c) shall be complied with —

    (a) where the tax due and payable in respect of any part of the gift is being paid by instalments under section 54, by the due payment of —

       (i) an amount which includes any instalment of tax which has fallen due prior to or on the date of the assessment of the tax referred to in subsection (2)(b), and

      (ii) any further instalments of such tax on the due dates in accordance with that section;

    (b) where the tax due and payable is inheritance tax which is being wholly or partly paid by the transfer of securities to the Minister for Finance under section 58, by —

       (i) delivering to the Commissioners with the return an application to pay all or part of the tax by such transfer,

      (ii) completing the transfer of the securities to the Minister for Finance within such time, not being less than 30 days, as may be specified by the Commissioners by notice in writing, and

    (iii) duly paying the excess, if any, of the amount of the tax referred to in subsection (2)(b), or in paragraph (a)(i), over the nominal face value of the securities tendered in payment of the tax in accordance with subparagraph (i).

(4) Subsection (2) applies to a charge for tax arising by reason of section 15 and to any other gift where —

    (a) the aggregate of the taxable values of all taxable gifts taken by the donee on or after 5 December 1991, which have the same group threshold (as defined in Schedule 2) as that other gift, exceeds an amount which is 80 per cent of the threshold amount (as defined in Schedule 2) which applies in the computation of tax on that aggregate, or

(b) the donee or, in a case to which section 32(2) applies, the transferee (within the meaning of, and to the extent provided for by, that section) is required by notice in writing by the Commissioners to deliver a return, and for the purposes of this subsection, a reference to a gift includes a reference to a part of a gift or to a part of a taxable gift, as the case may be.

(5) For the purposes of this section, the relevant date shall be—

(a) the valuation date, or

(b) where the donee or, in a case to which section 32(2) applies, the transferee (within the meaning of, and to the extent provided for by, that section) is required by notice in writing by the Commissioners to deliver a return, the date of the notice.

(6) Any person who is accountable for the payment of tax by virtue of subsection (2) or (9) of section 45 shall, if that person is required by notice in writing by the Commissioners to do so, comply with paragraphs (a), (b) and (c) of subsection (2) (as if that person were a person primarily accountable for the payment of tax by virtue of section 45(1)) within such time, not being less than 30 days, as may be specified in the notice.

(7) (a) Any accountable person shall, if that person is so required by the Commissioners by notice in writing, deliver and verify to the Commissioners within such time, not being less than 30 days, as may be specified in the notice—

(i) a statement (where appropriate, on a form provided, or approved of, by them) of such particulars relating to any property, and

(ii) such evidence as they require,

as may, in their opinion, be relevant to the assessment of tax in respect of the gift.

(b) The Commissioners may authorise a person to inspect—

(i) any property comprised in a gift, or

(ii) any books, records, accounts or other documents, in whatever form they are stored, maintained or preserved, relating to any property as may in their opinion be relevant to the assessment of tax in respect of a gift,

and the person having the custody or possession of that property, or of those books, records, accounts or documents, shall permit the person so authorised to make that inspection at such reasonable times as the Commissioners consider necessary.

(8) The Commissioners may by notice in writing require any accountable person to –

    (a) deliver to them within such time, not being less than 30 days, as may be specified in the notice, an additional return, if it appears to the Commissioners that a return made by that accountable person is defective in a material respect by reason of anything contained in or omitted from it,

    (b) notwithstanding section 49, make on that additional return an assessment of such amended amount of tax as, to the best of that person's knowledge, information and belief, ought to be charged, levied and paid on the relevant gift, and

    (c) duly pay the outstanding tax, if any, for which that person is accountable in respect of that gift,

and

    (i) the requirements of subparagraphs (ii), (iii) and (iv) of subsection (2)(a) shall apply to such additional return required by virtue of paragraph (a), and

    (ii) subsection (3) shall, with any necessary modifications, apply to any payment required by virtue of paragraph (c).

(9) Where any accountable person who has delivered a return or an additional return is aware or becomes aware at any time that the return or additional return is defective in a material respect by reason of anything contained in or omitted from it, that person shall, without application from the Commissioners and within 3 months of so becoming aware –

    (a) deliver to them an additional return,

    (b) notwithstanding section 49, make on that additional return an assessment of such amended amount of tax as, to the best of that person's knowledge, information and belief, ought to be charged, levied and paid on the relevant gift, and

    (c) duly pay the outstanding tax, if any, for which that person is accountable in respect of that gift, and

        (i) the requirements of subparagraphs (ii), (iii) and (iv) of subsection (2)(a) shall apply to such additional return required by virtue of paragraph (a), and

        (ii) subsection (3) shall, with any necessary modifications, apply to any payment required by virtue of paragraph (c).

(10) Any amount of tax payable by an accountable person in respect of an assessment of tax made by that accountable person on a return delivered by that accountable person (other than an amount of that tax payable by the transfer of securities to the Minister for Finance under section 56) shall accompany the return and be paid to the Collector.

(11) Any assessment or payment of tax made under this section shall include interest on tax payable in accordance with section 51.

(12) The Commissioners may by notice in writing require any person to deliver to them within such time, not being less than 30 days, as may be specified in the notice, a full and true return showing details of every taxable gift (including the property comprised in such gift) taken by that person during the period specified in the notice or, as the case may be, indicating that that person has taken no taxable gift during that period.

(13) As respects a taxable gift to which this subsection applies, any accountable person who is a disponer shall within 4 months of the valuation date deliver to the Commissioners a full and true return –

    (a) of all the property comprised in such gift on the valuation date,

    (b) of an estimate of the market value of such property on the valuation date, and

    (c) of such particulars as may be relevant to the assessment of tax in respect of the gift.

(14) Subsection (13) applies to a taxable gift, in the case where –

    (a) the taxable value of the taxable gift exceeds an amount which is 80 per cent of the group threshold (as defined in Schedule 2) which applies in relation to that gift for the purposes of the computation of the tax on that gift,

    (b) the taxable value of the taxable gift taken by the donee from the disponer increases the total taxable value of all taxable gifts and taxable inheritances taken on or after 5 December 1991 by the donee from the disponer from an amount less than or equal to the amount specified in paragraph (a) to an amount which exceeds the amount so specified, or

    (c) the total taxable value of all taxable gifts and taxable inheritances taken on or after 5 December 1991 by the donee from the disponer exceeds the amount specified in paragraph (a) and the donee takes a further taxable gift from the disponer.

(15) Where, under or in consequence of any disposition made by a person who is living and domiciled in the State at the date of the disposition, property becomes subject to a discretionary trust, the disponer shall within 4 months of the date of the disposition deliver to the Commissioners a full and true return of –

    (a) the terms of the discretionary trust,

    (b) the names and addresses of the trustees and objects of the discretionary trust, and

    (c) an estimate of the market value at the date of the disposition of the property becoming subject to the discretionary trust.

Section 47

[S.37, CATA, as amended]

Signing of returns, etc.

47. (1) A return or an additional return required to be delivered under this Act shall be signed by the accountable person who delivers the return or the additional return and shall include a declaration by the person signing it that the return or additional return is, to the best of that person's knowledge, information and belief, correct and complete.

(2) The Commissioners may require a return or an additional return to be made on oath.

(3) The Commissioners may, if they so think fit, accept a return or an additional return under this Act that has not been signed in accordance with this section and such return or additional return is deemed to be duly delivered to the Commissioners under this Act.

(4) (a) A return or additional return delivered under this Act shall—

   (i) be made on a form provided, or approved of, by the Commissioners, or

   (ii) except in a case to which subsection (2) relates but in a case where subsection (3) applies, be in a form approved of by the Commissioners and delivered by any electronic, photographic or other process approved of by them and in circumstances where the use of such process has been agreed by them and subject to such conditions as they may impose.

   (b) An affidavit, additional affidavit, account or additional account, delivered under this Act, shall be made on a form provided, or approved of, by the Commissioners.

(5) Any oath or affidavit to be made for the purposes of this Act may be made—

   (a) before the Commissioners,

   (b) before any officer or person authorised by the Commissioners in that behalf,

   (c) before any Commissioner for Oaths or any Peace Commissioner or Notary Public in the State, or

   (d) at any place outside the State, before any person duly authorised to administer oaths in that place.

Section 48

[S.38, CATA]

Affidavits and accounts.

48. (1)   In this section, "Inland Revenue affidavit" has the meaning assigned to it by section 22(1)(n) of the Finance Act 1894[1].

(2)   The Inland Revenue affidavit required for an application for probate or letters of administration shall extend to the verification of a statement of the following particulars:

(a)   details of all property in respect of which the grant of probate or administration is required and, in the case of a deceased person who died domiciled in the State, details of all property, wherever situate, the beneficial ownership of which, on that person's death, is affected —

(i)   by that person's will,

(ii)   by the rules for distribution on intestacy, or

(iii)   by Part IX or section 56 of the Succession Act 1965;

(b)   details of any property which was the subject matter of a disposition inter vivos made by the deceased person where the date of the disposition was within 2 years prior to that person's death or of a donatio mortis causa;

(c)   details of the inheritances arising under the will or intestacy of the deceased person or under Part IX or section 56 of the Succession Act 1965, or under the analogous law of another territory, together with a copy of any such will;

(d)   particulars of the inheritances (including the property comprised in such inheritances) other than those referred to in paragraphs (b) and (c), arising on the death of the deceased person;

(e)   the name and address of each person who takes an inheritance on the death of the deceased person and that person's relationship to the disponer; and

(f)   such other particulars as the Commissioners may require for the purposes of this Act.

(3)   Where the interest of the deceased person was a limited interest and that person died on or after the date of the passing of this Act, the trustee of the property in which the limited interest subsisted shall deliver an account which shall contain the following particulars —

(a)   details of each inheritance arising on the death of the deceased person under the disposition under which the limited interest of the deceased person arose, including the name and address of each person taking such inheritance and that person's relationship to the disponer, and

1149

(4) Notwithstanding subsection (2), interest is not payable on tax which is paid within 3 months of the valuation date, and where tax and interest, if any, on that tax is paid within 30 days of the date of assessment of that tax, interest shall not run on that tax for the period of 30 days from the date of the assessment or any part of that period, but, in relation to an assessment of tax made by an accountable person on a return delivered by that accountable person, interest is not payable on tax which is paid within 4 months of the valuation date.

(5) A payment on account of tax shall be applied —

   (a) if there is interest due on tax at the date of the payment, to the discharge, so far as may be, of the interest so due, and

   (b) if there is any balance of that payment remaining, to the discharge of so much tax as is equal to that balance,

   and a payment by an accountable person of tax is treated as a payment on account of tax for the purposes of this section, notwithstanding that the payment may be conditional or that the assessment of tax is incorrect.

(6) Subject to subsections (2), (4) and (5), payments on account may be made at any time, and when a payment on account is made, interest is not chargeable in respect of any period subsequent to the date of such payment on so much of the payment on account as is to be applied in discharge of the tax.

(7) In the case of a gift which becomes an inheritance by reason of its being taken under a disposition where the date of the disposition is within 2 years prior to the death of the disposer, this section has effect as if the references to the valuation date in subsections (1), (2), (3) and (4) were references to the date of death of the disposer.

(8) Where the value of a limited interest is to be ascertained in accordance with rule 8 of Schedule 1 as if it were a series of absolute interests, this section has effect, in relation to each of those absolute interests, as if the references to the valuation date in subsections (1), (2), (3) and (4) were references to the date of the taking of that absolute interest.

Section 52

[S.42, CATA]

Set-off of gift tax paid in respect of an inheritance.

52. Where an amount has been paid in respect of gift tax (or interest on such gift tax) on a gift which, by reason of the death of the disponer within 2 years after the date of the disposition under which the gift was taken, becomes an inheritance in respect of which inheritance tax is payable, the amount so paid is treated as a payment on account of the inheritance tax.

Section 53

[S.79, FA 1989]

Surcharge for undervaluation of property.

53. (1) In this section "ascertained value" means the market value subject to the right of appeal under section 66 or section 67.

(2) Where—

    (a) an accountable person delivers a return, and

    (b) the estimate of the market value of any asset comprised in a gift or inheritance and included in that return, when expressed as a percentage of the ascertained value of that asset, is within any of the percentages specified in column (1) of the Table to this section,

then the amount of tax attributable to the property which is that asset is increased by a sum (in this section referred to as the "surcharge") equal to the corresponding percentage, set out in column (2) of that Table opposite the relevant percentage in column (1), of that amount of tax.

(3) Interest is payable under section 51 on any surcharge as if the surcharge were tax, and the surcharge and any interest on that surcharge is chargeable and recoverable as if the surcharge and that interest were part of the tax.

(4) Any person aggrieved by the imposition on that person of a surcharge under this section in respect of any asset may, within 30 days of the notification to that person of the amount of such surcharge, appeal to the Appeal Commissioners against the imposition of such surcharge on the grounds that, having regard to all the circumstances, there were sufficient grounds on which that person might reasonably have based that person's estimate of the market value of the asset.

(5) The Appeal Commissioners shall hear and determine an appeal to them under subsection (4) as if it were an appeal to them against an assessment to tax, and the provisions of section 67 relating to an appeal or to the rehearing of an appeal or to the statement of a case for the opinion of the High Court on a point of law shall, with any

necessary modifications, apply accordingly.

TABLE

Estimate of the market value of the asset in the return, expressed as a percentage of the ascertained value of that asset	Surcharge
(1)	(2)
Equal to or greater than 0 per cent but less than 40 per cent	30 per cent
Equal to or greater than 40 per cent but less than 50 per cent	20 per cent
Equal to or greater than 50 per cent but less than 67 per cent	10 per cent

Section 54

[S.43, CATA]

Payment of tax by instalments.

54. (1) Subject to the payment of interest in accordance with section 51 and to the provisions of this section, the tax due and payable in respect of a taxable gift or a taxable inheritance may, at the option of the person delivering the return or additional return, be paid by 5 equal yearly instalments, the first of which is due at the expiration of 12 months from the date on which the tax became due and payable and the interest on the unpaid tax shall be added to each instalment and shall be paid at the same time as such instalment.

(2) An instalment not due may be paid at any time before it is due.

(3) In any case where and to the extent that the property of which the taxable gift or taxable inheritance consists is sold or compulsorily acquired, all unpaid instalments shall, unless the interest of the donee or successor is a limited interest, be paid on completion of the sale or compulsory acquisition and, if not so paid, shall be tax in arrear.

(4) This section shall not apply in any case where and to the extent to which a taxable gift or a taxable inheritance consists of personal property in which the donee, or the successor, or the transferee referred to in section 32(2), as the case may be, takes an absolute interest.

(5) In any case where the interest taken by a donee or a successor is an interest limited to cease on that person's death, and that person's death occurs before all the instalments of the tax in respect of the taxable gift or taxable inheritance would have fallen due if such tax were being paid by instalments, any instalment of such tax which would not have fallen due prior to the date of the death of that donee

or successor shall cease to be payable, and the payment, if made, of any such last-mentioned instalment is treated as an overpayment of tax for the purposes of section 57.

Section 55
[S.164, FA 1995, as amended]

Payment of tax on certain assets by instalments.

55. (1) In this section –

"agricultural property" has the meaning assigned to it by section 89;

"relevant business property" has the same meaning as it has in section 93, other than shares in or securities of a company (being shares or securities quoted on a recognised stock exchange) and without regard to sections 94 and 100(4).

(2) Where the whole or part of the tax which is due and payable in respect of a taxable gift or taxable inheritance is attributable to either or both agricultural property and relevant business property –

(a) section 54 shall apply to that whole or part of the tax notwithstanding subsection (3) or (4) of that section but where all or any part of that agricultural property or relevant business property, or any property which directly or indirectly replaces such property, is sold or compulsorily acquired and, by virtue of subsection (4) of section 89 or section 101, that sale or compulsory acquisition causes the taxable value of such a taxable gift or taxable inheritance to be increased, or would cause such increase if subsection (2) of section 89 or section 92 applied, all unpaid instalments referable to the property sold or compulsorily acquired shall, unless the interest of the donee or successor is a limited interest, be paid on completion of that sale or compulsory acquisition and, if not so paid, shall be tax in arrear, and

(b) notwithstanding subsection (2) of section 51 the rate at which interest is payable on that whole or part of the tax is 0.75 per cent or such other rate (if any) as stands prescribed by the Minister for Finance by regulations, for each month or part of a month instead of at the rate specified in that section and that section shall apply as regards that whole or part of the tax as if the rate so payable were substituted for the rate specified in that section, but the rate at which interest is payable on any overdue instalment of that whole or part of the tax, or on such part of the tax as would represent any such overdue instalment if that whole or part of the tax were being paid by instalments, shall continue to be at the rate specified in section 51.

(i) €6,345, and

(ii) the amount, or in the case of fraud, twice the amount, of the difference specified in subsection (5).

(4) Where any such return, additional return, statement, declaration, evidence or valuation as is mentioned in subsection (3) was delivered, made or furnished neither fraudulently nor negligently by a person and it comes to that person's notice that it was incorrect, then, unless the error is remedied without unreasonable delay, such matter is treated, for the purposes of this section, as having been negligently done by that person.

(5) The difference referred to in subsection (3) is the difference between –

(a) the amount of tax payable in respect of the taxable gift or taxable inheritance to which the return, additional return, statement, declaration, evidence or valuation relates, and

(b) the amount which would have been the amount so payable if the return, additional return, statement, declaration, evidence or valuation as made or submitted had been correct.

(6) For the purpose of subsection (3), where anything referred to in that subsection is delivered, made or furnished on behalf of a person, it is deemed to have been delivered, made or furnished by that person unless that person proves that it was done without that person's knowledge or consent.

(7) Any person who assists in or induces the delivery, making or furnishing for any purposes of the tax of any return, additional return, statement, declaration, evidence or valuation which that person knows to be incorrect shall be liable to a penalty of €1,265.

(8) This section shall not affect any criminal proceedings.

(9) Subject to this section, sections 987(4), 1061, 1062, 1063, 1064, 1065, 1066 and 1068 of the Taxes Consolidation Act 1997, shall, with any necessary modifications, apply to a penalty under this Act as if the penalty were a penalty under the Income Tax Acts.

Section 59

[S.44, CATA]

Postponement, remission and compounding of tax.

59. (1) Where the Commissioners are satisfied that tax leviable in respect of any gift or inheritance can not without excessive hardship be raised at once, they may allow payment to be postponed for such period, to such extent and on such terms (including the waiver of interest) as they think fit.

(2) If, after the expiration of the relevant period immediately following the date on which any tax became due and payable, the tax or any

part of that tax remains unpaid, the Commissioners may, if they think fit, remit the payment of any interest accruing after such expiration on the unpaid tax; and in this subsection, "relevant period" means the period at the end of which the interest on an amount payable in respect of tax would, at the rate from time to time chargeable during that period in respect of interest on tax, equal the amount of such tax.

(3) If, after the expiration of 20 years from the date on which any tax became due and payable, the tax or any part of that tax remains unpaid, the Commissioners may, if they think fit, remit the payment of such tax or any part of that tax and all or any interest on that tax.

(4) Where, in the opinion of the Commissioners, the complication of circumstances affecting a gift or inheritance or the value of that gift or inheritance or the assessment or recovery of tax on that gift or inheritance are such as to justify them in doing so, they may compound the tax payable on the gift or inheritance on such terms as they shall think fit, and may give a discharge to the person or persons accountable for the tax on payment of the tax according to such composition.

Section 60

[S.47, CATA]

Tax to be a charge.

60. (1) Tax due and payable in respect of a taxable gift or a taxable inheritance shall, subject to this section, be and remain a charge on the property (other than money or negotiable instruments) of which the taxable gift or taxable inheritance consists at the valuation date and the tax shall have priority over all charges and interests created by the donee or successor or any person claiming in right of the donee or successor or on that donee or successor's behalf, but where any settled property comprised in any taxable gift or taxable inheritance shall be subject to any power of sale, exchange, or partition, exercisable with the consent of the donee or successor, or by the donee or successor with the consent of another person, the donee or successor shall not be precluded by the charge of tax on that donee or successor's taxable gift or taxable inheritance from consenting to the exercise of such power, or exercising any power with proper consent, as the case may be; and where any such power is exercised, the tax shall be charged on the property acquired, in substitution for charging it on the property previously comprised in the gift or inheritance, and on all moneys arising from the exercise of any such power, and on all investments of such moneys.

(2) Property comprised in a taxable gift or taxable inheritance shall not, as against a bona fide purchaser or mortgagee for full consideration

in money or money's worth, or a person deriving title from or under such a purchaser or mortgagee, remain charged with or liable to the payment of tax after the expiration of 12 years from the date of the gift or the date of the inheritance.

(3) Tax shall not be a charge on property under subsection (1) as against a bona fide purchaser or mortgagee of such property for full consideration in money or money's worth without notice, or a person deriving title from or under such a purchaser or mortgagee.

Section 61

[S.48, CATA, as amended]

Receipts and certificates.

61. (1) When any amount in respect of tax is paid, the Commissioners shall give a receipt for the payment.

(2) The Commissioners shall, on application to them by a person who has paid the tax in respect of any property comprised in any taxable gift or taxable inheritance, give to the person a certificate, in such form as they think fit, of the amount of the tax paid by that person in respect of that property.

(3) The Commissioners shall, on application to them by a person who is an accountable person in respect of any of the property of which a taxable gift or taxable inheritance consists, if they are satisfied that the tax charged on the property in respect of the taxable gift or taxable inheritance has been or will be paid, or that there is no tax so charged, give a certificate to the person, in such form as they think fit, to that effect.

(4) Where a person who is an accountable person in respect of the property of which a taxable gift or taxable inheritance consists has—

    (a) delivered to the Commissioners, a full and true return of all the property comprised in the gift or inheritance on the valuation date and such particulars as may be relevant to the assessment of tax in respect of the gift or inheritance,

    (b) made on that return an assessment of such amount of tax as, to the best of that person's knowledge, information and belief, ought to be charged, levied and paid, and

    (c) duly paid the amount of such tax (if any),

the Commissioners may give a certificate to the person, in such form as they think fit, to the effect that the tax charged on the property in respect of the taxable gift or taxable inheritance has been paid or that there is no tax so charged.

(5) A certificate referred to in subsection (3) or (4) shall discharge the property from liability for tax (if any) in respect of the gift or

inheritance, to the extent specified in the certificate, but shall not discharge the property from tax in case of fraud or failure to disclose material facts and, in any case, shall not affect the tax payable in respect of any other property or the extent to which tax is recoverable from any accountable person or from the personal representatives of any accountable person, but a certificate purporting to be a discharge of the whole tax payable in respect of any property included in the certificate in respect of a gift or inheritance shall exonerate from liability for such tax a bona fide purchaser or mortgagee for full consideration in money or money's worth without notice of such fraud or failure and a person deriving title from or under such a purchaser or mortgagee.

(6) Subject to subsection (7), where tax is chargeable on the taxable value of a taxable gift or taxable inheritance and—

  (a) application is made to the Commissioners by any person (in this section referred to as "the applicant")—

    (i) who is a person accountable, but not primarily accountable, for the payment of the whole or part of the tax, or

    (ii) who is the personal representative of any person referred to in subparagraph (i),

  and

  (b) the applicant—

    (i) delivers to the Commissioners a full and true return of all the property comprised in the gift or inheritance and such particulars as may be relevant to the assessment of tax in respect of the gift or inheritance, and

    (ii) makes on that return an assessment of such amount of tax as, to the best of that person's knowledge, information and belief, ought to be charged, levied and paid,

the Commissioners may, on payment of the tax assessed by the applicant, give a certificate to the applicant which shall discharge the applicant from any other claim for tax in respect of the gift or inheritance.

(7) A certificate by the Commissioners under subsection (6) shall not discharge the applicant in the case of fraud or failure to disclose material facts within that applicant's own knowledge and shall not affect any further tax that may be payable by the applicant if any further property is afterwards shown to have been comprised in the taxable gift or taxable inheritance to which the certificate relates and in respect of which further property the applicant is liable for the tax.

Section 62

[S.146, FA 1994, as amended]

Certificate relating to registration of title based on possession.

62. (1) In this section —

"the Act of 1964" means the Registration of Title Act 1964;

"the Registrar" means the Registrar of Titles;

"relevant period", in relation to a person's application to be registered as owner of property, means the period commencing on 28 February 1974 and ending on the date as of which the registration was made, but —

(a) where the certificate referred to in subsection (2) is a certificate for a period ending prior to the date of the registration, the period covered by the certificate shall be deemed to be the relevant period if, at the time of the registration, the Registrar had no reason to believe that a death relevant to the application for registration occurred after the expiration of the period covered by the certificate, and

(b) where the registration of the person (if any) who, at the date of that application, was the registered owner of the property had been made as of a date after 28 February 1974, the relevant period shall commence on the date as of which that registration was made;

"the Rules of 1972" means the Land Registration Rules 1972 (S.I. No. 230 of 1972).

(2) A person shall not be registered as owner of property in a register of ownership maintained under the Act of 1964 on foot of an application made to the Registrar on or after the date of the passing of this Act which is —

(a) based on possession, and.

(b) made under the Rules of 1972, or any other rule made for carrying into effect the objects of the Act of 1964,

unless the applicant produces to the Registrar a certificate issued by the Commissioners to the effect that the Commissioners are satisfied —

(i) that the property did not become charged with gift tax or inheritance tax during the relevant period, or

(ii) that any charge for gift tax or inheritance tax to which the property became subject during that period has been discharged, or will (to the extent that it has not been discharged) be discharged within a time considered by the Commissioners to be reasonable.

(3) In the case of an application for registration in relation to which a solicitor's certificate is produced for the purpose of rule 19(3), 19(4) or 35 of the Rules of 1972, the Registrar may accept that the application

is not based on possession if the solicitor makes to the Registrar a declaration in writing to that effect.

(4) Where, on application to them by the applicant for registration, the Commissioners are satisfied that they may issue a certificate for the purpose of subsection (2), they shall issue a certificate for that purpose, and the certificate and the application for that certificate shall be on a form provided by the Commissioners.

(5) A certificate issued by the Commissioners for the purpose of subsection (2) shall be in such terms and subject to such qualifications as the Commissioners think fit, and shall not be a certificate for any other purpose.

(6) In subsection (2), the reference to a certificate issued by the Commissioners shall be construed as including a reference to a certificate to which subsection (7) relates, and subsection (2) shall be construed accordingly.

(7) (a) In this subsection—

"the relevant particulars" means the particulars of title to the relevant property which are required to be produced to the Registrar for the purposes of paragraph 2 of Form 5 of the Schedule of Forms referred to in the definition of "Forms" contained in rule 2(1) of the Rules of 1972;

"the relevant property" means the property in respect of which the application for registration is being made.

(b) A certificate to which this subsection relates is a certificate by the solicitor for the applicant for registration in which it is certified, on a form provided by the Commissioners, that the solicitor—

(i) is satisfied—

(I) in a case where the applicant is a statutory authority within the definition of "statutory authority" contained in section 3(1) of the Act of 1964, that the market value of the relevant property at the time of the application does not exceed €127,000, or

(II) in any other case, that—

(A) the area of the relevant property does not exceed 5 hectares, and

(B) the market value of the relevant property at the time of the application does not exceed €19,050,

and

(ii) having investigated the title to the relevant property, has no reason to believe that the relevant particulars, in so far as relating to the relevant property at any time during the relevant period, are particulars which related at that time to significant other real property, that is, real property which, if combined with the relevant property for the purposes of subparagraph (i), would cause a limit which applies to the relevant property by virtue of that subparagraph to be exceeded.

(8) Notwithstanding subsection (7), a certificate by the solicitor for the applicant for registration shall be a certificate to which subsection (7) relates if it certifies, on a form provided by the Commissioners, that the solicitor is satisfied that—

(a) the area of the property in respect of which the application for registration is being made does not exceed 500 square metres,

(b) the market value of that property at the time of the application does not exceed €2,540, and

(c) the application is not part of a series of related applications covering a single piece of property the total area of which exceeds 500 square metres or the market value of which at the time of the application exceeds €2,540.

Section 63

[S.49, CATA]

Recovery of tax and penalties.

63. (1) Any sum due and payable in respect of tax or interest on such tax and any penalty incurred in connection with tax or interest on such tax is deemed to be a debt due by the accountable person or, if that person is dead, by that person's personal representative, to the Minister for Finance for the benefit of the Central Fund and is payable to the Commissioners and may (without prejudice to any other mode of recovery of such tax and interest) be sued for and recovered by action, or other appropriate proceeding, at the suit of the Attorney General or the Minister for Finance or the Commissioners in any court of competent jurisdiction, notwithstanding anything to the contrary contained in the Inland Revenue Regulation Act 1890.

(2) Any person who, having received any sum of money as or for any tax, interest, or penalty under this Act, does not apply the money to the due payment of the tax, interest or penalty, and improperly withholds or detains the same, is accountable for the payment of the tax, interest or penalty to the extent of the amount so received by that person and the same is a debt due by that person to the Minister for Finance for the benefit of the Central Fund and is recoverable in like manner as a debt under subsection (1).

(3) If any accountable person is liable under section 46 to deliver to the Commissioners a return or an additional return and makes default in so doing, the Attorney General or the Minister for Finance or the Commissioners may sue by action or other appropriate proceeding in the Circuit Court for an order directing the person so making default

to deliver such return or additional return or to show cause to the contrary; and the Circuit Court may by order direct such accountable person to deliver such return or additional return within such time as may be specified in the order.

(4) Whenever property is subject to a charge by virtue of section 60, the Attorney General or the Minister for Finance or the Commissioners may sue by action or other appropriate proceeding in any court of competent jurisdiction for, and the court may make, an order directing the owner of the property to pay the tax with which the property is charged.

Section 64

[S.129, FA 1991, as amended]

Application of certain income tax provisions in relation to the collection and recovery of capital acquisitions tax, etc.

64. (1) In this section "functions" includes powers and duties.

(2) All sums due under this Act shall be paid to the Collector or to such person as may be nominated under this section.

(3) Section 928(1) and 964(2) of the Taxes Consolidation Act 1997, shall, with any necessary modifications, apply in relation to an assessment of tax, a correcting assessment of tax, or an additional assessment of tax as it applies in relation to assessments to income tax.

(4) The Collector shall collect and levy the tax from time to time charged in all assessments, correcting assessments and additional assessments of which particulars have been transmitted to the Collector under subsection (3).

(5) All the provisions of the Income Tax Acts relating to the collection and recovery of income tax shall, subject to any necessary modifications, apply in relation to tax as they apply in relation to income tax chargeable under Schedule D.

(6) (a) The Commissioners may nominate persons to exercise on behalf of the Collector any or all of the functions conferred on the Collector by this section and, accordingly, those functions, as well as being exercisable by the Collector, shall also be exercisable on the Collector's behalf by persons so nominated.

(b) A person shall not be nominated under this subsection unless that person is an officer or employee of the Commissioners.

Section 65

[S.50, CATA]

Evidence in proceedings for recovery of tax.

65. Section 39 of the Finance Act 1926[1], shall apply in any proceedings in the Circuit Court or the District Court for or in relation to the recovery of the tax.

Footnote
1   Reproduced on page 657.

PART 8
Appeals

Section 66

[S.51, CATA]

Appeals regarding value of real property.

66. (1)   If a person is aggrieved by the decision of the Commissioners as to the market value of any real property, that person may appeal against the decision in the manner prescribed by section 33 of the Finance (1909-10) Act 1910[1], and the provisions as to appeals under that section of that Act shall apply accordingly with any necessary modifications.

(2)   The particulars of any transfer or lease which are presented to or obtained by the Commissioners under section 12(2) of the Stamp Duties Consolidation Act 1999 shall, in any appeal under this section, be received as prima facie evidence of all matters and things stated in such particulars.

Footnote
1   Reproduced on page 655.

Section 67

[S.52, CATA, as amended]

Appeals in other cases.

67. (1) In this section —

"Appeal Commissioners" has the meaning assigned to it by section 850 of the Taxes Consolidation Act 1997;

"appellant" means a person who appeals to the Appeal Commissioners under subsection (2),

(2) Subject to the other provisions of this Act, a person who is called on by the Commissioners to pay an assessment of tax in respect of any property and who is aggrieved by the assessment may, in accordance with this section, appeal to the Appeal Commissioners against the assessment and the appeal shall be heard and determined by the Appeal Commissioners whose determination shall be final and conclusive unless the appeal is required to be reheard by a judge of the Circuit Court or a case is required to be stated in relation to it for the opinion of the High Court on a point of law.

(3) An appeal shall not lie under this section in relation to the market value of real property.

(4) A person who intends to appeal under this section against an assessment shall, within 30 days after the date of the assessment, give notice in writing to the Commissioners of that person's intention to appeal against the assessment.

(5) (a) Subject to this section, the provisions of the Income Tax Acts relating to —

(i) the appointment of times and places for the hearing of appeals,

(ii) the giving of notice to each person who has given notice of appeal of the time and place appointed for the hearing of that person's appeal,

(iii) the determination of an appeal by agreement between the appellant and an officer appointed by the Commissioners in that behalf,

(iv) the determination of an appeal by the appellant giving notice of that appellant's intention not to proceed with the appeal,

(v) the hearing and determination of an appeal by the Appeal Commissioners, including the hearing and determination of an appeal by one Appeal Commissioner,

(vi) the publication of reports of determinations of the Appeal Commissioners,

(vii) the determination of an appeal through the neglect or

refusal of a person who has given notice of appeal to attend before the Appeal Commissioners at the time and place appointed,

(viii) the extension of the time for giving notice of appeal and the readmission of appeals by the Appeal Commissioners and the provisions which apply where action by means of court proceedings has been taken,

(ix) the rehearing of an appeal by a judge of the Circuit Court and the statement of a case for the opinion of the High Court on a point of law,

(x) the payment of tax in accordance with the determination of the Appeal Commissioners notwithstanding that an appeal is required to be reheard by a judge of the Circuit Court or that a case for the opinion of the High Court on a point of law has been required to be stated or is pending,

(xi) the procedures for appeal,

(xii) the refusal of an application for an appeal hearing,

shall, with any necessary modifications, apply to an appeal under this section as if the appeal were an appeal against an assessment to income tax.

(b) The Commissioners shall, subject to their giving notice in writing in that behalf to the appellant within 10 days after the determination of an appeal by the Appeal Commissioners, have the same right as the appellant to have the appeal reheard by a judge of the Circuit Court.

(c) The rehearing of an appeal under this section by a judge of the Circuit Court shall be by a judge of the Circuit Court in whose circuit the appellant or one of the appellants resides or (in the case of a body corporate) has its principal place of business, but—

(i) in any case where no appellant is resident in or (in the case of a body corporate) has a place of business in the State, or

(ii) in any case where there is a doubt or a dispute as to the circuit,

the appeal shall be reheard by a judge of the Circuit Court assigned to the Dublin Circuit.

(6) (a) Where a notice or other document which is required or authorised to be served by this section is to be served on a body corporate, such notice shall be served on the secretary or other officer of the body corporate.

(b) Any notice or other document which is required or authorised by this section to be served by the Commissioners or by an appellant may be served by post and in the case of a notice or other document addressed to the Commissioners, shall be sent to the Secretaries, Revenue Commissioners, Dublin Castle, Dublin 2.

(c) Any notice or other document which is required or authorised to be served by the Commissioners on an appellant under this section may be sent to the solicitor, accountant or other agent of the appellant and a notice thus served shall be deemed to have been served on the appellant unless the appellant proves to the satisfaction of the Appeal Commissioners, or the Circuit Court, as the case may be, that that appellant had, before the notice or other document was served, withdrawn the authority of such solicitor, accountant or other agent to act on that appellant's behalf.

(7) Prima facie evidence of any notice given under this section by the Commissioners or by an officer of the Commissioners may be given in any proceedings by the production of a document purporting –

(a) to be a copy of the notice, or

(b) if the details specified in the notice are contained in an electronic, photographic or other record maintained by the Commissioners, to reproduce those details in so far as they relate to that notice,

and it shall not be necessary to prove the official position of the person by whom the notice purports to be given or, if it is signed, the signature, or that the person signing and giving it was authorised to do so.

(8) (a) The Commissioners may serve notice in writing, referring expressly to this subsection, on any person whom they have reason to believe to be accountable for the payment of tax, of any decision they have made which is relevant to such tax.

(b) Any person who is informed of a decision in accordance with paragraph (a) may appeal to the Appeal Commissioners against the decision.

(c) The Appeal Commissioners shall hear and determine an appeal to them under this subsection as if it were an appeal to them against an assessment to tax, and the provisions of this section relating to an appeal or to the rehearing of an appeal or to the statement of a case for the opinion of the High Court on a point of law shall, with any necessary modifications, apply accordingly.

Section 68

[S.52A, CATA]

Conditions before appeal may be made.

68. No appeal shall lie under section 66 or 67 until such time as the person aggrieved by the decision or assessment (as the case may be) complies with section 46(2) in respect of the gift or inheritance in relation to which

     (c)   under a disposition made by the spouse of the insured where the inheritance is taken only in the event of the insured not surviving the spouse by a period of up to 31 days,

and the relevant qualifying insurance policy is—

     (i)   a policy of insurance within the meaning of paragraphs (a), (b) and (c) of the definition of "insured" in this subsection, or

     (ii) a policy of insurance where the insured is an individual and the proceeds of the policy are payable only on the contingency of the insured surviving that spouse.

(2) (a) An interest in a qualifying insurance policy which is comprised in an inheritance taken under a disposition made by the insured is, to the extent that the proceeds of the policy are applied in paying relevant tax, exempt from tax in relation to that inheritance and is not taken into account in computing tax.

    (b) An interest in a qualifying insurance policy which is comprised in an inheritance taken under a disposition made by the insured is, to the extent that the proceeds of the policy are not applied in paying relevant tax, and notwithstanding the provisions of this Act, deemed to be taken on a day immediately after—

     (i)   the date of the death of the insured, or

     (ii) the latest date (if any) on which an inheritance is taken in respect of which that relevant tax is payable,

whichever is the later.

Section 73

[S.119, FA 1991]

Relief in respect of certain policies of insurance relating to tax payable on gifts.

73. (1) In this section—

"appointed date" means—

    (a) a date occurring not earlier than 8 years after the date on which a relevant insurance policy is effected, or

    (b) a date on which the proceeds of a relevant insurance policy become payable either on the critical illness or the death of the insured, or one of the insured in a case to which paragraph (b) of the definition of "insured" relates, being a date prior to the date to which paragraph (a) of this definition relates;

"insured" means—

    (a) where the insured is an individual, that individual, or

(b) where the insured is an individual and the spouse of that individual at the date the policy is effected, that individual and the spouse of that individual, jointly or separately, or the survivor of them, as the case may be;

"relevant insurance policy" means a policy of insurance –

(a) which is in a form approved by the Commissioners for the purposes of this section,

(b) in respect of which annual premiums are paid by the insured,

(c) the proceeds of which are payable on the appointed date, and

(d) which is expressly effected under this section for the purpose of paying relevant tax;

"relevant tax" means gift tax or inheritance tax, payable in connection with an inter vivos disposition made by the insured within one year after the appointed date, excluding gift tax or inheritance tax payable on an appointment out of an inter vivos discretionary trust set up by the insured.

(2) The proceeds of a relevant insurance policy are, to the extent that such proceeds are used to pay relevant tax, exempt from tax and are not taken into account in computing such tax.

(3) Subject to sections 70 and 76, where the insured makes an inter vivos disposition of the proceeds, or any part of the proceeds, of a relevant insurance policy other than in paying relevant tax, such proceeds are not exempt from tax.

(4) A relevant insurance policy is a qualifying insurance policy for the purposes of section 72 where the proceeds of such relevant insurance policy become payable on the death of the insured or one of the insured in a case to which paragraph (b) of the definition of "insured" relates, if such relevant insurance policy would have been a qualifying insurance policy if it had been expressly effected under that section.

(5) A qualifying insurance policy for the purposes of section 72 is a relevant insurance policy where the proceeds of such qualifying insurance policy are used to pay relevant tax arising under an inter vivos disposition made by the insured within one year after the appointed date.

Section 74

[S.133, FA 1993]

Exemption of certain policies of assurance.

74. (1) In this section –

"assurance company" has the meaning assigned to it by section 706 of the Taxes Consolidation Act 1997;

"new policy" means a contract entered into by an assurance company which is a policy of assurance on the life of any person issued on or after 1 January 2001;

"old policy" means a contract entered into by an assurance company in the course of carrying on a foreign life assurance business within the meaning of section 451 of the Taxes Consolidation Act 1997 and issued on or after 1 December 1992 and before 1 January 2001.

(2) Where any interest in a new policy or in an old policy is comprised in a gift or an inheritance, then any such interest –

  (a) is exempt from tax, and

  (b) is not taken into account in computing tax on any gift or inheritance taken by a donee or successor,

if it is shown to the satisfaction of the Commissioners that –

  (i) such interest is comprised in the gift or inheritance at the date of the gift or at the date of the inheritance,

  (ii) at the date of the disposition, the disponer is neither domiciled nor ordinarily resident in the State, and

  (iii) at the date of the gift or at the date of the inheritance, the donee or successor is neither domiciled nor ordinarily resident in the State.

(3) Where –

  (a) an interest in a new policy or in an old policy, as the case may be, which is comprised in a gift or inheritance came into the beneficial ownership of the disponer or became subject to the disposition prior to 15 February 2001, and

  (b) the conditions at subparagraphs (i) and (iii) of subsection (2) are complied with,

then that subsection shall apply to that interest in a new policy or in an old policy, as the case may be, if, at the date of the disposition, the proper law of the disposition was not the law of the State.

Section 75
[S.85, FA 1989, as amended, and s.224, FA 2001]

Exemption of specified collective investment undertakings.

75. In this section –

"investment undertaking" has the meaning assigned to it by section 739B of the Taxes Consolidation Act 1997;

"specified collective investment undertaking" has the meaning assigned to it by section 734 of the Taxes Consolidation Act 1997;

"unit", in relation to an investment undertaking, has the meaning assigned to it by section 739B of the Taxes Consolidation Act 1997;

"unit", in relation to a specified collective investment undertaking, has the meaning assigned to it by section 734 of the Taxes Consolidation Act 1997.

(2) Where any unit of an investment undertaking or of a specified collective investment undertaking is comprised in a gift or an inheritance, then such unit—

  (a) is exempt from tax, and

  (b) is not taken into account in computing tax on any gift or inheritance taken by the donee or successor,

  if it is shown to the satisfaction of the Commissioners that—.

  (i) the unit is comprised in the gift or inheritance—

    (I) at the date of the gift or at the date of the inheritance, and

    (II) at the valuation date,

  (ii) at the date of the disposition, the disponer is neither domiciled nor ordinarily resident in the State, and

  (iii) at the date of the gift or at the date of the inheritance, the donee or successor is neither domiciled nor ordinarily resident in the State.

(3) Where—

  (a) any unit of an investment undertaking or of a specified collective investment undertaking which is comprised in a gift or inheritance came into the beneficial ownership of the disponer or became subject to the disposition prior to 15 February 2001, and

  (b) the conditions at subparagraphs (i) and (iii) of subsection (2) are complied with,

  then that subsection shall apply to that unit of an investment undertaking or to that unit of a specified collective investment undertaking, as the case may be, comprised in a gift or inheritance, if at the date of the disposition, the proper law of the disposition was not the law of the State.

Section 76

[S.54, CATA, as amended]

Provisions relating to charities, etc.

76. (1) Where any person takes a benefit for public or charitable purposes that person is deemed—

  (a) for the purposes of sections 5(1) and 10(1), to have taken that benefit beneficially, and

  (b) for the purposes of Schedule 2, to have taken a gift or an inheritance accordingly to which the group threshold of €19,050 applies.

(2) A gift or an inheritance which is taken for public or charitable purposes is exempt from tax and is not taken into account in computing tax, to the extent that the Commissioners are satisfied that it has been, or will be, applied to purposes which, in accordance with the law of the State, are public or charitable.

(3) Except where provided in section 80(5), a gift or inheritance which a person takes on becoming entitled to any benefit on the application to public or charitable purposes of property (including moneys provided by the Oireachtas or a local authority) held for such purposes is exempt from tax and is not taken into account in computing tax.

Section 77

[S.55, CATA, as amended, and s.39, FA 1978, as amended]

Exemption of heritage property.

77. (1) This section applies to the following objects, that is, any pictures, prints, books, manuscripts, works of art, jewellery, scientific collections or other things not held for the purposes of trading—

   (a) which, on a claim being made to the Commissioners, appear to them to be of national, scientific, historic or artistic interest,

   (b) which are kept permanently in the State except for such temporary absences outside the State as are approved by the Commissioners, and

   (c) in respect of which reasonable facilities for viewing are allowed to members of the public or to recognised bodies or to associations of persons.

(2) (a) Any object to which this section applies and which, at the date of the gift or at the date of inheritance, and at the valuation date, is comprised in a gift or an inheritance taken by a person is exempt from tax in relation to that gift or inheritance, and the value of that gift or inheritance is not taken into account in computing tax on any gift or inheritance taken by that person unless the exemption ceases to apply under subsection (3) or (4).

   (b) Section 89(5) shall apply, for the purposes of this subsection, as it applies in relation to agricultural property.

(3) If an object exempted from tax by virtue of subsection (2) is sold within 6 years after the valuation date, and before the death of the donee or successor, the exemption referred to in subsection (2) shall cease to apply to such object, but if the sale of such object is a sale by private treaty to the National Gallery of Ireland, the National Museum of Science and Art or any other similar national institution, any university in the State or any constituent college of such university, a local authority or the Friends of the National Collections of Ireland, the exemption referred to in subsection (2) shall continue to apply.

(4) The exemption referred to in subsection (2) shall cease to apply to an object, if at any time after the valuation date and –

(a) before the sale of the object,

(b) before the death of the donee or successor, and

(c) before such object again forms part of the property comprised in a gift or an inheritance (other than an inheritance arising by virtue of section 20) in respect of which gift or inheritance an absolute interest is taken by a person other than the spouse of that donee or successor,

there has been a breach of any condition specified in paragraph (b) or (c) of subsection (1).

(5) Any work of art normally kept outside the State which is comprised in an inheritance which is charged to tax by virtue of section 11(1) (b) or 11(2)(c) is exempt from tax and is not taken into account in computing tax, to the extent that the Commissioners are satisfied that it was brought into the State solely for public exhibition, cleaning or restoration.

(6) Subsections (2) to (4) shall apply, as they apply to the objects specified in subsection (1), to a house or garden that is situated in the State and is not held for the purpose of trading and –

(a) which, on a claim being made to the Commissioners, appears to them to be of national, scientific, historic or artistic interest,.

(b) in respect of which reasonable facilities for viewing were allowed to members of the public during the 3 years immediately before the date of the gift or the date of the inheritance, and

(c) in respect of which reasonable facilities for viewing are allowed to members of the public,

with the modification that the reference in subsection (4) to subsection (1)(b) or (c) shall be construed as a reference to paragraph (c) of this subsection and with any other necessary modifications.

(7) Without prejudice to the generality of subsection (6), the provision of facilities for the viewing by members of the public of a house or garden is not regarded as reasonable in relation to any year which is taken into account for the purposes of paragraphs (b) and (c) of subsection (1), unless –

(a) Bord Fáilte Éireann (in this section referred to as "the Board") has, on or before 1 January in that year, been provided with particulars of –

(i) the name, if any, and address of the house or garden, and

(ii) the days and times during the year when access to the house or garden is afforded to the public and the price, if any, payable for such access,

that market value is attributable to such item of relevant heritage property.

(7) Notwithstanding subsections (5) and (6), the exemption referred to in subsection (2) shall continue to apply if the sale of the share referred to in subsection (5), or the sale of the item of relevant heritage property referred to in subsection (6), is a sale by private treaty to the National Gallery of Ireland, the National Museum of Science and Art or any other similar national institution, any university in the State or any constituent college of such university, a local authority or the Friends of the National Collections of Ireland.

Section 79
[S.165, FA 1995]

Exemption of certain inheritances taken by parents.
79. Notwithstanding any other provision of this Act, an inheritance taken by a person from a disponer is, where –

(a) that person is a parent of that disponer, and

(b) the date of the inheritance is the date of death of that disponer,

exempt from tax and is not taken into account in computing tax if that disponer took a non-exempt gift or inheritance from either or both of that disponer's parents within the period of 5 years immediately prior to the date of death of that disponer.

Section 80
[S.56, CATA]

Payments relating to retirement, etc.
80. (1) In this section –

"superannuation scheme" includes any arrangement in connection with employment for the provision of a benefit on or in connection with the retirement or death of an employee;

"employment" includes employment as a director of a body corporate and cognate words shall be construed accordingly.

(2) Subject to subsection (3), any payment to an employee or former employee by, or out of funds provided by, that employee's or former employee's employer or any other person, bona fide by means of retirement benefit, redundancy payment or pension is not a gift or an inheritance.

(3) Subsection (2) shall not apply in relation to a payment referred to in that subsection, and any such payment is deemed to be a gift or an inheritance where –

(a) (i) the employee is a relative of the employer or other disponer,

or

(ii) the employer is a private company within the meaning of section 27, and of which private company the employee is deemed to have control within the meaning of that section;

(b) the payment is not made under a scheme (relating to superannuation, retirement or redundancy) approved by the Commissioners under the Income Tax Acts; and

(c) the Commissioners decide that in the circumstances of the case the payment is excessive.

(4) The Commissioners shall serve on an accountable person a notice in writing of their decision referred to in subsection (3) and the accountable person concerned may appeal against such decision and section 67 shall apply with any necessary modifications in relation to such appeal as it applies in relation to an appeal against an assessment of tax.

(5) Any benefit taken by a person other than the person in respect of whose service the benefit arises, under the provisions of any superannuation fund, or under any superannuation scheme, established solely or mainly for persons employed in a profession, trade, undertaking or employment, and their dependants, is (whether or not any person had a right enforceable at law to the benefit) deemed to be a gift or an inheritance, as the case may be, derived under a disposition made by the person in respect of whose service the benefit arises and not by any other person.

Section 81

[S.57, CATA, as amended, s.135, FA 1997 and s.219, FA 2001]

Exemption of certain securities.

81. (1) In this section—

"security" means any security, stock, share, debenture, debenture stock, certificate of charge or other form of security issued, whether before, on or after the passing of this Act, and which by virtue of any enactment or by virtue of the exercise of any power conferred by any enactment is exempt from taxation when in the beneficial ownership of a person neither domiciled nor ordinarily resident in the State;

"unit trust scheme" means an authorised unit trust scheme within the meaning of the Unit Trusts Act 1990, whose deed expressing the trusts of the scheme restricts the property subject to those trusts to securities.

(2) Securities, or units (within the meaning of the Unit Trusts Act 1990) of a unit trust scheme, comprised in a gift or an inheritance are exempt from tax (and are not taken into account in computing tax on any gift or inheritance taken by the donee or successor) if it is shown to the satisfaction of the Commissioners that—

(a) the securities or units were comprised in the disposition continuously for a period of 6 years immediately before the

(b) The receipt by an incapacitated individual of the whole or any part of trust funds which are held on a qualifying trust, or of the income from such a qualifying trust, is not a gift or an inheritance.

(4) The receipt by a minor child of the disponer of money or money's worth for support, maintenance or education, at a time when the disponer and the other parent of that minor child are dead, is not a gift or an inheritance where the provision of such support, maintenance or education—

(a) is such as would be part of the normal expenditure of a person in the circumstances of the disponer immediately prior to the death of the disponer, and

(b) is reasonable having regard to the financial circumstances of the disponer immediately prior to the death of the disponer.

Section 83
[S.59, CATA]

Exemption where disposition was made by the donee or successor.

83. (1) In this section, "company" means a body corporate (wherever incorporated), other than a private company within the meaning of section 27.

(2) Tax is not chargeable on a gift or an inheritance taken by the donee or successor under a disposition made by that donee or successor.

(3) Where, at the date of the gift, 2 companies are associated in the manner described in subsection (4), a gift taken by one of them under a disposition made by the other is deemed to be a gift to which subsection (2) applies.

(4) For the purposes of subsection (3), 2 companies shall be regarded as associated if—

(a) one company would be beneficially entitled to not less than 90 per cent of any assets of the other company available for distribution to the owners of its shares and entitlements of the kind referred to in section 43(1) on a winding up, or

(b) a third company would be beneficially entitled to not less than 90 per cent of any assets of each of them available as in paragraph (a).

Section 84
[S.59A, CATA]

Exemption relating to qualifying expenses of incapacitated persons.

84. (1) In this section, "qualifying expenses" means expenses relating to medical care including the cost of maintenance in connection with such medical care.

(2) A gift or inheritance which is taken exclusively for the purpose of discharging qualifying expenses of an individual who is permanently incapacitated by reason of physical or mental infirmity is, to the extent that the Commissioners are satisfied that it has been or will be applied to such purpose, exempt from tax and is not taken into account in computing tax.

Section 85
[S.59B, CATA]

Exemption relating to retirement benefits.

85. (1) In this section, "retirement fund", in relation to an inheritance taken on the death of a disponer, means an approved retirement fund or an approved minimum retirement fund, within the meaning of section 784A or 784C of the Taxes Consolidation Act 1997, being a fund which is wholly comprised of all or any of the following, that is—

(a) property which represents in whole or in part the accrued rights of the disponer, or of a predeceased spouse of the disponer, under an annuity contract or retirement benefits scheme approved by the Commissioners for the purposes of Chapter 1 or Chapter 2 of Part 30 of that Act,

(b) any accumulations of income of such property, or

(c) property which represents in whole or in part those accumulations.

(2) The whole or any part of a retirement fund which is comprised in an inheritance which is taken on the death of a disponer is exempt from tax in relation to that inheritance and the value of that inheritance is not taken into account in computing tax, where—

(a) the disposition under which the inheritance is taken is the will or intestacy of the disponer, and

(b) the successor is a child of the disponer and had attained 21 years of age at the date of that disposition.

Section 86

[S.59C, CATA, as amended]

Exemption relating to certain dwellings.

86. (1) In this section—

"dwelling-house" means—

(a) a building or part (including an appropriate part within the meaning of section 5(5)) of a building which was used or was suitable for use as a dwelling, and

(b) the curtilage of the dwelling-house up to an area (exclusive of the site of the dwelling-house) of one acre but if the area of the curtilage (exclusive of the site of the dwelling-house) exceeds one acre then the part which comes within this definition is the part which, if the remainder were separately occupied, would be the most suitable for occupation and enjoyment with the dwelling-house;

"relevant period", in relation to a dwelling-house comprised in a gift or inheritance, means the period of 6 years commencing on the date of the gift or the date of the inheritance.

(2) In this section any reference to a donee or successor is construed as including a reference to the transferee referred to in section 32(2).

(3) Subject to subsections (4), (5), (6) and (7), a dwelling-house comprised in a gift or inheritance which is taken by a donee or successor who—

(a) has continuously occupied as that donee or successor's only or main residence—

(i) that dwelling-house throughout the period of 3 years immediately preceding the date of the gift or the date of the inheritance, or

(ii) where that dwelling-house has directly or indirectly replaced other property, that dwelling-house and that other property for periods which together comprised at least 3 years falling within the period of 4 years immediately preceding the date of the gift or the date of the inheritance,

(b) is not, at the date of the gift or at the date of the inheritance, beneficially entitled to any other dwelling-house or to any interest in any other dwelling-house, and

(c) continues to occupy that dwelling-house as that donee or successor's only or main residence throughout the relevant period,

is exempt from tax in relation to that gift or inheritance, and the value of that dwelling-house is not to be taken into account in computing tax on any gift or inheritance taken by that person unless the exemption ceases to apply under subsection (6) or (7).

(4) The condition in paragraph (c) of subsection (3) shall not apply where the donee or successor has attained the age of 55 years at the date of the gift or at the date of the inheritance.

(5) For the purpose of paragraph (c) of subsection (3), the donee or successor is deemed to occupy the dwelling-house concerned as that donee or successor's only or main residence throughout any period of absence during which that donee or successor worked in an employment or office all the duties of which were performed outside the State.

(6) If a dwelling-house exempted from tax by virtue of subsection (3) is sold or disposed of, either in whole or in part, within the relevant period, and before the death of the donee or successor (not being a donee or successor who had attained the age of 55 years at the date of the gift or inheritance), the exemption referred to in that subsection shall cease to apply to such dwelling-house unless the sale or disposal occurs in consequence of the donee or successor requiring long-term medical care in a hospital, nursing home or convalescent home.

(7) The exemption referred to in subsection (3) shall cease to apply to a dwelling-house, if at any time during the relevant period and—

(a) before the dwelling-house is sold or disposed of, and

(b) before the death of the donee or successor,

the condition specified in paragraph (c) of subsection (3) has not been complied with unless that non-compliance occurs in consequence of the donee or successor requiring long-term medical care in a hospital, nursing home or convalescent home, or in consequence of any condition imposed by the employer of the donee or successor requiring the donee or successor to reside elsewhere.

(8) Where a dwelling-house exempted from tax by virtue of subsection (3) (in this section referred to as the "first-mentioned dwelling house") is replaced within the relevant period by another dwelling house, the condition specified in paragraph (c) of subsection (3) is treated as satisfied if the donee or successor has occupied as that donee or successor's only or main residence the first-mentioned dwelling-house, that other dwelling-house and any dwelling-house which has within the relevant period directly or indirectly replaced that other dwelling-house for periods which together comprised at least 6 years falling within the period of 7 years commencing on the date of the gift or the date of the inheritance.

(9) Any period of absence which would satisfy the condition specified in paragraph (c) of subsection (3) in relation to the first-mentioned dwelling-house shall, if it occurs in relation to any dwelling-house which has directly or indirectly replaced that dwelling-house, likewise satisfy that condition as it has effect by virtue of subsection (8).

(10) Subsection (6) shall not apply to a case falling within subsection (8), but the extent of the exemption under this section in such a case shall, where the donee or successor had not attained the age of 55 years at the date of the gift or at the date of the inheritance, not exceed what it would have been had the replacement of one dwelling house by another referred to in subsection (8), or any one or more of such replacements, taken place immediately prior to that date.

Section 87
[S.98, FA 1982]

Exemption of certain benefits.

87. Where a gift or an inheritance is taken, by direction of the disponer, free of tax, the benefit taken is deemed to include the amount of tax chargeable on such gift or inheritance but not the amount of tax chargeable on such tax.

Section 88
[S.142, FA 1997, as amended]

Exemption of certain transfers from capital acquisitions tax following the dissolution of a marriage.

88. (1) Notwithstanding any other provision of this Act, a gift or inheritance taken by virtue or in consequence of an order to which this subsection applies by a spouse who was a party to the marriage concerned is exempt from tax and is not taken into account in computing tax.

(2) Subsection (1) applies —

(a) to a relief order or an order under section 25 of the Family Law Act 1995, made, following the dissolution of a marriage, or

(b) to a maintenance pending relief order made, following the granting of leave under section 23(3) of the Family Law Act 1995, to a spouse whose marriage has been dissolved,

(c) to an order referred to in section 41(a) of the Family Law Act 1995, or an order under section 42(1) of that Act made in addition to or instead of an order under section 41(a) of that Act, in favour of a spouse whose marriage has been dissolved,

(d) to an order under Part III of the Family Law (Divorce) Act 1996, and

(e) to an order or other determination to like effect, made on or after 10 February 2000, which is analogous to an order referred to in paragraph (a), (b), (c) or (d), of a court under the law of another territory made under or in consequence of the dissolution of a marriage, being a dissolution that is entitled to be recognised as valid in the State.

PART 10

Reliefs

CHAPTER 1

Agricultural Relief

Section 89

[S.19, CATA, as amended]

Provisions relating to agricultural property.

89. (1) In this section—

"agricultural property" means agricultural land, pasture and woodland situate in the State and crops, trees and underwood growing on such land and also includes such farm buildings, farm houses and mansion houses (together with the lands occupied with such farm buildings, farm houses and mansion houses) as are of a character appropriate to the property, and farm machinery, livestock and bloodstock on such property;

"agricultural value" means the market value of agricultural property reduced by 90 per cent of that value;

"farmer" in relation to a donee or successor, means an individual who is domiciled in the State and in respect of whom not less than 80 per cent of the market value of the property to which the individual is beneficially entitled in possession is represented by the market value of property in the State which consists of agricultural property, and, for the purposes of this definition—

    (a) no deduction is made from the market value of property for any debts or encumbrances, and

    (b) an individual is deemed to be beneficially entitled in possession to—

        (i) an interest in expectancy, notwithstanding the definition of "entitled in possession" in section 2, and

        (ii) property which is subject to a discretionary trust under or in consequence of a disposition made by the individual where the individual is an object of the trust.

  (2) Except where provided in subsection (6), in so far as any gift or inheritance consists of agricultural property—

    (a) at the date of the gift or at the date of the inheritance, and

    (b) at the valuation date,

and is taken by a donee or successor who is, on the valuation date and after taking the gift or inheritance, a farmer, section 28 (other than subsection (7)(b) of that section) shall apply in relation to agricultural property as it applies in relation to other property subject to the following modifications —

   (i) in subsection (1) of that section, the reference to market value shall be construed as a reference to agricultural value,

   (ii) where a deduction is to be made for any liability, costs or expenses in accordance with subsection (1) of that section only a proportion of such liability, costs or expenses is deducted and that proportion is the proportion that the agricultural value of the agricultural property bears to the market value of that property, and

   (iii) where a deduction is to be made for any consideration under subsection (2) or (4)(b) of that section, only a proportion of such consideration is deducted and that proportion is the proportion that the agricultural value of the agricultural property bears to the market value of that property.

(3) Where a taxable gift or a taxable inheritance is taken by a donee or successor subject to the condition that the whole or part of that taxable gift or taxable inheritance will be invested in agricultural property and such condition is complied with within 2 years after the date of the gift or the date of the inheritance, then the gift or inheritance is deemed, for the purposes of this section, to have consisted —

   (a) at the date of the gift or at the date of the inheritance, and

   (b) at the valuation date,

of agricultural property to the extent to which the gift or inheritance is subject to such condition and has been so invested.

(4) (a) The agricultural value shall cease to be applicable to agricultural property, other than crops, trees or underwood, if and to the extent that such property, or any agricultural property which directly or indirectly replaces such property —

     (i) is sold or compulsorily acquired within the period of 6 years after the date of the gift or the date of the inheritance, and

     (ii) is not replaced, within a year of the sale or within 6 years of the compulsory acquisition, by other agricultural property,

     and tax is chargeable in respect of the gift or inheritance as if the property were not agricultural property, but this paragraph shall not apply where the donee or successor dies before the property is sold or compulsorily acquired.

   (b) If an arrangement is made, in the administration of property subject to a disposition, for the appropriation of property in or towards the satisfaction of a benefit under the disposition, such arrangement is deemed not to be a sale or a compulsory acquisition for the purposes of paragraph (a).

   (c) The agricultural value in relation to a gift or inheritance referred to in subsection (2) shall cease to be applicable to agricultural property, other than crops, trees or underwood, if the donee or successor is not resident in the State for any of the 3 years of assessment immediately following the year of assessment in which the valuation date falls.

(5) For the purposes of subsection (2), if, in the administration of property subject to a disposition, property is appropriated in or towards the satisfaction of a benefit in respect of which a person is deemed to take a gift or an inheritance under the disposition, the property so appropriated, if it was subject to the disposition at the date of the gift or at the date of the inheritance, is deemed to have been comprised in that gift or inheritance at the date of the gift or at the date of the inheritance.

(6) Subsection (2) shall apply in relation to agricultural property which consists of trees or underwood as if the words "and is taken by a donee or successor who is, on the valuation date and after taking the gift or inheritance, a farmer," were omitted from that subsection.

(7) In this section, any reference to a donee or successor includes a reference to the transferee referred to in section 32(2).

CHAPTER 2
Business Relief

Section 90

[S.124, FA 1994, as amended]

Interpretation (Chapter 2).

90. (1) In this Chapter—

"agricultural property" has the meaning assigned to it by section 89;

"associated company" has the meaning assigned to it by section 16(1)(b) of the Companies (Amendment) Act 1986;.

"business" includes a business carried on in the exercise of a profession or vocation, but does not include a business carried on otherwise than for gain;

"excepted asset" shall be construed in accordance with section 100;

"full-time working officer or employee", in relation to one or more companies, means any officer or employee who devotes substantially the whole of such officer's or employee's time to the service of that company, or those companies taken together, in a managerial or technical capacity;

"holding company" and "subsidiary" have the meanings assigned to them, respectively, by section 155 of the Companies Act 1963;

"quoted", in relation to any shares or securities, means quoted on a recognised stock exchange and "unquoted", in relation to any shares or securities, means not so quoted;

"relevant business property" shall be construed in accordance with section 93.

(2) In this Chapter a reference to a gift shall be construed as a reference to a taxable gift and a reference to an inheritance shall be construed as a reference to a taxable inheritance.

(3) For the purposes of this Chapter a company and all its subsidiaries and any associated company of that company or of any of those subsidiaries and any subsidiary of such an associated company are members of a group.

(4) In this Chapter any reference to a donee or successor is construed as including a reference to the transferee referred to in section 32(2).

Section 91

[S.125, FA 1994]

Application (Chapter 2).

91. This Chapter shall apply in relation to gifts and inheritances, but shall not apply in relation to an inheritance taken by a discretionary trust by virtue of sections 15(1) or 20(1).

Section 92

[S.126, FA 1994, as amended]

Business relief.

92. Where the whole or part of the taxable value of any taxable gift or taxable inheritance is attributable to the value of any relevant business property, the whole or that part of the taxable value is, subject to the other provisions of this Chapter, treated as being reduced by 90 per cent.

Section 93

[S.127, FA 1994, as amended]

Relevant business property.

93. (1) In this Chapter and subject to the following provisions of this section and to sections 94, 96 and 100(4) "relevant business property" means, in relation to a gift or inheritance, any one or more of the following, that is:

(a) property consisting of a business or interest in a business,

(b) unquoted shares in or securities of a company whether incorporated in the State or otherwise to which paragraph (c) does not relate, and which on the valuation date (either by themselves alone or together with other shares or securities in that company in the absolute beneficial ownership of the donee or successor on that date) give control of powers of voting on all questions affecting the company as a whole which if exercised would yield more than 25 per cent of the votes capable of being exercised on those shares,

(c) unquoted shares in or securities of a company whether incorporated in the State or othewise which is, on the valuation date (after the taking of the gift or inheritance), a company controlled by the donee or successor within the meaning of section 27,

(d) unquoted shares in or securities of a company whether incorporated in the State or otherwise which do not fall within paragraph (b) or (c) and which on the valuation date (either by themselves alone or together with other shares or securities in that company in the absolute beneficial ownership of the donee or successor on that date) have an aggregate nominal value which represents 10 per cent or more of the aggregate nominal value of the entire share capital and securities of the company on condition that the donee or successor has been a fulltime working officer or employee of the company, or if that company is a member of a group, of one or more companies which are members of the group, throughout the period of 5 years ending on the date of the gift or inheritance,

(e) any land or building, machinery or plant which, immediately before the gift or inheritance, was used wholly or mainly for the purposes of a business carried on by a company of which the disponer then had control or by a partnership of which the disponer then was a partner and for the purposes of this paragraph a person is deemed to have control of a company at any time if that person then had control of powers of voting on all questions affecting the company as a whole which if exercised would have yielded a majority of the votes capable of being exercised on all such questions,

(f) quoted shares in or securities of a company which, but for the fact that they are quoted, would be shares or securities to which paragraph (b), (c) or (d) would relate on condition that such shares or securities, or other shares in or securities of the same company which are represented by those shares or securities, were in the beneficial ownership of the disponer immediately prior to the disposition and were unquoted at the date of the commencement of that beneficial ownership or at 23 May 1994, whichever is the later date.

(2) Where a company has shares or securities of any class giving powers of voting limited to either or both—

(a) the question of winding-up the company, and

(b) any question primarily affecting shares or securities of that class, the reference in subsection (1) to all questions affecting the company as a whole has effect as a reference to all such questions except any in relation to which those powers are capable of being exercised.

(3) A business or interest in a business, or shares in or securities of a company, is not relevant business property if the business or, as the case may be, the business carried on by the company consists wholly or mainly of one or more of the following, that is, dealing in. currencies, securities, stocks or shares, land or buildings, or making or holding investments.

(4) Subsection (3) shall not apply to shares in or securities of a company if the business of the company consists wholly or mainly in being a holding company of one or more companies whose business does not fall within that subsection.

(5) Any land, building, machinery or plant used wholly or mainly for the purposes of a business carried on as mentioned in subsection (1)(e) is not relevant business property in relation to a gift or inheritance, unless the disponer's interest in the business is, or shares in or securities of the company carrying on the business immediately before the gift or inheritance are, relevant business property in relation to the gift or inheritance or in relation to a simultaneous gift or inheritance taken by the same donee or successor.

(6) The references to a disponer in subsections (1)(e) and (5) include a reference to a person in whom the land, building, machinery or plant concerned is vested for a beneficial interest in possession immediately before the gift or inheritance.

(7) Where shares or securities are vested in the trustees of a settlement, any powers of voting which they give to the trustees of the settlement are, for the purposes of subsection (1)(e), deemed to be given to the person beneficially entitled in possession to the shares or securities except in a case where no individual is so entitled.

Section 94

[S.128, FA 1994]

Minimum period of ownership.

94. In relation to a gift or an inheritance, property shall not be relevant business property unless it was comprised in the disposition continuously —

(a) in the case of an inheritance, which is taken on the date of death of the disponer, for a period of 2 years immediately prior to the date of the inheritance, or

(b) in any other case, for a period of 5 years immediately prior to the date of the gift or inheritance,

and any period immediately before the date of the disposition during which the property was continuously in the beneficial ownership of the disponer, or of the spouse of the disponer, is deemed, for the purposes of this Chapter, to be a period or part of a period immediately before the date of the gift or inheritance during which it was continuously comprised in the disposition.

Section 95

[S.129, FA 1994]

Replacements.

95. (1) Property shall be treated as complying with section 94 if—

  (a) the property replaced other property and that property, that other property and any property directly or indirectly replaced by that other property were comprised in the disposition for periods which together comprised—

    (i) in a case referred to at paragraph (a) of section 94, at least 2 years falling within the 3 years immediately preceding the date of the inheritance, or

    (ii) in a case referred to at paragraph (b) of section 94, at least 5 years falling within the 6 years immediately preceding the date of the gift or inheritance,

  and

  (b) any other property concerned was such that, had the gift or inheritance been taken immediately before it was replaced, it would, apart from section 94, have been relevant business property in relation to the gift or inheritance.

(2) In a case to which subsection (1) relates, relief under this Chapter shall not exceed what it would have been had the replacement or any one or more of the replacements not been made.

(3) For the purposes of subsection (2) changes resulting from the formation, alteration or dissolution of a partnership, or from the acquisition of a business by a company controlled (within the meaning of section 27) by the former owner of the business, are disregarded.

Section 96

[S.130, FA 1994]

Succession.

96. For the purposes of sections 94 and 95, where a disponer became beneficially entitled to any property on the death of another person the disponer is deemed to have been beneficially entitled to it from the date of that death.

Section 97
[S.131, FA 1994]

Successive benefits.

97. (1) Where—

    (a) a gift or inheritance (in this section referred to as "the earlier benefit") was eligible for relief under this Chapter or would have been so eligible if such relief had been capable of being given in respect of gifts and inheritances taken at that time, and

    (b) the whole or part of the property which, in relation to the earlier benefit was relevant business property became, through the earlier benefit, the property of the person or of the spouse of the person who is the disponer in relation to a subsequent gift or inheritance (in this section referred to as "the subsequent benefit"), and

    (c) that property, or part, or any property directly or indirectly replacing it, would, apart from section 94, have been relevant business property in relation to the subsequent benefit, and

    (d) the subsequent benefit is an inheritance taken on the death of the disponer,

then the property which would have been relevant business property but for section 94 is relevant business property notwithstanding that section.

(2) Where the property which, by virtue of subsection (1), is relevant business property replaced the property or part referred to in subsection (1)(c), relief under this Chapter shall not exceed what it would have been had the replacement or any one or more of the replacements not been made, and section 95(3) shall apply with the necessary modifications for the purposes of this subsection.

(3) Where, in relation to the earlier benefit, the amount of the taxable value of the gift or inheritance which was attributable to the property or part referred to in subsection (1)(c) was part only of its value, a like part only of the value which, apart from this subsection, would fall to be reduced under this Chapter by virtue of this section is so reduced.

Section 98
[S.132, FA 1994]

Value of business.

98. For the purposes of this Chapter—

    (a) the value of a business or of an interest in a business is taken to be its net value,

    (b) subject to paragraph (c), the net value of a business shall be taken to be the market value of the assets used in the business (including goodwill) reduced by the aggregate market value of any liabilities incurred for the purposes of the business,

(c) in ascertaining the net value of an interest in a business, no regard is had to assets or liabilities other than those by reference to which the net value of the entire business would fall to be ascertained.

Section 99

[S.133, FA 1994]

Value of certain shares and securities.

99. (1) Where a company is a member of a group and the business of any other company which is a member of the group falls within section 93(3), then, unless that business consists wholly or mainly in the holding of land or buildings wholly or mainly occupied by members of the group whose business does not fall within section 93(3), the value of shares in or securities of the company is taken for the purposes of this Chapter to be what it would be if that other company were not a member of the group.

(2) (a) In this subsection "shares" include securities and "shares in a company" include other shares in the same company which are represented by those shares.

(b) Where unquoted shares in a company which is a member of a group are comprised in a gift or inheritance and shares in another company which is also a member of the group are quoted on the valuation date, the value of the first-mentioned shares is taken, for the purpose of this Chapter, to be what it would be if that other company were not a member of the group, unless those unquoted shares were in the beneficial ownership of the disponer immediately prior to the disposition and those quoted shares were unquoted —

(i) at some time prior to the gift or inheritance when they were in the beneficial ownership of the disponer or a member of that group, while being a member of such group, or

(ii) at 23 May 1994,

whichever is the later date.

Section 100

[S.134, FA 1994, as amended]

Exclusion of value of excepted assets.

100. (1) In determining for the purposes of this Chapter what part of the taxable value of a gift or inheritance is attributable to the value of relevant business property, so much of the last-mentioned value as is attributable to —

(a) any excepted assets within the meaning of subsection (2),or

(b) any excluded property within the meaning of subsection (7), is disregarded.

(2) An asset is an excepted asset in relation to any relevant business property if it was not used wholly or mainly for the purposes of the business concerned throughout the whole or the last 2 years of the relevant period; but where the business concerned is carried on by a company which is a member of a group, the use of an asset for the purposes of a business carried on by another company which at the time of the use and immediately prior to the gift or inheritance was also a member of that group is treated as use for the purposes of the business concerned, unless that other company's membership of the group is to be disregarded under section 99.

(3) The use of an asset for the purposes of a business to which section 93(3) relates is not treated as use for the purposes of the business concerned.

(4) Subsection (2) shall not apply in relation to an asset which is relevant business property by virtue only of section 93(1)(e), and an asset is not relevant business property by virtue only of that provision unless either—

(a) it was used in the manner referred to in that provision—

(i) in the case where the disponer's interest in the business or the shares in or securities of the company carrying on the business are comprised in an inheritance taken on the date of death of the disponer, throughout the 2 years immediately preceding the date of the inheritance, or

(ii) in any other case, throughout the 5 years immediately preceding the date of the gift or inheritance,

or

(b) it replaced another asset so used and it and the other asset and any asset directly or indirectly replaced by that other asset were so used for periods which together comprised—

(i) in the case referred to at paragraph (a)(i), at least 2 years falling within the 3 years immediately preceding the date of the inheritance, or

(ii) in any other case, at least 5 years falling within the 6 years immediately preceding the date of the gift or inheritance,

but where section 97 applies paragraphs (a) and (b) are deemed to be complied with if the asset, or that asset and the asset or assets replaced by it, was or were used throughout the period between the earlier and the subsequent benefit mentioned in that section, or throughout the part of that period during which it or they were in the beneficial ownership of the disponer or the disponer's spouse.

(5) Where part but not the whole of any land or building is used exclusively for the purposes of any business and the land or building would, but for this subsection, be an excepted asset, or, as the case may be, prevented by subsection (4) from being relevant business property, the part so used and the remainder are for the purposes of this section treated as separate assets, and the value of the part so used shall (if it would otherwise be less) be taken to be such proportion of the value of the whole as may be just.

(6) For the purposes of this section the relevant period, in relation to any asset, is the period immediately preceding the gift or inheritance during which the asset or, if the relevant business property is an interest in a business, a corresponding interest in the asset, was comprised in the disposition (within the meaning of section 94) or, if the business concerned is that of a company, was beneficially owned by that company or any other company which immediately before the gift or inheritance was a member of the same group.

(7) For the purposes of this section an asset is deemed not to have been used wholly or mainly for the purposes of the business concerned at any time when it was used wholly or mainly for the personal benefit of the disponer or of a relative of the disponer.

(8) Where, in relation to a gift or an inheritance —

    (a) relevant business property consisting of shares in or securities of a company are comprised in the gift or inheritance on the valuation date, and

    (b) property consisting of a business, or interest in a business, not falling within section 93(3) (in this section referred to as "company business property") is on that date beneficially owned by that company or, where that company is a holding company of one or more companies within the same group, by any company within that group,

that company business property shall, for the purposes of subsection (1), be excluded property in relation to those shares or securities unless it would have been relevant business property if —

    (i) it had been the subject matter of that gift or inheritance, and

    (ii) it had been comprised in the disposition for the periods during which it was in the beneficial ownership of that first-mentioned company or of any member of that group, while being such a member, or actually comprised in the disposition.

(9) In ascertaining whether or not company business property complies with paragraphs (i) and (ii) of subsection (7), section 95 shall, with any necessary modifications, apply to that company business property as to a case to which subsection (1) of section 95 relates.

Section 101

[S.135, FA 1994, as amended]

Withdrawal of relief.

101. (1)   In this section "relevant period", in relation to relevant business property comprised in a gift or inheritance, means the period of 6 years commencing on the date of the gift or inheritance.

(2)   The reduction which would fall to be made under section 92 in respect of relevant business property comprised in a gift or inheritance shall cease to be applicable if and to the extent that the property, or any property which directly or indirectly replaces it—

(a)   would not be relevant business property (apart from section 94 and the conditions attached to paragraphs (d) and (f) of subsection (1) of section 93 and other than by reason of bankruptcy or a bona fide winding-up on grounds of insolvency) in relation to a notional gift of such property taken by the same donee or successor from the same disponer at any time within the relevant period, unless it would be relevant business property (apart from section 94 and the conditions attached to paragraphs (d) and (f) of subsection (1) of section 93) in relation to another such notional gift taken within a year after the first-mentioned notional gift,

(b)   is sold, redeemed or compulsorily acquired within the relevant period and is not replaced, within a year of the sale, redemption or compulsory acquisition, by other property (other than quoted shares or securities or unquoted shares or securities to which section 99(2)(b) relates) which would be relevant business property (apart from section 94 and the condition attached to section 93(1)(d)) in relation to a notional gift of that other property taken by the same donee or successor from the same disponer on the date of the replacement,

and tax is chargeable in respect of the gift or inheritance as if the property were not relevant business property, but—

(i)   any land, building, machinery or plant which are comprised in the gift or inheritance and which qualify as relevant business property by virtue of section 93(1)(e) shall, together with any similar property which has replaced such property, continue to be relevant business property for the purposes of this section for so long as they are used for the purposes of the business concerned,

(ii)   this section shall not have effect where the donee or successor dies before the event which would otherwise cause the reduction to cease to be applicable.

Section 102
[S.135A, FA 1994]

Avoidance of double relief.

102. Where the whole or part of the taxable value of any taxable gift or taxable inheritance is attributable to agricultural property to which section 89(2) applies, such whole or part of the taxable value is not reduced under this Chapter.

CHAPTER 3
Miscellaneous Reliefs

Section 103
[S.61, FA 1985]

Relief from double aggregation.

103. (1) Property in respect of which tax is chargeable more than once on the same event is not included more than once in relation to that event in any aggregate referred to in Schedule 2.

(2) Paragraph 5 of Part 1 of Schedule 2 shall not have effect in ascertaining the tax payable in respect of property which is chargeable to tax as being taken more than once on the same day.

Section 104
[S.63, FA 1985, as amended]

Allowance for capital gains tax on the same event.

104. (1) Where gift tax or inheritance tax is charged in respect of property on an event happening on or after the date of the passing of this Act, and the same event constitutes for capital gains tax purposes a disposal of an asset (being the same property or any part of the same property), the capital gains tax, if any, chargeable on the disposal is not deducted in ascertaining the taxable value for the purposes of the gift tax or inheritance tax but, in so far as it has been paid, is deducted from the net gift tax or inheritance tax as a credit against the same; but, in relation to each asset, or to a part of each asset, so disposed of, the amount deducted is the lesser of—

(a) an amount equal to the amount of the capital gains tax attributable to such asset, or to the part of such asset, or

(b) an amount equal to the amount of the gift tax or inheritance tax attributable to the property which is that asset, or that part of that asset.

(2) For the purposes of any computation of the amount of capital gains tax to be deducted under this section, any necessary apportionments are made of any reliefs or expenditure and the method of apportionment adopted is such method as appears to the Commissioners, or on appeal to the Appeal Commissioners, to be just and reasonable.

Section 105

[S.34A, CATA]

Allowance for prior tax on the same event.

105. Where tax is charged more than once in respect of the same property on the same event, the net tax payable which is earlier in priority is not deducted in ascertaining the taxable value for the purposes of the tax which is later in priority, but is deducted from the tax which is later in priority as a credit against the same, up to the net amount of the same.

Section 106

[S.66, CATA]

Arrangements for relief from double taxation.

106. (1) If the Government by order declare that arrangements specified in the order have been made with the government of any territory outside the State in relation to affording relief from double taxation in respect of gift tax or inheritance tax payable under the laws of the State and any tax imposed under the laws of that territory which is of a similar character or is chargeable by reference to death or to gifts inter vivos and that it is expedient that those arrangements should have the force of law, the arrangements shall, notwithstanding anything in any enactment, have the force of law.

(2) Any arrangements to which the force of law is given under this section may include provision for relief from tax charged before the making of the arrangements and provisions as to property which is not itself subject to double tax, and the provisions of this section shall apply accordingly.

(3) For the purposes of subsection (1), arrangements made with the head of a foreign state are regarded as made with the government of that foreign state.

(4) Where any arrangements have the force of law by virtue of this section, the obligation as to secrecy imposed by any enactment shall not prevent the Commissioners from disclosing to any authorised officer of the government with which the arrangements are made such information as is required to be disclosed under the arrangements.

(5) (a) Any order made under this section may be revoked by a subsequent order and any such revoking order may contain such transitional provisions as appear to the Government to be necessary or expedient.

(b) Where an order is proposed to be made under this section, a draft of such order shall be laid before Dáil Éireann and the order shall not be made until a resolution approving of the draft has been passed by Dáil Éireann.

Section 107

[S.67, CATA, as amended]

Other relief from double taxation.

107. (1) (a) In this section –

"foreign tax" means any tax which is chargeable under the laws of any territory outside the State and is of a character similar to estate duty, gift tax or inheritance tax;

"event" means –

(i) a death, or

(ii) any other event,

by reference to which the date of the gift or the date of the inheritance is determined.

(b) For the purposes of this section, a reference to property situate in a territory outside the State is a reference to property situate in that territory at the date of the gift or the date of the inheritance, as the case may be, or to property representing such property.

(2) Where the Commissioners are satisfied that a taxable gift or taxable inheritance, taken under a disposition by a donee or successor on the happening of any event, is reduced by the payment of foreign tax which is chargeable in connection with the same event under the same disposition in respect of property which is situate in the territory outside the State in which that foreign tax is chargeable, they shall allow a credit in respect of that foreign tax against the gift tax or inheritance tax payable by that donee or successor on that taxable gift or taxable inheritance; but such credit shall not exceed –

(a) the amount of the gift tax or inheritance tax payable in respect of the same property by reason of such property being comprised in any taxable gift or taxable inheritance taken under that disposition on the happening of that event, or

(b) the amount of that foreign tax,

whichever is the lesser.

(3) This section is subject to any arrangement to which the force of law is given under section 106 and, if any such arrangement provides for the allowance of the amount of a tax payable in a territory outside the State as a credit against gift tax or inheritance tax, the provisions of the arrangement shall apply in relation to the tax payable in that territory in lieu of the provisions of subsection (2).

(4) Where the foreign tax in respect of property comprised in a taxable gift or a taxable inheritance taken under a disposition on the happening of an event is, under the terms of the disposition, directed to be paid out of a taxable gift or a taxable inheritance (taken under that disposition on the happening of the same event) other than the

taxable gift or taxable inheritance out of which it would be payable in the absence of such a direction, then, for the purposes of subsection (2), the taxable gift or taxable inheritance out of which the foreign tax would be payable in the absence of such a direction, and no other taxable gift or taxable inheritance, is treated as reduced by the payment of the foreign tax.

PART 11

Miscellaneous

Section 108

[S.60, CATA]

Certificates for probate.

108. (1) In this section "Inland Revenue affidavit" has the meaning referred to in section 48(1).

(2) Where an Inland Revenue affidavit has been delivered to the Commissioners and they are satisfied—

(a) that an adequate payment on account of inheritance tax in respect of the property passing under the deceased person's will or intestacy or Part IX or section 56 of the Succession Act 1965 has been made, or

(b) that the payment of inheritance tax in respect of such property may be deferred for the time being,

they shall certify in writing—

(i) that the Inland Revenue affidavit was delivered to them, and

(ii) (I) that a payment referred to in paragraph (a) has been made, or

(II) that the payment referred to in paragraph (b) has been deferred for the time being,

as the case may be.

(3) If, in the opinion of the Commissioners, the payment of inheritance tax in respect of the property passing under the deceased person's will or intestacy or Part IX or section 56 of the Succession Act 1965 can not be deferred for the time being without serious risk of such tax not being recovered, they may refuse to issue the certificate referred to in subsection (2) until the tax has been paid, or until such payment as is referred to in paragraph (a) of that subsection has been made.

(4) The certificate required by section 30 of the Customs and Inland Revenue Act 1881[1], to be made by the proper officer of the court, shall not be made until a certificate of the Commissioners issued under subsection (2) has been produced to such officer and shall (instead

of showing that the affidavit, if liable to stamp duty, has been duly stamped) show that the Commissioners have issued a certificate under subsection (2) and shall state the substance of the certificate so issued by the Commissioners.

(5) The form of certificate required to be given by the proper officer of the court under section 30 of the Customs and Inland Revenue Act 1881 may be prescribed by rule of court in such manner as may be necessary for giving effect to this Act.

Footnote
1   Reproduced on page 651.

Section 109
[S.61, CATA, as amended]

Payment of money standing in names of 2 or more persons.

109. (1) In this section—

"banker" means a person who carries on banking business in the State and includes a friendly society, an industrial and provident society, a building society, the Post Office Savings Bank, a trustee savings bank and any person with whom money is lodged or deposited;

"pay" includes transfer in the books of a banker and any dealings with any moneys which were lodged or deposited in the name of a person who died after the time of the lodgment or deposit and any other person or persons;

"current account" means an account which is customarily operated on by means of a cheque or banker's order;

"banking business" has the meaning assigned to it by section 2 of the Central Bank Act 1971;

references to moneys lodged or deposited include references to shares of a building society, friendly society or industrial and provident society.

(2) Where, either before or after the passing of this Act, a sum of money exceeding €31,750 is lodged or deposited (otherwise than on a current account) in the State with a banker, in the joint names of 2 or more persons, and one of such persons (in this section referred to as the deceased) dies on or after the date of the passing of this Act, the banker shall not pay such money or any part of such money to the survivor or all or any of the survivors of such persons, or to any other person, unless or until there is furnished to such banker a certificate by the Commissioners certifying that there is no outstanding claim for inheritance tax in connection with the death of the deceased in respect of such money or any part of such money or a consent in writing by the Commissioners to such payment pending the ascertainment and payment of such tax.

(3) Notwithstanding anything contained in this Act, tax chargeable on the death of the deceased is deemed for the purposes of this section to become due on the day of the death of the deceased.

(4) A banker who, after the passing of this Act, pays money in contravention of this section is liable to a penalty of €1,265.

(5) Where a penalty is demanded of a banker under this section, the onus of proving that such certificate or such consent as is mentioned in this section was furnished to such banker before that banker paid such money shall lie on such banker.

(6) Where a penalty is demanded of a banker under this section, it shall be a good defence to prove that, at the time when such banker paid such money, that banker had reasonable ground for believing that none of the persons in whose joint names such money was lodged or deposited with that banker was dead.

(7) This section shall not apply where the sum of money referred to in subsection (2) is lodged or deposited in the joint names of 2 persons, one of whom dies on or after the date of the passing of this Act and is at the time of that person's death the spouse of that other person.

Section 110
[S.62, CATA]
Court to provide for payment of tax.

110. Where any suit is pending in any court for the administration of any property chargeable with tax under this Act, such court shall provide, out of any such property which may be in the possession or control of the court, for the payment to the Commissioners of any of the tax or the interest on that tax which remains unpaid.

Section 111
[S.64, CATA]
Liability to tax in respect of certain sales and mortgages.

111. (1) In this section —

"death duties" has the meaning assigned to it by section 30 of the Finance Act 1971[1], and

"purchaser or mortgagee" includes a person deriving title from or under a purchaser or mortgagee in the case of such a sale or mortgage as is referred to in this section.

(2) Where an interest in expectancy has, prior to 1 April 1975, been bona fide sold or mortgaged for full consideration in money or money's worth, and that interest comes into possession on a death occurring on or after the date of the passing of this Act, the following provisions shall apply, that is —

(a) the purchaser or mortgagee shall not be liable in respect of inheritance tax on the inheritance referred to in paragraph (b) for an amount greater than that referred to in paragraph (c);

(b) the inheritance referred to in paragraph (a) is the inheritance of property in which the interest so sold or mortgaged subsists and which arises in respect of the interest of the remainderman referred to in section 32 so coming into possession;

(c) the amount referred to in paragraph (a) shall be the amount that would then have been payable by the purchaser or mortgagee in respect of death duties on the property in which the interest subsists as property passing under the same disposition as that under which the inheritance is taken, if the property, on so coming into possession, had been chargeable to death duties—

　(i) under the law in force, and

　(ii) at the rate or rates having effect,

　at the date of the sale or mortgage;

(d) where such an interest is so mortgaged, any amount of inheritance tax payable in respect of the inheritance referred to in paragraph (b), and from the payment of which the mortgagee is relieved under this section, shall, notwithstanding the priority referred to in section 60(1), rank, in relation to property charged with such tax under that section, as a charge subsequent to the mortgage;

(e) any person, other than the purchaser or mortgagee, who is accountable for the payment of so much of the inheritance tax as is not the liability of the purchaser or mortgagee by virtue of the relief given by this section, shall not be liable for the payment of any amount in respect of such inheritance tax in excess of the amount which is available to that person for such payment by reason of there being, at the time when the interest comes into possession, other property, or an equity of redemption, or both, subject to the same trusts, under the disposition referred to in paragraph (c), as the property in which the interest in expectancy subsists; and

(f) nothing in section 45(7) or (8) or section 60(1) shall be construed as derogating from the relief given by this section to a purchaser or mortgagee.

Footnote

1　Reproduced on page 679.

Section 112

[S.65, CATA]

References in deeds and wills, etc. to death duties.

112. In so far as a provision in a document refers (in whatever terms) to any death duty to arise on any death occurring on or after the date of the passing of this Act, it shall apply, as far as may be, as if the reference included a reference to inheritance tax –

(a) if that document was executed prior to 31 March 1976, and the reference is to legacy duty and succession duty or either of them,

(b) if that document was so executed, and the reference is to estate duty, and it may reasonably be inferred from all the circumstances (including any similarity of the incidence of inheritance tax to that of estate duty) that the inclusion of the reference to inheritance tax would be just, and

(c) whether the document was executed prior to, on or after 31 March 1976, if the reference is to death duties, without referring to any particular death duty.

Section 113

[S.68, CATA]

Tax, in relation to certain legislation.

113. (1) Inheritance tax shall not be a duty or a death duty for the purposes of section 9 of the Succession Act 1965, but it shall be a death duty for the purposes of –

(a) section 34(3) of that Act,

(b) the definition of pecuniary legacy in section 3(1) of that Act, and

(c) paragraph 8 of Part II of the First Schedule to that Act.

(2) Section 72 of the Registration of Title Act 1964 shall apply as if gift tax and inheritance tax were mentioned in that Act as well as estate duty and succession duty.

Section 114

[S.70, CATA]

Delivery, service and evidence of notices and forms, etc.

114. (1) Any notice which under this Act is authorised or required to be given by the Commissioners may be served by post.

(2) A notice or form which is to be served on a person may be either delivered to that person or left at that person's usual or last known place of abode.

(3) Prima facie evidence of any notice given under this Act by the Commissioners or by an officer of the Commissioners may be given in any proceedings by production of a document purporting –

(a) to be a copy of that notice, or

(b) if the details specified in that notice are contained in an electronic, photographic or other record maintained by the Commissioners, to reproduce those details in so far as they relate to that notice,

and it shall not be necessary to prove the official position of the person by whom the notice purports to be given or, if it is signed,. the signature, or that the person signing and giving it was authorised so to do.

(4) In any case where a time limit is specified by or under this Act, other than Part 8 of this Act, for the doing of any act required by or under this Act, other than Part 8 of this Act, to be done by any person other than the Commissioners, the Commissioners may, in their discretion, extend such time limit.

Section 115

[S.69, CATA]

Extension of certain Acts.

115. (1) Section 1 of the Provisional Collection of Taxes Act 1927[1] is hereby amended by the insertion of "and gift tax and inheritance tax" before "but no other tax or duty".

(2) Section 39 of the Inland Revenue Regulation Act 1890, is hereby amended by the insertion of "gift tax and inheritance tax," before "stamp duties".

Footnote
1   Reproduced on page 658.

Section 116

[S.71, CATA]

Regulations.

116. (1) The Commissioners shall make such regulations as seem to them to be necessary for the purpose of giving effect to this Act and of enabling them to discharge their functions under the Act.

(2) Every regulation made under this section shall be laid before Dáil Éireann as soon as may be after it is made and, if a resolution annulling the regulation is passed by Dáil Éireann within the next 21 days on which Dáil Éireann has sat after the regulation is laid before it, the regulation shall be annulled accordingly, but without prejudice to the validity of anything previously done under that regulation.

Section 117

[S.72, CATA]

Care and management.

117. (1) Tax is hereby placed under the care and management of the Commissioners.

(2) Subject to the direction and control of the Commissioners, any power, function or duty conferred or imposed on the Commissioners by this Act may be exercised or performed on their behalf by an officer of the Commissioners.

PART 12
Repeals, etc.

Section 118

Repeals

118. (1) Subject to subsection (2), the Capital Acquisitions Tax Act 1976 is hereby repealed.

(2) This Act shall not apply in relation to gifts and inheritances taken before the date of the passing of this Act, and the repealed enactments shall continue to apply in relation to such gifts and inheritances to the same extent that they would have applied if this Act had not been enacted.

(3) Notwithstanding subsection (1), any provision of the repealed enactments which imposes a fine, forfeiture, penalty or punishment for any act or omission shall, in relation to any act or omission which took place or began before the date of the passing of this Act, continue to apply in substitution for the provision of this Act to which it corresponds.

(4) Anything done under or in connection with the provisions of the repealed enactments which correspond to the provisions of this Act shall be deemed to have been done under or in connection with the provisions of this Act to which those provisions of the repealed enactments correspond; but nothing in this subsection shall affect the operation of section 120(3) and (4).

Section 119

Consequential amendments to other enactments.

119. Schedule 3, which provides for amendments to other enactments consequential on the passing of this Act, shall apply for the purposes of this Act.

Section 120

Transitional provisions.

120. (1) The Commissioners shall have all the jurisdictions, powers and duties in relation to capital acquisitions tax under this Act which they had before the passing of this Act.

(2) The continuity of the operation of the law relating to capital acquisitions tax shall not be affected by the substitution of this Act for the repealed enactments.

(3) Any reference, whether express or implied, in any enactment or document (including this Act and any Act amended by this Act) —

(a) to any provision of this Act, or

(b) to things done or to be done under or for the purposes of any provisions of this Act,

shall, if and in so far as the nature of the reference permits, be construed as including, in relation to the times, years or periods, circumstances or purposes in relation to which the corresponding provision in the repealed enactments applied or had applied, a reference to, or, as the case may be, to things done or to be done under or for the purposes of, that corresponding provision.

(4) Any reference, whether express or implied, in any enactment (including the repealed enactments and enactments passed after the passing of this Act) —

(a) to any provision of the repealed enactments, or

(b) to things done or to be done under or for the purposes of any provisions of the repealed enactments,

shall, if and in so far as the nature of the reference permits, be construed as including, in relation to the times, years or periods, circumstances or purposes in relation to which the corresponding provision of this Act applies, a reference to, or as the case may be, to things done or to be done under, or for the purposes of, that corresponding provision.

SCHEDULE 1

Valuation of Limited Interests

[First Schedule, CATA]

PART 1

Rules relating to the valuation of limited interests utilising Tables A and B in Parts 2 and 3 of this Schedule

1. The value of an interest for a single life in a capital sum shall be that sum multiplied by the factor, contained in column (3) or (4) respectively of

Table A, which is appropriate to the age and sex of the person in respect of the duration of whose life the interest is to be valued.

2. The value of an interest in a capital sum for the joint continuance of 2 lives shall be the value of an interest in that sum for the older life, ascertained in accordance with rule 1, multiplied by the joint factor in column (2) of Table A which is appropriate to the younger life.

3. The value of an interest in a capital sum for the joint continuance of 3 or more lives shall be the value of an interest in that sum for the joint continuance of the 2 oldest of those lives, ascertained in accordance with rule 2, multiplied by the joint factor of the youngest of those lives.

4. The value of an interest in a capital sum for the longer of 2 lives shall be ascertained by deducting from the total of the values of an interest in that sum for each of those lives, ascertained in accordance with rule 1, the value of an interest in the capital sum for the joint continuance of the same 2 lives, ascertained in accordance with rule 2.

5. Where an interest is given for the longest of more than 2 lives, it shall be valued, in accordance with rule 4, as if it were for the longer of the 2 youngest of those lives.

6. The value of an interest in a capital sum for a period certain shall be the aggregate of—

    (a) the value of the capital sum, multiplied by the factor in Table B which is appropriate to the number of whole years in that period (or zero if that period is less than a whole year); and

    (b) where the period is not an integral number of years, a fraction (of which the numerator is the number of days in excess of the number of whole years, if any, in that period and the denominator is 365) of the difference between—

        (i) the value of an interest in the capital sum for one year longer than the number of whole years, if any, in the period; and

        (ii) the value ascertained under the provisions of paragraph (a) (or zero, where so provided in that paragraph).

7. In the case of a limited interest where the interest is for a life or lives, but is guaranteed for a period certain, the value shall be the higher of—

    (a) the value of an interest for such life or lives, ascertained in accordance with the appropriate rule in this Part of this Schedule; and

    (b) the value of an interest for the period certain, ascertained in accordance with rule 6.

8. The value of a limited interest for which the other rules in this Part of this Schedule provide no method of valuing shall be ascertained as if the interest taken were a series of absolute interests in the property applied in satisfaction of the interest from time to time, taken as separate gifts or inheritances as the case may be.

PART 2

TABLE A

Years of age	Joint Factor	Value of an interest in a capital of €1 for a male life aged as in column 1	Value of an interest in a capital of €1 for a female life aged as in column 1
(1)	(2)	(3)	(4)
0	.99	.9519	.9624
1	.99	.9767	.9817
2	.99	.9767	.9819
3	.99	.9762	.9817
4	.99	.9753	.9811
5	.99	.9742	.9805
6	.99	.9730	.9797
7	.99	.9717	.9787
8	.99	.9703	.9777
9	.99	.9688	.9765
10	.99	.9671	.9753
11	.98	.9653	.9740
12	.98	.9634	.9726
13	.98	.9614	.9710
14	.98	.9592	.9693
15	.98	.9569	.9676
16	.98	.9546	.9657
17	.98	.9522	.9638
18	.98	.9497	.9617
19	.98	.9471	.9596
20	.97	.9444	.9572
21	.97	.9416	.9547
22	.97	.9387	.9521
23	.97	.9356	.9493
24	.97	.9323	.9464
25	.97	.9288	.9432
26	.97	.9250	.9399
27	.97	.9209	.9364
28	.97	.9165	.9328
29	.97	.9119	.9289
30	.96	.9068	.9248
31	.96	.9015	.9205
32	.96	.8958	.9159
33	.96	.8899	.9111

Years of age (1)	Joint Factor (2)	Value of an interest in a capital of €1 for a male life aged as in column 1 (3)	Value of an interest in a capital of €1 for a female life aged as in column 1 (4)
34	.96	.8836	.9059
35	.96	.8770	.9005
36	.96	.8699	.8947
37	.96	.8626	.8886
38	.95	.8549	.8821
39	.95	.8469	.8753
40	.95	.8384	.8683
41	.95	.8296	.8610
42	.95	.8204	.8534
43	.95	.8107	.8454
44	.94	.8005	.8370
45	.94	.7897	.8283
46	.94	.7783	.8192
47	.94	.7663	.8096
48	.93	.7541	.7997
49	.93	.7415	.7896
50	.92	.7287	.7791
51	.91	.7156	.7683
52	.90	.7024	.7572
53	.89	.6887	.7456
54	.89	.6745	.7335
55	.88	.6598	.7206
56	.88	.6445	.7069
57	.88	.6288	.6926
58	.87	.6129	.6778
59	.86	.5969	.6628
60	.86	.5809	.6475
61	.85	.5650	.6320
62	.85	.5492	.6162
63	.85	.5332	.6000
64	.85	.5171	.5830
65	.85	.5007	.5650
66	.85	.4841	.5462
67	.84	.4673	.5266
68	.84	.4506	.5070
69	.84	.4339	.4873
70	.83	.4173	.4679
71	.83	.4009	.4488

Years of age	Joint Factor	Value of an interest in a capital of €1 for a male life aged as in column 1	Value of an interest in a capital of €1 for a female life aged as in column 1
(1)	(2)	(3)	(4)
72	.82	.3846	.4301
73	.82	.3683	.4114
74	.81	.3519	.3928
75	.80	.3352	.3743
76	.79	.3181	.3559
77	.78	.3009	.3377
78	.76	.2838	.3198
79	.74	.2671	.3023
80	.72	.2509	.2855
81	.71	.2353	.2693
82	.70	.2203	.2538
83	.69	.2057	.2387
84	.68	.1916	.2242
85	.67	.1783	.2104
86	.66	.1657	.1973
87	.65	.1537	.1849
88	.64	.1423	.1730
89	.62	.1315	.1616
90	.60	.1212	.1509
91	.58	.1116	.1407
92	.56	.1025	.1310
93	.54	.0939	.1218
94	.52	.0858	.1132
95	.50	.0781	.1050
96	.49	.0710	.0972
97	.48	.0642	.0898
98	.47	.0578	.0828
99	.45	.0517	.0762
100 or over	.43	.0458	.0698

PART 3
TABLE B

(Column (2) shows the value of an interest in a capital of €1 for the number of years shown in column (1))

Number of years (1)	Value (2)	Number of years (1)	Value (2)
1	.0654	26	.8263
2	.1265	27	.8375
3	.1836	28	.8480
4	.2370	29	.8578
5	.2869	30	.8669
6	.3335	31	.8754
7	.3770	32	.8834
8	.4177	33	.8908
9	.4557	34	.8978
10	.4913	35	.9043
11	.5245	36	.9100
12	.5555	37	.9165
13	.5845	38	.9230
14	.6116	39	.9295
15	.6369	40	.9360
16	.6605	41	.9425
17	.6826	42	.9490
18	.7032	43	.9555
19	.7225	44	.9620
20	.7405	45	.9685
21	.7574	46	.9750
22	.7731	47	.9815
23	.7878	48	.9880
24	.8015	49	.9945
25	.8144	50 and over	1.0000

SCHEDULE 2
Computation of Tax

[Second Sch., CATA, as amended, s.59D and s.59E, CATA]

PART 1
Preliminary

1.   In this Schedule—

"group threshold", in relation to a taxable gift or a taxable inheritance taken on a particular day, means—

(a)   €381,000, where—

    (i)   the donee or successor is on that day the child, or minor child of a deceased child, of the disponer, or

    (ii)   the successor is on that day a parent of the disponer and—

        (I)   the interest taken is not a limited interest, and

        (II)   the inheritance is taken on the death of the disponer;

(b)   €38,100, where the donee or successor is on that day, a lineal ancestor, a lineal descendant (other than a child, or a minor child of a deceased child), a brother, a sister, or a child of a brother or of a sister of the disponer;

(c)   €19,050, where the donee or successor (who is not a spouse of the disponer) does not, on that day, stand to the disponer in a relationship referred to in subparagraph (a) or (b);

"the consumer price index number", in relation to a year, means the All Items Consumer Price Index Number for that year as compiled by the Central Statistics Office and expressed on the basis that the consumer price index number at mid-November 1996 is 100;

"Table" means the Table contained in Part 2 of this Schedule;

"threshold amount" in relation to the computation of tax on any aggregate of taxable values under paragraph 3, means the group threshold that applies in relation to all of the taxable gifts and taxable inheritances included in that aggregate but, in computing under this Schedule the tax chargeable on a taxable gift or taxable inheritance, that group threshold shall, for the purposes of this definition, be multiplied by the figure, rounded to the nearest third decimal place, determined by dividing by 104.8 the consumer price index number for the year immediately preceding the year in which that taxable gift or taxable inheritance is taken.

2.   In the Table "Value" means the appropriate aggregate referred to in paragraph 3.

3.   The tax chargeable on the taxable value of a taxable gift or a taxable inheritance (in this Schedule referred to as the first-mentioned gift or inheritance) taken by a donee or successor shall be of an amount equal to

the amount by which the tax computed on aggregate A exceeds the tax computed on aggregate B, where —

(a) aggregate A is the aggregate of the following:

    (i) the taxable value of the first-mentioned gift or inheritance, and

    (ii) the taxable value of each taxable gift and taxable inheritance taken previously by that donee or successor on or after 5 December 1991, which has the same group threshold as the first-mentioned gift or inheritance,

(b) aggregate B is the aggregate of the taxable values of all such taxable gifts and taxable inheritances so previously taken which have the same group threshold as the first-mentioned gift or inheritance, and

(c) the tax on an aggregate is computed at the rate or rates of tax applicable under the Table to that aggregate, but where —

    (i) in a case where no such taxable gift or taxable inheritance was so previously taken, the amount of the tax computed on aggregate B shall be deemed to be nil, and

    (ii) the amount of an aggregate that comprises only a single taxable value shall be equal to that value.

4. In the Table any rate of tax shown in the second column is that applicable to such portion of the value (within the meaning of paragraph 2) as is shown in the first column.

5. For the purposes of this Schedule, all gifts and inheritances which have the same group threshold and which are taken by a donee or successor on the same day shall count as one, and to ascertain the amount of tax payable on one such gift or inheritance of several so taken on the same day, the amount of tax computed under this Schedule as being payable on the total of such gifts and inheritances so taken on that day shall be apportioned rateably, according to the taxable values of the several taxable gifts and taxable inheritances so taken on that day.

6. Where any donee or successor is, at the date of the gift or at the date of the inheritance, the surviving spouse of a deceased person who, at the time of that deceased spouse's death, was of nearer relationship than such donee or successor to the disponer, then such donee or successor is, in the computation of the tax payable on such taxable gift or taxable inheritance, deemed to bear to the disponer the relationship of that deceased person.

7. (1) In this paragraph —

    "company" means a private company which, for the relevant period —

    (a) is a private company controlled by the disponer and of which the disponer is a director, and

    (b) is not a private non-trading company;

    "control", in relation to a company, is construed in accordance with section 27(4)(b);.

"investment income", in relation to a private company, means income which, if the company were an individual, would not be earned income within the meaning of section 3 of the Taxes Consolidation Act 1997;

"nominee" has the same meaning as it has in section 27;

"private company" has the meaning assigned to it by section 27;

"private company controlled by the disponer" means a private company that is under the control of any one or more of the following, that is—

(a) the disponer,

(b) nominees of the disponer,

(c) the trustees of a settlement made by the disponer;

"private non-trading company" means a private company—

(a) whose income (if any) in the 12 months preceding the date at which a share in that company is to be valued consisted wholly or mainly of investment income; and

(b) whose property, on the date referred to in paragraph (a), consisted wholly or mainly of property from which investment income is derived;

"relevant period" means—

(a) the period of 5 years ending on the date of the disposition; or

(b) where, at the date of the disposition,

  (i) an interest in possession in—

    (I) the property referred to in subparagraph (2)(a), or

    (II) the shares referred to in subparagraph (2)(b),

    as the case may be, is limited to the disponer under the disposition, and

  (ii) such property is not, or such shares are not, property consisting of the appropriate part of property, within the meaning of section 5(5), on which is charged or secured an annuity or other annual right limited to cease on the death of the disponer,

  the period of 5 years ending on the coming to an end of that interest,

subject, in relation to work, to the exclusion of reasonable periods of annual or sick leave from that period of 5 years.

(2) For the purpose of computing the tax payable on a gift or inheritance, the donee or successor is deemed to bear to the disponer the relationship of a child in any case where the donee or successor is a child of a brother, or a child of a sister, of the disponer and either—

(a) the donee or successor has worked substantially on a full-time basis for the disponer for the relevant period in carrying on, or in assisting in carrying on, the trade, business or profession of the disponer, and the gift or inheritance consists of property which was used in connection with that business, trade or profession; or

(b) the donee or successor has worked substantially on a full-time basis for a company for the relevant period in carrying on, or in assisting in carrying on, the trade, business or profession of the company, and the gift or inheritance consists of shares in that company.

(3) Without prejudice to the generality of subparagraph (2),a donee or successor is not deemed to be working substantially on a full-time basis for a disponer or a company unless –

(a) where the gift or inheritance consists of property which was used in connection with the business, trade or profession of the disponer, the donee or successor works –

(i) more than 24 hours a week for the disponer, at a place where that business, trade or profession, is carried on, or

(ii) more than 15 hours a week for the disponer, at a place where that business, trade or profession is carried on, and such business , trade or profession is carried on exclusively by the disponer, any spouse of the disponer, and the donee or successor,

or

(b) where the gift or inheritance consists of shares in the company, the donee or successor works –

(i) more than 24 hours a week for the company, at a place where the business, trade or profession of the company is carried on, or

(ii) more than 15 hours a week for the company, at a place where the business, trade or profession of the company is carried on, and such business, trade or profession is carried on exclusively by the disponer, any spouse of the disponer, and the donee or successor.

(4) This paragraph shall not apply to a gift or inheritance taken by a donee or successor under a discretionary trust.

8. (a) In this paragraph ''specified disposition'' means a disposition –

(i) the date of which is a date prior to 1 April 1975,

(ii) in relation to which the disponer is a grandparent of the donee or successor, and

(iii) in which the marriage of the parents of the donee or successor was, at the date of the disposition, expressed to be the consideration.

(b)   Where, on the cesser of a limited interest to which a parent of the donee or successor was entitled in possession, the donee or successor takes a gift or an inheritance under a specified disposition, then, for the purpose of computing the tax payable on the gift or inheritance, the donee or successor is deemed to bear to the disposer the relationship of a child.

9.   (1)   In this paragraph—

"the appropriate period" means periods which together comprised at least 5 years falling within the 18 years immediately following the birth of the donee or successor.

(2)   Where, on a claim being made to them in that behalf, the Commissioners are, subject to subparagraph (3), satisfied—

(a)   where the inheritance is taken by a successor on the date of death of the disponer, that the successor had, prior to the date of the inheritance, been placed in the foster care of the disponer under the Child Care (Placement of Children in Foster Care) Regulations 1995 (S.I. No. 260 of 1995), or the Child Care (Placement of Children with Relatives) Regulations 1995 (S.I. No. 261 of 1995), or

(b)   that throughout the appropriate period the donee or successor—

(i)   has resided with the disponer, and

(ii)   was under the care of and maintained by the disponer at the disponer's own expense,

then, subject to subparagraph (3), for the purposes of computing the tax payable on that gift or inheritance, that donee or successor is deemed to bear to that disponer the relationship of a child.

(3)   Relief under subparagraph (2) shall not apply where the claim for such relief is based on the uncorroborated testimony of one witness.

10.   Where, on a claim being made to them in that behalf, the Commissioners are satisfied that—

(a)   the donee or successor had at the date of the gift or the date of the inheritance been adopted in the manner referred to in paragraph (b) of the definition of "child" contained in section 2(1), and

(b)   the disponer is the natural mother or the natural father of the donee or successor,

then, notwithstanding section 2(5), for the purpose of computing the tax payable on that gift or inheritance, that donee or successor is deemed to bear to that disponer the relationship of a child.

11.   For the purposes of this Schedule, a reference to a gift or an inheritance, or to a taxable gift or a taxable inheritance, includes a reference to a part of a gift or an inheritance, or to a part of a taxable gift or a taxable inheritance, as the case may be.

PART 2

TABLE

Portion of Value	Rate of tax Per cent
The threshold amount	Nil
The balance	20

SCHEDULE 3

Consequential Amendments

In the enactments specified in column (1) of the following Table for the words set out or referred to in column (2), there shall be substituted the words set out in the corresponding entry in column (3).

Enactment Amended (1)	Words to be replaced (2)	Words to be substituted (3)
Value-Added Tax Act 1972:		
section 30(5)(b)(i)	section 38 of the Capital Acquisitions Tax Act 1976	section 48 of the Capital Acquisitions Tax Consolidation Act 2003
section 30(5)(b)(ii)	section 38	section 48
The Rules of the Superior Courts (S.I. No. 15 of 1986):		
Order 79, rule 84	Capital Acquisitions Tax Act 1976	Capital Acquisitions Tax Consolidation Act 2003
Order 80, rule 85	Capital Acquisitions Tax Act 1976	Capital Acquisitions Tax Consolidation Act 2003
Ethics in Public Office Act 1995:		
section 2(4)	Capital Acquisitions Tax Act 1976	Capital Acquisitions Tax Consolidation Act 2003
Taxes Consolidation Act 1997:		
section 8(1)(c)	Capital Acquisitions Tax Act 1976	Capital Acquisitions Tax Consolidation Act 2003
section 176(1)(b)(i)(I)	section 21 of the Capital Acquisitions Tax Act 1976	section 30 of the Capital Acquisitions Tax Consolidation Act 2003

Enactment Amended	Words to be replaced	Words to be substituted
(1)	(2)	(3)
section 577(5)(a)(ii)(I)	Capital Acquisitions Tax Act 1976	Capital Acquisitions Tax Consolidation Act 2003
section 577(5)(a)(ii)(II)	section 55 section 39 of the Finance Act 1978	section 77 section 77(6) and (7) of the Capital Acquisitions Tax Consolidation Act 2003
section 730GB	section 63 of the Finance Act 1985	section 104 of the Capital Acquisitions Tax Act 2003
section 739G(5)	section 63 of the Finance Act 1985	section 104 of the Capital Acquisitions Tax Consolidation Act 2003
section 747E(5)(a)	section 63 of the Finance Act 1985	section 104 of the Capital Acquisitions Tax Consolidation Act 2003
section 811(1)(a), in paragraph (iv) of the definition of "the Acts".	Capital Acquisitions Tax Act 1976	Capital Acquisitions Tax Consolidation Act 2003
section 818(c)	Capital Acquisitions Tax Act 1976	Capital Acquisitions Tax Consolidation Act 2003
section 825(1)(c)	Capital Acquisitions Tax Act 1976	Capital Acquisitions Tax Consolidation Act 2003
section 858(1)(a), in paragraph (vi) of the definition of "the Acts"	Capital Acquisitions Tax Act 1976	Capital Acquisitions Tax Consolidation Act 2003
section 859(1), in paragraph (f) of the definition of "the Revenue Acts"	Capital Acquisitions Tax Act 1976	Capital Acquisitions Tax Consolidation Act 2003
section 887(1), in paragraph (d) of the definition of "the Acts"	Capital Acquisitions Tax Act 1976	Capital Acquisitions Tax Consolidation Act 2003
section 912(1), in paragraph (f) of the definition of "the Acts"	Capital Acquisitions Tax Act 1976	Capital Acquisitions Tax Consolidation Act 2003

Enactment Amended	Words to be replaced	Words to be substituted
(1)	(2)	(3)
section 917D(1), in paragraph (e) of the definition of "the Acts"	Capital Acquisitions Tax Act 1976	Capital Acquisitions Tax Consolidation Act 2003
section 1002(1)(a), in paragraph (vi) of the definition of "the Acts"	Capital Acquisitions Tax Act 1976	Capital Acquisitions Tax Consolidation Act 2003
section 1003(1)(a), in paragraph (iii) of the definition of "the Acts"	Capital Acquisitions Tax Act 1976	Capital Acquisitions Tax Consolidation Act 2003
section 1006(1), in paragraph (d) of the definition of "the Acts"	Capital Acquisitions Tax Act 1976	Capital Acquisitions Tax Consolidation Act 2003
section 1006A(1), in paragraph (e) of the definition of "the Acts"	Capital Acquisitions Tax Act 1976	Capital Acquisitions Tax Consolidation Act 2003
section 1078(1), in paragraph (f) of the definition of "the Acts"	Capital Acquisitions Tax Act 1976	Capital Acquisitions Tax Consolidation Act 2003
section 1079(1), in paragraph (f) of the definition of "the Acts"	Capital Acquisitions Tax Act 1976	Capital Acquisitions Tax Consolidation Act 2003
section 1086(1), in paragraph (d) of the definition of "the Acts"	Capital Acquisitions Tax Act 1976	Capital Acquisitions Tax Consolidation Act 2003
section 1089(2)	section 41 of the Capital Acquisitions Tax Act 1976	section 51 of the Capital Acquisitions Tax Consolidation Act 2003
section 1104(5)	Capital Acquisitions Tax Act 1976	Capital Acquisitions Tax Consolidation Act 2003
Stamp Duties Consolidation Act 1999:		
section 19	section 15 of the Capital Acquisitions Tax Act 1976	section 26 of the Capital Acquisitions Tax Consolidation Act 2003
section 91(2)(b)(ii)	section 16 of the Capital Acquisitions Tax Act 1976	section 27 of the Capital Acquisitions Tax Consolidation Act 2003

Enactment Amended (1)	Words to be replaced (2)	Words to be substituted (3)
section 92(1)(b)(ii)	section 16 of the Capital Acquisitions Tax Act 1976	section 27 of the Capital Acquisitions Tax Consolidation Act 2003
section 92B(3)(b)(ii)	section 16 of the Capital Acquisitions Tax Act 1976	section 27 of the Capital Acquisitions Tax Consolidation Act 2003
Finance (No. 2) Act 2000:		
section 5(1), definition of "Act of 1976"	"Act of 1976" means the Capital Acquisitions Tax Act 1976	"Act of 2003" means the Capital Acquisitions Tax Consolidation Act 2003
section 5(1), in the definition of "date of the disposition"	section 2 of the Act of 1976	section 2 of the Act of 2003
section 5(1), in the definition of "discretionary trust"	section 2 of the Act of 1976	section 2 of the Act of 2003
section 5(1), in the definition of "disponer"	section 2 of the Act of 1976	section 2 of the Act of 2003
section 5(1), in the definition of "disposition"	section 2 of the Act of 1976	section 2 of the Act of 2003
section 5(1), in the definition of "donee"	section 2 of the Act of 1976	section 2 of the Act of 2003
section 5(1), in the definition of "entitled in possession"	section 2 of the Act of 1976	section 2 of the Act of 2003
section 5(1), in the definition of "gift"	section 2 of the Act of 1976	section 2 of the Act of 2003
section 5(1), in the definition of "interest in expectancy"	section 2 of the Act of 1976	section 2 of the Act of 2003
section 5(1), in the definition of "limited interest"	section 2 of the Act of 1976	section 2 of the Act of 2003
section 5(1), in the definition of "on a death"	section 3 of the Act of 1976	section 3 of the Act of 2003

FINANCE ACT 2003

Number 3 of 2003
(Enacted on 28th March, 2003)

PART 1
Income Tax, Corporation Tax and Capital Gains Tax

CHAPTER 3
Income Tax, Corporation Tax and Capital Gains Tax

Section 38

Exchange of information.

38. For the purposes of assisting the prevention and detection of tax evasion, by means of the exchange of information between the Revenue Commissioners and the tax authorities of certain other territories, [the Taxes Consolidation Act, 1997,] is amended -

(a) ....

(b) by inserting the following after section 912:

"Information for tax authorities in other territories.

912A. (1) In this section -

'foreign tax' means a tax chargeable under the laws of a territory in relation to which arrangements (in this section referred to as 'the arrangements') having the force of law by virtue of section 826 apply;

'liability to foreign tax', in relation to a person, means any liability in relation to foreign tax to which the person is or may be, or may have been, subject, or the amount of any such liability.

(2) For the purposes of complying with provisions with respect to the exchange of information contained in the arrangements, sections 900, 901, 902, 902A, 906A, 907 and 908 shall, subject to subsection (3), have effect -

(a) as if references in those sections to tax included references to foreign tax, and

(b) as if references in those sections to liability, in relation to a person, included references to liability to foreign tax, in relation to a person.

(3) Where sections 902A, 907 and 908 have effect by virtue only of this section, they shall have effect as if -

(a) there were substituted ' "a taxpayer" means a person;' for the definition of 'a taxpayer' in subsection (1) of each of those sections, and

(b) the references in those sections to -

(i) tax, were references to foreign tax, and

(ii) any provision of the Acts, were references to any provision of the law of a territory in accordance with which foreign tax is charged or collected.".

Section 57

Amendment of Part 26 (life inurance companies) of [the Taxes Consolidation Act, 1997].

57. The [Taxes Consolidation Act, 1997,] is amended in Part 26 -

(a) (i).......

(f) by substituting the following for section 730GB:

"Capital acquisitions tax; set-off.

730GB. Where on the death of a person, an assurance company is liable to account for appropriate tax (within the meaning of section 730F(1)) in connection with a gain arising on a chargeable event in relation to a life policy, the amount of such tax, in so far as it does not exceed the amount of appropriate tax to which the assurance company would be liable if that tax was calculated in accordance with section 730F(1)(a), shall be treated as an amount of capital gains tax paid for the purposes of section 63 of the Finance Act 1985."

PART 5

Capital Acquisitions Tax

Section 144

Interpretation (Part 5).

144. In this Part "Principal Act" means the Capital Acquisitions Tax Consolidation Act 2003.

Section 145

Time limits for capital acquisitions tax.

145. (1) [The Capital Acquisitions Tax Consolidation Act 2003] is amended—

(a) in section 18, by deleting subsection (5),

(b) in section 46, by inserting the following after subsection (7):

"(7A) The making of enquiries by the Commissioners for the purposes of subsection (7)(a) or the authorising of inspections by the Commissioners under subsection (7)(b) in connection with or in relation to a relevant return (within the meaning given in section 49(6A)(b)) may not be initiated after the expiry of 4 years commencing on the date that the relevant return is received by the Commissioners.

(7B) (a) The time limit referred to in subsection (7A) shall not apply where the Commissioners have reasonable grounds for believing that any form of fraud or neglect has been committed by or on behalf of any accountable person in connection with or in relation to any relevant return which is the subject of any enquiries or inspections.

(b) In this subsection 'neglect' means negligence or a failure to deliver a correct relevant return (within the meaning given in section 49(6A)(b)).",

(c) in section 49, by inserting the following after subsection (6):

"(6A) (a) For the purposes of subsection (6) an assessment, a correcting assessment or an additional assessment made in connection with or in relation to a relevant return may not be made after the expiry of 4 years from the date that the relevant return is received by the Commissioners.

(b) In this subsection 'relevant return' means a return within the meaning of section 21(e) or a return or an additional return within the meaning of section 46.

(6B) The time limit referred to in subsection (6A) shall not apply where the Commissioners have reasonable grounds for believing that any form of fraud or neglect (within the meaning given in section 46(7B)(b)) has been committed by or on behalf of any accountable person in connection with or in relation to any relevant return (within the meaning given in subsection (6A)) which is the subject of assessment.",

and

(d) by substituting the following for section 57:

"Overpayment of tax.

57. (1) In this section –

'relevant date', in relation to a repayment of tax means –

(a) the date which is 183 days after the date on which a valid claim in respect of the repayment is made to the Commissioners, or

(b) where the repayment is due to a mistaken assumption in the operation of the tax on the part of the Commissioners, the date which is the date of the payment of the tax which has given rise to that repayment;

'repayment' means a repayment of tax including a repayment of—

(a) any interest charged,

(b) any surcharge imposed,

(c) any penalty incurred,

under any provision of this Act in relation to tax;

'tax' includes interest charged, a surcharge imposed or a penalty incurred under any provision of this Act.

(2) Where, a claim for repayment of tax made to the Commissioners, is a valid claim, the Commissioners shall, subject to the provisions of this section, give relief by means of repayment of the excess or otherwise as is reasonable and just.

(3) Notwithstanding subsection (2), no tax shall be repaid to an accountable person in respect of a valid claim unless that valid claim is made within the period of 4 years commencing on the later of the valuation date or the date of the payment of the tax concerned.

(4) Subsection (3) shall not apply to a claim for repayment of tax arising by virtue of section 18(3), Article VI of the First Schedule to the Finance Act 1950[1], or Article 9 of the Schedule to the Double Taxation Relief (Taxes on Estates of Deceased Persons and Inheritances and on Gifts) (United Kingdom) Order 1978 (S.I. No. 279 of 1978)[2].

(5) Subsection (3) shall not apply to a claim for repayment of tax arising on or before the date of the passing of the Finance Act 2003, where a valid claim is made on or before 31 December 2004.

(6) Subject to the provisions of this section, where a person is entitled to a repayment, the amount of the repayment shall, subject to a valid claim in respect of the repayment being made to the Commissioners and subject to section 1006A(2A) of the Taxes Consolidation Act 1997, carry simple interest at the rate of 0.011 per cent, or such other rate (if any) prescribed by the Minister for Finance by order under subsection (11), for each day or part of a day for the period commencing on

the relevant date and ending on the date upon which the repayment is made.

(7) A claim for repayment under this section shall only be treated as a valid claim when—

    (a) it has been made in accordance with the provisions of the law (if any) relating to tax under which such claim is made, and

    (b) all information which the Commissioners may reasonably require to enable them determine if and to what extent a repayment is due, has been furnished to them.

(8) Interest shall not be payable under this section if it amounts to €10 or less.

(9) This section shall not apply in relation to any repayment or part of a repayment of tax in respect of which interest is payable under or by virtue of any provision of any other enactment.

(10) Income tax shall not be deductible on any payment of interest under this section and such interest shall not be reckoned in computing income for the purposes of the Tax Acts.

(11) (a) The Minister for Finance may, from time to time, make an order prescribing a rate for the purposes of subsection (6).

    (b) Every order made by the Minister for Finance under paragraph (a) shall be laid before Dáil Éireann as soon as may be after it is made and, if a resolution annulling the order is passed by Dáil Éireann within the next 21 days on which Dáil Éireann has sat after the order is laid before it, the order shall be annulled accordingly, but without prejudice to the validity of anything previously done under it.

(12) The Commissioners may make regulations as they deem necessary in relation to the operation of this section.".

(2) This section shall come into operation on such day or days as the Minister for Finance may by order or orders[3] appoint either generally or with reference to any particular purpose or provision and different days may be so appointed for different purposes or different provisions.

Footnotes

1   Reproduced on page 670.
2   Reproduced on page 1369.
3   See S.I. No 515 of 2003 at page 1379.

Section 146

Administrative changes.

146.(1) [The Capital Acquisitions Tax Consolidation Act 2003] is amended—

(a) by substituting the following for section 25:

"Penalty.

25. (1) Any person who contravenes or fails to comply with any requirement under section 21(e) is liable to a penalty of—

(a) €1,265, or

(b) twice the amount of tax payable in respect of the taxable inheritance to which the return relates,

whichever is the lesser.

(2) Where a person fails to comply with a requirement to deliver a return under section 21(e), by reason of fraud or neglect by that person, that person shall be liable to a penalty of—

(a) €1,265, and

(b) the amount, or in the case of fraud twice the amount, of the difference specified in subsection (3).

(3) The difference referred to in subsection (2)(b) is the difference between—

(a) the amount of tax paid by that person in respect of the taxable inheritance to which the return relates, and

(b) the amount of tax which would have been payable if the return had been delivered by that person and the return had been correct.",

(b) by inserting the following after section 45:

"Obligation to retain certain records.

45A. (1) In this section—

'records' includes books, accounts, documents, and any other data maintained manually or by any electronic, photographic or other process, relating to—

(a) property, of any description, which under or in consequence of any disposition, a person becomes beneficially entitled in possession to, otherwise than for full consideration in money or money's worth paid by that person,

(b) liabilities, costs and expenses properly payable out of that property,

     (c)   consideration given in good faith, in money or money's worth, paid by a person for that property,

     (d)   a relief or an exemption claimed under any provision of this Act, and

     (e)   the valuation, on the valuation date or other date, as the case may be, of property the subject of the disposition.

(2)   Every person who is an accountable person shall retain, or cause to be retained on his or her behalf, records of the type referred to in subsection (1) as are required to enable—

     (i)   a true return, additional return or statement to be made for the purposes of this Act, or

     (ii)   a claim to a relief or an exemption under any provision of this Act to be substantiated.

(3)   Records required to be retained by virtue of this section shall be retained—

     (a)   in written form in an official language of the State, or

     (b)   subject to section 887(2) of the Taxes Consolidation Act 1997, by means of any electronic, photographic or other process.

(4)   Records retained for the purposes of subsections (2) and (3) shall be retained by the person required to retain the records—

     (a)   where the requirements of section 21(e) or section 46(2), requiring the preparation and delivery of a return on or before the date specified in each of those provisions, are met, for the period of 6 years commencing on the valuation date of the gift or inheritance, or

     (b)   notwithstanding paragraph (a), where an accountable person fails to comply with the requirements of the provisions referred to in paragraph (a) in the manner so specified, or, where any person is required to deliver a return, additional return or statement under this Act other than the provisions referred to in paragraph (a), for the period of 6 years commencing on the date that the return, additional return or statement is received by the Commissioners.

(5)   Any person who fails to comply with subsection (2), (3) or (4) in respect of the retention of any records relating

to a gift or inheritance is liable to a penalty of €1,520; but a penalty shall not be imposed under this section on any person who is not liable to tax in respect of that gift or inheritance.'',

(c) by inserting the following after section 46:

''Expression of doubt.

46A. (1) Where an accountable person is in doubt as to the correct application of law to, or the treatment for tax purposes of, any matter to be included in a return or additional return to be delivered by such person under this Act, then that person may deliver the return or additional return to the best of that person's belief but that person shall draw the Commissioners' attention to the matter in question in the return or additional return by specifying the doubt and, if that person does so, that person shall be treated as making a full and true disclosure with regard to that matter.

(2) Subject to subsection (3), where a return or additional return, which includes an expression of doubt as to the correct application of law to, or the treatment for tax purposes of, any matter contained in the return or additional return, is delivered by an accountable person to the Commissioners in accordance with this section, then section 51(2) does not apply to any additional liability arising from a notification to that person by the Commissioners of the correct application of the law to, or the treatment for tax purposes of, the matter contained in the return or additional return the subject of the expression of doubt, on condition that such additional liability is accounted for and remitted to the Commissioners within 30 days of the date on which that notification is issued.

(3) Subsection (2) does not apply where the Commissioners do not accept as genuine an expression of doubt as to the correct application of law to, or the treatment for tax purposes of, any matter contained in the return or additional return and an expression of doubt shall not be accepted as genuine where the Commissioners are of the opinion that the person was acting with a view to the evasion or avoidance of tax.

(4) Where the Commissioners do not accept an expression of doubt as genuine they shall notify the accountable person accordingly within the period of 30 days after the date that the expression of doubt is received by the Commissioners, and the accountable person shall account for any tax, which was not correctly accounted

for in the return or additional return referred to in subsection (1) and section 51(2) applies accordingly.

(5) An accountable person who is aggrieved by a decision of the Commissioners that that person's expression of doubt is not genuine may, by giving notice in writing to the Commissioners within the period of 30 days after the notification of the said decision, require the matter to be referred to the Appeal Commissioners.",

and

(d) in section 58 —

(i) by inserting the following after subsection (1):

"(1A) Where a person fails to comply with a requirement to deliver a return or additional return under subsection (2), (6) or (8) of section 46, by reason of fraud or neglect by that person, that person is liable to a penalty of —

(a) €2,535, and

(b) the amount, or in the case of fraud twice the amount, of the difference specified in subsection (5A).",

and

(ii) by inserting the following after subsection (5):

"(5A) The difference referred to in paragraph (b) of subsection (1A) is the difference between —

(a) the amount of tax paid by that person in respect of the taxable gift or taxable inheritance to which the return or additional return relates, and

(b) the amount of tax which would have been payable if the return or additional return had been delivered by that person and that return or additional return had been correct.".

(2) This section shall come into effect on such day or days as the Minister for Finance may by order or orders[1], either generally or with reference to any particular purpose or provision, appoint and different days may be so appointed for different purposes or different provisions.

Footnote

1   See S.I. No. 466 of 2003 at page 1377.

Section 147

Amendment of section 47 (signing of returns, etc.) of [the Capital Acquisitions Tax Consolidation Act 2003].

147. Section 47 of [the Capital Acquisitions Tax Consolidation Act 2003] is amended by inserting the following after subsection (5):

"(6) For the purposes of this section, references to an oath shall be construed as including references to an affirmation and references in this section to the administration or making of an oath shall be construed accordingly."

Section 148

Amendment of section 55 (payment of tax on certain assets by instalments) of [the Capital Acquisitions Tax Consolidation Act 2003].

148. (1) Section 55(2)(b) of [the Capital Acquisitions Tax Consolidation Act 2003] is amended by substituting "0.0241 per cent or such other rate (if any) as stands prescribed by the Minister for Finance by regulations, for each day or part of a day" for "0.75 per cent or such other rate (if any) as stands prescribed by the Minister for Finance by regulations, for each month or part of a month".

(2) Subsection (1) applies on and from 1 September 2002 to interest payable under the provision mentioned in subsection (1) in respect of an amount due to be paid whether before, on or after that date in accordance with that provision.

Section 149

Amendment of section 69 (exemption of small gifts) of [the Capital Acquisitions Tax Consolidation Act 2003].

149. Section 69(2) of [the Capital Acquisitions Tax Consolidation Act 2003] is amended as respects relevant periods ending after 31 December 2002, by substituting "€3,000" for "€1,270".

Section 150

Amendment of section 81 (exemption of certain securities) of [the Capital Acquisitions Tax Consolidation Act 2003].

150. (1) Section 81 of [the Capital Acquisitions Tax Consolidation Act 2003] is amended —

(a) in subsection (2)(a), by substituting "15 years" for "6 years", and

(b) in subsection (4), by substituting "15 years" for "6 years".

(2) (a) Subsection (1)(a) has effect in relation to securities or units comprised in a gift or an inheritance where the date of the gift or the date of the inheritance is on or after 24 February 2003 and the securities or units —

(i)   come into the beneficial ownership of the disponer on or after 24 February 2003, or

(ii)   become subject to the disposition on or after that date without having been previously in the beneficial ownership of the disponer.

(b)   Subsection (1)(b) has effect as on and from 24 February 2003.

Section 151

Technical amendments (Part 5).

151. [The Capital Acquisitions Tax Consolidation Act 2003] is amended –

(a) in section 74(3), by substituting "paragraphs" for "subparagraphs" in paragraph (b), and

(b) in section 75(3), by substituting "paragraphs" for "subparagraphs" in paragraph (b).

Section 152

Amendment of section 100 (exclusion of value of excepted assets) of [the Capital Acquisitions Tax Consolidation Act 2003].

152. [The Capital Acquisitions Tax Consolidation Act 2003] is amended in section 100 –

(a) in subsection (1)(b), by substituting "subsection (8)" for "subsection (7)", and

(b) in subsection (9), by substituting "subsection (8)" for "subsection (7)".

Section 153

Transitional provisions (Part 5).

153. In this Part, any reference, whether express or implied –

(a) to any provision of [the Capital Acquisitions Tax Consolidation Act 2003], or

(b) to things done or to be done under or for the purposes of any provision of the [the Capital Acquisitions Tax Consolidation Act, 2003].

shall, if and in so far as the nature of the reference permits, be construed as including, in relation to the times, years or periods, circumstances or purposes in relation to which the corresponding provision in the repealed enactments applied or had applied, a reference to, or, as the case may be, to things done or to be done under or for the purposes of, that corresponding provision.

PART 7

Miscellaneous

Section 160

Amendment of section 1078 (revenue offences) of [the Taxes Consolidation Act, 1997].

160. (1) [The Taxes Consolidation Act, 1997,] is amended in section 1078(3)(a) by substituting "€3,000" for "€1,900".

(2) Subsection (1) applies as respects an offence committed on or after the day that this Act is passed.

Section 161

Amendment of Chapter 4 (revenue offences) of Part 47 of [the Taxes Consolidation Act, 1997].

161. [The Taxes Consolidation Act, 1997,] is amended in Chapter 4 of Part 47 by inserting the following after section 1078:

"Concealing facts disclosed by documents.

1078A. (1) Any person who —

    (a) knows or suspects that an investigation by an officer of the Revenue Commissioners into an offence under the Acts or the Waiver of Certain Tax, Interest and Penalties Act 1993 is being, or is likely to be, carried out, and

    (b) falsifies, conceals, destroys or otherwise disposes of material which the person knows or suspects is or would be relevant to the investigation or causes or permits its falsification, concealment, destruction or disposal,

    is guilty of an offence.

(2) Where a person —

    (a) falsifies, conceals, destroys or otherwise disposes of material, or

    (b) causes or permits its falsification, concealment, destruction or disposal,

in such circumstances that it is reasonable to conclude that the person knew or suspected —

    (i) that an investigation by an officer of the Revenue Commissioners into an offence under the Acts or the Waiver of Certain Tax, Interest and Penalties Act 1993 was being, or was likely to be, carried out, and

    (ii) that the material was or would be relevant to the investigation, the person shall be taken, for the purposes of this section, to have so known or suspected, unless the court or the jury, as the case may be, is satisfied having regard to all the evidence that there is a reasonable doubt as to whether the person so knew or suspected.

(3) A person guilty of an offence under this section is liable—

(a) on summary conviction to a fine not exceeding €3,000, or at the discretion of the court, to imprisonment for a term not exceeding 6 months or to both the fine and the imprisonment, or

(b) on conviction on indictment, to a fine not exceeding €127,000 or, at the discretion of the court, to imprisonment for a term not exceeding 5 years or to both the fine and the imprisonment.

Presumptions.

1078B. (1) In this section—

'return, statement or declaration' means any return, statement or declaration which a person is required to make under the Acts or the Waiver of Certain Tax, Interest and Penalties Act 1993.

(2) The presumptions specified in this section apply in any proceedings, whether civil or criminal, under any provision of the Acts or the Waiver of Certain Tax, Interest and Penalties Act 1993.

(3) Where a document purports to have been created by a person it shall be presumed, unless the contrary is shown, that the document was created by that person and that any statement contained therein, unless the document expressly attributes its making to some other person, was made by that person.

(4) Where a document purports to have been created by a person and addressed and sent to a second person, it shall be presumed, unless the contrary is shown, that the document was created and sent by the first person and received by the second person and that any statement contained therein—

(a) unless the document expressly attributes its making to some other person, was made by the first person, and

(b) came to the notice of the second person.

(5) Where a document is retrieved from an electronic storage and retrieval system, it shall be presumed unless the contrary is shown, that the author of the document is the person who ordinarily uses that electronic storage and retrieval system in the course of his or her business.

(6) Where an authorised officer in the exercise of his or her powers under subsection (2A) of section 905 has removed records (within the meaning of that section) from any place, gives

evidence in proceedings that to the best of the authorised officer's knowledge and belief, the records are the property of any person, the records shall be presumed unless the contrary is proved, to be the property of that person.

(7) Where in accordance with subsection (6) records are presumed in proceedings to be the property of a person and the authorised officer gives evidence that, to the best of the authorised officer's knowledge and belief, the records are records which relate to any trade, profession, or, as the case may be, other activity, carried on by that person, the records shall be presumed unless the contrary is proved, to be records which relate to that trade, profession, or, as the case may be, other activity, carried on by that person.

(8) In proceedings, a certificate signed by an inspector or other officer of the Revenue Commissioners certifying that a return, statement or declaration to which the certificate refers is in the possession of the Revenue Commissioners in such circumstances as to lead the officer to conclude that, to the best of his or her knowledge and belief it was delivered to an inspector or other officer of the Revenue Commissioners, it shall be presumed unless the contrary is proved, to be evidence that the said return, statement, or declaration was so delivered.

(9) In proceedings, a certificate, certifying the fact or facts referred to in subsection (8) and purporting to be signed as specified in that subsection, may be tendered in evidence without proof and shall be deemed until the contrary is proved to have been signed by a person holding, at the time of the signature, the office or position indicated in the certificate as the office or position of the person signing.

(10) References in this section to a document are references to a document in written, mechanical or electronic format and, for this purpose 'written' includes any form of notation or code whether by hand or otherwise and regardless of the method by which, or the medium in or on which, the document concerned is recorded.

Provision of information to juries.

1078C. (1) In a trial on indictment of an offence under the Acts or the Waiver of Certain Tax, Interest and Penalties Act 1993, the trial judge may order that copies of any or all of the following documents shall be given to the jury in any form that the judge considers appropriate:

(a) any document admitted in evidence at the trial,

(b) the transcript of the opening speeches of counsel,

(c) any charts, diagrams, graphics, schedules or agreed summaries of evidence produced at the trial,

    (d) the transcript of the whole or any part of the evidence given at the trial,

    (e) the transcript of the closing speeches of counsel,

    (f) the transcript of the trial judge's charge to the jury,

    (g) any other document that in the opinion of the trial judge would be of assistance to the jury in its deliberations including, where appropriate, an affidavit by an accountant or other suitably qualified person, summarising, in a form which is likely to be comprehended by the jury, any transactions by the accused or other persons which are relevant to the offence.

  (2) If the prosecutor proposes to apply to the trial judge for an order that a document mentioned in subsection (1)(g) shall be given to the jury, the prosecutor shall give a copy of the document to the accused in advance of the trial and, on the hearing of the application, the trial judge shall take into account any representations made by or on behalf of the accused in relation to it.

  (3) Where the trial judge has made an order that an affidavit by an accountant or other person mentioned in subsection (1)(g) shall be given to the jury, the accountant, or as the case may be, the other person so mentioned –

    (a) shall be summoned by the prosecution to attend at the trial as an expert witness, and

    (b) may be required by the trial judge, in an appropriate case, to give evidence in regard to any relevant procedures or principles within his or her area of expertise.".

Section 164

Mandatory electronic filing and payment of tax.

164. (1) [The Taxes Consolidation Act, 1997,] is amended –

    (a) in Chapter 6 of Part 38 by inserting the following after section 917E –

"Mandatory electronic filing and payment of tax.

917EA. (1) In this section –

        'electronic means' includes electrical, digital, magnetic, optical, electromagnetic, biometric, photonic means of transmission of data and other forms of related technology by means of which data is transmitted;

        'repayment of tax' includes any amount relating to tax which is to be paid or repaid by the Revenue Commissioners;

        'specified person' means any person, group of persons or class of persons specified in regulations made under this section for the purposes of either or both paragraphs (a) and (b) of subsection (3);

'specified return' means a return specified in regulations made under this section;

'specified tax liabilities' means liabilities to tax including interest on unpaid tax specified in regulations made under this section.

(2) Section 917D shall apply for the purposes of regulations made under this section in the same way as it applies for the purposes of this Chapter.

(3) The Revenue Commissioners may make regulations –

    (a) requiring the delivery by specified persons of a specified return by electronic means where an order under section 917E has been made in respect of that return,

    (b) requiring the payment by electronic means of specified tax liabilities by specified persons, and

    (c) for the repayment of any tax specified in the regulations to be made by electronic means.

(4) Regulations made under this section shall include provision for the exclusion of a person from the requirements of regulations made under this section where the Revenue Commissioners are satisfied that the person could not reasonably be expected to have the capacity to make a specified return or to pay the specified tax liabilities by electronic means, and allowing a person, aggrieved by a failure to exclude such person, to appeal that failure to the Appeal Commissioners.

(5) Regulations made under this section may, in particular and without prejudice to the generality of subsection (3), include provision for –

    (a) the electronic means to be used to pay or repay tax,

    (b) the conditions to be complied with in relation to the electronic payment or repayment of tax,

    (c) determining the time when tax paid or repaid using electronic means is to be taken as having been paid or repaid,

    (d) the manner of proving, for any purpose, the time of payment or repayment of any tax paid or repaid using electronic means, including provision for the application of any conclusive or other presumptions,

(e) notifying persons that they are specified persons, including the manner by which such notification may be made, and

(f) such supplemental and incidental matters as appear to the Revenue Commissioners to be necessary.

(6) The Revenue Commissioners may nominate any of their officers to perform any acts and discharge any functions authorised by regulation made under this section to be performed or discharged by the Revenue Commissioners.

(7) Where a specified person—

(a) makes a return which is a specified return for the purposes of regulations made under this section, or

(b) makes a payment of tax which is specified tax liabilities for the purposes of regulations made under this section,

in a form other than that required by any such regulation, the specified person shall be liable to a penalty of €1,520 and, for the purposes of the recovery of a penalty under this subsection, section 1061 applies in the same manner as it applies for the purposes of the recovery of a penalty under any of the sections referred to in that section.

(8) Every regulation made under this section shall be laid before Dáil Éireann as soon as may be after it is made and, if a resolution annulling the regulation is passed by Dáil Éireann within the next 21 days on which Dáil Éireann has sat after the regulation is laid before it, the regulation shall be annulled accordingly but without prejudice to the validity of anything previously done under the regulation.'',

(b) ....

and

(c) ....

(2) This section has effect from such day as the Minister for Finance may appoint by order.[1]

FINANCE ACT 2004

Number 8 of 2004
(Enacted on 25th March, 2004)

PART 5
Capital Acquisitions Tax

Section 76

Interpretation (Part 5).

76. In this Part "Principal Act" means the Capital Acquisitions Tax Consolidation Act 2003.

Section 77

Amendment of section 2 (general interpretation) of [the Capital Acquisitions Tax Consolidation Act 2003].

77. Section 2 of [the Capital Acqusitions Tax Consolidation Act 2003] is amended, in subsection (5), by deleting "in lawful wedlock".

Section 78

Amendment of section 93 (relevant business property) of [the Capital Acquisitions Tax Consolidation Act 2003].

78. (1) Section 93 of [the Capital Acquisitions Tax Consolidation Act 2003] is amended by substituting the following for subsection (4):

"(4) Subsection (3) shall not apply to shares in or securities of a company if—

(a) the business of the company consists wholly or mainly in being a holding company of one or more companies whose business does not fall within that subsection, or

(b) the value of those shares or securities, without having regard to the provisions of section 99, is wholly or mainly attributable, directly or indirectly, to businesses that do not fall within that subsection.".

(2) This section has effect in relation to gifts or inheritances taken on or after the date of the passing of this Act.

Section 79

Amendment of section 106 (arrangements for relief from double taxation) of [the Capital Acquisitions Tax Consolidation Act 2003].

79. Section 106 of [the Capital Acquisitions Tax Consolidation Act 2003] is amended by substituting the following for subsection (1):

"(1) If the Government by order declare that arrangements specified in the order have been made with the government of any territory outside the State in relation to—

(a) affording relief from double taxation in respect of gift tax or inheritance tax payable under the laws of the State and any tax imposed under the laws of that territory which is of a similar character or is chargeable by reference to death or to gifts inter vivos, or

(b) exchanging information for the purposes of the prevention and detection of tax evasion in respect of the taxes specified in paragraph (a),

and that it is expedient that those arrangements should have the force of law, the arrangements shall, notwithstanding anything in any enactment, have the force of law."

PART 6
Miscellaneous

Section 81

Sale of certain objects to Commissioners of Public Works in Ireland.

81. (1) Section 28(3) of the Finance Act 1931, the proviso to section 55(3) of the Capital Acquisitions Tax Act 1976 and section 77(3) of the Capital Acquisitions Tax Consolidation Act 2003 are amended by inserting "the Commissioners of Public Works in Ireland," after "national institution," in each place where it occurs.

(2) Subsection (1) is deemed to have applied as respects sales on or after 1 August 1994.

Section 82

Amendment of section 912A (information for tax authorities in other territories) of [the Taxes Consolidation Act, 1997]

82. Section 912A (inserted by the Finance Act 2003) of [the Taxes Consolidation Act, 1997,] is amended, in subsection (1), in the definition of "foreign tax" by inserting "or section 106 of the Capital Acquisitions Tax Consolidation Act 2003" after "section 826".

Section 85

Amendment of section 1003 (payment of tax by means of donation of heritage items of [the Taxes Consolidation Act, 1997].

85. Section 1003 of [the Taxes Consolidation Act, 1997,] is, as respects determinations made under subsection (2)(a) of that section on or after the passing of this Act, amended—

(a) in subsection (1) –

    (i) by substituting the following for paragraphs (i) to (vii) of the definition of "selection committee":

        "(i) an officer of the Minister for Arts, Sport and Tourism, who shall act as Chairperson of the committee,

        (ii) the Chief Executive of the Heritage Council,

        (iii) the Director of the Arts Council,

        (iv) the Director of the National Archives,

        (v) the Director of the National Gallery of Ireland,

        (vi) the Director of the National Library of Ireland,

        (vii) the Director of the National Museum of Ireland, and

        (viii) the Director and Chief Executive of the Irish Museum of Modern Art,",

    and

    (ii) by inserting, in paragraph (b), the following after subparagraph (ii):

    "(iii) For the purposes of making a decision in relation to an application made to it for a determination under subsection (2)(a), the selection committee shall not include the member of that committee who represents the approved body to which it is intended that the gift of the heritage item is to be made where that approved body is so represented but that member may participate in any discussion of the application by that committee prior to the making of the decision.",

    and

(b) in subsection (2) –

    (i) by substituting, in paragraph (a), "is, subject to the provisions of paragraphs (aa) and (ab), determined by the selection committee" for "is determined by the selection committee, after consideration of any evidence in relation to the matter which the person submits to the committee and after such consultation (if any) as may seem appropriate to the committee to be necessary with such person or body of persons as in the opinion of the committee may be of assistance to them,",

    (ii) by inserting the following after paragraph (a):

    "(aa) In considering an application under paragraph (a), the selection committee shall –

        (i) consider such evidence as the person making the application submits to it, and

        (ii) seek and consider the opinion in writing in relation to the application of –

> > (I) the approved body to which it is intended the gift is to be made, and
> >
> > (II) the Heritage Council, the Arts Council or such other person or body of persons as the committee considers to be appropriate in the circumstances.
>
> (ab) Where an application under paragraph (a) is in respect of a collection of items, the selection committee shall not make a determination under that paragraph in relation to the collection unless, in addition to the making of a determination in relation to the collection as a whole, the selection committee is satisfied that, on the basis of its consideration of the application in accordance with paragraph (aa), it could make a determination in respect of at least one item comprised in the collection, if such were required.",

and

> (iii) in paragraph (c) —
>
> > (I) by substituting the following for subparagraph (i):
> >
> > "(i) is less than,
> >
> > > (I) subject to clause (II), €150,000, and
> > >
> > > (II) in the case of at least one item comprised in a collection of items, €50,000, or",
> >
> > and
> >
> > (II) by substituting "€150,000" for "€100,000" in sub- paragraph (ii).

Section 87

Amendment of Chapter 4 (revenue powers) of Part 38 of [the Taxes Consolidation Act, 1997].

87. Chapter 4 of Part 38 of [the Taxes Consolidation Act, 1997,] is amended by inserting the following after section 908A:

"Application to High Court seeking order requiring information: associated institutions.

908B. (1) In this section —

> 'the Acts' has the meaning assigned to it by section 1078(1);
>
> 'associated institution', in relation to a financial institution, means a person that —
>
> (a) is controlled by the financial institution (within the meaning of section 432), and
>
> (b) is not resident in the State;
>
> 'authorised officer' means an officer of the Revenue Commissioners authorised by them in writing to exercise the powers conferred by this section;

'books, records or other documents' includes —

(a) any records used in the business of an associated institution, or used in the transfer department of an associated institution acting as registrar of securities, whether —

   (i) comprised in bound volume, loose-leaf binders or other loose-leaf filing system, loose-leaf ledger sheets, pages, folios or cards, or

   (ii) kept on microfilm, magnetic tape or in any non-legible form (by the use of electronics or otherwise) which is capable of being reproduced in a legible form,

(b) every electronic or other automatic means, if any, by which any such thing in non-legible form is so capable of being reproduced,

(c) documents in manuscript, documents which are typed, printed, stencilled or created by any other mechanical or partly mechanical process in use from time to time and documents which are produced by any photographic or photostatic process, and

(d) correspondence and records of other communications between an associated institution and its customers;

'financial institution' means —

(a) a person who holds or has held a licence under section 9 of the Central Bank Act 1971,

(b) a person referred to in section 7(4) of the Central Bank Act 1971, or

(c) a credit institution (within the meaning of the European Communities (Licensing and Supervision of Credit Institutions) Regulations 1992 (S.I. No. 395 of 1992)) which has been authorised by the Central Bank and Financial Services Authority of Ireland to carry on business of a credit institution in accordance with the provisions of the supervisory enactments (within the meaning of those Regulations);

'judge' means a judge of the High Court;

'liability' in relation to a person means any liability in relation to tax which the person is or may be, or may have been, subject, or the amount of such liability;

'tax' means any tax, duty, levy or charge under the care and management of the Revenue Commissioners;

'a taxpayer' means any person including a person whose identity is not known to the authorised officer, and a group or class of persons whose individual identities are not so known.

(2)   An authorised officer may, subject to this section, make an application to a judge for an order requiring a financial institution to do either or both of the following, namely—

(a)   to make available for inspection by the authorised officer, such books, records or other documents as are in the power, possession or procurement of an associated institution, in relation to the financial institution, as contain, or may (in the authorised officer's opinion formed on reasonable grounds) contain information relevant to a liability in relation to a taxpayer, or

(b)   to furnish to the authorised officer such information, explanations and particulars held by, or available from, the financial institution or an associated institution, in relation to the financial institution, as the authorised officer may reasonably require, being information, explanations or particulars that are relevant to any such liability,

and which are specified in the application.

(3)   An authorised officer shall not make an application under subsection (2) without the consent in writing of a Revenue Commissioner, and without being satisfied—

(a)   that there are reasonable grounds for suspecting that the taxpayer, or where the taxpayer is a group or class of persons, all or any one of those persons, may have failed or may fail to comply with any provision of the Acts,

(b)   that any such failure is likely to have led or to lead to serious prejudice to the proper assessment or collection of tax (having regard to the amount of a liability in relation to the taxpayer, or where the taxpayer is a group or class of persons, the amount of a liability, in relation to all or any one of them, that arises or might arise from such failure), and

(c)   that the information—

(i)   which is likely to be contained in the books, records or other documents to which the application relates, or

(ii)   which is likely to arise from the information, explanations and particulars to which the application relates,

is relevant to the proper assessment or collection of tax.

(4)   Where the judge, to whom an application is made under subsection (2), is satisfied that there are reasonable grounds for the application being made, then the judge may, subject to such conditions as he or she may consider proper and specify in the order, make an order requiring the financial institution—

(a)   to make available for inspection by the authorised officer, such books, records or other documents, and

(b) to furnish to the authorised officer such information, explanations and particulars,

as may be specified in the order.

(5) The persons who may be treated as a taxpayer for the purposes of this section include a company which has been dissolved and an individual who has died.

(6) Where in compliance with an order made under subsection (4) a financial institution makes available for inspection by an authorised officer, books, records or other documents, then the financial institution shall afford the authorised officer reasonable assistance, including information, explanations and particulars, in relation to the use of all the electronic or other automatic means, if any, by which the books, records or other documents, in so far as they are in a non-legible form, are capable of being reproduced in a legible form, and any data equipment or any associated apparatus or material.

(7) Where in compliance with an order made under subsection (4) a financial institution makes books, records or other documents available for inspection by the authorised officer, then the authorised officer may make extracts from or copies of all or any part of the books, records or other documents.

(8) Every hearing of an application for an order under this section and of any appeal in connection with that application shall be held in camera.''.

Section 88

Amendment of section 908A (revenue offence: power to obtain information from financial institutions) of [the Taxes Consolidation Act, 1997].

88. [The Taxes Consolidation Act, 1997,] is amended in section 908A by substituting the following for subsection (2) —

''(2)(a) In this subsection 'documentation' includes information kept on microfilm, magnetic tape or in any non-legible form (by use of electronics or otherwise) which is capable of being reproduced in a permanent legible form.

(b) If, on application made by an authorised officer, with the consent in writing of a Revenue Commissioner, a judge is satisfied, on information given on oath by the authorised officer, that there are reasonable grounds for suspecting —

(i) that an offence, which would result (or but for its detection would have resulted) in serious prejudice to the proper assessment or collection of tax, is being, has been, or is about to be committed (having regard to the amount of a liability in relation to any person which might be, or might have been, evaded but for the detection of the relevant facts), and

        (ii) that there is material in the possession of a financial institution specified in the application which is likely to be of substantial value (whether by itself or together with other material) to the investigation of the relevant facts,

the judge may make an order authorising the authorised officer to inspect and take copies of any entries in the books, records or other documents of the financial institution, and any documentation associated with or relating to an entry in such books, records or other documents, for the purposes of investigation of the relevant facts.''.

Section 89

Miscellaneous technical amendments in relation to tax.

89. The enactments specified in Schedule 3 are amended to the extent and in the manner specified in that Schedule.

SCHEDULE 3

Miscellaneous Technical Amendments in Relation to Tax.

1. ......

2. The Capital Acquisitions Tax Consolidation Act 2003 is amended in accordance with the following provisions:

    (a) in section 2(1) –

    (i) after the definition of "gift", by inserting the following definition:

    "'the Income Tax Acts' has the meaning assigned to it by section 2 of the Taxes Consolidation Act 1997;", and

    (ii) after the definition of "tax", by inserting the following definition:

    "'the Tax Acts' has the meaning assigned to it by section 2 of the Taxes Consolidation Act 1997;",

    (b) in section 6(1)(b), by substituting "disponer's" for "donee's" in each place where it occurs,

    (c) in section 46(3)(b), by substituting "section 56" for "section 58",

    (d) in section 72(1) –

    (i) in the definition of "insured", in paragraph (i), by substituting "are deemed" for "is deemed", and

    (ii) in the definition of "relevant tax", in paragraph (b), by substituting "death, or" for "death, and",

    (e) in section 75, by inserting "(1)" before "In this section –", and

    (f) in section 93(1) –

    (i) in paragraph (b), by substituting "all such questions" for "those shares", and

    (ii) in paragraph (c), by substituting "otherwise" for "othewise".

3. ......

5. (a) ......

    (b) Paragraph 2 is deemed to have come into force and have taken effect as on and from 21 February 2003.

FINANCE ACT 2005

Number 5 of 2005
(Enacted on 25th March, 2005)

PART 1

Income Tax, Corporation Tax and Capital Gains Tax

CHAPTER 3

PAYE: Electronic and Telephone Communications

Section 22

Amendment of Chapter 6 (electronic transmission of returns of income, profits, etc., and of other Revenue returns) of Part 38 of [the Taxes Consolidation Act, 1997].

22. With effect from the passing of this Act Chapter 6 (as amended by the Finance Act 2001) of Part 38 of the [Taxes Consolidation Act, 1997,] is amended—

    (a) in section 917D by inserting the following after the definition of "digital signature":

    "'electronic identifier', in relation to a person, means—

    (a) the person's digital signature, or

    (b) such other means of electronic identification as may be specified or authorized by the Revenue Commissioners for the purposes of this Chapter;",

    (b) in section 917F(1) by substituting the following for paragraph (c):

    "(c) the transmission bears the electronic identifier of that person, and",

    (c) in section 917G(1) by substituting "electronic identifiers" for "digital signatures",

    and

    (d) in section 917H—

        (i) in paragraph (b) of subsection (2) and paragraph (c) of subsection (3) by substituting "electronic identifier" for "digital signature", and

        (ii) by inserting the following after subsection (3):

        "(4) For the purposes of subsection (3), the Revenue Commissioners may determine different terms and conditions in relation to different returns or categories of a return, different categories of persons and different returns or categories of a return made by different categories of persons.".

PART 5
Capital Acquisitions Tax

Section 130

Interpretation (Part 5).

130. In this Part "Principal Act" means the Capital Acquisitions Tax Consolidation Act 2003.

Section 131

Amendment of section 48 (affidavits and accounts) of [the Capital Acquisitions Tax Consolidation Act 2003].

131. (1) Section 48 of the [Capital Acquisitions Tax Consolidation Act 2003] is amended, in subsection (2), by substituting the following for paragraph (a):

"(a) details of all property in respect of which the grant of probate or administration is required and, in the case of a deceased person who on the date of his or her death was—

(i) resident or ordinarily resident and domiciled in the State, or

(ii) resident or ordinarily resident and not domiciled in the State and who had been resident in the State for the 5 consecutive years of assessment immediately preceding the year of assessment in which the date of death falls,

details of all property, wherever situate, the beneficial ownership of which, on that person's death, is affected—

(I) by that person's will,

(II) by the rules for distribution on intestacy, or

(III) by Part IX or section 56 of the Succession Act 1965, or under the analogous law of another territory;".

(2) This section has effect in relation to Inland Revenue affidavits in respect of estates of deceased persons where those persons died on or after 1 December 2004.

Section 132

Amendment of section 58 (penalties) of [the Capital Acquisitions Tax Consolidation Act 2003].

132. (1) Section 58 of the [Capital Acquisitions Tax Consolidation Act 2003] is amended—

(a) in subsection (1A)(b) by deleting ", or in the case of fraud twice the amount," and

(b) in subsection (3)(ii) by deleting ", or in the case of fraud, twice the amount,".

(2) This section applies to returns, additional returns, statements, declarations, evidence or valuations delivered, made or, as the case may be, furnished on or after the passing of this Act.

Section 133

Amendment of section 72 (relief in respect of certain policies of insurance of [the Capital Acquisitions Tax Consolidation Act 2003].

133. (1) Section 72 of the [Capital Acquisitions Tax Consolidation Act 2003] is amended –

    (a) in subsection (1) –

        (i) before the definition of "insured", by inserting the following definition:

        "'approved retirement fund tax' means tax which a qualifying fund manager is obliged to deduct in accordance with the provisions of section 784A(4)(c) of the Taxes Consolidation Act 1997;" and

        (ii) in the definition of "relevant tax", by substituting "means approved retirement fund tax and inheritance tax" for "means inheritance tax",

    and

    (b) in subsection (2), by inserting the following after paragraph (b):

    "(c) For the purposes of this section, an amount of the proceeds of a qualifying insurance policy equal to the amount of approved retirement fund tax shall be treated as applied in paying relevant tax of that amount.".

(2) This section has effect in relation to relevant tax payable in respect of inheritances taken on or after 3 February 2005.

Section 134

Amendment of section 75 (exemption of specified collective investment undertakings) of [the Capital Acquisitions Tax Consolidation Act 2003].

134. (1) Section 75 of the [Capital Acquisitions Tax Consolidation Act 2003] is amended –

    (a) by substituting the following for subsection (1):

    "(1) In this section –

    'common contractual fund' has the meaning assigned to it by section 739I of the Taxes Consolidation Act 1997;

    'investment undertaking' has the meaning assigned to it by section 739B of the Taxes Consolidation Act 1997;

'unit', in relation to a common contractual fund, has the meaning assigned to it by section 739I of the Taxes Consolidation Act 1997;

'unit', in relation to an investment undertaking, has the meaning assigned to it by section 739B of the Taxes Consolidation Act 1997.'',

(b) in subsection (2), by substituting "common contractual fund" for "specified collective investment undertaking",

and

(c) by substituting the following for subsection (3):

"(3) Where—

(a) any unit of an investment undertaking which is comprised in a gift or inheritance came into the beneficial ownership of the disponer or became subject to the disposition prior to 15 February 2001, and

(b) the conditions at subparagraphs (i) and (iii) of subsection (2) are complied with,

then that subsection shall apply to that unit of an investment undertaking comprised in a gift or inheritance, if at the date of the disposition, the proper law of the disposition was not the law of the State.''.

(2) This section has effect in relation to gifts or inheritances taken on or after the passing of this Act.

Section 135

Amendment of section 89 (provisions relating to agricultural property) of [the Capital Acquisitions Tax Consolidation Act 2003].

135. (1) Section 89 of the [Capital Acquisitions Tax Consolidation Act 2003] is amended, in subsection (4) —

(a) by substituting the following for paragraph (a):

"(a) Where—

(i) all or any part of the agricultural property (other than crops, trees or underwood) comprised in a gift or inheritance is disposed of or compulsorily acquired within the period of 6 years after the date of the gift or inheritance, and

(ii) the proceeds from such disposal or compulsory acquisition are not fully expended in acquiring other agricultural property within a year of the disposal or within 6 years of the compulsory acquisition, then, except where the donee or successor dies before the property is disposed of or compulsorily acquired, all or, as the case may be, part of the agricultural property shall, for the purposes of subsection (2) and in accordance with paragraph (aa), be treated as property comprised in the gift or inheritance which is not agricultural property, and the taxable value of the gift or inheritance shall be determined accordingly (without regard to whether the donee or successor has ceased to be a farmer by virtue of the disposal or compulsory acquisition) and tax shall be payable accordingly.

(aa) For the purposes of paragraph (a) —

    (i)   the market value of agricultural property which is treated under paragraph (a) as not being agricultural property is determined by the following formula —

$$V1 \times \frac{N}{V2}$$

where —

V1 is the market value of all of the agricultural property on the valuation date without regard to paragraph (a),

V2 is the market value of that agricultural property immediately before the disposal or compulsory acquisition of all or, as the case may be, a part thereof, and

N is the amount of proceeds from the disposal or compulsory acquisition of all the agricultural property or, as the case may be, a part thereof, that was not expended in acquiring other agricultural property,

and

    (ii)   the proceeds from a disposal include an amount equal to the market value of the consideration (not being cash) received for the disposal.",

and

(b) in paragraph (b), by substituting "disposal" for "sale".

(2) This section has effect in relation to disposals or compulsory acquisitions of agricultural property occurring on or after 3 February 2005.

Section 136

Amendment of section 101 (withdrawal of relief) of [the Capital Acquisitions Tax Consolidation Act 2003].

136. (1) Section 101 of the [Capital Acquisitions Tax Consolidation Act 2003] is amended by inserting the following after subsection (2):

"(3) Notwithstanding subsection (2), where relevant business property (in this section referred to as 'original property') comprised in a gift or inheritance has been replaced directly or indirectly by other property and the market value of the original property is greater than the market value of that other property, then the reduction which would fall to be made under section 92 in respect of the original property shall be reduced in the same proportion as the market value of the other property bears to the market value of the original property.".

(2) This section has effect in relation to relevant business property which has been replaced by other property on or after 3 February 2005.

Section 137

Amendment of section 107 (other relief from double taxation) of [the Capital Acquisitions Tax Consolidation Act 2003].

137. (1) Section 107 of the Principal Act is amended by substituting the following for subsection (2):

"(2) Where the Commissioners are satisfied that a taxable gift or taxable inheritance, taken under a disposition by a donee or successor on the happening of any event, is reduced by the payment of foreign tax which is chargeable in connection with the same event under the same disposition in respect of property which is situate in any territory outside the State, they shall allow a credit in respect of that foreign tax against the gift tax or inheritance tax payable by that donee or successor on that taxable gift or taxable inheritance; but such credit shall not exceed —

(a) the amount of the gift tax or inheritance tax payable in respect of the same property by reason of such property being comprised in any taxable gift or taxable inheritance taken under that disposition on the happening of that event, or

(b) in so far as it has been paid, the amount of that foreign tax,

whichever is the lesser.".

(2) This section has effect in relation to gifts or inheritances taken on or after 1 December 2004.

PART 6

Miscellaneous

Section 142

Amendment of section 1078 (revenue offences) of Taxes Consolidation Act 1997.

142 The Taxes Consolidation Act 1997 is amended in section 1078 –

   (a) by inserting after subsection (1) the following subsection:

"(1A) (a) In this subsection –

     'facilitating' means aiding, abetting, assisting, inciting or inducing;

     'fraudulent evasion of tax by a person' means the person –

     (a) evading or attempting to evade any payment or deduction of tax required under the Acts to be paid by the person or, as the case may be, required under the Acts to be deducted from amounts due to the person, or

     (b) claiming or obtaining, or attempting to claim or obtain, relief or exemption from, or payment or repayment of, any tax, being relief, exemption, payment or repayment, to which the person is not entitled under the Acts,

     where, for those purposes, the person deceives, omits, conceals or uses any other dishonest means including –

     (i) providing false, incomplete or misleading information, or

     (ii) failing to furnish information,

     to the Revenue Commissioners or to any other person.

    (b) For the purposes of this subsection and subsection (5) a person (in this paragraph referred to as the 'first-mentioned person') is reckless as to whether or not he or she is concerned in facilitating –

     (i) the fraudulent evasion of tax by a person, being another person, or

     (ii) the commission of an offence under subsection (2) by a person, being another person,

     if the first-mentioned person disregards a substantial risk that he or she is so concerned, and for those purposes 'substantial risk' means a risk of such a nature and degree that, having regard to all the circumstances and the extent of the information available to the first-mentioned person, its disregard by that person involves culpability of a high degree.

(c) A person shall, without prejudice to any other penalty to which the person may be liable, be guilty of an offence under this section if the person—

   (i) is knowingly concerned in the fraudulent evasion of tax by the person or any other person,

   (ii) is knowingly concerned in, or is reckless as to whether or not the person is concerned in, facilitating—

     (I) the fraudulent evasion of tax, or

     (II) the commission of an offence under subsection (2) (other than an offence under paragraph (b) of that subsection),

   by any other person, or

   (iii) is knowingly concerned in the fraudulent evasion or attempted fraudulent evasion of any prohibition or restriction on importation for the time being in force, or the removal of any goods from the State, in contravention of any provision of the Acts.'',

(b) in subsection (2)—

   (i) by substituting for paragraph (f) the following paragraph:

   ''(f) fails to pay to the Collector-General appropriate tax (within the meaning of section 739E) within the time specified in that behalf in section 739F,'',

   (ii) in paragraph (i) by substituting ''by the Acts,'' for ''by the Acts, or'', and

   (iii) by inserting after paragraph (i) the following paragraph:

   ''(ii)(i) fails to deduct tax required to be deducted by the person under section 531(1), or

     (ii) fails, having made that deduction, to pay the sum deducted to the Collector-General within the time specified in that behalf in section 531(3A),

   or'',

and

(c) in subsection (5) by substituting ''to have been committed with the consent or connivance of or to be attributable to any recklessness (as provided for by subsection (1A)(b)) on the part of'' for ''to have been committed with the consent or connivance of''.

Section 143

Amendment of section 1086 (publication of names of tax defaulters) of Taxes Consolidation Act 1997.

143. (1) Section 1086 of the Taxes Consolidation Act 1997 is amended—

(a) in subsection (4)(c) by substituting " €30,000" for " €12,700", and

(b) by inserting the following subsection after subsection (4):

"(4A) (a) In this subsection—

'the consumer price index number' means the All Items Consumer Price Index Number compiled by the Central Statistics Office;

'the consumer price index number relevant to a year' means the consumer price index number at the mid-December before the commencement of that year expressed on the basis that the consumer price index at mid-December 2001 was 100;

'the Minister' means the Minister for Finance.

(b) The Minister shall, in the year 2010 and in every fifth year thereafter, by order provide, in accordance with paragraph (c), an amount in lieu of the amount referred to in subsection (4)(c), or where such an order has been made previously, in lieu of the amount specified in the last order so made.

(c) For the purposes of paragraph (b) the amount referred to in subsection (4)(c) or in the last previous order made under the said paragraph (b), as the case may be, shall be adjusted by—

(i) multiplying that amount by the consumer price index number relevant to the year in which the adjustment is made and dividing the product by the consumer price index number relevant to the year in which the amount was previously provided for, and

(ii) rounding the resulting amount up to the next €1,000.

(d) An order made under this subsection shall specify that the amount provided for by the order—

(i) takes effect from a specified date, being 1 January in the year in which the order is made, and

(ii) does not apply to any case in which the specified liability referred to in paragraphs (c) and (d) of subsection (2) includes tax, the liability in respect of which arose before, or which relates to periods which commenced before, that specified date.".

(2) Subsection (1)(a) shall not apply where the specified liability referred to in paragraphs (c) and (d) of subsection (2) of section 1086 of the Taxes Consolidation Act 1997 includes tax, the liability in respect of which arose before, or which relates to periods which commenced before, 1 January 2005.

Section 145

Interest on certain overdue tax.

145. (1) ....

(4) (a) Section 51 of the Capital Acquisitions Tax Consolidation Act 2003 is amended by substituting the following for subsection (2):

"(2) (a) Simple interest is payable, without the deduction of income tax, on the tax from the valuation date to the date of payment, and the amount of that interest shall be determined in accordance with paragraph (c).

(b) Interest payable in accordance with paragraph (a) is chargeable and recoverable in the same manner as if it were part of the tax.

(c) (i) In this paragraph—

'period of delay', in relation to any tax due and payable, means the period during which that tax remains unpaid;

'relevant period', in relation to a period of delay which falls into more than one of the periods specified in column (1) of Part 1 of the Table, means any part of the period of delay which falls into, or is the same as, a period specified in that column;

'Table' means the Table to this subsection.

(ii) The interest payable in accordance with paragraph (a), shall be—

(I) where one of the periods specified in column (1) of Part 1 of the Table includes or is the same as the period of delay, the amount determined by the formula—

$$T \times D \times P$$

where—

T is the tax due and payable which remains unpaid,

D is the number of days (including part of a day) forming the period of delay, and

P is the appropriate percentage in column (2) of the Table opposite the period specified in column (1) of Part 1 of the Table within which the period of delay falls or which is the same as the period of delay, and

(II) where a continuous period formed by 2 or more of the periods specified in column (1) of Part 1 of the Table, but not (as in subparagraph (I)) only one such period, includes or is the same as the period of delay, the aggregate of the amounts due in respect of each relevant period which forms part of the period of delay, and the amount due in respect of each such relevant period shall be determined by the formula —

$$T \times D \times P$$

where —

T is the tax due and payable which remains unpaid,

D is the number of days (including part of a day) forming the relevant period, and

P is the appropriate percentage in column (2) of Part 1 of the Table opposite the period specified in column (1) of Part 1 of the Table into which the relevant period falls or which is the same as the relevant period.

TABLE

Part 1

(Period)	(Percentage)
(1)	(2)
From 31 March 1976 to 31 July 1978	0.0492%
From 1 August 1978 to 31 March 1998	0.0410%
From 1 April 1998 to 31 March 2005	0.0322%
From 1 April 2005 to the date of payment	0.0273%

Part 2

(Period)	(Percentage)
(1)	(2)
From 8 February 1995 to 31 March 1998	0.0307%
From 1 April 1998 to 31 March 2005	0.0241%
From 1 April 2005 until the date of payment	0.0204%

(2A) For the purposes of calculating interest on the whole or the part of the tax to which section 55 applies, subsection (2) shall apply as if references in that subsection to Part 1 of the Table were references to Part 2 of the Table.''.

(b) Section 55 of the Capital Acquisitions Tax Consolidation Act 2003 is amended by substituting the following for paragraph (b) of subsection (2):

''(b) notwithstanding subsection (2) of section 51, the interest payable on that whole or part of the tax shall be determined –

(i) in accordance with that subsection as modified by subsection (2A) of that section, or

(ii) in such other manner as may be prescribed by the Minister for Finance by regulations,

instead of in accordance with subsection (2) of that section, and that section shall apply as regards that whole or part of the tax as if the interest so payable were determined under that section, but the interest payable on any overdue instalment of that whole or part of that tax, or on such part of the tax as would represent any such overdue instalment if that whole or part of the tax were being paid by instalments, shall continue to be determined in accordance with subsection (2) of section 51.''.

(5) (a) This subsection applies to interest payable under –

(i) .....

(iii) section 117 of the Finance Act 1993.

(b) Where any interest to which this subsection applies is chargeable on or after 1 April 2005 in respect of tax due to be paid whether before, on or after that date, then such interest shall, notwithstanding the provisions of any other enactment, be chargeable at the rate of 0.0273 per cent per day or part of a day instead of at the rate specified in that other enactment and the sections referred to in paragraph (a) shall have effect as if for interest so chargeable that rate were substituted for the rate specified in each of those sections.

(6) (a) The provisions set out in paragraph (b) are, in so far as they are not already repealed, repealed with effect from 1 April 2005 to the extent that they apply to interest chargeable or payable on income tax, corporation tax, capital gains tax, gift tax and inheritance tax that has not been paid before that date regardless of when that tax became due and payable.

(b) The provisions referred to in paragraph (a) are—

(i) .....

(v) section 41 of the Capital Acquisitions Tax Act 1976;

(vi) ....

(7) ....

(8) (a) ....

(d) Subsection (4) applies to any unpaid gift tax or inheritance tax, as the case may be, that has not been paid before 1 April 2005 regardless of when that tax becomes due and payable and notwithstanding anything to the contrary in any other enactment.

Section 147

Miscellaneous technical amendments in relation to tax.

147. The enactments specified in Schedule 6 are amended to the extent and in the manner specified in that Schedule.

SCHEDULE 6
Miscellaneous Technical Amendments in Relation to Tax

1. .....

2. The Capital Acquisitions Tax Consolidation Act 2003 is amended in section 45(2)(b)(i) by deleting "on or".

3. .....

4. (a) ....

(b) Paragraph 2 is deemed to have come into force and have taken effect as on and from 21 February 2003.

(c) ....

INTERPRETATION ACT 2005

Number 23 of 2005
(Enacted on 17th October, 2005)

Part 1
Preliminary and General

Section 1

Short title and commencement.

1. (1) This Act may be cited as the Interpretation Act 2005.

   (2) This Act comes into operation on 1 January 2006.

Section 2

Interpretation.

2. (1) In this Act—

   "Act" means—

   (a) an Act of the Oireachtas, and

   (b) a statute which was in force in Saorstát Éireann immediately before the date of the coming into operation of the Constitution and which continued in force by virtue of Article 50 of the Constitution;

   "enactment" means an Act or a statutory instrument or any portion of an Act or statutory instrument;

   "repeal" includes revoke, rescind, abrogate or cancel;

   "statutory instrument" means an order, regulation, rule, bye-law, warrant, licence, certificate, direction, notice, guideline or other like document made, issued, granted or otherwise created by or under an Act and references, in relation to a statutory instrument, to "made" or to "made under" include references to made, issued, granted or otherwise created by or under such instrument.

   (2) For the purposes of this Act, an enactment which has been replaced or has expired, lapsed or otherwise ceased to have effect is deemed to have been repealed.

Section 3

Repeals and savings.

3. (1) The following Acts are repealed:

    (a) the Interpretation Act 1889;

    (b) the Interpretation Act 1923;

    (c) the Interpretation Act 1937;

    (d) the Interpretation (Amendment) Act 1993.

(2) (a) The repeal by this Act of an Act which assigns a meaning to a word or expression in another enactment does not affect the meaning so assigned if—

    (i) in the absence of that meaning in this Act, or

    (ii) by the application to the other enactment of the meaning assigned by this Act to the same or a similar word or expression,

the other enactment would be changed in intent or become unclear or absurd.

(b) The repeal by this Act of an Act which provides for any matter (other than a matter to which paragraph (a) relates) in another enactment does not affect the matter so provided for if—

    (i) in the absence of that matter being provided for in this Act, or

    (ii) by the application to the other enactment of a matter provided for by this Act which corresponds to a matter provided for in the repealed Act concerned,

the other enactment would be changed in intent or become unclear or absurd.

Section 4

Application.

4. (1) A provision of this Act applies to an enactment except in so far as the contrary intention appears in this Act, in the enactment itself or, where relevant, in the Act under which the enactment is made.

(2) The provisions of this Act which relate to other Acts also apply to this Act unless the contrary intention appears in this Act.

PART 2
Miscellaneous Rules

Section 5

Construing ambiguous or obscure provisions, etc.

5. (1) In construing a provision of any Act (other than a provision that relates to the imposition of a penal or other sanction) —

    (a) that is obscure or ambiguous, or

    (b) that on a literal interpretation would be absurd or would fail to reflect the plain intention of —

        (i) in the case of an Act to which paragraph (a) of the definition of "Act" in section 2(1) relates, the Oireachtas, or

        (ii) in the case of an Act to which paragraph (b) of that definition relates, the parliament concerned,

    the provision shall be given a construction that reflects the plain intention of the Oireachtas or parliament concerned, as the case may be, where that intention can be ascertained from the Act as a whole.

    (2) In construing a provision of a statutory instrument (other than a provision that relates to the imposition of a penal or other sanction) —

    (a) that is obscure or ambiguous, or

    (b) that on a literal interpretation would be absurd or would fail to reflect the plain intention of the instrument as a whole in the context of the enactment (including the Act) under which it was made,

    the provision shall be given a construction that reflects the plain intention of the maker of the instrument where that intention can be ascertained from the instrument as a whole in the context of that enactment.

Section 6

Construing provisions in changing circumstances.

6. In construing a provision of any Act or statutory instrument, a court may make allowances for any changes in the law, social conditions, technology, the meaning of words used in that Act or statutory instrument and other relevant matters, which have occurred since the date of the passing of that Act or the making of that statutory instrument, but only in so far as its text, purpose and context permit.

Section 7

Supplemental provision to sections 5 and 6.

7. (1) In construing a provision of an Act for the purposes of section 5 or 6, a court may, notwithstanding section 18(g), make use of all matters that accompany and are set out in –

    (a) in the case of an Act of the Oireachtas, the signed text of such law as enrolled for record in the Office of the Registrar of the Supreme Court pursuant to Article 25.4.5° of the Constitution,

    (b) in the case of an Act of the Oireachtas of Saorstát Éireann, the signed text of such law as enrolled for record in the office of such officer of the Supreme Court of Saorstát Éireann as Dáil Éireann determined pursuant to Article 42 of the Constitution of the Irish Free State (Saorstát Éireann),

    (c) in the case of any other Act, such text of that Act as corresponds to the text of the Act enrolled in the manner referred to in paragraph (a) or (b).

    (2) For the purposes of subsection (1), it shall be presumed, until the contrary is shown, that a copy of the text of an Act that is required to be judicially noticed is a copy of the text to which subsection (1) relates.

Section 8

Reading provisions together as one and summary proceedings for offences.

8. Where –

    (a) an Act or portion of an Act (whenever passed) –

        (i) provides that summary proceedings for offences under it may be prosecuted by a specified person, and

        (ii) is subsequently read together as one with any provision of another Act,

    and

    (b) an offence is created under that provision which can be prosecuted in a summary manner but no express power is given to the specified person to so prosecute,

then, the specified person may bring summary proceedings for an offence under that other provision unless some other person is authorised by that other Act to bring such proceedings.

Section 9

References in enactments to Parts, etc.

9. (1) A reference in an enactment to a Part, Chapter, section, Schedule or other division, by whatever name called, shall be read as a reference

to a Part, Chapter, section, Schedule or other division of the enactment in which the reference occurs.

(2) A reference in an enactment to a subsection, paragraph, subparagraph, clause, subclause, article, subarticle or other division, by whatever name called, shall be read as a reference to a subsection, paragraph, subparagraph, clause, subclause, article, subarticle or other division of the provision in which the reference occurs.

Section 10

Enactment always speaking.

10. An enactment continues to have effect and may be applied from time to time as occasion requires.

Section 11

References in enactments to examples.

11. If under the heading –

(a) in the Irish language "Sampla" or "Samplaí", or

(b) in the English language "Example" or "Examples",

an enactment includes at the end of a provision or in a schedule relating to such provision an example of the operation of the provision, then the example –

(i) is not to be read as exhaustive of the provision, and

(ii) may extend, but does not limit, the meaning of the provision.

Section 12

Deviation from form.

12. Where a form is prescribed in or under an enactment, a deviation from the form which does not materially affect the substance of the form or is not misleading in content or effect does not invalidate the form used.

PART 3

Citation and Operation of Enactments

Section 13

Judicial notice.

13. An Act is a public document and shall be judicially noticed.

Section 14

Citation and references to amended enactments.

14. (1) An Act may be cited in any enactment or other document —

    (a) by the long title or short title of the Act,

    (b) where appropriate, by the consecutive number of the Act in the calendar year and by the calendar year in which it was passed, or

    (c) where the Act was passed prior to the enactment of the Constitution of the Irish Free State (Saorstát Éireann) Act 1922, by its regnal year and chapter number and, where there was more than one parliamentary session in the same regnal year, by reference to the session concerned.

  (2) A citation of or a reference to an enactment shall be read as a citation of or reference to the enactment as amended (including as amended by way of extension, application, adaptation or other modification of the enactment), whether the amendment is made before, on or after the date on which the provision containing the citation or reference came into operation.

  (3) In citing —

    (a) an Act by its short title, or

    (b) any other enactment by its citation (if any),

a comma immediately before a reference to a year and a comma immediately after such a reference that is not required for the purpose of punctuation may be omitted.

Section 15

Date of passing of Acts of Oireachtas.

15. (1) The date of the passing of an Act of the Oireachtas is the date of the day on which the Bill for the Act is signed by the President.

  (2) Immediately after the Bill for an Act of the Oireachtas is signed by the President, the Clerk of Dáil Éireann shall endorse on the Act immediately after the long title the date of the passing of the Act, and that date shall be taken to be part of the Act.

Section 16

Commencement.

16. (1) Subject to subsection (2), every provision of an Act comes into operation on the date of its passing.

(2) Where an Act or a provision of an Act is expressed to come into operation on a particular day (whether the day is before or after the date of the passing of the Act and whether the day is named in the Act or is to be fixed or ascertained in a particular manner), the Act or provision comes into operation at the end of the day before the particular day.

(3) Subject to subsection (4), every provision of a statutory instrument comes into operation at the end of the day before the day on which the statutory instrument is made.

(4) Where a statutory instrument or a provision of a statutory instrument is expressed to come into operation on a particular day (whether the day is before or after the date of the making of the statutory instrument and whether the day is named in the instrument or is to be fixed or ascertained in a particular manner), the statutory instrument or provision comes into operation at the end of the day before the particular day.

Section 17

Exercise of statutory powers before commencement of Act.

17. Where an Act or a provision of an Act is expressed to come into operation on a day subsequent to the date of the passing of the Act, the following provisions apply:

(a) if the day on which the Act or the provision comes into operation is to be fixed or ascertained in a particular manner, the statutory instrument, act or thing whereby the day is fixed or ascertained may, subject to any restriction imposed by the Act, be made or done at any time after the passing of the Act;

(b) if, for the purposes of the Act or the provision, the Act confers a power to make a statutory instrument or do any act or thing, the making or doing of which is necessary or expedient to enable the Act or provision to have full force and effect immediately on its coming into operation, the power may, subject to any restriction imposed by the Act, be exercised at any time after the passing of the Act.

PART 4

Meaning and Construction of Words and Expressions

Section 18

General rules of construction.

18. The following provisions apply to the construction of an enactment:

(a) Singular and plural. A word importing the singular shall be read as also importing the plural, and a word importing the plural shall be read as also importing the singular;

(b) Gender.

   (i) A word importing the masculine gender shall be read as also importing the feminine gender;

   (ii) In an Act passed on or after 22 December 1993, and in a statutory instrument made after that date, a word importing the feminine gender shall be read as also importing the masculine gender;

(c) Person. "Person" shall be read as importing a body corporate (whether a corporation aggregate or a corporation sole) and an unincorporated body of persons, as well as an individual, and the subsequent use of any pronoun in place of a further use of "person" shall be read accordingly;

(d) Adopted child. A reference, however expressed, to a child of a person shall be read as including—

   (i) in an Act passed after the passing of the Adoption Act 1976 a reference to a child adopted by the person under the Adoption Acts 1952 to 1998 and every other enactment which is to be construed together with any of those Acts, or

   (ii) in an Act passed on or after 14 January 1988 (the commencement of section 3 of the Status of Children Act 1987), a child to whom subparagraph (i) relates or a child adopted outside the State whose adoption is recognised by virtue of the law for the time being in force in the State;

(e) Distance. A word or expression relating to the distance between two points and every reference to the distance from or to a point shall be read as relating or referring to such distance measured in a straight line on a horizontal plane;

(f) Series description. Where a consecutive series is described by reference to the first and last in the series, the description shall be read as including the first and the last in the series;

(g) Marginal and shoulder notes, etc. Subject to section 7, none of the following shall be taken to be part of the enactment or be construed or judicially noticed in relation to the construction or interpretation of the enactment:

(i) a marginal note placed at the side, or a shoulder note placed at the beginning, of a section or other provision to indicate the subject, contents or effect of the section or provision,

(ii) a heading or cross-line placed in or at the head of or at the beginning of a Part, Chapter, section, or other provision or group of sections or provisions to indicate the subject, contents or effect of the Part, Chapter, section, provision or group;

(h) Periods of time. Where a period of time is expressed to begin on or be reckoned from a particular day, that day shall be deemed to be included in the period and, where a period of time is expressed to end on or be reckoned to a particular day, that day shall be deemed to be included in the period;

(i) Time. Where time is expressed by reference to a specified hour or to a time before or after a specified hour, that time shall be determined by reference to the Standard Time (Amendment) Act 1971;

(j) Offences by corporations. A reference to a person in relation to an offence (whether punishable on indictment or on summary conviction) shall be read as including a reference to a body corporate.

Section 19

Construction of statutory instruments.

19. A word or expression used in a statutory instrument has the same meaning in the statutory instrument as it has in the enactment under which the instrument is made.

Section 20

Interpretation provisions.

20. (1) Where an enactment contains a definition or other interpretation provision, the provision shall be read as being applicable except in so far as the contrary intention appears in —

(a) the enactment itself, or

(b) the Act under which the enactment is made.

(2) Where an enactment defines or otherwise interprets a word or expression, other parts of speech and grammatical forms of the word or expression have a corresponding meaning.

Section 21

Interpretation of words and expressions in Schedule.

21. (1) In an enactment, a word or expression to which a particular meaning, construction or effect is assigned in Part 1 of the Schedule has the meaning, construction or effect so assigned to it.

(2) In an enactment which comes into operation after the commencement of this Act, a word or expression to which a particular meaning, construction or effect is assigned in Part 2 of the Schedule has the meaning, construction or effect so assigned to it.

PART 5
Powers and Duties

Section 22

Powers under enactments.

22. (1) A power conferred by an enactment may be exercised from time to time as occasion requires.

(2) A power conferred by an enactment on the holder of an office as that holder shall be deemed to be conferred on, and may accordingly be exercised by, the holder for the time being of that office.

(3) A power conferred by an enactment to make a statutory instrument shall be read as including a power, exercisable in the like manner and subject to the like consent and conditions (if any), to repeal or amend a statutory instrument made under that power and (where required) to make another statutory instrument in place of the one so repealed.

Section 23

Duties under enactments.

23. (1) A duty imposed by an enactment shall be performed from time to time as occasion requires.

(2) A duty imposed by an enactment on the holder of an office as that holder shall be deemed to be imposed on, and shall accordingly be performed by, the holder for the time being of that office.

Section 24

Rules of court.

24. Where an enactment confers a new jurisdiction on a court or extends or varies an existing jurisdiction of a court, the authority having for the time being power to make rules or orders regulating the practice and procedure of the court has, and may at any time exercise, power to make rules or orders for regulating the practice and procedure of that court in the exercise of the jurisdiction so conferred, extended or varied.

Section 25

Service by post.

25. Where an enactment authorises or requires a document to be served by post, by using the word "serve", "give", "deliver", "send" or any other word or expression, the service of the document may be effected by properly addressing, prepaying (where required) and posting a letter containing the document, and in that case the service of the document is deemed, unless the contrary is proved, to have been effected at the time at which the letter would be delivered in the ordinary course of post.

PART 6
Amendment of Enactments, Etc.

Section 26

Repeals and substitutions.

26. (1) Where an enactment repeals another enactment and substitutes other provisions for the enactment so repealed, the enactment so repealed continues in force until the substituted provisions come into operation.

(2) Where an enactment ("former enactment") is repealed and re-enacted, with or without modification, by another enactment ("new enactment"), the following provisions apply:

(a) a person appointed under the former enactment shall continue to act for the remainder of the period for which the person was appointed as if appointed under the new enactment;

(b) a bond, guarantee or other security of a continuing nature given by a person under the former enactment remains in force, and data, books, papers, forms and things prepared or used under the former enactment may continue to be used as before the repeal;

(c) proceedings taken under the former enactment may, subject to section 27(1), be continued under and in conformity with the new enactment in so far as that may be done consistently with the new enactment;

(d) if after the commencement of this Act—

(i) any provision of a former enactment, that provided for the making of a statutory instrument, is repealed and re-enacted, with or without modification, as a new provision, and

(ii) such statutory instrument is in force immediately before such repeal and re-enactment,

then the statutory instrument shall be deemed to have been made under the new provision to the extent that it is not inconsistent with the new enactment, and remains in force until it is repealed or otherwise ceases to have effect;

(e) to the extent that the provisions of the new enactment express the same idea in a different form of words but are in substance the same as those of the former enactment, the idea in the new enactment shall not be taken to be different merely because a different form of words is used;

(f) a reference in any other enactment to the former enactment shall, with respect to a subsequent transaction, matter or thing, be read as a reference to the provisions of the new enactment relating to the same subject-matter as that of the former enactment, but where there are no provisions in the new enactment relating to the same subject-matter, the former enactment shall be disregarded in so far as is necessary to maintain or give effect to that other enactment.

Section 27

Effect of repeal of enactment.

27. (1) Where an enactment is repealed, the repeal does not—

(a) revive anything not in force or not existing immediately before the repeal,

(b) affect the previous operation of the enactment or anything duly done or suffered under the enactment,

(c) affect any right, privilege, obligation or liability acquired, accrued or incurred under the enactment,

(d) affect any penalty, forfeiture or punishment incurred in respect of any offence against or contravention of the enactment which was committed before the repeal, or

(e) prejudice or affect any legal proceedings (civil or criminal) pending at the time of the repeal in respect of any such right, privilege, obligation, liability, offence or contravention.

(2) Where an enactment is repealed, any legal proceedings (civil or criminal) in respect of a right, privilege, obligation or liability acquired, accrued or incurred under, or an offence against or contravention of, the enactment may be instituted, continued or enforced, and any penalty, forfeiture or punishment in respect of such offence or contravention may be imposed and carried out, as if the enactment had not been repealed.

SCHEDULE
PART 1

Interpretation of Particular Words and Expressions

"affidavit", in the case of a person for the time being allowed by law to declare instead of swearing, includes declaration;

"British statute" means an Act of the Parliament of the former United Kingdom of Great Britain and Ireland;

"Circuit Court" means the Circuit Court as established and for the time being maintained by law;

"commencement", when used in relation to an enactment, means the time at which the enactment comes into operation;

"Constitution" means the Constitution of Ireland enacted by the people on 1 July 1937, as amended;

"Dáil Éireann" means the House of the Oireachtas to which that name is given by section 1 of Article 15 of the Constitution;

"District Court" means the District Court as established and for the time being maintained by law;

"financial year", in relation to an exchequer financial year, means the period which is coextensive with a calendar year;

"Government" means the Government mentioned in Article 28 of the Constitution;

"Great Britain" does not include the Channel Islands or the Isle of Man;

"High Court" means the High Court as established and for the time being maintained by law pursuant to Article 34 of the Constitution;

"land" includes tenements, hereditaments, houses and buildings, land covered by water and any estate, right or interest in or over land;

"local financial year" means a period which is coextensive with a calendar year;

"midnight" means, in relation to a particular day, the point of time at which the day ends;

"Minister of the Government" means a member of the Government having charge of a Department of State;

"month" means a calendar month;

"oath", in the case of a person for the time being allowed by law to affirm or declare instead of swearing, includes affirmation or declaration;

"Oireachtas" means the National Parliament provided for by Article 15 of the Constitution;

"ordnance map" means a map made under the powers conferred by the Survey (Ireland) Acts 1825 to 1870;

"President" means the President of Ireland or any Commission, or other body or authority, for the time being lawfully exercising the powers and performing the duties of the President;

"pre-union Irish statute" means an Act passed by a Parliament sitting in Ireland at any time before the coming into force on 1 January 1801 of the Act entitled "An Act for the Union of Great Britain and Ireland";

"rateable valuation" means the valuation under the Valuation Act 2001 of the property concerned;

"rules of court" means rules made by the authority for the time being having power to make rules regulating the practice and procedure of the court concerned;

"Saorstát Éireann statute" means an Act of the Oireachtas of Saorstát Éireann;

"Saorstát Éireann" means the House of the Oireachtas to which that name is given by section 1 of Article 15 of the Constitution;

"statutory declaration" means a declaration made under the Statutory Declarations Act 1938;

"Supreme Court" means the Supreme Court as established and for the time being maintained by law pursuant to Article 34 of the Constitution;

"swear", in the case of a person for the time being allowed by law to affirm or declare instead of swearing, includes affirm and declare;

"week" means the period between midnight on any Saturday and midnight on the following Saturday;

"week-day" means a day which is not a Sunday;

"writing" includes printing, typewriting, lithography, photography, and other modes of representing or reproducing words in visible form and any information kept in a non-legible form, whether stored electronically or otherwise, which is capable by any means of being reproduced in a legible form;

"year", when used without qualification, means a period of 12 months beginning on the 1st day of January in any year.

PART 2

"Companies Acts" means the Companies Acts 1963 to 2001 and every other enactment which is to be read together with any of those Acts;

"full age", in relation to a person, means the time when the person attains the age of 18 years or sooner marries, or any time after either event;

"functions" includes powers and duties, and references to the performance of functions include, with respect to powers and duties, references to the exercise of the powers and the carrying out of the duties;

"Member State" means, where the context so admits, a Member State of the European Communities or of the European Union;

"Minister of State" means a person appointed under section 1 of the Ministers and Secretaries (Amendment) (No. 2) Act 1977 to be a Minister of State;

"public holiday" means a public holiday determined in accordance with the Organisation of Working Time Act 1997;

"Social Welfare Acts" means the Social Welfare (Consolidation) Act 1993 and every other enactment which is to be read together with that Act;

"working day" means a day which is not a Saturday, Sunday or public holiday.

FINANCE ACT 2006

Number 6 of 2006
(Enacted on 31st March, 2006)

PART 5
Capital Acquisitions Tax

Section 112

Interpretation (Part 5).

112. In this Part "Principal Act" means the Capital Acquisitions Tax Consolidation Act 2003.

Section 113

Amendment of section 6 (taxable gift) of [the Capital Acquisitions Tax Consolidation Act 2003].

113. (1) Section 6 of the [Capital Acquisitions Tax Consolidation Act 2003] is amended in subsection (5) by substituting the following for paragraph (b):

"(b) For the purposes of subsection (2)(d), so much of the market value of any share in a private company incorporated outside the State (which after taking the gift is a company controlled by the donee) as is attributable, directly or indirectly, to property situate in the State at the date of the gift shall be deemed to be a sum situate in the State.".

(2) This section shall apply to gifts taken on or after 2 February 2006.

Section 114

Amendment of section 11 (taxable inheritance) of [the Capital Acquisitions Tax Consolidation Act 2003].

114. (1) Section 11 of the [Capital Acquisitions Tax Consolidation Act 2003] is amended in subsection (5) by substituting the following for paragraph (b):

"(b) For the purposes of subsection (2)(c), so much of the market value of any share in a private company incorporated outside the State (which after taking the inheritance is a company controlled by the successor) as is attributable, directly or indirectly, to property situate in the State at the date of the inheritance shall be deemed to be a sum situate in the State.".

(2) This section shall apply to inheritances taken on or after 2 February 2006.

Section 115

Amendment of section 77 (exemption of heritage property) of [the Capital Acquisitions Tax Consolidation Act 2003].

115. Section 77 of the [Capital Acquisitions Tax Consolidation Act 2003] is amended in subsection (3) by inserting "the Trust (within the meaning of section 1003A of the Taxes Consolidation Act 1997)," after "the Commissioners of Public Works in Ireland,".

Section 116

Amendment of Chapter 3 (annual levy on discretionary trusts) of Part 3 of [the Capital Acquisitions Tax Consolidation Act 2003].

116. (1)　Chapter 3 of Part 3 of the [Capital Acquisitions Tax Consolidation Act 2003] is amended—

(a)　in section 19 by substituting the following for the definition of "chargeable date":

" 'chargeable date', in relation to any year, means—

(a)　in respect of the year 2006, 5 April and 31 December in that year, and

(b)　in respect of the year 2007 and subsequent years, 31 December in the year concerned;",

(b)　by substituting the following for section 23:

"Computation of tax.

23.　(1)　Subject to subsection (2), the tax chargeable on the taxable value of a taxable inheritance which is charged to tax by reason of section 20 is computed at the rate of one per cent of that taxable value.

(2)　The tax chargeable on the chargeable date that is 31 December 2006 shall be an amount equal to 73.97 per cent of the tax chargeable by virtue of subsection (1).",

and

(c)　in section 24 by inserting the following after subsection (1):

"(1A) Where the market value of property is on a valuation date determined in accordance with subsection (1) and that valuation date is 5 April 2006, then that market value as so determined shall be treated as the market value of the property on the valuation date that is 31 December 2006.".

(2)　This section shall apply as respects the year 2006 and subsequent years.

Section 117

Discretionary trusts: returns.

117. (1) The [Capital Acquisitions Tax Consolidation Act 2003] is amended—

  (a) in section 21—

  (i) by deleting paragraph (e), and

  (ii) in paragraph (f) by substituting "section 50 and section 81 and Schedule 2" for "section 46(2), (3), (4) and (5) and sections 50, 54, 56 and 81 and Schedule 2",

  (b) in section 46(2) by substituting "Any person who is primarily accountable for the payment of tax by virtue of paragraph (c) of section 16, paragraph (c) of section 21, or section 45(1)," for "Subject to paragraph (e) of section 21, any person who is primarily accountable for the payment of tax by virtue of section 45(1), or by virtue of paragraph (c) of section 16",

  (c) in section 46(3) by substituting "Subsection (2)(c) (other than in respect of tax arising by reason of section 20)" for "Subsection (2)(c)",

  (d) in section 46(4) by substituting "section 15 or 20" for "section 15",

  (e) in section 46(15) by substituting "a person who is resident or ordinarily resident in the State" for "a person who is living and domiciled in the State",

  (f) in section 46 by inserting the following after subsection (15):

  "(16) For the purposes of subsection (15), a person who is not domiciled in the State at the date of the disposition is treated as not resident and not ordinarily resident in the State on that date unless—

  (a) that person has been resident in the State for the 5 consecutive years of assessment immediately preceding the year of assessment in which that date falls, and

  (b) that person is either resident or ordinarily resident in the State on that date.",

  (g) in section 54(1) by substituting "the tax due and payable (other than tax arising by reason of section 20)" for "the tax due and payable", and

  (h) in section 56 by substituting "inheritance tax (other than tax arising by reason of section 20)" for "inheritance tax".

  (2) This section shall apply as respects the year 2006 and subsequent years.

Section 118

Amendment of Part 10 (reliefs) of [the Capital Acquisitions Tax Consolidation Act 2003].

118. (1) Part 10 of the [Capital Acquisitions Tax Consolidation Act 2003] is amended –

(a) in section 89(1) –

(i) by substituting the following for the definition of "agricultural property":

" 'agricultural property' means –

(a) agricultural land, pasture and woodland situate in the State and crops, trees and underwood growing on such land and also includes such farm buildings, farm houses and mansion houses (together with the lands occupied with such farm buildings, farm houses and mansion houses) as are of a character appropriate to the property, and farm machinery, livestock and bloodstock on such property, and

(b) a payment entitlement (within the meaning of Council Regulation (EC) No. 1782/2003 of 29 September 2003);",

and

(ii) in the definition of "farmer" by deleting "who is domiciled in the State and",

and

(b) by inserting the following Chapter after Chapter 2:

"CHAPTER 2A

Clawback of Agricultural Relief or Business Relief:
Development Land

Section 102A

Agricultural and business property: development land.

102A. (1) In this section –

'agricultural property' has the meaning assigned to it by section 89;

'current use value' –

(a) in relation to land at any particular time, means the amount which would be the market value of the land at that time if the market value were calculated on the assumption that it was at that time and would remain unlawful to carry out any development (within the meaning of section 3 of the Planning and Development Act 2000) in relation to the land other than development of a minor nature, and

(b) in relation to shares in a company at any particular time, means the amount which would be the value of the shares at that time if the market value were calculated on the same assumption, in relation to the land from which the shares derive all or part of their value, as is mentioned in paragraph (a);

'development land' means land in the State, the market value of which at the date of a gift or inheritance exceeds the current use value of that land at that date, and includes shares deriving their value in whole or in part from such land;

'development of a minor nature' means development (not being development by a local authority or statutory undertaker within the meaning of section 2 of the Planning and Development Act 2000) which, under or by virtue of section 4 of that Act, is exempted development for the purposes of that Act;

'relevant business property' shall be construed in accordance with section 93; '

'valuation date' shall be construed in accordance with section 30.

(2) Where—

(a) relief has been granted by virtue of section 89(2) or section 92 in respect of a gift or inheritance of agricultural property or, as the case may be, relevant business property,

(b) the property is comprised, in whole or in part, of development land, and

(c) the development land is disposed of in whole or in part by the donee or successor at any time in the period commencing 6 years after the date of the gift or inheritance and ending 10 years after that date,

then tax shall be re-computed at the valuation date of the gift or inheritance as if the amount by which the market value of the land disposed of exceeds its current use value at that date was the value of property which was not—

(i) agricultural property, or

(ii) relevant business property, as the case may be, and tax shall be payable accordingly.".

(2) (a) Subsection (1)(a)(i) is deemed to have applied as regards gifts and inheritances of agricultural property taken on or after 1 January 2005.

    (b) Subsections (1)(a)(ii) and (1)(b) shall apply to gifts and inheritances taken on or after 2 February 2006.

Section 119

Amendment of section 104 (allowance for capital gains tax on the same event) of [the Capital Acquisitions Tax Consolidation Act 2003].

119. (1) Section 104 of the [Capital Acquisitions Tax Consolidation Act 2003] is amended by inserting the following after subsection (2):

"(3) The deduction by virtue of subsection (1) of capital gains tax chargeable on the disposal of an asset against gift tax or inheritance tax shall cease to apply to the extent that the asset is disposed of within 2 years after the date of the gift or, as the case may be, the date of the inheritance.".

(2) This section shall apply to gifts and inheritances taken on or after 21 February 2006.

PART 6

Miscellaneous

Section 121

Amendment of section 1003 (payment of tax by means of donation of heritage items) of [the Taxes Consolidation Act, 1997].

121. Section 1003 of the [Taxes Consolidation Act, 1997,] is amended, as respects the year of assessment 2006 and subsequent years of assessment, by substituting the following for subsection (3)(a):

"(a) For the purposes of this section, the market value of any item or collection of items (in this subsection referred to as 'the property') shall, subject to paragraph (d), be estimated to be the lesser of —

(i) the price which, in the opinion of the Revenue Commissioners, the property would fetch if sold in the open market on the valuation date in such manner and subject to such conditions as might reasonably be calculated to obtain for the vendor the best price for the property, and

(ii) (I) the price which, in the opinion of the person making the gift of the property, the property would fetch on the valuation date if sold in the manner referred to in subparagraph (i), or

    (II) at the election of that person, the amount paid for the property by that person.".

Section 122

Payment of tax by means of donation of heritage property to an Irish heritage trust.

122. (1) The [Taxes Consolidation Act, 1997,] is amended in Chapter 5 of Part 42 by inserting the following after section 1003:

"1003A. (1) In this section—

'the Acts' means—

    (a) the Tax Acts (other than Chapter 8 of Part 6, Chapter 2 of Part 18 and Chapter 4 of this Part),

    (b) the Capital Gains Tax Acts, and

    (c) the Capital Acquisitions Tax Consolidation Act 2003, and the enactments amending or extending that Act,

and any instruments made thereunder;

'arrears of tax' means tax due and payable in accordance with any provision of the Acts (including any interest and penalties payable under any provision of the Acts in relation to such tax)—

    (a) in the case of income tax, corporation tax or capital gains tax, in respect of the relevant period, or

    (b) in the case of gift tax or inheritance tax, before the commencement of the calendar year in which the relevant gift is made,

which has not been paid at the time a relevant gift is made;

'contents of the building' means furnishings historically associated with the building and in respect of which the Minister is satisfied that they are important to establishing the historic or aesthetic context of the building;

'current liability' means—

    (a) in the case of income tax or capital gains tax, any liability to such tax arising in the year of assessment in which the relevant gift is made,

    (b) in the case of corporation tax, any liability to such tax arising in the accounting period in which the relevant gift is made,

    (c) in the case of gift tax or inheritance tax, any liability to such tax which becomes due and payable in the calendar year in which the relevant gift is made;

'heritage property' has the meaning assigned to it by subsection (2)(a);

'market value' has the meaning assigned to it by subsection (3);

'Minister' means the Minister for the Environment, Heritage and Local Government;

'relevant gift' means a gift of heritage property to the Trust in respect of which no consideration whatever (other than relief under this section) is received by the person making the gift, either directly or indirectly, from the Trust or otherwise;

'relevant period' means –

(a) in the case of income tax and capital gains tax, any year of assessment preceding the year in which the relevant gift is made, and

(b) in the case of corporation tax, any accounting period preceding the accounting period in which the relevant gift is made;

'tax' means income tax, corporation tax, capital gains tax, gift tax or inheritance tax, as the case may be, payable in accordance with any provision of the Acts;

'Trust' means the company designated for the purposes of this section by the order referred to in section 122(2) of the Finance Act 2006;

'valuation date' means the date on which an application is made to the Minister for a determination under subsection (2)(a).

(2) (a) In this section 'heritage property' means a building or a garden which, on application to the Minister in writing in that behalf by a person who owns the building or the garden is, subject to the provisions of paragraph (b), determined by the Minister to be a building or a garden which is –

(i) an outstanding example of the type of building or garden involved,

(ii) pre-eminent in its class,

(iii) intrinsically of significant scientific, historical, horticultural, national, architectural or aesthetic interest, and

(iv) suitable for acquisition by the Trust,

and, for the purposes of this section, a reference to 'building' includes –

(I) any associated outbuilding, yard or land where the land is occupied or enjoyed with the building as part of its garden or designed landscape and contributes to the appreciation of the building in its setting, and

(II) the contents of the building.

(b) In considering an application under paragraph (a), the Minister shall consider such evidence as the person making the application submits to the Minister.

(c) On receipt of an application for a determination under paragraph (a), the Minister shall request the Revenue Commissioners in writing to value the heritage property in accordance with subsection (3).

(d) The Minister shall not make a determination under paragraph (a) where the market value of the property, as determined by the Revenue Commissioners in accordance with subsection (3), at the valuation date exceeds an amount determined by the formula—

$$€6,000,000 - M$$

where M is an amount (which may be nil) equal to the market value at the valuation date of the heritage property (if any) or the aggregate of the market values at the respective valuation dates of all the heritage properties (if any), as the case may be, in respect of which a determination or determinations, as the case may be, under this subsection has been made by the Minister in any one calendar year and not revoked in that year.

(e) (i) A property shall cease to be a heritage property for the purposes of this section if—

(I) the property is sold or otherwise disposed of to a person other than the Trust,

(II) the owner of the property notifies the Trust in writing that it is not intended to make a gift of the property to the Trust, or

(III) the gift of the property is not made to the Trust within the calendar year following the year in which the determination is made under paragraph (a).

(ii) Where the Minister becomes aware, at any time within the calendar year in which a determination under paragraph (a) is made in respect of a property, that clause (I) or (II) of subparagraph (i) applies to the property, the Minister may revoke the determination with effect from that time.

(3) (a) For the purposes of this section, the market value of any property shall be estimated to be the lesser of —

(i) the price which, in the opinion of the Revenue Commissioners, the property would fetch if sold in the open market on the valuation date in such manner and subject to such conditions as might reasonably be calculated to obtain for the vendor the best price for the property, and

(ii) (I) the price which, in the opinion of the person making the gift of the property, the property would fetch on the valuation date if sold in the manner referred to in subparagraph (i), or

(II) at the election of that person, the amount paid for the property by that person.

(b) The market value of the property shall be ascertained by the Revenue Commissioners in such manner and by such means as they think fit, and they may authorise a person to inspect the property and report to them the value of the property for the purposes of this section, and the person having custody or possession of the property shall permit the person so authorised to inspect the property at such reasonable times as the Revenue Commissioners consider necessary.

(c) Where the Revenue Commissioners require a valuation to be made by a person authorised by them, the cost of such valuation shall be defrayed by the Revenue Commissioners.

(4) Where a relevant gift is made to the Trust —

(a) the Trust shall give a certificate to the person who made the relevant gift, in such form as the Revenue Commissioners may prescribe, certifying the receipt of that gift and the transfer of the ownership of the heritage property the subject of that gift to the Trust, and

(b) the Trust shall transmit a duplicate of the certificate to the Revenue Commissioners.

(5) Subject to this section, where a person has made a relevant gift the person shall, on submission to the Revenue Commissioners of the certificate given to the person in accordance with subsection (4), be treated as having made on the date of such submission a payment on account of tax of an amount equal to the market value of the relevant gift on the valuation date.

(6) A payment on account of tax which is treated as having been made in accordance with subsection (5) shall be set in so far as possible against any liability to tax of the person who is treated as having made such a payment in the following order—

(a) firstly, against any arrears of tax due for payment by that person and against an arrear of tax for an earlier period in priority to a later period, and for this purpose the date on which an arrear of tax became due for payment shall determine whether it is for an earlier or later period, and

(b) only then, against any current liability of the person which the person nominates for that purpose,

and such set-off shall accordingly discharge a corresponding amount of that liability.

(7) To the extent that a payment on account of tax has not been set-off in accordance with subsection (6), the balance remaining shall be set-off against any future liability to tax of the person who is treated as having made the payment which that person nominates for that purpose.

(8) Where a person has power to sell any heritage property in order to raise money for the payment of gift tax or inheritance tax, such person shall have power to make a relevant gift of that heritage property in or towards satisfaction of that tax and, except as regards the nature of the consideration and its receipt and application, any such relevant gift shall be subject to the same provisions and shall be treated for all purposes as a sale made in exercise of that power, and any conveyances or transfers made or purporting to be made to give

effect to such a relevant gift shall apply accordingly.

(9) A person shall not be entitled to any refund of tax in respect of any payment on account of tax made in accordance with this section.

(10) Interest shall not be payable in respect of any overpayment of tax for any period which arises directly or indirectly by reason of the set-off against any liability for that period of a payment on account of tax made in accordance with this section.

(11) Where a person makes a relevant gift and in respect of that gift is treated as having made a payment on account of tax, the person concerned shall not be allowed relief under any other provision of the Acts in respect of that gift.

(12) (a) The Revenue Commissioners shall as respects each year compile a list of the titles (if any), descriptions and values of the heritage properties (if any) in respect of which relief under this section has been given.

(b) Notwithstanding any obligation as to secrecy imposed on them by the Acts or the Official Secrets Act 1963, the Revenue Commissioners shall include in their annual report to the Minister for Finance the list (if any) referred to in paragraph (a) for the year in respect of which the report is made.".

(2) The Minister for Finance shall designate by order[1] the company (being a company incorporated under the Companies Acts) which is to be the Trust for the purposes of section 1003A of the Principal Act (inserted by subsection (1)).

(3) Subsection (1) comes into operation on such day as the Minister for Finance may appoint by order.[2]

Footnotes

1   See S.I. No. 521 of 2006 at page 1382.

2   See S.I. No. 520 of 2006 at page 1381.

Section 123

Prescribing of forms, etc.

123. (1) In this section –

"the Acts" means –

(a) the Tax Acts,

(b) the Capital Gains Tax Acts,

(c) the Capital Acquisitions Tax Consolidation Act 2003, and the enactments amending or extending that Act,

(d) the Stamp Duties Consolidation Act 1999, and the enactments amending or extending that Act, and

(e) Chapter IV of Part II of the Finance Act 1992,

and any instruments made thereunder;

"form or other document" includes a form or other document for use, or capable of use, in a machine readable form.

(2) Where a provision of the Acts requires that a form or other document used for any purpose of the Acts is to be prescribed, authorised or approved by the Revenue Commissioners, such form or other document may be prescribed, authorised or approved by –

(a) a Revenue Commissioner, or

(b) an officer of the Revenue Commissioners not below the grade or rank of Assistant Secretary authorised by them for that purpose.

(3) Nothing in this section shall be read as restricting section 12 of the Interpretation Act 2005.

Section 126

Transactions to avoid liability to tax: surcharge, interest and protective notifications.

126. The [Taxes Consolidation Act, 1997,] is amended –

(a) in section 811(1) –

(i) in paragraph (a) by substituting "In this section and section 811A –" for "In this section –", and

(ii) by inserting after paragraph (b) the following paragraph:

"(c) For the purposes of this section and section 811A, all appeals made under section 811(7) by, or on behalf of, a person against any matter or matters specified or described in the notice of opinion of the Revenue Commissioners that a transaction is a tax avoidance transaction, if they have not otherwise been so determined, shall be deemed to have been finally determined when –

(i)   there is a written agreement, between that person and an officer of the Revenue Commissioners, that the notice of opinion is to stand or is to be amended in a particular manner,

(ii) (I)   the terms of such an agreement that was not made in writing have been confirmed by notice in writing given by the person to the officer of the Revenue Commissioners with whom the agreement was made, or by such officer to the person, and

(II)   21 days have elapsed since the giving of the notice without the person to whom it was given giving notice in writing to the person by whom it was given that the first-mentioned person desires to repudiate or withdraw from the agreement, or

(iii) the person gives notice in writing to an officer of the Revenue Commissioners that the person desires not to proceed with an appeal against the notice of opinion.",

and

(b) by inserting the following after section 811:

"Transactions to avoid liability to tax: surcharge, interest and protective notification.

811A. (1) (a)   In this section references to tax being payable shall, except where the context requires otherwise, include references to tax being payable by a person to withdraw from that person so much of a tax advantage as is a refund of, or a payment of, an amount of tax, or an increase in an amount of tax, refundable, or otherwise payable, to the person.

(b)   For the purposes of this section the date on which the opinion of the Revenue Commissioners that a transaction is a tax avoidance transaction becomes final and conclusive is —

(i)   where no appeal is made under section 811(7) against any matter or matters specified or described in the notice of that opinion, 31 days after the date of the notice of that opinion, or

(ii)   the date on which all appeals made under section 811(7) against any such matter or matters have been finally determined and none of the appeals has been so determined by an order directing that the opinion of the Revenue Commissioners to the effect that the transaction is a tax avoidance transaction is void.

(c) This section shall be construed together with section 811 and shall have effect notwithstanding any of the provisions of section 811.

(2) Where, in accordance with adjustments made or acts done by the Revenue Commissioners under section 811(5), on foot of their opinion (as amended, or added to, on appeal where relevant) that a transaction is a tax avoidance transaction having become final and conclusive, an amount of tax is payable by a person that would not have been payable if the Revenue Commissioners had not formed the opinion concerned, then, subject to subsection (3) —

(a) the person shall be liable to pay an amount (in this section referred to as the 'surcharge') equal to 10 per cent of the amount of that tax and the provisions of the Acts, including in particular section 811(5) and those provisions relating to the collection and recovery of that tax, shall apply to that surcharge, as if it were such tax, and

(b) for the purposes of liability to interest under the Acts on tax due and payable, the amount of tax, or parts of that amount, shall be deemed to be due and payable on the day or, as respects parts of that amount, days specified in the notice of opinion (as amended, or added to, on appeal where relevant) in accordance with section 811(6)(a)(iii) construed together with subsection (4)(a) of this section,

and the surcharge and interest shall be payable accordingly.

(3) (a) Subject to subsection (6), neither a surcharge nor interest shall be payable by a person in relation to a tax avoidance transaction finally and conclusively determined to be such a transaction if the Revenue Commissioners have received from, or on behalf of, that person, on or before the relevant date (within the meaning of paragraph (c)), notification (referred to in this subsection and subsection (6) as a 'protective notification') of full details of that transaction.

(b) Where a person makes a protective notification, or a protective notification is made on a person's behalf, then the person shall be treated as making the protective notification —

(i) solely to prevent any possibility of a surcharge or interest becoming payable by the person by virtue of subsection (2), and

    (ii)   wholly without prejudice as to whether any opinion that the transaction concerned was a tax avoidance transaction, if such an opinion were to be formed by the Revenue Commissioners, would be correct.

(c)   Regardless of the type of tax concerned—

    (i)   where the whole or any part of the transaction, which is the subject of the protective notification, is undertaken or arranged on or after 2 February 2006, then the relevant date shall be—

        (I)   the date which is 90 days after the date on which the transaction commenced, or

        (II)   if it is later than the said 90 days, 2 May 2006,

    (ii)   where—

        (I)   the whole of the transaction is undertaken or arranged before 2 February 2006, and would give rise to, or would but for section 811 give rise to, a reduction, avoidance, or deferral of any charge or assessment to tax, or part thereof, and

        (II)   that charge or assessment would arise only by virtue of one or more other transactions carried out wholly on or after 2 February 2006,

    then the relevant date shall be the date which is 90 days after the date on which the first of those other transactions commenced, or

    (iii)   where—

        (I)   the whole of the transaction is undertaken or arranged before 2 February 2006, and would give rise to, or would but for section 811 give rise to, a refund or a payment of an amount, or of an increase in an amount of tax, or part thereof, refundable or otherwise payable to a person, and

        (II)   that amount or increase in the amount would, but for section 811, become first so refundable or otherwise payable to the person on a date on or after 2 February 2006,

    then the relevant date shall be the date which is 90 days after that date.

(d)   Notwithstanding the receipt by the Revenue Commissioners of a protective notice, paragraph (a) shall not apply to any interest, payable in relation to a tax avoidance transaction finally and conclusively determined to be such a transaction, in respect of days on or after the date on which the opinion of the Revenue Commissioners in relation to that transaction becomes final and conclusive.

(4) (a) The determination of tax consequences, which would arise in respect of a transaction if the opinion of the Revenue Commissioners, that the transaction was a tax avoidance transaction, were to become final and conclusive, shall, for the purposes of charging interest, include the specification of –

    (i) a date or dates, being a date or dates which is or are just and reasonable to ensure that tax is deemed to be due and payable not later than it would have been due and payable if the transaction had not been undertaken, disregarding any contention that another transaction would not have been undertaken or arranged to achieve the results, or any part of the results, achieved or intended to be achieved by the transaction, and

    (ii) the date which, as respects such amount of tax as is due and payable by a person to recover from the person a refund of or a payment of tax, including an increase in tax refundable or otherwise payable, to the person, is the day on which the refund or payment was made, set off or accounted for, and the date or dates shall be specified for the purposes of this paragraph without regard to –

        (I) when an opinion of the Revenue Commissioners that the transaction concerned was a tax avoidance transaction was formed,

        (II) the date on which any notice of that opinion was given, or

        (III) the date on which the opinion (as amended, or added to, on appeal where relevant) became final and conclusive.

(b) Where the grounds of an appeal in relation to tax consequences refer to such a date or dates as are mentioned in paragraph (a), subsection (7) of section 811 shall apply, in that respect, as if the following paragraph were substituted for paragraph (c) of that subsection:

'(c) the tax consequences specified or described in the notice of opinion, or such part of those consequences as shall be specified or described by the appellant in the notice of appeal, would not be just and reasonable to ensure that tax is deemed to be payable on a date or dates in accordance with subsection (4)(a)of section 811A'

and the grounds of appeal referred to in section 811(8)(a) shall be construed accordingly.

(5) A surcharge payable by virtue of subsection (2)(a) shall be due and payable on the date that the opinion of the Revenue Commissioners that a transaction is a tax avoidance transaction becomes final and conclusive and interest shall be payable in respect of any delay in payment of the surcharge as if the surcharge were an amount of that tax by reference to an amount of which the surcharge was computed.

(6) (a) A protective notification shall—

    (i) be delivered in such form as may be prescribed by the Revenue Commissioners and to such office of the Revenue Commissioners as—

        (I) is specified in the prescribed form, or

        (II) as may be identified, by reference to guidance in the prescribed form, as the office to which the notification concerned should be sent, and

    (ii) contain—

        (I) full details of the transaction which is the subject of the protective notification, including any part of that transaction that has not been undertaken before the protective notification is delivered,

        (II) full reference to the provisions of the Acts that the person, by whom, or on whose behalf, the protective notification is delivered, considers to be relevant to the treatment of the transaction for tax purposes, and

        (III) full details of how, in the opinion of the person, by whom, or on whose behalf, the protective notification is delivered, each provision, referred to in the protective notification in accordance with clause

(II), applies, or does not apply, to the transaction.

(b) Without prejudice to the generality of paragraph (a), the specifying, under—

(i) section 19B of the Value Added Tax Act 1972,

(ii) section 46A of the Capital Acquisitions Tax Consolidation Act 2003,

(iii) section 8 of the Stamp Duties Consolidation Act 1999, or

(iv) section 955(4) of this Act,

of a doubt as to the application of law to, or the treatment for tax purposes of, any matter to be contained in a return shall not be regarded as being, or being equivalent to, the delivery of a protective notification in relation to a transaction for the purposes of subsection (3).

(c) Where the Revenue Commissioners form the opinion that a transaction is a tax avoidance transaction and believe that a protective notification in relation to the transaction has not been delivered by a person in accordance with subsection (6)(a) by the relevant date (within the meaning of subsection (3)(c)) then, in giving notice under section 811(6)(a) to the person of their opinion in relation to the transaction, they shall give notice that they believe that a protective notification has not been so delivered by the person and section 811 shall be construed, subject to any necessary modifications, as if—

(i) subsection (7) of that section included as grounds for appeal that a protective notification in relation to the transaction was so delivered by the person, and

(ii) subsection (9) of that section provided that an appeal were to be determined, in so far as it is made on those grounds, by ordering that a protective notification in relation to the transaction was so delivered or that a protective notification in relation to the transaction was not so delivered.

(7) This section shall apply—

(a) as respects any transaction where the whole or any part of the transaction is undertaken or arranged on or after 2 February 2006, and

(b) as respects any transaction, the whole of which was undertaken or arranged before that date, in so far as it gives rise to, or would but for section 811 give rise to —

(i) a reduction, avoidance, or deferral of any charge or assessment to tax, or part thereof, where the charge or assessment arises only by virtue of another transaction or other transactions carried out wholly on or after 2 February 2006, or

(ii) a refund or a payment of an amount, or of an increase in an amount of tax, or part thereof, refundable or otherwise payable to a person where, but for section 811, that amount or increase in the amount would become first so refundable or otherwise payable to the person on or after 2 February 2006.".

Section 127

Miscellaneous technical amendments in relation to tax.

127. The enactments specified in Schedule 2 —

(a) are amended to the extent and in the manner specified in paragraphs 1 to 8 of that Schedule, and

(b) apply and come into operation in accordance with paragraph 9 of that Schedule.

SCHEDULE 2

Miscellaneous Technical Amendments in Relation to Tax

1. ....

2. The Capital Acquisitions Tax Consolidation Act 2003 is amended in section 77(7)(a) by substituting "the National Tourism Development Authority" for "Bord Fáilte Éireann (in this section referred to as "the Board")".

3. ....

9. (a) ....

(b) Paragraph 2 is deemed to have come into force and have taken effect as on and from 28 May 2003.

FINANCE ACT 2007

Number 11 of 2007
(Enacted on 2nd April, 2007)

PART 5
Capital Acquisitions Tax

Section 112

Interpretation (Part 5).

112. In this Part "Principal Act" means the Capital Acquisitions Tax Consolidation Act 2003.

Section 113

Amendment of section 18 (computation of tax) of [the Capital Acquisitions Tax Consolidation Act 2003].

113. (1) Section 18 of the [Capital Acquisitions Tax Consolidation Act 2003] is amended —

(a) by substituting the following for the definition of "relevant period" in subsection (1):

" 'relevant period' means —

(a) in relation to an earlier relevant inheritance, the period of 5 years commencing on the date of death of the disponer,

(b) in relation to a settled relevant inheritance, the period of 5 years commencing on the date of death of the life tenant concerned,

(c) in relation to a will trust relevant inheritance, the period of 5 years commencing on the date when property becomes subject to a discretionary trust which was created under the will of the disponer, and

(d) in relation to a later relevant inheritance, the period of 5 years commencing on the latest date on which a later relevant inheritance was deemed to be taken from the disponer;",

(b) by substituting the following for the definition of "the appropriate trust" in subsection (1):

" 'the appropriate trust', in relation to a relevant inheritance, means the trust by which the inheritance was deemed to have been taken;

'will trust relevant inheritance' means a relevant inheritance deemed to be taken when property becomes subject to a discretionary trust which was created under the will of the disponer.",

and

(c) by substituting the following for subsection (3):

"(3) Where, in the case of each earlier relevant inheritance, each settled relevant inheritance, each will trust relevant inheritance or each later relevant inheritance, as the case may be, taken from the same disponer, one or more objects of the appropriate trust became beneficially entitled in possession before the expiration of the relevant period to an absolute interest in the entire of the property of which that inheritance consisted on and at all times after the date of that inheritance (other than property which ceased to be subject to the terms of the appropriate trust by virtue of a sale or exchange of an absolute interest in that property for full consideration in money or money's worth), then, in relation to all such earlier relevant inheritances, all such settled relevant inheritances, all such will trust relevant inheritances or all such later relevant inheritances, as the case may be, the tax so chargeable is computed at the rate of 3 per cent.".

(2) This section applies to inheritances deemed to be taken on or after 1 February 2007.

Section 114

Amendment of section 21 (application of this Act) of [the Capital Acquisitions Tax Consolidation Act 2003].

114. (1) Section 21 of the [Capital Acquisitions Tax Consolidation Act 2003] is amended by substituting the following for paragraph (b):

"(b) the valuation date of the taxable inheritance is the relevant chargeable date;".

(2) This section applies to inheritances deemed to be taken on or after 1 February 2007.

Section 115

Amendment of section 51 (payment of tax and interest on tax) of [the Capital Acquisitions Tax Consolidation Act 2003].

115. (1) Section 51 of the [Capital Acquisitions Tax Consolidation Act 2003] is amended in subsection (3) by substituting the following for paragraph (e):

"(e) to the extent to which section 86(6) or (7) applies, for the duration of the period from the valuation date to the date the exemption ceases to apply,

(f) to the extent to which section 102A(2) applies, for the duration of the period from the valuation date to the date the development land is disposed of.".

(2) This section applies where the event that causes the exemption to cease to apply or the tax to be re-computed, as the case may be, occurs on or after 1 February 2007.

Section 116

Amendment of section 86 (exemption relating to certain dwellings) of [the Capital Acquisitions Tax Consolidation Act 2003].

116.(1) Section 86 of the [Capital Acquisitions Tax Consolidation Act 2003] is amended by inserting the following after subsection (3):

"(3A) For the purposes of subsection (3)(a), in the case of a gift—

(a) any period during which a donee occupied a dwelling house that was, during that period, the disponer's only or main residence, shall be treated as not being a period during which the donee occupied the dwelling house unless the disponer is compelled, by reason of old age or infirmity, to depend on the services of the donee for that period,

(b) where paragraph (a)(i) of subsection (3) applies, the dwelling house referred to in that paragraph is required to be owned by the disponer during the 3 year period referred to in that paragraph, and

(c) where paragraph (a)(ii) of subsection (3) applies, either the dwelling house or the other property referred to in that paragraph is required to be owned by the disponer during the 3 year period referred to in that paragraph.".

(2) This section applies to gifts taken on or after 20 February 2007.

Section 117

Amendment of section 89 (provisions relating to agricultural property) of [the Capital Acquisitions Tax Consolidation Act 2003].

117. (1) Section 89 of the [Capital Acquisitions Tax Consolidation Act 2003] is amended in subsection (1) by substituting the following for paragraph (a) of the definition of "farmer":

"(a) no deduction is made from the market value of property for any debts or encumbrances (except debts or encumbrances in respect of a dwelling house which is the only or main residence of the donee or successor and which is not agricultural property), and".

(2) This section applies to gifts and inheritances taken on or after 1 February 2007.

PART 7

Miscellaneous

Section 121

Amendment of provisions relating to interest on repayments.

121. (1) ....

(4) Paragraph (a) of the definition of "relevant date" in subsection (1) of section 57 (amended by the Finance Act 2003) of the Capital Acquisitions Tax Consolidation Act 2003 is amended by substituting "93 days" for "183 days".

(6) This section applies to interest payable under —

  (a) ....

  (d) section 57 of the Capital Acquisitions Tax Consolidation Act 2003, or

  (e) ....

  on repayments to which those sections apply made on or after the passing of this Act.

Section 122

Amendment of section 1003A (payment of tax by means of donation of heritage property to an Irish heritage trust) of [the Taxes Consolidation Act, 1997].

122.(1) Section 1003A of the [Taxes Consolidation Act, 1997,] is amended by inserting the following after subsection (11):

"(11A) (a) In the event that Fota House in County Cork is acquired by the Trust, either by way of a relevant gift under this section or otherwise, and the collection referred to in paragraph (b) is acquired by the Trust by way of gift, relief under this section shall, subject to paragraphs (c) and (d), be granted in respect of the collection on the basis that Fota House was acquired by the Trust by way of a relevant gift and the collection formed part of the contents of the building.

(b) The collection referred to in this paragraph (in this subsection referred to as the 'collection') is a collection —

  (i) of either or both Irish paintings and furniture which was displayed in Fota House in the period 1983 to 1990,

  (ii) which is to be housed by the Trust in Fota House, and

  (iii) in respect of which the Minister, after consulting with such person (if any) in the matter as the Minister may deem to be necessary, is satisfied that the collection is important to establishing the aesthetic context of Fota House.

(c) This subsection shall not apply unless the collection is gifted to the Trust before the end of 2007.

(d) Relief under this section, in respect of the market value of the collection as determined in accordance with subsection (3), shall, where this subsection applies, be granted to the person making the gift to the Trust of the collection, notwithstanding that that person is not the person from whom Fota House was acquired by the Trust.".

(2) Section 1003A of the [Taxes Consolidation Act, 1997,], as amended by subsection (1), applies as respects the year of assessment 2007 as if in subsection (2)(d) "€10,000,000" were substituted for "€6,000,000".

Section 123

Amendment of Part 38 (returns of income and gains, other obligations and returns, and revenue powers) of [the Taxes Consolidation Act, 1997].

123. The [Taxes Consolidation Act, 1997,] is amended in Part 38 —

(a) ....

(c) in section 910 by inserting the following after subsection (2):

"(3) Where information is to be provided to the Revenue Commissioners in accordance with subsection (1) it shall be provided, where the Revenue Commissioners so require, in an electronic format approved by them.",

and

(d) ....

Section 124

Amendment of Chapter 4 (revenue powers) of Part 38 of [the Taxes Consolidation Act, 1997].

124. The [Taxes Consolidation Act, 1997,] is amended in Chapter 4 of Part 38 —

(a) in section 905(2) —

(i) by substituting the following for paragraph (e):

"(e) An authorised officer shall not, without the consent of the occupier, enter any premises, or that portion of any premises, which is occupied wholly and exclusively as a private residence, except on production by the officer of a warrant issued under subsection (2A).",

and

(ii) by deleting paragraph (f),

(b) in section 905(2A)(c) by deleting "or for the purpose of any criminal proceedings", and

(c) by inserting the following after section 908B:

"Search warrants.

908C. (1) In this section—

'the Acts' means the Waiver of Certain Tax, Interest and Penalties Act 1993 together with the meaning assigned to it in section 1078(1);

'authorised officer' means an officer of the Revenue Commissioners authorised by them in writing to exercise the powers conferred by this section;

'commission', in relation to an offence, includes an attempt to commit the offence;

'computer' includes any electronic device capable of performing logical or arithmetical operations on data in accordance with a set of instructions;

'computer at the place which is being searched', includes any other computer, whether at that place or at any other place, which is lawfully accessible by means of that computer;

'information in non-legible form' means information which is kept (by electronic means or otherwise) on microfilm, microfiche, magnetic tape or disk or in any other non-legible form;

'material' means any books, documents, records or other things (including a computer);

'offence' means an offence under the Acts;

'place' includes any building (or part of a building), dwelling, vehicle, vessel, aircraft or hovercraft and any other place whatsoever;

'record' includes any information in non-legible form which is capable of being reproduced in a permanently legible form.

(2) If a judge of the District Court is satisfied by information given on oath by an authorised officer that there are reasonable grounds for suspecting—

(a) that an offence is being, has been or is about to be committed, and

(b) (i) that material which is likely to be of value (whether by itself or together with other information) to the investigation of the offence, or

(ii)   that evidence of, or relating to the commission of, the offence,

is to be found in any place,

the judge may issue a warrant for the search of that place, and of any thing and any persons, found there.

(3)   A warrant issued under this section shall be expressed and shall operate to authorise the authorised officer, accompanied by such other named officers of the Revenue Commissioners and such other named persons as the authorised officer considers necessary –

(a)   to enter, at any time or times within one month from the date of issuing of the warrant (if necessary by the use of reasonable force), the place named in the warrant,

(b)   to search, or cause to be searched, that place and any thing and any persons, found there, but no person shall be searched except by a person of the same sex unless express or implied consent is given,

(c)   to require any person found there –

(i)   to give his or her name, home address and occupation to the authorised officer, and

(ii)   to produce to the authorised officer any material which is in the custody or possession of that person,

(d)   to examine, seize and retain (or cause to be examined, seized and retained) any material found there, or in the possession of a person present there at the time of the search, which the authorised officer reasonably believes –

(i)   is likely to be of value (whether by itself or together with other information) to the investigation of the offence, or

(ii)   to be evidence of, or relating to the commission of, the offence, and

(e)   to take any other steps which may appear to the authorised officer to be necessary for preserving any such material and preventing interference with it.

(4)   The authority conferred by subsection (3)(d) to seize and retain (or to cause to be seized and retained) any material includes –

(a)   in the case of books, documents or records, authority to make and retain a copy of the books, documents or records, and

(b) where necessary, authority to seize and, for as long as necessary, retain, any computer or other storage medium in which records are kept and to copy such records.

(5) An authorised officer acting under the authority of a warrant issued under this section may —

(a) operate any computer at the place which is being searched or cause any such computer to be operated by a person accompanying the authorised officer, and

(b) require any person at that place who appears to the authorised officer to be in a position to facilitate access to the information held in any such computer or which can be accessed by the use of that computer —

(i) to give to the authorised officer any password necessary to operate it,

(ii) otherwise to enable the authorised officer to examine the information accessible by the computer in a form in which the information is visible and legible, or

(iii) to produce the information in a form in which it can be removed and in which it is, or can be made, visible and legible.

(6) A person who —

(a) obstructs or attempts to obstruct the exercise of a right of entry and search conferred by virtue of a warrant issued under this section,

(b) obstructs the exercise of a right so conferred to examine, seize and retain material,

(c) fails to comply with a requirement under subsection (3)(c) or gives to the authorised officer a name, address or occupation that is false or misleading, or

(d) fails to comply with a requirement under subsection (5)(b),

is guilty of an offence and is liable on summary conviction to a fine not exceeding €3,000 or imprisonment for a term not exceeding 6 months or to both the fine and the imprisonment.

(7) Where an authorised officer enters, or attempts to enter, any place in the execution of a warrant issued under subsection (2), the authorised officer may be accompanied by a member or members of the Garda Síochána, and any such member may arrest without warrant any person who is committing an offence under subsection (6) or whom

the member suspects, with reasonable cause, of having done so.

(8) Any material which is seized under subsection (3) which is required for the purposes of any legal proceedings by an officer of the Revenue Commissioners or for the purpose of any criminal proceedings, may be retained for so long as it is reasonably required for the purposes aforesaid.

Order to produce evidential material.

908D. (1) In this section—

'the Acts' means the Waiver of Certain Tax, Interest and Penalties Act 1993 together with the meaning assigned to it in section 1078(1);

'authorised officer' means an officer of the Revenue Commissioners authorised by them in writing to exercise the powers conferred by this section;

'commission', in relation to an offence, includes an attempt to commit the offence;

'computer' includes any electronic device capable of performing logical or arithmetical operations on data in accordance with a set of instructions;

'information in non-legible form' means information which is kept (by electronic means or otherwise) on microfilm, microfiche, magnetic tape or disk or in any other non-legible form;

'material' means any books, documents, records or other things (including a computer);

'offence' means an offence under the Acts;

'record' includes any information in non-legible form which is capable of being reproduced in a permanently legible form.

(2) If a judge of the District Court is satisfied by information given on oath by an authorised officer that there are reasonable grounds for suspecting—

(a) that an offence is being, has been or is about to be committed, and

(b) that material—

(i) which is likely to be of value (whether by itself or together with other information) to the investigation of the offence, or

(ii) which constitutes evidence of, or relating to the commission of, the offence, is in the possession or control of a person specified in the application,

the judge may order that the person shall —

(I) produce the material to the authorised officer for the authorised officer to take away, or

(II) give the authorised officer access to it,

either immediately or within such period as the order may specify.

(3) Where the material consists of or includes records contained in a computer, the order shall have effect as an order to produce the records, or to give access to them, in a form in which they are visible and legible and in which they can be taken away.

(4) An order under this section —

(a) in so far as it may empower an authorised officer to take away books, documents or records, or to be given access to them, shall also have effect as an order empowering the authorised officer to take away a copy of the books, documents or, as the case may be, records (and for that purpose the authorised officer may, if necessary, make a copy of them),

(b) shall not confer any right to production of, or access to, any document subject to legal privilege, and

(c) shall have effect notwithstanding any other obligation as to secrecy or other restriction on disclosure of information imposed by statute or otherwise.

(5) Any material taken away by an authorised officer under this section may be retained by the authorised officer for use as evidence in any criminal proceedings.

(6) (a) Information contained in books, documents or records which were produced to an authorised officer, or to which an authorised officer was given access, in accordance with an order under this section, shall be admissible in any criminal proceedings as evidence of any fact therein of which direct oral evidence would be admissible unless the information —

(i) is privileged from disclosure in such proceedings,

(ii) was supplied by a person who would not be compellable to give evidence at the instance of the prosecution,

(iii) was compiled for the purposes of, or in contemplation of, any —

   (I) criminal investigation,

   (II) investigation or inquiry carried out pursuant to or under any enactment,

   (III) civil or criminal proceedings, or

   (IV) proceedings of a disciplinary nature, or unless the requirements of the provisions mentioned in paragraph (b) are not complied with.

  (b) References in sections 7 (notice of documentary evidence to be served on accused), 8 (admission and weight of documentary evidence) and 9 (admissibility of evidence as to credibility of supplier of information) of the Criminal Evidence Act 1992 to a document or information contained in it shall be construed as including references to books, documents and records mentioned in paragraph (a) and the information contained in them, and those provisions shall have effect accordingly with any necessary modifications.

 (7) A judge of the District Court may, on the application of an authorised officer, or of any person to whom an order under this section relates, vary or discharge the order.

 (8) A person who without reasonable excuse fails or refuses to comply with an order under this section is guilty of an offence and liable on summary conviction to a fine not exceeding €3,000 or imprisonment for a term not exceeding 6 months or to both the fine and the imprisonment.".

Section 125

Amendment of section 1003 (payment of tax by means of donation of heritage items) of [the Taxes Consolidation Act, 1997].

125. Section 1003 of the [Taxes Consolidation Act, 1997,] is amended in subsection (1)(a) —

 (a) in the definition of "approved body" by inserting the following after subparagraph (iv):

  "(iva) the Crawford Art Gallery Cork Limited,",

  and

 (b) in the definition of "selection committee" by inserting the following after subparagraph (vi):

  "(via) the Director of the Crawford Art Gallery Cork Limited,".

Section 126

Amendment of section 1078 (revenue offences) of [the Taxes Consolidation Act, 1997].

126.Section 1078 of the [Taxes Consolidation Act, 1997,] is amended by inserting the following after subsection (1A):

"(1B)A person is guilty of an offence under this section if he or she, with the intention to deceive –

(a) purports to be, or

(b) makes any statement, or otherwise acts in a manner, that would lead another person to believe that he or she is,

an officer of the Revenue Commissioners.".

Section 128

Miscellaneous technical amendments in relation to tax.

128.The enactments specified in Schedule 4 –

(a) are amended to the extent and in the manner specified in paragraphs 1 to 5 of that Schedule, and

(b) apply and come into operation in accordance with paragraph 6 of that Schedule.

SCHEDULE 4

Miscellaneous Technical Amendments in Relation to Tax

1.   ....

2.   The Capital Acquisitions Tax Consolidation Act 2003 is amended in accordance with the following provisions:

(a) in section 25 –

(i) in subsection (1) by substituting "section 46(2)" for "section 21(e)", and

(ii) in subsection (2) by substituting "section 46(2)" for "section 21(e)";

(b) in section 45A(4)(a) by deleting "section 21(e) or"; and

(c) in section 49(6A)(b) by deleting "a return within the meaning of section 21(e) or".

3.   ....

6.   (a) ....

(b) Paragraph 2 is deemed to have come into force and have taken effect as respects the year 2006 and subsequent years.

(c) ....

FINANCE ACT 2008

Number 3 of 2008
(Enacted on 13th March, 2008)

PART 5
Capital Acquisitions Tax

Section 126

Interpretation (Part 5).
126. In this Part "Principal Act" means the Capital Acquisitions Tax Consolidation Act 2003.

Section 127

Amendment of section 57 (overpayment of tax) of [the Capital Acquisitions Tax Consolidation Act 2003].
127. (1) Section 57 of the [Capital Acquisitions Tax Consolidation Act] is amended in subsection (3) by substituting "the valuation date or the date of the payment of the tax concerned (where that tax has been paid within 4 months after the valuation date)" for "the later of the valuation date or the date of the payment of the tax concerned".

(2) This section applies to claims for repayment of tax made on or after 31 January 2008.

Section 128

Amendment of section 62 (certificate relating to registration of title based on possession) of [the Capital Acquisitions Tax Consolidation Act 2003].
128. (1) Section 62 of the [Capital Acquisitions Tax Consolidation Act 2003] is amended –

(a) in subsection (1) –

(i) by substituting the following for the definition of "the Act of 1964":

"'Act of 1964' means the Registration of Title Act 1964 as amended by the Registration of Deeds and Title Act 2006:"

(ii) by deleting the definition of "the Registrar",

(iii) by inserting the following after "Act of 1964":

"'Authority' means the Property Registration Authority established by section 9 of the Registration of Deeds and Title Act 2006:", and

        (iv) by substituting "Authority" for "Registrar" in paragraph (a) of the definition of "relevant period",

    and

    (b) in subsections (2), (3) and (7) by substituting "Authority" for "Registrar" in each place where it occurs.

(2) This section applies to applications to register property made on or after 4 November 2006.

Section 129

Amendment of section 106 (arrangements for relief from double taxation of [the Capital Acquisitions Tax Consolidation Act 2003].

129. (1) Section 106 of the [Capital Acquisitions Tax Consolidation Act 2003] is amended —

    (a) by substituting for "and that it is expedient that those arrangements should have the force of law, the arrangements shall, notwithstanding anything in any enactment, have the force of law." the following:

"and that it is expedient that those arrangements should have the force of law and the order so made is referred to in the Table to this section, the arrangements shall, notwithstanding anything in any enactment, have the force of law as if each such order were an Act of the Oireachtas on and from the date of —

    (i)   the insertion of the Table, or

    (ii) the insertion of a reference to the order in the Table,

whichever is the later."

    and

    (b) by inserting the following after subsection (5):

"TABLE

Part 1

ARRANGEMENTS MADE BY THE GOVERNMENT WITH THE GOVERNMENT OF ANY TERRITORY OUTSIDE THE STATE IN RELATION TO AFFORDING RELIEF FROM DOUBLE TAXATION AND EXCHANGING INFORMATION IN RELATION TO TAX

1.   The Double Taxation Relief (Taxes on Estates of Deceased Persons and Inheritances and on Gifts) (United Kingdom) Order 1978 (S.I. No. 279 of 1978).

ARRANGEMENTS IN RELATION TO THE EXCHANGE OF INFORMATION RELATING TO TAX AND IN RELATION TO OTHER MATTERS RELATING TO TAX".

(2) This section has effect from 31 January 2008.

PART VI
Miscellaneous

Section 131

Amendment of section 1003 (payment of tax by means of donation of heritage items) of [the Taxes Consolidation Act, 1997].

131. Section 1003 of the [Taxes Consolidation Act, 1997,] is amended—

(a) in subsection (2) by inserting the following after paragraph (ab):

"(ac) Paragraph (ab) shall not apply in the case of a collection of items, consisting wholly of archival material or manuscripts, which was either—

(i) created over time by one individual, family or organisation, or

(ii) was assembled by an individual, family or organisation,

and constitutes a collection of archival material or manuscripts where each item has been in such collection for a period of not less than 30 years and merits maintenance as a collection.".

(b) by inserting the following after subsection (2):

"(2A) Notwithstanding subsection (2)(c), the selection committee may make a determination in respect of an item or collection of items, consisting wholly of archival material or manuscripts, and the market value limit in respect of any one item in such a collection at the valuation date as set out in subsection (2) (c)(i)(II) shall not apply.".

Section 132

Amendment of section 1003A (payment of tax by means of donation of heritage property to Irish Heritage Trust) of [the Taxes Consolidation Act, 1997].

132. (1) Section 1003A of the [Taxes Consolidation Act, 1997,] is amended in subsection (11A)(c) (inserted by the Finance Act 2007) by substituting "2008" for "2007".

(2) Section 1003A of the [Taxes Consolidation Act, 1997,] as amended by subsection (1), applies as respects the year of assessment 2008 as if in subsection (2)(d) "€8,000,000" were substituted for "€6,000,000".

Section 135

Amendment of section 818 (interpretation (Part 34)) of [the Taxes Consolidation Act, 1997].

135. Section 818 of the [Taxes Consolidation Act, 1997,] is amended by substituting the following for the definition of "authorised officer":

"'authorised officer' means an officer of the Revenue Commissioners;".

Section 137

Miscellaneous amendments in relation to claims for repayment of tax.

137. The enactments specified in Schedule 6 —

(a) are amended to the extent and manner specified in paragraphs 1 and 2 of that Schedule, and

(b) apply as on and from 31 January 2008.

Section 138

Amendment of penalties on summary conviction for certain revenue offences.

138. (1) The [Taxes Consolidation Act, 1997,] is amended —

(a) . . . . . .

(b) in section 908C(6) by substituting "€5,000" for "€3,000",

(c) in section 908D(8) by substituting "€5,000" for "€3,000",

(d) in section 1078(3)(a) by substituting "€5,000" for "€3,000", and

(e) in section 1078A(3)(a) by substituting "€5,000" for "€3,000".

(2) Subsection (1) applies as respects an offence committed on a day after the passing of this Act.

Section 140

Amendment of section 811A (transactions to avoid liability to tax: surcharge , interest and protective notifications) of [the Taxes Consolidation Act, 1997].

140. (1) Section 811A of the [Taxes Consolidation Act, 1997,] is amended —

(a) by inserting the following after subsection (1) —

"(1A) Without prejudice to the generality of any provision of this section or section 811, sections 955(2)(a) and 956(1) (c), as construed together with section 950(2), shall not be construed as preventing an officer of the Revenue Commissioners from —

(a) making any enquiry, or

(b) taking any action,

at any time in connection with this section or section 811.

(1B)   Where the Revenue Commissioners have received from, or on behalf of, a person, on or before the relevant date (within the meaning of subsection (3)(c)) a notification (referred to in subsection (3) and (6) as a 'protective notification') of full details of a transaction, then the Revenue Commissioners shall not form the opinion that the transaction is a tax avoidance transaction pursuant to subsections (2) and (4) of that section after the expiry of the period of 2 years commencing at−

(a)   the relevant date, or

(b)   if earlier, the date on which the notification was received by the Revenue Commissioners,

but this subsection shall not be construed as preventing an officer of the Revenue Commissioners from making any enquiry at any time in connection with this section or section 811.

(1C)   Where the Revenue Commissioners have not received from, or on behalf of, a person, on or before the relevant date (within the meaning of subsection (3)(c)) a notification (referred to in subsection (3) and (6) as a 'protective notification') of full details of the transaction, then section 811 shall apply as respects that transaction, if it is a transaction specified or described in a notice of opinion given by the Revenue Commissioners, as if the following clauses were substituted for clauses (I) and (II) of subsection (9)(a)(i):

'(I)   consider that there are grounds on which the transaction specified or described in the notice of opinion or any part of that transaction could reasonably be considered to be a tax avoidance transaction, that the opinion or the opinion in so far as it relates to that part is to stand,

(II)   consider that, subject to such amendment or addition thereto as the Appeal Commissioners or the majority of them deem necessary and as they shall specify or describe, there are grounds on which the transaction, or any part of it, specified or described in the notice of opinion, could reasonably be considered to be a tax avoidance transaction, that the transaction or that part of it be so amended or added to and that, subject to the amendment or addition, the opinion or the opinion in so far as it relates to that part is to stand or',

and the provisions of section 811 shall be construed accordingly."

(b)   in subsection (2)(a) by substituting "20 per cent" for "10 percent",

(c)   in subsection (3) –

(i)   in subparagraph (b)(i) by inserting "the application of subsection (1C) to the transaction concerned or" after "solely to prevent any possibility of", and

(ii)   in subparagraph (c) by substituting –

(I)   "19 February 2008" for "2 February 2006", and

(II)   "19 May 2008" for "2 May 2006".

in each place where they occur,

(d)   in subsection (6)(b) by substituting "the purposes of subsection (1B) and (3)" for "the purposes of subsection (3)", and

(e)   in subsection (7) by substituting "19 February 2008" for "2 February 2006" in each place where it occurs.

(2)   This section applies –

(a)   as respects any transaction where the whole or any part of the transaction is undertaken or arranged on or after 19 February 2008, and

(b)   as respects any transaction, the whole of which was undertaken or arranged before that date, in so far as it gives rise to, or would but for section 811 of the [Taxes Consolidation Act, 1997,] give rise to –

(i)   a reduction, avoidance, or deferral of any charge or assessment to tax, or part thereof, where the charge or assessment arises only by virtue of another transaction or other transactions carried out wholly on or after 19 February 2008, or

(ii)   a refund or a payment of an amount, or of an increase in an amount of tax, or part thereof, refundable or otherwise payable to a person where, but for section 811 of the [Taxes Consolidation Act, 1997,] that amount or increase in the amount would become first so refundable or otherwise payable to the person on or after 19 February 2008,

but where as respects any transaction the Revenue Commissioners have before 19 February 2008 received from, or on behalf of, a person a notification (referred to in subsections (3) and (6) of section 811A of the [Taxes Consolidation Act, 1997,] as a "protective notification" and made on or before the relevant date, within the meaning of subsection (3) (c) of that section prior to any amendment made by this section) of full details of the transaction, then the said section 811A shall apply to that transaction as if this section had not been enacted.

Section 141

Miscellaneous technical amendments in relation to tax.

141. The enactments specified in Schedule 8 –

(a) are amended to the extent and in the manner specified in paragraphs 1 to 6 of that Schedule, and

(b) apply and come into operation in accordance with paragraph 7 of that Schedule.

SCHEDULE 6

Miscellaneous Amendments in Relation to Claims for Repayment of Tax

1. ......

2. The Capital Acquisitions Tax Consolidation Act 2003 is amended –

(a) in section 28, by inserting the following after subsection (5):

"(5A) Notwithstanding section 57(3), relief shall be given under subsection (5)(a) on a claim which shall be made within 4 years after the liability referred to in that paragraph has been paid.";

and

(b) in section 29, by inserting the following after subsection (1):

"(1A) Notwithstanding section 57(3), relief shall be given under subsection (1) on a claim which shall be made within 4 years after the entitlement referred to in that subsection ceases.".

SCHEDULE 8

Miscellaneous Technical Amendments in Relation to Tax

1. The Taxes Consolidation Act 1997 is amended in accordance with the following provisions:

(a) ...

(o) in section 730GB by substituting "Capital Acquisitions Tax Consolidation Act 2003." for "Capital Acquisitions Tax Act 2003.",

(p) ...

(q) in section 917D (1)-

(i) in paragraph (f) of the definition of "the Acts" by substituting "Stamp Duties Consolidation Act 1999," for "Stamp Act, 1891," and

(ii) in the definition of "authorised person" by substituting "section 917G(3)(a);" for "section 917G(3)(b);",

(r) ...

7. [a] as respects paragraph 1 –

(i) ...

(ii) subparagraphs (b) to (f), (i) to (o) and (q) to (v) have effect as on and from the passing of this Act, and

(iii) ...

[b] ...

FINANCE (NO. 2) ACT 2008

Number 25 of 2008
(Enacted on 24th December, 2008)

PART 1
Levies, Income Tax, Corporation Tax and Capital Gains Tax

CHAPTER 2
Levies

Section 2

Income levy.

2. The [Taxes Consolidation Act, 1997,] is amended —

(a) ....

(b) in section 1002, in the definition of "the Acts", by inserting the following after paragraph (iii):

"(iiia) Part 18A,",

(c) in section 1006, in the definition of "the Acts", by inserting the following after paragraph (a):

"(aa) Part 18A,",

(d) in section 1006A, in the definition of "the Acts", by inserting the following after paragraph (a):

"(aa) Part 18A,",

(e) in section 1078, in the definition of "the Acts", by inserting the following after paragraph (c):

"(ca) Part 18A,",

and

(f) in section 1079, in the definition of "the Acts", by inserting the following after paragraph (c):

"(ca) Part 18A,".

Section 3

Parking levy in urban areas.

3. (1) The [Taxes Consolidation Act, 1997,] is amended —

(a) ....

(b) in section 1002, in the definition of "the Acts", by inserting the following after paragraph (vii):

"(viii) Part 18B,",

    (c)   in section 1006, in the definition of "the Acts", by inserting the following after paragraph (e):

        "(f) Part 18B,",

    (d)   in section 1006A, in the definition of "Acts", by inserting the following after paragraph (h):

        "(i) Part 18B,",

        and

    (e)   in section 1078, in the definition of "the Acts", by inserting the following after paragraph (h):

        "(i) Part 18B,".

(2)   The Provisional Collection of Taxes Act 1927 is amended in the definition of "tax" in section 1 by inserting "and parking levy" after "stamp duties".

CHAPTER 3
Income Tax

Section 15

Amendment of section 819 (residence) of [the Taxes Consolidation Act, 1997].

15.   Section 819 of the [Taxes Consolidation Act, 1997,] is amended by substituting the following for subsection (4):

    "(4)   For the purposes of this section—

        (a)   as respects the year of assessment 2008 and previous years of assessment, an individual shall be deemed to be present in the State for a day if the individual is present in the State at the end of the day, and

        (b)   as respects the year of assessment 2009 and subsequent years of assessment, an individual shall be deemed to be present in the State for a day if the individual is present in the State at any time during that day.".

PART 5
Capital Acquisitions Tax

Section 88

Interpretation (Part 5).

88.   In this Part "Principal Act" means the Capital Acquisitions Tax Consolidation Act 2003.

Section 89

Amendment of section 89 (provisions relating to agricultural property) of [the Capital Acquisitions Tax Consolidation Act 2003].

89. (1) Section 89 of the [Capital Acquisitions Tax Consolidation Act 2003] is amended, in paragraph (a) of the definition of "agricultural property" in subsection (1) and in the definition of "farmer" in that subsection, by substituting "in a Member State" for "in the State".

(2) This section applies to gifts and inheritances taken on or after 20 November 2008.

Section 90

Capital acquisitions: rate of charge.

90. (1) The Table in Part 2 of Schedule 2 to the [Capital Acquisitions Tax Consolidation Act 2003] is amended by substituting "22" for "20",

(2) This section applies to gifts and inheritances taken on or after 20 November 2008.

PART 6
Miscellaneous

Section 92

Revenue powers.

92. The [Taxes Consolidation Act, 1997,] in amended —

(a) ....

(b) in section 900 by substituting the following for section (4):

"(4) Nothing in this section shall be construed as requiring any person to disclose to an authorised officer —

(a) information with respect to which a claim to legal professional privilege could be maintained in legal proceedings,

(b) information of a confidential medical nature, or

(c) professional advice of a confidential nature given to a client (other than advice given as part of a dishonest, fraudulent or criminal purpose).",

(c) in section 901 by substituting the following for subsection (3):

"(3) Nothing in this section shall be construed as requiring any person to disclose to an authorised officer —

(a) information with respect to which a claim to legal professional privilege could be maintained in legal proceedings,

    (b)   information of a confidential medical nature, or

    (c)   professional advice of a confidential nature given to a client (other than advice given as part of a dishonest, fraudulent or criminal purpose).",

(d) in section 902 by substituting the following for subsection (9):

    "(9) Nothing in this section shall be construed as requiring any person to disclose to an authorised officer —

        (a)   information with respect to which a claim to legal professional privilege could be maintained in legal proceedings,

        (b)   information of a confidential medical nature, or

        (c)   professional advice of a confidential nature given to a client (other than advice given as part of a dishonest, fraudulent or criminal purpose).",

(e) in section 902A by substituting the following for subsection (6):

    "(6) Nothing in this section shall be construed as requiring any person to disclose to an authorised officer —

        (a)   information with respect to which a claim to legal professional privilege could be maintained in legal proceedings,

        (b)   information of a confidential medical nature, or

        (c)   professional advice of a confidential nature given to a client (other than advice given as part of a dishonest, fraudulent or criminal purpose).",

(f) in section 905(2) by substituting the following for paragraph (c):

    "(c) Nothing in this section shall be construed as requiring any person to disclose to an authorised officer —

        (i)   information with respect to which a claim to legal professional privilege could be maintained in legal proceedings,

        (ii)   information of a confidential medical nature, or

        (iii) professional advice of a confidential nature given to a client (other than advice given as part of a dishonest, fraudulent or criminal purpose).",

(g) in section 906A(1) by substituting the following for paragraph (a) of the definition of "financial institution":

    "(a) a person who holds or has held a licence under section 9 of the Central Bank Act 1971, or a person who holds or has held a licence or other similar authorisation under the law of any other Member State of the European Communities which corresponds to a licence granted under that section,",

(h) in section 908A(1) by substituting the following for paragraph (a) of the definition of "financial institution":

"(a) a person who holds or has held a licence under section 9 of the Central Bank Act 1971, or a person who holds or has held a licence or other similar authorisation under the law of any other Member State of the European Communities which corresponds to a licence granted under that section,".

(i) in section 908B(1) by substituting the following for paragraph (a) of the definition of "financial institution":

"(a) a person who holds or has held a licence under section 9 of the Central Bank Act 1971, or a person who holds or has held a licence or other similar authorisation under the law of any other Member State of the European Communities which corresponds to a licence granted under that section,".

(j) in section 1002(1) by substituting the following for the definition of "financial institution":

"'financial institution' means—

(a) a person who holds or has held a licence under section 9 of the Central Bank Act 1971, or a person who holds or has held a licence or other similar authorisation under the law of any other Member State of the European Communities which corresponds to a licence granted under that section,

(b) a person referred to in section 7(4) of the Central Bank Act 1971,

(c) a credit institution (within the meaning of the European Communities (Licensing and Supervision of Credit Institutions) Regulations 1992 (S.I. No. 395 of 1992)) which has been authorised by the Central Bank and Financial Services Authority of Ireland to carry on business of a credit institution in accordance with the provisions of the supervisory enactments (within the meaning of those Regulations), or

(d) a branch of a financial institution which records deposits in its books as liabilities of the branch;".

and

(k) in section 1078(3B) by inserting "within a period of 30 days commencing in the day the order is made" after "in subsection (3A)".

Section 93

Returns in relation to settlements and trusts.

93. The [Taxes Consolidation Act, 1997,] is amended by inserting the following after section 896:

"896A. (1) In this section—

'authorised officer' means an officer of the Revenue Commissioners authorised by them in writing to exercise the powers conferred on them by this section;

'settlement' and 'settlor' have the same meanings respectively as in section 10.

(2) Where any person, in the course of a trade or profession carried on by that person, has been concerned with the making of a settlement and knows or has reason to believe that, at the time of the making of the settlement—

(a) the settlor was resident or ordinarily resident in the State, and

(b) the trustees of the settlement were not resident in the State,

then that person shall, within the period specified in subsection (3), deliver to the appropriate inspector (within the meaning assigned by section 894(1)) a statement specifying—

(i) the name and address of the settlor,

(ii) the names and addresses of the persons who are the trustees of the settlement, and

(iii) the date on which the settlement was made or created.

(3) The statement referred to in subsection (2) shall be delivered—

(a) in a case where the settlement is one made on or after the date of the passing of the Finance (No. 2) Act 2008, within 4 months of the date of the making of the settlement, or

(b) in a case where the settlement is one made within the 5 year period prior to the passing of the Finance (No. 2) Act 2008, within 6 months of the date of the passing of the Act.

(4) For the purposes of this section trustees of a settlement shall be regarded as not resident in the State unless the general administration of the settlement is ordinarily carried on in the State and the trustees or a majority of each class of trustees are for the time being resident in the State.

(5)   An authorised officer may be notice in writing require any person, whom the authorised officer has reason to believe has information relating to a settlement, to furnish to the authorised officer such information within such time as the authorised officer may direct.".

Section 94

Donations of heritage items and heritage property.

94.   (1)   Chapter 5 of Part 42 of the [Taxes Consolidation Tax Act, 1997,] is amended —

(a)   in section 1003(5) by substituting "an amount equal to 80 per cent of the market value" for "an amount equal to the market value", and

(b)   in section 1003A(5) by substituting "an amount equal to 80 per cent of the market value" for "an amount equal to the market value".

(2)   Subsection (1) applies —

(a)   in the case of paragraph (a) of that subsection, as respects any determination made under section 1003(2)(a) of the [Taxes Consolidation Act, 1997,] by the selection committee (within the meaning of that section), on or after 1 January 2009, and

(b)   in the case of paragraph (b) of that subsection, as respects any determination made under section 1003A(2)(a) of the [Taxes Consolidation Act, 1997,] by the Minister for the Environment, Heritage and Local Government, on or after 1 January 2009.

Section 95

Amendment of section 811A (transactions to avoid liability to tax: surcharge, interest and protective notification) of [the Taxes Consolidation Act, 1997].

95.   Section 811A of the [Taxes Consolidation Act, 1997,] is amended by inserting the following after subsection (6):

"(6A)   The Revenue Commissioners may nominate any of their officers to perform any acts and discharge any functions authorised by this section to be performed or discharged by the Revenue Commissioners, and references in this section to the Revenue Commissioners shall with any necessary modifications be construed as including references to an officer so nominated.".

Section 97

Miscellaneous amendments relating to collection and recovery of tax.

97.   The enactments specified in Schedule 4 are amended to the extent and manner specified in paragraphs 1 to 6 of, and the Table to, that Schedule.

Section 98

Miscellaneous amendments in relation to penalties.

98. (1) The enactments specified in Schedule 5 are amended or repealed to the extent and manner specified in that Schedule and, unless the contrary is stated, shall come into effect after the passing of this Act.

(2) Notwithstanding subsection (1), as respects subparagraph (ar) of paragraph 2 of Schedule 5—

(a) clauses (i), (iv), (v) and (vi) of that subparagraph shall apply as respects penalties, as are referred to in paragraphs (a) and (b) of section 1086(2), which are imposed or determined by a court on or after the passing of this Act, and

(b) clauses (ii) and (iii) of that subparagraph shall apply as respects specified sums, as are referred to in paragraphs (c) and (d) of section 1086(2), which the Revenue Commissioners accepted, or undertook to accept, in settlement of a specified liability on or after the passing of this Act.

Section 99

Miscellaneous technical amendments in relation to tax.

99. The enactments specified in Schedule 6—

(a) are amended to the extent and in the manner specified in paragraphs 1 to 6 of that Schedule, and

(b) apply and come into operation in accordance with paragraph 7 of that Schedule.

SCHEDULE 4

Provisions Relating to Collection and Recovery of Tax

1. The Taxes Consolidation Act 1997 is amended—

(a) in Chapter 1 of Part 39, by substituting the following for section 928:

"Transmission to Collector-General of particulars of sums to be collected.

928. (1) In this section—

'assessment' and 'Revenue officer' have, respectively, the same meanings as in Chapter 1A of Part 42;

'tax' means income tax, corporation tax, capital gains tax, value-added tax, excise duty, stamp duty, gift tax and inheritance tax.

(2) After assessments to tax have been made, the inspectors or other Revenue officers shall transmit particulars of the sums to be collected to the Collector-General or to a Revenue officer nominated in writing under section 960B for collection.

(3) The entering by an inspector or other Revenue officer of details of an assessment to tax and of the tax charged in such an assessment in an electronic, digital, magnetic, optical, electromagnetic, biometric, photonic, photographic or other record from which the Collector-General or a Revenue officer nominated in writing under section 960B may extract such details by electronic, digital, magnetic, optical, electromagnetic, biometric, photonic, photographic or other process shall constitute transmission of such details by the inspector or other Revenue officer to the Collector-General or to the Revenue officer nominated in writing under section 960B.",

(b) In Part 42—

(i) by inserting the following after Chapter 1:

"CHAPTER 1A

Interpretation

Interpretation.

960A. (1) In Chapters 1A, 1B and 1C, unless the contrary is expressly stated—

'Acts' means—

(a) the Tax Acts.

(b) the Capital Gains Tax Acts,

(c) the Value-Added Tax Act 1972, and the enactments amending and extending that Act,

(d) the statutes relating to the duties of excise and to the management of those duties and the enactments amending and extending those statutes,

(e) the Stamp Duties Consolidation Act 1999 and the enactments amending and extending that Act,

(f) the Capital Acquisitions Tax Consolidation Act 2003 and the enactments amending and extending that Act,

(g) Parts 18A and 18B (inserted by the Finance (No. 2) Act 2008).

and any instruments made under any of those Acts;

'assessment' means any assessment to tax made under any provision of the Acts, including any amended assessment, additional assessment, correcting assessment and any estimate made under section 990 or under Regulation 13 or 14 of the RCT

Regulations and any estimate made under section 22 of the Value-Added Tax Act 1972;

'emoluments' has the same meaning as in section 983;

'income tax month' has the same meaning as in section 983;

'PAYE Regulations' means regulations made under section 986;

'RCT Regulations' means the Income Tax (Relevant Contracts) Regulations 2000 (S.I. No. 71 of 2000);

'Revenue officer' means any officer of the Revenue Commissioners;

'tax' means any income tax, corporation tax, capital gains tax, value-added tax, excise duty, stamp duty, gift tax, inheritance tax or any other levy or charge which is placed under the care and management of the Revenue Commissioners and includes —

(a) any interest, surcharge or penalty relating to any such tax, duty, levy or charge,

(b) any clawback of a relief or an exemption relating to any such tax, duty, levy or charge, and

(c) any sum which is required to be deducted or withheld by any person and paid or remitted to the Revenue Commissioners or the Collector-General, as the case may be, under any provision of the Acts;

'tax due and payable' means tax due and payable under any provision of the Acts.

Discharge of Collector-Generals' functions.

960B.   The Revenue Commissioners may nominate in writing any Revenue officer to perform any acts and to discharge any functions authorised by Chapters 1B and 1C to be performed or discharged by the Collector-General other than the acts and functions referred to in subsections (1) to (4) of section 960N, and references in this part to 'Collector-General' shall be read accordingly.

CHAPTER 1B

Collection of tax, etc.

Tax to be due and payable to Revenue Commissioners.

960C.   Tax due and payable under the Acts shall be due and payable to the Revenue Commissioners

Tax to be debt due to Minister for Finance.

960D.   Tax due and payable to the Revenue Commissioners shall be treated as a debt due to the Minister for Finance for the benefit of the Central Fund.

Collection of tax, issue of demands, etc.

960E. (1) Tax due and payable to the Revenue Commissioners by virtue of section 960C shall be paid to and collected by the Collector-General, including tax charged in all assessments to tax, particulars of which have been given to the Collector-General under section 928.

(2) The Collector-General shall demand payment of tax that is due and payable but remaining unpaid by the person from whom that tax is payable.

(3) Where tax is not paid in accordance with the demand referred to in subsection (2), the Collector-General shall collect and levy the tax that is due and payable but remaining unpaid by the person from whom that tax is payable.

(4) On payment of tax, the Collector-General may provide a receipt to the person concerned in respect of that payment and such receipt shall consist of whichever of the following the Collector-General considers appropriate, namely —

(a) a separate receipt in respect of each such payment, or

(b) a receipt for all such payments that have been made within the period specified in the receipt.

Moneys received for capital acquisitions tax and stamp duties and not appropriated to be recoverable.

960F. (1) Any person who —

(a) having received a sum of money in respect of gift tax, inheritance tax or stamp duties, does not pay that sum to the Collector-General, and

(b) improperly withholds or detains such sum of money,

shall be accountable to the Revenue Commissioners for the payment of that sum to the extent of the amount so received by that person.

(2) The sum of money referred to in subsection (1) shall be treated as a debt due to the Minister for Finance for the benefit of the Central Fund and section 960I shall apply to any such sum as if it were tax due and payable.

Duty of taxpayer to identify liability against which payment to be set, etc.

960G. (1) Subject to subsection (2), every person who makes a payment to tax to the Revenue Commissioners or to the Collector-General shall identify the liability to tax against which he or she wishes the payment to be set.

(2) Where payment of tax is received by the Revenue Commissioners or the Collector-General and the payment is accompanied by a pay slip, a tax return, a tax demand or other document issued by the Revenue Commissioners or the Collector-General, the payment shall, unless the contrary intention is or has been clearly indicated, be treated as relating to the tax referred to in the document concerned.

(3) Where a payment is received by the Revenue Commissioners or the Collector-General from a person and it cannot reasonably be determined by the Revenue Commissioners or the Collector-General from the instructions, if any, which accompanied the payment which liabilities the person wishes the payment to be set against, then the Revenue Commissioners or the Collector-General may set the payment against any liability due by the person under the Acts.

Offset between taxes.

960H. (1) In this section—

'claim' means a claim that gives rise to either or both a repayment of tax and a payment of interest payable in respect of such a repayment and includes part of such a claim;

'liability' means any tax due and payable which is unpaid and includes any tax estimated to be due and payable;

'overpayment' means a payment or remittance (including part of such a payment or remittance) which is in excess of the amount of the liability against which it is credited.

(2) Where the Collector-General is satisfied that a person has not complied with the obligations imposed on the person in relation to either or both—

(a) the payment of tax that is due and payable, and

(b) the delivery of returns required to be made,

then the Collector-General may, in a case where a repayment is due to the person in respect of a claim or overpayment—

(i) where paragraph (a) applies, or where paragraphs (a) and (b) apply, instead of making the repayment, set the amount of the repayment against any liability, and

        (ii)   where paragraph (b) only applies, withhold making the repayment until such time as the returns required to be delivered have been delivered.

(3)   (a)   where a person (referred to in this subsection as the 'first-mentioned person') has assigned, transferred or sold a right to a claim or overpayment to another person (referred to in this subsection as the 'second-mentioned person') and subsection (2)(a) applies, then the Collector-General shall, in a case where a repayment would have been due to the first-mentioned person in respect of the claim or overpayment if he or she had not assigned, transferred or sold his or her right to the claim or overpayment, instead of making the repayment to the second-mentioned person, set that claim or over-payment against tax that is due and payable by that first-mentioned person.

      (b)   Where the first-mentioned person and the second-mentioned person are connected persons within the meaning of section 10, then the balance, if any, of the repayment referred to in paragraph (a) shall be set against tax due and payable by the second-mentioned person.

(4)   Where the Collector-General has set or withheld a repayment by virtue of subsection (2) or (3), then he or she shall give notice in writing to that effect to the person or persons concerned and, where subsection (2)(ii) applies, interest shall not be payable under any provision of the Acts from the date of such notice in respect of any repayment so withheld.

(5)   The Revenue Commissioners may make regulations for the purpose of giving effect to this section and, without prejudice to the generality of the foregoing, such regulations may provide for the order of priority of the liabilities to tax against which any claim or overpayment is to be set in accordance with subsection (2) or (3) or both.

(6)   Every regulation made under this section is to be laid before Dáil Éireann as soon as may be after it is made and, if a resolution annulling the regulation is passed by Dáil Éireann within the next 21 days on which Dáil Éireann has sat after the regulation is laid before it, the regulation shall be annulled accordingly, but without prejudice to the validity of anything previously done under the regulation.

(7) The Taxes (Offset of Repayments) Regulations 2002 (S.I. No. 471 of 2002) shall have effect as if they were made under subsection (5) and had complied with subsection (6).

CHAPTER 1C

Recovery provisions, evidential rules, etc.

Recovery of tax by way of civil proceedings.

960I. (1) Without prejudice to any other means by which payment of tax may be enforced, any tax due and payable or any balance of such tax may be sued for and recovered by proceedings taken by the Collector-General in any court of competent jurisdiction.

(2) All or any of the amounts of tax due from any one person may be included in the same summons.

(3) The rules of court for the time being applicable to civil proceedings commenced by summary summons, in so far as they relate to the recovery of tax, shall apply to proceedings under this section.

(4) The acceptance of a part payment or a payment on account in respect of tax referred to in a summons shall not prejudice proceedings for the recovery of the balance of the tax due and the summons may be amended accordingly.

(5) (a) Proceedings under this section may be brought for the recovery of the total amount which an employer is liable, under Chapter 4 and the PAYE Regulations, to pay to the Collector-General for any income tax month without—

(i) distinguishing the amounts for which the employer is liable to pay by reference to each employee, and

(ii) specifying the employees in question.

(b) For the purposes of the proceedings referred to in paragraph (a), the total amount shall be one single cause of action or one matter of complaint.

(c) Nothing in this subsection shall prevent the bringing of separate proceedings for the recovery of each of the several amounts which the employer is liable to pay by reference to any income tax month and to the employer's several employees.

(6) For the purposes of subsection (5), any amount of tax—

(a) estimated under section 989, or

    (b)   estimated under section 990 or any balance of tax so estimated but remaining unpaid,

is deemed to be an amount of tax which any person paying emoluments was liable, under Chapter 4 and the PAYE Regulations, to pay to the Collector-General.

Evidential and procedural rules.

960J (1)   In proceedings for the recovery of tax, a certificate signed by the Collector-General to the effect that, before the proceedings were instituted, any one or more of the following matters occurred:

    (a)   the assessment to tax, if any, was duly made,

    (b)   the assessment, if any, has become final and conclusive,

    (c)   the tax or any specified part of the tax is due and outstanding,

    (d)   demand for the payment of the tax has been duly made,

shall be evidence until the contrary is proved of such of those matters that are so certified by the Collector-General.

(2)   (a)   Subsection (1) shall not apply in the case of tax to which Chapter 4 applies.

    (b)   In proceedings for the recovery of tax to which Chapter 4 applies, a certificate signed by the Collector-General that a stated amount of income tax under Schedule E is due and outstanding shall be evidence until the contrary is proved that the amount is so due and outstanding.

(3)   In proceedings for the recovery of tax, a certificate purporting to be signed by the Collector-General certifying the matters or any of the matters referred to in subsection (1) or (2) may be tendered in evidence without proof and shall be deemed until the contrary is proved to have been duly signed by the person concerned.

(4)   If a dispute relating to a certificate referred to in subsection (1), (2) or (3) arises during proceedings for the recovery of tax, the judge may adjourn the proceedings to allow the Collector-General or the Revenue officer concerned to attend and give oral evidence in the proceedings and for any register, file or other record relating to the tax to be produced and put in evidence in the proceedings.

Judgments for recovery of tax.

960K. (1) In this section 'judgment' includes any order or decree.

(2) Where, in any proceedings for the recovery of tax, judgment is given against a person and a sum of money is accepted from the person against whom the proceedings were brought on account or in part payment of the amount of which the judgment was given, then—

    (a) such acceptance shall not prevent or prejudice the recovery under the judgment of the balance of that amount that remains unpaid,

    (b) the judgment shall be capable of being executed and enforced in respect of the balance as fully in all respects and by the like means as if the balance were the amount for which the judgment was given,

    (c) the law relating to the execution and enforcement of the judgment shall apply in respect of the balance accordingly, and

    (d) a certificate signed by the Collector-General stating the amount of the balance shall, for the purposes of the enforcement and execution of the judgment, be evidence until the contrary is proved of the amount of the balance.

Recovery by sheriff or county registrar.

960L (1) Where any person does not pay any sum in respect of tax for which he or she is liable under the Acts, the Collector-General may issue a certificate to the county registrar or sheriff of the county in which the person resides or has a place of business certifying the amount due and outstanding and the person from whom that amount is payable.

(2) (a) For the purposes of this subsection—

    'electronic' has the meaning assigned to it by the Electronic Commerce Act 2000 and an 'electronic certificate' shall be construed accordingly;

    'issued in non-paper format' includes issued in facsimile.

    (b) A certificate to be issued by the Collector-General under this section may—

        (i) be issued in an electronic or other format, and

        (ii) where the certificate is issued in a non-paper format, be reproduced in a paper format by the county registrar or sheriff or by persons authorised by the county registrar or sheriff to do so.

(c) A certificate issued in a non-paper format in accordance with paragraph (b) shall —

(i) constitute a valid certificate for the purposes of this section,

(ii) be deemed to have been made by the Collector-General, and

(iii) be deemed to have been issued on the date that the Collector-General caused the certificate to issue.

(d) (i) Where a certificate issued by the Collector-General is reproduced in a non-paper format in accordance with paragraph (b) (ii) and —

(I) the reproduction contains, or there is appended to it, a note to the effect that it is a copy of the certificate so issued, and

(II) the note contains the signature of the county registrar or sheriff or of the person authorised under paragraph (b) (ii) and the date of such signing,

then the copy of the certificate with the note so signed and dated shall, for all purposes, have effect as if it was the certificate itself.

(ii) A signature or date in a note, on a copy of, or appended to, a certificate issued in a non-paper format by the Collector-General, and reproduced in a paper format in accordance with paragraph (b) (ii), that —

(I) in respect of such signature, purports to be that of the county registrar or sheriff or of a person authorised to make a copy, shall be taken until the contrary is shown to be the signature of the county registrar or sheriff or of a person who at the material time was so authorised, and

(II) in respect of such date, shall be taken until the contrary is shown to have been duly dated.

(3)   (a)   Immediately on receipt of the certificate, the county registrar or sheriff shall proceed to levy the amount certified in the certificate to be in default by seizing all or any of the goods, animals or other chattels within his or her area of responsibility belonging to the defaulter.

    (b)   For the purposes of paragraph (a), the county registrar or sheriff shall (in addition to the rights, powers and duties conferred on him or her by this section) have all such rights, powers and duties as are for the time being vested in him or her by law in relation to the execution of a writ of fieri facias in so far as those rights, powers and duties are not inconsistent with the additional rights, powers and duties conferred on him or her by this section.

(4)   A county registrar or sheriff executing a certificate under this section shall be entitled —

    (a)   if the sum certified in the certificate is in excess of €19,050, to charge and (where appropriate) to add to that sum and (in any case) to levy under the certificate such fees and expenses, calculated in accordance to the scales appointed by the Minister for Justice. Equality and Law Reform under section 14(1)(a) of the Enforcement of Court Orders Act 1926 and for the time being in force, as the county registrar or sheriff would be entitled so to charge or add and to levy if the certificate were an execution order, within the meaning of the Enforcement of Court Orders Act 1926 (in this section referred to as an 'execution order'), of the High Court,

    (b)   if the sum referred to in the certificate to be in default exceeds €3,175 but does not exceed €19,050, to charge and (where appropriate) to add to that sum and (in any case) to levy under the certificate such fees and expenses, calculated according to the scales referred to in paragraph (a), as the county registrar or sheriff would be entitled so to charge or add and to levy if the certificate were an execution order of the Circuit Court, and

    (c)   if the sum certified in the certificate to be in default does not exceed €3,175 and (where appropriate) to add to that sum and (in any case) to levy under the certificate such fees and expenses, calculated according to the scales referred to in paragraph (a), as the county registrar or sheriff would be entitled so to charge or add and to levy if the certificate were an execution order of the District Court.

Taking by Collector-General of proceedings in bankruptcy.

960M. (1) The Collector-General may in his or her own name apply for the grant of a bankruptcy summons under section 8 of the Bankruptcy Act 1988 or present a petition for adjudication under section 11 of that Act in respect of tax (except corporation tax) due and payable or any balance of such tax.

(2) Subject to this section, the rules of court for the time being applicable and the enactments relating to bankruptcy shall apply to proceedings under this section.

Continuance of pending proceedings and evidence in proceedings.

960N. (1) Where the Collector-General has instituted proceedings under section 960I(1) or 960M(1) for the recovery of tax or any balance of tax and, while such proceedings are pending, such Collector-General ceases for any reason to hold that office, the proceedings may be continued in the name of that Collector-General by any person (in this section referred to as the 'successor') duly appointed to collect such tax in succession to that Collector-General or any subsequent Collector-General.

(2) In any case where subsection (1) applies, the successor shall inform the person or persons against whom the proceedings concerned are pending that those proceedings are being so continued and, on service of such notice, notwithstanding any rule of court, it shall not be necessary for the successor or obtain an order of court substituting him or her for the person who has instituted or continued proceedings.

(3) Any affidavit or oath to be made by a Collector-General for the purpose of the Judgment Mortgage (Ireland) Act 1850 or the Judgment Mortgage (Ireland) Act 1858 may be made by a successor.

(4) Where the Collector-General duly appointed to collect tax in succession to another Collector-General institutes or continues proceedings under section 960I(1) or 960M(1) for the recovery of tax or any balance of tax, then the person previously appointed as Collector-General shall for the purpose of the proceedings be deemed until the contrary is proved to have ceased to be the Collector-General appointed to collect the tax.

(5) Where a Revenue officer nominated in accordance with section 960B has instituted proceedings under

section 960I(1) or 960M(1) for the recovery of tax or the balance of tax, and while such proceedings are pending, such officer dies or otherwise ceases for any reason to be a Revenue officer –

(a) the right of such officer to continue proceedings shall cease and the right to continue proceedings shall vest in such other officer as may be nominated by the Revenue Commissioners,

(b) where such other officer is nominated he or she shall be entitled accordingly to be substituted as a party to the proceedings in the place of the first-mentioned officer, and

(c) where an officer is so substituted, he or she shall give notice in writing of the substitution to the defendant.

(6) In proceedings under section 960I(1) or 960M(1) taken by a Revenue officer nominated in accordance with section 960B, a certificate signed by the Revenue Commissioners certifying the following facts –

(a) that a person is an officer of the Revenue Commissioners,

(b) that he or she has been nominated by them in accordance with section 960B, and

(c) that he or she has been nominated by them in accordance with subsection (5)(a),

shall be evidence unless the contrary is proved of those facts.

(7) In proceedings under sections 960I(1) or 960M(1) taken by a Revenue officer nominated in accordance with section 960B, a certificate signed by the Revenue Commissioners certifying the following facts –

(a) that the plaintiff has ceased to be an officer of the Revenue Commissioners nominated by them in accordance with section 960B,

(b) that another person is a Revenue officer,

(c) that such other person has been nominated by them in accordance with section 960B, and

(d) that such other person has been nominated by them to take proceedings to recover tax,

shall be evidence until the contrary is proved of those facts.

960O. ...."

(ii) ....

2. Each enactment (in this Schedule referred to as the "repealed enactments") mentioned in the second column of Part 1 of the Table to this Schedule is repealed to the extent specified opposite that mentioned in the third column of that Part.

3. Part 2 of the Table to this Schedule, which provides for amendments to other enactments consequential on this Schedule coming into effect, shall have effect.

4. Any reference, whether express or implied, in any enactment or document (including the repealed enactments and enactments passed or documents made after this Schedule comes into effect) –

   (a) to any provision of the repealed enactments, or

   (b) to things done, or to be done under or for the purposes of any provision of the repealed enactments,

   shall, if and in so far as the nature of the reference permits, be construed as including, in relation to the times, years or periods, circumstances or purposes in relation to which the corresponding provision of this Schedule applies, a reference to, or as the case may be, to things done or deemed to be done or to be done under or for the purposes of, the corresponding provision.

5. All documents made or issued under a repealed enactment and in force immediately before this Schedule comes into effect shall continue in force as if made or issued under the provision inserted into the Taxes Consolidation Act 1997 by this Schedule which corresponds to the repealed enactment.

6. This Schedule comes into effect and applies as respects any tax that becomes due and payable on or after 1 March 2009.

TABLE

PART 1

REPEALS

Number and Year	Short Title	Extent of Repeal
....	....	....
No. 39 of 1997.	Taxes Consolidation Act 1997	.... Sections .... 1006A...
....	....	....
No. 1 of 2003.	Capital Acquisitions Tax Consolidation Act 2003	Subsections (1) and (2) of section 61, subsections 1 and 2 of section 63 and sections 64 and 65. In subsections (3) and (4) of section 63 the words "the Attorney General or the Minister for Finance or".

PART 2
CONSEQUENTIAL AMENDMENTS

Income tax, corporation tax, capital gains tax and related matters

Enactment amended	Words or references to be replaced	Words or references to be inserted
Tax Consolidation Act 1997:		
....	....	....
Section 1006(1), in the definitions of "certificate" and "fees"	section 962	section 960L
....	....	....

SCHEDULE 5
Miscellaneous Amendments in Relation to Penalties

PART 1
Amendment of Part 47 as respect penalties

1. The Taxes Consolidation Act 1997 is amended in Part 47 by the insertion of the following after Chapter 3:

"CHAPTER 3A

Determination of Penalties and Recovery of Penalties

Interpretation (Chapter 3A).

1077A. In this Chapter—

'the Acts' means—

(a) the Tax Acts,

(b) the Capital Gains Tax Acts,

(c) Parts 18A and 18B,

(d) the Value-Added Tax Act 1972, and the enactments amending or extending that Act,

(e) the Capital Acquisitions Tax Consolidation Act 2003, and the enactments amending or extending that Act,

(f) the Stamp Duties Consolidation Act 1999, and the enactments amending or extending that Act,

(g) the statutes relating to the duties of excise and to the management of those duties,

and any instrument made thereunder and any instrument made under any other enactment relating to tax;

'relevant court' means the District Court, the Circuit Court or the High Court, as appropriate, by reference to the jurisdictional limits for civil matters laid down in the Courts of Justice Act 1924, as amended, and the Courts (Supplemental Provisions) Act 1961, as amended;

'Revenue officer' means an officer of the Revenue Commissioners,

'tax' means any tax, duty, levy or charge under the care and management of the Revenue Commissioners.

Penalty notifications and determinations.

1077B. (1) Where—

(a) in the absence of any agreement between a person and a Revenue officer that the person is liable to a penalty under the Acts, or

(b) following the failure by a person to pay a penalty the person has agreed a liability to,

a Revenue officer is of the opinion that the person is liable to a penalty under the Acts, then that officer shall give notice in writing to the person and such notice shall identify—

(i) the provisions of the Acts under which the penalty arises.

(ii) the circumstances in which that person is liable to the penalty, and

(iii) the amount of the penalty to which that person is liable,

and include such other details as the Revenue officer considers necessary.

(2) A Revenue officer may at any time amend an opinion that a person is liable to a penalty under the Acts and shall give due notice of such amended opinion in like manner to the notice referred to in subsection (1).

(3) Where a person to whom a notice issued under subsection (1) or (2) does not, within 30 days after the date of such a notice—

(a) agree in writing with the opinion or amended opinion contained in such notice, and

(b) make a payment to the Revenue Commissioners of the amount of the penalty specified in such a notice.

then a Revenue officer may make an application to a relevant court for that court to determine whether—

(i) any action, inaction, omission or failure of, or

(ii) any claim, submission or delivery by,

the person in respect of whom the Revenue officer made the application gives rise to a liability to a penalty under the Acts on that person.

(4) A copy of any application to a relevant court for a determination under subsection (3) shall be issued to the person to whom the application relates.

(5) This section applies in respect of any act or omission giving rise to a liability to a penalty under the Acts whether arising before, on or after the passing of the Finance (No. 2) Act 2008 but shall not apply in respect of a penalty paid, or amounts paid in respect of a penalty, before the passing of that Act.

Recovery of penalties.

1077C. (1) Where a relevant court has made a determination that a person is liable to a penalty –

(a) that court shall also make an order as to the recovery of that penalty, and

(b) without prejudice to any other means of recovery, that penalty may be collected and recovered in like manner as an amount of tax.

(2) Where a person is liable to a penalty under the Acts, that penalty is due and payable from the date –

(a) it had been agreed in writing (or had been agreed in writing on that person's behalf) that the person is liable to that penalty,

(b) the Revenue Commissioners had agreed or undertaken to accept a specified sum of money in the circumstances mentioned in paragraph (c) and (d) of section 1086(2) from that individual, or

(c) a relevant court has determined that the person is liable to that penalty.

(3) This section applies in respect of any act or omission giving rise to a liability to a penalty under the Acts whether arising before, on or after the passing of the Finance (No. 2) Act 2008.

Proceedings against executor, administration or estate.

1077D. (1) Where before an individuals' death –

(a) that individual had agreed in writing (or it had been agreed in writing on his or her behalf) that he or she was liable to a penalty under the Acts,

(b) that individual had agreed in writing with an opinion or amended opinion of a Revenue officer that he or she was liable to a penalty under the Acts (or such opinion or amended opinion had been agreed in writing on his or her behalf),

(c) the Revenue Commissioners had agreed or undertaken to accept a specified sum of money in the circumstances mentioned in paragraph (c) or (d) of section 1086(2) from that individual, or

    (d) a relevant court has determined that the individual was liable to a penalty under the Acts,

then the penalty shall be due and payable and, subject to subsection (2), any proceedings for the recovery of such penalty under the Acts which have been, or could have been, instituted against that individual may be continued or instituted against his or her executor, administrator or estate, as the case may be, and any penalty awarded in proceedings so continued or instituted shall be a debt due from and payable out of his or her estate.

  (2) Proceedings may not be instituted by virtue of subsection (1) against the executor or administrator of a person at a time when by virtue of subsection (2) of section 1048 that executor or administrator is not assessable and chargeable under that section in respect of tax on profits or gains which arose or accrued to the person before his or her death.

CHAPTER 3B

....

PART 2

Amendment of the Taxes Consolidation Act 1997
as respects penalties

2.   The Taxes Consolidation Act 1999 is amended —

  (a) ....

  (j) in section 887(5)(b) by substituting "€3,000" for "€1,265",

  (k) ....

  (p) in section 900(7) by substituting "€4,000" for "€1,900",

  (q) in section 902(11) by substituting "€4,000" for "€1,900",

  (r) ....

  (t) in section 905(3) by substituting "€4,000" for "€1,265",

  (u) ....

  (ar) in section 1078(9) —

     (i) by inserting "subsections (9) and (17) of section 1077E," after "section 1053", and

    (ii) by substituting ",and section 27A(16) of the Value-Added Tax Act 1972, "for" and sections 26(6) and 27(7) of the Value-Added Tax Act, 1972,",

  (as) in section 1086 —

     (i) in subsection (2) —

        (I) in paragraph (a), by inserting "or determined" after "imposed",

(II) in paragraph (b), by inserting "or determined" after "imposed",

(III) in paragraph (d), by inserting "or determined" after "imposed",

(ii) by substituting the following for subsection(2A):

"(2A) For the purposes of subsection (2), the reference to a specified sum in paragraphs (c) and (d) of that subsection includes a references to a sum which is the full amount of the claim by the Revenue Commissioners in respect of the specified liability referred to in those paragraphs. Where the Revenue Commissioners accept or undertake to accept such a sum, being the full amount of their claim, then—

(a) they shall be deemed to have done so pursuant to an agreement, made with the person referred to in paragraph (c), whereby they refrained from initiating proceedings for the recovery of any fine or penalty of the kind mentioned in paragraphs (a) and (b) of subsection (2), and

(b) that agreement shall be deemed to have been made in the relevant period in which the Revenue Commissioners accepted or undertook to accept that full amount.".

(iii) in subsection (4) by substituting the following for paragraph (a):

(a) the Revenue Commissioners are satisfied that, before any investigation or inquiry had been started by them or by any of their officers into any matter occasioning a liability referred to in those paragraphs, the person had voluntarily furnished to them a qualifying disclosure (within the meaning of section 1077E, section 27A of the Value-Added Tax Act 1972 or section 134A of the Stamp Duties Consolidation Act 1999, as the case may be) in relation to and full particulars of that matter.".

(iv) by inserting the following after subsection (4A):

"(4B) Paragraphs (a) and (b) of subsection (2) shall not apply in relation to a person in whose case—

(a) the amount of a penalty determined by a court does not exceed 15 per cent of, as appropriate—

(i) the amount of the difference referred to in subsection (11) or (12), as the case may be, of section 1077E,

(ii) the amount of the difference referred to in subsection (11) or (12), as the case may be, of section 27A of the Value-Added Tax Act 1972, or

   (iii) the amount of the difference referred to in subsection (7), (8) or (9), as the case may be, of section 134A of the Stamp Duties Consolidation Act 1999,

  (b) the aggregate of the—

   (i) the tax due in respect of which the penalty is computed,

   (ii) except in the case of tax due by virtue of paragraphs (g) and (h) of the definition of 'the Acts' interest on that tax, and

   (iii) the penalty determined by a court,

   does not exceed €30,000, or

  (c) there has been a qualifying disclosure.",

 (v) in subsection (5)—

  (I) in paragraph (a), by inserting "or determined" after "imposed",

 and

  (II) in paragraph (b), by inserting "or determined" after "imposed".

 (vi) in subsection (5A)(a), by inserting "or determined" after "imposed".

(at)......

PART 3

....

PART 4
Capital Acquisitions Tax: Penalties

4. The Capital Acquisitions Tax Consolidation Act 2003 is amended—

 (a) by deleting section 25, and

 (b) in section 58—

  (i) by substituting "€3,000" for "€2,535" in subsections (1)(a) and (1A)(a),

  (ii) by substituting "€3,000" for "€1,265" in subsection (2),

  (iii) by inserting "deliberately or carelessly" before "fails" and by deleting ", by reason of fraud or neglect by that person," in subsection (1A),

  (iv) by substituting "deliberately or carelessly" for "fraudulently or negligently" in subsection (3),

  (v) by substituting "deliberately nor carelessly" for "fraudulently nor negligently" and "carelessly" for "negligently" in subsection (4),

  (vi) by substituting "€3,000" for "€1,265" in subsection (7), and

(vii) by substituting the following for subsection (9):

"(9) Subject to this section—

(a) sections 987(4), 1062, 1063, 1064, 1065, 1066 and 1068 of the Taxes Consolidation Act 1997 shall, with any necessary modifications, apply to a penalty under this Act as if the penalty were a penalty under the Income Tax Acts, and

(b) section 1077E (inserted by the Finance (No. 2) Act 2008) of the Taxes Consolidation Act 1997 shall, with any necessary modifications, apply to a penalty under this Act as if the penalty were a penalty relating to income tax, corporation tax or capital gains tax, as the case may be.".

PART 5

....

SCHEDULE 6

Miscellaneous Technical Amendments in Relation to Tax

1.   The Taxes Consolidation Act 1997 is amended—

(a)   ....

(c)   in section 1078 B(6) by inserting "or subsection (3) of section 908 C" after "of section 905", and

(d)   ....

2.   ....

3.   The Capital Acquisitions Tax Consolidation Act 2003 is amended in section 28(2) (a) by substituting, "donee on successor's" for "disponer's".

4.   ......

7. (a) as respects paragraph 1—

(i)   ....

(iii) subparagraphs (c) and (d) have effect as on and from the passing of this Act.

(b) ...

(c) Paragraph 3 is deemed to have came into force and have taken effect as on and from 21 February 2003.

(d) ....

FINANCE ACT 2009

Number 12 of 2009
(Enacted on 3rd June, 2009)

PART 5
Capital Acquisitions Tax

Section 23

Amendment of Schedule 2 (computation of tax) to Capital Acquisitions Tax Consolidation Act 2003.

27. (1) Schedule 2 to the Capital Acquisitions Tax Consolidation Act 2003 is amended—

    (a) in the definition of "group threshold" in paragraph 1 of Part 1—

        (i) in subparagraph (a) by substituting "€304,775" for "€381,000",

        (ii) in subparagraph (b) by substituting "€30,478" for "€38,100", and

        (iii) in subparagraph (c) by substituting "€15,239" for "€19,050".

    and

    (b) by substituting "25" for "22" in the Table in Part 2.

    (2) This section applies to gifts and inheritances taken on or after 8 April 2009.

PART 6
Miscellaneous

Section 29

Interest on certain overdue tax.

29. (1) The [Taxes Consolidation Act, 1997,] is amended ......

    (3) Section 51 of the Capital Acquisitions Tax Consolidation Act 2003 is amended in subsection (2) by substituting the following for the Table to that subsection:

"TABLE

Part 1

(Period) (1)	(Percentage) (2)
From 31 March 1976 to 31 July 1978	0.0492%
From 1 August 1978 to 31 March 1998	0.0410%
From 1 April 1998 to 31 March 2005	0.0322%
From 1 April 2005 to 30 June 2009	0.0273%
From 1 July 2009 to the date of payment	0.0219%

Part 2

(1)	(2)
From 8 February 1995 to 31 March 1998	0.0307%
From 1 April 1998 to 31 March 2005	0.0241%
From 1 April 2005 to 30 June 2009	0.0204%
From 1 July 2009 to the date of payment	0.0164%

"

Section 30

Miscellaneous technical amendments in relation to tax.

30. (1) .....

(2) Section 1077C(2)(b) (inserted by the Finance (No. 2) Act 2008) of the [Taxes Consolidation Act, 1997,] is amended by substituting "person" for "individual".

(4) The Finance (No. 2) Act 2008 is amended –

    (a) .....

    (b) in section 98(2) by substituting "subparagraph (as) of paragraph 2 of Schedule 5" for "subparagraph (ar) of paragraph 2 of Schedule 5".

(5) (a) .....

    (e) Subsection (4)(b) has effect as on and from the passing of this Act.

THIRD PART

(II) RULES, REGULATIONS AND ORDERS

For Contents of this Part, see page lxxxiv

(II) RULES, REGULATIONS AND ORDERS

S . R. & O., 1911. No. 414

THE LANDS VALUES (REFEREE)(IRELAND) RULES, 1911

In pursuance of section thirty-three of the Finance (1909–10) Act, 1910,[4] the Reference Committee for Ireland constituted under that section hereby make the following Rules: –

Rule 1

Short Title.

1. These rules may be cited as the Land Values (Referee) (Ireland) Rules, 1911.

Rule 2

Interpretation.

2. (1) In these rules, unless the context otherwise requires, –

    "The Act" means the Finance (1909-10) Act, 1910.[4]

    "The Commissioners" means the Revenue Commissioners.

    (2) The Interpretation Act, 1889, applies for the purpose of the interpretation of these rules as it applies for the purpose of the interpretation of an Act of Parliament.[5]

Rule 4

Withdrawal of appeal.

4. Notice of the withdrawal of an appeal may be in the form set out in the Schedule to these Rules or in a form to the like effect.

Rule 5

Time for notice of appeal.

5. The following provisions shall have effect as respects the time of giving notice of appeal: –

    (1) In the case of an appeal against total value or site value on a provisional valuation –

         (a) A notice of appeal shall not be treated as an effective notice of appeal if given sooner than thirty days after notice of objection to the provisional valuation has been given by the appellant;

(b) After the expiration of that time notice of the appeal may be given at any time unless notice is given by the Commissioners to the objector that they do not propose to amend their provisional valuation, or do not propose to make any further amendment in their provisional valuation to meet his objection, and in that case notice of appeal must be given within thirty days after notice is so given by the Commissioners.

(2) In the case of an appeal against any assessment of duty, or against any refusal of the Commissioners to make any allowance or to make the allowance claimed, or against any apportionment, or against the determination of any other matter by the Commissioners, notice of appeal must be given within thirty days after the Commissioners have given notice to the appellant of their assessment, refusal, apportionment, or determination, as the case may be.

Rule 6

Extension of time for giving notice by appellant.

6. (1) The Reference Committee may, on the application of any person desiring to appeal, extend the time for appeal prescribed by the foregoing rule as they, in their absolute discretion, think fit, and may so extend the time although the application is not made until after the expiration of the time prescribed.

(2) Any application for an extension of the time for appeal must be made in writing to the Reference Committee, and must state the grounds of the application, and a copy of the application must be sent to the Commissioners by the applicant.

(3) The Reference Committee shall give the Commissioners reasonable opportunity for laying before them in writing any objections which the Commissioners may have to any such application for an extension of time, and shall consider any such objections.

Rule 8

Consideration of appeal by referee.

8. (1) The referee selected shall, as soon as may be, proceed with the determination of the appeal, and arrange with the Commissioners and the appellant the time and place for consultation with the Commissioners and the appellant with respect thereto.

(2) The Reference Committee shall furnish the referee with a copy of the notice of appeal, and the Commissioners and the appellant shall furnish to the referee on his request any document or other information which it is in their or his power to furnish, and which the referee may require for the purpose of the determination of the appeal.

(3) Subject to the provisions of the Act and of these rules, the proceedings on the consideration of an appeal shall be such as the referee, subject to any special directions of the Reference Committee, may in his discretion direct.

(4) In this Rule any reference to the Commissioners or to the appellant includes a reference to any person nominated by the Commissioners or the appellant respectively under subsection (3) of section 33 of the Act.

Rule 9

Appellant limited to grounds of appeal.

9. The appellant shall not, on the consideration of his appeal, be allowed to rely upon any grounds of appeal not specifically set out in his notice of appeal, but the referee may, if he thinks it just under the circumstances, allow the notice of appeal to be amended at any time.

Rule 10

Decision of referee.

10. The decision of the referee shall be in the form contained in the Schedule to these rules, or in a form to the like effect, and the referee shall cause copies of his decision to be furnished to the Reference Committee, the Commissioners, and the appellant. Provided that in the event of any question of law being raised by any party to an appeal, the referee may, if he thinks fit, state his award in the form of a special case for the opinion of the Court.

Rule 12

Appearance of third parties.

12. (1) On the consideration of any appeal, the referee shall on the application of any person who appears to the referee to be interested in the land in respect of which the appeal is made, or to be otherwise interested in the matter of the appeal, give him an opportunity of putting his case before the referee in writing, and if necessary, of taking part in any consultation with reference to the appeal.

(2) The Commissioners, when they receive notice of any appeal against total or site value on a provisional valuation, shall give notice of the appeal to any person from whom a return has been required for the purpose of the valuation, and to any person who has applied to the Commissioners for a copy of the provisional valuation of the land under subsection (5) of section twenty-seven of the Act.

Rule 13

Alteration of valuation, &c., by Commissioners.

13. The Commissioners shall as soon as may be on receiving notice of the decision of the referee on any appeal make such alteration in the particular of any valuation, apportionments, reapportionments, assessments, or other documents as may be necessary to carry out the decisions of the referee.

Rule 15

Informalities not necessarily to invalidate proceedings.

15. Any failure on the part of any authority or any person to comply with the provisions of these rules shall not render the proceedings on a reference to a referee, or anything done in pursuance thereof, invalid, unless the referee so directs.

SCHEDULE[1]

I

FINANCE (1909-10) ACT, 1910

Notice of appeal to referee in respect of any matter other than total or site value on a provisional valuation.
County, Rural District and Townland or Town or City, Street and Number.
To the Reference Committee.
(Or, To the Commissioners of Inland Revenue.)
I hereby give notice of my intention to appeal against[2]
The particulars of my grounds of appeal are as follows-

Signed[3]:

Address:

Dated...

II
FINANCE (1909-10) ACT, 1910

Notice of withdrawal of appeal to referee in respect of any matter.
County,   Rural District and Townland or Town or City,   Street and Number.

To the Reference Committee.
(Or, To the Commissioners of Inland Revenue.)
I hereby withdraw my notice of appeal, dated the   19   against[2]

Signed[3]:

Address:

Dated..

III
FINANCE (1909-10) ACT, 1910
Decision of referee on appeal.

The decision on the appeal in respect of which the annexed notice of appeal
has been given is as follows:-

Signed:

Referee

Dated..

Footnotes

1   This Schedule should be construed having regard to the Property Values (Arbitrations and Appeals) Rules, 1961 – see page 1358.

2   Here insert the matter appealed against.

3   If an agent, the name and address of the principal on whose behalf he acts must be stated.

4   Reproduced on page 655.

5   But see now the Interpretation Act 2005 reproduced on page 1265.

S. I. No. 91 of 1961

PROPERTY VALUES (ARBITRATIONS AND APPEALS) RULES, 1961

We , the Reference Committee, in exercise of the powers conferred on us by section 33 of the Finance (1909-10) Act, 1910,[1] the Acquisition of Land (Assessment of Compensation) Act, 1919, and sections 3[2] and 4 of the Property Values (Arbitrations and Appeals) Act, 1960 (No. 45 of 1960), hereby make the following Rules, with the approval of the Minister for Finance in so far as they are made under the said section 33:

1. These Rules may be cited as the Property Values (Arbitrations and Appeals) Rules, 1961.

2. The Interpretation Act, 1937 (No. 38 of 1937)[3], applies to these Rules.

3. (1) In these Rules-

    "the Act of 1910" means the Finance (1909-10) Act 1910;[1]

    "the Act of 1919" means the Acquisition of Land (Assessment of Compensation) Act, 1919;

    "question" means a question referred to in section 1 of the Act of 1919;

    "the Reference Committee" means the Reference Committee established by section 1 of the Act of 1919, as amended by the Acquisition of Land (Reference Committee) Act, 1925 (No. 22 of 1925);

    "the Rules of 1911" means the Land Values (Referee) (Ireland) Rules, 1911;

    "the Rules of 1920" means the Acquisition of Land (Assessment of Compensation) Rules, 1920.

    (2) These Rules shall, in so far as they amend the Rules of 1911, be construed as one with the Rules of 1911 and shall, in so far as they amend the Rules of 1920, be construed as one with the Rules of 1920.

4. (1) As appeal under section 33 of the Act of 1910 to a property arbitrator may be made by sending to the Reference Committee and to the Revenue Commissioners within the period provided for by the Rules of 1911 a notice of appeal in the appropriate form set out in the Schedule to the Rules of 1911 or in a form to the like effect specifying the matter to which the appeal relates and giving particulars of the grounds of the appeal.

    (2) The Revenue Commissioners shall cause printed copies of the forms of notices of appeal set out in the Schedule to the Rules of 1911 to be furnished free of charge on application by any person to the

Revenue Commissioners or to any person authorised by the Revenue Commissioners to furnish the forms.

5.   Whenever the Reference Committee receives, pursuant to Rule 4 of these Rules, a notice of appeal in writing, it shall, as soon as may be, nominate a property arbitrator for the purpose of the reference and determination of the appeal to which the notice relates, and shall, as soon as it has nominated the property arbitrator, inform the Revenue Commissioners and the appellant of his name and address.

6.   In the Rules of 1911 –

(a)   references to the Reference Committee for Ireland constituted under section 33 of the Act of 1910, shall be construed as references to the Reference Committee,

(b)   references to a referee and the reference in Rule 8 to the referee selected shall be construed as references to a property arbitrator nominated under these Rules, and

(c)   Rules, 3, 7, 11 and 14 shall be revoked.

7.   (1)   Where a question has arisen, any party to or affected by, the acquisition in relation to which the question has arisen –

(a)   may, at any time after the expiration of fourteen days from the date on which notice to treat was served in relation to the acquisition, send to the Reference Committee an application in writing for the nomination of a property arbitrator for the purposes of the reference and determination of the question, and

(b)   shall, if he sends the application specified in paragraph (a) of this Rule, as soon as may be after such sending, send a copy thereof to every other party to, or affected by, the acquisition aforesaid.

(2)   An application under this Rule shall be in writing and shall specify the parties to, or affected by the acquisition, the land to be acquired, the nature of the question to which the application relates, the statutory provisions under which the question arises and, if compensation is claimed, the interest in respect of which it is claimed.

8.   Whenever the Reference Committee receives, pursuant to Rule 7 of these Rules, a valid application in writing for the appointment of a property arbitrator, it shall, as soon as may be, nominate a property arbitrator for the purpose of the reference and determination of the question to which the notice relates, and shall, as soon as it has nominated the property arbitrator, inform the parties to, or affected by, the acquisition in relation to which the question has arisen of his name and address.

9.   In the Rules of 1920 –

(a)   the definition of "arbitrator" in Rule 2 shall be deleted,

(b) "nomination" shall be substituted for "appointment" in each place where it occurs and "nominated" shall be substituted for "appointed" in each place where it occurs,

(c) references to an official arbitrator shall be construed as references to a property arbitrator nominated under these Rules, and

(d) Rules 3, 4, 6 and 9 and the Schedule shall be revoked.

10. The Reference Committee may, in the case of the death or incapacity of a property arbitrator nominated for the purposes of the reference and determination of an appeal under section 33 of the Act of 1910 or a question, or if it is shown to the Reference Committee that it is expedient so to do, in any other case, at any time before the determination of the appeal or question, as the case may be, revoke the nomination of the property arbitrator and nominate another property arbitrator for the purposes of the reference and determination of the appeal or question, as the case may be, and the Reference Committee shall as soon as it has nominated the other property arbitrator, inform –

(a) in the case of an appeal, the Revenue Commissioners and the appellant, and

(b) in the case of a question, every party to , or affected by, the acquisition to which the question relates,

of the name and address of the other property arbitrator.

11. Any notice or other document required or authorised by the Rules of 1911, the Rules of 1920 or these Rules to be sent to the Reference Committee or any other person shall be deemed to be duly sent by post –

(a) in the case of the Reference Committee, to the Secretary of the Reference Committee, Four Courts, Dublin, and

(b) in the case of any other person, to his usual address

12. These Rules shall not have effect in respect of –

(a) any appeal under section 33 of the Act of 1910 in relation to which a referee has been selected under the Rules of 1911 before the 21st day of December, 1960 or

(b) any question in relation to which an official arbitrator has been selected under the Rules of 1920 before the 21st day of December, 1960.

GIVEN this 29th day of April, 1961.

**CONCHUBHAR A. MAGUIDHIR
CAHIR DAVITT, P.
PADRAIG MULCAHY**

The Minister for Finance hereby approves of the foregoing Rules in so far as they are made under section 33 of the Finance (1909-10) Act, 1910.

GIVEN under the Official Seal of the Minister for Finance, this 29th day of April, 1961.

M. BREATHNACH.

Footnotes

1   Reproduced on page 655.

2   Reproduced on page 677.

3   But see now the Interpretation Act 2005 reproduced on page 1265.

S. I. No 309 of 1967

DEATH DUTIES (PAYMENT IN STOCK OF THE 6½ EXCHEQUER STOCK, 2000-2005) REGULATIONS, 1967[1]

I, CHARLES J. HAUGHEY, Minister for Finance, in exercise of the powers conferred on me by section 22 (5) of the Finance Act, 1954 (No. 22 of 1954),[2] hereby make the following regulations:

1. These Regulations may be cited as the Death Duties (Payment in Stock of the 6½ % Exchequer Stock, 2000-2005) Regulations, 1967.

2. Stock of the 6½ % Exchequer Stock, 2000-2005 (in these Regulations referred to as the Stock) shall be accepted in payment of any death duty subject to the following conditions:

    (a) the Stock shall only be accepted in payment or in part payment (as the case may be) of any death duty on the property passing under a will or intestacy if it is shown to the satisfaction of the Revenue Commissioners that the Stock formed part of that property at the death and that the deceased person had been the beneficial owner of the Stock continuously from the date of the original subscription in respect thereof up to the date of the death or for a period of not less than three months immediately preceding that date;

    (b) the Stock shall only be accepted in payment or in part payment (as the case may be) of any death duty on property passing or deemed to pass on a death under a title other than the will or intestacy of the deceased person if it is shown to the satisfaction of the Revenue Commissioners that the Stock formed part of the property passing or deemed to pass under that title and had formed part thereof continuously from the date of the original subscription in respect of Stock up to the date of the death or for a period of not less than three months immediately preceding that date.

3. In any case in which it is desired to pay any sum on account of any death duty by means of the transfer of the Stock in pursuance of these Regulations, application should be made to the Revenue Commissioners. The application should be addressed to the Revenue Commissioners (Estate Duty Branch). Dublin, and should specify the amount of the Stock tendered, whether the holding is subject to any lien or charge whatsoever and whether it is under the applicant's control, and it not, under whose control it is.

4. The Revenue Commissioners shall arrange with the applicant the procedure to be followed in each particular case for the transfer of the Stock.

5. The value of the Stock tendered, calculated in accordance with section 22 (3) (a) of the Finance Act, 1954, shall not exceed the amount of the duty payable.

6. In all cases, the Stock shall be accepted subject to such verification as may be necessary, and subject to an undertaking to the Revenue Commissioners that all steps necessary to complete the transfer will be taken by or on behalf of the applicant, and the Revenue Commissioners may require such security as they think fit to be given for the completion of the transfer.

7. The Revenue Commissioners shall forward to the Central Bank of Ireland particulars of any holding of the Stock which has been tendered to them under these Regulations, and the Central Bank of Ireland shall be and is hereby authorised to decline to permit any dealing with, or accept any direction with regard to, such holding except upon the instruction of the Revenue Commissioners.

8. For the purposes of section 22(1) of the Finance Act, 1954[2], the prescribed account of the Minister for Finance shall be the account entitled "Account of the Minister for Finance – Stock accepted in payment of Death Duties".

GIVEN under my Official Seal,
this 29th day of December , 1967

CHARLES J. HAUGHEY
Minister for Finance

Footnotes

1 At the date of publication of this book, this was the last security available for payment of inheritance tax and was redeemed on 27th June, 2000.

2 Reproduced on page 673.

S. I. No. 279 of 1978

DOUBLE TAXATION RELIEF (TAXES ON ESTATES OF DECEASED PERSONS AND INHERITANCES AND ON GIFTS) (UNITED KINGDOM) ORDER, 1978

WHEREAS it is enacted by section 66 (1) of the Capital Acquisitions Tax Act. 1976 (No. 8 of 1976), that if the Government by order declare that arrangements specified in the order have been made with the government of any territory outside the State in relation to affording relief from double taxation in respect of gift tax or inheritance tax payable under the laws of the State and any tax imposed under the laws of that territory which is of a similar character or is chargeable by reference to death or to gifts inter vivos and that it is expedient that those arrangements should have the force of law, the arrangements shall, notwithstanding anything in any enactment, have the force of law:

AND WHEREAS it is further enacted by section 66(5) of that Act that, where such an order is proposed to be made, a draft thereof shall be laid before Dáil Eireann and the order shall not be made until a resolution approving of the draft has been passed by Dáil Eireann:

AND WHEREAS a draft of this Order has been laid before Dáil Eireann and a resolution approving of the draft has been passed by Dáil Eireann:

NOW, the Government, in exercise of the powers conferred on them by section 66 of the Capital Acquisitions Tax Act, 1976, hereby order as follows:

1. This Order may be cited as the Double Taxation Relief (Taxes on Estates of Deceased Persons and Inheritances and on Gifts) (United Kingdom) Order, 1978.

2. It is hereby declared –

    (a) that the arrangements specified in the Convention set out in the Schedule to this Order have been made with the Government of the United Kingdom in relation to affording relief from double taxation in respect of gift tax and inheritance tax payable under the laws of the State and any tax imposed under the laws of the United Kingdom which is of a similar character, and

    (b) that it is expedient that those arrangements should have the force of law.

SCHEDULE

CONVENTION BETWEEN THE GOVERNMENT OF IRELAND AND THE GOVERNMENT OF THE UNITED KINGDOM FOR THE AVOIDANCE OF DOUBLE TAXATION AND THE PREVENTION OF FISCAL EVASION WITH RESPECT TO TAXES ON ESTATES OF DECEASED PERSONS AND INHERITANCES AND ON GIFTS

The Government of Ireland and the Government of the United Kingdom;
Desiring to conclude a Convention for the avoidance of double taxation and the prevention of fiscal evasion with respect to taxes on estates of deceased persons and inheritances and on gifts;
Have agreed as follows:

ARTICLE 1

Scope

This Convention shall apply to any person who is within the scope of a tax which is the subject of this Convention, and to any property by reference to which there is a charge to such a tax.

ARTICLE 2

Taxes covered

(1) The taxes which are the subject of this Convention are:

    (a) in Ireland

        (i)   the gift tax, and

        (ii) the inheritance tax;

    (b) in the United Kingdom, the capital transfer tax.

(2) This Convention shall also apply to any identical or substantially similar taxes which are imposed by either Contracting State after the date of signature of this Convention in addition to, or in place of, the existing taxes.

ARTICLE 3

General definitions

(1) In this Convention, unless the context otherwise requires:

    (a) the term "nationals" means:

        (i)   in relation to Ireland, all citizens of Ireland and all legal persons, associations or other entities deriving their status as such from the law in force in Ireland;

        (ii) in relation to the United Kingdom, citizens of the United Kingdom and Colonies, British subjects under Section 2 of the

British Nationality Act 1948 whose notices given under that Section have been acknowledged before the date of signature of this Convention, British subjects by virtue of Section 13 (1) or Section 16 of the British Nationality Act 1948 or Section 1 of the British Nationality Act 1965, and British protected persons within the meaning of the British Nationality Act 1948; and all legal persons, associations or other entities deriving their status as such from the law in force in the United Kingdom;

(b) the term "tax" means the gift tax or the inheritance tax imposed in Ireland or the capital transfer tax imposed in the United Kingdom, as the context requires;

(c) the term "a Contracting State" and "the other Contracting State" mean Ireland or the United Kingdom, as the context requires;

(d) the term "person" includes an individual, a company and any other body of persons;

(e) the term "company" means any body corporate or any entity which is treated as a body corporate for tax purposes;

(f) the term "competent authority" means, in the case of the United Kingdom, the Commissioners of Inland Revenue or their authorised representative, and in the case of Ireland, the Revenue Commissioners or their authorised representative;

(g) the term "event" includes a death.

(2) As regards the application of this Convention by a Contracting State any term not otherwise defined shall, unless the context otherwise requires, have the meaning which it has under the law of that Contracting State relating to the taxes which are the subject of this Convention.

ARTICLE 4

Fiscal domicile

(1) For the purposes of this Convention, the question whether a person is, or was at any material time, domiciled in a Contracting State shall be determined by whether he is, or was at that time, domiciled in that Contracting State in accordance with the law of that Contracting State or is or was treated as so domiciled for the purposes of a tax which is the subject of this Convention.

(2) Where by reason of the provisions of paragraph (1) a person is, or was at any material time, domiciled in both Contracting States, then this question shall be determined in accordance with the following rules:

(a) he shall be deemed to be domiciled in the Contracting State in which he has, or had at the material time, a permanent home available to him. If he has or had a permanent home available to him in both Contracting States, the domicile shall be deemed to be in the

Contracting State with which his personal and economic relations are, or were at the material time, closer (centre of vital interests);

(b) if the Contracting State in which he has or had his centre of vital interests cannot be determined, or if he has not or had not a permanent home available to him in either Contracting State, the domicile shall be deemed to be in the Contracting State in which he has, or had at the material time, an habitual abode;

(c) if he has or had an habitual abode in both Contracting States or in neither of them, the domicile shall be deemed to be in the Contracting State of which he is, or was at the material time, a national;

(d) if he is or was a national of both Contracting States or of neither of them, the competent authorities of the Contracting States shall settle the question by mutual agreement.

ARTICLE 5

Taxing rights

(1) Subject to the following provisions of this Convention, each Contracting State shall retain the right to tax which it would have under its own law apart from this Convention.

(2) For the purposes of paragraph (2) of Article 6 and paragraph (2) of Article 8, the Contracting State with subsidiary taxing rights shall be determined as follows:

(a) in relation to property other than property comprised in a settlement, where a person's domicile has been determined under paragraph (2) of Article 4, that Contracting State shall be the Contracting State in which the person is or was, by virtue of that paragraph, not domiciled;

(b) in relation to property comprised in a settlement:

(i) where the proper law of the settlement as regards that property at the time when the settlement was made was the law of Ireland and the settlor's domicile at the time when the settlement was made has been determined under paragraph (1) of Article 4 as being in the United Kingdom, then that Contracting State shall be the United Kingdom;

(ii) where the proper law of the settlement as regards that property at the time when the settlement was made was not the law of Ireland and the settlor's domicile at that time has been determined under paragraph (1) of Article 4 as being in the United Kingdom but under its own law Ireland would impose tax on property outside its territory because at some later time either the proper law of the settlement as regards that property was the law of Ireland or the settlor's domicile has been determined under the said paragraph as being in Ireland, then that Contracting State shall be Ireland;

(iii) subject to paragraph (ii) of this subparagraph, where the proper law of the settlement as regards that property at the time when the settlement was made was not the law of Ireland and the settlor's domicile at that time has been determined under paragraph (2) of Article 4, then that Contracting State shall be the Contracting State in which the settlor was, by virtue of that paragraph, not domiciled at that time.

(3) In subparagraph (a) of paragraph (2) of this Article, the term "person" means, in Ireland the disponer, and in the United Kingdom the transferor.

(4) In paragraph (2) of this Article, "settlement" has the meaning which it has under the law of the United Kingdom relating to capital transfer tax and for the purposes of that paragraph a settlement is made when property first becomes comprised in it.

ARTICLE 6

Situs

(1) For the purposes of this Convention, the situs of any property shall be determined by each Contracting State under its own law, except that, where part of the value by reference to which tax is imposed in the United Kingdom is represented by a liability to tax which is satisfied out of property situated outside the United Kingdom, then that part of the value shall be deemed to be attributable to that property.

(2) If the situs of any property as determined by one Contracting State under paragraph (1) of this Article is not the same as that so determined by the other Contracting State, and the credit to be allowed under Article 8 is thereby affected, then the question shall be determined exclusively under the law of the Contracting State which, by virtue of paragraph (2) of Article 5, has subsidiary taxing rights or, if there is no such Contracting State, shall be determined by mutual agreement.

ARTICLE 7

Deduction of debts

In determining the amount on which tax is to be computed, permitted deductions shall be allowed under the law in force in the Contracting State in which the tax is imposed.

ARTICLE 8

Elimination of double taxation

(1) Where a Contracting State imposes tax on an event by reference to any property which is not situated in that Contracting State but is situated

in the other Contracting State, the former Contracting State shall allow against so much of its tax (as otherwise computed) as is attributable to that property a credit (not exceeding the amount of tax so attributable) equal to so much of the tax imposed in the other Contracting State on the same event as is attributable to such property.

(2) Where both Contracting States impose tax on an event by reference to any property which is not situated in either Contracting State but is situated in a third territory, the Contracting State which, by virtue of paragraph (2) of Article 5, has subsidiary taxing rights shall allow against so much of its tax (as otherwise computed) as is attributable to that property a credit (not exceeding the amount of tax so attributable) equal to so much of the tax imposed in the other Contracting State on the same event as is attributable to such property.

(3) Any credit to be allowed in Ireland under this Article in relation to gifts or inheritances shall be allowed only so as to relieve the tax imposed in Ireland on the gift or inheritance which is reduced by the payment of the tax in respect of which that credit is to be allowed; and a gift which in the United Kingdom is a chargeable transfer shall be treated as reduced by the amount of tax imposed in the United Kingdom on that gift and borne by the transferor.

(4) For the purposes of this Article:

(a) the tax attributable to any property imposed in a Contracting State is tax as reduced by the amount of any credit allowed by that Contracting State in respect of tax attributable to that property imposed in a territory other than a Contracting State;

(b) tax is imposed in a Contracting State or a territory if it is chargeable under the law of that Contracting State or territory and duly paid; and

(c) property includes property representing property.

ARTICLE 9

Time limit

Any claim for a credit or for a repayment of tax founded on the provisions of this Convention shall be made within six years from the date of the event in respect of which the claim was made.

ARTICLE 10

Non-discrimination

(1) The nationals of a Contracting State shall not be subjected in the other Contracting State to any taxation or any requirement connected therewith which is other or more burdensome that the taxation and connected requirements to which nationals of that Contracting State in the same circumstances are or may be subjected.

(2) The taxation on a permanent establishment which an enterprise of a Contracting State has in the other Contracting State shall not be less favourably levied in that other Contracting State than the taxation levied on enterprises of that other Contracting State carrying on the same activities.

(3) Enterprises of a Contracting State, the capital of which is wholly or partly owned or controlled, directly or indirectly, by one or more residents of the other Contracting State, shall not be subjected in the first-mentioned Contracting State to any taxation or any requirement connected therewith which is other or more burdensome that the taxation and connected requirements to which other similar enterprises of that first-mentioned Contracting State are or may be subjected.

(4) Nothing contained in this Article shall be construed as obliging either Contracting State to grant to individuals not domiciled in that Contracting State, any of the personal allowances, relief, and reductions for tax purposes which are granted to individuals so domiciled.

(5) In this Article the term "taxation" means taxes covered by this Convention.

ARTICLE 11

Mutual agreement procedure

(1) Where a person considers that the actions of one or both of the Contracting States result or will result for him in taxation not in accordance with the provisions of this Convention, he may, irrespective of the remedies provided by the domestic laws of those Contracting States, present his case to the competent authority of either Contracting State.

(2) The competent authority shall endeavour, if the objection appears to it to be justified and if it is not itself able to arrive at a satisfactory solution, to resolve the case by mutual agreement with the competent authority of the other Contracting State, with a view to the avoidance of taxation which is not in accordance with the provisions of this Convention.

(3) The competent authorities of the Contracting States shall endeavour to resolve by mutual agreement any difficulties or doubts arising as to the interpretation or application of this Convention.

(4) The competent authorities of the Contracting States may communicate with each other directly for the purpose of reaching an agreement in the sense of the preceding paragraphs.

ARTICLE 12

Exchange of information

(1) The competent authorities of the Contracting States shall exchange such information as is necessary for carrying out the provisions of this

Convention and the domestic laws of the Contracting States concerning taxes covered by this Convention in so far as the taxation thereunder is in accordance with this Convention. Any information so exchanged shall be treated as secret and shall not be disclosed to any persons other than persons (including a Court or administrative body) concerned with the assessment or collection of, or prosecution in respect of, or the determination of appeals in relation to, the taxes which are the subject of this Convention.

(2) In no case shall the provisions of paragraph (1) be construed so as to impose on the competent authority of either Contracting State the obligation:

(a) to carry out administrative measures at variance with the laws or administrative practice prevailing in either Contracting State;

(b) to supply particulars which are not obtainable under the laws or in the normal course of the administration of that or of the other Contracting State;

(c) to supply information which would disclose any trade, business, industrial, commercial or professional secret or trade process, or information, the disclosure of which would be contrary to public policy.

ARTICLE 13

Diplomatic and consular officials

Nothing in this Convention shall affect the fiscal privileges of diplomatic or consular officials under the general rules of international law or under the provisions of special agreements.

ARTICLE 14

Entry into force

This Convention shall enter into force on the exchange of Notes confirming that the necessary steps have been taken to give it the force of law in Ireland and in the United Kingdom and shall thereupon have effect:

(a) In Ireland:

(i) in respect of gift tax, from 28 February 1974;

(ii) in respect of inheritance tax, from 1 April 1975;

(b) In the United Kingdom:

(i) in respect of capital transfer tax other than capital transfer tax on a death, from 27 March 1974;

(ii) in respect of capital transfer tax on a death, from 13 March 1975.

ARTICLE 15

Termination

This Convention shall remain in force until terminated by one of the Contracting States. Either Contracting States may terminate the Convention, through the diplomatic channel, by giving notice of termination at least six months before the end of any calendar year after the year 1980. In such event the Convention shall cease to have effect at the end of the calendar year in which the notice is given but shall continue to apply in respect of property by reference to which there was a charge to tax which arose before the end of that calendar year.

In witness thereof the undersigned, duly authorised thereto by their respective Governments, have signed this Convention.

Done in two originals at London this 7th day of December, 1977.

For the Government of Ireland: **PAUL J. KEATING**

For the Government of the
United Kingdom: **FRANK JUDD**

S.I. No 28 of 1987

CAPITAL ACQUISITIONS TAX (HERITAGE HOUSES AND GARDENS) REGULATIONS, 1987

The Revenue Commissioners, in exercise of the powers conferred on them by section 71 of the Capital Acquisitions Tax Act, 1976 (No. 8 of 1976), hereby make the following Regulations:

1. These Regulations may be cited as the Capital Acquisitions Tax (Heritage Houses and Gardens) Regulations, 1987.

2. These Regulations shall apply to a house or garden to which, by virtue of section 39 of the Finance Act, 1978 (No. 21 of 1978), section 55 of the Capital Acquisitions Tax Act, 1976 (No. 8 of 1976), applies.

3. These Regulations shall have effect in relation to any gift or inheritance taken on or after the 1st day of February, 1987.

4. Without prejudice to the generality of section 39 (which provides for the extension of section 55 of the Capital Acquisitions Tax Act, 1976) of the Finance Act, 1978, the provision of facilities for the viewing by members of the public of a house or garden shall not be regarded as reasonable in relation to any year, which is the year 1987 or any subsequent year and which is taken into account for the purposes of subsections (1) (b) and (1) (c) of the said section 39, unless, in the opinion of the Revenue Commissioners –

   (a) subject to such temporary closure necessary for the purpose of the repair, maintenance or restoration of the house or garden as is reasonable, access to the house or garden is afforded for not less than ninety days (including not less than sixty days during the period commencing on the 1st day of May and ending on the 30th day of September) in that year;

   (b) on each day on which access to the house or garden is afforded, the access is afforded in a reasonable manner and at reasonable times for a period, or periods in the aggregate, of not less than four hours;

   (c) access to the whole or to a substantial part of the house or garden is afforded at the same time;

   (d) the price, if any, paid by members of the public in return for that access is reasonable in amount and does not operate to preclude members of the public from seeking access to the house or garden; and

   (e) adequate notice of the right of access to the house or garden and of the price, if any, payable for such access is given, by advertisement or otherwise, to members of the public.

GIVEN this 28th day of January, 1987.

L. REASON – Revenue Commissioner

S. I. No. 176 of 1990

PAYMENT OF INTEREST ON OVERPAID TAX REGULATIONS, 1990

I, Albert Reynolds, Minister for Finance, in exercise of the powers conferred on me by section 429 of the Income Tax Act, 1967 (No. 6 of 1967), as amended by section 114 of the Finance Act, 1986 (No. 13 of 1986), section 30 of the Finance Act, 1976 (No. 16 of 1976), as so amended, section 107 of the Finance Act, 1983 (No. 15 of 1983), as so amended, and section 46 of the Capital Acquisitions Tax Act, 1976 (No 8 of 1976), as amended by section 109 of the Finance Act, 1986, hereby make the following Regulations:

1. These Regulations may be cited as the Payment of Interest on Overpaid Tax Regulations, 1990.

2. These Regulations shall come into operation on the 1st day of August, 1990.

3. The rate of 0.6 per cent is hereby prescribed for the purposes of:

    (a) paragraph (a) of the proviso to subsection (4) of section 429 of the Income Tax Act, 1967 (No. 6 of 1967), as amended by section 114 of the Finance Act, 1986 (No. 13 of 1986),

    (b) subsection (4) of section 30 of the Finance Act, 1976 (No. 16 of 1976), as amended by the said section 114,

    (c) subsection (2) of section 107 of the Finance Act, 1983 (No. 15 of 1983), as amended by the said section 114, and

    (d) subsection (1) of section 46 of the Capital Acquisitions Tax Act, 1976 (No. 8 of 1976), as amended by section 109 of the Finance Act, 1986.

GIVEN under my Official Seal, this 13th day of July, 1990.

Albert Reynolds.

S. I. No. 443 of 2003

TAXES (ELECTRONIC TRANSMISSION OF CAPITAL ACQUISITIONS TAX RETURNS) (SPECIFIED PROVISIONS AND APPOINTED DAY) ORDER 2003

The Revenue Commissioners in exercise of the powers conferred on them by section 917E (inserted by section 209 of the Finance Act 1999 (No. 2 of 1999)) of the Taxes Consolidation Act 1997 (No. 39 of 1997) order as follows:

1. The Order may be cited as the Taxes (Electronic Transmission of Capital Acquisitions Tax Returns) (Specified Provisions and Appointed Day) Order 2003.

2. Section 46 of the Capital Acquisitions Tax Consolidation Act 2003 (No. 1 of 2003) apart from subsections (3), (7), (13) and (15) is specified for the purpose of Chapter 6 of Part 38 of the Taxes Consolidation Act 1997.

3. The 28th day of September 2003 is appointed in relation to returns to be made under the provisions specified in Article 2 of this Order.

GIVEN under my hand,
23 September 2003.

Josephine Feehily,
Revenue Commissioner.

Explanatory Note (issued by the Revenue Commissioners)

(This note is not part of the Instrument and does not purport to be a legal interpretation.)

This order applies the legislation governing the electronic filing of tax information to the principal capital acquisitions tax returns, and appoints a day, namely, 28th September, 2003, in relation to such returns, which ensures that the electronic filing legislation applies to returns of capital acquisitions tax which are filed on or after 29th September, 2003.

Chapter 6 of Part 38 of the Taxes Consolidation Act, 1997, provides the legislative framework whereby tax related information, required by law to be provided to the Revenue Commissioners, may be supplied electronically. The legislation only applies to information where the provision under which the information is supplied is specified in an order made by the Revenue Commissioners. Where a provision is so specified, the legislation applies to information supplied under that provision after the day appointed in the order in relation to the provision concerned. The reason for this procedure is to allow the Revenue Commissioners to manage the roll-out of the system for receiving tax related information electronically. The system will be extended to further informational items as the necessary developmental work, in relation to the electronic receipt of particular items, is completed.

S.I. No. 466 of 2003

FINANCE ACT 2003 (SECTION 146)(COMMENCEMENT) ORDER 2003

I, Charlie McCreevy, Minister for Finance, in exercise of the powers conferred on me by section 146(2) of the Finance Act 2003 (No. 3 of 2003), hereby order as follows:

1. This Order may be cited as the Finance Act 2003 (Section 146) (Commencement) Order 2003.

2. The 1st day of October 2003 is appointed as the day on which section 146 of the Finance Act 2003 (No. 3 of 2003) comes into operation.

GIVEN under my Official Seal,
25 September 2003

Charlie McCreevy

Minister for Finance

Explanatory Note (issued by the Minister for Finance)

This Order appoints the coming into effect of paragraphs (a), (b), (c) and (d) of subsection (1) of section 146 of the Finance Act, 2003, on 1st October, 2003.

Paragraph (a) of subsection (I) substitutes a new section 25 of the Capital Acquisitions Tax Consolidation Act, 2003. The new section imposes penalties based on the tax due in a tax return, in respect of the annual 1% charge imposed on the property in certain discretionary trusts, where a person, fraudulently or negligently, fails to submit a return in respect of that 1% charge to the Revenue Commissioners.

Paragraph (b) of subsection (I) inserts a new section (section 45A) into the Capital Acquisitions Tax Consolidation Act, 2003. The new section imposes an obligation on taxpayers to retain records in respect of a gift or an inheritance for a period of 6 years after the valuation date of the gift or inheritance where the taxpayer has complied with his obligations to file on time in accordance with section 46(2) of the Capital Acquisitions Tax Consolidation Act, 2003. Otherwise, they must retain records for a period of 6 years from the date that a return, additional return or statement is received by the Revenue Commissioners.

Paragraph (c) of subsection (I) inserts a new section (section 46A) into the Capital Acquisitions Tax Consolidation Act, 2003. The new section introduces an expression of doubt facility in relation to capital acquisitions tax returns. This enables a taxpayer to express doubt on a technical point, without being penalised with interest, if the taxpayer's view on the tax treatment of the point at issue is not accepted.

Paragraph (d) of subsection (1) inserts two new subsections (subsections (1A) and (5A)) into section 58 of the Capital Acquisitions Tax Consolidation Act, 2003. The new subsections impose penalties based on the tax due in a tax return where a person, fraudulently or negligently, fails to submit a capital acquisitions tax return to the Revenue Commissioners.

S.I. No. 515 of 2003

FINANCE ACT 2003 (COMMENCEMENT OF SECTION 145) ORDER 2003

I, Charlie McCreevy, Minister for Finance, in exercise of the powers conferred on my by section 145(2) of the Finance Act 2003 (No. 3 of 2003), hereby order as follows:

1. This Order may be cited as the Finance Act 2003 (Commencement of Section 145) Order 2003.

2. The 1st day of November 2003 is appointed as the day on which –

   (a) paragraph (a) of section 145(1) of the Finance Act 2003, and

   (b) paragraph (d) of section 145(1) of the Finance Act 2003 in so far as it relates to section 57 (other than subsections (2) to (5)) of the Capital Acquisitions Tax Consolidation Act 2003 (No. 1 of 2003), as respects repayments made on or after that day (except repayments in respect of claims for repayment made before that date not being claims for repayment made by virtue of section 18(3) of the Capital Acquisitions Tax Consolidation Act 2003),

   come into operation.

3. The 1st day of January 2005 is appointed as the day on which paragraphs (b) and (c) of section 145(1) come into operation.

4. The date of the making of this Order is appointed as the day on which paragraph (d) of section 145(1) of the Finance Act 2003 in so far as it relates to subsections (2) to (5) of section 57 of the Capital Acquisitions Tax Consolidation Act 2003 comes into operation.

GIVEN under my Official Seal,
31 October 2003.

Charlie McCreevy,
Minister for Finance.

Explanatory Note (issued by the Minister for Finance)
This Order appoints the coming into operation of section 145(1) of the Finance Act, 2003, in the following manner:

(a) as regards paragraph (a) of that subsection, on 1st November, 2003. That paragraph deletes section 18(5) of the Capital Acquisitions Tax Consolidation Act, 2003, which provides that, notwithstanding section 57 of that Act, interest shall not be payable on any repayment of tax which arises by virtue of section 18(3) of that Act. Section 18(3) of the Act provides that the 6 per cent charge imposed on the property comprised in certain discretionary trusts is reduced to 3 per cent in specific circumstances;

(b)   as regards paragraphs (b) and (c) of that subsection, on 1st January, 2005. Those paragraphs restrict the period within which the Revenue Commissioners may make enquiries or raise assessments in relation to underpayments of capital acquisitions tax to a period of 4 years from the date of receipt of the return by the Revenue Commissioners. This restriction will not apply where the underpayment arises from fraud or neglect on the part of the taxpayer;

(c)   as regards paragraph (d) of that subsection, in so far as it relates to section 57(2) to (5) of the Capital Acquisitions Tax Consolidation Act, 2003, on the date this Order is made (31st October, 2003). Those subsections restrict the repayment of capital acquisitions tax to valid claims made within 4 years of the later of the valuation date or the date of payment on the tax concerned. A valid claim is one where the Revenue Commissioners have been provided with all the information to enable them establish the extent of the overpayment. This measure is being introduced subject to traditional arrangements.

Paragraph (d) will come into effect other than in relation to section 57(2) to (5) of the Capital Acquisitions Tax Consolidation Act, 2003, as respects repayments of capital acquisitions tax made on or after 1st November, 2003. The new provisions will also apply to repayments made on or after 1st November, 2003, in respect of claims for repayment made by virtue of section 18(3) of the Capital Acquisitions Tax Consolidation Act, 2003. The existing provisions for interest on repayments will apply to claims for repayment made before 1st November, 2003.

Under the new section 57, interest on a repayment will only be paid where the repayment has not been made by the Revenue Commissioners within the period of 183 days of receipt of a valid claim for repayment and then only from the expiration of that period. An exception to this general rule is that interest will be paid from the date of the event giving rise to the repayment for valid claims made where the Revenue Commissioners have made an error in the operation of capital acquisitions tax. The rate of interest on such repayments will be 0.011 per cent per day or part of a day.

S.I. No. 520 of 2006

FINANCE ACT 2006 (COMMENCEMENT OF SECTION 122(1)) ORDER 2006

I, Brian Cowen, Minister for Finance, in exercise of the powers conferred on me by section 122(3) of the Finance Act 2006 (No. 6 of 2006), hereby order as follows:

1. This Order may be cited as the Finance Act 2006 (Commencement of Section 122(1)) Order 2006.

2. The 5th day of October 2006 is appointed as the day on which section 122(1) of the Finance Act 2006 (No. 6 of 2006) comes into operation.

GIVEN under my Official Seal,
5th October 2006.

Brian Cowen
Minister for Finance.

S.I. No. 521 of 2006

FINANCE ACT 2006 (SECTION 122(2)) (DESIGNATION OF COMPANY) ORDER 2006

I, Brian Cowen, Minister for Finance, in exercise of the powers conferred on me by section 122(2) of the Finance Act 2006 (No. 6 of 2006), hereby order as follows:

1. This Order may be cited as the Finance Act 2006 (Section 122(2)) (Designation of Company) Order 2006.

2. The company designated to be the Trust for the purposes of section 1003A (inserted by section 122(1) of the Finance Act 2006 (No. 6 of 2006)) of the Taxes Consolidation Act 1997 (No. 39 of 1997) is the company incorporated under the Companies Act on 30 June 2006 as The Irish Heritage Trust Limited.

GIVEN under my Official Seal,
5th October 2006.

Brian Cowen
Minister for Finance.

FOURTH PART

This Part contains sections enacted in various Finance Acts, which sections are relevant to taxes in general, including capital acquisitions tax as contained in the Capital Acquisitions Tax Act, 1976. These sections are shown, as and where amended, as they existed on 6th April, 1997, on which date they were repealed and re-enacted in the Taxes Consolidation Act, 1997.

For Contents of this Part, see page lxxxv

FINANCE ACT, 1928

Number 11 of 1928
(Enacted on 17th July, 1928)

PART V
Miscellaneous and General

Section 34[1]

Care and management of taxes and duties.

34.   (1)   . . . .

(2)   Any information acquired, whether before or after the passing of this Act, by the Revenue Commissioners in connection with any tax or duty under their care and management may be used by them for any purpose connected with any other tax or duty under their care and management.

Footnote

1   S.34(2) was unamended before it was repealed and re-enacted in s.872(1), TCA, with effect as on and from 6th April, 1997.

FINANCE ACT, 1976

Number 16 of 1976
(Enacted on 27 May, 1976)

PART I - CHAPTER VI
Income Tax, Sur-Tax, Corporation Profits Tax, Corporation Tax and Capital Gains Tax

Section 29[1]

Interest on unpaid wealth tax and capital acquisitions tax.

29. Interest payable under section 18 of the Wealth Tax Act, 1975, or section 41 of the Capital Acquisitions Tax Act, 1976, shall not be allowed in computing any income, profits or losses for any of the purposes of the Tax Acts or of any of the enactments relating to corporation profits tax.

Footnote

1   S.29 took effect as on and from 6th April, 1976, and was unamended before it was repealed and re-enacted in s.1089(2), TCA, with effect as on and from 6th April, 1997.

Section 34[1]

Inspection of documents and records.

34.   (1)   In this section—

"authorised officer" means an officer of the Revenue Commissioners authorised by them in writing to exercise the powers conferred by this section;

"property" means any asset relating to a tax liability;

"records" means any document, or any other written or printed material in any form including any information stored, maintained or preserved by means of any mechanical or electronic device, whether or not stored, maintained or preserved in a legible form, which a person is obliged by any provision relating to tax to keep, to retain, to issue, to produce for inspection or which may be inspected under any provision relating to tax;

"tax" means any tax, duty, levy or charge under the care and management of the Revenue Commissioners;

"tax liability" means any existing liability to tax or further liability to tax which may be established by an authorised officer following the exercise or performance of his powers or duties under this section.

(2) (a) An authorised officer may at all reasonable times enter any premises or place where he has reason to believe that—

    (i) any trade or profession or other activity, the profits or gains of which are chargeable to tax, is or has been carried on,

    (ii) anything is or has been done in connection with any trade, profession or other activity the profits or gains of which are chargeable to tax,

    (iii) any records relating to—

        (I) any trade, profession, other source of profits or gains or chargeable gains,

        (II) any tax liability, or

        (III) any repayments of tax in regard to any person

    are or may be kept, or

    (iv) any property is or has been located,

and may

    (A) require any person who is on those premises or in that place, other than a person who is there to purchase goods or to receive a service, to produce any records or property,

    (B) if he has reason to believe that any of the records or property which he has required to be produced to him under the provisions of this subsection have not been produced, search on those premises or in that place for those records or property,

    (C) examine any records or property and take copies of or extracts from any records,

    (D) remove any records and retain them for a reasonable time for the purposes of their further examination or for the purposes of any legal proceedings instituted by an officer of the Revenue Commissioners, or for the purposes of any criminal proceedings, and

    (E) examine property listed in any records.

(b) An authorised officer may, in the exercise or performance of his powers or duties under this section, require any person, whom he has reason to believe—

    (i) is or was carrying on any trade, profession or other activity the profits or gains of which are chargeable to tax,

    (ii) is or was liable to any tax, or

(iii) has information relating to any tax liability,

to give the authorised officer all reasonable assistance including providing information and explanations or furnishing documents and making available for inspection property as required by the authorised officer in relation to any tax liability or any repayment of tax in regard to any person.

(c) Nothing in this subsection shall be construed as requiring any person carrying on a profession, or any person employed by any person carrying on a profession, to produce to an authorised officer any documents relating to a client, other than such documents—

(i) as pertain to the payment of fees to the person carrying on the profession or to other financial transactions of the person carrying on the profession,

(ii) as are otherwise material to the tax liability of the person carrying on the profession, or

(iii) as are already required to be provided following a request issued under the provisions of section 16 (inserted by section 101 of the Finance Act, 1991) of the Stamp Act, 1891,

and, in particular, he shall not be required to disclose any information or professional advice of a confidential nature given to a client.

(d) This subsection shall not apply to any premises or place where a banking business, within the meaning of the Central Bank Act, 1971, is carried on or to any person, or an employee of any person, carrying on such a business.

(e) (i) An authorised officer shall not, without the consent of the occupier, enter any premises, or that portion of any premises, which is occupied wholly and exclusively as a private residence, except on production by such officer of a warrant issued by a Judge of the District Court expressly authorising the authorised officer to so enter.

(ii) A Judge of the District Court may issue a warrant under subparagraph (i), if satisfied by information on oath that it is proper for him to do so for the purposes of this section.

(3) A person who does not comply with any requirement of an authorised officer in the exercise or performance of his powers

or duties under this section shall be liable to a penalty of £1,000.

(4) An authorised officer, when exercising or performing his powers or duties under this section, shall on request show his authorisation for the purposes of this section.

Footnote

1   S.34 took effect as on and from 6th April, 1976. It was substituted in full by s.232, FA 1992, with effect as on and from 28th May, 1992, and was repealed and re-enacted in s.905, TCA, with effect as on and from 6th April, 1997.

FINANCE ACT, 1977

Number 18 of 1977
(Enacted on 1st June, 1977)

PART V
Miscellaneous

Section 53[1]

Residence treatment of donors of gifts to the State.

53.   (1)   In this section—

"the Acts" means—

(a)   the Tax Acts,

(b)   the Capital Gains Tax Act, 1975,

(c)   the Wealth Tax Act, 1975, and

(d)   the Capital Acquisitions Tax Act, 1976;

"donor" means an individual who makes a gift to the State;

"gift" means a gift of property to the State which, upon acceptance of the gift by the Government pursuant to the State Property Act, 1954, becomes vested, pursuant to that Act, in a State authority within the meaning of that Act;

"Irish tax" means any tax imposed by the Acts;

"property" includes interests and rights of any description;

"relevant date", in relation to an individual (being a donor or spouse of a donor), means the date (being a date not earlier than the 1st day of September, 1974) on which he leaves the State for the purpose of residence (other than occasional residence) outside the State;

"tax in that country" means any tax imposed in that country which is identical with or substantially similar to Irish tax;

"visits" means—

(a)   in relation to a donor, visits by him to the State after the relevant date for the purpose of advising on the management of the property which is the subject of the gift, being visits that are, in the aggregate, less than 182 days in any year of assessment in which they are made, and

(b)   in relation to the spouse of a donor, visits by the said spouse when accompanying the donor on visits of the kind referred to in paragraph (a).

(2)   Where, for any year of assessment, a person (being a donor or the spouse of a donor) is resident in a country outside the State for the purposes of tax in that country and is chargeable to that tax without

any limitation as to chargeability, then, notwithstanding anything to the contrary in the Tax Acts—

(a) as respects the year of assessment in which the relevant date occurs, that person shall not, as from the relevant date, be regarded as ordinarily resident in the State for the purposes of Irish tax, and

(b) as respects any subsequent year of assessment, in determining whether that person is resident or ordinarily resident in the State for the purposes of Irish tax, visits shall be disregarded.

Footnote

1   S.53 took effect as on and from 1st June, 1977, and was unamended before it was repealed and re-enacted in s.825, TCA, with effect as on and from 6th April, 1997.

FINANCE ACT, 1981

Number 16 of 1981
(Enacted on 28th May, 1981)

PART VI
Miscellaneous

Section 52[1]

Disclosure of information to the Ombudsman.

52. Any obligation to maintain secrecy or other restriction upon the disclosure or production of information (including documents) obtained by or furnished to the Revenue Commissioners, or any person on their behalf, for taxation purposes, shall not apply to the disclosure or production of information (including documents) to the Ombudsman for the purposes of an examination or investigation by the Ombudsman, under the Ombudsman Act, 1980, of any action (within the meaning of the Ombudsman Act, 1980) taken by or on behalf of the Revenue Commissioners, being such an action taken in the performance of administrative functions in respect of any tax or duty under the care and management of the Revenue Commissioners.

Footnote

1   S.52 took effect as on and from 28th May, 1981, and was unamended before it was repealed and re-enacted in s.1093, TCA, with effect as on and from 6th April, 1997.

FINANCE ACT, 1983

Number 15 of 1983
(Enacted on 8th June, 1983)

PART I - CHAPTER IV
Anti-Avoidance and Anti-Evasion

Section 19A[1]

Anonymity.

19A. (1) In this section—

"authorised officer" means an officer of the Revenue Commissioners nominated by them to be a member of the staff of the body;

"the body" has the same meaning as in section 19;

"proceedings" includes any hearing before the Appeal Commissioners (within the meaning of the Revenue Acts);

"the Revenue Acts" means the Acts within the meaning of section 94 of this Act together with Chapter IV of Part II of the Finance Act, 1992, and any instruments made thereunder and any instruments made under any other enactment and relating to tax;

"tax" means any tax, duty, levy or charge under the care and management of the Revenue Commissioners.

(2) Notwithstanding any requirement made by or under any enactment or any other requirement in administrative and operational procedures, including internal procedures, all reasonable care shall be taken to ensure that the identity of an authorised officer shall not be revealed.

(3) In particular and without prejudice to the generality of subsection (2)—

[(a) where, for the purposes of exercising or performing his or her powers or duties under the Revenue Acts in pursuance of the functions of the body, an authorised officer may, apart from this section, be required to produce or show any written authority or warrant of appointment under those Acts or otherwise to identify himself or herself, the authorised officer shall—

(i) not be required to produce or show any such authority or warrant of appointment or to so identify himself or herself, for the purposes of exercising or performing his or her powers or duties under those Acts, and

(ii) be accompanied by a member of the Garda Síochána who shall, on request, by a person affected identify himself or herself as a member of the Garda Síochána and shall state that he or she is accompanied by an authorised officer,]²

(b)   where, in pursuance of the functions of the body, an authorised officer exercises or performs in writing any of his or her powers or duties under the Revenue Acts or any provisions of any other enactment, whenever passed, which relate to Revenue, such exercise or performance of his or her powers or duties shall be done in the name of the body and not in the name of the individual authorised officer involved, notwithstanding any provision to the contrary in any of those enactments,

(c)   in any proceedings arising out of the exercise or performance, in pursuance of the functions of the body, of powers or duties by an authorised officer, any documents relating to such proceedings shall not reveal the identity of any authorised officer, notwithstanding any requirements in any provision to the contrary, and in any proceedings the identity of such officer other than as an authorised officer shall not be revealed other than to the judge or the Appeal Commissioner, as the case may be, hearing the case,

(d)   where, in pursuance of the functions of the body, an authorised officer is required, in any proceedings, to give evidence and the judge or the Appeal Commissioner, as the case may be, is satisfied that there are reasonable grounds in the public interest to direct that evidence to be given by such authorised officer should be given in the hearing and not in the sight of any person, he or she may so direct.

Footnotes

1   S.19A was inserted by s.12, DCITPA, with effect as on and from 30th July, 1996. It was repealed and re-enacted in S.859, TCA, with effect as on and from 6th April, 1997.

2   As substituted by s.23, CABA, with effect as on and from 11th October, 1996.

Section 23[1]

Publication of names of tax defaulters.

23.   (1)   In this section "the Acts" means –

(a)   the Tax Acts,

(b)   the Capital Gains Tax Acts,

(c)   the Value-Added Tax Act, 1972, and the enactments amending or extending that Act,

(d)   the Capital Acquisitions Tax Act, 1976, and the enactments amending or extending that Act,

(e)   the statutes relating to stamp duty and to the management of that duty, and

(f)   Part VI,

and any instruments made thereunder.

[(2) The Revenue Commissioners shall, as respects each relevant period (being the period beginning on the 1st day of January, 1997, and ending on the 30th day of June, 1997, and each subsequent period of three months beginning with the period ending on the 30th day of September, 1997), compile a list of names and addresses and the occupations or descriptions of every person—

(a)   upon whom a fine or other penalty was imposed by a court under any of the Acts during that relevant period,

(b)   upon whom a fine or other penalty was otherwise imposed by a court during that relevant period in respect of an act or omission by the person in relation to tax, or

(c)   in whose case the Revenue Commissioners, pursuant to an agreement made with the person in that relevant period, refrained from initiating proceedings for recovery of any fine or penalty of the kind mentioned in paragraphs (a) and (b) and, in lieu of initiating such proceedings, accepted, or undertook to accept, a specified sum of money in settlement of any claim by the Revenue Commissioners in respect of any specified liability of the person under any of the Acts for—

    (i)   payment of any tax,

    (ii)   payment of interest thereon, and

    (iii) a fine or other monetary penalty in respect thereof.][2]

[(3) Notwithstanding any obligation as to secrecy imposed on them by the Acts or the Official Secrets Act, 1963—

(a)   the Revenue Commissioners shall, before the expiration of three months from the end of each relevant period, cause each such list referred to in subsection (2) in relation to that period to be published in Iris Oifigiúil, and

(b)   the Revenue Commissioners may, at any time, cause any such list referred to in subsection (2) to be publicised in such manner as they shall consider appropriate.][3]

(4) Paragraph (c) of subsection (2) does not apply in relation to a person in whose case—

(a)   the Revenue Commissioners are satisfied that, before any investigation or inquiry had been commenced by them or by any of their officers into any matter occasioning a liability referred to in the said paragraph of the person, the person had voluntarily furnished to them complete information in relation to and full particulars of the said matter, or [(aa) the provisions of section 72 of the Finance Act, 1988, or section 3 of the Waiver of Certain Tax, Interest and Penalties Act, 1993, apply, or][4]

(b) the specified sum referred to in the said paragraph (c) does not exceed £10,000 or was paid on or before the 31st day of December, 1983.

(5) Any such list as is referred to in subsection (2) shall specify in respect of each person named in the list such particulars as the Revenue Commissioners think fit—

(a) of the matter occasioning the fine or penalty of the kind referred to in subsection (2) imposed on the person or, as the case may be, the liability of that kind to which the person was subject, and

(b) of any interest, fine or other monetary penalty, and of any other penalty or sanction, to which that person was liable, or which was imposed on him by a court, and which was occasioned by the said matter.

(6) In this section "tax" means income tax, capital gains tax, corporation tax, value-added tax, gift tax, inheritance tax, residential property tax and stamp duty.

Footnotes

1   S.23, as originally enacted, applied to the year 1984 and subsequent years. It was repealed and re-enacted in s.1086, TCA, with effect as on and from 6th April, 1997.

2   S.23(2) was extended by s.240 (a), FA 1992, as respects the year 1992 and subsequent years and was substituted in full by s.158(a), FA 1997, as respects the year 1997 and subsequent years.

3   S.23(3) was extended by s.240(b), FA 1992, as respects the year 1992 and subsequent years and was substituted in full by s.158(b), FA 1997, as respects the year 1997 and subsequent years.

4   S.23(4)(aa) was enacted by s.72(7), FA 1988, with effect as on and from 25th May, 1988, to include the provisions of s.72, FA 1988, and was extended by s.3(7), WCTIPA, with effect as on and from 14th July, 1993, to include the provisions of s.3, WCTIPA.

PART V
Revenue Offences

Section 94[1]

Revenue offences.

94.   (1)   In this Part—

"the Acts" means

(a)   the Customs Acts,

(b)   the statutes relating to the duties of excise and to the management of those duties,

(c)   the Tax Acts,

(d)   the Capital Gains Tax Acts,

(e)   the Value-Added Tax Act, 1972, and the enactments amending or extending that Act,

(f)   the Capital Acquisitions Tax Act, 1976, and the enactments amending or extending that Act,

(g)   the statutes relating to stamp duty and to the management of that duty, and

(h)   Part VI,

and any instruments made thereunder and any instruments made under any other enactment and relating to tax;

["an authorised officer" means an officer of the Revenue Commissioners authorised by them in writing to exercise any of the powers conferred by the Acts;][2]

"tax" means any tax, duty, levy or charge under the care and management of the Revenue Commissioners.

(2)   A person shall, without prejudice to any other penalty to which he may be liable, be guilty of an offence under this section if, after the date of the passing of this Act, he—

(a)   knowingly or wilfully delivers any incorrect return, statement or accounts or knowingly or wilfully furnishes any incorrect information in connection with any tax,

(b)   knowingly aids, abets, assists, incites or induces another person to make or deliver knowingly or wilfully any incorrect return, statement or accounts in connection with any tax,

(c)   claims or obtains relief or exemption from, or repayment of, any tax, being a relief, exemption or repayment to which, to his knowledge, he is not entitled,

(d)   knowingly or wilfully issues or produces any incorrect invoice, receipt, instrument or other document in connection with any tax,

[(dd) (i)   fails to make any deduction required to be made by him under section 32 (1) of the Finance Act, 1986,

(ii)   fails, having made the deduction, to pay the sum deducted to the Collector-General within the time specified in that behalf in section 33 (3) of that Act, or

(iii)   fails to pay to the Collector-General an amount on account of appropriate tax (within the meaning of Chapter IV of Part I of that Act) within the time specified in that behalf in section 33 (4) of that Act,][3] [(ddd) (i) fails to make any deduction required to be made by him under section 18 (5) of the Finance Act, 1989, or

(ii) fails, having made the deduction, to pay the sum deducted to the Collector-General within the time specified in paragraph 1 (3) of the First Schedule to that Act.][4]

(e) knowingly or wilfully fails to comply with any provision of the Acts requiring –

(i) the furnishing of a return of income, profits or gains, or of sources of income, profits or gains, for the purposes of any tax,

(ii) the furnishing of any other return, certificate, notification, particulars, or any statement or evidence, for the purposes of any tax,

(iii) the keeping or retention of books, records, accounts or other documents for the purposes of any tax, or

(iv) the production of books, records, accounts or other documents, when so requested, for the purposes of any tax,

[(ee) knowingly or wilfully, and within the time limits specified for their retention, destroys, defaces, or conceals from an authorised officer –

(i) any documents, or

(ii) any other written or printed material in any form, including any information stored, maintained or preserved by means of any mechanical or electronic device, whether or not stored, maintained or preserved in a legible form, which a person is obliged by any provision of the Acts to keep, to issue or to produce for inspection,][5]

(f) fails to remit any income tax payable pursuant to Chapter IV of Part V of the Income Tax Act, 1967, and the regulations thereunder, or section 7 of the Finance Act, 1968, and the said regulations, or value-added tax within the time specified in that behalf in relation to income tax or value-added tax, as the case may be, by the Acts, or

(g) obstructs or interferes with any officer of the Revenue Commissioners, or any other person, in the exercise or performance of powers or duties under the Acts for the purposes of any tax.

(3) A person guilty of an offence under this section shall be liable —

[(a) on summary conviction to a fine of £1,000 which may be mitigated to not less than one fourth part thereof or, at the discretion of the court, to imprisonment for a term not exceeding 12 months or to both the fine and the imprisonment, or][6]

(b) on conviction on indictment, to a fine not exceeding £10,000 or, at the discretion of the court, to imprisonment for a term not exceeding 5 years or to both the fine and the imprisonment.

(4) Section 13 of the Criminal Procedure Act, 1967, shall apply in relation to an offence under this section as if, in lieu of the penalties specified in subsection (3) of the said section 13, there were specified therein the penalties provided for by subsection (3) (a) of this section, and the reference in subsection (2) (a) of the said section 13 to the penalties provided for in the said subsection (3) shall be construed and have effect accordingly.

(5) Where an offence under this section is committed by a body corporate and the offence is shown to have been committed with the consent or connivance of any person who, when the offence was committed, was a director, manager, secretary or other officer of the body corporate, or a member of the committee of management or other controlling authority of the body corporate, that person shall also be deemed to be guilty of the offence and may be proceeded against and punished accordingly.

(6) In any proceedings under this section, a return or statement delivered to an inspector or other officer of the Revenue Commissioners under any provision of the Acts and purporting to be signed by any person shall be deemed, until the contrary is proved, to have been so delivered, and to have been signed, by that person.

(7) Notwithstanding the provisions of any other enactment, proceedings in respect of an offence under this section may be instituted within 10 years from the date of the commission of the offence or incurring of the penalty (as the case may be).

(8) Section 1 of the Probation of Offenders Act, 1907, shall not apply in relation to offences under this section.

(9) The provisions of sections 128 (4), 500 (4), 501 (3), 502 (3), 506 and 507 of the Income Tax Act, 1967, and sections 26 (6) and 27 (7) of the Value-Added Tax Act, 1972, shall, with any necessary modifications, apply for the purposes of this section as they apply for the purposes of those provisions, including, in the case of such of those provisions as were applied by the Capital Gains Tax Act,

1975, the Corporation Tax Act, 1976, or Part VI, the purposes of those provisions as so applied.

Footnotes

1   S.94 took effect after 8th June, 1983, and was repealed and re-enacted in s.1078, TCA, with effect as on and from 6th April, 1997.

2   As inserted by s.243(a)(i), FA 1992, with effect as on and from 28th May, 1992.

3   As inserted by s.40(2), FA 1986, with effect as on and from 6th April, 1986.

4   As inserted by para. 3(2), First Sch., FA 1989, with effect as on and from 24th May, 1989.

5   As inserted by para. 13(2), Fifth Sch., Part I, FA 1996, with effect as on and from 6th April, 1996 (replacing a similar provision erroneously inserted in s.94(1) by s.243(a)(ii), FA 1992).

6   As amended by s.243(b), FA 1992, with effect as on and from 28th May, 1992.

FINANCE ACT, 1986

Number 13 of 1986
(Enacted on 27th May, 1986)

PART VI
Miscellaneous

Section 112[1]

Application of Age of Majority Act, 1985.

112. (1) Notwithstanding the provisions of subsection (4) of [section 2 of the Age of Majority Act, 1985][2], subsections (2) and (3) of the said section 2 shall, subject to subsection (2), apply and have effect for the purposes of the Income Tax Acts and any other statutory provision (within the meaning of the said Act) dealing with the imposition, repeal, remission, alteration or regulation of any tax or other duty under the care and management of the Revenue Commissioners and accordingly subparagraph (vii) of paragraph (b) of the said subsection (4) shall cease to have effect.

(2) Nothing in subsection (1) shall affect a claimant's entitlement to a deduction under section 138A (inserted by the Finance Act, 1985) or section 141 (inserted by this Act) of the Income Tax Act, 1967.

(3) This section shall be deemed to have come into force and shall take effect as on and from the 6th day of April, 1986, and so far as it relates to gift tax or inheritance tax shall have effect in relation to gifts and inheritances taken on or after that date.

Footnotes

1   S.112 was unamended before it was repealed and re-enacted in s.7, TCA, with effect as on and from 6th April, 1997.

2   Reproduced on page 782.

Section 113[1]

Use of electronic data processing.

113. (1) In this section—

"the Acts" means—

(a) the Tax Acts,

(b) the Capital Gains Tax Acts,

(c) [the Value-Added Tax Act, 1972,][2]

    (d) the Capital Acquisitions Tax Act, 1976, and the enactments amending or extending that Act, and

    (e) Part VI of the Finance Act, 1983,

and any instruments made thereunder;

"records" means documents which a person is obliged by any provision of the Acts to keep, to issue or to produce for inspection, and any other written or printed material;

"tax" means income tax, corporation tax, capital gains tax, value-added tax or residential property tax, as the case may be.

(2) Subject to the agreement of the Revenue Commissioners, records may be stored, maintained, transmitted, reproduced or communicated, as the case may be, by any electronic, photographic or other process approved of by the Revenue Commissioners, and in circumstances where the use of such process has been agreed by them and subject to such conditions as they may impose.

(3) Where, in pursuance of subsection (2), records are preserved by electronic, photographic or other process, a statement contained in a document produced by any such process shall, subject to the rules of court, be admissible in evidence in any proceedings, whether civil or criminal, to the same extent as the records themselves.

(4) ....[3]

Footnotes

1   S.113 took effect as on and from 27th May, 1986. It was repealed and re-enacted in s.887, TCA, with effect as on and from 6th April, 1997.

2   As amended by s.99, FA 1993, with effect as on and from 17th June, 1993.

3   This and subsequent subsections do not relate to CAT.

FINANCE ACT, 1988

Number 12 of 1988
(Enacted on 25th May, 1988)

PART VI
Miscellaneous

Section 71[1]

Poundage and certain other fees.

71. (1) (a) In this section –

"the Acts" means –

(a) the Tax Acts,

(b) the Capital Gains Tax Acts,

(c) the Value-Added Tax Act, 1972, and the enactments amending or extending that Act,

(d) the Capital Acquisitions Tax Act, 1976, and the enactments amending or extending that Act, and

(e) Part VI of the Finance Act, 1983, and the enactments amending or extending that Part,

and any instruments made thereunder;

"certificate" means a certificate issued under section 485 of the Income Tax Act, 1967;

"county registrar" means a person appointed to be a county registrar under section 35 of the Court Officers Act, 1926;

"defaulter" means a person specified or certified in an execution order or certificate upon whom a relevant amount specified or certified in the order or certificate is leviable;

"execution order" has the same meaning as in the Enforcement of Court Orders Act, 1926;

"fees" means the fees known as poundage fees payable under section 14 (1) of the Enforcement of Court Orders Act, 1926, and orders made thereunder for services in or about the execution of an execution order directing or authorising the execution of an order of a court by the seizure and sale of a person's property or, as may be appropriate, the fees, corresponding to the fees aforesaid, payable under section 485 of the Income Tax Act, 1967, for the execution of a certificate;

"interest on unpaid tax" means interest that has accrued under any provision of the Acts providing for the charging of interest in respect of unpaid tax including interest on an undercharge of tax which is attributable to fraud or neglect;

"relevant amount" means an amount of tax or interest on unpaid tax;

"tax" means any tax, duty, levy or charge which, in accordance with any provision of the Acts, is placed under the care and management of the Revenue Commissioners.

(b) References, as respects an execution order, to a relevant amount include references to any amount of costs specified in the order.

(2) (a) Where—

    (i) an execution order or certificate specifying or certifying a defaulter and relating to a relevant amount is lodged, whether before or after the passing of this Act, with the appropriate sheriff or county registrar for execution,

    (ii) the sheriff or, as the case may be, the county registrar gives notice to the defaulter of the lodgement or of his intention to execute the execution order or certificate by seizure of the property of the defaulter to which it relates, or demands payment by the defaulter of the relevant amount, and

    (iii) the whole or part of the relevant amount is paid to the sheriff or, as the case may be, the county registrar or to the Collector-General, after the giving of the notice or the making of the demand, aforesaid,

then, for the purpose of the liability of the defaulter for the payment of fees and of the exercise of any rights or powers in relation to the collection of fees for the time being vested by law in sheriffs and county registrars—

    (I) the sheriff or, as the case may be, the county registrar shall be deemed to have entered, in the execution of the execution order or certificate, into possession of the property aforesaid, and

    (II) the payment mentioned in subparagraph (iii) shall be deemed to have been levied, in the execution of the execution order or certificate, by the sheriff or, as the case may be, the county registrar,

and fees shall be payable by the defaulter to such sheriff or, as the case may be, county registrar accordingly in respect of the payment mentioned in subparagraph (iii).

(b) Paragraph (a) shall, with any necessary modifications, apply also in a case in which such a notice or demand as is mentioned in subparagraph (ii) of that paragraph was given or made before the passing of this Act if the fees concerned were paid to the sheriff or county registrar concerned before such passing.

Footnote

1   S.71 took effect as on and from 25th May, 1988, and was unamended before it was repealed and re-enacted in s.1006, TCA, with effect as on and from 6th April, 1997.

Section 73[1]

Deductions from payments due to defaulters of amounts due in relation to tax.

73. (1) (a) This section shall apply and have effect as on and from the 1st day of October, 1988.

(b) In this section, except where the context otherwise requires —

["the Acts" means —

(i) the Customs Acts,

(ii) the statutes relating to the duties of excise and to the management of those duties,

(iii) the Tax Acts,

(iv) the Capital Gains Tax Acts,

(v) the Value-Added Tax Act, 1972, and the enactments amending or extending that Act,

(vi) the Capital Acquisitions Tax Act, 1976, and the enactments amending or extending that Act, and

(vii) the Stamp Act, 1891, and the enactments amending or extending that Act,

and any instrument made thereunder;][1]

"additional debt" means, in relation to a relevant person who has received a notice of attachment in respect of a taxpayer, any amount which, at any time after the time of the receipt by the relevant person of the notice of attachment but before the end of the relevant period in relation to the notice, would be a debt due by him to the taxpayer if a notice of attachment were received by him at that time;

"debt" means, in relation to a notice of attachment given to a relevant person in respect of a taxpayer and in relation to the said relevant person and tax payer, the amount or aggregate amount of any money which, at the time the notice of attachment is received by the relevant person, is due by the relevant person (whether on his own account, or as an agent or trustee) to the taxpayer, irrespective of whether the taxpayer has applied for the payment (to himself or any other person) or for the withdrawal of all or part of the money:

Provided that —

[(i) where a relevant person is a financial institution, any amount or aggregate amount of money, including interest thereon, which at that time is a deposit held by the relevant person —

(I) to the credit of the taxpayer for his sole benefit,

or

(II)   to the credit of the taxpayer and any other person or persons for their joint benefit,

shall be regarded as a debt due by the relevant person to the taxpayer at that time,]²

(ii)   any amount of money due by the relevant person to the taxpayer as emoluments under a contract of service shall not be so regarded, and

(iii)   where there is a dispute as to an amount of money which is due by the relevant person to the taxpayer, the amount in dispute shall be disregarded for the purposes of determining the amount of the debt;

[Provided also that, in the case of paragraph (i) of the preceding proviso, a deposit held by a relevant person which is a financial institution to the credit of the taxpayer and any other person or persons (hereafter referred to in this proviso as "the other party or parties") for their joint benefit shall be deemed (unless evidence to the contrary is produced to the satisfaction of the relevant person within 10 days of the giving of the notices specified in paragraph (c) of subsection (2)) to be held to the benefit of the taxpayer and the other party or parties to the deposit equally and, accordingly, only the portion thereof so deemed shall be regarded as a debt due by the relevant person to the taxpayer at that time and where such evidence is produced within the specified time only so much of the deposit as is shown to be held to the benefit of the taxpayer shall be regarded as a debt due by the relevant person to the taxpayer at that time;]³

"deposit" means a sum of money paid to a financial institution on terms under which it will be repaid with or without interest and either on demand or at a time or in circumstances agreed by or on behalf of the person making the payment and the person to whom it is made;

"emoluments" means anything assessable to income tax under Schedule E;

"financial institution" means a holder of a licence issued under section 9 of the Central Bank Act, 1971, or a person referred to in section 7 (4) of that Act and includes a branch of a financial institution that records deposits in its books as liabilities of the branch;

"further return" means a return made by a relevant person under subsection (4);

["interest on unpaid tax", in relation to a specified amount specified in a notice of attachment, means interest, that has accrued to the date on which the notice of attachment is given, under any provision of the Acts providing for the charging of interest in respect of the unpaid tax, including interest on an undercharge of tax which is attributable to fraud or neglect, specified in the notice of attachment;][4]

"notice of attachment" means a notice under subsection (2);

"notice of revocation" means a notice under subsection (10);

"penalty" means a monetary penalty imposed on a taxpayer under a provision of the Acts;

"relevant period", in relation to a notice of attachment, means, as respects the relevant person to whom the notice of attachment is given, the period commencing at the time at which the notice is received by the relevant person and ending on —

(i)   the date on which he completes the payment to the Revenue Commissioners out of the debt, or the aggregate of the debt and any additional debt, due by him to the taxpayer named in the notice, of an amount equal to the specified amount in relation to the taxpayer,

(ii)   the date on which he receives a notice of revocation of the notice of attachment, or

(iii) where he or the taxpayer named in the notice is —

(I)   declared bankrupt, the date he or the taxpayer is so declared, or

(II)   a company which commences to be wound up, the "relevant date" within the meaning of section 285 of the Companies Act, 1963, in relation to the winding up,

whichever is the earliest;

"relevant person" means, in relation to a taxpayer, a person in respect of whom the Revenue Commissioners have reason to believe that he may have, at the time a notice of attachment is received by him in respect of a taxpayer, a debt due to the taxpayer;

"return" means a return made by a relevant person under subsection (2) (a) (iii);

"specified amount" has the meaning assigned to it by subsection (2) (a) (ii);

"tax" means any tax, duty, levy or charge which, in accordance with any provision of the Acts, is placed under the care and management of the Revenue Commissioners;

"taxpayer" means a person who is liable to pay, remit or account for tax to the Revenue Commissioners under the Acts.

(2) (a) Subject to subsection (3), where a taxpayer has made default, whether before or after the passing of this Act, in paying, remitting, or accounting for, any tax, interest on unpaid tax, or penalty to the Revenue Commissioners, the Revenue Commissioners may, if the taxpayer has not made good the default, give to a relevant person in relation to the taxpayer a notice in writing (in this section referred to as "the notice of attachment") in which is entered –

    (i)   the taxpayer's name and address,

    [(ii) (I)   the amount or aggregate amount, or

          (II) in a case where more than one notice of attachment is given to a relevant person or relevant persons in respect of a taxpayer, a portion of the amount or aggregate amount,

of the taxes, interest on unpaid taxes and penalties in respect of which the taxpayer is in default at the time of the giving of the notice or notices of attachment (the said amount, aggregate amount, or portion of the amount or aggregate amount, as the case may be, being referred to in this section as "the specified amount"),][5]

    (iii) a direction to the relevant person –

          (I)   to deliver to the Revenue Commissioners, within the period of 10 days from the time at which the notice of attachment is received by him, a return in writing specifying whether or not any debt is due by him to the taxpayer at the time the notice is received by him, and if any debt is so due, specifying the amount of the debt:

Provided that where the amount of the debt due by the relevant person to the taxpayer is equal to or greater than the specified amount in relation to the taxpayer, the amount of the debt specified in the return shall be an amount equal to the specified amount,

[Provided also that where the relevant person is a financial institution and the debt due by the relevant person to the taxpayer is part of a deposit held to the credit of the taxpayer and any other person or persons to their joint benefit the said return shall be made within a period of 10 days from –

          (A) the expiry of the period specified in the notices to be given under paragraph (c), or

          (B) the production of the evidence referred to in paragraph (c) (II),][6]

        and

(II) if the amount of any debt is so specified to pay to the Revenue Commissioners within the period aforesaid a sum equal to the amount of the debt so specified.

(b) A relevant person to whom a notice of attachment has been given shall comply with the direction in the notice.

[(c) Where a relevant person which is a financial institution is given a notice of attachment and the debt due by the relevant person to the taxpayer is part of a deposit held by the relevant person to the credit of the taxpayer and any other person or persons (hereafter in this paragraph referred to as "the other party or parties") for their joint benefit, the relevant person shall, on receipt of the notice of attachment, give to the taxpayer and the other party or parties to the deposit a notice in writing in which is entered —

(i) the taxpayer's name and address,

(iii) the name and address of the person to whom a notice under this paragraph is given,

(iii) the name and address of the relevant person, and

(iv) the specified amount,

and which states that —

(I) a notice of attachment under this section has been received in respect of the taxpayer,

(II) under this section, a deposit is deemed (unless evidence to the contrary is produced to the satisfaction of the relevant person within 10 days of the giving of the notice under this paragraph) to be held to the benefit of the taxpayer and the other party or parties to the deposit equally, and

(III) unless such evidence is produced within the period specified in the notice given under this paragraph, a sum equal to the amount of the deposit so deemed to be held to the benefit of the taxpayer, and, accordingly, regarded as a debt due to the taxpayer by the relevant person, shall be paid to the Revenue Commissioners where that amount is equal to or less than the specified amount and where that amount is greater than the specified amount an amount equal to the specified amount shall be paid to the Revenue Commissioners.][7]

(3) An amount in respect of tax, interest on unpaid tax or a penalty, as respects which a taxpayer is in default as specified in subsection (2) shall not be entered in a notice of attachment unless —

(a) a period of one month has expired from the date on which such default commenced, and [(b) the Revenue Commissioners have given the taxpayer a notice in writing (whether or not the document containing the notice also contains other information being communicated by the Revenue Commissioners to the taxpayer), not later than 7 days before the date of the receipt by the relevant person or relevant persons concerned of a notice of attachment, stating that, if the amount is not paid, it may be specified in a notice or notices of attachment and recovered under this section from a relevant person or relevant persons in relation to the taxpayer.][8]

(4) If, when a relevant person receives a notice of attachment, the amount of the debt due by him to the taxpayer named in the notice is less than the specified amount in relation to the taxpayer or no debt is so due and, at any time thereafter before the end of the relevant period in relation to the notice, an additional debt becomes due by the relevant person to the taxpayer, the relevant person shall, within 10 days of that time –

  (a) if the aggregate of the amount of any debt so due and the additional debt so due is equal to or less than the specified amount in relation to the taxpayer –

    (i) deliver a further return to the Revenue Commissioners specifying the additional debt, and

    (ii) pay to the Revenue Commissioners the amount of the additional debt,

and so on for each subsequent occasion during the relevant period in relation to the notice of attachment on which an additional debt becomes due by the relevant person to the taxpayer until the aggregate amount of the debt and the additional debt or debts so due equals the specified amount in relation to the taxpayer or the provisions of paragraph (b) apply in relation to an additional debt, and

  (b) if the aggregate amount of any debt and the additional debt or debts so due to the taxpayer is greater than the specified amount in relation to the taxpayer –

    (i) deliver a further return to the Revenue Commissioners specifying such portion of the latest additional debt as when added to the aggregate of the debt and any earlier additional debts is equal to the specified amount in relation to the taxpayer, and

    (ii) pay to the Revenue Commissioners the said portion of the additional debt.

(5) Where a relevant person delivers, either fraudulently or negligently, an incorrect return or further return that purports to be a return or further return made in accordance with this section, he shall be

deemed to be guilty of an offence under section 94 of the Finance
Act, 1983.

(6) (a) Where a notice of attachment has been given to a relevant
person in respect of a taxpayer, the relevant person shall not,
during the relevant period in relation to the notice, make
any disbursements out of the debt, or any additional debt,
due by him to the taxpayer save to the extent that any such
disbursement—

  (i) will not reduce the debt or the aggregate of the debt and
  any additional debts so due to an amount that is less than
  the specified amount in relation to the taxpayer, or

  (ii) is made pursuant to an order of a court.

(b) For the purposes of this section, a disbursement made by a
relevant person contrary to paragraph (a) shall be deemed not
to reduce the amount of the debt or any additional debts due
by him to the taxpayer.

(7) (a) Sections 500 and 503 of the Income Tax Act, 1967, shall apply
to a failure by a relevant person to deliver a return required
by a notice of attachment within the time specified in the
notice or to deliver a further return within the time specified
in subsection (4) as they apply to a failure to deliver a return
referred to in the said section 500 and Schedule 15 to the
said Act is hereby amended by the insertion in Column 1 of
"Finance Act, 1988, paragraph (a) (iii) (I) of subsection (2) and
paragraphs (a) (i) and (b) (i) of subsection (4) of section 73".

(b) A certificate signed by an officer of the Revenue Commissioners
which certifies that he has examined the relevant records and
that it appears from them that, during a specified period, a
specified return was not received from a relevant person shall
be evidence until the contrary is proved that the relevant person
did not deliver the return during that period and a certificate
certifying as provided by this paragraph and purporting to be
signed by an officer of the Revenue Commissioners may be
tendered in evidence without proof and shall be deemed until
the contrary is proved to have been so signed.

(8) Where a relevant person to whom a notice of attachment in respect
of a taxpayer has been given—

(a) delivers the return required to be delivered by the said notice
but fails to pay to the Revenue Commissioners, within the
time specified in the notice, the amount specified in the return
or any part of that amount, or

(b) delivers a further return under subsection (4) but fails to pay
to the Revenue Commissioners, within the time specified in
the said subsection (4), the amount specified in the further
return or any part of that amount,

the amount specified in the return or further return, or the part of that amount, as the case may be, which he has failed to pay to the Revenue Commissioners may, if the notice of attachment has not been revoked by a notice of revocation, be sued for and recovered by action, or other appropriate proceedings, at the suit of an officer of the Revenue Commissioners in any court of competent jurisdiction.

(9) Nothing in this section shall be construed as rendering any failure by a relevant person to make a return or further return required by this section, or pay to the Revenue Commissioners the amount or amounts required by this section to be paid by him, liable to be treated as a failure to which section 94 of the Finance Act, 1983, applies.

(10) (a) A notice of attachment given to a relevant person in respect of a taxpayer may be revoked by the Revenue Commissioners, at any time, by notice in writing given to the relevant person and shall be revoked forthwith if the taxpayer has paid the specified amount to the Revenue Commissioners.

(b) Where, in pursuance of this section, a relevant person pays any amount to the Revenue Commissioners out of a debt or an additional debt due by him to the taxpayer and, at the time of the receipt by the Revenue Commissioners of the said amount, the taxpayer has paid the [amount or aggregate amount of the taxes, interest on unpaid taxes and penalties in respect of which the taxpayer is in default at the time of the giving of the notice or notices of attachment][9] to the Revenue Commissioners, the first-mentioned amount shall be refunded by the Revenue Commissioners forthwith to the taxpayer.

(11) If a notice of attachment or a notice of revocation is given to a relevant person in relation to a taxpayer a copy thereof shall be given by the Revenue Commissioners to the taxpayer forthwith.

(12) (a) If, in pursuance of this section, any amount is paid to the Revenue Commissioners by a relevant person, the relevant person shall forthwith give the taxpayer concerned a notice in writing specifying the payment, its amount and the reason for which it was made.

(b) On the receipt by the Revenue Commissioners of an amount paid in pursuance of this section, the Revenue Commissioners shall forthwith notify the taxpayer and the relevant person in writing of such receipt.

(13) If, in pursuance of this section, a relevant person pays to the Revenue Commissioners the whole or part of the amount of a debt, or an additional debt, due by him to a taxpayer, or any portion of such an amount, the taxpayer shall allow such payment and the relevant person shall be acquitted and discharged of the amount of the payment as if it had been paid to the taxpayer.

(14) If, in pursuance of this section, a relevant person is prohibited from making any disbursement out of a debt, or an additional debt, due to a taxpayer, no action shall lie against the relevant person in any court by reason of a failure to make any such disbursement.

(15) Any obligation on the Revenue Commissioners to maintain secrecy or any other restriction upon the disclosure of information by the Revenue Commissioners shall not apply in relation to information contained in a notice of attachment.

(16) A notice of attachment in respect of a taxpayer shall not be given to a relevant person at a time when the relevant person or the taxpayer is an undischarged bankrupt or a company being wound up.

(17) ....[10]

(18) The Revenue Commissioners may nominate any of their officers to perform any acts and discharge any functions authorised by this section to be performed or discharged by the Revenue Commissioners.

Footnotes

1   S.73 was extended by s.130, FA 1991, to the CATA and to the Stamp Act, 1891, with effect as on and from 1st October, 1991. S.73 was extended by s.241(a)(i), FA 1992, to the Customs Acts and to the statutes relating to the duties of excise, with effect as on and from 28th May, 1992.

     S.73 was repealed and re-enacted in s.1002, TCA, with effect as on and from 6th April, 1997.

2   As substituted by s.241(a)(ii), FA 1992, with effect as on and from 28th May, 1992.

3   As inserted by s.241(a)(iii), FA 1992, with effect as on and from 28th May, 1992.

4   As substituted by s.241(a)(iv), FA 1992, with effect as on and from 28th May, 1992.

5   As substituted by s.241(b)(i), FA 1992, with effect as on and from 28th May, 1992.

6   As inserted by s.241(b)(ii), FA 1992, with effect as on and from 28th May, 1992.

7   As inserted by s.241(b)(iii), FA 1992, with effect as on and from 28th May, 1992.

8   As substituted by s.241(c), FA 1992, with effect as on and from 28th May, 1992.

9   As substituted by s.241(d), FA 1992, with effect as on and from 28th May, 1992.

10   S.73(17) was deleted by s.241(e), FA 1992, with effect as on and from 28th May, 1992.

Section 74[1]

Construction of certain Acts in accordance with Status of Children Act, 1987.

74.   (1)   In this section "the Acts" means—

(i)   the Tax Acts,

(ii)   the Capital Gains Tax Acts,

(iii)   the Capital Acquisitions Tax Act, 1976, and the enactments amending or extending that Act, and

(iv)   the statutes relating to stamp duty,

and any instruments made thereunder.

(2)   Notwithstanding any provision of the Acts or the dates on which they were passed, in deducing any relationship between persons for

the purposes of the Acts, the Acts shall be construed in accordance
with [section 3 of the Status of Children Act, 1987].[2]

(3) This section shall have effect—

    (i)   in relation to the Tax Acts, as respects the year 1987-88 and
subsequent years of assessment or accounting periods ending
on or after the 14th day of January, 1988, as the case may be,

    (ii)   in relation to the Capital Gains Tax Acts, as respects disposals
made on or after the 14th day of January, 1988,

    (iii) in relation to the Capital Acquisitions Tax Act, 1976, as
respects gifts and inheritances taken on or after the 14th day of
January, 1988, and

    (iv) in relation to the statutes relating to stamp duties, as respects
any instrument executed on or after the 14th day of January,
1988.

Footnotes

1   S.74 was unamended before it was repealed and re-enacted in s.8, TCA, with effect as
on and from 6th April, 1997.

2   Reproduced on page 799.

FINANCE ACT, 1989

Number 10 of 1989
(Enacted on 24th May, 1989)

PART VI
Anti-Avoidance

Section 86[1]

Transactions to avoid liability to tax.

86. (1) (a) In this section —

"the Acts" means —

(i)   the Tax Acts,

(ii) the Capital Gains Tax Acts,

(iii) the Value-Added Tax Act, 1972, and the enactments amending or extending that Act,

(iv) the Capital Acquisitions Tax Act, 1976, and the enactments amending or extending that Act,

(v)   Part VI of the Finance Act, 1983, and the enactments amending or extending that Part, and

(vi) the statutes relating to stamp duty,

and any instrument made thereunder;

"business" means any trade, profession or vocation;

"notice of opinion" means a notice given by the Revenue Commissioners under the provisions of subsection (6);

"tax" means any tax, duty, levy or charge which, in accordance with the provisions of the Acts, is placed under the care and management of the Revenue Commissioners and any interest, penalty or other amount payable pursuant to those provisions;

"tax advantage" means —

(i)   a reduction, avoidance or deferral of any charge or assessment to tax, including any potential or prospective charge or assessment, or

(ii) a refund of or a payment of an amount of tax, or an increase in an amount of tax, refundable or otherwise payable to a person, including any potential or prospective amount so refundable or payable,

arising out of, or by reason of, a transaction, including a transaction where another transaction would not have been undertaken or arranged to achieve the results, or any part of the results, achieved or intended to be achieved by the transaction;

"tax avoidance transaction" has the meaning assigned to it by subsection (2);

"tax consequences" means, in relation to a tax avoidance transaction, such adjustments and acts as may be made and done by the Revenue Commissioners pursuant to subsection (5) in order to withdraw or deny the tax advantage resulting from the tax avoidance transaction;

"transaction" means—

(i) any transaction, action, course of action, course of conduct, scheme, plan or proposal, and

(ii) any agreement, arrangement, understanding, promise or undertaking, whether express or implied and whether or not enforceable or intended to be enforceable by legal proceedings, and

(iii) any series of or combination of the circumstances referred to in paragraphs (i) and (ii) ,

whether entered into or arranged by one person or by two or more persons—

(I) whether acting in concert or not, or

(II) whether or not entered into or arranged wholly or partly outside the State, or

(III) whether or not entered into or arranged as part of a larger transaction or in conjunction with any other transaction or transactions.

(b) In subsections (2) and (3), for the purposes of the hearing or rehearing under subsection (8) of an appeal made under subsection (7) or for the purposes of the determination of a question of law arising on the statement of a case for the opinion of the High Court, the references to the Revenue Commissioners shall, subject to any necessary modifications, be construed as references to the Appeal Commissioners or to a judge of the Circuit Court or, to the extent necessary, to a judge of the High Court, as appropriate.

(2) For the purposes of this section and subject to subsection (3), a transaction is a "tax avoidance transaction" if, having regard to any one or more of the following, that is to say—

(a) the results of the transaction,

(b) its use as a means of achieving those results, and

(c) any other means by which the results or any part of the results could have been achieved, the Revenue Commissioners form the opinion that—

(i) it gives rise to, or, but for this section, would give rise to, a tax advantage, and

(ii) the transaction was not undertaken or arranged primarily for purposes other than to give rise to a tax advantage,

and references in this section to the Revenue Commissioners forming an opinion that a transaction is a tax avoidance transaction shall be construed as references to them forming an opinion with regard to the transaction in accordance with the provisions of this subsection.

(3) Without prejudice to the generality of the provisions of subsection (2), in forming an opinion in accordance with that subsection and subsection (4), as to whether or not a transaction is a tax avoidance transaction, the Revenue Commissioners shall not regard the transaction as being a tax avoidance transaction if they are satisfied that—

(a) notwithstanding that the purpose or purposes of the transaction could have been achieved by some other transaction which would have given rise to a greater amount of tax being payable by the person, the transaction—

(i) was undertaken or arranged by a person with a view, directly or indirectly, to the realisation of profits in the course of the business activities of a business carried on by the person, and

(ii) was not undertaken or arranged primarily to give rise to a tax advantage,

or

(b) the transaction was undertaken or arranged for the purpose of obtaining the benefit of any relief, allowance or other abatement provided by any provision of the Acts and that transaction would not result directly or indirectly in a misuse of the provision or an abuse of the provision having regard to the purposes for which it was provided:

Provided that, in forming an opinion as aforesaid in relation to any transaction, the Revenue Commissioner shall have regard to—

(I) the form of that transaction,

(II) the substance of that transaction,

(III) the substance of any other transaction or transactions which that transaction may reasonably be regarded as being directly or indirectly related to or connected with, and

(IV) the final outcome and result of that transaction and any combination of those other transactions which are so related or connected.

(4) Subject to the provisions of this section, the Revenue Commissioners, as respect any transaction, may, at any time –

(a) form the opinion that the transaction is a tax avoidance transaction,

(b) calculate the tax advantage which they consider arises, or which, but for this section, would arise, from the transaction,

(c) determine the tax consequences which they consider would arise in respect of the transaction if their opinion were to become final and conclusive in accordance with subsection (5) (e), and

(d) calculate the amount of any relief from double taxation which they would propose to give to any person in accordance with the provisions of subsection (5) (c).

(5) (a) Where the opinion of the Revenue Commissioner that a transaction is a tax avoidance transaction becomes final and conclusive they may, notwithstanding any other provision of the Acts, make all such adjustments and do all such acts as are just and reasonable (in so far as those adjustments and acts have been specified or described in a notice of opinion given under subsection (6) and subject to the manner in which any appeal made under subsection (7) against any matter specified or described in the notice of opinion has been finally determined, including any adjustments and acts not so specified or described in the notice of opinion but which form part of a final determination of any appeal as aforesaid) in order that the tax advantage resulting from a tax avoidance transaction shall be withdrawn from or denied to any person concerned.

(b) Subject to, but without prejudice to the generality of paragraph (a), the Revenue Commissioners may –

(i) allow or disallow, in whole or in part, any deduction or other amount which is relevant in computing tax payable, or any part thereof,

(ii) allocate or deny to any person any deduction, loss, abatement, relief, allowance, exemption, income or other amount, or any part thereof, or

(iii) recharacterize for tax purposes the nature of any payment or other amount.

(c) Where the Revenue Commissioners make any adjustment or do any act for the purposes of paragraph (a), they shall afford relief from any double taxation which they consider would, but for this paragraph, arise by virtue of any adjustment made or act done by them pursuant to the foregoing provisions of this subsection.

(d) Notwithstanding any other provision of the Acts, where –

    (i) pursuant to subsection (4)(c), the Revenue Commissioners determine the tax consequences which they consider would arise in respect of a transaction if their opinion, that the transaction is a tax avoidance transaction, were to become final and conclusive, and

    (ii) pursuant to that determination, they specify or describe in a notice of opinion any adjustment or act which they consider would be, or be part of, the said tax consequences,

then, in so far as any right of appeal lay under subsection (7) against any such adjustment or act so specified or described, no right or further right of appeal shall lie under the Acts against that adjustment or act when it is made or done in accordance with the provisions of this subsection or against any adjustment or act so made or done that is not so specified or described in the notice of opinion but which forms part of the final determination of any appeal made under the said subsection (7) against any matter specified or described in the notice of opinion.

(e) For the purposes of this subsection an opinion of the Revenue Commissioners that a transaction is a tax avoidance transaction shall be final and conclusive –

    (i) if, within the time limited, no appeal is made under subsection (7) against any matter or matters specified or described in a notice or notices of opinion given pursuant to that opinion, or

    (ii) as and when all appeals made under the said subsection (7) against any such matter or matters have been finally determined and none of the appeals has been so determined by an order directing that the opinion of the Revenue Commissioners to the effect that the transaction is a tax avoidance transaction is void.

(6) (a) Where, pursuant to subsections (2) and (4), the Revenue Commissioners form the opinion that a transaction is a tax avoidance transaction, they shall immediately thereupon give notice in writing of the opinion to any person from whom a tax advantage would be withdrawn or to whom a tax advantage would be denied or to whom relief from double taxation would be given, if the opinion became final and conclusive, and the notice shall, specify or describe –

      (i) the transaction which in the opinion of the Revenue Commissioners is a tax avoidance transaction,

      (ii) the tax advantage, or part thereof, calculated by the Revenue Commissioners which would be withdrawn from or denied to the person to whom the notice is given,

      (iii) the tax consequences of the transaction determined by the Revenue Commissioners, in so far as they would refer to the person, and

      (iv) the amount of any relief from double taxation calculated by the Revenue Commissioners which they would propose to give to the person in accordance with subsection (5) (c).

  (b) Section 542 of the Income Tax Act, 1967, shall, with any necessary modifications, apply for the purposes of a notice given under this subsection, or subsection (10), as if it were a notice given under that Act.

(7) Any person aggrieved by an opinion formed or, in so far as it refers to the person, a calculation or determination made by the Revenue Commissioners pursuant to subsection (4) may, by notice in writing given to the Revenue Commissioners within 30 days of the date of the notice of opinion, appeal to the Appeal Commissioners on the grounds and, notwithstanding any other provision of the Acts, only on the grounds that, having regard to all of the circumstances, including any fact or matter which was not known to the Revenue Commissioners when they formed their opinion or made their calculation or determination, and to the provisions of this section—

  (a) the transaction specified or described in the notice of opinion is not a tax avoidance transaction, or

  (b) the amount of the tax advantage, or the part thereof, specified or described in the notice of opinion which would be withdrawn from or denied to the person is incorrect, or

  (c) the tax consequences specified or described in the notice of opinion, or such part thereof as shall be specified or described by the appellant in the notice of appeal, would not be just and reasonable in order to withdraw or to deny the tax advantage, or part thereof, specified or described in the notice of opinion, or

  (d) the amount of relief from double taxation which the Revenue Commissioners propose to give to the person is insufficient or incorrect.

(8) The Appeal Commissioners shall hear and determine an appeal made to them under subsection (7) as if it were an appeal against an assessment to income tax and, subject to subsection (9), all the

provisions of the Income Tax Act, 1967, relating to the rehearing of an appeal and the statement of a case for the opinion of the High Court on a point of law shall apply accordingly with any necessary modifications:

Provided that on the hearing or rehearing of the appeal –

(a) it shall not be lawful to go into any grounds of appeal other than those specified in subsection (7), and

(b) at the request of the appellants, two or more appeals made by two or more persons pursuant to the same opinion, calculation or determination formed or made by the Revenue Commissioners pursuant to subsection (4) may be heard or reheard together.

(9) (a) On the hearing of an appeal made under subsection (7) the Appeal Commissioners shall have regard to all matters to which the Revenue Commissioners may or are required to have regard under the provisions of this section and –

(i) in relation to an appeal made on the grounds referred to in paragraph (a) of subsection (7), they shall determine the appeal, in so far as it is made on those grounds, by ordering, if they, or a majority of them –

(I) consider that the transaction specified or described in the notice of opinion, or any part of that transaction, is a tax avoidance transaction, that the opinion, or the opinion in so far as it relates to that part, is to stand good, or

(II) consider that, subject to such amendment or addition thereto as the Appeal Commissioners, or the said majority of them, deem necessary and as they shall specify or describe the transaction, or any part of it, specified or described in the notice of opinion, is a tax avoidance transaction, that the transaction, or that part of it, be so amended or added to and that, subject to the amendment or addition, the opinion, or the opinion in so far as it relates to that part, is to stand good, or

(III) do not so consider as referred to in clause (I) or (II), that the opinion is void,

or

(ii) in relation to an appeal made on the grounds referred to in paragraph (b) of subsection (7), they shall determine the appeal, in so far as it is made on those grounds, by ordering that the amount of the tax advantage, or the part thereof, specified or described in the notice of opinion be increased or reduced by such amount as they shall direct or that it shall stand good,

or

(iii) in relation to an appeal made on the grounds referred to in paragraph (c) of subsection (7), they shall determine the appeal, in so far as it is made on those grounds, by ordering that the tax consequences specified or described in the notice of opinion shall be altered or added to in such manner as they shall direct or that they shall stand good,

or

(iv) in relation to an appeal made on the grounds referred to in paragraph (d) of subsection (7), they shall determine the appeal, in so far as it is made on those grounds, by ordering that the amount of the relief from double taxation specified or described in the notice of opinion shall be increased or reduced by such amount as they shall direct or that it shall stand good.

(b) The provisions of this subsection shall, subject to any necessary modifications, apply to the rehearing of an appeal by a judge of the Circuit Court and, to the extent necessary, to the determination by the High Court of any question or questions of law arising on the statement of a case for the opinion of the High Court.

(10) The Revenue Commissioners may, at any time, amend, add to or withdraw any matter specified or described in a notice of opinion by giving notice (hereafter in this subsection referred to as the "notice of amendment") in writing of the amendment, addition or withdrawal to each and every person affected thereby, in so far as the person is so affected, and the foregoing provisions of this section shall apply in all respects as if the notice of amendment were a notice of opinion and any matter specified or described in the notice of amendment were specified or described in a notice of opinion:

Provided that no such amendment, addition or withdrawal may be made so as to set aside or alter any matter which has become final and conclusive on the determination of an appeal made with regard to that matter under subsection (7).

(11) Where pursuant to subsections (2) and (4), the Revenue Commissioners form the opinion that a transaction is a tax avoidance transaction and, pursuant to that opinion, notices are to be given under subsection (6) to two or more persons, any obligation on the Revenue Commissioners to maintain secrecy or any other restriction upon the disclosure of information by the Revenue Commissioners shall not apply with respect to the giving of the notices as aforesaid or to the performance of any acts or the discharge of any functions authorised by this section to be performed or discharged by them or to the performance of any act or the discharge of any functions,

including any act or function in relation to an appeal made under subsection (7), which is directly or indirectly related to the acts or functions so authorised.

(12) The Revenue Commissioners may nominate any of their officers to perform any acts and discharge any functions, including the forming of an opinion, authorised by this section to be performed or discharged by the Revenue Commissioners and references in this section to the Revenue Commissioners shall, with any necessary modifications, be construed as including references to an officer so nominated.

(13) This section shall apply as respects any transaction where the whole or any part of the transaction is undertaken or arranged on or after the 25th day of January, 1989, and as respects any transaction undertaken or arranged wholly before that date in so far as it gives rise to, or would, but for this section, give rise to –

    (a) a reduction, avoidance or deferral of any charge or assessment to tax, or part thereof, where the charge or assessment arises by virtue of any other transaction carried out wholly on or after a date, or

    (b) a refund or a payment of an amount, or of an increase in an amount, of tax, or part thereof, refundable or otherwise payable to a person where that amount, or increase in the amount, would otherwise become first so refundable or otherwise payable to the person on a date,

which could not fall earlier than the said 25th day of January, 1989, as the case may be.

Footnote

1   S.86(13) provides a commencement date of 25th January, 1989. S.86 was unamended before it was repealed and re-enacted in s.811, TCA, with effect as on and from 6th April, 1997.

FINANCE ACT, 1991

Number 13 of 1991
(Enacted on 29th May, 1991)

PART I – Chapter VIII

Taxation of Acquisition by a Company of its Own Shares

Section 61[1]

Purchase of unquoted shares by issuing company or its subsidiary.

61. (1) Notwithstanding any provision of Part IX of the Act of 1976, references in the Tax Acts to distributions of a company, other than any such references in sections 101 and 162 of the Act of 1976, shall be construed so as not to include references to a payment made on or after the relevant day by a company on the redemption, repayment or purchase of its own shares if the company is an unquoted trading company or the unquoted holding company of a trading group and either –

    (a) (i) the redemption, repayment or purchase –

        (I) is made wholly or mainly for the purpose of benefiting a trade carried on by the company or by any of its 51 per cent. subsidiaries, and

        (II) does not form part of a scheme or arrangement the main purpose or one of the main purposes of which is to enable the owner of the shares to participate in the profits of the company or of any of its 51 per cent. subsidiaries without receiving a dividend,

    and

      (ii) the conditions specified in sections 62 to 66, so far as applicable, are satisfied in relation to the owner of the shares, or

    (b) the person to whom the payment is made –

      (i) applies the whole, or substantially the whole, of the payment (apart from any sum applied in discharging his liability to capital gains tax, if any, in respect of the redemption, repayment or purchase) to discharging,

        (I) within 4 months of the valuation date of a taxable inheritance of the company's shares taken by him, a liability to inheritance tax in respect of that inheritance, or

(II) within one week of the day on which the payment is made, a debt incurred by him for the purpose of discharging the said liability to inheritance tax,

and

(ii) could not, without undue hardship, have otherwise discharged that liability to inheritance tax and, where appropriate, the debt so incurred.

(2) Where subsection (1) would apply to a payment, made on or after the relevant day by a company which is a subsidiary (within the meaning of section 155 of the Companies Act, 1963) of another company on the acquisition of shares of the other company, if, for all the purposes of the Tax Acts other than this subsection –

(a) the payment were to be treated as a payment by the other company on the purchase of its own shares, and

(b) the acquisition by the subsidiary of the shares were to be treated as a purchase by the other company of its own shares,

then, notwithstanding any provision of Part IX of the Act of 1976, references in the Tax Acts to distributions of a company, other than references in sections 101 and 162 of the Act of 1976, shall be construed so as not to include references to the payment made by the subsidiary.

(3) In subsection (1) (b) (i) "valuation date" has the meaning assigned to it by section 21 of the Capital Acquisitions Tax Act, 1976.

Footnote

1   S.61 took effect as on and from 6th April, 1991, and was unamended before it was repealed and re-enacted in s.176, TCA, with effect as on and from 6th April, 1997.

FINANCE ACT, 1992

Number 9 of 1992
(Enacted on 28th May, 1992)

PART VII
Anti-Avoidance and Anti-Evasion

Section 236[1]

Authorised officers and Garda Síochána.

236. Where an authorised officer (within the meaning of section 127A (inserted by this Act) of the Income Tax Act, 1967, section 17A (as so inserted) of the Finance Act, 1970, or section 34 (as so inserted) of the Finance Act, 1976, as the case may be) in accordance with the said section 127A, 17A or 34 enters any premises or place, he may be accompanied by a member or members of the Garda Síochána and any such member may arrest without warrant any person who obstructs or interferes with the authorised officer in the exercise or performance of his powers or duties under any of the said sections.

Footnote

1   S.236 took effect as on and from 28th May, 1992, and was unamended before it was repealed and re-enacted in s.906, TCA, with effect as on and from 6th April, 1997.

Section 237[1]

Inspection of computer documents and records.

237. (1)   In this section—

"the Acts" means—

(a)   the Customs Acts,

(b)' the statutes relating to the duties of excise and to the management of those duties,

(c)   the Tax Acts,

(d)   the Capital Gains Tax Acts,

(e)   the Value-Added Tax Act, 1972, and the enactments amending or extending that Act,

(f)   the Capital Acquisitions Tax Act, 1976, and the enactments amending or extending that Act, and

(g)   Part VI of the Finance Act, 1983,

and any instruments made thereunder;

"data" means information in a form in which it can be processed;

"data equipment" means any electronic, photographic, magnetic, optical or other equipment for processing data;

"processing" means performing automatically logical or arithmetical operations on data, or the storing, maintenance, transmission, reproduction or communication of data;

"records" means documents which a person is obliged by any provision of the Acts to keep, to issue or to produce for inspection, and any other written or printed material;

"software" means any sequence of instructions used in conjunction with data equipment for the purpose of processing data or controlling the operation of the data equipment.

(2) Any provision under the Acts which –

    (a)   requires a person to keep, retain, issue or produce any records or cause any records to be kept, retained, issued or produced,

    or

    (b)   permits an officer of the Revenue Commissioners –

        (i)   to inspect any records,

        (iii) to enter premises and search for any records, or

        (iii) to take extracts from or copies of or remove any records,

shall, where the records are processed by data equipment, apply to the data equipment together with any associated software, data, apparatus or material as it applies to the records.

(3) An officer of the Revenue Commissioners may, in the exercise or performance of his powers or duties, require –

    (a)   the person by or on whose behalf the data equipment is or has been used, or

    (b)   any person having charge of, or otherwise concerned with the operation of, the data equipment or any associated apparatus or material,

to afford him all reasonable assistance in relation thereto.

Footnote

1   S.237 took effect as on and from 28th May, 1992, and was unamended before it was repealed and re-enacted in s.912, TCA, with effect as on and from 6th April, 1997.

FINANCE ACT, 1994

Number 13 of 1994
(Enacted on 23rd May, 1994)

PART VII
Miscellaneous

CHAPTER I
Provisions Relating to Residence of Individuals

Section 149[1]

Interpretation (Chapter I).

149. In this Part—

"the Acts" means—

    (a)   the Income Tax Acts,

    (b)   the Corporation Tax Acts,

    (c)   the Capital Gains Tax Acts, and

    (d)   the Capital Acquisitions Tax Act, 1976, and the enactments amending or extending that Act,

and any instrument made thereunder;

"authorised officer" means an officer of the Revenue Commissioners authorised by them in writing for the purposes of this Chapter;

"present in the State", in relation to an individual, means the personal presence of the individual in the State;

"tax" means any tax payable in accordance with any provision of the Acts.

Footnote

1   S.149 took effect as shown in s.158 on page 1430, and was unamended before it was repealed and re-enacted in s.818, TCA, with effect as on and from 6th April, 1997.

Section 150[1]

Residence.

150. (1) For the purposes of the Acts, an individual is resident in the State for a year of assessment if the individual is present in the State—

    (a)   at any one time or several times in the year of assessment for a period in the whole amounting to 183 days or more, or

    (b)   at any one time or several times—

(i)   in the year of assessment, and

(ii) in the preceding year of assessment,

for a period (being a period comprising in the aggregate the number of days on which the individual is present in the State in the year of assessment and the number of days on which the individual was present in the State in the preceding year of assessment) in the whole amounting to 280 days or more:

Provided that, notwithstanding paragraph (b), where for a year of assessment an individual is present in the State at any one time or several times for a period in the whole amounting to not more than 30 days —

(a)   the individual shall not be resident in the State for the year of assessment, and

(b)   no account shall be taken of the period for the purposes of the aggregate mentioned in paragraph (b).

(2) (a) Notwithstanding subsection (1), an individual —

(i)   who is not resident in the State for a year of assessment, and

(ii) to whom paragraph (b) applies,

may, at any time, elect to be treated as resident in the State for that year and, where an individual so elects, the individual shall, for the purposes of the Acts, be deemed to be resident in the State for that year.

(b)   This paragraph applies to an individual who satisfies an authorised officer that the individual is in the State —

(i)   with the intention, and

(ii) in such circumstances,

that the individual will be resident in the State for the following year of assessment.

(3) For the purposes of this section, an individual shall be deemed to be present in the State for a day if the individual is present in the State at the end of the day.

Footnote

1 S.150 took effect as shown in s.158 on page 1430, and was unamended before it was repealed and re-enacted in s.819, TCA, with effect as on and from 6th April, 1997.

Section 151[1]

Ordinary residence.

151. (1) For the purposes of the Acts, an individual is ordinarily resident in the State for a year of assessment if the individual has been resident

---

> in the State for each of the 3 years of assessment preceding that year.

(2) An individual who is ordinarily resident in the State shall not, for the purposes of the Acts, cease to be ordinarily resident in the State for a year of assessment unless the individual has not been resident in the State in each of the 3 years of assessment preceding that year.

Footnote

1   S.151 took effect as shown in s.158 on page 1430, and was unamended before it was repealed and re-enacted in s.820, TCA, with effect as on and from 6th April, 1997.

Section 153[1]

Split year residence.

153. (1) For the purposes of a charge to tax on any income, profits or gains from an employment, where, during a year of assessment ("the relevant year")—

(a) (i) an individual who has not been resident in the State for the preceding year of assessment, satisfies an authorised officer that the individual is in the State—

(I) with the intention, and

(II) in such circumstances,

that the individual will be resident in the State for the following year of assessment, or

(ii) an individual who is resident in the State, satisfies an authorised officer that the individual is leaving the State, other than for a temporary purpose,

(I) with the intention, and

(II) in such circumstances,

that the individual will not be resident in the State for the following year of assessment,

and

(b) the individual would, but for the provisions of this section, be resident in the State for the relevant year,

subsection (2) shall apply in relation to the individual.

(2) (a) An individual to whom paragraphs (a) (i) and (b) of subsection (1) apply, shall be deemed to be resident in the State for the relevant year only from the date of his or her arrival in the State.

(b) An individual to whom paragraphs (a) (ii) and (b) of subsection (1) apply, shall be deemed to be resident in the State for the relevant year only up to and including the date of his or her leaving the State.

(3) Where, by virtue of this section, an individual is resident in the State for part of a year of assessment, all the provisions of the Acts shall apply as if—

(a) income arising during that part of the year or, in a case to which the provisions of section 76 (3) of the Income Tax Act, 1967, apply, amounts received in the State during that part of the year, were income arising or amounts received for a year of assessment in which the individual is resident in the State, and

(b) income arising or, as the case may be, amounts received in the remaining part of the year, were income arising or amounts received in a year of assessment in which the individual is not resident in the State.

Footnote

1   S.153 took effect as shown in s.158 on page 1430, and was unamended before it was repealed and re-enacted in S.822, TCA, with effect as on and from 6th April, 1997.

Section 156[1]

Appeals.

156. (1) An individual who is aggrieved by the decision of an authorised officer on any question arising under those provisions of this Chapter which require an individual to satisfy an authorised officer on such a question may, by notice in writing to that effect given to the authorised officer within two months from the date on which notice of the decision is given to the individual, make an application to have the question heard and determined by the Appeal Commissioners.

(2) Where an application is made under subsection (1), the Appeal Commissioners shall hear and determine the question concerned in like manner as an appeal made to them against an assessment and all the provisions of the Acts relating to such an appeal (including the provisions relating to the rehearing of an appeal and to the statement of a case for the opinion of the High Court on a point of law) shall apply accordingly with any necessary modifications.

Footnote

1   S.153 took effect as shown in s.158 on page 1430, and was unamended before it was repealed and re-enacted in S.824, TCA, with effect as on and from 6th April, 1997.

Section 158

Commencement (Chapter I).

158. (1) Subject to subsection (2), this Chapter shall apply as respects the year 1994-95 and subsequent years of assessment.

(2) Where in any case an individual –

(a) was resident in the State for the year of assessment 1991-92 but not resident in the State for the years of assessment 1992-93 and 1993-94, or

(b) was resident in the State for the year of assessment 1992-93 but not resident in the State for the year of assessment 1993-94, or

(c) was resident in the State for the year of assessment 1993-94 and would not, but for section 150, be resident in the State in the year of assessment 1994-95, or

(d) left the State in the years of assessment 1992-93 or 1993-94 for the purpose of commencing a period of ordinary residence outside the State and did not recommence ordinary residence in the State prior to the end of the year of assessment 1993-94,

section 150 and section 157, in so far as it relates to the repeal of section 4 of the Finance Act, 1987, shall apply as respects the year 1995-96 and subsequent years of assessment in that case.

FINANCE ACT, 1995

Number 8 of 1995
(Enacted on 2nd June, 1995)

PART VII
Miscellaneous

CHAPTER II
General

Section 172¹

Duties of a relevant person in relation to certain revenue offences.

172. (1) In this section —

"the Acts" means —

(a) the Customs Acts,

(b) the statutes relating to the duties of excise and to the management of those duties,

(c) the Tax Acts,

(d) the Capital Gains Tax Acts,

(e) the Value-Added Tax Act, 1972, and the enactments amending or extending that Act,

(f) the Capital Acquisitions Tax Act, 1976, and the enactments amending or extending that Act,

(g) the statutes relating to stamp duty and to the management of that duty,

and any instruments made thereunder and any instruments made under any other enactment and relating to tax;

"appropriate officer" means any officer nominated by the Revenue Commissioners to be an appropriate officer for the purposes of this section;

"company" means any body corporate;

"relevant person", in relation to a company, means a person who —

(a) (i) is an auditor to the company appointed in accordance with section 160 of the Companies Act, 1963 (as amended by the Companies Act, 1990), or

(ii) in the case of an industrial and provident society or a friendly society, is a public auditor to the society for the purposes of the Industrial and Provident Societies Acts,

1893 to 1978, and the Friendly Societies Acts, 1896 to 1977,

or

(b) with a view to reward assists or advises the company in the preparation or delivery of any information, declaration, return, records, accounts or other document which he or she knows will be, or is likely to be, used for any purpose of tax:

Provided that a person who would, but for this proviso, be treated as a relevant person in relation to a company shall not be so treated if the person assists or advises the company solely in the person's capacity as an employee of the said company, and a person shall be treated as assisting or advising the company in that capacity where the person's income from assisting or advising the company consists solely of emoluments to which Chapter IV of Part V of the Income Tax Act, 1967, applies;

"relevant offence" means an offence committed by a company which consists of the company –

(a) knowingly or wilfully delivering any incorrect return, statement or accounts or knowingly or wilfully furnishing or causing to be furnished any incorrect information in connection with any tax,

(b) knowingly or wilfully claiming or obtaining relief or exemption from, or repayment of, any tax, being a relief, exemption or repayment to which there is no entitlement,

(c) knowingly or wilfully issuing or producing any incorrect invoice, receipt, instrument or other document in connection with any tax,

(d) knowingly or wilfully failing to comply with any provision of the Acts requiring the furnishing of a return of income, profits or gains, or of sources of income, profits or gains, for the purposes of any tax:

Provided that an offence under this paragraph committed by a company shall not be a relevant offence if the company has made a return of income, profits or gains to the Revenue Commissioners in respect of an accounting period falling wholly or partly into the period of 3 years immediately preceding the accounting period in respect of which the offence was committed;

"tax" means tax, duty, levy or charge under the care and management of the Revenue Commissioners.

(2) If, having regard solely to information obtained in the course of examining the accounts of a company, or in the course of assisting or advising a company in the preparation or delivery of any information, declaration, return, records, accounts or other document for the purposes of tax, as the case may be, a person who

is a relevant person in relation to the company becomes aware that the company has committed, or is in the course of committing, one or more relevant offences, the person shall, if the offence or offences are material —

(a) communicate particulars of the offence or offences in writing to the company without undue delay and request the company to —

    (i) take such action as is necessary for the purposes of rectifying the matter, or

    (ii) notify an appropriate officer of the offence or offences,

not later than 6 months after the time of communication, and

(b) (i) unless it is established to the person's satisfaction that the necessary action has been taken or notification made, as the case may be, under paragraph (a), cease to act as the auditor to the company or to assist or advise the company in such preparation or delivery as is specified in paragraph (b) of the definition of relevant person, and

    (ii) shall not so act, assist or advise before a time which is —

        (I) 3 years after the time at which the particulars were communicated under paragraph (a), or

        (II) the time at which it is established to the person's satisfaction that the necessary action has been taken or notification made, as the case may be, under paragraph (a),

whichever is the earlier:

Provided that nothing in this paragraph shall prevent a person from assisting or advising a company in preparing for, or conducting, legal proceedings, either civil or criminal, which are extant or pending at a time which is 6 months after the time of communication under paragraph (a).

(3) Where a person, being in relation to a company a relevant person within the meaning of paragraph (a) of the definition of relevant person, ceases under the provisions of this section to act as auditor to the company, then the person shall deliver —

(a) a notice in writing to the company stating that he or she is so resigning, and

(b) a copy of the notice to an appropriate officer not later than 14 days after he or she has delivered the notice to the company.

(4) A person shall be guilty of an offence under this section if the person —

(a) fails to comply with subsection (2) or (3), or

    (b)   knowingly or wilfully makes a communication under subsection (2) which is incorrect.

(5) Where a relevant person is found guilty of an offence under this section the person shall be liable —

    (a)   on summary conviction to a fine of £1,000 which may be mitigated to not less than one-fourth part thereof, or

    (b)   on conviction on indictment, to a fine not exceeding £5,000 or, at the discretion of the court, to imprisonment for a term not exceeding 2 years or to both the fine and the imprisonment.

(6) Section 13 of the Criminal Procedure Act, 1967, shall apply in relation to this section as if, in lieu of the penalties specified in subsection (3) of the said section 13, there were specified therein the penalties provided for by subsection (5) (a) of this section, and the reference in subsection (2) (a) of the said section 13 to the penalties provided for in the said subsection (3) shall be construed and have effect accordingly.

(7) Notwithstanding the provisions of any other enactment, proceedings in respect of this section may be instituted within 6 years from the time at which a person is required under subsection (2) to communicate particulars of an offence or offences in writing to a company.

(8) It shall be a good defence in a prosecution for an offence under subsection (4) (a) in relation to a failure to comply with subsection (2) for an accused (being a person who is a relevant person in relation to a company) to show that he or she was, in the ordinary scope of professional engagement, assisting or advising the company in preparing for legal proceedings and would not have become aware that one or more relevant offences had been committed by the company if he or she had not been so assisting or advising.

(9) If a person who is a relevant person takes any action required by subsection (2) or (3), no duty to which the person may be subject shall be regarded as contravened and no liability or action shall lie against the person in any court for so doing.

(10) The Revenue Commissioners may nominate an officer to be an appropriate officer for the purposes of this section and the name of an officer so nominated and the address to which copies of notices under subsection (2) or (3) shall be delivered shall be published in the *Iris Oifigiúil*.

(11) This section shall have effect as respects a relevant offence committed by a company in respect of tax which is —

    (a)   assessable by reference to accounting periods, for any accounting period beginning after the 30th day of June, 1995,

    (b)   assessable by reference to years of assessment, for the year of assessment 1995-96 and subsequent years,

(c) payable by reference to a taxable period, for a taxable period beginning after the 30th day of June, 1995,

(d) chargeable on gifts or inheritances taken on or after the 30th day of June, 1995,

(e) chargeable on instruments executed on or after the 30th day of June, 1995, or

(f) payable in any other case, on or after the 30th day of June, 1995.

Footnote

1   See s.172(11)(d) which applies the section to a relevant offence committed by a company in respect of tax which is chargeable on gifts or inheritances taken on or after 30th June, 1995.

S. 172 was unamended before it was repealed and re-enacted in s.1079, TCA, with effect as on and from 6th April, 1997

Section 175[1]

Power to obtain information.

175. (1) For the purposes of the assessment, charge, collection and recovery of any tax or duty placed under their care and management, the Revenue Commissioners may, by notice in writing, request any Minister of the Government to provide them with such information in the possession of the Minister in relation to payments for any purposes made by the Minister, whether on his own behalf or on behalf of any other person, to such persons or classes of persons as the Revenue Commissioners may specify in the notice and a Minister so requested shall provide such information as may be specified.

(2) The Revenue Commissioners may nominate any of their officers to perform any acts and discharge any functions authorised by this section to be performed or discharged by the Revenue Commissioners.

Footnote

1   S.175 took effect as on and from 2nd June, 1995, and was unamended before it was repealed and re-enacted in s.910, TCA, with effect as on and from 6th April, 1997.

Section 176[1]

Relief for donations of heritage items.

176. (1) (a) In this section —

"the Acts" means —

(i) the Tax Acts (other than Chapter IV of Part V of the Income Tax Act, 1967, section 17 of the Finance Act, 1970, and Chapter VII of Part I of the Finance Act, 1983),

(ii)   the Capital Gains Tax Acts, and

(iii) the Capital Acquisitions Tax Act, 1976, and the enactments amending or extending that Act,

and any instrument made thereunder;

"approved body" means –

(i)   the National Archives,

(ii)   the National Gallery of Ireland,

(iii) the National Library of Ireland,

(iv) the National Museum of Ireland,

(v)   the Irish Museum of Modern Art, or

(vi) in relation to the offer of a gift of a particular item or collection of items, any other such body (being a body owned, or funded wholly or mainly, by the State or by any public or local authority) as may be approved, with the consent of the Minister for Finance, by the Minister for Arts, Culture and the Gaeltacht for the purposes of this section;

"arrears of tax" means tax due and payable in accordance with any provision of the Acts (including any interest and penalties payable under any provision of the Acts in relation to such tax) –

(i)   in the case of income tax, corporation tax or capital gains tax, in respect of the relevant period, or

(ii)   in the case of gift tax or inheritance tax, prior to the commencement of the calendar year in which the relevant gift is made,

which has not been paid at the time a relevant gift is made;

"current liability" means –

(i)   in the case of income tax or capital gains tax, any liability to such tax arising in the year of assessment in which the relevant gift is made, or

(ii)   in the case of corporation tax, any liability to such tax arising in the accounting period in which the relevant gift is made, or

(iii) in the case of gift tax or inheritance tax, any liability to such tax which becomes due and payable in the calendar year in which the relevant gift is made;

"designated officer" means –

(i)   the member of the selection committee who represents the appropriate approved body on that committee where the approved body is so represented, or

(ii) in any other case, a person nominated in that behalf by the Minister for Arts, Culture and the Gaeltacht;

"heritage item" has the meaning assigned to it by subsection (2) (a);

"market value" has the meaning assigned to it by subsection (3);

"relevant gift" means a gift of a heritage item to an approved body which is made on or after the date of the passing of this Act and in respect of which no consideration whatsoever (other than relief under this section) is received by the person making the gift, either directly or indirectly, from the approved body or otherwise;

"relevant period" means—

(i) in the case of income tax and capital gains tax, any year of assessment preceding the year in which the relevant gift is made, and

(ii) in the case of corporation tax, any accounting period preceding the accounting period in which the relevant gift is made;

"selection committee" means a committee consisting of the Chairperson of the Heritage Council, the Director of the Arts Council, the Director of the National Archives, the Director of the National Gallery of Ireland, the Director of the National Library of Ireland, the Director of the National Museum of Ireland and the Director of the Irish Museum of Modern Art and includes any person duly acting in the capacity of any of the foregoing as a result of the member concerned being unable to fulfil his or her duties for any of the reasons set out in paragraph (b) (ii);

"tax" means income tax, corporation tax, capital gains tax, gift tax or inheritance tax, as the case may be, payable in accordance with any provision of the Acts;

"valuation date" means the date on which an application is made, to the selection committee, for a determination under subsection (2) (a).

(b) (i) The selection committee may act notwithstanding one or more vacancies among its members and may regulate its own procedure.

(ii) If and so long as a member of the selection committee is unable through illness, absence or other cause to fulfil his or her duties, a person nominated in that behalf by the member shall act as the member of the committee in the place of the member.

(2) (a) In this section "heritage item" means any kind of cultural item including—

   (i) any archaeological item, archive, book, estate record, manuscript and painting, and

   (ii) any collection of cultural items and any collection thereof in their setting,

which, on application to the selection committee in writing in that behalf by a person who owns the item or collection of items (as the case may be) is determined by the selection committee, after consideration of any evidence in relation to the matter which the person submits to the committee and after such consultation (if any) as may seem to the committee to be necessary with such person or body of persons as in the opinion of the committee may be of assistance to them, to be an item or collection of items—

   (I) which is an outstanding example of the type of item involved, pre-eminent in its class, whose export from the State would constitute a diminution of the accumulated cultural heritage of Ireland, and

   (II) suitable for acquisition by an approved body.

(b) On receipt of an application for a determination under paragraph (a) the selection committee shall request the Revenue Commissioners in writing to value the item or collection of items, as the case may be, in accordance with the provisions of subsection (3).

(c) The selection committee shall not make a determination under paragraph (a) where the market value of the item or collection of items (as the case may be), as determined by the Revenue Commissioners in accordance with subsection (3), at the valuation date—

   (i) is less than £75,000, or

   (ii) exceeds an amount (which shall not be less than £75,000) determined by the formula—

$$[£750,000]^2 - M$$

where M is an amount (which may be nil) equal to the market value at the valuation date of the heritage item (if any) or the aggregate of the market values at the respective valuation dates of all the heritage items (if any), as the case may be, in respect of which a determination or determinations, as the case may be, under this subsection has been made by the selection committee in any one calendar year and not revoked in that year.

(d) (i) An item or collection of items shall cease to be a heritage item for the purposes of this section if the item or collection of items —

    (I) is sold or otherwise disposed of to a person other than an approved body, or

    (II) the owner thereof notifies the selection committee in writing that it is not intended to make a gift thereof to an approved body, or

    (III) the gift of the item or collection of items is not made to an approved body within the calendar year following the year in which the determination is made under paragraph (a).

(ii) Where the selection committee becomes aware, at any time within the calendar year in which a determination under paragraph (a) is made in respect of an item or collection of items, that clause (I) or (II) of subparagraph (i) applies to the item or collection of items the selection committee may revoke its determination with effect from that time.

(3) (a) For the purposes of this section, the market value of any item or collection of items (hereafter in this subsection referred to as "the property") shall be estimated to be the price which, in the opinion of the Revenue Commissioners, the property would fetch if sold in the open market on the valuation date in such manner and subject to such conditions as might reasonably be calculated to obtain for the vendor the best price for the property.

(b) The market value of the property shall be ascertained by the Revenue Commissioners in such manner and by such means as they think fit, and they may authorise a person to inspect the property and report to them the value thereof for the purposes of this section, and the person having custody or possession of the property shall permit the person so authorised to inspect the property at such reasonable times as the Revenue Commissioners consider necessary.

(c) Where the Revenue Commissioners require a valuation to be made by a person authorised by them, the cost of such valuation shall be defrayed by the Revenue Commissioners.

(4) Where a relevant gift is made to an approved body —

(a) the designated officer of that body shall give a certificate to the person who made the relevant gift, in such form as the Revenue Commissioners may prescribe, certifying the receipt of that gift and the transfer of the ownership of the heritage item the subject of that gift to the approved body, and

(b) the designated officer shall transmit a duplicate of the certificate to the Revenue Commissioners.

(5) Subject to the provisions of this section, where a person has made a relevant gift the person shall, on submission to the Revenue Commissioners of the certificate given to the person in accordance with subsection (4), be treated as having made on the date of such submission a payment on account of tax of an amount equal to the market value of the relevant gift on the valuation date.

(6) A payment on account of tax which is treated as having been made in accordance with the provisions of subsection (5) shall be set, so far as possible, against any liability to tax of the person who is treated as having made such a payment in the following order –

(a) firstly, against any arrears of tax due for payment by that person and against an arrear of tax for an earlier period in priority to a later period and, for this purpose, the date on which an arrear of tax became due for payment shall determine whether it is for an earlier or later period, and

(b) then, and only then, against any current liability of the person which the person nominates for that purpose,

and such set-off shall accordingly discharge a corresponding amount of that liability.

(7) Where and to the extent that a payment on account of tax has not been set off in accordance with the provisions of subsection (6), the balance remaining shall be set off against any future liability to tax of the person who is treated as having made the payment which that person nominates for that purpose.

(8) Where a person has power to sell any heritage item in order to raise money for the payment of gift tax or inheritance tax, such person shall have power to make a relevant gift of that heritage item in or towards satisfaction of that tax and, except as regards the nature of the consideration and its receipt and application, any such relevant gift shall be subject to the same provisions and shall be treated for all purposes as a sale made in exercise of that power and any conveyances or transfers made or purporting to be made to give effect to such a relevant gift shall have effect accordingly.

(9) A person shall not be entitled to any refund of tax in respect of any payment on account of tax made in accordance with the provisions of this section.

(10) Interest shall not be payable in respect of any overpayment of tax for any period which arises directly or indirectly due to the set-off against any liability for that period of a payment on account of tax made in accordance with the provisions of this section.

(11) Where a person makes a relevant gift and in respect of that gift is treated as having made a payment on account of tax the person

concerned shall not be allowed relief under any other provision of the Acts in respect of that gift.

(12) (a) The Revenue Commissioners shall, as respects each year (being the calendar year 1995 and subsequent calendar years), compile a list of the names (if any), descriptions and values of the heritage items (if any) in respect of which relief under this section has been given.

(b) Notwithstanding any obligation as to secrecy imposed on them by the Acts or the Official Secrets Act, 1963, the Revenue Commissioners shall include in their annual report to the Minister for Finance, commencing with the report for the year 1995, the list (if any) referred to in paragraph (a) for the year in respect of which the report is made.

Footnotes

1   S.176 took effect as on and from 2nd June, 1995. The section was repealed and re-enacted in s.1003, TCA, with effect as on and from 6th April, 1997.

2   "£750,000" substituted for "£500,000" for the calendar year 1996 and subsequent calendar years – s.139, FA 1996.

FINANCE ACT, 1997

Number 22 of 1997
(Enacted on 10th May, 1997)

PART VIII
Miscellaneous

Section 159[1]

Evidence of authorisation.

159. (1) In this section, except where the context otherwise requires—

"the Acts" means—

    (a)   (i)   the Customs Acts,

        (ii)   the statutes relating to the duties of excise and to the management of those duties,

        (iii)   the Tax Acts,

        (iv)   the Capital Gains Tax Acts,

        (v)   the Value-Added Tax Act, 1972, and the enactments amending or extending that Act,

        (vi)   the Capital Acquisitions Tax Act, 1976, and the enactments amending or extending that Act,

        (vii)   the statutes relating to stamp duty and to the management of that duty,

and any instruments made thereunder or under any other enactment and relating to tax, and

    (b)   the European Communities (Intrastat) Regulations, 1993 (S.I. No. 136 of 1993);

"authorised officer" means an officer of the Revenue Commissioners who is authorised, nominated or appointed under any provision of the Acts, to exercise or perform any functions under any of the specified provisions, and "authorised" and "authorisation" shall be construed accordingly;

"functions" includes powers and duties;

"identity card", in relation to an authorised officer, means a card which is issued to the officer by the Revenue Commissioners and which contains—

    (a)   a statement to the effect that the officer—

        (i)   is an officer of the Revenue Commissioners, and

      (ii) is an authorised officer for the purposes of the specified provisions,

(b) a photograph and signature of the officer,

(c) a hologram showing the logo of the Office of the Revenue Commissioners,

(d) the facsimile signature of a Revenue Commissioner, and

(e) particulars of the specified provisions under which the officer is authorised;

"specified provisions", in relation to an authorised officer, means either or both the provisions of the Acts under which the authorised officer —

(a) is authorised and which are specified on his or her identity card, and

(b) exercises or performs functions under the Customs Acts or any statutes relating to the duties of excise and to the management of those duties;

"tax" means any tax, duty, levy, charge under the care and management of the Revenue Commissioners.

(2) Where, in the exercise or performance of any functions under any of the specified provisions in relation to him or her, an authorised officer is requested to produce or show his or her authorisation for the purposes of that provision, the production by the authorised officer of his or her identity card —

(a) shall be taken as evidence of authorisation under that provision, and

(b) shall satisfy any obligation under that provision which requires the authorised officer to produce such authorisation on request.

(3) This section shall come into operation on such day as the Minister for Finance may appoint by order.

Footnote

1   S.159 never took effect as no order was made under s.159(3). The section was repealed and re-enacted in s.858, TCA, with effect as on and from 6th April, 1997.

FIFTH PART

Probate tax was introduced in Chapter I, Part VI, of the Finance Act, 1993, and had effect in relation to persons dying after 17th June, 1993. The tax was imposed in the form of an inheritance tax on an absolute interest in a deceased person's estate deemed to be taken by his personal representatives, and was governed by the Capital Acquisitions Tax Act, 1976.

This Fifth Part contains sections of the various Finance Acts relating to probate tax, as and where amended, as they existed immediately before probate tax was abolished by section 225 of the Finance Act, 2001, in relation to persons dying on or after 6th December, 2000. However:

(i)   section 117(b) of the Finance Act, 1993, dealing with the rate of interest on unpaid tax, has been amended by section 129(5) of the Finance Act, 2002, with effect from 1st September, 2002, to 31st March 2005, and by section 145(5) of the Finance Act, 2005, with effect from 1st April, 2005, and

(ii)   section 115 of the Finance Act, 1993, dealing with the incidence of probate tax, has been amended by section 16 of the Courts and Court Officers Act, 2002, which, at the date of publication of this book, has not yet become operative.

For Contents of this Part, see page lxxxvii

FINANCE ACT, 1993

Number 13 of 1993
(Enacted on 17th June, 1993)

PART VI
Capital Acquisitions Tax

CHAPTER I
Taxation of Assets passing on Inheritance (Probate Tax)

Section 109

Interpretation (Chapter I).

109. (1) In this Chapter, except where the context otherwise requires —

"the Act of 1965" means the Succession Act, 1965;

["agricultural property" has the same meaning as it has in section 19 (as amended by the Finance Act, 1994) of [the Capital Acquisitions Tax Act, 1976,] but excluding farm machinery, livestock and bloodstock;

"agricultural value" means the market value of agricultural property reduced by 30 per cent. of that value;][1]

"the consumer price index number" means the All Items Consumer Price Index Number for a year as compiled by the Central Statistics Office and expressed on the basis that the consumer price index number at [mid-November 1996],[2] is 100;

"the deceased", in relation to the disposition referred to in section 110 (1), means the disponer;

"dependent child", in relation to the deceased, means a child who at the time of the deceased's death —

(a) was living and had not attained the age of 18 years, or

(b) was receiving full-time education or instruction at any university, college, school or other educational establishment and was under the age of 21 years or, if over the age of 21 years, was receiving such full-time education or instruction continuously since before attaining the age of 21 years;

"dependent relative", in relation to the deceased, has the meaning assigned to it by [subsection (11) of section 604 of the Taxes Consolidation Act, 1997.][3]

"the dwelling-house" means —

(a)   a dwelling-house, or part of a dwelling-house, which was occupied by the deceased as his only or principal place of residence, at the date of his death,

(b)   the curtilage of the dwelling-house which the deceased had for his own use and enjoyment with that dwelling-house up to an area (exclusive of the site of the dwelling-house) of one acre, and

(c)   furniture and household effects being the normal contents of the dwelling-house:

Provided that—

(i)   in the case of a dwelling-house, part of which was used mainly for the purpose of a trade, business, profession or vocation or was let, this definition shall not apply to the part so used or let, and

(ii) in a case where more than one dwelling-house is included in the estate of the deceased, and more than one such dwelling-house is used equally as a place of residence this definition shall apply only to one dwelling-house so used;

"the estate of the deceased" means the real and personal estate of the deceased as defined by section 10 (4) of the Act of 1965;

"the net market value of the dwelling-house" means the market value of the dwelling-house at the date of death of the deceased or, if less, that market value less the market value at that date of any sum which is charged or secured on the dwelling-house by the will, or other testamentary disposition, of the deceased and which is comprised in the share of an object of the relevant trust in the estate of the deceased, other than the share of a person whose place of normal residence was at that date the dwelling-house and who was on that date a dependent child or dependent relative of the deceased;

"object", in relation to a relevant trust, means a person entitled to a share in the estate of the deceased (otherwise than as a creditor);

"occupied", in relation to a dwelling-house or part of a dwelling-house, means having the use thereof, whether actually used or not;

"the Principal Act" means the Capital Acquisitions Tax Act, 1976;

["relevant threshold" means—

(a)   £40,000, where the death of the deceased occurred on or before 31 December 2000, and

(b)   in any other case, £40,000 multiplied by the figure, rounded up to the nearest third decimal place, determined by dividing by 104.8 the consumer price index number for the year immediately preceding the year in which the death of the deceased occurred;][4]

"relevant trust" means –

(a) any trust under which, by virtue of the provisions of section 10 (3) of the Act of 1965, the executors of a deceased person hold the estate of the deceased as trustees for the persons by law entitled thereto, or

(b) any trust of which, by virtue of section 110 (3), the President of the High Court is deemed to be a trustee;

"share", in relation to the estate of the deceased, includes any share or interest, whether arising—

(a) under a will or other testamentary disposition, or

(b) on intestacy, or

(c) as a legal right under section 111 of the Act of 1965, or

(d) as the subject of an order under section 117 (as amended by the Status of Children Act, 1987) of the Act of 1965. or

(e) in accordance with the law of another country,

and includes also the right to the entire of the estate of the deceased.

(2) A reference in this Act or in any Act of the Oireachtas passed after the passing of this Act to probate tax shall, unless the contrary intention appears, be construed as a reference to the tax chargeable on the taxable value of a taxable inheritance which is charged to tax by virtue of section 110.

Footnotes

1   As inserted by s.137, FA 1994, which has effect retrospectively in relation to persons dying after 17th June, 1993.

2   Substituted for "mid-November, 1989" by s.147(1)(a), FA 2000, in relation to persons dying on or after 1st December, 1999.

3   Substituted for "subsection (9A)(a) (inserted by the Finance Act, 1979) of section 25 of the Capital Gains Tax Act, 1975" by s.1100, TCA, with effect from 6th April, 1997.

4   As substituted by s.147(1)(b), FA 2000, in relation to persons dying on or after 1st December, 1999. The actual relevant thresholds for all dates of death are set out at footnote 1 to section 113 on page 1457.

Commentary

A   See the Revenue Information Leaflet CAT3 in relation to probate tax.

B   See articles on probate tax by Kieran Twomey in the *Irish Tax Review* of September 1993, page 645, and by Richard Grogan in the *Irish Tax Review* of November 1993, page 695. As to "reasonable funeral expenses", see Commentary A under s.111, FA 1993, on page 1455.

Section 110

Acquisitions by relevant trusts.

110. (1) Where, under or in consequence of any disposition, property becomes subject to a relevant trust on the death of a person dying after the date of the passing of this Act (in this section referred to as "the disponer") the trust shall be deemed on the date of death of the disponer to become beneficially entitled in possession to an absolute interest in that property and to take an inheritance accordingly as if the trust, and the trustees as such for the time being of the trust, were together a person for the purposes of [the Capital Acquisitions Tax Act, 1976,] and that date shall be the date of the inheritance.

(2) The provisions of subsection (1) shall not prejudice any charge for tax in respect of any inheritance affecting the same property or any part of it taken under the disposition referred to in subsection (1) –

(a) by an object of the relevant trust referred to in subsection (1), or

(b) by a discretionary trust by virtue of section 106 (1) of the Finance Act, 1984,

and any such inheritance shall, except for the purposes of subsections (3) and (4) of section 55 of [the Capital Acquisitions Tax Act, 1976], be deemed to be taken after the inheritance referred to in subsection (1).

(3) Where, under the provisions of section 13 of the Act of 1965, the estate of a deceased person vests on the date of death of the deceased in the President of the High Court, then, for the purpose of subsection (1), the President of the High Court shall be deemed to hold that estate as a trustee in trust for the persons by law entitled thereto, and the estate of the deceased shall be deemed to be property which became subject to that trust on that date.

(4) The provisions of sections 10 and 13 of the Act of 1965, shall, for the purposes of subsection (1), be deemed to apply irrespective of the domicile of the deceased or the locality of the estate of the deceased.

Section 111

Application of [the Capital Acquisitions Act, 1976].

111. In relation to a charge for tax arising by virtue of section 110 –

(a) the valuation date of the taxable inheritance shall be the date of the inheritance;

(b) a reference in section 16 of [the Capital Acquisitions Tax Act, 1976] (as amended by the Finance Act, 1993) to a company controlled by the successor and the definition in that section of "group of shares" shall be construed as if (for the purpose of that reference) the list of persons contained in subsection (3) of that section and (for the purpose of that definition) the list of persons contained in that definition included the following persons, that is to say, the trustees of the relevant trust, the relatives of the deceased, the nominees of those trustees or of those relatives, and the trustees of a settlement whose objects include the relatives of the deceased;

(c) a person who is a personal representative of the deceased shall be a person primarily accountable for the payment of the tax;

(d) every person entitled for an interest in possession to a share in the estate of the deceased, and every person to whom or for whose benefit any of the property subject to the relevant trust is applied or appointed, shall also be accountable for the payment of the tax and [the Capital Acquisitions Tax Act, 1976,] shall have effect, in its application to that charge for tax, as if each of those persons were a person referred to in section 35 (2) of [the Capital Acquisitions Tax Act, 1976];

(e) where the total taxable value referred to in paragraph (a) of the proviso to section 113 exceeds the relevant threshold, section 36 (2) of [the Capital Acquisitions Tax Act, 1976] (inserted by the Finance Act, 1989) shall have effect, in the application of [the Capital Acquisitions Tax Act, 1976,] to any such charge for tax as aforesaid, as if —

  (i) the reference in that subsection to four months were construed as a reference to nine months, and

  (ii) the reference in that subsection to a person primarily accountable for the payment of tax were construed as including a reference to a person primarily accountable by virtue of paragraph (c) of this section;

(f) sections 19, 21, 35 (1), 36 (4) and 40, subsections (1) to (3) of section 41, and section 43 of, and the Second Schedule to, [the Capital Acquisitions Tax Act, 1976,] shall not apply;

(g) section 18 of [the Capital Acquisitions Tax Act, 1976,] shall have effect, in the application of [the Capital Acquisitions Tax Act, 1976,] to any such charge for tax as aforesaid, as if —

  (i) liabilities, costs or expenses incurred after the death of the deceased, other than reasonable funeral expenses, were not an allowable deduction,

  (ii) any bona fide consideration paid prior to the death of the deceased by an object of the relevant trust, in return for a share in the estate of the deceased, were consideration paid by the relevant trust on the date on which it was paid by the object,

  [(iia) in so far as the inheritance consists of agricultural property, the reference to market value in subsection (1) of the said section 18 were a reference to agricultural value, and][1]

  (iii) where the property which is exempt from such tax is the dwelling-house, or a part thereof, the restriction on the deduction of any liability referred to in subsection (5) (e) of the said section 18 did not apply;

[Provided that nothing in this subparagraph shall have effect so as to reduce the tax which would but for this subparagraph be borne by property which at the date of death of the deceased represented the share in the estate of the deceased of a person who was not on that date a dependent child or a dependent relative of the deceased;][2]

(h) section 60 of [the Capital Acquisitions Tax Act, 1976,] shall apply with the modification that, notwithstanding subsection (3) of that section, the Commissioners may refuse to issue the certificate referred to in subsection (1) of that section—

(i) in a case where the tax is being wholly or partly paid by the transfer of securities to the Minister for Finance under the provisions of section 45 of [the Capital Acquisitions Tax Act, 1976], until such security as they think fit has been given for the completion of the transfer of the securities to the Minister for Finance, or

(ii) in a case where payment of such tax has been postponed under the provisions of section 44 (1) of [the Capital Acquisitions Tax Act, 1976], or under section 118, until such tax as has not been so postponed has been paid together with the interest, if any, thereon, or

(iii) in any other case, until the tax has been paid together with the interest, if any, thereon;

(i) section 2 (a) of section 57 of [the Capital Acquisitions Tax Act, 1976] (inserted by the Finance Act, 1978) shall not apply and subsection (2) (c) of that section shall be construed as if the reference therein to the donee or successor were a reference to the deceased;

(j) subsection (6) of section 36 of [the Capital Acquisitions Tax Act, 1976] (inserted by the Finance Act, 1989) shall have effect, in the application of [the Capital Acquisitions Tax Act, 1976,] to any such charge for tax as aforesaid, as if the reference in that subsection to a person primarily accountable for the payment of tax by virtue of section 35 (1) were a reference to a person primarily accountable by virtue of paragraph (c) of this section;

(k) section 55 of [the Capital Acquisitions Tax Act, 1976,] shall be construed as if the reference in subsection (4) of that section to the successor were a reference to the person who would be the successor for the purpose of that subsection if this Chapter had not been enacted; and

(l) section 63 of [the Capital Acquisitions Tax Act, 1976] (as amended by the Finance Act, 1989) shall have effect, in the application of [the Capital Acquisitions Tax Act, 1976,] to any such charge for tax as aforesaid, as if—

(i) [€1.265][3] were substituted for [€6,345][3] in subsection (3) of that section,

(ii) [€505]³ were substituted for [€2,535]³ in subsection (1) (a) of that section,

(iii) [€250]³ were substituted for [€1,265]³ in subsections (2) and (7) of that section, and

(iv) [€6]³ were substituted for [€30]³ in subsection (1) (b) of that section.

Footnotes

1   As inserted by s.138(1)(a), FA 1994, which has effect retrospectively in relation to persons dying after 17th June, 1993.

2   As inserted by s.138(1)(b), FA 1994, which has effect retrospectively in relation to persons dying after 17th June, 1993.

3   For any act or omission which takes place on or after 1st January, 2002, s.240(2)(k) and Part 5 of the Fifth Sch., FA 2001, substituted (a) "€1,265" for "£1,000", (b) "€6,345" for "£5,000"; (c) "€505" for "£400", (d) "€2,535" for "£2,000", (e) "€250" for "£200"; (f) "€6" for "£5", and (g) "€30" for "£25".

Commentary

A   As to s.111(g)(i), see articles in the *Irish Tax Review* of September 1994 by Frank Carr (page 1064) and Richard Grogan (page 1071) in which it is stated that Revenue has advised that "reasonable funeral expenses" include reasonable disbursements on foot of funeral meals and grave/headstone expenses.

Section 112

Exemptions.¹

112. The following property shall be exempt from tax (and shall not be taken into account in computing tax) in relation to a charge for tax arising by virtue of section 110 —

(a) any right to receive any benefit —

(i) under —

(A) any sponsored superannuation scheme within the meaning of [section 783(1) of the Taxes Consolidation Act, 1997],² but excluding any scheme or arrangement which relates to matters other than service in particular offices or employments, or

(B) a trust scheme or part of a trust scheme approved under the said [section 784 or section 785]³ of the said Act; or

(ii) under any scheme for the provision of superannuation benefits on retirement established by or under any enactment; or

(iii) under a contract approved by the Commissioners for the purposes of granting relief for the purposes of [section 787 of the Taxes Consolidation Act, 1997],⁴ in respect of the premiums payable in respect thereof;

(b) property given by the will of the deceased for public or charitable purposes to the extent that the Commissioners are satisfied that it has been, or will be, applied to purposes which, in accordance with the law of the State, are public or charitable;

(c) .... [5]

[(d) the dwelling-house comprised in an inheritance which, on the date of death of the deceased, is taken under the will or other testamentary disposition or under the intestacy of the deceased, by a person who was on that date a dependent child of the deceased or a dependent relative of the deceased and whose place of normal residence was on that date the dwelling-house:

Provided that –

(i) the total income from all sources of that dependent child or that dependent relative, for income tax purposes, in the year of assessment ending on the 5th day of April next before that date, did not exceed the "specified amount" referred to in [subsection (1) of section 466 of the Taxes Consolidation Act, 1997],[6]

(ii) the amount of the exemption shall (subject, with any necessary modifications, to the provisions of section 18(4) (a) of [the Capital Acquisitions Act, 1976,] in the case of a limited interest, and to the provisions of section 20 of that Act in the case of a contingency) be the whole or, as the case may be, the appropriate part (within the meaning of section 5 (5) of [the Capital Acquisitions Act, 1976]) of the net market value of the dwelling-house, and

(iii) the amount of the exemption shall not be reduced by virtue of the provisions of section 20 of [the Capital Acquisitions Tax Act, 1976,] where an entitlement ceasing within the meaning of that section ceases because of an enlargement of that entitlement.] [7]

Footnotes

1   A further exemption relating to retirement benefits is contained in s.59B, CATA, in relation to persons dying on or after 25th March, 1999. See page 1465.

2   Substituted for "section 235(9) of the Income Tax Act, 1967" by s.1100, TCA, with effect from 6th April, 1997.

3   Substituted for "section 235 or section 235A" by s.1100, TCA, with effect from 6th April, 1997.

4   Substituted for "section 236 of the Income Tax Act, 1967" by s.1100, TCA, with effect from 6th April, 1997.

5   The words "the dwelling-house, in a case where the deceased is survived by the spouse" were deleted by s.139(1)(a), FA 1994, which has effect in relation to persons dying on or after 23rd May, 1994.

6   Substituted for "subsection 1(A) of section 142 of the Income Tax Act, 1967" by s.1100, TCA, with effect from 6th April, 1997. The actual specified amounts are as follows –

	£
year ending 5th April, 1993	3,877
year ending 5th April, 1994	4,023
year ending 5th April, 1995	4,149
year ending 5th April, 1996	4,270
year ending 5th April, 1997	4,440
year ending 5th April, 1998	4,601
year ending 5th April, 1999	4,740
year ending 5th April, 2000	4,848
year ending 5th April, 2001	4,968.

7   As substituted by s.139(1)(b) FA 1994, which has effect in relation to persons dying on or after 23rd May, 1994.

Commentary

A   See an article on the Law and Taxation of Charities by John H. Hickson in the Irish Tax Review of November 1996, page 377.

Section 113

Computation of tax.

113.   The tax chargeable on the taxable value of a taxable inheritance which is charged to tax by virtue of section 110 shall be computed at the rate of two per cent. of such taxable value:

Provided that—

(a)   where the total taxable value on which tax is chargeable by virtue of section 110 on the death of the deceased does not exceed the relevant threshold, that tax shall be nil, and

(b)   where that total taxable value exceeds the relevant threshold, that tax shall not exceed the amount by which that total taxable value exceeds the relevant threshold.

Footnote

1   The actual relevant thresholds are as follows for person dying –

	£
in the calendar year 1993	10,000
in the calendar year 1994	10,150
in the calendar year 1995	10,390
in the calendar year 1996	10,650
in the calendar year 1997	10,820
in the calendar year 1998	10,980
in the calendar year 1999, prior to 1st December, 1999	11,250
on or after 1st December, 1999	40,000.

Section 114

Relief in respect of quick succession.

114.   Where by virtue of section 110 tax is payable in respect of any property on the death of one party to a marriage, then a charge to tax shall not

arise by virtue of that section in respect of that property, or in respect of any property representing that property, on the death of the other party to the marriage within—

(a) one year after the death of the first-mentioned party, or

(b) 5 years after the death of the first-mentioned party, if that other party is survived by a dependent child of that other party.

Section 115

Incidence.

115. In relation to a charge for tax arising by virtue of section 110, property which, at the date of death of the deceased, represents any share in the estate of the deceased, shall, save to the extent that it is exempt from or not chargeable to such tax, bear its due proportion of such tax, and any dispute as to the proportion of tax to be borne by any such property, or by property representing any such property, may be determined upon application by any person interested in manner directed by rules of court, either by the High Court, or, where the amount in dispute is less than [e100,000][1], by the Circuit Court in whose circuit the person recovering the same resides, or the property in respect of which the tax is paid is situate.

Footnote

1   Amended from "£15,000" by s.16, Courts and Court Officers Act, 2002, reproduced on page 1093. The amendment will operate on such day as the Minister for Justice, Equality and Law Reform may appoint by order. At the date of publication of this book, no order had been made.

Section 115A[1]

Abatement and postponement of tax.

115A. (1) Where the spouse of a deceased survives the deceased, probate tax chargeable by virtue of section 110 which is borne by property which, at the date of death of the deceased, represents the share of that spouse in the estate of the deceased, shall be abated to a nil amount:

Provided that—

(a) where the same property represents more than one person's share in the estate of the deceased and that spouse's interest in that property at that date is not a limited interest to which paragraph (b) relates, only a proportion of the probate tax borne by that property shall be abated to a nil amount and that proportion shall be the proportion which the value of that interest at that date bears to the total value of the property at that date, and for this purpose the value of that interest at that date shall not include the value of any interest in expectancy created by the will or other testamentary disposition of the deceased;

(b) where a limited interest to which that spouse became beneficially entitled in possession on that date was created by the will or other testamentary disposition of the deceased, probate tax borne by the property in which that limited interest subsisted on that date shall not be abated to a nil amount, but, notwithstanding section 117 (a), that tax shall not become due and payable until the date of the cesser of that limited interest and every person who (on the cesser of that limited interest) takes an inheritance which consists of all or part of the property in which that limited interest subsisted immediately prior to that cesser (hereinafter in this proviso referred to as "the said property") and every trustee or other person in whose care the said property or the income therefrom is placed at the date of that cesser and every person in whom the said property is vested after that date, other than a bona fide purchaser or mortgagee for full consideration in money or money's worth, or a person deriving title from or under such a purchaser or mortgagee shall, notwithstanding any other provision to the contrary, be the only persons accountable for the payment of that tax and that tax shall be a charge on the said property in all respects as if the date of the inheritance in respect of which that tax is chargeable were the date of such cesser and the said property were property of which, for the purpose of section 47 of [the Capital Acquisitions Tax Act, 1976], that inheritance consisted at that date;

(c) if consideration in money or money's worth is paid to that spouse on the coming to an end of the limited interest referred to in paragraph (b) of this proviso before the event on which that interest was limited to cease, an appropriate proportion of the probate tax borne by the said property shall be abated to a nil amount and that proportion shall be the proportion which the value of that consideration bears to the value of the said property at the date of the cesser.

(2) Where the spouse of a deceased survives the deceased, probate tax chargeable by virtue of section 110 which is borne by the dwelling-house, or by any part thereof, shall, notwithstanding subsection (1) and section 117 (a), not become due and payable until the date of death of that spouse and, notwithstanding any provision to the contrary, the only persons who shall be accountable for that tax shall be the following, that is to say —

(a) any person who takes an inheritance under the will or other testamentary disposition of the deceased which consists in whole or in part of the dwelling-house, or part thereof, or which consists of property which represents that dwelling-house or part; and

(b) any trustee in whom the property comprised in any such inheritance is vested at the date of death of that spouse or at any time thereafter and any other person in whom the property comprised in any such inheritance becomes vested for a beneficial interest in possession at any time thereafter, other than a bona fide purchaser or mortgagee for full consideration in money or money's worth, or a person deriving title from or under such a purchaser or mortgagee.

(3) Where the date upon which tax becomes due and payable is postponed by virtue of subsection (1) (b) or subsection (2), then, notwithstanding paragraph (b) of section 117, interest upon that tax shall not be payable in respect of the period commencing on the valuation date and ending 9 months after the date on which that tax actually becomes due and payable.

Footnote

1   As inserted by s.140, FA 1994, which has effect retrospectively in relation to persons dying after 17th June, 1993.

Section 116

Payment of tax.

116. (1) The person applying for probate or letters of administration of the estate of the deceased shall—

(a) notwithstanding the provisions of section 36 (inserted by the Finance Act, 1989) or section 39 of [the Capital Acquisitions Tax Act, 1976], make, on a form provided by the Commissioners, an assessment of the tax arising on the death of the deceased by virtue of section 110, and that assessment shall include the interest, if any, payable on the tax in accordance with paragraph (b) of section 117, and shall be of such amount as to the best of the said person's knowledge, information and belief, ought to be charged, levied and paid, and the form on which the assessment is made shall accompany the Inland Revenue Affidavit which is required to be delivered to the Commissioners, and

(b) on delivering the Inland Revenue Affidavit to the Commissioners, duly pay the amount of such tax and interest,

and the Inland Revenue Affidavit and the form on which the assessment is made shall together, for the purpose of section 36 (2) of [the Capital Acquisitions Tax Act, 1976], be deemed, in relation to the tax arising by virtue of section 110, to be a return delivered by a person primarily accountable.

(2) The provisions of section 36 (3) (b) of [the Capital Acquisitions Tax Act, 1976] (inserted by the Finance Act, 1989) shall, with any

necessary modifications, apply to any payment required by virtue of this section.

Commentary

A   In an article on page 227 of the *Irish Tax Review* of May 2000, Richard Grogan has advised that, because of difficulties in paying probate tax, Bank of Ireland has agreed that, where a solicitor produces a copy of the self-assessment probate tax return and a letter requesting a draft payable to the Revenue Commissioners, Bank of Ireland branches can release up to £10,000 (2% on an estate of £500,000) where there are sufficient funds in the deceased's account. Requests for larger amounts will be referred by branches to their line management.

Section 117

Interest on tax.

117.   In relation to a charge for tax arising by virtue of section 110 –

(a)   the tax shall be due and payable on the valuation date;

(b)   simple interest to the date of payment of the tax shall, from the first day after the expiration of the period of 9 months commencing on the valuation date, be payable upon the tax at the rate of [0.0273 per cent per day or part of a day]1, without deduction of Income Tax, and shall be chargeable and recoverable in the same manner as if it were part of the tax;

(c)   notwithstanding the provisions of paragraph (a), where, during the said period of 9 months, a payment is made on foot of the tax, the tax due at the time of the payment shall be discounted by an amount appropriate to the payment, such discount being calculated on tax at a rate per cent. equal to [one per cent.]2 multiplied by the number of months in the period from the date of payment to the date of the expiration of the said period of 9 months, and for this purpose a month shall include a part of a month:

Provided that insofar as the payment is repaid by the Commissioners in accordance with the provisions of section 46 of [the Capital Acquisitions Tax Act, 1976], no discount shall be appropriate to the payment;

(d)   notwithstanding the provisions of paragraph (b), the interest payable upon the tax shall not exceed the amount of the tax.

Footnotes

1   The original rate of interest in s.117(b) was 1.25% per month or part of a month. This was amended to 1% per month, or part of a month, by s.127(1)(a), FA 1998, in relation to the probate tax due before, on or after 27th March, 1998, where the period in respect of which interest is to be charged commences on or after 27th March, 1998, and before 1st September, 2002. S.129(5), FA 2002, amends the rate of interest to 0.0322 per cent per day or part of a day, and applies to interest charged from 1st September, 2002.

S.145(5), FA 2005, further amends the rate of interest from "0.0322" to "0.0273" where such interest is chargeable on or after 1st April, 2005, in respect of tax due to be paid whether before, on or after that date.

2   Substituted for "one and one-quarter per cent" by s.127(1)(b), FA 1998, which has effect
     in relation to probate tax due before, on or after 27th March, 1998, where the period in
     respect of which a discount falls to be made, commences on or after 27th March, 1998.
     With the abolition of probate tax in respect of persons dying on or after 6th December,
     2000, s.117(c) is obsolete.

Commentary

A   See Part 11A of the Revenue CAT Work Manual regarding the interpretation of the
     word "month".

Section 118

Postponement of tax.

118. Where the Commissioners are satisfied that there are insufficient liquid
      assets comprised in the estate of the deceased to meet any tax arising by
      virtue of section 110, they may allow payment to be postponed for such
      period, to such extent and on such terms as they think fit.

Commentary

A   According to the Revenue Information Leaflet CAT3, when the estate is illiquid, the
     Revenue Commissioners will postpone payment until after the grant has been extracted.
     Relief under s.44, CATA, is also available as probate tax is imposed in the form of tax on
     a deemed inheritance.

Section 119

Application of section 85 of Finance Act, 1989, and section 133 of Finance Act,
1993.

119. In relation to a charge for tax arising by virtue of section 110,
      section 85 (2) (b) (iii) of the Finance Act, 1989, and section 133 (2) (b) (iii)
      shall not apply.

FINANCE ACT, 1997

Number 22 of 1997
(Enacted on 10th May, 1997)

―――

PART VI
Capital Acquisitions Tax

Section 143[1]

Abatement and postponement of probate tax on certain property.

143. (1) Subsection (1) of section 115A of the Finance Act, 1993 (which was inserted by the Finance Act, 1994, and provides for the abatement or postponement of probate tax payable by a surviving spouse) –

 (a) shall apply to a spouse in whose favour an order has been made –

  (i) under section 25 of the Family Law Act, 1995, [. . . . . . .][2]

  (ii) under section 18 of the Family Law (Divorce) Act, [1996, or][2]

  [(iii) to an order or other determination to like effect, which is analogous to an order referred to in subparagraph (i) or (ii), of a court under the law of another territory made under or in consequence of the dissolution of a marriage, being a dissolution that is entitled to be recognised as valid in the State.][2]

  as it applies to a spouse referred to in the said section 115A, and

 (b) shall apply to property or an interest in property the subject of such an order as it applies to the share of a spouse referred to in the said section 115A in the estate of a deceased referred to in that section or the interest of such a spouse in property referred to in that section,

 with any necessary modifications.

 (2) Section 53 of the Family Law Act, 1995, and section 36 of the Family Law (Divorce) Act, 1996, are hereby repealed.

―――

Footnotes

1 This section has effect from 10th May, 1997. It re-enacts the provisions of s.53, Family Law Act, 1995 (which came into force on 1st August, 1996 – see page 925) and of s.36, Family Law (Divorce) Act, 1996 (which was enacted on 27th November, 1996 – see page 938) both of which sections 53 and 36 are now repealed by this section.

2 In relation to an order or other determination to like effect made on or after 10th February, 2000, s.150, FA 2000, provides that –

(i) the word "or" is deleted at the end of subsection (1)(a)(i),

(ii) the words "1996, or" are substituted for "1996" at the end of subsection (1)(a)(ii), and

(iii) subsection (1)(a)(iii) is inserted.

CAPITAL ACQUISITIONS TAX ACT, 1976

Number 8 of 1976
(Enacted on 31st March, 1976)

PART X
Miscellaneous

Section 59B[1]

Exemption relating to retirement benefits.

59B. (1) The whole or any part of a retirement fund which is comprised in an inheritance which is taken upon the death of a disponer dying on or after the date of the passing of the Finance Act, 1999, shall be exempt from tax in relation to that inheritance and in relation to a charge for tax arising on that death by virtue of section 110 of the Finance Act, 1993, and the value thereof shall not be taken into account in computing tax, where —

(a) the disposition under which the inheritance is taken is the will or intestacy of the disponer, and

(b) the successor is a child of the disponer and had attained 21 years of age at the date of that disposition.

(2) In this section "retirement fund", in relation to an inheritance taken on the death of a disponer, means an approved retirement fund or an approved minimum retirement fund, within the meaning of section 784A or 784C of the Taxes Consolidation Act, 1997, being a fund which is wholly comprised of all or any of the following, that is to say —

(a) property which represents in whole or in part the accrued rights of the disponer, or of a predeceased spouse of the disponer, under an annuity contract or retirement benefits scheme approved by the Revenue Commissioners for the purposes of Chapter 1 or Chapter 2 of Part 30 of that Act,

(b) any accumulations of income thereof, or

(c) property which represents in whole or in part those accumulations.

Footnote

1   As inserted by s.206, FA 1999, which Act was enacted on 25th March, 1999. See s.112, FA 1993, for other exemptions from probate tax, at page 1455.

INDEX

This index relates to the First Part of this book only, and the numbers refer to pages of that Part.

Each provision of the Capital Acquisitions Tax Consolidation Act 2003 contained in this First Part shows, under the section or Schedule number, the corresponding legislation source of that section or Schedule. By using this source, one may trace where a reference in this Index is available in the Second Part of this book dealing directly with capital acquisitions tax. For example, the definition of "farmer" shown in this Index at page 118 is also in section 19, Capital Acquisitions Tax Act, 1976, in the Second Part, and the definition of "relevant business property" shown in this Index at page 123 is also in section 127, Finance Act, 1994, in the Second Part, under the heading of Business Relief.

INDEX